D1567147

EVIDENCE

ASPEN PUBLISHERS

EVIDENCE
CASES, COMMENTARY, AND PROBLEMS

Second Edition

David Alan Sklansky
University of California, Berkeley, School of Law

Wolters Kluwer
Law & Business

AUSTIN   BOSTON   CHICAGO   NEW YORK   THE NETHERLANDS

Aspen Publishers
Attn: Permissions Department
76 Ninth Avenue, 7th Floor
New York, NY 10011-5201

To contact Customer Care, e-mail customer.care@aspenpublishers.com,
call 1-800-234-1660, fax 1-800-901-9075, or mail correspondence to:

Aspen Publishers
Attn: Order Department
PO Box 990
Frederick, MD 21705

Printed in the United States of America.

1 2 3 4 5 6 7 8 9 0

ISBN 978-0-7355-6562-3

Library of Congress Cataloging–in–Publication Data

Sklansky, David A., 1959–
    Evidence : cases, commentary, and problems / David A. Sklansky. — 2nd ed.
      p. cm.
    ISBN 978-0-7355-6562-3 (casebook : alk. paper)   1. Evidence (Law)—United States.
    I. Title
    KF8935.S54   2008
    347.73′6—dc22

                                                    2008015519

About Wolters Kluwer Law & Business

Wolters Kluwer Law & Business is a leading provider of research information and workflow solutions in key specialty areas. The strengths of the individual brands of Aspen Publishers, CCH, Kluwer Law International and Loislaw are aligned within Wolters Kluwer Law & Business to provide comprehensive, in-depth solutions and expert-authored content for the legal, professional and education markets.

CCH was founded in 1913 and has served more than four generations of business professionals and their clients. The CCH products in the Wolters Kluwer Law & Business group are highly regarded electronic and print resources for legal, securities, antitrust and trade regulation, government contracting, banking, pension, payroll, employment and labor, and healthcare reimbursement and compliance professionals.

Aspen Publishers is a leading information provider for attorneys, business professionals and law students. Written by preeminent authorities, Aspen products offer analytical and practical information in a range of specialty practice areas from securities law and intellectual property to mergers and acquisitions and pension/benefits. Aspen's trusted legal education resources provide professors and students with high-quality, up-to-date and effective resources for successful instruction and study in all areas of the law.

Kluwer Law International supplies the global business community with comprehensive English-language international legal information. Legal practitioners, corporate counsel and business executives around the world rely on the Kluwer Law International journals, loose-leafs, books and electronic products for authoritative information in many areas of international legal practice.

Loislaw is a premier provider of digitized legal content to small law firm practitioners of various specializations. Loislaw provides attorneys with the ability to quickly and efficiently find the necessary legal information they need, when and where they need it, by facilitating access to primary law as well as state-specific law, records, forms and treatises.

Wolters Kluwer Law & Business, a unit of Wolters Kluwer, is headquartered in New York and Riverwoods, Illinois. Wolters Kluwer is a leading multinational publisher and information services company.

To Deborah, again

SUMMARY OF CONTENTS

CONTENTS

3   HEARSAY   43

PREFACE

Evidence law is steeped in the drama of trials. It is critically important for any lawyer who might ever set foot in a courtroom. And it is just plain fascinating. For all these reasons, I love teaching the subject, and most students seem to enjoy learning it.

But students also tend to find evidence law difficult. The rules of evidence are notoriously complicated and confusing. Much of evidence law makes sense only against the backdrop of Anglo-American trial procedure, with which law students typically have only limited familiarity. And students, along with lawyers and judges, often are puzzled by the very nature of evidence law. Is it statutory, judge-made, or a matter of applied logic?

I have tried in this book to capitalize on the inherent attractions of evidence law and to minimize its difficulty. Because actual cases are more interesting and more memorable than made-up problems, the book has more cases than problems. The cases have been selected to illustrate the central concepts and controversies of evidence law, not to provide encyclopedic coverage of the subject, and they have been edited tightly. Problems have been used selectively, sometimes to test students' understanding of the rules, sometimes to highlight ambiguities, and sometimes to encourage reflection on what the rules are trying to accomplish and how well they succeed. Many of the problems are drawn from real cases. Because the Federal Rules of Evidence provide a convenient and now pervasive framework for thinking about evidence law, the structure of the book tracks, wherever possible, the structure of the federal rules. The major exceptions to the ban on hearsay, for example, are addressed in the same order here as in the Federal Rules of Evidence. Because the legislative history of the federal rules, particularly the Advisory Committee's Notes, have proved so highly influential, the cases are accompanied by edited excerpts from the Advisory Committee Notes and, where relevant, congressional reports and floor debates. Because academic commentary has played such a large role in the development of evidence law—and because much of that commentary is so interesting—I have added excerpts from the writings of a wide range of scholars. Wigmore and Morgan are here, but so are Mirjan Damaška and Jennifer Mnookin. These excerpts, too, have been edited tightly, in part to allow room for multiple perspectives.

For this second edition, I have significantly reorganized and revised the materials on hearsay, taking into account the Supreme Court's recent reinterpretation of the Confrontation Clause. I have also added new materials, new problems, and new editorial text throughout the book. The book is still designed, though, so that it can be presented cover to cover in a four-unit course. The topics are arranged in the order that I address them when I teach evidence law, but other instructors may choose to vary the sequence. In view of the steadily increasing importance of scientific evidence, probabilistic proof, expert testimony, and demonstrative exhibits, I have included more materials on these topics than evidence casebooks typically contain. I also have included readings on certain other topics traditionally slighted in evidence courses, such as questioning by the judge and by the jury. I have found that students enjoy studying all of these issues, and I think they are sufficiently important to warrant the space I have given them. But instructors who disagree can easily skip those portions of the book or assign readings from them selectively.

My greatest debt by far is recorded in the dedication. But I also owe some other thanks. Paul Bergman, Ken Graham, Eleanor Swift, Jan Vetter, and John Wiley taught me much of what I know about teaching evidence. My parents, Jack and Gloria Sklansky, taught me much of what I know, period. Hundreds of law students at UCLA, Berkeley, and Harvard have sharpened my understanding of evidence law and made teaching the subject a joy. Several students, in particular, gave countless hours of their time to help me improve this book and its supporting materials: on the first edition, Carolyn Hoff, Christina Johnson, Hien Nguyn, Meghan Habersack, Robert Horton, and Jonathan Phillips; on the second edition, Katie Wozencroft. My editors at Aspen—Lynn Churchill, Anne Brunell, Barbara Roth, and the incomparable Carol McGeehan—have been a joy to work with. Steven Clymer, Daniel Richman, and several anonymous reviewers criticized early drafts of the first edition of this book perceptively and constructively. Michael Beach graciously helped me with the "probability primer" in Chapter 9. A number of instructors who used the first edition of the book gave me sound and valuable advice for revising it; I owe special thanks in this regard to James Tomkovicz and to the late Welsh White. Conversations with Scott Brewer and Alex Whiting also helped me significantly in revising the book. And I have been blessed at UCLA, at Berkeley, and at Harvard with terrific librarians and strong clerical support. Jan Qashat, in particular, made the process of preparing the second edition far easier than it deserved to be, much as Tal Grietzer worked wonders with the first edition.

My son Joseph continues to educate me in the complexities of proof and persuasion. More important, he has kept his parents smiling through two editions of this book.

David Alan Sklansky

June 2008

ACKNOWLEDGMENTS

Excerpts from the following, copyrighted materials are reprinted with permission. Except where noted, the publication date is also the copyright date.

Mirko Bagaric & Kumar Amarasekara, The Prejudice Against Similar Fact Evidence, 5 Int'l J. Evid. & Proof 71 (2001). Reprinted with permission of Vathek Publishing

Vaughn C. Ball, The Myth of Conditional Relevance, 14 Ga. L. Rev. 435 (1980). Reprinted with permission of the Georgia Law Review.

Benjamin H. Barton, Do Judges Systematically Favor the Interests of the Legal Profession?, 59 Alabama L. Rev. (2008). Reprinted with permission of the author and the Alabama Law Review.

Robert D. Brain & Daniel J. Broderick, The Derivative Use of Demonstrative Evidence: Charting Its Proper Evidentiary Status, copyright © 1992 by Robert D. Brain & Daniel J. Broderick; published in 25 U.C. Davis L. Rev. 957 (1992), copyright © 1992 by the Regents of the University of California. Reprinted with permission of the authors and the Regents of the University of California.

Kenneth S. Broun, ed., McCormick on Evidence (6th ed. 2006), published by West Group. Copyright © 1954, 1972, 1984, 1987, 1999 by West Publishing Co.; copyright © 2006 by West Group. Reprinted with permission of the publisher.

Simon A Cole, Suspect Identities: A History of Fingerprinting and Criminal Identification (2001), published by Harvard University Press, Cambridge, Mass. Copyright © 2001 by the President and Fellows of Harvard College. Reprinted by permission of the publisher.

Mirjan Damaška, Evidence Law Adrift (1997), published by Yale University Press. Copyright © 1997 by Yale University. Reprinted with permission of the publisher.

James J. Duane, The New Federal Rules of Evidence on Prior Acts of Accused Sex Offenders, published by West Publishing Co. in 157 F.R.D. 95 (1994). Reprinted with permission of the publisher.

David L. Faigman, David H. Kaye, Michael J. Saks & Joseph Sanders, How Good Is Good Enough? Expert Evidence Under *Daubert* and *Kumho*, 50 Case W. Res. L. Rev. 645 (2000). Reprinted with permission of the authors and Case Western Law Review

G. Michael Fenner, The Residual Exception to the Hearsay Rule, 33 Creighton L. Rev. 265 (2000). Reprinted with permission of the author.

Richard D. Friedman, Character Impeachment Evidence: The Asymmetrical Interaction Between Personality and Situation, 43 Duke L.J. 826 (1994). Reprinted with permission of the author and Duke Law Journal

Richard D. Friedman, "E" Is for Eclectic: Multiple Perspectives on Evidence, 87 Va. L. Rev. 2029 (2001). Reprinted with permission.

Victor Gold, Do the Federal Rules of Evidence Matter?, 25 Loyola L.A. L. Rev. 909 (1992). Reprinted with permission of the author and Loyola of Los Angeles Law Review.

Robert H. Hutchins & Donald Slesinger, Some Observations on the Law of Evidence. This article originally appeared at 28 Colum. L. Rev. 432 (1928). Reprinted with permission of Columbia Law Review.

Edward J. Imwinkelried, The Use of Evidence of an Accused's Uncharged Misconduct to Prove Mens Rea. Originally published in 51 Ohio St. L.J. 575 (1990). Reprinted with permission of the author and Ohio State Law Journal.

Jonathan J. Koehler, DNA Matches and Statistics: Important Questions, Surprising Answers, 76 Judicature 222 (1993). Reprinted with permission of the author and the American Judicature Society.

Jonathan J. Koehler, On Conveying the Probative Value of DNA Evidence: Frequencies, Likelihood Ratios, and Error Rates, 67 U. Colo. L. Rev. 859 (1996). Reprinted with permission of the author.

John H. Langbein, Historical Foundations of the Law of Evidence: A View from the Ryder Sources. This article originally appeared at 96 Colum. L. Rev. 1168 (1996). Reprinted with permission of the author and Columbia Law Review

Joseph H. Levie, Hearsay and Conspiracy, 52 Mich. L. Rev. 1159 (1954). Reprinted with permission of the author and Michigan Law Review.

Graham C. Lilly, An Introduction to the Law of Evidence (3d ed. 1996), published by West Publishing Co. Copyright © 1996 by West Publishing Co. Reprinted with permission of the publisher.

Brooks W. MacCracken, The Case of the Anonymous Corpse, published in American Heritage (1968). Copyright © 1968 by American Heritage, Inc. Reprinted by permission of American Heritage, Inc.

Jennifer McMenamin, Judge Bars Use of Fingerprints in Murder Trial, Balt. Sun, Oct. 23, 2007. Reprinted with permission of the Baltimore Sun.

Kevin C. McMunigal & Calvin William Sharpe, Reforming Extrinsic Impeachment, 33 Conn. L. Rev. 363 (2001). Reprinted with permission of the authors and Connecticut Law Review.

Thomas M. Mengler, The Theory of Discretion in the Federal Rules of Evidence, 74 Iowa L. Rev. 413 (1989). Reprinted with permission of the author and Iowa Law Review.

Jennifer Mnookin, The Image of Truth: Photographic Evidence and the Power of Analogy, 10 Yale J.L. & Human. 1 (1998). Reprinted with permission of the author.

Edmund M. Morgan, Admissions, 1 UCLA L. Rev. 18 (1953). Reprinted with permission.

Edmund M. Morgan, Basic Problems of Evidence (1961), published by the Joint Committee on Continuing Legal Education of the American Law Institute and the American Bar Association. Copyright © 1954, 1957, 1961 by the American Law Institute. Reprinted with the permission of the American Law Institute–American Bar Association Committee on Continuing Professional Education.

Andrew J. Morris, Federal Rule of Evidence 404(B): The Fictitious Ban on Character Reasoning from Other Crime Evidence. Published originally in 17 Rev. Litig. 181 (1998). Copyright © 1998 by the University of Texas Law School Publications, Inc. Reprinted with permission of the publisher.

Robert P. Mosteller, Testing the Testimonial Concept and Exceptions to Confrontation: "A Little Child Shall Lead Them," 82 Ind. L.J. 917 (2007). Reprinted with permission of the author and Indiana Law Journal.

Christopher B. Mueller & Laird C. Kirkpatrick, Evidence (2003). Copyright © 2003 by Aspen Publishers. Reprinted with permission.

Erin Murphy, The New Forensics: Criminal Justice, False Certainty, and the Second Generation of Scientific Evidence, 95 Cal. L. Rev. 721 (2007). Reprinted with permission of the author and California Law Review.

Dale A. Nance, The Best Evidence Principle, 73 Iowa L. Rev. 227 (1998). Reprinted with permission of the author and Iowa Law Review.

Aviva Orenstein, No Bad Men: A Feminist Analysis of Character Evidence in Rape Trials, 49 Hastings L.J. 663 (1998). Copyright © 1998 by the University of California, Hastings College of the Law. Reprinted with permission of the author and Hastings Law Journal.

Roger C. Park, The Crime Bill of 1994 and the Law of Character Evidence: Congress Was Right About Consent Defense Cases. This excerpt was originally published in the Fordham Urban Law Journal as Roger C. Park, The Crime Bill of 1994 and the Law of Character Evidence: Congress Was Right About Consent Defense Cases, 22 Fordham Urban L.J. 271 (1995). Reprinted with permission of the author and Fordham Urban Law Journal.

Roger C. Park, Evidence Scholarship, Old and New, 75 Minn. L. Rev. 849 (1991). Reprinted with permission of the author and Minnesota Law Review

Roger C. Park, David P. Leonard & Steven H. Goldberg, Evidence Law (1998), published by West Group. Copyright © 1998 by West Group. Reprinted with permission of the publisher.

Merrill D. Peterson, Lincoln in American Memory (1994), published by Oxford University Press. Copyright © 1994 by Merrill Peterson. Used by permission of Oxford University Press, Inc.

Daniel C. Richman, Old Chief v. United States: Stipulating Away Prosecutorial Accountability?, 83 Va. L. Rev. 939 (1997). Reprinted with permission of the author.

D. Michael Riseinger, Navigating Expert Reliability: Are Criminal Standards of Certainty Being Left on the Dock?, 64 Albany L. Rev. 99 (2000). Reprinted with permission of the authors and Albany Law Review.

Paul F. Rothstein, Intellectual Coherence in an Evidence Code, 28 Loyola L.A. L. Rev. 1295 (1995). Reprinted with permission of the author and Loyola of Los Angeles Law Review.

Michael J. Saks, Banishing Ipse Dixit: The Impact of *Kumbo Tire* on Forensic Identification Science, 57 Wash. & Lee L. Rev. 879 (2000). Reprinted with permission of the author and Washington & Lee Law Review.

Michael J. Saks & Jonathan J. Koehler, What DNA "Fingerprinting" Can Teach the Law About the Rest of Forensic Science, 13 Cardozo L. Rev. 361 (1991). Reprinted with permission of the authors and Cardozo Law Review.

Steven A. Saltzberg, Michael M. Martin & Daniel J. Capra, Federal Rules of Evidence Manual (7th ed. 1998), published by Lexis Law Publishing. Copyright © 1998 by Matthew Bender & Company, Inc., a member of the LexisNexis Group. Reprinted with permission of the publisher.

William H. Simon: The Kaye Scholer Affair: The Lawyer's Duty of Candor and the Bar's Temptations of Evasion and Apology, 23 Law & Soc. Inquiry 243 (1998) by the University of Chicago Press. Copyright © 1998 by the American Bar Foundation. Reprinted with permission.

David A. Sklanksy & Stephen C. Yeazell, Comparative Law Without Leaving Home: What Civil Procedure Can Teach Criminal Procedure and Vice Versa, 94 Geo. L.J. 683 (2006). Reprinted with permission the authors and Georgetown Law Review.

Christopher Slobogin, Doubts About Daubert: Psychiatric Anecdata as a Case Study, 57 Wash. & Lee L. Rev. 919 (2000). Reprinted with permission of the author and Washington & Lee Law Review.

Christopher Slobogin, The Story of Rule 410 and United States v. Mezzanatto: Using Plea Statements at Trial in Evidence Stories (2006), Foundation Press. Reprinted with permission of Foundation Press.

State Bar of California, California Bar Examination (1998). Reprinted with permission of the publisher.

John W. Strong, Consensual Modifications of the Rules of Evidence: The Limits of Party Autonomy in an Adversary System, 80 Neb. L. Rev. 159 (2001). Reprinted with permission of Nebraska Law Review.

John W. Strong, ed., McCormick on Evidence (5th ed. 1999), published by West Group. Copyright © 1954, 1972, 1984, 1987 by West Publishing Co.; copyright © 1999 by West Group. Reprinted with permission of the publisher.

Eleanor Swift, One Hundred Years of Evidence Law Reform: Thayer's Triumph, 88 Cal. L. Rev. 2437 (2000). Copyright © 2000 by the California Law Review. Reprinted by permission of the author and the University of California, Berkeley.

Laurence H. Tribe, Triangulating Hearsay, 87 Harv. L. Rev. 957 (1974). Copyright © 1974 by the Harvard Law Review Association. Reprinted with permission of the author and the Harvard Law Review Association.

Jon R. Waltz, The Present-Sense Impression Exception to the Rule Against Hearsay: Origins and Attributes, 66 Iowa L. Rev. 869 (1981). Reprinted with permission of the author and Iowa Law Review.

Glen Weissenberger, The Former Testimony Exception: A Study in Rulemaking, Judicial Revisionism, and the Separation of Powers, 67 N.C. L. Rev. 295 (1989). Reprinted with permission of the author.

Glen Weissenberger & James J. Duane, Federal Rules of Evidence (5th ed. 2007). Reprinted with permission. Copyright 2007 Matthew Bender & Company, Inc., a member of the LexisNexis Group. All rights reserved.

John Shepard Wiley Jr., Taming Patent: Six Steps for Surviving Scary Patent Cases, UCLA L. Rev. 1413 (2002). Reprinted with permission of the author.

Charles Alan Wright & Kenneth W. Graham Jr., Federal Practice and Procedure: Evidence (1980), published by West Publishing Co. Copyright © 1980 by West Publishing Co. Reprinted with permission of West Publishing Co.

EVIDENCE

INTRODUCTION TO
EVIDENCE LAW

*"I took aim, pulled the trigger, and then,
suddenly, shots rang out."*

A. GOOD NEWS AND BAD NEWS

The Law of Evidence, which I now propose to investigate, is also one of the landmarks of civilization which it is impossible for the philosophical inquirer to overlook.

> John George Phillimore, *The History and Principles of the Law of Evidence as Illustrating Our Social Progress* (1850)

[T]he system, taken in the aggregate, is repugnant to the ends of justice; and . . . this is true of almost every rule that has ever been laid down on the subject of evidence.

> Jeremy Bentham, *Rationale of Judicial Evidence* (1827)

Nobody can fairly pretend to make the Anglo-American law of evidence easy, because it is essentially very difficult.

> John MacArthur Maguire, *Evidence: Common Sense and Common Law* (1947)

[F]oreigners complain that its doctrines and practices are arcane and that they deviate too far from ordinary modes of investigating facts. But even in these laments there is a soupçon of uneasy respect for the exotic charms of the common law.

> Mirjan R. Damaška, *Evidence Law Adrift* (1997)

Foreigners are not the only ones intrigued by the Anglo-American law of evidence. Every night on television screens across the nation, fictional lawyers squabble over arcane rules of proof, captivating viewers who may never have dreamed of attending law school. Contributory negligence and implied warranties rarely surface in prime time, but hearsay doctrine and testimonial privileges come up regularly. Evidence law is a fixture of popular culture.

And for excellent reason. The rules of evidence dictate how and when facts may be proved or disproved at a trial. They regulate, that is to say, our most dramatic and most heavily ritualized process for untangling human affairs gone wrong—a process to which many lawyers happily devote much of their careers. Evidence law constitutes the end product of centuries of effort to make that process as fair, as accurate, and as conclusive as possible. Opinions differ regarding the success of those efforts. But as social artifacts alone the rules of evidence hold a lasting fascination.

For lawyers, of course, the interest is more than academic. The rules of evidence are the nuts and bolts of courtroom work. Mastering them hardly turns you into a skilled trial lawyer. That takes a good deal more. But without a basic knowledge of evidence law, you cannot even begin to find your way around a courtroom.

Not all lawyers try cases. But all lawyers need familiarity with the rules of evidence, and not just to pass the bar exam. Litigators, even if they are not trial lawyers, need to understand what happens if a case goes to trial. And every lawyer, even one who never litigates, works in the shadow of litigation. All effective legal work is informed in part by the contingency of litigation, the contingency of litigation is in part the contingency of trial, and the contingency of trial is strongly shaped by evidence law.

Then, too, careers in the law often take unexpected turns. It always pays to be prepared. Trial work is undeniably exciting, and even lawyers who plan never to see the inside of a courtroom can wind up trying cases and enjoying it. It happened, for example, to the author of this book.

The rules of evidence are thus critically important, particularly for lawyers, and of extraordinary intellectual interest. They may not be "impossible for the philosophical inquirer to overlook," but they amply reward study. And evidence cases can be entertaining, too. They are rooted, after all, in the drama of the courtroom. For all these reasons, few students find evidence law boring, and many greatly enjoy learning it.

That is the good news.

Now for the bad news. Evidence has a reputation as a particularly challenging subject, and the reputation is not entirely undeserved. Several features of evidence law can make it difficult to study. You might as well know about them from the start.

First, evidence law often operates in technical and counterintuitive ways. Some evidence doctrines do take the mushy form familiar to you from other law school courses: "Do X when it is sensible." But many other rules of evidence are considerably more complicated, and they often produce surprising results. The hearsay rule, in particular, can make even treacherous doctrines like the rule against perpetuities look commonsensical by comparison. (That is one reason why the hearsay chapter is by far the longest chapter in this book.)

Second, the rules of evidence frequently cannot be applied without reference to the substantive law governing a particular dispute—the law of contracts, torts, property, or crimes. You have probably already studied these areas of the law, but your knowledge may be rusty or incomplete. This can make it difficult to follow the application of evidence law to specific fact patterns, either real or hypothetical.

Third, there is the terminology. All fields of law employ specialized vocabularies. Evidence law is not unusual in this respect. But the specialized vocabulary of evidence law is particularly large, and the same word or phrase often has two or three completely different meanings. Even the most basic terms of evidence law—terms like "relevant," "competent," "collateral," or "inissue"—sometimes show a maddening slipperiness. Lawyers and judges talking about evidence law sometimes use these terms in their ordinary, everyday senses, and sometimes use them in narrower, more technical ways. It can be hard to keep the definitions straight.

Fourth, beyond matters of terminology, the nature of evidence law itself can seem slippery. At times it can be hard to know exactly what you are studying. What exactly *is* evidence law? Is it a set of common law doctrines? Statutory rules? Constitutional dictates? Applied logic?

A few decades ago this kind of confusion was less likely. Evidence law was almost entirely judge-made and operated within few constitutional constraints. Since then the constitutional constraints have increased, but not by much. The larger change has been the advent of modern codes of evidence. Following years of study, California enacted a comprehensive and influential code of evidence rules in 1965. That same year, an Advisory Committee of judges, lawyers, and law professors appointed by the Supreme Court began drafting federal rules of evidence, much as similar committees earlier had worked out the Federal Rules of Civil Procedure and the Federal Rules of Criminal Procedure. The result was the Federal Rules of Evidence, which were endorsed by the Supreme Court in 1972, enacted by Congress (with significant amendments) in 1974, and signed into law in 1975. Most states now have evidence codes modeled closely on the federal rules. California has retained its own code, though, and in a few states—New York, for example—evidence law remains uncodified.

When studying evidence law you can therefore be at sea regarding what you should be learning, particularly if you plan to practice in a state, like California or New York, that does not have an evidence code tracking the Federal Rules of Evidence. Should you concentrate on the federal rules, which have become so widely influential? Should you focus on the common law doctrines those rules codify? Should you pay greatest attention to the rules in your own state?

Nor is this all. Most questions regarding the admissibility of evidence are resolved by trial judges without written opinions, and appellate reversals of these decisions are relatively rare. Many evidence rules expressly vest broad discretion in trial judges to admit or exclude evidence, and even when appellate judges conclude that a trial judge erred, they frequently deem the error harmless. Therefore the law on the books often matters less than the law as trial judges apply it. As Professor Maguire put it, "evidence is essentially a matter to be threshed out between counsel and judge in the trial court. The wheat stays there; what goes up in the appellate record seems pretty much chaff." What, then, should you care about: what appellate courts say, or how trial courts act?

There is a fifth and final reason why evidence law can be particularly hard to learn. The rules of evidence operate against the backdrop of a more basic set of rules regarding the structure of the Anglo-American trial: rules about the sequence of proof, when and how the lawyers may address the jury, and so on. These rules are matters more of convention than of law, and they have remained largely uncodified. The rules of evidence, and cases applying those rules, often assume familiarity with these conventions without explaining them. This is fine for the principal users of evidence law: trial judges and trial lawyers. They know how trials are conducted. But you may not have had a separate course in trial procedure. You probably have a rough acquaintance with trials. You have read about them and have seen them dramatized. But without a somewhat firmer grasp of Anglo-American trial conventions, the rules of evidence can be hard to decipher.

Now for more good news. The special difficulties surrounding the study of evidence are surmountable, particularly when they are recognized from the outset. Evidence law is easier to learn if you expect it sometimes to operate in technical and counterintuitive ways; if you understand that evidence rules often cannot be applied without reference to the substantive law of contracts, torts, property, and crimes; and if you keep on the lookout for terms with multiple definitions. This is why these sources of confusion have been described at the very beginning of this book. Forewarned is forearmed.

Some additional background will also help. Evidence instructors generally provide their own guidance regarding where students should focus their attention, but following that guidance—or making one's way without it—requires a certain basic comprehension of the nature and development of evidence law. And it helps also to understand, at the outset, the rudimentary conventions of Anglo-American trials, as well as certain implications of those conventions. The remainder of this chapter takes up each of these matters.

B. THE NATURE AND DEVELOPMENT OF EVIDENCE LAW

Evidence law today is overwhelmingly statutory. Evidentiary questions in federal court are governed by the Federal Rules of Evidence, adopted in 1975 and since periodically amended. The vast majority of states have enacted codes of evidence rules closely modeled on the federal rules; typically even the numbering of the rules is the same. The influence of the Federal Rules of Evidence, like that of the Federal Rules of Civil Procedure, therefore extends far beyond the world of federal litigation. So any sensible study of evidence law today must focus first and foremost on the Federal Rules of Evidence. (They are also on the Multistate Bar Examination.)

Those rules, however, do not come out of a vacuum. To study the Federal Rules of Evidence intelligently and to make full sense of them, it helps to understand their complicated origin.

Until a few decades ago, American rules of evidence were almost entirely a matter of common law, hammered out by generations of judges and lawyers. Efforts to organize and systematize this mass of rulings began in the early twentieth century with the writings of James Bradley Thayer, who taught evidence and constitutional law at Harvard Law School. Those efforts picked up steam with the work of Thayer's student, John Henry Wigmore, who was for many years Dean of Northwestern University Law School. Wigmore's mammoth treatise on the law of evidence is not only the most famous work ever written in the field, it is widely thought to be the most influential treatise ever written on *any* branch of American law. Wigmore also tried his hand at codifying the rules of evidence, but the long, detailed result attracted little attention.

In 1942 the American Law Institute—the same group that later produced the Model Penal Code—published a Model Code of Evidence. The drafter, Edmund Morgan, taught evidence at Harvard along with John Maguire, the scholar who memorably described evidence law as "essentially very difficult." Professor Morgan's Model Code was heavily reformist. Like the Model Penal Code, it sought not to restate the law but to rationalize it.

It largely eliminated, for example, the hearsay rule. But the Model Code of Evidence was never adopted anywhere. Nor did it leave any lingering mark on evidence law.

In 1953 the National Commissioners on Uniform State Laws—the organization that had collaborated with the American Law Institute on the Uniform Commercial Code—proposed Uniform Rules of Evidence, which largely codified existing law without seeking to reform it. The Uniform Rules were endorsed by the American Bar Association and, more significantly, they inspired and served as the model for comprehensive evidence codes actually adopted in a few states—among them, eventually, California. The California Code of Evidence, enacted by the legislature 1965, followed a decade of study by the state's Law Revision Commission. It stuck even closer to prior law than the Uniform Rules and proved even more influential.

Meanwhile, the Judicial Conference of the United States—a nationwide group of federal judges that meets annually by congressional command— began in 1961 to urge the promulgation of Federal Rules of Evidence, to supplement the Federal Rules of Civil Procedure and the Federal Rules of Criminal Procedure. The Supreme Court had issued each of these earlier sets of rules pursuant to the Rules Enabling Act of 1934 after each had been drafted by an Advisory Committee appointed by the Court. In 1965 the Court, acting through Chief Justice Earl Warren, likewise appointed an Advisory Committee of judges, lawyers and law professors to draft Federal Rules of Evidence.

The principal task of drafting both the rules and the official commentary fell to the Committee's Reporter, Professor Edward Cleary of the University of Illinois College of Law. Learning from earlier efforts at codification, Cleary and the Advisory Committee sought to simplify and to clarify existing law but not to alter it dramatically. Following several preliminary drafts, two rounds of public comments, and approval by the Judicial Conference, the Committee gave its final product to the Supreme Court in 1972, and early the following year the Court forwarded the rules to Congress.

Under the Rules Enabling Act, the rules were to become effective 90 days after their transmittal by the Court, barring objection from both Houses of Congress. This is how the Federal Rules of Civil Procedure and the Federal Rules of Criminal Procedure had become law. But Congress was uneasy about the proposed rules of evidence, particularly those concerning privileges—a controversial topic in early 1973, with the Watergate scandal unfolding and President Nixon aggressively asserting executive privilege. Congress therefore declared that the evidence rules would not take effect unless and until Congress expressly approved them. Both Houses then held hearings on the rules and amended them substantially and in different ways. Both Houses dropped most of the privilege rules. A Conference Committee reconciled the two bills, and the resulting rules were approved by both Houses in December 1974 and signed into law by President Ford in January 1975. They became effective July 1, 1975.

Since 1975, the Federal Rules of Evidence have been amended repeatedly. In some instances Congress has amended the rules on its own, acting through new federal legislation. In other cases amendments have been proposed by a new Advisory Committee on the Federal Rules of Evidence, created in 1993 and appointed by the Judicial Conference rather than the

Supreme Court. By statute, amendments proposed by the Advisory Committee must be approved by the Judicial Conference and the Supreme Court. And the Rules Enabling Act now contains a permanent exception, codified at 28 U.S.C. §2074(b), to the general principle that procedural rules proposed by the Supreme Court take effect unless Congress objects: Rules regarding evidentiary privilege "have no force or effect unless approved by Act of Congress."

This story has been told in detail here to make several important points. First, although modern evidence law is overwhelmingly statutory, the most influential statute—the Federal Rules of Evidence—largely codifies preexisting common law. So understanding evidence law under the federal rules and their state counterparts often will require examination of common law materials predating codification. Second, these materials will include both judicial decisions and scholarly commentary, because law professors—especially Wigmore—have played an unusually prominent role in the development of evidence law. Third, the recent history of evidence law is littered with unsuccessful attempts at codification, including the privilege provisions that Congress dropped from the Federal Rules of Evidence. These rejected rules play an ambiguous role in evidence law. Sometimes they are consulted as thoughtful and persuasive statements of what the law is or should be, and sometimes just the opposite—because the rules ultimately did not find favor, they are taken as good indications of what the law is not and should not be.

How then is a topic of evidence law best studied? Start, obviously, with the pertinent provisions of the Federal Rules of Evidence. Your instructor may also ask you to examine the corresponding sections of the California Evidence Code, to highlight what is distinctive in the federal rules. Most sections of this book therefore begin with citations to the applicable provisions of the Federal Rules of Evidence (abbreviated "F.R.E.") and the California Evidence Code ("C.E.C."). The citations are typically followed by excerpts from the legislative history of the federal rule: the official commentary of the Advisory Committee, or pertinent portions of the congressional reports, or both. These materials are important both because they often clarify the thinking behind the rule, and because courts often treat them as authoritative—although that practice recently has grown more controversial.

Like most rules, though, evidence rules cannot be grasped in the abstract, even with the guidance of their legislative history. To understand a rule one must see it in application, and preferably in several applications. With evidence law, this means seeing both how trial courts use the rule and how appellate courts review those uses. This book therefore includes excerpts from lots of cases. Generally the excerpts are short, on the theory that it is more helpful to see the rough outline of three applications than one application in detail. Partly this is because different fact patterns can raise different problems, and partly it is because different judges can see the rule in different ways.

The book also includes frequent excerpts from scholarly commentary on the rules of evidence, both treatises and law review articles. Sometimes this material is included because it summarizes the cases or explains a principle better than any single judicial opinion can do, or even a series of judicial opinions. Sometimes it is included because it sets forth a viewpoint that has been particularly influential in the development of evidence law, even if the current rules reject it. And sometimes it is included simply to provide food for thought regarding the wisdom of the rules of evidence in their current form.

Many of the sections in this book conclude with problems. The problems range in difficulty. Some simply test understanding of the rules and ability to apply them in straightforward situations. Others highlight ambiguities in the rules and seek to provoke reflection on how they should best be applied.

All of the materials in this book—the legislative history, the cases, the scholarly commentary, and the problems—aim to help you understand the origins of the modern rules, the manner in which the rules are applied, and the continuing controversies surrounding the rules. The materials are best studied with a copy of the applicable rules always at the side. This is one reason why the rules themselves, despite their centrality, are not reprinted here; another reason is that the rules are frequently amended, and you should consult the most recent versions.

C. THE ANGLO-AMERICAN TRIAL

Many of the doctrines now codified in federal and state rules of evidence are intelligible only by reference to the distinctive features of the Anglo-American trial. The rules of evidence were crafted largely by generations of trial judges and trial lawyers, who were hammering out basic conventions of trial practice at the same time. It is often difficult to understand one without knowing something about the other.

The basic rules of trial practice—who asks questions when, and so on—generally have remained matters of custom rather than law. For the most part the law lets trial judges conduct trials the way they see fit. The Federal Rules of Evidence, in particular, say very little about the stages of a trial beyond instructing, in Rule 611, that trial judges should "exercise reasonable control over the mode and order of interrogating witnesses." Chapter Six of this book examines in detail the few requirements that the Federal Rules of Evidence *do* impose on the overall conduct of trials. At the outset, though, it will help to have a more general sense of what traditionally happens at a trial.

Before the trial actually begins, the judge often hears motions pertaining to how it will proceed. Often these are requests to rule certain evidence admissible or inadmissible. Evidentiary motions heard before trial are called motions *in limine*, to distinguish them from objections raised during the trial, when the evidence is actually presented. ("*In limine*" is Latin for "at the threshold.") Not all motions *in limine* are actually resolved before trial.

Sometimes the judge defers decision, because he or she wants to see how the rest of the evidence unfolds.

After the pretrial motions have been addressed and either resolved or deferred, jury selection typically starts—if there is to be a jury. If the parties agree not to use a jury, or if neither side has a right to a jury, the judge holds a *bench trial*, rendering the verdict himself or herself. But most trials of serious matters in the United States, whether criminal or civil, involve a jury. The jury usually is picked through a process called *voir dire*, from the old law French for "to speak the truth." (The same term is used for preliminary questioning of witnesses to see whether they are competent to testify.) Potential jurors are questioned about their backgrounds and outlooks, sometimes by the judge and sometimes by the lawyers. Each side then can exercise a certain number of "peremptory challenges" to disqualify jurors without giving any reason, and can ask the judge to disqualify other jurors "for cause"—i.e., because they appear biased or otherwise unfit for service. Once 12 jurors have passed through this screening, the jury takes an oath to carry out its duties faithfully and is deemed "empanelled." At this point the judge may give the jury some preliminary instructions about the law they will be asked to apply. Then the trial proper begins.

The first stage is *opening statements*. The prosecutor or the lawyer for the plaintiff tells the jury what he or she expects the evidence to show, and then the lawyer for the defendant has the opportunity to make a similar statement or to delay it until later. If there is more than one plaintiff or more than one defendant and they have separate counsel, the lawyers for the plaintiffs all give their opening statements first, and then the lawyers for the defendants.

In theory, an opening statement is not evidence. Indeed, juries are routinely instructed that *nothing* the lawyers say during the trial is evidence. The point of an opening statement is just to give the jury a roadmap of the evidence, not to supply evidence itself. And in theory an opening statement must be descriptive rather than argumentative. "The defendant shot him" is permitted. "The defendant shot him in cold blood, like swatting a fly" is not. In practice, of course, the line between description and argument is often indistinct, and different judges draw the line in different ways.

After opening statements, the prosecutor or the plaintiff's lawyer presents his or her *case in chief*. The lawyer does this by calling witnesses to the stand, questioning them under oath, and often also by offering *physical evidence*—documents, photographs, contraband, bloody clothing, etc. The order in which witnesses are called is generally decided by the lawyer. After the lawyer finishes questioning a witness he or she has called, the lawyer or lawyers for the other side have a chance to do the same. The questioning by the lawyer who called the witness is called "direct examination," and the questioning by the other side is called "cross-examination." After cross-examination, the lawyer who called the witness can ask further questions; this is called "redirect examination." Redirect examination is followed by "re-cross-examination," and then, if necessary, by further redirect examination, and so on.

With important exceptions, which will be taken up in Chapter Six, leading questions are allowed on cross-examination and re-cross-examination
but not on direct examination or redirect examination. A leading question
is a question that suggests the desired answer, like, "Did your father then
throw the computer through the window?" or, "She ate her cereal with a fork,
didn't she?" The scope of cross-examination, though, is limited to the credibility of the witness and to any matters raised on direct examination. The
scope of redirect examination likewise is limited to the scope of cross-
examination, and so on. Leading questions and the scope of interrogation
are among the few issues of trial procedure that the Federal Rules of Evidence
do address, albeit quite loosely. The pertinent provisions are in Rule 611 and
are discussed in Chapter Six.

When lawyers object to questions posed by opposing lawyers or
answers given by witnesses, they often do so in language that only loosely
tracks the doctrines of evidence law. Some standard objections, like "leading" or "hearsay," refer directly to particular rules of evidence. But other
standard objections, like "argumentative" or "asked and answered," appeal
first and foremost to traditions of trial practice, and only indirectly to the
codified rules embracing those traditions.

Physical evidence will be discussed in detail in Chapter Eleven, but a
word or two more should be said about it now. A physical object, whether a
business letter or a bag of cocaine, is introduced into evidence in two steps.
First it is *marked for identification*, for example as "Plaintiff's Exhibit 3."
This can take place before trial or during trial, but it generally must occur
before the item is shown to a witness. Marking the exhibit not only makes
reference to it easier; it also makes the exhibit a permanent part of the record
in the case, available for inspection by reviewing courts. But it does not entitle
the parties to show the exhibit to the jury. That requires *introducing* the
exhibit. Once the necessary predicate has been established—what lawyers
call "laying the foundation"—the party seeking to use a marked exhibit as
proof asks the judge to admit it into evidence. What constitutes the necessary
predicate, and the possible grounds for objection to the admission of physical
evidence, are matters taken up in Chapter Eleven. (Judges and trial lawyers
often speak of "laying the foundation" for testimony, as well as for physical
evidence. In either case, the phrase refers to the process of satisfying whatever
requirements the rules set for introduction of the evidence.)

Evidentiary objections raised during trial may be resolved in a variety of
ways, depending on the judge and on the complexity of the issues involved.
The judge may simply sustain or deny the objection. The judge may ask
opposing counsel for a brief response and then make a ruling. The judge
may ask the parties to accompany the court reporter to "sidebar"—i.e., the
side of the judge's bench opposite the jury, where the judge can confer with
the lawyers out of the jury's earshot. Or the judge may defer consideration
of the matter until the jury is out of the courtroom.

After the prosecutor or plaintiff's lawyer announces to the judge that
the case in chief is concluded, the defendant's lawyer may move to dismiss

the case for insufficient evidence. To grant the motion the judge must conclude not just that the evidence is unconvincing, but that no rational jury could find that it satisfies the applicable standard of proof: "beyond a reasonable doubt" in a criminal case, and either "preponderance of the evidence" or "clear and convincing" in a civil case.

If the motion is denied, the defendant then presents his or her case. If the defendant's lawyer did not make an opening statement at the outset of the trial, he or she can do so now. The defendant's case then goes forward much as the plaintiff's or prosecutor's case proceeded: direct examination, cross-examination, redirect examination, etc.

After the defendant's case is concluded, the prosecutor or plaintiff typically presents a *rebuttal case.* In theory the evidence here must respond to evidence presented in the defendant's case, just as redirect examination is limited to the scope of cross-examination. But trial judges sometimes waive these limitations. Judges also sometimes give defendants the opportunity to present a *surrebuttal case*, responding to the rebuttal case, and the plaintiff or prosecutor may then be allowed to present evidence responding to the surrebuttal case.

After all the evidence has been presented, the lawyers make *closing arguments*. Typically the prosecutor or plaintiff's lawyer goes first, then the defendant's lawyer argues, and then the prosecutor or plaintiff's lawyer gives a *rebuttal argument.* Unlike opening statements, closing arguments are not restricted even in theory to factual statements, but they *are* restricted to claims based on the evidence that has been introduced. Following closing statements, the judge typically gives the jury additional instructions. The jury then deliberates in secret and, if it can, agrees on a verdict.

Several distinctive features of the Anglo-American trial have important implications for evidence law. The first is the jury. Although the rules of evidence apply to bench trials as well as to jury trials, many of the rules seem shaped by concern that certain kinds of proof might unduly influence amateur fact finders—and perhaps also by the need to avoid long interruptions in the trial, given that jurors serve only temporarily. The second is a strong preference for *viva voce* proof—i.e., testimony from live, sworn witnesses, who are subject to cross-examination and whose demeanor the jury can observe.

The third is the pervasive control lawyers exercise over the conduct of the trial. Subject only to generally loose supervision by the judge, lawyers decide what witnesses to call, what questions to ask, what physical evidence to introduce, and in what order to proceed. Most evidence rules take this control for granted, and some actually strengthen it. For example, the introduction of evidence forbidden by the rules generally will not be ground for reversal unless the lawyer for the opposing party knows to raise an objection at trial and chooses to do so; trial lawyers can effectively waive rules of evidence they do not wish to enforce. The system assumes that fair trials and accurate verdicts are best secured by giving trained advocates substantial leeway in assembling the evidence. Of course that leeway also serves the professional interests of trial lawyers, and perhaps also of trial judges—the two groups most responsible for our current rules of evidence and trial practice. So keep a certain skepticism about the extraordinary power and responsibility our system vests in trial lawyers.

D. The Role of the Trial Judge

There is a fourth and final distinctive feature of Anglo-American trials worth noting at the outset of a course in evidence law: the central role of the presiding judge. Anglo-American trial lawyers have wide latitude to craft their cases as they see fit, but there are important constraints on that latitude, and those constraints are imposed by the trial judge. Evidence law, in particular, grants the trial judge both extensive authority and extensive discretion. The rules describing the role of the trial judge are fundamental to the operation of the entire system.

1. The Trial Judge's Authority

[F.R.E. 104(a); C.E.C. §§310, 400, 405]

ADVISORY COMMITTEE NOTE TO F.R.E. 104(a)

The applicability of a particular rule of evidence often depends upon the existence of a condition. Is the alleged expert a qualified physician? Is a witness whose former testimony is offered unavailable? Was a stranger present during a conversation between attorney and client? In each instance the admissibility of evidence will turn upon the answer to the question of the existence of the condition. Accepted practice, incorporated in the rule, places on the judge the responsibility for these determinations. . . .

If the question is factual in nature, the judge will of necessity receive evidence pro and con on the issue. The rule provides that the rules of evidence in general do not apply to this process. McCormick §53, p. 123, n. 8, points out that the authorities are "scattered and inconclusive," and observes:

> Should the exclusionary law of evidence, "the child of the jury system" in Thayer's phrase, be applied to this hearing before the judge? Sound sense backs the view that it should not, and that the judge should be empowered to hear any relevant evidence, such as affidavits or other reliable hearsay.

This view is reinforced by practical necessity in certain situations. An item, offered and objected to, may itself be considered in ruling on admissibility, though not yet admitted in evidence. Thus, the content of an asserted declaration against interest must be considered in ruling whether it is against interest. Again, common practice calls for considering the testimony of a witness, particularly a child, in determining competency. . . .

2. The Trial Judge's Discretion

[F.R.E. 103; C.E.C. §§353, 354]

ROGER C. PARK, DAVID P. LEONARD & STEVEN H. GOLDBERG, EVIDENCE LAW

§§12.03 & 12.04, at 543-548 (1998)

The Federal Rules of Evidence, Federal Rules of Civil Procedure, and Federal Rules of Criminal Procedure all mandate that courts disregard errors that do not "affect the substantial rights of the parties." Thus, reversible or prejudicial errors are those which affect the substantial rights of parties. . . . The definition of substantial rights is vague and courts review the entire record in making the determination of prejudice. . . . Courts differ on what degree of certainty that the error did not affect the outcome is required to find an error harmless. . . . For example, the Ninth Circuit uses a "more probably harmless than not" test for nonconstitutional errors. The Third Circuit standard is more onerous, requiring reversal unless it is "highly probable" that the verdict would have been the same if the error had not occurred. In the Fifth Circuit, reversal is required unless the court is "sure that the error did not influence the jury, or had but slight effect." In the case of constitutional errors, the Supreme Court has held that the prosecution has the burden of proving that the error was harmless beyond a reasonable doubt.

Courts generally apply the same standard for harmless error in civil cases as in criminal cases, although some cases argue that the standard should differ in accordance with the differing standards of proof applicable to civil and criminal cases. . . .

When no objection was made at trial, the appellate court will reverse only if it finds "plain error." . . . Plain error is not easily defined and allows for substantial judicial discretion. Courts employing the doctrine have found plain error when . . . [for example,] the error was "particularly egregious," a "miscarriage of justice" resulted from the error, or the error deprived the defendant of a fair trial. . . . Some courts require that the error be obvious in the record.

STEPHEN A. SALTZBURG, MICHAEL M. MARTIN & DANIEL J. CAPRA, FEDERAL RULES OF EVIDENCE MANUAL

1:103-10–103-11 (9th ed. 2006)

Most appellants do not even get the opportunity to test the harmfulness of error because the deferential standard of review employed . . . makes it extremely difficult to prove error on an evidentiary question in

14   Chapter 1.   Introduction to Evidence Law

the first place. While pure issues of Rule construction are reviewed *de novo*, there are very few such issues that arise in practice. Mixed questions of law and fact are also reviewed *de novo*, and they arise with somewhat more frequency than pure questions of law; for example, the question whether a communication is protected by a privilege is usually a mixed question of law and fact. Still, the vast majority of evidentiary rulings are reviewed under the Trial-Court-friendly abuse of discretion standard, even where the claim of error has been properly preserved. . . . All in all, the chances of reversal on the ground of an evidentiary error are slim indeed.

UNITED STATES v. WALTON

217 F.3d 443 (7th Cir. 2000)

COFFEY, Circuit Judge.

We review a trial judge's determination of the admissibility of evidence under the abuse of discretion standard. "We afford great deference to the trial court's determination of the admissibility of evidence because of the trial judge's first-hand exposure to the witnesses and the evidence as a whole, and because of the judge's familiarity with the case and ability to gauge the impact of the evidence in the context of the entire proceeding." *United States v. Van Dreel*, 155 F.3d 902, 905 (7th Cir. 1998). Indeed, "[a]ppellants who challenge evidentiary rulings of the district court are like rich men who wish to enter the Kingdom: their prospects compare with those of camels who wish to pass through the eye of the needle." [*United States v. Glecier*, 923 F.2d 496, 503 (7th Cir.) (Bauer, J.), *cert. denied*, 502 U.S. 810 (1991).]

BANDERA v. CITY OF QUINCY

344 F.3d 47 (1st Cir. 2003)

BOUDIN, Chief Judge.

This is an appeal by the City of Quincy from a jury verdict against the city in favor of [the former executive director of its Community Policing Commission,] Kathleen Bandera. The jury awarded Bandera $135,000 in punitive damages for sexual harassment. . . .

At trial, Bandera testified in detail as to her experience and . . . also adduced testimony from a number of witnesses including Nancy Coletta, a female police officer in the Quincy Police Department . . . who had filed then-pending sexual harassment claims of her own against the police department. . . .

Prior to trial, when Coletta was identified as a witness for Bandera, defendants anticipated that Coletta among others would be asked to describe her own experiences with the police and thus moved *in limine* for an order limiting or excluding such testimony on the ground that it was irrelevant or, if relevant, unduly prejudicial under Federal Rule of Evidence 403. The district judge denied the motion without discussion.

At trial Coletta gave testimony of two different types. Primarily, she described the harassment to which she herself had been subject. . . . In addition, Coletta was allowed to testify over objections by the defense as to how Coletta felt about, and assessed, Bandera's own allegations. . . .

Coletta's recitation of her own experiences was relevant . . . to show liability on the part of supervisory officers . . . and also on the city for a pattern of knowing toleration of harassment by its subordinates. . . . Coletta's testimony as to her own assessment of Bandera's experience is quite a different matter. . . . [S]o far as it appears, Coletta had no actual knowledge of what had happened to Bandera, and her assessments of what Bandera reported to have happened and the psychological impact on Bandera were wholly inappropriate opinion testimony. Fed. R. Evid. 701. . . . Coletta was not qualified as an expert on anything and her assessments were not the limited kind of opinion testimony deemed helpful to a jury (*e.g.*, an estimate of car speed or whether a defendant was intoxicated) but simply jury argument offered from the witness stand. The testimony should certainly not have been admitted.

If the basic objection—improper opinion testimony by a lay witness—had been preserved, we might be tempted to reverse. Quite possibly this phase of the testimony had fairly limited impact: Coletta's assessment of Bandera's situation was nothing like so graphic as Coletta's admissible testimony as to her own experience; her opinions as to Bandera's experience were mildly phrased; and the jury was far more likely to base its judgment on Bandera's own detailed recitation of what had happened to her. Still, whether the testimony's admission could be described safely as harmless error is open to doubt.

But the objection was not in our view properly preserved. Admittedly, the newly amended Federal Rules of Evidence sensibly provide that an objection resolved by a definitive *in limine* ruling admitting evidence need not be renewed at trial. Fed. R. Evid. 103(a) (2000). But if the district judge ruled definitively on anything, it was that Coletta and similar witnesses could testify about their own experience and not that they could assess that of Bandera. This is evident from the *in limine* motion itself.

Then at trial when the opinion testimony was offered, defense counsel said "objection" on several occasions; but few of the objections were explained and the ones that were had to do with time frame. Given earlier general attacks on Coletta's testimony based on relevance and prejudice, we do not think that it was at all necessarily obvious to the magistrate judge that the new objections were to impermissible lay witness opinion. . . .

The law is clear that an objection, if its basis is not obvious, is not preserved unless the ground is stated. Fed. R. Evid. 103(a)(1). . . . This case is a perfect illustration of why that rule is a sound one. Coletta's opinion testimony, although clearly inappropriate, was at the tag end of other testimony to which different objections had been litigated pretrial. If counsel had explained why this new testimony differed and was in no way covered by the district court's *in limine* ruling, there is a good chance that the magistrate judge would have excluded it.

This is not a criticism of counsel. Trials are a rough and ready business; snap judgments as to unexpected testimony have to be made all the time. However, the failure to preserve the objection means review is at most for plain error. Fed. R. Evid. 103(d). As we have noted, it is far from clear that the opinion testimony was harmful. This doubt alone is enough to bar reversal under the plain error doctrine: although the error is plain in retrospect, there is no showing that it probably infected the outcome or caused a miscarriage of justice. . . . [Remanded on other grounds.]

2

RELEVANCE

"I'm Virgo with the moon in Aries, if that will help you any."

A. RELEVANCE AND IRRELEVANCE

The two most basic principles of modern evidence law are that all irrelevant evidence should be excluded and that relevant evidence should, as a rule, be admitted. The first of these principles has no exceptions, but the second has very many exceptions. The rest of evidence law, in fact, can be understood as a series of qualifications to the broad proposition that relevant evidence is admissible. That is how James Bradley Thayer thought about evidence law, and here as elsewhere his thinking remains highly influential.

As Thayer used the terms, the relevance or irrelevance of a piece of evidence is determined by logic and experience, not by legal rules. Evidence is relevant if it is rationally probative in any way, and irrelevant if it is not. This means that evidence need have very little probative force to be relevant. Even extremely weak evidence is relevant as long as it rationally can be given *some* probative value. The low threshold for relevance is part of the explanation for the absence of any exceptions to the prohibition on irrelevant evidence. The other part of the explanation is that, as Thayer pointed out, the prohibition reflects the legal system's fundamental commitment to basing adjudication on reason.

[F.R.E. 401 & 402; C.E.C. §§210, 350, 351]

ADVISORY COMMITTEE NOTE TO F.R.E. 401

Problems of relevancy call for an answer to the question whether an item of evidence, when tested by the processes of legal reasoning, possesses sufficient probative value to justify receiving it in evidence. Thus, assessment of the probative value of evidence that a person purchased a revolver shortly prior to a fatal shooting with which he is charged is a matter of analysis and reasoning. . . .

Relevancy is not an inherent characteristic of any item of evidence but exists only as a relation between an item of evidence and a matter properly provable in the case. Does the item of evidence tend to prove the matter sought to be proved? Whether the relationship exists depends upon principles evolved by experience or science, applied logically to the situation at hand. The rule summarizes this relationship as a "tendency to make the existence" of the fact to be proved "more probable or less probable."

The standard of probability under the rule is "more . . . probable than it would be without the evidence." Any more stringent requirement is unworkable and unrealistic. As McCormick §152, p. 317, says, "A brick is not a wall," or, as Falknor, Extrinsic Policies Affecting Admissibility, 10 Rutgers L. Rev. 574, 576 (1956), quotes Professor McBaine, ". . . [I]t is not to be supposed that every witness can make a home run." Dealing with probability in the language of the rule has the added virtue of avoiding confusion between questions of admissibility and questions of the sufficiency of the evidence.

The rule uses the phrase "fact that is of consequence to the determination of the action" to describe the kind of fact to which proof may properly be directed. The language is that of California Evidence Code §210; it has the advantage of avoiding the loosely used and ambiguous word "material." The fact to be proved may be ultimate, intermediate, or evidentiary; it matters not, so long as it is of consequence in the determination of the action.

The fact to which the evidence is directed need not be in dispute. While situations will arise which call for the exclusion of evidence offered to prove a point conceded by the opponent, the ruling should be made on the basis of such considerations as waste of time and undue prejudice (see Rule 403), rather than under any general requirement that evidence is admissible only if directed to matters in dispute. Evidence which is essentially background in nature can scarcely be said to involve disputed matter, yet it is universally offered and admitted as an aid to understanding. Charts, photographs, views of real estate, murder weapons, and many other items of evidence fall in this category. A rule limiting admissibility to evidence directed to a controversial point would invite the exclusion of this helpful evidence, or at least the raising of endless questions over its admission. Cf. California Evidence Code §210, defining relevant evidence in terms of tendency to prove a disputed fact.

ADVISORY COMMITTEE NOTE TO F.R.E. 402

The provisions that all relevant evidence is admissible, with certain exceptions, and that evidence which is not relevant is not admissible are "a presupposition involved in the very conception of a rational system of evidence." Thayer, preliminary Treatise on Evidence 264 (1898). They constitute the foundation upon which the structure of admission and exclusion rests. . . .

KNAPP v. STATE

79 N.E. 1076 (Ind. 1907)

GILLET, J.

Appellant appeals from a judgment in the above-entitled cause, under which he stands convicted of murder in the first degree. Error is assigned on the overruling of a motion for new trial.

Appellant as a witness in his own behalf, offered testimony tending to show a killing in self-defense. He afterwards testified, presumably for the purpose of showing that he had reason to fear the deceased, that before the killing he had heard that the deceased, who was the marshal of Hagerstown, had clubbed and seriously injured an old man in arresting him, and that he died a short time afterwards. On appellant being asked, on cross-examination, who told him this, he answered: "Some people around Hagerstown there. I can't say as to who it was now." The state was permitted, on rebuttal, to prove by a physician over the objection and exception of the defense, that the old man died of senility and alcoholism, and that there were no bruises or marks on his person. Counsel for appellant contend that it was error to admit this testimony; that the question was as to whether he had, in fact, heard the story, and not as to its truth or falsity. While it is laid down in the books that there must be an open and visible connection between the fact under inquiry and the evidence by which it is sought to be established, yet the connection thus required is in the logical processes only, for to require an actual connection between the two facts would be to exclude all pre-sumptive evidence. Within settled rules, the competency of testimony depends largely upon its tendency to persuade the judgment. . . .

We are of opinion that the testimony referred to was competent. While appellant's counsel are correct in their assertion that the question was whether appellant had heard a story to the effect that the deceased had offered serious violence to the old man, yet it does not follow that the testimony complained of did not tend to negative the claim of appellant as to what he had heard. One of the first principles of human nature is the impulse to speak the truth. "This principle," says Dr. Reid, whom Professor Greenleaf quotes at length in his work on Evidence (volume 1, §7n), "has a powerful operation, even in the greatest liars; for where they lie once they speak truth 100 times." Truth speaking preponderating, it follows that to show that there was no basis in fact for the statement appellant claims to have heard had a tendency to make it less probable that his testimony on this point was true. . . . [W]e do not perceive how, without the possibility of a gross perversion of right, the state could be denied the opportunity to meet in the manner indicated the evidence of the defendant as to what he had heard, where he, cunningly perhaps, denies that he can remember who gave him the information. The fact proved by the state tended to discredit appellant, since it showed that somewhere between the fact and the testi-mony there was a person who was not a truth speaker, and, appellant being unable to point to his informant, it must at least be said that the testimony complained of had a tendency to render his claim as to what he had heard less probable. . . . Judgment affirmed.

UNITED STATES v. DOMINGUEZ

907 F.2d 216 (1st Cir. 1990)
(sub nom. United States v. Maravilla)

BREYER, Circuit Judge.

[Rafael Dominguez was a U.S. Customs officer. A jury found Domin-guez and a fellow officer guilty of kidnapping, robbing, and murdering Yamil Mitri when Mitri attempted to carry $700,000 into the United States.]

After presenting evidence that a gunshot killed Mitri, the government introduced evidence showing (a) that Dominguez owned a gun, (b) that a week after Mitri's death, he asked a friend to bring his gun to a Miami gun shop to have the barrel replaced, (c) that the shopowner saw scratches on the barrel, which could have been left by an attempt to remove it, and (d) that the shopowner repaired the barrel but did not replace it. The defendants point out that Dominguez, as a customs officer, had to own a gun. They argue, in light of that fact, that the evidence presented of owner-ship and about barrel replacement was irrelevant and prejudicial.

We do not see how one could say the evidence is irrelevant. Relevant evidence is evidence "having any tendency to make the existence of any fact that is of consequence . . . more probable or less probable than it would be without the evidence." Fed. R. Evid. 401. Obviously, the fact that Dominguez owned a gun makes his guilt somewhat more probable than if he did not own a gun. The fact that he might have had a good reason, consistent with innocence, for owning a gun, makes the evidence less probative, not irrelevant. Regardless, the government had to show that Dominguez owned a gun in order to show that he tried to have the barrel replaced. The effort to replace, in turn, suggests an effort to eliminate features of the gun that might have linked it with a bullet eventually found in, or near, Mitri's body. And any such effort suggests consciousness of guilt. Given this set of logical connections, the replacement effort makes guilt more probable than had there been no replacement effort; and the evidence, consequently, is relevant.

The defendants point out that the chain of inferences is far weaker than if the government had introduced the gun itself into evidence, for then experts could have tested it to see if it matched the bullet that killed Mitri. The record provides no basis, however, for concluding that the government ever found the bullet. . . . Regardless, the government is perfectly free to introduce weak, as well as strong, evidence. *See, e.g.*, Fed. R. Evid. 401 advisory committee's note ("The standard of probability under the rule is 'more . . . probable than it would be without the evidence.' Any more stringent requirement is unworkable and unrealistic."); Cleary, *McCormick on Evidence* §185, at 542-43 (3rd ed. 1984) ("Under our system, molded by the tradition of jury trial and predominantly oral proof, a party offers his evidence not *en masse*, but item by item. An item of evidence . . . need not prove conclusively the proposition for which it is offered. . . . A brick is not a wall.") (citations omitted). No one claimed that this particular piece of evidence *proved* guilt. It was merely one piece of evidence among many. . . . *Affirmed in part and reversed in part [on other grounds].*

STATE v. LARSON

843 P.2d 777 (Mont. 1992)

McDONOUGH, Justice.

This is an appeal from a judgment of the First Judicial District Court, Lewis and Clark County, convicting Larson of negligent endangerment. . . . On July 21, 1991, five-year-old Brenda Perry suffered fatal injuries when a horse she and Myron Larson were riding reared and fell backward, crushing Brenda. . . . She died a short time later of internal bleeding. . . .

The accident occurred during a barbecue at a rural home near Helena. [Larson had borrowed the horse from its owner and had then allowed Perry to ride seated behind him. The owner of the horse had warned Larson that the horse was "inexperienced" and "hot-blooded." Three hours after the accident, armed law enforcement officers took a blood sample from Larson.] . . . Lynn Kurtz, a forensic scientist for the State Crime Lab, measured Larson's blood alcohol content at .17 grams of alcohol per 100 milliliters of

blood. Kurtz estimated that Larson had a blood alcohol content between
.20 and .27 at the time of the accident.

At trial, . . . [the court] permitted Kurtz to compare Larson's blood
alcohol level with the level that the scientific community has determined
will impair a person's ability to drive a motor vehicle. Kurtz testified that the
scientific community has determined that a blood alcohol level of .08 grams
of alcohol per 100 milliliters of blood will impair a person's ability to safely
operate a motor vehicle. . . .

The prosecution argued that Larson made mistakes in judgment due to
his alcohol consumption. In closing, the prosecution mentioned to the jury
that Larson's blood alcohol level at the time of the accident was three times
the level that will impair a person's ability to drive an automobile. The prosecution also argued that a person who is too impaired to drive an automobile
safely is too impaired to ride a horse safely, and certainly is too impaired
to allow a five-year-old child on a high-spirited horse with him. . . .

Larson . . . contends that the level of blood alcohol which will impair a
person's ability to drive is irrelevant to his conduct relative to a high-spirited
young horse. On the contrary, "[r]elevant evidence means evidence having
any tendency to make the existence of any fact that is of consequence to the
determination of the action more probable or less probable than it would
be without the evidence." Rule 401, M.R. Evid.

> The test of relevance is whether an item of evidence will have any value, as
> determined by logic and experience, in proving the proposition for which it is
> offered. The standard used to measure this acceptable probative value is "any
> tendency to make the existence of any fact . . . more probable or less probable
> than it would be without the evidence."

State v. Fitzpatrick (1980), 186 Mont. 187, 207 (quoting M.R. Evid. Commission Comments).

At Larson's trial, the prosecution offered his blood alcohol level to
show that alcohol had impaired his reactions and judgment when he
chose to ride double on a high-spirited horse with a young girl. Larson's
blood alcohol level on the day of the accident is relevant.

The comparison of Larson's blood alcohol level with that which the
scientific community has determined will impair a person's ability to drive a
motor vehicle is also relevant. The comparison aided the jury in evaluating
Larson's level of intoxication. It allowed the jurors to apply their experience
and logic to determine whether Larson's level of intoxication clouded his
judgment and impaired his reactions, and its probative value outweighs any
prejudice to the defendant. We hold that the court did not abuse its discretion in admitting the comparison. . . . Affirmed.

EDMUND M. MORGAN, BASIC PROBLEMS OF EVIDENCE

185-188 (1961)

In the following example it is not meant to assert that each proposition
is more probably true than not, but that it is more probably true than an

identical proposition concerning a man as to whom nothing is known. Assume that X has met his death by violence; the proposition to be proved is that Y killed him; the offered item of evidence is a love letter written by Y to X's wife. The series of inferences is about as follows: From Y's letter, (A), to Y's love of X's wife, (B), to Y's desire for the exclusive possession of X's wife, (C), to Y's desire to get rid of X, (D), to Y's plan to get rid of X, (E), to Y's execution of the plan by killing X, (F). The unarticulated premise, (M), conjoined with (A) is "A man who writes a love letter to a woman is probably in love with her"; that, (N), conjoined with (B) is, "A man who loves a woman probably desires her for himself alone"; that, (O), conjoined with (C) is, "A man who loves a married woman and desires her for himself alone desires to get rid of her husband"; that, (P), conjoined with (D) is, "A man who desires to get rid of the husband of the woman he loves probably plans to do so"; and that, (Q), conjoined with (E) is, "A man who plans to get rid of the husband of the woman he loves is probably the man who killed him." If an arrow represents the drawing of an inference, the series may be represented thus:

```
A)
+) →  B)
M)    +) →  C)
   N)    +) →  D)
      O)    +) →  E)
         P)    +) →  F
            Q)
```

Now it must be obvious that the value of item A as probative of F varies with the degree of probability of the existence of each presumed fact and inversely with the number of inferences between A and F. . . . [A] distinction must be drawn between the relevance of A as evidence of F on the one hand and its weight on the other. Obviously A standing by itself would not justify the inference of F; indeed, it might not justify even D or E. But the proponent of A may offer another item or several other items, each of which will begin a series of inferences leading to F. . . . [T]he greater the number of items, the stronger will be the foundation for the ultimate inference. Nevertheless, no matter how numerous the items or how short the series of inferences required for each of them, they will never produce certainty. . . . On the other hand, no matter how great the number of items established, they will never make the existence of the ultimate fact a question for the trier unless the total would justify reasonable men in concluding that the existence of the ultimate fact is more probable than its nonexistence.

GRAHAM C. LILLY, AN INTRODUCTION TO THE LAW OF EVIDENCE

§2.2, at 31-32 (3d ed. 1996)

Note that even if most links were strong, probative force would always be limited by the weakest link. . . . Some of the inferential links [in Professor

Morgan's example] are comparatively strong (e.g., from love letters to deep affection), yet others are comparatively weak (e.g., from the desire to possess to a plan to kill). Does the love letter still pass the test of relevance? It does because it increases somewhat the likelihood that [the defendant] committed the murder. Of course, whether the prosecution can establish beyond a reasonable doubt that the accused committed the offense charged is an entirely different matter which depends upon the combined probative effect of all of the inculpatory evidence introduced at trial. . . . At the conclusion of the prosecutor's evidence, the judge must decide if a reasonable trier could conclude from all of the evidence that [the defendant] was the murderer.

B. PROBATIVE VALUE AND PREJUDICE

If, as Thayer thought, the vast bulk of evidence law consists of exceptions to the general proposition that relevant evidence is admissible, none of those exceptions is more important than the rule giving trial judges broad discretion to exclude evidence that is more trouble than it is worth—either because it likely will impair rather than assist the jury's search for the truth, or because it simply will take up too much time. Probably more evidence is excluded under this flexible rule than under the rest of the rules of evidence combined, and the authority the rule gives to trial judges creates in each court-room a kind of parallel, discretionary law of evidence, working alongside the law set forth in the remaining rules.

[F.R.E. 105, 403; C.E.C. §§352, 355]

ADVISORY COMMITTEE NOTE TO F.R.E. 403

The case law recognizes that certain circumstances call for the exclusion of evidence which is of unquestioned relevance. These circumstances entail risks which range all the way from inducing decision on a purely emotional basis, at one extreme, to nothing more harmful than merely wasting time, at the other extreme. Situations in this area call for balancing the probative value of and need for the evidence against the harm likely to result from its admission. The rules which follow in this Article are concrete applications evolved for particular situations. However, they reflect the policies underlying the present rule, which is designed as a guide for the handling of situations for which no specific rules have been formulated.

Exclusion for risk of unfair prejudice, confusion of issues, misleading the jury, or waste of time, all find ample support in the authorities. "Unfair prejudice" within its context means an undue tendency to suggest decision on an improper basis, commonly, though not necessarily, an emotional one.

The rule does not enumerate surprise as a ground for exclusion, in this respect following Wigmore's view of the common law. 6 Wigmore §1849. Cf. McCormick §152, p. 320, n. 29, listing unfair surprise as a ground for exclusion but stating that it is usually "coupled with the danger of prejudice and confusion of issues." . . . While it can scarcely be doubted that claims of unfair surprise may still be justified despite procedural requirements of notice and instrumentalities of discovery, the granting of a continuance is a more appropriate remedy than exclusion of the evidence. . . .

In reaching a decision whether to exclude on grounds of unfair prejudice, consideration should be given to the probable effectiveness or lack of effectiveness of a limiting instruction. . . . The availability of other means of proof may also be an appropriate factor.

ELEANOR SWIFT, ONE HUNDRED YEARS OF EVIDENCE LAW REFORM: THAYER'S TRIUMPH

88 Cal. L. Rev. 2437, 2446-2447 (2000)

There are both benefits and costs to granting discretion to the trial judge to admit or exclude evidence. Some commentators argue that deferential appellate review of trial court discretion promotes judicial economy by reducing appellate expenditure of time and energy. Proponents of discretion also contend that many questions that arise in litigation, including the decision to admit or exclude evidence, require individualized and flexible decision making based on the particular context of the case; "they involve multifarious, fleeting, special, narrow facts that utterly resist generalization. . . ." [Maurice Rosenberg, *Judicial Discretion of the Trial Court, Viewed from Above*, 22 Syr. L. Rev. 635, 662 (1971).] Shoe-horning such decisions into rigid rules would promote error and injustice. And once the need for individualized decision making is acknowledged, trial courts are in a superior position to make decisions that require taking the context and specific facts of a case into account. This serves a truth-seeking function, as "rules allowing room for a trial judge's sensitivity to the complexity and uniqueness of a particular case necessarily should promote truth more than rules providing for only mechanical application of a closed and complete system." [Thomas M. Mengler, *The Theory of Discretion in the Federal Rules of Evidence*, 74 Iowa L. Rev. 413, 460 (1989).]

The costs of discretion and deferential review are also well known. There are fears that discretionary power will be exercised arbitrarily and unfairly; that broad and ambiguous principles make evidentiary rulings unpredictable to parties preparing for trial and result in inconsistent outcomes; and that the perceived unfairness of inconsistent outcomes, or outcomes dependent on the personality of the judge one happens to draw, could lead to a loss of confidence in the judicial system. Even more troubling, perhaps, is the fear that trial judges, although closer to the context and facts of the case, simply are not capable of making the subtle and profound judgments that rules like Federal Rule 403 require.

UNITED STATES v. NORIEGA

117 F.3d 1206 (11th cir. 1997)

KRAVITCH, Senior Circuit Judge:

On February 4, 1988, a federal grand jury for the Southern District of Florida indicted Manuel Antonio Noriega on drug-related charges. At that time, Noriega served as commander of the Panamanian Defense Forces in the Republic of Panama. [The indictment charged that Noriega had used his position of authority to help Columbian drug traffickers smuggle cocaine through Panama and into the United States.] Shortly thereafter, Panama's president, Eric Arturo Delvalle, formally discharged Noriega from his military post, but Noriega refused to accept the dismissal. Panama's legislature then ousted Delvalle from power. The United States, however, continued to acknowledge Delvalle as the constitutional leader of Panama. Later, after a disputed presidential election in Panama, the United States recognized Guillermo Endara as Panama's legitimate head of state.

On December 15, 1989, Noriega publicly declared that a state of war existed between Panama and the United States. Within days of this announcement by Noriega, President George [H.W.] Bush directed United States armed forces into combat in Panama for the stated purposes of "safeguarding American lives, restoring democracy, preserving the Panama Canal treaties, and seizing Noriega to face federal drug charges in the United States." *United States v. Noriega*, 746 F. Supp. 1506, 1511 (S.D. Fla. 1990). The ensuing military conflagration resulted in significant casualties and property loss among Panamanian civilians. Noriega lost his effective control over Panama during this armed conflict, and he surrendered to United States military officials on January 3, 1990. Noriega then was brought to Miami to face the pending federal charges.

Following extensive pre-trial proceedings and a lengthy trial, a jury found Noriega guilty of eight counts in the indictment and not guilty of the remaining two counts. The district court entered judgments of conviction against Noriega upon the jury's verdict and sentenced him to consecutive imprisonment terms of 20, 15 and five years, respectively. . . .

[Before trial,] Noriega gave notice of his intent to use classified information regarding his intelligence work for the United States to rebut the government's assertion that he had unexplained wealth. The government objected to any disclosure of the purposes for which the United States had paid Noriega. In pre-trial proceedings, the government offered to stipulate that Noriega had received approximately $320,000 from the United States Army and the Central Intelligence Agency. Noriega insisted that the actual figure approached $10,000,000, and that he should be allowed to disclose the tasks he had performed for the United States.

The district court held that information about the content of the discrete operations in which Noriega had engaged in exchange for the alleged payments was irrelevant to his defense. Alternatively, it ruled that the tendency of such evidence to confuse the issues before the jury substantially out-weighed any probative value it might have had. The district court's . . . ruling, however, left Noriega free to present evidence of the fact, amounts, time, source and method of conveyance of money he alleged he had received from the United States. At trial, Noriega declined to submit evidence regarding monies he allegedly received from the United States, because, he now contends, it would not have appeared credible to the jury absent the excluded details regarding the actual services he had performed. . . .

Our review leads us to conclude that information regarding the purposes for which the United States previously paid Noriega potentially had some probative value. Specifically, had Noriega testified that he had received $10,000,000 from the United States, and had the government then rebutted that testimony by presenting evidence that it had paid Noriega $320,000, evidence regarding what Noriega did for the United States might have helped the jury determine which of the two payment totals was more credible. To the extent that the proffered evidence on the intelligence operations showed that the United States had engaged Noriega to carry out significant duties, the jury might have inferred that he had received the higher figure, rather than the lower sum. Thus, the district court may have overstated the case when it declared evidence of the purposes for which the United States allegedly paid Noriega wholly irrelevant to his defense.

The potential probative value of this material, however, was relatively marginal. Evidence of the purposes for which monies allegedly are given does not aid significantly in the determination of the fact and amount of such purported payments. Further, and more importantly, the district court correctly recognized that the admission of evidence regarding the nature of Noriega's assistance to the United States would have shifted unduly the focus of the trial from allegations of drug trafficking to matters of geo-political intrigue. Accordingly, we cannot conclude that the district court abused its discretion when it determined that the probative value of the proffered material was outweighed substantially by the confusion of issues its admission would have caused. *See* Fed. R. Evid. 403.

. . . Noriega's convictions are AFFIRMED, and the district court's order denying Noriega's motion for a new trial is AFFIRMED.

UNITED STATES v. FLITCRAFT

803 F.2d 184 (5th Cir. 1986)

JOHNSON, Circuit Judge:

Robert W. Flitcraft and his wife Rebecca appeal their convictions for failing to file tax returns and filing false withholding exemption certificates. . . . At trial, the Flitcrafts admitted that their income was high enough to make them liable for tax and that they had in fact signed the false withholding forms and failed to file returns. They contested only the Government's contention that these acts were done willfully. Mrs. Flitcraft stated

that she had trusted her husband when he told her that he had researched
the question and that they owed no tax. Mr. Flitcraft testified that he had
read cases and articles that convinced him that his wages were not income,
merely an even exchange of money for time. The trial judge, a United States
magistrate, refused to allow Flitcraft to introduce the legal materials on
which he claimed to have relied, but did allow him to testify about them
orally. . . . The Flitcrafts now argue that the jury would have been more
likely to credit the sincerity of the Flitcrafts' belief that they were not subject
to filing a return if it had seen the documents.

The Federal Rules of Evidence provide that evidence, though relevant,
"may be excluded if its probative value is substantially outweighed by the
danger of . . . confusion of the issues, or misleading the jury, or by consideration of undue delay, waste of time, or needless presentation of cumulative evidence." Fed. R. Evid. 403. A district court's ruling under Rule 403
will not be disturbed except for an abuse of discretion.

In the present case the introduction of the cases and documents relied
on by Flitcraft would have been cumulative because Flitcraft testified to the
documents he relied on and their contents. The introduction of the documents themselves would have had little further probative value. In addition,
the documents presented a danger of confusing the jury by suggesting that
the law is unsettled and that it should resolve such doubtful questions of
law. . . . [Reversed on other grounds.]

ABERNATHY v. SUPERIOR HARDWOODS, INC.

704 F.2d 963 (7th Cir. 1983)

POSNER, Circuit Judge.

One day in 1978 Robert Abernathy drove a flatbed truck loaded with
logs to a sawmill in Indiana owned by Superior Hardwoods. The logs were
fastened to the bed of the truck with four chains. Abernathy released each
chain but before he could stow them all in the cab of the truck Superior
Hardwoods' forklift began unloading the logs and one tumbled off and hit
Abernathy in the back. Abernathy and his wife sued Superior Hardwoods
for negligence, basing federal jurisdiction on diversity of citizenship, and
got a jury verdict. . . .

The president of Superior Hardwoods made a videotape with his
home videotape system showing a forklift unloading logs from a truck at
the sawmill. The videotape was not a tape of the accident, of course—it
was made several years later—or even an attempt to reconstruct the accident. It was an attempt (in the defendant's words) "to fairly and accurately
depict the method in which log trucks are routinely unloaded at" its sawmill. The district judge allowed the tape to be shown to the jury but only
with the sound turned off. Yet according to the defendant the soundtrack
proves that Abernathy should have heard the forklift beginning to unload
the logs.

The levels both of background noise and of forklift operating noise
were relevant to the defense of contributory negligence, and there is no

objection in principle to presenting evidence of noise levels through a sound recording, even one made long after the accident. But to be admissible—at least as a matter of law, rather than in the trial judge's discretion—the recording must, of course, meet minimum standards of reliability. This one did not. The microphone was not placed where Abernathy had been standing when he was hit by the log, though it easily could have been; the recording was made by an amateur, using amateur's equipment; and there is no indication that in the courtroom the video recorder's volume control would have been adjusted to produce the same decibel level as the sounds actually recorded.

Although all of these points could have been brought out on cross-examination if the soundtrack had been played to the jury, a district judge is not required to encumber a trial with evidence of slight probative value merely because effective cross-examination might expose its weakness. Fed. R. Evid. 403. . . . Juries have a tough enough time deciding cases intelligently even when they are not assailed by evidence of tangential relevance, and federal trials already take up enough time without being prolonged to receive such evidence. Nor can a district judge rely on counsel's self-interest not to offer worthless evidence. A lawyer with a weak case may throw in a lot of evidence just to confuse the jury—a tactic sometimes called "serving up a muddle." As the federal courts become ever busier, the need for district judges to manage trials with a firm hand becomes ever greater. The district judge in this case is to be commended rather than criticized for not taking the easy way out, which would have been to let in all the minimally relevant nonprivileged evidence either party cared to offer . . . [Affirmed in relevant part.]

UNITED STATES v. McRAE

593 F.2d 700 (5th Cir. 1979)

Gee, Circuit Judge:

About two years ago, appellant McRae killed his wife Nancy by shooting her through the head with his deer rifle at point-blank range. That he did so is admitted; his sole defense at trial was that the shooting was not malicious but accidental. The offense having occurred on the Fort Bliss military reservation, McRae was indicted for second-degree murder under 18 U.S.C. §1111. A jury trial resulted in his conviction and sentence to life imprisonment. . . .

[On appeal the defendant objects to] the admission of various photographs of the deceased and of the death scene. It is said that these should have been excluded under Rule 403, Federal Rules of Evidence, as relevant matter the probative value of which is substantially outweighed by the danger of unfair prejudice. Two of these color prints are indeed as the trial court characterized them gross, distasteful and disturbing. Exhibit 29 is a view of Mrs. McRae's corpse, clothed in her bloody garments, bent forward so as to display an exit wound in the back of her skull produced by part of McRae's dum-dum bullet, which exploded in her brain. Exhibit 22 shows a front view of her body, seated in the chair where she died, her left eye disfigured by the bullet's entry and her head broken by its force. By comparison with these, the other photographs are mild; but these are not pretty even to the hardened eye. Neither, however, was the crime, and these exhibits are not flagrantly or deliberately gruesome depictions of it. The trial court carefully reviewed the government's photographic exhibits, excluding some of little probative value. It found those admitted important to establishing elements of the offense such as Mrs. McRae's position and that of the rifle when it was fired, as bearing on McRae's defense of accident.

Relevant evidence is inherently prejudicial; but it is only *unfair* prejudice, *substantially* outweighing probative value, which permits exclusion of relevant matter under Rule 403. Unless trials are to be conducted on scenarios, on unreal facts tailored and sanitized for the occasion, the application of Rule 403 must be cautious and sparing. Its major function is limited to excluding matter of scant or cumulative probative force, dragged in by the heels for the sake of its prejudicial effect. As to such, Rule 403 is meant to relax the iron rule of relevance, to permit the trial judge to preserve the fairness of the proceedings by exclusion despite its relevance. It is not designed to permit the court to "even out" the weight of the evidence, to mitigate a crime, or to make a contest where there is little or none. Here was no parade of horrors. We refuse to interfere with the trial court's exercise of its discretion. . . . AFFIRMED.

OLD CHIEF v. UNITED STATES

519 U.S. 172 (1997)

Justice SOUTER delivered the opinion of the Court.

. . . In 1993, petitioner, Old Chief, was arrested after a fracas involving at least one gunshot. The ensuing federal charges included not only assault with a dangerous weapon and using a firearm in relation to a crime of violence but violation of 18 U.S.C. §922(g)(1). This statute makes it unlawful for anyone "who has been convicted in any court of a crime punishable by imprisonment for a term exceeding one year" to "possess in or affecting commerce, any firearm. . . ." "[A] crime punishable by imprisonment for a term exceeding one year" is defined to exclude "any Federal or State offenses pertaining to antitrust violations, unfair trade practices, restraints of trade, or other similar offenses relating to the regulation of business practices" and "any State offense classified by the laws of the State as a misdemeanor and punishable by a term of imprisonment of two years or less." §921(a)(20).

The earlier crime charged in the indictment against Old Chief was assault causing serious bodily injury. Before trial, he moved for an order requiring the Government "to refrain from mentioning—by reading the Indictment, during jury selection, in opening statement, or closing argument—and to refrain from offering into evidence or soliciting any testimony from any witness regarding the prior criminal convictions of the Defendant, *except* to state that the Defendant has been convicted of a crime punishable by imprisonment exceeding one (1) year." He said that revealing the name and nature of his prior assault conviction would unfairly tax the jury's capacity to hold the Government to its burden of proof beyond a reasonable doubt on current charges of assault, possession, and violence with a firearm, and he offered to "solve the problem here by stipulating, agreeing and requesting the Court to instruct the jury that he has been convicted of a crime punishable by imprisonment exceeding one (1) yea[r]." He argued that the offer to stipulate to the fact of the prior conviction rendered evidence of the name and nature of the offense inadmissible under Rule 403 of the Federal Rules of Evidence, the danger being that unfair prejudice from that evidence would substantially outweigh its probative value. . . .

The Assistant United States Attorney refused to join in a stipulation, insisting on his right to prove his case his own way, and the District Court agreed, ruling orally that, "If he doesn't want to stipulate, he doesn't have to." At trial, over renewed objection, the Government introduced the order of judgment and commitment for Old Chief's prior conviction. This document disclosed that on December 18, 1988, he "did knowingly and unlawfully assault Rory Dean Fenner, said assault resulting in serious bodily injury," for which Old Chief was sentenced to five years' imprisonment. The jury found Old Chief guilty on all counts, and he appealed. [The Ninth Circuit affirmed.] . . .

As a threshold matter, there is Old Chief's erroneous argument that the name of his prior offense as contained in the record of conviction is irrelevant to the prior-conviction element, and for that reason inadmissible under Rule 402 of the Federal Rules of Evidence. Rule 401 defines relevant evidence as having "any tendency to make the existence of any fact that is of consequence to the determination of the action more probable or less probable than it would be without the evidence." To be sure, the fact that Old Chief's prior conviction was for assault resulting in serious bodily injury rather than, say, for theft was not itself an ultimate fact, as if the statute had specifically required proof of injurious assault. But its demonstration was a step on one evidentiary route to the ultimate fact, since it served to place Old Chief within a particular sub-class of offenders for whom firearms possession is outlawed by §922(g)(1). A documentary record of the conviction for that named offense was thus relevant evidence in making Old Chief's §922(g)(1) status more probable than it would have been without the evidence.

Nor was its evidentiary relevance under Rule 401 affected by the availability of alternative proofs of the element to which it went, such as an admission by Old Chief that he had been convicted of a crime "punishable by imprisonment for a term exceeding one year" within the meaning of the statute. The 1972 Advisory Committee Notes to Rule 401 make this point directly:

> "The fact to which the evidence is directed need not be in dispute. While situations will arise which call for the exclusion of evidence offered to prove a

point conceded by the opponent, the ruling should be made on the basis of such considerations as waste of time and undue prejudice (see Rule 403), rather than under any general requirement that evidence is admissible only if directed to matters in dispute."

If, then, relevant evidence is inadmissible in the presence of other evidence related to it, its exclusion must rest not on the ground that the other evidence has rendered it "irrelevant," but on its character as unfairly prejudicial, cumulative or the like, its relevance notwithstanding.

The principal issue is the scope of a trial judge's discretion under Rule 403, which authorizes exclusion of relevant evidence when its "probative value is substantially outweighed by the danger of unfair prejudice, confusion of the issues, or misleading the jury, or by considerations of undue delay, waste of time, or needless presentation of cumulative evidence." Old Chief relies on the danger of unfair prejudice.

The term "unfair prejudice," as to a criminal defendant, speaks to the capacity of some concededly relevant evidence to lure the factfinder into declaring guilt on a ground different from proof specific to the offense charged. . . . Such improper grounds certainly include the one that Old Chief points to here: generalizing a defendant's earlier bad act into bad character and taking that as raising the odds that he did the later bad act now charged (or, worse, as calling for preventive conviction even if he should happen to be innocent momentarily). As then-Judge Breyer put it, "Although . . . 'propensity evidence' is relevant, the risk that a jury will convict for crimes other than those charged—or that, uncertain of guilt, it will convict anyway because a bad person deserves punishment—creates a prejudicial effect that outweighs ordinary relevance." *United States v. Moccia*, 681 F.2d 61, 63 (C.A.1 1982). Justice Jackson described how the law has handled this risk:

> "Courts that follow the common-law tradition almost unanimously have come to disallow resort by the prosecution to any kind of evidence of a defendant's evil character to establish a probability of his guilt. Not that the law invests the defendant with a presumption of good character, but it simply closes the whole matter of character, disposition and reputation on the prosecution's case-in-chief. The state may not show defendant's prior trouble with the law, specific criminal acts, or ill name among his neighbors, even though such facts might logically be persuasive that he is by propensity a probable perpetrator of the crime. The inquiry is not rejected because character is irrelevant; on the contrary, it is said to weigh too much with the jury and to so overpersuade them as to prejudge one with a bad general record and deny him a fair opportunity to defend against a particular charge. The overriding policy of excluding such evidence, despite its admitted probative value, is the practical experience that its disallowance tends to prevent confusion of issues, unfair surprise and undue prejudice." *Michelson v. United States*, 335 U.S. 469, 475-476 (1948) (footnotes omitted).

Rule of Evidence 404(b) reflects this common-law tradition by addressing propensity reasoning directly: "Evidence of other crimes, wrongs, or acts is not admissible to prove the character of a person in order to show action in conformity therewith." There is, accordingly, no question that propensity would be an "improper basis" for conviction and that evidence of a prior conviction is subject to analysis under Rule 403 for relative probative value and for prejudicial risk of misuse as propensity evidence. Cf. 1 J. Strong, McCormick on Evidence 780 (4th ed. 1992) (hereinafter McCormick) (Rule 403 prejudice may occur, for example, when "evidence of convictions for prior, unrelated crimes may lead a juror to think that since the defendant already has a criminal record, an erroneous conviction would not be quite as serious as would otherwise be the case"). . . .

[A] reading of the companions to Rule 403, and of the commentaries that went with them to Congress, makes it clear that what counts as the Rule 403 "probative value" of an item of evidence, as distinct from its Rule 401 "relevance," may be calculated by comparing evidentiary alternatives. The Committee Notes to Rule 401 explicitly say that a party's concession is pertinent to the court's discretion to exclude evidence on the point conceded. Such a concession, according to the Notes, will sometimes "call for the exclusion of evidence offered to prove [the] point conceded by the opponent. . . ." As already mentioned, the Notes make it clear that such rulings should be made not on the basis of Rule 401 relevance but on "such considerations as waste of time and undue prejudice (see Rule 403). . . ." The Notes to Rule 403 then take up the point by stating that when a court considers "whether to exclude on grounds of unfair prejudice," the "availability of other means of proof may . . . be an appropriate factor." The point gets a reprise in the Notes to Rule 404(b), dealing with admissibility when a given evidentiary item has the dual nature of legitimate evidence of an element and illegitimate evidence of character: "No mechanical solution is offered. The determination must be made whether the danger of undue prejudice outweighs the probative value of the evidence in view of the availability of other means of proof and other facts appropriate for making decision of this kind under 403. Thus the notes leave no question that when Rule 403 confers discretion by providing that evidence "may" be excluded, the discretionary judgment may be informed not only by assessing an evidentiary item's twin tendencies, but by placing the result of that assessment alongside similar assessments of evidentiary alternatives. See 1 McCormick 782, and n. 41 (suggesting that Rule 403's "probative value" signifies the "marginal probative value" of the evidence relative to the other evidence in the case); 22 C. Wright & K. Graham, Federal Practice and Procedure §5250, pp. 546-547 (1978) ("The probative worth of any particular bit of evidence is obviously affected by the scarcity or abundance of other evidence on the same point").

In dealing with the specific problem raised by §922(g)(1) and its prior conviction element, there can be no question that evidence of the name or nature of the prior offense generally carries a risk of unfair prejudice to the defendant. That risk will vary from case to case, for the reasons already given, but will be substantial whenever the official record offered by the Government would be arresting enough to lure a juror into a sequence of bad character reasoning. Where a prior conviction was for a gun crime or one similar to other charges in a pending case the risk of unfair prejudice would be especially obvious, and Old Chief sensibly worried that the prejudicial effect of his prior assault conviction, significant enough with respect to the current gun charges alone, would take on added weight from the related assault charge against him.[8]

The District Court was also presented with alternative, relevant, admissible evidence of the prior conviction by Old Chief's offer to stipulate, evidence necessarily subject to the District Court's consideration on the motion to exclude the record offered by the Government. Although Old Chief's formal offer to stipulate was, strictly, to enter a formal agreement with the Government to be given to the jury, even without the Government's acceptance his proposal amounted to an offer to admit that the prior-conviction element was satisfied, and a defendant's admission is, of course, good evidence. See Fed. Rule Evid. 801(d)(2)(A).

Old Chief's proffered admission would, in fact, have been not merely relevant but seemingly conclusive evidence of the element. The statutory language in which the prior-conviction requirement is couched shows no congressional concern with the specific name or nature of the prior offense beyond what is necessary to place it within the broad category of qualifying felonies, and Old Chief clearly meant to admit that his felony did qualify, by stipulating "that the Government has proven one of the essential elements of the offense." As a consequence, although the name of the prior offense may have been technically relevant, it addressed no detail in the definition of the prior-conviction element that would not have been covered by the stipulation or admission. Logic, then, seems to side with Old Chief.

There is, however, one more question to be considered before deciding whether Old Chief's offer was to supply evidentiary value at least equivalent to what the Government's own evidence carried. In arguing that the stipulation or admission would not have carried equivalent value, the Government invokes the familiar, standard rule that the prosecution is entitled to prove its case by evidence of its own choice, or, more exactly, that a criminal defendant may not stipulate or admit his way out of the full evidentiary force of the case as the Government chooses to present it. The authority usually cited for this rule is *Parr v. United States*, 255 F.2d 86 (CA5), cert. denied, 358 U.S. 824 (1958), in which the Fifth Circuit explained that the "reason for the rule is to permit a party 'to present to the jury a picture of the events relied upon. To substitute for such a picture a naked admission might have the effect to rob the evidence of much of its fair and legitimate weight.'" 255 F.2d, at 88 (quoting *Dunning v. Maine Central R. Co.*, 91 Me. 87, 39 A. 352, 256 (1897)).

---

8. It is true that a prior offense may be so far removed in time or nature from the current gun charge and any others brought with it that its potential to prejudice the defendant unfairly will be minimal. Some prior offenses, in fact, may even have some potential to prejudice the Government's case unfairly. Thus an extremely old conviction for a relatively minor felony that nevertheless qualifies under the statute might strike many jurors as a foolish basis for convicting an otherwise upstanding member of the community of otherwise legal gun possession. Since the Government could not, of course, compel the defendant to admit formally the existence of the prior conviction, the Government would have to bear the risk of jury nullification, a fact that might properly drive the Government's charging decision.

This is unquestionably true as a general matter. The "fair and legitimate weight" of conventional evidence showing individual thoughts and acts amounting to a crime reflects the fact that making a case with testimony and tangible things not only satisfies the formal definition of an offense, but tells a colorful story with descriptive richness. Unlike an abstract premise, whose force depends on going precisely to a particular step in a course of reasoning, a piece of evidence may address any number of separate elements, striking hard just because it shows so much at once; the account of a shooting that establishes capacity and causation may tell just as much about the triggerman's motive and intent. Evidence thus has force beyond any linear scheme of reasoning, and as its pieces come together a narrative gains momentum, with power not only to support conclusions but to sustain the willingness of jurors to draw the inferences, whatever they may be, necessary to reach an honest verdict. This persuasive power of the concrete and particular is often essential to the capacity of jurors to satisfy the obligations that the law places on them. Jury duty is usually unsought and sometimes resisted, and it may be as difficult for one juror suddenly to face the findings that can send another human being to prison, as it is for another to hold out conscientiously for acquittal. When a juror's duty does seem hard, the evidentiary account of what a defendant has thought and done can accomplish what no set of abstract statements ever could, not just to prove a fact but to establish its human significance, and so to implicate the law's moral underpinnings and a juror's obligation to sit in judgment. Thus, the prosecution may fairly seek to place its evidence before the jurors, as much to tell a story of guiltiness as to support an inference of guilt, to convince the jurors that a guilty verdict would be morally reasonable as much as to point to the discrete elements of a defendant's legal fault.

But there is something even more to the prosecution's interest in resisting efforts to replace the evidence of its choice with admissions and stipulations, for beyond the power of conventional evidence to support allegations and give life to the moral underpinnings of law's claims, there lies the need for evidence in all its particularity to satisfy the jurors' expectations about what proper proof should be. Some such demands they bring with them to the courthouse, assuming, for example, that a charge of using a firearm to commit an offense will be proven by introducing a gun in evidence. A prosecutor who fails to produce one, or some good reason for his failure, has something to be concerned about. "If [jurors'] expectations are not satisfied, triers of fact may penalize the party who disappoints them by drawing a negative inference against that party." Saltzburg, A Special Aspect of Relevance: Countering Negative Inferences Associated with the Absence of Evidence, 66 Calif. L. Rev. 1011, 1019 (1978) (footnotes omitted). Expectations may also arise in jurors' minds simply from the experience of a trial itself. The use of witnesses to describe a train of events naturally related can raise the prospect of learning about every ingredient of that natural sequence the same way. If suddenly the prosecution presents some occurrence in the series differently, as by announcing a stipulation or admission, the effect may be like saying, "never mind what's behind the door," and jurors may well wonder what they are being kept from knowing. A party seemingly responsible for cloaking something has reason for apprehension, and the prosecution with its burden of proof may prudently demur at a defense request to interrupt the flow of evidence telling the story in the usual way.

In sum, the accepted rule that the prosecution is entitled to prove its case free from any defendant's option to stipulate the evidence away rests on good sense. A syllogism is not a story, and a naked proposition in a courtroom may be no match for the robust evidence that would be used to prove it. People who hear a story interrupted by gaps of abstraction may be puzzled at the missing chapters, and jurors asked to rest a momentous decision on the story's truth can feel put upon at being asked to take responsibility knowing that more could be said than they have heard. A convincing tale can be told with economy, but when economy becomes a break in the natural sequence of narrative evidence, an assurance that the missing link is really there is never more than second best.

This recognition that the prosecution with its burden of persuasion needs evidentiary depth to tell a continuous story has, however, virtually no application when the point at issue is a defendant's legal status, dependent on some judgment rendered wholly independently of the concrete events of later criminal behavior charged against him. As in this case, the choice of evidence for such an element is usually not between eventful narrative and abstract proposition, but between propositions of slightly varying abstraction, either a record saying that conviction for some crime occurred at a certain time or a statement admitting the same thing without naming the particular offense. . . . Nor can it be argued that the events behind the prior conviction are proper nourishment for the jurors' sense of obligation to vindicate the public interest. The issue is not whether concrete details of the prior crime should come to the jurors' attention but whether the name or general character of that crime is to be disclosed. Congress, however, has made it plain that distinctions among generic felonies do not count for this purpose; the fact of the qualifying conviction is alone what matters under the statute. . . . The most the jury needs to know is that the conviction admitted by the defendant falls within the class of crimes that Congress thought should bar a convict from possessing a gun, and this point may be made readily in a defendant's admission and underscored in the court's jury instructions. Finally, the most obvious reason that the general presumption that the prosecution may choose its evidence is so remote from application here is that proof of the defendant's status goes to an element entirely outside the natural sequence of what the defendant is charged with thinking and doing to commit the current offense. Providing status without telling exactly why that status was imposed leaves no gap in the story of a defendant's subsequent criminality, and its demonstration by stipulation or admission neither displaces a chapter from a continuous sequence of conventional evidence nor comes across as an officious substitution, to confuse or offend or provoke reproach.

Given these peculiarities of the element of felony-convict status and of admissions and the like when used to prove it, there is no cognizable difference between the evidentiary significance of an admission and of the legitimately probative component of the official record the prosecution would prefer to place in evidence. For purposes of the Rule 403 weighing of the probative against the prejudicial, the functions of the competing evidence are distinguishable only by the risk inherent in the one and wholly absent from the other. In this case, as in any other in which the prior conviction is for an offense likely to support conviction on some improper ground, the only reasonable conclusion was that the risk of unfair prejudice did substantially out-weigh the discounted probative value of the record of conviction, and it was an abuse of discretion to admit the record when an admission was available.[10] What we have said shows why this will be the general rule when proof of convict status is at issue, just as the prosecutor's choice will generally survive a Rule 403 analysis when a defendant seeks to force the substitution of an admission for evidence creating a coherent narrative of his thoughts and actions in perpetrating the offense for which he is being tried.

The judgment is reversed, and the case is remanded to the Ninth Circuit for further proceedings consistent with this opinion.[11]

Justice O'CONNOR, with whom THE CHIEF JUSTICE, Justice SCALIA, and Justice THOMAS join, dissenting.

. . . Federal Rule of Evidence 105 provides that when evidence is admissible for one purpose, but not another," the court, upon request, shall restrict the evidence to its proper scope and instruct the jury accordingly." Indeed, on petitioner's own motion in this case, the District Court instructed the jury that it was not to "consider a prior conviction as evidence of guilt of the crime for which the defendant is now on trial." The jury is presumed to have followed this cautionary instruction, see *Shannon v. United States*, 512 U.S. 537, 585 (1994), and the instruction offset whatever prejudice might have arisen from the introduction of petitioner's prior conviction. . . .

A jury is as likely to be puzzled by the "missing chapter" resulting from a defendant's stipulation to his prior felony conviction as it would be by the defendant's conceding any other element of the crime. The jury may wonder why it has not been told the name of the crime, or it may question why the defendant's firearm possession was illegal, given the tradition of lawful gun ownership in this country. . . .

. . . I cannot agree that it "unfairly" prejudices a defendant for the Government to prove his prior conviction with evidence that reveals the name or basic nature of his past crime. Like it or not, Congress chose to

---

10. There may be yet other means of proof besides a formal admission on the record that, with a proper objection, will obligate a district court to exclude evidence of the name of the offense. A redacted record of conviction is the one most frequently mentioned. Any alternative will; of course, require some jury instruction to explain it (just as it will require some discretion when the indictment is read). A redacted judgment in this case, for example, would presumably have revealed to the jury that Old Chief was previously convicted in federal court and sentenced to more than a year's imprisonment, but it would not have shown whether his previous conviction was for one of the business offenses that do not count, under §921(a)(20). Hence, an instruction, with the defendant's consent, would be necessary to make clear that the redacted judgment was enough to satisfy the status element remaining in the case. The Government might, indeed, propose such a redacted judgment for the trial court to weigh against a defendant's offer to admit, as indeed the Government might do even if the defendant's admission had been received into evidence.

11. In remanding, we imply no opinion on the possibility of harmless error, an issue not passed upon below.

make a defendant's prior criminal conviction one of the two elements of the
§922(g)(1) offense. Moreover, crimes have names; a defendant is not
convicted of some indeterminate, unspecified "crime." Nor do I think that
Federal Rule of Evidence 403 can be read to obviate the well accepted
principle, grounded in both the Constitution and in our precedent, that
the Government may not be forced to accept a defendant's concession
to an element of a charged offense as proof of that element. I respectfully
dissent.

DANIEL C. RICHMAN, *OLD CHIEF v. UNITED STATES:* STIPULATING AWAY PROSECUTORIAL ACCOUNTABILITY?

83 Va. L. Rev. 939, 952-953 (1997)

Although the Court appears willfully blind to the effects of its rule on
the government's prospects at trial, Justice Souter's analysis is far more
convincing when read, not as description of jury behavior, but as a determination that prosecutors must accept the consequences of a statute that
reaches far too many cases that do not comport with popular notions of
criminality. . . . Jurors might indeed take §922(g)(1) prosecutions less
seriously, and consequently be less likely to return guilty verdicts, when
precluded from learning the particulars of defendants' prior records. But if
Congress is going to legislate so broadly, the Court suggests, perhaps §922
(g)(1) offenses *ought* to be taken less seriously.

PROBLEM

2.1. A criminal defendant is charged in federal court with three counts
of being a felon in possession of a firearm. The defendant claims he is not a
"felon" within the meaning of the federal prohibition. The prosecutor seeks
to introduce into evidence three high-powered, military-style rifles found in
the defendant's basement. Defense counsel objects on grounds of relevance
and offers to stipulate that three weapons satisfying the statutory definition
of "firearm" were found the defendant's basement. The prosecutor says
she does not want to stipulate to this fact but prefers to prove it, in part
by introducing the guns into evidence. Does the judge have discretion to
overrule the objection?

C. CONDITIONAL RELEVANCE

Many rules of evidence make the admissibility of a particular item of proof
depend on the answer to a "preliminary question" of fact. The attorney-client

privilege, for example, applies only to "confidential" communications. Most preliminary questions of this kind are answered by the trial judge. To apply the attorney-client privilege, for example, the judge simply decides whether he or she believes the communication in question was "confidential."

But when the rule being applied is the ban on irrelevant evidence, things get more complicated. Suppose a piece of evidence—say, in a reckless driving prosecution, the speed of a certain car—is relevant only if some "preliminary fact" is true—say, that the defendant was driving the car. (As you will see, not everyone believes that situations like this actually arise, given the low threshold for relevance. But suppose for the moment that they do.) It seems wrong for the judge to decide whether he or she *personally* believes the defendant was driving the car; if that fact is in dispute, it seems like something the jury should decide.

So the rules direct the judge to allow the speed of the car to be proved as long as there is sufficient evidence to permit *a reasonable jury* to conclude that the defendant was driving the car. The judge applies a "sufficiency" standard, rather than simply deciding for himself or herself whether the preponderance of the evidence suggests that the defendant was at the wheel. The preliminary question the judge has to answer is whether there is sufficient evidence to allow the jury to find the defendant was the driver.

Situations of this kind are instances of "conditional relevance." Lawyers and judges sometimes say loosely that that questions of conditional relevance are for the jury rather than the judge, but that is misleading. The judge still decides on the admissibility of the evidence, and the judge does so by considering a preliminary question of fact. It is just that the preliminary question the judge asks in the case of conditional relevance is not whether the preliminary fact is *actually* true, but whether a reasonable jury could *think* so, given the other evidence in the case.

[F.R.E. 104(b); C.E.C. §403]

EDMUND M. MORGAN, BASIC PROBLEMS OF EVIDENCE

45-46 (1961)

It often happens that upon an issue as to existence of fact C, a combination of facts A and B will be highly relevant but that either without the other will have no relevance. For example, if M is charged with having caused the death of X, the fact that X carried life insurance in favor of M is entirely irrelevant unless M knew of it. Or if P sues D for breach of contract, and offers evidence of an oral offer made to X and acceptance thereof by X in behalf of D, the offer and acceptance are irrelevant unless X's authority to act for D also exists. In each of these situations fact A is irrelevant without fact B. It is impossible to offer evidence through witnesses of both simultaneously. . . . If the proponent can make the existence of B a question for the judge by first offering evidence of the existence of A, he can make the existence of A determinable by the judge by first offering evidence of the existence of B. Consequently where the only objection is lack of relevance, it seems clear that the function of the judge should be to see to it only that sufficient evidence of each is introduced to justify a finding of its existence and the jury should determine the dispute as to each under proper instructions from the judge.

ADVISORY COMMITTEE NOTE TO F.R.E. 104(b)

In some situations, the relevancy of an item of evidence, in the large sense, depends upon the existence of a particular preliminary fact. Thus when a spoken statement is relied upon to prove notice to X, it is without probative value unless X heard it. Or if a letter purporting to be from Y is relied upon to establish an admission by him, it has no probative value unless Y wrote or authorized it. Relevance in this sense has been labelled "conditional relevancy." Morgan, Basic Problems of Evidence 45-46 (1962). Problems arising in connection with it are to be distinguished from problems of logical relevancy, e.g., evidence in a murder case that accused on the day before purchased a weapon of the kind used in the killing, treated in Rule 401.

If preliminary questions of conditional relevancy were determined solely by the judge, as provided in [Rule 104(a)], the functioning of the jury as a trier of fact would be greatly restricted and in some cases virtually destroyed. These are appropriate questions for juries. Accepted treatment, as provided in the rule, is consistent with that given fact questions generally. The judge makes a preliminary determination whether the foundation evidence is sufficient to support a finding of fulfillment of the condition. If so, the item is admitted. If, after all the evidence on the issue is in, pro and con, the jury could reasonably conclude that fulfillment of the condition is not established, the issue is for them. If the evidence is not such as to allow a finding, the judge withdraws the matter from their consideration. . . . The order of proof here, as generally, is subject to the control of the judge.

STATE v. McNEELY

8 P.3d 212 (Or. 2000)

Van Hoomissen, J.

[Defendant McNeely was convicted of aggravated murder. A fellow jail inmate, Thompson, testified at trial about statements McNeely had made to him.]

Defendant contends . . . that the trial court erred in denying his motion to exclude Thompson's testimony, because Thompson was unable to identify defendant at trial as the man with whom he had spoken in jail. . . . The state responds that Thompson's testimony was "conditionally relevant," citing OEC 104,[5] and, thus, was properly admitted.

Defendant's assignment of error presents a question of conditional relevancy. . . . When dealing with a matter of conditional relevancy under OEC 104(2), the judge determines whether the foundation evidence is sufficient for the jury reasonably to find that the condition on which relevance depends has been fulfilled. If so, the evidence is admitted; if not, the evidence is not admitted. After the judge decides that the foundation evidence is sufficient for the jury reasonably to find the contested fact under OEC 104(2), either party may introduce evidence before the jury that is relevant to the weight and credibility of the evidence.

At trial, Thompson testified that he had spoken with a man in jail who had admitted choking and killing the victim. If defendant were that man, then Thompson's testimony was relevant evidence. There also was evidence at trial that Thompson and defendant had met in jail in 1993. Thompson testified:

> "I spoke to somebody that represented himself as being [defendant] or was represented by somebody else as being [defendant]."

Thompson related several incriminating conversations that he had with that man. Moreover, there also was evidence that defendant had gained 25 pounds and had shaved off his moustache since the time when he and Thompson were in jail together.

Despite Thompson's inability to identify defendant at trial, the trial court determined that a reasonable juror could find that defendant was the person with whom Thompson had spoken in jail. The record supports that conclusion. We agree with the trial court. Thompson's inability to identify defendant at trial went to the weight the jury might give to his testimony, not to its admissibility. It follows that the trial court did not err in leaving the matter to the jury. . . . [Affirmed.]

---

5. OEC 104 provides in part:

"(1) Preliminary questions concerning the qualification of a person to be a witness, the existence of a privilege or the admissibility of evidence shall be determined by the court, subject to the provisions of subsection (2) of this section. In making its determination the court is not bound by the rules of evidence except those with respect to privileges."

"(2) When the relevancy of evidence depends upon the fulfillment of a condition of fact, the court shall admit it upon, or subject to, the introduction of evidence sufficient to support a finding of the fulfillment of the condition."

Conditional relevancy means a situation where one fact is relevant only if another fact is proven. Laird C. Kirkpatrick, *Oregon Evidence* 31 (2d ed. 1989 & Supp. 1999).

VAUGHN C. BALL, THE MYTH
OF CONDITIONAL RELEVANCE

14 Ga. L. Rev. 435, 440-446, 453, 467 (1980)

[L]et us consider one of Professor Morgan's illustrations, the case of the oral contract alleged to have been entered into by P and by X as agent for D. Almost all of the illustrations can be cast into a parallel form. In Morgan's formulation, fact A is: offer by P and acceptance by X on behalf of D, all treated as one fact. Fact B is authorization of X to contract for D. "[T]he offer and acceptance are irrelevant unless X's authority to act for D also exists." . . .

[But] problems of evidence . . . deal with *probabilities*, not with truths or falsehoods. . . . The definition of relevancy adopted in all modern writing on the subject and in the Federal Rules recognizes this. . . . [13]

. . . [Whatever the probability of B,] there [is] some possibility of a contract when A occur[s], but by definition no probability of a contract when A [does] not occur. . . . [Therefore,] the probability of a contract [is] greater if A occur[s] than if it [does] not. And evidence which raise[s] A's probability thus change[s] the probability of a contract . . . and thus [is] relevant to the proposition of contract.

The failure to notice and deal with the obvious relation between no offer and acceptance and no contract is what shows that the received doctrine, after paying lip-service to the definition or relevancy based on probability, slips back into the true-false groove, which is so useful in analyzing the substantive law, and so misleading in analyzing evidence. . . . [T]here does not appear to be any scope for the operation of Rule 104(b) at all.

PROBLEM

2.2. The prosecution in a murder case wishes to demonstrate motive by proving that, a week before his death, the victim assaulted the defendant's cousin. Defense counsel objects on grounds of relevance. How should the judge rule? Does it matter whether the judge believes (a) that the defendant knew about the assault, or (b) that the jury could reasonably conclude the defendant knew about the assault?

---

13. Rule 401 says "any" tendency to make more probable or less probable than it would be without the evidence; and the Note says: "Any more stringent requirement is unworkable and unrealistic," quoting McCormick, who points out that "a brick is not a wall." Everyone recognizes that a brick is not a wall at some point in these analyses. The difficulties of the current doctrine of conditional relevancy stem from the inability to recognize a brick.

3

Hearsay

"I heard he came into money and moved to a portobello."

A. The Hearsay Rule and Its Rationale

1. Introduction

Wigmore called the hearsay prohibition "the most characteristic rule of the Anglo-American law of Evidence" and said it was second only to jury trial as "the greatest contribution of that eminently practical legal system to the world's methods of procedures." Few commentators since have been so charitable. The general attitude today is probably best summed

up by the English evidence scholar Peter Murphy: "There should probably
be an organisation called 'Hearsay Anonymous.' Membership would be
open to those judges, practitioners and students (not to mention occasional
law teachers) to whom the rule against hearsay has always been an awesome
and terrifying mystery. Like its partner in terror, the rule against perpetuities, the rule against hearsay ranks as one of the law's most celebrated
nightmares."

For better or worse, the hearsay rule and its exceptions are unrivalled
for complexity by any other part of American evidence law—or, probably, by
any part of the evidence law of any other nation. Hearsay law is complicated
not only because the prohibition against hearsay has many exceptions, but
also because the prohibition itself can be difficult to comprehend. At its
core, though, the hearsay rule expresses a very simple notion: Factual disputes in criminal and civil cases should be decided based on live, sworn
testimony, not secondhand accounts of what other people said outside of
court. Opinions differ on the merits of this notion, but no one doubts its
importance. It reflects the strong and distinctive preference our system of
adjudication has historically had for *vive voce* evidence, and a continuing
faith that juries are best able to sort truth from falsehood by hearing directly
from sworn witnesses subject to cross-examination.

[F.R.E. 801(a)-(c), 802; C.E.C. §§225, 1200]

TRIAL OF SIR WALTER RALEIGH, KNIGHT, FOR HIGH TREASON, BY A SPECIAL COMMISION OF OYER AND TERMINER, AT WINCHESTER, 17TH NOVEMBER, 1603, 2 JAMES I

1 Criminal Trials 400, 427, 434-436, 441-442, 449, 451, 511
(David Jardine ed., 1850)

[Raleigh was charged with conspiring with Lord Cobham and others to
kill James I and to place Lady Arabella Stuart on the throne. Cobham was
interrogated in the Tower of London and signed a sworn confession,
which he later recanted. His confession was the chief evidence against
Raleigh.]

Sir W. Raleigh. . . . But it is strange to see how you press me still with
my Lord Cobham, and yet will not produce him; it is not for gaining of time
or prolonging my life that urge this; he is the house hard by and may soon be
brought hither; let him be produced, and if he will yet accuse me or avow
this Confession of his, it shall convict me and ease you of further proof.

Lord Cecil. Sir Walter Raleigh presseth often that my Lord Cobham
should be brought face to face; if he ask as a thing of grace or favour,
they must come from him only who can give them; but if he ask a matter
of law, then, in order that we, who sit here as commissioners, may be satisfied, I desire to hear the opinions of my Lords, the Judges, whether it may
be done by law.

The Judges all answered, that in respect it might be a mean to cover many with treasons, and it might be prejudicial to the King, therefore by the law it was not sufferable.

Sir W. Raleigh. Good my Lords, let my accuser come face to face, and be deposed. Were the case but for a small copyhold, you would have witnesses or good proof to lead the jury to a verdict; and I am here for my life!

Popham, C.J. There must not such a gap be opened for the destruction of the King as would be if we should grant this; you plead hard for yourself, but the laws plead as hard for the King. Where no circumstances do concur to make a matter probable, then an accuser may be heard; but so many circumstances agreeing and confirming the accusation in this case, the accuser is not to be produced; for having first confessed against himself voluntarily, and so charged another person, if we shall now hear him again in person, he may for favour or fear retract what formerly he hath said, and the jury may, by that means, be inveigled. . . .

Sir Walter Raleigh. I have already often urged the producing of my Lord Cobham, but it is still denied me. I appeal now once more to your Lordships in this: my Lord Cobham is the only one that hath accused me, for all the treasons urged upon me are by reflection from him. It is now clear that he hath since retracted; therefore since his accusation is recalled by himself, let him now by word of mouth convict or condemn me. Campion, the Jesuit, was not denied to have his accusers face to face. And if that be true which hath been some labored all this day, that I have been the setter-on of my Lord Cobham, his instigator, and have *infused* these treasons upon him, as hath been said, then have I been the efficient cause of his destruction; all his honours, houses, lands, and good, and all he hath, are lost by me; against whom, then, should he seek revenge but upon me? And the world knoweth him as revengeful of nature as any man living. Besides, a dying man is ever presumed to speak truth: now Cobham is absolutely in the King's mercy; to excuse me cannot avail him, by accusing me he may hope for favour. It is you, then, Mr. Attorney, that should press his testimony, and I ought to fear his producing, if all that be true which you have alleged.

Lord Henry Howard. Sir Walter, you have heard that it cannot be granted; pray importune us no longer.

Sir Walter Raleigh. Nay, my Lord, it toucheth my life, which I value at as a high a rate as your Lordship does yours.

Lord Cecil. I am afraid my often speaking may give opinion to the hearers that I have delight to hear myself talk. Sir Walter Raleigh has often urged, and still doth urge, the producing of my Lord Cobham, I would know of my Lords the Judges, if it might not stand with the order of our proceedings to take a further time, and know his Majesty's pleasure in that which is desired.

The Judges resolved that the Proceedings must go on and receive an end. . . .

Attorney-General. I shall now produce a witness *viva voce.*

He then produced one Dyer, a pilot, who being sworn said, Being at Lisbon, there came to me a Portugal gentleman who asked me how the King of England did, and whether he was crowned? I answered him that I hoped our noble King was well and crowned by this, but the time was not come when I came from the coast for Spain. "Nay," says he, "your King shall never be crowned, for Don Cobham and Don Raleigh will cut his throat before he come to be crowned." And this in time was found to be spoken in mid July.

Sir W. Raleigh. This is the saying of some wild Jesuit or beggarly Priest; but what proof is it against me?

Attorney-General. It must per force arise out of some preceding intelligence, and shows that your treason had wings. . . .

The Evidence now seemed at an end; whereupon Sir Walter Raleigh addressed himself to the Jury, and used a speech to this effect:—

Sir W. Raleigh. You, Gentlemen of the Jury . . . if you yourselves would like to be hazarded in your lives, disabled in your posterities,—your lands, goods, and all you have confiscated,—your wives, children, and servants left crying to the world; if you would be content all this should befall you upon a trial by suspicions and presumptions,—upon an accusation not subscribed by your accuser,—without the open testimony of a single witness, then so judge me as you would yourselves be judged. . . .

This ended, the jury were willed to go together; who departed, and stayed not a quarter of an hour, when they returned, bringing in their verdict of Guilty of Treason. . . . The Lord Chief Justice then delivered the judgment of the Court in the usual form in cases of high treason. . . .

The conduct of the Judges on the trial of Sir Walter Raleigh at Winchester has been warmly censured by his numerous biographers, and by most modern historians who have related the transaction: and, undoubtedly, the injustice of the course of evidence and of the conviction is so flagrant, that unprofessional writers and readers are naturally led into the belief, that the whole proceedings must have been, even at that time, grossly contrary to law. Unfortunately, and in spite of the general assertion of lawyers to the contrary, the rules of law are not, even in the present improved state of society, always founded upon the principles of reason and justice; still less were they so in the reign of James I.

LEAKE v. HAGERT

175 N.W.2d 675 (N.D. 1970)

PAULSON, J.

This is an appeal by the plaintiff, Allen Leake, from a judgment of dismissal of his cause of action entered in the District Court of Grand Forks County, North Dakota, and from an order of the trial court denying his motion for a new trial.

Allen Leake's complaint was predicated upon the alleged negligence of the defendant, Charlotte Hagert, in her operation of a motor vehicle on

October 25, 1966, wherein she negligently and carelessly drove her automobile into the rear of the plow being towed by a tractor which Leake was operating, causing injuries to Leake and damages to his plow and tractor. Leake's complaint included allegations of damages for hospital and doctor bills; for permanent injuries to his chest and right arm; for pain and suffering; and for damages to his plow and tractor; and he prayed for a judgment against Charlotte Hagert in the sum of $27,600. Charlotte Hagert, in her answer, admitted that the collision occurred, but, as a defense, denied that the collision was proximately caused by her negligence in the operation of her motor vehicle, and she alleged that the sole and proximate cause of the collision was the negligence of the plaintiff in the maintenance and operation of his tractor and plow, upon a public highway after sunset, without proper lights, reflectors, or other warnings. Charlotte Hagert counterclaimed for damages caused by the alleged negligence of Allen Leake for permanent injuries, for pain and suffering, for hospitalization and medical expenses, and for damages to her 1966 Plymouth automobile; and she prayed for a judgment against him in the sum of $32,000.

All claims and defenses of both Allen Leake and Charlotte Hagert were submitted to a jury, which returned a verdict dismissing the complaint of Allen Leake as well as dismissing the counterclaim of Charlotte Hagert. . . .

[Leake appealed but Hagert did not.]

Leake's first contention on appeal is that certain errors at law occurred during the course of the trial, at the time that the trial court overruled objections to the admission of certain evidence. The evidence objected to was certain testimony adduced from Edward Gross, an adjuster who investigated the accident. Gross testified that Allen Leake's son told him, with reference to the small rear light on the tractor, that the red lens had been out for some time. Edward Gross's testimony concerning the statement of Allen Leake's son was hearsay.

The hearsay rule prohibits use of a person's assertion, as equivalent to testimony of the fact asserted, unless the assertor is brought to testify in court on the stand, where he may be probed and cross-examined as to the grounds of his assertion and his qualifications to make it. *Grand Forks B. & D. Co. v. Iowa Hardware Mut. Ins. Co.*, 31 N.W.2d 495 (1948). *See* 5 Wigmore on Evidence (3d ed.) §§ 1361, 1364. . . . Leake's son did not testify in the present action; he was not a party to the action; his statement was not made under oath; his statement was not subject to cross-examination; and he was not available as a witness at the time of trial because he was in the Army and overseas. We find that it was error for the trial court to admit into evidence the testimony concerning what Leake's son said to Edward Gross; the son's statement was hearsay and should have been excluded.

Having found that the trial court erred in admitting the statement of Allen Leake's son into evidence, we must determine on this appeal whether such an erroneous admission was prejudicial and constitutes reversible error. Under Rule 61, N.D.R. Civ. P., error in the admission of evidence is not a ground for a new trial unless such error affects the substantial rights of the parties. . . . Other witnesses testified during the trial as to the condition of the taillight and whether the light had a red lens. Curtis Hagert, Myron Larson, and Edward Gross testified to the fact that the rear light was painted or covered with some reddish substance and that there was nothing which would indicate that the red lens had been shattered by the accident. In addition, a statement taken by Edward Gross, from Allen Leake's summary of circumstances surrounding the accident, included a statement that the lens had been out for some time before the accident. This statement was introduced by Allen Leake. Reviewing the record concerning the testimony submitted with reference to the condition of the light and the lens at the time of the accident, we find that the hearsay statement of Allen Leake's son was erroneously admitted by the trial court, but that such error was not prejudicial. . . . [The judgment is affirmed.]

McCORMICK ON EVIDENCE
§245, at 2:125-127 (Kenneth S. Broun, ed., 6th ed. 2006)

The factors upon which the value of testimony depends are the perception, memory, narration, and sincerity of the witness. (1) *Perception*. Did the witness perceive what is described and perceive it accurately? (2) *Memory*. Has the witness retained an accurate impression of that perception? (3) *Narration*. Does the witness' language convey that impression accurately? (4) *Sincerity*. Is the witness, with varying degrees of intention, testifying falsely?

In order to encourage witnesses to put forth their best efforts and to expose inaccuracies that might be present with respect to any of the foregoing factors, the Anglo-American tradition evolved three conditions under which witnesses ordinarily are required to testify: oath, personal presence at the trial, and cross-examination. The rule against hearsay is designed to insure compliance with these ideal conditions, and when one of them is absent, the hearsay objection becomes pertinent.

In the hearsay situation, two "witnesses" are involved. The first complies with all three of the ideal conditions for the giving of testimony but merely reports what the second "witness" said. The second "witness" is the out-of-court declarant whose statement was not given in compliance with the ideal conditions but contains the critical information.

Oath. Among the earliest of the criticisms of hearsay, and one often repeated in judicial opinions down to the present, is the objection that the out-of-court declarant who made the hearsay statement commonly speaks or writes without the solemnity of the oath administered to witnesses in a court of law. The oath may be important in two aspects. As a ceremonial and religious symbol, it may induce a feeling of special obligation to speak the truth, and it may also impress upon the witness the danger of criminal punishment for perjury, to which the judicial oath of an equivalent solemn affirmation would be a prerequisite condition. . . .

Personal presence at trial. Another long-asserted objection is the lack of opportunity for observation of the out-of-court declarant's demeanor, with the light that this may shed on credibility. In addition, the solemnity of the occasion and possibility of public disgrace can scarcely fail to impress the witness, and testifying falsely becomes more difficult if the person against whom it is directed is present. . . .

Cross-examination. The lack of any opportunity for the adversary to cross-examine the absent declarant whose out-of-court statement is reported is today accepted as the main justification for the exclusion of hearsay. As early as 1668, hearsay was rejected because "the other party could not cross-examine the witness sworn." . . . Cross-examination, as Bentham pointed out, was a distinctive feature of the English trial system, and the one that most contributed to the prestige of the institution of jury trial. He called it "a security for the correctness and completeness of testimony." The nature of this safeguard which hearsay lacks is indicated by Chancellor Kent: "Hearsay testimony is from the very nature of it attended with all such doubts and difficulties and it cannot clear them up. 'A person who relates a hearsay is not obliged to enter into any particulars, to answer any questions, to solve any difficulties, to reconcile any contradictions, to explain any obscurities, to remove any ambiguities; he entrenches himself in the simple assertion that he was told so, and leaves the burden entirely on his dead or absent author.'" In perhaps his most famous remark, Wigmore described cross-examination as "beyond any doubt the greatest legal engine ever invented for the discovery of truth."

LAURENCE H. TRIBE, TRIANGULATING HEARSAY

87 Harv. L. Rev. 957, 958-961 (1974)

The basic hearsay problem is that of forging a reliable chain of inferences, from an act or utterance of a person not subject to contemporaneous in-court cross-examination about that act or utterance, to an event that the act or utterance is supposed to reflect. Typically, the first link in the required chain of inferences is the link from the act or utterance to the belief it is thought to express or indicate. It is helpful to think of this link as involving a "trip" into the head of the person responsible for the act or utterance (the declarant) to see what he or she was really thinking when the act occurred. The second link is the one from the declarant's assumed belief to a conclusion about some external event that is supposed to have triggered the belief, or that is linked to the belief in some other way. This link involves a trip out of the head of the declarant, in order to match the declarant's assumed belief with the external reality sought to be demonstrated.

The trier must obviously employ such a chain of inferences whenever a witness testifies in court. But the process has long been regarded as particularly suspect when the act or utterance is not one made in court, under oath, by a person whose demeanor at the time is witnessed by the trier, and under circumstances permitting immediate cross-examination by counsel in order to probe possible inaccuracies in the inferential chain. These inaccuracies are usually attributed to the four testimonial infirmities of ambiguity, insincerity, faulty perception, and erroneous memory. In the absence of special reasons, the perceived untrustworthiness of such an out-of-court act or utterance has led the Anglo-Saxon legal system to exclude it as hearsay despite its potentially probative value.

There exists a rather simple way of schematizing all of this in terms of an elementary geometric construct that serves to structure its several related elements. The construct might be called the Testimonial Triangle. By making graphic the path of inferences, and by functionally grouping the problems encountered along the path, the triangle makes it easier both to identify when a hearsay problem exists and to structure consideration of the appropriateness of exceptions to the rule that bars hearsay inferences.

The diagram is as follows:

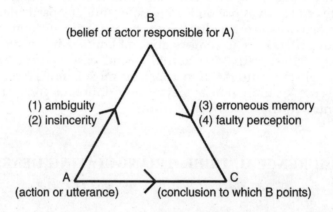

B
(belief of actor responsible for A)

(1) ambiguity   (3) erroneous memory
(2) insincerity   (4) faulty perception

A   C
(action or utterance)   (conclusion to which B points)

If we use the diagram to trace the inferential path the trier must follow, we begin at the lower left vertex of the triangle (A), which represents the declarant's (X's) act or assertion. The path first takes us to the upper vertex (B), representing X's belief in what his or her act or assertion suggests, and then takes us to the lower right vertex (C), representing the external reality suggested by X's belief. When "A" is used to prove "C" along the path through "B," a traditional hearsay problem exists and the use of the act or assertion as evidence is disallowed upon proper objection in the absence of some special reason to permit it.

It is of course a simple matter to locate the four testimonial infirmities on the triangle to show where and how they might impede the process of inference. To go from "A" to "B," the declarant's belief, one must remove the obstacles of (1) ambiguity and (2) insincerity. To go from "B" to "C," the external fact, one must further remove the obstacles of (3) erroneous memory and (4) faulty perception. . . . By contrast, when the trier's inference can proceed from "A" directly to "C," the infirmities of hearsay do not arise. For example, the out-of-court statement "I can speak" would be admissible as nonhearsay to prove that the declarant was capable of speech, for it is the fact of his speaking rather than the content of the statement which permits the inference, and that involves no problems of the statement's ambiguity, or of sincerity, memory, or perception.

PROBLEM

3.1. In February and March 1857, a Glasgow clerk named Emile L'Angelier suffered three attacks of internal pain and vomiting. The third attack killed him. An autopsy found arsenic in his stomach. Several months later L'Angelier's former lover, Madeleine Smith, was tried before the High Court of Justiciary in Edinburgh for his murder. The jury returned a verdict of "not proven," and Smith was set free. The outcome was widely attributed to an evidence ruling by the three presiding judges:

> Amongst L'Angelier's effects was found a little pocket-book. . . . There are various entries of no particular interest, then comes: "Thursday, 19th February. Saw Mimi a few moments. Was very ill during the night. Friday, 20th February. Passed two pleasant hours with Mimi in the drawing room. Saturday, 21st February. Did not feel very well. Sunday, 22nd February. Saw Mimi in drawing room. Promised me French Bible. Taken very ill." These dates cover . . . the dates of the first two illnesses. . . .
>
> The defence, quite rightly, fought hard to obtain the exclusion of this pocket-book from the evidence. The Lord Justice-Clerk, Lord Handyside, and Lord Ivory had to decide this vital question of the pocket-book. The Lord Justice-Clerk and Lord Handyside held that it was not admissible. Lord Ivory disagreed with them. The Lord Justice-Clerk said that he was unable to admit such evidence. "It might relax the sacred laws of evidence to an extent that the mind could hardly contemplate. One could not tell how many documents might exist and be found in the repositories of a deceased person. A man might have threatened another, he might have hatred against him and be determined to revenge himself, and what entries might he not make in a diary for this purpose?" Lord Handyside pointed out that, had the writer of the memoranda still been alive, they could not have been used for evidence. . . . It was generally felt dangerous to admit as evidence memoranda on which no examination could in the nature of things be possible. The pocket-book was therefore ruled out as evidence. . . .

F. Tennyson Jesse, *Trial of Madeleine Smith* 35 (1927). As a result of this ruling, "the prosecution failed to adduce the smallest vestige of evidence that Madeleine met L'Angelier before any of the three occasions on which he was taken ill." *Id.* at 32.

Was the diary hearsay? Were the judges right to exclude it?

2. Nonhearsay Uses of Out-of-Court Statements

The canonical formulation of the hearsay rule bars the use of "out-of-court statements to prove the truth of the matter asserted." The term "out-of-court" is shorthand for any statement other than one made under oath and in front of the factfinder during the same proceeding in which it is being offered in evidence. Testimony in an earlier trial, for example, counts as an "out-of-court" statement for purposes of the hearsay rule.

The traditional definition of hearsay raises two problems. One is figuring out what constitutes a "statement," and the other is figuring out what it means for a statement to be introduced "for the truth of the matter asserted." Of these two problems, the second causes by far the most trouble and it is the subject of this section. The first problem, the definition of "statement," is taken up in the section following this one.

The easiest way to grasp what it means to introduce a statement "to prove the truth of the matter asserted" is to consider *other* things a statement can be used to prove, *aside* from "the truth of the matter asserted." The cases that follow provide illustrations of such nonhearsay uses of out-of-court statements.

In reading these cases—and the remainder of this chapter—you can avoid a great deal of confusion if you keep in mind several points of terminology.

First, in the definition of hearsay, the "matter asserted" means the matter asserted *in the statement offered into evidence,* not the matter "asserted" by the party offering the evidence. *All* evidence presumably is offered to prove the truth of claims made by the party offering the evidence.

Second, evidence typically is introduced to support not just one proposition but a series of propositions, linked together in a chain of inference. Evidence of an out-of-court statement thus may tend to prove A, which in turn makes more likely B, which in turn suggests C. (Recall the love letter discussed by Professor Morgan in Chapter Two.) If *any one* of the propositions in this chain of inference is "the truth of the matter asserted" in the out-of-court statement, the evidence falls within the traditional definition of hearsay.

Third, the words "witness" and "declarant" have specialized meanings in hearsay law. In everyday parlance, the word "witness" often means someone who sees or observes something, and the word "declarant" is often used for someone who says something under oath. But in hearsay law the term "witness" is reserved for someone who testifies under oath, from the witness stand, and the term "declarant" refers to someone who makes a statement of any kind, whether or not under oath, and whether in or out of court.

Most potential hearsay situations involve two statements. The second one is made under oath in court by a "witness," and it describes the first statement. The person who makes the first statement is called the "declarant." Thus, in *Leake v. Hagert*, Edward Gross was the witness, and Allan Leake's son was the declarant. In *Raleigh's Case*, Dyer was a witness, but the "Portugal gentleman" was just a declarant.

Not all potential hearsay situations involve two statements, because not all out-of-court statements are introduced through the testimony of a live witness. When an out-of-court statement is written—like Cobham's confession in *Raleigh's Case*—the written document itself typically is introduced. When the statement is electronically recorded, the recording is usually offered into evidence. But most out-of-court statements are introduced through the testimony of a witness, so most hearsay situations involve two statements: an in-court statement, by a "witness," about an out-of-court statement, by a "declarant."

ADVISORY COMMITTEE NOTE TO F.R.E. 801(C)

The definition follows along familiar lines in including only statements offered to prove the truth of the matter asserted. McCormick § 225; 5 Wigmore § 1361, 6 id. § 1766. If the significance of an offered statement lies solely in the fact that it was made no issue is raised as to the truth of anything asserted, and the statement is not hearsay. Emich Motors Corp. v. General Motors Corp., 181 F.2d 70 (7th Cir 1950), rev'd on other grounds 340 U.S. 558, letters of complaint from customers offered as a reason for cancellation of dealer's franchise, to rebut contention that franchise was revoked for refusal to finance sales through affiliated finance company. The effect is to exclude from hearsay the entire category of "verbal acts" and "verbal parts of an act," in which the statement itself affects the legal rights of the parties or is a circumstance bearing on conduct affecting their rights.

LYONS PARTNERSHIP v. MORRIS COSTUMES, INC.

243 F.3d 789 (4th Cir. 2001)

NIEMEYER, Circuit Judge:

. . . Lyons Partnership, L.P., ("Lyons"), a Texas limited partnership, owns all of the intellectual property rights to the character "Barney," the well-stuffed Tyrannosaurus Rex with a green chest and stomach, friendly mien, green spots on its back, and yellow "toeballs." Barney is readily recognizable to young children, who repeatedly parrot his song, "I Love You," often testing the patience of nearby adults. . . . [T]he "Barney and Friends" show is viewed weekly by 14 million children, and over 50 million copies of Barney-related videos have been sold. . . . Lyons has registered approximately 25 trademarks and obtained hundreds of copyrights with respect to the name "Barney" and the character's depiction.

. . . Lyons commenced this action against Morris Costumes, . . . a retail costume-rental establishment in Charlotte, North Carolina. . . . [The complaint alleged, among other things, that Morris Costumes rented a "Duffy the Dragon" costume that infringed Lyons's trademarks in Barney.] After a four-day bench trial, the district court entered judgment in favor of the defendants on all claims. . . .

The district court found . . . that Lyons had not demonstrated a likelihood of confusion between the Duffy costume and the Barney character. It reached its conclusion, however, only after disregarding most of the evidence of actual confusion. . . . Although the court stated that "[t]here is no evidence on which to support a finding concerning actual confusion of children," ample evidence presented at trial would have supported such a finding. . . . [T]he principal at an elementary school testified that when she wore the Duffy costume at a school rally, the children shouted "Barney. Barney. Barney," and parents testified that when they rented the Duffy costume for their children's birthday parties, the children believed that the person dressed as Duffy was in fact Barney. In addition, Lyons offered newspaper clippings that evidenced actual confusion between Duffy and

Barney, not only by the children who were the subject of the articles, but by the reporters themselves, who erroneously described Duffy as "Barney."

Despite initially admitting that evidence, the district court's final opinion dismissed it as "unreliable hearsay." If the district court disregarded this evidence because it was hearsay, we believe that this conclusion was erroneous. Lyons did not offer the children's statements or the newspaper articles to prove the truth of the matter asserted—i.e., that the persons wearing the Duffy costume were in fact Barney—but rather merely to prove that the children and the newspaper reporters *expressed their belief* that those persons were Barney. This was direct evidence of the children's and the reporters' reactions and not hearsay. . . . Because such evidence was highly probative of actual confusion and the existence of actual confusion is often dispositive to a trademark infringement analysis, we . . . vacate the district court's judgment as to the Duffy-related trademark claim. . . .

UNITED STATES v. PARRY

649 F.2d 292 (5th Cir. 1981)

Lewis R. Morgan, Circuit Judge.

The question in this case is whether the district court erred in excluding certain testimony by the appellant's mother as inadmissible hearsay. We conclude that the evidence should have been admitted and therefore reverse appellant's convictions and remand for a new trial.

Scott Parry was tried before a jury and convicted in consolidated cases of conspiring to distribute phenycyclidine hydrochloride (PCP) and of possessing with intent to distribute PCP and dimethamphetamine hydrochloride. . . . Parry did not deny that he had participated in the drug transactions described by [two undercover narcotics] agents but argued that, during each of these transactions, he had proceeded upon the good faith belief that he was working for the agents, assisting them in locating drug dealers. . . .

In support of his position that he had known from the outset of the agents' identities, Parry related a conversation he had had with his mother shortly after he met [one of the agents] in October 1974 and well in advance of his arrest in January 1975. Parry testified that, in response to his mother's inquiry, he had stated that the person who had frequently telephoned her home asking to speak to Parry was a narcotics agent with whom he was then working. In an effort to corroborate his story, Parry called his mother as a witness. . . . Although the government voiced no objection to the proffered testimony, the court ruled that Parry's mother could not testify to "any conversations that she had with her son or that her son had with her." . . .

Rule 801(c) of the Federal Rules of Evidence defines hearsay as "a statement, other than one made by the declarant while testifying at the trial or hearing, offered in evidence to prove the truth of the matter asserted." The reasons for excluding hearsay are clear: when an out-of-court statement is offered as a testimonial assertion of the truth of the matter stated, we are vitally interested in the credibility of the out-of-court declarant. Because a statement made out of court is not exposed to the normal credibility safeguards of oath, presence at trial, and cross-examination, the jury has no basis for evaluating the declarant's trustworthiness and thus his statement is considered unreliable. Implicit in both the definition and justification for the rule, however, is the recognition that whenever an out-of-court statement is offered for some purpose other than to prove the truth of the matter asserted, the value of the statement does not rest upon the declarant's credibility and, therefore, is not subject to attack as hearsay. . . .

Parry's mother sought to testify that her son had stated that the person who had been telephoning her home was a narcotics agent and that he, Parry, was working with the agent. As Parry explained to the district court, this statement was not offered to prove that the caller was a narcotics agent or that Parry was working with the agent, but to establish that Parry had knowledge of the agent's identity when he spoke. In other words, Parry offered the statement as the basis for a circumstantial inference by the jury that, if this statement was in fact made—a question which the in-court witness could testify to while under oath, before the jury, and subject to cross-examination—then Parry probably knew of the agent's identity. Using an out-of-court utterance as circumstantial evidence of the declarant's knowledge of the existence of some fact, rather than as testimonial evidence of the truth of the matter asserted, does not offend the hearsay rule. . . . Contrary to the government's position, the danger that the jury could improperly use the out-of-court statement as an assertion to be believed does not render the statement inadmissible. Where evidence is admissible for one purpose but not for another, the accepted practice is to admit the evidence with instructions that the jury consider the evidence only for the permissible purpose. A different rule applies only where the probative value of the evidence when used for its allowable purpose is outweighed by the prejudice that would result if the evidence were used for its improper purpose. In this case the dangers associated with the jury's possible misuse of the out-of-court statement are not sufficient to require that the evidence be excluded. The court should admit the statement and give a limiting instruction that the statement is admissible only as circumstantial evidence of Parry's knowledge and not as evidence of the truth of the matter asserted. . . .

Rather than being merely cumulative, the excluded testimony was the only available evidence that could corroborate Parry's story that he had known of the agents' identities, a story the jury may have found self-serving if not farfetched. . . . Moreover, the jury may well have assumed that because Parry did not ask his mother to confirm the existence of the critical conversation, the conversation probably never occurred. Because we are unable to say with fair assurance that the jury was not substantially influenced by the error, we must reverse Parry's conviction and remand for a new trial.

SUBRAMANIAM v. PUBLIC PROSECUTOR

1 W.L.R. 965 (Privy Council 1956)

Their Lordships' reasons for allowing the appeal were delivered by Mr. L. M. D. DE SILVA. This is an appeal, by special leave, from a judgment of the Supreme Court of the Federation of Malaya dismissing an appeal against a conviction in the High Court of Jahore Bahru whereby the appellant was found guilty of being in possession on April 29, 1955, of 20 rounds of ammunition contrary to regulation 4(1)(*b*) of the Emergency Regulations, 1951, and sentenced to death. . . .

It was common ground that . . . the appellant was found in a wounded condition by certain members of the security forces; that when he was searched there was found around his waist a leather belt with three pouches containing 20 live rounds of ammunition; no weapon of any description was found upon him or in the immediate vicinity.

The defence put forward on behalf of appellant was that he had been captured by terrorists, that at all material times he was acting under duress, and that at the time of his capture by the security forces he had formed the intention to surrender, with which intention he had come to the place where he was found. . . .

The appellant gave evidence in defence. . . . He described how he was forced to accompany the terrorists, one of whom walked in front and two behind, who told him he was being taken to their leader. At this stage an intervention by the trial judge is recorded thus:-

> "*Court*: I tell Murugason hearsay evidence is not admissible and all the conversation with the bandits is not admissible unless they are called."

Murugason was counsel assigned to defend the appellant.

In ruling out peremptorily the evidence of conversation between the terrorists and the appellant the trial judge was in error. Evidence of a statement made to a witness by a person who is not himself called as a witness may or may not be hearsay. It is hearsay and inadmissible when the object of the evidence is to establish the truth of what is contained in the statement. It is not hearsay and is admissible when it is proposed to be established by the evidence, not the truth of the statement, but the fact that it was made. The fact that the statement was made, quite apart from its truth, is frequently relevant in considering the mental state and conduct thereafter of the witness or of some other person in whose presence the statement was made. In the case before their Lordships statements could have been made to the appellant by the terrorists, which, whether true or not, if they had been believed by the appellant, might reasonably have induced in him an apprehension of instant death if he failed to conform to their wishes. . . . Their Lordships feel unable to hold with any confidence that had the excluded evidence, which goes to the very root of the defence of duress, been admitted the result of the trial would probably have been the same.

For the reasons which have been given their Lordships have humbly advised Her Majesty that the appeal be allowed.

SOUTHERLAND v. SYCAMORE COMMUNITY SCHOOL DISTRICT

No. 03-4189 (6th Cir., Dec. 17, 2004)

Sutton, Circuit Judge.

Sycamore Community School District challenges a $50,000 jury verdict in favor of Cheryl Southerland, a bus driver for the school district, who accused the district of sexual harassment and negligent retention. . . . From April of 1999 through January of 2000, Southerland was the victim of several instances of harassing conduct by another bus driver, Ralph Smith. . . . [The evidence indicated that Smith stalked Southerland, tailgated her bus, stared and leered at her, spread a rumor that he was sexually involved with her, and ignored repeated instructions from company officers to stay away from her. Southerland suffered depression requiring medication, became so distraught she rear-ended a car, was hospitalized for chest pains, and was forced to take medical leave. Finally, in February 2000, Sycamore suspended Smith, and, following a disciplinary hearing, he resigned.]

Sycamore . . . argues that testimony regarding . . . rumors floating around the bus compound that Smith and Southerland were having a relationship . . . amounted to inadmissible hearsay. . . . [W]e do not agree.

" 'Hearsay' is a statement, other than one made by the declarant while testifying at the trial or hearing, offered in evidence to prove the truth of the matter asserted." Fed. R. Evid. 801(c). The rumor testimony and notes were not offered to prove the truth of the matters they asserted; they were used to show that Sycamore officials had knowledge of the problem, which was an essential element of the negligent-retention claim. Attempting to eliminate any confusion over the relevance of this testimony, the district court gave a limiting instruction on at least six separate occasions to this effect. The following admonition is illustrative:

> Now, the objections that you are hearing this morning relate to certain things that were heard by Mr. Buchholz in his job as a counselor at the Sycamore School District on sexual harassment matters in its investigation and the determination of whether the school district did everything it should in this situation to protect Mrs. Southerland, which was its obligation. And Counsel is asking Mr. Buchholz of information he obtained, and it is going to determine what was done in regard to that information. The information that Mr. Buchholz is relating that he heard is not being offered for the truth of what the person told Mr. Buchholz. It is being offered to show what Mr. Buchholz had in his mind when he was deciding or recommending to his superior what should be done in this case.

. . . [N]o error occurred. . . . [W]e affirm.

UNITED STATES v. JOHNSON

71 F.3d 539 (6th Cir. 1995)

KENNEDY, Circuit Judge.

A jury convicted defendant Keithley Johnson on nine counts of distribution of controlled substances in violation of 21 U.S.C. § 841(a)(1), and four counts of mail fraud in violation of 18 U.S.C. § 1341. . . . The government's theory at trial was that Drs. Johnson and Uppal, who together ran the Neighborhood Health Clinic ("Clinic"), were engaged in the distribution of controlled substances and illegal medical billing practices. . . .

Defendant . . . argues that the District Court erroneously admitted hearsay evidence. At trial, a former employee of the Clinic, Tina Chapman, testified that pharmacies would telephone the Clinic about prescriptions written by defendant. Chapman testified that she told Dr. Uppal of these phone calls, . . . [and] that on one occasion she heard Dr. Uppal tell defendant over the telephone that "he was going to have to stop writing prescriptions like that." . . .

Hearsay is "a statement, other than one made by the declarant while testifying at the trial or hearing, offered in evidence to prove the truth of the matter asserted." Fed. R. Evid. 801(c). Chapman's testimony of the telephone conversation she overheard is not hearsay because it was not offered to prove the truth of the matter asserted. Rather, as the government argues, this testimony is evidence of defendant's knowledge that he was prescribing medication without a legitimate medical purpose and outside the course of professional practice. As defendant's state of mind is an element of the offense, this evidence is relevant. . . . [Convictions affirmed.]

UNITED STATES v. JEFFERSON

650 F.2d 854 (6th Cir. 1981)

NATHANIEL R. JONES, Circuit Judge.

Louis Charles Jefferson appeals from his conviction for possession with intent to distribute heroin and bond jumping. . . . The district court properly admitted a letter and two mailgrams into evidence to show that Jefferson had been sent notice of the hearing he failed to attend. These were not offered to prove the truth of the matter asserted, but only to show that Jefferson had been sent notice of the hearings. [Conviction for bond jumping affirmed.]

UNITED STATES v. SAAVEDRA

684 F.2d 1293 (9th Cir. 1982)

EAST, District Judge:

Saavedra appeals from her judgments of conviction for conspiracy to commit wire fraud in violation of 18 U.S.C. § 371, and three substantive counts of wire fraud in violation of 18 U.S.C. § 1343. . . . The underlying fraud involved wrongfully charging Western Union money orders to improperly obtained Master Charge numbers. The principal architects of the fraud were inmates in . . . the Los Angeles County Jail. The inmates would telephone individuals whose numbers had been obtained from the city phone book, and would pose as law enforcement or bank security personnel checking on credit card problems. The inmate would have the person read off his or her credit card number to "verify" it, and would then call Western Union and order a money order, charging it to the misappropriated credit card number. The inmate would direct the money order to a specific Western Union office, made out to someone on the outside who would pick it up. . . . Saavedra, using the names Carlotta Santana and Charlotte Carpenter, acted as one of these outside persons. . . .

Saavedra . . . contends that the District Court erred in admitting hearsay evidence against her. She complains of the admission of the testimony of three victims of the credit card fraud scheme. These witnesses testified that in the fall of 1977 they received telephone calls from unknown males who identified themselves as law enforcement officers and elicited the victims' credit card numbers. . . .

Fed. R. Evid. 801(c) defines hearsay as "a statement, other than one made by the declarant while testifying at the trial or hearing, offered in evidence to prove the truth of the matter asserted." The testimony objected to here was not offered to prove that the statements made by the unidentified callers were true; i.e., that they were in fact law enforcement officials investigating credit card "problems." Instead, this testimony was introduced to show how the credit card numbers were fraudulently obtained by persons posing as law enforcement officers, thus providing circumstantial evidence that the later unauthorized use of those numbers to purchase money orders was intentional, and that others besides Saavedra were involved in the scheme to defraud. . . . AFFIRMED.

HANSON v. JOHNSON

201 N.W. 322 (Minn. 1924)

WILSON, C.J.

Action in conversion. Appeal from judgment by defendants. Case was tried to the court without a jury.

It is claimed that the court erred in the reception of evidence. Plaintiff owned and leased a farm to one Schrik under a written lease, the terms of which gave plaintiff two-fifths of the corn grown. The tenant gave a mortgage to defendant bank on his share of the crops. The tenant's mortgaged property was sold at auction by the bank with his permission. At this sale a crib of corn containing 393 bushels was sold by the bank to defendant Johnson. If plaintiff owned the corn it was converted by defendants.

In an effort to prove that the corn was owned by plaintiff, and that it was a part of his share, he testified over the objection of hearsay . . . that when the tenant was about through husking corn he was on the farm and the tenant pointed out the corn in question (and a double crib of corn) and said: "Mr. Hanson, here is your corn for this year, this double crib here and this single crib here is your share for this year's corn; this belongs to you, Mr. Hanson."

A bystander was called, and against the same objection testified to having heard the talk in substantially the same language.

There is no question but that plaintiff owned some corn. It was necessary to identify it. The division made his share definite. This division and identity was made by the acts of tenant in husking the corn and putting it in separate cribs and then his telling Hanson which was his share, and the latter's acquiescence therein. The language of the tenant was the very fact necessary to be proved. The verbal part of the transaction between plaintiff and the tenant was necessary to prove the fact. The words were the verbal acts. They aid in giving legal significance to the conduct of the parties. They accompanied the conduct. There could be no division without words or gestures identifying the respective shares. This was a fact to be shown in the chain of proof of title. It was competent evidence. It was not hearsay. . . . Affirmed.

CREAGHE v. IOWA HOME MUTUAL CASUALTY CO.

323 F.2d 981 (10th Cir. 1963)

SETH, Circuit Judge.

The plaintiff-appellant has an unsatisfied judgment against Muril J. Osborn obtained in a damage action which arose from a collision between the plaintiff's car and Osborn's truck. In the case at bar, appellant alleges that the appellee insurance company was the insurer of Osborn's truck at the time of the accident, and seeks to collect this judgment from it. The appellee admits that at one time it issued a liability policy to Osborn, but asserts that he cancelled it shortly before the accident. Osborn was not a party to this suit and did not appear as a witness. . . .

Appellant challenges the action of the trial court in admitting the testimony of the agent of appellee and his employee . . . that the insured stated he wanted the policy cancelled, also that his check for some of the premiums in addition to those initially made was then returned. Appellant asserts that this testimony was hearsay.

The hearsay rule does not exclude relevant testimony as to what the contracting parties said with respect to the making or the terms of an oral agreement. The presence or absence of such words and statements of themselves are part of the issues in the case. This use of such testimony does not require a reliance by the jury or the judge upon the competency of the person who originally made the statements for the truth of their content. Neither the truth of the statements nor their accuracy are then involved. In the case at bar we are not concerned with whether the insured was truthful or not when he told the agent he wanted the policy cancelled and that he did not need it any more. It is enough for the issues here presented to determine only whether or not he made such statements to the agent. The fact that these statements were made was testified to by the agent, and his competency and truthfulness as to this testimony was subject to testing through cross-examination by counsel for appellant, and this was done at considerable length. The fact that the statements with which we are here concerned related to an oral termination of a written contract does not lead to a rule different from that prevailing for the formation of an oral agreement. The reasons for the rule permitting such testimony are the same in both instances. . . .

[T]he testimony with which we are here concerned is admissible since it is part of, or is the oral agreement to cancel the insurance policy. Oral agreements can only be established by testimony as to the conversation which was had between the parties. This testimony may be given by a witness to such conversation, as was the agent of the appellee in this instance. . . . Affirmed.

UNITED STATES v. MONTANA

199 F.3d 947 (7th Cir. 1999)

POSNER, Chief Judge.

The defendant was convicted of bank robbery and related offenses and given a very long sentence—almost 30 years. James Dodd committed the actual robbery; Montana drove the getaway car. Dodd pleaded guilty, and testified at Montana's trial, as Montana's witness, that Montana had not known that Dodd was planning to rob the bank. Shortly before the end of the trial, Dodd gave Montana's lawyer a note for Montana's mother, who after she read it told the lawyer that the note demanded money in exchange for Dodd's having testified favorably to Montana. The following morning, a deputy U.S. marshal heard Dodd tell Montana to tell Montana's father that "it's going to be $10,000" for the favorable testimony. The district judge allowed the marshal to testify to what he had heard. . . .

[Montana complains the marshal's testimony about Dodd's out-of-court statement was hearsay.] The government argues that it was admissible as a "verbal act," thus echoing the linguist's distinction between performative and illocutionary utterances. The latter narrate, describe, or otherwise convey information, and so are judged by their truth value (information is useful only if true—indeed is *information* only if it is true); the former—illustrated by a promise, offer, or demand—commit the speaker to a course of action. Performative utterances are not within the scope of the hearsay rule, because they do not make any truth claims. Had the marshal overheard Dodd tell Montana, "your father has promised me $10,000," Dodd's overheard statement would have been hearsay, because its value as evidence would have depended on its being truthful, that is, on such a promise having actually been made. But what in fact was overheard was merely a demand—in effect, "give me $10,000"—and so the only issue of credibility was whether the marshal was reporting the demand correctly, and *his* testimony was not hearsay. AFFIRMED.

PROBLEMS

3.2. The defendant in a prosecution for assault with a deadly weapon testifies that he shot the victim after the victim pulled out a hunting knife and said, "I'm going to slit your throat." Is the victim's statement hearsay?

3.3. After a gossip magazine describes a soap opera actress as "perpetually intoxicated," the actress sues for libel, and seeks to introduce a copy of the magazine. Is the magazine hearsay?

3.4. To prove falsity, the actress seeks to introduce a newspaper article describing her as "well known for shunning drugs and alcohol." Is the article hearsay?

3.5. To prove absence of malice, the gossip magazine calls one of its reporters, who testifies that a director who worked with the actress told the reporter the actress "always has booze on her breath." Is the director's statement hearsay?

3.6. A patient injured during surgery sues the surgeon and the hospital. To prove negligence by the hospital, the plaintiff seeks to prove that, a year before her surgery, a nurse told the hospital that the surgeon was incompetent. Is the nurse's statement hearsay?

3.7. A developer brings an action to quiet title to a tract of farmland. A farmer intervenes, claiming that she owns the land. To prove adverse possession, the farmer seeks to call witnesses who have heard her refer to the land as hers. Would this testimony recount hearsay?

3.8. The plaintiff in an automobile collision case calls the police officer who investigated the accident. The plaintiff seeks to have the officer testify that an eyewitness, who can no longer be located, told the officer in a tape-recorded interview that the other driver was speeding. The plaintiff also seeks to play the tape for the jury. Does any of this evidence involve hearsay?

3.9. The strength of an alibi offered by a criminal defendant depends on when the defendant arrived at a bar. The prosecution calls a waitress at the bar, who testifies that, shortly before the defendant arrived, the waitress asked the bartender what time it was, and the bartender said, "Nine thirty." Is the bartender's statement hearsay? What if the bartender testifies, in addition to the waitress, and explains that, although he did not see the defendant arrive, he recalls that the waitress asked him for the time at 9:30? Would there be a hearsay problem?

3.10. To prove that a testator was incompetent, his son seeks to prove that the testator claimed to have a summer house on Mars. Is the testator's claim hearsay?

3.11. To prove that a testator was incompetent, his son seeks to prove that the testator's coworkers complained that the testator kept dead fish in his desk. Are the complaints hearsay?

3. Implied Assertions

Sometimes people "communicate" without trying. They put on sweaters, for example, and thereby signal that they are cold. Or they leave a theater and thereby indicate that the play is over. Judges sometimes have treated evidence of this kind of conduct as hearsay when it is offered to prove the truth of what it seems to suggest—i.e., that it was cold, or that the play was over. But the Federal Rules of Evidence and most state codes of evidence have defined hearsay to include only "statements" offered to prove the truth of what they assert. "Statements" are in turn defined to include nonverbal conduct only when it is *intended* as a form of communication.

What about *verbal expressions* that reveal something other than what the speaker intended to communicate? They, too, are generally treated as nonhearsay, either on the ground that they are not offered to prove "the truth of the matter asserted," or—as in the influential opinion in

United States v. Zenni—on the ground that there *is* no "matter asserted." But this result is more controversial, as *State v. Dullard* and the excerpt from Professor Tribe's article illustrate.

UNITED STATES v. ZENNI

492 F. Supp. 464 (E.D. Ky. 1980)

BERTELSMAN, District Judge.

This prosecution for illegal bookmaking activities presents a classic problem in the law of evidence, namely, whether implied assertions are hearsay. The problem was a controversial one at common law, the discussion of which has filled many pages in the treatises and learned journals. Although the answer to the problem is clear under the Federal Rules of Evidence, there has been little judicial treatment of the matter, and many members of the bar are unfamiliar with the marked departure from the common law the Federal Rules have effected on this issue.

The relevant facts are simply stated. While conducting a search of the premises of the defendant, Ruby Humphrey, pursuant to a lawful search warrant which authorized a search for evidence of bookmaking activity, government agents answered the telephone several times. The unknown callers stated directions for the placing of bets on various sporting events. The government proposes to introduce this evidence to show that the callers believed that the premises were used in betting operations. The existence of such belief tends to prove that they were so used. The defendants object on the ground of hearsay. . . .

[T]he utterances of the absent declarants are not offered for the truth of the words,[7] and the mere fact that the words were uttered has no relevance of itself.[8] Rather they are offered to show the declarants' belief in a fact sought to be proved. At common law this situation occupied a controversial no-man's land. It was argued on the one hand that the out-of-court utterance was not hearsay, because the evidence was not offered for any truth stated in it, but for the truth of some other proposition inferred from it. On the other hand, it was also argued that the reasons for excluding hearsay applied, in that the evidence was being offered to show declarant's belief in the implied proposition, and he was not available to be cross-examined. Thus, the latter argument was that there existed strong policy reasons for ruling that such utterances were hearsay.

---

7. That is, the utterance, "Put $2 to win on Paul Revere in the third at Pimlico," is a direction and not an assertion of any kind, and therefore can be neither true nor false.

8. Cf. United States v. McLennan, 593 F.2d 943 (9th Cir. 1977), in a criminal case, the defense was advice of counsel. Statements made by counsel to the defendant were not hearsay, because it was relevant what the advice was. Of a similar nature would be a policeman's statement, "Go through the stop sign," if it were illegal to go through it unless directed by an officer. Other examples of expression admissible as non-hearsay, because they are verbal acts, relevant merely because they occurred, are "I agree" offered to show a contract was made; or "He took a bribe," offered to show a slander was published.

The classic case, which is discussed in virtually every textbook on evidence, is *Wright v. Tatham*, 7 Adolph. & E. 313, 386, 112 Eng. Rep. 488 (Exch. Ch. 1837), and 5 Cl. & F. 670, 739, 47 Rev. Rep. 136 (H.L. 1838). Described as a "celebrated and hard-fought cause,"[10] *Wright v. Tatham* was a will contest, in which the will was sought to be set aside on the grounds of the incompetency of the testator at the time of its execution. The proponents of the will offered to introduce into evidence letters to the testator from certain absent individuals on various business and social matters. The purpose of the offer was to show that the writers of the letters believed the testator was able to make intelligent decisions concerning such matters, and thus was competent.

One of the illustrations advanced in the judicial opinions in *Wright v. Tatham* is perhaps even more famous than the case itself. This is Baron Parke's famous sea captain example. Is it hearsay to offer as proof of the seaworthiness of a vessel that its captain, after thoroughly inspecting it, embarked on an ocean voyage upon it with his family?

The court in *Wright v. Tatham* held that implied assertions[11] of this kind were hearsay. The rationale, as stated by Baron Parke, was as follows:

"The conclusion at which I have arrived is, that proof of a particular fact which is not of itself a matter in issue, but which is relevant only as implying a statement or opinion of a third person on the matter in issue, is inadmissible in all cases where such a statement or opinion not on oath would be of itself inadmissible; and, therefore, in this case the letters which are offered only to prove the competence of the testator, that is the truth of the implied statements therein contained, were properly rejected, as the mere statement or opinion of the writer would certainly have been inadmissible."

This was the prevailing common law view, where the hearsay issue was recognized. But frequently, it was not recognized. . . .

The common law rule that implied assertions were subject to hearsay treatment was criticized by respected commentators. . . . In a frequently cited article the following analysis appears:

"But ought the hearsay rule be deemed applicable to evidence of conduct? As McCormick has observed, the problem 'has only once received any adequate discussion in any decided case,' *i.e.*, in *Wright v. Tatham*, already referred to. And even in that case the court did not pursue its inquiry beyond the point of concluding that evidence of an 'implied' assertion must necessarily be excluded wherever evidence of an 'express' assertion would be inadmissible. But as has been pointed out more than once (although I find no *judicial* recognition of the difference), the 'implied' assertion is, from the hearsay standpoint, not nearly as vulnerable as an express assertion of the fact which the evidence is offered to establish.

10. McCormick [on Evidence] § 250 [(2d ed. 1972)]. This case "entailed no less than four separate trials, hundreds of pages of published transcript, numerous appeals, vast amounts of money, and the participation of most of England's high judiciary, before it was finally concluded in 1838." [Weinstein's Evidence] ¶ 801(a)(01) at 801-54.

11. The problem is the same whether the relevant assertion is implied from verbal expression, such as that of the betters in the instant case or the letter writers in Wright, or from conduct, as in the sea captain example. See F. R. Ev. 801(a). . . .

"This is on the assumption that the conduct was 'nonassertive' that the passers-by had their umbrellas up for the sake of keeping dry, not for the purpose of telling anyone it was raining; that the truck driver started up for the sake of resuming his journey, not for the purpose of telling anyone that the light had changed; that the vicar wrote the letter to the testator for the purpose of settling the dispute with the latter, rather than with any idea of expressing his opinion of the testator's sanity. And in the typical 'conduct as hearsay' case this assumption will be quite justifiable.

"On this assumption, it is clear that evidence of conduct must be taken as freed from at least one of the hearsay dangers, i.e., mendacity. A man does not lie to himself. Put otherwise, if in doing what he does a man has no intention of asserting the existence or non-existence of a fact, it would appear that the trustworthiness of evidence of this conduct is the same whether he is an egregious liar or a paragon of veracity. Accordingly, the lack of opportunity for cross-examination in relation to his veracity or lack of it, would seem to be of no substantial importance. Accordingly, the usual judicial disposition to equate the 'implied' to the 'express' assertion is very questionable."[16]

The drafters of the Federal Rules agreed with the criticisms of the common law rule that implied assertions should be treated as hearsay and expressly abolished it. They did this by providing that no oral or written expression was to be considered as hearsay, unless it was an "assertion" concerning the matter sought to be proved and that no nonverbal conduct should be considered as hearsay, unless it was intended to be an "assertion" concerning said matter.[18] . . .

The Advisory Committee note concerning this problem states:

"The definition of 'statement' assumes importance because the term is used in the definition of hearsay in subdivision (c) [of Rule 801]. *The effect of the definition of 'statement' is to exclude from the operation of the hearsay rule all evidence of conduct, verbal or nonverbal, not intended as an assertion. The key to the definition is that nothing is an assertion unless intended to be one.*

"It can scarcely be doubted that an assertion made in words is intended by the declarant to be an assertion. Hence verbal assertions readily fall into the category of 'statement.' Whether nonverbal conduct should be regarded as a statement for purposes of defining hearsay requires further consideration. Some nonverbal conduct, such as the act of pointing to identify a suspect in a lineup, is clearly the equivalent of words, assertive in nature, and to

16. Falknor, [*The "Hear-say" Rule as a "See-Do" Rule: Evidence of Conduct*, 33 Rocky Mt. L. Rev. 133,] 136 [(1961)]. The context makes clear that the author would apply the same analysis "where the conduct, although 'verbal,' is relevant, not as tending to prove the truth of what was said, but circumstantially, that is, as manifesting a belief in the existence of the fact the evidence is offered to prove." *Id.* at 134.

18. *See* the sea captain illustration discussed, *supra.* In an unpublished ruling this court recently held admissible as non-hearsay the fact that a U.S. mining inspector ate his lunch in an area in a coal mine now alleged to have been unsafe, and that other inspectors who observed operations prior to a disastrous explosion issued no citations, when it would have been their duty to do so, if there had been safety violations. These non-assertive acts would have been hearsay under the rule of *Wright v. Tatham* but are not hearsay under Rule 801 of the Federal Rules of Evidence, because the inspectors did not intend to make assertions under the circumstances. *Boggs v. Blue Diamond Coal Company* (E.D. Ky. No. 77-69, Pikeville Division).

be regarded as a statement. Other nonverbal conduct, however, may be offered as evidence that the person acted as he did because of his belief in the existence of the condition sought to be proved, from which belief the existence of the condition may be inferred. This sequence is, arguably, in effect an assertion of the existence of the condition and hence properly includable within the hearsay concept. . . . Admittedly evidence of this character is untested with respect to the perception, memory, and narration (or their equivalents) of the actor, *but the Advisory Committee is of the view that these dangers are minimal in the absence of an intent to assert and do not justify the loss of the evidence on hearsay grounds*. No class of evidence is free of the possibility of fabrication, but the likelihood is less with nonverbal than with assertive verbal conduct. The situations giving rise to the nonverbal conduct are such as virtually to eliminate questions of sincerity. Motivation, the nature of the conduct, and the presence or absence of reliance will bear heavily upon the weight to be given the evidence. . . . *Similar considerations govern nonassertive verbal conduct and verbal conduct which is assertive but offered as a basis for inferring something other than the matter asserted*, also excluded from the definition of hearsay by the language of subdivision (c)." (Emphasis added).

This court, therefore, holds that, "Subdivision (a)(2) of Rule 801 removes implied assertions from the definition of statement and consequently from the operation of the hearsay rule."[20]

Applying the principles discussed above to the case at bar, this court holds that the utterances of the betters telephoning in their bets were nonassertive verbal conduct, offered as relevant for an implied assertion to be inferred from them, namely that bets could be placed at the premises being telephoned. The language is not an assertion on its face, and it is obvious these persons did not intend to make an assertion about the fact sought to be proved or anything else.

As an implied assertion, the proffered evidence is expressly excluded from the operation of the hearsay rule by Rule 801 of the Federal Rules of Evidence, and the objection thereto must be overruled. An order to that effect has previously been entered.

STATE v. DULLARD

668 N.W.2d 585 (Iowa 2003)

Cady, Justice.

[Brett Dullard was convicted of possession of ephedrine or pseudoephedrine with intent to use it as a precursor, after a search of his home revealed three unopened boxes of Benadryl (an allergy medicine containing pseudoephedrine) and other materials and equipment commonly used to manufacture methamphetamine.] The police also found a small spiral

---

20. Weinstein, ¶ 801(a)(01) at 801-56; McCormick § 250 at 599.

notebook in a wooden desk located in the garage. It contained a handwritten note from an unidentified person. The note read as follows:

> B—
> I had to go inside to pee + calm my nerves somewhat down.
> When I came out to go get Brian I looked over to the street North of here +
> there sat a black + white w/ the dude out of his car facing our own direction—
> no one else was with him

     . . . The handwritten note was also introduced into evidence over Dullard's hearsay objection. The State argued the note was not offered to prove the truth of the matters it asserted but to connect Dullard to the items in the garage used to manufacture methamphetamine and the Benadryl. The State argued the note was written to Dullard based on the first letter of his first name. . . .

     Hearsay "is a statement, other than one made by the declarant while testifying at the trial . . . offered in evidence to prove the truth of the matter asserted." Iowa R. Evid. 5.801(c). Hearsay is not admissible unless it is exempt from the rule or falls within one of the exceptions. *See id.* 5.802. . . .

     A statement is defined under our rules of evidence as "(1) an oral or written assertion or (2) nonverbal conduct of a person, if it is intended by the person as an assertion." Iowa R. Evid. 5.801(a). The term assertion is not similarly defined in the Iowa or federal rules of evidence. Nevertheless, it is generally recognized to be a statement of fact or belief. . . .

     Under the State's argument in this case, the author of the note asserts he or she is nervous and that the police are watching the house. The State acknowledges this note constitutes a written assertion under the rule, but claims it was not hearsay because it was not offered to prove the truth of the assertion, but a different proposition inferred from the words of warning. The State maintains it was offered to show the declarant's belief that the recipient of the note needed to be told of the events because he was involved in the drug activity in the garage and was in possession of the drug lab materials. . . .

     [T]he resolution of this issue requires us to examine the concept of implied assertions and the extent to which they constitute statements under our definition of hearsay. . . . The issue we confront has been imbedded in debate and controversy throughout the development of the common law, and has continued to be debated to a large degree following the adoption of the federal rules of evidence. *See United States v. Zenni,* 492 F. Supp. 464, 465 (E.D. Ky. 1980). . . . Despite the wealth of legal commentary and some scholarly court decisions on the subject, no clear answer or approach has emerged. In truth, many courts have not engaged in a serious examination of the subject of implied assertions as hearsay, while those who have follow divergent paths. Legal scholars advocate a variety of positions, with a slight preference, perhaps, to favor an approach that would include most implied assertions within the definition of hearsay, at least where the declarant intended to some degree to assert the proposition. The United States Supreme Court has never squarely addressed the issue . . . [and the] federal circuit courts of appeals are fairly evenly divided. . . .

Federal rule of evidence 801(a) appears to support the departure from the common law, evidenced more by the advisory committee note accompanying the rule than the language of the rule itself. . . . The thrust of the advisory committee note is that the same considerations that justify the specific exclusion of nonverbal conduct not intended as an assertion from the definition of a statement under rule 801(a)—the minimal dangers resulting from the inability to cross-examine the declarant—support, by analogy, the similar exclusion of nonassertive verbal conduct, as well as assertive verbal conduct offered as a basis for inferring something other than the asserted matter. . . .

Generally, a position taken by the advisory committee on federal rules is persuasive authority for determining the meaning of our Iowa rules of evidence. This is because the federal definition of hearsay and the defined terms within the definition are nearly identical to the corresponding Iowa rules. Thus, in the same manner, we typically follow federal decisions interpreting rules closely aligned to the Iowa rules and we look for guidance to the United States Supreme Court advisory committees' notes. On the other hand, the persuasiveness of the committee notes on implied assertions is undermined by the clear split of authority among the federal circuit courts, as well as many legal scholars. . . .

The circumstances of this case, as well as other cases, can make it tempting to minimize hearsay dangers when a declaration is assertive but offered as a basis for inferring a belief of the declarant that most likely was not a significant aspect of the communication process at the time the declaration was made. Absent unusual circumstances, the unknown declarant likely would not have thought about communicating the implied belief at issue, and this lack of intent arguably justifies excluding the assertion from the hearsay rule. Nevertheless, we are not convinced that the absence of intent necessarily makes the underlying belief more reliable, especially when the belief is derived from verbal conduct as opposed to nonverbal conduct.

Four dangers are generally identified to justify the exclusion of out-of-court statements under the hearsay rule: erroneous memory, faulty perception, ambiguity, and insincerity or misrepresentation. Yet, the distinction drawn between intended and unintended conduct or speech only implicates the danger of insincerity, based on the assumption that a person who lacks an intent to assert something also lacks an intent to misrepresent. The other "hearsay dangers," however, remain viable, giving rise to the need for cross-examination. Moreover, even the danger of insincerity may continue to be present in those instances where the reliability of the direct assertion may be questioned. If the expressed assertion is insincere, such as a fabricated story, the implied assertion derived from the expressed assertion will similarly be unreliable. Implied assertions can be no more reliable than the predicate expressed assertion. Paul R. Rice, *Should Unintended Implications of Speech be Considered Nonhearsay? The Assertive/Nonassertive Distinction Under Rule 801(a) of the Federal Rules of Evidence*, 65 Temp. L. Rev. 529, 538 (1992).

The consequence of the committee's approach is to admit into evidence a declarant's belief in the existence of a fact the evidence is offered to prove, without cross-examination, just as if the declarant had explicitly stated the belief. Yet, if the declarant of the written note in this case had intended to declare his or her belief that Dullard had knowledge and possession of drug lab materials, the note would unquestionably constitute hearsay. Implied assertions from speech intended as communication clearly come within the definition of a statement under rule 5.801(a)(1). Unlike the committee, however, we do not believe indirect or unintentional assertions in speech are reliable enough to avoid the hearsay rule. We think the best approach is to evaluate the relevant assertion in the context of the purpose for which the evidence is offered.

We recognize this approach will have a tendency to make most implied assertions hearsay. *See* Christopher B. Mueller, *Incoming Drug Calls and Performative Words: They're Not Just Talking About It, Baron Parke!*, 16 Miss. C. L. Rev. 117, 121-22 (1995). However, we view this in a favorable manner because it means the evidence will be judged for its admission at trial based on accepted exceptions or exclusions to the hearsay rule. It also establishes a better, more straightforward rule for litigants and trial courts to understand and apply.

Additionally, we interpret legislative enactments consistent with common law principles when the language used by the legislature does not specifically negate the common law. Clearly, there is no explicit language in our definition of hearsay under rule 5.801(a) and (c), as with the federal rule, that categorizes implied assertions from oral or written words as nonhearsay. The rule only expressly excludes unintended conduct. The characterization arrived at by the committee is achieved by analogy to nonverbal conduct. Yet, the specific exclusion under the rule of nonverbal conduct as nonhearsay, in the absence of the specific exclusion of nonassertive verbal conduct or assertive verbal conduct offered to infer something other than the matter asserted from the definition of a statement, tends to indicate that the legislature may not have intended to exclude such implied assertions from the hearsay rule. *See* [David E. Seidelson, *Implied Assertions and Federal Rule of Evidence 801: A Continuing Quandary for Federal Courts*, 16 Miss. C. L. Rev. 33 (1995)]. Thus, the rule should be read to incorporate our common law approach. . . .

Having determined the note to be hearsay, we next consider whether it would be admissible, as secondarily argued by the State, under the exemption to the hearsay rule applicable to the statements by co-conspirators pursuant to Iowa Rule of Evidence 5.801(d)(2)(E). . . . Proof of a conspiracy must include evidence independent of the co-conspirator's statement. *State v. Florie*, 411 N.W.2d 689, 696 (Iowa 1987). In addition to the statement, "the circumstances surrounding the statement, such as the identity of the speaker, the context in which the statement was made, or evidence corroborating the content of the statement" must be considered. Fed. R. Evid. 801 advisory committee's note, 1997 amendment. In this case, there was insufficient evidence to establish the speaker's identity, the time and place the expressed or implied assertions were made, and any other circumstances supporting a conspiracy between the unknown declarant and Dullard.

Without elaborating in great detail, we also fail to find any other exception to the hearsay rule that would allow the note to be admitted. . . . Accordingly, the note was improperly admitted. . . . [P]rejudice is apparent because the admission of the note played a pivotal role in establishing the possession element of the crime and Dullard was unable to cross-examine the declarant to overcome this prejudice. This is not a case in which there is otherwise overwhelming evidence of guilt. . . . We conclude the judgment and sentence of the district court must be reversed based on the error in admitting the hearsay evidence. The case shall be remanded for a new trial.

LAURENCE H. TRIBE, TRIANGULATING HEARSAY

87 Harv. L. Rev. 957, 972 (1974)

Rule 801(a), by defining a "statement" as *assertive* verbal or nonverbal conduct, eliminates from the very definition of hearsay in Rule 801(c) any seemingly nonassertive conduct of a party. Even apart from the well-known difficulty that it is question-begging to define conduct as nonassertive when the very issue may be whether or not it was designed to deceive a viewer, the justification for this treatment of apparently nonassertive conduct seems dubious. The best that can be said for it is that, if the conduct is truly nonassertive, there is no possibility of its insincerity. But the problem of ambiguity is, if anything, greater. . . . And, of course, [the risks of erroneous memory and faulty perception are as significant] here as in any hearsay situation. In terms of both theory and result, it is thus hard to justify the exclusion of such utterances from the very definition of hearsay. . . .

PROBLEMS

3.12. A criminal defendant charged with murder claims that the victim's husband killed her. He seeks to introduce evidence that the victim's husband fled the country after the victim was found dead. Would this evidence involve hearsay under the view expressed by Baron Parke in *Wright v. Tatham?* Would it involve hearsay in federal court today?

3.13. A traveler contracts pneumonia after a three-hour bus trip through upstate New York in January. He sues the bus company for the cost of his hospitalization, claiming that he got sick because the driver failed to keep the bus adequately heated. The bus company seeks to prove that none of the other passengers on the bus complained about the temperature, and that two passengers took off their sweaters midway through the trip. Would any of this evidence involve hearsay under *Wright v. Tatham?* Under the Federal Rules of Evidence?

3.14. A police officer testifies in a murder case that when she asked the victim who shot him, the victim pointed to a picture of his wife. Would Baron Parke treat this evidence as hearsay? Would the Federal Rules of Evidence?

3.15. The prosecution in a burglary case seeks to prove that a blood-hound, after sniffing a pair of gloves left at the crime scene, led the police to the defendant's house, and then barked quietly when the defendant answered the doorbell. The dog's handler offers to testify that the dog is trained to bark quietly when confronted with the source of the scent the dog has been tracking. Would any of this evidence involve hearsay under Baron Parke's view? Under the Federal Rules of Evidence?

3.16. Consider the following remarks by Lord Ackner in *Regina v. Kearley*, 2 App. Cas. 228 (H.L. 1992):

> Following the appellant's arrest and when he was either not at his home nor within earshot, a number of telephone calls were made to his home which were answered by the police, in which the caller inquired whether he could speak to Chippie (the appellant's nickname), and asked to be supplied with drugs. Later, while the police were still on the premises, a number of persons arrived at the house, some with money, also asking to be supplied with drugs. It is these requests that certain police officers were allowed to recount in evidence, none of those who made the inquiries being called by the prosecution.
>
> Each of those requests was, of course, evidence of the state of mind of the person making the request. He wished to be supplied with drugs and thought that the appellant would so supply him. It was not evidence of the fact that the appellant had supplied or could or would supply the person making the request. But the state of mind of the person making the request was not an issue at the trial; accordingly evidence of his request was irrelevant and therefore inadmissible. . . .
>
> It will be apparent from what I have already stated that the application of the hearsay rule does not, on the facts so far recited, fall for consideration. The evidence is not admissible because it is irrelevant. It is as simple as that. . . .

Partly on these grounds and partly on grounds of hearsay—citing *Wright v. Tatham*—the House of Lords held for the defendant in *Kearley*. Was Lord Ackner right that the evidence was inadmissible even if it was not hearsay, because it was irrelevant? If so, was *United States v. Zenni* wrongly decided?

3.17. Britain's Criminal Justice Act 2003 restricts the definition of hearsay to statements that appear to have been intended by the speaker "(a) to cause another person to believe the matter, or (b) to cause another person to act . . . on the basis that the matter is as stated." § 115(3). Does this provision effectively overrule *Wright v. Tatham*? Is the definition of hearsay in Britain now the same as under the Federal Rules of Evidence?

B. HEARSAY AND CONFRONTATION

The Sixth Amendment to the United States Constitution gives every criminal defendant the right "to be confronted with the witnesses against him." Like the hearsay rule, the Confrontation Clause was a reaction against the kind of procedures used, infamously, against Sir Walter Raleigh. It is clear that the two rules partly overlap. But the Supreme Court has found it difficult to say exactly *how* the two prohibitions overlap, and in what ways the constitutional right to confrontation diverges from the hearsay rule.

Three limitations on the reach of the Confrontation Clause are uncontroversial, because they flow directly from the constitutional language. The first is that the clause applies only in "criminal prosecutions." The second is that the clause grants a right of confrontation only to "the accused." And the third is that the right is satisfied if the accused is "confronted." There is disagreement about what "confrontation" necessarily entails, but there is broad consensus that the requirement is fully satisfied by in-court testimony, in the presence of the defendant, subject to cross-examination.

These three, straightforward limits on the reach of the Confrontation Clause mean that the clause has no implications for three large categories of hearsay: hearsay in civil cases, hearsay introduced against the prosecution in criminal cases, and hearsay declarations from someone who winds up testifying in open court, subject to cross-examination. The remaining question, which has generated much controversy, is when the Constitution prohibits the introduction, against a criminal defendant, of hearsay from a declarant who does not testify.

In *Ohio v. Roberts*, 448 U.S. 56 (1980), the Supreme Court read the Confrontation Clause to allow hearsay of this kind, so long as the evidence fell within a well established exception to hearsay rule or carried comparable "indicia of reliability." The Court stuck with this interpretation for almost a quarter-century. More recently, however, the Court has rejected the *Roberts* approach, and has announced a different test for determining when hearsay violates the Confrontation Clause. What matters, the Court now says, is whether the out-of-court statement was "testimonial." The key decisions explaining and justifying this new approach—*Crawford v. Washington*, 541 U.S. 36 (2004), and *Davis v. Washington,* 126 U.S. 226 (2006)—are excerpted below.

The overruling of *Roberts* means that a good deal of hearsay not excluded by the hearsay rule (because, for example, it falls within one of the exceptions addressed later in this chapter) is now nonetheless inadmissible if offered against a criminal defendant. And even when evidence in a criminal case *is* excluded by the hearsay rule, it can be important to know whether it is also barred by the Confrontation Clause. For one thing, the harmless error rules are less forgiving of evidence admitted in violation of the Constitution. Under *Chapman v. California*, 386 U.S. 18 (1967), a constitutional error generally requires reversal of a defendant's conviction unless the prosecution can show that the error was harmless "beyond a reasonable doubt." As we saw in Chapter One, courts apply varying criteria for determining whether an ordinary evidentiary error was harmless, but these criteria are almost always easier to satisfy than the *Chapman* standard. Even more important, the Supreme Court has sharply restricted the use of limiting instructions to avoid violations of the Confrontation Clause. That restriction, announced in *Bruton v. United States*, 391 U.S. 123 (1968), is taken up later in this chapter.

CRAWFORD v. WASHINGTON

541 U.S. 36 (2004)

Justice SCALIA delivered the opinion of the Court.

... On August 5, 1999, Kenneth Lee was stabbed at his apartment. Police arrested petitioner [Michael Crawford] later that night. After giving petitioner and his wife [Sylvia] *Miranda* warnings, detectives interrogated each of them twice. Petitioner eventually confessed that he and Sylvia had gone in search of Lee because he was upset over an earlier incident in which Lee had tried to rape her. The two had found Lee at his apartment, and a fight ensued. ... Sylvia generally corroborated petitioner's story about the events leading up to the fight, but her account of the fight itself was arguably different—particularly with respect to whether Lee had drawn a weapon before petitioner assaulted him. ...

The State charged petitioner with assault and attempted murder. At trial, he claimed self-defense. Sylvia did not testify because of the state marital privilege, which generally bars a spouse from testifying without the other spouse's consent. See Wash. Rev. Code § 5.60.060(1) (1994). In Washington, this privilege does not extend to a spouse's out-of-court statements admissible under a hearsay exception, see *State v. Burden,* [841 P.2d 758, 761 (Wash. 1992)], so the State sought to introduce Sylvia's tape-recorded statements to the police as evidence that the stabbing was not in self-defense. Noting that Sylvia had admitted she led petitioner to Lee's apartment and thus had facilitated the assault, the State invoked the hearsay exception for statements against penal interest, Wash. Rule Evid. 804(b)(3) (2003).

Petitioner countered that, state law notwithstanding, admitting the evidence would violate his federal constitutional right to be "confronted with the witnesses against him." Amdt. 6. ... The trial court here admitted the statement. ... The prosecution played the tape for the jury and relied on it in closing, arguing that it was "damning evidence" that "completely refutes [petitioner's] claim of self-defense." The jury convicted petitioner of assault. The Washington Court of Appeals reversed ... [but the] Washington Supreme Court reinstated the conviction. ...

The Sixth Amendment's Confrontation Clause provides that, "[i]n all criminal prosecutions, the accused shall enjoy the right ... to be confronted with the witnesses against him." We have held that this bedrock procedural guarantee applies to both federal and state prosecutions. ... We must ... turn to the historical background of the Clause to understand its meaning.

The right to confront one's accusers is a concept that dates back to Roman times. The founding generation's immediate source of the concept, however, was the common law. English common law has long differed from continental civil law in regard to the manner in which witnesses give testimony in criminal trials. The common-law tradition is one of live testimony in court subject to adversarial testing, while the civil law condones examination in private by judicial officers. See 3 W. Blackstone, Commentaries on the Laws of England 373-374 (1768).

Nonetheless, England at times adopted elements of the civil-law practice. Justices of the peace or other officials examined suspects and witnesses before trial. These examinations were sometimes read in court in lieu of live testimony, a practice that "occasioned frequent demands by the prisoner to have his 'accusers,' *i.e.*, the witnesses against him, brought before him face to face." 1 J. Stephen, History of the Criminal Law of England 326 (1883). In some cases, these demands were refused. See 9 W. Holdsworth, History of English Law 216-217, 228 (3d ed. 1944); *e.g.*, *Raleigh's Case,* 2 How. St. Tr. 1, 15-16, 24 (1603); *Throckmorton's Case,* 1 How. St. Tr. 869, 875-876 (1554); cf. *Lilburn's Case,* 3 How. St. Tr. 1315, 1318-1322, 1329 (Star Chamber 1637).

Pretrial examinations became routine under two statutes passed during the reign of Queen Mary in the 16th century, 1 & 2 Phil. & M., c. 13 (1554), and 2 & 3 *id.*, c. 10 (1555). These Marian bail and committal statutes required justices of the peace to examine suspects and witnesses in felony cases and to certify the results to the court. It is doubtful that the original purpose of the examinations was to produce evidence admissible at trial. See J. Langbein, Prosecuting Crime in the Renaissance 21-34 (1974). Whatever the original purpose, however, they came to be used as evidence in some cases, see 2 M. Hale, Pleas of the Crown 284 (1736), resulting in an adoption of continental procedure. See 4 Holdsworth, *supra,* at 528-530.

The most notorious instances of civil-law examination occurred in the great political trials of the 16th and 17th centuries. One such was the 1603 trial of Sir Walter Raleigh for treason. Lord Cobham, Raleigh's alleged accomplice, had implicated him in an examination before the Privy Council and in a letter. At Raleigh's trial, these were read to the jury. Raleigh argued that Cobham had lied to save himself: "Cobham is absolutely in the King's mercy; to excuse me cannot avail him; by accusing me he may hope for favour." 1 D. Jardine, Criminal Trials 435 (1832). Suspecting that Cobham would recant, Raleigh demanded that the judges call him to appear, arguing that "[t]he Proof of the Common Law is by witness and jury: let Cobham be here, let him speak it. Call my accuser before my face. . . ." 2 How. St. Tr., at 15-16. The judges refused, and, despite Raleigh's protestations that he was being tried "by the Spanish Inquisition," the jury convicted, and Raleigh was sentenced to death.

One of Raleigh's trial judges later lamented that "'the justice of England has never been so degraded and injured as by the condemnation of Sir Walter Raleigh.'" 1 Jardine, *supra,* at 520. Through a series of statutory and judicial reforms, English law developed a right of confrontation that limited these abuses. For example, treason statutes required witnesses to confront the accused "face to face" at his arraignment. Courts, meanwhile, developed relatively strict rules of unavailability, admitting examinations only if the witness was demonstrably unable to testify in person. Several authorities also stated that a suspect's confession could be admitted only against himself, and not against others he implicated.

One recurring question was whether the admissibility of an unavailable witness's pretrial examination depended on whether the defendant had had an opportunity to cross-examine him. In 1696, the Court of King's Bench answered this question in the affirmative, in the widely reported misdemeanor libel case of *King v. Paine,* 5 Mod. 163, 87 Eng. Rep. 584. The court ruled that, even though a witness was dead, his examination was not admissible where "the defendant not being present when [it was] taken before the mayor . . . had lost the benefit of a cross-examination." . . . [B]y 1791 (the year the Sixth Amendment was ratified), courts were applying the cross-examination rule even to examinations by justices of the peace in felony cases. . . .

Controversial examination practices were also used in the Colonies. . . . [Partly as a result, many] declarations of rights adopted around the time of the Revolution guaranteed a right of confrontation. The proposed Federal Constitution, however, did not. At the Massachusetts ratifying convention, Abraham Holmes objected to this omission precisely on the ground that it would lead to civil-law practices. . . . Similarly, a prominent Antifederalist writing under the pseudonym Federal Farmer criticized the use of "written evidence." . . . The First Congress responded by including the Confrontation Clause in the proposal that became the Sixth Amendment.

This history supports two inferences about the meaning of the Sixth Amendment.

First, the principal evil at which the Confrontation Clause was directed was the civil-law mode of criminal procedure, and particularly its use of *ex parte* examinations as evidence against the accused. It was these practices that the Crown deployed in notorious treason cases like Raleigh's; that the Marian statutes invited; that English law's assertion of a right to confrontation was meant to prohibit; and that the founding-era rhetoric decried. The Sixth Amendment must be interpreted with this focus in mind.

Accordingly, we once again reject the view that the Confrontation Clause applies of its own force only to in-court testimony, and that its application to out-of-court statements introduced at trial depends upon "the law of Evidence for the time being." 3 Wigmore § 1397, at 101; accord, *Dutton v. Evans,* 400 U.S. 74, 94 (1970) (Harlan, J., concurring in result). Leaving the regulation of out-of-court statements to the law of evidence would render the Confrontation Clause powerless to prevent even the most flagrant inquisitorial practices. Raleigh was, after all, perfectly free to confront those who read Cobham's confession in court.

This focus also suggests that not all hearsay implicates the Sixth Amendment's core concerns. An off-hand, overheard remark might be unreliable evidence and thus a good candidate for exclusion under hearsay rules, but it bears little resemblance to the civil-law abuses the Confrontation Clause targeted. On the other hand, *ex parte* examinations might sometimes be admissible under modern hearsay rules, but the Framers certainly would not have condoned them.

The text of the Confrontation Clause reflects this focus. It applies to "witnesses" against the accused—in other words, those who "bear testimony." 2 N. Webster, An American Dictionary of the English Language (1828). "Testimony," in turn, is typically "[a] solemn declaration or affirmation made for the purpose of establishing or proving some fact." *Ibid.* An accuser who makes a formal statement to government officers bears testimony in a sense that a person who makes a casual remark to an acquaintance does not. The constitutional text, like the history underlying the common-law right of confrontation, thus reflects an especially acute concern with a specific type of out-of-court statement.

Various formulations of this core class of "testimonial" statements exist: "*ex parte* in-court testimony or its functional equivalent—that is, material such as affidavits, custodial examinations, prior testimony that the defendant was unable to cross-examine, or similar pretrial statements that declarants would reasonably expect to be used prosecutorially," Brief for Petitioner 23; "extrajudicial statements . . . contained in formalized testimonial materials, such as affidavits, depositions, prior testimony, or confessions," *White v. Illinois,* 503 U.S. 346, 365 (1992) (THOMAS, J., joined by SCALIA, J., concurring in part and concurring in judgment); "statements that were made under circumstances which would lead an objective witness reasonably to believe that the statement would be available for use at a later trial," Brief for National Association of Criminal Defense Lawyers et al. as *Amici Curiae* 3. These formulations all share a common nucleus and then define the Clause's coverage at various levels of abstraction around it. Regardless of the precise articulation, some statements qualify under any definition—for example, *ex parte* testimony at a preliminary hearing.

Statements taken by police officers in the course of interrogations are also testimonial under even a narrow standard. Police interrogations bear a striking resemblance to examinations by justices of the peace in England. The statements are not *sworn* testimony, but the absence of oath was not dispositive. Cobham's examination was unsworn, see 1 Jardine, Criminal Trials, at 430, yet Raleigh's trial has long been thought a paradigmatic confrontation violation. Under the Marian statutes, witnesses were typically put on oath, but suspects were not. See 2 Hale, Pleas of the Crown, at 52. Yet Hawkins and others went out of their way to caution that such unsworn confessions were not admissible against anyone but the confessor.

That interrogators are police officers rather than magistrates does not change the picture either. Justices of the peace conducting examinations under the Marian statutes were not magistrates as we understand that office today, but had an essentially investigative and prosecutorial function. See 1 Stephen, Criminal Law of England, at 221; Langbein, Prosecuting Crime in the Renaissance, at 34-45. England did not have a professional police force until the 19th century, see 1 Stephen, *supra,* at 194-200, so it is not surprising that other government officers performed the investigative functions now associated primarily with the police. The involvement of government officers in the production of testimonial evidence presents the same risk, whether the officers are police or justices of the peace.

In sum, even if the Sixth Amendment is not solely concerned with testimonial hearsay, that is its primary object, and interrogations by law enforcement officers fall squarely within that class. . . .

The historical record also supports a second proposition: that the Framers would not have allowed admission of testimonial statements of a witness who did not appear at trial unless he was unavailable to testify, and the defendant had had a prior opportunity for cross-examination. The text of the Sixth Amendment does not suggest any open-ended exceptions from the confrontation requirement to be developed by the courts. Rather, the "right . . . to be confronted with the witnesses against him," Amdt. 6, is most naturally read as a reference to the right of confrontation at common law, admitting only those exceptions established at the time of the founding. As the English authorities above reveal, the common law in 1791 conditioned admissibility of an absent witness's examination on unavailability and a prior opportunity to cross-examine. The Sixth Amendment therefore incorporates those limitations. The numerous early state decisions applying the same test confirm that these principles were received as part of the common law in this country. . . .

We do not read the historical sources to say that a prior opportunity to cross-examine was merely a sufficient, rather than a necessary, condition for admissibility of testimonial statements. They suggest that this requirement was dispositive, and not merely one of several ways to establish reliability. This is not to deny, as THE CHIEF JUSTICE notes, that "[t]here were always exceptions to the general rule of exclusion" of hearsay evidence. Several had become well established by 1791. But there is scant evidence that exceptions were invoked to admit *testimonial* statements against the accused in a *criminal* case.[6] Most of the hearsay exceptions covered statements that by their nature were not testimonial—for example, business records or statements in furtherance of a conspiracy. We do not infer from these that the Framers thought exceptions would apply even to prior testimony. . . .[7]

Our caselaw has been largely consistent with these two principles . . .[8] . . . [but] the same cannot be said of our rationales. [*Ohio v. Roberts*, 448 U.S. 56 (1980),] conditions the admissibility of all hearsay evidence on whether it falls under a "firmly rooted hearsay exception" or bears "particularized guarantees of trustworthiness." This test departs from the historical principles identified above in two respects. First, it is too broad: It applies the same mode of analysis whether or not the hearsay

6. The one deviation we have found involves dying declarations. The existence of that exception as a general rule of criminal hearsay law cannot be disputed. See, *e.g., Mattox v. United States,* 156 U.S. 237, 243-244 (1895); *King v. Reason,* 16 How. St. Tr. 1, 24-38 (K.B. 1722); 1 D. Jardine, Criminal Trials 435 (1832); . . . 1 G. Gilbert, Evidence 211 (C. Lofft ed. 1791); see also F. Heller, The Sixth Amendment 105 (1951) (asserting that this was the *only* recognized criminal hearsay exception at common law). Although many dying declarations may not be testimonial, there is authority for admitting even those that clearly are. . . . We need not decide in this case whether the Sixth Amendment incorporates an exception for testimonial dying declarations. If this exception must be accepted on historical grounds, it is *sui generis.*

7. We cannot agree with THE CHIEF JUSTICE that the fact "[t]hat a statement might be testimonial does nothing to undermine the wisdom of one of these [hearsay] exceptions." Involvement of government officers in the production of testimony with an eye toward trial presents unique potential for prosecutorial abuse—a fact borne out time and again throughout a history with which the Framers were keenly familiar. This consideration does not evaporate when testimony happens to fall within some broad, modern hearsay exception, even if that exception might be justifiable in other circumstances.

8. . . . [W]e reiterate that, when the declarant appears for cross-examination at trial, the Confrontation Clause places no constraints at all on the use of his prior testimonial statements. See *California v. Green,* 399 U.S. 149, 162 (1970) . . . . The Clause also does not bar the use of testimonial statements for purposes other than establishing the truth of the matter asserted. See *Tennessee v. Street,* 471 U.S. 409, 414 (1985).

consists of *ex parte* testimony. This often results in close constitutional scrutiny in cases that are far removed from the core concerns of the Clause. At the same time, however, the test is too narrow: It admits statements that *do* consist of *ex parte* testimony upon a mere finding of reliability. This malleable standard often fails to protect against paradigmatic confrontation violations. . . .

Where testimonial statements are involved, we do not think the Framers meant to leave the Sixth Amendment's protection to the vagaries of the rules of evidence, much less to amorphous notions of "reliability." Certainly none of the authorities discussed above acknowledges any general reliability exception to the common-law rule. Admitting statements deemed reliable by a judge is fundamentally at odds with the right of confrontation. To be sure, the Clause's ultimate goal is to ensure reliability of evidence, but it is a procedural rather than a substantive guarantee. It commands, not that evidence be reliable, but that reliability be assessed in a particular manner: by testing in the crucible of cross-examination. The Clause thus reflects a judgment, not only about the desirability of reliable evidence (a point on which there could be little dissent), but about how reliability can best be determined. Cf. 3 Blackstone, Commentaries, at 373 ("This open examination of witnesses . . . is much more conducive to the clearing up of truth"); M. Hale, History and Analysis of the Common Law of England 258 (1713) (adversarial testing "beats and bolts out the Truth much better").

The *Roberts* test allows a jury to hear evidence, untested by the adversary process, based on a mere judicial determination of reliability. It thus replaces the constitutionally prescribed method of assessing reliability with a wholly foreign one. In this respect, it is very different from exceptions to the Confrontation Clause that make no claim to be a surrogate means of assessing reliability. For example, the rule of forfeiture by wrongdoing (which we accept) extinguishes confrontation claims on essentially equitable grounds; it does not purport to be an alternative means of determining reliability. See *Reynolds v. United States,* 98 U.S. 145, 158-159 (1879).

The Raleigh trial itself involved the very sorts of reliability determinations that *Roberts* authorizes. In the face of Raleigh's repeated demands for confrontation, the prosecution responded with many of the arguments a court applying *Roberts* might invoke today: that Cobham's statements were self-inculpatory, 2 How. St. Tr., at 19, that they were not made in the heat of passion, *id.*, at 14, and that they were not "extracted from [him] upon any hopes or promise of Pardon," *id.*, at 29. It is not plausible that the Framers' only objection to the trial was that Raleigh's judges did not properly weigh these factors before sentencing him to death. Rather, the problem was that the judges refused to allow Raleigh to confront Cobham in court, where he could cross-examine him and try to expose his accusation as a lie.

Dispensing with confrontation because testimony is obviously reliable is akin to dispensing with jury trial because a defendant is obviously guilty. This is not what the Sixth Amendment prescribes. . . .

Roberts' failings were on full display in the proceedings below. Sylvia Crawford made her statement while in police custody, herself a potential suspect in the case. Indeed, she had been told that whether she would be released "depend[ed] on how the investigation continues." In response to often leading questions from police detectives, she implicated her husband in Lee's stabbing and at least arguably undermined his self-defense claim. Despite all this, the trial court admitted her statement, listing several reasons why it was reliable. In its opinion reversing, the Court of Appeals listed several *other* reasons why the statement was *not* reliable. Finally, the State Supreme Court relied exclusively on the interlocking character of the statement and disregarded every other factor the lower courts had considered. The case is thus a self-contained demonstration of *Roberts'* unpredictable and inconsistent application.

Each of the courts also made assumptions that cross-examination might well have undermined. The trial court, for example, stated that Sylvia Crawford's statement was reliable because she was an eyewitness with direct knowledge of the events. But Sylvia at one point told the police that she had "shut [her] eyes and . . . didn't really watch" part of the fight, and that she was "in shock." The trial court also buttressed its reliability finding by claiming that Sylvia was "being questioned by law enforcement, and, thus, the [questioner] is . . . neutral to her and not someone who would be inclined to advance her interests and shade her version of the truth unfavorably toward the defendant." The Framers would be astounded to learn that *ex parte* testimony could be admitted against a criminal defendant because it was elicited by "neutral" government officers. But even if the court's assessment of the officer's motives was accurate, it says nothing about Sylvia's perception of her situation. Only cross-examination could reveal that.

The State Supreme Court gave dispositive weight to the interlocking nature of the two statements—that they were both ambiguous as to when and whether Lee had a weapon. The court's claim that the two statements were *equally* ambiguous is hard to accept. Petitioner's statement is ambiguous only in the sense that he had lingering doubts about his recollection: "A. I could a swore I seen him goin' for somethin' before, right before everything happened. . . . [B]ut I'm not positive." Sylvia's statement, on the other hand, is truly inscrutable, since the key timing detail was simply assumed in the leading question she was asked: "Q. Did Kenny do anything to fight back from this assault?" Moreover, Sylvia specifically said Lee had nothing in his hands after he was stabbed, while petitioner was not asked about that.

The prosecutor obviously did not share the court's view that Sylvia's statement was ambiguous—he called it "damning evidence" that "completely refutes [petitioner's] claim of self-defense." We have no way of knowing whether the jury agreed with the prosecutor or the court. Far from obviating the need for cross-examination, the "interlocking" ambiguity of the two statements made it all the more imperative that they be tested to tease out the truth.

We readily concede that we could resolve this case by simply reweighing the "reliability factors" under *Roberts* and finding that Sylvia Crawford's statement falls short. But we view this as one of those rare cases in which the result below is so improbable that it reveals a fundamental failure on our part to interpret the Constitution in a way that secures its intended constraint on judicial discretion. Moreover, to reverse the Washington Supreme Court's decision after conducting our own reliability analysis would perpetuate, not avoid, what the Sixth Amendment condemns. The Constitution prescribes a procedure for determining the reliability of testimony in criminal trials, and we, no less than the state courts, lack authority to replace it with one of our own devising. . . .

Vague standards are manipulable, and, while that might be a small concern in run-of-the-mill assault prosecutions like this one, the Framers had an eye toward politically charged cases like Raleigh's—great state trials where the impartiality of even those at the highest levels of the judiciary might not be so clear. It is difficult to imagine *Roberts* providing any meaningful protection in those circumstances.

Where nontestimonial hearsay is at issue, it is wholly consistent with the Framers' design to afford the States flexibility in their development of hearsay law—as does *Roberts,* and as would an approach that exempted such statements from Confrontation Clause scrutiny altogether. Where testimonial evidence is at issue, however, the Sixth Amendment demands what the common law required: unavailability and a prior opportunity for cross-examination. We leave for another day any effort to spell out a comprehensive definition of "testimonial." Whatever else the term covers, it applies at a minimum to prior testimony at a preliminary hearing, before a grand jury, or at a former trial; and to police interrogations. These are the modern practices with closest kinship to the abuses at which the Confrontation Clause was directed. . . . Where testimonial statements are at issue, the only indicium of reliability sufficient to satisfy constitutional demands is the one the Constitution actually prescribes: confrontation.

The judgment of the Washington Supreme Court is reversed. . . .

Chief Justice REHNQUIST, with whom Justice O'CONNOR joins, concurring in the judgment.

I dissent from the Court's decision to overrule *Ohio v. Roberts*, 448 U.S. 56 (1980). . . . Between 1700 and 1800 the rules regarding the admissibility of out-of-court statements were still being developed. There were always exceptions to the general rule of exclusion, and it is not clear to me that the Framers categorically wanted to eliminate further ones. . . . It is an odd conclusion indeed to think that the Framers created a cut-and-dried rule with respect to the admissibility of testimonial statements when the law during their own time was not fully settled. . . .

Exceptions to confrontation have always been derived from the experience that some out-of-court statements are just as reliable as cross-examined in-court testimony due to the circumstances under which they were made. . . . That a statement might be testimonial does nothing to undermine the wisdom of one of these exceptions. . . .

"[I]n a given instance [cross-examination may] be superfluous; it may be sufficiently clear, in that instance, that the statement offered is free enough from the risk of inaccuracy and untrustworthiness, so that the test of cross-examination would be a work of supererogation." 5 Wigmore § 1420, at 251. In such a case, as we noted over 100 years ago, "The law in its wisdom declares that the rights of the public shall not be wholly sacrificed in order that an incidental benefit may be preserved to the accused." *Mattox,* 156 U.S., at 243. By creating an immutable category of excluded evidence, the Court adds little to a trial's truth-finding function and ignores this long-standing guidance. . . .

In *Idaho v. Wright*, 497 U.S. 805 (1990), we held that an out-of-court statement was not admissible simply because the truthfulness of that statement was corroborated by other evidence at trial. As the Court notes, the Supreme Court of Washington gave decisive weight to the "interlocking nature of the two statements." No re-weighing of the "reliability factors," which is hypothesized by the Court, is required to reverse the judgment here. A citation to *Idaho v. Wright* would suffice. . . . I believe that this would be a far preferable course for the Court to take here.

DAVIS v. WASHINGTON
126 S. Ct. 226 (2006)

Justice SCALIA delivered the opinion of the Court.

These cases require us to determine when statements made to law enforcement personnel during a 911 call or at a crime scene are "testimonial" and thus subject to the requirements of the Sixth Amendment's Confrontation Clause. . . .

The relevant statements in *Davis v. Washington,* No. 05-5224, were made to a 911 emergency operator on February 1, 2001. When the operator answered the initial call, the connection terminated before anyone spoke. She reversed the call, and Michelle McCottry answered. In the ensuing conversation, the operator ascertained that McCottry was involved in a domestic disturbance with her former boyfriend Adrian Davis, the petitioner in this case:

> "*911 Operator:* Hello.
> "*Complainant:* Hello.
> "*911 Operator:* What's going on?
> "*Complainant:* He's here jumpin' on me again.
> "*911 Operator:* Okay. Listen to me carefully. Are you in a house or an apartment?
> "*Complainant:* I'm in a house.
> "*911 Operator:* Are there any weapons?
> "*Complainant:* No. He's usin' his fists.
> "*911 Operator:* Okay. Has he been drinking?
> "*Complainant:* No.
> "*911 Operator:* Okay, sweetie. I've got help started. Stay on the line with me, okay?
> "*Complainant:* I'm on the line.
> "*911 Operator:* Listen to me carefully. Do you know his last name?
> "*Complainant:* It's Davis.
> "*911 Operator:* Davis? Okay, what's his first name?
> "*Complainant:* Adrian.
> "*911 Operator:* What is it?
> "*Complainant:* Adrian.

> "*911 Operator:*   Adrian?
> "*Complainant:*   Yeah.
> "*911 Operator:*   Okay. What's his middle initial?
> "*Complainant:*   Martell. He's runnin' now."

As the conversation continued, the operator learned that Davis had "just r[un] out the door" after hitting McCottry, and that he was leaving in a car with someone else. McCottry started talking, but the operator cut her off, saying, "Stop talking and answer my questions." She then gathered more information about Davis (including his birthday), and learned that Davis had told McCottry that his purpose in coming to the house was "to get his stuff," since McCottry was moving. McCottry described the context of the assault, after which the operator told her that the police were on their way. "They're gonna check the area for him first," the operator said, "and then they're gonna come talk to you."

The police arrived within four minutes of the 911 call and observed McCottry's shaken state, the "fresh injuries on her forearm and her face," and her "frantic efforts to gather her belongings and her children so that they could leave the residence." 154 Wash. 2d 291, 296 (2005) (en banc).

The State charged Davis with felony violation of a domestic no-contact order. "The State's only witnesses were the two police officers who responded to the 911 call. Both officers testified that McCottry exhibited injuries that appeared to be recent, but neither officer could testify as to the cause of the injuries." McCottry presumably could have testified as to whether Davis was her assailant, but she did not appear. Over Davis's objection, based on the Confrontation Clause of the Sixth Amendment, the trial court admitted the recording of her exchange with the 911 operator, and the jury convicted him. The Washington Court of Appeals affirmed. The Supreme Court of Washington, with one dissenting justice, also affirmed. . . .

In *Hammon v. Indiana,* No. 05-5705, police responded late on the night of February 26, 2003, to a "reported domestic disturbance" at the home of Hershel and Amy Hammon. They found Amy alone on the front porch, appearing " 'somewhat frightened,' " but she told them that " 'nothing was the matter.' " She gave them permission to enter the house, where an officer saw "a gas heating unit in the corner of the living room" that had "flames coming out of the . . . partial glass front. There were pieces of glass on the ground in front of it and there was flame emitting from the front of the heating unit."

Hershel, meanwhile, was in the kitchen. He told the police "that he and his wife had 'been in an argument' but 'everything was fine now' and the argument 'never became physical.' " By this point Amy had come back inside. One of the officers remained with Hershel; the other went to the living room to talk with Amy, and "again asked [her] what had occurred." Hershel made several attempts to participate in Amy's conversation with the police, but was rebuffed. The officer later testified that Hershel "became angry when I insisted that [he] stay separated from Mrs. Hammon so that we can investigate what had happened." After hearing Amy's account, the officer "had her fill out and sign a battery affidavit." Amy handwrote the following: "Broke our Furnace & shoved me down on the floor into the broken glass. Hit me in the chest and threw me down. Broke our lamps & phone. Tore up my van where I couldn't leave the house. Attacked my daughter."

The State charged Hershel with domestic battery and with violating his probation. Amy was subpoenaed, but she did not appear at his subsequent bench trial. The State called the officer who had questioned Amy, and asked him to recount what Amy told him and to authenticate the affidavit. Hershel's counsel repeatedly objected to the admission of this evidence. At one point, after hearing the prosecutor defend the affidavit because it was made "under oath," defense counsel said, "That doesn't give us the opportunity to cross examine [the] person who allegedly drafted it. Makes me mad." Nonetheless, the trial court admitted the affidavit as a "present sense impression," and Amy's statements as "excited utterances" that "are expressly permitted in these kinds of cases even if the declarant is not available to testify." The officer thus testified that Amy

> "informed me that she and Hershel had been in an argument. That he became irrate [sic] over the fact of their daughter going to a boyfriend's house. The argument became . . . physical after being verbal and she informed me that Mr. Hammon, during the verbal part of the argument was breaking things in the living room and I believe she stated he broke the phone, broke the lamp, broke the front of the heater. When it became physical he threw her down into the glass of the heater.
> "She informed me Mr. Hammon had pushed her onto the ground, had shoved her head into the broken glass of the heater and that he had punched her in the chest twice I believe."

The trial judge found Hershel guilty on both charges, and the Indiana Court of Appeals affirmed in relevant part. The Indiana Supreme Court also affirmed. . . .

Without attempting to produce an exhaustive classification of all conceivable statements—or even all conceivable statements in response to police interrogation—as either testimonial or nontestimonial, it suffices to decide the present cases to hold as follows: Statements are nontestimonial when made in the course of police interrogation under circumstances objectively indicating that the primary purpose of the interrogation is to enable police assistance to meet an ongoing emergency. They are testimonial when the circumstances objectively indicate that there is no such ongoing emergency, and that the primary purpose of the interrogation is to establish or prove past events potentially relevant to later criminal prosecution.[1]

---

1. Our holding refers to interrogations because, as explained below, the statements in the cases presently before us are the products of interrogations—which in some circumstances tend to generate testimonial responses. This is not to imply, however, that statements made in the absence of any interrogation are necessarily nontestimonial. The Framers were no more willing to exempt from cross-examination volunteered testimony or answers to open-ended questions than they were to exempt answers to detailed interrogation. (Part of the evidence against Sir Walter Raleigh was a letter from Lord Cobham that was plainly *not* the result of sustained questioning. *Raleigh's Case,* 2 How. St. Tr. 1, 27 (1603).) And of course even when interrogation exists, it is in the final analysis the declarant's statements, not the interrogator's questions, that the Confrontation Clause requires us to evaluate.

In *Crawford* [*v. Washington*, 541 U.S. 36 (2004)], it sufficed for resolution of the case before us to determine that "even if the Sixth Amendment is not solely concerned with testimonial hearsay, that is its primary object, and interrogations by law enforcement officers fall squarely within that class." . . . [T]he facts of that case spared us the need to define what we meant by "interrogations." The *Davis* case today does not permit us this luxury of indecision. The inquiries of a police operator in the course of a 911 call[2] are an interrogation in one sense, but not in a sense that "qualifies under any conceivable definition." We must decide, therefore, whether the Confrontation Clause applies only to testimonial hearsay; and, if so, whether the recording of a 911 call qualifies.

The answer to the first question was suggested in *Crawford*, even if not explicitly held:

"The text of the Confrontation Clause reflects this focus [on testimonial hearsay]. It applies to 'witnesses' against the accused—in other words, those who 'bear testimony.' 1 N. Webster, An American Dictionary of the English Language (1828). 'Testimony,' in turn, is typically 'a solemn declaration or affirmation made for the purpose of establishing or proving some fact.' *Ibid.* An accuser who makes a formal statement to government officers bears testimony in a sense that a person who makes a casual remark to an acquaintance does not."

A limitation so clearly reflected in the text of the constitutional provision must fairly be said to mark out not merely its "core," but its perimeter.

We are not aware of any early American case invoking the Confrontation Clause or the common-law right to confrontation that did not clearly involve testimony as thus defined. Well into the 20th century, our own Confrontation Clause jurisprudence was carefully applied only in the testimonial context. . . .

Most of the American cases applying the Confrontation Clause or its state constitutional or common-law counterparts involved testimonial statements of the most formal sort—sworn testimony in prior judicial proceedings or formal depositions under oath—which invites the argument that the scope of the Clause is limited to that very formal category. But the English cases that were the progenitors of the Confrontation Clause did not limit the exclusionary rule to prior court testimony and formal depositions. . . . In any event, we do not think it conceivable that the protections of the Confrontation Clause can readily be evaded by having a note-taking policeman *recite* the unsworn hearsay testimony of the declarant, instead of having the declarant sign a deposition. Indeed, if there is one point for which no case—English or early American, state or federal—can be cited, that is it.

_____

2. If 911 operators are not themselves law enforcement officers, they may at least be agents of law enforcement when they conduct interrogations of 911 callers. For purposes of this opinion (and without deciding the point), we consider their acts to be acts of the police. As in *Crawford v. Washington*, 541 U.S. 36 (2004), therefore, our holding today makes it unnecessary to consider whether and when statements made to someone other than law enforcement personnel are "testimonial."

The question before us in *Davis*, then, is whether, objectively considered, the interrogation that took place in the course of the 911 call produced testimonial statements. When we said in *Crawford* that "interrogations by law enforcement officers fall squarely within [the] class" of testimonial hearsay, we had immediately in mind (for that was the case before us) interrogations solely directed at establishing the facts of a past crime, in order to identify (or provide evidence to convict) the perpetrator. The product of such interrogation, whether reduced to a writing signed by the declarant or embedded in the memory (and perhaps notes) of the interrogating officer, is testimonial. It is, in the terms of the 1828 American dictionary quoted in *Crawford*, " '[a] solemn declaration or affirmation made for the purpose of establishing or proving some fact.' " (The solemnity of even an oral declaration of relevant past fact to an investigating officer is well enough established by the severe consequences that can attend a deliberate falsehood. See, *e.g., United States v. Stewart*, 433 F.3d 273, 288 (C.A.2 2006) (false statements made to federal investigators violate 18 U.S.C. § 1001); *State v. Reed*, 280 Wis. 2d 68 (state criminal offense to "knowingly giv[e] false information to [an] officer with [the] intent to mislead the officer in the performance of his or her duty").) A 911 call, on the other hand, and at least the initial interrogation conducted in connection with a 911 call, is ordinarily not designed primarily to "establis[h] or prov[e]" some past fact, but to describe current circumstances requiring police assistance.

The difference between the interrogation in *Davis* and the one in *Crawford* is apparent on the face of things. In *Davis*, McCottry was speaking about events *as they were actually happening*, rather than "describ[ing] past events," *Lilly v. Virginia*, 527 U.S. 116, 137 (1999) (plurality opinion). Sylvia Crawford's interrogation, on the other hand, took place hours after the events she described had occurred. Moreover, any reasonable listener would recognize that McCottry (unlike Sylvia Crawford) was facing an ongoing emergency. Although one *might* call 911 to provide a narrative report of a crime absent any imminent danger, McCottry's call was plainly a call for help against bona fide physical threat. Third, the nature of what was asked and answered in *Davis*, again viewed objectively, was such that the elicited statements were necessary to be able to *resolve* the present emergency, rather than simply to learn (as in *Crawford*) what had happened in the past. That is true even of the operator's effort to establish the identity of the assailant, so that the dispatched officers might know whether they would be encountering a violent felon. . . . And finally, the difference in the level of formality between the two interviews is striking. Crawford was responding calmly, at the station house, to a series of questions, with the officer-interrogator taping and making notes of her answers; McCottry's frantic answers were provided over the phone, in an environment that was not tranquil, or even (as far as any reasonable 911 operator could make out) safe.

We conclude from all this that the circumstances of McCottry's interrogation objectively indicate its primary purpose was to enable police assistance to meet an ongoing emergency. She simply was not acting as a *witness;* she was not *testifying*. What she said was not "a weaker substitute for live testimony" at trial, *United States v. Inadi*, 475 U.S. 387, 394 (1986), like Lord Cobham's statements in *Raleigh's Case*, 2 How. St. Tr. 1 (1603), or Jane Dingler's *ex parte* statements against her husband in *King v. Dingler*, 2 Leach 561, 168 Eng. Rep. 383 (1791), or Sylvia Crawford's statement in *Crawford*. In each of those cases, the *ex parte* actors and the evidentiary products of the *ex parte* communication aligned perfectly with their courtroom analogues. McCottry's emergency statement does not. No "witness" goes into court to proclaim an emergency and seek help. . . .

This is not to say that a conversation which begins as an interrogation to determine the need for emergency assistance cannot, as the Indiana Supreme Court put it, "evolve into testimonial statements," once that purpose has been achieved. In this case, for example, after the operator gained the information needed to address the exigency of the moment, the emergency appears to have ended (when Davis drove away from the premises). The operator then told McCottry to be quiet, and proceeded to pose a battery of questions. It could readily be maintained that, from that point on, McCottry's statements were testimonial, not unlike the "structured police questioning" that occurred in *Crawford*. This presents no great problem. Just as, for Fifth Amendment purposes, "police officers can and will distinguish almost instinctively between questions necessary to secure their own safety or the safety of the public and questions designed solely to elicit testimonial evidence from a suspect," *New York v. Quarles*, 467 U.S. 649, 658-59 (1984), trial courts will recognize the point at which, for Sixth Amendment purposes, statements in response to interrogations become testimonial. Through *in limine* procedure, they should redact or exclude the portions of any statement that have become testimonial, as they do, for example, with unduly prejudicial portions of otherwise admissible evidence. Davis's jury did not hear the *complete* 911 call, although it may well have heard some testimonial portions. We were asked to classify only McCottry's early statements identifying Davis as her assailant, and we agree with the Washington Supreme Court that they were not testimonial. That court also concluded that, even if later parts of the call were testimonial, their admission was harmless beyond a reasonable doubt. Davis does not challenge that holding, and we therefore assume it to be correct.

Determining the testimonial or nontestimonial character of the statements that were the product of the interrogation in *Hammon* is a much easier task, since they were not much different from the statements we found to be testimonial in *Crawford*. It is entirely clear from the circumstances that the interrogation was part of an investigation into possibly criminal past conduct—as, indeed, the testifying officer expressly acknowledged. There was no emergency in progress; the interrogating officer testified that he had heard no arguments or crashing and saw no one throw or break anything. When the officers first arrived, Amy told them that things were fine, and there was no immediate threat to her person. When the officer questioned Amy for the second time, and elicited the challenged statements, he was not seeking to determine (as in *Davis*) "what is happening," but rather "what happened." Objectively viewed, the primary, if not indeed the sole, purpose of the interrogation was to investigate a possible crime—which is, of course, precisely what the officer *should* have done.

It is true that the *Crawford* interrogation was more formal. It followed a *Miranda* warning, was tape-recorded, and took place at the station house. While these features certainly strengthened the statements' testimonial aspect—made it more objectively apparent, that is, that the purpose of the exercise was to nail down the truth about past criminal events—none was essential to the point. It was formal enough that Amy's interrogation was conducted in a separate room, away from her husband (who tried to intervene), with the officer receiving her replies for use in his "investigat[ion]." What we called the "striking resemblance" of the *Crawford* statement to civil-law *ex parte* examinations is shared by Amy's statement here. Both declarants were actively separated from the defendant—officers forcibly prevented Hershel from participating in the interrogation. Both statements deliberately recounted, in response to police questioning, how potentially criminal past events began and progressed. And both took place some time after the events described were over. Such statements under official interrogation are an obvious substitute for live testimony, because they do precisely *what a witness does* on direct examination; they are inherently testimonial.[5]

Both Indiana and the United States as *amicus curiae* argue that this case should be resolved much like *Davis.* For the reasons we find the comparison to *Crawford* compelling, we find the comparison to *Davis* unpersuasive. The statements in *Davis* were taken when McCottry was alone, not only unprotected by police (as Amy Hammon was protected), but apparently in immediate danger from Davis. She was seeking aid, not telling a story about the past. McCottry's present-tense statements showed immediacy; Amy's narrative of past events was delivered at some remove in time from the danger she described. And after Amy answered the officer's questions, he had her execute an affidavit, in order, he testified, "[t]o establish events that have occurred previously."

Although we necessarily reject the Indiana Supreme Court's implication that virtually any "initial inquiries" at the crime scene will not be testimonial, we do not hold the opposite—that *no* questions at the scene will yield nontestimonial answers. We have already observed of domestic disputes that "[o]fficers called to investigate . . . need to know whom they are dealing with in order to assess the situation, the threat to their own safety, and possible danger to the potential victim." [*Hiibel v. Sixth Judicial Dist. Court*, 542 U.S. 177, 186 (2004)]. Such exigencies may *often* mean that "initial inquiries" produce nontestimonial statements. But in cases like this

5. The dissent . . . charge[s] that our holding is not a "targeted attempt to reach the abuses forbidden by the [Confrontation] Clause," which the dissent describes as the depositions taken by Marian magistrates, characterized by a high degree of formality. . . . We do not dispute that formality is indeed essential to testimonial utterance. But we no longer have examining Marian magistrates; and we do have, as our 18th-century forebears did not, examining police officers, see L. Friedman, Crime and Punishment in American History 67-68 (1993)—who perform investigative and testimonial functions once performed by examining Marian magistrates, see J. Langbein, The Origins of Adversary Criminal Trial 41 (2003). It imports sufficient formality, in our view, that lies to such officers are criminal offenses. Restricting the Confrontation Clause to the precise forms against which it was originally directed is a recipe for its extinction. Cf. *Kyllo v. United States*, 533 U.S. 27 (2001).

one, where Amy's statements were neither a cry for help nor the provision of information enabling officers immediately to end a threatening situation, the fact that they were given at an alleged crime scene and were "initial inquiries" is immaterial.[6]

Respondents in both cases, joined by a number of their *amici,* contend that the nature of the offenses charged in these two cases—domestic violence—requires greater flexibility in the use of testimonial evidence. This particular type of crime is notoriously susceptible to intimidation or coercion of the victim to ensure that she does not testify at trial. When this occurs, the Confrontation Clause gives the criminal a windfall. We may not, however, vitiate constitutional guarantees when they have the effect of allowing the guilty to go free. Cf. *Kyllo v. United States*, 533 U.S. 27 (2001) (suppressing evidence from an illegal search). But when defendants seek to undermine the judicial process by procuring or coercing silence from witnesses and victims, the Sixth Amendment does not require courts to acquiesce. While defendants have no duty to assist the State in proving their guilt, they *do* have the duty to refrain from acting in ways that destroy the integrity of the criminal-trial system. We reiterate what we said in *Crawford*: that "the rule of forfeiture by wrongdoing . . . extinguishes confrontation claims on essentially equitable grounds." That is, one who obtains the absence of a witness by wrongdoing forfeits the constitutional right to confrontation.

We take no position on the standards necessary to demonstrate such forfeiture, but federal courts using Federal Rule of Evidence 804(b)(6), which codifies the forfeiture doctrine, have generally held the Government to the preponderance-of-the-evidence standard, see, *e.g., United States v. Scott,* 284 F.3d 758, 762 (C.A.7 2002). State courts tend to follow the same practice, see, *e.g., Commonwealth v. Edwards,* 444 Mass. 526, 542 (2005). Moreover, if a hearing on forfeiture is required, *Edwards,* for instance, observed that "hearsay evidence, including the unavailable witness's out-of-court statements, may be considered." . . .

We have determined that, absent a finding of forfeiture by wrongdoing, the Sixth Amendment operates to exclude Amy Hammon's affidavit. The Indiana courts may (if they are asked) determine on remand whether such a claim of forfeiture is properly raised and, if so, whether it is meritorious.

We affirm the judgment of the Supreme Court of Washington in No. 05-5224. We reverse the judgment of the Supreme Court of Indiana in No. 05-5705, and remand the case to that Court for proceedings not inconsistent with this opinion.

---

6. Police investigations themselves are, of course, in no way impugned by our characterization of their fruits as testimonial. Investigations of past crimes prevent future harms and lead to necessary arrests. While prosecutors may hope that inculpatory "nontestimonial" evidence is gathered, this is essentially beyond police control. Their saying that an emergency exists cannot make it be so. The Confrontation Clause in no way governs police conduct, because it is the trial *use* of, not the investigatory *collection* of, *ex parte* testimonial statements which offends that provision. But neither can police conduct govern the Confrontation Clause; testimonial statements are what they are.

Justice THOMAS, concurring in the judgment in part and dissenting in part.

. . . [T]he history surrounding the right to confrontation supports the conclusion that it was developed to target particular practices that occurred under the English bail and committal statutes passed during the reign of Queen Mary, namely, the "civil-law mode of criminal procedure, and particularly its use of *ex parte* examinations as evidence against the accused." [*Crawford v. Washington*, 541 U.S. 36, 50 (2004)] . . . "The predominant purpose of the [Marian committal] statute was to institute *systematic* questioning of the accused and the witnesses." J. Langbein, Prosecuting Crime in the Renaissance 23 (1974) (emphasis added). The statute required an oral examination of the suspect and the accusers, transcription within two days of the examinations, and physical transmission to the judges hearing the case. These examinations came to be used as evidence in some cases, in lieu of a personal appearance by the witness. *Crawford, supra*; 9 W. Holdsworth, A History of English Law 223-229 (1926). . . .

Neither the 911 call at issue in *Davis* nor the police questioning at issue in *Hammon* is testimonial under the appropriate framework. Neither the call nor the questioning is itself a formalized dialogue.[5] Nor do any circumstances surrounding the taking of the statements render those statements sufficiently formal to resemble the Marian examinations; the statements were neither Mirandized nor custodial, nor accompanied by any similar indicia of formality. Finally, there is no suggestion that the prosecution attempted to offer the women's hearsay evidence at trial in order to evade confrontation. See 829 N.E.2d 444, 447 (Ind. 2005) (prosecution subpoenaed Amy Hammon to testify, but she was not present); 154 Wash. 2d 291, 296 (2005) (en banc) (State was unable to locate Michelle McCottry at the time of trial). Accordingly, the statements at issue in both cases are nontestimonial and admissible under the Confrontation Clause. . . .

Because the standard adopted by the Court today is neither workable nor a targeted attempt to reach the abuses forbidden by the Clause, I concur only in the judgment in *Davis v. Washington*, No. 05-5224, and respectfully dissent from the Court's resolution of *Hammon v. Indiana*, No. 05-5705.

PROBLEMS

3.18. In a prosecution of Richard for bank robbery, the defense seeks to call a private investigator, who will testify about an interview she conducted with a waitress. The waitress told the investigator that Richard was in her restaurant at the time of the robbery. Is this evidence hearsay? Would its introduction violate the Confrontation Clause?

---

5. Although the police questioning in *Hammon* was ultimately reduced to an affidavit, all agree that the affidavit is inadmissible *per se* under our definition of the term "testimonial." Brief for Respondent in No. 05-5705, p. 46; Brief for United States as *Amicus Curiae* in No. 05-5705, p. 14.

3.19. In a murder prosecution, the prosecutor seeks to introduce the written report of the victim's autopsy, to prove the victim was killed by a bullet that entered through the back of the victim's head. The coroner who conducted the autopsy and prepared the report has since died. Is the report hearsay? Would its introduction violate the Confrontation Clause?

3.20. In a statutory rape prosecution of Devon, the prosecutor seeks to call Warrington, who will testify that he was present when Devon met the victim, and that the victim told Devon that she was underage. Is this evidence hearsay? Would its introduction violate the Confrontation Clause?

C. Exceptions to the Hearsay Rule

LAURENCE H. TRIBE, TRIANGULATING HEARSAY

87 Harv. L. Rev. 957, 957 (1974)

As long ago as 1937, Edmund Morgan lamented that "the hearsay rule in its present form is the result of a conglomeration of conflicting considerations modified by historical accident." And Charles McCormick even earlier criticized "the mitigation of a rigid rule by numerous rigid exceptions." But while the British have seen fit to virtually abandon the hearsay rule in civil cases, progress in the United States has been exceedingly slow.

ADVISORY COMMITTEE NOTE TO ARTICLE VIII OF THE F.R.E.

Common sense tells that much evidence which is not given [under oath, in the presence of the trier of fact, and subject to cross-examination] may be inherently superior to much that is. Moreover, when the choice is between evidence which is less than best and no evidence at all, only clear folly would dictate an across-the-board policy of doing without. The problem thus resolves itself into effecting a sensible accommodation between these considerations and the desirability of giving testimony under the ideal conditions.

The solution evolved by the common law has been a general rule excluding hearsay but subject to numerous exceptions under circumstances supposed to furnish guarantees of trustworthiness. Criticisms of this scheme are that it is bulky and complex, fails to screen good from bad hearsay realistically, and inhibits the growth of the law of evidence. . . .

Abandonment of the system of class exceptions in favor of individual treatment in the setting of the particular case, accompanied by procedural safeguards, has been impressively advocated. Admissibility would be determined by weighing the probative force of the evidence against the possibility of prejudice, waste of time, and the availability of more satisfactory evidence. . . . Procedural safeguards would consist of notice of intention to use hearsay, free comment by the judge on the weight of the evidence, and a greater measure of authority in both trial and appellate judges to deal with evidence on the basis of weight. The Advisory Committee has rejected this approach to hearsay as involving too great a measure of judicial discretion, minimizing the predictability of rulings, enhancing the difficulties of preparation for trial, adding a further element to the already over-complicated congeries of pretrial procedures, and requiring substantially different rules for civil and criminal cases. The only way in which the probative force of hearsay differs from the probative force of other testimony is in the absence of oath, demeanor, and cross-examination as aids in determining credibility. For a judge to exclude evidence because he does not believe it has been described as "altogether atypical, extraordinary. . . ." Chadbourn, Bentham and the Hearsay Rule—A Benthamic View of Rule 63(4)(c) of the Uniform Rules of Evidence, 75 Harv. L. Rev. 932, 947 (1962).

The approach to hearsay in these rules is that of the common law, i.e., a general rule excluding hearsay, with exceptions under which evidence is not required to be excluded even though hearsay. The traditional hearsay exceptions are drawn upon . . . [and supplemented with] provision for hearsay statements not within one of the specified exceptions "but having comparable [equivalent] circumstantial guarantees of trustworthiness." This plan is submitted as calculated to encourage growth and development in this area of the law, while conserving the values and experience of the past as a guide to the future.

1. Prior Statements by Witnesses

The Federal Rules of Evidence usefully divide most of the myriad exceptions to the hearsay rule into two categories: exceptions that apply whether or not the declarant is available to testify in court, codified in Rule 803, and exceptions that apply only if the declarant is unavailable, codified in Rule 804. Rule 804 also describes the various ways in which a witness can be "unavailable." Before getting to any of that, though, the federal rules except two special classes of statements from the hearsay rule by declaring them "not hearsay"—even though they satisfy the traditional definition of hearsay. The first of these special classes consists of certain out-of-court statements by declarants who testify as witnesses, in court and under oath, in the very proceedings in which their earlier statements are offered as evidence.

In studying each of the various exceptions to the hearsay rule addressed in this chapter, it is important to ask whether the statements it exempts from the hearsay ban are nonetheless inadmissible against a criminal defendant by virtue of the Confrontation Clause. For prior statements by witnesses, the answer will generally be no, because the declarant's appearance in court as a witness in the trial satisfies the requirement of confrontation. For other exceptions, the answer will often be less clear.

[F.R.E. 801(d)(1); C.E.C. §§1235-36, 1238]

ALBERT v. McKAY & CO.

174 Cal. 451 (1917)

SLOSS, J.

For some years prior to March 10, 1913, Frank H. Albert had been in the employ of the defendant, McKay & Co., a corporation owning and operating a lumber mill at Eureka, in Humboldt county. On the day named, Albert's clothing was caught in an appliance attached to one of the shafts used in the transmission of power for the mill machinery, his body was drawn against the rapidly revolving shaft, and he received injuries which caused his death. He was survived by a widow and a minor child. This action was brought by the widow, as administratrix of his estate, to recover damages for the alleged negligent killing of her intestate. Upon the trial the plaintiff recovered a verdict in the sum of $8,000, and judgment was entered accordingly. The defendant appeals from the judgment, bringing up the evidence by means of a bill of exceptions.

. . . [The plaintiff alleged] that the machinery was negligently started after Albert had begun to work. . . . [But t]estimony of numerous witnesses is unanimous to the effect that the machinery, including the shaft in question, was running before Albert went to the lower floor, and that it was not stopped until the discovery of his body on the shaft. There was no competent evidence in contradiction of this. . . . [The plaintiff points to the testimony of] one Elener, a blacksmith in defendant's employ [who testified on direct examination that the machinery had been running continuously]. The proper foundation having been laid by cross-examination, the plaintiff sought to impeach him by calling in rebuttal a witness who testified that Elener had said, shortly after the accident, that the machinery had not been running, and that somebody must have left the tightener down after Albert had started working. When a witness is impeached by proof of prior inconsistent statements, the effect is merely to discredit him as a witness. The former statements made by him are incompetent for any other purpose. They do not constitute evidence of the truth of the facts so stated by him. 2 Wigmore on Evidence, § 1018; *Keyes v. Geary Street, etc., R. R. Co.*, 152 Cal. 437, 441, 93 Pac. 88; *Worley v. Spreckels Bros. Com. Co.*, 163 Cal. 60, 71, 124 Pac. 697.

In the absence of any conflict, the jury had no right to find a verdict based upon the theory that the machinery had been negligently started after Albert had placed himself in close proximity to the shaft. This is not a case in which such negligence can be inferred under the doctrine of *res ipsa loquitur*. The rule has no application to the facts of this case. The plaintiff charged . . . that Albert's death was caused by the negligent starting of the machinery. If there had been any evidence to show that the machinery was started after Albert took his position near the shaft, it might be said that the mere occurrence of the accident warranted an inference that the defendant had been negligent in setting the shaft in motion. But such inference cannot, of course, be indulged in face of the undisputed testimony that the machinery had not been started at all and therefore could not have been started negligently. . . . The judgment is reversed.

ADVISORY COMMITTEE NOTE TO F.R.E. 801(D)(1)

Considerable controversy has attended the question whether a prior out-of-court statement by a person now available for cross-examination concerning it, under oath and in the presence of the trier of fact, should be classed as hearsay. If the witness admits on the stand that he made the statement and that it was true, he adopts the statement and there is no hearsay problem. The hearsay problem arises when the witness on the stand denies having made the statement or admits having made it but denies its truth. The argument in favor of treating these latter statements as hearsay is based upon the ground that the conditions of oath, cross-examination, and demeanor observation did not prevail at the time the statement was made and cannot adequately be supplied by the later examination. The logic of the situation is troublesome. So far as concerns the oath, its mere presence has never been regarded as sufficient to remove a statement from the hearsay category, and it receives much less emphasis than cross-examination as a truth-compelling device. . . . [T]he fact is that, of the many common law exceptions to the hearsay rule, only that for reported testimony has required the statement to have been made under oath. Nor is it satisfactorily explained why cross-examination cannot be conducted subsequently with success. The decisions contending most vigorously for its inadequacy in fact demonstrate quite thorough exploration of the weaknesses and doubts attending the earlier statement. . . . In respect to demeanor, as Judge Learned Hand observed in DiCarlo v. United States, 6 F.2d 364 (2d Cir. 1925), when the jury decides that the truth is not what the witness says now, but what he said before, they are still deciding from what they see and hear in court. The bulk of the case law nevertheless has been against allowing prior statements of witnesses to be used generally as substantive evidence. Most of the writers and Uniform Rule 63(1) have taken the opposite position.

The position taken by the Advisory Committee in formulating this part of the rule is founded upon an unwillingness to countenance the general use of prior prepared statements as substantive evidence, but with a recognition that particular circumstances call for a contrary result. The judgment is one more of experience than of logic. The rule requires in each instance, as a general safeguard, that the declarant actually testify as a witness, and it then enumerates three situations in which the statement is excepted from the category of hearsay. Compare Uniform Rule 63(1) which allows any out-of-court statement of a declarant who is present at the trial and available for cross-examination.

Prior inconsistent statements traditionally have been admissible to impeach but not as substantive evidence. Under the rule they are substantive evidence. As has been said by the California Law Revision Commission with respect to a similar provision:

"Section 1235 admits inconsistent statements of witnesses because the dangers against which the hearsay rule is designed to protect are largely non-existent. The declarant is in court and may be examined and cross-examined in regard to his statements and their subject matter. In many cases, the inconsistent statement is more likely to be true than the testimony of the witness at the trial because it was made nearer in time to the matter to which it relates and is less likely to be influenced by the controversy that gave rise to the litigation. The trier of fact has the declarant before it and can observe his demeanor and the nature of his testimony as he denies or tries to explain away the inconsistency. Hence, it is in as good a position to determine the truth or falsity of the prior statement as it is to determine the truth or falsity of the inconsistent testimony given in court. Moreover, Section 1235 will provide a party with desirable protection against the 'turncoat' witness who changes his story on the stand and deprives the party calling him of evidence essential to his case." Comment, California Evidence Code § 1235. . . . Moreover, the requirement that the statement be inconsistent with the testimony given assures a thorough exploration of both versions while the witness is on the stand and bars any general and indiscriminate use of previously prepared statements.

Prior consistent statements traditionally have been admissible to rebut charges of recent fabrication or improper influence or motive but not as substantive evidence. Under the rule they are substantive evidence. The prior statement is consistent with the testimony given on the stand, and, if the opposite party wishes to open the door for its admission in evidence, no sound reason is apparent why it should not be received generally.

The admission of evidence of identification finds substantial support, although it falls beyond a doubt in the category of prior out-of-court statements. . . . The basis is the generally unsatisfactory and inconclusive nature of courtroom identifications as compared with those made at an earlier time under less suggestive conditions. . . .

REPORT OF THE SENATE JUDICIARY COMMITTEE
S. Rep. 93-1277 (1974)

As submitted by the Supreme Court, subdivision (d)(1)(A) made admissible as substantive evidence the prior statement of a witness inconsistent with his present testimony. The House severely limited the admissibility of prior inconsistent statements by adding a requirement that the prior statement must have been subject to cross-examination, thus precluding even the use of grand jury statements. . . . [W]e think the House amendment should be rejected and the rule as submitted by the Supreme Court reinstated.

REPORT OF THE CONFERENCE COMMITTEE

Conf. Rep. No. 93-1597 (1974)

The House bill provides that a statement is not hearsay if the declarant testifies and is subject to cross-examination concerning the statement and if the statement is inconsistent with his testimony and was given under oath subject to cross-examination and subject to the penalty of perjury at a trial or hearing or in a deposition. The Senate amendment drops the requirement that the prior statement be given under oath subject to cross-examination and subject to the penalty of perjury at a trial or hearing or in a deposition.

The Conference adopts the Senate amendment with an amendment, so that the rule now requires that the prior inconsistent statement be given under oath subject to the penalty of perjury at a trial, hearing, or other proceeding, or in a deposition. The rule as adopted covers statements before a grand jury. Prior inconsistent statements may, of course, be used for impeaching the credibility of a witness. When the prior inconsistent statement is one made by a defendant in a criminal case, it is covered by Rule 801(d)(2).

REPORT OF THE SENATE JUDICIARY COMMITTEE

S. Rep. No. 94-199 (1975)

In . . . Gilbert v. California, 388 U.S. 263, 272 n. 3 (1967), the Supreme Court, noting the split of authority in admitting prior out-of-court identifications, stated, "The recent trend, however, is to admit the prior identification under the exception [to the hearsay rule] that admits as substantive evidence a prior communication by a witness who is available for cross-examination at the trial." And the Federal Courts of Appeals have generally admitted these identifications. . . .

In the course of processing the Rules of Evidence in the final weeks of the 93d Congress, the provision excluding such statements of identification from the hearsay category was deleted . . . . Concern was . . . expressed that a conviction could be based upon such unsworn, out-of-court testimony. Upon further reflection . . . it appears the rule is desirable. Since these identifications take place reasonably soon after an offense has been committed, the witness' observations are still fresh in his mind. The identification occurs before his recollection has been dimmed by the passage of time. Equally as important, it also takes place before the defendant or some other party has had the opportunity, through bribe or threat, to influence the witness to change his mind.

Both experience and psychological studies suggest that identifications consisting of nonsuggestive lineups, photographic spreads, or similar identifications, made reasonably soon after the offense, are more reliable than in-court identifications. Admitting these prior identifications therefore provides greater fairness to both the prosecution and defense in a criminal trial.

UNITED STATES v. OWENS

484 U.S. 554 (1988)

Justice SCALIA delivered the opinion of the Court.

On April 12, 1982, John Foster, a correctional counselor at the federal prison in Lompoc, California, was attacked and brutally beaten with a metal pipe. His skull was fractured, and he remained hospitalized for almost a month. As a result of his injuries, Foster's memory was severely impaired. When Thomas Mansfield, an FBI agent investigating the assault, first attempted to interview Foster, on April 19, he found Foster lethargic and unable to remember his attacker's name. On May 5 Mansfield again spoke to Foster, who was much improved and able to describe the attack. Foster named respondent as his attacker and identified respondent from an array of photographs.

Respondent was tried . . . for assault with intent to commit murder under . . . . At trial, Foster recounted his activities just before the attack, and described feeling the blows to his head and seeing blood on the floor. He testified that he clearly remembered identifying respondent as his assailant during his May 5th interview with Mansfield. On cross-examination, he admitted that he could not remember seeing his assailant. He also admitted that, although there was evidence that he had received numerous visitors in the hospital, he was unable to remember any of them except Mansfield, and could not remember whether any of these visitors had suggested that respondent was the assailant. Defense counsel unsuccessfully sought to refresh his recollection with hospital records, including one indicating that Foster had attributed the assault to someone other than respondent. Respondent was convicted and sentenced to 20 years' imprisonment to be served consecutively to a previous sentence. . . .

Rule 801(d)(1)(C) defines as not hearsay a prior statement "of identification of a person made after perceiving the person," if the declarant "testifies at the trial or hearing and is subject to cross-examination concerning the statement." . . . It seems to us that the more natural reading of "subject to cross-examination concerning the statement" includes what was available here. Ordinarily a witness is regarded as "subject to cross-examination" when he is placed on the stand, under oath, and responds willingly to questions. . . . [L]imitations on the scope of examination by the trial court or assertions of privilege by the witness may undermine the process to such a degree that meaningful cross-examination within the intent of the Rule no longer exists. But that effect is not produced by the witness' assertion of memory loss—which . . . is often the very result sought to be produced by cross-examination, and can be effective in destroying the force of the prior statement. Rule 801(d)(1)(C), which specifies that the cross-examination need only "concer[n] the statement," does not on its face require more. . . .

The premise for Rule 801(d)(1)(C) was that, given adequate safeguards against suggestiveness, out-of-court identifications were generally preferable to courtroom identifications. Advisory Committee's Notes on Rule 801. Thus, despite the traditional view that such statements were hearsay, the

Advisory Committee believed that their use was to be fostered rather than discouraged. Similarly, the House Report on the Rule noted that since, "[a]s time goes by, a witness' memory will fade and his identification will become less reliable," minimizing the barriers to admission of more contemporaneous identification is fairer to defendants and prevents "cases falling through because the witness can no longer recall the identity of the person he saw commit the crime." H.R. Rep. No. 94-355, p. 3 (1975). See also S. Rep. No. 94-199, p. 2 (1975). To judge from the House and Senate Reports, Rule 801(d)(1)(C) was in part directed to the very problem here at issue: a memory loss that makes it impossible for the witness to provide an in-court identification or testify about details of the events underlying an earlier identification. . . .

[For similar reasons, the court found no violation of the confrontation clause, which the court reaffirmed requires only "an *opportunity* for effective cross-examination, not cross-examination that is effective in whatever way, and to what extent, the defense might wish." Conviction upheld. Justice Brennan, joined by Justice Marshall, filed a dissenting opinion. Justice Kennedy took no part in deciding the case.]

PROBLEMS

3.21. How would *Albert v. McKay Co.* be decided today under the Federal Rules of Evidence? Under the California Evidence Code?

3.22. In an assault prosecution, the victim testifies and identifies the defendant from the witness stand as her assailant. The prosecution then seeks to have the victim testify that she earlier picked the defendant out of a lineup. Is the victim's testimony about the earlier identification barred by the hearsay rule? By the Confrontation Clause?

3.23. Following a bank robbery, a customer picks a suspect out of a lineup and identifies him as the robber. The customer does not testify at trial, but the government seeks to have a police officer who was present at the lineup testify about the identification. Is this testimony barred by the hearsay rule? By the Confrontation Clause?

3.24. Suppose the customer does testify at trial but no longer recognizes the defendant: When asked whether the robber is present in court, the customer says he is unsure. May a police officer who was present at the lineup testify that the customer identified the defendant as the robber?

3.25. In 2003, prosecutors associated with the International Criminal Tribunal for the former Yugoslavia (ICTY) were investigating allegations, ultimately substantiated, that members of the Kosovo Liberation Army (KLA) had tortured and murdered civilians at a prison camp in the village of Llapushnik. In formal, videotaped interviews, two former members of the KLA said that Fatmir Limaj, another KLA member, had commanded soldiers at the camp. When Limaj was prosecuted at the ICTY in 2005, the witnesses recanted, and the prosecutors moved to introduce the videotaped interviews both for impeachment and as "substantive evidence" of Limaj's role as a commander. The three-judge panel presiding over the trial granted the motion, relying on an ICTY rule that gave trial judges discretion to admit hearsay that was relevant and had sufficient indicia of reliability. Months later, though, the same judges acquitted Limaj, finding insufficient evidence that he exercised authority over the soldiers who carried out the tortures and murders. In their written ruling, the judges noted they were "not persuaded . . . that the prior inconsistent statements of these two witnesses can safely be relied upon as the sole or principal basis for proof of a material fact," especially "because each witness, in oral evidence, disavowed, in very material respects, what previously had been stated in the interview." *Prosecutor v. Limaj et al.*, No. IT-03-66-T (ICTY, Nov. 30, 2005); *see* Pascale Chifflet, *The First Trial of Former Members of the Kosovo Liberation Army: Prosecutor v. Fatmir Limaj, Haradin Bala, and Isak Musliu*, 19 Leiden J. Int'l L. 459, 466-469 (2006). Would this evidence be handled differently under the Federal Rules of Evidence? How *should* it be handled?

2. Admissions by Party-Opponents

Two classes of statements are deemed "not hearsay" under Federal Rule of Evidence 801 even though they satisfy the traditional definition of hearsay. The first, discussed above, consists of certain statements by declarants who also give sworn, in-court testimony in the trial in which their statements are offered into evidence. The second class of statements given this special treatment consists of various kinds of "admissions by party-opponents." When an out-of-court statement is offered into evidence against the person who made it, the statement qualifies as an "admission" and therefore is exempt from the hearsay rule—regardless whether the statement seems on its face to "admit" anything contrary to the declarant's interest. What matters is not the content of the statement but the identity of the declarant and the party against whom it is introduced.

The admissions doctrine is not limited to statements made directly by the party against whom they are introduced. It also applies when, for any of several other reasons, it seems somehow right to hold the party against whom the evidence is offered at least partially responsible for the out-of-court statement.

Unlike most of the exceptions to the hearsay rule, which find their justification largely in considerations of reliability, the admissions doctrine is rooted, at least nominally, in notions of adversarial fairness. Whether those notions, or any others, can justify the breadth of the admissions doctrine remains controversial.

It is also unclear whether the Supreme Court's reinterpretation of the Confrontation Clause in *Crawford v. Washington* and *Davis v. Washington* will require reconsidering the admissibility, in criminal cases, of some statements previously introduced as admissions. Direct admissions will not be affected: the defendant cannot persuasively claim he has had no chance to "confront" himself. And most co-conspirator admissions will probably qualify as nontestimonial, and thus escape Confrontation Clause scrutiny—as the Supreme Court itself pointed out in *Crawford*. This will likely be true also of many if not most adopted admissions, authorized admissions, and employee admissions. Some statements in the latter categories, though, may wind up being deemed "testimonial," throwing into doubt their admissibility against any criminal defendant who has not previously had an opportunity to cross-examine the declarant.

a. Direct Admissions

i. Generally

[F.R.E. 801(d)(2)(A); C.E.C. §1220]

SALVITTI v. THROPPE

23 A.2d 445 (Pa. 1942)

STERN, Justice.

[Joseph Salvitti and his wife were injured when the car Salvitti was driving hit a tree. Salvitti claimed he swerved to avoid a negligently driven truck. He and his wife sued Throppe, the truck driver's employer.]

Plaintiffs testified that defendant and the driver of the truck visited them, admitted that the accident was their fault, and promised that "everything would be taken care of." The acknowledgment by a party that it was he who was at fault is admissible as a declaration against interest. Defendant, while conceding this to be the general rule, urges that in the present case the testimony should have been rejected because he was not present at the time of the accident and could have based his remark only on what his driver told him. Personal knowledge, however, is not required in the case of an admission by a party. It is said in Wigmore on Evidence, 3d Ed., volume 4, pp. 12, 13, sec. 1053: "Since a party may make a claim and file averment of pleadings without regard to personal knowledge of the facts, it would be fallacious to exact, in his contrary admissions, an element of personal knowledge which is not required for the original advancement of his claim. . . . Add to this that, in the psychology of testimony, a person's assertions regarding his own affairs have always some testimonial value regardless of the exactness of his personal observation of the data leading to his belief." Of course, the weight to be attributed by the jury to such an admission would naturally depend upon whether it was made by defendant on the basis of his own knowledge or of information imparted to him by others.

Judgment affirmed.

ADVISORY COMMITTEE NOTE TO F.R.E. 801(d)(2)

Admissions by a party-opponent are excluded from the category of hearsay on the theory that their admissibility in evidence is the result of the adversary system rather than satisfaction of the conditions of the hearsay rule. Strahorn, A Reconsideration of the Hearsay Rule and Admissions, 85 U. Pa. L. Rev. 484, 564 (1937); Morgan, Basic Problems of Evidence 265 (1962); 4 Wigmore § 1048. No guarantee of trustworthiness is required in the case of an admission. The freedom which admissions have enjoyed from technical demands of searching for an assurance of truthworthiness in some against-interest circumstance, and from the restrictive influences of the opinion rule and the rule requiring firsthand knowledge, when taken with the apparently prevalent satisfaction with the results, calls for generous treatment of this avenue to admissibility.

EDMUND MORGAN, ADMISSIONS

1 UCLA L. Rev. 18, 19 (1953)

The admissibility of an admission made by the party himself rests not upon any notion that the circumstances in which it was made furnish the trier means of evaluating it fairly, but upon the adversary theory of litigation. A party can hardly object that he had no opportunity to cross-examine himself or that he is unworthy of credence save when speaking under the sanction of an oath. His adversary may use against him anything which he has said or done. Originally he had no chance to make an explanation, but since about the middle of the 1800's, he has been competent as a witness and can furnish the trier with all pertinent information within his knowledge. Consequently the orthodox decisions refuse to apply to evidence of personal admissions restrictions usually applicable to testimonial evidence.

UNITED STATES v. McGEE

189 F.3d 626 (7th Cir. 1999)

Ripple, Circuit Judge.

A jury found John Earl McGee guilty of one count of bank robbery. . . . He claims that . . . the district court erred in admitting under Federal Rule of Evidence 801(d)(2)(A) his statement to the police. . . .

The prosecution . . . called Detective Carl Buschmann of the Milwaukee Police Department to testify that he interviewed Mr. McGee on August 20, 1997, concerning the July 5 robbery of North Shore Bank. Detective Buschmann testified that, during the interview, Mr. McGee provided three different versions of the events of July 5, 1997. First, Mr. McGee said that he had taken a bus to the North Shore Bank that day to open an account but left the bank when he was told he would need two forms of identification. After Mr. McGee was informed that co-defendants Natasha Williams and Bridget Womack had provided statements implicating him in the robbery, he admitted that he had lied about taking the bus and decided to change his story. [He then said Womack had driven him to the bank. He gave two different accounts of how he had returned home. He continued to deny any involvement in or knowledge of the robbery.]

Mr. McGee contends that his statement to Detective Buschmann is not admissible under Rule 801(d)(2) as an admission by a party-opponent because it was not inculpatory. . . . We cannot accept this submission. . . . [No] Seventh Circuit case of which we are aware establishes a requirement that admissions by a party-opponent be inculpatory in order to be admissible as nonhearsay under Rule 801. Nor does the case law from the other circuits indicate that an admission must be inculpatory; the courts that have addressed the issue have held that, in accordance with the language of Rule 801(d)(2) the statement need only be made by the party against whom it is offered.

We agree with the other circuits that Rule 801(d)(2)(A) should be interpreted on its face to require only a party's own statement offered against the party. We therefore reject Mr. McGee's contention that the district court erred in admitting his statement to Detective Buschmann. . . . [T]he judgment of the district court is affirmed.

McCORMICK ON EVIDENCE

§254, at 2:181-182 (Kenneth S. Broun, ed., 6th ed. 2006)

A type of evidence with which admissions may be confused is evidence of declarations against interest. The latter, treated under a separate exception to the hearsay rule, must have been against the declarant's interest when made. Although most admissions are against interest when made, no such requirement is applied to admissions. For example, if a person states that a note is forged and then later acquires the note and sues upon it, the previous statement may be introduced as an admission although the party had no interest when he or she made the statement. Hence the common phrase "admissions against interest" is an invitation to confuse two separate theories of admitting hearsay and erroneously engraft an against-interest requirement on admissions.

UNITED STATES v. PHELPS

572 F. Supp. 262 (E.D. Ky. 1983)

BERTELSMAN, District Judge:

. . . The case arises out of the prosecution of the defendants for willful possession of 169 pounds of marijuana and a pound-and-a-half of cocaine with intent to distribute, which conduct is prohibited by 21 U.S.C. §841(a)(1). . . . At a bench conference, counsel for defendant Phelps advised the court that he was going to seek to introduce through the testimony of one of the officers, that, when the officers discovered the cocaine in the gym bag, Phelps had stated, "That is my gym bag, but Taylor put it in the trunk." The unusual feature concerning the introduction of this statement was that the statement was sought to be introduced by Phelps himself and the objection to the testimony was made, not by the United States, but by the co-defendant Taylor. . . .

Although the proponent of the testimony was the declarant himself, the testimony constituted hearsay under F.R. Ev. 801. . . . Further, it is equally clear that the statement was not excluded from the definition of hearsay by the fact that it was an admission. . . . The statement of a party may be introduced as an admission only when offered *against* that party. This principle is reflected by the standard but often unanalyzed objection that such testimony by a party constitutes a "self-serving declaration." 6 J. Wigmore, *Evidence* § 1732 (1976). Some confusion arises by reason of the fact that, to be admissible, a party's out-of-court statement need not have been against his interest when made. But it may not be offered in his *favor*, but only *against* him. . . . Therefore, the court sustained the objection and excluded the testimony.

ii. Admissions and Multiple Hearsay

[F.R.E. 805; C.E.C. §1201]

REED v. McCORD
54 N.E. 737 (N.Y. 1899)

MARTIN, J.

This action was to recover damages for personal injuries to the plaintiff's intestate which occasioned his death, and was based upon the alleged negligence of the defendant. The plaintiff had a verdict, which was not directed by the court. From the judgment entered thereon an appeal was taken. . . .

Upon the trial of this action the official stenographer for the board of coroners was called and permitted, under the defendant's objection and exception, to testify that upon the hearing before the coroner the defendant gave evidence to the effect that all machines of the make of the one in use when the decedent was killed were alike; that at the time of the injury the dog of the machine was not in position, which caused the accident; and that "the man who had charge of it supposed the dog was in position, and he released his hold on the thing, and it commenced to revolve, and then he got down so as to put his foot on it, and it was going so rapidly that it slipped past." It was admitted that the defendant was not present when the accident occurred, and hence, it is obvious that his statement before the coroner was not based upon his personal knowledge, but upon what he had learned as to the situation and how the accident occurred. The contention of the appellant is that, as his admissions were not based upon his personal knowledge, proof of them should have been excluded, and that his exception to their admission was well taken.

The defendant being a party to this action, his admissions against his own interest were evidence in favor of his adversary, if of a fact material to the issue. If he had merely admitted that he heard that the accident occurred in the manner stated, it would have been inadmissible, as then it would only have amounted to an admission that he had heard the statement which he repeated, and not to an admission of the facts included in it. That would have been in no sense an admission of any fact pertinent to the issue, but a mere admission of what he had heard, without adoption or indorsement. Such evidence is clearly inadmissible. But the admissions proved in this case were not of that character. They were plain admissions of facts and circumstances which attended the intestate's injury. In a civil action the admissions by a party of any fact material to the issue are always competent evidence against him, wherever, whenever, or to whomsoever made. . . . Judgment affirmed.

FOSTER v. COMMISSIONER OF INTERNAL REVENUE

80 T.C. 34 (1983), vacated in part on other grounds,
756 F.2d 1430 (9th Cir. 1985)

Dawson, Judge:

Although Fed. R. Evid. 805 does not technically apply because admissions do not constitute hearsay statements under Fed. R. Evid. 801(d)(2), . . . hearsay within an admission is subject to objection, unless, of course, an exception to the hearsay rule applies. However . . . there is a difference between offering as an admission a party's out-of-court statement that "A said that x is a fact" for the purpose of proving that x is a fact, and offering as an admission a party's out-of-court statement that "x is a fact" for that same purpose. . . . [A] party's lack of personal knowledge that x is a fact does not render inadmissible his statement to that effect. Returning to our example, even though a party's out-of-court statement that "x is a fact" is based on A's having told him that fact rather than on his personal knowledge, the statement is still admissible as an admission. Of course, a party is entitled to try to lessen the *weight* of an admission by introducing evidence that it was not based on personal knowledge.

STEPHEN A. SALTZBURG, MICHAEL M. MARTIN & DANIEL J. CAPRA, FEDERAL RULES OF EVIDENCE MANUAL

4:805-2–805-3 (9th ed. 2006)

[A]dmissions under Rule 801(d)(2) and certain prior statements of available witnesses under Rule 801(d)(1) are defined as not hearsay. . . . But, Courts have held that the technical difference between Rule 801(d) "not hearsay" and Rule 803, 804, and 807 "hearsay subject to exception" cannot control the application of Rule 805's limitation on multiple hearsay. As one Court put it: "For the purpose of the hearsay-within-hearsay principle expressed in Rule 805, non-hearsay statements under Rule 801(d) . . . should be considered in analyzing a multiple-hearsay statement as the equivalent of a level of the combined statements that conforms with an exception to the hearsay rule." Thus, the mere fact that one level of a multiple level statement qualifies as exempt from the hearsay rule does not excuse the other levels from satisfying the Rule 805 requirement that each level satisfy the hearsay rule. Conversely, a statement admissible under Rule 801(d) can be admitted when included in another hearsay statement if the other hearsay statement qualifies as an exception.

iii. Admissions and Completeness

[F.R.E. 106; C.E.C. §356]

BEECH AIRCRAFT CORP. v. RAINEY

488 U.S. 153 (1988)

Justice BRENNAN delivered the opinion of the Court.

In this action we address . . . whether, on the facts of this litigation, the trial court abused its discretion in refusing to admit, on cross-examination, testimony intended to provide a more complete picture of a document about which the witness had testified on direct.

This litigation stems from the crash of a Navy training aircraft at Middleton Field, Alabama, on July 13, 1982, which took the lives of both pilots on board, Lieutenant Commander Barbara Ann Rainey and Ensign Donald Bruce Knowlton. . . . The two pilots' surviving spouses brought a product liability suit against petitioners Beech Aircraft Corporation, the plane's manufacturer, and Beech Aerospace Services, which serviced the plane under contract with the Navy. The plaintiffs alleged that the crash had been caused by a loss of engine power, known as "rollback," due to some defect in the aircraft's fuel control system. The defendants, on the other hand, advanced the theory of pilot error, suggesting that the plane had stalled during [an] abrupt avoidance maneuver. . . .

Five or six months after the accident, plaintiff John Rainey, husband of the deceased pilot and himself a Navy flight instructor, sent a detailed letter to Lieutenant Commander Morgan. [Morgan had investigated the accident for the Navy and had written a report concluding that pilot error probably caused the collision.] Based on Rainey's own investigation, the letter took issue with some of [Morgan's] findings and outlined Rainey's theory that "[t]he most probable primary cause factor of this aircraft mishap is a loss of useful power (or rollback) caused by some form of pneumatic sensing/fuel flow malfunction, probably in the fuel control unit."

At trial Rainey did not testify during his side's case in chief, but he was called by the defense as an adverse witness. On direct examination he was asked about two statements contained in his letter. The first was to the effect that his wife had unsuccessfully attempted to cancel the ill-fated training flight because of a variety of adverse factors including her student's fatigue. The second question concerned a portion of Rainey's hypothesized scenario of the accident:

"Didn't you say, sir, that after Mrs. Rainey's airplane rolled wings level, that Lieutenant Colonel Habermacher's plane came into view unexpectedly at its closest point of approach, although sufficient separation still existed between the aircraft. However, the unexpected proximitely [*sic*] of Colonel Habermacher's plane caused one of the aircrew in Mrs. Rainey's plane to react instinctively and abruptly by initiating a hard right turn away from Colonel Habermacher's airplane?"

Rainey admitted having made both statements. On cross-examination, Rainey's counsel asked the following question: "In the same letter to which Mr. Toothman made reference to in his questions, sir, did you also say that the most probably [*sic*] primary cause of this mishap was rollback?" Before Rainey answered, the court sustained a defense objection on the ground that the question asked for Rainey's opinion. Further questioning along this line was cut off.

Following a 2-week trial, the jury returned a verdict for petitioners. . . . [T]he Eleventh Circuit reversed and remanded for a new trial [in part based on a violation of Federal Rule of Evidence 106]. . . . We agree with the unanimous holding of the Court of Appeals en banc that the District Court erred in refusing to permit Rainey to present a more complete picture of what he had written to Morgan.

We have no doubt that the jury was given a distorted and prejudicial impression of Rainey's letter. The theory of Rainey's case was that the accident was the result of a power failure, and, read in its entirety, his letter to Morgan was fully consistent with that theory. While Rainey did discuss problems his wife had encountered the morning of the accident which led her to attempt to cancel the flight, and also agreed that her airplane had violated pattern integrity in turning left prematurely, the thrust of his letter was to challenge Morgan's theory that the crash had been caused by a stall that took place when the pilots turned sharply right and pitched up in attempting to avoid the other plane. Thus Rainey argued that Morgan's hypothesis was inconsistent with the observations of eyewitnesses, the physical findings in the wreckage, and the likely actions of the two pilots. He explained at length his theory of power failure and attempted to demonstrate how the various pieces of evidence supported it. What the jury was told, however, through the defendants' direct examination of Rainey as an adverse witness, was that Rainey had written six months after the accident (1) that his wife had attempted to cancel the flight, partly because her student was tired and emotionally drained, and that "unnecessary pressure" was placed on them to proceed with it; and (2) that she or her student had abruptly initiated a hard right turn when the other aircraft unexpectedly came into view. It is plausible that a jury would have concluded from this information that Rainey did not believe in his theory of power failure and had developed it only later for purposes of litigation. Because the court sustained defense counsel's objection, Rainey's counsel was unable to counteract this prejudicial impression by presenting additional information about the letter on cross-examination.

The common-law "rule of completeness," which underlies Federal Rule of Evidence 106, was designed to prevent exactly the type of prejudice of which Rainey complains. In its aspect relevant to this litigation, the rule of completeness was stated succinctly by Wigmore: "[T]he opponent, against whom a part of an utterance has been put in, may in his turn complement it by putting in the remainder, in order to secure for the tribunal a complete understanding of the total tenor and effect of the utterance." 7 J. Wigmore, Evidence in Trials at Common Law § 2113, p. 653 (J. Chadbourn rev. 1978). The Federal Rules of Evidence have partially codified the doctrine of completeness in Rule 106:

> "When a writing or recorded statement or part thereof is introduced by a party, an adverse party may require the introduction at that time of any other part or any other writing or recorded statement which ought in fairness to be considered contemporaneously with it."

In proposing Rule 106, the Advisory Committee stressed that it "does not in any way circumscribe the right of the adversary to develop the matter on cross-examination or as part of his own case." Advisory Committee's Notes on Fed. Rule Evid. 106. We take this to be a reaffirmation of the obvious: that when one party has made use of a portion of a document, such that misunderstanding or distortion can be averted only through presentation of another portion, the material required for completeness is *ipso facto* relevant and therefore admissible under Rule 401 and 402. The District Court's refusal to admit the proffered completion evidence was a clear abuse of discretion.

While much of the controversy in this suit has centered on whether Rule 106 applies, we find it unnecessary to address that issue. Clearly the concerns underlying Rule 106 are relevant here, but, as the general rules of relevancy permit a ready resolution to this litigation, we need go no further in exploring the scope and meaning of Rule 106. . . . [W]e hold that on the facts of this litigation the District Court abused its discretion in restricting the scope of cross-examination of respondent Rainey by his counsel, and to that extent we affirm the Court of Appeals' judgment. . . .

[Chief Justice Rehnquist, joined by Justice O'Connor, filed an opinion dissenting from this part of the Court's opinion.]

PROBLEMS

3.26. The owners of all rights to the animated character "Seymour the Super Spaniel" bring a trademark infringement suit against the manufacturer of a "plush toy" that looks similar to Seymour. To prove that children are likely to confuse the defendant's toy with Seymour, the plaintiffs seek to prove that the defendant has made the following statements to wholesale purchasers: (a) "Kids can't tell this thing apart from Seymour." (b) "I showed the dog to my six-year-old niece, and she said, 'Oh, it's Seymour!' " (c) "My bookkeeper tells me we run out of inventory every time a new

Seymour movie comes out." Which if any of these statements are barred by the hearsay rule?

3.27. In a murder prosecution, a police officer testifies for the government that, when arrested, the defendant said, "I did it. I shot him." On cross-examination of the officer, the defense seeks to elicit that, immediately after making those statements, the defendant said, "It was self-defense. He tried to kill me." The government objects on grounds of hearsay. How should the judge rule?

b. Adoptive Admissions

[F.R.E. 801(d)(2)(B); C.E.C. §1221]

ADVISORY COMMITTEE NOTE TO F.R.E. 801(d)(2)(B)

Under established principles an admission may be made by adopting or acquiescing in the statement of another. While knowledge of contents would ordinarily be essential, this is not inevitably so: "X is a reliable person and knows what he is talking about." Adoption or acquiescence may be manifested in any appropriate manner. When silence is relied upon, the theory is that the person would, under the circumstances, protest the statement made in his presence, if untrue. The decision in each case calls for an evaluation in terms of probable human behavior. In civil cases, the results have generally been satisfactory. In criminal cases, however, troublesome questions have been raised by decisions holding that failure to deny is an admission: the inference is a fairly weak one, to begin with; silence may be motivated by advice of counsel or realization that "anything you say may be used against you"; unusual opportunity is afforded to manufacture evidence; and encroachment upon the privilege against self-incrimination seems inescapably to be involved. However, recent decisions of the Supreme Court relating to custodial interrogation and the right to counsel appear to resolve these difficulties. Hence the rule contains no special provisions concerning failure to deny in criminal cases.

UNITED STATES v. FORTES

619 F.2d 108 (5th Cir. 1980)

LEVIN H. CAMPBELL, Circuit Judge.

Following a jury trial in the District Court for the District of Massachusetts appellants Fortes and Jemison were convicted of armed robbery under 18 U.S.C. § 2113(d). . . . In order to link Fortes and Jemison with this robbery, the government relied heavily on the testimony of Anton Ward, who at the time of trial was serving a three-year prison sentence for conspiracy to commit bank robbery imposed by the United States District Court for the District of Connecticut. . . .

Jemison challenges the district court's admission, against her, of certain statements made by Fortes [in a conversation with Ward two days after the robbery]. . . . Ward stated that both Fortes and Jemison were present during the conversation. Ward testified that at this time he asked appellants "if they did a bank robbery," and that Fortes answered affirmatively, providing details of the robbery. Fortes' recitation, according to Ward, contained a description of Jemison's participation, including the information that she had taken the bank's money while Fortes held a shotgun and that she had difficulty separating the "red money" from the "regular money." Jemison objected repeatedly to the admission of Fortes' statements against her. . . .

This testimony was properly received against Jemison under Fed. R. Evid. 801(d)(2)(B), which allows the introduction of so-called adoptive admissions, including admissions by silence or acquiescence. See IV Wigmore § 1071 (Chadbourn rev. 1972). The general rule has been stated as follows:

> " 'When a statement tending to incriminate one accused of committing a crime is made in his presence and hearing and such statement is not denied, contradicted, or objected to by him, both the statement and the fact of his failure to deny are admissible in a criminal prosecution against him, as evidence of his acquiescence in its truth' . . . if made 'under such circumstances as would warrant the inference that he would naturally have contradicted them if he did not assent to their truth.' "

Arpan v. United States, 260 F.2d 649, 655 (8th Cir. 1958) (citations omitted). *See Sparf v. United States*, 156 U.S. 51 (1895).

. . . [W]e have no difficulty in concluding that an inquiry of two persons as to whether they had "done a bank robbery," followed by an affirmative response by one of them describing his participation with the other in the crime, is the type of exchange to which the silence of the unresponsive accomplice, assuming he is present and conscious of the conversation, "gives consent." IV Wigmore § 1071, at 102 (Chadbourn rev. 1972). Further, sufficient facts were introduced preliminarily to show, by way of foundation, that Jemison heard the statements detailing her conduct in the robbery and comprehended them. Ward testified several times that Jemison was present during the conversation and implied that he had directed his questions to both Jemison and Fortes, asking "if they did a bank robbery." We thus do not have the situation which existed in cases cited by Jemison where no evidence was offered to show that the defendant against whom the statements were introduced had any relation to the conversation in issue, although he might have been somewhere present in the room in which the conversation took place. We note also that Jemison failed to object to this line of questioning specifically on the grounds of insufficient foundation, see Fed. R. Evid. 103(a)(1); she likewise did not request that the government elicit fuller preliminary information; and on cross-examination of Ward, Jemison did not attempt to rebut the foundation laid by the government as to her presence at the time of the conversation or her ability to hear or understand Fortes' incriminating comments. In these circumstances, we find that Fortes' inculpatory remarks, recounted by Ward, were properly admitted against Jemison. The ultimate weight given them was, of course, a matter for the jury. . . . [Convictions affirmed.]

SOUTHERN STONE CO. v. SINGER

665 F.2d 698 (5th Cir. Unit B 1982)

R. LANIER ANDERSON, III, Circuit Judge:

[Southern Stone Co. was never paid for limestone rock it sold to S&M Materials Co., and was unable to collect on a judgment it obtained against S&M. Seeking to pierce the corporate veil,] Southern Stone brought this action against Thomas D. Moore, Sam M. Singer and Susan M. Singer, the officers, directors and shareholders of S&M, and against The Singer Company, a corporation wholly owned by Sam Singer at all times relevant to this action. . . . The jury returned a verdict in favor of Susan Singer and The Singer Company, but against appellants Sam Singer and Moore. We reverse and remand for a new trial as to Sam Singer's and Moore's liability because of the prejudicial effect of the erroneous admission of a letter written by Southern Stone's counsel to Moore. . . .

After S&M stopped doing business, Moore started his own corporation, TM, Inc. ("TM"), in order to continue in the business of hauling and selling lime purchased from Southern Stone. This new corporation eventually ran up a sizeable account with Southern Stone. . . . The district court permitted the introduction into evidence of a letter written on December 8, 1977, to Moore by Southern Stone's counsel.[4] The letter purports to relate several statements made by Moore to Southern Stone's counsel concerning the activities of Moore and Sam Singer in the final months of S&M's operation and concerning the date Singer decided to end S&M's business. . . .

Southern Stone argues that the letter is admissible under Fed. R. Evid. 801(d)(2)(B) as a statement in which Moore manifested his adoption or his belief in its truth. Although Southern Stone's counsel, not Moore, wrote the letter, Southern Stone argues that Moore's failure to respond to the letter, in the face of a postscript requesting a reply if the letter incorrectly recounted Moore's remarks, sufficiently indicates Moore's adoption or belief in the truth of the letter's contents, in effect transforming the letter into Moore's own statement about what he said during the conversation. However, the mere failure to respond to a letter does not indicate an

---

4. The body of the letter reads as follows:

This will confirm our conversation this date at which time you told me that Mr. Singer instructed you to buy on account, all the lime that you could from Southern Stone Company's quarry in Lee County, Alabama, and if necessary to even lease other truck [sic] if S&M's trucks were otherwise busy and to haul the lime from Lee County quarry of Southern Stone Company to S&M Materials Co. in Russell County and at a place that S&M Materials Co. had leased for the special purposes of stockpiling lime outside of Phenix City, Alabama. At the time the instructions were given to you to buy all the lime that you could on the account of S&M from Southern Stone Company, Inc., Mr. Singer had made the decision on behalf of S&M Materials Company 2 or 3 months before the business closed that S&M Materials Company was going out of business as of December 31, 1976.

I believe this is the same information that you relayed to Mr. Mark C. Gallups sometime ago.

P.S. If any of the above is incorrect, please advise me.

adoption unless it was reasonable under the circumstances for the sender to expect the recipient to respond and to correct erroneous assertions. . . . All the circumstances surrounding this letter do not support a reasonable expectation of any response. The only reason Moore went to the office of Southern Stone's counsel was to sign a personal note for the account that TM owed Southern Stone. Southern Stone introduced no evidence indicating that Moore was there to discuss any matters relating to his former involvement with S&M, which was the entire subject matter of the letter. Indeed, S&M had ceased operations nearly a year prior to the meeting between Moore and Southern Stone's counsel. Moore testified that the reason he never responded to the letter was that at the time, he was no longer involved with S&M, "didn't care what was going on" and considered that "the corporation was gone." Moore also testified that he could remember nothing about the conversation. Because of Southern Stone's failure to lay a foundation for the introduction of the letter more solid than Moore's mere failure to respond, the letter did not meet the requirements of Rule 801(d)(2)(B) and could not be admitted on that basis.

Once stripped of its asserted status as, in effect, Moore's own admission as to what he said in the conversation, the letter can be viewed only as a hearsay declaration of Southern Stone's counsel as to what Moore said. The letter involves two levels of hearsay: the letter says that Southern Stone's counsel said (first level) that Moore made certain admissions (second level). Even if Moore's declarations are not hearsay under Fed. R. Evid. 801(d)(2)(A) (statements of a party offered against the party), the first level of hearsay still exists. In attempting to explain why its counsel did not personally testify as to his conversation with Moore, Southern Stone stated that it might be improper for the attorney representing Southern Stone in the trial of this case also to testify on Southern Stone's behalf. Southern Stone should have engaged other trial counsel if it had any reservations about placing its trial attorney on the witness stand. Southern Stone cannot create its own exception to the hearsay rule by failing to retain such other counsel. Because we perceive no other applicable hearsay exception for which Southern Stone laid an adequate foundation, the letter was inadmissible. . . . REVERSED AND REMANDED.

c. Authorized Admissions

[F.R.E. 801(d)(2)(C); C.E.C. §1222]

HANSON v. WALLER

888 F.2d 806 (11th Cir. 1989)

MARCUS, District Judge:

. . . Appellants brought this action on behalf of the deceased, Alfaretta Spina ("Spina") who died of injuries sustained after being struck by a truck driven by Appellee Ralph Waller ("Waller"). . . . Appellants contend that it was error to allow the Defendant at trial to put into evidence, a letter from Appellants' first attorney Mr. Thompson to Defendant's attorney Mr. Dorsey. The letter, as read into the evidence, indicated the following:

> Dear Mr. Dorsey: As per my previous letter to you of June the 29th, 1987, enclosed herewith please find copies of the photographs taken from the scene of the accident along with photographs taken from the same type truck the Defendant Waller was driving, which shows it impossible for him to see Ms. Spina if in crossing the street she had reached a position directly in front of the truck when the traffic light changed. If you care to discuss the matter with me, please feel free to call and with kindest personal regards, I remain, Very truly yours, Thomas L. Thompson, Jr.

... Rule 801(d)(2)(C) specifically excludes statements used against a party which were made by another person authorized by the party to make a statement concerning the subject, from the definition of hearsay. This provision has been applied to allow in evidence statements made by attorneys in a representational capacity. *See, e.g., United States v. Ojala*, 544 F.2d 940, 946 (8th Cir. 1976); *Williams v. Union Carbide Co.*, 790 F.2d 552, 555-56 (6th Cir.1986). Although an attorney does not have authority to make an out-of-court admission for his client in all instances, he does have authority to make admissions which are directly related to the management of litigation. *United States v. Dolleris*, 408 F.2d 918, 921 (6th Cir. 1969), *cert. denied*, 395 U.S. 943 (1968). In the instant case, the letter sent by Mr. Thompson to Mr. Dorsey was clearly related to the management of the Appellants' litigation. Therefore, the contents of the letter fall within the hearsay exclusion provided by Rule 801(d)(2)(C). Finally, we observe that the Appellants have not demonstrated that the revelation of the contents of the letter was harmful to their case at trial. Accordingly, we find no error. . . .

ADVISORY COMMITTEE NOTE
TO F.R.E. 801(d)(2)(C)

No authority is required for the general proposition that a statement authorized by a party to be made should have the status of an admission by the party. However, the question arises whether only statements to third persons should be so regarded, to the exclusion of statements by the agent to the principal. The rule is phrased broadly so as to encompass both. While it may be argued that the agent authorized to make statements to his principal does not speak for him, Morgan, Basic Problems of Evidence 273 (1962), communication to an outsider has not generally been thought to be an essential characteristic of an admission. Thus a party's books or records are usable against him, without regard to any intent to disclose to third persons. 5 Wigmore § 1557. . . . Cf. Uniform Rule 63(8)(a) and California Evidence Code § 1222 which limit status as an admission in this regard to statements authorized by the party to be made "for" him, which is perhaps an ambiguous limitation to statements to third persons.

PROBLEM

3.28. The plaintiffs in a product liability lawsuit against a bicycle manufacturer seek to introduce evidence that a spokesperson for the company
admitted that "the design of that particular bike has proven defective." The
company claims that it fired the spokesperson hours before she made that
statement; the plaintiffs claim the spokesperson was dismissed shortly *after*
making the statement. After hearing conflicting testimony on this question,
the judge concludes that it is impossible to tell which side is right, but that
the evidence slightly favors the company's account. Should the jury be told
about the spokesperson's statement?

d. Agent and Employee Admissions

[F.R.E. 801(d)(2)(D); C.E.C. §§1224, 1225]

ADVISORY COMMITTEE NOTE TO F.R.E. 801(d)(2)(D)

The tradition has been to test the admissibility of statements by agents,
as admissions, by applying the usual test of agency. Was the admission made
by the agent acting in the scope of his employment? Since few principals
employ agents for the purpose of making damaging statements, the usual
result was exclusion of the statement. Dissatisfaction with this loss of
valuable and helpful evidence has been increasing. A substantial trend
favors admitting statements related to a matter within the scope of the
agency or employment.

MAHLANDT v. WILD CANID SURVIVAL & RESEARCH CENTER, INC.

588 F.2d 626 (8th Cir. 1978)

VAN SICKLE, District Judge.

This is a civil action for damages arising out of an alleged attack by a
wolf on a child. The sole issues on appeal are as to the correctness of three
rulings which excluded conclusionary statements against interest. Two of
them were made by a defendant, who was also an employee of the corporate defendant; and the third was in the form of a statement appearing in the
records of a board meeting of the corporate defendant.

On March 23, 1973, Daniel Mahlandt, then 3 years, 10 months, and 8
days old, was sent by his mother to a neighbor's home on an adjoining street
to get his older brother, Donald. Daniel's mother watched him cross the
street, and then turned into the house to get her car keys. Daniel's path took
him along a walkway adjacent to the Poos' residence. Next to the walkway
was a five foot chain link fence to which Sophie had been chained with a

six foot chain. In other words, Sophie was free to move in a half circle having a six foot radius on the side of the fence opposite from Daniel.

Sophie was a bitch wolf, 11 months and 28 days old, who had been born at the St. Louis Zoo, and kept there until she reached 6 months of age, at which time she was given to the Wild Canid Survival and Research Center, Inc. It was the policy of the Zoo to remove wolves from the Children's Zoo after they reached the age of 5 or 6 months. Sophie was supposed to be kept at the Tyson Research Center, but Kenneth Poos, as Director of Education for the Wild Canid Survival and Research Center, Inc., had been keeping her at his home because he was taking Sophie to schools and institutions where he showed films and gave programs with respect to the nature of wolves. Sophie was known as a very gentle wolf who had proved herself to be good natured and stable during her contacts with thousands of children, while she was in the St. Louis Children's Zoo.

Sophie was chained because the evening before she had jumped the fence and attacked a beagle who was running along the fence and yapping at her.

A neighbor who was ill in bed in the second floor of his home heard a child's screams and went to his window, where he saw a boy lying on his back within the enclosure, with a wolf straddling him. The wolf's face was near Daniel's face, but the distance was so great that he could not see what the wolf was doing, and did not see any biting. Within about 15 seconds the neighbor saw Clarke Poos, about seventeen, run around the house, get the wolf off of the boy, and disappear with the child in his arms to the back of the house. Clarke took the boy in and laid him on the kitchen floor.

Clarke had been returning from his friend's home immediately west when he heard a child's cries and ran around to the enclosure. He found Daniel lying within the enclosure, about three feet from the fence, and Sophie standing back from the boy the length of her chain, and wailing. An expert in the behavior of wolves stated that when a wolf's wail is a sign of compassion, and an effort to get attention, not a sign of attack. No witness saw or knew how Daniel was injured.

Clarke and his sister ran over to get Daniel's mother. She says that Clarke told her, "a wolf got Danny and he is dying." Clarke denies that statement. The defendant, Mr. Poos, arrived home while Daniel and his mother were in the kitchen. After Daniel was taken in an ambulance, Mr. Poos talked to everyone present, including a neighbor who came in. Within an hour after he arrived home, Mr. Poos went to Washington University to inform Owen Sexton, President of Wild Canid Survival and Research Center, Inc., of the incident. Mr. Sexton was not in his office so Mr. Poos left the following note on his door:

> Owen, would call me at home, 727-5080? Sophie bit a child that came in our back yard. All has been taken care of. I need to convey what happened to you.

Denial of admission of this note is one of the issues on appeal.

Later that day, Mr. Poos found Mr. Sexton at the Tyson Research Center and told him what had happened. Denial of plaintiff's offer to prove that Mr. Poos told Mr. Sexton that, "Sophie had bit a child that day," is the second issue on appeal.

A meeting of the Directors of the Wild Canid Survival and Research Center, Inc., was held on April 4, 1973. Mr. Poos was not present at that meeting. The minutes of that meeting reflect that there was a "great deal of discussion . . . about the legal aspects of the incident of Sophie biting the child." Plaintiff offered an abstract of the minutes containing that reference. Denial of the offer of that abstract is the third issue on appeal.

Daniel had lacerations of the face, left thigh, left calf, and right thigh, and abrasions and bruises of the abdomen and chest. Mr. Mahlandt was permitted to state that Daniel had indicated that he had gone under the fence. Mr. Mahlandt and Mr. Poos, about a month after the incident, examined the fence to determine what caused Daniel's lacerations. Mr. Mahlandt felt that they did not look like animal bites. The parallel scars on Daniel's thigh appeared to match the configuration of the barbs or tines on the fence. The expert as to the behavior of wolves opined that the lacerations were not wolf bites or wounds caused by wolf claws. Wolves have powerful jaws and a wolf bite will result in massive crushing or severing of a limb. He stated that if Sophie had bitten Daniel there would have been clear apposition of teeth and massive crushing of Daniel's hands and arms which were not injured. Also, if Sophie had pulled Daniel under the fence, tooth marks on the foot or leg would have been present, although Sophie possessed enough strength to pull the boy under the fence.

The jury brought in a verdict for the defense.

The trial judge's rationale for excluding the note, the statement, and the corporate minutes, was the same in each case. He reasoned that Mr. Poos did not have any personal knowledge of the facts, and accordingly, the first two admissions were based on hearsay; and the third admission contained in the minutes of the board meeting was subject to the same objection of hearsay, and unreliability because of lack of personal knowledge.

. . . [T]he statement in the note pinned on the door is not hearsay, and is admissible against Mr. Poos. It was his own statement, and as such was clearly different from the reported statement of another. . . . It was also a statement of which he had manifested his adoption or belief in its truth. And the same observations may be made of the statement made later in the day to Mr. Sexton that, "Sophie had bit a child. . . ."

Are these statements admissible against Wild Canid Survival and Research Center, Inc.? They were made by Mr. Poos when he was an agent or servant of the Wild Canid Survival and Research Center, Inc., and they concerned a matter within the scope of his agency, or employment, i.e., his custody of Sophie, and were made during the existence of that relationship.

Defendant argues that Rule 801(d)(2) does not provide for the admission of "in house" statements; that is, it allows only admissions made to third parties. The notes of the Advisory Committee on the Proposed Rules . . . discuss the problem of "in house" admissions with reference to Rule 801(d)(2)(C) situations. This is not a (C) situation because Mr. Poos was not authorized or directed to make a statement on the matter by anyone. But the rationale developed in that comment does apply to this (D) situation. Mr. Poos had actual physical custody of Sophie. His conclusions, his opinions, were obviously accepted as a basis for action by his principal. . . .

Weinstein states categorically that although an express requirement of personal knowledge on the part of the declarant of the facts underlying his statement is not written into [Rule 801(d)(2)(D)], it should be. He feels that is mandated by Rules 805 and 403. . . . [N]either rule mandates the introduction into Rule 801(d)(2)(D) of an implied requirement that the declarant have personal knowledge of the facts underlying his statement. So we conclude that the two statements made by Mr. Poos were admissible against Wild Canid Survival and Research Center, Inc.

As to the entry in the records of a corporate meeting, the directors as primary officers of the corporation had the authority to include their conclusions in the record of the meeting. So the evidence would fall within 801(d)(2)(C) as to Wild Canid Survival and Research Center, Inc., and be admissible. The "in house" aspect of this admission has already been discussed. . . .

But there was no servant, or agency, relationship which justified admitting the evidence of the board minutes as against Mr. Poos. None of the conditions of 801(d)(2) cover the claim that minutes of a corporate board meeting can be used against a non-attending, non-participating employee of that corporation. The evidence was not admissible as against Mr. Poos.

There is left only the question of whether the trial court's rulings which excluded all three items of evidence are justified under Rule 403. He clearly found that the evidence was not reliable, pointing out that none of the statements were based on the personal knowledge of the declarant.

Again, that problem was faced by the Advisory Committee on Proposed Rules. In its discussion of 801(d)(2) exceptions to the hearsay rule, the Committee said:

> The freedom which admissions have enjoyed from technical demands of searching for an assurance of trustworthiness in some against-interest circumstances, and from the restrictive influences of the opinion rule and the rule requiring first hand knowledge, when taken with the apparently prevalent satisfaction with the results, calls for generous treatment of this avenue to admissibility.

So here, remembering that relevant evidence is usually prejudicial to the cause of the side against which it is presented, and that the prejudice which concerns us is unreasonable prejudice; and applying the spirit of Rule 801(d)(2), we hold that Rule 403 does not warrant the exclusion of the evidence of Mr. Poos' statements as against himself or Wild Canid Survival and Research Center, Inc. But the limited admissibility of the corporate minutes, coupled with the repetitive nature of the evidence and the low probative value of the minute record, all justify supporting the judgment of the trial court under Rule 403.

The judgment of the District Court is reversed and the matter remanded to the District Court for a new trial consistent with this opinion.

SEA-LAND SERVICE, INC. v. LOZEN
INTERNATIONAL, LLC

285 F.3d 808 (9th Cir. 2002)

GRABER, Circuit Judge:

Plaintiff Sea-Land Service, Inc. (Sea-Land), brought this action against Defendant Lozen International, LLC (Lozen), to recover money owed under a shipping contract. Lozen counterclaimed for damages resulting from Sea-Land's failure to timely deliver one of the shipments at issue. The parties settled and dismissed Sea-Land's claim, but they were unable to reach an agreement with respect to Lozen's counterclaims. As to those, the district court entered summary judgment in favor of Sea-Land. . . .

Lozen appeals, arguing . . . that the district court improperly excluded Exhibit 4, an internal company e-mail authored by one Sea-Land employee and forwarded to Lozen by a second Sea-Land employee. The district court excluded this evidence on the ground that Lozen "makes no argument, nor does it present any evidence indicating the identity or job title of [the] employee" who authored the forwarded e-mail. Lozen argues that the e-mail is admissible and is not hearsay because it is an admission by a party opponent. Fed. R. Evid. 801(d)(2)(D). . . .

Exhibit 4 is an admission by a party opponent. The original e-mail, an internal company memorandum, closes with an electronic "signature" attesting that the message was authored by "Mike Jacques," Sea-Land's "Rail Reefer Services Coordinator" at the time the e-mail was written. Jacques is listed as one of Sea-Land's employees in Exhibit 9, a letter from Sea-Land to Lozen that the district court *did* admit into evidence. The original e-mail also appears to concern a matter within the scope of Jacques' employment.

More importantly, however, Jacques' original e-mail was forwarded to Lozen by Laurie Martinez, a second Sea-Land employee. She copied the entire body of Jacques' internal memorandum into her e-mail and prefaced it with the statement, "Yikes, Pls note the rail screwed us up. . . ." Martinez thereby incorporated and adopted the contents of Jacques' original message, because her remark "manifested an adoption or belief in [the] truth" of the information contained in the original e-mail. Fed. R. Evid. 801(d)(2)(B); . . . *cf. Alvord-Polk, Inc. v. F. Schumacher & Co.*, 37 F.3d 996, 1005 n. 6 (3d Cir.1994) (holding that statements of company president, which were reprinted in company publications, were not hearsay but were instead admissible as adoptive admissions). Further, there is evidence in the record that Martinez was one of Sea-Land's employees at the time her message was written and that the contents of the e-mail were within the scope of her employment. Her admission (including the incorporated portion) therefore conforms to the requirements of Rule 801(d)(2)(D).

For these reasons, the district court abused its discretion when it excluded the e-mail. . . . REVERSED and REMANDED for proceedings consistent with this opinion.

PROBLEMS

3.29. A delivery company fires a driver after his truck collides with a motorcycle. The driver then telephones the motorcyclist and admits that he was speeding. The motorcyclist sues the driver and the delivery company for negligence, proceeding against the delivery company on a theory of *respondeat superior*. Is the driver's statement admissible against the driver? Against the company?

3.30. A newspaper reports that the "old time marinade" advertised by a fast food chain is mayonnaise and food coloring. The chain sues for libel. The newspaper seeks to have its reporter testify that she was told the ingredients by the chain's Vice President for Menus and Recipes. Is the testimony admissible to prove lack of malice? To prove the actual ingredients?

3.31. During a circus performance, a lion escapes and mauls a spectator to death. Hours later the lion tamer tells his supervisor that the latch on the lion's cage was rusty and weak. The circus company, Amazing Inc., is prosecuted in state court for criminally negligent homicide. The state code of evidence is substantially identical to the Federal Rules of Evidence. Assume the lion tamer does not testify at trial. Would the hearsay rule or the Confrontation Clause bar the introduction of his statement against Amazing Inc.?

e. Co-Conspirator Admissions

[F.R.E. 801(d)(2)(E); C.E.C. §1223]

ADVISORY COMMITTEE NOTE TO F.R.E. 801(d)(2)(E)

The limitation upon the admissibility of statements of co-conspirators to those made "during the course and in furtherance of the conspiracy" is in the accepted pattern. While the broadened view of agency taken in [Rule 801(d)(2)(D)] might suggest wider admissibility of statements of co-conspirators, the agency theory of conspiracy is at best a fiction and ought not to serve as a basis for admissibility beyond that already established. See Levie, Hearsay and Conspiracy, 52 Mich. L. Rev. 1159 (1954); Comment, U. Chi. L. Rev. 520 (1958). The rule is consistent with the position of the Supreme Court in denying admissibility to statements made after the objectives of the conspiracy have either failed or been achieved. Krulewitch v. United States, 336 U.S. 440 (1949);Wong Sun v. United States, 371 U.S. 471, 490 (1963).

REPORT OF THE SENATE JUDICIARY COMMITTEE
S. Rep. No. 93-1277 (1974)

While [proposed Rule 801(d)(2)(E)] refers to a coconspirator, it is this committee's understanding that the rule is meant to carry forward the universally accepted doctrine that a joint venturer is considered as a coconspirator for the purposes of this rule even though no conspiracy has been charged. United States v. Rinaldi, 393 F.2d 97, 99 (2d Cir.), cert. denied, 393 U.S. 913 (1968); United States v. Spencer, 415 F.2d 1301, 1304 (7th Cir. 1969).

JOSEPH H. LEVIE, HEARSAY AND CONSPIRACY

52 Mich. L. Rev. 1159, 1161-1166 (1954)

The odd thing about this exception to the hearsay rule is its very existence. Why single out conspiracies for preferential treatment? . . . The usual reason given for the co-conspirators' exception is the classical agency rationale that co-conspirators are co-agents and, as such, liable for each other's declarations. . . . [This] begs the question. The rules of agency govern the substantive law of conspiracy; they decide who is a member of the conspiracy. As such they are involved in determining *against whom* the evidence may be admitted. . . . [T]hey are not relevant in determining *why* it should be admitted.

Wigmore's theory that such declarations are admitted because they are trustworthy (and accordingly the need for cross-examination is less acute) fares no better. Wigmore argues that since the interest of all conspirators is identical, an admission of one against his interest is against the interest of each. This fails to distinguish between declarations showing the existence of a conspiracy and declarations concerning the membership or aims. Of course sane men do not falsely admit to conspiracy. Conspirators' declarations are good to prove that some conspiracy exists and less trustworthy to show its aims and membership. The conspirator's interest is likely to lie in misleading the listener into believing the conspiracy stronger with more members (and different members) and other aims than it in fact has. It is no victory for common sense to make a belief that criminals are notorious for their veracity the basis for law.

. . . The true reason for the exception explains both its growth and the parallelism of that expansion to the expansion of the law of conspiracy. That reason is simply: There is great probative need for such testimony. Conspiracy is a hard thing to prove. The substantive law of conspiracy has vastly expanded. This created a tension solved by relaxation in the law of evidence. Conspirators' declarations are admitted out of necessity.

BOURJAILY v. UNITED STATES

483 U.S. 171 (1987)

Chief Justice Rehnquist delivered the opinion of the Court.

Federal Rule of Evidence 801(d)(2)(E) provides: "A statement is not hearsay if . . . [t]he statement is offered against a party and is . . . a statement by a coconspirator of a party during the course and in further-ance of the conspiracy." We granted certiorari to answer three questions regarding the admission of statements under Rule 801(d)(2)(E): (1) whether the court must determine by independent evidence that the conspiracy existed and that the defendant and the declarant were mem-bers of this conspiracy; (2) the quantum of proof on which such deter-minations must be based; and (3) whether a court must in each case examine the circumstances of such a statement to determine its reliability.

In May 1984, Clarence Greathouse, an informant working for the Federal Bureau of Investigation (FBI), arranged to sell a kilogram of cocaine to Angelo Lonardo. Lonardo agreed that he would find individuals to distribute the drug. When the sale became imminent, Lonardo stated in a tape-recorded telephone conversation that he had a "gentleman friend" who had some questions to ask about the cocaine. In a subsequent telephone call, Greathouse spoke to the "friend" about the quality of the drug and the price. Greathouse then spoke again with Lonardo, and the two arranged the details of the purchase. They agreed that the sale would take place in a designated hotel parking lot, and Lonardo would transfer the drug from Greathouse's car to the "friend," who would be waiting in the parking lot in his own car. Greathouse proceeded with the transaction as planned, and FBI agents arrested Lonardo and petitioner immediately after Lonardo placed a kilogram of cocaine into petitioner's car in the hotel parking lot. In petitioner's car, the agents found over $20,000 in cash.

Petitioner was charged with conspiring to distribute cocaine, in viola-tion of 21 U.S.C. § 846, and possession of cocaine with intent to distribute, a violation of 21 U.S.C. § 841(a)(1). The Government introduced, over peti-tioner's objection, Angelo Lonardo's telephone statements regarding the participation of the "friend" in the transaction. The District Court found that, considering the events in the parking lot and Lonardo's statements over the telephone, the Government had established by a preponderance of the evidence that a conspiracy involving Lonardo and petitioner existed, and that Lonardo's statements over the telephone had been made in the course of and in furtherance of the conspiracy. Accordingly, the trial court held that Lonardo's out-of-court statements satisfied Rule 801(d)(2)(E) and were not hearsay. Petitioner was convicted on both counts and sentenced to 15 years. The United States Court of Appeals for the Sixth Circuit affir-med. . . . We affirm.

Before admitting a co-conspirator's statement over an objection that it does not qualify under Rule 801(d)(2)(E), a court must be satisfied that the statement actually falls within the definition of the Rule. There must be evidence that there was a conspiracy involving the declarant and the non-offering party, and that the statement was made "during the course and in furtherance of the conspiracy." Federal Rule of Evidence 104(a) provides: "Preliminary questions concerning . . . the admissibility of evidence shall be determined by the court." Petitioner and the Government agree that the existence of a conspiracy and petitioner's involvement in it are preliminary questions of fact that, under Rule 104, must be resolved by the court. The

Federal Rules, however, nowhere define the standard of proof the court must observe in resolving these questions.

We are therefore guided by our prior decisions regarding admissibility determinations that hinge on preliminary factual questions. We have traditionally required that these matters be established by a preponderance of proof. Evidence is placed before the jury when it satisfies the technical requirements of the evidentiary Rules, which embody certain legal and policy determinations. The inquiry made by a court concerned with these matters is not whether the proponent of the evidence wins or loses his case on the merits, but whether the evidentiary Rules have been satisfied. Thus, the evidentiary standard is unrelated to the burden of proof on the substantive issues, be it a criminal case, see *In re Winship*, 397 U.S. 358 (1970), or a civil case. The preponderance standard ensures that before admitting evidence, the court will have found it more likely than not that the technical issues and policy concerns addressed by the Federal Rules of Evidence have been afforded due consideration. As in *Lego v. Twomey*, 404 U.S. 477, 488 (1972), we find "nothing to suggest that admissibility rulings have been unreliable or otherwise wanting in quality because not based on some higher standard." We think that our previous decisions in this area resolve the matter. See, *e.g., Colorado v. Connelly*, [479 U.S. 157 (1986)] (preliminary fact that custodial confessant waived rights must be proved by preponderance of the evidence); *Nix v. Williams*, 467 U.S. 431, 444, n. 5 (1984) (inevitable discovery of illegally seized evidence must be shown to have been more likely than not); *United States v. Matlock*, 415 U.S. 164 (1974) (voluntariness of consent to search must be shown by preponderance of the evidence); *Lego v. Twomey, supra* (voluntariness of confession must be demonstrated by a preponderance of the evidence). Therefore, we hold that when the preliminary facts relevant to Rule 801(d)(2)(E) are disputed, the offering party must prove them by a preponderance of the evidence.[1]

Even though petitioner agrees that the courts below applied the proper standard of proof with regard to the preliminary facts relevant to Rule 801(d)(2)(E), he nevertheless challenges the admission of Lonardo's statements. Petitioner argues that in determining whether a conspiracy exists and whether the defendant was a member of it, the court must look only to independent evidence—that is, evidence other than the statements sought to be admitted. Petitioner relies on *Glasser v. United States*, 315 U.S. 60 (1942), in which this Court first mentioned the so-called "bootstrapping rule." The relevant issue in *Glasser* was whether Glasser's counsel, who also represented another defendant, faced such a conflict

---

1. We intimate no view on the proper standard of proof for questions falling under Federal Rule of Evidence 104(b) (conditional relevancy). We also decline to address the circumstances in which the burden of coming forward to show that the proffered evidence is inadmissible is appropriately placed on the nonoffering party. . . . Finally, we do not express an opinion on the proper order of proof that trial courts should follow in concluding that the preponderance standard has been satisfied in an ongoing trial.

of interest that Glasser received ineffective assistance. Glasser contended that conflicting loyalties led his lawyer not to object to statements made by one of Glasser's co-conspirators. The Government argued that any objection would have been fruitless because the statements were admissible. The Court rejected this proposition:

> "[S]uch declarations are admissible over the objection of an alleged coconspirator, who was not present when they were made, only if there is proof *aliunde* that he is connected with the conspiracy. . . . Otherwise, hearsay would lift itself by its own bootstraps to the level of competent evidence."

The Court revisited the bootstrapping rule in *United States v. Nixon*, 418 U.S. 683 (1974), where again, in passing, the Court stated: "Declarations by one defendant may also be admissible against other defendants upon a sufficient showing, *by independent evidence*, of a conspiracy among one or more other defendants and the declarant and if the declarations at issue were in furtherance of that conspiracy" (emphasis added) (footnote omitted). Read in the light most favorable to petitioner, *Glasser* could mean that a court should not consider hearsay statements at all in determining preliminary facts under Rule 801(d)(2)(E). Petitioner, of course, adopts this view of the bootstrapping rule. *Glasser*, however, could also mean that a court must have *some* proof *aliunde*, but may look at the hearsay statements themselves in light of this independent evidence to determine whether a conspiracy has been shown by a preponderance of the evidence. The Courts of Appeals have widely adopted the former view and held that in determining the preliminary facts relevant to co-conspirators' out-of-court statements, a court may not look at the hearsay statements themselves for their evidentiary value.

Both *Glasser* and *Nixon*, however, were decided before Congress enacted the Federal Rules of Evidence in 1975. . . . Petitioner concedes that Rule 104, on its face, appears to allow the court to make the preliminary factual determinations relevant to Rule 801(d)(2)(E) by considering any evidence it wishes, unhindered by considerations of admissibility. That would seem to many to be the end of the matter. Congress has decided that courts may consider hearsay in making these factual determinations. Out-of-court statements made by anyone, including putative co-conspirators, are often hearsay. Even if they are, they may be considered, *Glasser* and the bootstrapping rule notwithstanding. But petitioner nevertheless argues that the bootstrapping rule, as most Courts of Appeals have construed it, survived this apparently unequivocal change in the law unscathed and that Rule 104, as applied to the admission of co-conspirator's statements, does not mean what it says. We disagree.

Petitioner claims that Congress evidenced no intent to disturb the bootstrapping rule, which was embedded in the previous approach, and we should not find that Congress altered the rule without affirmative evidence so indicating. It would be extraordinary to require legislative history to *confirm* the plain meaning of Rule 104. The Rule on its face allows the trial judge to consider any evidence whatsoever, bound only by the rules of privilege. We think that the Rule is sufficiently clear that to the extent that it is inconsistent with petitioner's interpretation of *Glasser* and *Nixon*, the Rule prevails.[2]

Nor do we agree with petitioner that this construction of Rule 104(a) will allow courts to admit hearsay statements without any credible proof of the conspiracy, thus fundamentally changing the nature of the co-conspirator exception. Petitioner starts with the proposition that co-conspirators' out-of-court statements are deemed unreliable and are inadmissible, at least until a conspiracy is shown. Since these statements are unreliable, petitioner contends that they should not form any part of the basis for establishing a conspiracy, the very antecedent that renders them admissible. . . .

Even if out-of-court declarations by co-conspirators are presumptively unreliable, trial courts must be permitted to evaluate these statements for their evidentiary worth as revealed by the particular circumstances of the case. Courts often act as factfinders, and there is no reason to believe that courts are any less able to properly recognize the probative value of evidence in this particular area. The party opposing admission has an adequate incentive to point out the shortcomings in such evidence before the trial court finds the preliminary facts. If the opposing party is unsuccessful in keeping the evidence from the factfinder, he still has the opportunity to attack the probative value of the evidence as it relates to the substantive issue in the case. See, *e.g.*, Fed. R. Evid. 806 (allowing attack on credibility of out-of-court declarant).

We think that there is little doubt that a co-conspirator's statements could themselves be probative of the existence of a conspiracy and the participation of both the defendant and the declarant in the conspiracy. Petitioner's case presents a paradigm. The out-of-court statements of Lonardo indicated that Lonardo was involved in a conspiracy with a "friend." The statements indicated that the friend had agreed with Lonardo to buy a kilogram of cocaine and to distribute it. The statements also revealed that the friend would be at the hotel parking lot, in his car, and would accept the cocaine from Greathouse's car after Greathouse gave Lonardo the keys. Each one of Lonardo's statements may itself be

---

2. The Advisory Committee Notes show that the Rule was not adopted in a fit of absentmindedness. The Note to Rule 104 specifically addresses the process by which a federal court should make the factual determinations requisite to a finding of admissibility:

"If the question is factual in nature, the judge will of necessity receive evidence pro and con on the issue. The rule provides that the rules of evidence in general do not apply to this process. McCormick § 53, p. 123, n. 8, points out that the authorities are 'scattered and inconclusive,' and observes:

"'Should the exclusionary law of evidence, "the child of the jury system" in Thayer's phrase, be applied to this hearing before the judge? Sound sense backs the view that it should not, and that the judge should be empowered to hear *any relevant evidence*, such as affidavits *or other reliable hearsay*.'" (emphasis added).

The Advisory Committee further noted: "An item, offered and objected to, *may itself be considered in ruling on admissibility*, though not yet admitted in evidence" (emphasis added). We think this language makes plain the drafters' intent to abolish any kind of bootstrapping rule. Silence is at best ambiguous, and we decline the invitation to rely on speculation to import ambiguity into what is otherwise a clear rule.

unreliable, but taken as a whole, the entire conversation between Lonardo and Greathouse was corroborated by independent evidence. The friend, who turned out to be petitioner, showed up at the prearranged spot at the prearranged time. He picked up the cocaine, and a significant sum of money was found in his car. On these facts, the trial court concluded, in our view correctly, that the Government had established the existence of a conspiracy and petitioner's participation in it.

We need not decide in this case whether the courts below could have relied solely upon Lonardo's hearsay statements to determine that a conspiracy had been established by a preponderance of the evidence. . . . It is sufficient for today to hold that a court, in making a preliminary factual determination under Rule 801(d)(2)(E), may examine the hearsay statements sought to be admitted. As we have held in other cases concerning admissibility determinations, "the judge should receive the evidence and give it such weight as his judgment and experience counsel." *United States v. Matlock,* 415 U.S., at 175. The courts below properly considered the statements of Lonardo and the subsequent events in finding that the Government had established by a preponderance of the evidence that Lonardo was involved in a conspiracy with petitioner. We have no reason to believe that the District Court's factfinding of this point was clearly erroneous. We hold that Lonardo's out-of-court statements were properly admitted against petitioner. . . . *Affirmed.*

[Justice Stevens filed a concurring opinion.]

Justice BLACKMUN, with whom Justice BRENNAN and Justice MARSHALL join, dissenting.

. . . By all accounts, the [common-law co-conspirator] exemption was based upon agency principles, the underlying concept being that a conspiracy is a common undertaking where the conspirators are all agents of each other and where the acts and statements of one can be attributed to all. As Judge Learned Hand explained this in a frequently quoted remark:

> "When men enter into an agreement for an unlawful end, they become ad hoc agents for one another, and have made a 'partnership in crime.' What one does pursuant to their common purpose, all do, and, as declarations may be such acts, they are competent against all." *Van Riper v. United States*, 13 F.2d 961, 967 (CA2), cert. denied *sub nom. Ackerson v. United States*, 273 U.S. 702 (1926).

. . . [D]espite the recognized need by prosecutors for co-conspirator statements, these statements often have been considered to be somewhat unreliable. It has long been understood that such statements in some cases may constitute, at best, nothing more than the "idle chatter" of a declarant or, at worst, malicious gossip. Moreover, when confronted with such a statement, an innocent defendant would have a difficult time defending himself against it, for, if he were not in the conspiracy, he would have no idea why the conspirator made the statement. . . . Because of this actual "real world" experience with the possible unreliability of these statements, the Advisory Committee retained the agency rationale for this exemption in Rule 801(d)(2)(E), as well as the safeguards, albeit limited, against unreliability that this rationale provided the defendant. The independent-evidence requirement was one such safeguard. If this requirement is set aside, then one of the exemption's safeguards is lost. . . .

ADVISORY COMMITTEE NOTE TO 1997 AMENDMENT TO F.R.E. 801(d)(2)

Rule 801(d)(2) has been amended in order to respond to three issues raised by *Bourjaily v. United States*, 483 U.S. 171 (1987). First, the amendment codifies the holding in *Bourjaily* by stating expressly that a court shall consider the contents of a coconspirator's statement in determining "the existence of the conspiracy and the participation therein of the declarant and the party against whom the statement is offered." . . .

Second, the amendment resolves an issue on which the Court had reserved decision. It provides that the contents of the declarant's statement do not alone suffice to establish a conspiracy in which the declarant and the defendant participated. The court must consider in addition the circumstances surrounding the statement, such as the identity of the speaker, the context in which the statement was made, or evidence corroborating the contents of the statement in making its determination as to each preliminary question. This amendment is in accordance with existing practice. Every court of appeals that has resolved this issue requires some evidence in addition to the contents of the statement.

Third, the amendment extends the reasoning of *Bourjaily* to statements offered under subdivisions (C) and (D) of Rule 801(d)(2). . . .

PROBLEM

3.32. Following his arrest, a bank robber waives his *Miranda* rights and tells the police that an employee of the bank disabled the security cameras for him. Is this statement admissible against the employee in a prosecution for aiding and abetting bank robbery, or in a civil suit brought against the employee by the bank?

f. Admissions and the *Bruton* Rule

When two or more defendants are tried together, a prior statement by one of the defendants will be admissible against that defendant as an admission, but typically cannot be introduced against the other defendant or defendants without violating both the hearsay rule and the Confrontation Clause. You know by now that the usual way of dealing with situations like this, where evidence is admissible against one party to a case but inadmissible against other parties, is with a limiting instruction. But the Supreme Court has deemed this procedure unacceptable when the evidence in question is an incriminating statement by a codefendant. As you will see, the lines the Court has drawn have been controversial.

BRUTON v. UNITED STATES

391 U.S. 123 (1968)

Mr. Justice BRENNAN delivered the opinion of the Court.

This case presents the question, last considered in *Delli Paoli v. United States*, 352 U.S. 232 whether the conviction of a defendant at a joint trial should be set aside although the jury was instructed that a codefendant's confession inculpating the defendant had to be disregarded in determining his guilt or innocence.

A joint trial of petitioner and one Evans in the District Court for the Eastern District of Missouri resulted in the conviction of both by a jury on a federal charge of armed postal robbery, 18 U.S.C. § 2114. A postal inspector testified that Evans orally confessed to him that Evans and petitioner committed the armed robbery. The postal inspector obtained the oral confession, and another in which Evans admitted he had an accomplice whom he would not name, in the course of two interrogations of Evans at the city jail in St. Louis, Missouri, where Evans was held in custody on state criminal charges. Both petitioner and Evans appealed their convictions to the Court of Appeals for the Eighth Circuit. That court set aside Evans' conviction on the ground that [under *Miranda v. Arizona*, 384 U.S. 436 (1966)] his oral confessions to the postal inspector should not have been received in evidence against him. However, the court, relying upon *Delli Paoli*, affirmed petitioner's conviction because the trial judge instructed the jury that although Evans' confession was competent evidence against Evans it was inadmissible hearsay against petitioner and therefore had to be disregarded in determining petitioner's guilt or innocence.[2] ... We hold that, because of the substantial risk that the jury, despite instructions to the contrary, looked to the

---

2. At the close of the Government's direct case, the trial judge cautioned the jury that Evans' admission implicating petitioner "if used, can only be used against the defendant Evans. It is hearsay insofar as the defendant George William Bruton is concerned, and you are not to consider it in any respect to the defendant Bruton, because insofar as he is concerned it is hearsay."

The instructions to the jury included the following:

"A confession made outside of court by one defendant may not be considered as evidence against the other defendant, who was not present and in no way a party to the confession. Therefore, if you find that a confession was in fact voluntarily and intentionally made by the defendant Evans, you should consider it as evidence in the case against Evans, but you must not consider it, and should disregard it, in considering the evidence in the case against the defendant Bruton. . . .

"It is your duty to give separate, personal consideration to the cause of each individual defendant. When you do so, you should analyze what the evidence shows with respect to that individual, leaving out of consideration entirely any evidence admitted solely against some other defendant. Each defendant is entitled to have his case determined from his own acts and statements and the other evidence in the case which may be applicable to him."

incriminating extrajudicial statements in determining petitioner's guilt, admission of Evans' confession in this joint trial violated petitioner's right of cross-examination secured by the Confrontation Clause of the Sixth Amendment. We therefore overrule *Delli Paoli* and reverse.

The basic premise of *Delli Paoli* was that it is "reasonably possible for the jury to follow" sufficiently clear instructions to disregard the confessor's extrajudicial statement that his codefendant participated with him in committing the crime. If it were true that the jury disregarded the reference to the codefendant, no question would arise under the Confrontation Clause, because by hypothesis the case is treated as if the confessor made no statement inculpating the nonconfessor. But since *Delli Paoli* was decided this Court has effectively repudiated its basic premise.[3] . . . True, the repudiation was not in the context of the admission of a confession inculpating a codefendant but in the context of a New York rule which submitted to the jury the question of the voluntariness of the confession itself. *Jackson v. Denno*, 378 U.S. 368. Nonetheless the message of *Jackson* for *Delli Paoli* was clear. We there held that a defendant is constitutionally entitled at least to have the trial judge first determine whether a confession was made voluntarily before submitting it to the jury for an assessment of its credibility. More specifically, we expressly rejected the proposition that a jury, when determining the confessor's guilt, could be relied on to ignore his confession of guilt should it find the confession involuntary. Significantly, we supported that conclusion in part by reliance upon the dissenting opinion of Mr. Justice Frankfurter for the four Justices who dissented in *Delli Paoli*.

That dissent challenged the basic premise of *Delli Paoli* that a properly instructed jury would ignore the confessor's inculpation of the nonconfessor in determining the latter's guilt. "The fact of the matter is that too often such admonition against misuse is intrinsically ineffective in that the effect of such a nonadmissible declaration cannot be wiped from the brains of the jurors. The admonition therefore becomes a futile collocation of words and fails of its purpose as a legal protection to defendants against whom such a declaration should not tell." The dissent went on to say, as quoted . . . in *Jackson*, "The Government should not have the windfall of having the jury be influenced by evidence against a defendant which, as a matter of law, they should not consider but which they cannot put out of their minds." To the same effect, and also cited in the *Jackson* note, is the statement of Mr. Justice Jackson in his concurring opinion in *Krulewitch v. United States*, 336 U.S. 440, 453: "The naive assumption that prejudicial effects can be overcome by instructions to the jury . . . all practicing lawyers know to be unmitigated fiction. . . ."

3. We emphasize that the hearsay statement inculpating petitioner was clearly inadmissible against him under traditional rules of evidence. . . . There is not before us, therefore, any recognized exception to the hearsay rule insofar as petitioner is concerned and we intimate no view whatever that such exceptions necessarily raise questions under the Confrontation Clause.

The significance of *Jackson* for *Delli Paoli* was suggested by Chief Justice Traynor in *People v. Aranda*, 63 Cal. 2d 518, 528-29, 47 Cal. Rptr. 353, 358-59:

> "Although *Jackson* was directly concerned with obviating any risk that a jury might rely on an unconstitutionally obtained confession in determining the defendant's guilt, its logic extends to obviating the risks that the jury may rely on any inadmissible statements. If it is a denial of due process to rely on a jury's presumed ability to disregard an involuntary confession, it may also be a denial of due process to rely on a jury's presumed ability to disregard a codefendant's confession implicating another defendant when it is determining that defendant's guilt or innocence.
>
> "Indeed, the latter task may be an even more difficult one for the jury to perform than the former. Under the New York procedure, which *Jackson* held violated due process, the jury was only required to disregard a confession it found to be involuntary. If it made such a finding, then the confession was presumably out of the case. In joint trials, however, when the admissible confession of one defendant inculpates another defendant, the confession is never deleted from the case and the jury is expected to perform the over-whelming task of considering it in determining the guilt or innocence of the declarant and then of ignoring it in determining the guilt or innocence of any codefendants of the declarant. A jury cannot 'segregate evidence into separate intellectual boxes.' . . . It cannot determine that a confession is true insofar as it admits that A has committed criminal acts with B and at the same time effectively ignore the inevitable conclusion that B has committed those same criminal acts with A."

. . . Those who have defended reliance on the limiting instruction in this area have cited several reasons in support. Judge Learned Hand, a particularly severe critic of the proposition that juries could be counted on to disregard inadmissible hearsay,[8] wrote the opinion for the Second Circuit which affirmed Delli Paoli's conviction. In Judge Hand's view the limiting instruction, although not really capable of preventing the jury from considering the prejudicial evidence, does as a matter of form provide a way around the exclusionary rules of evidence that is defensible because it "probably furthers, rather than impedes, the search for truth. . . ." *Nash v. United States*, 2 Cir., 54 F.2d 1006, 1007. Insofar as this implies the prosecution ought not to be denied the benefit of the confession to prove the confessor's guilt, however, it overlooks alternative ways of achieving that benefit without at the same time infringing the nonconfessor's right

---

8. Judge Hand addressed the subject several times. The limiting instruction, he said, is a "recommendation to the jury of a mental gymnastic which is beyond, not only their powers, but anybody's else," *Nash v. United States*, 2 Cir., 54 F.2d 1006, 1007; "Nobody can indeed fail to doubt whether the caution is effective, or whether usually the practical result is not to let in hearsay," *United States v. Gottfried*, 2 Cir., 165 F.2d 360, 367; "it is indeed very hard to believe that a jury will, or for that matter can, in practice observe the admonition," *United States v. Delli Paoli*, 2 Cir., 229 F.2d 319, 321. Judge Hand referred to the instruction as a "placebo," medically defined as "a medicinal lie." Judge Jerome Frank suggested that its legal equivalent "is a kind of 'judicial lie': It undermines a moral relationship between the courts, the jurors, and the public; like any other judicial deception, it damages the decent judicial administration of justice." *United States v. Grunewald*, 2 Cir., 233 F.2d 556, 574. . . .

of confrontation.[10] Where viable alternatives do exist, it is deceptive to rely on the pursuit of truth to defend a clearly harmful practice.

Another reason cited in defense of *Delli Paoli* is the justification for joint trials in general, the argument being that the benefits of joint proceedings should not have to be sacrificed by requiring separate trials in order to use the confession against the declarant. Joint trials do conserve state funds, diminish inconvenience to witnesses and public authorities, and avoid delays in bringing those accused of crime to trial. But the answer to this argument was cogently stated by Judge Lehman of the New York Court of Appeals, dissenting in *People v. Fisher*, 249 N.Y. 419, 432, 164 N.E. 336, 341:

> "We still adhere to the rule that an accused is entitled to confrontation of the witnesses against him and the right to cross-examine them. . . . We destroy the age-old rule which in the past has been regarded as a fundamental principle of our jurisprudence by a legalistic formula, required of the judge, that the jury may not consider any admissions against any party who did not join in them. We secure greater speed, economy and convenience in the administration of the law at the price of fundamental principles of constitutional liberty. That price is too high."

Finally, the reason advanced by the majority in *Delli Paoli* was to tie the result to maintenance of the jury system. "Unless we proceed on the basis that the jury will follow the court's instructions where those instructions are clear and the circumstances are such that the jury can reasonably be expected to follow them, the jury system makes little sense." We agree that there are many circumstances in which this reliance is justified. Not every admission of inadmissible hearsay or other evidence can be considered to be reversible error unavoidable through limiting instructions; instances occur in almost every trial where inadmissible evidence creeps in, usually inadvertently. . . . "A defendant is entitled to a fair trial but not a perfect one." *Lutwak v. United States*, 344 U.S. 604, 619. It is not unreasonable to conclude that in many such cases the jury can and will follow the trial judge's instructions to disregard such information. Nevertheless, as was recognized in *Jackson v. Denno, supra*, there are some contexts in which the risk that the jury will not, or cannot, follow instructions is so great, and the consequences of failure so vital to the defendant, that the practical and human limitations of the jury system cannot be ignored. Such a context is presented here, where the powerfully incriminating extrajudicial statements of a codefendant, who stands accused side-by-side with the defendant, are deliberately spread before the jury in a joint trial. Not only are the incriminations devastating to the defendant but their credibility is inevitably suspect, a fact recognized when accomplices do take the stand and the jury is instructed to weigh their testimony

---

10. Some courts have required deletion of references to codefendants where practicable. For criticisms suggesting that deletions (redaction) from the confession are ineffective, *see, e.g.*, Note, 72 Harv. L. Rev. 920, 990 (1959); Comment, 24 U. Chi. L. Rev. 710, 713 (1957); Note, 74 Yale L.J. 553, 564 (1965). . . .

carefully given the recognized motivation to shift blame onto others. The unreliability of such evidence is intolerably compounded when the alleged accomplice, as here, does not testify and cannot be tested by cross-examination. It was against such threats to a fair trial that the Confrontation Clause was directed.

. . . Despite the concededly clear instructions to the jury to disregard Evans' inadmissible hearsay evidence inculpating petitioner, in the context of a joint trial we cannot accept limiting instructions as an adequate substitute for petitioner's constitutional right of cross-examination. The effect is the same as if there had been no instruction at all.

Reversed.

Mr. Justice WHITE, dissenting.

. . . Here we deal with a codefendant's confession which is admitted only against the codefendant and with a firm instruction to the jury to disregard it in determining the defendant's guilt or innocence. That confession cannot compare with the defendant's own confession in evidentiary value. As to the defendant, the confession of the codefendant is wholly inadmissible. It is hearsay, subject to all the dangers of inaccuracy which characterize hearsay generally. Furthermore, the codefendant is no more than an eyewitness, the accuracy of whose testimony about the defendant's conduct is open to more doubt than would be the defendant's own account of his actions. More than this, however, the statements of a codefendant have traditionally been viewed with special suspicion. Due to his strong motivation to implicate the defendant and to exonerate himself, a codefendant's statements about what the defendant said or did are less credible than ordinary hearsay evidence. Whereas the defendant's own confession possesses greater reliability and evidentiary value than ordinary hearsay, the codefendant's confession implicating the defendant is intrinsically much less reliable.

The defendant's own confession may not be used against him if coerced, not because it is untrue but to protect other constitutional values. The jury may have great difficulty understanding such a rule and following an instruction to disregard the confession. In contrast, the codefendant's admissions cannot enter into the determination of the defendant's guilt or innocence because they are unreliable. This the jury can be told and can understand. Just as the Court believes that juries can reasonably be expected to disregard ordinary hearsay or other inadmissible evidence when instructed to do so, I believe juries will disregard the portions of a codefendant's confession implicating the defendant when so instructed. Indeed, if we must pick and choose between hearsay as to which limiting instructions will be deemed effective and hearsay the admission of which cannot be cured by instructions, codefendants' admissions belong in the former category rather than the latter, for they are not only hearsay but hearsay which is doubly suspect. If the Court is right in believing that a jury can be counted on to ignore a wide range of hearsay statements which it is told to ignore, it seems very odd to me to question its ability to put aside the codefendant's hearsay statements about what the defendant did. . . .

GRAY v. MARYLAND

523 U.S. 185 (1998)

Justice BREYER delivered the opinion of the Court.

. . . In 1993, Stacy Williams died after a severe beating. Anthony Bell gave a confession, to the Baltimore City police, in which he said that he (Bell), Kevin Gray, and Jacquin "Tank" Vanlandingham had participated in the beating that resulted in Williams' death. Vanlandingham later died. A Maryland grand jury indicted Bell and Gray for murder. The State of Maryland tried them jointly.

The trial judge, after denying Gray's motion for a separate trial, permitted the State to introduce Bell's confession into evidence at trial. But the judge ordered the confession redacted. Consequently, the police detective who read the confession into evidence said the word "deleted" or "deletion" whenever Gray's name or Vanlandingham's name appeared. Immediately after the police detective read the redacted confession to the jury, the prosecutor asked, "after he gave you that information, you subsequently were able to arrest Mr. Kevin Gray; is that correct?" The officer responded, "That's correct." The State also introduced into evidence a written copy of the confession with those two names omitted, leaving in their place blank white spaces separated by commas. The State produced other witnesses, who said that six persons (including Bell, Gray, and Vanlandingham) participated in the beating. Gray testified and denied his participation. Bell did not testify.

When instructing the jury, the trial judge specified that the confession was evidence only against Bell; the instructions said that the jury should not use the confession as evidence against Gray. The jury convicted both Bell and Gray. Gray appealed.

Maryland's intermediate appellate court accepted Gray's argument that *Bruton* [*v. United States*, 391 U.S. 123 (1968),] prohibited use of the confession and set aside his conviction. Maryland's highest court disagreed and reinstated the conviction. We granted certiorari. . . .

In deciding whether *Bruton*'s protective rule applies to the redacted confession before us, we must consider both *Bruton*, and a later case, *Richardson v. Marsh*, 481 U.S. 200 (1987), which limited *Bruton*'s scope. . . . [*Richardson*] involved a joint murder trial of Marsh and Williams. The State had redacted the confession of one defendant, Williams, so as to "omit all reference" to his codefendant, Marsh—"indeed, to omit all indication that anyone other than . . . Williams" and a third person had "participated in the crime." The trial court also instructed the jury not to consider the confession against Marsh. As redacted, the confession indicated that Williams and the third person had discussed the murder in the front seat of a car while they traveled to the victim's house. The redacted confession contained no indication that Marsh—or any other person—was in the car. Later in the trial, however, Marsh testified that she was in the back seat of the car. For that reason, in context, the confession still could have helped convince the jury that Marsh knew about the murder in advance and therefore had participated knowingly in the crime.

The Court held that this redacted confession fell outside *Bruton*'s scope and was admissible (with appropriate limiting instructions) at the joint trial. The Court distinguished Evans' confession in *Bruton* as a confession that was "incriminating on its face," and which had "expressly implicat[ed]" Bruton. By contrast, Williams' confession amounted to "evidence requiring linkage" in that it "became" incriminating in respect to Marsh "only when linked with evidence introduced later at trial." The Court held "that the Confrontation Clause is not violated by the admission of a nontestifying codefendant's confession with a proper limiting instruction when, as here, the confession is redacted to eliminate not only the defendant's name, but any reference to his or her existence." The Court added: "We express no opinion on the admissibility of a confession in which the defendant's name has been replaced with a symbol or neutral pronoun."

. . . [U]nlike *Richardson*'s redacted confession, [the confession in this case] refers directly to the "existence" of the nonconfessing defendant. The State has simply replaced the nonconfessing defendant's name with a kind of symbol, namely the word "deleted" or a blank space set off by commas. The redacted confession, for example, responded to the question "Who was in the group that beat Stacey," with the phrase, "Me,   , and a few other guys." And when the police witness read the confession in court, he said the word "deleted" or "deletion" where the blank spaces appear. We therefore must decide a question that *Richardson* left open, namely whether redaction that replaces a defendant's name with an obvious indication of deletion, such as a blank space, the word "deleted," or a similar symbol, still falls within *Bruton*'s protective rule. We hold that it does.

Bruton, as interpreted by *Richardson*, holds that certain "powerfully incriminating extrajudicial statements of a codefendant"—those naming another defendant—considered as a class, are so prejudicial that limiting instructions cannot work. Unless the prosecutor wishes to hold separate trials or to use separate juries or to abandon use of the confession, he must redact the confession to reduce significantly or to eliminate the special prejudice that the *Bruton* Court found. Redactions that simply replace a name with an obvious blank space or a word such as "deleted" or a symbol or other similarly obvious indications of alteration, however, leave statements that, considered as a class, so closely resemble *Bruton*'s unredacted statements that, in our view, the law must require the same result.

For one thing, a jury will often react similarly to an unredacted confession and a confession redacted in this way, for the jury will often realize that the confession refers specifically to the defendant. This is true even when the State does not blatantly link the defendant to the deleted name, as it did in this case by asking whether Gray was arrested on the basis of information in Bell's confession as soon as the officer had finished reading the redacted statement. Consider a simplified but typical example, a confession that reads "I, Bob Smith, along with Sam Jones, robbed the bank." To replace the words "Sam Jones" with an obvious blank will not likely fool anyone. A juror somewhat familiar with criminal law would know immediately that the blank, in the phrase "I, Bob Smith, along with   , robbed the bank," refers to defendant Jones. A juror who does not know the law and who therefore wonders to whom the blank might refer need only lift his eyes to Jones, sitting at counsel table, to find what will seem the obvious answer, at least if the juror hears the judge's instruction not to consider the confession as evidence against Jones, for that instruction will provide an obvious reason for the blank. A more sophisticated juror, wondering if the blank refers to someone else, might also wonder how, if it did, the prosecutor could argue the confession is reliable, for the prosecutor, after all, has been arguing that Jones, not someone else, helped Smith commit the crime.

For another thing, the obvious deletion may well call the jurors' attention specially to the removed name. By encouraging the jury to speculate about the reference, the redaction may overemphasize the importance of the confession's accusation—once the jurors work out the reference. That is why Judge Learned Hand, many years ago, wrote in a similar instance that blacking out the name of a codefendant not only "would have been futile. . . . [T]here could not have been the slightest doubt as to whose names had been blacked out," but "even if there had been, that blacking out itself would have not only laid the doubt, but underscored the answer." *United States v. Delli Paoli*, 229 F.2d 319, 321 (CA2 1956), *aff'd*, 352 U.S. 232 (1957), *overruled by Bruton v. United States*, 391 U.S. 123 (1968). *See also Malinski v. New York*, 324 U.S. 401, 430 (1945) (Rutledge, J., dissenting) (describing substitution of names in confession with "X" or "Y" and other similar redactions as "devices . . . so obvious as perhaps to emphasize the identity of those they purported to conceal").

Finally, *Bruton*'s protected statements and statements redacted to leave a blank or some other similarly obvious alteration, function the same way grammatically. They are directly accusatory. Evans' statement in *Bruton* used a proper name to point explicitly to an accused defendant. And Bruton held that the "powerfully incriminating" effect of what Justice Stewart called "an out-of-court accusation," 391 U.S., at 138 (Stewart, J., concurring), creates a special, and vital, need for cross-examination—a need that would be immediately obvious had the codefendant pointed directly to the defendant in the courtroom itself. The blank space in an obviously redacted confession also points directly to the defendant, and it accuses the defendant in a manner similar to Evans' use of Bruton's name or to a testifying codefendant's accusatory finger. By way of contrast, the factual statement at issue in *Richardson*—a statement about what others said in the front seat of a car—differs from directly accusatory evidence in this respect, for it does not point directly to a defendant at all.

. . . We concede that *Richardson* placed outside the scope of *Bruton*'s rule those statements that incriminate inferentially. We also concede that the jury must use inference to connect the statement in this redacted confession with the defendant. But inference pure and simple cannot make the critical difference, for if it did, then *Richardson* would also place outside *Bruton*'s scope confessions that use shortened first names, nicknames, descriptions as unique as the "red-haired, bearded, one-eyed man-with-a-limp," *United States v. Grinnell Corp.*, 384 U.S. 563, 591 (1966) (Fortas, J., dissenting), and perhaps even full names of defendants who are always known by a nickname. This Court has assumed, however, that nicknames and specific descriptions fall inside, not outside, *Bruton*'s protection.

See Harrington v. California, 395 U.S. 250, 253 (1969) (assuming *Bruton* violation where confessions describe codefendant as the "white guy" and give a description of his age, height, weight, and hair color). The Solicitor General, although supporting Maryland in this case, concedes that this is appropriate.

That being so, *Richardson* must depend in significant part upon the kind of, not the simple fact of, inference. *Richardson*'s inferences involved statements that did not refer directly to the defendant himself and which became incriminating "only when linked with evidence introduced later at trial." The inferences at issue here involve statements that, despite redaction, obviously refer directly to someone, often obviously the defendant, and which involve inferences that a jury ordinarily could make immediately, even were the confession the very first item introduced at trial. Moreover, the redacted confession with the blank prominent on its face, in *Richardson*'s words, "facially incriminat[es]" the codefendant. Like the confession in *Bruton* itself, the accusation that the redacted confession makes "is more vivid than inferential incrimination, and hence more difficult to thrust out of mind." 481 U.S., at 208.

Nor are the policy reasons that *Richardson* provided in support of its conclusion applicable here. *Richardson* expressed concern lest application of *Bruton*'s rule apply where "redaction" of confessions, particularly "confessions incriminating by connection," would often "not [be] possible," thereby forcing prosecutors too often to abandon use either of the confession or of a joint trial. Additional redaction of a confession that uses a blank space, the word "delete," or a symbol, however, normally is possible. Consider as an example a portion of the confession before us: The witness who read the confession told the jury that the confession (among other things) said,

> "*Question:* Who was in the group that beat Stacey?
> "*Answer:* Me, deleted, deleted, and a few other guys."

Why could the witness not, instead, have said:

> "*Question:* Who was in the group that beat Stacey?
> "*Answer:* Me and a few other guys."

Richardson itself provides a similar example of this kind of redaction. The confession there at issue had been "redacted to omit all reference to respondent—indeed, to omit all indication that anyone other than Martin and Williams participated in the crime," and it did not indicate that it had been redacted. *But cf. post* (SCALIA, J., dissenting) (suggesting that the Court has "never before endorsed . . . the redaction of a statement by some means other than the deletion of certain words, with the fact of the deletion shown").

The *Richardson* Court also feared that the inclusion, within *Bruton*'s protective rule, of confessions that incriminated "by connection" too often would provoke mistrials, or would unnecessarily lead prosecutors to abandon the confession or joint trial, because neither the prosecutors nor the judge could easily predict, until after the introduction of all the evidence, whether or not *Bruton* had barred use of the confession. To include the use of blanks, the word "delete," symbols, or other indications of redaction, within *Bruton*'s protections, however, runs no such risk. Their use is easily identified prior to trial and does not depend, in any special way, upon the other evidence introduced in the case. We also note that several Circuits have interpreted *Bruton* similarly for many years, yet no one has told us of any significant practical difficulties arising out of their adminis- tration of that rule.

. . . The judgment of the Court of Appeals is vacated, and the case is remanded for further proceedings not inconsistent with this opinion. . . .

Justice SCALIA, with whom THE CHIEF JUSTICE, Justice KENNEDY, and Justice THOMAS join, dissenting.

. . . The almost invariable assumption of the law is that jurors follow their instructions. This rule "is a pragmatic one, rooted less in the absolute certitude that the presumption is true than in the belief that it represents a reasonable practical accommodation of the interests of the state and the defendant in the criminal justice process." *Richardson*. We have held, for example, that the state may introduce evidence of a defendant's prior con- victions for the purpose of sentencing enhancement, or statements elicited from a defendant in violation of *Miranda v. Arizona*, 384 U.S. 436 (1966), for the purpose of impeachment, so long as the jury is instructed that such evidence may not be considered for the purpose of determining guilt. *Spen- cer v. Texas*, 385 U.S. 554 (1967); *Harris v. New York*, 401 U.S. 222 (1971). The same applies to codefendant confessions: "a witness whose testimony is introduced at a joint trial is not considered to be a witness 'against' a defendant if the jury is instructed to consider that testimony only against a codefendant." *Richardson, supra*. In *Bruton*, we recognized a "narrow exception" to this rule: "We held that a defendant is deprived of his Sixth Amendment right of confrontation when the facially incriminating confes- sion of a nontestifying codefendant is introduced at their joint trial, even if the jury is instructed to consider the confession only against the codefen- dant." 481 U.S., at 207. We declined in *Richardson*, however, to extend *Bruton* to confessions that incriminate only by inference from other evidence. When incrimination is inferential, "it is a less valid generalization that the jury will not likely obey the instruction to disregard the evidence." 481 U.S., at 208. Today the Court struggles to decide whether a confession redacted to omit the defendant's name is incriminating on its face or by inference. On the one hand, the Court "concede[s] that the jury must use inference to connect the statement in this redacted confession with the defendant," but later asserts, on the other hand, that "the redacted confes- sion with the blank prominent on its face . . . 'facially incriminat[es].' " The Court should have stopped with its concession: the statement "Me, deleted, deleted, and a few other guys" does not facially incriminate anyone but the speaker. The Court's analogizing of "deleted" to a physical description that clearly identifies the defendant . . . does not survive scrutiny. By "facially incriminating," we have meant incriminating independent of other evidence introduced at trial. Since the defendant's appearance at counsel table is not evidence, the description "red-haired, bearded, one-eyed man-with-a-limp" would be facially incriminating—unless, of course, the defendant had dyed his hair black and shaved his beard before trial, and the prosecution introduced evidence concerning his former appearance. Similarly, the statement "Me, Kevin Gray, and a few other guys" would be facially incriminating, unless the defendant's name set forth in the indictment was not Kevin Gray, and evidence was introduced to the effect that he sometimes used "Kevin Gray" as an alias. By contrast, the person to whom "deleted" refers in "Me, deleted, deleted, and a few other guys" is not apparent from anything the jury knows independent of the evidence at trial. Though the jury may speculate, the statement expressly implicates no one but the speaker.

Of course the Court is correct that confessions redacted to omit the defendant's name are more likely to incriminate than confessions redacted to omit any reference to his existence. But it is also true—and more relevant here—that confessions redacted to omit the defendant's name are less likely to incriminate than confessions that expressly state it. The latter are "powerfully incriminating" as a class; the former are not so. Here, for instance, there were two names deleted, five or more participants in the crime, and only one other defendant on trial. The jury no doubt may "speculate about the reference," as it speculates when evidence connects a defendant to a confession that does not refer to his existence. The issue, however, is not whether the confession incriminated petitioner, but whether the incrimination is so "powerful" that we must depart from the normal presumption that the jury follows its instructions. I think it is not—and I am certain that drawing the line for departing from the ordinary rule at the facial identification of the defendant makes more sense than drawing it anywhere else.

The Court's extension of *Bruton* to name-redacted confessions "as a class" will seriously compromise "society's compelling interest in finding, convicting, and punishing those who violate the law." *Moran v. Burbine*, 475 U.S. 412, 426 (1986). We explained in *Richardson* that forgoing use of codefendant confessions or joint trials was "too high" a price to insure that juries never disregard their instructions. The Court minimizes the damage that it does by suggesting that "[a]dditional redaction of a confession that uses a blank space, the word 'delete,' or a symbol . . . normally is possible." In the present case, it asks, why could the police officer not have testified that Bell's answer was "Me and a few other guys"? The answer, it seems obvious to me, is because that is not what Bell said. Bell's answer was "Me, Tank, Kevin and a few other guys." Introducing the statement with full disclosure of deletions is one thing; introducing as the complete statement what was in fact only a part is something else. And of course even concealed deletions from the text will often not do the job that the Court demands. For inchoate offenses—conspiracy in particular—redaction to delete all reference to a confederate would often render the confession nonsensical. If the question was "Who agreed to beat Stacey?", and the answer was "Me and Kevin," we might redact the answer to "Me and [deleted]" or perhaps to "Me and somebody else," but surely not to just "Me"—for that would no longer be a confession to the conspiracy charge, but rather the foundation for an insanity defense. To my knowledge we have never before endorsed—and to my strong belief we ought not endorse—the redaction of a statement by some means other than the deletion of certain words, with the fact of the deletion shown. The risk to the integrity of our system (not to mention the increase in its complexity) posed by the approval of such free-lance editing seems to me infinitely greater than the risk posed by the entirely honest reproduction that the Court disapproves.

. . . For these reasons, I would affirm the judgment of the Court of Appeals of Maryland.

3. Spontaneous and Contemporaneous Statements

Unlike the admissions doctrine, most exceptions to the hearsay rule pertain to out-of-court statements that for one reason or another are thought particularly reliable. Most of these exceptions apply regardless whether the declarant is also available to testify as a witness, and are codified in Federal Rule of Evidence 803. The first two exceptions listed in Rule 803 derive from common-law decisions allowing the introduction of statements made contemporaneously with the events they describe; often the events had placed the declarant under some kind of emotional strain. There is a long-standing debate about whether it was chiefly the contemporaneity or the emotional strain that justified an exception to the hearsay rule. The Federal Rules of Evidence sidestep the debate by creating two separate exceptions, one tied to contemporaneity and one requiring emotional stress.

Many statements that fall within these exceptions may nonetheless be inadmissible against a criminal defendant under *Crawford v. Washington* and *Davis v. Washington*. The latter case, in fact, dealt directly with statements introduced under state-law versions of Fed. R. Evid. 803(1) and (2).

[F.R.E. 803(1), (2); C.E.C. §§1240, 1241]

ADVISORY COMMITTEE NOTE TO F.R.E. 803

The exceptions are phrased in terms of nonapplication of the hearsay rule, rather than in positive terms of admissibility, in order to repel any implication that other possible grounds for exclusion are eliminated from consideration.

The present rule proceeds upon the theory that under appropriate circumstances a hearsay statement may possess circumstantial guarantees of trustworthiness sufficient to justify nonproduction of the declarant in person at the trial even though he may be available. The theory finds vast support in the many exceptions to the hearsay rule developed by the common law in which unavailability of the declarant is not a relevant factor. The present rule is a synthesis of them, with revision where modern developments and conditions are believed to make that course appropriate.

In a hearsay situation, the declarant is, of course, a witness, and neither this rule nor Rule 804 dispenses with the requirement of firsthand knowledge. It may appear from his statement or be inferable from circumstances. See Rule 602.

Exceptions (1) and (2).   In considerable measure these two examples overlap, though based on somewhat different theories. The most significant practical difference will lie in the time lapse allowable between event and statement.

The underlying theory of Exception (1) is that substantial contemporaneity of event and statement negate the likelihood of deliberate or conscious misrepresentation. Moreover, if the witness is the declarant, he may be examined on the statement. If the witness is not the declarant, he may be examined as to the circumstances as an aid in evaluating the statement.

The theory of Exception (2) is simply that circumstances may produce a condition of excitement which temporarily stills the capacity of reflection and produces utterances free of conscious fabrication. Spontaneity is the key factor in each instance, though arrived at by somewhat different routes. Both are needed in order to avoid needless niggling.

While the theory of Exception (2) has been criticized on the ground that excitement impairs accuracy of observation as well as eliminating conscious fabrication, Hutchins and Slesinger, Some Observations on the Law of Evidence: Spontaneous Exclamations, 28 Colum. L. Rev. 432 (1928), it finds support in cases without number. See cases in 6 Wigmore § 1750; Annot. 53 A.L.R.2d 1245 (statements as to cause of or responsibility for motor vehicle accident); Annot., 4 A.L.R.3d 149 (accusatory statements by homicide victims). Since unexciting events are less likely to evoke comment, decisions involving Exception (1) are far less numerous. . . .

With respect to the *time element*, Exception (1) recognizes that in many, if not most, instances precise contemporaneity is not possible and hence a slight lapse is allowable. Under Exception (2) the standard of measurement is the duration of the state of excitement. "How long can excitement prevail? Obviously there are no pat answers and the character of the transaction or event will largely determine the significance of the time factor." Slough, Spontaneous Statements and State of Mind, 46 Iowa L. Rev. 224, 243 (1961). . . .

Participation by the declarant is not required: a non-participant may be moved to describe what he perceives, and one may be startled by an event in which he is not an actor. . . . Whether *proof of the startling event* may be made by the statement itself is largely an academic question, since in most cases there is present at least circumstantial evidence that something of a startling nature must have occurred . . . [e.g.,] the condition of the declarant (injuries, state of shock). . . . Nevertheless, on occasion the only evidence may be the content of the statement itself, and rulings that it may be sufficient are described as "increasing," Slough, supra at 246, and as the "prevailing practice," McCormick § 272, p. 579. . . . Moreover, under Rule 104(a) the judge is not limited by the hearsay rule in passing upon preliminary questions of fact.

Proof of declarant's perception by his statement presents similar considerations when declarant is identified. However, when declarant is an unidentified bystander, the cases indicate hesitancy in upholding the statement alone as sufficient, a result which would under appropriate circumstances be consistent with the rule.

Permissible *subject matter* of the statement is limited under Exception (1) to description or explanation of the event or condition, the assumption being that spontaneity, in the absence of a starting event, may extend no farther. In Exception (2), however, the statement need only "relate" to the startling event or condition, thus affording a broader scope of subject matter coverage. . . . See Sanitary Grocery Co. v. Snead, 67 App. D.C. 129, 90 F.2d 374 (1937), slip-and-fall case sustaining admissibility of clerk's statement. "That has been on the floor for a couple of hours," and Murphy Auto Parts Co., Inc. v. Ball, 101 U.S. App. D.C. 416, 249 F.2d 508 (1957), upholding admission, on issue of driver's agency, of his statement that he had to call on a customer and was in a hurry to get home. . . .

UNITED STATES v. OBAYAGBONA

627 F. Supp. 329 (E.D.N.Y. 1985)

WEINSTEIN, Chief Judge:

[A jury found defendant Florence Obayagbona guilty of conspiring to sell heroin to an undercover FBI agent, Michael Turner. She moved to set aside the verdict, arguing that hearsay had been improperly introduced against her. Equipped with a hidden tape recorder and using the pseudonym "Joe," Turner had negotiated the purchase from another woman, Clara Onaiwu, in the presence of Obayagbona and an informant who had introduced Turner to Onaiwu. Obayagbona wore a black-and-white dress; "Onaiwu was more colorfully attired." According to Turner's testimony at trial, Obayagbona took a sample of heroin out of her purse and handed it to him. Other agents then arrested both women, as well as Turner and the informant. Obayagbona testified she had nothing to do with the deal, and that Onaiwu gave the sample to Turner. Onaiwu, who pleaded guilty, corroborated Obayagbona's account.]

Agent Turner, "under arrest" for the sake of the scenario, was handcuffed and thus unable to touch the controls of his tape recorder. While the machine continued to record, his fellow agents asked about the heroin. . . . After the testimony of Onaiwu and the defendant, the government sought on rebuttal to introduce the tape of Agent Turner's statement made contemporaneously with the arrest: "The girl in the black and white handed it to me out of her purse." Over objection, the court allowed the tape to be played. According to a stipulation, "14 minutes and 25 seconds" elapsed between the receipt of the sample by Special Agent Turner and his taped statement. . . .

Under Rule 803(2), a statement "relating to a startling event or condition made while the declarant was under the stress of excitement caused by the event or condition" is not excluded by the hearsay rule.

When a statement is offered as an excited utterance, the trial court must find two conditions: "First, there must be an occurrence or event sufficiently startling to render inoperative the normal reflective thought processes of an observer. Second, the statement of the declarant must have been a spontaneous reaction to the occurrence or event and not the result of reflective thought." McCormick, Evidence § 297, at 85455 (Cleary, 3d ed. 1984). Under Rule 104(a) of the Federal Rules of Evidence, the trial court makes the determination as to the existence of excitement and the applicability of this exception.

Determination of excitement is facilitated by the recording. On tape Agent Turner's voice is exultant—he has just completed his job, a successful arrest has been made, and the pent-up tension of his performance in the role of "Joe" has just come to an abrupt end. Testimony, and Turner's recording, depict a quick and somewhat chaotic arrest that would continue the excitement of receiving and testing the sample. Such a situation engenders excitement. Listening to the tape, the court determined that there were valid psychological guarantees against fabrication. It is not likely that the witness was deliberately fabricating evidence. He was too excited to do so.

The fact that the excited witness was a law enforcement agent does not preclude admissibility under the excited utterance exception. Law officers are subject to strain and excitement, much like people in other walks of life.

Agent Turner's statement is admissible as well under Rule 803(1). It is a statement "describing or explaining an event or condition made while the declarant was perceiving the event or condition, or immediately thereafter." . . .

Illustrative of the Rule's application is *United States v. Andrews*, 765 F.2d 1491, 1500 (11th Cir. 1985). The government there introduced in rebuttal a tape that a police officer made, recording his impressions of what he saw while looking through the defendant's window. Defendant argued on appeal that this was self-serving hearsay recorded out of the presence of the defendant, and was repetition rather than rebuttal. Both the district and the appellate courts found that this recording fell within the exception for present sense impressions.

Although the *Andrews* statement was somewhat more contemporaneous than Turner's, similar circumstances create a similar guarantee of trustworthiness. Rule 803(1) provides that "immediately thereafter" must be close enough to allow an inference of spontaneity. The Advisory Committee's notes recognize that "precise contemporaneity" is often not possible. A few minutes' pause after the moment at which the statement could have been made is within the period contemplated in Rule 803(1).

Where a precisely contemporaneous declaration cannot be made, near contemporaneity fulfills the requirements of 803(1). Agent Turner spoke at his first opportunity. His declaration was as spontaneous as possible: there had elapsed only two minutes and 25 seconds after the arrest and less than 15 minutes after delivery of the sample. By its nature the statement could not have been made in the presence of Onaiwu or the defendant. It was repressed and then exploded almost as a reflex as soon as Agent Turner was free to speak. . . . The motion for a new trial or for a judgment of acquittal is denied.

BEMIS v. EDWARDS

45 F.3d 1369 (9th Cir. 1995)

D.W. NELSON, Circuit Judge:

Appellant Ronald E. Bemis brought a civil rights action under 42 U.S.C. § 1983 against police officers Tim Edwards, Leo Lotito, Perry Aldrich, and the City of Bend, Oregon ("Appellees") in which he claimed that the police had used excessive force against him. In his appeal from a jury verdict for the Appellees, Bemis argues that the trial judge improperly excluded from evidence portions of a tape recording of [a 911 emergency call made by Gary Estep, in front of whose house Bemis had been arrested]. . . .

In one part of the tape . . . Estep reported, "Now there's a cop beating the shit out of the guy now," and then:

> "There's five units—I got a scanner here in my house, so—but it's kind of getting ridiculous guys. I mean, the cop's beating the shit out of the guy right now. The guy's got a gun, though. I guess it's legal."

. . . Under certain circumstances, [statements made in a 911 emergency call] may qualify as either a "present sense impression," Fed. R. Evid. 803(1), or an "excited utterance," Fed. R. Evid. 803(2). *See United States v. Mejia-Valez*, 855 F. Supp. 607, 613-14 (E.D.N.Y. 1994) (admitting under either exception a tape of 911 call made by an eyewitness immediately following a shooting); *United States v. Campbell*, 782 F. Supp. 1258, 1260-61 (N.D. Ill. 1991) (admitting under either exception a 911 tape of an eyewitness's description of a gunman). Certainly, a statement by a 911 caller who is witnessing the violent arrest of a suspect by the police could qualify under either exception. . . .

[T]o qualify under either exception, an out-of-court statement must be nearly contemporaneous with the incident described and made with little chance for reflection.[1] Although the Estep Statement satisfies these requirements, it does not meet the further requirement of personal knowledge of the events described. Generally, a witness must have "personal knowledge of the matter" to which she testifies. Fed. R. Evid. 602. In the context of hearsay, the declarant must also have personal knowledge of what she describes.[2] Fed. R. Evid. 803 advisory committee's note ("In a hearsay situation, the declarant is, of course, a witness, and neither this rule nor Rule 804 dispenses with the requirement of firsthand knowledge.") . . .

As the proponent of the evidence, Bemis had the burden of establishing personal perception by a preponderance of the evidence. Estep's

---

1. In the case of an excited utterance, the contemporaneity requirement refers to temporal proximity to the "startling event." Although the subject matter of an excited utterance is frequently a description of the "startling event," the statement need only "relat[e] to" the startling event. Fed. R. Evid. 803(2); *See United States v. Napier*, 518 F.2d 316, 318 (9th Cir.) (admitting statement identifying the defendant as the declarant's assailant when made as a spontaneous reaction to the "startling event" of viewing a picture of the defendant two months after the assault), *cert. denied*, 423 U.S. 895 (1975).

2. A witness who merely testifies to the fact that a declarant made the statement, however, need only have firsthand knowledge that the statement was made, not of the events described in the statement. Fed. R. Evid. 602 advisory committee's note. . . .

proximity to the scene at the time of the incident provided some circumstantial evidence of firsthand knowledge, which ordinarily may be sufficient to satisfy the foundational requirement in the context of a statement by a phone caller. *See First State Bank of Denton v. Maryland Casualty Co.*, 918 F.2d 38, 41-42 (5th Cir. 1990) (admitting declarant's assertion over the phone that a party was not at home when statement was made from phone at the home at the relevant time); *Miller v. Crown Amusements, Inc.*, 821 F. Supp. 703, 705-06 (S.D. Ga. 1993) (admitting unidentified 911 caller's description of hit-and-run accident because it was made in close physical and temporal proximity to the accident and the caller indicated that she had seen the accident); *see also* Fed. R. Evid. 803 advisory committee's note (stating that firsthand knowledge "may appear from [the declarant's] statement or be inferable from circumstances").

The district court, however, correctly noted that the record in this case gives an articulable basis to suspect that Estep did not witness the events he described, but instead had relayed to the 911 operator descriptions by other people who had been observing from the windows of Estep's house. Not only did Estep admit at one point that he could not describe what was happening outside, but he also could be heard repeating the words of an unidentified voice in the background. Although Estep was available to testify as to the circumstances surrounding his statements, Bemis declined to offer his testimony. Because there are affirmative indications that the declarant lacked firsthand knowledge of the events he described, we hold that the district court did not abuse its discretion in refusing to admit the Estep Statement. . . . AFFIRMED.

UNITED STATES v. ELEM

845 F.2d 170 (8th Cir. 1988)

McMILLIAN, Circuit Judge.

Appellant, Jimmy Dean Elem, appeals from the district court's judgment entered on a jury verdict convicting him for possession of a firearm by a convicted felon in violation of Title 18 U.S.C. app § 1202(a)(1) (West Supp. 1984). . . . [A]ppellant challenges the district court's ruling upon the government's pre-trial *in limine* motion to exclude certain exculpatory statements made by the appellant to the police at the time he was taken into custody. Appellant, in response to a police question about whether the gun was his, answered, "No," and in response to a police inquiry about the flourishing of a weapon, appellant answered, "You won't be able to make that." Appellant now contends that these statements were admissible as a part of the *res gestae* or as excited utterances under Fed. R. Evid. 803(2). The district court disagreed and excluded both statements as impermissible hearsay.

The doctrine of *res gestae* has an undistinguished past. According to Wigmore, courts in general have reduced the term "*res gestae*" to a useless and misleading shibboleth by embracing within it two separate and distinct categories of verbal statements, one of which is truly an exception to the hearsay rule and the other of which is not, the two being admissible in evidence under different principles. 6 Wigmore, *Evidence* § 1767, at 255

(Chadbourn rev. 1976). When the utterance of certain words constitutes or is part of the details of an act, occurrence or transaction which in itself is relevant and provable, the utterance may be proved as a verbal act, just as may be a visual observation of an event. This is not hearsay evidence; it is not admitted for the purpose of proving the truth of what was said, but for the purpose of describing the relevant details of what took place. . . .

The character of utterance that is admissible as a genuine exception to the hearsay rule, also under the customary label of "*res gestae*," is a spontaneous exclamation, which may or may not be exactly contemporaneous with the provable act or event. *Id.* § 1745 *et seq.* . . . This type of statement is received in a testimonial capacity as evidence of the truth of the fact asserted.

> This general principle is based on the experience that, under certain external circumstances a physical shock, of stress of nervous excitement may be produced which stills the reflective faculties and removes their control, so that the utterance which then occurs is a spontaneous and sincere response to the actual sensations and perceptions already produced by the external shock. Since this utterance is made under the immediate and uncontrolled domination of the senses, and during the brief period when considerations of self-interest could not have been brought fully to bear by reasoned reflection, the utterance may be taken as particularly trustworthy (or at least as lacking the usual grounds of untrustworthiness), and thus as expressing the real tenor of the speaker's belief as to the facts just observed by him; and may therefore be received as testimony to those facts.

Id. § 1747, at 195. . . .

In his brief appellant cites both prongs of what has been defined by courts as coming under the aegis of the *res gestae* doctrine, i.e., the verbal acts doctrine, and the excited utterance doctrine. Appellant seems to rely, however, not on the verbal acts doctrine but on the excited utterance doctrine. . . . [I]t is the excitement and the spontaneity that supply the indicia of trustworthiness and reliability which supports the admission of hearsay under this exception. Here we find nothing in the record to support appellant's contention that he was unduly excited so as to alter any of his conscious reflections. . . . [Conviction affirmed.]

GRAHAM C. LILLY, AN INTRODUCTION TO THE LAW OF EVIDENCE

§7.9, at 279 (3d ed. 1996)

The phrase "res gestae" still appears in judicial opinions despite widespread condemnation. A declaration is said to be admissible despite the hearsay rule if it constitutes a part of the "the thing done." Often, the term is used to signify the admission of a statement having independent legal significance (a "verbal act"), that is, a statement that is consequential simply because it was uttered and regardless of its truth. . . . [S]uch a statement is not hearsay and thus need not be entered under an exception. Unfortunately, the res gestae label is sometimes indiscriminately applied to hearsay declarations that fit within the exceptions of excited utterance, present sense impression, physical condition, or state of mind. . . . The imprecision of the term, coupled with careless usage by the courts, has been a source of perplexity for students and lawyers. Fortunately, the res gestae label continues to lose favor; the term is not included in the Federal Rules of Evidence or their counterpart, the Revised Uniform Rules of Evidence. Some lawyers may lament its omission. "If you wish to tender inadmissible evidence," Lord Blackburn reminds us, "say it is part of the res gestae." Tregarthen, The Law of Hearsay Evidence 21 (1915).

ROBERT M. HUTCHINS & DONALD SLESINGER, SOME OBSERVATIONS ON THE LAW OF EVIDENCE

28 Colum. L. Rev. 432, 437-439 (1928)

One need not be a psychologist to distrust an observation made under emotional stress; everyone accepts such statements with mental reservation. M. Gorphe cites the case of an excited witness to a horrible accident who erroneously declared that the coachman deliberately and vindictively ran down a helpless woman. Fiore tells of an emotionally upset man who testified that hundreds were killed in an accident; that he had seen their heads rolling from their bodies. In reality only one man was killed, and five others injured. . . .

That participants, as well as bystanders, have their perceptions clouded by strong emotions will not be doubted. When a carriage containing the inevitable psychologist upset, that worthy gentleman amused himself and his companions by taking depositions while they awaited assistance. He had no known reality to check their stories against, but it was obvious that if any one was right, all the rest were wrong. That even trained observers are fallible is well brought out in an editorial in the *New York World* in which several accounts of newspaper reports of the striking of Kerensky on his recent visit to America are printed. Though the reporters were all experts, and situated close to the platform, each told a different story of what must have been a fairly simple event.[1]

---

1. These are descriptions of the manner in which the young woman struck her blow:

> WORLD: "Slashed him viciously across the cheek with her glove."
> NEWS: "Struck him on the left cheek with the bouquet."
> AMERICAN: "Dropped her flowers and slapped him in the face with her gloves."
> TIMES: "Slapped his face vigorously with her gloves three times."
> HERALD TRIBUNE: "Beat him on the face and head . . . a half-dozen blows."
> EVENING WORLD: Struck him across the face "several times."
> MIRROR: Struck him a single time.
> POST: "Vigorously and accurately slapped him."

And this is what happened next:

> AMERICAN: Kerensky "reeled back."
> EVENING WORLD: "He stood unmoved."
> NEWS: "He stepped back, maintaining a calm pose."
> WORLD: He stood still, but used his arms to "wave back his friends."
> HERALD TRIBUNE: He stood still, with his arms "thrown back."
> JOURNAL: "He reeled."
> POST: "He remained unmoved."
> MIRROR: "He reeled from the blow. His supporters were stemmed by a handful of royalists. Fists flew; noses ran red; shirts and collars were torn."

What emotion gains by way of overcoming the desire to lie, it loses by impairing the declarant's power of observation. . . . [A]ccording to this view, the best evidence of all is a statement made in immediate response to an external stimulus which produces no shock or nervous excitement whatever.

JON R. WALTZ, THE PRESENT-SENSE IMPRESSION EXCEPTION TO THE RULE AGAINST HEARSAY: ORIGINS AND ATTRIBUTES
66 Iowa L. Rev. 869, 875 (1981)

It was Dean Wigmore, in the 1904 edition of his evidence treatise, who argued that contemporaneousness of event and descriptive statement, without more, was an insufficient guarantor of trustworthiness. He substituted as the essential ingredient a spontaneity born of shock or excitement induced by the perceived event or condition. In typically imperial terms, Wigmore . . . assert[ed] that "[t]o admit hearsay simply because it was uttered at the time something else was going on is to introduce an arbitrary and unreasoned test and to remove all limits of principle. . . ." Such was the impact of Wigmore's treatise on bench and bar that for most of this century the debatable exception for excited utterances has enjoyed at least grudging acceptance while the arguably more defensible exception for calm, contemporaneous observations languished.

PROBLEMS

3.33. Pauline sues Devon for damages caused when their cars collided. Devon's wife, Wilma, was a passenger in Devon's car at the time of accident. Pauline seeks to testify that, immediately following the accident, Wilma told her in a state of great agitation that Devon had "been sleeping terribly all week long." Does the hearsay rule prohibit this testimony?

3.34. Dumbarton is charged with murdering Vasquez. The prosecution seeks to have a witness testify that she spoke with Vasquez by telephone on the night he died, and that he ended the conversation by saying, "Oh, there's the door. It must be Dumbarton. Talk to you later." The defense objects on grounds of hearsay and confrontation. How should the judge rule?

4. State of Mind

[F.R.E. 803(3); C.E.C. §§1250-1252, 1260]

a. Generally

When an out-of-court statement is used as circumstantial proof of the declarant's state of mind, the hearsay rule is not implicated, because the statement is not offered to prove the truth of what it asserts. Think of the children yelling "Barney, Barney, Barney!" in *Lyons Partnership v. Morris Costumes, Inc.* or the defendant in *United States v. Parry* telling his mother that he was working with a narcotics agent. But sometimes a statement *explicitly* describes the speaker's state of mind: "Hey, I think that's Barney!" or "I think she's an undercover cop," or "I hate him." Statements of this kind seem to qualify as hearsay when used to prove what the declarants believed, knew, or felt. But they fall within a longstanding exception for statements describing the declarant's state of mind.

ADVISORY COMMITTEE NOTE TO F.R.E. 803(3)

Exception (3)   This is essentially a specialized application of Exception (1), presented separately to enhance its usefulness and accessibility. See McCormick §§ 265, 268. . . .

UNITED STATES v. HARRIS

733 F.2d 994 (2d Cir. 1984)

GEORGE C. PRATT, Circuit Judge:

George Harris and Angelo Mamone appeal from judgments entered on jury verdicts . . . convicting them of conspiracy to distribute heroin . . . and attempting to possess heroin with the intent to distribute in violation. . . .

The prosecution of Harris and Mamone was largely the product of an arrangement between the government and one Mahlon Steward, a narcotics dealer with a lengthy criminal record, who agreed to act as an informant and undercover operative for the federal Drug Enforcement Administration (DEA) following his most recent arrest in May 1981. Posing as a prospective heroin purchaser, Steward led the DEA to Harris, who, in turn, eventually led the DEA to Mamone. . . . The government built its case around the testimony of Steward and tape recordings of telephone conversations that Steward initiated with Harris. . . . [T]he defense sought to portray Harris's conversations with Steward as "an eventually doomed and misguided attempt to maintain his parole status without jeopardizing his life." The defense thus attempted to establish that Harris knew Steward was an informant and only played along with him out of fear of what would happen to him if he refused. . . .

[C]ounsel for Harris proposed at the completion of the government's case to call Rafael Hernandez, Harris's parole officer from Detroit, as his first defense witness. According to Harris's written offer of proof, submitted at the request of the district judge: [Hernandez would testify that] "during the period of time of the time charged in the Indictment, George Harris expressed to Rafael Hernandez that the Government and people were after him and trying to set him up." . . .

After hearing brief argument, the district judge excluded this proffer, reasoning that "[i]t is plainly blatantly hearsay, unreliable and self-serving."

When counsel for Harris then made an oral offer of proof with respect to similar proposed testimony by Ira Auslander, Harris's Detroit counsel, the district judge ruled "I would exclude that on the same ground. . . . If I am wrong, I am sure the Second Circuit knows their cases." . . .

Because of the manner in which these matters were handled, it is not clear precisely how either of these witnesses would have testified. Though both witnesses were present at trial, the district judge made his rulings without first requiring a *voir dire* of either witness. . . . [W]e are left with only the written offer of proof of the parole officer, quoted above, which is susceptible to varying interpretations, particularly as to time, and defense counsel's oral representations that Harris's Detroit attorney would testify "that exactly around the time of the Super Bowl . . . Mr. Harris told him that Mr. Steward had brought an agent to him, that he believed he brought an agent to him."

Taking these offers of proof at face value, as unfortunately we must on this record, we believe the district judge erred in excluding the proffered testimony as hearsay. Depending on the precise phraseology used by each witness, their testimony would have been admissible either as nonhearsay, or under the then existing state of mind hearsay exception. To the extent that Harris told either witness that he had "an encounter with some people who could cause him trouble"; that "the Government and people were after him and trying to set him up"; that "the Government was trying to set him up" (written offer of proof of Rafael Hernandez); and/or that "Mr. Steward had brought an agent to him" (oral offer of proof of attorney Auslander), the district judge erred in characterizing these statements as hearsay under Fed. R. Evid. 801(c). These statements were admissible, not for their truth, but instead as circumstantial evidence of Harris's state of mind—his knowledge of Steward's cooperation. On the other hand, to the extent that Harris told either his parole officer or attorney "that he *believed* [Steward] brought an agent to him" (emphasis added) (oral offer of proof of attorney Auslander), this statement would indeed have been hearsay under Fed. R. Evid. 801(c), since its evidentiary significance depended on the truth of the matter asserted—Harris's belief. However, such a "statement of the declarant's then existing state of mind" should have been admitted as a hearsay exception under Fed. R. Evid. 803(3). *See United States v. DiMaria*, 727 F.2d 265 at 271 (2d Cir. 1984) (citing cases). . . .

The government's attempt to avoid these conclusions is unpersuasive. The government . . . suggests that "[r]ather than focusing on academic analyses intent on rigid classification, it would be more profitable to analyze the probative value of the statement and to examine the dangers stemming from its admission in light of other factors." The "other factor" the government deems most significant is whether "the circumstances indicate plainly a motive to deceive.". . . .

As Judge Friendly observed [in *DiMaria*]:

It is doubtless true that all the hearsay exceptions in Rules 803 and 804 rest on a belief that declarations of the sort there described have "some particular assurance of credibility." . . . But the scheme of the Rules is to determine that issue by categories; if a declaration comes within a category defined as an exception, the declaration is admissible without any preliminary finding of probable credibility by the judge, save for the "catch-all" exceptions of Rules 803(24) and 804(b)(5) and the business records exception of Rule 803(6) ("unless the source of information or the method or circumstance of preparation indicate lack of trustworthiness"). As Judge Weinstein has stated, "the scheme adopted for the hearsay article in the federal rules is that of a system of class exceptions coupled with an open-ended provision in Rules 803(24) and 804(b)(5), and with the exemption of certain prior statements from the definition of hearsay" . . . , even though this excludes certain hearsay statements with a high degree of trustworthiness and admits certain statements with a low one. This evil was doubtless thought preferable to requiring preliminary determinations of the judge with respect to trustworthiness, with attendant possibilities of delay, prejudgment and encroachment on the province of the jury. (Citations omitted.)

We realize that under certain circumstances a *defendant* may object on the ground of probable unreliability to admission of a declaration of a nonwitness which is within an exception to the hearsay rule or is not hearsay. . . . This, however, is because of a defendant's special rights under the confrontation clause of the sixth amendment—a protection not extended to the government. . . . [Reversed.]

b. The *Hillmon* Doctrine

Over a century ago, in the most famous hearsay case in American history, the Supreme Court extended the state-of-mind exception to statements of intent offered to prove that the declarants actually did what they said they would. Modern evidence codes retain this rule, although controversy continues over its justification and proper scope.

MUTUAL LIFE INS. CO. v. HILLMON

145 U.S. 285 (1892)

On July 13, 1880, Sallie E. Hillmon, a citizen of Kansas, brought an action against the Mutual Life Insurance Company, a corporation of New York, on a policy of insurance, dated December 10, 1878, on the life of her husband, John W. Hillmon, in the sum of $10,000, payable to her within 60 days after notice and proof of his death. On the same day the plaintiff brought two other actions,—the one against the New York Life Insurance Company, a corporation of New York, on two similar policies of life insurance, dated, respectively, November 30, 1878, and December 10, 1878, for the sum of $5,000 each; and the other against the Connecticut Mutual Life Insurance Company, a corporation of Connecticut, on a similar policy, dated March 4, 1879, for the sum of $5,000.

In each case the declaration alleged that Hillmon died on March 17, 1879, during the continuance of the policy, but that the defendant, though duly notified of the fact, had refused to pay the amount of the policy, or any part thereof; and the answer denied the death of Hillmon, and alleged that he, together with John H. Brown and divers other persons, on or before November 30, 1878, conspiring to defraud the defendant, procured the issue of all the policies, and afterwards, in March and April, 1879, falsely pretended and represented that Hillmon was dead, and that a dead body which they had procured was his, whereas in reality he was alive and in hiding.

. . . On February 29, 1988, after two trials at which the jury had disagreed, the three cases on for trial, under the [trial court's] order of consolidation. . . . [P]laintiff introduced evidence tending to show that on or about March 5, 1879, Hillmon and Brown left Wichita, in the state of Kansas, and traveled together through southern Kansas in search of a site for a cattle ranch; that on the night of March 18th, while they were in camp at a place called "Crooked Creek," Hillmon was killed by the accidental discharge of a gun; that Brown at once notified persons living in the neighborhood, and that the body was thereupon taken to a neighboring town, where, after an inquest, it was buried. The defendants introduced evidence tending to show that the body found in the camp at Crooked Creek on the night of March 18th was not the body of Hillmon, but was the body of one Frederick Adolph Walters. Upon the question whose body this was there was much conflicting evidence, including photographs and descriptions of the corpse, and of the marks and scars upon it, and testimony to its likeness to Hillmon and to Walters.

The defendants introduced testimony that Walters left his home at Ft. Madison, in the state of Iowa, in March, 1878, and was afterwards in Kansas in 1878, and in January and February, 1879; that during that time his family frequently received letters from him, the last of which was written from Wichita; and that he had not been heard from since March, 1879. The defendants also offered the following evidence:

Elizabeth Rieffenach testified that she was a sister of Frederick Adolph Walters, and lived at Ft. Madison; and thereupon, as shown by the bill of exceptions, the following proceedings took place:

> "Witness further testified that she had received a letter written from Wichita, Kansas, about the 4th or 5th day of March, 1879, by her brother Frederick Adolph; that the letter was dated at Wichita, and was in the handwriting of her brother; that she had searched for the letter, but could not find the same, it being lost; that she remembered and could state the contents of the letter.
>
> "Thereupon the defendants' counsel asked the question, 'State the contents of that letter;' to which the plaintiff objected, on the ground that the same is incompetent, irrelevant, and hearsay. The objection was sustained, and the defendants duly excepted. The following is the letter as stated by witness:
>
> "Wichita, Kansas, March 4th or 5th or 3d or 4th,—I don't know,—1879. Dear Sister and All: I now in my usual style drop you a few lines to let you know that I expect to leave Wichita on or about March the 5th with a certain Mr. Hillmon, a sheep trader, for Colorado, or parts unknown to me. I expect to see the country now. News are of no interest to you, as you are not acquainted here. I will close with compliments to all inquiring friends. Love to all. I am truly your brother, FRED. ADOLPH WALTERS."

Alvina D. Kasten testified that she was 21 years of age, and resided in Ft. Madison; that she was engaged to be married to Frederick Adolph Walters; that she last saw him on March 24, 1878, at Ft. Madison; that he left there at that time, and had not returned; that she corresponded regularly with him, and received a letter about every two weeks until March 3, 1879, which was the last time she received a letter from him; that this letter was dated at Wichita, March 1, 1879, and was addressed to her at Ft. Madison, and the envelope was postmarked "Wichita, Kansas, March 2, 1879"; and that she had never heard from or seen him since that time.

The defendants put in evidence the envelope with the postmark and address, and thereupon offered to read the letter in evidence. The plaintiff objected to the reading of the letter. The court sustained the objection, and the defendants excepted.

This letter was dated "Wichita, March 1, 1879," was signed by Walters, and began as follows:

"Dearest Alvina: Your kind and ever welcome letter was received yesterday afternoon about an hour before I left Emporia. I will stay here until the fore part of next week, and then will leave here to see a part of the country that I never expected to see when I left home, as I am going with a man by the name of Hillmon, who intends to start a sheep ranch, and, as he promised me more wages than I could make at anything else, I concluded to take it, for a while at least, until I strike something better. There is so many folks in this country that have got the Leadville fever, and if I could not of got the situation that I have now I would have went there myself; but as it is at present I get to see the best portion of Kansas, Indian Territory, Colorado, and Mexico. The route that we intend to take would cost a man to travel from $150 to $200, but it will not cost me a cent; besides, I get good wages. I will drop you a letter occasionally until I get settled down. Then I want you to answer it."

. . . The jury, being instructed by the court to return a separate verdict in each case, returned verdicts for the plaintiff against the three defendants respectively for the amounts of their policies and interest, upon which separate judgments were rendered. The defendants sued out four writs of error, one jointly in the three cases as consolidated, and one in each case separately.

Mr. Justice GRAY, after stating the case as above, delivered the opinion of the court.

[The judgments are reversed because the trial court allowed each of the three defendants to exercise only one peremptory challenge during jury selection. By statute, each defendant was entitled to three peremptory challenges.]

. . . There is, however, one question of evidence so important, so fully argued at the bar, and so likely to arise upon another trial, that it is proper to express an opinion upon it.

This question is of the admissibility of the letters written by Walters on the first days of March, 1879, which were offered in evidence by the defendants, and excluded by the court. . . . The position taken at the bar that the letters were competent evidence . . . as memoranda made in the ordinary course of business, cannot be maintained, for they were clearly not such.

But upon another ground suggested they should have been admitted. A man's state of mind or feeling can only be manifested to others by countenance, attitude, or gesture, or by sounds or words, spoken or written. The nature of the fact to be proved is the same, and evidence of its proper tokens is equally competent to prove it, whether expressed by aspect or conduct, by voice or pen. . . .

The existence of a particular intention in a certain person at a certain time being a material fact to be proved, evidence that he expressed that intention at that time is as direct evidence of the fact as his own testimony that he then had that intention would be. After his death there can hardly be any other way of proving it, and while he is still alive his own memory of his state of mind at a former time is no more likely to be clear and true than a bystander's recollection of what he then said, and is less trustworthy than letters written by him at the very time and under circumstances precluding a suspicion of misrepresentation.

The letters in question were competent not as narratives of facts communicated to the writer by others, nor yet as proof that he actually went away from Wichita, but as evidence that, shortly before the time when other evidence tended to show that he went away, he had the intention of going, and of going with Hillmon, which made it more probable both that he did go and that he went with Hillmon than if there had been no proof of such intention. In view of the mass of conflicting testimony introduced upon the question whether it was the body of Walters that was found in Hillmon's camp, this evidence might properly influence the jury in determining that question.

The rule applicable to this case has been thus stated by this court: "Wherever the bodily or mental feelings of an individual are material to be proved, the usual expressions of such feelings are original and competent evidence. Those expressions are the natural reflexes of what it might be impossible to show by other testimony. If there be such other testimony, this may be necessary to set the facts thus developed in their true light, and to give them their proper effect. As independent, explanatory, or corroborative evidence it is often indispensable to the due administration of justice. Such declarations are regarded as verbal acts, and are as competent as any other testimony, when relevant to the issue. Their truth or falsity is an inquiry for the jury." *Insurance Co. v. Mosley*, 8 Wall. 397, 404, 405.

. . . Upon principle and authority, therefore, we are of opinion that the two letters were competent evidence of the intention of Walters at the time of writing them, which was a material fact bearing upon the question in controversy; and that for the exclusion of these letters, as well as for the undue restriction of the defendants' challenges, the verdicts must be set aside, and a new trial had . . . .

Judgment reversed, and case remanded to the circuit court, with directions to set aside the verdict and to order a new trial.

BROOKS W. MacCRACKEN, THE CASE OF THE ANONYMOUS CORPSE

Am. Heritage, June 1968, at 51, 75-77

[T]he insurance-company attorneys apparently presented no sound theory by which the Walters letters could have been held admissible, and we are told that the point was "miserably argued." Nevertheless, the Supreme Court justices voted unanimously to decide in favor of the insurance companies on general principles. . . . The preparation of the Supreme Court's opinion was assigned to Justice Horace Gray, who could be relied upon to find a precedent for the decision if anyone could do so. He was the most learned and resourceful member of the court—a Harvard graduate, former chief justice of Massachusetts, an heir to wealth, and a thorough Bostonian. Typically, his opinions were larded with judicial citations and legal principles. Yet we are reliably told that even he was in "dense darkness" about how to justify the admission of Walters' letters, until a suggestion came from his young legal secretary's father, James Bradley Thayer, professor of evidence at Harvard Law School. Together Justice Gray and Thayer brought forth a new legal theory and adorned it with their authority. . . . [N]o court would have allowed Walters' letter to be admitted in evidence if he had written his sweetheart saying, "I have left Wichita with Hillmon the sheep trader." Such a letter would indisputably have been hearsay. But the learned professor suggested that there was a logical difference between a hearsay account of a past fact and Walters' personal expression of his then present intent; the Supreme Court agreed. . . .

[N]o one ever found Hillmon. Walters never showed up either. . . . Between 1892 and 1897 two more trials were held (the fourth and fifth of the series) and two more juries disagreed. . . . By this time New York Life . . . thought it wise to settle with Sallie Hillmon, but . . . Mutual Life and Connecticut Mutual continued to contest the case. [The sixth trial resulted in a verdict for the plaintiff, but was reversed—again on evidentiary grounds—by the Supreme Court in 1903.] A seventh trial was then too much to contemplate even for the parties themselves; and a settlement with the last of the insurance companies was finally reached. (Counting accumulated interest, the "widow" eventually received a total of $35,700 from the three companies.) She had been for some years happily remarried, with no apparent apprehensions of bigamy. . . . The truth in the Hillmon case is as debatable today as it was when it began.

SHEPARD v. UNITED STATES

290 U.S. 96 (1933)

Mr. Justice CARDOZO delivered the opinion of the Court.

The petitioner, Charles A. Shepard, a major in the medical corps of the United States Army, has been convicted of the murder of his wife, Zenana Shepard, at Fort Riley, Kan., a United States military reservation.

The jury having qualified their verdict by adding thereto the words "without capital punishment" (18 U.S.C. § 567), the defendant was sentenced to imprisonment for life. The judgment of the United States District Court has been affirmed by the Circuit Court of Appeals for the Tenth Circuit, one of the judges of that court dissenting. A writ of certiorari brings the case here.

The crime is charged to have been committed by poisoning the victim with bichloride of mercury. The defendant was in love with another woman, and wished to make her his wife. There is circumstantial evidence to sustain a finding by the jury that to win himself his freedom he turned to poison and murder. Even so, guilt was contested, and conflicting inferences are possible. The defendant asks us to hold that by the acceptance of incompetent evidence the scales were weighted to his prejudice and in the end to his undoing.

The evidence complained of was offered by the government in rebuttal when the trial was nearly over. On May 22, 1929, there was a conversation in the absence of the defendant between Mrs. Shepard, then ill in bed, and Clara Brown, her nurse. The patient asked the nurse to go to the closet in the defendant's room and bring a bottle of whisky that would be found upon a shelf. When the bottle was produced, she said that this was the liquor she had taken just before collapsing. She asked whether enough was left to make a test for the presence of poison, insisting that the smell and taste were strange. And then she added the words, "Dr. Shepard has poisoned me."

The conversation was proved twice. After the first proof of it, the government asked to strike it out, being doubtful of its competence, and this request was granted. A little later, however, the offer was renewed; the nurse having then testified to statements by Mrs. Shepard as to the prospect of recovery. "She said she was not going to get well; she was going to die." With the aid of this new evidence, the conversation already summarized was proved a second time. There was a timely challenge of the ruling.

She said, "Dr. Shepard has poisoned me." The admission of this declaration, if erroneous, was more than unsubstantial error. As to that the parties are agreed. The voice of the dead wife was heard in accusation of her husband, and the accusation was accepted as evidence of guilt. If the evidence was incompetent, the verdict may not stand. . . .

Witnesses for the defendant had testified to declarations by Mrs. Shepard which suggested a mind bent upon suicide, or at any rate were thought by the defendant to carry that suggestion. More than once before her illness she had stated in the hearing of these witnesses that she had no wish to live, and had nothing to live for, and on one occasion she added that she expected some day to make an end to her life. . . . This testimony opened the door, so it is argued, to declarations in rebuttal that she had been poisoned by her husband. They were admissible, in that view, not as evidence of the truth of what was said, but as betokening a state of mind inconsistent with the presence of suicidal intent.

The testimony was neither offered nor received for the strained and narrow purpose now suggested as legitimate. . . . Aside, however, from this objection, the accusatory declaration must have been rejected as evidence of a state of mind, though the purpose thus to limit it had been brought to light upon the trial. The defendant had tried to show by Mrs. Shepard's declarations to her friends that she had exhibited a weariness of life and a readiness to end it, the testimony giving plausibility to the hypothesis of suicide. Wigmore, § 1726; *Commonwealth v. Trefethen*, 157 Mass. 180, 31 N.E. 961. By the proof of these declarations evincing an unhappy state of mind, the defendant opened the door to the offer by the government of declarations evincing a different state of mind, declarations consistent with the persistence of a will to live. The defendant would have no grievance if the testimony in rebuttal had been narrowed to that point. What the government put in evidence, however, was something very different. It did not use the declarations by Mrs. Shepard to prove her present thoughts and feelings, or even her thoughts and feelings in times past. It used the declarations as proof of an act committed by some one else, as evidence that she was dying of poison given by her husband. This fact, if fact it was, the government was free to prove, but not by hearsay declarations. It will not do to say that the jury might accept the declarations for any light that they cast upon the existence of a vital urge, and reject them to the extent that they charged the death to some one else. Discrimination so subtle is a feat beyond the compass of ordinary minds. The reverberating clang of those accusatory words would drown all weaker sounds. It is for ordinary minds, and not for psychoanalysts, that our rules of evidence are framed. They have their source very often in considerations of administrative convenience, of practical expediency, and not in rules of logic. When the risk of confusion is so great as to upset the balance of advantage, the evidence goes out. Thayer, Preliminary Treatise on the Law of Evidence, 266, 516; Wigmore, Evidence, §§ 1421, 1422, 1714.

These precepts of caution are a guide to judgment here. There are times when a state of mind, if relevant, may be proved by contemporaneous declarations of feeling or intent. *Mutual Life Ins. Co. v. Hillmon*, 145 U.S. 285, 295; *Shailer v. Bumstead*, 99 Mass. 112; Wigmore, §§ 1725, 1726, 1730. Thus, in proceedings for the probate of a will, where the issue is undue influence, the declarations of a testator are competent to prove his feelings for his relatives, but are incompetent as evidence of his conduct or of theirs. *Throckmorton v. Holt*, 180 U.S. 552, 571, 572, 573: *Waterman v. Whitney*, 11 N.Y. 157, 62 Am. Dec. 71; *Matter of Kennedy*, 167 N.Y. 163, 172, 60 N.E. 442. In suits for the alienation of affections, letters passing between the spouses are admissible in aid of a like purpose. Wigmore, § 1730; *Ash v. Prunier (C.C.A.)*, 105 F. 722; *Mutual Life Ins. Co. v. Hillmon, supra*, page 297; *Jameson v. Tully*, 178 Cal. 380, 173 P. 577; *Cottle v. Johnson*, 179 N.C. 426, 102 S.E. 769; *Curtis v. Miller*, 269 Pa. 509, 512, 112 A. 747. In damage suits for personal injuries, declarations by the patient to bystanders or physicians are evidence of sufferings or symptoms (Wigmore, §§ 1718, 1719), but are not received to prove the acts, the external circumstances, through which the injuries came about. Wigmore, § 1722; *Amys v. Barton*, (1912) 1 K.B. 40; *Chicago & A.R.R. Co. v. Industrial Board*, 274 Ill. 336, 113 N.E. 629; *Peoria Cordage Co. v. Industrial Board*, 284 Ill. 90, 119 N.E. 996; *Larrabee's Case*, 120 Me. 242, 113 A. 268; *Maine v. Maryland Casualty Co.*,

172 Wis. 350, 178 N.W. 749. Even statements of past sufferings or symptoms are generally excluded (Wigmore, § 1722(b); *Cashin v. New York, N.H. & H.R.R. Co.*, 185 Mass. 543, 70 N.E. 930), though an exception is at times allowed when they are made to a physician (*Roosa v. Loan Co.*, 132 Mass. 439, 440; *Cleveland, C., C. & I.R. Co. v. Newell*, 104 Ind. 264, 271, 3 N.E. 836; *contra, Davidson v. Cornell*, 132 N.Y. 228, 237, 30 N.E. 573). So also in suits upon insurance policies, declarations by an insured that he intends to go upon a journey with another may be evidence of a state of mind lending probability to the conclusion that the purpose was fulfilled. *Mutual Life Ins. Co. v. Hillmon, supra*. The ruling in that case marks the high-water line beyond which courts have been unwilling to go. It has developed a substantial body of criticism and commentary.[2] Declarations of intention, casting light upon the future, have been sharply distinguished from declarations of memory, pointing backwards to the past. There would be an end, or nearly that, to the rule against hearsay if the distinction were ignored.

The testimony now questioned faced backward and not forward. This at least it did in its most obvious implications. What is even more important, it spoke to a past act, and, more than that, to an act by some one not the speaker. Other tendency, if it had any, was a filament too fine to be disentangled by a jury.

The judgment should be reversed and the cause remanded to the District Court for further proceedings in accordance with this opinion.

ADVISORY COMMITTEE NOTE TO F.R.E. 803(3)

. . . The exclusion of "statements of memory or belief to prove the fact remembered or believed" is necessary to avoid the virtual destruction of the hearsay rule which would otherwise result from allowing state of mind, provable by a hearsay statement, to serve as the basis for an inference of the happening of the event which produced the state of mind. Shepard v. United States, 290 U.S. 96 (1933); Maguire, The Hillmon Case—Thirty-three Years After, 38 Harv. L. Rev. 709, 719-731 (1925); Hinton, States of Mind and the Hearsay Rule, 1 U. Chi. L. Rev. 394, 421-423 (1934). The rule of Mutual Life Ins. Co. v. Hillmon, 145 U.S. 285 (1892), allowing evidence of intention as tending to prove the doing of the act intended, is, of course, left undisturbed.

The carving out, from the exclusion mentioned in the preceding paragraph, of declarations relating to the execution, revocation, identification, or terms of declarant's will represents an ad hoc judgment which finds ample reinforcement in the decisions, resting on practical grounds of necessity and expediency rather than logic. McCormick § 271, pp. 577-578; Annot. 34 A.L.R.2d 588, 62 A.L.R.2d 855. A similar recognition of the

---

2. Maguire, *The Hillmon Case*, 38 Harvard Law Review, 709, 721, 727; Seligman, *An Exception to the Hearsay Rule*, 26 Harvard Law Review, 146; Chafee, *Review of Wigmore's Treatise*, 37 Harvard Law Review, 513, 519.

need for and practical value of this kind of evidence is found in California Evidence Code § 1260.

REPORT OF THE HOUSE JUDICIARY COMMITTEE

Rule 803(3) was approved in the form submitted by the Court to Congress. However, the Committee intends that the Rule be construed to limit the doctrine of Mutual Life Insurance Co. v. Hillmon, 145 U.S. 285, 295-300 (1892), so as to render statements of intent by a declarant admissible only to prove his future conduct, not the future conduct of another person.

UNITED STATES v. HOULIHAN

871 F. Supp. 1495 (D. Mass. 1994)

YOUNG, District Judge.

In the early morning hours of Monday, March 2, 1992, James Boyden Jr. was found dead in the vicinity of Spice Street, Charlestown. He had been shot in the back of the head. . . . As he was leaving [his sister's apartment the previous evening], he allegedly told his sister that he was going out "to meet Billy Herd." [Herd and others were charged with Boyden's murder and related offenses.]

As the trial unfolded, the government . . . [sought] to admit the statement of James Boyden Jr. to his sister that he intended to meet Herd as relevant circumstantial evidence that it was Herd who killed him later that evening. The government argued that this statement is admissible because it constitutes a statement of a then existing mental or emotional condition under Federal Rule of Evidence 803(3). Over objection, the Court admitted the statement and Marie Boyden Connors was allowed so to testify. This memorandum explains the Court's reasoning.

This case presents an issue of first impression in the First Circuit, namely, whether the out-of-court statement of a victim-declarant of an intention to meet with a defendant on the evening of the victim's murder can be admitted at trial as circumstantial evidence of the meeting. . . . Prior to the adoption of the Federal Rules of Evidence, the Supreme Court addressed this issue in the famous case of *Mutual Life Insurance Co. of New York v. Hillmon*, 145 U.S. 285 (1892). In *Hillmon*, an insurance company sought to introduce out-of-court statements by a declarant, Walters, that he intended to travel with the insured, Hillmon. The hearsay statement was used as the principal proof that Hillmon had actually traveled with Walters. . . . Thus, under *Hillmon*, out-of-court statements of a declarant are admissible to prove the subsequent conduct of others. . . . The question for this Court, then, is whether in enacting Rule 803(3) Congress codified in full the reasoning of *Hillmon*, or whether it sought to limit the case's application. . . .

Unfortunately, the legislative history of Rule 803(3) only serves to obfuscate the analysis. While the Advisory Committee's Note to Rule

803(3) states that "the rule of *Mutual Life Insurance Co. v. Hillmon*, allow-ing evidence of intention as tending to prove the doing of the act intended, is, of course, left undisturbed," the Report of the House Judiciary Commit-tee states that "the committee intends that the rule be construed to limit the doctrine of *Mutual Life Insurance Co. v. Hillmon*, so as to render state-ments of intent by a declarant admissible only to prove his future conduct, not the future conduct of another person." The Senate Report and the Conference Report are silent on this point.

Courts that have had the opportunity to consider the application of Rule 803(3) are divided. . . . Some courts have held that a declarant's state-ment of intent may be admitted against a non-declarant only when there is independent evidence connecting the declarant's statement with the non-declarant's conduct. *See United States v. Jenkins*, 579 F.2d 840, 842-43 (4th Cir.), *cert. denied*, 439 U.S. 967 (1978) (declarant's statement of intent is not admissible to prove subsequent conduct of third party, but is admissible to prove why third party acted as he did where there exists independent evidence that third party did in fact engage in the alleged conduct).

Similarly, the Second Circuit has held that "declarations of intentions or future plans are admissible against a nondeclarant when they are linked with independent evidence that corroborates the declaration." *United States v. Nersesian*, 824 F.2d 1294, 1325 (2d Cir.), *cert. denied*, 484 U.S. 958 (1987). . . . A district judge in the Northern District of Illinois has likewise adopted this approach. *See United States v. York*, No. 86 CR 315, 1987 WL 5938, at *7 (N.D. Ill. Jan. 12, 1987) (hearsay testimony held inadmissible where victim-declarant's statement that she intended to meet with the defendant at a particular time could not be corroborated with particularity). *But cf. Johnson v. Chrans*, 844 F.2d 842, 846 n. 4 (7th Cir.), *cert. denied*, 488 U.S. 835 (1988) (explaining that in some circumstances the Seventh Circuit has been willing to admit a declarant's out-of-court state-ments to prove conduct of another person, despite opposite result under Illinois state law). . . .

To the contrary, the Ninth Circuit has held that statements of a declar-ant's intent are admissible under Rule 803(3) to prove subsequent conduct of a person other than the declarant without corroborating evidence. *See United States v. Pheaster*, 544 F.2d 353, 374-80 (9th Cir. 1976), *cert. denied sub nom. Inciso v. United States*, 429 U.S. 1099 (1977) *(in kidnapping prosecution, trial court did not err in admitting testimony of a friend of the victim that shortly before the victim disappeared he told his friend that he was going to meet a person with the same name as the defendant). In holding statements of intent admissible against third parties, the Phea-ster* court recognized that such testimony could be unreliable, but rejected this as grounds for its exclusion. The Ninth Circuit explained that

> [t]he inference from a statement of present intention that the act intended was in fact performed is nothing more than an inference. . . . The possible unreliability of the inference to be drawn from the present intention [of the declarant] is a matter going to the weight of the evidence which might be argued to the trier of fact, but it should not be a ground for completely excluding the admittedly relevant evidence.

The court also acknowledged the "theoretical awkwardness" of applying a state of mind exception to prove conduct, but dismissed this objection because of the impressive array of authority favoring such application. . . .

The language of Rule 803(3) clearly says that statements of intent are admissible. Thus, because it does not by its terms limit the class of persons against whom such statements of intent may be admitted, this Court rules that Rule 803(3) codifies *Hillmon* as written and does not disturb its conclusion or its reasoning. . . . [H]ad Congress intended to limit the admissibility of such statements, it presumably would have done so. This Court will not venture to graft a limitation where none exists.

As Rule 803(3) is unambiguous, this Court is unpersuaded by appeals to legislative history. . . . Even if the Court were properly to engage in an examination of Rule 803(3)'s legislative history, the conflicting nature of that evidence would nevertheless lead us right back to the text. . . . [W]hile the approach adopted by the Second and Fourth Circuits may seem practical and fair, it is really little more than judicial policymaking. . . . For the reasons set forth above, on December 14, 1994, during the twenty-third day of trial, Marie Boyden Connors was permitted to testify, over timely objection, that as her brother James Boyden Jr. left her apartment for the last time, he said, he "was going to meet Billy Herd."

PROBLEMS

3.35. Sam is arrested when he tries to enter the United States from Mexico and cocaine is found underneath his car. At his trial on charges of attempted smuggling, he wishes to elicit testimony from the arresting officer that, when the cocaine was discovered, Sam said, "I don't know where that came from." The prosecutor objects on grounds of hearsay. How should the judge rule?

3.36. Henry Jumpertz was acquitted in 1859 of the murder of his mistress, Sophie Werner. The prosecutors argued Jumpertz had killed Werner to rid himself of her, and Jumpertz claimed Werner had committed suicide. To show that Werner was suicidal and to rebut the prosecution's claim of motive, Jumpertz introduced a letter that he said he had received from Werner shortly before she died. In the letter Werner declared she soon would "renounce[] the world" and be "in the grave." Jumpertz also called two witnesses who testified they had discussed the letter with him shortly after he had received it. *See* Jennifer L. Mnookin, *Scripting Expertise: The History of Handwriting Identification Evidence and the Judicial Construction of Reliability*, 87 Va. L. Rev. 1723 (2001). Should this evidence have been admitted?

3.37. Former football star O.J. Simpson was charged in Los Angeles in 1994 with the murders of his former wife, Nicole Brown Simpson, and her friend, Ronald Goldman. The prosecution sought to introduce evidence that shortly before her death Nicole Brown Simpson told relatives and friends that her ex-husband was stalking her and that she was afraid of him. The trial judge excluded the testimony on grounds of hearsay. *See* Gerald F. Uelmen, *The O.J. Files* 102-104 (1998). Following

Simpson's acquittal, relatives of the victims won a civil judgment against
him for wrongful death. The judge in the civil case admitted, to prove
state of mind, the statements excluded in the criminal case. The civil
plaintiffs argued (but the prosecutors did not) that Nicole's state of
mind was relevant to support the claim that she made a final break
with him on the day of the murders, which in turn gave him the motive
to kill her. Was the ruling in either the criminal or the civil case erroneous? (The ruling in the civil case was affirmed on appeal. *See* Rufo v.
Simpson, 103 Cal. Rptr. 2d 492 (Cal. App. 2001).) If the criminal case
were tried today, would the stalking statements be excluded under the
Confrontation Clause?

5. Injury Reports

Codifying common-law decisions, the Federal Rule of Evidence 803(4)
exempts from the hearsay rule a broad range of statements made to physicians or others for purpose of medical diagnosis. The theory is that self-
interest tends to keep a patient honest. But, controversially, the federal rule
expands the exception to cover many statements made to physicians hired
not for treatment but simply for diagnosis with an eye to litigation. Debate
has also surrounded the use of Rule 803(4) and its state-law analogs to allow
into evidence out-of-court statements identifying the perpetrators of sexual
abuse, particularly of children.

The Supreme Court's revised interpretation of the Confrontation
Clause, announced in *Crawford v. Washington*, has created an additional
layer of uncertainty about when the Constitution permits out-of-court
injury reports to be introduced against a criminal defendant. In many
cases, the answer will depend on whether the statement is deemed
"testimonial."

[F.R.E. 803(4); C.E.C. §§1251, 1253, 1370]

ADVISORY COMMITTEE NOTE TO F.R.E. 803(4)

Even those few jurisdictions which have shied away from generally
admitting statements of present condition have allowed them if made to
a physician for purposes of diagnosis and treatment in view of the patient's
strong motivation to be truthful. The same guarantee of trustworthiness
extends to statements of past conditions and medical history, made for
purposes of diagnosis or treatment. It also extends to statements as to causation, reasonably pertinent to the same purposes, in accord with the
current trend. Statements as to fault would not ordinarily qualify under
this latter language. Thus a patient's statement that he was struck by an
automobile would qualify but not his statement that the car was driven
through a red light. Under the exception the statement need not have

been made to a physician. Statements to hospital attendants, ambulance drivers, or even members of the family might be included.

Conventional doctrine has excluded from the hearsay exception, as not within its guarantee of truthfulness, statements to a physician consulted only for the purpose of enabling him to testify. While these statements were not admissible as substantive evidence, the expert was allowed to state the basis of his opinion, including statements of this kind. The distinction thus called for was one most unlikely to be made by juries. The rule accordingly rejects the limitation. This position is consistent with the provision of Rule 703 that the facts on which expert testimony is based need not be admissible in evidence if of a kind ordinarily relied upon by experts in the field.

ROCK v. HUFFCO GAS & OIL CO.

922 F.2d 272 (5th Cir. 1991)

THORNBERRY, Circuit Judge:

... This litigation stems from two accidents allegedly suffered by Richard D. Rock while employed as a steward/cook for Offshore Food Service, Inc. of Houma, Louisiana. Offshore Food Service provides food catering services to offshore drilling platforms and vessels in the Gulf of Mexico.

On July 13, 1987, Rock was assigned to work on the Huffco Fixed Platform 206A, which was located in the High Island Region off the coast of Galveston, Texas. On the morning following his arrival, as he was leaving his sleeping quarters, Rock claimed that his foot fell through a rusted part of a step located just outside of his doorway causing him to sprain his ankle. There were no witnesses to the accident. . . . Doctors reported that Rock had a tender and swollen right ankle and described the injury as a moderate sprain. The ankle was placed in a six inch plaster splint, and Rock was instructed not to put any weight on the ankle, to walk with crutches, and to elevate the ankle when possible.

On July 21, 1987, after a few days of rest, Rock returned to work. . . . [O]n August 26, 1987, Rock claimed to have re-injured his ankle by slipping in some grease on the floor of [a jack-up rig owned by the Dual Drilling Company]. The only potential witness to the accident was Barry Breaux, another Offshore Food's employee assigned to work with Rock. During his deposition, Breaux reported that he was in the galley at the time of the accident but did not see Rock fall. In fact, Breaux claims that Rock had previously advised him of a plan to fake such an accident. . . .

Because of his ankle's worsening condition, Rock consulted Dr. A. Delmar Walker on September 17th and 27th of 1987. As part of those examinations, Rock provided the doctor with a history of the injury to his ankle including a description of the two incidents discussed above. On October 1, 1987, Dr. Walker referred Rock to a vascular surgeon, Dr. Fritz J. Rau, who again asked Rock for a history of the injury to his ankle. . . .

Apparently, as a result of the injury to his ankle, Rock was suffering from a condition known as venous insufficiency. This occurs when the veins in the lower legs fail to return blood to the torso. Several surgeries were performed on Rock in an attempt to restore normal blood flow, but his condition deteriorated. In addition to his vascular condition, Rock developed infections, possibly resulting from the surgical procedures themselves. Rock died from a heart attack on December 12, 1988. . . .

After Rock's death, surviving members of his family . . . pursued negligence claims against the defendants. . . . [The district court granted summary judgment to the defendants, on the ground that there was no admissible evidence that Rock had injured himself on the rig.] Specifically, the court concluded that the evidence offered by plaintiffs constituted hearsay, which did not fall within any of the recognized exceptions to the hearsay rule. . . .

Appellants . . . suggest that written and testimonial evidence concerning the history of Rock's alleged accidents, which were given by Rock to the doctors treating his ankle, should be admissible under Federal Rule of Evidence 803(4). This rule provides that otherwise inadmissible hearsay should not be excluded if the statement was initially "made for purposes of medical diagnosis or treatment and describ[es] medical history, or past or present symptoms, pain, or sensations, or the inception or general character of the cause or external source thereof insofar as *reasonably pertinent to diagnosis or treatment.*" Fed. R. Evid. 803(4) (emphasis added).

Admissibility of a statement made to one's physician turns on the guarantee of the absent declarant's trustworthiness. *See* Fed. R. Evid. 803(4) advisory committee's note. Therefore, before admitting such hearsay statements, the court should determine whether the statements were reasonably considered by the declarant as being pertinent to the diagnosis or treatment sought. Details of the injury not necessary for treatment but serving only to suggest fault "would not ordinarily qualify" as an exception to the hearsay rule under Rule 803(4). *See id.* A case cited by plaintiffs, *Ramrattan v. Burger King Corp.*, 656 F. Supp. 522 (D. Md. 1987), illustrates the application of this rule. In *Ramrattan*, the district court held that a statement made to a physician that the defendant's car struck his vehicle was admissible under Rule 803(4), but that "statements concerning who ran the red light or the fault of the parties are not pertinent to diagnosis or treatment."

The plaintiffs argue that Drs. Walker and Rau considered the cause of Rock's injury pertinent to their diagnosis, however, deposition transcripts do not bear this out. . . . The doctors stated that they only needed to know that Rock had twisted his ankle; they did not need to know the additional detail that Rock may have twisted the ankle while stepping through a rusted-out or defective step or by slipping in some grease in order to diagnose or treat Rock's injury. . . . [T]he district court was correct in ruling Rock's statements to his doctors as inadmissible under Federal Rule of Evidence 803(4). . . . [Affirmed.]

STATE v. MOSES

119 P.3d 906 (Wash. App. 2005)

SCHINDLER, J.

A jury convicted Jeffrey Duane Moses of murder in the second degree for the shooting death of his wife, Jennifer Moses [in September 2002]. . . . Moses contends admission of the out-of-court hearsay statements made by Jennifer and her son, F.M., concerning a prior 2001 incident of domestic violence violated his Confrontation Clause rights. . . . In the early morning of November 1, 2001, Jennifer's neighbor called 911. The neighbor reported Moses had hit and kicked Jennifer. After the police arrived, over the course of an approximately forty-minute interview, Jennifer described the assault. She was then transported to the hospital for treatment of her injuries. The children, F. and F.M., went with Jennifer to the hospital emergency room (ER). Jennifer told the treating ER doctor and the hospital social worker that Moses hit her and kicked her in the face. The trial court admitted statements made by Jennifer to the police, the ER doctor and the social worker as excited utterances.

The hospital social worker also interviewed Jennifer's sons, F. and F.M., about the assault. Based on F.M.'s report that his dad kicked his mom, the social worker called Child Protective Services (CPS). The social worker testified at trial about what F.M. told her and that she reported the domestic violence assault to CPS. . . .

Under [Washington Evidence Rule] 803(a)(4), "[s]tatements made for purposes of medical diagnosis or treatment and describing medical history, or past or present symptoms, pain, or sensations, or the inception or general character of the cause or external source thereof insofar as reasonably pertinent to diagnosis or treatment" are admissible. . . . Although statements attributing fault are generally not relevant to diagnosis or treatment, this court has found statements attributing fault to an abuser in a domestic violence case are an exception because the identity of the abuser is pertinent and necessary to the victim's treatment. . . .

Courts that have addressed *Crawford*'s impact on statements admitted under the medical diagnosis and treatment exception focus on the purpose of the declarant's encounter with the health care provider. In *State v. Fisher*, 108 P.3d 1262, 1269 (Wash. App. 2005), the court held that the statement made by a victim of child abuse to a physician was not testimonial. The victim made the statement the morning after the assault, when the physician asked the child what happened. In concluding the victim's statement was not testimonial, the court noted that the doctor was not a government employee and there was no indication of a purpose to prepare testimony for trial. In *State v. Vaught*, 682 N.W.2d 284 (Neb. 2004), the Nebraska Supreme Court held that a four-year-old's identifying statements to a doctor were not testimonial. The court determined that the only purpose of the medical examination was to provide medical treatment and there was no indication of a purpose to develop testimony for trial. Similarly, in *State v. Scacchetti*, 690 N.W.2d 393, 396 (Minn. Ct. App. 2005), the court held a statement made by a three-year-old victim of sexual abuse to a nurse was not testimonial. The victim's statement was in response to the nurse's question about whether anything happened. The court noted that the nurse sought information to provide a medical diagnosis and was not working on behalf of, or in conjunction with, investigating police officers or other government officials for the purpose of developing testimony for prosecution.

In cases where courts have found statements to health care providers are testimonial, the prosecutorial purpose of the medical examination has been clear. *People v. Vigil*, 104 P.3d 258, 265 (Colo. App. 2004); *In re T.T.*, 815 N.E.2d 789 (Ill. App. 2004). In *Vigil*, the case relied on by Moses, a seven-year-old child made a statement identifying the perpetrator of a sexual assault to a doctor. The court in *Vigil* found the victim's statement was testimonial because the doctor was a member of a child protection team that provided consultation services in cases of suspected child abuse, and the doctor performed a "forensic sexual abuse examination." In *T.T.*, the court held that the victim's statement identifying the perpetrator was testimonial because the medical examination was done six months after the assault, for the purpose of pursuing a prosecution.

This case is more similar to *Fisher* and *Vaught*. Jennifer was taken to the emergency room of the hospital shortly after the assault for serious injuries. The ER doctor, Dr. Appleton, testified that he questioned Jennifer in order to provide treatment. Dr. Appleton examined Jennifer and asked her what had happened and then ordered x-rays of Jennifer's jaw. And unlike *Vigil* and *T.T.*, the purpose of Dr. Appleton's examination was for medical diagnosis and treatment of Jennifer's significant injuries. Dr. Appleton had no role in the investigation of the assault and he was not working on behalf of or in conjunction with the police or governmental officials to develop testimony for the prosecution. There is also nothing in the record to indicate Jennifer believed or had reason to believe that her statements to Dr. Appleton would be used at a subsequent trial. We conclude that Jennifer's statements to Dr. Appleton were not testimonial under *Crawford.* . . .

An out-of-court statement to a social worker is also admissible if made in the course of diagnosis and treatment. Two post-*Crawford* cases have addressed statements to social workers, each holding that the statements were testimonial. . . . In both [cases], the social workers were interviewing children on behalf of the State for the express purpose of gathering evidence for a future prosecution or developing the children's testimony for prosecution.

Here, the hospital social worker, Muller, testified that while Jennifer was sleeping off the effects of the pain medication, she interviewed the children. F.M. told Muller that he saw Moses kick Jennifer. Both children reported regular fights between Moses and Jennifer that caused them to hide under their beds. After talking to the children, Muller called CPS to report the assault. When Jennifer woke up, Muller interviewed her. Muller testified that Jennifer was initially reluctant to talk about the assault, but was generally cooperative. Jennifer identified Moses as her assailant, and told

Muller that Moses kicked her in the jaw. At some point during the interview, Muller told Jennifer that she had contacted CPS to report domestic violence.

Because the trial occurred prior to the Supreme Court's decision in *Crawford*, the record is not clear when Jennifer identified Moses as her assailant during the course of the interview with Muller. Nor is it clear when Muller told Jennifer that she had contacted CPS. Like Dr. Appleton, Muller was providing treatment to Jennifer and statements in that context are not testimonial. But once Muller told Jennifer that she had contacted CPS, Jennifer would have been aware of the potential implications of her statements to Muller, and, under those circumstances, Muller's testimony about Moses' assault could be impermissible testimonial hearsay under *Crawford*.

The State contends that F.M.'s statement to the social worker is not testimonial hearsay because it was not offered to prove the truth of the matter asserted. The *Crawford* Court explicitly excluded testimonial statements that were not introduced for the truth of the matter asserted from a Confrontation Clause analysis. . . . At trial, the State asked Muller why she contacted CPS. Muller testified that she contacted CPS because F.M. told her that his dad kicked his mom. We conclude that F.M.'s statement was not introduced for the truth of the matter asserted, but to show why Muller contacted CPS. F.M.'s statement did not implicate *Crawford*, and the trial court did not err in admitting this testimony. . . .

[The court concluded that Jennifer's statements to the police were testimonial under *Crawford* and should not have been admitted. Nonetheless, the introduction of this evidence and any testimonial statements Jennifer made to the social worker was harmless error, because the "untainted evidence" was "so overwhelming that it necessarily [led] to a finding of guilt."]

We affirm the conviction. . . .

ROBERT P. MOSTELLER, TESTING THE TESTIMONIAL CONCEPT AND EXCEPTIONS TO CONFRONTATION: "A LITTLE CHILD SHALL LEAD THEM"
82 Ind. L.J. 917, 950-951, 952 (2007)

[S]tatements of children to doctors and nurses who are the first to examine the child after the report of assault are almost universally treated as nontestimonial. . . . The only exception is the specific issue of the identity of the perpetrator, with a few cases treating the part of the child's statement that names the perpetrator as testimonial based on its accusatory nature. . . .

In all or almost all jurisdictions, a doctor who finds substantial evidence of sexual or physical abuse of a child is required by law to report the findings to authorities for possible prosecution. In most jurisdictions, some and often all of what is conveyed will be admissible under the hearsay rules. There is every reason to assume that the vast majority of doctors and nurses are aware both of reporting requirements and the admissibility of many statements made to them during the examination process. The medical examination thus always has the potential to feed directly into the criminal process, and use of the statements at trial is an obvious possibility.

The legal requirement imposed upon doctors in most states to report reasonable suspicion of abuse would seem to have some bearing on the testimonial issue. However, in none of the lower court opinions has a court ruled that the reporting requirement renders the statement automatically testimonial. Indeed, the reporting requirement has no impact at all.

PROBLEMS

3.38. A woman brings her infant daughter into the emergency room and tells the intake clerk, "My boyfriend burned her with a cigarette. He gets nasty when he's been drinking." Is all or part of this statement admissible against the boyfriend in a subsequent prosecution for battery?

3.39. Along with his wife, a miner sues his employer for causing his respiratory illness. Their lawyer hires a physician as an expert witness, and the miner tells the doctor, "My lungs started to hurt ten years ago, a month or so after I started working in the mine." The miner dies before trial. Is his statement to the doctor admissible to prove when the disease began to manifest itself?

6. Recorded Recollection

Suppose an eyewitness to an accident appears at trial as a witness but can no longer remember what happened. If the witness previously wrote down her recollections, modern evidence law follows Wigmore in distinguishing two different ways in which the record may be used. The doctrine of "past recollection recorded" allows the record, in certain cases, to be introduced into evidence—or, in federal court and in many states, read to the jury—to prove the truth of what it asserts, notwithstanding the hearsay rule. Past recollection recorded is therefore an exception to the hearsay rule. It is often confused with what Wigmore called "present recollection revived" and other writers have sometimes called "present recollection refreshed." This is a technique not for introducing a document, nor even for having it read to the jury, but rather for jogging the memory of a forgetful witness, and thereby allowing the witness to testify from "present recollection."

There is room for debate whether witnesses commonly distinguish as Wigmore did between having their memory refreshed and simply repeating what they previously wrote. But the rules of evidence and conventional trial practice assume that they do. Moreover, conventional practice allows *anything* to be used to revive the recollection of a forgetful witness, as long as it is first shown to opposing counsel—and subject, of course, to the judge's general authority to regulate trial procedures in the interests of fairness and efficiency.

[F.R.E. 612, 803(5); C.E.C. §1237]

ADVISORY COMMITTEE NOTE TO F.R.E. 803(5)

A hearsay exception for recorded recollection is generally recognized and has been described as having "long been favored by the federal and practically all the state courts that have had occasion to decide the question." United States v. Kelly, 349 F.2d 720, 770 (2d Cir. 1965). . . . The guarantee of trustworthiness is found in the reliability inherent in a record made while events were still fresh in mind and accurately reflecting them.

The principal controversy attending the exception has centered, not upon the propriety of the exception itself, but upon the question whether a preliminary requirement of impaired memory on the part of the witness should be imposed. The authorities are divided. If regard be had only to the accuracy of the evidence, admittedly impairment of the memory of the witness adds nothing to it and should not be required. Nevertheless, the absence of the requirement, it is believed, would encourage the use of statements carefully prepared for purposes of litigation under the supervision of attorneys, investigators, or claim adjusters. Hence the example includes a requirement that the witness not have "sufficient recollection to enable him to testify fully and accurately." To the same effect are California Evidence Code § 1237 and New Jersey Rule 63(1)(b), and this has been the position of the federal courts. . . .

No attempt is made in the exception to spell out the method of establishing the initial knowledge or the contemporaneity and accuracy of the record, leaving them to be dealt with as the circumstances of the particular case might indicate. Multiple person involvement in the process of observing and recording, as in Rathbun v. Brancatella, 93 N.J. L. 222, 107 A. 279 (1919), is entirely consistent with the exception.

Locating the exception at this place in the scheme of the rules is a matter of choice. There were two other possibilities. The first was to regard the statement as one of the group of prior statements of a testifying witness which are excluded entirely from the category of hearsay by Rule 801(d)(1). That category, however, requires that declarant be "subject to cross-examination," as to which the impaired memory aspect of the exception raises doubts. The other possibility was to include the exception among those covered by Rule 804. Since unavailability is required by that rule and lack of memory is listed as a species of unavailability by the definition of the term in Rule 804(a)(3), that treatment at first impression would seem appropriate. The fact is, however, that the unavailability requirement of the exception is of a limited and peculiar nature. Accordingly, the exception is located at this point rather than in the context of a rule where unavailability is conceived of more broadly.

FISHER v. SWARTZ

130 N.E.2d 575 (Mass. 1955)

SPALDING, Justice.

In this action of contract to recover for labor and materials alleged to have been furnished to the defendant, the plaintiff had a verdict. The case is here on the defendant's exception to a ruling on evidence.

The plaintiff testified that he furnished certain labor and materials in repairing a house owned by the defendant. While testifying he "refresh[ed] his recollection" from a carbon copy of an itemized statement of charges made for the labor and materials furnished by him.

The statement contained more than a hundred items. The original of this statement had been sent to the defendant. Following the use of the copy to aid his testimony, the plaintiff offered it in evidence and the defendant objected. . . . [T]he copy was admitted in evidence subject to the defendant's exception.

In support of the ruling the plaintiff argues that the statement contained business entries which were admissible under G.L. (Ter. Ed.) c. 233, § 78. But there is lacking here the preliminary finding by the judge of the statutory prerequisites. . . . It is apparent from the record that no attempt was made to bring the statement within the statute and that counsel and the judge dealt with it on the basis of a memorandum which had aided the plaintiff while testifying. . . .

If the evidence is admissible it must be on other grounds. A writing may be used by a witness in different ways. He may use it to revive or stimulate a present recollection, or, having no present recollection even with the aid of the writing, he may use it merely as a record of his past knowledge. Professor Wigmore has classified these situations as "present recollection revived" and "past recollection recorded" and several courts in recent years have employed these designations. In order to decide whether the statement in question was admissible it becomes necessary to determine to which of these classifications it belongs, for the legal consequences are not the same. In a case of "present recollection revived" the witness, although he may use the writing to refresh his recollection, must testify to the fact as he remembers it and he may not read or show the writing to the jury. But in a case of "past recollection recorded" the judge in his discretion may permit a witness "to incorporate in his testimony a writing expressive of his past knowledge, and to read it and even to show it to the jury." Bendett v. Bendett, 315 Mass. 59, 64 [1943]. . . . While the record in the case at bar is not as clear as it might be, we think that it may fairly be inferred that the writing was a record of the witness' past recollection and was treated as such by counsel and the trial judge. . . .

The defendant does not argue that the statement was not a record of past recollection. His position in substance is that it is not admissible in any event, and he relies on Bendett v. Bendett, cited above. That that case sustains the defendant's contention cannot be gainsaid. There the plaintiff while testifying had used a diary kept in the usual course of business to "refresh his recollection." It is not clear from the opinion—and an inspection of the original papers furnishes no additional light—whether the memorandum revived a present memory or was a record of past recollection. The opinion dealt with the question on the basis that it might have been the latter. So treated, the court said that it saw "no reason for denying to the trial judge discretion to permit a witness to incorporate in his testimony a writing expressive of his past knowledge, and to read it and even to show it to the jury." But, as the court pointed out, the judge went further and admitted the writing as independent evidence and not as a part of the testimony of the plaintiff. This was held to be error. The court recognized that in some jurisdictions, "because of the slight practical difference between the incorporation of a writing in the testimony of a witness and the admission of the writing as evidence by itself, a written record of the past knowledge of a witness is held admissible in evidence." The court, nevertheless, was of opinion that "such a writing under some circumstances might have some inherent evidential weight independently of its adoption by the witness as the expression and embodiment of his testimony. In such a case, neither party would be entitled to have that weight thrown into the scale, on the merits of the case, unless the writing should be admissible on some other ground."

In view of the importance of this question in the trial of causes we are disposed to reconsider it. Further study of the question has convinced us that both reason and authority lead to the conclusion that the writing ought to be admissible as evidence. It is to be noted that in the Bendett case a majority of the court was of opinion that, although it was error to permit the memorandum to be put in evidence, the error, nevertheless, was harmless. The reason was that the witness had testified with respect to the items contained in the memorandum and had been cross-examined about them. "Thus," said the court, "the jury had been made familiar with everything material that was contained in the book. The admission of the book in evidence merely put before their eyes what they knew already. So far as appears there was nothing in the sight of the items in the book that was more convincing than the testimony of the plaintiff that they were the items in an account that he knew to be true. We do not see how the defendant was harmed." But that would be the case in most if not all situations where a memorandum of past recollection was put in evidence. Prior to its admission the witness would usually have read to the court or jury the contents of the memorandum, and its admission as evidence, since it would have added little or nothing, would generally be treated as harmless error. We prefer a less squeamish approach to the question. Rather than to say the admission of the writing is error, but error that does no harm, we think that it is better to say that there is no error at all.

This is the prevailing view elsewhere and is favored by distinguished scholars in the field of evidence. . . . Wigmore on Evidence (3d ed.) § 754; McCormick on Evidence, § 278. See Maguire, Evidence, Common Sense & Common Law, pages 37-39. See also . . . Model Code of Evidence, Rule 504. As the Supreme Court of Errors aptly said in a well-considered opinion, "It seems to us to be pressing the use of a legal fiction too far for a court to permit the statement made by such paper to be read as evidence, while holding that the law forbids the admission as evidence of the paper which is the original and only proof of the statement admitted." Curtis v.

Bradley, 65 Conn. 99, 109 [1894]. Accordingly we are of opinion that the judge in the case at bar did not err in admitting the statement in question and that to the extent that the Bendett case is opposed to this view we decline to follow it. . . . Exceptions overruled.

UNITED STATES v. RICCARDI

174 F.2d 883 (3d Cir. 1949)

KALODNER, Circuit Judge.

The defendant was [convicted of] . . . wilfully, unlawfully and feloniously having transported or having caused to be transported in interstate commerce certain chattels of the value of $5,000 or more. . . . We are not here primarily concerned with the particular fraudulent representations which the defendant made. Rather we are called upon to decide the propriety of the method utilized at the trial to prove what chattels the defendant obtained and transported, and their value. In short, the principal question is whether the witnesses who testified to these essentials were properly permitted to refresh their memory. . . .

The chattels involved are numerous items of bric-a-brac, linens, silverware, and other household articles of quality and distinction. They were the property of Doris Farid es Sultaneh, and were kept in her home at Morristown, New Jersey, from which the defendant is alleged to have transported them to Arizona in a truck and station wagon. The defendant did not deny receiving some of the lady's chattels, but did deny both the quantity and quality alleged. . . .

To prove the specific chattels involved, the government relied on the testimony of Doris Farid; to prove their value, it relied on the testimony of an expert, one Leo Berlow.

Farid testified that as the chattels were being moved from the house, she made longhand notes, and that later she copied these notes on her typewriter. Only one of the original notes was produced, and became part of the evidence of the case, a search by Farid having failed to disclose the others. The government sought to have Farid testify with respect to the chattels by using the typewritten notes for the purpose of refreshing her recollection.[2] Although the defendant's objection was overruled, the

2. At pages 114a-115a of Appellant's Appendix, the following appears:

"The Court: That isn't the question. When you look at that typewritten sheet, does that refresh your recollection as to the items therein mentioned?
"The Witness: It does.
"The Court: In what way?
"The Witness: Well, every item here—for instance: '2 Chinese vases octagonal shape Satsuma, light for mantel' I remember.
"The Court: You remember those items individually as packed?
"The Witness: Individually, each one.
"The Court: I will allow her to refresh her recollection, but I will expect you to produce the original notes."

government, on the next day of the trial, submitted to Farid lists of chattels taken out of a copy of the indictment, but from which had been deleted such information as dates and values. With the aid of these lists, the witness testified that her recollection was refreshed[4] and that she presently recognized and could identify each item. She was then permitted to read the lists aloud, and testified that she knew that the items were loaded on the truck or station wagon, as the case was. The lists were neither offered nor received in evidence.

The expert, Berlow, testified that he had visited Doris Farid's home on numerous occasions in his professional capacity as dealer in antiques, bric-a-brac, etc.; that he was very familiar with the furnishings therein, having examined the household for the purpose of buying items from Farid or selling them for her on commission. He was shown the same lists which Farid had used to refresh her recollection, and with their aid testified that he could recall the items individually, with some exceptions; that he remembered them to the extent that he could not only describe the items, but in many instances could state where in the house he had seen them; and that he could give an opinion as to their value. This he was permitted to do.

. . . It is [the defendant's] position that the lists should not have been used because they were not made by the witnesses at or shortly after the time of the transaction while the facts were fresh in memory. It is further contended that . . . what Farid did, in fact, was to read off the lists as proof of the actual articles loaded on the vehicles.

The government, on the other hand, asserts that the witnesses gave their independent recollection, which is admissible, albeit refreshed, because it is the recollection and not the writing which is the evidence. It goes further, and urges that where the witness has an independent recollection, anything may be used to stimulate and vitalize that recollection with regard to source or origin.[5]

---

4. For example, at page 140a of Appellant's Appendix:

"The Court: Well, Madam, as you look at that list does it refresh your recollection?
"The Witness: I lived with these things, your Honor, I know them.
"The Court: You lived with them yourself?
"The Witness: I did.
"The Court: So when you look at that paper, it does refresh your recollection?
"The Witness: Absolutely."

5. This is in paraphrase of Lord Ellenborough's statement in Henry v. Lee, 2 Chitty 124: "If upon looking at any document he can so far refresh his memory as to recollect a circumstance, it is sufficient; and it makes no difference that the memorandum is not written by himself, for it is not the memorandum that is the evidence but the recollection of the witness."

Refreshing the recollection of a witness is not an uncommon trial practice, but as a theory of evidentiary law its content and application are far from clear. . . . An analysis as good and trustworthy as presently exists appears in Chapter XXVIII, 3 Wigmore on Evidence (3rd ed. 1940). Professor Wigmore separated, broadly, what he called "past recollection recorded" from "present recollection revived," attributing much of the confusion in the cases to a failure to make this distinction and to the use of the phrase "refreshing the recollection" for both classes of testimony. The primary difference between the two classifications is the ability of the witness to testify from present knowledge: where the witness' memory is revived, and he presently recollects the facts and swears to them, he is obviously in a different position from the witness who cannot directly state the facts from present memory and who must ask the court to accept a writing for the truth of its contents because he is willing to swear, for one reason or another, that its contents are true. . . .

The difference between present recollection revived and past recollection recorded has a demonstrable effect upon the method of proof. In the instance of past recollection recorded, the witness, by hypothesis, has no present recollection of the matter contained in the writing. Whether the record is directly admitted into evidence, or indirectly by the permissive parroting of the witness, it is nevertheless a substitute for his memory and is offered for the truth of its contents. It assumes a distinct significance as an independent probative force, and is therefore ordinarily required to meet certain standards. . . .

In the case of present recollection revived, the witness, by hypothesis, relates his present recollection, and under oath and subject to cross-examination asserts that it is true; his capacities for memory and perception may be attacked and tested; his determination to tell the truth investigated and revealed; protestations of lack of memory, which escape criticism and indeed constitute a refuge in the situation of past recollection recorded, merely undermine the probative worth of his testimony. It is in recognition of these factors that we find:

> "The law of contemporary writing or entry qualifying it as primary evidence has no application. The primary evidence here is not the writing. It was not introduced in evidence. It was not offered. The primary evidence is the oral statement of the hostile witness. It is not so important when the statement was made or by whom if it serves the purpose to refresh the mind and unfold the truth." Hoffman v. United States, 9 Cir., 1937, 87 F.2d 410, 411.
>
> "When a party uses an earlier statement of his own witness to refresh the witness' memory, the only evidence recognized as such is the testimony so refreshed. . . . Anything may in fact revive a memory; a song, a scent, a photograph, an allusion, even a past statement known to be false. When a witness declares that any of these has evoked a memory, the opposite party may show, either that it has not evoked what appears to the witness as a memory, or that, although it may so appear to him, the

memory is a phantom and not a reliable record of its content. When the evoking stimulus is not itself an account of the relevant occasion, no question of its truth can arise; but when it is an account of that occasion, its falsity, if raised by the opposing party, will become a relevant issue if the witness has declared that the evoked memory accords with it. . . ." United States v. Rappy, 2 Cir., 1947, 157 F.2d 964, 967-968, certiorari denied 329 U.S. 806.

In the instant case, the learned trial judge determined that both Farid and the expert, Berlow, testified from present recollection. On the record, we cannot say that it was plainly not so. Both witnesses stated that they knew the chattels and could identify them. Farid, who testified that she was present and helped to pack them, said she could remember which were transported; Berlow said he could give an opinion of their value. On a number of occasions the trial judge investigated the foundations of their claim to present recollection and satisfied himself as to its bona fides. . . . [T]he trial judge immediately recognized that the items of property involved were so numerous that in the ordinary course of events no one would be expected to recite them without having learned a list by rote memory. On the other hand, the items were such that a person familiar with them reasonably could be expected to recognize them and tell what he knows. Under these circumstances, the District Judge might well have permitted the government, in lieu of the procedure followed, to ask Farid leading questions, directing her attention to specific items, and asking her whether she knew what happened to them. This is especially true of Berlow, who did not purport to have any knowledge of the movement of the articles. Clearly, it would have been pointless to ask him to give the value of every article he had ever seen in Farid's home. The same result could have been achieved legitimately without the use of the lists by orally directing his attention to any specific article previously identified by Farid and asking him whether he had seen it, presently remembered it, and could give an opinion as to its value. By the use of lists, nothing more or different was accomplished.

Moreover, we think the procedure followed lay within the discretion of the trial court, and that no prejudicial error ensued. . . . The defense had at its disposal the customary opportunities and all the necessary material to test the witness' recollection and other testimonial qualifications, including the single original longhand list which Farid located, the typewritten lists which she said were made at the time of the events involved, and the lists the prosecution used. It might very well have put Farid through severe cross-examination with respect to each chattel she identified on direct examination, but chose instead to attack the reliability of her memory by other means.

Accordingly, it is our conclusion that the learned trial judge did not abuse his discretion, either in determining that the witnesses testified from present recollection, or in permitting the use of the lists described herein. . . . [T]he judgment of the District Court will be affirmed.

"Perhaps *this* will refresh your memory."

PROBLEM

3.40. An eyewitness to a hit-and-run accident calls his wife fifteen minutes later, tells her the license plate number of the car he saw leave the scene, and asks her to write it down. She does so. Under what circumstances will her note be admissible in a later prosecution of the driver? Under what circumstances may it be shown to the jury? Under what circumstances may it be used to refresh the recollection of the husband or the wife?

7. Business Records

The business records exception to the hearsay rule applies to more than simply "businesses" as that term is usually understood, but it finds its roots in common-law decisions allowing litigants to prove commercial transactions through carefully maintained records rather than by requiring testimony from all of the employees involved. Historically, the exception has been defended by appeal both to the reliability of such records and to the practical necessities of litigation. As with other exceptions to the hearsay rule, opinions differ regarding whether the original rationales for the business records rule justify the exception in its current form.

[F.R.E. 803(6), 803(7); C.E.C. §§1270-1272]

a. Generally

ADVISORY COMMITTEE NOTES TO F.R.E. 803(6)

Exception (6) This represents an area which has received much attention from those seeking to improve the law of evidence. The Commonwealth Fund Act was the result of a study completed in 1927 by a distinguished committee under the chairmanship of Professor Morgan. With changes too minor to mention, it was adopted by Congress in 1936 as the rule for federal courts. 28 U.S.C. § 1732. A number of states took similar action. . . . These reform efforts were largely within the context of business and commercial records, as the kind usually encountered, and concentrated considerable attention upon relaxing the requirement of producing as witnesses, or accounting for the nonproduction of, all participants in the process of gathering, transmitting, and recording information which the common law had evolved as a burdensome and crippling aspect of using records of this type. . . . The element of unusual reliability of business records is said variously to be supplied by systematic checking, by regularity and continuity which produce habits of precision, by actual experience of business in relying upon them, or by a duty to make an accurate record as part of a continuing job or occupation. . . .

STATE v. ACQUISTO

463 A.2d 122 (R.I. 1983)

Weisberger, Justice.

This case comes before us on the defendant's appeal from a judgment of conviction of first-degree sexual assault entered against him in the Superior Court. . . . The defendant presented evidence of alibi. Two of the alibi witnesses were defendant's mother, Mrs. Julia Griffin, and Mrs. Ann Callahan, both of whom were employed as stipendiary volunteers (senior companions) at the Institute of Mental Health (IMH) during the period in issue. . . . [They testified that they saw the defendant at the home he shared with his mother on the morning of September 27, 1979, when the assault took place, and] that they were home that morning since the employees of the IMH were on strike and therefore they were not able to go to work.

In rebuttal the state presented Mrs. Marie C. Judge who testified that she was the custodian of records for the Department of Elderly Affairs. Part of her duties included the handling of payroll records for senior companions. Mrs. Judge testified that she received payroll vouchers from the IMH which were signed by Mrs. Griffin and Mrs. Callahan. These vouchers were offered in evidence and tended to show that Mrs. Griffin and Mrs. Callahan worked during the morning of September 27. These vouchers further indicated that the strike at the IMH was not in progress on September 27 but had in fact occurred the prior week, September 17 through September 19. The defendant challenges the receipt of these records in evidence on the ground that they do not meet the common-law standards for introduction of business records. The defendant cites *Quint v. Pawtuxet Valley Bus Lines*, 114 R.I. 473, 481, 335 A.2d 328, 333 (1975), as setting forth the following common-law requirements for admissibility of business records:

> "The record maker and each human link in the chain of information, if living and competent, had to testify that the entry was made in the regular course of business in his handwriting or under his immediate supervision and each provider of information contained in the report had to testify. If any necessary witness such as the maker was deemed incompetent or was absent from the jurisdiction at trial time, other witnesses had to identify the record and explain how and by whom it was kept. *State v. Mace*, 6 R.I. 85 (1859)."

. . . The restriction of the common law in introduction of business records has been roundly criticized by Professor Wigmore in 5 Wigmore, *Evidence* § 1530 at 451-52 (Chadbourn rev. 1974):

> "In such a case, it should be sufficient if the books were verified on the stand by a supervising officer who knew them to be the books of regular entries kept in that establishment; thus the production on the stand of a battalion of bookkeepers, salesmen, shipping clerks, teamsters, foremen, or other employees, should be dispensed with. . . .
>
> "Such entries are dealt with in that way in the most important undertakings of mercantile and industrial life. They are the ultimate basis of calculation, investment, and general confidence in every business enterprise. Nor does the practical impossibility of obtaining constantly and permanently the verification of every employee affect the trust that is given to such books. It would seem that expedients which the entire commercial world recognizes as safe could be sanctioned, and not discredited, by courts of justice."

Similarly, in commenting upon the common-law requirement of authentication, Professor McCormick suggests that

> "[i]n light of present business practices, the common law requirement is clearly unreasonable. The complex nature of modern business organizations is such that all participants in the preparation of a record can most often not be identified or, if they can be pinpointed, could not reasonably be expected to have any helpful recollection concerning the specific transactions at issue. Moreover, production of the large numbers of participants that would be

required would be a substantial burden on the offering party, a burden not likely to be justified by the benefits to be derived from requiring production of all participants." *McCormick's Handbook of the Law of Evidence* § 312 at 729 (2d ed. Cleary 1972).

A most reasonable balance has been struck in the Federal Rules of Evidence dealing with the introduction of business records. . . . [W]e believe that the common-law requirement adds nothing to the reliability of the record to be introduced, given the business practices of the twentieth century. Therefore, we adopt the standards set forth in Federal Rule 803(6) for the introduction of business records as evidence in criminal cases. . . .

Applying the standards set forth in Federal Rule 803(6), the foundation laid for introduction of these exhibits was adequate. Mrs. Judge was the custodian of the records. She was responsible for administering payroll. The claim for payment made by the two senior companions and approved by their supervisor was the type of information upon which her payroll records and authorization for payment were based. This is not unlike the circumstances described in 5 Wigmore, *supra*, at § 1530, wherein the custodian of records makes entries on the basis of information given by others. The defendant further objects to the receiving of these payroll vouchers into evidence because they were prepared prior to the making up of the payroll. This circumstance does not constitute a violation of the standards set forth in Federal Rule 803(6). It is specifically provided that a memorandum in any form of acts, events, or conditions made "at or near the time by, or from information transmitted by, a person with knowledge," may be admitted into evidence. In the instant case Mrs. Judge testified that although the vouchers were made up in advance, she would be notified before the payroll was completed in the event that any information contained on the voucher should be changed. In this case no such change was transmitted. Consequently, the trial justice was not in error in admitting the payroll vouchers into evidence. . . . [T]he judgment of conviction is affirmed. . . .

ADVISORY COMMITTEE NOTE TO THE 2000 AMENDMENT TO F.R.E. 803(6)

The amendment provides that the foundation requirements of Rule 803(6) can be satisfied under certain circumstances without the expense and inconvenience of producing time-consuming foundation witnesses. Under current law, courts have generally required foundation witnesses to testify. See, e.g., Tongil Co., Ltd. v. Hyundai Merchant Marine Corp., 968 F.2d 999 (9th Cir. 1992)(reversing a judgment based on business records where a qualified person filed an affidavit but did not testify). Protections are provided by the authentication requirements of Rule 902(11) for domestic records, Rule 902(12) for foreign records in civil cases, and 18 U.S.C. § 3505 for foreign records in criminal cases.

b. Qualifying "Businesses"

REPORT OF THE HOUSE JUDICIARY COMMITTEE

H.R. Rep. No. 93-650 (1973)

Rule 803(6) as submitted by the Court permitted a record made "in the course of a regularly conducted activity" to be admissible in certain circumstances. The Committee believed there were insufficient guarantees of reliability in records made in the course of activities falling outside the scope of "business" activities as that term is broadly defined in 28 U.S.C. 1732. Moreover, the Committee concluded that the additional requirement of Section 1732 that it must have been the regular practice of a business to make the record is a necessary further assurance of its trustworthiness. The Committee accordingly amended the Rule to incorporate these limitations.

REPORT OF THE CONFERENCE COMMITTEE

Conf. Rep. No. 93-1597 (1974)

The House bill provides in subsection (6) that records of a regularly conducted "business" activity qualify for admission into evidence as an exception to the hearsay rule. "Business" is defined as including "business, profession, occupation and calling of every kind." The Senate amendment drops the requirement that the records be those of a "business" activity and eliminates the definition of "business." The Senate amendment provides that records are admissible if they are records of a regularly conducted "activity."

The Conference adopts the House provision that the records must be those of a regularly conducted "business" activity. The Conferees changed the definition of "business" contained in the House provision in order to make it clear that the records of institutions and associations like schools, churches and hospitals are admissible under this provision. The records of public schools and hospitals are also covered by Rule 803(8), which deals with public records and reports.

KEOGH v. COMMISSIONER OF INTERNAL REVENUE

713 F.2d 496 (9th Cir. 1983)

DUNIWAY, Circuit Judge:

In this case we review the tax court's finding of income tax deficiencies against a Las Vegas casino employee. . . . Appellant husband here, petitioner in the tax court, was employed at the Dunes Hotel & Country Club, in Las Vegas. He worked in the casino, where he dealt blackjack or ran "big wheel" or roulette games and was known as a 21 dealer. The 21 dealers earned regular wages paid semimonthly. In addition, 21 players sometimes gave them tips or "tokes" in the form of coins or casino chips. . . . The tax court found that during the years in question, 1969-1971, all 21 dealers at the Dunes pooled their tokes, and that the pool was divided equally once a day among all the dealers who had worked during that day's three shifts. . . .

The Commissioner asserted that the Keoghs had underreported tip income in 1969, 1970, and 1971. He calculated Keogh's toke income through a statistical analysis based on entries in a diary kept by one John Whitlock, Jr., not a party to this action, who worked at the Dunes from March 4, 1967 to May 7, 1970. In the diary, the date of the month and the day of the week were listed on the left side of each page, and separate vertical columns were designated "gross," "net," "tax," and "tips." Beginning in January, 1968, there was an additional column designated "F.I.C.A.," and beginning in April, 1969, a further column designated "insurance." Wage entries were made in the notebook approximately every two weeks in amounts that were the same as those in the Dunes' payroll records for Whitlock. An entry of "off," "sick," "vac," or a dollar amount was made in the diary in the "tips" column for each day. . . . [I]t is undisputed that Whitlock had, as the tax court found, "a poor reputation for honesty and truthfulness," was dismissed by the Dunes for unsatisfactory work, and had been convicted, with his wife, of receiving stolen property. . . .

At trial before the tax court, the principal evidence was a photocopy of the Whitlock diary and testimony by Barbara Mikle, by then Whitlock's former wife. Whitlock, though subpoenaed by the Commissioner, failed to appear. . . .

The Whitlock diary, offered in evidence to prove the truth of its contents as they related to tokes received by Dunes 21 dealers, was hearsay and thus inadmissible unless excepted by one or more rules of evidence. F. R. Evid. 801, 802. . . . [W]e find the diary admissible under Rule 803(6). . . .

[The Keoghs argue] that Rule 803(6) does not apply to the diary because it was not a business record. They argue that the diary was Whitlock's personal record, not a record of the business enterprise involved, the Dunes. But Whitlock's diary, even though personal to him, shows every indication of being kept "in the course of" his own "business activity," "occupation, and calling." *See* 4 Weinstein's Evidence § 803(6)[03] (1981 ed.) at 803-155: "[P]ersonal records kept for business reasons may be able to qualify. A housekeeper's records kept neatly and accurately for purposes of balancing bank statements, keeping strict budgets and preparing income tax returns could qualify under the statute."

The reliability usually found in records kept by business concerns may be established in personal business records if they are systematically checked and regularly and continually maintained. *See United States v. Hedman*, 7 Cir., 1980, 630 F.2d 1184, 1197-98 (diary of payoffs by extortion victim); *United States v. McPartlin*, 7 Cir., 1979, 595 F.2d 1321, 1347-1350 (desk calendar-appointment diary, and cases there cited); Weinstein, *supra* (reliability determined from "testimony indicating that they were kept meticulously"); Advisory Committee Note to Rule 803(6). . . .

Here, Mikle testified that she saw Whitlock and only Whitlock make entries in the diary; that he usually made them after night shifts of work; that when he made no entries for three to four days, he would copy entries for those days from a record kept in his wallet; that he usually made no entries in the diary on his days off; and that she understood the diary to contain a record of tokes he received from his work as a dealer. . . .

[T]here is no evidence that Whitlock's motives in making the entries were suspect. The diary contained his own personal financial records; there is no reason put forward for him to have lied to himself. The reliability of the tip entries is corroborated by the fact that other entries corresponded with Dunes' payroll records, and that reliability is not tarnished by the fact that Whitlock, as the Keoghs are alleged to have done, reported to the government smaller amounts of tip income than he in fact received and recorded in the diary. Neither is Rule 803(6) made inapplicable by the fact that Mikle, not Whitlock, testified to lay the foundation for the diary. She testified adequately as to the regularity of the entries.

The Keoghs contend that the testimony of Whitlock as custodian of the diary was required because only he could speak to his reliance on the records kept there. But the record gives us no reason to believe that Whitlock did not rely on his personal financial diary; therefore, we do not find that the tax court abused its discretion in admitting it without Whitlock's personal testimony. . . . Affirmed.

UNITED STATES v. GIBSON

711 F.2d 871 (9th Cir. 1982) (sub nom. United States v. Foster)

ALARCON, Circuit Judge:

[Johnnie Gibson and several codefendants were convicted of heroin trafficking.] . . . Over Gibson's objection, [cooperating prosecution witness Minyon] Logan's ledger was admitted into evidence under the business record exception of Fed. R. Evid. 803(6). The ledger, which contained records of drug transactions, implicated Gibson in the conspiracy. Gibson contends that the ledger was improperly admitted because the records were not kept in the course of regularly conducted business activity and because the entries were untrustworthy.

To be admissible as a business record under Rule 803(6), the record must have been kept in the "regular course" of a business activity. . . . Logan testified that she kept a record of most of her large drug transactions. She stated that it was her regular practice to enter into the ledger the number of balloons that went out on a particular day and how much money she took in. The transactions were recorded contemporaneously, and Logan relied on them. This evidence was sufficient to satisfy Rule 803(6).

The fact that the ledger was an incomplete record of Gibson's drug dealings and contained several blank pages and unrelated entries did not render the ledger inadmissible. The accuracy of the remaining pages was not altered simply because Logan did not record every heroin sale that occurred. Nor does the fact that the entries were made out of sequence destroy their accuracy. The entries were made at or near the time of the events described and they satisfied the regularity requirement. Their sequence was therefore irrelevant.

Gibson argues that the entries were nonetheless untrustworthy. However, because Logan had to rely on the entries, there would have been little reason for her to distort or falsify them. . . . All appellants' convictions on all counts are AFFIRMED.

c. Qualifying Records

PALMER v. HOFFMAN

318 U.S. 109 (1943)

Mr. Justice DOUGLAS delivered the opinion of the Court.

This case arose out of a grade crossing accident which occurred in Massachusetts. . . . The accident occurred on the night of December 25, 1940. On December 27, 1940, the engineer of the train, who died before the trial, made a statement at a freight office of petitioners where he was interviewed by an assistant superintendent of the road and by a representative of the Massachusetts Public Utilities Commission. This statement was offered in evidence by petitioners under the Act of June 20, 1936, 49 Stat. 1561, 28 U.S.C. § 695.[1] They offered to prove (in the language of the Act) that the statement was signed in the regular course of business, it being the regular course of such business to make such a statement. Respondent's objection to its introduction was sustained.

We agree with the majority view below that it was properly excluded. . . . [T]he fact that a company makes a business out of recording its employees' versions of their accidents does not put those statements in the class of records made "in the regular course" of the business within the meaning of the Act. If it did, then any law office in the land could follow the same course, since business as defined in the Act includes the professions. We would then have a real perversion of a rule designed to facilitate admission of records which experience has shown to be quite trustworthy. Any business by installing a regular system for recording and preserving its version of accidents for which it was potentially liable could qualify those reports under the Act. . . . The probability of trustworthiness of records because they were routine reflections of the day to day operations of a business would be forgotten as the basis of the rule. . . . [I]t is manifest that in this case those reports are not for the systematic conduct of the

---

1. "In any court of the United States and in any court established by Act of Congress, any writing or record, whether in the form of an entry in a book or otherwise, made as a memorandum or record of any act, transaction, occurrence, or event, shall be admissible as evidence of said act, transaction, occurrence, or event, if it shall appear that it was made in the regular course of any business, and that it was the regular course of such business to make such memorandum or record at the time of such act, transaction, occurrence, or event or within a reasonable time thereafter. All other circumstances of the making of such writing or record, including lack of personal knowledge by the entrant or maker, may be shown to affect its weight, but they shall not affect its admissibility. The term 'business' shall include business, profession, occupation, and calling of every kind."

enterprise as a railroad business. Unlike payrolls, accounts receivable, accounts payable, bills of lading and the like these reports are calculated for use essentially in the court, not in the business. Their primary utility is in litigating, not in railroading. . . . Affirmed.

LEWIS v. BAKER

526 F.2d 470 (2d Cir. 1975)

WATERMAN, Circuit Judge:

Plaintiff, Clifford J. Lewis, Jr., brought this action . . . alleging he suffered a disabling injury while employed by the Penn Central Railroad. Judgment was entered in favor of defendants after a jury trial. Plaintiff appeals. . . .

On the date of his injury, October 26, 1969, plaintiff was employed as a freight brakeman or car dropper in the Penn Central railroad freight yard in Morrisville, Pennsylvania. . . . [He claimed he was injured when the hand-brake on a boxcar he was moving failed to hold.] At the trial, defendants sought to rebut plaintiff's allegations of a faulty brake with evidence that the brake had functioned properly immediately prior to the accident when the plaintiff tested it, and immediately after the accident when it was checked in connection with the preparation of an accident report. It was the defendants' contention that plaintiff improperly set, or forgot to set, a necessary brake handle. . . .

In support of their interpretation of the events, defendants offered into evidence a "personal injury report" and an "inspection report." Frank Talbott, a trainmaster, testified that the personal injury report was signed by him and prepared under his supervision. The information had been provided to him by William F. Campbell, the night trainmaster. Talbott confirmed the authenticity of the record and testified that he was required to make out such reports of injuries as part of the regular course of business. At the trial David W. Halderman, an assistant general foreman for the defendants, identified the inspection report which had been prepared by Campbell and by Alfred Zuchero, a gang foreman. This report was based upon an inspection of the car Campbell and Zuchero had conducted less than four hours after the accident. Halderman testified that Zuchero was dead and that Campbell was employed by a railroad in Virginia. The latter was thus beyond the reach of subpoena. Halderman also confirmed that following every accident involving injury to an employee his office was required to complete inspection reports, and that such reports were regularly kept in the course of business. Over objection, the court admitted both reports into evidence . . . under the Federal Business Records Act. . . .[1]

---

1. 28 U.S.C. § 1732 provides, insofar as is applicable:

Record made in regular course of business . . .

(a) In any court of the United States and in any court established by Act of Congress, any writing or record, whether in the form of an entry in a book or otherwise, made as a memorandum or record of any act, transaction, occurrence, or event, shall be admissible as evidence of such act, transaction, occurrence, or

Appellant argues . . . the Supreme Court's decision in *Palmer v. Hoffman*, 318 U.S. 109 (1943), precludes their admission into evidence. . . . In *Palmer v. Hoffman*, the engineer preparing the report had been personally involved in the accident, and as Circuit Judge Frank stated in his opinion for the Court of Appeals, the engineer knew "at the time of making it that he [was] very likely, in a probable law suit relating to that accident, to be charged with wrongdoing as a participant in the accident, so that he [was] almost certain, when making the memorandum or report, to be sharply affected by a desire to exculpate himself and to relieve himself or his employer of liability." 129 F.2d 976, 991 (2d Cir. 1942) (italics omitted). Here there could have been no similar motivation on the part of Talbott, Campbell or Zuchero, for not one of them was involved in the accident, or could have possibly been the target of a lawsuit by Lewis. . . . In the absence of a motive to fabricate, a motive so clearly spelled out in *Palmer v. Hoffman*, the holding in that case is not controlling to emasculate the Business Records Act. Therefore the trial court must look to those earmarks of reliability which otherwise establish the trustworthiness of the record. . . .

As we stated in *Taylor v. Baltimore & Ohio R.R. Co.*, [344 F.2d 281 (2d Cir. 1965),] "[i]t would ill become a court to say that the regular making of reports required by law is not in the regular course of business." In addition to their use by the railroad in making reports to the ICC, the reports here were undoubtedly of utility to the employer in ascertaining whether the equipment involved was defective so that future accidents might be prevented. These factors, we think, are sufficient indicia of trustworthiness to establish the admissibility of the reports into evidence under the Federal Business Records Act. . . . Affirmed.

ADVISORY COMMITTEE NOTE TO F.R.E. 803(6)

. . . Amplification of the kinds of activities producing admissible records has given rise to problems which conventional business records by their nature avoid. . . . Entries in the form of opinions were not encountered in traditional business records in view of the purely factual nature of the items recorded, but they are now commonly encountered with respect to medical diagnoses, prognoses, and test results, as well as occasionally in other areas. . . . [T]he rule specifically includes both diagnoses and opinions, in addition to acts, events, and conditions, as proper subjects of admissible entries.

Problems of the motivation of the informant have been a source of difficulty and disagreement. In Palmer v. Hoffman, 318 U.S. 109 (1943),

---

event, if made in regular course of any business, and if it was the regular course of such business to make such memorandum or record at the time of such act, transaction, occurrence, or event or within a reasonable time thereafter.

All other circumstances of the making of such writing or record, including lack of personal knowledge by the entrant or maker, may be shown to affect its weight, but such circumstances shall not affect its admissibility.

The term "business," as used in this section, includes business, profession, occupation, and calling of every kind.

exclusion of an accident report made by the since deceased engineer, offered by defendant railroad trustees in a grade crossing collision case, was upheld. The report was not "in the regular course of business," not a record of the systematic conduct of the business as a business, said the Court. The report was prepared for use in litigating, not railroading. While the opinion mentions the motivation of the engineer only obliquely, the emphasis on records of routine operations is significant only by virtue of impact on motivation to be accurate. Absence of routineness raises lack of motivation to be accurate. The opinion of the Court of Appeals had gone beyond mere lack of motive to be accurate: the engineer's statement was "dripping with motivations to misrepresent." Hoffman v. Palmer, 129 F.2d 976, 991 (2d Cir. 1942). The direct introduction of motivation is a disturbing factor, since absence of motive to misrepresent has not traditionally been a requirement of the rule; that records might be self-serving has not been a ground for exclusion. As Judge Clark said in his dissent, "I submit that there is hardly a grocer's account book which could not be excluded on that basis." A physician's evaluation report of a personal injury litigant would appear to be in the routine of his business. If the report is offered by the party at whose instance it was made, however, it has been held inadmissible, Yates v. Bair Transport, Inc., 249 F. Supp. 681 (S.D.N.Y. 1965), otherwise if offered by the opposite party, Korte v. New York, N.H. & H.R. Co., 191 F.2d 86 (2d Cir. 1951), cert. denied 342 U.S. 868.

The decisions hinge on motivation and which party is entitled to be concerned about it. Professor McCormick believed that the doctor's report or the accident report were sufficiently routine to justify admissibility. Yet hesitation must be experienced in admitting everything which is observed and recorded in the course of a regularly conducted activity. Efforts to set a limit are illustrated by Hartzog v. United States, 217 F.2d 706 (4th Cir. 1954), error to admit worksheets made by since deceased deputy collector in preparation for the instant income tax evasion prosecution, and United States v. Ware, 247 F.2d 698 (7th Cir. 1957), error to admit narcotics agents' records of purchases. . . . Some decisions have been satisfied as to motivation of an accident report if made pursuant to statutory duty, since the report was oriented in a direction other than the litigation which ensued. The formulation of specific terms which would assure satisfactory results in all cases is not possible. Consequently the rule proceeds from the base that records made in the course of a regularly conducted activity will be taken as admissible but subject to authority to exclude if "the sources of information or other circumstances indicate lack of trustworthiness."

Occasional decisions have reached for enhanced accuracy by requiring involvement as a participant in matters reported. . . . The rule includes no requirement of this nature. Wholly acceptable records may involve matters merely observed, e.g. the weather.

The form which the "record" may assume under the rule is described broadly as a "memorandum, report, record, or data compilation, in any form." The expression "data compilation" is used as broadly descriptive of any means of storing information other than the conventional words and figures in written or documentary form. It includes, but is by no means limited to, electronic computer storage. . . .

d. Sources of Information

ADVISORY COMMITTEE NOTE TO F.R.E. 803(6)

. . . Sources of information presented no substantial problem with ordinary business records. All participants, including the observer or participant furnishing the information to be recorded, were acting routinely, under a duty of accuracy, with employer reliance on the result, or in short "in the regular course of business." If, however, the supplier of the information does not act in the regular course, an essential link is broken; the assurance of accuracy does not extend to the information itself, and the fact that it may be recorded with scrupulous accuracy is of no avail. An illustration is the police report incorporating information obtained from a bystander: the officer qualifies as acting in the regular course but the informant does not. The leading case, *Johnson v. Lutz*, 253 N.Y. 124, 170 N.E. 517 (1930), held that a report thus prepared was inadmissible. Most of the authorities have agreed with the decision. The point is not dealt with specifically in the Commonwealth Fund Act, the Uniform Act, or Uniform Rule 63(13). However, Model Code Rule 514 contains the requirement "that it was the regular course of that business for one with personal knowledge . . . to make such a memorandum or record or to transmit information thereof to be included in such a memorandum or record. . . . "The rule follows this lead in requiring an informant with knowledge acting in the course of the regularly conducted activity. . . .

WILSON v. ZAPATA OFF-SHORE CO.

939 F.2d 260 (5th Cir. 1991)

GARWOOD, Circuit Judge:

[Plaintiff Elizabeth Wilson appealed from adverse judgments in her suits against her former employer, Zapata Off-Shore Co., for sex discrimination and emotional distress.] Wilson left Zapata in October 1984 because she was experiencing emotional problems, which she claims were caused by a hostile work environment aboard the rig. She was admitted to Riverside Hospital in Jackson, Mississippi on October 16, 1984, where she was treated for anxiety-related disorders. . . .

Wilson . . . challenges the district court's refusal to exclude portions of hospital records reporting a statement by Wilson's sister, Laird, to a social worker, who recorded that "informant reports that the patient is a habitual liar and has been all of her life." . . . Wilson is correct that the hospital record contains double hearsay. Double hearsay in the context of a business record exists when the record is prepared by an employee with information supplied by another person. If both the source and the recorder of the information, as well as every other participant in the chain producing the record, are acting in the regular course of business, the multiple hearsay is excused by Rule 803(6). *United States v. Baker*, 693 F.2d 183, 188 (D.C. Cir. 1982).

However, if the source of the information is an outsider, as in the facts before us, Rule 803(6) does not, by itself, permit the admission of the business record. The outsider's statement must fall within another hearsay exception to be admissible because it does not have the presumption of accuracy that statements made during the regular course of business have. Further, Federal Rule of Evidence 805 requires that all levels of hearsay satisfy exception hearsay requirements before the statement is admissible.

Rule 803(6) provides a hearsay exception for records kept in the course of *any* regularly conducted business activity, which would include hospitals. . . . The second level of hearsay presents a closer question. The out-of-court statements by Laird were offered to prove the truth of the matter asserted, and thus were classic hearsay. Zapata argues that Laird's statements fall within Fed. R. Evid. 803(4), which excepts from the hearsay rule statements made for purposes of medical diagnosis or treatment. The test, when examining whether statements contained in medical records relating to a patient's condition are admissible hearsay, is whether such statements are of the type pertinent to a physician in providing treatment. Courts have construed Rule 803(4) to include statements made for psychiatric diagnosis. *See, e.g., Morgan v. Foretich*, 846 F.2d 941, 949 (4th Cir. 1988) (allowing statements made by child abuse victim to psychiatrist). Moreover, Rule 803(4) does not always require that the out-of-court statements refer to the condition of the declarant. McCormick, *McCormick on Evidence*, § 292 at pp. 840-41 (1984). It is apparent that the treating psychiatrists in this case were concerned with learning about Wilson's background, lifestyle and history of psychiatric treatment. Further, it was obviously important for the psychiatrists to know whether Wilson was a credible informant. Statements by Wilson's sister, recorded two days after Wilson's admission to the hospital, could be appropriate and helpful background information for the psychiatrists to consider in the diagnosis and treatment of Wilson's complaints. The value of the statements, however, would appear to be somewhat compromised by their total generality and conclusory nature. . . .

We pretermit determination of whether admission of the records was error. Even [if] it were, we will not reverse if we find that the error was harmless. We conclude that it is highly probable that the admission of these medical reports did not affect Wilson's substantial rights. We note that Wilson's sister was called to testify and denied making the statements to the social worker. There was abundant other evidence casting serious doubt on Wilson's credibility, as well as directly contradicting her version of the crucial events on which she based her suit. . . . AFFIRMED.

e. Absence of Record

ADVISORY COMMITTEE NOTE TO F.R.E. 803(7)

Failure of a record to mention a matter which would ordinarily be mentioned is satisfactory evidence of its nonexistence. While probably not hearsay as defined in Rule 801, supra, decisions may be found which class the evidence not only as hearsay but also as not within any exception. In order to set the question at rest in favor of admissibility, it is specifically treated here.

UNITED STATES v. GENTRY

925 F.2d 186 (7th Cir. 1991)

EASTERBROOK, Circuit Judge.

[Defendant Kevin Gentry] told fellow employees—plus the security force of the mall where he worked—that he had bit into a pin when he ate M & M candy bought from a vending machine. One of Gentry's fellow employees found some metal embedded in the candy. Sheriff's deputies who investigated the report found Gentry's claim hard to believe and asked him to take a polygraph test. Gentry did; the examiner concluded that he was lying; after the examiner switched off the machine, Gentry confessed that he had put the pin in the candy and made the report to get attention. He was prosecuted for [making a false report of food tampering in violation of 18 U.S.C.] § 1365(c)(1) and received a sentence of 12 months' imprisonment. . . .

Gentry . . . objects to testimony from an employee of the manufacturer that there were no other reports of pins in M & M candy. The testimony was relevant; it implies that the pin came from Gentry rather than the factory (or a tamperer other than Gentry). And Fed. R. Evid. 803(7) allows this use of business records to show the nonoccurrence of an event. . . . The conviction is affirmed. . . .

PROBLEM

3.41. An author hurt in an automobile collision sues the other driver for negligence and seeks compensation for money she lost because her injuries prevented her from finishing a novel. She seeks to introduce copies of daily e-mail messages she sent to her brother before the accident, describing her progress on the novel. Do the messages qualify as business records?

8. Public Records

The public records exception of Federal Rule of Evidence 803(8) is narrower than the business records exception codified in Rule 803(6), and in fact consists of three separate exceptions. Federal courts have struggled with the wording of Rule 803(8), and with the problem of public records that fail to satisfy the requirements of that exception but fall within another exception. The latter problem arises particularly often in connection with the business records rule, because most if not all public agencies qualify as "businesses" for purposes of that exception.

In reading the materials below, consider how the Confrontation Clause, as reinterpreted by the Supreme Court in *Crawford v. Washington*, now affects the admissibility of public records in criminal cases.

[F.R.E. 803(8)-803(10); C.E.C. §§1280, 1281, 1284]

ADVISORY COMMITTEE NOTE TO F.R.E. 803(8)

Public records are a recognized hearsay exception at common law and have been the subject of statues without number. . . . Justification for the exception is the assumption that a public official will perform his duty properly and the unlikelihood that he will remember details independently of the record. As to items (a) and (b), further support is found in the reliability factors underlying records of regularly conducted activities generally.

(a) Cases illustrating the admissibility of records of the office's or agency's own activities are numerous. Chesapeake & Delaware Canal Co. v. United States, 250 U.S. 123 (1919), Treasury records of miscellaneous receipts and disbursements; Howard v. Perrin, 200 U.S. 71 (1906), General Land Office records; Ballew v. United States, 160 U.S 187 (1895), Pension Office records.

(b) Cases sustaining admissibility of records of matters observed are also numerous. United States v. Van Hook, 284 F.2d 489 (7th Cir. 1960), remanded for resentencing 365 U.S. 609, letter from induction officer to District Attorney, pursuant to army regulations, stating fact and circumstances of refusal to be inducted; T'Kach v. United States, 242 F.2d 937 (5th Cir.1957), affidavit of White House personnel officer that search of records showed no employment of accused, charged with fraudulently representing himself as an envoy of the President; Minnehaha County v. Kelley, 150 F.2d 356 (8th Cir. 1945); Weather Bureau records of rainfall; United States v. Meyer, 113 F.2d 387 (7th Cir. 1940), cert. denied 311 U.S. 706, map prepared by government engineer from information furnished by men working under his supervision.

(c) The more controversial area of public records is that of the so-called "evaluative" report. The disagreement among the decisions has been due in part, no doubt, to the variety of situations encountered, as well as to differences in principle. . . . Various kinds of evaluative reports are admissible under federal statutes. . . . While these statutory exceptions to the hearsay rule are left undisturbed, Rule 802, the willingness of Congress to recognize a substantial measure of admissibility for evaluative reports is a helpful guide.

Factors which may be of assistance in passing upon the admissibility of evaluative reports include: (1) the timeliness of the investigation, (2) the special skill or experience of the official, (3) whether a hearing was held and the level at which conducted, (4) possible motivation problems suggested by Palmer v. Hoffman, 318 U.S. 109 (1943). Others no doubt could be added.

The formulation of an approach which would give appropriate weight to all possible factors in every situation is an obvious impossibility. Hence the rule, as in Exception (6), assumes admissibility in the first instance but with ample provision for escape if sufficient negative factors are present. In one respect, however, the rule with respect to evaluative reports under item (c) is very specific: they are admissible only in civil cases and against the government in criminal cases in view of the almost certain collision with confrontation rights which would result from their use against the accused in a criminal case.

BEECH AIRCRAFT CORP. v. RAINEY

488 U.S. 153 (1988)

Justice BRENNAN delivered the opinion of the Court.

In this action we address a longstanding conflict among the Federal Courts of Appeals over whether Federal Rule of Evidence 803(8)(C), which provides an exception to the hearsay rule for public investigatory reports containing "factual findings," extends to conclusions and opinions contained in such reports. . . . This litigation stems from the crash of a Navy training aircraft at Middleton Field, Alabama, on July 13, 1982, which took the lives of both pilots on board, Lieutenant Commander Barbara Ann Rainey and Ensign Donald Bruce Knowlton. . . . The two pilots' surviving spouses brought a product liability suit against petitioners Beech Aircraft Corporation, the plane's manufacturer, and Beech Aerospace Services, which serviced the plane under contract with the Navy. The plaintiffs alleged that the crash had been caused by a loss of engine power, known as "rollback," due to some defect in the aircraft's fuel control system. The defendants, on the other hand, advanced the theory of pilot error, suggesting that the plane had stalled during [an] abrupt avoidance maneuver.

. . . One piece of evidence presented by the defense was an investigative report prepared by Lieutenant Commander William Morgan on order of the training squadron's commanding officer and pursuant to authority granted in the Manual of the Judge Advocate General. This "JAG Report," completed during the six weeks following the accident, was organized into sections labeled "finding of fact," "opinions," and "recommendations," and was supported by some 60 attachments. The "finding of fact" included statements like the following:

"13. At approximately 1020, while turning crosswind without proper interval, 3E955 crashed, immediately caught fire and burned. . . .
"27. At the time of impact, the engine of 3E955 was operating but was operating at reduced power."

Among his "opinions" Lieutenant Commander Morgan stated, in paragraph 5, that due to the deaths of the two pilots and the destruction of the aircraft "it is almost impossible to determine exactly what happened to Navy 3E955 from the time it left the runway on its last touch and go until it impacted the ground." He nonetheless continued with a detailed reconstruction of a possible set of events, based on pilot error, that could have caused the accident. The next two paragraphs stated a caveat and a conclusion:

"6. Although the above sequence of events is the most likely to have occurred, it does not change the possibility that a 'rollback' did occur.
"7. The most probable cause of the accident was the pilots [*sic*] failure to maintain proper interval."

The trial judge initially determined, at a pretrial conference, that the JAG Report was sufficiently trustworthy to be admissible, but that it "would be admissible only on its factual findings and would not be admissible insofar as any opinions or conclusions are concerned." The day before trial, however, the court reversed itself and ruled, over the plaintiffs' objection, that certain of the conclusions would be admitted. Accordingly, the court admitted most of the report's "opinions," including the first sentence of paragraph 5 about the impossibility of determining exactly what happened, and paragraph 7, which opined about failure to maintain proper interval as "[t]he most probable cause of the accident." On the other hand, the remainder of paragraph 5 was barred as "nothing but a possible scenario," and paragraph 6, in which investigator Morgan refused to rule out rollback, was deleted as well.[3]

. . . Following a 2-week trial, the jury returned a verdict for petitioners. A panel of the Eleventh Circuit reversed and remanded for a new trial. . . . Considering itself bound by the Fifth Circuit precedent of *Smith v. Ithaca Corp.*, 612 F.2d 215 (1980), the panel agreed with Rainey's argument that Federal Rule of Evidence 803(8)(C), which excepts investigatory reports from the hearsay rule, did not encompass evaluative conclusions or opinions. Therefore, it held, the "conclusions" contained in the JAG Report should have been excluded. . . .

Federal Rule of Evidence 803 provides that certain types of hearsay statements are not made excludable by the hearsay rule, whether or not the declarant is available to testify. Rule 803(8) defines the "public records and reports" which are not excludable, as follows:

"Records, reports, statements, or data compilations, in any form, of public offices or agencies, setting forth (A) the activities of the office or agency, or (B) matters observed pursuant to duty imposed by law as to which matters there was a duty to report, . . . or (C) in civil actions and proceedings and against the Government in criminal cases, factual findings resulting from an investigation made pursuant to authority granted by law, unless the sources of information or other circumstances indicate lack of trustworthiness."

Controversy over what "public records and reports" are made not excludable by Rule 803(8)(C) has divided the federal courts from the beginning. In the present litigation, the Court of Appeals followed the "narrow" interpretation of *Smith v. Ithaca, supra*, which held that the term "factual findings" did not encompass "opinions" or "conclusions." Courts of Appeals other than those of the Fifth and Eleventh Circuits, however, have generally adopted a broader interpretation. For example,

3. The record gives no indication why paragraph 6 was deleted. Neither at trial nor on appeal have respondents raised any objection to the deletion of paragraph 6.

the Court of Appeals for the Sixth Circuit, in *Baker v. Elcona Homes Corp.*, 588 F.2d 551 (1978), cert. denied, 441 U.S. 933 (1979), held that "factual findings admissible under Rule 803(8)(C) may be those which are made by the preparer of the report from disputed evidence . . . ."[6] The other Courts of Appeals that have squarely confronted the issue have also adopted the broader interpretation. We agree and hold that factually based conclusions or opinions are not on that account excluded from the scope of Rule 803(8)(C).

. . . We begin with the language of the Rule itself. Proponents of the narrow view have generally relied heavily on a perceived dichotomy between "fact" and "opinion" in arguing for the limited scope of the phrase "factual findings." *Smith v. Ithaca Corp.* contrasted the term "factual findings" in Rule 803(8)(C) with the language of Rule 803(6) (records of regularly conducted activity), which expressly refers to "opinions" and "diagnoses." "Factual findings," the court opined, must be something other than opinions.

For several reasons, we do not agree. In the first place, it is not apparent that the term "factual findings" should be read to mean simply "facts" (as opposed to "opinions" or "conclusions"). A common definition of "finding of fact" is, for example, "[a] conclusion by way of reasonable inference from the evidence." Black's Law Dictionary 569 (5th ed. 1979). To say the least, the language of the Rule does not compel us to reject the interpretation that "factual findings" includes conclusions or opinions that flow from a factual investigation. Second, we note that, contrary to what is often assumed, the language of the Rule does not state that "factual findings" are admissible, but that "*reports* . . . setting forth . . . factual findings" (emphasis added) are admissible. On this reading, the language of the Rule does not create a distinction between "fact" and "opinion" contained in such reports.

Turning next to the legislative history of Rule 803(8)(C), we find no clear answer to the question of how the Rule's language should be interpreted. Indeed, in this litigation the legislative history may well be at the origin of the dispute. Rather than the more usual situation where a court must attempt to glean meaning from ambiguous comments of legislators who did not focus directly on the problem at hand, here the Committees in both Houses of Congress clearly recognized and expressed their opinions on the precise question at issue. Unfortunately, however, they took diametrically opposite positions. Moreover, the two Houses made no effort to reconcile their views, either through changes in the Rule's language or through a statement in the Report of the Conference Committee.

---

6. *Baker* involved a police officer's report on an automobile accident. While there was no direct witness as to the color of the traffic lights at the moment of the accident, the court held admissible the officer's conclusion on the basis of his investigations at the accident scene and an interview with one of the drivers that "apparently . . . unit#2 . . . entered the intersection against a red light."

The House Judiciary Committee, which dealt first with the proposed rules after they had been transmitted to Congress by this Court, included in its Report but one brief paragraph on Rule 803(8):

"The Committee approved Rule 803(8) without substantive change from the form in which it was submitted by the Court. The Committee intends that the phrase 'factual findings' be strictly construed and that evaluations or opinions contained in public reports shall not be admissible under this Rule." H.R. Rep. No. 93-650, p. 14 (1973).

The Senate Committee responded at somewhat greater length, but equally emphatically:

"The House Judiciary Committee report contained a statement of intent that 'the phrase "factual findings" in subdivision (c) be strictly construed and that evaluations or opinions contained in public reports shall not be admissible under this rule.' The committee takes strong exception to this limiting understanding of the application of the rule. We do not think it reflects an understanding of the intended operation of the rule as explained in the Advisory Committee notes to this subsection. . . . We think the restrictive interpretation of the House overlooks the fact that while the Advisory Committee assumes admissibility in the first instance of evaluative reports, they are not admissible if, as the rule states, 'the sources of information or other circumstances indicate lack of trustworthiness'. . . .

"The committee concludes that the language of the rule together with the explanation provided by the Advisory Committee furnish sufficient guidance on the admissibility of evaluative reports." S. Rep. No. 93-1277, p. 18 (1974).

Clearly this legislative history reveals a difference of view between the Senate and the House that affords no definitive guide to the congressional understanding. It seems clear however that the Senate understanding is more in accord with the wording of the Rule and with the comments of the Advisory Committee.[9]

The Advisory Committee's comments are notable, first, in that they contain no mention of any dichotomy between statements of "fact" and "opinions" or "conclusions." What was on the Committee's mind was simply whether what it called "evaluative reports" should be admissible. Illustrating the previous division among the courts on this subject, the Committee cited numerous cases in which the admissibility of such reports had been both sustained and denied. It also took note of various federal statutes that made certain kinds of evaluative reports admissible in evidence. What is striking about all of these examples is that these were *reports that stated conclusions. E.g., Moran v. Pittsburgh-Des Moines Steel Co.*, 183 F.2d 467, 472-473 (CA3 1950) (report of Bureau of Mines concerning the cause of a gas tank explosion admissible); *Franklin v. Skelly Oil Co.*, 141 F.2d 568, 571-572 (CA10 1944) (report of state fire marshal on the cause of a gas explosion inadmissible); 42 U.S.C. § 269(b) (bill of health by appropriate official admissible as prima facie evidence of vessel's sanitary

9. As Congress did not amend the Advisory Committee's draft in any way that touches on the question before us, the Committee's commentary is particularly relevant in determining the meaning of the document Congress enacted.

history and condition). The Committee's concern was clearly whether reports of this kind should be admissible. Nowhere in its comments is there the slightest indication that it even considered the solution of admitting only "factual" statements from such reports. Rather, the Committee referred throughout to "reports," without any such differentiation regarding the statements they contained. What the Committee referred to in the Rule's language as "reports . . . setting forth . . . factual findings" is surely nothing more or less than what in its commentary it called "evaluative reports." Its solution as to their admissibility is clearly stated in the final paragraph of its report on this Rule. That solution consists of two principles: First, "the rule . . . assumes admissibility in the first instance. . . ." Second, it provides "ample provision for escape if sufficient negative factors are present."

That "provision for escape" is contained in the final clause of the Rule: evaluative reports are admissible "unless the sources of information or other circumstances indicate lack of trustworthiness." This trustworthiness inquiry—and not an arbitrary distinction between "fact" and "opinion"—was the Committee's primary safeguard against the admission of unreliable evidence, and it is important to note that it applies to all elements of the report. Thus, a trial judge has the discretion, and indeed the obligation, to exclude an entire report or portions thereof—whether narrow "factual" statements or broader "conclusions"—that she determines to be untrustworthy. Moreover, safeguards built into other portions of the Federal Rules, such as those dealing with relevance and prejudice, provide the court with additional means of scrutinizing and, where appropriate, excluding evaluative reports or portions of them. And of course it goes without saying that the admission of a report containing "conclusions" is subject to the ultimate safeguard—the opponent's right to present evidence tending to contradict or diminish the weight of those conclusions.

Our conclusion that neither the language of the Rule nor the intent of its framers calls for a distinction between "fact" and "opinion" is strengthened by the analytical difficulty of drawing such a line. It has frequently been remarked that the distinction between statements of fact and opinion is, at best, one of degree:

> "All statements in language are statements of opinion, i.e., statements of mental processes or perceptions. So-called 'statements of fact' are only more specific statements of opinion. What the judge means to say, when he asks the witness to state the facts, is: 'The nature of this case requires that you be more specific, if you can, in your description of what you saw.' " W. King & D. Pillinger, Opinion Evidence in Illinois 4 (1942) (footnote omitted), quoted in 3 J. Weinstein & M. Berger, Weinstein's Evidence § 701[01], p. 701-6 (1988).

See also E. Cleary, McCormick on Evidence 27 (3d ed. 1984) ("There is no conceivable statement however specific, detailed and 'factual', that is not in some measure the product of inference and reflection as well as observation and memory");R. Lempert & S. Saltzburg, A Modern Approach to Evidence 449 (2d ed. 1982) ("A factual finding, unless it is a simple report of something observed, is an opinion as to what more basic facts imply"). Thus, the traditional requirement that lay witnesses give statements of fact rather than opinion may be considered, "[l]ike the hearsay and original documents rules . . . a 'best evidence' rule." McCormick, Opinion Evidence in Iowa, 19 Drake L. Rev. 245,246 (1970).

In the present action, the trial court had no difficulty in admitting as a factual finding the statement in the JAG Report that "[a]t the time of impact, the engine of 3E955 was operating but was operating at reduced power." Surely this "factual finding" could also be characterized as an opinion, which the investigator presumably arrived at on the basis of clues contained in the airplane wreckage. Rather than requiring that we draw some inevitably arbitrary line between the various shades of fact/opinion that invariably will be present in investigatory reports, we believe the Rule instructs us—as its plain language states—to admit "reports . . . setting forth . . . factual findings." The Rule's limitations and safeguards lie elsewhere: First, the requirement that reports contain factual findings bars the admission of statements not based on factual investigation. Second, the trustworthiness provision requires the court to make a determination as to whether the report, or any portion thereof, is sufficiently trustworthy to be admitted.

A broad approach to admissibility under Rule 803(8)(C), as we have outlined it, is also consistent with the Federal Rules' general approach of relaxing the traditional barriers to "opinion" testimony. Rules 702-705 permit experts to testify in the form of an opinion, and without any exclusion of opinions on "ultimate issues." And Rule 701 permits even a lay witness to testify in the form of opinions or inferences drawn from her observations when testimony in that form will be helpful to the trier of fact. We see no reason to strain to reach an interpretation of Rule 803(8)(C) that is contrary to the liberal thrust of the Federal Rules.

We hold, therefore, that portions of investigatory reports otherwise admissible under Rule 803(8)(C) are not inadmissible merely because they state a conclusion or opinion. As long as the conclusion is based on a factual investigation and satisfies the Rule's trustworthiness requirement, it should be admissible along with other portions of the report.[13] As the trial judge in this action determined that certain of the JAG Report's conclusions were trustworthy, he rightly allowed them to be admitted into evidence. We therefore reverse the judgment of the Court of Appeals in respect of the Rule 803(8)(C) issue. . . .

UNITED STATES v. OATES

560 F.2d 45 (2d Cir. 1977)

WATERMAN, Circuit Judge:

This is an appeal from a judgment of the United States District Court for the Eastern District of New York convicting appellant, following a six-day

---

13. We emphasize that the issue in this litigation is whether Rule 803(8)(C) recognizes any difference between statements of "fact" and "opinion." There is no question here of any distinction between "fact" and "law." We thus express no opinion on whether legal conclusions contained in an official report are admissible as "findings of fact" under Rule 803(8)(C).

jury trial, of possession of heroin with intent to distribute, and of conspiracy to commit that substantive offense. . . . [Defendant claims] that the trial court incorrectly admitted into evidence at trial the official report and work-sheet of the chemist who analyzed the substance seized from [codefendant Isaac] Daniels. . . .

At trial the government had planned upon calling as one of its final witnesses a Mr. Milton Weinberg, a retired United States Customs Service chemist who allegedly had analyzed the white powder seized from Isaac Daniels. It seems that Mr. Weinberg had been present on the day the trial had been scheduled to commence but he was not able to testify then because of a delay occasioned by the unexpected length of the pretrial suppression hearing. . . . [I]t appears that Weinberg called the United States Attorney's office to inform them of his unavailability and that subsequently the Assistant United States Attorney attempted to speak to Weinberg personally but was able, for some reason, to speak only to Weinberg's wife who advised that Weinberg had "some type of bronchial infection." . . .

When Weinberg became "unavailable," the government decided to call another Customs chemist, Shirley Harrington, who, although she did not know Weinberg personally, was able to testify concerning the regular practices and procedures used by Customs Service chemists in analyzing unknown substances. Through Mrs. Harrington the government was successful in introducing Exhibits 13 and 12 which purported to be, respectively, the handwritten worksheet used by the chemist analyzing the substance seized from Daniels and the official typewritten report of the chemical analysis. . . .

Although at trial the government placed some reliance on FRE 803(8), the so-called "public records and reports" exception to exclusion, in its brief in this court it completely ignores the provision, apparently abandoning any reliance on it for reasons we shall discuss below. Instead, it urges us to find that the challenged evidence falls easily within the scope of what has traditionally been labeled the "business records exception" to the hearsay exclusionary rule, the codification of which in the Federal Rules of Evidence is found in FRE 803(6). . . . [A]lthough as a general rule there is no question that hearsay evidence failing to meet the requirements of one exception may nonetheless satisfy the standards of another exception, and there thus might be no need to examine FRE 803(8) at all, we agree with appellant that both the language of Rule 803(8) and the congressional intent, as gleaned from the explicit language of the rule and from independent sources, which impelled that language have impact that extends beyond the immediate confines of exception (8) itself. . . .

That the chemist's report and worksheet could not satisfy the requirements of the "public records and reports" exception seems evident merely from examining, on its face, the language of FRE 803(8). . . . While there may be no sharp demarcation between the records covered by exception 8(B) and those referenced in exception 8(C), and indeed there may in some cases be actual overlap, we conclude without hesitation that surely the language of item (C) is applicable to render the chemist's documents inadmissible as evidence in this case, and they might also be within the ambit of the terminology of item (B), a claim appellant argues to us persuasively.

It is manifest from the face of item (C) that "factual findings resulting from an investigation made pursuant to authority granted by law" are not shielded from the exclusionary effect of the hearsay rule by "the public records exception" if the government seeks to have those "factual findings" admitted against the accused in a criminal case. It seems indisputable to us that the chemist's official report and worksheet in the case at bar can be characterized as reports of "factual findings resulting from an investigation made pursuant to authority granted by law." The "factual finding" in each instance, the conclusion of the chemist that the substance analyzed was heroin, obviously is the product of an "investigation," supposedly involving on the part of the chemist employment of various techniques of scientific analysis. Furthermore, in view of its reliance on the chemist's report at trial and its representation to the district court that "chemical analys[e]s of unidentified substances are indeed a regularly conducted activity of the Customs laboratory of Customs chemists," the government here is surely in no position to dispute the fact that the analyses regularly performed by United States Customs Service chemists on substances lawfully seized by Customs officers are performed pursuant to authority granted by law.

Though with less confidence, we believe that the chemist's documents might also fail to achieve status as public records under FRE 803(8)(B) because they are records of "matters observed by police officers and other law enforcement personnel." . . . [T]he difficult question would be whether the chemists making the observations could be regarded as "other law enforcement personnel." We think this phraseology must be read broadly enough to make its prohibitions against the use of government-generated reports in criminal cases coterminous with the analogous prohibitions contained in FRE 803(8)(C). We would thus construe "other law enforcement personnel" to include, at the least, any officer or employee of a governmental agency which has law enforcement responsibilities. Applying such a standard to the case at bar, we easily conclude that full-time chemists of the United States Customs Services are "law enforcement personnel." . . .

Our conclusion that the chemist's report and worksheet do not satisfy the standards of FRE 803(8) comports perfectly with what we discern to be clear legislative intent not only to exclude such documents from the scope of FRE 803(8) but from the scope of FRE 803(6) as well. . . . [A]n overriding concern of the Advisory Committee was that the rules be formulated so as to avoid impinging upon a criminal defendant's right to confront the witnesses against him. . . . This preoccupation with preserving the confrontation rights of criminal defendants was shared by a Congress which established enhanced protection for those rights by substantially amending the proposed language of FRE 803(8)(B). An amendment offered by Representative David Dennis added important qualifying language to item (B) which before the amendment deemed as "public records" under FRE 803(8) "matters observed pursuant to duty imposed by law as to which matters there was a duty to report." The amendment qualified the foregoing language by adding "excluding, however, in criminal cases matters observed by police officers and other law enforcement personnel." In the debate that followed the offer of this amendment, the accused's right to confront the witnesses against him was advanced as the impetus for the proposal. . . . [We] think it manifest that it was the clear intention of Congress to make evaluative and law enforcement reports absolutely inadmissible against defendants in criminal cases. Just as importantly, it must have been the unquestionable belief of Congress that the language of FRE 803(8)(B) and (C) accomplished that very result. . . .

[T]he only way to construe FRE 803(6) so that it is reconcilable with this intended effect is to interpret FRE 803(6) and the other hearsay exceptions in such a way that police and evaluative reports not satisfying the standards of FRE 803(8)(B) and (C) may not qualify for admission under FRE 803(6) or any of the other exceptions to the hearsay rule. . . . The prosecution's utilization of any hearsay exception to achieve admission of evaluative and law enforcement reports would serve to deprive the accused of the opportunity to confront his accusers as effectively as would reliance on a "public records" exception. . . .

We are not the first court to indulge in a less than literal construction of a hearsay exception so as to effectuate congressional intent. An issue addressed by the D.C. Circuit in *United States v. Smith*, [521 F.2d 957 (D.C. Cir. 1975),] was whether the police reports of FRE 803(8)(B) are admissible against the government. While conceding that "[o]n its face, 803(8)(B) appears to [say that they are not, the court was] convinced, however, that 803(8)(B) should be read, in accordance with the obvious intent of Congress and in harmony with 803(8)(C) to authorize the admission of the reports of police officers and other law enforcement personnel at the request of the defendant in a criminal case." The "obvious intent of Congress" in enacting FRE 803(8)(B) was found to be that "use of reports against defendants would be unfair." "Since there [was] no apparent reason to allow defendants to use the reports admitted by 803(8)(C) but not those governed by 803(8)(B)[, the court concluded] that a police report . . . is an exception to the new hearsay rules when introduced at the request of the defense." . . . Our approach in the case at bar closely parallels that taken by the D. C. Circuit in *Smith*. . . .

[I]n criminal cases reports of public agencies setting forth matters observed by police officers and other law enforcement personnel and reports of public agencies setting forth factual findings resulting from investigations made pursuant to authority granted by law cannot satisfy the standards of any hearsay exception if those reports are sought to be introduced against the accused. Inasmuch as the chemist's documents here can be characterized as governmental reports which set forth matters observed by law enforcement personnel or which set forth factual findings resulting from an authorized investigation, they were incapable of qualifying under any of the exceptions to the hearsay rule specified in FRE 803 and 804. The documents were crucial to the government's case, they were, of course, hearsay, and, inasmuch as they were ineligible to qualify for any exception to the hearsay rule, their admission at trial against appellant was prejudicial error. . . . [A]ccordingly, we reverse the judgment of conviction and remand for a new trial.

UNITED STATES v. BROWN

9 F.3d 907 (11th Cir. 1993)

PER CURIAM:

The appellant, Cary Brown, appeals his conviction and sentence for possession of a firearm by a convicted felon, in violation of 18 U.S.C. § 922(g)(1). . . .

On February 11, 1991, Miami Police Officers Raymond Socorro and Wayne Cooper approached the appellant, Cary Brown, at an intersection in Coconut Grove, Florida. After following Brown on foot for several blocks, Officer Cooper called out to him, and Brown began to run. In the ensuing chase, Officer Socorro saw the defendant pull an object from his waistband and throw it to the ground. Socorro retrieved the object, a .38 caliber Taurus revolver, but was unable to apprehend Brown. Socorro took the weapon to the Miami Police Department's property unit, and a property receipt was prepared. Because no arrest was made and the suspect was unknown, the property was classified as found property, rather than evidence.

About two weeks later, Officers Socorro and Cooper identified Brown at a nearby intersection. The officers arrested Brown and took him into custody. Following the arrest, Officer Socorro never returned to the property room to reclassify the Taurus revolver as evidence. As a result, the weapon was later destroyed by the police department, pursuant to standard policy.

. . . Over Brown's objection, the government introduced as evidence the property receipt for the weapon. The government also called Willard Delancy, a crime scene technician, who testified that he inspected the weapon and found no latent fingerprints. Brown's sole defense was the alibi of his mother, who testified that Brown was in his room on the night of February 11 at the time in question. . . .

We reject Brown's argument that the government failed to establish a proper foundation for admitting the property receipt under the business records exception. Before introducing the property receipt into evidence, the government established that its regular and customary procedure was to fill out a property receipt for any type of evidence. The police custodian testified that for every piece of evidence, he filled out a property receipt containing the case number, date, location the property was found, and a description of the evidence. Brown's argument that the government must establish that it was customary to list the make and serial number of the gun takes the foundation requirement to unwarranted extremes.

Brown also argues that Rule 803(6) cannot be used to admit evidence that would otherwise be barred by the language of Rule 803(8)(B) excluding from the public records exception matters observed by law enforcement personnel. The former Fifth Circuit has held that the business records exception cannot be used as a "back door" to introduce evidence that would not be admissible under Rule 803(8)(B). *United States v. Cain*, 615 F.2d 380, 382 (5th Cir. 1980) (per curiam); *accord United States v. Oates*, 560 F.2d 45, 68 (2d Cir. 1977). At trial, however, Brown failed to raise this basis for his objection. Therefore, we review this issue on appeal only for plain error.

Although Rule 803(6) cannot be used as a back door to admit evidence excluded by Rule 803(8)(B), we believe that the property receipt in the instant case is not the type of evidence contemplated by the exclusion of Rule 803(8)(B). In excluding from the public records exception those matters observed by police officers and other law enforcement personnel, Congress was concerned about the adversarial nature of the relationship between law enforcement officials and defendants in criminal proceedings. S. Rep. No. 1277, 93d Cong., 2d Sess. (1974). Congress was aware of the inherent bias that might exist in reports prepared by law enforcement officials in anticipation of trial. . . .

Many courts, however, have drawn a distinction between police records prepared in a routine, non-adversarial setting and those resulting from a more subjective investigation and evaluation of a crime. *E.g., United States v. Quezada*, 754 F.2d 1190, 1194 (5th Cir. 1985); *United States v. Grady*, 544 F.2d 598, 604 (2d Cir. 1976). As the Fifth Circuit stated in *Quezada*:

> In the case of documents recording routine, objective observations, made as part of the everyday function of the preparing official or agency, the factors likely to cloud the perception of an official engaged in the more traditional law enforcement functions of observation and investigation of crime are simply not present. Due to the lack of any motivation on the part of the recording official to do other than mechanically register an unambiguous factual matter . . . , such records are, like other public documents, inherently reliable.

We are persuaded by this reasoning. The police custodian in the instant case had no incentive to do anything other than mechanically record the relevant information on the property receipt. We believe that this is the type of reliable public record envisioned by the drafters of Rule 803(8). We therefore hold that the trial court's admission of the property receipt did not constitute plain error. . . . [Affirmed.]

UNITED STATES v. OROZCO

590 F.2d 789 (9th Cir. 1979)

CHOY, Circuit Judge:

Appellants Jose Liva-Corona and Maria Orozco appeal from their convictions for possession of cocaine and heroin with intent to distribute in violation of 21 U.S.C. § 841(a)(1). [The heroin was found in a car Liva-Corona had been seen exiting. When officers had approached Liva-Corona, Orozco had stepped out of a second car, parked in a nearby driveway. Orozco had told the officers she owned both cars, and that she and

Liva-Corona had just returned from a double date in the car parked in the driveway.] On appeal, appellants contend . . . that the trial court abused its discretion by admitting into evidence computer data cards from the Treasury Enforcement Communications System (TECS). The TECS cards indicated that the car in the driveway, said to have been used on a double date in Los Angeles on the night of the arrest, had been recorded crossing the Mexican border at San Ysidro on the same night. . . .

At trial, customs officials explained the procedure for recording the license plate numbers of vehicles passing through the border at San Ysidro. The procedure is a relatively simple one. As vehicles approach the border station, the primary customs inspector enters the license plate number into a computer. The computer then scans its system to determine whether that license number has appeared within the previous 72-hour period.

While the district court admitted these computer cards under the "business records" exception, we feel that the proper inquiry is directed toward the "public records" exception of rule 803(8). While governmental functions could be included within the broad definition of "business" in rule 803(6), such a result is obviated by rule 803(8), which is the "business records" exception for public records such as those in issue here. . . .

In excluding "matters observed by . . . law enforcement personnel" from the coverage of [803(8)(B)], Congress did not intend to exclude records of routine, nonadversarial matters such as those in question here. The legislative history indicates that

> [o]stensibly, the reason for this exclusion is that observations by police officers at the scene of the crime or the apprehension of the defendant are not as reliable as observations by public officials in other cases because of the adversarial nature of the confrontation between the police and the defendant in criminal cases.

S. Rep. No. 1277, 93d Cong., 2d Sess. The customs inspector is one of the "law enforcement personnel" included in rule 803(8). However, the simple recordation of license numbers of all vehicles which pass his station is not of the adversarial confrontation nature which might cloud his perception. The Second Circuit has noted that

> [i]n adopting this exception, Congress was concerned about prosecutors attempting to prove their cases in chief simply by putting into evidence police officers' reports of their contemporaneous observations of crime. . . . The reports admitted here were not of this nature; they did not concern observations by the [police] of the appellants' commission of crimes. Rather, they simply related to the routine function of recording serial numbers. . . .

United States v. Grady, 544 F.2d 598, 604 (2d Cir. 1976).

Therefore, the TECS cards were admissible "unless the sources of information or other circumstances indicate lack of trustworthiness." Fed. R. Evid. 803(8). There was testimony at trial that as the license numbers are entered, they appear on the computer's screen, allowing the inspector to see if a mistake has been made in his entry. The customs agents have no motive to fabricate entries into the computer and the possibility of an inaccurate entry is no greater here than it would be in any other recording system. The reliability of computers has been demonstrated in similar contexts. Since nothing about this recording procedure indicates a "lack of trustworthiness," we hold that the district court did not abuse its discretion in admitting the TECS cards into evidence. . . . AFFIRMED.

STATE v. FORTE

629 S.E.2d 137 (N.C. 2006)

EDMUNDS, Justice.

[Defendant Linwood Earl Forte was convicted of sexually assaulting and murdering three elderly women, Eliza Jones, Hattie Bonner, and Thelma Bowen.] The jury recommended a sentence of death . . . and the trial court entered judgment accordingly. . . .

Analysis of the DNA samples obtained in each of these incidents indicated that one person was responsible for all three attacks. During the 1990s, defendant was incarcerated on other, unrelated charges and his DNA was recorded in the SBI database. In 2001, after defendant had been released, his DNA was matched with the DNA recovered from the unsolved cases. . . .

Defendant . . . contends that the trial court erred in allowing the State to introduce certain [State Bureau of Investigation] reports as substantive evidence because the law enforcement investigator who prepared the reports did not testify. The investigator in question, SBI Special Agent D.J. Spittle, . . . would receive samples of blood and bodily fluids sent to the laboratory for analysis, examine the samples and identify the fluids, and then refer the material to other investigators in the laboratory for further analysis. His records reflected both the results of his investigation and his disposition of the evidence. . . . Agent Spittle left his employment with the SBI in 2001 and did not testify at defendant's trial. His reports were introduced into evidence through Agent Nelson, who had been Agent Spittle's supervisor in the 1990s. . . .

Under the Supreme Court's analysis [in *Crawford*], the reports at issue here are not testimonial. They do not fall into any of the categories that the Supreme Court defined as unquestionably testimonial. These unsworn reports, containing the results of Agent Spittle's objective analysis of the evidence, along with routine chain of custody information, do not bear witness against defendant. Instead, they are neutral, having the power to exonerate as well as convict. Although we acknowledge that the reports were prepared with the understanding that eventual use in court was possible or even probable, they were not prepared exclusively for trial and Agent Spittle had no interest in the outcome of any trial in which the records might be used.

Consistent with this interpretation, the Supreme Court in *Crawford* indicated in dicta that business records are not testimonial. ("Most of the hearsay exceptions covered statements that by their nature were not testimonial—for example, business records or statements in furtherance of a conspiracy.") The distinction between business records and testimonial evidence is readily seen. Among other attributes, business records are neutral, are created to serve a number of purposes important to the creating organization, and are not inherently subject to manipulation or abuse. . . .

Agent Nelson was Agent Spittle's supervisor and was responsible for creating and implementing laboratory polices regarding record-keeping. Agent Nelson testified that Agent Spittle created the reports contemporaneously with his work as part of the regular practice of the agency and within the ordinary course of agency business. Accordingly, we agree with the trial court that the reports are business records under Rule 803(6) [of the North Carolina Rules of Evidence].

However, our determination that the reports in question can be considered business records does not end our inquiry. Under [North Carolina Rule of Evidence] 803(8),

> [t]he following are not excluded by the hearsay rule, even though the declarant is available as a witness: . . .
>   (8) Public Records and Reports. Records, reports, statements, or data compilations, in any form, of public offices or agencies, setting forth (A) the activities of the office or agency, or (B) matters observed pursuant to duty imposed by law as to which matters there was a duty to report, excluding, however, in criminal cases matters observed by police officers and other law-enforcement personnel, or (C) in civil actions and proceedings and against the State in criminal cases, factual findings resulting from an investigation made pursuant to authority granted by law, unless the sources of information or other circumstances indicate lack of trustworthiness.

The SBI reports in question also fall under the definition of public records set out in this rule, and "[p]ublic records and reports that are not admissible under Exception (8) are not admissible as business records under Exception (6)." Rule 803(8) Cmt. As a result, we must determine whether these reports are admissible under Rule 803(8) before we can decide whether they are admissible as business records.

Defendant contends that the provision in Rule 803(8)(C) that findings from an investigation made under authority of law are admissible "against the State" means that these laboratory reports are inadmissible when offered by the State against defendant. However, in interpreting the public records exception to the hearsay rule, the Oregon Court of Appeals held that

> in adopting FRE 803(8)(B), Congress did not intend to change the common law rule allowing admission of public records of purely "ministerial observations." Rather, Congress intended to prevent prosecutors from attempting to prove their cases through police officers' reports of their observations during the investigation of crime. *United States v. Grady*, 544 F.2d 598, 604 (2d Cir. 1976). We infer that the state legislature adopted [Oregon Evidence Code Section] 803(8)(b) with the same intent.

State v. Smith, 675 P.2d 510, 512 (Ore. App. 1984). We cited this language with approval in reaching a similar result as to business records in a case dealing with reports of breathalyzer testing. *State v. Smith*, 323 S.E.2d 316, 327-28 (N.C. 1984); *see also Crawford*, 541 U.S. at 68 ("Where nontestimonial hearsay is at issue, it is wholly consistent with the Framers' design to

afford the States flexibility in their development of hearsay law. . . .").
Accordingly, if Agent Spittle's reports fall under this exception for "purely
'ministerial observations,'" they are not inadmissible under either Rule
803(6) or 803(8).

Here, the reports concern routine, nonadversarial matters. Although
the record is silent, common experience tells us that such reports are
prepared for a number of purposes, including statistical analysis and construction of databases. Thus, potential use in court was only one purpose
among several served by the creation and compilation of Agent Spittle's
reports. Agent Spittle's analysis of the evidence on hand also facilitated
further examination of the evidence within the SBI laboratory. Therefore,
these reports are records of purely ministerial observations that do not
offend the public records exception and were properly admitted as business
records. . . . [Affirmed in relevant part.]

HINOJOS-MENDOZA v. PEOPLE

169 P.3d 662 (Colo. 2007)

Justice Rice delivered the Opinion of the Court.

Hinojos-Mendoza was convicted of unlawful possession with intent
to distribute a schedule II controlled substance, cocaine (more than one
thousand grams), and sentenced to 16 years in the Department of Corrections. At Hinojos-Mendoza's trial, the People introduced into evidence a
Colorado Bureau of Investigation lab report that identifies the substance
found in Hinojos-Mendoza's vehicle to be cocaine. The lab report lists
Hinojos-Mendoza's name under a section entitled "suspect(s)." The
report describes the exhibit at issue as a "tan tape wrapped block containing 1004.5 grams of compressed white powder." Under the "results"
section, the report states: "[a]nalysis disclosed the presence of cocaine,
schedule II."

The People introduced the lab report into evidence without calling as a
witness the technician who prepared the report. Defense counsel objected
to the admission of the report on general hearsay grounds. . . . The trial
court . . . overruled the objection and admitted the report pursuant
to . . . [Colorado Revised Statutes] section 16-3-309(5), which states in relevant part:

> Any report or copy thereof . . . of the criminalistics laboratory shall be
> received in evidence in any court . . . in the same manner and with the
> same force and effect as if the employee or technician of the criminalistics
> laboratory who accomplished the requested analysis, comparison, or identi-
> fication had testified in person. Any party may request that such employee or
> technician testify in person at a criminal trial on behalf of the state before a
> jury or to the court, by notifying the witness and other party at least ten days
> before the date of such criminal trial.

. . . Hinojos-Mendoza argues that lab reports are testimonial
under *Crawford,* and therefore that section 16-3-309(5) is facially

unconstitutional. . . . The court of appeals concluded that the lab report is nontestimonial, and thus does not implicate *Crawford.* The court of appeals based its analysis in part on its holding that a lab report qualifies as a business record under the Colorado rules of evidence. The court further noted that Hinojos-Mendoza did not dispute at trial that the substance was cocaine but only disputed the weight of the cocaine. Because weighing an incoming substance is "a routine laboratory procedure," the technician who prepared the report would "merely have authenticated the document." Finally, the court of appeals distinguished cases holding similar lab reports to be testimonial by finding that the report in this case is not an affidavit, was not "prepared at the express direction of the prosecutor for the purpose of litigation," and contains "no directly accusatorial statements against [Hinojos-Mendoza]." We disagree.

Some state courts have held that laboratory reports constitute nontestimonial hearsay after *Crawford. See, e.g., . . . Perkins v. State*, 897 So. 2d 457, 462-65 (Ala. Crim. App. 2004) (autopsy report); *People v. Johnson*, 121 Cal. App. 4th 1409, 18 Cal. Rptr. 3d 230, 233 (Cal. Ct. App. 2004) (lab report analyzing a rock of cocaine); *Commonwealth v. Verde*, 444 Mass. 279, 827 N.E.2d 701, 706 (Mass. 2005) (drug certificate); *State v. Dedman*, 136 N.M. 561, 102 P.3d 628, 635-36 (N.M. 2004) (blood alcohol report). Many of these courts based their conclusion on dictum in *Crawford* which suggested that, historically, business records fall outside the scope of testimonial hearsay. ("Most of the hearsay exceptions [in 1791] covered statements that by their nature were not testimonial—for example, business records or statements in furtherance of a conspiracy.")

These decisions, as well as the court of appeals' opinion in this case, erroneously focus on the reliability of the reports and whether the reports fall within the business or public records hearsay exceptions. *See, e.g., Perkins*, 897 So. 2d at 464 (autopsy report nontestimonial because it fell under a firmly rooted hearsay exception); *Johnson*, 18 Cal. Rptr. 3d at 233 (lab report was simply "routine documentary evidence"); *Verde*, 827 N.E.2d at 705 ("Certificates of chemical analysis . . . merely state the results of a well-recognized scientific test. . . ."); *Dedman*, 102 P.3d at 635 (blood alcohol report admissible as a public record). The Supreme Court in *Crawford*, however, abrogated reliability as the proper inquiry and divorced Confrontation Clause analysis from the rules of evidence. . . . Moreover, *Crawford's* dictum regarding the historic business records hearsay exception does not mean that any document which falls within the modern-day business records exception is automatically nontestimonial.

We therefore find that the better reasoned cases reject the reliability and business record rationale, and instead hold that laboratory reports are testimonial statements subject to *Crawford. See, e.g., Thomas*, 914 A.2d at 12-15 (DEA chemist's report identifying substance as cocaine); *People v. Lonsby*, 707 N.W.2d 610, 618-21 (Mich. Ct. App. 2005) (notes and lab report of crime lab serologist); *State v. Caulfield*, 722 N.W.2d 304, 309-10 (Minn. 2006) (lab report identifying substance as cocaine); *March*, 216 S.W.3d at 665-67 (lab report identifying substance as cocaine); *City of Las Vegas v. Walsh*, 124 P.3d 203, 207-08 (Nev. 2005) (affidavit of registered nurse who completed blood draw); *State v. Kent*, 918 A.2d 626, 636-40 (N.J. Super. Ct.

App. Div. 2007) (State Police chemist's lab report and a blood test certificate); *State v. Smith*, No. 1-05-39 (Ohio Ct. App. Apr. 3, 2006) (lab reports identifying substance as crack cocaine); *State v. Miller*, 144 P.3d 1052, 1058 (Or. Ct. App. 2006) (lab reports identifying the presence of methamphetamine); *Deener v. State*, 214 S.W.3d 522, 526 (Tex. Crim. App. 2006) (chain of custody affidavit and certificate of analysis identifying substance as cocaine).

... [T]he specific lab report at issue in this case ... was prepared at the direction of the police and a copy of the report was transmitted to the district attorney's office. There can be no serious dispute that the sole purpose of the report was to analyze the substance found in Hinojos-Mendoza's vehicle in anticipation of criminal prosecution. The report states "offense: 3530—cocaine—sell" and lists Hinojos-Mendoza as the suspect. Moreover, the report was introduced at trial to establish the elements of the offense with which Hinojos-Mendoza was charged. Under such circumstances, the lab report is testimonial in nature. *Crawford*, 541 U.S. at 2 (including in the core class of testimonial statements those made under circumstances "which would lead an objective witness reasonably to believe that the statement would be available for use at a later trial"). ...

[W]e hold that the lab report is testimonial hearsay under *Crawford*, and we therefore reverse that portion of the court of appeals' opinion. Nonetheless, we hold that Hinojos-Mendoza waived his right to confront the technician who prepared the report at trial by failing to comply with [Colorado Revised Statutes] section 16-3-309(5), [which requires a party to object at least ten days prior to trial to the introduction of a lab technician's report in lieu of the technician's in-court testimony]. ... The court of appeals' holding that the trial court did not err in admitting the lab report without the testimony of the technician who prepared the report is therefore affirmed on other grounds.

9. Former Testimony

Federal Rule of Evidence 804 collects several exceptions to the hearsay rule that traditionally have applied only when, for any of several specified reasons, the declarant is unavailable to testify in the trial in which his or her statements are offered as evidence. The first of these exceptions pertains to testimony previously given by the declarant in another trial or proceeding—including a deposition or earlier hearing in the same case. The precise circumstances in which Rule 804 allows the introduction of former testimony remains, in some respects, controversial.

One confusion should be avoided from the outset. The breadth of the former testimony exception depends in part on whether the proceeding in which the exception is invoked is criminal or civil. What matters is the nature of the *second* proceeding, not the nature of the proceeding in which the declarant originally testified. The exception can be invoked in a criminal case only if the criminal defendant was a party to the earlier proceeding, and had an opportunity and a "similar motive" to cross-examine the now unavailable declarant. Even if the rules themselves did not impose this restriction, the Confrontation Clause would, because whatever else counts as "testimonial" within the meaning of *Crawford v. Washington* and *Davis v. Washington*, actual testimony in an earlier proceeding plainly falls within that category.

[F.R.E. 804(A) & (B)(1); C.E.C. §§1290-1292]

ADVISORY COMMITTEE NOTE TO F.R.E. 804

. . . Rule 803, supra, is based upon the assumption that a hearsay statement falling within one of its exceptions possesses qualities which justify the conclusion that whether the declarant is available or unavailable is not a relevant factor in determining admissibility. The instant rule proceeds upon a different theory: hearsay which admittedly is not equal in quality to testimony of the declarant on the stand may nevertheless be admitted if the declarant is unavailable and if his statement meets a specified standard. The rule expresses preferences: testimony given on the stand in person is preferred over hearsay, and hearsay, if of the specified quality, is preferred over complete loss of the evidence of the declarant. The exceptions evolved at common law with respect to declarations of unavailable declarants furnish the basis for the exceptions enumerated in the proposal. . . .

Former testimony does not rely upon some set of circumstances to substitute for oath and cross-examination, since both oath and opportunity to cross-examine were present in fact. The only missing one of the ideal conditions for the giving of testimony is the presence of trier and opponent ("demeanor evidence"). This is lacking with all hearsay exceptions. Hence it may be argued that former testimony is the strongest hearsay and should be included under Rule 803, supra. However, opportunity to observe demeanor is what in a large measure confers depth and meaning upon oath and cross-examination. Thus in cases under Rule 803 demeanor lacks the significance which it possesses with respect to testimony. In any event, the tradition, founded in experience, uniformly favors production of the witness if he is available. The exception indicates continuation of the policy. This preference for the presence of the witness is apparent also in rules and statutes on the use of depositions, which deal with substantially the same problem. . . .

The common law did not limit the admissibility of former testimony to that given in an earlier trial of the same case, although it did require identity of issues as a means of insuring that the former handling of the witness was the equivalent of what would now be done if the opportunity were presented. Modern decisions reduce the requirement to "substantial" identity. Since identity of issues is significant only in that it bears on motive and interest in developing fully the testimony of the witness, expressing the matter in the latter terms is preferable. . . .

As a further assurance of fairness in thrusting upon a party the prior handling of the witness, the common law also insisted upon identity of parties, deviating only to the extent of allowing substitution of successors in a narrowly construed privity. Mutuality as an aspect of identity is now generally discredited, and the requirement of identity of the offering party disappears except as it might affect motive to develop the testimony. The question remains whether strict identity, or privity, should continue as a requirement with respect to the party against whom offered. The rule departs to the extent of allowing substitution of one with the right and opportunity to develop the testimony with similar motive and interest. This position is supported by modern decisions. . . .

ROGER C. PARK, DAVID P. LEONARD & STEVEN H. GOLDBERG, EVIDENCE LAW

§7.47, at 328-330 (1998)

A typical instance of the operation of the former testimony exception can arise after a case has been reversed on appeal and remanded for a new trial. If a witness at the first trial is unavailable for the second, then the witness' testimony is admissible under this exception.

When the testimony is offered in the form of a transcript of the prior trial, there are two levels of hearsay. First, the transcript is the statement of the court reporter about what was said on the witness stand at the prior trial. The public records exception creates an exception for this statement. Many jurisdictions have statutes that provide specific exceptions for statements of court reporters. Second, the witness' testimony at the prior trial is also hearsay, at least under the federal definition. The present exception applies to allow it to be received.

Former testimony often comes into evidence through some route other than this exception. For example, former testimony can be used to impeach a witness with a prior inconsistent statement . . . . Federal Rule of Evidence 801(d)(1)(A) provides the basis for receiving the testimony. Similarly, former testimony of the opposing party is admissible against that party under Rule 801(d)(2) without the need for laying the foundation for the current exception. . . .

UNITED STATES v. BOLLIN

264 F.3d 391 (4th Cir. 2001)

CYNTHIA HOLCOMB HALL, Senior Circuit Judge.

[Defendant Gary Bollin was convicted of participating in an investment fraud scheme.] Bollin contends that the district court abused its discretion when it allowed the Government to present a redacted version of his grand jury testimony but refused to allow him to present the omitted portions under the rule of completeness or the former testimony exception to the hearsay rule. We find no abuse of discretion.

Federal Rule of Evidence 804(b)(1) provides an exception to the hearsay rule for the former testimony of a declarant where the declarant is unavailable as a witness.[16] A declarant is "unavailable" when the declarant "is exempted by ruling of the court on the ground of privilege from testifying concerning the subject matter of the declarant's statement." Bollin contends that he was "unavailable" because he had invoked his Fifth Amendment privilege against self-incrimination.

A criminal defendant who invokes his Fifth Amendment privilege makes himself unavailable to any other party. Rule 804(a) provides, however, that "[a] declarant is not unavailable as a witness if exemption, refusal, claim of lack of memory, inability, or absence is due to the procurement or wrongdoing of the proponent of a statement for the purpose of preventing the witness from attending or testifying." By invoking his Fifth Amendment privilege, Bollin made himself unavailable for the purpose of preventing his testimony, and he therefore cannot invoke the exception in Rule 804(b)(1). *Accord United States v. Peterson*, 100 F.3d 7, 13 (2d Cir. 1996) (holding that a defendant who exercises his privilege not to testify at a second trial of his case is not entitled to introduce the testimony he gave at the first trial); *United States v. Kimball*, 15 F.3d 54, 55-56 (5th Cir. 1994) (same).

Bollin identifies several portions of his grand jury testimony that he contends should have been admitted under [the "rule of completeness" codified in Federal Rule of Evidence 106]. We have reviewed Bollin's grand jury testimony as admitted and his unredacted grand jury testimony. Like the district court, we conclude that the omitted testimony was not necessary to avoid misleading the jury or otherwise place the admitted testimony in context. The fact that some of the omitted testimony arguably was exculpatory does not, without more, make it admissible under the rule of completeness. . . . *AFFIRMED*.

KIRK v. RAYMARK INDUSTRIES, INC.

61 F.3d 147 (3d Cir. 1995)

COWEN, Circuit Judge.

. . . Alfred Kirk ("decedent"), a retired painter, died on July 5, 1988 at the age of 65 from malignant asbestos-induced mesothelioma. Mrs. Sarah Kirk ("Kirk"), suing on behalf of herself and her deceased husband's estate, filed this diversity action against eight defendants, including Owens-Corning Fiberglas Corporation ("Owens-Corning"). Kirk alleged that her husband's mesothelioma was caused by exposure to dust from asbestos products during his employment at the New York Shipyard in Camden, New Jersey, during the late 1950's and early 1960's. . . .

---

16. Bollin also argues that his grand jury statements are not hearsay. His statements to the grand jury were made out of court, and Bollin would introduce them to prove the truth of the matter asserted. They are hearsay. *See* Fed. R. Evid. 801(c). The statements were admissible by the Government as admissions under Rule 801(d)(2).

During the liability phase of the trial, Owens-Corning offered the expert testimony of Dr. Harry Demopoulos to prove that the overwhelming majority of asbestos-induced mesotheliomas are caused by crocidolite asbestos fiber. This testimony supported Owens-Corning's defense that its product, Kaylo, which did not contain crocidolite fiber, could not have caused the decedent's mesothelioma. Over Owens-Corning's objection, Kirk was permitted to read to the jury the prior trial testimony of Dr. Louis Burgher from an unrelated New Jersey State Court asbestos action in 1992. In that case, Dr. Burgher had been an expert witness for Owens-Corning and testified on cross-examination that it was possible for mesothelioma to be caused by chrysotile fibers contaminated with tremolite. Kirk was clearly attempting to discredit Owens-Corning's defense offered through Dr. Demopoulos by revealing to the jury that Owens-Corning's expert witness in a previous case voiced a different and contradictory opinion as to which asbestos fibers cause mesothelioma. . . .

Owens-Corning argues that the district court erred in allowing the jury to hear this evidence in light of the fact that it was hearsay. Although the record is at best vague as to what the district court's basis was for allowing such testimony, Kirk attempts to justify its admission under two distinct theories—either the testimony was not hearsay pursuant to Rule 801(d)(2)(C) of the Federal Rules of Evidence or it was hearsay, but subject to an exception pursuant to Rule 804(b)(1).[18]

Kirk first attempts to justify the district court's admission of the prior trial testimony of Dr. Burgher by arguing it is an admission by a party opponent since it is a statement by a person authorized by Owens-Corning to speak concerning mesothelioma and is thus not hearsay. *See* Fed. R. Evid. 801(d)(2)(C). . . . Because an expert witness is charged with the duty of giving *his or her* expert *opinion* regarding the matter before the court, we fail to comprehend how an expert witness, who is not an agent of the party who called him, can be authorized to make an admission for that party. . . . Accordingly, we find Dr. Burgher's prior trial testimony to be hearsay in the context of the present trial.

Because the testimony of Dr. Burgher is hearsay, we must next inquire whether it falls within any of the hearsay exceptions enumerated in the Federal Rules of Evidence. Kirk argues that Dr. Burgher's testimony falls within the former testimony hearsay exception of Rule 804(b)(1). . . . [I]t is the proponent of the statement offered under Rule 804 who bears the burden of proving the unavailability of the declarant. We can find nothing in the record that indicates any "reasonable means" employed by Kirk to procure the services of Dr. Burgher so that he might testify at trial. *See McCormick* [*on Evidence*] § 253, at 134 [(4th ed. 1992)] (mere absence of the declarant, standing alone, does not establish unavailability); *see also Moore v. Mississippi*

---

18. Alternatively, Kirk argues that assuming *arguendo* it was error to admit the testimony of Dr. Burgher, it was harmless error because the weight of the medical testimony of Kirk's other witnesses was overwhelming. In light of our decision to remand for a new trial because the jury was improperly constituted, we need not address whether any evidentiary errors may be harmless.

Valley State University, 871 F.2d 545, 552 (5th Cir. 1989) (deposition inadmissible in civil trial where no evidence to establish unavailability offered).

Kirk claims that Dr. Burgher, who is a resident of Nebraska, was beyond her ability to subpoena and was thus unavailable. However, Kirk made no independent attempt to contact Dr. Burgher, offer him his usual expert witness fee, and request his attendance at trial. Because Dr. Burgher was never even as much as contacted, Kirk has failed to prove that she used "reasonable means" to enlist his services. . . . [Reversed.]

CLAY v. JOHNS-MANVILLE SALES CORP.

722 F.2d 1289 (6th Cir. 1984)

GEORGE CLIFTON EDWARDS, JR., Circuit Judge.

In these two cases plaintiffs John Ed Clay and Curtis Bailey, each joined by his wife, brought actions for damages against defendants Johns-Manville Sales Corporation and Raybestos-Manhattan, Inc., on the basis of products liability claims resulting from plaintiffs' exposure to asbestos containing products manufactured by the defendants. The cases were tried in the United States District Court for the Eastern District of Tennessee and ended in jury verdicts for the defendants.

Appellants urge that . . . the District Judge erred in excluding a deposition taken from a witness, Dr. Kenneth Wallace Smith, in *DeRocco v. Forty-eight Installation, Inc.*, No. 7880 (W.D. Pa. 1974). At the time of the *DeRocco* proceeding, Dr. Smith was 63 years of age and had acquired his knowledge about asbestos disease in the employment of the Johns-Manville Corporation, the largest asbestos manufacturer in the field. Serving Johns-Manville during a good portion of his 22 years of employment as the only full-time physician in the organization, Dr. Smith's deposition is peculiarly relevant to the extent of the knowledge possessed by manufacturers of the hazards of asbestos containing products during the years when appellants Clay and Bailey allege they were exposed to asbestos.

Dr. Smith had died before the trial of this case. The key question in relation to the admissibility of this evidence is posed by the language of Rule 804(b)(1) of the Federal Rules of Evidence, which [exempts from the hearsay rule, when the declarant is unavailable, testimony] "given as a witness at another hearing of the same or a different proceeding, or in a deposition taken in compliance with law in the course of the same or another proceeding, if the party against whom the testimony is now offered, or, in a civil action or proceeding, a predecessor in interest, had an opportunity and similar motive to develop the testimony by direct, cross, or redirect examination."

To ascertain the meaning of "predecessor in interest," an examination of legislative history is necessary. As originally proposed by the Supreme Court, Rule 804(b)(1) would have admitted prior testimony of an unavailable witness if the party against whom it is offered or a person "with a motive and interest" similar to him had an opportunity to examine that witness. The House of Representatives substituted the current "predecessor in interest" language. The House Committee on the Judiciary offered the following explanation for the alteration:

> The Committee considered that it is generally unfair to impose upon the party against whom the hearsay evidence is being offered responsibility for the manner in which the witness was previously handled by another party. The sole exception to this, in the Committee's view, is when a party's predecessor in interest in a civil action or proceeding had an opportunity and similar motive to examine the witness. The Committee amended the Rule to reflect these policy determinations.

H.R. Rep. No. 650, [93d Cong., 1st Sess. 15 (1973)].

Although the Senate accepted the change proposed by the House, the Senate Committee on the Judiciary made the following observation about the import of the House actions: . . .

> The House amended the rule to apply only to a party's predecessor in interest. Although the committee recognizes considerable merit to the rule submitted by the Supreme Court, a position which has been advocated by many scholars and judges, we have concluded that the difference between the two versions is not great and we accept the House amendment.

S. Rep. No. 1277, 93d Cong., 2d Sess. 28 (1974).

We join the Third Circuit in agreeing with the Senate Committee that the difference between the ultimate revision and the Rule, as originally proposed, is "not great." *Lloyd v. American Export Lines, Inc.*, 580 F.2d 1179, 1185 (3d Cir.), *cert. denied*, 439 U.S. 969 (1978). Accordingly, we adopt the position taken by the *Lloyd* court which it expressed in the following language:

> While we do not endorse an extravagant interpretation of who or what constitutes a "predecessor in interest," we prefer one that is realistically generous over one that is formalistically grudging. We believe that what has been described as "the practical and expedient view" expresses the congressional intention: "if it appears that in the former suit a party having a like motive to cross-examine about the same matters as the present party would have, was accorded an adequate opportunity for such examination, the testimony may be received against the present party." Under these circumstances, the previous party having like motive to develop the testimony about the same material facts is, in the final analysis, a predecessor in interest to the present party.

See also Rule v. International Association of Bridge, Structural Ornamental Iron Workers, Local 396, 568 F.2d 558, 569 (8th Cir. 1977); *Weinstein & Berger, Evidence* § 804(b)(1) [04] at 804-67 (1969) ("[C]ases decided since the enactment of Rule 804(b)(1) for the most part indicate a reluctance to interpret 'predecessor in interest' in its old, narrow, and substantive law sense, of privity"). *Contra In re IBM Peripheral EDP Devices Antitrust Litigation*, 444 F. Supp. 110 (N.D. Cal. 1978).

Our examination of the record submitted in this case satisfies us that defendants in the DeRocco case had a similar motive in confronting Dr. Smith's testimony, both in terms of appropriate objections and searching cross-examination, to that which Raybestos has in the current litigation. . . . [Reversed and remanded for retrial.]

GLEN WEISSENBERGER, THE FORMER TESTIMONY HEARSAY EXCEPTION: A STUDY IN RULEMAKING, JUDICIAL REVISIONISM, AND THE SEPARATION OF POWERS

67 N.C. L. Rev. 295, 316, 320 (1989)

[T]he House left the term "predecessor in interest" undefined. As a result, courts have been inconsistent in their interpretations of this language—at times to the point of ignoring it. Initial interpretations of language by commentators suggested that the "predecessor in interest" language denotes the "traditional rule," which at common law meant privity. As Professor Lilly explains:

> Although the phrase "predecessor in interest" (which the courts frequently use interchangeably with the phrase "persons in privity") has an exasperating inexactness about it, the expression generally refers to the predecessor from whom the present party received the right, title, interest or obligation that is at issue in the current litigation. For example, a decedent is a predecessor in interest to ("in privity with") both his personal representative and those, such as heirs and legatees, who take from him; so, too, is a grantor of property a predecessor to his grantee, as is a principal to his surety.

Professor Lilly's interpretation of "predecessor in interest" is consistent with the House committee's overriding policy emphasis on fairness in modifying the advisory committee's version of rule 804(b)(1), which contained no such limitation. . . .

While numerous federal courts have followed the *Lloyd* reasoning . . . judicial interpretations of rule 804(b)(1) have been far from uniform. Some courts have emphasized that Congress intended rule 804(b)(1) to be strictly construed because of fairness considerations. Other courts have not specifically focused on the legislative history of rule 804(b)(1) or expressly followed *Lloyd*, but have excluded prior testimony evidence on the basis of absence of the appropriate motive. Other courts have concluded that former testimony may be admitted when a substantial identity of issues existed in the two actions, coupled with a similar motive and meaningful opportunity to cross examine the witness. . . .

UNITED STATES v. SALERNO

505 U.S. 317 (1992)

Justice THOMAS delivered the opinion of the Court.

Federal Rule of Evidence 804(b)(1) states an exception to the hearsay rule that allows a court, in certain instances, to admit the former testimony of an unavailable witness. We must decide in this case whether the Rule permits a criminal defendant to introduce the grand jury testimony of a witness who asserts the Fifth Amendment privilege at trial.

The seven respondents, Anthony Salerno, Vincent DiNapoli, Louis DiNapoli, Nicholas Auletta, Edward Halloran, Alvin O. Chattin, and Aniello

Migliore, allegedly took part in the activities of a criminal organization known as the Genovese Family of La Cosa Nostra (Family) in New York City. In 1987, a federal grand jury in the Southern District of New York indicted the respondents and four others on the basis of these activities. The indictment charged the respondents with a variety of federal offenses, including 41 acts constituting a "pattern of illegal activity" in violation of the Racketeer Influenced and Corrupt Organizations Act (RICO), 18 U.S.C. § 1962(b).

Sixteen of the alleged acts involved fraud in the New York construction industry in the 1980's. According to the indictment and evidence later admitted at trial, the Family used its influence over labor unions and its control over the supply of concrete to rig bidding on large construction projects in Manhattan. The Family purportedly allocated contracts for these projects among a so-called "Club" of six concrete companies in exchange for a share of the proceeds.

Much of the case concerned the affairs of the Cedar Park Concrete Construction Corporation (Cedar Park). Two of the owners of this firm, Frederick DeMatteis and Pasquale Bruno, testified before the grand jury under a grant of immunity. In response to questions by the United States, they repeatedly stated that neither they nor Cedar Park had participated in the Club. At trial, however, the United States attempted to show that Cedar Park, in fact, had belonged to the Club by calling two contractors who had taken part in the scheme and by presenting intercepted conversations among the respondents. The United States also introduced documents indicating that the Family had an ownership interest in Cedar Park.

To counter the United States' evidence, the respondents subpoenaed DeMatteis and Bruno as witnesses in the hope that they would provide the same exculpatory testimony that they had presented to the grand jury. When both witnesses invoked their Fifth Amendment privilege against self-incrimination and refused to testify, the respondents asked the District Court to admit the transcripts of their grand jury testimony. . . . The District Court refused. . . . It observed that Rule 804(b)(1) permits admission of former testimony against a party at trial only when that party had a "similar motive to develop the testimony by direct, cross, or redirect examination." The District Court held that the United States did not have this motive, stating that the "motive of a prosecutor in questioning a witness before the grand jury in the investigatory stages of a case is far different from the motive of a prosecutor in conducting the trial." A jury subsequently convicted the respondents of the RICO counts and other federal offenses.

The United States Court of Appeals for the Second Circuit reversed, holding that the District Court had erred in excluding DeMatteis' and Bruno's grand jury testimony. Although the Court of Appeals recognized that "the government may have had no motive . . . to impeach . . . Bruno or DeMatteis" before the grand jury, it concluded that "the government's motive in examining the witnesses . . . was irrelevant." The Court of Appeals decided that, in order to maintain "adversarial fairness" Rule 804(b)(1)'s similar motive element should "evaporat[e]" when the Government obtains immunized testimony in a grand jury proceeding from a witness who refuses to testify at trial. We granted certiorari, and now reverse and remand. . . .

When Congress enacted the prohibition against admission of hearsay in Rule 802, it placed 24 exceptions in Rule 803 and 5 additional exceptions in Rule 804. Congress thus presumably made a careful judgment as to what hearsay may come into evidence and what may not. To respect its determination, we must enforce the words that it enacted. The respondents, as a result, had no right to introduce DeMatteis' and Bruno's former testimony under Rule 804(b)(1) without showing a "similar motive." This Court cannot alter evidentiary rules merely because litigants might prefer different rules in a particular class of cases.

The respondents' argument for a different result takes several forms. They first assert that adversarial fairness requires us to infer that Rule 804(b)(1) contains implicit limitations. They observe, for example, that the Advisory Committee Note to Rule 804 makes clear that the former testimony exception applies only to statements made under oath or affirmation, even though the Rule does not state this restriction explicitly. The respondents maintain that we likewise may hold that Rule 804(b)(1) does not require a showing of similar motive in all instances.

The respondents' example does not persuade us to change our reading of Rule 804(b)(1). If the Rule applies only to sworn statements, it does so not because adversarial fairness implies a limitation, but simply because the word "testimony" refers only to statements made under oath or affirmation. See Black's Law Dictionary 1476 (6th ed. 1990). We see no way to interpret the text of Rule 804(b)(1) to mean that defendants sometimes do not have to show "similar motive."

The respondents also assert that courts often depart from the Rules of Evidence to prevent litigants from presenting only part of the truth. For example, citing *United States v. Miller*, 600 F.2d 498 (CA5 1979), the respondents maintain that, although parties may enjoy various testimonial privileges, they can forfeit these privileges by "opening the door" to certain subjects. . . . Even assuming that we should treat the hearsay rule like the rules governing testimonial privileges, we would not conclude that a forfeiture occurred here. Parties may forfeit a privilege by exposing privileged evidence, but do not forfeit one merely by taking a position that the evidence might contradict. In *Miller*, for example, the court held that a litigant, "after giving the jury his version of a privileged communication, [could not] prevent the cross-examiner from utilizing *the communication itself* to get at the truth" (emphasis added). In this case, by contrast, the United States never presented to the jury any version of what DeMatteis and Bruno had said in the grand jury proceedings. Instead, it attempted to show Cedar Park's participation in the Club solely through other evidence available to the respondents. . . .

The respondents finally argue that adversarial fairness may prohibit suppression of exculpatory evidence produced in grand jury proceedings. They note that, when this Court required disclosure of a grand jury transcript in *Dennis v. United States*, 384 U.S. 855 (1966), it stated that "it is rarely justifiable for the prosecution to have exclusive access" to relevant facts. They allege that the United States nevertheless uses the following tactics to develop evidence in a one-sided manner: If a witness inculpates a defendant during the grand jury proceedings, the United States immunizes him and calls him at trial; however, if the witness exculpates the defendant, as Bruno and DeMatteis each did here, the United States refuses to immunize him and attempts to exclude the testimony as hearsay. The respondents assert that dispensing with the "similar motive" requirement would limit these tactics.

We again fail to see how we may create an exception to Rule 804(b)(1). The *Dennis* case, unlike this one, did not involve a question about the admissibility of evidence. Rather, it concerned only the need to disclose a transcript to the defendants. Moreover, in *Dennis*, we did not hold that adversarial fairness required the United States to make the grand jury transcript available. Instead, we ordered disclosure under the specific language of Federal Rule of Criminal Procedure 6(e). In this case, the language of Rule 804(b)(1) does not support the respondents. Indeed, the respondents specifically ask us to ignore it. Neither *Dennis* nor anything else that the respondents have cited provides us with this authority.

The question remains whether the United States had a "similar motive" in this case. The United States asserts that the District Court specifically found that it did not and that we should not review its factual determinations. It also argues that a prosecutor generally will not have the same motive to develop testimony in grand jury proceedings as he does at trial. A prosecutor, it explains, must maintain secrecy during the investigatory stages of the criminal process and therefore may not desire to confront grand jury witnesses with contradictory evidence. It further states that a prosecutor may not know, prior to indictment, which issues will have importance at trial and accordingly may fail to develop grand jury testimony effectively.

The respondents disagree with both of the United States' arguments. They characterize the District Court's ruling as one of law, rather than fact, because the District Court essentially ruled that a prosecutor's motives at trial always differ from his motives in grand jury proceedings. The respondents contend further that the grand jury transcripts in this case actually show that the United States thoroughly attempted to impeach DeMatteis and Bruno. They add that, despite the United States' stated concern about maintaining secrecy, the United States revealed to DeMatteis and Bruno the identity of the major witnesses who testified against them at trial.

The Court of Appeals, as noted, erroneously concluded that the respondents did not have to demonstrate a similar motive in this case to make use of Rule 804(b)(1). It therefore declined to consider fully the arguments now presented by the parties about whether the United States had such a motive. Rather than to address this issue here in the first instance, we think it prudent to remand the case for further consideration.

It is so ordered.

Justice BLACKMUN, concurring.

... Because "similar motive" does not mean "identical motive," the similar-motive inquiry, in my view, is inherently a *factual* inquiry, depending in part on the similarity of the underlying issues and on the context of the grand jury questioning. It cannot be that the prosecution either *always or never* has a similar motive for questioning a particular witness with respect to a particular issue before the grand jury as at trial. . . . Because this case involves factual issues unusual in complexity and in number and because neither the District Court nor the Court of Appeals apparently engaged in the type of factual inquiry appropriate for resolution of the similar-motive inquiry, I join the majority in remanding the case for further consideration.

Justice STEVENS, dissenting.

. . . As the Court explains, the grand jury testimony of Bruno and DeMatteis was totally inconsistent with the Government's theory of the alleged RICO conspiracy to rig bids on large construction projects in Manhattan. . . . It is therefore clear that before the grand jury the Government had precisely the same interest in establishing that Bruno's and DeMatteis' testimony was false as it had at trial. Thus, when the prosecutors doubted Bruno's and DeMatteis' veracity before the grand jury—as they most assuredly did—they unquestionably had an "opportunity and similar motive to develop the testimony by direct, cross, or redirect examination" within the meaning of Rule 804(b)(1). . . .

[A party] might decide—for tactical reasons or otherwise—not to engage in a rigorous cross-examination, or even in any cross-examination at all. In such a case, however, I do not believe that it is accurate to say that the party lacked a similar motive to cross-examine the witness; instead, it is more accurate to say that the party had a similar motive to cross-examine the witness (*i.e.*, to undermine the false or misleading testimony) but chose not to act on that motive. Although the Rules of Evidence allow a party to make that choice about whether to engage in cross-examination, they also provide that she must accept the consequences of that decision—including the possibility that the testimony might be introduced against her in a subsequent proceeding. . . .

I am therefore satisfied that the Government had an "opportunity and similar motive" to develop the grand jury testimony of witnesses Bruno and DeMatteis; consequently, the transcript of that testimony was admissible against the Government at respondents' trial under Rule 804(b)(1). For that reason, I would affirm the judgment of the Court of Appeals.

PROBLEMS

3.42. A newspaper reports that a local hospital illegally disposes of hazardous materials. The hospital sues for libel. At trial the newspaper elicits testimony from a janitorial employee of the hospital that the hospital director had him pour toxic waste into a storm drain. Under what circumstances, if any, will the transcript of this testimony be admissible in a subsequent criminal case against the hospital director for illegal dumping?

3.43. The manager of a gasoline station is prosecuted for illegally burying engine oil in a vacant field. A mechanic who works at the station testifies that, at the manager's direction, she buried engine oil in the field. The jury returns a verdict of not guilty. Under what circumstances, if any, may the mechanic's testimony be introduced in a subsequent civil suit for cleanup costs, brought by the city against the company that owns the gasoline station?

10. Dying Declarations

One of the oldest of the exceptions to the hearsay rule allows the introduction of certain "dying declarations." Like the business records doctrine, the exception for dying declarations has traditionally been justified on grounds both of reliability and practical necessity.

[F.R.E. 804(B)(2); C.E.C. §1242]

McCORMICK ON EVIDENCE

§309, at 2:363 (Kenneth S. Broun, ed., 6th ed. 2006)

Of the doctrines that authorize the admission of special classes of hearsay, the doctrine relating to dying declarations is the most mystical in its theory and traditionally among the most arbitrary in its limitations. The notion of the special likelihood of truthfulness of deathbed statements was widespread long before the recognition of a general rule against hearsay in the early 1700s. Not surprisingly, nearly as soon as we find a hearsay rule, we also find an exception for dying declarations.[4]

SHEPARD v. UNITED STATES

290 U.S. 96 (1933)

Mr. Justice Cardozo delivered the opinion of the Court.

[The defendant was convicted of the murder of his wife. At trial, the decedent's nurse testified that Mrs. Shepard told her on May 22, 1929, "Dr. Shepard has poisoned me." Before making this statement, Mrs. Shepard allegedly asked the nurse to bring a bottle of whiskey from her room, identified it as liquor she drank just before collapsing, said it had smelled and tasted strange, and asked if it could be tested for poison. The nurse also

---

4. . . . The classic statement of the basis of the rule was made by Chief Baron Eyre in Rex v. Woodcock, 1 Leach 500, 168 Eng. Rep. 352 (K.B. 1789):

Now the general principle on which this species of evidence is admitted is, that they are declarations made in extremity, when the party is at the point of death, and when every hope of this world is gone; when every motive to falsehood is silenced, and the mind is induced by the most powerful considerations to speak the truth; a situation so solemn, and so awful, is considered by the law as creating an obligation equal to that which is imposed by a positive oath administered in a Court of Justice. . . .

testified that Mrs. Shepard "said she was not going to get well; she was going to die."]

. . . Upon the hearing in this court the government finds its main prop in the position that what was said by Mrs. Shepard was admissible as a dying declaration. This is manifestly the theory upon which it was offered and received. The prop, however, is a broken reed. To make out a dying declaration, the declarant must have spoken without hope of recovery and in the shadow of impending death. The record furnishes no proof of that indispensable condition. . . .

[The declarant's] illness began on May 20. She was found in a state of collapse, delirious, in pain, the pupils of her eyes dilated, and the retina suffused with blood. The conversation with the nurse occurred two days later. At that time her mind had cleared up, and her speech was rational and orderly. There was as yet no thought by any of her physicians that she was dangerously ill, still less that her case was hopeless. To all seeming she had greatly improved, and was moving forward to recovery. There had been no diagnosis of poison as the cause of her distress. Not till about a week afterwards was there a relapse, accompanied by an infection of the mouth, renewed congestion of the eyes, and later hemorrhages of the bowels. Death followed on June 15.

Nothing in the condition of the patient on May 22 gives fair support to the conclusion that hope had then been lost. She may have thought she was going to die and have said so to her nurse, but this was consistent with hope, which could not have been put aside without more to quench it. Indeed, a fortnight later, she said to one of her physicians, though her condition was then grave, "You will get me well, won't you?" Fear or even belief that illness will end in death will not avail of itself to make a dying declaration. There must be "a settled hopeless expectation" (Willes, J. in *Reg. v. Peel*, 2 F. & F. 21, 22) that death is near at hand, and what is said must have been spoken in the hush of its impending presence. *Mattox v. United States*, 146 U.S. 140, 151; *Carver v. United States*, 160 U.S. 553; *Id.*, 164 U.S. 694; *R. v. Perry*, (1909) 2 K.B. 697; *People v. Sarzano*, 212 N.Y. 231, 235, 106 N.E. 87; 3 Wigmore on Evidence, §§ 1440, 1441, 1442, collating the decisions. Despair of recovery may indeed be gathered from the circumstances if the facts support the inference. There is no unyielding ritual of words to be spoken by the dying. Despair may even be gathered, though the period of survival outruns the bounds of expectation. What is decisive is the state of mind. Even so, the state of mind must be exhibited in the evidence, and not left to conjecture. The patient must have spoken with the consciousness of a swift and certain doom.

What was said by this patient was not spoken in that mood. There was no warning to her in the circumstances that her words would be repeated and accepted as those of a dying wife, charging murder to her husband, and charging it deliberately and solemnly as a fact within her knowledge. To the focus of that responsibility her mind was never brought. She spoke as one ill, giving voice to the beliefs and perhaps the conjectures of the moment. The liquor was to be tested, to see whether her beliefs were sound. She did not speak as one dying, announcing to the survivors a definitive conviction, a legacy of knowledge on which the world might act when she had gone.

The petitioner insists that the form of the declaration exhibits other defects that call for its exclusion, apart from the objection that death was not imminent and that hope was still alive. Homicide may not be imputed to a defendant on the basis of mere suspicions, though they are the suspicions of the dying. To let the declaration in, the inference must be permissible that there was knowledge or the opportunity for knowledge as to the acts that are declared. Wigmore, § 1445(2). . . . The form is not decisive, though it be that of a conclusion, a statement of the result with the antecedent steps omitted. Wigmore, § 1447. "He murdered me," does not cease to be competent as a dying declaration because in the statement of the act there is also an appraisal of the crime. One does not hold the dying to the observance of all the niceties of speech to which conformity is exacted from a witness on the stand. What is decisive is something deeper and more fundamental than any difference of form. The declaration is kept out if the setting of the occasion satisfies the judge, or in reason ought to satisfy him, that the speaker is giving expression to suspicion or conjecture, and not to known facts. The difficulty is not so much in respect of the governing principle as in its application to varying and equivocal conditions. In this case, the ruling that there was a failure to make out the imminence of death and the abandonment of hope relieves us of the duty of determining whether it is a legitimate inference that there was the opportunity for knowledge. We leave that question open. . . . [Reversed.]

UNITED STATES v. SACASAS

381 F.2d 451 (2d Cir. 1967)

WATERMAN, Circuit Judge:

This is an appeal from a judgment of conviction [for bank robbery] entered in the United States District Court for the Southern District of New York after a three-day trial by jury. . . . On the day fixed for imposition of sentence appellant moved for a new trial based upon newly discovered evidence. The motion was denied; the purported evidence, if true, would not have been admissible. The ruling is appealed from, though appellant practically concedes it to have been correct. According to one Boyle, a fellow-inmate of the Federal House of Detention with Richard L. Mahan, who had been indicted with appellant, and who, there awaiting trial, died before trial, [Mahan] told Boyle ten minutes before Mahan finally lost consciousness, "If anything happens to me tell them that the Greek had nothing to do with the job." Appellant seeks to persuade that this hearsay evidence should be admissible under the "dying declaration" exception to the exclusion of hearsay. Of course the exception is inapplicable here—Mahan was not dying following a homicidal attack, and neither appellant, "the Greek," nor Mahan had been prosecuted for a homicide. 5 Wigmore, Evidence §§ 1432-1434 (2d ed. 1940). Conviction affirmed.

ADVISORY COMMITTEE NOTE TO F.R.E. 804(B)(2)

The exception is the familiar dying declaration of the common law, expanded somewhat beyond its traditionally narrow limits. While the original religious justification for the exception may have lost its conviction for some persons over the years, it can scarcely be doubted that powerful psychological pressures are present. See 5 Wigmore § 1443 and the classic statement of Chief Baron Eyre in Rex v. Woodcock, 1 Leach 500, 502, 168 Eng. Rep. 352, 353 (K.B. 1789).

The common law required that the statement be that of the victim, offered in a prosecution for criminal homicide. Thus declarations by victims in prosecutions for other crimes, e.g. a declaration by a rape victim who dies in childbirth, and all declarations in civil cases were outside the scope of the exception. An occasional statute has removed these restrictions . . . or has expanded the area of offenses to include abortions. Kansas by decision extended the exception to civil cases. While the common law exception no doubt originated as a result of the exceptional need for the evidence in homicide cases, the theory of admissibility applies equally in civil cases and in prosecutions for crimes other than homicide. The same considerations suggest abandonment of the limitation to circumstances attending the event in question, yet when the statement deals with matters other than the supposed death, its influence is believed to be sufficiently attenuated to justify the limitation. Unavailability is not limited to death. See subdivision (a) of this rule. Any problem as to declarations phrased in terms of opinion is laid at rest by Rule 701, and continuation of a requirement of firsthand knowledge is assured by Rule 602.

REPORT OF THE HOUSE JUDICIARY COMMITTEE

H.R. Rep. No. 93-650, at 15 (1973)

[Rule 804] as submitted by the Court . . . proposed to expand the traditional scope of the dying declaration exception (i.e. a statement of the victim in a homicide case as to the cause or circumstances of his believed imminent death) to allow such statements in all criminal and civil cases. The Committee did not consider dying declarations as among the most reliable forms of hearsay. Consequently, it amended the provision to limit their admissibility in criminal cases to homicide prosecutions, where exceptional need for the evidence is present. This is existing law. At the same time, the Committee approved the expansion to civil actions and proceedings where the stakes do not involve possible imprisonment, although noting that this could lead to forum shopping in some instances.

STATE v. LEWIS

235 S.W.3d 136 (Tenn. 2007)

WADE, J.

[Sabrina Lewis was convicted of criminally negligent homicide and facilitation of attempted aggravated robbery in connection with the failed robbery of an antiques store, during which the store's owner, Gary Finchum, was fatally shot. Lewis was alleged to have helped to set up the robbery by making an appointment to bring in two vases for Finchum to appraise. On the morning of the shooting, Finchum telephoned his wife and told her "I believe the woman with the vases is coming in." Approximately an hour later, employees at a pharmacy adjacent to the antiques store heard loud crashes and ran next door. Finchum told them he had been "shot in the heart" and asked them to call 911. Finchum's breathing was shallow, and the pharmacy employees thought he would likely die before the ambulance arrived.]

Detective Mike Chastain of the Metro Police Department Armed Robbery unit arrived at the scene prior to the paramedics and observed the victim lying on the floor at the rear of the store. The victim, who was in "obvious pain" and "blood[-]soaked," identified himself to the detective and when asked if he had been robbed, responded, "[H]e tried to." He described his assailant as a "young male black" and showed the detective a blue, "floppy" hat that he had left behind. When the paramedics arrived and initiated treatment, the victim pointed with both of his hands and said, "[O]fficer, officer, the lady's information is on the desk." When asked about what "lady" to whom he was referring, the victim responded, "[T]he lady with the vases." On further questioning about whether the "lady" was connected to the robbery and shooting, the victim stated, "I know she is." Another detective found a piece of paper on the counter bearing the name "Sabrina Lewis," what appeared to be a driver's license number, and the words "two vases." . . .

It is our view that the victim's statement to Detective Chastain, that he "knew" that "the lady with the vases" was involved in the offenses, qualifies as testimonial.[6] The assailant had left the store. . . . The 911 call had already been made. . . . While the victim's statements here took place at the crime scene, they were responses to inquiries by the investigating officers. Even though the victim was in a state of distress from his wounds, his comments did not describe an "ongoing emergency," as defined in *Crawford*, and were instead descriptions of recent, but past, criminal activity. . . . Because the statements were testimonial, we must . . . consider whether they should have been excluded under the rule in *Crawford*[,] which not only requires

---

6. Although the victim made other statements to Detective Chastain, including providing a description of the shooter and identifying the hat he wore, the Defendant does not challenge the admissibility of these statements. Her challenge is, instead, confined to the victim's statement, "I know she is," given in response to Detective Chastain's question of whether "the lady with the vases" was involved in the shooting and robbery attempt.

the unavailability of the declarant, which was obviously satisfied, but the opportunity for cross-examination, which was not.

. . . [T]he trial court admitted the victim's statements under the dying declaration exception to the hearsay rule. In *Crawford*, the Court included a footnote, describing the dying declaration as historically unique in the prosecution of homicide and hinting at the admissibility of such statements, even if testimonial:

> The one deviation we have found involves dying declarations. The existence of that exception as a general rule of criminal hearsay law cannot be disputed. *Although many dying declarations may not be testimonial, there is authority for admitting even those that clearly are.* We need not decide in this case whether the Sixth Amendment incorporates an exception for testimonial dying declarations. If this exception must be accepted on historical grounds, it is *sui generis.*

Crawford, 541 U.S. at 56 n.6 (citations omitted) (emphasis added). Since *Crawford*, we found no jurisdiction that has excluded a testimonial dying declaration. Several states have specifically allowed the declaration as an exception to the rule in *Crawford*. *See, e.g., Wallace v. State*, 836 N.E.2d 985, 992-96 (Ind. Ct. App. 2005); *State v. Young*, 710 N.W.2d 272, 283-84 (Minn. 2006). Because the admissibility of the dying declaration is also deeply entrenched in the legal history of this state, it is also our view that this single hearsay exception survives the mandate of *Crawford* regardless of its testimonial nature.[8] . . .

Rule 804(b)(2) of the Tennessee Rules of Evidence, effective January 1, 1990, is the common law embodiment of the dying declaration:

> Statement Under Belief of Impending Death.—In a prosecution for homicide, a statement made by the victim while believing that the declarant's death was imminent and concerning the cause or circumstances of what the declarant believed to be impending death.

The Advisory Commission Comments to the rule confirm that "[t]he rule retains Tennessee's common law limitations." Long ago, this Court more specifically addressed the reason behind the rule:

> [W]hen the party is at the point of death, and when every hope of this world is gone, when every motive to falsehood is silenced, and the mind is induced by the most powerful consideration to speak the truth, a situation, so solemn and so awful, is considered by the law as creating an obligation equal to that which is imposed by a positive oath administered in a court of justice.

Smith v. State, 28 Tenn. (9 Hum.) 9, 19 (1848). . . .

---

8. There is a historical and literary basis for the Supreme Court's recognition of the exception. As early as the twelfth century, dying declarations merited special treatment in the courts. 5 John H. Wigmore, *Evidence in Trials at Common Law* § 1430 n. 8 (James H. Cadbourn rev. 1974). Some authorities suggest the rule is of Shakespearean origin. In "The Life and Death of King John," Shakespeare has Lord Melun utter what a "hideous death within my view, [r]etaining but a quantity of life, [w]hich bleeds away, . . . los[t] the use of all deceit" and asked, "Why should I then be false, since it is true [t]hat I must die here and live hence by truth?" William Shakespeare, *The Life and Death of King John*, act. 5, sc. 2, lines 22-29.

The Defendant . . . argues that the victim's statement should have been excluded because it is an opinion rather than an assertion of fact. . . . Cases pre-dating the adoption of our rules of evidence have been understandably inconsistent when considering the admissibility of an opinion expressed as part of a dying declaration. The traditional authorities have recognized that the general rule, which allows a statement of fact but precludes a mere opinion, often created confusion in the effort to separate one from the other. D.E. Evins, Annotation, *Admissibility in criminal trial of dying declarations involving an asserted opinion or conclusion*, 86 A.L.R.2d 905 (1962). Nevertheless, the prevailing standard at common law permitted an opinion or conclusion "as to the identity of the assailant . . . where it was determined that such a statement was reasonable in view of the surrounding circumstances." *Id.* at § 2. In contrast, an expression of opinion as to identity has been excluded when the circumstances established that the victim "could not have known whether [the defendant] fired the fatal shots." *Stevens v. Commonwealth*, 298 S.W. 678, 679 (Ky. 1927).

Because a dying declaration is essentially a substitute for the testimony of the victim, the admissible evidence is limited to that to which the victim could have testified if present. Applying this reasoning, lay opinion should not be allowed simply because it is in the form of a dying declaration but it must not be unduly restricted when reasonably based. This historical perspective comports with Rule 701 of the Tennessee Rules of Evidence, which specifically governs the admission of opinion evidence by a lay witness:

> If a witness is not testifying as an expert, the witness's testimony in the form of opinions or inferences is limited to those opinions or inferences which are
>
> (1) rationally based on the perception of the witness and
> (2) helpful to a clear understanding of the witness's testimony or the determination of a fact in issue.

Here, the record suggests that the victim's identification of the Defendant is "rationally based upon the perception" of the victim. . . . If the victim had lived, he would have been permitted to offer this testimony at trial. Under these circumstances, it is our view that the statement, while an expression of opinion and testimonial in nature, was admissible as a dying declaration, an evidentiary rule which has thus far survived *Crawford* and its progeny. . . . [Affirmed.]

PROBLEM

3.44. Summoned to the scene of a shooting, Officer Rachel Raskin finds the victim, Eugene Engels, bleeding badly and gasping for breath. Engels tells Raskin that he was shot by Larry Libby, to prevent him from testifying about a shooting the previous week. Engels says, "I was with Mike Mallon when he shot Casey Carleton—that kid on Acorn Avenue. Libby is Mallon's cousin. They're like brothers. Libby thought I might snitch. I told him I wouldn't. He didn't trust me." Shortly after speaking with Raskin, Engels loses consciousness. Paramedics take him to the hospital, and he is placed on life support. He survives but does not regain consciousness. Five months

later, Mallon is on trial for Carleton's murder. Engels is still on life support
and still in a coma. Can the prosecutor call Raskin to testify about what
Engels told her?

11. Declarations Against Interest

Unlike the admissions doctrine, the exception for declarations against
interest applies to statements by anyone, not just statements made by or
attributable to the party against whom they are introduced. But, again
unlike the admissions doctrine, the present exception applies only to statements that are obviously contrary to the interest of the declarant—so
contrary, in fact, that a "reasonable person" would make the statement
only if it were true. The major controversies associated with this exception
have concerned its application to declarations that appear to subject the
declarant to criminal liability.

[F.R.E. 804(B)(3); C.E.C. §1230]

ADVISORY COMMITTEE NOTE TO F.R.E. 804(B)(3)

The circumstantial guaranty of reliability for declarations against
interest is the assumption that persons do not make statements which
are damaging to themselves unless satisfied for good reason that they are
true. If the statement is that of a party, offered by his opponent, it comes in
as an admission, Rule [801(d)(2)], and there is no occasion to inquire
whether it is against interest, this not being a condition precedent to admissibility of admissions by opponents.

The common law required that the interest declared against be pecuniary or proprietary but within this limitation demonstrated striking inge-
nuity in discovering an against-interest aspect. The exception discards the
common law limitation and expands to the full logical limit. One result is to
remove doubt as to the admissibility of declarations tending to establish a
tort liability against the declarant or to extinguish one which might be
asserted by him, in accordance with the trend of the decisions in this
country. Another is to allow statements tending to expose declarant to
hatred, ridicule, or disgrace, the motivation here being considered to be
as strong as when financial interests are at stake. And finally, exposure to
criminal liability satisfies the against-interest requirement. The refusal of the
common law to concede the adequacy of a penal interest was no doubt
indefensible in logic, but one senses in the decisions a distrust of evidence
of confessions by third persons offered to exculpate the accused arising
from suspicions of fabrication either of the fact of the making of the confession or in its contents, enhanced in either instance by the required unavailability of the declarant. . . . The requirement of corroboration is
included in the rule in order to effect an accommodation between these
competing considerations. When the statement is offered by the accused by

way of exculpation, the resulting situation is not adapted to control by rulings as to the weight of the evidence, and hence the provision is cast in terms of a requirement preliminary to admissibility. The requirement of corroboration should be construed in such a manner as to effectuate its purpose of circumventing fabrication.

Ordinarily the third-party confession is thought of in terms of exculpating the accused, but this is by no means always or necessarily the case: it may include statements implicating him, and under the general theory of declarations against interest they would be admissible as related statements. . . . Whether a statement is in fact against interest must be determined from the circumstances of each case. Thus a statement admitting guilt and implicating another person, made while in custody, may well be motivated by a desire to curry favor with the authorities and hence fail to qualify as against interest. . . . On the other hand, the same words spoken under different circumstances, e.g., to an acquaintance, would have no difficulty in qualifying. The rule does not purport to deal with questions of the right of confrontation.

REPORT OF THE HOUSE JUDICIARY COMMITTEE

H.R. Rep. No. 93-650 16 (1974)

The Court's Rule . . . proposed to expand the hearsay limitation from its present federal limitation to include statements subjecting the declarant to criminal liability and statements tending to make him an object of hatred, ridicule, or disgrace. The Committee eliminated the latter category from the subdivision as lacking sufficient guarantees of reliability. As for statements against penal interest, the Committee shared the view of the Court that some such statements do possess adequate assurances of reliability and should be admissible. It believed, however, as did the Court, that statements of this type tending to exculpate the accused are more suspect and so should have their admissibility conditioned upon some further provision insuring trustworthiness. The proposal in the Court Rule to add a requirement of simple corroboration was, however, deemed ineffective to accomplish this purpose since the accused's own testimony might suffice while not necessarily increasing the reliability of the hearsay statement. The Committee settled upon the language "unless corroborating circumstances clearly indicate the trustworthiness of the statement" as affording a proper standard and degree of discretion.

UNITED STATES v. DURAN SAMANIEGO

345 F.3d 1280 (11th Cir. 2003)

CARNES, Circuit Judge.

[Between 1972 and 1989, Roberto Duran Samaniego won four world boxing championships. He retired in 2002.] Duran claims that his championship belts were stolen from his house in Panama by his brother-in-law, Bolivar Iglesias, in September of 1993. . . . It is undisputed that Duran's championship belts ultimately came into the hands of Luis Gonzalez Baez, a Miami businessman, and that Baez attempted to sell the belts to undercover FBI agents (who had set up a sting operation) for $200,000. Baez was arrested, but he claimed that the belts had not been stolen. The government confiscated the belts and filed an interpleader action in federal district court to determine whether Duran or Baez is the rightful owner of the belts. The case was tried to a jury, which returned a verdict in favor of Duran. This is Baez's appeal from the judgment the district court entered in accordance with that verdict.

Baez's principal contention on appeal is that the district court should not have admitted testimony about a purported apology from Bolivar Iglesias. Over Baez's objection, the district court permitted a number of witnesses, including Duran and some of his family members, to testify that Iglesias apologized in their presence for stealing the belts. Baez contends that testimony is inadmissible hearsay. The district court allowed it on the theory that the out-of-court statement described an existing state of mind or emotion, and for that reason fit within the hearsay exception set out in Federal Rule of Evidence 803(3). . . . The question, as Baez's argument frames it, is whether Iglesias's apology falls within the exclusion from Rule 803(3) admissibility because it is a "statement of memory or belief to prove the fact remembered or believed."

An apology is evidence of a then-existing state of mind or emotion: remorse. Iglesias's apology is admissible to prove the truth of the matter asserted—that Iglesias felt remorse at the time he made the apologetic statement. That is not the problem. The problem is . . . that "the state-of-mind exception does not permit the witness to relate any of the declarant's statements as to why he held the particular state of mind, or what he might have believed that would have induced the state of mind." United States v. Cohen, 631 F.2d 1223, 1225 (5th Cir. 1980). . . . [T]he purpose of the exclusion from Rule 803(3) admissibility is "to narrowly limit those admissible statements to declarations of condition—'I'm scared'—and not belief—'I'm scared because [someone] threatened me.' " Id.

The testimony admitted in this case was not limited to the fact that Iglesias had expressed remorse, but also included the fact that he said he apologized for and asked forgiveness for having stolen the belts. The testimony most often came in response to questions from Duran's counsel about how the witness knew Iglesias had stolen the belts. What Iglesias said was offered to show not only that he was remorseful, but also that he had stolen the belts. Rule 803(3) expressly prohibits the use of a statement of then-existing state of mind in this way. That prohibition, the committee notes explain, is necessary "to avoid the virtual destruction of the hearsay rule which would otherwise result from allowing state of mind, provable by a hearsay statement, to serve as the basis for an inference of the happening of the event which produced the state of mind."

Our conclusion that Iglesias's apology was not properly admitted under Rule 803(3) does not end the matter. Although the district court admitted the statement under Rule 803(3), Duran offered the testimony

concerning the apology as a statement against interest by a declarant unavailable at trial, which is admissible under Rule 804(b)(3). The district court
did not reach that alternative ground for admissibility, but we do because
we will not hold that the district court abused its discretion where it reached
the correct result even if it did so for the wrong reason. The part of Iglesias's
apology in which he admitted having stolen Duran's belts is a statement
against interest, because it would "subject the declarant to civil or criminal
liability'" within the meaning of Rule 804(b)(3). For a statement against
interest to be admissible under Rule 804, however, the declarant must have
been unavailable at the time of the trial within the meaning of Rule 804(a).

Iglesias was not present at the trial, but that does not mean he was
unavailable for Rule 804 purposes. Subsection (a) of that rule tells us a
witness should be considered unavailable in five separate circumstances,
only one of which is relevant in this case: The declarant is unavailable if he
"is absent from the hearing and the proponent of a statement has been
unable to procure the declarant's attendance (or in the case of a hearsay
exception under subdivision (b)(2), (3), or (4), the declarant's attendance
or testimony) by process or other reasonable means."

Duran could not procure Iglesias's attendance or testimony by process
because Iglesias, a citizen of Panama, apparently was living in that country at
the time of the trial, and "foreign nationals located outside the United
States . . . are beyond the subpoena power of the district court." United
States v. Drogoul, 1 F.3d 1546, 1553 (11th Cir. 1993). Duran did enlist
the help of Iglesias's immediate family in an attempt to locate him and
persuade him to return to the United States and testify. Iglesias's sister,
who is Duran's wife, testified that she and her mother had tried to locate
Iglesias on five different occasions, but finding him had proven impossible.
Iglesias's mother testified that she had tried to contact him in order to get
him to come back and testify but was unable to get Iglesias.

Using the efforts of Iglesias's sister and mother, as Duran did, is a
reasonable means of attempting to locate Iglesias in Panama and persuade
him to travel to the United States to testify. It follows that Duran did establish Iglesias was unavailable to testify under Rule 804(a)(5), so the out-of-
court statement Iglesias made was admissible under Rule 804(b)(3) as a
statement against interest. The district court did not abuse its discretion
in admitting the statement, albeit on the wrong ground. . . . The judgment
entered on the jury's verdict stands, and under it Roberto Duran is entitled
to regain his championship belts.

UNITED STATES v. JACKSON

335 F.3d 170 (2d Cir. 2003)

McLaughlin, Circuit Judge.

. . . [A] jury found defendant Charles L. Jackson guilty of conspiring to
import 5 kilograms or more of cocaine into the United States. . . . Jackson
challenges his conviction on evidentiary grounds. He contends that the
court abused its discretion in refusing to admit the entire plea allocution

of co-conspirator Steve Brown. . . . Specifically, Jackson challenges the exclusion of Brown's statement that Brown never supervised Jackson. . . .

Under Rule 804(b)(1), an unavailable witness's testimony from a prior hearing or proceeding is not barred by the hearsay rule "if the party against whom the testimony is now offered . . . had an opportunity and similar motive to develop the testimony by direct, cross, or redirect examination." . . . Here, both sides concede that Brown was unavailable at Jackson's trial because he had properly invoked his Fifth Amendment right against self-incrimination. . . . [The issue] is whether the Government had an opportunity and similar motive to examine Brown at his plea allocution. . . . Under Fed. R. Crim. P. 11, the purpose of a plea proceeding is to ensure that the defendant's plea is knowing, voluntary, and grounded on a proper factual basis. . . . [A] plea proceeding is conducted solely by the district court judge who is primarily responsible for ensuring that the requirements of Rule 11 are satisfied. On the rare occasion where the prosecutor is permitted to address the defendant, the questions posed are usually formulaic and perfunctory. The Government's role at a plea proceeding is quite limited, and certainly does not include the opportunity to engage in the type of examination contemplated by Rule 804(b)(1). . . . Moreover, [w]e agree with the Third and Seventh Circuits that the Government does not have the same motive to examine the defendant at a plea hearing as it does at other proceedings. *See United States v. Lowell*, 649 F.2d 950, 965 (3d Cir. 1981); *United States v. Powell*, 894 F.2d 895, 901 (7th Cir. 1990). Here, the Government had no reason to cross-examine Brown at his plea allocution about his supervision over Jackson. That Brown's plea colloquy may have included misstatements or inaccuracies did not preclude it from providing an adequate factual basis for the plea. The district court, therefore, did not abuse its discretion in excluding Brown's plea allocution under Rule 804(b)(1).

Jackson's contention that Brown's plea allocution might be admissible under Rule 804(b)(3) is a stronger argument, but it too is ultimately without merit. Rule 804(b)(3) allows the admission of a hearsay statement by an unavailable witness if that statement "at the time of its making . . . so far tended to subject the declarant to civil or criminal liability . . . that a reasonable person in the declarant's position would not have made the statement unless believing it to be true." This exception rests on the notion that "reasonable people, even reasonable people who are not especially honest, tend not to make self-inculpatory statements unless they believe them to be true." *Williamson v. United States*, 512 U.S. 594, 599 (1994).

Rule 804(b)(3) further requires that, if the statement exposes the declarant (*i.e.*, Brown) to criminal liability and is offered to exculpate the accused (*i.e.*, Jackson), the proponent of the statements must identify "corroborating circumstances [that] clearly indicate the trustworthiness of the statement." *Id.* at 605. The purpose of this corroboration requirement is to "circumvent[] fabrication" by the declarant. *See* Fed. R. Evid. 804(b)(3) Advisory Committee Notes. . . .

Although we have recognized that statements from a guilty plea allocution can be admitted under Rule 804(b)(3) . . . their admission is strictly circumscribed by the Supreme Court's holding in *Williamson v. United States* . . . that Rule 804(b)(3) "does not allow admission of non-self-inculpatory statements, even if they are made within a broader narrative that is generally self-inculpatory." . . . [E]ach particular hearsay statement offered under Rule 804(b)(3) must be separately parsed and must, itself, be self-inculpatory. . . .

[T]he statements by Brown that Jackson sought to introduce at trial were not themselves self-inculpatory as to Brown. They did not, therefore, satisfy *Williamson.* Brown's statements that he never supervised Jackson and never asked Jackson to go to Jamaica to smuggle drugs did not in any way inculpate Brown or expose him to criminal liability. Accordingly, the separate guarantee of trustworthiness required by Rule 804(b)(3) is non-existent as to these statements. If anything, these statements were probably exculpatory as to Brown as they minimized the number of people that he supervised during the conspiracy.

Moreover, even if Brown's statements could be construed as self-inculpatory, Jackson has failed to satisfy the corroboration requirement of Rule 804(b)(3). . . . [D]uring his plea allocution Brown made conflicting assertions about Jackson's role in the conspiracy. For example, Brown first asserted that Jackson was a person with whom he had arrangements to smuggle drugs into the country. At another point, however, Brown claimed that Jackson smuggled cocaine into the country only for Guthrie. . . . [And] Brown's own motives for making the statements excul-pating Jackson were highly suspect. Because Brown was aware at the time of his plea that there was a possibility that he could be called upon to testify at Jackson's trial (he was on the Government's witness list), the district court sagely noted that Brown's apparent attempt to exculpate Jackson may well have been an effort to avoid testifying against one of his co-conspirators.

Accordingly, the district court did not abuse its discretion in failing to admit Brown's plea allocution statements under the Rule 804(b)(3) exception to the hearsay rule. . . . [Affirmed in relevant part.]

PROBLEMS

3.45. Dwight, charged with armed robbery of a bank, seeks to elicit testimony from Sarah that her husband told her, just before he died of injuries he suffered in an automobile accident, "I'm not going to make it. There's something you've got to make right. That stickup job they're putting on Dwight—it was me." Is Sarah's testimony admissible? Does it matter whether some of the money from the robbery was later found in her husband's car?

3.46. As part of its case against Dwight, the prosecution seeks to introduce testimony from Frank that, while Frank was on a fishing trip with Greg, Greg boasted of planning a bank robbery and having someone else carry it out. Frank will further testify that he asked Greg who carried out the robbery, and that Greg said it was Dwight. Greg cannot now be located. Is the testimony from Frank admissible? Does it matter whether a large cash deposit was made to Greg's bank account on the day after the robbery?

12. Forfeiture by Wrongdoing

Rule 804(b)(6) was added in 1997 to codify a common-law exception aimed at preventing use of the hearsay rule by a party who purposely and wrongfully causes a declarant's unavailability.

[F.R.E. 804(B)(6); C.E.C. §§1231, 1350]

ADVISORY COMMITTEE NOTE TO 1997
AMENDMENT TO F.R.E. 804

. . . Rule 804(b)(6) has been added to provide that a party forfeits the right to object on hearsay grounds to the admission of a declarant's prior statement when the party's deliberate wrongdoing or acquiescence therein procured the unavailability of the declarant as a witness. This recognizes the need for a prophylactic rule to deal with abhorrent behavior "which strikes at the heart of the system of justice itself." *United States v. Mastrangelo*, 693 F.2d 269, 273 (2d Cir. 1982), cert. denied, 467 U.S. 1204 (1984). The wrongdoing need not consist of a criminal act. The rule applies to all parties, including the government.

Every circuit that has resolved the question has recognized the principle of forfeiture by misconduct, although the tests for determining whether there is a forfeiture have varied. . . . The usual Rule 104(a) preponderance of the evidence standard has been adopted in light of the behavior the new Rule 804(b)(6) seeks to discourage.

GILES v. CALIFORNIA
554 U.S. _____ (2008)

Justice SCALIA delivered the opinion of the Court. . . .

[Dwayne Giles fatally shot his ex-girlfriend, Brenda Avie. A jury convicted him of murder, rejecting his claim of self-defense. Among the evidence at trial were] statements that Avie had made to a police officer responding to a domestic-violence report about three weeks before the shooting. Avie, who was crying when she spoke, told the officer that Giles had accused her of having an affair, and that after the two began to argue, Giles grabbed her by the shirt, lifted her off the floor, and began to choke her. According to Avie, when she broke free and fell to the floor, Giles punched her in the face and head, and after she broke free again, he opened a folding knife, held it about three feet away from her, and threatened to kill her if he found her cheating on him. Over Giles' objection, the trial court admitted these statements into evidence under a provision of California law that permits admission of out-of-court statements describing the infliction or threat of physical injury on a declarant when the declarant is unavailable to testify at trial and the prior statements are deemed trustworthy. Cal. Evid. Code Ann. § 1370. . . .

The State does not dispute here, and we accept without deciding, that Avie's statements accusing Giles of assault were testimonial. But it maintains (as did the California Supreme Court) that the Sixth Amendment did not prohibit prosecutors from introducing the statements because an exception to the confrontation guarantee permits the use of a witness's unconfronted testimony if a judge finds, as the judge did in this case, that the defendant committed a wrongful act that rendered the witness unavailable to testify at trial. We held in *Crawford* that the Confrontation Clause is "most naturally read as a reference to the right of confrontation at common law, admitting only those exceptions established at the time of the founding." We therefore ask whether the theory of forfeiture by wrongdoing accepted by the California Supreme Court is a founding-era exception to the confrontation right.

We have previously acknowledged that two forms of testimonial statements were admitted at common law even though they were unconfronted. The first of these were declarations made by a speaker who was both on the brink of death and aware that he was dying. See, *e.g.*, *King* v. *Woodcock,* 168 Eng. Rep. 352, 353–354 (1789). . . . Avie did not make the unconfronted statements admitted at Giles' trial when she was dying, so her statements do not fall within this historic exception.

A second common-law doctrine, which we will refer to as forfeiture by wrongdoing, permitted the introduction of statements of a witness who was "detained" or "kept away" by the "means or procurement" of the defendant. . . . The terms used to define the scope of the forfeiture rule suggest that the exception applied only when the defendant engaged in conduct *designed* to prevent the witness from testifying. . . . We are aware of no case in which the exception was invoked although the defendant had not engaged in conduct designed to prevent a witness from testifying, such as offering a bribe. . . . In cases where the evidence suggested that the defendant had caused a person to be absent, but had not done so to prevent the person from testifying—as in the typical murder case involving accusatorial statements by the victim—the testimony was excluded unless it was confronted or fell within the dying-declaration exception. Prosecutors do not appear to have even *argued* that the judge could admit the unconfronted statements because the defendant committed the murder for which he was on trial.

Consider *King* v. *Woodcock.* William Woodcock was accused of killing his wife, Silvia, who had been beaten and left near death. A Magistrate took Silvia Woodcock's account of the crime, under oath, and she died about 48 hours later. The judge stated that "[g]reat as a crime of this nature must always appear to be, yet the inquiry into it must proceed upon the rules of evidence." Aside from testimony given at trial in the presence of the prisoner, the judge said, there were "two other species which are admitted by law: The one is the dying declaration of a person who has received a fatal blow; the other is the examination of a prisoner, and the depositions of the witnesses who may be produced against him" taken under the Marian bail and committal statutes. Silvia Woodcock's statement could not be admitted pursuant to the Marian statutes because it was unconfronted—the defendant had not been brought before the examining Magistrate and "the prisoner therefore had no opportunity of contradicting the facts it contains." Thus, the statements were admissible only if the witness "apprehended that she was in such a state of mortality as would inevitably oblige her soon to answer before her Maker for the truth or falsehood of her assertions." Depending on the account one credits, the court either instructed the jury to consider the statements only if Woodcock was "in fact under the apprehension of death," 168 Eng. Rep., at 354, or determined for itself that Woodcock was "quietly resigned and submitting to her fate" and admitted her statements into evidence, 1 E. East, Pleas of the Crown 356 (1803). . . . Many other cases excluded victims' statements when there was insufficient evidence that the witness was aware he was about to die. . . .

The State and the dissent note that common-law authorities justified the wrongful-procurement rule by invoking the maxim that a defendant should not be permitted to benefit from his own wrong. See, *e.g.*, G. Gilbert, Law of Evidence 140–141 (1756) (if a witness was "detained and kept back from appearing by the means and procurement" testimony would be read because a defendant "shall never be admitted to shelter himself by such evil Practices on the Witness, that being to give him Advantage of his own Wrong"). But as the evidence amply shows, the "wrong" and the "evil Practices" to which these statements referred was conduct *designed* to prevent a witness from testifying. The absence of a forfeiture rule covering this sort of conduct would create an intolerable incentive for defendants to bribe, intimidate, or even kill witnesses against them. There is nothing mysterious about courts' refusal to carry the rationale further. The notion that judges may strip the defendant of a right that the Constitution deems essential to a fair trial, on the basis of a prior *judicial* assessment that the defendant is guilty as charged, does not sit well with the right to trial by jury. It is akin, one might say, to "dispensing with jury trial because a defendant is obviously guilty." *Crawford*, 541 U.S., at 62.

Not only was the State's proposed exception to the right of confrontation plainly not an "exceptio[n] established at the time of the founding," *id.*, at 54; it is not established in American jurisprudence *since* the founding. American courts never—prior to 1985—invoked forfeiture outside the context of deliberate witness tampering. . . . In 1997, this Court approved a Federal Rule of Evidence, entitled "Forfeiture by wrongdoing," which applies only when the defendant "engaged or acquiesced in wrongdoing that was intended to, and did, procure the unavailability of the declarant as a witness." Fed. Rule of Evid. 804(b)(6). We have described this as a rule "which codifies the forfeiture doctrine." *Davis* v. *Washington*, 547 U.S. 813, 833 (2006). Every commentator we are aware of has concluded the requirement of intent "means that the exception applies only if the defendant has in mind the particular purpose of making the witness unavailable."[2] The commentators come out this way because the dissent's claim

---

2. Only a single state evidentiary code appears to contain a forfeiture rule broader than our holding in this case (and in *Crawford*) allow. . . . These rules cast more than a little doubt on the dissent's assertion that the historic forfeiture rule creates intolerable problems of proof. The lone forfeiture exception whose text reaches more broadly than the rule we adopt is an Oregon rule adopted in 2005.

that knowledge is sufficient to show intent is emphatically *not* the modern view.

In sum, our interpretation of the common-law forfeiture rule is supported by (1) the most natural reading of the language used at common law; (2) the absence of common-law cases *admitting* prior statements on a forfeiture theory when the defendant had not engaged in conduct designed to prevent a witness from testifying; (3) the common law's uniform exclusion of unconfronted inculpatory testimony by murder victims (except testimony given with awareness of impending death) in the innumerable cases in which the defendant was on trial for killing the victim, but was not shown to have done so for the purpose of preventing testimony; (4) a subsequent history in which the dissent's broad forfeiture theory has not been applied. The first two and the last are highly persuasive; the third is in our view conclusive. . . .

The dissent closes by pointing out that a forfeiture rule which ignores *Crawford* would be particularly helpful to women in abusive relationships—or at least particularly helpful in punishing their abusers. Not as helpful as the dissent suggests, since only *testimonial* statements are excluded by the Confrontation Clause. Statements to friends and neighbors about abuse and intimidation, and statements to physicians in the course of receiving treatment would be excluded, if at all, only by hearsay rules, which are free to adopt the dissent's version of forfeiture by wrongdoing. In any event, we are puzzled by the dissent's decision to devote its peroration to domestic abuse cases. Is the suggestion that we should have one Confrontation Clause (the one the Framers adopted and *Crawford* described) for all other crimes, but a special, improvised, Confrontation Clause for those crimes that are frequently directed against women? Domestic violence is an intolerable offense that legislatures may choose to combat through many means—from increasing criminal penalties to adding resources for investigation and prosecution to funding awareness and prevention campaigns. But for that serious crime, as for others, abridging the constitutional rights of criminal defendants is not in the State's arsenal.

The domestic-violence context is, however, relevant for a separate reason. Acts of domestic violence often are intended to dissuade a victim from resorting to outside help, and include conduct designed to prevent testimony to police officers or cooperation in criminal prosecutions. Where such an abusive relationship culminates in murder, the evidence may support a finding that the crime expressed the intent to isolate the victim and to stop her from reporting abuse to the authorities or cooperating with a criminal prosecution—rendering her prior statements admissible under the forfeiture doctrine. Earlier abuse, or threats of abuse, intended to dissuade the victim from resorting to outside help would be highly relevant to this inquiry, as would evidence of ongoing criminal proceedings at which the victim would have been expected to testify. . . .

The state courts in this case did not consider the intent of the defendant because they found that irrelevant to application of the forfeiture doctrine. This view of the law was error, but the court is free to consider evidence of the defendant's intent on remand. . . . The judgment of the California Supreme Court is vacated. . . .

Justice THOMAS, concurring.

I write separately to note that I adhere to my view that statements like those made by the victim in this case do not implicate the Confrontation Clause. . . . Nonetheless, in this case respondent does not argue that the contested evidence is nontestimonial, the court below noted "no dispute" on the issue, and it is outside the scope of the question presented. Because the Court's opinion accurately reflects our Confrontation Clause jurisprudence where the applicability of that Clause is not at issue, I join the Court in vacating the decision below.

Justice ALITO, concurring.

I join the Court's opinion, but I write separately to make clear that, like Justice THOMAS, I am not convinced that the out-of-court statement at issue here fell within the Confrontation Clause in the first place. . . .

Justice SOUTER, with whom Justice GINSBURG joins, concurring in [relevant] part.

. . . The historical record as revealed by the exchange simply does not focus on what should be required for forfeiture when the crime charged occurred in an abusive relationship or was its culminating act; today's understanding of domestic abuse had no apparent significance at the time of the Framing, and there is no early example of the forfeiture rule operating in that circumstance. Examining the early cases and commentary, however, reveals two things that count in favor of the Court's understanding of forfeiture when the evidence shows domestic abuse. The first is the substantial indication that the Sixth Amendment was meant to require some degree of intent to thwart the judicial process before thinking it reasonable to hold the confrontation right forfeited; otherwise the right would in practical terms boil down to a measure of reliable hearsay, a view rejected in *Crawford* v. *Washington*, 541 U.S. 36 (2004). The second is the absence from the early material of any reason to doubt that the element of intention would normally be satisfied by the intent inferred on the part of the domestic abuser in the classic abusive relationship, which is meant to isolate the victim from outside help, including the aid of law enforcement and the judicial process. If the evidence for admissibility shows a continuing relationship of this sort, it would make no sense to suggest that the oppressing defendant miraculously abandoned the dynamics of abuse the instant before he killed his victim, say in a fit of anger. The Court's conclusion . . . thus fits the rationale that equity requires and the historical record supports.

Justice BREYER, with whom Justice STEVENS and Justice KENNEDY join, dissenting.

... [A]n examination of the forfeiture rule's basic purposes and objectives indicates that the rule applies here. At the time of the founding, a leading treatise writer described the forfeiture rule as designed to assure that the prisoner "shall never be admitted to shelter himself by such evil Practices on the Witness, that being to give him Advantage of his own Wrong." [1 G. Gilbert, Law of Evidence 214–215 (1791).] ... What more "evil practice" ... than to murder the witness? And what greater evidentiary "advantage" could one derive from that wrong than thereby to prevent the witness from testifying, *e.g.*, preventing the witness from describing a history of physical abuse that is not consistent with the defendant's claim that he killed her in self-defense?

... [T]he defendant here knew that murdering his ex-girlfriend would keep her from testifying; and that knowledge is sufficient to show the *intent* that law ordinarily demands. ... With a few criminal law exceptions not here relevant, the law holds an individual responsible for consequences known likely to follow just as if that individual had intended to achieve them. A defendant, in a criminal or a civil case, for example, cannot escape criminal or civil liability for murdering an airline passenger by claiming that his purpose in blowing up the airplane was to kill only a single passenger for her life insurance, not the others on the same flight. ... [T]he law does not often turn matters of responsibility upon *motive*, rather than *intent*. And there is no reason to believe that application of the rule of forfeiture constitutes an exception to this general legal principle. ... [T]o turn application of the forfeiture rule upon proof of the defendant's *purpose* (rather than *intent*), as the majority does, creates serious practical evidentiary problems ...
[and] cannot be squared with the exception's basically ethical objective. ...

Each year, domestic violence results in more than 1,500 deaths and more than 2 million injuries; it accounts for a substantial portion of all homicides; it typically involves a history of repeated violence; and it is difficult to prove in court because the victim is generally reluctant or unable to testify. ... Regardless of a defendant's purpose, threats, further violence, and ultimately murder, can stop victims from testifying. See [Lininger, Prosecuting Batterers After *Crawford*, 91 Va. L. Rev. 747, 769 (2005)] (citing finding that batterers threaten retaliatory violence in as many as half of all cases, and 30 percent of batterers assault their victims again during the prosecution). A *constitutional* evidentiary requirement that insists upon a showing of purpose (rather than simply intent or probabilistic knowledge) may permit the domestic partner who made the threats, caused the violence, or even murdered the victim to avoid conviction for earlier crimes by taking advantage of later ones. ... [T]he Court ... grants the defendant not fair treatment, but a windfall. I can find no history, no underlying purpose, no administrative consideration, and no constitutional principle that requires this result. Insofar as Justice SOUTER's [concurrence] in effect presumes "purpose" based on no more than evidence of a history of domestic violence, I agree with it. In all other respects, however, I must respectfully dissent.

13. Residual Exception

The residual or "catchall" exception to the federal hearsay rule allows the introduction of certain out-of-court statements that seem reliable and highly probative but are not "covered" by other exceptions. The major controversy associated with its application has concerned the meaning of the word "covered"—and, by implication, the degree of freedom trial courts should have to expand or to supplement the traditional hearsay exceptions on a case-by-case basis.

[F.R.E. 807]

ADVISORY COMMITTEE NOTE TO RULE 807

The contents of Rule 803(24) and Rule 804(b)(5) have been combined and transferred to a new Rule 807. This was done to facilitate additions to Rules 803 and 804. No change in meaning is intended.

GLEN WEISSENBERGER & JAMES J. DUANE, FEDERAL RULES OF EVIDENCE
§807.1, at 618 (5th ed. 2007)

The legislative history of former Rules 803(24) and 804(b)(5) illustrates that the exceptions contained therein represented a compromise between the competing goals of allowing flexibility in the development of the hearsay system on the one hand and ensuring some degree of certainty for trial preparation on the other. Although the Supreme Court approved the Advisory Committee's draft, the Judiciary Committee deleted the residual exceptions from Rules 803 and 804 as "injecting too much uncertainty into the law of evidence and impairing the ability of practitioners to prepare for trial." The Committee believed that "if additional hearsay exceptions are to be created, they should be by amendments to the Rules, not on a case-by-case basis."

The Senate Judiciary Committee reinstated the residual exceptions, but added several restrictions to narrow their scope. While the Senate's draft was intended to provide room for growth in the hearsay rules, the Committee nevertheless cautioned that "[i]t is intended that the residual hearsay exceptions will be used very rarely, and only in exceptional circumstances." The Conference Committee approved the Senate's version of the Rules, but added a requirement that the proponent of the evidence offered under one of the residual exceptions must give his opponent sufficient notice before trial to enable him to prepare to meet the evidence. As enacted, Rules 803(24) and 804(b)(5) adopted the approach taken by some pre-Rules decisions which evaluated the trustworthiness of and need for a particular hearsay statement rather than the strict applicability of a specific exception. The residual exception now embodied in Rule 807 continues to allow courts to follow this approach to the admission of hearsay.

UNITED STATES v. LASTER

258 F.3d 525 (6th Cir. 2001)

Siler, Circuit Judge.

Defendants Jerry Lear and James M. Laster appeal their convictions and sentences for drug offenses [pertaining to the manufacture of methamphetamine. At trial the government introduced records of the Wilson Oil Company showing sales of hydriodic acid, a component of methamphetamine, to Laster. Mr. Wilson, the owner and operator of Wilson Oil Company, died before the trial began.] ... The district court held that the Wilson Oil Company records were admissible under either the business records hearsay exception of Fed. R. Evid. 803(6) or the residual exception of Fed. R. Evid. 807. [James Acquisto, a detective for a state drug task force,] was determined to be a qualified witness under Fed. R. Evid. 803(6), and was permitted to lay the foundation upon which the records were admitted. . . .

Acquisto did not examine the books or ledger sheets of Wilson Oil Company, nor did he know whether Wilson had an accountant or bookkeeper. Neither did Acquisto ask Wilson whether these documents were prepared simultaneously with the transactions reflected thereon. . . . Other than a few conversations between Acquisto and Wilson, there is no evidence that Acquisto was familiar with the record-keeping system of Wilson Oil Company. Therefore, the evidence was not admissible under Fed. R. Evid. 803(6).

However, the district court did not err in admitting the purchase orders and other related documents under the residual hearsay exception of Fed. R. Evid. 807 as there was "no indication" that the records were not reliable. This rule finds an equally trustworthy statement "not specifically covered by Rule 803 or 804," admissible if it is "material," "more probative on the point for which it is offered than any other evidence which the proponent can procure through reasonable efforts," and its admission best serves the interests of justice.

Although some courts have held that if proffered evidence fails to meet the requirements of the Fed. R. Evid. 803 hearsay exception, it cannot qualify for admission under the residual exception, the court declines to adopt this narrow interpretation of Fed. R. Evid. 807 as suggested by defendants. Rather, this court interprets Fed. R. Evid. 807, along with the majority of circuits, to mean that "if a statement is admissible under one of the hearsay exceptions, that exception should be relied on instead of the residual exception." 5 Jack B. Weinstein & Margaret A. Berger, *Weinstein's Federal Evidence* § 807.03(4) (2d ed. 2000). We endorse the reasoning in *United States v. Earles*, 113 F.3d 796 (8th Cir. 1997), which held that "the phrase 'specifically covered' [by a hearsay exception] means only that if a statement is *admissible* under one of the [803] exceptions, such . . . subsection should be relied upon" instead of the residual exception. Therefore, the analysis of a hearsay statement should not end when a statement fails to qualify as a prior inconsistent statement, but should be evaluated under the residual hearsay exception. . . . The district court did not err in admitting the records of Wilson Oil Company as these records were admissible under Fed. R. Evid. 807. . . . AFFIRMED.

KAREN NELSON MOORE, Circuit Judge, dissenting.

. . . Despite the plain language of the rule, which states that it applies only to statements "*not specifically covered* by Rule 803 or Rule 804," some courts have applied Rule 807 to statements *not admissible* under either Rule 803 or 804. Under this approach, out-of-court statements inadmissible under either Rule 803 or 804 may still be admissible under Rule 807, even when they are of a sort "specifically covered" by Rule 803 or 804, if they possess "equivalent circumstantial guarantees of trustworthiness." Thus, for example, although grand jury testimony is arguably former testimony, and thus specifically covered (and inadmissible) under Rule 804(b)(1), a number of circuits, including this one, have held that the grand jury testimony of an unavailable witness is admissible under the residual exception when it bears the "equivalent circumstantial guarantees of trustworthiness." *See United States v. Barlow*, 693 F.2d 954, 961-63 (6th Cir. 1982), *cert. denied*, 461 U.S. 945 (1983). *See also, e.g., United States v. Earles*, 113 F.3d 796, 800 (8th Cir. 1997) (holding that grand jury testimony, although inadmissible under other hearsay exceptions, "may . . . be considered for admission under the catch-all exception"), *cert. denied*, 522 U.S. 1075 (1998); *United States v. Marchini*, 797 F.2d 759, 764 (9th Cir. 1986) (holding that grand jury testimony was admissible under the residual exception), *cert. denied*, 479 U.S. 1085 (1987). *But see United States v. Vigoa*, 656 F. Supp. 1499, 1506 (D.N.J. 1987) (concluding "that admission of grand jury testimony under [the residual exception] is a perversion of the Federal Rules of Evidence and should not be condoned"), *aff'd*, 857 F.2d 1467 (3d Cir. 1988).

The contrary (minority) view of the residual exception is that the residual exception means what it says—i.e., that it applies to those exceptional cases in which an established exception to the hearsay rule does not apply but in which circumstantial guarantees of trustworthiness, equivalent to those existing for the established hearsay exceptions, are present. *See Conoco Inc. v. Dep't of Energy*, 99 F.3d 387, 393-93 (Fed. Cir. 1997) (holding that summaries by certain purchasers, made long after the purchases had been made, were not admissible under the residual exception because such summaries were not as trustworthy as either business records, which are covered by Fed. R. Evid. 803(6), or market reports and commercial publications, covered by Fed. R. Evid. 803(17)). Not only is this minority approach consistent with the plain language of the rule, *see United States v. Dent*, 984 F.2d 1453, 1465-66 (7th Cir.) (Easterbrook, J., concurring, joined by Bauer, C.J.) ("Rule [807] reads more naturally if we understand the introductory clause to mean that evidence of a kind specifically addressed ("covered") by one of the . . . other [exceptions] must satisfy the conditions laid down for its admission, and that other kinds of evidence not covered (because the drafters could not be exhaustive) are admissible if the evidence is approximately as reliable as evidence that would be admissible under the specific [exceptions].”), *cert. denied*, 510 U.S. 858 (1993), but it is also consistent with the legislative history of the residual exception, *see* S. Rep. No. 93-1277, at 20 (1974), *reprinted in* 1974 U.S.C.C.A.N. 7051, 7066 (“It is intended that the residual hearsay exceptions will be *used very rarely, and only in exceptional circumstances*. The committee *does not intend to establish a broad license for trial judges to admit hearsay statements that do not fall within one of the other exceptions* contained in rules 803 and 804. . . .”) (emphases added), and the original Advisory Committee Note to Rule 807’s predecessors, *see* Fed. R. Evid. 803(24), Advisory Committee Note (1975 Adoption) (repealed 1997) (“It would . . . be presumptuous to assume that all possible desirable exceptions to the hearsay rule have been catalogued. . . . Exception (24) and its companion provision . . . are accordingly included. They do not contemplate an unfettered exercise of judicial discretion, but they do provide for treating *new and presently unanticipated situations* which demonstrate a trustworthiness within the spirit of the specifically stated exceptions.”) (emphasis added).

This plain-language interpretation of the residual exception is sometimes described by its detractors as the “near-miss theory” of the residual exception: “[t]he doctrine that a ‘near miss’ under a specified exception . . . renders evidence inadmissible under [the] residual exception.” *United States v. Clarke*, 2 F.3d 81, 84 (4th Cir. 1993), *cert. denied*, 510 U.S. 1166 (1994). In the same vein, however, the majority approach might be called the “close-enough” theory of the residual exception, i.e., the doctrine that hearsay is admissible under the residual exception even when it just misses admissibility under an established exception. Such an approach makes little sense given the listing of explicit hearsay exceptions in Rules 803 and 804, exceptions that the drafters of the residual exception thought sufficient to cover anticipated (in other words, common) hearsay situations. *See United States v. Turner*, 104 F.3d 217, 221 (8th Cir. 1997) (“Allowing Turner to introduce the medical texts under [the residual exception], when Federal Rule of Evidence 803(18) specifically deals with the admissibility of this type of evidence, would circumvent the general purposes of the rules.”). . . .

The majority’s holding . . . appears to make it unnecessary ever to call a sponsoring witness to establish the admissibility of business records, at least so long as there is “ ‘no indication’ that the records [are] not reliable.” This cannot be squared with the language of Rule 803(6), which requires “the testimony of the custodian [of the records] or other qualified witness” to vouch for the existence of the other elements of the business records exception. Nor is it clear how, as a general matter, business records introduced without the testimony of a qualified sponsoring witness can be said to have “circumstantial guarantees of trustworthiness” equivalent to those that exist when a qualified sponsoring witness testifies to the trustworthiness of the records in question.

In sum, under the majority’s “close-enough” approach, the residual exception swallows all the other exceptions, as well as the rule. This court should not join the other circuits in expanding the residual hearsay exception to cover hearsay situations clearly anticipated by the drafters of the Federal Rules of Evidence. It should certainly not do so in the present case, in which an established hearsay exception clearly applied but rendered the documents inadmissible.

G. MICHAEL FENNER, THE RESIDUAL EXCEPTION TO THE HEARSAY RULE: THE COMPLETE TREATMENT
33 Creighton L. Rev. 265, 266, 273-276 (2000)

The residual exception is an expression of the need for flexibility in the rules. . . . Excluding near-miss evidence from the residual exception would place the rules of evidence back in the straightjacket from which the residual exception was intended to free them.[38]
. . . "Specifically covered" by one of the exceptions in Rule 803 or 804 . . . seems to mean falling within one of those exceptions. It does not seem to mean falling outside the exception. No matter how close it came, a miss is still a miss. . . . That is, each exception has certain foundational elements, and if there is sufficient evidence of each foundational element for any one exception then the statement is "specifically covered" by the exception. It is specifically covered by this exception whether it fits under any other exception or not. And, if one of the foundational elements is missing, then it is not "specifically covered" by this exception—no matter how close it comes. In fact, in this latter situation, the statement is specifically not covered by the barely missed exception. . . . " '[S]pecifically covered' means exactly what it says: if a statement does not meet all of the requirements for admissibility under one of the prior exceptions, then it is not 'specifically covered.' "[49]

14. Review

PROBLEMS FROM THE MULTISTATE BAR EXAMINATION*

[The following fact patterns are excerpts from publicly disclosed questions appearing on past Multistate Bar Examinations and from sample

---

38. Additionally, excluding near-miss evidence from the hearsay rule "promises much litigation over how close a statement can come [to a specified objection] before it is rendered inadmissible." United States v. Clarke, 2 F.3d 81, 84 (4th Cir. 1993). "Both litigants and courts spend their time more productively in analyzing the trustworthiness of the particular statement, rather than debating the abstract question of 'How close is too close?' to a specified hearsay exception." Id.

49. Clarke, 2 F.3d at 83.

*Copyright © 1992 (questions 3.57-3.69), 1995 (questions 3.70-3.72), 1996 (questions 3.47-3.54), and 2000 (questions 3.55 and 3.56) by the National Conference of Bar Examiners. All rights reserved.

questions distributed by the National Conference of Bar Examiners. In each case, is the offered evidence admissible, and, if so, for what purposes?]

3.47. Pawn sued Dalton for injuries received when she fell down a stairway in Dalton's apartment building. Pawn, a guest in the building, alleged that she caught the heel of her shoe in a tear in the stair carpet. Pawn calls Witt, a tenant, to testify that Young, another tenant, had said to him a week before Pawn's fall: "When I paid my rent this morning, I told the manager he had better fix that torn carpet."

3.48. Dahle is charged with possession of heroin. Prosecution witness Walker, an experienced dog trainer, testified that he was in the airport with a dog trained to detect heroin. As Dahle approached, the dog immediately became alert and pawed and barked frantically at Dahle's briefcase. Dahle managed to run outside and throw his briefcase into the river, from which it could not be recovered. After Walker's experience is established, he is asked to testify as an expert that the dog's reaction told him that Dahle's briefcase contained heroin.

3.49. Pamela sued Driver for damages for the death of Pamela's husband Ronald, resulting from an automobile collision. At trial, Driver calls Ronald's doctor to testify that the day before his death, Ronald, in great pain, said, "It was my own fault; there's nobody to blame but me."

3.50. In an automobile collision case brought by Poe against Davies, Poe introduced evidence that Ellis made an excited utterance that Davies ran the red light. Davies called Witt to testify that later Ellis, a bystander, now deceased, told Witt that Davies went through a yellow light.

3.51. Prine sued Dover for an assault that occurred March 5 in California. To support his defense that he was in Utah on that date, Dover identifies and seeks to introduce a letter he wrote to his sister a week before the assault in which he stated that he would see her in Utah on March 5.

3.52. Plaza Hotel sued Plaza House Hotel for infringement of its trade name. To establish a likelihood of name confusion, Plaintiff Plaza Hotel offers a series of memoranda which it had asked its employees to prepare at the end of each day listing instances during the day in which telephone callers, cab drivers, customers, and others had confused the two names.

3.53. Defendant was prosecuted for bankruptcy fraud. Defendant's wife, now deceased, had testified adversely to Defendant during earlier bankruptcy proceedings that involved similar issues. Although the wife had been cross-examined, no serious effort was made to challenge her credibility despite the availability of significant impeachment information. At the fraud trial, the prosecutor offers into evidence the testimony given by Defendant's wife at the bankruptcy proceeding.

3.54. Dove is on trial for theft. At trial, the prosecutor called John and May Wong. They testified that, as they looked out their apartment window, they saw thieves across the street break the window of a jewelry store, take jewelry, and leave in a car. Mrs. Wong telephoned the police and relayed to them the license number of the thieves' car as Mr. Wong looked out the window with binoculars and read it to her. Neither of them has any present memory of the number. The prosecutor offers as evidence a properly authenticated police tape recording of May Wong's telephone call with her voice giving the license number, which is independently shown to belong to Dove's car.

3.55. In a civil action for personal injury, Paul alleges that he was beaten up by Donald during an altercation in a crowded bar. Donald's defense is that he was not the person who hit Paul. To corroborate his testimony about the cause of his injuries, Paul seeks to introduce, through the hospital records custodian, a notation in a regular medical record made by an emergency room doctor at the hospital where Paul was treated for his injuries. The notation is: "Patient says he was attacked by Donald."

3.56. Pedestrian died from injuries caused when Driver's car struck him. Executor, Pedestrian's executor, sued Driver for wrongful death. At trial, Executor calls Nurse to testify that two days after the accident, Pedestrian said to Nurse, "The car that hit me ran the red light." Fifteen minutes thereafter, Pedestrian died. As a foundation for introducing evidence of Pedestrian's statement, Executor offers to the court Doctor's affidavit that Doctor was the intern on duty the day of Pedestrian's death and that several times that day Pedestrian had said that he knew he was about to die.

3.57. Dean, charged with murder, was present with her attorney at a preliminary examination when White, who was the defendant in a separate prosecution for concealing the body of the murder victim, testified for the prosecution against Dean. When called to testify at Dean's trial, White refused to testify, though ordered to do so. The prosecution offers evidence of White's testimony at the preliminary examination.

3.58. In a prosecution of Dale for murdering Vera, Dale testified that the killing had occurred in self-defense when Vera tried to shoot him. In rebuttal, the prosecution seeks to call Walter, Vera's father, to testify that the day before the killing Vera told Walter that she loved Dale so much she could never hurt him.

3.59. In Peck's antitrust suit against manufacturers of insulation, Peck's interrogatories asked for information concerning total sales of insulation by each of the defendant manufacturers in a particular year. The defendants replied to the interrogatories by referring Peck to the *Insulation Manufacturer's Annual Journal* for the information. . . . [A]t trial, Peck offers the annual as evidence of the sales volume.

3.60. Peters sues Davis for $100,000 for injuries received in a traffic accident. Davis charges Peters with contributory negligence and alleges that Peters failed to have his lights on at a time when it was dark enough to require them. Davis calls Bystander to testify that Passenger, who was riding in Peters' automobile and who also was injured, confided to him at the scene of the accident that "we should have had our lights on."

3.61. Davis offers to have Bystander testify that he was talking to Witness when he heard the crash and heard Witness, now deceased, exclaim, "That car doesn't have any lights on."

3.62. Perez sue[s] Dawson for damages arising out of an automobile collision. At trial, Perez call[s] Minter, an eyewitness to the collision. Perez expect[s] Minter to testify that she . . . observed Dawson's automobile for five seconds prior to the collision and estimated Dawson's speed at the time of the collision to [be] 50 miles per hour. Instead, Minter testifie[s] that she estimated Dawson's speed to [be] 25 miles per hour. . . . Perez then call[s] Wallingford, a police officer, to testify that Minter . . . told him during his investigation of the accident scene that Dawson "was doing at least 50."

3.63. Drew is charged with the murder of Pitt. The prosecutor introduced testimony of a police officer that Pitt told a priest, administering the last rites, "I was stabbed by Drew. Since I am dying, tell him I forgive him." Thereafter, Drew's attorney offers the testimony of Wall that the day before, when Pitt believed he would live, he stated that he had been stabbed by Jack, an old enemy.

3.64. Dray [is] prosecuted for bank robbery. At trial, the bank teller, Wall, [is] unable to identify Dray, now bearded, as the bank robber. The prosecutor then show[s] Wall a group of photographs, and [offers Wall's testimony] that she had previously told the prosecutor that the middle picture (concededly a picture of Dray before he grew his beard) was a picture of the bank robber.

3.65. Deetz [is] prosecuted for homicide. He testifie[s] that he shot in self-defense. In rebuttal, Officer Watts testifie[s] that he came to the scene in response to a telephone call from Deetz. Watts offers to testify that he asked, "What is the problem here, sir?" and Deetz replied, "I was cleaning my gun and it went off accidentally."

3.66. While crossing Spruce Street, Pesko was hit by a car that she did not see. Pesko sued Dorry for her injuries. At trial, Pesko calls Williams, a police officer, to testify that, ten minutes after the accident, a driver stopped him and said, "Officer, a few minutes ago I saw a hit-and-run accident on Spruce Street involving a blue convertible, which I followed to the drive-in restaurant at Oak and Third," and that a few seconds later Williams saw Dorry sitting alone in a blue convertible in the drive-in restaurant's parking lot.

3.67. An issue in Parker's action against Daves for causing Parker's back injury was whether Parker's condition had resulted principally from a similar occurrence five years before, with which Daves had no connection. Parker called Watts, his treating physician, who offered to testify that when she saw Parker after the latest occurrence, Parker told her that before the accident he had been working full time, without pain or limitation of motion, in a job that involved lifting heavy boxes.

3.68. West, a witness in a contract case, testified on direct examination that four people attended a meeting. When asked to identify them, she gave the names of three but despite trying was unable to remember the name of the fourth person. The attorney who called her as a witness seeks to show her his handwritten notes of the part of his pretrial interview with her in which she provided all four names.

3.69. Patty sues Mart Department Store for personal injuries, alleging that while shopping she was knocked to the floor by a merchandise cart being pushed by Handy, a stock clerk, and that as a consequence her back was injured. Handy testified that Patty fell near the cart but was not struck by it. Thirty minutes after Patty's fall, Handy, in accordance with regular practice at Mart, had filled out a printed form, "Employee's Report of Accident—Mart Department Store," in which he stated that Patty had been leaning over to spank her young child and in so doing had fallen near his cart. Counsel for Mart offers in evidence the report, which had been given him by Handy's supervisor.

3.70. Park sued Dunlevy for copyright infringement for using in Dunlevy's book some slightly disguised house plans on which Park held the copyright. Park is prepared to testify that he heard Dunlevy's executive assistant for copyright matters say that Dunlevy had obtained an advance copy of the plans from Park's office manager.

3.71. In a medical malpractice suit by Payne against Dr. Dock, Payne seeks to introduce a properly authenticated photocopy of Payne's hospital chart. The chart contained a notation made by a medical resident that an aortic clamp had broken during Payne's surgery. The resident made the notation in the regular course of practice, but had no personal knowledge of the operation, and cannot remember which of the operating physicians gave him the information.

3.72. Roberta Monk, a famous author, had a life insurance policy with Drummond Life Insurance Company. Her son, Peter, was beneficiary. Roberta disappeared from her residence in the city of Metropolis two years ago and has not been seen since. On the day that Roberta disappeared, Sky Airlines Flight 22 left Metropolis for Rio de Janeiro and vanished; the plane's passenger list included a Roberta Rector. Peter is now suing Drummond Life Insurance Company for the proceeds of his mother's policy. At trial, Peter offers to testify that his mother told him that she planned to write her next novel under the pen name of Roberta Rector.

D. HEARSAY AND DUE PROCESS

The Constitution places two significant constraints on hearsay law.

First, as we have seen, the Confrontation Clause of the Sixth Amendment, made applicable to the states through the Due Process Clause of the Fourteenth Amendment, prohibits the use of certain hearsay evidence against a criminal defendant. This prohibition may apply even to evidence that is otherwise admissible under the rules of evidence. Even when statements are rendered inadmissible by the hearsay rule, it can be important to know whether the Confrontation Clause also bars their introduction. For one thing, a constitutional violation, unlike like a mere violation of the hearsay rule, will not be harmless unless the government can demonstrate beyond a reasonable doubt that it did not affect the verdict. More importantly, inadmissibility under the Confrontation Clause triggers the *Bruton* doctrine—the special prohibition the Supreme Court has crafted against relying on limiting instructions to cure the prejudice created in a joint trial when a confession by one defendant would violate the Confrontation Clause if introduced against the other defendant.

The second constitutional supplement to hearsay law, discussed below, stems from the Due Process Clauses of the Fifth and Fourteenth Amendments. The Supreme Court has held that due process can require the admission of some evidence *offered* by a criminal defendant, even if the hearsay rule (or other rules of evidence) would otherwise prohibit use of the statements. Few statements, though, appear to fall within this category.

CHAMBERS v. MISSISSIPPI

410 U.S. 284 (1973)

Mr. Justice POWELL delivered the opinion of the Court.

Petitioner, Leon Chambers, was tried by a jury in a Mississippi trial court and convicted of murdering a policeman. The jury assessed punishment at life imprisonment, and the Mississippi Supreme Court affirmed, one justice dissenting. . . . [T]he petition for certiorari was granted to consider whether petitioner's trial was conducted in accord with principles of due process under the Fourteenth Amendment. We conclude that it was not.

I

The events that led to petitioner's prosecution for murder occurred in the small town of Woodville in southern Mississippi. On Saturday evening, June 14, 1969, two Woodville policemen, James Forman and Aaron 'Sonny' Liberty, entered a local bar and pool hall to execute a warrant for the arrest of a youth named C. C. Jackson. Jackson resisted and a hostile crowd of some 50 or 60 persons gathered. The officers' first attempt to handcuff Jackson was frustrated when 20 or 25 men in the crowd intervened and wrestled him free. Forman then radioed for assistance and Liberty removed his riot gun, a 12-gauge sawed-off shotgun, from the car. Three deputy sheriffs arrived shortly thereafter and the officers again attempted to make their arrest. Once more, the officers were attacked by the onlookers and during the commotion five or six pistol shots were fired. Forman was looking in a different direction when the shooting began, but immediately saw that Liberty had been shot several times in the back. Before Liberty died, he turned around and fired both barrels of his riot gun into an alley in the area from which the shots appeared to have come. The first shot was wild and high and scattered the crowd standing at the face of the alley. Liberty appeared, however, to take more deliberate aim before the second shot and hit one of the men in the crowd in the back of the head and neck as he ran down the alley. That man was Leon Chambers.

Officer Forman could not see from his vantage point who shot Liberty or whether Liberty's shots hit anyone. One of the deputy sheriffs testified at trial that he was standing several feet from Liberty and that he saw Chambers shoot him. Another deputy sheriff stated that, although he could not see whether Chambers had a gun in his hand, he did see Chambers 'break his arm down' shortly before the shots were fired. The officers who saw Chambers fall testified that they thought he was dead but they made no effort at that time either to examine him or to search for the murder weapon.

Instead, they attended to Liberty, who was placed in the police car and taken to a hospital where he was declared dead on arrival. A subsequent autopsy showed that he had been hit with four bullets from a .22-caliber revolver.

Shortly after the shooting, three of Chambers' friends discovered that he was not yet dead. James Williams,[1] Berkley Turner, and Gable McDonald loaded him into a car and transported him to the same hospital. Later that night, when the county sheriff discovered that Chambers was still alive, a guard was placed outside his room. Chambers was subsequently charged with Liberty's murder. He pleaded not guilty and has asserted his innocence throughout.

The story of Leon Chambers is intertwined with the story of another man, Gable McDonald. McDonald, a lifelong resident of Woodville, was in the crowd on the evening of Liberty's death. Sometime shortly after that day, he left his wife in Woodville and moved to Louisiana and found a job at a sugar mill. In November of that same year, he returned to Woodville when his wife informed him that an acquaintance of his, known as Reverend Stokes, wanted to see him. Stokes owned a gas station in Natchez, Mississippi, several miles north of Woodville, and upon his return McDonald went to see him. After talking to Stokes, McDonald agreed to make a statement to Chambers' attorneys, who maintained offices in Natchez. Two days later, he appeared at the attorneys' offices and gave a sworn confession that he shot Officer Liberty. He also stated that he had already told a friend of his, James Williams, that he shot Liberty. He said that he used his own pistol, a nine-shot .22-caliber revolver, which he had discarded shortly after the shooting. In response to questions from Chambers' attorneys, McDonald affirmed that his confession was voluntary and that no one had compelled him to come to them. Once the confession had been transcribed, signed, and witnessed, McDonald was turned over to the local police authorities and was placed in jail.

One month later, at a preliminary hearing, McDonald repudiated his prior sworn confession. He testified that Stokes had persuaded him to confess that he shot Liberty. He claimed that Stokes had promised that he would not go to jail and that he would share in the proceeds of a lawsuit that Chambers would bring against the town of Woodville. On examination by his own attorney and on cross-examination by the State, McDonald swore that he had not been at the scene when Liberty was shot but had been down the street drinking beer in a cafe with a friend, Berkley Turner. When he and Turner heard the shooting, he testified, they walked up the street and found Chambers lying in the alley. He, Turner, and Williams took Chambers to the hospital. McDonald further testified at the preliminary hearing that he did not know what had happened, that there was no discussion about the shooting either going to or coming back from the hospital, and that it was not until the next day that he learned that Chambers had been felled by a blast from Liberty's riot gun. In addition, McDonald stated that while he once owned a .22-caliber pistol he had lost it many

---

1. James Williams was indicted along with Chambers. The State, however, failed to introduce any evidence at trial implicating Williams in the shooting. At the conclusion of the State's case-in-chief, the trial court granted a directed verdict in his favor.

months before the shooting and did not own or possess a weapon at that time. The local justice of the peace accepted McDonald's repudiation and released him from custody. The local authorities undertook no further investigation of his possible involvement.

Chambers' case came on for trial in October of the next year. At trial, he endeavored to develop two grounds of defense. He first attempted to show that he did not shoot Liberty. Only one officer testified that he actually saw Chambers fire the shots. Although three officers saw Liberty shoot Chambers and testified that they assumed he was shooting his attacker, none of them examined Chambers to see whether he was still alive or whether he possessed a gun. Indeed, no weapon was ever recovered from the scene and there was no proof that Chambers had ever owned a .22-caliber pistol. One witness testified that he was standing in the street near where Liberty was shot, that he was looking at Chambers when the shooting began, and that he was sure that Chambers did not fire the shots.

Petitioner's second defense was that Gable McDonald had shot Officer Liberty. He was only partially successful, however, in his efforts to bring before the jury the testimony supporting this defense. Sam Hardin, a life-long friend of McDonald's, testified that he saw McDonald shoot Liberty. A second witness, one of Liberty's cousins, testified that he saw McDonald immediately after the shooting with a pistol in his hand. In addition to the testimony of these two witnesses, Chambers endeavored to show the jury that McDonald had repeatedly confessed to the crime. Chambers attempted to prove that McDonald had admitted responsibility for the murder on four separate occasions, once when he gave the sworn statement to Chambers' counsel and three other times prior to that occasion in private conversations with friends.

In large measure, he was thwarted in his attempt to present this portion of his defense by the strict application of certain Mississippi rules of evidence. Chambers asserts in this Court, as he did unsuccessfully in his motion for new trial and on appeal to the State Supreme Court, that the application of these evidentiary rules rendered his trial fundamentally unfair and deprived him of due process of law. It is necessary, therefore, to examine carefully the rulings made during the trial.

II

Chambers filed a pretrial motion requesting the court to order McDonald to appear. . . . The trial court granted the motion. . . . At trial, after the State failed to put McDonald on the stand, Chambers called McDonald, laid a predicate for the introduction of his sworn out-of-court confession, had it admitted into evidence, and read it to the jury. The State, upon cross-examination, elicited from McDonald the fact that he had repudiated his prior confession. McDonald further testified, as he had at the preliminary hearing, that he did not shoot Liberty, and that he confessed to the crime only on the promise of Reverend Stokes that he would not go to jail and would share in a sizable tort recovery from the town. He also retold his own story of his actions on the evening of the shooting, including his visit to the cafe down the street, his absence from the scene during the critical period, and his subsequent trip to the hospital with Chambers.

At the conclusion of the State's cross-examination, Chambers renewed his motion to examine McDonald as an adverse witness. The trial court denied the motion, stating: "He may be hostile, but he is not adverse in the sense of the word, so your request will be overruled." On appeal, the State Supreme Court upheld the trial court's ruling, finding that "McDonald's testimony was not adverse to appellant" because "[n]owhere did he point the finger at Chambers."

Defeated in his attempt to challenge directly McDonald's renunciation of his prior confession, Chambers sought to introduce the testimony of the three witnesses to whom McDonald had admitted that he shot the officer. The first of these, Sam Hardin, would have testified that, on the night of the shooting, he spent the late evening hours with McDonald at a friend's house after their return from the hospital and that, while driving McDonald home later that night, McDonald stated that he shot Liberty. The State objected to the admission of this testimony on the ground that it was hearsay. The trial court sustained the objection.[4]

Berkley Turner, the friend with whom McDonald said he was drinking beer when the shooting occurred, was then called to testify. In the jury's presence, and without objection, he testified that he had not been in the cafe that Saturday and had not had any beers with McDonald. The jury was then excused. In the absence of the jury, Turner recounted his conversations with McDonald while they were riding with James Williams to take Chambers to the hospital. When asked whether McDonald said anything regarding the shooting of Liberty, Turner testified that McDonald told him that he "shot him." Turner further stated that one week later, when he met McDonald at a friend's house, McDonald reminded him of their prior conversation and urged Turner not to "mess him up." Petitioner argued to the court that, especially where there was other proof in the case that was corroborative of these out-of-court statements, Turner's testimony as to McDonald's self-incriminating remarks should have been admitted as an exception to the hearsay rule. Again, the trial court sustained the State's objection.

The third witness, Albert Carter, was McDonald's neighbor. They had been friends for about 25 years. Although Carter had not been in Woodville on the evening of the shooting, he stated that he learned about it the next morning from McDonald. That same day, he and McDonald walked out to a well near McDonald's house and there McDonald told him that he was the one who shot Officer Liberty. Carter testified that McDonald also told him that he had disposed of the .22-caliber revolver later that night. He further testified that several weeks after the shooting, he accompanied McDonald to Natchez where McDonald purchased another .22 pistol to replace the one

---

4. Hardin's testimony, unlike the testimony of the other two men who stated that McDonald had confessed to them, was actually given in the jury's presence. After the State's objection to Hardin's account of McDonald's statement was sustained, the trial court ordered the jury to disregard it.

he had discarded.[5] The jury was not allowed to hear Carter's testimony. Chambers urged that these statements were admissible, the State objected, and the court sustained the objection. On appeal, the State Supreme Court approved the lower court's exclusion of these witnesses' testimony on hearsay grounds.

In sum, then, this was Chambers' predicament. As a consequence of the combination of Mississippi's "party witness" or "voucher" rule and its hearsay rule, he was unable either to cross-examine McDonald or to present witnesses in his own behalf who would have discredited McDonald's repudiation and demonstrated his complicity. Chambers had, however, chipped away at the fringes of McDonald's story by introducing admissible testimony from other sources indicating that he had not been seen in the cafe where he said he was when the shooting started, that he had not been having beer with Turner, and that he possessed a .22 pistol at the time of the crime. But all that remained from McDonald's own testimony was a single written confession countered by an arguably acceptable renunciation. Chambers' defense was far less persuasive than it might have been had he been given an opportunity to subject McDonald's statements to cross-examination or had the other confessions been admitted.

III

The right of an accused in a criminal trial to due process is, in essence, the right to a fair opportunity to defend against the State's accusations. The rights to confront and cross-examine witnesses and to call witnesses in one's own behalf have long been recognized as essential to due process. . . . Both of these elements of a fair trial are implicated in the present case.

A

Chambers was denied an opportunity to subject McDonald's damning repudiation and alibi to cross-examination. He was not allowed to test the witness' recollection, to probe into the details of his alibi, or to "sift" his conscience so that the jury might judge for itself whether McDonald's testimony was worthy of belief. *Mattox v. United States*, 156 U.S. 237, 242-243 (1895). The right of cross-examination is more than a desirable rule of trial procedure. It is implicit in the constitutional right of confrontation, and helps assure the "accuracy of the truth-determining process." *Dutton v. Evans*, 400 U.S. 74, 89 (1970); *Bruton v. United States*, 391 U.S. 123, 135-37 (1968). It is, indeed, "an essential and fundamental requirement for the kind of fair trial which is this country's constitutional goal." *Pointer v. Texas*, 380 U.S. 400, 405 (1965). Of course, the right to confront and to

---

5. A gun dealer from Natchez testified that McDonald had made two purchases. The witness' business records indicated that McDonald purchased a nine-shot .22-caliber revolver about a year prior to the murder. He purchased a different style .22 three weeks after Liberty's death.

cross-examine is not absolute and may, in appropriate cases, bow to accommodate other legitimate interests in the criminal trial process. But its denial or significant diminution calls into question the ultimate "integrity of the fact-finding process" and requires that the competing interest be closely examined. *Berger v. California*, 393 U.S. 314, 315 (1969).

In this case, petitioner's request to cross-examine McDonald was denied on the basis of a Mississippi common-law rule that a party may not impeach his own witness. The rule rests on the presumption—without regard to the circumstances of the particular case—that a party who calls a witness "vouches for his credibility." *Clark v. Lansford*, 191 So. 2d 123, 125 (Miss. 1966). Although the historical origins of the "voucher" rule are uncertain, it appears to be a remnant of primitive English trial practice in which "oath-takers" or "compurgators" were called to stand behind a particular party's position in any controversy. Their assertions were strictly partisan and, quite unlike witnesses in criminal trials today, their role bore little relation to the impartial ascertainment of the facts.[7]

Whatever validity the "voucher" rule may have once enjoyed, and apart from whatever usefulness it retains today in the civil trial process, it bears little present relationship to the realities of the criminal process.[8] It might have been logical for the early common law to require a party to vouch for the credibility of witnesses he brought before the jury to affirm his veracity. Having selected them especially for that purpose, the party might reasonably be expected to stand firmly behind their testimony. But in modern criminal trials, defendants are rarely able to select their witnesses: they must take them where they find them. Moreover, as applied in this case, the "voucher" rule's[9] impact was doubly harmful to Chambers' efforts to develop his defense. Not only was he precluded from cross-examining McDonald, but, as the State conceded at oral argument, he was also restricted in the scope of his direct examination by the rule's corollary requirement that the party calling the witness is bound by anything he might say. He was, therefore, effectively prevented from exploring the circumstances of McDonald's three prior oral confessions and from challenging the renunciation of the written confession. . . .

The argument that McDonald's testimony was not "adverse" to, or "against," Chambers is not convincing. The State's proof at trial excluded the theory that more than one person participated in the shooting of Liberty. To the extent that McDonald's sworn confession tended to incriminate him, it tended also to exculpate Chambers. And, in the circumstances of this case, McDonald's retraction inculpated Chambers to the same extent that it exculpated McDonald. It can hardly be disputed that McDonald's testimony

---

7. 3A J. Wigmore, Evidence § 896, pp. 658-660 (J. Chadbourn ed. 1970); C. McCormick, Evidence § 38, pp. 75-78 (2d ed. 1972).

8. The "voucher" rule has been condemned as archaic, irrational, and potentially destructive of the truth-gathering process, C. McCormick, *supra*, n. 7; E. Morgan, Basic Problems of Evidence 70-71 (1962); 3A J. Wigmore, *supra*, n. 7, § 898, p. 661.

9. The "voucher" rule has been rejected altogether by the newly proposed Federal Rules of Evidence, Rule 607, Rules of Evidence for United States Courts and Magistrates (approved Nov. 20, 1972, and transmitted to Congress to become effective July 1, 1973, unless the Congress otherwise determines).

was in fact seriously adverse to Chambers. The availability of the right to confront and to cross-examine those who give damaging testimony against the accused has never been held to depend on whether the witness was initially put on the stand by the accused or by the State. We reject the notion that a right of such substance in the criminal process may be governed by that technicality or by any narrow and unrealistic definition of the word "against." The "voucher" rule, as applied in this case, plainly interfered with Chambers' right to defend against the State's charges.

B

We need not decide, however, whether this error alone would occasion reversal since Chambers' claimed denial of due process rests on the ultimate impact of that error when viewed in conjunction with the trial court's refusal to permit him to call other witnesses. The trial court refused to allow him to introduce the testimony of Hardin, Turner, and Carter. Each would have testified to the statements purportedly made by McDonald, on three separate occasions shortly after the crime, naming himself as the murderer. The State Supreme Court approved the exclusion of this evidence on the ground that it was hearsay.

The hearsay rule, which has long been recognized and respected by virtually every State, is based on experience and grounded in the notion that untrustworthy evidence should not be presented to the triers of fact. Out-of-court statements are traditionally excluded because they lack the conventional indicia of reliability: they are usually not made under oath or other circumstances that impress the speaker with the solemnity of his statements; the declarant's word is not subject to cross-examination; and he is not available in order that his demeanor and credibility may be assessed by the jury. A number of exceptions have developed over the years to allow admission of hearsay statements made under circumstances that tend to assure reliability and thereby compensate for the absence of the oath and opportunity for cross-examination. Among the most prevalent of these exceptions is the one applicable to declarations against interest—an exception founded on the assumption that a person is unlikely to fabricate a statement against his own interest at the time it is made. Mississippi recognizes this exception but applies it only to declarations against pecuniary interest. It recognizes no such exception for declarations, like McDonald's in this case, that are against the penal interest of the declarant.

This materialistic limitation on the declaration-against-interest hearsay exception appears to be accepted by most States in their criminal trial processes, although a number of States have discarded it. Declarations against penal interest have also been excluded in federal courts under the authority of *Donnelly v. United States*, 228 U.S. 243, 272-273 (1913), although exclusion would not be required under the newly proposed Federal Rules of Evidence. Exclusion, where the limitation prevails, is usually premised on the view that admission would lead to the frequent presentation of perjured testimony to the jury. It is believed that confessions of criminal activity are often motivated by extraneous considerations and, therefore, are not as inherently reliable as statements against pecuniary or proprietary interest.

While that rationale has been the subject of considerable scholarly criticism, we need not decide in this case whether, under other circumstances, it might serve some valid state purpose by excluding untrustworthy testimony.

The hearsay statements involved in this case were originally made and subsequently offered at trial under circumstances that provided considerable assurance of their reliability. First, each of McDonald's confessions was made spontaneously to a close acquaintance shortly after the murder had occurred. Second, each one was corroborated by some other evidence in the case—McDonald's sworn confession, the testimony of an eyewitness to the shooting, the testimony that McDonald was seen with a gun immediately after the shooting, and proof of his prior ownership of a .22-caliber revolver and subsequent purchase of a new weapon. The sheer number of independent confessions provided additional corroboration for each. Third, whatever may be the parameters of the penal-interest rationale,[20] each confession here was in a very real sense self-incriminatory and unquestionably against interest. McDonald stood to benefit nothing by disclosing his role in the shooting to any of his three friends and he must have been aware of the possibility that disclosure would lead to criminal prosecution. Indeed, after telling Turner of his involvement, he subsequently urged Turner not to "mess him up." Finally, if there was any question about the truthfulness of the extrajudicial statements, McDonald was present in the courtroom and was under oath. He could have been cross-examined by the State, and his demeanor and responses weighed by the jury. The availability of McDonald significantly distinguishes this case from the prior Mississippi precedent, *Brown v. State, supra*, and from the *Donnelly*-type situation, since in both cases the declarant was unavailable at the time of trial.[21]

20. The Mississippi case which refused to adopt a hearsay exception for declarations against penal interest concerned an out-of-court declarant who purportedly stated that he had committed the murder with which his brother had been charged. The Mississippi Supreme Court believed that the declarant might have been motivated by a desire to free his brother rather than by any compulsion of guilt. The Court also noted that the declarant had fled, was unavailable for cross-examination, and might well have known at the time he made the statement that he would not suffer for it. *Brown v. State*, 99 Miss. 719, 55 So. 961 (1911). There is, in the present case, no such basis for doubting McDonald's statements.

21. McDonald's presence also deprives the State's argument for retention of the penal-interest rule of much of its force. In claiming that "[t]o change the rule would work a travesty on justice," the State posited the following hypothetical:

"If the rule were changed, A could be charged with the crime; B could tell C and D that he committed the crime; *B could go into hiding* and at A's trial C and D would testify as to B's admission of guilt; A could be acquitted and B would return to stand trial; B could then provide several witnesses to testify as to his whereabouts at the time of the crime. The testimony of those witnesses along with A's statement that he really committed the crime could result in B's acquittal. A would be barred from further prosecution because of the protection against double jeopardy. No one could be convicted of perjury as A did not testify at his first trial, B did not lie under oath, and C and D were truthful in their testimony." Brief for Respondent 7 n. 3 (emphasis supplied).

Obviously, B's absence at trial is critical to the success of the justice-subverting ploy.

Few rights are more fundamental than that of an accused to present witnesses in his own defense. In the exercise of this right, the accused, as is required of the State, must comply with established rules of procedure and evidence designed to assure both fairness and reliability in the ascertainment of guilt and innocence. Although perhaps no rule of evidence has been more respected or more frequently applied in jury trials than that applicable to the exclusion of hearsay, exceptions tailored to allow the introduction of evidence which in fact is likely to be trustworthy have long existed. The testimony rejected by the trial court here bore persuasive assurances of trustworthiness and thus was well within the basic rationale of the exception for declarations against interest. That testimony also was critical to Chambers' defense. In these circumstances, where constitutional rights directly affecting the ascertainment of guilt are implicated, the hearsay rule may not be applied mechanistically to defeat the ends of justice.

We conclude that the exclusion of this critical evidence, coupled with the State's refusal to permit Chambers to cross-examine McDonald, denied him a trial in accord with traditional and fundamental standards of due process. In reaching this judgment, we establish no new principles of constitutional law. Nor does our holding signal any diminution in the respect traditionally accorded to the States in the establishment and implementation of their own criminal trial rules and procedures. Rather, we hold quite simply that under the facts and circumstances of this case the rulings of the trial court deprived Chambers of a fair trial. . . .

Reversed and remanded.

[Justice White filed a concurring opinion. Justice Rehnquist filed a dissenting opinion.]

FORTINI v. MURPHY

257 F.3d 39 (1st Cir. 2001)

BOUDIN, Chief Judge.

This is an appeal by Robert Fortini from a federal district court order dismissing Fortini's petition for a writ of habeas corpus. Fortini is currently serving a life sentence, having been convicted in state court of second degree murder [for the shooting death of Ceasar Monterio. At trial, Fortini argued self-defense. The trial judge excluded evidence that the victim, Ceasar Monterio, assaulted four men on a basketball court shortly before his confrontation with Fortini. He argued in his habeas petition that this ruling violated *Chambers v. Mississippi*.]

Fortini's constitutional claim presents a difficult issue that cannot be said to be directly governed by existing Supreme Court precedent. . . . Although *Chambers* unquestionably remains "the law," *e.g., Crane v. Kentucky*, 476 U.S. 683, 690 (1986), the Court has rarely used it to overturn convictions and in recent years has made clear that it can be invoked only in extreme cases. Most recently, a majority of the Court said that a state law justification for exclusion will prevail unless it is "arbitrary or disproportionate" and "infringe[s] upon a weighty interest of the accused," *United States v. Scheffer*, 523 U.S. 303, 308 (1998). *See also Montana v. Egelhoff*, 518 U.S. 37, 53 (1996) (plurality opinion suggestion that any justification is sufficient to satisfy due process).

Inevitably, the lower federal courts have tended to "balance" incommensurate competing interests, taking account of the importance of the testimony to the defense, its inherent strength and reliability, and various kinds of countervailing reasons for excluding it offered by the state. Nevertheless, in cases less powerful than *Chambers*, a defendant whose proffer of evidence was rejected for any conventionally plausible reason or rule usually has an uphill struggle.

Admittedly, Fortini has a strong argument that the evidence in question should have been admitted under conventional evidence rules. . . . Although the evidence of the basketball court episode was certainly not relevant to *Fortini*'s state of mind (since he did not then know about the fight), it was relevant to Monterio's state of mind, making it more likely than it would be without the evidence that Monterio lunged at Fortini, as the latter claimed. . . . [I]t might look as if the basketball court incident was merely character evidence, tending to portray Monterio as a violent man. Such evidence is commonly excluded by courts because of its remoteness and tendency to prejudice the jury. Fed. R. Evid. 404. . . . But in a federal court, and so far as we can tell under Massachusetts law, the basketball court incident was so close in time to the shooting as to suggest that it might fall within the exceptions that admit (where pertinent) acts demonstrating state of mind and emotion of the actor, here Monterio. . . .

Even highly relevant evidence can be excluded if it is unduly prejudicial. The evidence in question was certainly prejudicial in the pertinent sense, that is, it invited the jury to acquit because it made Monterio out to be a violent and dangerous man of whom the world was well rid. But the state court did not exclude the evidence on grounds of undue prejudice and there is no certainty that it would have done so if it had appreciated the relevance of the evidence. Nor did the Appeals Court mention prejudice of this kind.

It might thus be argued that there was *no* valid justification invoked for excluding the evidence. The Appeals Court itself assumed *arguendo* that the evidence should not have been excluded. Although the [Supreme Judicial Court] has never squarely addressed the issue, it is hard for us to see why—assuming relevance—such bad acts would be categorically inadmissible where offered to show the state of mind of the victim rather than the state of mind of the defendant. . . .

Yet not every *ad hoc* mistake in applying state evidence rules, even in a murder case, should be called a violation of due process; otherwise every significant state court error in excluding evidence offered by the defendant would be a basis for undoing the conviction. The few Supreme Court cases that actually undid convictions based on a *Chambers* analysis involved far more egregious situations; and the more recent decisions of the Court we have cited create serious doubts that the Court is interested in carrying the doctrine beyond egregious cases.

Chambers and *Crane* both involved highly probative evidence absolutely critical to the defense. . . . By contrast, in the present case the defendant offered direct testimony on the pertinent issue—whether Monterio lunged at him. The basketball court incident that was excluded is at best indirect evidence which does no more than add to existing proof that Monterio was in a mood to lunge. . . .

[W]e conclude that the exclusion of evidence in question does not rise to the level of a *Chambers* violation. The evidence at best lies on the margin of a blurred line that divides character evidence, commonly but not always excluded, *cf.* Fed. R. Evid. 404, from state-of-mind evidence; the evidence at best does no more than increase somewhat the likelihood of a lunge, already the subject of Fortini's direct testimony; and the risk of unfair prejudice to the prosecution was real even if many courts would not have chosen to exclude the evidence on this ground.

It is very difficult to predict the evolution of Chambers because in over 30 years it has been used by the Supreme Court only a handful of times to overturn convictions; and the Supreme Court's standards are quite vague, although understandably so in a due process matter. Although this is a close case, exclusion of the evidence does not in our view add up to the kind of fundamental unfairness that warrants a federal court in finding a violation of due process. The exclusion in our view was error but it was not constitutional error. . . . [T]he judgment of the district court is affirmed. . . .

4

CHARACTER EVIDENCE

"*Wait a minute. I thought I was on trial here—
not my vented spoonbill cap.*"

A. THE BASIC RULE AND ITS EXCEPTIONS

A longstanding principle of Anglo-American evidence law prohibits proving a person's character to support an inference that the person acted in conformity with his character on a particular occasion. The prosecutor in a murder case, for example, generally cannot rely on evidence that the defendant has a violent temper. The rule customarily is justified on the ground that evidence of this sort, while probative, is likely to be unduly prejudicial.

Like the hearsay rule, the character evidence rule depends in its application on the purpose for which the challenged evidence is offered. Just as
out-of-court statements are barred by the hearsay rule only if they are
offered to prove the truth of what they assert, so evidence of a character
trait is barred only if it is offered to prove conduct in conformity with the
trait. But unlike the hearsay rule, with its myriad exceptions, the character
evidence rule has only three exceptions: one for the character of a criminal
defendant, one for the character of the victim or alleged victim of a criminal
offense, and one for the character of a witness. The first two exceptions
generally must be first invoked by a criminal defendant; once the defendant
chooses to open up the question of his or her character, or the character of
the victim or alleged victim, the prosecution can follow suit.

Despite being simpler than the hearsay doctrine, the system of rules
that has emerged for character evidence is no less controversial. Wigmore
praised the character evidence ban as "a revolution in the theory of criminal
trials, and . . . one of the peculiar features, of vast moment, which distinguishes the Anglo-American from the Continental system of Evidence." But
more recent reviews are more mixed. Professor Richard Uviller complained
a quarter-century ago that "today, character evidence most often appears
either in burlesque of its function, or as a product of an arcane legalistic
wordplay, or as a cruel and senseless shard of forgotten dogma." Many
critics agree.

The following cases and excerpts address the rationale of the character
evidence rule, its basic operation, and the exceptions for the character of a
criminal defendant and the character of a victim or alleged victim. The third
exception to the rule, concerning the character of witness, authorizes a
form of impeachment and rehabilitation. It is taken up in Chapter Seven
of this book.

[F.R.E. 404(a); C.E.C. §§1101(a), 1102-1103]

PEOPLE v. ZACKOWITZ

172 N.E. 466 (N.Y. 1930)

CARDOZO, C. J.

On November 10, 1929, shortly after midnight, the defendant in Kings
county shot Frank Coppola and killed him without justification or excuse.
A crime is admitted. What is doubtful is the degree only.

Four young men, of whom Coppola was one, were at work repairing
an automobile in a Brooklyn street. A woman, the defendant's wife, walked
by on the opposite side. One of the men spoke to her insultingly, or so at
least she understood him. The defendant, who had dropped behind to buy a
newspaper, came up to find his wife in tears. He was told she had been
insulted, though she did not then repeat the words. Enraged, he stepped
across the street and upbraided the offenders with words of coarse

profanity. He informed them, so the survivors testify, that "if they did not get out of there in five minutes, he would come back and bump them all off." Rejoining his wife, he walked with her to their apartment house located close at hand. He was heated with liquor which he had been drinking at a dance. Within the apartment he induced her to tell him what the insulting words had been. A youth had asked her to lie with him, and had offered her $2. With rage aroused again, the defendant went back to the scene of the insult and found the four young men still working at the car. In a statement to the police, he said that he had armed himself at the apartment with a .25-caliber automatic pistol. In his testimony at the trial he said that this pistol had been in his pocket all the evening. Words and blows followed, and then a shot. The defendant kicked Coppola in the stomach. There is evidence that Coppola went for him with a wrench. The pistol came from the pocket, and from the pistol a single shot, which did its deadly work. The defendant walked away and at the corner met his wife who had followed him from the home. The two took a taxicab to Manhattan, where they spent the rest of the night at the dwelling of a friend.

On the way the defendant threw his pistol into the river. He was arrested on January 7, 1930, about two months following the crime.

At the trial the vital question was the defendant's state of mind at the moment of the homicide. Did he shoot with a deliberate and premeditated design to kill? Was he so inflamed by drink or by anger or by both combined that, though he knew the nature of his act, he was the prey to sudden impulse, the fury of the fleeting moment? If he went forth from his apartment with a preconceived design to kill, how is it that he failed to shoot at once? How to reconcile such a design with the drawing of the pistol later in the heat and rage of an affray? These and like questions the jurors were to ask themselves and answer before measuring the defendant's guilt. Answers consistent with guilt in its highest grade can reasonably be made. Even so, the line between impulse and deliberation is too narrow and elusive to make the answers wholly clear. The sphygmograph records with graphic certainty the fluctuations of the pulse. There is no instrument yet invented that records with equal certainty the fluctuations of the mind. At least, if such an instrument exists, it was not working at midnight in the Brooklyn street when Coppola and the defendant came together in a chance affray. With only the rough and ready tests supplied by their experience of life, the jurors were to look into the workings of another's mind, and discover its capacities and disabilities, its urges and inhibitions, in moments of intense excitement. Delicate enough and subtle is the inquiry, even in the most favorable conditions, with every warping influence excluded. There must be no blurring of the issues by evidence illegally admitted and carrying with it in its admission an appeal to prejudice and passion.

Evidence charged with that appeal was, we think, admitted here. Not only was it admitted, and this under objection and exception, but the changes were rung upon it by prosecutor and judge. Almost at the opening of the trial the people began the endeavor to load the defendant down with the burden of an evil character. He was to be put before the jury as a man of murderous disposition. To that end they were allowed to prove that at the time of the encounter and at that of his arrest he had in his apartment, kept there in a radio box, three pistols and a tear-gas gun. There was no claim that he had brought these weapons out at the time of the affray, no claim that with any of them he had discharged the fatal shot. He could not have done so, for they were all of different caliber. The end to be served by laying the weapons before the jury was something very different. The end was to bring persuasion that here was a man of vicious and dangerous propensities, who because of those propensities was more likely to kill with deliberate and premeditated design than a man of irreproachable life and amiable manners. Indeed, this is the very ground on which the introduction of the evidence is now explained and defended. The district attorney tells us in his brief that the possession of the weapons characterized the defendant as "a desperate type of criminal," a "person criminally inclined." . . . The weapons were not brought by the defendant to the scene of the encounter. They were left in his apartment where they were incapable of harm. In such circumstances, ownership of the weapons, if it has any relevance at all, has relevance only as indicating a general disposition to make use of them thereafter, and a general disposition to make use of them thereafter is without relevance except as indicating a "desperate type of criminal," a criminal affected with a murderous propensity.

. . . If a murderous propensity may be proved against a defendant as one of the tokens of his guilt, a rule of criminal evidence, long believed to be of fundamental importance for the protection of the innocent, must be first declared away. Fundamental hitherto has been the rule that character is never an issue in a criminal prosecution unless the defendant chooses to make it one. Wigmore, Evidence, vol. 1, §§55, 192. In a very real sense a defendant starts his life afresh when he stands before a jury, a prisoner at the bar. There has been a homicide in a public place. The killer admits the killing, but urges self-defense and sudden impulse. Inflexibly the law has set its face against the endeavor to fasten guilt upon him by proof of character or experience predisposing to an act of crime. The endeavor has been often made, but always it has failed. At times, when the issue has been self-defense, testimony has been admitted as to the murderous propensity of the deceased, the victim of the homicide, but never of such a propensity on the part of the killer. The principle back of the exclusion is one, not of logic, but of policy. There may be cogency in the argument that a quarrelsome defendant is more likely to start a quarrel than one of milder type, a man of dangerous mode of life more likely than a shy recluse. The law is not blind to this, but equally it is not blind to the peril to the innocent if character is accepted as probative of crime. "The natural and inevitable tendency of the tribunal—whether judge or jury—is to give excessive weight to the vicious record of crime thus exhibited, and either to allow it to bear too strongly on the present charge, or to take the proof of it as justifying a condemnation irrespective of guilt of the present charge." Wigmore, Evidence, vol. 1, §194, and cases cited.

A different question would be here if the pistols had been bought in expectation of this particular encounter. They would then have been admissible as evidence of preparation and design. A different question would be here if they were so connected with the crime as to identify the perpetrator, if he had dropped them, for example, at the scene of the affray. They would then have been admissible as tending to implicate the possessor (if identity was disputed), no matter what the opprobrium attached to his possession. Different, also, would be the question if the defendant had been shown to have gone forth from the apartment with all the weapons on his person. To be armed from head to foot at the very moment of an encounter may be a circumstance worthy to be considered, like acts of preparation generally, as a proof of preconceived design. There can be no such implication from the ownership of weapons which one leaves behind at home.

The endeavor was to generate an atmosphere of professional criminality. It was an endeavor the more unfair in that, apart from the suspicion attaching to the possession of these weapons, there is nothing to mark the defendant as a man of evil life. He was not in crime as a business. He did not shoot as a bandit shoots in the hope of wrongful gain. He was engaged in a decent calling, an optician regularly employed, without criminal record, or criminal associates. If his own testimony be true, he had gathered these weapons together as curious, a collection that interested and amused him. Perhaps his explanation of their ownership is false. There is nothing stronger than mere suspicion to guide us to an answer. Whether the explanation be false or true, he should not have been driven by the people to the necessity of offering it. Brought to answer a specific charge, and to defend himself against it, he was placed in a position where he had to defend himself against another, more general and sweeping. He was made to answer to the charge, pervasive and poisonous even if insidious and covert, that he was a man of murderous heart, of criminal disposition.

. . . The judgment of conviction should be reversed, and a new trial ordered.

CLEGHORN v. NEW YORK CENTRAL & HUDSON RIVER R.R. CO.

56 N.Y. 44 (1874)

CHURCH, Ch. J. The accident was caused by the carelessness of the switchman, in neglecting to close the switch after the stock train had passed on to the side track, and in giving a false signal to the approaching passenger train, that the track was all right. . . . It is insisted that the court erred in admitting evidence of the intemperate habits of the switchman, and that the case of *Warner v. N.Y.C. R.R. Co.* (44 N.Y., 465) is a direct authority against it. That was a case of injury at a road crossing. It was proved that the flagman neglected to give the customary signal, and was intoxicated at the time. The Commission of Appeals held it error to show previous habits of intemperance known to the officers of the company, upon the ground that such evidence had no bearing upon the question of negligence at the time. In that view the decision was right. Previous intoxication would not tend to establish an omission to give the signal on the occasion of the accident. In this case it was sought to be proved, not only that Hartman was intoxicated at the time of the accident, but that he was a man of intemperate habits, which were known by the agent of the company, having the power to employ and discharge him and other subordinates, with a view of claiming exemplary damages. For this purpose the evidence was competent. It is unnecessary in this connection, to speak of the strength of the proof upon which a claim for exemplary damages was made in this case. It is sufficient to say that the evidence was competent upon the question of gross negligence on the part of the defendant in employing or continuing the employment of a subordinate known to be unfit for his position by reason of intoxication. [Judgment for plaintiff reversed on other grounds.]

BERRYHILL v. BERRYHILL

410 So. 2d 416 (Ala. 1982)

BEATTY, Justice.

. . . During the course of the custody proceeding, the petitioner asked the respondent if he had ever killed anyone. Although that question may be considered overbroad, we disagree with the conclusion by the Court of Civil Appeals that the relevancy of the question was not shown.

If character or reputation becomes a matter in issue in a civil suit, evidence with reference to such a party's reputation or character is admissible. . . . In a child custody proceeding, character is obviously in issue and "evidence touching the character, conduct, and reputation of the parties, or any other evidence tending to throw light on their fitness to be the custodian of the child, is admissible." *Milner v. Gatlin*, 143 Ga. 816, 85 S.E. 1045, 1047 (1915). . . . Thus, the question directed toward the respondent asking whether he had ever killed anyone would be relevant as an attempt to show a specific act of bad character bearing on the "fitness" of the respondent. . . . For these reasons the judgment of the Court of Civil Appeals is reversed. . . .

LARSON v. KLAPPRODT

231 N.W.2d 370 (S.D. 1975) (sub nom. Walkon Carpet Corp. v. Klapprodt)

COLER, Justice.

. . . In his counterclaim defendant alleged that the plaintiff Larson had slandered him in telling certain persons that he both drank to excess and was sexually promiscuous. The trial court may properly have considered from the development of the evidence on that count and from other evidence in the record that the reputation of the defendant was not such, in its tarnished state, as to have been materially damaged by the slander of the plaintiff. Since damage to reputation was at least part of Klapprodt's claim, evidence of his reputation or past misdeeds was admissible both in establishing truth, *Tokmakian v. Fritz*, 1949, 75 R.I. 496, 67 A.2d 834, and in mitigating damages. *Kruglak v. Landre*, 1965, 23 A.D.2d 758, 258 N.Y.S.2d 550. The Restatement of Torts, Explanatory Notes §621, comment d, at 287 (Tent. Draft No. 20, 1974), supports this view. "In determining the amount of an award of general damages, the jury or other trier of fact may consider the character of the plaintiff and his general standing in the community as affecting the loss which he has sustained or will sustain." . . . Judgment is affirmed.

ADVISORY COMMITTEE NOTE TO F.R.E. 404(a)

Character questions arise in two fundamentally different ways. (1) Character may itself be an element of a crime, claim, or defense. A situation of this kind is commonly referred to as "character in issue." Illustrations are: the chastity of the victim under a statute specifying her chastity as an element of the crime of seduction, or the competency of the driver in an action for negligently entrusting a motor vehicle to an incompetent driver. No problem of the general relevancy of character evidence is involved, and the present rule therefore has no provision on the subject. . . . (2) Character evidence is susceptible of being used for the purpose of suggesting an inference that the person acted on the occasion in question consistently with his character. This use of character is often described as "circumstantial." Illustrations are: evidence of a violent disposition to prove that the person was the aggressor in an affray, or evidence of honesty in disproof of a charge of theft. . . .

In most jurisdictions today, the circumstantial use of character is rejected but with important exceptions: (1) an accused may introduce pertinent evidence of good character (often misleadingly described as "putting his character in issue"), in which event the prosecution may rebut with evidence of bad character; (2) an accused may introduce pertinent evidence of the character of the victim, as in support of a claim of self-defense to a charge of homicide or consent in a case of rape, and the prosecution may introduce similar evidence in rebuttal of the character evidence, or, in a homicide case, to rebut a claim that deceased was the first aggressor, however proved; and (3) the character of a witness may be gone into as bearing on his credibility. This pattern is incorporated in the rule. While its basis lies more in history and experience than in logic an underlying justification can fairly be found in terms of the relative presence and absence of prejudice in the various situations. In any event, the criminal rule is so deeply imbedded in our jurisprudence as to assume almost constitutional proportions and to override doubts of the basic relevancy of the evidence.

. . . The argument is made that circumstantial use of character ought to be allowed in civil cases to the same extent as in criminal cases, i.e. evidence of good (nonprejudicial) character would be admissible in the first instance, subject to rebuttal by evidence of bad character. . . . The difficulty with expanding the use of character evidence in civil cases is set forth by the California Law Revision Commission . . . : "Character evidence is of slight probative value and may be very prejudicial. It tends to distract the trier of fact from the main question of what actually happened on the particular occasion. It subtly permits the trier of fact to reward the good man and to punish the bad man because of their respective characters despite what the evidence in the case shows actually happened."

McCORMICK ON EVIDENCE

§§191-192, at 1:768-769 n. 2, 776-777 (Kenneth S. Broun, ed., 6th ed. 2006)

The difference in the [character evidence] rule as regards the prosecution and the defense has been characterized as an amelioration of the "brutal rigors" of the early criminal law. Maguire, Evidence—Common Sense and Common Law 204 (1947). But to say that the defendant deserves the benefit of all reasonable doubts and that good character may produce a reasonable doubt assumes what should be demonstrated—that the doubt is not the product of unfair prejudice. . . . Thus, one must consider whether a parade of character witnesses convinces most jurors that the defendant has led an exemplary life even when his past is not so unblemished and whether many defendants with checkered backgrounds will be in a position to produce such witnesses. Furthermore, to the extent that the ability to collect impressive character witnesses is concentrated among those accused of white collar rather than street crimes, one may question the fairness of an asymmetrical rule. . . .

[When] the character of the *victim* is being proved . . . [t]here is . . . a risk of a different form of prejudice. Learning of the victim's bad character could lead the jury to think that the victim merely "got what he deserved" and to acquit for that reason. Nevertheless, at least in murder and perhaps in battery cases as well, when the identity of the first aggressor is really in doubt, the probative value of the evidence ordinarily justifies taking this risk.

PROBLEMS

4.1. A criminal defendant charged with heroin trafficking admits selling heroin to an undercover agent but claims to have been entrapped. Under federal law the defense of entrapment is unavailable to a defendant who was "predisposed" to commit the offense. The government seeks to call a rebuttal witness who will describe buying heroin from the defendant a month before the undercover purchase. Is the testimony barred by F.R.E. 404(a)?

4.2. A civil defendant, sued in federal court for wrongful death, claims he shot the victim in self-defense. In order to support his testimony that the victim attacked him, may the defendant introduce evidence that the victim had an explosive temper? In order to support his testimony that he reasonably feared for his life, may the defendant introduce evidence that the victim had a reputation for brutality?

4.3. A criminal defendant charged with murder testifies that he shot the victim only after the victim lunged at him with a knife. May the prosecution introduce evidence of the victim's peaceful character? May the prosecution introduce evidence of the defendant's violent character?

4.4. A criminal defendant charged with murder claims self-defense and introduces evidence that the victim was prone to violence. May the prosecution introduce evidence of the victim's peaceful character? May the prosecution introduce evidence of the defendant's violent character?

4.5. In an extortion prosecution, the government proves the defendant made vaguely menacing statements to the victim. In order to show that the defendant intended the statements as threats of physical harm, and that the statements put the victim in reasonable fear for his safety, may the government prove that the defendant has a well known proclivity toward violence?

B. Methods of Proving Character

The hearsay rule and its exceptions pay little attention to how an out-of-court statement is proved. All that matters, generally, is the nature of the statement itself and the purpose for which it is offered. The character evidence rule is different. When one of the three exceptions to the character evidence rule applies, it typically applies only to certain kinds of evidence of character—namely, testimony about a person's reputation, or a witness's own opinion about the person's character. What remains excluded, typically, is what many people would find the best proof of a person's character: evidence of how the person has actually acted on other occasions. The following materials discuss the rationale and operation of this counterintuitive rule.

[F.R.E. 405, 803(21); C.E.C. §§1102-1103, 1324]

MICHELSON v. UNITED STATES

335 U.S. 469 (1948)

Mr. Justice Jackson delivered the opinion of the Court.

In 1947 petitioner Michelson was convicted of bribing a federal revenue agent. The Government proved a large payment by accused to the agent for the purpose of influencing his official action. The defendant, as a witness on his own behalf, admitted passing the money but claimed it was done in response to the agent's demands, threats, solicitations, and inducements that amounted to entrapment. It is enough for our purposes to say that determination of the issue turned on whether the jury should believe the agent or the accused.

. . . Defendant called five witnesses to prove that he enjoyed a good reputation. Two of them testified that their acquaintance with him extended over a period of about thirty years and the others said they had known him at least half that long. A typical examination in chief was as follows:

"*Q.* Do you know the defendant Michelson? *A.* Yes.
"*Q.* How long do you know Mr. Michelson? *A.* About 30 years.
"*Q.* Do you know other people who know him? *A.* Yes.
"*Q.* Have you had occasion to discuss his reputation for honesty and truthfulness and for being a law-abiding citizen? *A.* It is very good.
"*Q.* You have talked to others? *A.* Yes.
"*Q.* And what is his reputation? *A.* Very good."

These are representative of answers by three witnesses; two others replied, in substance, that they never had heard anything against Michelson.

. . . To four of these witnesses the prosecution also addressed the question the allowance of which, over defendant's objection, is claimed to be reversible error:

"Did you ever hear that on October 11th, 1920, the defendant, Solomon Michelson, was arrested for receiving stolen goods?"

None of the witnesses appears to have heard of this.

The trial court asked counsel for the prosecution, out of presence of the jury, "Is it a fact according to the best information in your possession that Michelson was arrested for receiving stolen goods?" Counsel replied that it was, and to support his good faith exhibited a paper record which defendant's counsel did not challenge.

The judge also on three occasions warned the jury, in terms that are not criticized, of the limited purpose for which this evidence was received.[3]

3. In ruling on the objection when the question was first asked, the Court said: ". . . I instruct the jury that what is happening now is this: the defendant has called character witnesses, and the basis for the evidence given by those character witnesses is the reputation of the defendant in the community, and since the defendant tenders the issue of his reputation the prosecution may ask the witness if she has heard of various incidents in his career. I say to you that regardless of her answer you are not to assume that the incidents asked about actually took place. All that is happening is that this witness' standard of opinion of the reputation of the defendant is being tested. Is that clear?"

In overruling the second objection to the question the Court said: "Again I say to the jury there is no proof that Mr. Michelson was arrested for receiving stolen goods in 1920, there isn't any such proof. All this witness has been asked is whether he had heard of that. There is nothing before you on that issue. Now would you base your decision on the case fairly in spite of the fact that that question has been asked? You would? All right."

The charge included the following: "In connection with the character evidence in the case I permitted a question whether or not the witness knew that in 1920 this defendant had been arrested for receiving stolen goods. I tried to give you the instruction then that that question was permitted only to test the standards of character evidence that these character witnesses seemed to have. There isn't any proof in the case that could be produced before

Defendant-petitioner challenges the right of the prosecution so to cross-examine his character witnesses. The Court of Appeals held that it was permissible. The opinion, however, points out that the practice has been severely criticized and invites us, in one respect, to change the rule. Serious and responsible criticism has been aimed, however, not alone at the detail now questioned by the Court of Appeals but at common-law doctrine on the whole subject of proof of reputation or character.[5] It would not be possible to appraise the usefulness and propriety of this cross-examination without consideration of the unique practice concerning character testimony, of which such cross-examination is a minor part.

Courts that follow the common-law tradition almost unanimously have come to disallow resort by the prosecution to any kind of evidence of a defendant's evil character to establish a probability of his guilt. Not that the law invests the defendant with a presumption of good character, but it simply closes the whole matter of character, disposition and reputation on the prosecution's case-in-chief. The State may not show defendant's prior trouble with the law, specific criminal acts, or ill name among his neighbors, even though such facts might logically be persuasive that he is by propensity a probable perpetrator of the crime. The inquiry is not rejected because character is irrelevant; on the contrary, it is said to weigh too much with the jury and to so overpersuade them as to prejudge one with a bad general record and deny him a fair opportunity to defend against a particular charge. The overriding policy of excluding such evidence, despite its admitted probative value, is the practical experience that its disallowance tends to prevent confusion of issues, unfair surprise and undue prejudice.

But this line of inquiry firmly denied to the State is opened to the defendant because character is relevant in resolving probabilities of guilt. He may introduce affirmative testimony that the general estimate of his character is so favorable that the jury may infer that he would not be likely to commit the offense charged. This privilege is sometimes valuable to a defendant for this Court has held that such testimony alone, in some circumstances, may be enough to raise a reasonable doubt of guilt and that in the federal courts a jury in a proper case should be so instructed.

---

you legally within the rules of evidence that this defendant was arrested in 1920 for receiving stolen goods, and that fact you are not to hold against him; nor are you to assume what the consequences of that arrest were. You just drive it from your mind so far as he is concerned, and take it into consideration only in weighing the evidence of the character witnesses."

5. A judge of long trial and appellate experience has uttered a warning which, in the opinion of the writer, we might well have heeded in determining whether to grant certiorari here: ". . . evidence of good character is to be used like any other, once it gets before the jury, and the less they are told about the grounds for its admission, or what they shall do with it, the more likely they are to use it sensibly. The subject seems to gather mist which discussion serves only to thicken, and which we can scarcely hope to dissipate by anything further we can add." L. Hand in *Nash v. United States*, 2 Cir., 54 F.2d 1006, 1007.

In opening its cyclopedic review of authorities from many jurisdictions, CORPUS JURIS SECUNDUM summarizes that the rules regulating proof of character "have been criticized as illogical, unscientific, and anomalous, explainable only as archaic survivals of compurgation or of states of legal development when the jury personally knew the facts on which their verdict was based." 32 C.J.S., Evidence, §433.

When the defendant elects to initiate a character inquiry, another anomalous rule comes into play. Not only is he permitted to call witnesses to testify from hearsay, but indeed such a witness is not allowed to base his testimony on anything but hearsay. . . . The witness may not testify about defendant's specific acts or courses of conduct or his possession of a particular disposition or of benign mental and moral traits; nor can he testify that his own acquaintance, observation, and knowledge of defendant leads to his own independent opinion that defendant possesses a good general or specific character, inconsistent with commission of acts charged. The witness is, however, allowed to summarize what he has heard in the community, although much of it may have been said by persons less qualified to judge than himself. The evidence which the law permits is not as to the personality of defendant but only as to the shadow his daily life has cast in his neighborhood. This has been well described in a different connection as "the slow growth of months and years, the resultant picture of forgotten incidents, passing events, habitual and daily conduct, presumably honest because disinterested, and safer to be trusted because prone to suspect. . . . It is for that reason that such general repute is permitted to be proven. It sums up a multitude of trivial details. It compacts into the brief phrase of a verdict the teaching of many incidents and the conduct of years. It is the average intelligence drawing its conclusion." Finch J., in *Badger v. Badger*, 88 N.Y. 546, 552, 42 Am. Rep. 263.

While courts have recognized logical grounds for criticism of this type of opinion-based-on-hearsay testimony, it is said to be justified by "overwhelming considerations of practical convenience" in avoiding innumerable collateral issues which, if it were attempted to prove character by direct testimony, would complicate and confuse the trial, distract the minds of jurymen and befog the chief issues in the litigation. *People v. Van Gaasbeck*, 189 N.Y. 408, 418, 82 N.E. 718.

. . . Thus the law extends helpful but illogical options to a defendant. Experience taught a necessity that they be counterweighted with equally illogical conditions to keep the advantage from becoming an unfair and unreasonable one. The price a defendant must pay for attempting to prove his good name is to throw open the entire subject which the law has kept closed for his benefit and to make himself vulnerable where the law otherwise shields him. The prosecution may pursue the inquiry with contradictory witnesses to show that damaging rumors, whether or not well-grounded, were afloat—for it is not the man that he is, but the name that he has which is put in issue.[16] Another hazard is that his own witness is

---

16. A classic example in the books is a character witness in a trial for murder. She testified she grew up with defendant, knew his reputation for peace and quiet, and that it was good. On cross-examination she was asked if she had heard that the defendant had shot anybody and, if so, how many. She answered, "Three or four," and gave the names of two but could not recall the names of the others. She still insisted, however, that he was of "good character." The jury seems to have valued her information more highly than her judgment, and on appeal from conviction the cross-examination was held proper. *People v. Laudiero*, 192 N.Y. 304, 309, 85 N.E. 132.

subject to cross-examination as to the contents and extent of the hearsay on which he bases his conclusions, and he may be required to disclose rumors and reports that are current even if they do not affect his own conclusion. It may test the sufficiency of his knowledge by asking what stories were circulating concerning events, such as one's arrest, about which people normally comment and speculate. Thus, while the law gives defendant the option to show as a fact that his reputation reflects a life and habit incompatible with commission of the offense charged, it subjects his proof to tests of credibility designed to prevent him from profiting by a mere parade of partisans.

To thus digress from evidence as to the offense to hear a contest as to the standing of the accused, at its best opens a tricky line of inquiry as to a shapeless and elusive subject matter. At its worst it opens a veritable Pandora's box of irresponsible gossip, innuendo and smear. . . . Wide discretion is accompanied by heavy responsibility on trial courts to protect the practice from any misuse. The trial judge was scrupulous to so guard it in the case before us. He took pains to ascertain, out of presence of the jury, that the target of the question was an actual event, which would probably result in some comment among acquaintances if not injury to defendant's reputation. He satisfied himself that counsel was not merely taking a random shot at a reputation imprudently exposed or asking a groundless question to waft an unwarranted innuendo into the jury box. . . . [The question permitted by the trial court] was proper cross-examination because reports of [Michelson's] arrest for receiving stolen goods, if admitted, would tend to weaken the assertion that he was known as an honest and law-abiding citizen.

. . . We do not overlook or minimize the consideration that "the jury almost surely cannot comprehend the Judge's limiting instructions," which disturbed the Court of Appeals. The refinements of the evidentiary rules on this subject are such that even lawyers and judges, after study and reflection, often are confused, and surely jurors in the hurried and unfamiliar movement of a trial must find them almost unintelligible. However, limiting instructions on this subject are no more difficult to comprehend or apply than those upon various other subjects. . . . [W]e think defendants in general and this defendant in particular have no valid complaint at the latitude which existing law allows to the prosecution to meet by cross-examination an issue voluntarily tendered by the defense.

. . . We concur in the general opinion of courts, textwriters and the profession that much of this law is archaic, paradoxical and full of compromises and compensations by which an irrational advantage to one side is offset by a poorly reasoned counter-privilege to the other. But somehow it has proved a workable even if clumsy system when moderated by discretionary controls in the hands of a wise and strong trial court. To pull one misshapen stone out of the grotesque structure is more likely simply to upset its present balance between adverse interests than to establish a rational edifice. . . . The judgment is affirmed.

[Justice Frankfurter filed a concurring opinion. Justice Rutledge, joined by Justice Murphy, filed a dissenting opinion.]

ADVISORY COMMITTEE NOTE TO F.R.E. 405

Of the three methods of proving character provided by the rule, evidence of specific instances of conduct is the most convincing. At the same time it possesses the greatest capacity to arouse prejudice, to confuse, to surprise, and to consume time. Consequently the rule confines the use of evidence of this kind to cases in which character is, in the strict sense, in issue and hence deserving of a searching inquiry. When character is used circumstantially and hence occupies a lesser status in the case, proof may be only by reputation and opinion. These latter methods are also available when character is in issue. This treatment is, with respect to specific instances of conduct and reputation, conventional contemporary common law doctrine. McCormick §153.

In recognizing opinion as a means of proving character, the rule departs from usual contemporary practice in favor of that of an earlier day. See 7 Wigmore §1986, pointing out that the earlier practice permitted opinion and arguing strongly for evidence based on personal knowledge and belief as contrasted with "the secondhand, irresponsible product of multiplied guesses and gossip which we term 'reputation'." It seems likely that the persistence of reputation evidence is due to its largely being opinion in disguise. Traditionally character has been regarded primarily in moral overtones of good and bad: chaste, peaceable, truthful, honest. Nevertheless, on occasion nonmoral considerations crop up, as in the case of the incompetent driver, and this seems bound to happen increasingly. If character is defined as the kind of person one is, then account must be taken of varying ways of arriving at the estimate. These may range from the opinion of the employer who has found the man honest to the opinion of the psychiatrist based upon examination and testing. No effective dividing line exists between character and mental capacity, and the latter traditionally has been provable by opinion.

According to the great majority of cases, on cross-examination inquiry is allowable as to whether the reputation witness has heard of particular instances of conduct pertinent to the trait in question. Michelson v. United States, 335 U.S. 469 (1948); Annot., 47 A.L.R.2d 1258. The theory is that, since the reputation witness relates what he has heard, the inquiry tends to shed light on the accuracy of his hearing and reporting. Accordingly, the opinion witness would be asked whether he knew, as well as whether he had heard. The fact is, of course, that these distinctions are of slight if any practical significance, and the second sentence of subdivision (a) eliminates them as a factor in formulating questions. This recognition of the propriety of inquiring into specific instances of conduct does not circumscribe inquiry otherwise into the bases of opinion and reputation testimony.

The express allowance of inquiry into specific instances of conduct on cross-examination in subdivision (a) and the express allowance of it as part of a case in chief when character is actually in issue in subdivision (b) contemplate that testimony of specific instances is not generally permissible on the direct examination of an ordinary opinion witness to character. . . .

ADVISORY COMMITTEE NOTE TO F.R.E. 803(21)

Exception (21) recognizes the traditional acceptance of reputation evidence as a means of proving human character. The exception deals only with the hearsay aspect of this kind of evidence. Limitations upon admissibility based on other grounds will be found in Rules 404, relevancy of character evidence generally, and 608, character of witness. The exception is in effect a recitation, in the context of hearsay, of Rule 405(a). . . .

GOVERNMENT OF THE VIRGIN ISLANDS v. ROLDAN

612 F.2d 775 (3d Cir. 1979)

GARTH, Circuit Judge.

This is an appeal from a conviction for murder in the first degree under V.I. Code tit. 14, §922(a)(1). . . . Testimony included that of Luz Maria Cruz, the wife of Roldan's nephew. Cruz was called by the Government. Defense counsel's cross-examination began as follows:

> Q. Mrs. Cruz, I am a lawyer for Mr. Roldan, I am going to ask you a few questions. Now, have you known Mr. Roldan for two or three years?
> A. Yes. I am married to my husband since 1961, ever since I know him.
> Q. Do you ever see people other than Mr. Roldan going to his house?
> A. No.
> Q. Would you say that he is a lonely unsociable fellow?
> A. He is a man that never bother anybody.

This line of questioning was not continued. . . .

On redirect examination, Cruz was asked the following questions by the Government:

> Q. Mrs. Cruz, you are aware, are you not, that the Defendant was convicted previously of murder in the 1st degree?
> MR. JOHNSON: (defense counsel) I object to the question and ask that it be stricken and the jury instructed to disregard.
> THE COURT: I will overrule the objection on the grounds I previously stated.
> A. (By the witness) Yes, I knew about that.
> Q. (By Mr. Schwartz (Assistant U.S. Attorney)) You knew he was convicted of murder in the 1st degree?
> A. Yes, sir, I have known of that.
> Q. And you would still say he is a man who never bothers anyone?
> A. Now, yes, I have to say that.

Roldan argues that it was error for the district court to have allowed the Government to inquire whether Cruz knew that Roldan had been convicted previously of first degree murder, since evidence of prior bad acts is generally inadmissible. . . . The district court determined that by asking the questions about Roldan's social habits, Roldan's counsel had put Roldan's character in issue. We agree. The last two questions which Roldan's counsel asked Cruz, are apparently directed toward establishing that Roldan had little contact with anyone and would therefore be unlikely to have reason to murder anyone. We do not think that Cruz' answer, "He is a man that never bother anybody," was a gratuitous, unsolicited remark; on the contrary, it was precisely the type of answer called for by defense counsel. The court's admission of the Government's impeachment testimony was thus proper.

Roldan objects further to the form of the impeachment questions, arguing that it was improper to use the phrases, "you are aware, are you not," and "[y]ou knew," rather than the form, "have you heard." . . . Even if Roldan has preserved this point for appeal, we find no error. Roldan's argument is predicated on *Michelson v. United States*, 335 U.S. 469, 482 (1948). . . . [T]the Advisory Committee Note to rule 405 implies that rule 405 overruled this aspect of *Michelson*. . . . There is thus no basis in the form of the impeachment questions for reversing Roldan's conviction. . . . We will therefore affirm the district court's March 16, 1979 judgment of sentence imposed upon Roldan.

UNITED STATES v. KRAPP

815 F.2d 1183 (8th Cir. 1987)

Ross, Circuit Judge.

Patricia E. Krapp appeals her conviction of three counts of making false record entries with intent to mislead, deceive or defraud the United States in violation of 18 U.S.C. §2073. . . . We affirm.

Krapp was the postmaster of the Pocahontas, Iowa post office from November 1983 to February 1986. An investigation by United States Postal Inspectors in January 1986 revealed a shortage of 100 coils of 22 cent stamps ($2200) at the Pocahontas post office. Krapp admitted to the inspectors that she had discovered the shortage in late November or early December 1985, but had failed to accurately reflect the shortage on certain postal forms and reports which she was required to fill out in connection with her duties as postmaster. Krapp stated that she did not report the shortage because she was investigating the incident and because she lacked expertise in filling out the postal forms. Krapp was charged with three counts of making false record entries with intent to defraud the United States.

At trial, Krapp presented a character witness who testified that Krapp had a reputation as "an honest, trustworthy person." On cross-examination the Assistant United States Attorney asked the witness "Are you aware that Pat Krapp's husband with her knowledge omitted cash income that he had on his—on their tax returns?" Before the witness answered, Krapp's attorney objected to the question and moved for a mistrial on the basis that the question was improper. Although refusing to grant a mistrial, the trial court sustained the objection and admonished the jury to disregard the question. Krapp now argues that a mistrial should have been granted because the question was asked without good faith and served only to prejudice the jury.

... This court has previously recognized the possible prejudicial impact of "did you know" type impeachment questions if they have no basis in fact. *See Gross v. United States*, 394 F.2d. 216, 219 (8th Cir. 1968). *See also United States v. Nixon*, 777 F.2d 958, 970 (5th Cir. 1985). In *Gross*, we noted:

> The rule permitting the cross-examiner to ask the character witness whether he "has heard" of other particular crimes of accused involving the same trait is pregnant with possibilities of destructive prejudice. The mere asking by a respected official of such a question, however answered, may well suggest to the jury that the imputation is true.

Id. at 221 n. 1 (quoting McCormick, Evidence (1954) §158, pp. 336, 337). Further, "[u]nless circumscribed by rules of fairness and grounded in demonstrated good faith on the part of the prosecution, the result could be most prejudicial to the defendant and make for a miscarriage of justice." *Id.* at 219 (citations omitted).

When asked by the trial judge outside the hearing of the jury what his good faith basis was for asking the question, the prosecutor stated that the notes of one of the postal inspectors reflected that Krapp had told the inspector that her husband received cash income which he did not report on their tax return. Further, the prosecutor had seen the tax returns and he believed them to be joint returns. Krapp replied that the postal inspector's notes concerned her 1985 tax return which the prosecutor knew had not been filed.

The trial court, in sustaining Krapp's objection, stated that he was not impugning any bad faith on the part of the prosecutor in asking the question, but found that the prejudicial effect of the question outweighed its probative value. We also make no determination as to whether the question was asked in good faith, although we find the issue to be a close one. Instead, we determine that even if the question were improper, when viewed in the context of the whole trial it was not so offensive as to warrant a mistrial. The question was asked only once, was unanswered, and the subject matter of the question was never brought up again before the jury. Further, the district court immediately admonished the jury to disregard the question. Also, from a review of the record we determine that there was substantial other evidence on which the jury could base Krapp's conviction such that the question did not have a substantial adverse impact on the verdict. Therefore, we find no abuse of discretion by the trial court in refusing to grant a mistrial.

However, we admonish the Assistant United States Attorney for asking Krapp's character witness about the Krapps' tax returns in front of the jury without first raising the matter with the trial judge. Before an attempt at impeachment of a character witness with "did you know" type questions such as this, the trial judge should have the opportunity, out of the hearing of the jury, to rule on the propriety of the questions. By failing to raise the matter first with the trial judge, the Assistant United States Attorney created the risk of mistrial after substantial time had been invested in the trial. . . .

UNITED STATES v. SETIEN

929 F.2d 610 (11th Cir. 1991) (sub nom.
United States v. Camejo)

DYER, Senior Circuit Judge:

[Luis Setien and four other employees of Eastern Airlines were convicted of conspiracy to import cocaine.] Setien's witness Max Mermelstein made a proffer of his testimony outside the presence of the jury. He testified that during the period that Setien was accused of having been involved in the cocaine importation conspiracy, they met regularly as social friends. During that time, Mermelstein was involved as a high level importer and distributor of cocaine throughout the United States. He offered Setien the lure of easy money if he would quit his job as an Eastern Airlines baggage handler and just hang around Mermelstein while he conducted his narcotics business. Setien refused to involve himself in the narcotics business and repeatedly reminded Mermelstein of the damage he was doing to society. . . . The court ruled that the testimony was irrelevant under Rule 405(b) and was not admissible under Rule 404(b). We agree.

Evidence of good conduct is not admissible to negate criminal intent. *Michelson v. United States*, 335 U.S. 469, 477 (1948); *United States v. Russell*, 703 F.2d 1243, 1249 (11th Cir. 1983). Mermelstein's proffered testimony was merely an attempt to portray Setien as a good character through the use of prior "good acts". The trial judge properly exercised his discretion in excluding this testimony as inadmissible character evidence. . . . AFFIRMED.

McCORMICK ON EVIDENCE

§187, at 746-747 (Kenneth S. Broun, ed., 6th ed. 2006)

The phrase "character in issue" sometimes invites confusion. A defendant in a criminal case generally can bring in evidence of good character to show that he is not the type of person who would have committed the offense charged. Although courts sometimes speak loosely of this strategy as putting the defendant's character in issue, the defendant is using character solely as circumstantial evidence. When the defendant makes his character an issue in this manner, it merely means that the prosecution is allowed to bring forth certain kinds of rebuttal evidence of bad character.

It does not justify evidence of specific acts, opinion, and reputation by either party. That freewheeling approach to character evidence is limited to the unusual situation in which an offense, claim, or defense for which character is an essential element is pled.

PROBLEMS

4.6. May a criminal defendant charged with tax evasion call his sister to testify that she thinks the defendant is thoroughly honest? May he call a neighbor to testify that he has a reputation as ethical and law-abiding? May he call a police officer to testify that the defendant turned in an expensive watch he found on the street? May the defendant himself testify about turning in the watch?

4.7. A criminal defendant charged with murder calls his minister, who testifies that the defendant is "gentle" and "wouldn't hurt anyone." Can the prosecution call a rebuttal witness who will testify that the defendant attacked him in a supermarket checkout line a year before the killing? Can the prosecutor ask the minister on cross-examination, "Are you aware that the defendant attacked someone in a supermarket checkout line?" Can the prosecutor ask the minister, "Have you heard that the defendant attacked someone in a supermarket checkout line?"

4.8. Henry Jumpertz was acquitted in 1859 of the murder of his mistress, Sophie Werner. Jumpertz claimed Werner had killed herself, and he "offered the testimony of witness suggesting that Sophie had suicidal tendencies and had earlier attempted suicide several times." *See* Jennifer L. Mnookin, *Scripting Expertise: The History of Handwriting Identification Evidence and the Judicial Construction of Reliability*, 87 Va. L. Rev. 1723, 1748-1751 (2001). Should this evidence have been admitted?

C. OTHER USES OF SPECIFIC CONDUCT

As we have seen, evidence of a defendant's character generally is inadmissible to prove his or her conduct in conformity with that character, unless the defendant chooses to place his or her character in controversy. And even if the defendant does choose to open that door, his or her character generally must be proved with opinion or reputation evidence, not with evidence of his or her conduct on other, specific occasions. Despite these rules, evidence of uncharged misconduct by defendants is routinely admitted in criminal cases. The evidence comes in on the theory that it is being used to prove something other than the defendant's character, so that the character evidence rule does not come into play at all. Despite (or perhaps because of) its widespread use and its explicit endorsement in modern evidence codes, this theory of admissibility remains highly controversial.

1. Permissible Purposes

[F.R.E. 404(b); C.E.C. §1101(b)]

UNITED STATES v. BEECHUM

582 F.2d 898 (5th Cir. 1978) (en banc)

TJOFLAT, Circuit Judge:

... A jury convicted Orange Jell Beechum, a substitute letter carrier for the United States Postal Service, of unlawfully possessing an 1890 silver dollar that he knew to be stolen from the mails, in violation of 18 U.S.C. §1708 (1976). To establish that Beechum intentionally and unlawfully possessed the silver dollar, the Government introduced into evidence two Sears, Roebuck & Co. credit cards found in Beechum's wallet when he was arrested. Neither card was issued to Beechum, and neither was signed. The Government also introduced evidence indicating that the cards had been mailed some ten months prior to Beechum's arrest to two different addresses on routes he had serviced. . . . We hold that the credit cards were properly admissible.

... [Rule 404(b)] follows the venerable principle that evidence of extrinsic offenses should not be admitted solely to demonstrate the defendant's bad character. Even though such evidence is relevant, because a man of bad character is more likely to commit a crime than one not, the principle prohibits such evidence because it is inherently prejudicial. *See, e.g., Michelson v. United States*, 335 U.S. 469, 475-76 (1948). Without an issue other than mere character to which the extrinsic offenses are relevant, the probative value of those offenses is deemed insufficient in all cases to outweigh the inherent prejudice. Where, however, the extrinsic offense evidence is relevant to an issue such as intent, it may well be that the evidence has probative force that is not substantially outweighed by its inherent prejudice. If this is so, the evidence may be admissible.

What the rule calls for is essentially a two-step test. First, it must be determined that the extrinsic offense evidence is relevant to an issue other than the defendant's character. Second, the evidence must possess probative value that is not substantially outweighed by its undue prejudice and must meet the other requirements of rule 403. . . . The task for the court in its ascertainment of probative value and unfair prejudice under rule 403 calls for a commonsense assessment of all the circumstances surrounding the extrinsic offense. As the Advisory Committee Notes to rule 404(b) state: "No mechanical solution is offered. The determination must be made whether the danger of undue prejudice outweighs the probative value of the evidence in view of the availability of other means of proof and other facts appropriate for making decision of this kind under Rule 403."

... [T]he credit card evidence is relevant to Beechum's intent with respect to the silver dollar. That Beechum possessed the credit cards with illicit intent diminishes the likelihood that at the same moment he intended to turn in the silver dollar. . . . We move now to the second step of the rule 404(b) analysis, the application of rule 403. . . . From the very inception of trial, it was clear that the crucial issue in the case would be Beechum's intent in possessing the silver dollar. He took the stand to proclaim that he intended to surrender the coin to his supervisor. The issue of intent was therefore clearly drawn, and the policies of justice that require a defendant to explain evidence that impugns his exculpatory testimony were in full force. . . . The credit card evidence bore directly on the plausibility of Beechum's story; justice called for its admission.

That the posture of this case demanded the admission of the credit card evidence is reinforced by the nature of the Government's proof on the issue of intent apart from that evidence. This proof consisted of the following. The Government called Cox, Beechum's supervisor, who testified that Beechum had had several opportunities to surrender the coin to him. Beechum denied this, and called two fellow employees who testified that Beechum had asked them if they had seen Cox. Absent the credit card evidence, the issue would have been decided wholly by the jury's assessment of the credibility of these witnesses. The Government, therefore, did not make out such a strong case of criminal intent that the credit card evidence would have been of little incremental probity. In fact, the credit card evidence may have been determinative.

. . . The probity of the credit card evidence in this case is augmented by the lack of temporal remoteness. Although Beechum may have obtained the cards as much as ten months prior to his arrest for the possession of the silver dollar, he kept the cards in his wallet where they would constantly remind him of the wrongfulness of their possession. In effect, Beechum's state of mind with respect to the credit cards continued through his arrest. He maintained contemporaneously the wrongful intent with respect to the cards and the intent as regards the coin. The force of the probity of this circumstance is illustrated by what Beechum would have had to convince the jury in order to avoid it. He would have been forced to argue that his state of mind was schizoid that he intended at the same time to relinquish the coin but to keep the cards. This situation does not differ significantly from one in which a thief is caught with a bag of loot, is charged with the larceny as to one of the items, but claims that he intended to return that item. Would any reasonable jury believe this story when it is established that he had stolen the rest of the loot?

The remaining considerations under rule 403 do not alter our conclusion as to the admissibility of the extrinsic offense evidence in this case. The extrinsic offense here is not of a heinous nature; it would hardly incite the jury to irrational decision by its force on human emotion. The credit card evidence was no more likely to confuse the issues, mislead the jury, cause undue delay, or waste time than any other type of extrinsic offense evidence. Since the need for the evidence in this case was great, it can hardly be said that the admission of the cards constituted "needless presentation of cumulative evidence."

It is significant that the court was careful to allay, as much as limiting instructions can, the undue prejudice engendered by the credit card evidence. It gave extensive instructions to the jury on the limited use of extrinsic offense evidence employed to prove unlawful intent.[23]

. . . [W]e conclude that the credit card evidence meets the requirements of rule 403. Therefore, the conditions imposed by the second step of the analysis under rule 404(b) have been met, and the extrinsic offense evidence in this case was properly admitted at trial. . . . AFFIRMED.

UNITED STATES v. BOYD

53 F.3d 631 (4th Cir. 1995)

HAMILTON, Circuit Judge:

Richard Edison Boyd appeals his conviction [for marijuana trafficking]. . . . Boyd argues the district court abused its discretion in admitting . . . testimony that Boyd personally used marijuana and cocaine. According to Boyd, such evidence was only admitted to show he had a bad character, and, therefore, must have committed the crimes of which he was charged. *See* Fed. R. Evid. 404(b) ("[E]vidence of other crimes,

---

23. The Advisory Committee Notes to rule 403 require the judge to consider the effectiveness of a limiting instruction in reducing the prejudicial impact of evidence: "In reaching a decision whether to exclude on grounds of unfair prejudice, consideration should be given to the probable effectiveness or lack of effectiveness of a limiting instruction."

This is a context in which limiting instructions are of substantial efficacy, and we think the judge adequately admonished the jury to consider the credit card evidence solely on the issue of Beechum's intent. We reproduce below the instructions he gave.

> During the course of this trial certain evidence has been presented concerning an alleged transaction similar to that charged in the indictment, to wit, the possession by the Defendant of the two Sears credit cards, admitted in evidence as Government Exhibits 6 and 7.
> This evidence, if you choose to accept it, is admitted for the limited purpose of assisting you in determining the intent with which a defendant may have acted. In this regard, you are instructed that evidence of an alleged similar transaction may not be considered by the jury in determining whether an accused committed the acts or participated in the activity alleged in the indictment.
> Nor may evidence of such an alleged similar transaction of a like nature be considered for any other purpose whatever unless the jury first finds that the other evidence in the case, standing alone, establishes beyond a reasonable doubt that the accused participated in the activity alleged in the indictment.
> If the jury should find beyond a reasonable doubt from other evidence in the case that the accused participated in the activity alleged in the indictment, then the jury may consider evidence as to transactions of a like nature, in determining the state of mind or intent with which the accused did the act charged in the indictment.
> I want to instruct you very explicitly and unequivocally as to the very limited extent to which you may consider this evidence as to a similar offense.
> As I just instructed you, you may consider such evidence of another transaction of a like nature in determining the state of mind or intent with which the accused may have done the act charged in the indictment, but only if you first find that the other evidence standing alone establishes beyond a reasonable doubt that the defendant committed the act alleged in the indictment.

wrongs, or acts is not admissible to show action in conformity therewith."). We disagree.

. . . The government's theory was that Boyd participated in the charged conspiracies in order to support his personal drug use. *See United States v. Templeman*, 965 F.2d 617, 619 (8th Cir.) ("Evidence of [defendant's] personal use of cocaine indicates potential motives for his distribution of cocaine: to finance his own use of the drug and to insure himself of a ready supply."), *cert. denied*, 506 U.S. 980, 113 S. Ct. 482, 121 L. Ed.2d 387 (1992). . . . [E]vidence of Boyd's personal marijuana and cocaine use would be admissible under Rule 404(b) as proof of his motive for participating in the charged conspiracies.

. . . Nor was its probative value substantially outweighed by its prejudicial effect. *See* Fed. R. Evid. 403. Of course, in one sense all incriminating evidence is inherently prejudicial. "The proper question under Rule 404(b), however, is whether such evidence has the potential to cause undue prejudice, and if so, whether the danger of such undue prejudice substantially outweighs its probative value." [*United States v. Mark*, 943 F.2d 444, 449 (4th Cir. 1991).] In this case, the balancing test undeniably weighs in favor of admitting the evidence, because the evidence of Boyd's personal use of marijuana and cocaine did not involve conduct any more sensational or disturbing than the crimes with which he was charged. [T]he jury heard and credited evidence that Boyd supplied hundreds of pounds of marijuana. . . . We conclude that Boyd's personal drug use was far less prejudicial than this evidence, the admission of which Boyd has not challenged on appeal. The evidence at issue was, therefore, admissible. . . . AFFIRMED.

UNITED STATES v. DEJOHN

638 F.2d 1048 (7th Cir. 1981)

HARLINGTON WOOD, JR., Circuit Judge.

Defendant John DeJohn appeals from a jury conviction on the charge of uttering and publishing two United States Treasury checks in violation of 18 U.S.C. §495. [The payees and defendant all lived at the same YMCA.] . . . Defendant objects to testimony by a YMCA security guard who stated that he "arrested" the defendant when he found him behind a reception desk at the YMCA in violation of the establishment's rules. Defendant also objects to the testimony of a Chicago police officer that in the course of searching defendant at police headquarters on an occasion unrelated to the offense for which defendant was on trial, the officer found checks, one of them a Treasury check, made out to a payee named Michael Dore. The officer testified that defendant stated he had obtained the checks from a mailbox behind the reception desk at the YMCA and was holding them for safekeeping. Police were unable to locate the payee of the checks and no charges were filed against defendant as a result of the checks found in the search.

As applied to the defendant in a criminal case, Rule 404 prevents any effort to prove that the defendant acted in the criminal manner as charged by the introduction of evidence showing the defendant acted in a similar way at some other time not charged. As part (b) of the rule indicates, though, evidence of similar actions generally is admissible when introduced for purposes other than those which (under the rule) improperly show propensity to commit the crime. Here, the testimony of the security officer and the policeman was highly probative of the defendant's opportunity to gain access to the mailboxes and obtain the checks that he cashed at a later time knowing the checks to contain forged endorsements. This circumstantial evidence was properly admissible.

The issue of opportunity became material to the trial once defense counsel set forth the theory in opening argument that it was not their client who uttered the forged checks. Defendant's opportunity to gain access to the checks thus became a key issue. . . . AFFIRMED.

LEWIS v. UNITED STATES

771 F.2d 454 (10th Cir. 1985)

WILLIAM E. DOYLE, Circuit Judge.

Defendant Jermaine Lewis appeals his conviction for burglary of a post office, a violation of 18 U.S.C. §2115, and for destruction of government property, a violation of 18 U.S.C. §1361. . . . [D]efendant maintains that the district court erred in admitting into evidence testimony that defendant had participated in the burglary of a garage store earlier on the evening of the post office burglary. . . . Evidence of defendant's participation in a burglary several hours before the post office burglary with which defendant was charged falls squarely within Rule 404(b) as establishing defendant's plan and intent. The evidence was especially probative because defendant allegedly took from the store some equipment needed for the post office burglary. Therefore the district court did not abuse its discretion in admitting the evidence. . . . Affirmed.

UNITED STATES v. CROCKER

788 F.2d 802 (5th Cir. 1986)

CEREZO, District Judge.

Gerald James Crocker was convicted by a jury on one count of a two-count indictment for conspiring to commit bank theft, 18 U.S.C. Sections 371 and 2113(b), and was sentenced to three years imprisonment. . . . This particular conspiracy consisted of cashing counterfeit checks in various banks in the New England area from on or about January 1984 to May 3, 1984. . . . Besides obtaining and preparing checks, appellant's role was to drive a co-conspirator to the banks where the checks would be cashed and the proceeds split equally.

Crocker claims that the admission of evidence related to his 1977 arrest violated Fed. R. Evid. 404(b). . . . Defendant's "knowing" participation in the conspiracy was a crucial element which if not clearly established could have left the jury with the impression that defendant was merely driving his friend Gaeta to several New England banks. *Cf. United States v. Zeuli*, 725 F.2d 813-816 (1st Cir. 1984) ("In every conspiracy case . . . a not guilty plea renders the defendant's intent a material issue and imposes a difficult burden on the government.") The fact that defendant had been arrested before with co-conspirator Gaeta while in an automobile with counterfeit checks was highly probative of his knowledge that Gaeta's checks and his trips to the banks were for an illicit purpose. The district court did not abuse its discretion in admitting this evidence after balancing its probative value against its potential prejudice. . . . [Reversed on other grounds.]

UNITED STATES v. DOSSEY

558 F.2d 1336 (8th Cir. 1977)

HENLEY, Circuit Judge.

Debra Lynn Dossey appeals her conviction by a jury of armed bank robbery in violation of 18 U.S.C. §2113(d). We affirm.

On July 12, 1976 appellant was indicted for the robbery of the Capitol Branch of the First National Bank in Little Rock, Arkansas. At trial the teller at the bank testified that on February 27, 1976 she was approached by a young white female, who produced a pistol and demanded money. The teller complied with the demand and the robber fled. The teller described the robber as being a blond, about 22 or 23 years of age, weighing about 115 or 120 pounds, and being about 5'3" tall. At the time of the robbery the robber was dressed in a blue plaid shirt and blue jeans and wore rose-colored, wire-framed glasses. The teller could not positively identify appellant as the robber, but testified that appellant "looks like" the robber.

Other testimony placed appellant and a companion, James Weaver, in Little Rock on the day of the robbery. The day after the robbery appellant and Weaver flew from Little Rock to Phoenix, Arizona.

. . . Ann Louise Jagow testified that she first met appellant in Phoenix, Arizona, in March, 1976. She testified that she had a conversation with appellant during which appellant admitted having done robberies in Little Rock. Appellant told Jagow that she was wearing a wig and her tinted glasses during one bank robbery, that she was armed, and that she made her escape by going over a brick wall and riding off with Weaver in her El Camino.

Miss Jagow further testified that she, along with appellant, Weaver and others planned and executed a bank robbery in Mesa, Arizona. She testified that appellant wore a blond wig and a blue T-shirt during the robbery, along with pinkish-tinted, wire-framed glasses. Finally, Miss Jagow testified that appellant had admitted committing bank robbery in Minnesota.

. . . We are of the opinion that the evidence of the Arizona robbery was admissible to prove identification of the person who robbed the Little Rock bank, an issue that was important due to the teller's inability positively to identify appellant. Miss Jagow testified that appellant, armed with a pistol, entered the Arizona bank alone, wearing a blond wig, a blue shirt and pinkish-tinted, wire-framed glasses. The similarity in modus operandi and disguise is great and the incidents were close in time. The substantial pro-bative value of this evidence was not outweighed by the possibility of unfair prejudice and it was properly admitted.

It is questionable whether the district court should have admitted Miss Jagow's testimony about the Minnesota robberies. This testimony was of very limited probative value because its only connection with the Little Rock robbery was appellant's statement that she wore disguises in Minnesota. However, this testimony was limited to two brief answers and was not again referred to by the government. The district court also gave appropriate limiting instructions.* In these circumstances, we are convinced that the error, if any, was harmless beyond a reasonable doubt. . . .

UNITED STATES v. WRIGHT

901 F.2d 68 (7th Cir. 1990)

POSNER, Circuit Judge.

A jury found Stanley Wright guilty of two counts of distributing cocaine and two of distributing it within a thousand feet of a school. 21 U.S.C. §§841(a)(1), 845a. The judge sentenced him to seven years in prison. The principal question raised by the appeal is whether the trial was con-taminated by evidence of other criminal activity by Wright.

On two different days in May 1988, three plainclothes police officers bought a total of four bags of "crack" at $20 a bag from a man who sold it to the officers at curbside on a Chicago street a few blocks from Hyde Park, handing the bags through the window of the unmarked police car. The sales occurred in daylight, and from police photographs the officers identified

---

* ["Immediately after Jagow's testimony concerning the Arizona robbery, the trial court instructed the jury as follows: 'Now the Court has permitted in certain evidence that might suggest or indicate to the jury either other wrongs or other crimes in Arizona. Now you are not concerned with any other wrongs or crimes in Arizona, but the Court has admitted that only as it might bear upon the issue of identity of the people involved or person or persons involved in the robbery in Little Rock, Arkansas on February 27 and the modus operandi or the planning which might also go along with the question of identity. The jury may feel it is of no importance and disregard it entirely, but it has been admitted only because of its potential relevance on the issue of identity, plan and modus operandi and not for any other reason. You should not be concerned about whether there was any wrong or any other crime committed in Arizona.'" *United States v. Weaver*, 565 F.2d 129, 133-34 (8th Cir. 1977).]

the man as Stanley Wright. No arrest was made, however, and instead the police waited six months and then with court authorization placed a wiretap on Wright's telephone line in November 1988. The tap intercepted a conversation between Wright and an unidentified woman in which Wright bragged about being a drug dealer. At trial, over Wright's objection, the judge let the government play a tape recording of portions of the conversation to the jury. . . .

Wright did not admit in the recorded conversation making the sales— which had occurred six months earlier—that he is charged in this case with having made. He did admit committing other drug crimes. The admissibility of evidence of other crimes is governed by Rule 404(b) of the Federal Rules of Evidence, which provides that such evidence may not be used to prove a person's bad character or his propensity to commit crimes in conformity with that character, but may be used "for other purposes, such as proof of motive, opportunity, intent, preparation, plan, knowledge, or absence of mistake or accident." The judge admitted the conversation to establish identity and intent, and told the jury to limit their consideration of the conversation to those issues. There was, however, no issue of intent in this case—no question, for example, whether Wright knew what was in the packages that he sold the plainclothes officers. So the jury, if it obeyed the judge's instructions, could have used the recorded conversation only in connection with the issue of identity, that is, only to help decide whether Wright was the man who had sold the crack to the plainclothes officers.

By "identity," the district judge must have meant "guilt," and that is an impermissible equation. The intercepted telephone conversation may well show that Wright is more likely to be guilty of the crime with which he is charged than the average man on the street, who is not a drug dealer, but it does not in the least show that the man who had sold the plainclothes officers four bags of crack six months earlier was correctly identified as Stanley Wright. It would tend to show this if for example the conversation had indicated that Wright was at that time selling drugs on streets near where the transactions occurred, or if he had said something that only a party to those transactions would know. The conversation indicated neither of these things. . . .

The only relevance of the tape was to depict Wright as a drug dealer (and a brazen and boastful one at that), and, against this, the limiting instruction was not limiting at all. It told the jurors that they could consider the tape for what light it cast on the identity and intent of the man who had sold crack to the officers. The implication was that a drug dealer is more likely than someone who is not a drug dealer to sell drugs, even if at a different level of distribution from his accustomed one. No doubt this is true. "The inquiry [into previous criminal acts] is not rejected because character is irrelevant; on the contrary, it is said to weigh too much with the jury and to so overpersuade them as to prejudge one with a bad general record and deny him a fair opportunity to defend against a particular charge." *Michelson v. United States*, 335 U.S.469, 475-76(1948). The logic of the district court's ruling is that a drug defendant's prior drug convictions are admissible *per se*, even if they do not help to clear up a question of identification or establish a modus operandi or otherwise illuminate the particular conduct of which the defendant is accused, and even if he does not take the stand, which would lay him open to being impeached by his prior convictions. The use of evidence of other crimes to establish a propensity to commit the type of crime charged is the use of such evidence that Rule 404(b) forbids.

Some of that evidence has no probative value at all. If Wright were accused of a criminal violation of the securities laws, the fact that he may once have been found guilty of child molestation would not increase the probability that he was guilty of the securities offense. To exclude such evidence, however, Rule 404(b) is not necessary; irrelevant evidence of any kind is made inadmissible by Rules 402 and 403. The purpose of Rule 404(b) is to exclude a type of evidence—evidence that the defendant had previously engaged in a broadly similar criminal activity—which has some probative value but the admission of which would tend as a practical matter to deprive a person with a criminal record of the protection, in future prosecutions, of the government's burden of proving guilt beyond a reasonable doubt. As Justice Jackson pointed out in *Michelson*, a jury is not likely to insist on the government's satisfying so demanding a standard of proof if the defendant is a thoroughly bad sort who even if not clearly guilty of the crime with which he is charged is no doubt guilty of some similar crime or crimes for which he may never have been caught or, if caught, may not have been punished adequately.

. . . The government's back-up argument that the admission of the tape was, if error, a harmless one because the three officers positively identified Wright has no merit. Identification evidence is not infallible, and police officers are not disinterested witnesses. If the government's case were as airtight as the government now says it is, one wonders why it pressed so hard for the admission of the recorded conversation.

The judgment is reversed with instructions to grant the defendant a new trial.

ADVISORY COMMITTEE NOTE TO 1991 AMENDMENT TO F.R.E. 404

Rule 404(b) has emerged as one of the most cited Rules in the Rules of Evidence. And in many criminal cases evidence of an accused's extrinsic acts is viewed as an important asset in the prosecution's case against an accused. Although there are a few reported decisions on use of such evidence by the defense, *see, e.g., United States v. McClure*, 546 F.2d 670 (5th Cir. 1990) (acts of informant offered in entrapment defense), the overwhelming number of cases involve introduction of that evidence by the prosecution. The amendment to Rule 404(b) adds a pretrial notice requirement in criminal cases and is intended to reduce surprise and promote early resolution on the issue of admissibility. . . .

EDWARD J. IMWINKELRIED, THE USE OF EVIDENCE OF AN ACCUSED'S UNCHARGED MISCONDUCT TO PROVE *MENS REA*: THE DOCTRINES WHICH THREATEN TO ENGULF THE CHARACTER EVIDENCE PROHIBITION

51 Ohio St. L.J. 575, 576-578, 602 (1990)

The admissibility of uncharged misconduct evidence is the single most important issue in contemporary criminal evidence law. . . . Rule 404(b) has generated more published opinions than any other subsection of the Federal Rules. In many jurisdictions, alleged errors in the admission of uncharged misconduct evidence are the most common ground for appeal in criminal cases. In some jurisdictions, errors in the introduction of uncharged misconduct are the most frequent basis for reversal in criminal cases.

. . . Some commentators have argued that the distinction between character and noncharacter theories of relevance is illusory; according to this argument, even the purportedly noncharacter theories entail assumptions about the accused's tendencies and disposition. Alternatively, other commentators have contended that an accused's uncharged crimes can be so highly probative even on a character theory that it would be irrational to exclude them. . . . To date, the direct attacks on the character evidence prohibition have been unsuccessful. . . . Notwithstanding the failure of the direct attacks, the ban is imperiled. The threat to the ban arises from . . . emerging lines of case law governing the use of an accused's uncharged misconduct to prove the accused's mens rea. The use of the defendant's other crimes to prove intent is already the most widely used basis for admitting uncharged misconduct evidence . . . [N]ew lines of authority, however, threaten to expand the admissibility of uncharged misconduct to establish mens rea to the point that this use of the evidence may substantially undermine the character evidence prohibition.

. . . Following the example of the United Kingdom, our courts may one day relax the character evidence prohibition in criminal cases. Distinguished American commentators have called for that relaxation. However, at least for the interim, the American courts seem determined to adhere to the conventional prohibition. . . . If we are going to modify or abolish the prohibition, it should be done explicitly in a straightforward fashion—not by legerdemain.

ANDREW J. MORRIS, FEDERAL RULE OF EVIDENCE 404(b): THE FICTITIOUS BAN ON CHARACTER REASONING FROM OTHER CRIME EVIDENCE

17 Rev. Litig. 181, 189-192, 196, 199 (1998)

To comply with the plain words of Rule 404(b), courts must refuse to admit any evidence whose relevance depends on propensity reasoning.

Even a quick run through the case reports, however, turns up abundant evidence that courts routinely admit such evidence. . . . [In drug cases, for example,] evidence of prior drug activity pours in unexamined on the rationale that, as long as the evidence is probative of "intent," the evidence does not involve the forbidden reasoning. . . . Courts even go as far as to repeatedly generalize that evidence of "the use of prior drug involvement to show plan, motive or intent in a drug trafficking offense is appropriate." Despite the courts' repetition of this principle, it is fatally flawed; its application almost always violates Rule 404(b). What chain of reasoning can link the prior drug history of [a defendant] to the charged crime other than one that infers that the defendant has a drug-related propensity, and that based on this propensity, the jury can disbelieve him when he denies criminal intent as to the latest drug incident? There is no propensity-free chain. The earlier drug use, which is behavioral evidence, can be relevant only if we assume that the defendant's behavior forms an unchanging pattern. In the words of Rule 404(b), the drug history is relevant only because it "prove[s] the character of" the defendant and supports the inference that, in the case at issue, the defendant acted consistent with that character.

. . . [Similarly, in "identity" or "modus operandi" cases,] the relevance of bad acts evidence depends on propensity reasoning. In these cases, evidence of an earlier crime is relevant because it shares critical but unusual features with the charged crime, thus suggesting that the defendant committed both. . . . It goes without saying that the identification of defendants using fingerprints or blood samples depends on the assumption that physical characteristics remain constant across time. In precisely the same way, identification based on bad acts needs an unchanging feature for the reasoning to work; in those cases, the assumed continuity of the defendant's character serves the role that the immutable nature of physical characteristics plays in the physical evidence cases. Without this assumption of continuity of character, we could not use other crimes evidence for purposes of identification any more than we could identify defendants by using fingerprints if they changed over time.

PAUL F. ROTHSTEIN, INTELLECTUAL COHERENCE IN AN EVIDENCE CODE

28 Loy. L.A. L. Rev. 1259, 1260, 1265 (1995)

It is inescapable that the first sentence of Rule 404(b), the prohibitory sentence, is inconsistent with the second sentence, the permissive sentence, at least as those sentences are currently interpreted. The first sentence commands, in effect, "Thou shalt not use other crimes, wrongs, or acts to prove character in order to prove an act in conformity with that character." The second sentence, however, says, in effect, "Yes, but you may use those other crimes, wrongs, or acts in order to prove such facts as knowledge, intent, motive, identity, plan, or absence of mistake or accident." The standard interpretation of these two sentences is that evidence is excluded by the first sentence if it is offered on a "propensity" theory—

that is, that the defendant's prior acts demonstrate a tendency to behave the same way in the future. But, under the second sentence, the evidence may be admissible if the relevance of the evidence does not depend on a propensity inference. This dichotomy does not hold up under closer examination. The first and second sentences cannot be construed consistently in light of their interpretation in case law. Both describe evidence offered on a propensity theory.

... [A] more promising way to produce intellectual coherence between the two sentences of Rule 404(b) ... [is to assume that] the first sentence of 404(b) bans propensity, but only when it is the general and morally tinged propensity known as character. In other words, character, the word used and banned in the first sentence of the Rule, is not synonymous with "propensity." Instead, character is just one type of propensity—the amorphous, general, morally-tinged kind—that presents the specter of the several dangers the character rule worries about: that the propensity is too amorphous and general to lead to a solid inference of specific behavior; that the jury may not realize this; and that they might be induced to make prejudicial moral judgments of the person or relax the rigor of their scrutiny of the facts based on their willingness to punish for general or past "badness." The second sentence, the permissive sentence of Rule 404(b), licenses another kind of propensity. This is not character, which is excluded, but the more specific kind of propensity that may not be attended by the same dangers in the same degree. Finally, there is habit, governed by Rule 406, which licenses an even more specific and compelling kind of propensity. ...

MIRKO BAGARIC & KUMAR AMARASEKARA, THE PREJUDICE AGAINST SIMILAR FACT EVIDENCE

5 Int'l J. Evid. & Proof 71, 93-95, 97-98 (2001)

[P]revious conduct is of little weight in predicting if a particular individual will commit a criminal offence. However, we suggest that previous conduct assumes considerable weight where it is *known* that a criminal act has been committed and the only fact in issue is by whom or whether the culprit had the requisite criminal intent. ... Thereupon the issue is not whether the agent will re-offend. It is whether he or she is the perpetrator (or had the necessary guilty mind), given that the agent has demonstrated a behavioural capacity for committing that type of offence. In such circumstances, evidence of prior misconduct is highly relevant because fortunately the vast majority of us are not willing to rob banks or sexually abuse others under *any* circumstances. Evidence of prior similar misconduct places the accused in the small category of individuals who have a capacity for engaging in the relevant misconduct. ...

[A]lthough experiments on simulated juries show that disclosure of a similar previous conviction increases the probability of a finding of guilt ... there is nothing to show that juries give *too much* weight to this type of consideration. ... To assume that similar fact evidence must inevitably prejudice the jury not only accords insufficient weight to the collective intelligence of such a body, but also discounts entirely the effect of defence counsel's cross-examination as well as the trial judge's caution. . . . [S]imilar fact evidence should be *prima facie* admissible as being relevant to the *mens reas* of the offence or the identity of the culprit. . . . [T]his would represent a considerable improvement on the present approach, which demonstrates an irrational prejudice against such evidence and substantially subverts the principal aim of the criminal trial process: to identify and punish those responsible for criminal offences.

2. Requisite Proof

Before introducing evidence of uncharged misconduct by the defendant, should the prosecution be required to prove to the court's satisfaction that the misconduct actually occurred? In *Huddleston v. United States*, excerpted below, the Supreme Court held that the Federal Rules of Evidence impose no such requirement.

When reading *Huddleston*, ask yourself the following questions. Does it make sense to allow charged misconduct to be proven with evidence of uncharged misconduct that is itself contested? And what drives the Court's analysis in *Huddleston*—the language of the rules, the legislative history, or the Court's own sense of what will tend to make trials fair?

HUDDLESTON v. UNITED STATES

485 U.S. 681 (1988)

Chief Justice Rehnquist delivered the opinion of the Court.

. . . This case presents the question whether [under Federal Rule of Evidence 404(b)] the district court must itself make a preliminary finding that the Government has proved the "other act" by a preponderance of the evidence before it submits the evidence to the jury. We hold that it need not do so.

Petitioner, Guy Rufus Huddleston, was charged with one count of selling stolen goods in interstate commerce, 18 U.S.C. §2315, and one count of possessing stolen property in interstate commerce, 18 U.S.C. §659. The two counts related to two portions of a shipment of stolen Memorex videocassette tapes that petitioner was alleged to have possessed and sold, knowing that they were stolen.

The evidence at trial showed that a trailer containing over 32,000 blank Memorex videocassette tapes with a manufacturing cost of $4.53 per tape was stolen from the Overnight Express yard in South Holland, Illinois, sometime between April 11 and 15, 1985. On April 17, 1985, petitioner contacted Karen Curry, the manager of the Magic Rent-to-Own in Ypsilanti, Michigan, seeking her assistance in selling a large number of blank

Memorex videocassette tapes. After assuring Curry that the tapes were not stolen, he told her he wished to sell them in lots of at least 500 at $2.75 to $3 per tape. Curry subsequently arranged for the sale of a total of 5,000 tapes, which petitioner delivered to the various purchasers—who apparently believed the sales were legitimate.

There was no dispute that the tapes which petitioner sold were stolen; the only material issue at trial was whether petitioner knew they were stolen. The District Court allowed the Government to introduce evidence of "similar acts" under Rule 404(b), concluding that such evidence had "clear relevance as to [petitioner's knowledge]." The first piece of similar act evidence offered by the Government was the testimony of Paul Toney, a record store owner. He testified that in February 1985, petitioner offered to sell new 12" black and white televisions for $28 apiece. According to Toney, petitioner indicated that he could obtain several thousand of these televisions. Petitioner and Toney eventually traveled to the Magic Rent-to-Own, where Toney purchased 20 of the televisions. Several days later, Toney purchased 18 more televisions.

The second piece of similar act evidence was the testimony of Robert Nelson, an undercover FBI agent posing as a buyer for an appliance store. Nelson testified that in May 1985, petitioner offered to sell him a large quantity of Amana appliances—28 refrigerators, 2 ranges, and 40 ice-makers. Nelson agreed to pay $8,000 for the appliances. Petitioner was arrested shortly after he arrived at the parking lot where he and Nelson had agreed to transfer the appliances. A truck containing the appliances was stopped a short distance from the parking lot, and Leroy Wesby, who was driving the truck, was also arrested. It was determined that the appliances had a value of approximately $20,000 and were part of a shipment that had been stolen.

Petitioner testified that the Memorex tapes, the televisions, and the appliances had all been provided by Leroy Wesby, who had represented that all of the merchandise was obtained legitimately. Petitioner stated that he had sold 6,500 Memorex tapes for Wesby on a commission basis. Petitioner maintained that all of the sales for Wesby had been on a commission basis and that he had no knowledge that any of the goods were stolen.

In closing, the prosecution explained that petitioner was not on trial for his dealings with the appliances or the televisions. The District Court instructed the jury that the similar acts evidence was to be used only to establish petitioner's knowledge, and not to prove his character. The jury convicted petitioner on the possession count only. . . .

Before this Court, petitioner argues that the District Court erred in admitting Toney's testimony as to petitioner's sale of the televisions. . . . Petitioner acknowledges that this evidence was admitted for the proper purpose of showing his knowledge that the Memorex tapes were stolen. He asserts, however, that the evidence should not have been admitted because the Government failed to prove to the District Court that the televisions were in fact stolen.

Petitioner argues from the premise that evidence of similar acts has a grave potential for causing improper prejudice. For instance, the jury may choose to punish the defendant for the similar rather than the charged act, or the jury may infer that the defendant is an evil person inclined to violate the law. Because of this danger, petitioner maintains, the jury ought not to be exposed to similar act evidence until the trial court has heard the evidence and made a determination under Federal Rule of Evidence 104(a) that the defendant committed the similar act. Rule 104(a) provides that "[p]reliminary questions concerning the qualification of a person to be a witness, the existence of a privilege, or the admissibility of evidence shall be determined by the court, subject to the provisions of subdivision (b)." According to petitioner, the trial court must make this preliminary finding by at least a preponderance of the evidence.

We reject petitioner's position, for it is inconsistent with the structure of the Rules of Evidence and with the plain language of Rule 404(b). Article IV of the Rules of Evidence deals with the relevancy of evidence. Rules 401 and 402 establish the broad principle that relevant evidence— evidence that makes the existence of any fact at issue more or less probable—is admissible unless the Rules provide otherwise. Rule 403 allows the trial judge to exclude relevant evidence if, among other things, "its probative value is substantially outweighed by the danger of unfair prejudice." Rules 404 through 412 address specific types of evidence that have generated problems. Generally, these latter Rules do not flatly prohibit the introduction of such evidence but instead limit the purpose for which it may be introduced. Rule 404(b), for example, protects against the introduction of extrinsic act evidence when that evidence is offered solely to prove character. The text contains no intimation, however, that any preliminary showing is necessary before such evidence may be introduced for a proper purpose. If offered for such a proper purpose, the evidence is subject only to general strictures limiting admissibility such as Rules 402 and 403.

Petitioner's reading of Rule 404(b) as mandating a preliminary finding by the trial court that the act in question occurred not only superimposes a level of judicial oversight that is nowhere apparent from the language of that provision, but it is simply inconsistent with the legislative history behind Rule 404(b). The Advisory Committee specifically declined to offer any "mechanical solution" to the admission of evidence under 404(b). Advisory Committee's Notes on Fed. Rule Evid. 404(b). Rather, the Committee indicated that the trial court should assess such evidence under the usual rules for admissibility: "The determination must be made whether the danger of undue prejudice outweighs the probative value of the evidence in view of the availability of other means of proof and other factors appropriate for making decisions of this kind under Rule 403." *Ibid*; see also S. Rep. No. 93-1277, p. 25 (1974) ("[I]t is anticipated that with respect to permissible uses for such evidence, the trial judge may exclude it only on the basis of those considerations set forth in Rule 403, i.e. prejudice, confusion or waste of time").

Petitioner's suggestion that a preliminary finding is necessary to protect the defendant from the potential for unfair prejudice is also belied by the Reports of the House of Representatives and the Senate. The House made clear that the version of Rule 404(b) which became law was intended to "plac[e] greater emphasis on admissibility than did the final Court version." H.R. Rep. No. 93-650, p. 7 (1973). The Senate echoed this theme: "[T]he use of the discretionary word 'may' with respect to the admissibility of evidence of crimes, wrongs, or other acts is not intended to confer any arbitrary discretion on the trial judge." S. Rep. No. 93-1277, supra, at 24. Thus, Congress was not nearly so concerned with the potential prejudicial effect of Rule 404(b) evidence as it was with ensuring that restrictions would not be placed on the admission of such evidence.

We conclude that a preliminary finding by the court that the Government has proved the act by a preponderance of the evidence is not called for under Rule 104(a). This is not to say, however, that the Government may parade past the jury a litany of potentially prejudicial similar acts that have been established or connected to the defendant only by unsubstantiated innuendo. Evidence is admissible under Rule 404(b) only if it is relevant. . . . In the Rule 404(b) context, similar act evidence is relevant only if the jury can reasonably conclude that the act occurred and that the defendant was the actor. *See United States v. Beechum*, 582 F.2d 898, 912-913 (CA5 1978) (en banc). In the instant case, the evidence that petitioner was selling the televisions was relevant under the Government's theory only if the jury could reasonably find that the televisions were stolen.

Such questions of relevance conditioned on a fact are dealt with under Federal Rule of Evidence 104(b). Rule 104(b) provides: "When the relevancy of evidence depends upon the fulfillment of a condition of fact, the court shall admit it upon, or subject to, the introduction of evidence sufficient to support a finding of the fulfillment of the condition." In determining whether the Government has introduced sufficient evidence to meet Rule 104(b), the trial court neither weighs credibility nor makes a finding that the Government has proved the conditional fact by a preponderance of the evidence. The court simply examines all the evidence in the case and decides whether the jury could reasonably find the conditional fact—here, that the televisions were stolen—by a preponderance of the evidence. The trial court has traditionally exercised the broadest sort of discretion in controlling the order of proof at trial, and we see nothing in the Rules of Evidence that would change this practice. Often the trial court may decide to allow the proponent to introduce evidence concerning a similar act, and at a later point in the trial assess whether sufficient evidence has been offered to permit the jury to make the requisite finding. If the proponent has failed to meet this minimal standard of proof, the trial court must instruct the jury to disregard the evidence.

We emphasize that in assessing the sufficiency of the evidence under Rule 104(b), the trial court must consider all evidence presented to the jury. "[I]ndividual pieces of evidence, insufficient in themselves to prove a point, may in cumulation prove it. The sum of an evidentiary presentation may well be greater than its constituent parts." *Bourjaily v. United States*, 483 U.S. 171, 179-180 (1987). In assessing whether the evidence was sufficient to support a finding that the televisions were stolen, the court here was required to consider not only the direct evidence on that point—the low price of the televisions, the large quantity offered for sale, and petitioner's inability to produce a bill of sale—but also the evidence concerning petitioner's involvement in the sales of other stolen merchandise obtained from

Wesby, such as the Memorex tapes and the Amana appliances. Given this evidence, the jury reasonably could have concluded that the televisions were stolen, and the trial court therefore properly allowed the evidence to go to the jury.

We share petitioner's concern that unduly prejudicial evidence might be introduced under Rule 404(b). See *Michelson v. United States*, 335 U.S. 469, 475-476 (1948). We think, however, that the protection against such unfair prejudice emanates not from a requirement of a preliminary finding by the trial court, but rather from four other sources: first, from the requirement of Rule 404(b) that the evidence be offered for a proper purpose; second, from the relevancy requirement of Rule 402—as enforced through Rule 104(b); third, from the assessment the trial court must make under Rule 403 to determine whether the probative value of the similar acts evidence is substantially outweighed by its potential for unfair prejudice; and fourth, from Federal Rule of Evidence 105, which provides that the trial court shall, upon request, instruct the jury that the similar acts evidence is to be considered only for the proper purpose for which it was admitted. . . . Affirmed.

PROBLEMS

4.9. On June 30, 1915, George Joseph Smith was convicted in London of murdering Bessie Mundy. Three years earlier Mundy had married Smith (who unbeknownst to her was already married), had executed a will leaving him all her property, and then had drowned in her bath. Smith claimed the drowning had been accidental, but at trial the prosecution proved that, following Mundy's death, two other women had died in their baths after going through marriage ceremonies with Smith and making out wills in his favor. The introduction of this evidence was the principal issue on appeal:

> Mr. Marshall Hall carried the appeal before [Lord Chief] Justice Darling and his brother judges on July 29, 1915. "All I say is 'not guilty'," he told the Court. "Until the prosecution has proved this death was not by accident they cannot proceed." He contended that the evidence of the other two deaths should never have been admitted, and that without it there was not a prima facie case to go to the jury.
>
> "Why, after all, can't lawyers act as sensible people?" demanded Mr. Justice Darling. That remark was typical of him. His practical common sense cut right through legal quibbles and got down to the true basis of true justice.
>
> "It would be difficult to believe," persisted counsel, "that the same number could come up on a roulette table five times in succession, but if it happened you would not be entitled to convict the croupier as a dishonest man."
>
> "If I saw it happen," observed the Lord Chief Justice, "and the same people were at the table all the time I should grow suspicious."
>
> After the three judges had consulted together for nearly half an hour the Lord Chief Justice delivered the judgment. The Court had decided that there was a prima facie case on the death of Bessie Mundy, without taking the other deaths into account at all. Therefore, they upheld Mr. Justice Scutton's decision to admit the evidence. . . . The appeal was dismissed. George Joseph Smith was executed without having confessed on August 13, 1915.

Dudley Barker, *Lord Darling's Famous Cases* 82 (1936); *see Rex v. Smith*, 11 Crim. App. 229, 84 K.B. 2153, [1914-15] All E.R. 262 (1915).

Would the evidence of the other deaths be admissible under the Federal Rules of Evidence? What if without that evidence there was no prima facie case—i.e., what if the proof regarding Mundy's death, standing alone, would not allow a rational jury to find Smith guilty of murder?

4.10. A Nevada jury found Horace Tucker guilty of murdering Omar Evans, who was found shot to death on Tucker's couch in October 1963. Tucker claimed that he fell asleep and woke up to find Evans dead. At trial the prosecution proved that in 1957 another man, Earl Kaylor, had been found shot to death on Tucker's floor; on that occasion, too, Tucker claimed that he had been sleeping and awoke to find the corpse. Both times Tucker appeared to the police to have been drinking. The Nevada Supreme Court reversed Tucker's conviction, ruling that the trial judge should have excluded evidence of the 1957 death:

> There is nothing in this record to establish that Tucker killed Kaylor. Anonymous crimes can have no relevance in deciding whether the defendant committed the crime with which he is charged. Kaylor's assailant remains unknown. A fortiori, evidence of that crime cannot be received in the trial for the murder of Evans. . . . Here there was only conjecture and suspicion, aroused by the fact that Kaylor was found dead in Tucker's home. . . . [B]efore evidence of a collateral offense is admissible for any purpose, the prosecution must first establish by plain, clear and convincing evidence, that the defendant committed that offense. . . . Fundamental fairness demands this standard in order to preclude verdicts which might otherwise rest on false assumptions.

Tucker v. State, 412 P.2d 970, 972 (Nev. 1966). Would the result be the same under the Federal Rules of Evidence?

D. CHARACTER AND HABIT

Although evidence of character generally is *not* admissible to prove conduct in conformity with character on a particular occasion, evidence of habit *is* admissible to prove conduct in conformity with habit on a particular occasion. The habit rule gives rise to two mysteries: where the line is drawn between habit and character, and why the two are treated so differently.

[F.R.E. 406; C.E.C. §§1104-1105]

ADVISORY COMMITTEE NOTE TO F.R.E. 406

An oft-quoted paragraph, McCormick, §162, p. 340, describes habit in terms effectively contrasting it with character. "Character and habit are close akin. Character is a generalized description of one's disposition, or of one's disposition in respect to a general trait, such as honesty, temperance, or peacefulness. 'Habit,' in modern usage, both lay and psychological, is more specific. It describes one's regular response to a repeated specific situation. If we speak of character for care, we think of the person's tendency to act prudently in all the varying situations of life, in business, family life, in handling automobiles and in walking across the street. A habit, on the other hand, is the person's regular practice of meeting a particular kind of situation with a specific type of conduct, such as the habit of going down a particular stairway two stairs at a time, or of giving the hand-signal for a left turn, or of alighting from railway cars while they are moving. The doing of the habitual acts may become semi-automatic."

Equivalent behavior on the part of a group is designated "routine practice of an organization" in the rule.

Agreement is general that habit evidence is highly persuasive as proof of conduct on a particular occasion. Again quoting McCormick §162, p. 341: "Character may be thought of as the sum of one's habits though doubtless it is more than this. But unquestionably the uniformity of one's response to habit is far greater than the consistency with which one's conduct conforms to character or disposition. Even though character comes in only exceptionally as evidence of an act, surely any sensible man in investigating whether X did a particular act would be greatly helped in his inquiry by evidence as to whether he was in the habit of doing it."

When disagreement has appeared, its focus has been upon the question what constitutes habit, and the reason for this is readily apparent. The extent to which instances must be multiplied and consistency of behavior maintained in order to rise to the status of habit inevitably gives rise to differences of opinion. While adequacy of sampling and uniformity of response are key factors, precise standards for measuring their sufficiency for evidence purposes cannot be formulated.

The rule is consistent with prevailing views. Much evidence is excluded simply because of failure to achieve the status of habit. Thus, evidence of intemperate "habits" is generally excluded when offered as proof of drunkenness in accident cases, Annot., 46 A.L.R.2d 103, and evidence of other assaults is inadmissible to prove the instant one in a civil assault action, Annot., 66 A.L.R.2d 806. In Levin v. United States, 119 U.S. App. D.C. 156, 338 F.2d 265 (1964), testimony as to the religious "habits" of the accused, offered as tending to prove that he was at home observing the Sabbath rather than out obtaining money through larceny by trick, was held properly excluded: "It seems apparent to us that an individual's religious practices would not be the type of activities which would lend themselves to the characterization of 'invariable regularity.' [1 Wigmore 520.] Certainly the very volitional basis of the activity raises serious questions as to its invariable nature, and hence its probative value."

These rulings are not inconsistent with the trend towards admitting evidence of business transactions between one of the parties and a third person as tending to prove that he made the same bargain or proposal in the litigated situation. Nor are they inconsistent with such cases as Whittemore v. Lockheed Aircraft Corp., 65 Cal. App. 2d 737, 151 P.2d 670 (1944), upholding the admission of evidence that plaintiff's intestate had on four other occasions flown planes from defendant's factory for delivery to his employer airline, offered to prove that he was piloting rather than a guest on a plane which crashed and killed all on board while en route for delivery. . . .

REPORT OF THE HOUSE JUDICIARY COMMITTEE

Rule 406 as submitted to Congress contained a subdivision (b) providing that the method of proof of habit or routine practice could be "in the form of an opinion or by specific instances of conduct sufficient in number to warrant a finding that the habit existed or that the practice was routine." The Committee deleted this subdivision believing that that the method of proof of habit and routine practice should be left to the courts to deal with on a case-by-case basis. At the same time, the Committee does not intend that its action be construed as sanctioning a general authorization of opinion evidence in this area.

LOUGHAN v. FIRESTONE TIRE & RUBBER CO.

749 F.2d 1519 (11th Cir. 1985)

HATCHETT, Circuit Judge:

. . . On July 24, 1974, John F. Loughan, the appellant, while employed as a tire mechanic by Slutz-Seiberling Tire Company in Fort Lauderdale, Florida, was mounting and dismounting a Firestone multi-piece rim wheel assembly to a trailer axle. Loughan sustained injuries when, in the process of remounting, a part of the three part rim wheel assembly separated with explosive force, striking Loughan in the head. . . . Loughan brought this diversity personal injury action against Firestone Tire and Rubber Company, appellee, asserting theories of negligence and strict liability in tort for the defective design of the multi-piece truck wheel components. After granting Firestone's motion for a directed verdict on the issue of warning, the district court submitted the remainder of the case to the jury, which returned a special verdict in favor of Firestone. Loughan asserts that the district court committed reversible error in admitting into evidence prior instances of Loughan's drinking of alcoholic beverages. The district court held that the evidence of Loughan's drinking was sufficiently regular to constitute habit evidence admissible pursuant to Federal Rule of Evidence 406. . . .

Our determination of whether the references to Loughan's drinking introduced by the defendant represent evidence admissible to prove habit begins with a review of the Fifth Circuit's decision in *Reyes v. Missouri Railroad Co.*, 589 F.2d 791 (5th Cir. 1979). In *Reyes*, a Missouri Pacific railroad train ran over Joel Reyes as he lay on the railroad tracks. Reyes sued the railroad alleging negligence on the part of the railroad's employees in failing to discover him as he lay on the tracks. The district court permitted the railroad to support its defense of contributory negligence by introducing into evidence Reyes' four prior misdemeanor convictions for public intoxication.

The Fifth Circuit reversed the district court and held that the four prior convictions for intoxication were inadmissible under Federal Rule of Evidence 404. The evidence was inadmissible because it was proffered to prove that Reyes acted in conformity with his character on the night of the accident; the court held that the four convictions failed to constitute habit evidence. The court stated: "Although a precise formula cannot be proposed for determining when the behavior may become so consistent as to rise to the level of habit, 'adequacy of sampling and uniformity of response' are controlling considerations." *Reyes*, 589 F.2d at 795 (quoting Notes of Advisory Committee on Proposed Rules, Fed. R. Evid. 406). . . . The court found that four prior convictions for public intoxication spanning a three and one-half year period are of insufficient regularity to rise to the level of "habit" evidence.

. . . Prior to admitting testimony of Loughan's drinking, the district court discussed with counsel admission of the evidence in light of the *Reyes* decision and rule 406. The court distinguished the inadmissible evidence in *Reyes* from the evidence introduced by Firestone. The court stated that in *Reyes* the evidence consisted of four particular incidents; whereas, Firestone offered evidence of Loughan's drinking over an extended period of time, coupled with evidence of Loughan's regular practice of carrying a cooler of beer at or about the time of the accident. The district court relied on the cumulative effect of the evidence in measuring its sufficiency to establish a drinking habit under rule 406.

Evidence adduced from three sources, taken together, demonstrates a uniform pattern of behavior. Loughan admitted that he carried a cooler of beer on his truck while employed by Slutz and that he would drink beer at some time between the hours of 9 a.m. and 5 p.m. Orr, Loughan's supervisor at Slutz, testified that Loughan routinely carried a cooler of beer on his truck and that he was in the habit of drinking on the job. Orr stated that complaints had been made by customers regarding Loughan's drinking while working on their equipment and that Loughan "normally" had something to drink in the early morning hours. Thompson, Loughan's former employer, further corroborated Loughan's habit when he testified that he fired Loughan because, based on his general observations and complaints from customers, he believed Loughan drank beer on the job. Thompson's observations of Loughan while under his employ between 1969 and 1971 are consistent with Orr's testimony regarding Loughan's behavior in Florida between 1971 and 1974. These recounts establish a pattern of drinking over a period of time.

. . . We do not attempt here to develop a precise threshold of proof necessary to transform one's general disposition into a "habit"; on a close call, we will find the district court's admission of evidence relating to Loughan's drinking on the job rose to the level of habit pursuant to rule 406. District courts exercise broad discretion in determining the admissibility of evidence and will be reversed only if discretion has been abused. We find no abuse of discretion. . . . AFFIRMED.

BURCHETT v. COMMONWEALTH

98 S.W.3d 492 (Ky. 2003)

Opinion of the Court by Justice JOHNSTONE.

As the result of a fatal automobile collision, Appellant, George Burchett, Jr., was convicted by a Green Circuit Court jury of reckless homicide, for which he received a sentence of five years' imprisonment. . . . We granted discretionary review to consider . . . whether evidence that a defendant smoked marijuana on a daily basis is admissible to prove that he smoked marijuana on the day of the collision. For the reasons discussed below, we hold this evidence to be inadmissible; accordingly, we reverse and remand. . . .

At the time of the collision, Appellant was on his way to the Taylor County Hospital to visit his girlfriend, . . . who had given birth to their child the previous day. . . . [He ran a stop sign and collided with the victim's truck; the victim had the right of way.]

Appellant was indicted for second-degree manslaughter. This offense requires proof of a wanton mental state. One way to prove wantonness is to show that the defendant in a vehicle-homicide case was driving while intoxicated. Consequently, the prosecutor intended to show that Appellant was under the influence of marijuana or other drugs at the time of his collision. . . . While Appellant did not contest admission of evidence that he smoked a marijuana cigarette the day before the collision, Appellant did contest the admission of any evidence that he had a habit of drinking alcohol or smoking marijuana every day. . . . [T]he [trial] court ruled that evidence concerning Appellant's daily drinking would not be admitted. But the court also ruled that evidence of Appellant's daily use of marijuana was admissible.

This evidence was first introduced during the prosecution's direct examination of the emergency room nurse, who read the notes she took after assessing Appellant in the ER: "Patient states I smoke one joint in the morning and one at night." The nurse later read the physician's notes: "[Patient a]dmits to one joint this morning. Two joints daily." . . . [A]t trial [Appellant] denied that he smoked marijuana the morning of the collision. . . .

In 1990, the General Assembly sought to permit habit evidence when it enacted KRS 422A.0406, which would have created a state counterpart to the federal rule permitting habit evidence. But KRS 422A.0406 was subject to the approval of this Court and, consistent with our longstanding case law, we rejected that legislation, which was subsequently repealed. . . . Most states have adopted a version of FRE 406, either by rule or by statute. Kentucky is one of the few jurisdictions in the United States that does not currently admit such evidence. Instead of unquestioningly following our sister jurisdictions, we examine the soundness of the rule and the ramifications of adopting it.

While habit evidence has an intuitive appeal, close scrutiny reveals numerous difficulties with its use. . . . It is easy to recognize the prejudice to the defendant if the prosecutor is permitted to attach the label of "habit" to his actions. E.g., John Doe has the "habit" of watching pornographic videos after work in front of his minor daughters. Or, John Doe has the "habit" of beating his wife on the weekends. Simply characterizing the defendant's actions as a "habit" attaches excessive significance in the minds of jurors. . . . The label becomes a scarlet letter. . . . In this case, the prosecutor used the term in just this inflammatory manner when he declared: "You're just pretty much a one joint morning [sic] and one joint at night, that's just your habit."

Confusion of the issues and delay are additional unwanted, but unavoidable, byproducts of habit evidence. In deciding whether certain conduct constitutes habit, [courts consider, among factors, how often and how regularly the conduct has occurred]. . . . The Advisory Committee underscored the idea that "adequacy of sampling and uniformity of response are key factors" for measuring the sufficiency of the evidence. But proof of these occurrences requires numerous collateral inquiries, which leads to delay and jury confusion. . . . Even in cases where the habit evidence is ultimately excluded, the attorneys must still prepare the evidence and the judge must still examine it.

This kind of extensive "habit" testimony occurred in *Perrin v. Anderson*, 784 F.2d 1040 (8th Cir. 1986). Perrin was killed by two police officers after they attempted to question him about an automobile accident. According to the officers, Perrin attacked them during the questioning. The defendant-officers made an offer of proof that other police officers would testify about numerous violent encounters instigated by Perrin against these officers. Ultimately, four officers were permitted to testify about five such incidents. The Tenth Circuit agreed with the trial court that this evidence was properly admitted as evidence of habit tending to prove that Perrin was the first aggressor. Aside from the fact that the testimony of these officers appears to be impermissible character evidence and not evidence of habit, it is clear that to establish the "habit," four witnesses were examined and cross-examined. . . . All of this testimony about habit could have easily distracted the jury from the central issue in the case: Did Perrin attack the police officers and threaten their lives on that particular day?

In the present case, even though Appellant testified about his own habit, there were numerous collateral evidentiary issues related to his marijuana use that were not explored, but likely could have been. These issues could easily have involved other witnesses. Appellant testified that he slept at the hospital the night before the collision and he drove directly to work the next morning. . . . How much evidence could Appellant introduce that he never kept marijuana in his truck but only at his home? Or that when he spent the night away from home, he did not smoke marijuana in the morning? Could Appellant offer evidence that he did not have marijuana when other important family events occurred, like the death of a parent or sibling? Or that he typically ran out of marijuana on a particular day of the week? Or that he met his supplier on a typical day? This is the type of evidence that delays trials and confuses jurors—an exorbitant price to pay for evidence that fails to even address the critical issue. . . .

Of course one of the most compelling reasons to exclude habit evidence is presented by the facts of this case. Appellant stated that, in addition to smoking marijuana daily, it was his normal routine to drink one-half to three-quarters of a gallon of vodka daily. If habit evidence were admissible, Appellant's drinking practice would have been admissible as substantive evidence that Appellant had likely been drinking on the day of the collision. That evidence would undoubtedly weigh heavily on the minds of the jurors. But that evidence would have been utterly false. In fact, Appellant did not drink any alcohol that day, as was confirmed by the blood alcohol test, which was the only reason the evidence of Appellant's drinking "habit" was excluded. Unfortunately for Appellant, his blood sample could not be tested and the drug test results could not corroborate his testimony that he did not smoke marijuana that morning, so evidence of his daily smoking was admitted. This scenario ferrets out the dangerous non sequitur that the habit evidence rule encourages: because a defendant regularly performs a particular act, he also did so on this particular occasion. In light of these difficulties, this Court chooses to avoid the introduction of such specious evidence into the courtrooms of this Commonwealth. . . .

[T]he evidence of Appellant's marijuana use should have been excluded. This error by the trial court was not harmless. Accordingly, we reverse and remand this case to the Green Circuit Court for a new trial consistent with this Opinion.

KELLER, Justice, Concurring.

[W]hile I acknowledge that Justice Johnstone has outlined some valid concerns regarding the potential malleability of the habit label, I believe that those concerns could be allayed with an appropriately narrow definition and/or interpretation of habit, and thus I would support this Court's adoption of an evidentiary rule permitting the introduction of habit evidence for the purpose of proving conforming action on a particular occasion. I vote to reverse Appellant's convictions and to remand this indictment for a new trial, however, because, in my opinion, before Kentucky trial courts may permit the introduction of habit evidence, this Court must amend the Kentucky Rules of Evidence. . . .

COOPER, Justice, Dissenting.

Both character evidence and habit evidence are offered as circumstantial evidence of conforming conduct. The element of habit evidence that distinguishes it from character evidence is the element of specificity, as opposed to mere disposition. Thus, evidence that Appellant is a "drunkard" would be character evidence, whereas evidence that he drinks "one-half to three-quarters of a gallon a day of vodka" is evidence of a habit. . . . Forty-three of the fifty states have adopted [analogues of FRE 406]. . . . Five additional states have common law rules admitting evidence of habit to prove conduct with some variation. . . . Except for Kentucky, Massachusetts is the only jurisdiction that purports to preclude evidence of habit to prove conforming conduct. . . . Nevertheless, the Massachusetts Supreme Court has clarified that habit evidence is not inadmissible in all circumstances. "Massachusetts draws a distinction between evidence of personal habit and evidence of business habit or custom. . . . [E]vidence of business habits or customs is admissible to prove that an act was performed in accordance with the habit." *Palinkas v. Bennett*, 620 N.E.2d 775, 777 (1993). . . . Thus, Kentucky is the only jurisdiction that precludes, under all circumstances, admission of evidence of individual habit or of the routine practice of an organization as circumstantial evidence of conforming conduct on a specific occasion.

All of the cases applying Kentucky's common law rule of exclusion are more than fifty years old and many involved what is more correctly categorized as character evidence, not habit evidence. *Dawson v. Shannon*, 9 S.W.2d 998, 998-99 (Ky. 1928) ("habit" of drinking); *Louisville & N.R. Co. v. Adams' Adm'r*, 265 S.W. 623, 627 (Ky. 1924) (habit of being a "careful and prudent driver"); *City of Madisonville v. Stewart*, 121 S.W. 421, 423 (Ky. 1909) ("habit" of drunkenness); *Louisville & N.R. Co. v. Taylors' Adm'r*, 104 S.W. 776, 778 (Ky. 1907) ("custom" of reckless driving). Nevertheless, there are other cases where the excluded evidence was properly treated as evidence of habit. *Cincinnati, N.O. & T.P. Ry. Co. v. Hare's Adm'r*, 178 S.W.2d 835, 838 (1944) (evidence that the deceased driver always looked both ways before entering a railroad crossing, used his lowest gear, and always crossed slowly); *Louisville & N.R. Co. v. Gardner's Adm'r*, 131 S.W. 787, 788 (1910) (evidence that the deceased had never been known to be intoxicated); *Lexington Ry. Co. v. Herring*, 96 S.W. 558, 560-61 (1906) (evidence that the plaintiff habitually boarded and departed street cars while they were still in motion); *Chesapeake Y O. Ry. Co. v. Riddle's Adm'x*, 72 S.W. 22, 23 (1903) (evidence that the plaintiff had never taken an alcoholic drink in his life).

The evidence excluded in those cases would satisfy today's definition of relevant evidence, *i.e.*, "evidence having any tendency to make the existence of any fact that is of consequence to the determination of the action more probable or less probable than it would be without the evidence." Under [Kentucky Rule of Evidence] 402, all relevant evidence is admissible unless excluded by "the Constitutions of the United States and the Commonwealth of Kentucky, by acts of the General Assembly of the Commonwealth of Kentucky, by these rules, or by other rules adopted by the Supreme Court of Kentucky." . . . Presumably, [this rule] has already superseded our common law exclusionary rule with respect to evidence of habit and routine practice. If not, then we should take this occasion to overrule our outdated precedents and bring Kentucky into the mainstream of American jurisprudence. . . . Accordingly, I dissent and would affirm the judgment of the Green Circuit Court in all respects.

THOMAS M. MENGLER, THE THEORY OF DISCRETION IN THE FEDERAL RULES OF EVIDENCE

74 Iowa L. Rev. 413, 417, 423-424 (1989)

Rule 406 . . . exemplifies well the drafters' conscious decision to provide trial courts with maneuvering room. . . . [A]t least regarding those rules designed to balance an item's probative value against its potentially harmful effects, the Federal Rules are misnamed. The drafters of the Federal Rules did not consider them as rigid rules to be mechanically applied, but rather as flexible principles for both trial and appellate courts.

The Committee's Note to Rule 406 contains two analytically distinct understandings of habit. The first understanding—described by some as the "psychological theory"—focuses on the nonvolitional or semiautomatic nature of a habit. The second understanding—which has been labeled the "probability theory"—focuses entirely on a person's regular response to a specific situation.

Regularity in responding to a specific situation is a requirement not only of the probability theory, but also of the psychological theory. In order for a response to be considered semiautomatic, it must uniformly follow a stimulus. But uniformity is just one aspect of the psychological theory. The other feature is that the individual's response must be unconsciously mechanical—Pavlovian. Thus, on this psychological theory, the routine practice of reading a novel before going to bed, while customary, could not be habitual because it is volitional. In contrast, the regular practice of turning the pages of the novel with one's left hand could be habitual because of its mechanical or automatic nature. . . .

[T]he Committee advanced two theories, not because of entrenched disagreement or indecision among Committee members, but from a deliberate design to build flexibility into the Federal Rules of Evidence. The Committee's primary reason for advancing two theories of habit was to promote trial court discretion. . . . The drafters, in effect, provided flexibility within the parameters of the Rule itself. For example, presented with evidence that a litigant regularly reads mystery novels before going to bed to prove the litigant was doing so on the night in question, a trial court either could exclude it under the psychological theory, since reading is volitional, or admit it under the probability theory, since the litigant's behavior was specific and sufficiently regular.

PROBLEM

4.11. Stan is being prosecuted for perjury. In her case in chief, the prosecutor seeks to introduce evidence from Stan's former employer that Stan "has a habit of telling lies whenever the truth seems inconvenient." Stan objects. Is the testimony admissible? Would the answer be different if the prosecutor sought to prove the habit by introducing specific examples of lies that Stan told his employer?

E. Sexual Assault and Child Molestation

The character evidence rule and its exceptions used to take the same general shape in cases of sexual assault and child molestation as in other cases: The character of a criminal defendant was off-limits unless and until the defendant chose to make it admissible, and the defendant also had the option to make evidence of the victim's character admissible. But the rules no longer work this way in sex offense cases.

The first rules to change were those pertaining to evidence of the victim's character. "Rape shield statutes," adopted at the federal level and by most states in the 1970s, significantly curtail the ability of defendants in rape cases to offer evidence of the victim's character in an effort to prove consent. These statutes responded to widespread perceptions that the admissibility of such evidence unduly harassed rape victims, discouraged victims from reporting rapes, and tended to be greatly overvalued by juries.

More recently, the Federal Rules of Evidence and some state codes have been amended to allow prosecutors and plaintiffs in cases of sexual assault and child molestation to offer evidence of the defendant's character in the case-in-chief. Again, the amendments respond to perceived differences between cases of this kind and other cases. These new amendments remain highly controversial, for reasons that will become clear.

1. Character of the Victim

Evidence of the victim's character, and specifically her chastity or lack thereof, used to be a staple of rape trials, in a way that was wholly unparalleled in other criminal prosecutions. As the older materials excerpted suggest, courts and commentators found such evidence highly probative on the question of consent, and sometimes admitted it even when consent was not issue. These materials also suggest the reasons that evidence of a rape victim's sexual history was, and remains, so problematical. Juries—as well as judges and commentators—were apt to overvalue the evidence, treating it as more probative of consent than it actually was. What is more, the evidence was apt to be misused—treated as grounds for not worrying much about the rape, even if it did occur. Then, too, the admissibility of such evidence tended to transform rape trials into trials of the victim, brutalizing her and powerfully discouraging other rape victims from coming forward.

Growing recognition of these problems eventually led, in the 1970s, to the widespread adoption of "rape shield statutes" in most states and at the federal level. The terms of these laws vary widely, but broadly speaking they ban the use of character evidence to prove the victim's consent. F.R.E. 412 is the federal version.

[F.R.E. 412; C.E.C. §§1103(c), 1106]

JOHN HENRY WIGMORE, A TREATISE ON
THE ANGLO-AMERICAN SYSTEM OF EVIDENCE
IN TRIALS AT COMMON LAW
§62, at 1:279-282 (2d ed. 1923)

The reasons of Auxiliary Policy which affect the use of a defendant's character by the prosecution are peculiar to that use, and do not affect the use of character *as against other persons* in a criminal case wherever it may be relevant.

One of those relevant uses is that of the character of a *rape-complainant* for chastity. The non-consent of the complainant is here a material element; and the character of the woman as to chastity is of considerable probative value in judging the likelihood of that consent: . . .

> 1856, Isham, J., in *State v. Johnson*, 28 Vt. 514: "In all cases of this character, the assent of the witness to the act is the material matter in issue, and on that question the defense generally rests on circumstantial testimony. In determining that question, which is purely a mental act, it is important to ascertain whether her consent would from her previous habits be the natural result of her mind, of whether it would be inconsistent with her previous life and repugnant to all her moral feelings. Such habits as are imputed to the witness by this inquiry have a tendency to show consent as the natural operation of her propensities, and rebut the inference or necessity of actual violence."
>
> 1895, Garoutte, J., in *People v. Johnson*, 106 Cal. 289: "This class of evidence is admissible for the purpose of tending to show the non-probability of resistance upon the part of the prosecutrix; for it is certainly more probable that a woman who has done these things voluntarily in the past would be much more likely to consent than one whose past reputation was without blemish, and whose general conduct could not truthfully be assailed. In other words, this class of evidence goes to the question of consent only."

The admissibility, on a *rape* charge, of the complainant's *character for chastity or unchastity* is generally conceded; and her *habits as a prostitute* are usually regarded as equivalent to a general trait of character. . . . The only difficulty in applying the principle is to distinguish between the use of Character, as bearing on consent, and the use of *specific acts of unchastity* as a means of evidencing the character itself. The latter kind of evidence being in many jurisdictions excluded, the woman's character as evidenced by reputation is alone admissible in those jurisdictions. . . .

GRAHAM v. STATE

67 S.W.2d 296 (Tex. Crim. App. 1933)

CHRISTIAN, J.

The offense is rape by force; the punishment, confinement in the penitentiary for fifty years. . . . [Appellant sought unsuccessfully to introduce testimony] that the general reputation of the prosecutrix for chastity was bad . . . [and] that prosecutrix habitually spent the night in her apartment with various men.

. . . Appellant having expressly declared that he did not have an act of intercourse with prosecutrix, there was no issue as to consent. Hence the general rule that, on the issue of consent, proof is admissible that prosecutrix' general reputation for chastity was bad, and that she had engaged in previous acts of intercourse with the accused, would have no application. . . . [But] it occurs to us that proof that prosecutrix bore the general reputation of being unchaste and had habitually engaged in acts of sexual intercourse with others was admissible as shedding light on the transaction. In its absence, it would appear that appellant's version of the transaction might be deemed incredible; whereas, if the jury had had such proof before them, the conclusion might have been reached that the condition of the prosecutrix resulted from a fight in which she was the aggressor. In other words, the jury might have concluded that she sought to bestow carnal favors, which were rejected, and that, as a result, a fight ensued in which she received the injuries described in the testimony. . . . The judgment is reversed, and the cause remanded.

REMARKS OF REP. ELIZABETH HOLTZMAN

124 Cong. Rec. H 11944 (Oct. 10, 1978)

[Representative Holtzman was the principal sponsor of H.R. 4727, which added Rule 412 to the Federal Rules of Evidence.]

Ms. HOLTZMAN. . . . Too often in this country victims of rape are humiliated and harassed when they report and prosecute the rape. Bullied and cross-examined about their prior sexual experiences, many find the trial almost as degrading as the rape itself. Since rape trials become inquisitions into the victim's morality, not trials of the defendant's innocence or guilt, it is not surprising that it is the least reported crime. It is estimated that as few as one in ten rapes is ever reported.

Mr. Speaker, over 30 States have taken some action to limit the vulnerability of rape victims to such humiliating cross-examination of their past sexual experiences and intimate personal histories. In federal courts, however, it is permissible still to subject rape victims to brutal cross-examination about their past sexual histories. H.R. 4727 would rectify this problem in Federal courts and I hope, also serve as a model to suggest to the remaining states that reform of existing rape laws is important to the equity of our criminal justice system. . . . It will protect women from both injustice and indignity.

ADVISORY COMMITTEE NOTE TO 1994
AMENDMENTS TO RULE 412

Rule 412 has been revised to diminish some of the confusion engendered by the original rule and to expand the protection afforded alleged victims of sexual misconduct. Rule 412 applies to both civil and criminal proceedings. The rule aims to safeguard the alleged victim against the invasion of privacy, potential embarrassment and sexual stereotyping that is associated with public disclosure of intimate sexual details and the infusion of sexual innuendo into the factfinding process. By affording victims protection in most instances, the rule also encourages victims of sexual misconduct to institute and to participate in legal proceedings against alleged offenders.

Rule 412 seeks to achieve these objectives by barring evidence relating to the alleged victim's sexual behavior or alleged sexual predisposition, whether offered as substantive evidence or for impeachment, except in designated circumstances in which the probative value of the evidence significantly outweighs possible harm to the victim.

The revised rule applies in all cases involving sexual misconduct without regard to whether the alleged victim or person accused is a party to the litigation. Rule 412 extends to "pattern" witnesses in both criminal and civil cases whose testimony about other instances of sexual misconduct by the person accused is otherwise admissible. When the case does not involve alleged sexual misconduct, evidence relating to a third-party witness' alleged sexual activities is not within the ambit of Rule 412. The witness will, however, be protected by other rules such as Rules 404 and 608, as well as Rule 403.

The terminology "alleged victim" is used because there will frequently be a factual dispute as to whether sexual misconduct occurred. It does not connote any requirement that the misconduct be alleged in the pleadings. Rule 412 does not, however, apply unless the person against whom the evidence is offered can reasonably be characterized as a "victim of alleged sexual misconduct." When this is not the case, as for instance in a defamation action involving statements concerning sexual misconduct in which the evidence is offered to show that the alleged defamatory statements were true or did not damage the plaintiff's reputation, neither Rule 404 nor this rule will operate to bar the evidence; Rules 401 and 403 will continue to control. Rule 412 will, however, apply in a Title VII action in which the plaintiff has alleged sexual harassment.

The reference to a person "accused" is also used in a non-technical sense. There is no requirement that there be a criminal charge pending against the person or even that the misconduct would constitute a criminal offense. Evidence offered to prove allegedly false prior claims by the victim is not barred by Rule 412. However, the evidence is subject to the requirements of Rule 404.

. . . Past sexual behavior connotes all activities that involve actual physical conduct, i.e. sexual intercourse or sexual contact. *See, e.g., United States v. Galloway*, 937 F.2d 542 (10th Cir. 1991), *cert. denied*, 113 S. Ct. 418 (1992) (use of contraceptives inadmissible since use implies sexual activity); *United States v. One Feather*, 702 F.2d 736 (8th Cir. 1983) (birth of an illegitimate child inadmissible); *State v. Carmichael*, 727 P.2d 918, 925 (Kan. 1986) (evidence of venereal disease inadmissible). In addition, the word "behavior" should be construed to include activities of the mind, such as fantasies of dreams. *See* 23C. Wright and K. Graham, Jr., Federal Practice and Procedure, §5384 at p. 548 (1980) ("While there may be some doubt under statutes that require 'conduct,' it would seem that the language of Rule 412 is broad enough to encompass the behavior of the mind.").

The rule has been amended to also exclude all other evidence relating to an alleged victim of sexual misconduct that is offered to prove a sexual predisposition. This amendment is designed to exclude evidence that does not directly refer to sexual activities or thoughts but that the proponent believes may have a sexual connotation for the factfinder. Admission of such evidence would contravene Rule 412's objectives of shielding the alleged victim from potential embarrassment and safeguarding the victim against stereotypical thinking. Consequently, unless the (b)(2) exception is satisfied, evidence such as that relating to the alleged victim's mode of dress, speech, or life-style will not be admissible.

. . . The reason for extending the rule to all criminal cases is obvious. The strong social policy of protecting a victim's privacy and encouraging victims to come forward to report criminal acts is not confined to cases that involve a charge of sexual assault. The need to protect the victim is equally great when a defendant is charged with kidnapping, and evidence is offered, either to prove motive or as background, that the defendant sexually assaulted the victim.

The reason for extending Rule 412 to civil cases is equally obvious. The need to protect alleged victims against invasions of privacy, potential embarrassment, and unwarranted sexual stereotyping, and the wish to encourage victims to come forward when they have been sexually molested do not disappear because the context has shifted from a criminal prosecution to a claim for damages or injunctive relief. There is a strong social policy in not only punishing those who engage in sexual misconduct, but in also providing relief to the victim. Thus, Rule 412 applies in any civil case in which a person claims to be the victim of sexual misconduct, such as actions for sexual battery or sexual harassment.

. . . Subdivision (b)(2) governs the admissibility of otherwise proscribed evidence in civil cases. It employs a balancing test rather than the specific exceptions stated in subdivision (b)(1) in recognition of the difficulty of foreseeing future developments in the law. Greater flexibility is needed to accommodate evolving causes of action such as claims for sexual harassment.

The balancing test requires the proponent of the evidence, whether plaintiff or defendant, to convince the court that the probative value of the proffered evidence "substantially outweighs the danger of harm to any victim and of unfair prejudice of any party." This test for admitting evidence offered to prove sexual behavior or sexual propensity in civil cases differs in three respects from the general rule governing admissibility set forth in Rule 403. First, it reverses that usual procedure spelled out in Rule 403 by shifting the burden to the proponent to demonstrate admissibility rather than making the opponent justify exclusion of the evidence. Second, the standard expressed in subdivision (b)(2) is more stringent than in the original rule; it raises the threshold for admission by requiring that the probative value of the evidence substantially outweigh the specified dangers. Finally, the Rule 412 test puts "harm to the victim" on the scale in addition to prejudice to the parties. . . .

UNITED STATES v. SAUNDERS

943 F.2d 388 (4th Cir. 1991)

NIEMEYER, Circuit Judge:

Henry Saunders was convicted by a jury of aggravated sexual abuse under 18 U.S.C. §2241(a) and was sentenced as a career offender to 360 months imprisonment. On appeal he contends that the district court erred in excluding evidence, under Fed. R. Evid. 412, that the complaining witness [Patricia Duckett] was a "skeezer" (a prostitute who trades sex for drugs). . . .

On Saunders' pretrial motion to offer evidence at trial about Patricia Duckett's past sexual conduct with him and with his friend, Kenneth Smith, the district court conducted an in camera hearing pursuant to Fed. R. Evid. 412. At the hearing, Saunders testified to his own prior sexual encounters with Duckett and to a conversation with Kenneth Smith one week prior to the alleged rape, in which Smith said that Duckett was a "skeezer" and that Smith had had sex with Duckett in exchange for drugs. Smith confirmed that he had, in fact, had sex with Duckett, but he invoked the Fifth Amendment when asked if he had exchanged drugs for sex. The district court ruled that Saunders could testify to his own prior sexual relations with Duckett but that Smith could not testify to his experience with her.

Saunders argues that the court erred in excluding Smith's testimony. He argues that the testimony was relevant to his state of mind that he knew of Duckett's reputation at the time of the alleged rape. He relies on *Doe v. United States*, 666 F.2d 43 (4th Cir. 1981). In *Doe*, when confronted with the question of whether "evidence of the defendant's 'state of mind as a result of what he knew of [the victim's] reputation' " was admissible under Fed. R. Evid. 412(a), the court concluded, "There is no indication, however, that this evidence was intended to be excluded when offered solely to show the accused's state of mind." The government argues that *Doe* is an incorrect application of Rule 412.

Notwithstanding a question of whether the decision in *Doe*, regarding reputation evidence under 412(a), is correct,[1] we find that the district court's ruling in this case was proper.

Section (a) of the rule, which applies to reputation and opinion testimony of past sexual behavior, prohibits the evidence in every rape trial under Title 18, Chapter 109A (which includes 18 U.S.C. §2241(a), applicable here), regardless of the circumstances under which it is offered. Section

---

1. *Doe* has been criticized for reading an exception into the flat prohibition of Fed. R. Evid. 412(a), when relevant to the defendant's state of mind. *See* Spector & Foster, *Rule 412 and the* Doe *Case: The Fourth Circuit Turns Back the Clock*, 35 Okla. L. Rev. 87, 96-97 (1982): "[T]he court arrogated to itself the authority to declare that the categorical mandate expressed in the rule did not fully articulate Congress' intent. Furthermore, the court fashioned and propounded its own exception to the rule's explicit ban on previous sexual behavior, an exception unauthorized by legislative fiat that is of such magnitude that its very existence threatens to . . . vitiate the utility of Rule 412 as a means of implementing the federal legislative purposes motivating its enactment." *But see* Galvin, *Shielding Rape Victims in the State and Federal Courts: A Proposal for the Second Decade*, 70 Minn. L. Rev. 763, 890-93 (1986).

(b), which applies to other evidence of past sexual behavior, also prohibits the evidence except in three limited circumstances: (1) when the evidence is constitutionally required to be admitted . . . , (2) when the defendant claims that he was not the source of the semen or injury . . . , and (3) when the defendant claims that the victim consented, in which case he may testify only to his prior relations with the victim. . . . Thus, the scheme of Rule 412 is that reputation and opinion evidence about a victim's past sexual behavior are never admissible, and evidence of specific prior acts is limited (to the extent constitutionally permitted) to directly probative evidence. *United States v. Torres*, 937 F.2d 1469, 1471 (9th Cir. 1991); *United States v. Duran*, 886 F.2d 167, 168 n.3 (8th Cir. 1989). Rule 412 is an express limitation on the general rules of admissibility of evidence about the prior conduct of witnesses otherwise applicable.

In this case, the district judge ruled that Saunders' testimony about his own past sexual relationship with Patricia Duckett was admissible . . . and that Smith's testimony, "I had her [Patricia Duckett] home for three days," was inadmissible because it was testimony of specific sexual behavior that did not come within one of the three exceptions. . . . The only exception arguably applicable to Smith's testimony is that the evidence would be constitutionally required. . . . The defendant has a constitutional right to present admissible evidence that is probative of his innocence by showing the government's failure to prove the offense charged, by establishing a defense, or by attacking the credibility or fair mindedness of a witness. *See, e.g., Olden v. Kentucky*, 488 U.S. 227 (1988); *Chambers v. Mississippi*, 410 U.S. 284 (1973); *Torres*, 937 F.2d at 1471-72. We can discern no constitutional basis, however, that requires the admission of evidence about a three-day relationship between the victim and some third person.

Saunders contends that his knowledge that Duckett was a "skeezer" or prostitute corroborated his belief that she consented. A defendant's reasonable, albeit mistaken, belief that the victim consented may constitute a defense to rape. *See* W. LaFave & A. Scott, Handbook on Criminal Law, §47, at 357-58 (1972). When consent is the issue, however, [Rule 412] permits only evidence of the defendant's past experience with the victim. The rule manifests the policy that it is unreasonable for a defendant to base his belief of consent on the victim's past sexual experiences with third persons, since it is intolerable to suggest that because the victim is a prostitute, she automatically is assumed to have consented with anyone at any time. If we were to require admission of Smith's testimony about his affair with Duckett, we would eviscerate the clear intent of the rule to protect victims of rape from being exposed at trial to harassing or irrelevant inquiry into their past sexual behavior, an inquiry that, prior to the adoption of the rule, had the tendency to shield defendants from their illegal conduct by discouraging victims from testifying.

In this case even the district court's admission of evidence that Duckett had prior sexual relations with the defendant was of marginal relevance because consent was not the basis of Saunders' defense. Saunders was charged with a rape that occurred while he and Duckett were in an automobile parked at Fort Belvoir. Instead of contending that Duckett consented, Saunders testified that no sexual intercourse took place at this time and place. His state of mind that Duckett was a "skeezer" is hardly relevant to that defense. Saunders did, however, provide an explanation for the presence of semen based on a consensual affair. He contended that he and Duckett had consensual sexual intercourse earlier in the evening at Saunders' house. For that reason Saunders could justify evidence of his own prior sexual conduct with Duckett. . . . [W]e find no reversible error in the conduct of the trial and affirm Saunders' conviction.

OLDEN v. KENTUCKY

488 U.S. 227 (1988)

PER CURIAM.

Petitioner James Olden and his friend Charlie Ray Harris, both of whom are black, were indicted for kidnapping, rape, and forcible sodomy. The victim of the alleged crimes, Starla Matthews, a young white woman, gave the following account at trial: She and a friend, Regina Patton, had driven to Princeton, Kentucky, to exchange Christmas gifts with Bill Russell, petitioner's half brother. After meeting Russell at a local car wash and exchanging presents with him, Matthews and Patton stopped in J.R's, a "boot-legging joint" serving a predominantly black clientele, to use the restroom. Matthews consumed several glasses of beer. As the bar became more crowded, she became increasingly nervous because she and Patton were the only white people there. When Patton refused to leave, Matthews sat at a separate table, hoping to demonstrate to her friend that she was upset. As time passed, however, Matthews lost track of Patton and became somewhat intoxicated. When petitioner told her that Patton had departed and had been in a car accident, she left the bar with petitioner and Harris to find out what had happened. She was driven in Harris' car to another location, where, threatening her with a knife, petitioner raped and sodomized her. Harris assisted by holding her arms. Later, she was driven to a dump, where two other men joined the group. There, petitioner raped her once again. At her request, the men then dropped her off in the vicinity of Bill Russell's house.

On cross-examination, petitioner's counsel focused on a number of inconsistencies in Matthews' various accounts of the alleged crime. Matthews originally told the police that she had been raped by four men. Later, she claimed that she had been raped by only petitioner and Harris. At trial, she contended that petitioner was the sole rapist. Further, while Matthews testified at trial that petitioner had threatened her with a knife, she had not previously alleged that petitioner had been armed.

Russell, who also appeared as a State's witness, testified that on the evening in question he heard a noise outside his home and, when he went out to investigate, saw Matthews get out of Harris' car. Matthews immediately told Russell that she had just been raped by petitioner and Harris.

Petitioner and Harris asserted a defense of consent. According to their testimony, Matthews propositioned petitioner as he was about to leave the bar, and the two engaged in sexual acts behind the tavern. Afterwards, on

Matthews' suggestion, Matthews, petitioner, and Harris left in Harris' car in search of cocaine. When they discovered that the seller was not at home, Matthews asked Harris to drive to a local dump so that she and petitioner could have sex once again. Harris complied. Later that evening, they picked up two other men, Richard Hickey and Chris Taylor, and drove to an establishment called The Alley. Harris, Taylor, and Hickey went in, leaving petitioner and Matthews in the car. When Hickey and Harris returned, the men gave Hickey a ride to a store and then dropped Matthews off, at her request, in the vicinity of Bill Russell's home.

Taylor and Hickey testified for the defense and corroborated the defendants' account of the evening. While both acknowledged that they joined the group later than the time when the alleged rape occurred, both testified that Matthews did not appear upset. Hickey further testified that Matthews had approached him earlier in the evening at J.R.'s and told him that she was looking for a black man with whom to have sex. An independent witness also appeared for the defense and testified that he had seen Matthews, Harris, and petitioner at a store called Big O's on the evening in question, that a policeman was in the store at the time, and that Matthews, who appeared alert, made no attempt to signal for assistance.

Although Matthews and Russell were both married to and living with other people at the time of the incident, they were apparently involved in an extramarital relationship. By the time of trial the two were living together, having separated from their respective spouses. Petitioner's theory of the case was that Matthews concocted the rape story to protect her relationship with Russell, who would have grown suspicious upon seeing her disembark from Harris' car. In order to demonstrate Matthew's motive to lie, it was crucial, petitioner contended, that he be allowed to introduce evidence of Matthew's and Russell's current cohabitation. Over petitioner's vehement objections, the trial court nonetheless granted the prosecutor's motion in limine to keep all evidence of Matthews' and Russell's living arrangement from the jury. Moreover, when the defense attempted to cross-examine Matthews about her living arrangements, after she had claimed during direct examination that she was living with her mother, the trial court sustained the prosecutor's objection.

Based on the evidence admitted at trial, the jury acquitted Harris of being either a principal or an accomplice to any of the charged offenses. Petitioner was likewise acquitted of kidnaping and rape. However, in a somewhat puzzling turn of events, the jury convicted petitioner alone of forcible sodomy. He was sentenced to 10 years' imprisonment.

Petitioner appealed, asserting, inter alia, that the trial court's refusal to allow him to impeach Matthews' testimony by introducing evidence supporting a motive to lie deprived him of his Sixth Amendment right to confront witnesses against him. The Kentucky Court of Appeals upheld the conviction. The court specifically held that evidence that Matthews and Russell were living together at the time of trial was not barred by the State's rape shield law. Moreover, it acknowledged that the evidence in question was relevant to petitioner's theory of the case. But it held, nonetheless, that the evidence was properly excluded as "its probative value [was] outweighed by its possibility for prejudice." By way of explanation, the court stated: "[T]here were the undisputed facts of race; Matthews was white and Russell was black. For the trial court to have admitted into evidence testimony that Matthews and Russell were living together at the time of the trial may have created extreme prejudice against Matthews." Judge Clayton, who dissented but did not address the evidentiary issue, would have reversed petitioner's conviction both because he believed the jury's verdicts were "manifestly inconsistent," and because he found Matthews' testimony too incredible to provide evidence sufficient to uphold the verdict.

The Kentucky Court of Appeals failed to accord proper weight to petitioner's Sixth Amendment right "to be confronted with the witnesses against him." That right, incorporated in the Fourteenth Amendment and therefore available in state proceedings, *Pointer v. Texas*, 380 U.S. 400 (1965), includes the right to conduct reasonable cross-examination. *Davis v. Alaska*, 415 U.S. 308, 315-316 (1974).

In *Davis v. Alaska*, we observed that, subject to "the broad discretion of a trial judge to preclude repetitive and unduly harassing interrogation . . . , the cross-examiner has traditionally been allowed to impeach, i.e., discredit, the witness." We emphasized that "the exposure of a witness' motivation in testifying is a proper and important function of the constitutionally protected right of cross-examination." Recently, in *Delaware v. Van Arsdall*, 475 U.S. 673 (1986), we reaffirmed *Davis*, and held that "a criminal defendant states a violation of the Confrontation Clause by showing that he was prohibited from engaging in otherwise appropriate cross-examination designed to show a prototypical form of bias on the part of the witness, and thereby 'to expose to the jury the facts from which jurors . . . could appropriately draw inferences relating to the reliability of the witness.'" 475 U.S., at 680, *quoting Davis, supra*, 415 U.S., at 318.

In the instant case, petitioner has consistently asserted that he and Matthews engaged in consensual sexual acts and that Matthews—out of fear of jeopardizing her relationship with Russell—lied when she told Russell she had been raped and has continued to lie since. It is plain to us that "[a] reasonable jury might have received a significantly different impression of [the witness'] credibility had [defense counsel] been permitted to pursue his proposed line of cross-examination." *Delaware v. Van Arsdall, supra*, 475 U.S., at 680.

The Kentucky Court of Appeals did not dispute, and indeed acknowledged, the relevance of the impeachment evidence. Nonetheless, without acknowledging the significance of, or even adverting to, petitioner's constitutional right to confrontation, the court held that petitioner's right to effective cross-examination was outweighed by the danger that revealing Matthews' interracial relationship would prejudice the jury against her. While a trial court may, of course, impose reasonable limits on defense counsel's inquiry into the potential bias of a prosecution witness, to take account of such factors as "harassment, prejudice, confusion of the issues, the witness' safety, or interrogation that [would be] repetitive or only marginally relevant," *Delaware v. Van Arsdall, supra*, at 679, the limitation here was beyond reason. Speculation as to the effect of jurors' racial biases cannot justify exclusion of cross-examination with such strong potential to demonstrate the falsity of Matthews' testimony.

In *Delaware v. Van Arsdall, supra*, we held that "the constitutionally improper denial of a defendant's opportunity to impeach a witness for bias, like other Confrontation Clause errors, is subject to *Chapman* [*v. California*, 386 U.S. 18 (1967)] harmless-error analysis." Thus we stated: "The correct inquiry is whether, assuming that the damaging potential of the cross-examination were fully realized, a reviewing court might nonetheless say that the error was harmless beyond a reasonable doubt. Whether such an error is harmless in a particular case depends upon a host of factors, all readily accessible to reviewing courts. These factors include the importance of the witness' testimony in the prosecution's case, whether the testimony was cumulative, the presence or absence of evidence corroborating or contradicting the testimony of the witness on material points, the extent of cross-examination otherwise permitted, and, of course, the overall strength of the prosecution's case."

Here, Matthews' testimony was central, indeed crucial, to the prosecution's case. Her story, which was directly contradicted by that of petitioner and Harris, was corroborated only by the largely derivative testimony of Russell, whose impartiality would also have been somewhat impugned by revelation of his relationship with Matthews. Finally, as demonstrated graphically by the jury's verdicts, which cannot be squared with the State's theory of the alleged crime, and by Judge Clayton's dissenting opinion below, the State's case against petitioner was far from overwhelming. In sum, considering the relevant *Van Arsdall* factors within the context of this case, we find it impossible to conclude "beyond a reasonable doubt" that the restriction on petitioner's right to confrontation was harmless.

The motion for leave to proceed in forma pauperis and the petition for certiorari are granted, the judgment of the Kentucky Court of Appeals is reversed, and the case is remanded for further proceedings not inconsistent with this opinion.

It is so ordered.

Justice MARSHALL, dissenting.

I continue to believe that summary dispositions deprive litigants of a fair opportunity to be heard on the merits and create a significant risk that the Court is rendering an erroneous or ill-advised decision that may confuse the lower courts. I therefore dissent from the Court's decision today to reverse summarily the decision below.

2. Character of the Defendant

Rape shield statutes, as we have seen, are motivated in part by versions of the same concerns that have traditionally motivated the character evidence rule, particularly the danger that the jury will overvalue or misuse the evidence. In stark contrast, the new federal rules regarding evidence of prior similar misconduct in sexual assault and child molestation cases are motivated by a *rejection* of those concerns, at least in this special set of cases.

The new rules were adopted in the face of strong and nearly universal condemnation by lawyers, scholars, and judges. The flavor of that opposition is suggested by some of the materials that follow. When reading these materials, ask yourself whether the new rules are as bad as their critics make them out to be, and whether, in particular, it makes sense to criticize these rules—as many commentators have—for being excessively "political." Should politicians stay away from evidence law? It is worth recalling that F.R.E. 412, the rape shield statute, also originated through the political process. And if the new rules are inconsistent with traditional thinking about character evidence, is this a reason to reject the new rules or to rethink the older, more general rules about character evidence?

[F.R.E. 413-415; C.E.C. §§1108-1109]

REMARKS OF REP. SUSAN MOLINARI

140 Cong. Rec. H8991-92 (Aug. 21, 1994)

[Rep. Molinari was the principal House sponsor of the legislation adding Rules 413-15 to the Federal Rules of Evidence.]

Ms. MOLINARI. Mr. Speaker, the revised conference bill contains a critical reform that I have long sought to protect the public from crimes of sexual violence—general rules of admissibility in sexual assault and child molestation cases for evidence that the defendant has committed offenses of the same type on other occasions. The enactment of this reform is first and foremost a triumph for the public—for the women who will not be raped and the children who will not be molested because we have strengthened the legal system's tools for bringing the perpetrators of these atrocious crimes to justice.

. . . We have agreed to a temporary deferral of the effective date of the new rules, pending a report by the Judicial Conference, in order to accommodate procedural objections raised by opponents of the reform. However, regardless of what the Judicial Conference may recommend, the new rules will take effect within at most 300 days of the enactment of this legislation, unless repealed or modified by subsequent legislation.

. . . The new rules will supersede in sex offense cases the restrictive aspects of Federal Rule of Evidence 404(b). In contrast to Rule 404(b)'s general prohibition of evidence of character or propensity, the new rules for sex offense cases authorize admission and consideration of evidence of an uncharged offense for its bearing "on any matter to which it is relevant." This includes the defendant's propensity to commit sexual assault or child molestation offenses, and assessment of the probability or improbability that the defendant has been falsely or mistakenly accused of such an offense.

In other respects, the general standards of the rules of evidence will continue to apply, including the restrictions on hearsay evidence and the court's authority under Evidence Rule 403 to exclude evidence whose probative value is substantially outweighed by its prejudicial effect. Also, the government (or the plaintiff in a civil case) will generally have to disclose to the defendant any evidence that is to be offered under the new rules at least 15 days before trial.

The proposed reform is critical to the protection of the public from rapists and child molesters, and is justified by the distinctive characteristics of the cases it will affect. In child molestation cases, for example, a history of similar acts tends to be exceptionally probative because it shows an unusual disposition of the defendant—a sexual or sadosexual interest in children—that simply does not exist in ordinary people. Moreover, such cases require reliance on child victims whose credibility can readily be attacked in the absence of substantial corroboration. In such cases, there is a compelling public interest in admitting all significant evidence that will illumine the credibility of the charge and any denial by the defense.

Similarly, adult-victim sexual assault cases are distinctive, and often turn on difficult credibility determinations. Alleged consent by the victim is rarely an issue in prosecutions for other violent crimes—the accused mugger does not claim that the victim freely handed over [his] wallet as a gift—but the defendant in a rape case often contends that the victim engaged in consensual sex and then falsely accused him. Knowledge that the defendant has committed rapes on other occasions is frequently critical in assessing the relative plausibility of these claims and accurately deciding cases that would otherwise become unresolvable swearing matches.

The practical effect of the new rules is to put evidence of uncharged offenses in sexual assault and child molestation cases on the same footing as other types of relevant evidence that are not subject to a special exclusionary rule. The presumption is in favor of admission. The underlying legislative judgment is that the evidence admissible pursuant to the proposed rules is typically relevant and probative, and that its probative value is normally not outweighed by any risk of prejudice or other adverse effects.

In line with this judgment, the rules do not impose arbitrary or artificial restrictions on the admissibility of evidence. Evidence of offenses for which the defendant has not previously been prosecuted or convicted will be admissible, as well as evidence of prior convictions. No time limit is imposed on the uncharged offenses for which evidence may be admitted; as a practical matter, evidence of other sex offenses by the defendant is often probative and properly admitted, notwithstanding very substantial lapses of time in relation to the charged offense or offenses. *See, e.g., United States v. Hadley*, 918 F.2d 848, 850-51 (9th Cir. 1990), *cert. dismissed*, 113 S. Ct. 486 (1992) (evidence of offenses occurring up to 15 years earlier admitted); *State v. Plymate*, 345 N.W.2d 327 (Neb. 1984) (evidence of defendant's commission of other child molestations more than 20 years earlier admitted).

Finally, the practical efficacy of these rules will depend on faithful execution by judges of the will of Congress in adopting this critical reform. To implement the legislative intent, the courts must liberally construe these rules to provide the basis for a fully informed decision of sexual assault and child molestation cases, including assessment of the defendant's propensities and questions of probability in light of the defendant's past conduct.

REPORT OF THE JUDICIAL CONFERENCE OF THE UNITED STATES ON THE ADMISSION OF CHARACTER EVIDENCE IN CERTAIN SEXUAL MISCONDUCT CASES

159 F.R.D. 51 (1995)

This report is transmitted to Congress in accordance with the Violent Crime Control and Law Enforcement Act of 1994, Pub. L. No. 103-322 (September 13, 1994). . . . Under the Act, new Rules 413, 414, and 415 would be added to the Federal Rule of Evidence. . . . [T]he Judicial Conference was provided 150 days within which to make and submit to Congress alternative recommendations. . . .

[T]he Judicial Conference's . . . Advisory Committee on Evidence Rules sent out a notice soliciting comments. . . . The notice was sent to the courts, including all federal judges, about 900 evidence law professors, 40 women's rights organizations, and 1,000 other individuals and interested organizations. . . . [The committee received back] 84 written comments, representing 112 individuals, 8 local and 8 national organizations. The overwhelming majority of the judges, lawyers, law professors, and legal organizations who responded opposed the new Evidence Rules 413, 414, and 415. . . . The [advisory] committee's report was unanimous except for a dissenting vote by the representative of the Department of Justice. The advisory committee believed that the concerns expressed by Congress and embodied in new Evidence Rules 413, 414, and 415 are already adequately addressed in the existing Federal Rules of Evidence. In particular, Evidence Rule 404(b) now allows the admission of evidence against a criminal defendant of the commission of prior crimes, wrongs, or acts for specified purposes, including to show intent, plan, motive, preparation, identity, knowledge, or absence of mistake or accident.

Furthermore, the new rules, which are not supported by empirical evidence, could diminish significantly the protections that have safeguarded persons accused in criminal cases and parties in civil cases against undue prejudice. These protections form a fundamental part of American jurisprudence and have evolved under long-standing rules and case law. A significant concern identified by the committee was the danger of convicting a criminal defendant for past, as opposed to charged, behavior or for being a bad person.

In addition, the advisory committee concluded that, because prior bad acts would be admissible even though not the subject of a conviction, mini-trials within trials concerning those acts would result when a defendant seeks to rebut such evidence. . . .

The Advisory Committees on Criminal and Civil Rules unanimously, except for representatives of the Department of Justice, also opposed the new rules . . . After the advisory committees reported, the Standing Committee [on Rules of Practice and Procedure] unanimously, again except for the representative of the Department of Justice, agreed with the view of the advisory committees.

It is important to note the highly unusual unanimity of the members of the Standing and Advisory Committees, composed of over 40 judges, practicing lawyers, and academicians, in taking the view that Rules 413-415 are undesirable. Indeed, the only supporters of the Rules were representatives of the Department of Justice. . . .

The Judicial Conference concurs with the views of the Standing Committee and urges that Congress reconsider its policy determinations underlying Evidence Rules 413-415. In the alternative, . . . amendments to Evidence Rules 404 and 405 are recommended, in lieu of new Evidence Rules 413, 414, and 415.

STEPHEN A. SALTZBURG, MICHAEL M. MARTIN & DANIEL J. CAPRA, FEDERAL RULES OF EVIDENCE MANUAL

2:413-12 (9th ed. 2006)

[T]he Judicial Conference submitted its report concerning the proposed rules on February 9, 1995. . . . Congress neither followed the Conference's recommendations nor otherwise altered the proposed rules. As a result, [pursuant to the enacting legislation], the proposed rules became effective on July 9, 1995.

UNITED STATES v. LECOMPTE

131 F.3d 767 (8th Cir. 1997)

Richard S. Arnold, Chief Judge.

Before the trial of Leo LeCompte for the alleged sexual abuse of his wife's 11-year-old niece, "C.D.," under 18 U.S.C. §§2244(a)(1) and 2246(3) (1994), the defendant moved *in limine* to exclude evidence of prior uncharged sex offenses against another niece by marriage, "T.T." . . . In LeCompte's first trial, the government offered the evidence under Rule 404(b). It was not then able to offer the evidence under Rule 414 because of its failure to provide timely notice of the offer, as required by Rule 414. The District Court admitted the evidence, and the jury convicted LeCompte. On appeal, this Court held that the District Court's admission of the evidence under Rule 404(b) was improper, and reversed LeCompte's conviction. We now consider the admissibility of T.T.'s testimony in LeCompte's retrial, under Rule 414, the government having given timely notice the second time around.

On remand . . . [t]he District Court ruled that T.T.'s testimony was potentially admissible under Rule 414, but excluded by Rule 403. It noted that although the evidence's only relevance was as to LeCompte's propensity to commit child sexual abuse, Rule 414 expressly allowed its use on that basis. The Court then turned to a Rule 403 analysis of the evidence. As to the evidence's probative value, the Court recognized the similarities between C.D.'s and T.T.'s accounts: they were both young nieces of LeCompte at the time he molested them, he forced them both to touch him, he touched them both in similar places, and he exposed himself to both of them. The Court found that the evidence's probative value was limited, however, by several differences. First, the acts allegedly committed against C.D. occurred with her siblings present, while the acts against T.T. occurred in isolation. Second, LeCompte had not played games with C.D. immediately before molesting her, as he had with T.T. Finally, the acts against C.D. and T.T. were separated by a period of eight years. The District Court concluded that the probative value of T.T.'s testimony was limited.

On the other hand, it found that the risk of unfair prejudice was high, reasoning that "T.T.'s testimony is obviously highly prejudicial evidence against defendant. . . . 'child sexual abuse deservedly carries a unique stigma in our society; such highly prejudicial evidence should therefore carry a very high degree of probative value if it is to be admitted.' " The Court therefore excluded the evidence under Rule 403. [The government took an interlocutory appeal pursuant to 18 U.S.C. §3731.]

. . . This Court has recognized that evidence otherwise admissible under Rule 414 may be excluded under Rule 403's balancing test. *United States v. Summer*, 119 F.3d 658, 661 (8th Cir. 1997). However, Rule 403 must be applied to allow Rule 414 its intended effect. . . . In light of the strong legislative judgment that evidence of prior sexual offenses should ordinarily be admissible, we think the District Court erred in its assessment that the probative value of T.T.'s testimony was substantially outweighed by the danger of unfair prejudice. The sexual offenses committed against T.T. were substantially similar to those allegedly committed against C.D. By comparison, the differences were small. In particular, the District Court itself acknowledged that the time lapse between incidents "may not be as significant as it appears at first glance, because defendant was imprisoned for a portion of the time between 1987 and 1995, which deprived defendant of the opportunity to abuse any children."

Moreover, the danger of unfair prejudice noted by the District Court was that presented by the "unique stigma" of child sexual abuse, on account of which LeCompte might be convicted not for the charged offense, but for his sexual abuse of T.T. This danger is one that all propensity evidence in such trials presents. It is for this reason that the evidence was previously excluded, and it is precisely such holdings that Congress intended to overrule. *Compare United States v. Fawbush*, 900 F.2d 150 (8th Cir. 1990) (prior acts of child sexual abuse inadmissible to show propensity under Rule 404(b)). . . . On balance, then, we hold that the motion in limine should not have been granted.

The order of the District Court is reversed, and the cause remanded for further proceedings not inconsistent with this opinion.

JAMES JOSEPH DUANE, THE NEW FEDERAL RULES OF EVIDENCE ON PRIOR ACTS OF ACCUSED SEX OFFENDERS: A POORLY DRAFTED VERSION OF A VERY BAD IDEA

157 F.R.D. 95, 108-110 (1994)

... The legislative history of the new rules contains no acknowledgment of the undeniable fact that they can possibly lead to additional convictions only in the case of those defendants who (1) are acquitted under current law, and (2) have some sort of alleged history of sexual assault. Given that inevitable reality, would that change result in a net improvement or reduction in the overall accuracy and integrity of our system for determining guilt and innocence? The answer to that crucial question—which was barely even mentioned in the Congressional debates leading to the passage of the rules—depends entirely on one's assumptions about the group of accused sex offenders who are acquitted under current law but have a suspect background: how many of them are innocent, and how many are guilty? Even if only 10% of that group are actually innocent, increasing the chances of convicting them all runs afoul of our society's fundamental constitutional value determination "that it is far worse to convict an innocent man than to let a guilty man go free."

... Under new Rule 413, prosecutors ... are free to use even unproven (and perhaps false) allegations of sexual misconduct that may be many years old. Old convictions admittedly cannot be created out of whole cloth after a suspect has been accused, but antagonistic accusers with stale, uncertain, and possibly false allegations can easily come out of the woodwork after it becomes widely known that an accused rapist is heading for trial on either civil or criminal charges. Moreover, ... in the common case where the defendant maintains that the victim has simply identified the wrong man—which includes virtually all rape cases in which the victim has been threatened with a weapon or caused serious physical injury—it is altogether likely that an innocent accused who has been mistakenly identified as the victim's rapist or abuser would also have a record of similar criminal accusations or convictions. Such a scenario would hardly amount to a "coincidence" if, as is often the case, the wrong man first became a suspect because he was known to the police (and then brought to the attention of the victim) due to his record of prior complaints, arrests, or convictions. ...

AVIVA ORENSTEIN, NO BAD MEN! A FEMINIST ANALYSIS OF CHARACTER EVIDENCE IN RAPE TRIALS

49 Hastings L.J. 663, 692-695 (1998)

... [T]he traditional evidence critique of Rule 413 can be informed and enhanced by feminist insight. As a logical matter, a feminist would argue that given the tolerance for rape and its widespread perpetration throughout society, evidence that the accused has raped someone before is not necessarily probative in determining whether a rape occurred in the principal case. To use an overstated analogy, if witnesses established that the perpetrator wore a baseball hat while committing a crime, how probative would it be if the person accused of the crime also wore a baseball hat sometimes? Not very. It might have some minuscule probative value, but given the number of people who wear hats, it wouldn't tell you much. Tragically, the magnitude and extent of rape in the population warrants a similar conclusion. The fact that a man raped once before is not necessarily probative given the number of men who rape.

On the other side of the evidentiary balance, however, information concerning the prior rape is extraordinarily prejudicial and unfair. This prejudice derives from traditional sources, such as the tendency of the jury to overvalue the evidence, the desire of the jury to punish the accused for past crimes, and the willingness of the jury to ignore the high threshold of reasonable doubt. A feminist analysis adds another crucial insight, citing a unique source of potential unfairness: the jury's willingness to be swayed by evidence of a prior rape is heightened because of its own misconceptions about the prevalence of rape. The prejudice plays on the notion inherent in the new rules that only a few rotten deviants are terrorizing women. . . . By relying on the antifeminist assumption that rapists are a small group of sick, dangerous men, Rule 413 prejudices the accused by offering up someone who has already been branded as a member of that small anti-social set.

[In addition], Rule 413 may soon become yet another barrier to prosecuting rape cases. After a few years of Rule 413, how long will it be before a prosecutor tells a woman that her case is no good—or at least unwinnable—because there doesn't seem to be any other evidence of prior rape by the defendant? What starts as a boon to women easily transforms into a requirement or a litmus test. . . .

[F]eminists must be on the lookout for differences in the law that may cross the line from acknowledging women's different voice and experience to patronizing women by providing them increased "protection." One hint that Rule 413 may be more paternalistic than feminist is the fact that its wording is nearly identical to Rule 414, which deals with children. Feminists would not necessarily presume, as the Federal Rules seem to, that the rule should be the same for women and children—what I call the "lifeboat syndrome" (women and children first). Instead, a feminist analysis would inquire into the special circumstances of crimes against children and the particular needs of child witnesses. The melding of the two categories of victims suggests an infantilization of women. . . .

ROGER C. PARK, THE CRIME BILL OF 1994 AND THE LAW OF CHARACTER EVIDENCE: CONGRESS WAS RIGHT ABOUT CONSENT DEFENSE CASES

22 Fordham Urb. L.J. 271, 273, 275-278 (1995)

I believe that state reformers should wholeheartedly embrace the feature of Congress's recent reform package that makes evidence of other sexual assaults freely receivable in cases in which the accused raises a defense of consent.[3] . . . There is no danger [in these cases] that letting in character evidence will detract from the development of better evidence. These cases often boil down to a credibility contest between the victim and the defendant. Aside from the testimony of these two people, the uncharged misconduct evidence is likely to be the best evidence available. . . .

Even with the protection of rape shield laws, victims of rape must endure an unusual second ordeal when the accused presents a consent defense. The defense will likely investigate the complainant's sexual history and attempt to put in evidence about it. That process can be intrusive and embarrassing even if the judge excludes the evidence in a pretrial hearing. The defense will also try to show that the victim is lying. A defense counsel who ordinarily would prefer to try to show that a crime victim is honestly mistaken rather than lying is, in a consent-defense rape case, forced to attack the truthfulness of the victim. The need to make that attack will lead to a search for evidence (sexual or not) that portrays the victim as a liar. The defense will also try to show that the victim provoked the sexual event. It may try to portray her behavior just before the rape as brazen, or her clothing and manner as provocative. In addition, the defendant may seek a psychiatric examination or psychiatric records in an attempt to impeach the victim's credibility as a witness. In some jurisdictions the defense would be allowed to put in expert testimony of absence of rape trauma syndrome to cast doubt upon the victim's veracity. In short, the defense will try to cast the victim in the role of a solitary, mentally unstable woman who behaved irresponsibly and provocatively, and who is now lying under oath.

One approach to reducing victim ordeal is through the exclusion of evidence that embarrasses the victim. We may, however, be approaching the limits of that approach. Due process requires that the defendant be allowed to question the veracity of the victim and to put in evidence of her behavior with the accused. Another approach is to allow the victim to have the support of other women who testify that they have had the same experience with the defendant. That is an approach that does not restrict the evidence that the jury will hear or result in the exclusion of evidence that a rational fact-finder would want to consider. . . .

[E]vidence about a victim's sexual history is less probative than evidence about the defendant's prior sex offenses because the victim evidence cuts both ways. If the victim frequently consented to casual sex, that fact tends to show, however slightly, that she is more likely to have consented to casual sex on a particular occasion than another woman who never consents. It also tends, however, to show that she does not readily make accusations of rape.

3. . . . The question whether a defendant's previous sex offenses should automatically be received in evidence in cases involving allegations of child sexual abuse is beyond the scope of this Essay. I do not favor allowing free proof of prior sex offenses in adult "stranger rape" cases where the defense is misidentification. Allowing free proof of propensity to rape in stranger rape cases would create a startling anomaly in the law of evidence. It would mean that in stranger-on-stranger rape cases, evidence of other rapes would be freely admissible to show propensity to rape, but that in stranger-on-stranger robbery, murder or mayhem cases, evidence of other crimes would not be admissible to show propensity to rob, murder or assault. Nothing in common sense or systematic study justifies that distinction.

Otherwise, why didn't she accuse one of her many other partners of rape? The defendant's history of other rapes does not cut both ways. It simply tends to show that the defendant is a rapist who is more likely to be guilty in this case than he would be without the evidence.

UNITED STATES v. CUNNINGHAM

103 F.3d 553 (7th Cir. 1996)

POSNER, Chief Judge.

. . . "Propensity" evidence and "motive" evidence need not overlap. They do not, for example, when past drug convictions are used to show that the defendant in a robbery case in an addict and his addiction is offered as the motive for the robbery. *See, e.g., People v. McConnell*, 335 N.W.2d 226, 230 (Mich. App. 1983); *cf. People v. Moreno*, 132 Cal. Rptr. 569 (1976) (man's theft of a woman's underwear). . . . They do overlap when the crime is motivated by a taste for engaging in that crime or a compulsion to engage in it (an "addiction"), rather than by a desire for pecuniary gain or for some other advantage to which the crime is instrumental in the sense that it would not be committed if the advantage could be obtained as easily by a lawful route. Sex crimes provide a particularly clear example. Most people do not have a taste for sexually molesting children. As between two suspected molesters, then, only one of whom has a history of such molestation, the history establishes a motive that enables the two suspects to be distinguished. In 1994, Rule 414 was added to the Federal Rules of Evidence to make evidence of prior acts of child molestation expressly admissible, without regard to Rule 404(b). But the principle that we are discussing is not limited to sex crimes. A "firebug"—one who commits arson not for insurance proceeds or revenge or to eliminate a competitor, but for the sheer joy of watching a fire—is, like the sex criminal, a person whose motive to commit the crime with which he is charged is revealed by his past commission of the same crime. No special rule analogous to Rules 413 through 415 is necessary to make the evidence of the earlier crime admissible, because 404(b) expressly allows evidence of prior wrongful acts to establish motive. . . .

5

OTHER FORBIDDEN INFERENCES

"*Your honor, we find the defendant not guilty, because the prosecution simply didn't do its homework.*"

The hearsay rule and the character evidence rule share a similar structure: each forbids a certain kind of proof used for a certain kind of purpose. Neither rule operates when the proof in question is offered for some other purpose—when, that is to say, an out-of-court statement is introduced for some purpose other than proving the truth of what it asserts, or when evidence of a character trait is offered for some purpose other than proving action in conformity with the trait.

Several other, more minor rules of evidence law also have this structure. Evidence of subsequent remedial measures is typically inadmissible to prove fault. Settlement efforts generally cannot be proved to show the merit or weakness of a civil claim or criminal charge. Humanitarian payments typically are inadmissible to demonstrate liability. And the presence or absence of liability insurance generally cannot be proved to show fault or lack of fault.

Each of these rules is addressed in this chapter.

A.   SUBSEQUENT REMEDIAL MEASURES

[F.R.E. 407; C.E.C. §1151]

ADVISORY COMMITTEE NOTE TO F.R.E. 407

The rule incorporates conventional doctrine which excludes evidence of subsequent remedial measures as proof of an admission of fault. The rule rests on two grounds. (1) The conduct is not in fact an admission, since the conduct is equally consistent with injury by mere accident or through contributory negligence. Or, as Baron Bramwell put it, the rule rejects the notion that "because the world gets wiser as it gets older, therefore it was foolish before." Hart v. Lancashire & Yorkshire Ry. Co., 21 L.T.R. N.S. 261, 263 (1869). Under a liberal theory of relevancy this ground alone would not support exclusion as the inference is still a possible one. (2) The other, and more impressive, ground for exclusion rests on a social policy of encouraging people to take, or at least not discouraging them from taking, steps in furtherance of added safety. The courts have applied this principle to exclude evidence of subsequent repairs, installation of safety devices, changes in company rules, and discharge of employees, and the language of the present rule is broad enough to encompass all of them.

The second sentence of the rule directs attention to the limitations of the rule. Exclusion is called for only when the evidence of subsequent remedial measures is offered as proof of negligence or culpable conduct. In effect it rejects the suggested inference that fault is admitted. Other purposes are, however, allowable, including ownership or control, existence of duty, and feasibility of precautionary measures, if controverted, and impeachment. Two recent federal cases are illustrative. Boeing Airplane Co. v. Brown, 291 F.2d 310 (9th Cir. 1961), an action against an airplane manufacturer for using an allegedly defectively designed alternator shaft which caused a plane crash, upheld the admission of evidence of subsequent design modification for the purpose of showing that design changes and safeguards were feasible. And Powers v. J.B. Michael & Co., 329 F.2d 674 (6th Cir. 1964), an action against a road contractor for negligent failure to put out warning signs, sustained the admission of evidence that defendant subsequently put out signs to show that the portion of the road in question was under defendant's control. The requirement that the other purpose be controverted calls for automatic exclusion unless a genuine issue be present and allows the opposing party to lay the groundwork for exclusion by making an admission. Otherwise the factors of undue prejudice, confusion of issues, misleading the jury, and waste of time remain for consideration under Rule 403.

CLAUSEN v. STORAGE TANK DEVELOPMENT CORP.

21 F.3d 1181 (1st Cir. 1994) (sub nom. Clausen v. Sea-3, Inc.)

LEVIN H. CAMPBELL, Senior Circuit Judge.

On February 6, 1989, Eric Clausen ("Clausen"), plaintiff-appellee, slipped, fell, and injured his back while working as a pile driver at a job site at a fuel terminal facility on the Piscataqua River, Portsmouth Harbor, Newington, New Hampshire. A Massachusetts resident, Clausen sued for negligence, under the diversity jurisdiction, in the United States District Court for the District of New Hampshire. Defendants were the owner of the facility, Storage Tank Development Corp. ("Storage Tank"), a New Hampshire corporation, and the occupier of the facility, Sea-3, Inc. ("Sea-3"), a Texas corporation. Defendants filed third-party complaints against Clausen's employer, Goudreau Construction Corp. ("Goudreau").

. . . Storage Tank owns docking facilities along the Piscataqua River in Newington, New Hampshire. These include a walkway-pier that first extends perpendicularly from the shore line into the water, and then turns ninety degrees to the left and extends upstream. A concrete mooring cell, referred to as Cell Three, is located in the water beyond the end of the walkway-pier. Cell Three, at the time of Clausen's injury, was connected to the end of the walk way-pier by the ramp upon which Clausen slipped and fell. . . .

Storage Tank complains of the allowance of evidence that, in 1992, Storage Tank, at Sea-3's request, replaced the ramp on which Clausen fell with a set of steps. . . . Because Storage Tank failed timely to object at trial to the admission of evidence of the subsequent alteration to the ramp in 1992, we review the district court's decision to allow such evidence only for plain error. . . . It is utterly clear that the district court's decision to permit the evidence of the changes made to the ramp in 1992, whether right or wrong, was not plain error.

Although Fed. R. Evid. 407 proscribes the admission of evidence of subsequent remedial measures to "prove negligence or culpable conduct," it allows such evidence . . . "when offered for another purpose, such as proving . . . control." The parties agree that control of the ramp area where Clausen's injury occurred was a material issue in this case. According to the appellant, one aspect of the control issue arose because both Storage Tank and Sea-3 asserted that Goudreau was in control of the work site and was, therefore, responsible for clearing and sanding the area where the plaintiff fell. Clausen points out that a second aspect of the control issue in this case, not alluded to by Storage Tank, involved whether Storage Tank, Sea-3, or both jointly, controlled the area where Clausen fell if Goudreau, at that time, did not control the ramp.

To be sure, Storage Tank argues that the evidence that it made changes to the ramp at the request of Sea-3 subsequent to Clausen's accident was inadmissible under the control exception to Fed. R. Evid. 407 because the evidence failed to satisfy the independent requirements of Fed. R. Evid. 403. Storage Tank maintains that, because the ramp was replaced in 1992, approximately three years after Clausen's fall, the evidence is not probative of whether Storage Tank or Sea-3 controlled the ramp, either separately or jointly, in 1989, particularly since, according to Storage Tank, the area had been exclusively occupied by Goudreau when Clausen's injury occurred. Whatever can be said for such arguments had Storage Tank preserved its right to argue the merits, they do not come close to demonstrating that it was plain error for the district court to believe that the evidence carried at least some probative weight as to who controlled the ramp in 1989.

Storage Tank also suggests that it was greatly prejudiced because the jury may have used the evidence of the ramp's replacement for an improper purpose. The judge, however, instructed the jury that "[e]vidence of the subsequent installation of stairs in 1992 is evidence relevant only on the issue of control. It is not to be considered evidence of liability or fault." According to the advisory committee's notes to Fed. R. Evid. 403, "[i]n reaching a decision whether to exclude on grounds of unfair prejudice, consideration should be given to the probable effectiveness or lack of effectiveness of a limiting instruction." Although limiting instructions may not always be effective, the inadequacy of the one in this situation is scarcely so patent as to support a finding of plain error. We do not readily assume that a jury disregards clear directions. . . . [Affirmed.]

IN RE ASBESTOS LITIGATION

995 F.2d 343 (2d Cir. 1993)

McLaughlin, Circuit Judge:

John Crane-Houdaille, Inc. ("Crane") appeals from a personal injury and wrongful death judgment, jointly entered on July 31, 1992 by the United States District Courts for the Eastern and Southern Districts of New York (Charles P. Sifton, Judge), following a consolidated asbestos jury trial. . . . [The judgment was awarded to Anne McPadden, whose late husband, Martin McPadden, had worked with encapsulated asbestos valve packing manufactured by Crane.]

We find it necessary to focus on only one evidentiary error that seriously prejudiced the liability verdict. The district court erred in admitting evidence that Crane placed warnings on its asbestos product after decedent's last exposure. The warnings were subsequent remedial measures and, as such, inadmissible under Fed. R. Evid. 407. . . .

In denying Crane's post-trial motion, the district court concluded that "plaintiff's use of the label evidence focused on the statement that no warning labels were placed on the products at the time of McPadden's exposure, not that the labels were placed on the products later because Crane recognized the danger." McPadden contends that this distinction salvages the evidence because Rule 407 permits the admission of subsequent warnings to prove feasibility. We are not persuaded.

"Feasibility" is not an open sesame whose mere invocation parts Rule 407 and ushers in evidence of subsequent repairs and remedies. To read it that casually will cause the exception to engulf the rule. Rule 407 states that a defendant must first contest the feasibility of a warning before the subsequent warning would become admissible. The record is clear that Crane at no point argued that it was unable to issue a warning. Instead, it vigorously denied that its product required a warning or was defective without a warning. Because our review of the record convinces us that feasibility was not a contested issue, it was error to permit McPadden to read into evidence . . . deposition testimony concerning post-exposure warnings that were placed on the product more than 12 years after McPadden was last exposed to Crane's asbestos products. . . . [Reversed.]

B. SETTLEMENT EFFORTS

1. Civil Cases

[F.R.E. 408; C.E.C. §§1152, 1154]

ADVISORY COMMITTEE NOTE TO F.R.E. 408

As a matter of general agreement, evidence of an offer to compromise a claim is not receivable in evidence as an admission of, as the case may be, the validity or invalidity of the claim. As with evidence of subsequent remedial measures, dealt with in Rule 407, exclusion may be based on two grounds. (1) The evidence is irrelevant, since the offer may be motivated by a desire for peace rather than from any concession of weakness of position. The validity of this position will vary as the amount of the offer varies in relation to the size of the claim and may also be influenced by other circumstances. (2) A more consistently impressive ground is promotion of the public policy favoring the compromise and settlement of disputes. McCormick §§ 76, 251. While the rule is ordinarily phrased in terms of offers of compromise, it is apparent that a similar attitude must be taken with respect to completed compromises when offered against a party thereto. This latter situation will not, of course, ordinarily occur except when a party to the present litigation has compromised with a third person. . . .

The practical value of the common law rule has been greatly diminished by its inapplicability to admissions of fact, even though made in the course of compromise negotiations, unless hypothetical, stated to be "without prejudice," or so connected with the offer as to be inseparable from it. McCormick § 251, pp. 540-541. An inevitable effect is to inhibit freedom of communication with respect to compromise, even among lawyers. Another effect is the generation of controversy over whether a given statement falls within or without the protected area. These considerations account for the expansion of the rule herewith to include evidence of conduct or statements made in compromise negotiations, as well as the offer or completed compromise itself. . . .

The policy considerations which underlie the rule do not come into play when the effort is to induce a creditor to settle an admittedly due amount for a lesser sum. McCormick § 251, p. 540. Hence the rule requires that the claim be disputed as to either validity or amount.

The final sentence of the rule serves to point out some limitations upon its applicability. Since the rule excludes only when the purpose is proving the validity or invalidity of the claim or its amount, an offer for another purpose is not within the rule. . . .

RAMADA DEVELOPMENT CO. v. RAUCH

644 F.2d 1097 (5th Cir. Unit B 1981)

TUTTLE, Circuit Judge:

On December 13, 1972, Martin Rauch signed a contract in which the Ramada Development Company agreed to design, furnish, and construct a 160-unit Ramada Inn Motor Hotel and Restaurant in Venice, Florida. . . . On January 31, 1975, approximately one year after Rauch occupied the motel and refused to make further payments to Ramada, Ramada brought this diversity action against Rauch for the balance due under the contract. . . . The defendant answered, denying liability and alleging a counterclaim against Ramada for failure to perform according to the contract and for negligence in planning and construction of the project. . . .

[T]he jury . . . gave a verdict that was basically favorable to Ramada. . . .

[Rauch challenges] the district court's exclusion of a document referred to as the Goldsmith Report. Goldsmith was an architect employed by Ramada in 1974 to study the defects that Rauch had alleged at that time. Rauch claims that he sought to introduce this report as "a part of his case in chief," because it confirmed the majority of the alleged defects. The district court heard testimony regarding the origins of the report and concluded that it was inadmissible under Federal Rule of Evidence 408 because the report was a tool used in an unsuccessful settlement attempt. Rauch contends that this ruling was in error because Rule 408 does not exclude all evidence presented in settlement attempts and there was the lack of any pre-trial understanding that the report could not be used in evidence. Rauch's claim of error is without merit.

Rule 408 . . . is designed to encourage settlements by fostering free and full discussion of the issues. The previous common law rule held that admissions of fact made in negotiations were admissible "unless hypothetical, stated to be 'without prejudice,' or so connected with the offer as to be inseparable from it." Advisory Committee Notes [to] Rule 408. After the House Committee rejected a proposed deviation from the common law rule, the Senate Committee [reverted to the Advisory Committee's proposal,] because

> The real impact of this [House] amendment however, is to deprive the rule of much of its salutory effect. The exception for factual admissions was believed by the Advisory Committee to hamper free communication between parties and thus to constitute an unjustifiable restraint upon efforts to negotiate settlements the encouragement of which is the purpose of the rule. Further, by protecting hypothetically phrased statements, it constituted a preference for the sophisticated, and a trap for the unwary.

S. Rep. No. 1277, 93d Cong., 2d Sess. (1974). The present rule fosters free discussion in connection with such negotiations and eliminates the need to determine whether the statement if not expressly qualified "falls within or without the protected area of compromise"; the question under the rule is "whether the statements or conduct were intended to be part of the negotiations toward compromise." 2J. Weinstein & M. Berger, Weinstein's Evidence ¶ 408(03), at 408-20 to -21 (1980). The rule does not indicate that there must be a pre-trial understanding or agreement between the parties regarding the nature of the report. Indeed, Rauch's assertions in this regard would partially revive the common law rule that a party assert that his statement is made "without prejudice."

The Goldsmith Report, thus, appears to fit squarely within the exclusionary scope of rule 408. The only indication given by the parties of the report's origins is the testimony of Leonard Gilbert whose testimony can only be construed as supporting the position that Goldsmith was commissioned by Ramada to prepare a report that would function as a basis of settlement negotiations regarding the alleged defects in the motel. The report was to identify arguable defects that could then be discussed in monetary terms in the negotiations. The Goldsmith Report, as described by Mr. Gilbert, thus represents a collection of statements made in the course of an effort to compromise, and the district court properly held it inadmissible under the main provision of rule 408.

Rauch raises numerous reasons why the Goldsmith Report is admissible under the exceptions in rule 408. First, he argues that the report falls into the exception to rule 408 which holds that the rule "does not require the exclusion of any evidence otherwise discoverable merely because it is presented in the course of compromise negotiations." This sentence was intended to prevent one from being able to "immunize from admissibility documents otherwise discoverable merely by offering them in a compromise negotiation." S. Rep. No. 1277, 93d Cong., 2d Sess. (1974). Clearly such an exception does not cover the present case where the document, or statement, would not have existed but for the negotiations, hence the negotiations are not being used as a device to thwart discovery by making existing documents unreachable. Second, Rauch contends that the report was not only offered to prove the existence of defect but also to prove Ramada's notice of the alleged defects. Rule 408 "does not require exclusion when the evidence is offered for another purpose (other than proving the existence of defects)," but this provision, surely, was not intended to completely undercut the policy behind the rule. See 2 J. Weinstein & M. Berger, supra, ¶ 408(05), at 408-25 to -26 (court "should weigh the need for such evidence against the potentiality of discouraging future settlement negotiations"). This Court, in a pre-rules case, recognized that this exception, as codified in rule 408, must be balanced against the policy of encouraging settlements and the district court's judgment in this regard will be upset only for abuse of discretion. We cannot say that the district court abused its discretion; notice could be effectively proved by means less in conflict with the policy behind rule 408.[9] The exclusion of the Goldsmith Report under rule 408 must stand. . . . [Affirmed in relevant part.]

CARNEY v. AMERICAN UNIVERSITY

151 F.3d 1090 (D.C. Cir. 1998)

TATEL, Circuit Judge:

. . . A senior administrator at The American University since 1981, appellant Darion Carney became Director of Student Service in 1988, the highest ranking African American at the University. A year later, she became Acting Dean of Students, serving in that capacity for two years while the University searched for a permanent Dean. She applied for the permanent position, but the University selected someone else. She then returned to her former position as Director of Student Services. Two years later, the University commenced "downsizing," a process which resulted in the elimination of Carney's position and her dismissal.

Soon after she lost her job, Carney informed the University by letter that she intended to sue. About the same time, a question arose as to whether she might be entitled to an additional three months' severance pay on top of her existing severance package. The University did not give her the extra three months' pay.

. . . Carney filed suit in the United States District Court for the District of Columbia, claiming that the University discriminated against her on the basis of her race when it did not select her for the Dean of Students position, and again when it eliminated her position. She also claimed that the University withheld extra severance pay in retaliation for exercising her civil rights. In defense, the University asserted that it had legitimate, nondiscriminatory reasons for not hiring her and for subsequently eliminating her position. With respect to her retaliation claim, the University argued first that it crafted Carney's severance package before it knew that she intended to sue, and second, that all evidence of linkage between the extra severance pay and her lawsuit is contained in inadmissible settlement correspondence.

The district court granted summary judgment for the University. [We affirm as to the discrimination claims but reverse and remand as to the claim of retaliation.]

Carney contends that the University withheld extra severance pay in retaliation for having signaled her intention to file suit. In a settlement letter

9. For example, the Court exhibits contain a series of letters dated in October, 1974 between counsel for both sides, referring to a list of complaints given to Goldsmith apparently at approximately the same time. These letters accompanied by the list which was not included in the exhibit could have proved this notice issue without prejudice to Ramada.

from the University's lawyer dated December 12, 1994, responding to a letter from Carney's attorney, the University acknowledged that under certain interpretations of its personnel manuals, Carney might "arguably [be] entitl[ed] . . . to an additional three months' pay." . . . According to the University, the extra severance pay amounted to nothing more than a settlement offer.

Granting summary judgment for the University, the district court found that Carney failed to present evidence of causation, reasoning that the University crafted her initial severance package containing only seven months' severance pay before it knew that Carney intended to sue. The court also held that Rule 408 of the Federal Rules of Evidence prohibited Carney from relying on settlement correspondence to establish causation.

We disagree with the district court for two reasons. First, apart from the settlement letters, [Carney offered] evidence from which a jury could conclude that the University retaliated against Carney either by refusing to give her any extra pay or refusing even to consider it. . . . Second, although settlement letters are inadmissible to prove liability or amount, they are admissible "when the evidence is offered for another purpose." Fed. R. Evid. 408. In particular, such correspondence can be used to establish an independent violation (here, retaliation) unrelated to the underlying claim which was the subject of the correspondence (race discrimination). *See Eisenberg v. University of N.M.*, 911 F.2d 1131, 1134 (10th Cir. 1991) (affidavit obtained in settlement negotiations admissible to impose Rule 11 liability); *Urico v. Parnell Oil Co.*, 708 F.2d 852, 854-55 (1st Cir. 1983) (evidence of settlement negotiations admissible to show interference with efforts to mitigate damages); *Resolution Trust Corp. v. Blasdell*, 154 F.R.D. 675, 681 (D. Ariz. 1993) (evidence of settlement negotiations admissible to prove retaliatory motive); *see also* 23 Charles Alan Wright & Kenneth W. Graham, Jr., Federal Practice and Procedure § 5314, at 282 (1980) ("Rule 408 is [ ] inapplicable when the claim is based upon some wrong that was committed in the course of settlement discussions; e.g., libel, assault, breach of contract, unfair labor practice, and the like."). Carney offered the settlement correspondence not to prove that the University discriminated against her, but to show that the University committed an entirely separate wrong by conditioning her benefits on a waiver of her rights. The letters were therefore admissible. . . .

2. Criminal Cases

[F.R.E. 410; C.E.C. §1153]

ADVISORY COMMITEE NOTE TO F.R.E. 410

Withdrawn pleas of guilty were held inadmissible in federal prosecutions in Kercheval v. United States, 274 U.S. 220 (1927). The Court pointed out that to admit the withdrawn plea would effectively set at naught the allowance of withdrawal and place the accused in a dilemma utterly inconsistent with the decision to award him a trial. The New York Court of Appeals, in People v. Spitaleri, 9 N.Y.2d 168, 212 N.Y.S.2d 53, 173 N.E.2d 35 (1961), re-examined and overturned its earlier decisions which had allowed admission. In addition to the reasons set forth in Kercheval, which was quoted at length, the court pointed out that the effect of admitting the plea was to compel defendant to take the stand by way of explanation and to open the way for the prosecution to call the lawyer who had represented him at the time of entering the plea. . . .

Pleas of *nolo contendere* are recognized by Rule 11 of the Rules of Criminal Procedure, although the law of numerous States is to the contrary. The present rule gives effect to the principal traditional characteristic of the *nolo* plea, i.e. avoiding the admission of guilt which is inherent in pleas of guilty. . . .

Exclusion of offers to plead guilty or *nolo* has as its purpose the promotion of disposition of criminal cases by compromise. As pointed out in McCormick § 251, p. 543: "Effective criminal law administration in many localities would hardly be possible if a large proportion of the charges were not disposed of by such compromises." . . . As with compromise offers generally, Rule 408, free communication is needed, and security against having an offer of compromise or related statement admitted in evidence effectively encourages it.

Limiting the exclusionary rule to use against the accused is consistent with the purpose of the rule, since the possibility of use for or against other persons will not impair the effectiveness of withdrawing pleas or the freedom of discussion which the rule is designed to foster. . . .

UNITED STATES v. MEZZANATTO

513 U.S. 196 (1995)

Justice THOMAS delivered the opinion of the Court.

Federal Rule of Evidence 410 and Federal Rule of Criminal Procedure 11(e)(6) provide that statements made in the course of plea discussions between a criminal defendant and a prosecutor are inadmissible against the defendant. The court below held that these exclusionary provisions may not be waived by the defendant. We granted certiorari to resolve a conflict among the Courts of Appeals, and we now reverse.

[Respondent Gary Mezzanatto was arrested after selling methamphetamine to an undercover agent.] On October 17, 1991, respondent and his attorney asked to meet with the prosecutor to discuss the possibility of cooperating with the Government. The prosecutor agreed to meet later that day. At the beginning of the meeting, the prosecutor informed respondent that he had no obligation to talk, but that if he wanted to cooperate he would have to be completely truthful. As a condition to proceeding with the discussion, the prosecutor indicated that respondent would have to agree that any statements he made during the meeting could be used to impeach any contradictory testimony he might give at trial if the case proceeded that far. Respondent conferred with his counsel and agreed to proceed under the prosecutor's terms.

Respondent then admitted knowing that the package he had attempted to sell to the undercover police officer contained methamphetamine, but insisted that he had dealt only in "ounce" quantities of methamphetamine prior to his arrest. Initially, respondent also claimed that he was acting merely as a broker for [another trafficker, Gordon Shuster,] and did not know that Shuster was manufacturing methamphetamine at his residence, but he later conceded that he knew about Shuster's laboratory. Respondent attempted to minimize his role in Shuster's operation by claiming that he had not visited Shuster's residence for at least a week before his arrest. At this point, the Government confronted respondent with surveillance evidence showing that his car was on Shuster's property the day before the arrest, and terminated the meeting on the basis of respondent's failure to provide completely truthful information.

Respondent eventually was tried on the methamphetamine charge and took the stand in his own defense. He maintained that he was not involved in methamphetamine trafficking and that he had thought Shuster used his home laboratory to manufacture plastic explosives for the CIA. He also denied knowing that the package he delivered to the undercover officer contained methamphetamine. Over defense counsel's objection, the prosecutor cross-examined respondent about the inconsistent statements he had made during the October 17 meeting. Respondent denied having made certain statements, and the prosecutor called one of the agents who had attended the meeting to recount the prior statements. The jury found respondent guilty, and the District Court sentenced him to 170 months in prison.

A panel of the Ninth Circuit reversed, over the dissent of Chief Judge Wallace. The Ninth Circuit held that respondent's agreement to allow admission of his plea statements for purposes of impeachment was unenforceable and that the District Court therefore erred in admitting the statements for that purpose. . . .

Federal Rule of Evidence 410 and Federal Rule of Criminal Procedure 11(e)(6) (Rules or plea-statement Rules) are substantively identical. Rule 410 provides:

> "Except as otherwise provided in this rule, evidence of the following is not, in any civil or criminal proceeding, admissible against the defendant who . . . - was a participant in the plea discussions: . . . (4) any statement made in the course of plea discussions with an attorney for the prosecuting authority which do not result in a plea of guilty. . . ."

The Ninth Circuit noted that these Rules are subject to only two express exceptions, neither of which says anything about waiver, and thus concluded that Congress must have meant to preclude waiver agreements such as respondent's. In light of the "precision with which these rules are generally phrased," the Ninth Circuit declined to "write in a waiver in a waiverless rule."

The Ninth Circuit's analysis is directly contrary to the approach we have taken in the context of a broad array of constitutional and statutory provisions. Rather than deeming waiver presumptively unavailable absent some sort of express enabling clause, we instead have adhered to the opposite presumption. . . . The presumption of waivability has found specific application in the context of evidentiary rules. Absent some "overriding procedural consideration that prevents enforcement of the contract," courts have held that agreements to waive evidentiary rules are generally enforceable even over a party's subsequent objections. 21 C. Wright & K. Graham, Federal Practice and Procedure § 5039, pp. 207-208 (1977) (hereinafter Wright & Graham). Courts have "liberally enforced" agreements to waive various exclusionary rules of evidence. Note, *Contracts to Alter the Rules of Evidence*, 46 Harv. L. Rev. 138, 139-140 (1933). Thus, at the time of the adoption of the Federal Rules of Evidence, agreements as to the admissibility of documentary evidence were routinely enforced and held to preclude subsequent objections as to authenticity. See, *e.g., Tupman Thurlow Co. v. S.S. Cap Castillo*, 490 F.2d 302, 309 (CA2 1974); *United States v. Wing*, 450 F.2d 806, 811 (CA9 1971). And although hearsay is inadmissible except under certain specific exceptions, we have held that agreements to waive hearsay objections are enforceable. See *Sac and Fox Indians of Miss. in Iowa v. Sac and Fox Indians of Miss. in Okl.*, 220 U.S. 481, 488-489 (1911); see also *United States v. Bonnett*, 877 F.2d 1450, 1458-1459 (CA10 1989) (party's stipulation to admissibility of document precluded hearsay objection at trial).

Indeed, evidentiary stipulations are a valuable and integral part of everyday trial practice. Prior to trial, parties often agree in writing to the admission of otherwise objectionable evidence, either in exchange for stipulations from opposing counsel or for other strategic purposes. Both the Federal Rules of Civil Procedure and the Federal Rules of Criminal Procedure appear to contemplate that the parties will enter into evidentiary agreements during a pretrial conference. See Fed. Rule Civ. Proc. 16(c)(3); Fed. Rule Crim. Proc. 17.1. During the course of trial, parties frequently decide to waive evidentiary objections, and such tactics are routinely honored by trial judges. See 21 Wright & Graham § 5032, at 161 ("It is left to the parties, in the first instance, to decide whether or not the rules are to be enforced. . . . It is only in rare cases that the trial judge will . . . exclude evidence they are content to see admitted"); see also *United States v. Coonan*, 938 F.2d 1553, 1561 (CA2 1991) (criminal defendant not entitled "to evade the consequences of an unsuccessful tactical decision" made in welcoming admission of otherwise inadmissible evidence).

. . . There may be some evidentiary provisions that are so fundamental to the reliability of the factfinding process that they may never be waived without irreparably "discredit[ing] the federal courts." See 21 Wright & Graham § 5039, at 207-208; see also *Wheat v. United States*, 486 U.S. 153, 162, 108 S. Ct. 1692, 1698-1699, 100 L. Ed. 2d 140 (1988) (court may decline a defendant's waiver of his right to conflict-free counsel); *United States v. Josefik*, 753 F.2d 585, 588 (CA7 1985) ("No doubt there are limits to waiver; if the parties stipulated to trial by 12 orangutans the defendant's conviction would be invalid notwithstanding his consent, because some minimum of civilized procedure is required by community feeling regardless of what the defendant wants or is willing to accept"). But enforcement of agreements like respondent's plainly will not have that effect. The admission of plea statements for impeachment purposes enhances the truth-seeking function of trials and will result in more accurate verdicts. . . . Under any view of the evidence, the defendant has made a false statement, either to the prosecutor during the plea discussion or to the jury at trial; making the jury aware of the inconsistency will tend to increase the reliability of the verdict without risking institutional harm to the federal courts.

. . . Respondent also contends that waiver is fundamentally inconsistent with the Rules' goal of encouraging voluntary settlement. . . . We need not decide whether and under what circumstances substantial "public policy" interests may permit the inference that Congress intended to override the presumption of waivability, for in this case there is no basis for concluding that waiver will interfere with the Rules' goal of encouraging plea bargaining. . . . [A]lthough the availability of waiver may discourage some defendants from negotiating, it is also true that prosecutors may be unwilling to proceed without it.

Prosecutors may be especially reluctant to negotiate without a waiver agreement during the early stages of a criminal investigation, when prosecutors are searching for leads and suspects may be willing to offer information in exchange for some form of immunity or leniency in sentencing. In this "cooperation" context, prosecutors face "painfully delicate" choices as to "whether to proceed and prosecute those suspects against whom the already produced evidence makes a case or whether to extend leniency or full immunity to some suspects in order to procure testimony against other, more dangerous suspects against whom existing evidence is flimsy or nonexistent." Hughes, *Agreements for Cooperation in Criminal Cases*, 45 Vand. L. Rev. 1, 15 (1992). Because prosecutors have limited resources and must be able to answer "sensitive questions about the credibility of the testimony" they receive before entering into any sort of cooperation agreement, *id.*, at 10, prosecutors may condition cooperation discussions on an agreement that the testimony provided may be used for impeachment purposes. If prosecutors were precluded from securing such agreements, they might well decline to enter into cooperation discussions in the first place and might never take this potential first step toward a plea bargain.

. . . Respondent asserts that there is a "gross disparity" in the relative bargaining power of the parties to a plea agreement and suggests that a waiver agreement is "inherently unfair and coercive." . . . The dilemma flagged by respondent is indistinguishable from any of a number of difficult choices that criminal defendants face every day. The plea bargaining process necessarily exerts pressure on defendants to plead guilty and to abandon a series of fundamental rights, but we have repeatedly held that the government "may encourage a guilty plea by offering substantial benefits in return for the plea." *Corbitt v. New Jersey*, 439 U.S. 212, 219 (1978). . . . The mere potential for abuse of prosecutorial bargaining power is an insufficient basis for foreclosing negotiation altogether. "Rather, tradition and experience justify our belief that the great majority of prosecutors will be faithful to their duty." *Newton v. Rumery*, 480 U.S. 386, 397 (1987) (plurality opinion). Thus, although some waiver agreements "may not be the product of an informed and voluntary decision," this possibility "does not justify invalidating all such agreements." *Newton*, 480 U.S. at 393 (majority opinion). Instead, the appropriate response to respondent's predictions of abuse is to permit case-by-case inquiries into whether waiver agreements are the product of fraud or coercion. We hold that absent some affirmative indication that the agreement was entered into unknowingly or involuntarily, an agreement to waive the exclusionary provisions of the plea-statement Rules is valid and enforceable. . . . Accordingly, the judgment of the Court of Appeals is reversed.

Justice GINSBURG, with whom Justice O'CONNOR and Justice BREYER join, concurring.

The Court holds that a waiver allowing the Government to impeach with statements made during plea negotiations is compatible with Congress' intent to promote plea bargaining. It may be, however, that a waiver to use such statements in the case in chief would more severely undermine a defendant's incentive to negotiate, and thereby inhibit plea bargaining. As the Government has not sought such a waiver, we do not here explore this question.

Justice SOUTER, with whom Justice STEVENS joins, dissenting.

. . . Already, standard forms indicate that many federal prosecutors routinely require waiver of Rules 410 and 11(e)(6) rights before a prosecutor is willing to enter into plea discussions. . . . As the Government conceded during oral argument, defendants are generally in no position to challenge demands for these waivers, and the use of waiver provisions as contracts of adhesion has become accepted practice. Today's decision can only speed the heretofore illegitimate process by which the exception has been swallowing the Rules. . . .

It is true that many (if not all) of the waiver forms now employed go only to admissibility for impeachment. But although the erosion of the Rules has begun with this trickle, the majority's reasoning will provide no principled limit to it. The Rules draw no distinction between use of a statement for impeachment and use in the Government's case in chief. If objection can be waived for impeachment use, it can be waived for use as affirmative evidence, and if the Government can effectively demand waiver in the former instance, there is no reason to believe it will not do so just as successfully in the latter. When it does, there is nothing this Court will legitimately be able to do about it. The Court is construing a congressional Rule on the theory that Congress meant to permit its waiver. Once that point is passed, as it is today, there is no legitimate limit on admissibility of a defendant's plea negotiation statements beyond what the Constitution may independently impose or the traffic may bear. Just what the traffic may bear is an open question, but what cannot be denied is that the majority opinion sanctions a demand for waiver of such scope that a defendant who gives it will be unable even to acknowledge his desire to negotiate a guilty plea without furnishing admissible evidence against himself then and there. In such cases, the possibility of trial if no agreement is reached will be reduced to fantasy. The only defendant who will not damage himself by even the most restrained candor will be the one so desperate that he might as well walk into court and enter guilty plea. It defies reason to think that Congress intended to invite such a result, when it adopted a Rule said to promote candid discussion in the interest of encouraging compromise.

CHRISTOPHER SLOBOGIN, THE STORY OF RULE 410 AND *UNITED STATES v. MEZZANATTO:* USING PLEA STATEMENTS AT TRIAL

Evidence Stories 103, 121-122 (Richard Lempert ed., 2006)

Most courts that have considered the issue [after *Mezzanatto*] have approved waiver agreements permitting use of *any* statements, including even preliminary "proffers," for *any* rebuttal of the defense's case, including impeachment of defense witnesses other than the defendant and statements by the defense attorney, and some courts have explicitly allowed plea agreements to be used in the prosecution's case-in-chief. Consistent with Justice Souter's prediction, *Mezzanatto* is well on the way to making Rule 410 and Rule 11(g) "dead letters."

JOHN W. STRONG, CONSENSUAL MODIFICATIONS OF THE RULES OF EVIDENCE: THE LIMITS OF PARTY AUTONOMY IN AN ADVERSARY SYSTEM

80 Neb. L. Rev. 159, 159-164 (2001)

I start from the proposition, well known to all those trained in the Anglo-American legal tradition, that we have an adversary system, which is quite different from those employed in much of the non-English speaking world. The distinctiveness of the adversary system, as its name would suggest, lies in its allocation to the adversaries in the dispute the basic responsibility for discovering, marshalling, and presenting the facts of the case to the decision maker, either judge or jury, rather than assigning these tasks to a non-partisan official. Essentially two complementary justifications have been presented for this mode of proceeding. First, the adversary system is a sort of analog of laissez-faire economics, in the sense that as according to Adam Smith, individual pursuit of personal economic advantage will ultimately redound to the general public benefit. This places the burden of fact development and presentation upon those most interested in the result and will tend to ensure the fullest and ultimately most accurate depiction of the facts. A second justification sometimes asserted is that this allocation of responsibility is essentially fair, in the sense that those most immediately affected by judicial decisions should be given every reasonable opportunity to participate in the resolution process.

Consistent with these rationales, parties to litigation are, for the most part, given great latitude in the manner in which they choose to assert their rights in court. This autonomy is slightly less in criminal matters, where it is said that the state possesses a significant interest. But even here, the over-riding interest in allowing self-determination will often prevail even to the extent of allowing the criminal defendant to make choices which would generally be thought to be undesirable and even foolish.

Not surprisingly, the rules of evidence, which are themselves part and parcel of the adversary system, generally also operate upon the principle of party responsibility. By that I mean it is usually the responsibility of the parties to see that the rules are applied. This responsibility is most clearly embodied in the so-called contemporaneous objection rule, which requires the party wishing to see a rule of evidence enforced to lodge an objection as soon as an impending violation of the rule is reasonably to be anticipated. Failure to make an objection will, in the great majority of instances, mean that the rule goes unenforced at trial. In addition, such a violation of the rule will provide no ground for claiming error on appeal. In other words, the usual result is that any rule not insisted upon by a party wishing to see it applied is waived.

And, of course, in addition to waiver, there are several other avenues by which the parties may forego enforcement of the usual rules. Foremost among these are pre-dispute contracts in which the parties specify what rules will apply in the event a dispute develops between them, and stipula-tions, which will sometimes constitute an agreed modification of the rules or represent mutual acceptance of a fact which otherwise would need to be established by ordinary evidentiary means. . . .

A seeming majority of courts have now retreated from the position, earlier common, that the parties are powerless to affect the rules by con-sensual agreement. . . . Today, though a contrariety of statements can still be found, the most common judicial formulation is that the parties are allowed wide discretion in determining what rules of evidence are to be enforced in a judicial proceeding, but may not by party agreement violate pubic policy. Beyond this very general statement, the decisions give only sketchy suggestions as to what the limitations of public policy may be.

C. MEDICAL PAYMENTS AND LIABILITY INSURANCE

[F.R.E. 409, 411; C.E.C. §1155]

ADVISORY COMMITTEE NOTE TO F.R.E. 409

The considerations underlying this rule parallel those underlying Rules 407 and 408, which deal respectively with subsequent remedial mea-sures and offers of compromise. As stated in Annot., 20 A.L.R.2d 291, 293: "[G]enerally, evidence of payment of medical, hospital, or similar expenses of an injured party by the opposing party, is not admissible, the reason often given being that such payment or offer is usually made from humane impulses and not from an admission of liability, and that to hold otherwise would tend to discourage assistance to the injured person."

Contrary to Rule 408, dealing with offers of compromise, the present rule does not extend to conduct or statements not a part of the act of furnishing or offering or promising to pay. This difference in treatment arises from fundamental difference in nature. Communication is essential if compromises are to be effected, and consequently broad protection of statements is needed. This is not so in cases of payments or offers or promises to pay medical expenses, where factual statements may be expected to be incidental in nature. . . .

ADVISORY COMMITTEE NOTE TO F.R.E. 411

The courts have with substantial unanimity rejected evidence of liability insurance for the purpose of proving fault, and absence of liability insurance as proof of lack of fault. At best the inference of fault from the fact of insurance coverage is a tenuous one, as is its converse. More important, no doubt, has been the feeling that knowledge of the presence of liability insurance would induce juries to decide cases on improper grounds. The rule is drafted in broad terms so as to include contributory negligence or other fault of a plaintiff as well as fault of a defendant. The second sentence points out the limits of the rule, using well established illustrations.

CHARTER v. CHLEBORAD

551 F.2d 246 (8th Cir. 1977)

Per Curiam.

This is a diversity action to recover damages for alleged medical malpractice. In June of 1973, plaintiff was struck by a truck while working as a highway flagman. The accident caused extensive injuries to both of plaintiff's legs. Plaintiff was hospitalized and placed under the care of a general practitioner and defendant, a surgeon. Surgery was performed on both legs. As a result of severe complications plaintiff was transferred to another hospital where both legs were amputated above the knee. The trial of the matter resulted in a jury verdict for defendant and the district court denied plaintiff's motion for a new trial. . . .

[At trial p]laintiff offered the testimony of Dr. Joseph Lichtor, M.D., a Kansas City, Missouri orthopedic surgeon. . . . Dr. Lichtor testified that the cause of the complications and subsequent amputations was defendant's negligence. As a part of his rebuttal case, defendant offered the testimony of John J. Alder, an attorney from the Kansas City area. Mr. Alder testified that Dr. Lichtor's reputation for truth and veracity in the Kansas City area was bad. On cross-examination Mr. Alder testified that he did some defense work in medical malpractice cases. He also stated that some of his clients in those cases were insurance companies.

Plaintiff's counsel then asked him to name some of those companies and defendant objected to the relevancy of the matter. After a conference at the Bench the district court refused to allow further questioning on the subject of insurance. As plaintiff stated in his motion for a new trial, Mr. Alder was employed in part by the same liability carrier who represents defendant in this action.

It is well established that the existence of a liability insurance policy is not admissible to show one's negligence or other wrongful conduct. Fed. R. Evid. 411 (1975); C. McCormick, Evidence s 201, at 479 (2d ed. 1972). This rule has its belief that such evidence is of questionable probative value or relevance and is often prejudicial. Evidence of the existence of insurance may be offered for other purposes, however.

In this case the fact that defendant's insurer employed Mr. Alder was clearly admissible to show possible bias of that witness. . . . Plaintiff's claim rested for the most part on the credibility of his witness. When defendant undertook to impeach that witness plaintiff was entitled to attempt to show possible bias of Mr. Alder as surrebuttal. Considering the importance of expert testimony in this case we cannot conclude that the trial court's exclusionary ruling was mere harmless error. . . . Accordingly, the judgment of the district court is reversed and the action is remanded with directions to grant the plaintiff a new trial.

HIGGINS v. HICKS CO.

756 F.2d 681 (8th Cir. 1985)

FAGG, Circuit Judge.

This lawsuit is the result of two separate motorcycle accidents that occurred on a four-lane divided highway in South Dakota. The accidents occurred after sunset on a stretch of Interstate 90 that was under construction. The Hicks Company, under contract with the State of South Dakota, was resurfacing the interstate with asphalt. On the day of the accident, there was a 5.4 mile stretch of highway that had been resurfaced on the passing lane of eastbound I-90 but not on the driving lane. This left a 3-4 inch ridge over which a driver had to maneuver to move from the driving lane to the passing lane. Steven Martinez lost control of his motorcycle when moving from the driving lane to the passing lane and was fatally injured. Mallard Teal also lost control of his vehicle when changing lanes on this 5.4 mile stretch and claims damages as a result of the injuries he sustained.

Plaintiffs claim that The Hicks Company and the State of South Dakota were negligent in opening both eastbound lanes on I-90 at this 5.4 mile stretch without adequate warning signs. Defendants deny any negligence and claim Martinez and Teal were contributorially negligent in operating their motorcycles at a speed greater than was reasonable under the circumstances and in failing to keep a proper lookout. The jury returned a verdict favorable to The Hicks Company and the State of South Dakota.

[P]laintiffs contend that it was error for the district court to refuse to admit evidence that the State of South Dakota carries liability insurance. Plaintiffs contend that evidence of the state's liability insurance was admissible to eliminate any bias of the jurors as taxpayers of the State of South Dakota. We cannot agree.

Evidence of liability insurance may be admitted if relevant to an issue in the case or to prove bias or prejudice of a witness. Fed. R. Evid. 411. It is not admissible to prove negligence of the insured person. *Id.* The advisory committee note to Federal Rule 411 indicates that "knowledge of the presence or absence of liability insurance would induce juries to decide cases on improper grounds." We believe that evidence of the state's liability insurance was irrelevant to any issues in this case and that the evidence was properly excluded by the district court. . . . Affirmed.

CHARLES ALAN WRIGHT & KENNETH W. GRAHAM, JR. FEDERAL PRACTICE AND PROCEDURE, EVIDENCE

23 §5362 (1980)

The writers, almost without exception, have been critical of the "archaic legal principle" upon which Rule 411 is based; indeed, it has been buried by an "avalanche of authoritative criticism." The mildest critic was Wigmore, who thought the common law rule "impracticable" because the benefits were so clearly outweighed by the costs of administering it. McCormick called the rule "a hollow shell" because of the many ways in which it could be evaded, while Morgan thought that enforcement of the rule led courts to "indulge in a lot of nonsense." An early critic saw the rule as a "coddling" of insurance companies, a view shared by a venerated torts scholar who referred to the "fantastic efforts which have been made by courts of the country to develop protection for indemnity insurers."

. . . [I]t is probably true that it is an "absurd hypothesis" that the existence of insurance will foster "a 'devil-may-care' attitude" on the part of the average driver, but it is doubtful that this hypothesis would be advanced in the case of the average driver; there are, however, drivers who would "court self-destruction" where they did not risk financial ruin and the evidence is clearly relevant in such cases. Moreover, in many cases the defendant is not the driver of an automobile; the instinct for self-preservation is not likely to figure prominently in the decision to, say permit a driver of questionable skills to borrow one's vehicle. Similarly, the argument that the procuring of insurance shows prudence rather than recklessness confuses care in looking out for oneself with care in attending to the interests of others. It certainly does not seem implausible to suggest that the decision of whether to leave one's fireside to remove ice from the front walk on a winter day in South Dakota might be influenced by the presence or absence of personal liability to strangers who might fall.

... The need for a rule dealing with the admissibility of evidence of insurance arises because the insurance company is permitted to litigate disguised as its insured. Viewed from this perspective, the rule of evidence is not so much a doctrine of relevance as it is part of an arsenal of weapons that courts have developed to perpetuate the fiction that the insurance company is not a party though it controls the litigation and will pay the judgment. ... Viewing the evidence rule from this broader perspective has made it seem even less defensible to the critics. The goal of the rule is seen as "impracticable" because the existence of insurance can be made known to the jury as early as voir dire examination under the law in most jurisdictions. Moreover, at least in automobile litigation, modern jurors are likely to assume the existence of insurance, with the result that the evidence rule is of little benefit to insurance companies but works substantial prejudice to uninsured defendants. Finally, the attempt to enforce the rule puts the trial court on the horns of a dilemma. Rigorous enforcement is very expensive in terms of mistrials, the costs of adjudicating blame if that factor is relevant to reversal, and the waste of time spent trying to usher witnesses past the insurance company without their remarking its presence. If, on the other hand, the rule is loosely enforced it may give an unwarranted advantage to counsel who are sufficiently clever or unscrupulous enough to take advantage of such lax enforcement. In sum, if the goal is to prevent excessive verdicts against insurance companies, there are procedural devices—remittitur, for example—that are better suited to this purpose than a rule of evidence barring a party from proving what the jury already knows or suspects.

PROBLEMS

5.1. Following a traffic accident one driver says to the other, "I don't want to litigate this. I'll pay for the damage to your car, and I'll pay if you need to see a doctor." If the second driver later sues the first for negligence, is the first driver's statement admissible to prove fault?

5.2. An appliance repairer requires his customers to sign a contract providing that in any lawsuit brought against him, his lack of liability insurance will be admissible "without limitation." A clothes dryer he repairs catches fire and causes extensive damage to the customer's home. The customer sues the repairer for negligence. May the defendant introduce proof that he carries no liability insurance?

5.3. A bicycle company requires all its customers to sign a contract agreeing that in any lawsuit alleging a product defect, evidence that the defect was later remedied will be inadmissible for any purpose, including proof of feasibility. The brakes fail on a bicycle sold by the company, and the customer is injured. She sues alleging defective design. At trial the company claims the brakes could not feasibly have been made more reliable, and the customer seeks to counter that claim with evidence that, following her accident, the company changed the design of the brakes in a way that made them more reliable. Is the evidence admissible?

5.4. Consider the following fact pattern from the July 1998 California Bar Examination: "A car driven by Dunn collided with Empire Trucking Co.'s truck. . . . Dunn and Dunn's passenger, Paul, were seriously injured. Paul sued Empire for personal injuries [and called Dunn as a witness]. Empire asked Dunn on cross-examination: 'Q. Isn't it true your insurance carrier reached a settlement with Paul and as part of that written agreement, you agreed to testify on Paul's behalf today?' " Should Paul's objection to this question be sustained?

6

TRIAL MECHANICS

"I'm going to ask the jury to hold its applause until all the evidence has been introduced."

Evidence law leaves most questions regarding the mechanics of trial—the order of proof and the mode of examining witnesses—to the discretion of the trial judge. Nonetheless, several loose constraints are placed on that discretion, some by rule and others by tradition. This chapter addresses both kinds of constraints.

A. Order of Proof

A traditional rule of trial practice, codified in the Federal Rules of Evidence and its state counterparts, generally restricts cross-examination to the subjects addressed in direct examination, and redirect examination to the subjects raised on cross-examination. But trial judges have broad discretion to depart from that rule, and from other traditional practices regarding the order of proof.

1. Generally

[F.R.E. 611(a) & (b); C.E.C. §§760-763, 765(a), 772-774]

ADVISORY COMMITTEE NOTE TO F.R.E. 611

Spelling out detailed rules to govern the mode and order of interrogating witnesses and presenting evidence is neither desirable nor feasible. The ultimate responsibility for the effective working of the adversary system rests with the judge. The rule sets forth the objectives which he should seek to attain. . . .

The tradition in the federal courts and in numerous state courts has been to limit the scope of cross-examination to matters testified to on direct, plus matters bearing upon the credibility of the witness. . . . [T]he matter is essentially one of the order of presentation and not one in which involvement at the appellate level is likely to prove fruitful. . . . The provision of the second sentence [of subsection (b)], that the judge may in the interests of justice limit inquiry into new matters on cross-examination, is designed for those situations in which the result otherwise would be confusion, complication, or protraction of the case, not as a matter of rule but as demonstrable in the actual development of the particular case. . . .

ROGER C. PARK, DAVID P. LEONARD & STEVEN H. GOLDBERG, EVIDENCE LAW

§1.09, at 34-35 (1998)

As a general proposition, lawyers are allowed to conduct subsequent interrogations of a witness until everything the witness can offer is before the jury. The direct examiner's subsequent examinations of the witness are called redirect examination and the cross-examiner's subsequent examinations of the witness are called re-cross examinations. How many layers of redirect and re-cross are necessary to present the full testimony to the jury is entirely within the discretion of the trial judge.

The language of Rule 611(b) addresses only cross-examination, but the principle expressed in the Rule—that the subsequent examination is limited to the subject matter of the preceding examination—is usually applied to redirect examinations, as well as to cross and re-cross examinations. The judge's discretion, pursuant to Rule 611(a), to promote the orderly presentation of evidence by restricting redirect examination to the scope of the cross-examination can, of course, be exercised in the other direction. The judge can allow the proponent on redirect to repair omissions in the direct examination, by allowing questions that go beyond the scope of the cross-examination.

STONE v. PEACOCK

968 F.2d 1163 (11th Cir. 1992)

PER CURIAM:

Plaintiff Calvin J. Stone lost a jury verdict . . . in his suit against officers of the Georgia Department of Corrections claiming they terminated his employment in retaliation for his speaking out about the improper use of public property and funds. . . . At the beginning of trial, the district court required Stone to testify first so that some chronology would be laid out at the beginning of the case. This initial testimony was not subject to cross-examination at that time. Stone's counsel protested the court's reordering of the witnesses. Federal Rules of Evidence Rule 611(a), however, gives courts reasonable control over the order and presentation of evidence. There may have been some error, but perhaps harmless in this case, if the court did not give Stone proper notice. The court's witness order requirement alone, however, is not reversible error absent some showing of harm. Although it does not appear that Stone has shown harm, we need not make this determination. If there is a retrial, the plaintiff will be on notice that he may be required by the court to testify at the beginning of the case. . . . [Vacated and remanded in part on other grounds.]

ELGABRI v. LEKAS

964 F.2d 1255 (1st Cir. 1992)

STAHL, District Judge.

. . . Plaintiff-appellant Dr. Tarek H. Elgabri alleged various violations of state and federal antitrust laws, as well as a common law claim of tortious interference with prospective business relationships, against various doctors affiliated at four Rhode Island hospitals. The jury found for defendants on all counts. . . .

Dr. Elgabri argues that his ability to call defendants during his case-in-chief was improperly limited by the trial court. He contends that he has an "unfettered right to call the adverse party on direct examination as part of his case-in-chief and to interrogate by leading questions without restrictions."

As part of his case-in-chief, Dr. Elgabri called defendant Dr. Lekas. After some examination of the witness, the court informed plaintiff during a recess that "it's unfair sometimes for a Plaintiff to prove his case through the mouth of the Defendant." Dr. Elgabri then continued his examination of Dr. Lekas.

After the day's testimony, the court decided to limit plaintiff's examination of defendants in his case-in-chief to subject matter that could not be obtained in any other fashion. The court suggested that plaintiff could prove the essential nature of a defendant's testimony in a proffer prior to the examination of each defendant. Defendants promised that they would take the stand as part of their case-in-chief and the court indicated that plaintiff would have ample opportunity to cross-examine them at that time. The court further indicated that no limits would be placed on the scope of cross-examination. Plaintiff thereafter made no further proffers and vigorously cross-examined the other defendants during their presentations. . . .

We find that plaintiff did not have an "unfettered right" to call defendants during his case-in-chief. Rule 611(a) of the Federal Rules of Evidence [places the] . . . mode and order of questioning . . . in the trial court's discretion. We do not disturb decisions regarding courtroom management unless these decisions amount to an abuse of discretion that prejudices appellant's case. *Loinaz v. EG & G, Inc.*, 910 F.2d 1, 6 (1st Cir. 1990); *see also* 3 Jack B. Weinberg & Margaret A. Berger, *Weinstein's Evidence* 611[01] at 611-17 (1991) ("Once the judge exercises his power, his decision is virtually immune to attack and will be overturned only in the rare case where the appellate court finds a clear abuse of discretion that seriously damaged a party's right to a fair trial.").

Dr. Elgabri argues that Fed. R. Evid. 611(c), which allows for leading questions of adverse parties on direct examination, requires the court to allow direct examination of defendants in his case-in-chief. Rule 611(c) does not, however, impose such a requirement. Rather, Rule 611(c) only requires that the court allow a plaintiff who calls an adverse party on direct to use leading questions in his examination because the witness is presumed hostile. *See* Fed. R. Evid. 611(c), advisory committee's note; *see also* 3 *Weinstein's Evidence* 611[05] at 611-82 to 611-83.

In this case, the court reasonably held that plaintiff's examination of defendants should be limited in the described manner in order to make the presentation of evidence effective and to avoid needless consumption of time. Further, plaintiff does not argue that he failed to obtain evidence as a result of the district court's limiting of his presentation of his case; he only objects to the order of presentation. We therefore find no reversible error. . . .

UNITED STATES v. WILFORD

710 F.2d 439 (8th Cir. 1983)

LAY, Chief Judge.

[Wilford and three codefendants were convicted of extorting drivers at a waste treatment construction site in Cedar Rapids to join a Teamsters

Union local.] ... The defendants argue that a witness presented by the government during its rebuttal brought forward new facts not raised earlier, and that the defendants were entitled to present evidence on surrebuttal to counter the witness' testimony and to impeach his credibility. The trial court sustained the government's objection to surrebuttal by the defendants.

The witness, an investigator for the [National Labor Relations Board], testified as to his observation of events taking place at the Pittsburgh-Des Moines Steel Co. site. The government's stated purpose in offering the investigator's testimony was to show the similarity of the Pittsburgh-Des Moines incident to the incident for which the defendants were being tried. The defendants argue that they were entitled to present evidence in surrebuttal because the witness intimated that a violent act took place in connection with the stopping of a truck driven by a non-union driver, and because the defendants were entitled to show the investigator's bias against the Teamsters Union.

The decision whether to allow a party to present evidence in surrebuttal is committed to the sound discretion of the trial court. *United States v. Burgess*, 691 F.2d 1146, 1153 (4th Cir. 1982); *Kines v. Butterwoth*, 669 F.2d 6, 13 (1st Cir. 1981), *cert. denied*, 456 U.S. 980 (1982); *United States v. Greene*, 497 F.2d 1068, 1083 (7th Cir. 1974), *cert. denied*, 420 U.S. 909 (1975). In this case we find no abuse of discretion by the trial judge in his refusal to allow the defendants' surrebuttal. . . . [E]ven though a party is normally entitled to impeach the credibility of an opponent's key witness, in this case the investigator was not a key government witness, and in light of other evidence adduced at trial, his testimony regarding the similarity of the Pittsburgh-Des Moines incident to the incident for which the defendants were being tried was merely cumulative. Thus, it was not unfairly prejudicial for the trial court to refuse to allow the defendants to present evidence in surrebuttal. As the Seventh Circuit noted in *United States v. Greene*:

> When the point of completion of a trial has been reached, which was the situation here, the trial judge should be vested with substantial discretionary powers to bring the evidentiary phase to a close, or to put it another way, to curb the natural tendency of vigorous counsel to get in the final word.

We find no prejudicial error in the trial court's ruling. . . . [T]he defendants' convictions are affirmed.

UNITED STATES v. CARTER

910 F.2d 1524 (7th Cir. 1990)

CRABB, Chief District Judge.

Defendant Steven Carter was charged in a two-count indictment under 18 U.S.C. §2113(a) with robbing the Acme Continental Credit Union in [the CNA Insurance building in] Chicago on January 9, 1989 and again on January 20, 1989. The jury returned verdicts of guilty on both counts. . . .

Defendant argues that the trial court improperly allowed the government to exceed the scope of direct examination when it cross-examined Lashan Riggins.

The government did not call Riggins as a witness in its case in chief. Defendant called her as a defense witness. On cross-examination, the government exceeded the scope of direct examination by inquiring into the following subjects: (1) defendant's statement to her that he committed the robberies, made to her in the holding room at the police station after he confessed to the authorities; (2) her recollection of the clothing defendant wore when he left Indianapolis for Chicago on January 20, 1989; and (3) her recognition of the clothing discarded following the January 9 robbery as similar to clothing owned by defendant. Defendant objected to these questions at trial on the ground that they were prohibited by Fed. R. Evid. 611(b), but in each instance the trial court invoked its discretion under the rule to permit the questions.

The district court did not act improperly in so ruling. Although Fed. R. Evid. 611(b) limits cross-examination to the subject matter of direct examination, it grants the trial court discretion to "permit inquiry into additional matters as if on direct examination." A district court's evidentiary rulings are not subject to reversal unless the defendant can show a clear abuse of discretion. Moreover, because the management of cross-examination is peculiarly committed to the district court's discretion, "[t]he effect is to confine the matter largely to the trial level and to remove it from the area of profitable appellate review." *McCormick on Evidence*, §24 n. 6 (3d ed. 1984).

Despite this deferential appellate standard, defendant argues that the court's decision to allow Riggins to be questioned on such matters constitutes an abuse of discretion because it enabled the government to present evidence that it chose not to offer in its case in chief and that would not have been proper rebuttal. Although defendant is correct in these assertions, he must show more than this to establish that the trial court abused its discretion. The testimony elicited challenged some of the alibis that defendant was presenting, such as his contention that he was not at the CNA building on January 9, 1989 and that he was misidentified as the robber on January 20, 1989. In light of the probative value of this evidence, the trial judge did not abuse his discretion by allowing the government to exceed the scope of Riggins's direct examination. . . . AFFIRMED.

2. Rule of Completeness

[F.R.E. 106; C.E.C. §356]

ADVISORY COMMITTEE NOTE TO F.R.E. 106

The rule is an expression of the rule of completeness. . . . The rule is based on two considerations. The first is the misleading impression created by taking matters out of context. The second is the inadequacy of repair work when delayed to a point later in the trial. The rule does not in any way circumscribe the right of the adversary to develop the matter on cross-examination or as part of his own case. For practical reasons, the rule is limited to writings and recorded statements and does not apply to conversations.

STEPHEN A. SALTZBURG, MICHAEL M. MARTIN & DANIEL J. CAPRA, FEDERAL RULES OF EVIDENCE MANUAL

1:106-109 (9th ed. 2006)

Rule 106 is one of the rare examples of an evidence rule that permits one party to require another party to introduce more evidence than the latter desires to offer, or at least to have the latter party's case-in-chief interrupted while additional evidence is offered. Contrast Rule 106 with the typical approach to oral trial testimony. Questions asked on direct examination may produce a story that is shaded to the advantage of the party calling the witness. Yet, clarification does not occur until cross-examination. Thus, the Rule provides protection against initial offers of incomplete writings and recordings that is not provided against initial offers of incomplete testimony. The reason for limiting the Rule to writings and recordings, at least as to timing, was that a process of immediate interruption was thought to be unwieldy for witness testimony. The broader principle of completeness applies to writings, recordings, and oral testimony . . . but the more limited principle of contemporaneous presentation embodied in the Rule can be applied only to writings and recordings.

B. Mode of Questioning

Traditional Anglo-American trial practice allows leading questions on cross-examination but generally forbids them on direct examination. A "leading" question is a question phrased in such a way as to suggest the desired answer. There are long-standing exceptions to the general prohibition of leading questions on direct examination. The most important of these exceptions allows leading questions when necessary to develop the testimony—for example, when the witness's recollection needs refreshing, when the witness is a young child, or when the witness appears hostile or can be presumed to have sympathies aligned with the opposing party. Similarly, when cross-examination really amounts to direct examination—when, for example, one defendant cross-examines a friendly witness called by a co-defendant—the traditional rule is that cross-examination must proceed without leading questions.

[F.R.E. 611(c); C.E.C. §§764, 767]

ADVISORY COMMITTEE NOTE TO F.R.E. 611

. . . The rule continues the traditional view that the suggestive powers of the leading question are as a general proposition undesirable. Within this tradition, however, numerous exceptions have achieved recognition: The witness who is hostile, unwilling, or biased; the child witness or the adult with communication problems; the witness whose recollection is exhausted; and undisputed preliminary matters. 3 Wigmore §§774-778. An almost total unwillingness to reverse for infractions has been manifested by appellate courts. The matter clearly falls within the area of control by the judge over the mode and order of interrogation and presentation and accordingly is phrased in words of suggestion rather than command.

The rule also conforms to tradition in making the use of leading questions on cross-examination a matter of right. The purpose of the qualification "ordinarily" is to furnish a basis for denying the use of leading questions when the cross-examination is cross-examination in form only and not in fact, as for example the "cross-examination" of a party by his own counsel after being called by the opponent (savoring more of re-direct) or of an insured defendant who proves to be friendly to the plaintiff.

The final sentence deals with categories of witnesses automatically regarded and treated as hostile. Rule 43(b) of the Federal Rules of Civil Procedure has included only "an adverse party or an officer, director, or managing agent of a public or private corporation or of a partnership or association which is an adverse party." This limitation virtually to persons whose statements would stand as admissions is believed to be an unduly narrow concept of those who may safely be regarded as hostile without further demonstration. . . . The phrase of the rule, "witness identified with" an adverse party, is designed to enlarge the category of persons thus callable.

UNITED STATES v. NABORS

762 F.2d 642 (10th Cir. 1985)

Sachs, District Judge.

The defendant brothers, Charles Bruce Nabors and John Calvin Nabors, Jr., appeal from a final judgment entered in the district court after a jury verdict finding each of them guilty of bank robbery by means of a deadly weapon and conspiracy to commit bank robbery. . . . Key testimony connecting the defendants to the bank robbery was provided by twelve-year-old Tray Campbell, a nephew by marriage of John Nabors. . . . [Following the robbery, Tray discovered the defendants in the basement of his mother's home,] laughing and giggling about an amount of money that they had gotten. . . .

On direct examination of Tray Campbell, the Government's attorney asked the boy whether either of the defendants said anything immediately after they saw Tray for the first time in the . . . basement. The boy's initial reply was that John Nabors "turned around to his brother and said Tray's here." Counsel for John Nabors objected after the prosecutor continued this line of inquiry by asking, "Tray, exactly what did he say?" The trial court rejected the contention that the Government was asking improper leading questions and instead stated that "I think perhaps what he's doing is repeating what the witness has said essentially, and of course given the circumstances here which are quite obvious, the court is going to overrule the objection." The following inquiry then occurred:

> Q. (Prosecutor) Tray, have you told me before what they said?
> A. (Tray) Yes, sir.
> Q. And what did you tell me that John said?
> A. Can I say it?
> Q. Yes, you can say it.
> A. He said, he said, "Oh, shit, Tray's here."

Defendant characterizes this entire line of questioning as "an improper and extremely prejudicial method of interrogation of a child witness." We do not agree with this description. Although leading questions are not ordinarily permitted on direct examination except "as may be necessary to develop . . . testimony," (Federal Rule of Evidence 611(c)), the Notes of the Advisory Committee describe a long-recognized exception—"the child witness or the adult with communication problems." In this case the prosecutor did not suggest the language used, although he did press for a repetition of words previously used. Tray's hesitation in using a "naughty" word in a formal proceeding was understandable. The wording of that statement did tend to implicate the defendants in the bank robbery in that it indicated some alarm at being discovered; it was thus proper for the prosecutor to attempt to elicit its precise language. The trial court's ruling deserves deference because the court was in the best position to evaluate the emotional condition of the child witness and his hesitancy to testify. . . . [W]e affirm the judgments as to both defendants.

ELLIS v. CITY OF CHICAGO

667 F.2d 606 (7th Cir. 1981)

CUDAHY, Circuit Judge.

[Chicago Police Officer Frank Kusar entered plaintiffs' home based on a telephone tip and fatally shot plaintiffs' dog, allegedly after the dog lunged at him. Plaintiffs sued Kusar and the city for damages, claiming violation of their civil rights. The jury found for defendants, and plaintiffs appealed.]

. . . [P]laintiffs claim that the trial court erred in refusing to permit counsel for plaintiffs to use leading questions during his direct examinations of Officer Calandra and Sergeant Holub, police officers employed by the City of Chicago. Since 1975, the use of leading questions has been governed by Rule 611(c) of the Federal Rules of Evidence. This rule provides that while leading questions should not normally be used on direct examination, they may be employed "[W]hen a party calls a hostile witness, an adverse party, or a witness identified with an adverse party." Plaintiffs argue that the trial judge committed reversible error by refusing to recognize Officer Calandra and Sergeant Holub as witnesses identified with an adverse party for purposes of this Rule.

Before the adoption of Rule 611(c), the use of leading questions on direct examination required either a showing of actual hostility or a determination that the witness being examined was an adverse party, or an officer, director, or managing agent of such an adverse party. These limitations were designed to guard against the risk of improper suggestion inherent in examining friendly witnesses through the use of leading questions. The drafters of Rule 611(c), however, determined that these limitations represented "an unduly narrow concept of those who may safely be regarded as hostile without further demonstration." Fed. R. Evid. 611(c) (Advisory Committee Notes). The new rule was thus designed to enlarge the categories of witnesses automatically regarded as adverse, and therefore subject to interrogation by leading questions without further showing of actual hostility. *Id.*

We agree with plaintiffs that the district court should have permitted leading questions during plaintiffs' direct examinations of Officer Calandra and Sergeant Holub. These police officers were employees of defendant City of Chicago at all times during the litigation and were each present during portions of the incident which gave rise to this lawsuit. Moreover, the record indicates that both officers had worked closely with defendant Frank Kusar during the period of their employment. Officer Calandra and Sergeant Holub thus clearly qualified as "witness(es) identified with an adverse party" for purposes of Rule 611(c).

We do not believe, however, that this conclusion requires reversal of the judgment. In essence, Rule 611(c) codifies the traditional mode of dealing with leading questions. It acknowledges that they are generally undesirable on direct examination, that they are usually permissible on cross-examination, and that there are exceptions to both of these propositions. Although not explicitly stated, the rule is consistent with what has long been the law—that in the use of leading questions "much must be left to the sound discretion of the trial judge who sees the witness and can, therefore, determine in the interest of truth and justice whether the circumstances justify leading questions to be propounded to a witness by the party producing them." *St. Clair v. United States*, 154 U.S. 134 (1894). Such a decision will not be reversed absent a clear showing of prejudice to the complaining party.

Plaintiffs here have made no such showing of prejudice. Indeed, the record indicates that counsel for plaintiffs examined both Officer Calandra and Sergeant Holub at length without the use of leading questions and that neither witness was evasive or antagonistic. Moreover, defendants called Sergeant Holub as their own witness, thus permitting plaintiffs to ask leading questions on cross-examination. Finally, and most importantly, nowhere in their briefs do plaintiffs indicate what additional testimony they would have elicited had they been permitted to employ leading questions in their direct examinations of Officer Calandra and Sergeant Holub. Under these circumstances, any harm to plaintiffs from the district court's ruling is purely speculative. . . . Affirmed.

PROBLEMS

6.1. Two brothers, Dan and Doug, are charged with robbing a bank and are tried together. Dan calls their sister Wendy as a witness and elicits testimony that she went to the beach with both defendants on the day of the robbery. Following direct examination, Doug's lawyer cross-examines Wendy. He asks her, "The trip to beach lasted all day, didn't it?" The prosecutor objects that "counsel is leading the witness." Should the objection be sustained? What if Doug were unrelated to Dan and Wendy?

6.2. Elaine, an eyewitness to a collision between a passenger car and a delivery van, tells a police officer who reports to the scene that the car entered the intersection first and then was struck by the van. The car driver later sues the van driver for negligence and calls Elaine as a witness. On direct examination, plaintiff's counsel asks Elaine whether the car or the van entered the intersection first. Elaine says she cannot remember. Plaintiff's counsel then asks, "Do you remember talking to a police officer about the accident?" Elaine says she does. Plaintiff's counsel asks, "Do you remember telling the officer that the van entered the intersection first?" Defense counsel objects on grounds of hearsay and improper leading. How should the judge rule?

6.3. Suppose Elaine's memory does not fail her at trial; she testifies that the passenger car entered the intersection and then was struck by the van. On cross-examination, counsel for the van driver asks Elaine whether she is related by marriage to the plaintiff. Plaintiff's counsel objects that this is beyond the scope of direct examination. How should the judge rule?

C. SEQUESTERING WITNESSES

The practice of excluding witnesses from the courtroom until they testify—commonly known as "sequestering" witnesses—is centuries old. A celebrated illustration both of the practice and of its traditional rationale appears in the Apocryphal story of Susanna and the Elders. Susanna is falsely accused of adultery and condemned to death. The prophet Daniel saves her by questioning the two elders who claim to have witnessed the liaison. Unable to coordinate their lies, they tell conflicting stories about where it occurred.

[F.R.E. 615; C.E.C. §777]

ADVISORY COMMITTEE NOTE TO F.R.E. 615

The efficacy of excluding or sequestering witnesses has long been recognized as a means of discouraging and exposing fabrication, inaccuracy, and collusion. 6 Wigmore §§1837-1838. The authority of the judge is admitted, the only question being whether the matter is committed to his discretion or one of right. The rule takes the latter position. No time is specified for making the request.

REPORT OF THE SENATE JUDICIARY COMMITTEE

S. Rep. 93-1277 (1974)

Many district courts permit government counsel to have an investigative agent at counsel table throughout the trial although the agent is or may be a witness. The practice is permitted as an exception to the rule of exclusion and compares with the situation defense counsel finds himself in—he always has the client with him to consult during the trial. The investigative agent's presence may be extremely important to government counsel, especially when the case is complex or involves some specialized subject matter. The agent, too, having lived with the case for a long time, may be able to assist in meeting trial surprises where the best-prepared counsel would otherwise have difficulty. Yet, it would not seem the Government could often meet the burden under rule 615 of showing that the agent's presence is essential. Furthermore, it could be dangerous to use the agent as a witness as early in the case as possible, so that he might then help counsel as a nonwitness, since the agent's testimony could be needed in rebuttal. Using another, nonwitness agent from the same investigative agency would not generally meet government counsel's needs.

This problem is solved if it is clear that investigative agents are within the group specified under the second exception made in the rule, for "an officer or employee of a party which is not a natural person designated as its representative by its attorney." It is our understanding that this was the intention of the House committee. It is certainly this committee's construction of the rule.

UNITED STATES v. MACHOR

879 F.2d 945 (1st Cir. 1989)

TORRUELLA, Circuit Judge.

After a joint jury trial, the four appellants . . . were convicted under 21 U.S.C. §841(a)(1) for aiding and abetting each other in the possession with intent to distribute cocaine. [They were arrested after trying to sell a kilo-gram of cocaine to an undercover agent and a confidential informant.] . . .

[Two of the appellants] argue that the trial court abused its discretion when it denied defendant's motion to exclude agent Rivera while the infor-mant testified. In the alternative, Carrasco and Allen claim that the court abused its discretion by not ordering agent Rivera to testify before the informant.

Fed. R. Evid. 615 requires that the trial court sequester witnesses at the request of a party. There are several exceptions to this rule, however. The most common is that a party who is a natural person cannot be excluded from the courtroom. As an extension of this basic principle, Fed. R. Evid. 615(2) provides that, when a party is not a natural person, its designated representative is also exempted from the sequestration rule. It seems clear that a case agent representing the government is within this exception. . . .

Defendants maintain, however, that even after the promulgation of the new Federal Rules of Evidence, the court retained discretion to exclude a person who falls within the 615(2) exception. The courts are divided on this issue. Some cases support defendants' view that the trial court has discre-tion to exclude the government case agent. *United States v. Thomas*, 835 F.2d 219, 223 (9th Cir. 1987), *cert. denied*, 486 U.S. 1010 (1988); *United States v. Woody*, 588 F.2d 1212, 1213 (8th Cir. 1978), *cert. denied*, 440 U.S. 928 (1979).

The majority view, however, is that Fed. R. Evid. 615(2) has severely curtailed the discretion of the trial court to sequester the government's case agent. *See 3 Weinstein's Evidence*, §615[02], n. 8 and cases therein cited. The practical and policy concerns inherent in the promulgation of the rule support this view.[2] *See Senate Report [93-1277]*. Thus, we reject defendants' argument. . . . Appellants' convictions are *affirmed*.

D. QUESTIONING BY JUDGE

The Federal Rules of Evidence and most of their state counterparts expressly authorize trial judges to call their own witnesses and to interrogate wit-nesses called by the parties. But as the case excerpted below illustrates, judges risk reversal when they ask questions that seem to reveal their own assessment of the evidence. The underlying idea is that jurors must be shielded from the views of judges, because they would defer improperly to those views. In particular, appellate courts expect trial judges to avoid revealing what they think about witnesses; otherwise, it is feared, we will sacrifice the principle that juries, not judges, should be assessing credibility.

---

2. We are not holding however, that the rule withdraws all discretion from the trial court to exclude a case agent in an exceptional case. Because this is not such a special circumstance, we need not decide the point.

Those expectations and assumptions are thoroughly ingrained in most practicing lawyers and judges. They explain not only why questioning by judges can be reversible error, but also why most states no longer permit judges to comment directly on the evidence, and why even judges who *are* permitted to comment on the evidence—such as those in federal court and in California state courts—risk reversal if their remarks are too pointed. Judges used to have far more freedom to comment on the evidence; they still have that freedom in the United Kingdom. We have grown accustomed to the view that fair trials require judges who keep their thoughts about witnesses largely to themselves, and that the only ones offering juries guidance about whom to believe should be the lawyers. When reading the materials below, ask yourself whether those assumptions are justified.

[F.R.E. 614; C.E.C. §775]

ADVISORY COMMITTEE NOTE TO F.R.E. 614

. . . While exercised more frequently in criminal than in civil cases, the authority of the judge to call witnesses is well established. . . . [T]he judge is not imprisoned within the case as made by the parties.

. . . The authority of the judge to question witnesses is also well established. The authority is, of course, abused when the judge abandons his proper role and assumes that of advocate, but the manner in which interrogation should be conducted and the proper extent of its exercise are not susceptible of formulation in a rule. The omission in no sense precludes courts of review from continuing to reverse for abuse. . . . The provision relating to objections is designed to relieve counsel of the embarrassment attendant upon objecting to questions by the judge in the presence of the jury, while at the same time assuring that objections are made in apt time to afford the opportunity to take possible corrective measures. . . .

UNITED STATES v. TILGHMAN

134 F.3d 414 (D.C. Cir. 1998)

Tatel, Circuit Judge.

Convicted of lying in order to obtain disability benefits, appellant argues that the trial judge's repeated questioning of him prejudiced the jury and denied him a fair trial. . . . [We] reverse and remand for a new trial.

[Tilghman took disability leave from the government in 1983 and the next year incorporated Tilghman Enterprises Ltd. ("TEL"), which bid on federal agency contracts to investigate employment discrimination complaints. To receive disability payment he had to report his earnings each year on Department of Labor Form 1032. For every year but 1991, Tilghman reported no earnings.]

. . . Tilghman testified that he had no intention of defrauding the government. He told the jury that he honestly believed that he had no obligation to report his . . . investigative work on Form 1032 because TEL operated at a loss, because he never received any salary . . . and because a DOL employee told him over the telephone that he could earn up to $300 a month without reporting it.

During the first of Tilghman's two days on the stand, the district judge questioned him extensively in the presence of the jury. Defense counsel offered no objection. On the morning of the second day and before trial began, defense counsel moved for a mistrial, arguing that the judge's questioning influenced the jury and deprived Tilghman of a fair trial. The district judge denied the motion and continued to question Tilghman. Defense counsel objected to four questions and renewed his motion for mistrial at the close of the case. . . .

Rule 614(b) of the Federal Rules of Evidence expressly permits judges to question witnesses. Judges may do so repeatedly and aggressively to clear up confusion and manage trials or where " 'testimony is inarticulately or reluctantly given.' " *United States v. Norris*, 873 F.2d 1519, 1525-26 (D.C. Cir. 1989) (upholding judge's participation in questioning defendant, although perhaps more extensive than it should have been, because it aimed at clarifying evidence) (quoting *United States v. Barbour*, 420 F.2d 1319, 1321 (D.C. Cir. 1969)).

District court authority to question witnesses and manage trials, however, has limits. Because juries, not judges, decide whether witnesses are telling the truth, and because judges wield enormous influence over juries, judges may not ask questions that signal their belief or disbelief of witnesses. *United States v. Wyatt*, 442 F.2d 858, 859-61 (D.C. Cir. 1971) (court's questioning of defendant and his alibi witnesses damaged defendant's credibility and therefore was reversible error). Because such questions can usurp the jury's factfinding function, cast the judge in the role of advocate, and "breach []the atmosphere of judicial evenhandedness that should pervade the courtroom," they can deprive defendants of fair trials. *Barbour*, 420 F.2d at 1321. Judges must therefore strive to preserve an appearance of impartiality and " 'err on the side of [a]bstention from intervention.' " *Norris*, 873 F.2d at 1526. . . . We have reversed when judicial interrogation "may have damaged the appellant's credibility in the eyes of the jury" or "may have given the jury the impression that the judge doubted the defendant's credibility." *Wyatt*, 442 F.2d at 860, 861. We have sustained judicial questioning where the case was not "close" and the issues addressed by the judge were "peripheral to the main issues in the case." *United States v. Mangum*, 100 F.3d 164, 174 (D.C. Cir. 1996).

. . . [W]e need not decide whether the Day Two mistrial motion was sufficiently timely under Rule 614(c) to permit harmless error review of Day One questions. Counsel's objections were timely with respect to all Day Two questions; as the government concedes, moreover, when reviewing Day Two questions we must review the record as a whole, including Day One questions. . . .

. . . Central to his defense, Tilghman asserted that DOL employee Julio Mendez told him in a 1984 telephone call that he had no obligation to report earnings of up to $300 per month. While the prosecution questioned Tilghman about this claim [on Day Two], the following colloquy occurred:

THE COURT:	You didn't put this on any form, did you?
DEFENDANT:	Did I put it on a form? No sir; this was a telephone conversation.
THE COURT:	Did this Julio Mendez put it on a form?
DEFENDANT:	I don't know, sir.
THE COURT:	We just have to take your word for it?
DEF. COUNSEL:	Objection, Your Honor.
THE COURT:	Overruled. Is that right?
DEFENDANT:	I'm sworn to tell the truth, sir.
THE COURT:	I know, but we have to take your word for it; is that right?
DEFENDANT:	I don't know if he has any record of it or not.

Focusing on the absence of any evidence of this phone call, the prosecutor then questioned Tilghman for several transcript pages.

Earlier that same day, while Tilghman described for the jury his understanding of DOL Form 1032, the judge questioned him as follows:

THE COURT:	You were an employee of Tilghman Enterprises?
DEFENDANT:	That is correct, sir.
THE COURT:	Doesn't that fit in the paragraph Employment other than self-Employment? Under this heading, you must report all employment.
DEFENDANT:	For which you receive wages.
DEF. COUNSEL:	Objection, Your Honor.
THE COURT:	It goes on to say if you perform work for which you were not paid, you must show a rate of pay of what it would have cost. You didn't put that in any of them?
DEFENDANT:	I felt that was not applicable, sir, because there was no way to compute those figures.
DEF. COUNSEL:	Your Honor, if I may just renew my objection.
THE COURT:	The objection is over-ruled.
PROSECUTOR:	In other words, Mr. Tilghman, it is your belief that the Department of Labor had to specifically ask you, Okay, Mr. Tilghman, asterisks, we want to know about your corporation?
DEFENDANT:	No. It was my belief that I had to answer carefully, accurately, and honestly; and I did so.

. . . [W]e think these questions "may have given the jury the impression that the judge doubted the defendant's credibility." *Wyatt*, 442 F.2d at 861. The judge's questions could have been particularly damaging because the indictment charged Tilghman with lying, making his credibility unusually critical to his defense. The jury could have interpreted the Mendez question—"[W]e have to take your word for it; is that right?"—as signaling that the judge considered Tilghman's oath irrelevant and his word suspect.

Even the government conceded at oral argument that the judge should not have asked this question, calling it "unfortunate." From the second set of questions, the jury could have inferred that the judge accepted the government's theory of the case that Tilghman should have checked off the "self-employment" box on Form 1032.

Turning to Day One, the judge's questions reinforce our perception that the Day Two questions may have colored the jury's assessment of Tilghman's veracity. For example, as Tilghman explained to the jury how a bank officer had instructed him to fill out a loan application, the following exchange took place:

> *THE COURT:* You're an educated man, aren't you? You have a master's degree, and you did work for a doctorate. Is that right?
> *DEFENDANT:* That's correct, sir.
> *THE COURT:* Now, this is supposed to get a loan from the bank, and you put down as annual income $45,000 and expenditures $14,000. On the basis of that, they were going to give you a loan, right?
> *DEFENDANT:* I would assume so, yes.
> *THE COURT:* And those figures aren't accurate because the chairman of the board told you to put them in. . . .
> *DEFENDANT:* In essence, he did tell me what to put in.
> *THE COURT:* Do you think that any sane bank would give somebody a loan on figures that are totally made up? I mean, as an educated man who's been in business off and on, and government business, private business. Do you think [a] bank would give a loan to somebody on the basis of figures that are just made up by the chairman of the board?

Later on Day One, Tilghman described the bidding process for [employment discrimination] investigative contracts, stating that he and other investigators routinely lost money or broke even:

> *THE COURT:* Other people who [bid] in the same ball park with you, and they all must have lost money, too, is that right?
> *DEFENDANT:* I'm assuming so, sir, yes, sir, because [a] lot of them went out of business.
> *THE COURT:* I see. It's a peculiar business where everybody stays in for years and loses money all the time.
> *DEFENDANT:* All I can—the only thing I know to relate it to—
> *THE COURT:* Wouldn't you agree it's a peculiar business? . . .
> *DEFENDANT:* Not necessarily. I taught for years, and I could have made much more money doing something else.

A moment later, the judge interjected:

> *THE COURT:* Just a minute. Something occurred to me. You were not in the business of making money out of these contracts. You were perfectly content to lose money on these contracts.

DEFENDANT: I was—
THE COURT: You were a philanthropist; you wanted to help these
   people.
DEFENDANT: No, I was hoping I could at least break even.

Like the questions on Day Two, these inquiries could have suggested
to the jury that the judge disbelieved Tilghman. From the first set of questions, particularly the judge's reference to "any sane bank," the jury could
have inferred that the judge thought Tilghman was lying about the basis of
the loan. The judge's reference to philanthropy likewise could have suggested to the jury that he did not believe that Tilghman was losing money, as
he testified. Having heard these Day One questions and the judge's Day Two
challenge to Tilghman's honesty under oath, the jury could well have concluded that the judge considered Tilghman an untruthful witness. . . . Because the jury could reasonably have interpreted the judge's pointed
comments as reflecting his personal disbelief of Tilghman, we cannot
find that the government has "prove[n] beyond a reasonable doubt that
[the judge's commentary] did not contribute to the verdict obtained."
[*Chapman v. California*, 386 U.S. 18, 24 (1967).]
     The government argues that because the judge also asked intrusive ques-
tions of government witnesses and badgered the prosecutor about her handling of exhibits, the jury could have perceived him as evenhanded. The
record shows that the district judge did criticize the prosecution's case, implying, for example, that some government witnesses were unclear, confused, or
inept. After questioning one government witness, the judge said to the prosecutor, "You better ask the questions. I don't know what she's talking about."
To other witnesses he made such comments as: "You have never said just 'no'
or 'yes.' You always go on and on and make a whole speech," 5/15 Tr. at 41,
"Never mind, never mind. You are not helping me," and "Just answer the
question. . . . We don't need an encyclopedia in response to every question."
He also commented on the prosecution's evidence. When granting a defense
objection, for example, he said: "I don't see any relevance whatever. I am
surprised nobody has objected before," and during the prosecution's examination of a character witness he asked, "Are you finished with this line of
questioning? . . . Or are you dredging up some more?" In addition, the judge
criticized the prosecution's inefficient handling of exhibits. "I want to con-
gratulate you," he said at one point, "[t]his is actually marked with a sticker."
     . . . [W]e think the nature of the judge's treatment of the prosecution
differed fundamentally from his questioning of Tilghman. Indeed, comparing the two illustrates the difference between appropriate, active, even
aggressive judicial management and prejudicial judicial questioning. . . . It
is one thing to criticize counsel about exhibits; it is quite another to
question the defendant's credibility on the stand when the central issue
is whether he is telling the truth. The judge's comments on the confusing
quality of government testimony could not possibly undermine the prosecution's case in the same way that his questioning of Tilghman could have
punctured the heart of the defense.
     The government argues finally that the judge's instructions to the jury
cured any improprieties. Having explained that the jury bears sole

responsibility for determining the facts, the district judge instructed the jury as follows:

> And if I say anything about the facts, which normally I don't, you just disregard it because I don't have any responsibility, any obligation on the facts. It's entirely up to you. And if I say something, if I said something in the trial or say something in this closing charge about the facts, you just disregard it because you are [as] much judges on the facts as I am judge on the law. I hope you understand that. And that applies to anything I said in the course of the trial, the questions I may have asked or rulings I may have made, they're all not designed, and you should not take them as being my opinion on the facts because it's your opinion on the facts that counts.

This instruction was too little, too late. Although jury instructions can cure certain irregularities, at least under the plain error standard, we agree with the Second Circuit that where, as here, the trial judge asked questions, objected to by counsel, that could have influenced the jury's assessment of the defendant's veracity, such interference with jury fact-finding cannot be cured by standard jury instructions. *United States v. Filani*, 74 F.3d 378, 386 (2d Cir. 1996). We need not consider whether special instructions or other measures might cure such errors, for none was employed here. . . . [W]e reverse defendant's conviction and remand for a new trial. . . .

E. QUESTIONING BY JURORS

A slowly but steadily increasing number of judges, rebelling against the received wisdom that fairness requires jurors to listen passively throughout the trial, are experimenting with procedures that allow jurors to ask questions of witnesses. But they remain very much in the minority. Most judges, and most trial lawyers, remain deeply uncomfortable with the notion of jurors playing an active role in the trial, even in the most limited of ways. When reading the materials below, ask yourself what accounts for this discomfort, and whether it is justified.

UNITED STATES v. HERNANDEZ

176 F.3d 719 (3d Cir. 1999)

McKee, Circuit Judge.

Julio Hernandez appeals his conviction for conspiring to obstruct interstate commerce by robbery . . . and receiving or possessing goods stolen from commerce. . . . This case arises from the highjacking of a tractor trailer truck containing 494 cases of cigarettes. . . .

We turn first to Hernandez' challenge to the District Court's practice of allowing jurors to participate in questioning witnesses during the course of the trial. The District Court allowed jurors to pose questions by handing the court written questions for the court's review. . . . [T]he court would then allow the attorneys to see the question so that counsel could make whatever objections they deemed appropriate, and the court could thus determine the admissibility and propriety of a question outside the hearing of the jury before asking the question.

One juror did submit a question in this manner. The juror asked: "[w]hat kind of rear doors are on the rear of the trailer?" However, the court did not ask the question of the witness. Rather, the court allowed the attorneys to decide what, if any, response each would make to the question.

The court then gave the following explanation to the jury:

Let me just say with regard to questions that are presented by a witness,—by a juror, it well may be a particular witness who is on the stand at the time may not be the person to whom such a question would be addressed because he may not be a witness who may be in a position to answer the question.

We appreciate having your questions because now the attorneys on both sides know what inquiries you would make and either they may address them through their closing arguments, or they know if they wish to bring any additional witnesses to address the question, that would be up to them.

. . . [Defendant's] challenge to the propriety of allowing juror questioning is an issue of first impression in this circuit. . . . Although we have not previously addressed this issue, several other courts of appeal have. Although those courts have consistently expressed concern over the dangers of the practice, they have refused to adopt a rule prohibiting juror questioning of witnesses during the course of a criminal trial. We take this opportunity to approve of the practice so long as it is done in a manner that insures the fairness of the proceedings, the primacy of the court's stewardship, and the rights of the accused.

. . . In *United States v. Bush*, [47 F.3d 511 (2d Cir. 1995),] jurors directly questioned witnesses, including the defendant. Defense counsel failed to object, and even engaged in a dialogue with the jurors. The practice of allowing such questioning was therefore reviewed for plain error. The court first noted that "[w]e have already held . . . that direct questioning by jurors is a 'matter within the judge's discretion, like witness-questioning by the judge himself.'" The court noted that "[e]very circuit court that has addressed this issue agrees. State courts, moreover, have overwhelmingly placed juror questioning of witnesses within the trial judge's discretion, and indeed its common law roots are deeply entrenched." Nevertheless, the court expressed concern over this practice. "Although we reaffirm our earlier holding . . . that juror questioning of witnesses lies within the trial judge's discretion, we strongly discourage its use." The court listed several dangers endemic to the practice including "turning jurors into advocates, compromising their neutrality," the "risk that jurors will ask prejudicial or otherwise improper questions," and counsel's inability to respond for fear of antagonizing, alienating, or embarrassing a juror. The court noted that

[b]alancing the risk that a juror's question may be prejudicial against the benefit of issue-clarification will almost always lead trial courts to disallow juror questioning, in the absence of extraordinary or compelling circumstances.

However, the court affirmed the conviction because the challenged questioning had been "limited and controlled" and because the defendant could not demonstrate prejudice.

In *United States v. Sutton*, 970 F.2d 1001 (1st Cir. 1992), the court voiced similar concerns about allowing jurors to question witnesses even though the procedure used involved the court asking questions that the jurors had submitted in writing. Once again, the court allowed the practice though it was clearly troubled by it. "Although we think this practice may frequently court unnecessary trouble, we find no error in the circumstances of this case." There, at the beginning of the trial, the trial court had informed the jurors that they could ask questions by handing written questions to the jury foreman who would then give them to the judge. "If your question even possibly could make any legal difference . . . if it's relevant as the lawyers say, I'll ask it for you." On appeal, the court stated:

> Allowing jurors to pose questions during a criminal trial is a procedure fraught with perils. In most cases, the game will not be worth the candle. Nevertheless, we are fully committed to the principle that trial judges should be given wide latitude to manage trials. We are, moreover, supportive of reasoned efforts by the trial bench to improve the truth seeking attributes of the jury system. Consistent with this overall approach, and mindful that the practice . . . may occasionally be advantageous, especially in complex cases and under carefully controlled conditions, we hold that allowing juror-inspired questions in a criminal case is not prejudicial per se, but is a matter committed to the sound discretion of the trial court.

Although the court allowed the practice, it was quick to discourage it. "We hasten to add that the practice, while not forbidden, should be employed sparingly and with great circumspection." The court also added to the list of concerns enunciated in *Bush*, though it acknowledged that the practice could further the search for truth by allowing jurors to clear up confusion. The court also recognized that allowing jurors to participate in questioning could enhance the attentiveness of jurors. Nevertheless, the court concluded "in most situations, the risks inherent in the practice will outweigh its utility."

In *United States v. Ajmal*, [67 F.3d 12, 14 (2d Cir. 1995),] the court did reverse a conviction based upon juror questioning of witnesses [including the defendant himself]. . . . The trial judge there had taken precautions. He had required questions to be in writing, and the court, rather than the attorneys, asked the questions. In addition, the court only asked those questions that it believed were proper under the Federal Rules of Evidence. Nevertheless, the Court of Appeals held that the trial judge had abused his discretion. . . . [A]lthough the court was once again concerned with the practice of allowing juror questioning absent circumstances sufficient to justify the risk inherent in the procedure, the court . . . based its reversal upon the trial court's encouragement of such questioning, and the frequency with which jurors had accepted the judge's invitation.

Here, the court received only one question from the jury. It was a fact question that was not even asked. We do not think that one fact question which is submitted to a judge in writing, but not even asked, can be labeled an abuse of discretion. . . .

We agree that a trial judge who allows . . . questioning [by jurors] in a given case should adopt a procedure to first screen the questions. However, we conclude that the danger of allowing jurors to ask questions orally far outweighs any perceived benefit of allowing juror questioning of witnesses. Thus, the judge should ask any juror-generated questions, and he or she should do so only after allowing attorneys to raise any objection out of the hearing of the jury.

The procedure utilized here is consistent with our admonitions and consistent with the sound exercise of judicial discretion. The court did not surrender its discretion as to whether to allow a given question to be asked, and the judge, not the attorneys (and certainly not the jurors), was to have asked any questions posed by a juror. This procedure is consistent with the holding of every court of appeals that has addressed this issue. We hold that the trial judge did not abuse her discretion. . . . [Reversed on other grounds.]

STATE v. FISHER

789 N.E.2d 222 (Ohio 2003)

Moyer, C.J.

Defendant-appellant, Michael A. Fisher, appeals from the judgment of the Tenth District Court of Appeals, which affirmed his conviction for felonious assault with a firearm specification. . . .

Prior to the presentation of evidence, the trial court informed the jurors that they would be permitted to ask questions of the witnesses that testified at trial. The trial judge instructed the jurors to submit their questions in writing to the bailiff, whereupon the judge and the attorneys would review the questions in a sidebar conference. The trial judge would then determine whether the questions were admissible under the rules of evidence and would read the admissible questions aloud to the witnesses.

In accordance with the foregoing procedure, the jurors submitted 23 questions to six of the eight witnesses that testified at trial. The trial court disallowed five questions on evidentiary grounds and rephrased two questions for clarification. After reading a juror question, the trial court allowed the prosecution and defense counsel an opportunity to ask follow-up questions. Although defense counsel did not object to the particular questions that were read to the witnesses, counsel entered a continuing objection to the general practice of allowing jurors to submit questions. . . .

Every federal circuit that has addressed the issue has concluded that the practice of allowing jurors to question witnesses is a matter within the discretion of the trial court. Several of the federal circuits, however, discourage the practice. . . . The vast majority of state courts have also concluded that juror questioning is a matter committed to the sound discretion of the trial court. . . . Nevertheless, several jurisdictions permit juror questioning only where procedural safeguards are employed. Other jurisdictions have relegated the procedure by which jurors submit questions to the discretion of the trial court.

Only five jurisdictions prohibit jurors from questioning witnesses. . . . Among these jurisdictions, however, Georgia, Mississippi, and Nebraska have concluded that such error may be either forfeited or harmless beyond a reasonable doubt. . . . [O]nly two states—Texas and Minnesota—have held that juror questioning is not subject to harmless error analysis. . . .

The hallmark of the American trial is the pursuit of truth. Such truth—and, in the end, justice—is attainable only if counsel successfully communicates evidence to the jury. History has nonetheless relegated the jury to a passive role that dictates a one-way communication system—a system that, in its traditional form, is not amenable to resolving juror confusion. The practice of allowing jurors to question witnesses provides for two-way communication through which jurors can more effectively fulfill their fundamental role as factfinders.

In *United States v. Callahan*, 588 F.2d at 1086 [1979], the United States Court of Appeals for the Fifth Circuit articulated the paramount benefit of such communication: "There is nothing improper about the practice of allowing occasional questions from jurors to be asked of witnesses. If a juror is unclear as to a point in the proof, it makes good common sense to allow a question to be asked about it. If nothing else, the question should alert trial counsel that a particular factual issue may need more extensive development. Trials exist to develop truth. It may sometimes be that counsel are so familiar with a case that they fail to see problems that would naturally bother a juror who is presented with the facts for the first time."

Juror questioning not only enhances the ability of jurors to discern truth but also may provide counsel an opportunity to better comprehend jurors' thought processes and their perception of case weaknesses. Recognizing a similar advantage of juror questioning, the . . . Court of Appeals for the District of Columbia has observed: "Questions by jurors also may bring to the court's and counsel's attention *improper* concerns which can be promptly addressed with cautionary instructions, admonishing the juror who asked the question that the matter is not relevant to the case and should not be brought to the attention of other jurors or play any part in the inquiring juror's consideration of the case." *Yeager* [*v. Greene*, 502 A.2d 980, 998 (D.C. 1985).]

Furthermore, the practice of allowing jurors to question witnesses may increase juror attentiveness at trial. The D.C. Court of Appeals, acknowledging such a benefit, has observed that "there is reason to believe that permitting receivers of information, *e.g.*, jurors, to ask questions enhances not only their ability to understand what is being communicated, but results in their putting forth more effort to listen and to understand because they *know* they may ask questions. A concomitant benefit predictable from these effects might well be a reduced likelihood that the court will be required to intervene to question witnesses or elucidate issues that are clarified by juror questions." [*Id.* at 998-1000.]

Finally, empirical research suggests that jurors who are allowed to question witnesses are more satisfied with their service and more confident with their verdicts. As one Ohio jurist has noted, "Allowing jurors to ask questions makes jurors feel more like a part of the judiciary, and less like helpless outsiders trying to penetrate a sanctimonious institution. This type of change can only bring us closer to the ultimate goal of our legal system: justice." Valen, Jurors Asking Questions: Revolutionary or Evolutionary? (1993), 20 N. Ky. L. Rev. 423, 439.

Although we are cognizant of the potential benefits of juror questioning, we are also mindful of the concerns associated with the practice. Courts have identified four principal dangers inherent in juror questioning: (1) jurors may submit inadmissible questions, (2) counsel may refrain from objecting to improper questions for fear of offending jurors, (3) juror interruptions may disrupt courtroom decorum, and (4) such questioning may distort juror impartiality. The extent to which these dangers affect the trial process depends, in great part, upon the manner in which such questioning is conducted.

In the instant case, the procedural safeguards applied by the trial court operated to circumvent many of the foregoing dangers. These safeguards included (1) requiring the jurors to submit their questions in writing to the court, whereupon the judge could review and exclude improper questions, (2) providing counsel an opportunity to object at sidebar, thereby eliminating the danger that a juror would be affronted by an objection, and (3) specifying the precise time at which jurors should submit questions to prevent interference with attorney questioning and courtroom decorum.

The final concern associated with juror questioning lies in the potential distortion of the adversary system. Appellant argues that "by allowing jurors to question witnesses, the role of the jury is fundamentally changed" from neutral factfinder to partial advocate. Such an argument, however, rests on the erroneous premise that one must be passive to be impartial. To the contrary, [Ohio] Evid. R. 614(B) expressly authorizes the trial court—the factfinder in a bench trial—to "interrogate witnesses, in an impartial manner, whether called by itself or by a party." Consequently, the ability of a factfinder to question witnesses is not inconsistent with the duty of impartiality. . . .

The issue of whether juror questions are aimed at advocacy rather than clarification cannot be answered in the abstract, but instead requires courts to examine the nature of each question in the overall context of a trial. We conclude that the trial court is in the best position to render such a determination and, within its sound discretion, disallow improper juror questions. . . .

To minimize the danger of prejudice, however, trial courts that permit juror questioning should (1) require jurors to submit their questions to the court in writing, (2) ensure that jurors do not display or discuss a question with other jurors until the court reads the question to the witness, (3) provide counsel an opportunity to object to each question at sidebar or outside the presence of the jury, (4) instruct jurors that they should not draw adverse inferences from the court's refusal to allow certain questions, and (5) allow counsel to ask follow-up questions of the witnesses.

Our nation's profound commitment to trial by jury is founded on competing principles that, in one sense, foster the development of truth and, in another sense, stifle it. Such is the great paradox of the criminal justice system. To balance these principles in the assortment of cases with which a trial court is faced—dissimilar as one case is from another—appellate courts generally defer to the discretion of the trial court, rather than attempting to account for the infinite array of circumstances that may arise with a categorical rule. A less prudent approach would eviscerate that discretion at the first sign of abuse—or, worse yet, at the mere potential for it. . . .

[W]e hold that the decision to allow jurors to question witnesses is a matter within the discretion of the trial court and should not be disturbed on appeal absent an abuse of that discretion. The judgment of the court of appeals is affirmed.

IMPEACHMENT AND REHABILITATION

"Your witness"

A. INTRODUCTION

Impeachment and rehabilitation are ways in which evidence can be relevant. Evidence qualifies as impeachment if it is relevant because it suggests that a certain witness lacks credibility and therefore that his or her testimony should be disregarded. Evidence qualifies as rehabilitation if it is relevant because it rebuts impeachment evidence—i.e., because it suggests that a witness who has been impeached is in fact credible and should be believed. Impeachment and rehabilitation evidence is subject to all the rules of evidence examined elsewhere in this book, and also to some special restrictions, which are the subject of this chapter.

It is important not to confuse impeachment and rehabilitation with cross-examination and redirect examination. Much, perhaps most, impeachment goes on in cross-examination, and much, perhaps most, rehabilitation occurs in redirect examination. But cross-examination is often used for purposes other than impeachment, and redirect examination is often used for purposes other than rehabilitation. Lawyers often use cross-examination, for example, to elicit information that is helpful to their clients and that does not involve discrediting the witness; redirect examination is often used not to rehabilitate the witness, but to bring out additional facts known to the witness that are helpful to the party that called the witness. And just as cross-examination is not limited to impeachment and redirect examination is not limited to rehabilitation, so impeachment is not limited to cross-examination, and rehabilitation can occur outside of redirect examination.

As the materials below explain, there are special terms for distinguishing between, on the one hand, impeachment or rehabilitation that occurs through the testimony of the witness being impeached or rehabilitated, and, on the other hand, impeachment or rehabilitation that occurs through the use of other evidence—i.e., physical exhibits, or testimony from other witnesses. There are special terms, too, for distinguishing between different "modes" of impeachment—between, that is to say, different kinds of facts that can undermine the credibility of a witness. All of this terminology turns out to be important, because—as we will see later in this chapter—several of the special rules for impeachment and rehabilitation vary in their application depending on the manner and mode of attacking a witness's credibility.

[F.R.E. 607, 806; C.E.C. §§780, 785, 1202]

McCORMICK ON EVIDENCE

§33 (Kenneth S. Broun, ed., 6th ed. 2006)

There are five main modes of attack upon a witness's credibility. The first, and probably most frequently employed, is self contradiction. That technique consists of proof that the witness on a previous occasion has made statements inconsistent with his present testimony. The second is an attack showing that the witness is partial on account of emotional influences such as kinship for one party or hostility to another, or motives of pecuniary interest, whether legitimate or corrupt. The third is an attack on the witness's character, but lack of religious belief is not available as a basis of attack on credibility. The fourth is an attack showing a defect of the witness's capacity to observe, remember, or recount the matters testified about. The fifth is specific contradiction, that is, proof by other witnesses that material facts are otherwise than as testified to by the witness being impeached. Some of these attacks, such as bias, are not specifically or completely treated by the Federal or Revised Uniform Rules of Evidence, but nevertheless they are authorized by those rules. Article VI of the Federal Rules contains several provisions expressly regulating impeachment techniques such as proof of prior inconsistent statements, and the proof of other facts logically relevant to witness credibility is governed by the general analytic framework set out in Federal Rules 401-03.

The process of impeachment may proceed in two different stages. First, the facts discrediting the witness of his testimony may be elicited from the witness himself on cross-examination. A good faith basis for the inquiry is required. Certain modes of attack are limited to this stage; the shorthand expression is, "You must take his answer." When the mode of attack is limited in this manner, the cross-examiner is sometimes said to be restricted to "intrinsic" impeachment. Second, in other situations, the facts discrediting the witness may be proved by extrinsic evidence; the assailant waits until the time for putting on his own case in rebuttal, and then proves by a second witness or documentary evidence, the facts discrediting the testimony of the witness attacked.

. . . In general, today there is less emphasis on impeachment of witnesses today than formerly. The elaborate system of rules regulating impeachment that developed in the past is now applied with less strictness. The system has been simplified by relying less on rules and more on judicial discretion. Again, Article VI of the Federal Rules contains only a handful of provisions expressly regulating impeachment techniques. In the case of all other impeachment techniques, a federal judge applies the general relevancy principles codified in Federal Rules 401-03.

B. CHARACTER FOR UNTRUTHFULNESS

The following materials address the special rules that govern impeachment for dishonesty—or, as the federal rules put it, "untruthfulness." This mode of impeachment is a variety of character evidence, because it involves proving the character of a person—in this case, a witness—in order to suggest that the person likely acted in conformity with his or her character on a particular occasion—in this case, that the witness has lied because it is his or her nature to lie. As we saw in Chapter Four, the character evidence rule generally prohibits this kind of proof. There is a traditional exception to the character evidence rule for evidence used to impeach a witness. But that exception, codified in F.R.E. 404(a)(3), carries with it some important limitations.

1. In General

[F.R.E. 608, 610; C.E.C. §§786-787, 789]

ADVISORY COMMITTEE NOTE TO F.R.E. 608

In Rule 404(a) the general position is taken that character evidence is not admissible for the purpose of proving that the person acted in conformity therewith, subject, however, to several exceptions, one of which is character evidence of a witness as bearing upon his credibility. The present rule develops that exception.

In accordance with the bulk of judicial authority, the inquiry is strictly limited to character for veracity, rather than allowing evidence as to character generally. The result is to sharpen relevancy, to reduce surprise, waste of time, and confusion, and to make the lot of the witness somewhat less unattractive.

The use of opinion and reputation evidence as means of proving the character of witnesses is consistent with Rule 405(a). While the modern practice has purported to exclude opinion, witnesses who testify to reputation seem in fact often to be giving their opinions, disguised somewhat misleadingly as reputation. And even under the modern practice, a common relaxation has allowed inquiry as to whether the witnesses would believe the principal witness under oath.

. . . In conformity with Rule 405, which forecloses use of evidence of specific incidents as proof in chief of character unless character is an issue in the case, the present rule generally bars evidence of specific instances of conduct of a witness for the purpose of attacking or supporting his credibility. . . . Conviction of crime as a technique of impeachment is treated in detail in Rule 609, and here is merely recognized as an exception to the general rule excluding evidence of specific incidents for impeachment purposes. Particular instances of conduct, though not the subject of criminal conviction, may be inquired into on cross-examination of the principal witness himself or of a witness who testifies concerning his character for truthfulness. Effective cross-examination demands that some allowance be made for going into matters of this kind, but the possibilities of abuse are substantial. Consequently safeguards are erected in the form of specific requirements that the instances inquired into be probative of truthfulness or its opposite and not remote in time. Also, the overriding protection of Rule 403 requires that probative value not be outweighed by danger of unfair prejudice, confusion of issues, or misleading the jury, and that of Rule 611 bars harassment and undue embarrassment. . . .

ADVISORY COMMITTEE NOTE TO F.R.E. 610

While the rule forecloses inquiry into the religious beliefs or opinions of a witness for the purpose of showing that his character for truthfulness is affected by their nature, an inquiry for the purpose of showing interest or bias because of them is not within the prohibition. Thus disclosure of affiliation with a church which is a party to the litigation would be allowable under the rule. . . .

UNITED STATES v. LOLLAR

606 F.2d 587 (5th Cir. 1979)

JAMES C. HILL, Circuit Judge:

Howard Lollar appeals from his conviction for interstate transportation of stolen property valued in excess of $5,000, 18 U.S.C.A. § 2314. The property was alleged to have been stolen by appellant and several of his employees from a warehouse in West Milford, New Jersey. We affirm.

After appellant testified at trial, the government recalled one of its witnesses and asked him whether he would believe appellant under oath. Defense counsel's objection was overruled, and the witness, a former employer, answered the question in the negative. Appellant now argues that it was error to allow the witness to offer his opinion on appellant's veracity.

Although a criminal defendant cannot be compelled to take the stand in his own defense, once he chooses to testify "he places his credibility in issue as does any other witness." *United States v. Jackson*, 588 F.2d 1046, 1055 (5th Cir. 1979). While the defendant's decision to testify does not open the door to attacks on his general character, it does free the government to offer evidence bearing on the defendant's believability as a witness. Historically, the most widely used method of impeaching a defendant's credibility was to call witnesses to testify that the defendant's reputation for truth and veracity was bad. The propriety of asking a more direct question, such as "would you believe this person under oath," caused a great deal of conflict among the courts and the commentators. Early cases in this Circuit adopted the position that such testimony could be used to impeach a witness' credibility. *See Miller v. United States*, 288 F. 816, 818 (5th Cir. 1923); *Held v. United States*, 260 F. 932, 933 (5th Cir. 1919). While this was the minority view among the courts, many commentators agreed that "the exclusion of opinion evidence was 'historically unsound.'" 3 Weinstein's Evidence ¶ 608 [04], at 608-20 (1978); *see* McCormick, Evidence § 44, at 95 (1954); 7 Wigmore, Evidence §§ 1981-1986 (3d ed. 1940); Ladd, Techniques of Character Testimony, 24 Iowa L. Rev. 498, 509-13 (1939). This conflict was resolved in 1976 with the enactment of Rule 608(a) of the Federal Rules of Evidence. . . .

> Witnesses may now be asked directly to state their opinion of the principal witness' character for truthfulness and they may answer for example, "I think X is a liar." The rule imposes no prerequisite conditioned upon long acquaintance or recent information about the witness; cross-examination can be expected to expose defects of lack of familiarity and to reveal reliance on isolated or irrelevant instances of misconduct or the existence of feelings of personal hostility towards the principal witness.

Weinstein's Evidence ¶ 608[04], at 608-20 (1978).

Accordingly, we hold that the district court was acting well within its discretion in overruling defense counsel's objection. . . . AFFIRMED.

UNITED STATES v. ROSA

891 F.2d 1063 (3d Cir. 1989)

STAPLETON, Circuit Judge:

[Joseph Rosa and 27 other defendants were charged with cocaine trafficking in a 113-count indictment. All but two of the defendants, Kostrick and Romano, pleaded guilty. Rosa testified for the government.]

Kostrick and Romano both contend that the district court improperly prohibited their cross-examination of Joseph Rosa . . . regarding certain prior criminal conduct because Rosa had not been convicted for that conduct. This simply did not occur. The record reveals that the trial judge, in accordance with Federal Rules of Evidence 608 and 609, prohibited defendants' attorneys from questioning Rosa about criminal conduct for which he had not been convicted because that conduct was not probative of truthfulness or untruthfulness. The judge permitted defense counsel to question Rosa concerning his conspiratorial oath of loyalty to his crime family to the extent that it bore on truthfulness. Similarly, the trial judge correctly allowed cross-examination concerning a fraudulent insurance claim Rosa had filed, since fraud is one of the offenses that bears on a witness's credibility. The only subject on which the trial judge prohibited cross-examination was Rosa's alleged involvement in a bribe of public officials in connection with his insurance fraud. Bribery, however, is not the kind of conduct which bears on truthfulness or untruthfulness. Moreover, even if we regarded bribery as minimally probative of those matters, given the extensive examination permitted on the underlying fraud, we could not say that the trial judge abused his discretion in limiting cross-examination with respect to Rosa's alleged bribery. . . . The judgments with respect to Kostrick and Romano will be affirmed. . . .

UNITED STATES v. LING

581 F.2d 1118 (4th Cir. 1978)

BOREMAN, Senior Circuit Judge:

Roger T. Ling, II, was convicted of conspiring to violate the federal narcotics laws, 21 U.S.C. § 846, and manufacturing a Schedule I non-narcotic controlled substance, 21 U.S.C. § 841(a)(1). . . . Ling admitted that he agreed to manufacture an illegal drug known as DMT (dimethyltryptamine) for the "Pagans," a motorcycle gang. . . . Ling took the witness stand in his own defense and testified that although he did participate in the manufacture of the drug, he intended to sabotage that manufacture before it was completed. Evidence adduced at trial showed that Ling was not popular with the Pagans and, in fact, his apartment had been burglarized by them and he had been severely beaten by them. On direct examination Ling admitted that he had an extensive gun collection and that he sometimes carried a gun, but he denied ever shooting anyone or using his guns to threaten anyone. Ling also testified that he did not drink alcoholic beverages because of an allergy. However, he did admit on direct examination that he did "drink on occasion."

On cross-examination, in an attempt to impeach defendant's credibility, the prosecutor asked Ling if he ever fired any of his guns on a public street and Ling answered "never." Based upon Ling's denial, the government introduced rebuttal testimony from Officer McKenny, a Baltimore police officer, who testified that he had arrested Ling for discharging a firearm in a public place, possession of a handgun and driving while under the influence of alcohol. According to Officer McKenny's testimony, Ling was given a breathalyzer test at the time of his arrest on these charges which test indicated a .04 reading and the drunk driving charge was subsequently dismissed. Officer McKenny also testified that Ling at all times denied firing a gun, the charge of discharging a firearm was dismissed and defendant received "probation before judgment" as to the charge of possession of a handgun a disposition that carries no penalty and is not considered a conviction under Maryland law.

. . . It is a well-settled rule that a defendant who voluntarily offers himself as a witness and testifies in his own behalf subjects himself to legitimate and pertinent cross-examination to test his veracity and credibility. However, when a defendant is cross-examined for the purpose of impeaching his credibility by proof of specific acts of past misconduct not the subject of a conviction, the examiner must be content with the witness' answer. The examiner may not, over objection, produce independent proof to show the falsity of such answer. This court has summarized the no extrinsic evidence rule by stating "the interrogator is bound by [the witness'] answers and may not contradict him." *United States v. Whiting*, 311 F.2d 191, 196 (4 Cir. 1962), *cert. denied*, 372 U.S. 935 (1963). Although the cross-examiner may continue to press the defendant for an admission, he cannot call other witnesses to prove the misconduct after defendant's denial. In the instant case the prosecutor should have accepted Ling's answer that he never fired a gun on a public street and should not have attempted to impeach defendant's credibility on this collateral issue by use of the police officer's rebuttal testimony.[2] . . . The introduction of the police officer's rebuttal testimony violated well-established rules of evidence and interjected an inflammatory collateral issue into Ling's trial. We conclude, in all fairness, that the appellant is entitled to a new trial. . . .

2. Although Ling's trial took place before the effective date of the new Federal Rules of Evidence, the new Rules would also have prohibited the introduction of the police officer's rebuttal testimony. . . .

UNITED STATES v. WHITE

972 F.2d 590 (5th Cir. 1992)

W. EUGENE DAVIS, Circuit Judge:

John Sennett White and John Michael Wilson appeal their convictions on charges of possession with intent to distribute cocaine and conspiracy to commit the same offense. . . . White and Wilson sought to invoke Rule 404(b), along with Rules 405(b) and 406, to introduce evidence of extrinsic offenses committed by Northcutt, the government's star witness. They proffered testimony by Northcutt's prior attorney that Northcutt had previously offered to fabricate testimony against an individual in exchange for government leniency in charges pending against him.

The defendants argue that Northcutt's testimony was admissible under Rule 404(b) to show Northcutt's intent to fabricate evidence in order to gain favorable consideration from the government in his own case. The district court, relying on Rule 608(b), ruled that the defendants could elicit the evidence of Northcutt's credibility only on cross-examination of Northcutt, not through an extrinsic source. We agree.

. . . [E]xcept for his credibility, Northcutt's intent was not an issue in the case. . . . This evidence could have served only one function: to demonstrate that Northcutt had a proclivity to lie and therefore was probably lying in this case. Rule 404(b) prohibits the use of extrinsic act evidence for this purpose. The use of evidence to attack a witness's credibility is subject to the limitations of Rule 608. Under that rule, specific instances of misconduct of a witness for that purpose can not be proved by extrinsic evidence. The trial court did not abuse its discretion by excluding the proffered testimony. . . . [Reversed in part on other grounds.]

UNITED STATES v. APONTE

31 F.3d 86 (2d Cir. 1994)

WINTER, Circuit Judge:

Michael Aponte appeals from a conviction and sentence entered by Judge Dominick L. DiCarlo, following a jury trial. The jury convicted Aponte of conspiracy to rob a United States Postal Service truck, in violation of 18 U.S.C. § 371, and aiding and abetting the armed robbery of a Postal Service truck, in violation of 18 U.S.C. §§ 2, 2114. . . . [W]ith regard to the exclusion as hearsay of a sworn statement containing fabrications by government witness Gregory Quiles and of other documents giving false descriptions of "robbers" provided by Quiles, the district court may have applied the wrong evidentiary rule, but the statements were nevertheless properly excluded. Quiles' fabricated statement and false descriptions were not offered for the truth of the matter asserted and therefore were not hearsay. Fed. R. Evid. 801(c). Rather, the documents were offered to show Quiles' capacity for deception. However, the statements were excludable as extrinsic evidence of the character and conduct of Quiles. "Specific instances of the conduct of a witness, for the purpose of attacking or supporting the witness' credibility . . . may not be proved by extrinsic evidence." Fed. R. Evid. 608(b). . . . AFFIRMED.

PROBLEMS

7.1. If the defendant in a tax fraud prosecution testifies in her own defense, can the government ask her on cross-examination about a deceptive resume she sent to a prospective employer ten years ago? Under what circumstances, if any, can the government introduce the resume itself?

7.2. Suppose the defendant chooses not to testify but calls a character witness who testifies that he knows the defendant well and that she is "upright and extremely ethical." Can the government ask the witness whether he knows about the deceptive resume? Under what circumstances, if any, can the government introduce the resume itself?

7.3. In a prosecution of Gerald for bank robbery, Gerald's neighbor Max testifies that Gerald boasted of carrying out the robbery. Gerald later testifies he had nothing to do with the robbery, and he denies boasting about it. On cross-examination of Gerald, the prosecutor seeks to elicit that Gerald knew about, and did nothing to stop, a plan by Gerald's business associate Oscar to threaten to disclose that Max was sexually abused as a child if Max testified against Gerald. Defense counsel objects to this line of cross-examination. How should the judge rule?

7.4. Harry Potter is on trial at the Ministry of Magic for unauthorized use of magic by an underage sorcerer. Potter claims he acted in self-defense. The chief defense witness, Albus Dumbledore, is asked whether Potter previously tried to cover up his use of magic on a different occasion by falsely claiming that the magic was performed by an elf. Dumbledore says the elf was in fact responsible for the magic and would admit it if called to court to testify. The court disallows the elf's testimony. Would that be the right result under the Federal Rules of Evidence? See J.K. Rowling, *Harry Potter and the Order of the Phoenix* 139-149 (2003).

2. Prior Criminal Convictions

The upshot of the general rules regarding impeachment for dishonesty is that a witness can be impeached with evidence that it is in his or her nature to be deceitful, but not by extrinsic evidence of specific acts of dishonesty. The ban on impeachment with extrinsic evidence of specific acts of deception is waived, though, for certain criminal convictions. Which criminal convictions? The answer given by common-law courts was "felonies." But the modern, federal rule is more complicated.

a. Admissible and Inadmissible Convictions

[F.R.E. 609; C.E.C. §788]

UNITED STATES v. WONG

703 F.2d 65 (3d Cir. 1983)

PER CURIAM:

This case presents the issue whether a district court has any discretion to exclude, as unduly prejudicial, evidence that a witness had previously been convicted of a crime involving dishonesty or false statement. The district court held that it had no discretion to weight the probative value of the prior conviction against its prejudicial effect. Agreeing with every other circuit to consider the matter, we affirm.

John Barry Wong was charged with seventeen counts of violation of the mail fraud statute, 18 U.S.C. § 1341 (1976), and two counts of violation of the Racketeer Influenced and Corrupt Organizations statute, 18 U.S.C. §§ 1961-68 (1976 & Supp. V 1981). A jury found him guilty on all counts, and he was sentenced to seven years' imprisonment followed by five years' probation and ordered to make restitution of $100,000.

Wong had previously been convicted at least twice—a 1978 mail fraud conviction in a federal court in Pennsylvania and a 1981 Medicare fraud conviction in a federal court in Hawaii. At trial in this case, prior to putting his client on the stand, counsel for Wong moved to preclude use of these convictions for impeachment. The trial court stated that the probative value of the convictions did not outweigh their prejudicial effect. The trial court held, however, that since the two convictions were crimes involving dishonesty or false statement [so-called *crimen falsi*], under Fed. R. Evid. 609(a)(2) no balancing of prejudice against probative value was appropriate. Wong then took the stand; during his cross-examination the two convictions were introduced against him.

Wong now attacks as erroneous the legal conclusion of the trial judge that *crimen falsi* under Fed. R. Evid. 609(a)(2) are admissible as impeachment without reference to their prejudicial effect.

. . . Rule 609(a) differentiates on its face between convictions for crimes punishable by imprisonment of more than one year, which are admissible under 609(a)(1), and convictions for *crimen falsi*, which are admissible under 609(a)(2). The former may be admitted only if the trial court determines that their probative value outweighs their prejudicial effect. The latter simply "shall be admitted."

Wong suggests that the apparently mandatory admission of *crimen falsi* under Fed. R. Evid. 609(a)(2) is qualified by the general balancing test of Fed. R. Evid. 403. Wong asserts that the trial court therefore has the power to exclude *crimen falsi* convictions if it determines that their probative force is substantially outweighed by their prejudicial effect.

We disagree. As the First Circuit has recently noted, Rule 403 was not designed to override more specific rules; rather it was "designed as a guide for the handling of situations for which no specific rules have been formulated." *United States v. Kiendra*, 663 F.2d 349, 354 (1st Cir. 1981) (quoting Fed. R. Evid. 403 advisory committee note). Rule 609(a) is such a specific rule. It was the product of extensive Congressional attention and considerable legislative compromise, clearly reflecting a decision that judges were to have no discretion to exclude *crimen falsi.*

In an earlier draft, Rule 609 included a subsection, 609(a)(3), which would have allowed the court to exclude either convictions carrying an imprisonment of more than one year or *crimen falsi* convictions if it determined that their probative value was substantially outweighed by their prejudicial effect. Subsection (a)(3) was described as a particularized application of Rule 403.

Proposed section 609(a)(3) was severely criticized by Senator McClellan of Arkansas on the floor of the Senate. Thereafter, when the Supreme Court officially promulgated the Federal Rules of Evidence and transmitted them to the Congress, section 609(a)(3) had disappeared; at that point there was no reference in the section to any weighing by the trial judge of probative value against prejudicial effect.

Rule 609(a) then came under considerable scrutiny in Congress. Various ways of treating impeachment by conviction were proposed. The compromise that resulted in the final version of Rule 609(a) came in the Conference Committee and was described in the following terms by the Chairman of the Subcommittee on Criminal Justice of the House Judiciary Committee:

> The House version of the rule permitted the use of convictions for crimes of dishonesty or false statement. The Senate version permitted the use of convictions for any felony or for any crime of dishonesty or false statement. . . .
>
> The conference rule strikes a middle ground between the two versions, but a ground as close or closer to the House version than to the Senate's. *The conference rule provides that evidence of a conviction of a crime involving dishonesty or false statement may always be used to impeach.* . . . This constitutes no change from either the House or Senate version. The conference rule further provides that evidence of a prior felony conviction may be used for impeachment but only if the court determines that the probative value of the conviction outweighs its prejudicial effect to the defendant.

120 Cong. Rec. 40,891 (1974) (Statement of Rep. Hungate presenting the Conference Report on H.R. 5463 to the House for final consideration) (emphasis added).

The Conference Report is likewise clear:

> The admission of prior convictions involving dishonesty and false statement is not within the discretion of the Court. Such convictions are peculiarly probative of credibility and, under this rule, are always to be admitted.

H.R. Rep. No. 1597, 93d Cong., 2d. Sess. 9.

Thus the legislative history of Rule 609(a)(2) unambiguously demonstrates that a judge has no authority to prohibit the government's effort to impeach the credibility of a witness by questions concerning a prior *crimen falsi* conviction. In light of this clear Congressional judgment we hold that the general balancing test of Fed. R. Evid. 403 is not applicable to impeachment by *crimen falsi* convictions under Fed. R. Evid. 609(a)(2). The judgment of the district court will be affirmed.

UNITED STATES v. AMAECHI

991 F.2d 374 (7th Cir. 1993)

CUMMINGS, Circuit Judge.

[Defendant Ihuoma Amaechi was convicted of narcotics trafficking based on evidence that he had taken delivery of suitcase containing half a kilogram of heroin. Among the prosecution witnesses was Doreen Bennett, who had taken the suitcase to Amaechi.]

Defendant . . . suggests that the court erred in excluding evidence of Doreen Bennett's conviction for shoplifting. Bennett pleaded guilty on April 19, 1989 in Cook County Circuit Court to stealing less than $150, a misdemeanor, and was sentenced to a three-month term of supervision. Federal Rule of Evidence 609 allows evidence of a witness's prior conviction for impeachment if, among other things, the punishment could have exceeded one year (Bennett's did not), or if the crime involves dishonesty or false statement no matter how long the sentence. . . . Illinois law clearly contemplates that a sentence of supervision does not constitute a conviction for evidentiary purposes. *People v. Schuning*, 476 N.E.2d 423, 426 (Ill. 1985); *see also People v. Leeks*, 492 N.E.2d 920, 923 (Ill. 1986). Since Bennett's shoplifting did not result in a conviction, it may not be admitted to attack her credibility under Rule 609(a)(2).

The government also urges us to adopt the reasoning of nine circuits that shoplifting is not a crime of dishonesty unless committed in a fraudulent or deceitful manner. Shoplifting, of course, does involve dishonesty of a certain kind; the question is whether it involves the kind contemplated by Congress in drafting the Rules of Evidence—i.e., whether it indicates that a person may be more likely to commit perjury. The calculus underlying this realm of evidence law—that people who lie in other contexts are more likely to perjure themselves than people who steal—is empirically questionable on a number of levels. Some people who falsify forms, for example, would stop short of committing the crime of perjury, while many thieves may be incorrigible liars. Yet the drafters of the Rules of Evidence explicitly intended that Rule 609 be limited to crimes involving "some element of misrepresentation or other indication of a propensity to lie and excluding those crimes which, bad though they are, do not carry with them a tinge of falsification." [*United States v. Ortega*, 561 F.2d 803, 806 (9th Cir. 1977).] Having made the initial questionable assumption that some people are more given to perjury than others based on past conduct, we agree with nine other circuits that to include shoplifting as a crime of dishonesty would swallow the rule and allow any past crime to be admitted for impeachment purposes. Therefore, we hold that petty shoplifting does not in and of itself quality as a crime of dishonesty under Rule 609. The district judge correctly prohibited Amaechi's counsel from impeaching Bennett with her shoplifting conviction. . . . [Defendant's conviction is affirmed.]

UNITED STATES v. SANDERS

964 F.2d 295 (4th Cir. 1992)

PHILLIPS, Circuit Judge:

Carlos Sanders appeals his convictions for assault with a dangerous weapon with intent to do bodily harm in violation of 18 U.S.C. § 113(c), and for possession of contraband (a shank used in the assault) in violation of Virginia Code § 53.1-203(4), as assimilated by 18 U.S.C. § 13. . . . Sanders and Ricky Alston, both inmates at Lorton Reformatory, were indicted for . . . assaulting fellow inmate Bobby Jenkins with a shank on April 7, 1989.

Before trial, Sanders filed a motion *in limine* to exclude evidence of his prior convictions. Although the district court granted this motion in part by prohibiting the government from questioning Sanders about a stabbing for which he was acquitted and an armed robbery for which his conviction was reversed, the court declined to preclude the government from cross-examining Sanders about his prior assault and contraband possession convictions. The court ruled that the assault and contraband convictions were admissible under Federal Rules of Evidence 609(a) and 404(b).

After hearing the evidence, the jury acquitted Alston on the assault count and convicted Sanders of possession of a shank. The jury was unable to reach a verdict on the assault count against Sanders, however. . . . [In a subsequent retrial,] Sanders testified that he had acted in self-defense, claiming that Jenkins had attacked him first. The government cross-examined Sanders about his prior convictions as follows:

Q: You testified on direct that you are a convicted felon.
A: Yes, sir.
Q: And in fact you were convicted in 1988 for committing an assault in Lorton, weren't you?
A: Yes, sir.
Q: And you were also convicted of prisoner in possession of contraband at that time?
A: Yes, sir.
Q: You were convicted because you stabbed an inmate named Silas Horn (phonetic).

At this point, Sanders' counsel objected to any further questioning about the nature of the prior convictions and the district court sustained the objection. Trial was concluded in a half a day; the jury deliberated the rest of that day and into the next before returning a verdict of the lesser included offense of assault with a dangerous weapon with intent to do bodily harm. This appeal followed. Sanders challenges both his conviction of contraband possession on the first trial and of assault on the second.

. . . Sanders' convictions for assault and possession of contraband fall under 609(a)(1), and the district court therefore was required to balance the probative value of the evidence against its prejudicial effect in assessing its admissibility. Here, although evidence of the prior convictions may be thought somehow generally probative of Sanders' lack of credibility, they were extremely prejudicial since they involved the exact type of conduct for which Sanders was on trial.

We have recognized the prejudice that results from admitting evidence of a similar offense under Rule 609:

> Admission of evidence of a similar offense often does little to impeach the credibility of a testifying defendant while undoubtedly prejudicing him. The jury, despite limiting instructions, can hardly avoid drawing the inference that the past conviction suggests some probability that defendant committed the similar offense for which he is currently charged. The generally accepted view, therefore, is that evidence of similar offenses for impeachment purposes under Rule 609 should be admitted sparingly if at all.

United States v. Beahm, 664 F.2d 414, 418-19 (4th Cir. 1981) (footnote omitted). . . . It is unclear whether and how the district court may have sought to balance the probative value of this evidence against its prejudicial effect, since at the hearing on Sanders' motion in limine the district judge simply stated, "[t]hey [the government] are entitled to go into that [Sanders' prior convictions] both on the question of intent and impeachment." Even if the district court had explicitly conducted a balancing inquiry before admitting this evidence, we would find the evidence inadmissible under Rule 609(a) because of the high likelihood of prejudice that accompanies the admission of such similar prior convictions. As we stated in *Beahm*,

> [W]here as here the offense sought to be admitted against defendant had little bearing on his propensity to tell the truth, the district court should have recognized that the substantial likelihood of prejudice outweighed the minimal impeachment value of the evidence, and refused to admit the evidence, . . . or at the very least limited disclosure to the fact of conviction without revealing its nature.

. . . In the alternative, the district court held that Sanders' prior convictions were admissible under Rule 404(b) to show Sanders' intent to commit both crimes charged. . . . Since Sanders admitted the stabbing and claimed only that in doing so he acted in self-defense, the only factual issue in the case was whether that was the reason for the admitted act. The fact that Sanders had committed an assault on another prisoner and possessed contraband one year earlier had nothing to do with his reason for—his intent in—stabbing Jenkins. All that the evidence of the prior conviction of assault could possibly show was Sanders' propensity to commit assaults on other prisoners or his general propensity to commit violent crimes. The total lack of any probative value in the contraband possession conviction, except to show general criminal disposition, is even more stark. This is exactly the kind of propensity inference that Rule 404(b)'s built-in limitation was designed to prevent. . . . Because Sanders' prior convictions could only "prove the character of [Sanders] in order to show action and conformity therewith," we hold that the district court erred in admitting this evidence under Rule 404(b).

. . . The admission of Sanders' prior convictions was not harmless error as to his assault conviction. The assault prosecution turned essentially upon the jury's assessment of the relative credibility of Sanders and Jenkins, the direct protagonists, who gave widely conflicting versions of the stabbing. In such a situation, evidence having no possible basis except to show a propensity for violence on the part of the defendant obviously has the capacity to tip the balance in such a swearing contest. . . . We conclude, however, that the error in admitting the evidence of the prior convictions was harmless as to the possession count for which Sanders was convicted on his first trial. As opposed to the closeness of the case on the assault count—with the outcome depending upon the jury's assessment of conflicting testimony on Sanders' self-defense theory—the case on the possession count was not comparably close. As to that count, Sanders of course admitted possession of the shank used to stab Jenkins, he simply denied ownership, ascribing that to Jenkins. The evidence was not sufficiently strong in comparison to the Government's evidence that the shank was Sanders' to convince us that his conviction on that count was "substantially swayed" by the admission of this prior-conviction evidence.

We therefore affirm Sanders' conviction on the possession count, but reverse and remand for a new trial on the assault count. . . .

UNITED STATES v. OAXACA

569 F.2d 518 (9th Cir. 1978)

Duniway, Circuit Judge:

Oaxaca was charged in a one-count indictment alleging a single armed bank robbery. He was convicted after a jury trial. . . . At trial Oaxaca chose to testify in his own behalf. The prosecutor sought to impeach Oaxaca by introducing evidence that he had suffered two prior felony convictions. The defense attempted to bar any inquiry into the precise nature of the priors but the district judge, refusing to so limit the questioning, permitted the prosecutor to establish that Oaxaca had been convicted of burglary in 1967, and of bank robbery in 1972.

On appeal, Oaxaca acknowledges, as he must, that the district court had "wide discretion in deciding whether to exclude evidence of prior convictions as more prejudicial than probative of lack of credibility." *United States v. Prewitt*, 9 Cir., 1976, 534 F.2d 200, 201. While conceding that the court acted within its discretion in permitting inquiry into his criminal record generally, Oaxaca argues that evidence of the specific nature of his prior convictions was more prejudicial than probative and on this ground ought to have been excluded.

We find no abuse of discretion. The convictions were for crimes which reflected adversely on the defendant's honesty and integrity. As such they were relevant to the question of Oaxaca's credibility, which, in light of his alibi defense, was a key issue in the case.

The 1972 bank robbery conviction was not inadmissible per se, merely because the offense involved was identical to that for which Oaxaca was on trial. In *United States v. Wilson*, 9 Cir., 1976, 536 F.2d 883, we held that prior convictions for attempted robbery and receiving stolen property were properly admitted against a defendant charged with bank robbery, in light of their impeachment value. In *United States v. Hatcher*, 9 Cir., 1974, 496 F.2d 529, 530, we concluded that a defendant charged with violating the Dyer Act was properly impeached with evidence of three prior Dyer Act convictions, noting, "[t]he convictions were for theft which is more indicative of credibility than, say, convictions for crimes of violence." . . . AFFIRMED.

UNITED STATES v. HERNANDEZ

106 F.3d 737 (7th Cir. 1997)

RIPPLE, Circuit Judge.

Salvador Hernandez was convicted by a jury of conspiracy to kidnap in violation of 18 U.S.C. § 1201(c) and of kidnaping in violation of 18 U.S.C. § 1201(a). . . . [He] submits that the district court erred in admitting the evidence of a prior conviction for the possession of cocaine and marijuana. . . . [H]e points out that the prior conviction was for possession of cocaine and marijuana and that the current charges also were related to drugs because the ransom money was meant to pay back a drug deal. The admission of the similar prior conviction would suggest, he submits, his bad character or a willingness to commit this drug-related kidnaping. . . .

[W]e discern no abuse of discretion. At the outset, we note that the prior conviction occurred five years earlier and therefore was well within the time period of Rule 609. The district court ultimately determined that the evidence ought to be admitted because of its value in assessing the credibility of the defendant. The court was well aware that there was a similarity between the two crimes, a factor that requires caution on the part of the district court to avoid the possibility of the jury's inferring guilt on a ground not permissible under Rule 404(b). Nevertheless, the court acted within its discretion when it determined that, given the importance of the credibility issue in this case, evidence of the earlier conviction ought to be admitted. See *United States v. Causey*, 9 F.3d 1341, 1344-45 (7th Cir. 1993) (noting the danger of admitting evidence of similar crimes, but holding that a district court may nevertheless determine that the importance of the credibility determination requires admission of the previous conviction), *cert. denied*, 511 U.S. 1024 (1994). Finally, we note that the court's instruction cautioned the jury that the conviction was to be considered solely to assess the credibility of the defendant. . . . AFFIRMED.

RICHARD D. FRIEDMAN, CHARACTER IMPEACHMENT EVIDENCE: THE ASYMMETRIAL INTERACTION BETWEEN PERSONALITY AND SITUATION

43 Duke L.J. 816 (1994)

In my view, character impeachment evidence cannot substantially alter a rational juror's assessment of a criminal defendant's inclination to lie unless the juror follows a train of thought something like the following: "At first I thought it was very unlikely that, if Defoe committed robbery, he would be willing to lie about it. But now that I know he committed forgery a year before, that possibility seems substantially more likely." It seems plain, however, that it is highly improbable that a rational juror would follow such a train of thought. . . .

Character impeachment of criminal defendants should be eliminated, and all other character impeachment evidence, including proof of prior convictions, should be subject to a discretionary rule. In terms of the Federal Rules of Evidence, these changes could be accomplished quite simply. First, Rule 608, the discretionary rule that applies to all types of character impeachment evidence except for prior convictions, should be expanded to apply to that type of evidence as well but narrowed to exclude character impeachment of criminal defendants. Second, Rule 609, which now prescribes in substantial detail situations in which the trial court must, may, and may not admit evidence of prior convictions, should be eliminated. . . . We would no longer deal with the charade of evidence supposedly offered to prove that the accused is unworthy of belief but actually having little value in the circumstances to prove that proposition and really offered to show that the accused is a bad person with a propensity for criminal behavior. Nor would the prospect of such evidence scare the accused off the stand; not facing an overwhelming disincentive to testify, he would have an unobstructed opportunity to tell his side of the story under oath to a jury that could assess his testimony fully aware of his self-interest. . . .

b. Preserving Claims of Error

LUCE v. UNITED STATES

469 U.S. 38 (1984)

Chief Justice Burger delivered the opinion of the Court.

. . . Petitioner was indicted on charges of conspiracy, and possession of cocaine with intent to distribute, in violation of 21 U.S.C. §§ 846 and 841(a)(1). During his trial in the United States District Court for the Western District of Tennessee, petitioner moved for a ruling to preclude the Government from using a 1974 state conviction to impeach him if he testified. There was no commitment by petitioner that he would testify if the motion were granted, nor did he make a proffer to the court as to what his testimony would be. In opposing the motion, the Government represented that the conviction was for a serious crime—possession of a controlled substance.

The District Court ruled that the prior conviction fell within the category of permissible impeachment evidence under Federal Rule of Evidence 609(a). The District Court noted, however, that the nature and scope of petitioner's trial testimony could affect the court's specific evidentiary rulings; for example, the court was prepared to hold that the prior conviction would be excluded if petitioner limited his testimony to explaining his attempt to flee from the arresting officers. However, if petitioner took the stand and denied any prior involvement with drugs, he could then be impeached by the 1974 conviction. Petitioner did not testify, and the jury returned guilty verdicts.

The United States Court of Appeals for the Sixth Circuit affirmed. . . . The Court of Appeals held that when the defendant does not testify, the court will not review the District Court's in limine ruling.

. . . Any possible harm flowing from a district court's *in limine* ruling permitting impeachment by a prior conviction is wholly speculative. The ruling is subject to change when the case unfolds, particularly if the actual testimony differs from what was contained in the defendant's proffer. Indeed even if nothing unexpected happens at trial, the district judge is free, in the exercise of sound judicial discretion, to alter a previous in limine ruling. On a record such as here, it would be a matter of conjecture whether the District Court would have allowed the Government to attack petitioner's credibility at trial by means of the prior conviction.

When the defendant does not testify, the reviewing court also has no way of knowing whether the Government would have sought to impeach with the prior conviction. If, for example, the Government's case is strong, and the defendant is subject to impeachment by other means, a prosecutor might elect not to use an arguably inadmissible prior conviction.

Because an accused's decision whether to testify "seldom turns on the resolution of one factor," *New Jersey v. Portash*, 440 U.S. 450, 467 (1979) (Blackmun, J., dissenting), a reviewing court cannot assume that the adverse ruling motivated a defendant's decision not to testify. In support of his motion a defendant might make a commitment to testify if his motion is granted; but such a commitment is virtually risk free because of the difficulty of enforcing it.

Even if these difficulties could be surmounted, the reviewing court would still face the question of harmless error. Were *in limine* rulings under Rule 609(a) reviewable on appeal, almost any error would result in the windfall of automatic reversal; the appellate court could not logically term "harmless" an error that presumptively kept the defendant from testifying. Requiring that a defendant testify in order to preserve Rule 609(a) claims will enable the reviewing court to determine the impact any erroneous impeachment may have had in light of the record as a whole; it will also tend to discourage making such motions solely to "plant" reversible error in the event of conviction.

... We hold that to raise and preserve for review the claim of improper impeachment with a prior conviction, a defendant must testify. Accordingly, the judgment of the Court of Appeals is affirmed.

[Justice Brennan, joined by Justice Marshall, filed a concurring opinion. Justice Stevens took no part in the case.]

OHLER v. UNITED STATES

529 U.S. 753 (2000)

CHIEF JUSTICE REHNQUIST delivered the opinion of the Court.

Petitioner, Maria Ohler, was arrested and charged with importation of marijuana and possession of marijuana with the intent to distribute. The District Court granted the Government's motion *in limine* seeking to admit evidence of her prior felony conviction as impeachment evidence under Federal Rule of Evidence 609(a)(1). Ohler testified at trial and admitted on direct examination that she had been convicted of possession of methamphetamine in 1993. The jury convicted her of both counts, and the Court of Appeals for the Ninth Circuit affirmed. We agree with the Court of Appeals that Ohler may not challenge the in limine ruling of the District Court on appeal.

... Generally, a party introducing evidence cannot complain on appeal that the evidence was erroneously admitted. *See* 1 J. Weinstein & M. Berger, Weinstein's Federal Evidence § 103.14, 103-30 (2d ed. 2000). *Cf.* 1 J. Strong, McCormick on Evidence § 55, p. 246 (5th ed. 1999) ("If a party who has objected to evidence of a certain fact himself produces evidence from his own witness of the same fact, he has waived his objection."). ... Ohler argues that it would be unfair to apply such a waiver rule in this situation because it compels a defendant to forgo the tactical advantage of preemptively introducing the conviction in order to appeal the *in limine* ruling. She argues that if a defendant is forced to wait for evidence of the conviction to be introduced on cross-examination, the jury will believe that the defendant is less credible because she was trying to conceal the conviction. The Government disputes that the defendant is unduly disadvantaged by waiting for the prosecution to introduce the conviction on cross-examination. First, the Government argues that it is debatable whether jurors actually perceive a defendant to be more credible if she introduces a conviction herself. Second, even if jurors do consider the defendant more credible, the Government suggests that it is an unwarranted advantage because the jury does not realize that the defendant disclosed the conviction only after failing to persuade the court to exclude it.

Whatever the merits of these contentions, they tend to obscure the fact that both the Government and the defendant in a criminal trial must make choices as the trial progresses. For example, the defendant must decide whether or not to take the stand in her own behalf. If she has an innocent or mitigating explanation for evidence that might otherwise incriminate, acquittal may be more likely if she takes the stand. . . . But once the defendant testifies, she is subject to cross-examination, including impeachment by prior convictions, and the decision to take the stand may prove damaging instead of helpful. A defendant has a further choice to make if she decides to testify, notwithstanding a prior conviction. The defendant must choose whether to introduce the conviction on direct examination and remove the sting or to take her chances with the prosecutor's possible elicitation of the conviction on cross-examination.

The Government, too, in a case such as this, must make a choice. If the defendant testifies, it must choose whether or not to impeach her by use of her prior conviction. Here the trial judge had indicated he would allow its use, but the Government still had to consider whether its use might be deemed reversible error on appeal. This choice is often based on the Government's appraisal of the apparent effect of the defendant's testimony. If she has offered a plausible, innocent explanation of the evidence against her, it will be inclined to use the prior conviction; if not, it may decide not to risk possible reversal on appeal from its use. . . .

Petitioner's submission would deny to the Government its usual right to decide, after she testifies, whether or not to use her prior conviction against her. She seeks to short-circuit that decisional process by offering the conviction herself (and thereby removing the sting) and still preserve its admission as a claim of error on appeal.

But here petitioner runs into the position taken by the Court in a similar, but not identical, situation in *Luce v. United States*, 469 U.S. 38 (1984), that "[a]ny possible harm flowing from a district court's in limine ruling permitting impeachment by a prior conviction is wholly speculative." Only when the government exercises its option to elicit the testimony is an appellate court confronted with a case where, under the normal rules of trial, the defendant can claim the denial of a substantial right if in fact the district court's in limine ruling proved to be erroneous. In our view, there is nothing "unfair," as petitioner puts it, about putting petitioner to her choice in accordance with the normal rules of trial.

For these reasons, we conclude that a defendant who preemptively introduces evidence of a prior conviction on direct examination may not on appeal claim that the admission of such evidence was error. The judgment of the Court of Appeals for the Ninth Circuit is therefore affirmed.

[Justice Souter filed a dissenting opinion, joined by Justice Stevens, Justice Ginsburg, and Justice Breyer.]

PROBLEMS

7.5. A defendant prosecuted for felony tax fraud has previously been convicted of the same offense. If the defendant testifies, does the judge have discretion to exclude impeachment with the prior conviction?

7.6. A defendant prosecuted in federal court for embezzlement moves before trial to exclude evidence of his prior felony conviction in state court for shoplifting. The trial judge rules that the evidence is admissible as proof of intent and also, if the defendant testifies, for impeachment. Must the defendant testify in order to challenge this ruling on appeal?

C. PRIOR INCONSISTENT STATEMENTS

Just as there are special rules that govern impeachment for dishonesty, there are special rules that govern impeachment for inconsistency—that is to say, impeachment by showing the witness has told a different story in the past. But there are not as many rules on this subject as there used to be. In fact F.R.E. 613, which addresses impeachment with prior inconsistent statements, starts off by rejecting an old, common-law restriction: the "rule in *Queen's Case*," which provided that before a prior, written statement could be used to impeach a witness, it had to be shown to the witness. F.R.E. 613 does preserve, though, a looser requirement that "extrinsic evidence" of a witness's prior inconsistent statement is inadmissible only if the witness is given a chance to explain or deny it, and the opposing party is given a chance to ask the witness about it.

It is easy to be confused about the relationship between this requirement and the hearsay rule. F.R.E. 613 and its state analogs set forth procedural prerequisites for the introduction of a prior inconsistent statement used to impeach a witness, but do not address the separate question of under what circumstances the prior inconsistent statement can be used not just for impeachment but also to prove the truth of the matter asserted. That question is addressed in Chapter Three of this book.

[F.R.E. 613, 801(d)(1); C.E.C. §§769-770, 1235]

ADVISORY COMMITTEE NOTE TO F.R.E. 613

The Queen's Case, 2 Br. & B. 284, 129 Eng. Rep. 976 (1820), laid down the requirement that a cross-examiner, prior to questioning the witness about his own prior statement in writing, must first show it to the witness. Abolished by statute in the country of its origin, the requirement nevertheless gained currency in the United States. The rule abolishes this useless impediment to cross-examination. . . .

The familiar foundation requirement that an impeaching statement first be shown to the witness before it can be proved by extrinsic evidence is preserved but with some modifications. The traditional insistence that the witness be directed to the statement on cross-examination is relaxed in favor of simply providing the witness an opportunity to explain and the opposite party an opportunity to examine on the statement, with no specification of any particular time or sequence. Under this procedure, several collusive witnesses can be examined before disclosure of a joint prior inconsistent statement. . . . Also, dangers of oversight are reduced.

In order to allow for such eventualities as the witness becoming unavailable by the time the statement is discovered, a measure of discretion is
conferred upon the judge. . . . Under principles of *expression unius* the rule
does not apply to impeachment by evidence of prior inconsistent conduct.
The use of inconsistent statements to impeach a hearsay declaration is
treated in Rule 806.

UNITED STATES v. LEBEL

622 F.2d 1054 (2d Cir. 1979) (sub nom. United States v. Praetorius)

KELLEHER, District Judge:

[Kenneth Lebel and several codefendants were convicted of conspiring
to import heroin from Thailand into the United States.]

Lebel contends that the district court erred in disallowing evidence
that witness Laws failed to identify him at the first trial. Laws had testified
on direct examination at that trial that he met eight of the conspirators in
Bangkok, and then identified them in the courtroom, with the exception of
Lebel. He did, however, identify Lebel the following day. At the second trial,
Lebel's counsel attempted to elicit this fact of non-identification of his client
by examining Special Agent Yaniello, the D.E.A. case agent (who had been
present at the first trial). The trial judge refused to allow the introduction of
the non-identification testimony unless and until Laws was given a chance
to explain or deny the statement on the witness stand. The judge relied
upon F.R.E. Rule 613(b). . . .

Lebel's first contention is that the failure to identify was not a "statement"
within the meaning of that term in the rule. The advisory committee note to
the rule provides that the rule does not apply to evidence of prior inconsistent
conduct. The only definition of "statement" to be found in the Federal Rules is
the definition in Rule 801(a): "(a statement includes) nonverbal conduct of a
person, if it is intended by him as an assertion." Under that definition, the
identification or non-identification of persons in a courtroom can be termed a
statement. Lebel's contention to the contrary is without merit.

Lebel, however, correctly points out that the trial judge was misinter-
preting the rule in requiring that Laws be confronted with the "statement"
immediately. The rule does not specify any particular order of calling witnesses, and so the defense should have been able to introduce the evidence
during the examination of Agent Yaniello. . . .

Having determined that it was error to refuse to admit the evidence, the
next inquiry must be whether that error was harmless, or if a new trial is
mandated. An error is harmless only if it did not influence the jury, or had but
very slight effect. Here, it does not appear that the error committed requires
reversal. First, it was impeachment testimony as to a collateral matter, Laws'
credibility. Second, counsel for Lebel always had the opportunity of calling
Laws to the witness stand and confronting him with the identification or non-
identification; that was never done. Third, Laws was on the witness stand for
two and one half days of cross-examination, and counsel did not inquire at

that time about the failure to identify Lebel at the first trial. Under all these circumstances, we must conclude that the error was harmless. . . . The judgments of conviction are affirmed in all respects and as to each defendant.

UNITED STATES v. DENNIS

625 F.2d 782 (8th Cir. 1980)

McMillian, Circuit Judge.

Willie H. Dennis appeals his conviction on twelve counts of an eighteen-count indictment charging seventeen violations of the Extortionate Credit Transactions Act (ECT), 18 U.S.C. §§ 892, 894 (1976), and one obstruction of justice under 18 U.S.C. § 1503.

. . . Dennis objects to the trial court's admission of prior inconsistent statements before the grand jury by complaining witness Charles Miller (count nine) for purposes of impeachment because of confusion of the issues and misleading the jury under Rule 403, Federal Rules of Evidence. . . . Miller had testified before the grand jury that he had seen Dennis with a gun; that Dennis had lent him money at "25 cents on the dollar" and that Dennis had told him not to tell the grand jury; that he was afraid to go to Dennis's house because he was worried about his family or dying; and that he was afraid to testify against Dennis because, even if Dennis were incarcerated, "there might be somebody else out there that would knock me off." Yet on direct examination at trial, Miller not only denied the underlying facts, but also either denied making or claimed not to recall having made the above statements. Often, his denials in court went beyond the questions asked and inadvertently revealed his recollection of his previous testimony. For example, when asked, "Did Willie Dennis charge you interest?", he replied, "No, he haven't. He didn't charge me 25 cents on the dollar. No, he didn't." On cross-examination, excerpts from the first few minutes of Miller's grand jury testimony to the effect that he hadn't been threatened were read, and Miller admitted having made them. Dennis also implied that the grand jury had asked Miller leading questions.

The government prosecutor complained that Miller had changed his testimony at trial and asked permission to impeach him by prior inconsistent statements in the grand jury transcript. The judge noted that Miller was obviously frightened at trial and that the prosecutor had been surprised by his testimony.[6] However, the judge considered Miller's grand jury

---

6. At common law, the party calling a witness at trial could not impeach his credibility unless the party could show both surprise and substantial harm. But Rule 607 of the Federal Rules of Evidence allows impeachment of one's own witness. So long as prior inconsistent statements are otherwise admissible, they may be used for impeachment; and surprise is no longer a prerequisite to their use. The prosecution's ability to impeach its witness with prior inconsistent statements is crucial in cases where the "turncoat" witness is afraid, *United States v. Gerry*, 515 F.2d 130, 139-40 (2d Cir. 1975) (loansharking prosecution), or hostile, *United States v. Rogers*, 549 F.2d 490 (8th Cir. 1976) (charged with the same offense).

testimony weak or confused, so he read the transcript himself and determined which portions could be called to the jury's attention. . . .

Statements made before a grand jury are within the Rule 801(d)(1)(A) exception for statements given under oath and subject to the penalty of perjury. This is so even if the statements were elicited by means of leading questions. The trial judge has considerable discretion in determining whether testimony is "inconsistent" with prior statements; inconsistency is not limited to diametrically opposed answers but may be found in evasive answers, inability to recall, silence, or changes of position. . . .

Miller's grand jury testimony was clearly not hearsay according to the criteria in Rule 801(d)(1)(A). . . . The trial judge correctly determined that Miller's denials of and inability to recall grand jury testimony were "inconsistent" with his trial testimony. Because Miller denied or could not recall the prior inconsistent statements, reading them to the jury was the proper method of putting them in evidence. Limiting use of the prior inconsistent statements to impeachment was within the trial judge's sound discretion.

. . . We hold that the trial judge correctly admitted Miller's prior inconsistent statements before the grand jury. Dennis gives no clue as to what collateral issues he feels were injected by their admission. The prior inconsistent statements would have gone directly to the elements of extortionate extension of credit. The judge, however, limited their use to impeachment. Moreover, the trial judge admitted only those prior inconsistent statements which he found reliable. These discretionary judgments by the trial court fulfilled Rule 403's purpose minimizing the evidentiary costs while protecting parties from undue prejudice. . . . Accordingly, the judgment of the district court is affirmed.

UNITED STATES v. INCE

21 F.3d 576 (4th Cir. 1994)

MURNAGHAN, Circuit Judge:

Appellant Nigel D. Ince was convicted by a jury for assault with a dangerous weapon, with intent to do bodily harm. Because the United States' only apparent purpose for impeaching one of its own witnesses was to circumvent the hearsay rule and to expose the jury to otherwise inadmissible evidence of Ince's alleged confession, we reverse.

[Ince was arrested on suspicion of having fired a pistol at trucks leaving a concert on the grounds of Fort Belvoir, Virginia. Angela Neumann was with Ince at the time of his arrest.] As part of the investigation that followed, Military Policeman Roger D. Stevens interviewed and took a signed, unsworn statement from Neumann. She recounted that Ince had admitted to firing the shots, but said he no longer had the gun.

. . . At Ince's trial the Government called Neumann to the stand. When her memory supposedly failed her, the prosecution attempted to refresh her recollection with a copy of the signed statement that she had given Stevens on the night of the shooting. Even with her recollection refreshed, she testified that she could no longer recall the details of her conversation with Ince. Following Neumann's testimony, the Government excused her and called Stevens, who testified (over the objection of defense counsel) as to what Neumann had told him shortly after the shooting. The trial ended with a dead-locked jury.

At the second trial, the Government again called Neumann. She again acknowledged that she had given the military police a signed statement describing what Ince had told her immediately after the shooting. But she repeatedly testified that she could no longer recall the details of Ince's remarks, despite the prosecution's effort to refresh her recollection with a copy of the statement. . . . Over defense counsel's repeated objections, the Government again called MP Stevens to the stand, supposedly to impeach Neumann as to her memory loss. He testified that, within hours of the shooting, Neumann had told him that Ince had confessed to firing the gun. The Government also called two eyewitnesses who identified Ince as the gunman.

The defense's theory of the case was mistaken identity: Frank Kelly, not Nigel Ince, had fired the shots. . . . In an attempt to undermine the defense's theory of the case, the prosecution, in its closing argument, reminded the jurors that they had "heard testimony that Ms. Neumann made a statement to an MP [immediately following the shooting]. And she told [him] at that time that the defendant said, 'Frank didn't shoot the gun; I shot the gun.' "

The second time around, the jury convicted Ince. The district judge sentenced him to forty-one months in prison, plus two years of supervised release. . . . [T]he sole question presented on appeal is whether the admission of Stevens's testimony constituted reversible error.

Rule 607 of the Federal Rules of Evidence provides that "[t]he credibility of a witness may be attacked by any party, including the party calling the witness." One method of attacking the credibility of (*i.e.*, impeaching) a witness is to show that he has previously made a statement that is inconsistent with his present testimony. Even if that prior inconsistent statement would otherwise be inadmissible as hearsay, it may be admissible for the limited purpose of impeaching the witness. At a criminal trial, however, there are limits on the Government's power to impeach its own witness by presenting his prior inconsistent statements. *See United States v. Morlang*, 531 F.2d 183 (4th Cir. 1975). In *Morlang*, we reversed the defendant's conviction for conspiracy to bribe and bribery because the Government had employed impeachment by prior inconsistent statement "as a mere subterfuge to get before the jury evidence not otherwise admissible."

At Morlang's trial the Government had called Fred Wilmoth, an original codefendant who had subsequently pleaded guilty, as its first witness despite the fact that his previous statements to the Government suggested he would be hostile. The real purpose for calling Wilmoth was apparently to elicit a denial that he had ever had a conversation with a fellow prisoner in which he had implicated Morlang. Having obtained the expected denial, the Government then called Raymond Crist, another prisoner, to impeach Wilmoth with the alleged prior inconsistent statement. As expected, Crist testified that his fellow inmate Wilmoth had made a conclusory statement from which one could only infer Morlang's guilt. As expected, the jury delivered a guilty verdict.

In reversing Morlang's conviction, Judge Widener explained that courts must not "permit the government, in the name of impeachment, to present testimony to the jury by indirection which would not otherwise be admissible." "To permit the government in this case to supply testimony which was a naked conclusion as to Morlang's guilt in the name of impeachment," he explained, would be tantamount to convicting a defendant on the basis of hearsay:

> Foremost among [the notions of fairness upon which our system is based] is the principle that men should not be allowed to be convicted on the basis of unsworn testimony. . . .
>
> We must be mindful of the fact that prior unsworn statements of a witness are mere hearsay and are, as such, generally inadmissible as affirmative proof. The introduction of such testimony, even where limited to impeachment, necessarily increases the possibility that a defendant may be convicted on the basis of unsworn evidence, for despite proper instructions to the jury, it is often difficult for [jurors] to distinguish between impeachment and substantive evidence. . . . Thus, the danger of confusion which arises from the introduction of testimony under circumstances such as are presented here is so great as to upset the balance and [to] warrant continuation of the rule of exclusion.

Id.

. . . In the case at bar, MP Stevens testified that Ince had *admitted* to firing the gun—the critical element of the crime for which he was being tried. It is hard to imagine any piece of evidence that could have had a greater prejudicial impact than such a supposed naked confession of guilt. . . .

Given the likely prejudicial impact of Steven's testimony, the trial judge should have excluded it absent some extraordinary probative value. Because evidence of Neumann's prior inconsistent statement was admitted solely for purposes of impeachment, its probative value must be assessed solely in terms of its impeaching effect upon Neumann's testimony or overall credibility. Our review of the record below, however, shows that the probative value of Stevens's testimony *for impeachment purposes* was nil. Unlike the classic "turncoat" witness, Neumann certainly had not shocked the Government with her "loss of memory" at the second trial, as she had made it plain during the first trial that she would not readily testify to the alleged confession of her friend, Nigel Ince.

Furthermore, Neumann's actual in-court testimony did not affirmatively damage the Government's case; she merely refused to give testimony that the Government had hoped she would give. Thus, the prosecution had no need to attack her credibility. . . . She testified that, immediately after the shooting, as they left the scene of the crime but before the military police pulled them over, (1) Ince stated that Frank Kelly—the person whom Ince's lawyer identified at trial as the likely perpetrator of the crime—was *not* the person who had fired the gun, (2) Ince stated that "he didn't have [the gun] with him," and (3) Ince instructed Neumann to tell the military police that she knew nothing about the events of the evening. She presented no evidence affirming or denying Ince's alleged confession. Taken as a whole, then, Neumann's testimony probably *strengthened* the Government's case. Therefore, evidence attacking her credibility had no probative value *for impeachment purposes*.

Because Stevens's so-called "impeachment" testimony was both highly prejudicial and devoid of probative value as impeachment evidence, the trial judge should have recognized the Government's tactic for what it was—an attempt to circumvent the hearsay rule and to infect the jury with otherwise inadmissible evidence of Ince's alleged confession. Instead, the judge allowed Stevens's testimony to come before the jury in clear violation of *Morlang* and its progeny, notwithstanding defense counsel's proper and timely objections. . . . Accordingly, we reverse the conviction of Nigel D. Ince and remand the case for a new trial.

UNITED STATES v. WEBSTER

734 F.2d 1191 (7th Cir. 1984)

POSNER, Circuit Judge.

The defendant, Webster, was convicted of aiding and abetting the robbery of a federally insured bank and receiving stolen bank funds, was sentenced to nine years in prison, and appeals. Only one issue need be discussed. The government called the bank robber, King (who had pleaded guilty and been given a long prison term), as a witness against Webster. King gave testimony that if believed would have exculpated the defendant, where-upon the government introduced prior inconsistent statements that King had given the FBI inculpating Webster. Although the court instructed the jury that it could consider the statements only for purposes of impeachment, Webster argues that this was not good enough, that the government should not be allowed to get inadmissible evidence before the jury by calling a hostile witness and then using his out-of-court statements, which would otherwise be inadmissible hearsay, to impeach him.

Rule 607 of the Federal Rules of Evidence provides: "The credibility of a witness may be attacked by any party, including the party calling him." But it would be an abuse of the rule, in a criminal case, for the prosecution to call a witness that it knew would not give it useful evidence, just so it could introduce hearsay evidence against the defendant in the hope that the jury would miss the subtle distinction between impeachment and substantive evidence—or, if it didn't miss it, would ignore it. The purpose would not be to impeach the witness but to put in hearsay as substantive evidence against the defendant, which Rule 607 does not contemplate or authorize. We thus agree that "impeachment by prior inconsistent statement may not be permitted where employed as a mere subterfuge to get before the jury evidence not otherwise admissible." *United States v. Morlang*, 531 F.2d 183, 190 (4th Cir. 1975). Although *Morlang* was decided before the Federal Rules of Evidence became effective, the limitation that we have quoted on the prosecutor's rights under Rule 607 has been accepted in all circuits that have considered the issue.

But it is quite plain that there was no bad faith here. Before the prosecutor called King to the stand she asked the judge to allow her to examine him outside the presence of the jury, because she didn't know what he would say. The defendant's counsel objected and the voir dire was not held. We do not see how in these circumstances it can be thought that the prosecutor put King on the stand knowing he would give no useful evidence. If she had known that, she would not have offered to voir dire him, as the voir dire would have provided a foundation for defense counsel to object, under *Morlang*, to the admission of King's prior inconsistent statements. . . . The judgment of conviction is Affirmed.

PEOPLE v. FREEMAN

20 Cal. Rptr. 717 (Cal. Ct. App. 1971)

FRIEDMAN, Acting P.J.

[Defendant Norman Freeman was convicted of serving as the getaway driver in an armed robbery in which Foster served as a gunman. Freeman claimed at trial that he spent the morning of the robbery asleep at the home of his fiancée, Brenda Banks.] Claims of error arise from the testimony of Mrs. Anna Duckworth and Fred Knipp, a district attorney's investigator. Both were prosecution rebuttal witnesses, and both testified over defense objections. With reference to the Saturday morning in question, Mrs. Duckworth testified that about 7 a.m. she had gone to the nearby house of her daughter, Annette, girl friend of Foster. She testified that Foster was frequently at Annette's house but she did not know whether he was there on this particular morning. While Mrs. Duckworth was outside the house, a man came to the house. She heard her daughter greet the man with the words, "Hi, Norman." Several days later Knipp, the investigator, interviewed her. She admitted telling Knipp that her daughter had greeted a man by the name of Norman; denied telling Knipp that Foster had been in bed at Annette's house on the morning in question; denied telling Knipp that Norman twice came to the house that morning and, on the second occasion, had left the house in company with Foster; denied identifying the man as Norman Freeman.

Over objection the prosecutor called Knipp, who testified that he had interviewed Mrs. Duckworth, who told him that on the Saturday morning in question a man had twice come to the daughter's house, where Lee Foster was in bed; that on the second occasion Foster and the man had left the house together; that the man was Norman Freeman.

Without analysis and without citation of authority, defendant charges that Mrs. Duckworth's "Hi, Norman" testimony was hearsay. It was not hearsay, because not offered to prove the statement's truth or falsity but as evidence of the fact that the statement was made. Where the fact that a statement was made is relevant regardless of its truth or falsity, the statement is admissible. Thus Wigmore states: "Utterances serving to *identify* are admissible as any other circumstance of identification would be." Norman Freeman's presence at the home of Annette Duckworth (at a time when he said he was asleep at the home of his fiancée, Brenda Banks) was itself a relevant fact. The fact that the statement "Hi, Norman" was made tended to prove circumstantially that one Norman had come to the house of a person associated with Foster, the alleged associate of Norman Freeman in the armed robbery.

Defendant argues that the prosecution could not place Mrs. Duckworth on the stand, elicit her version of statements to Knipp as a device for getting in Knipp's inconsistent version of these statements, ostensibly as impeachment but really to prove the truth of the latter version. The argument is supported by *People v. Taylor*, 4 Cal. App. 2d 220, 223, a case antedating Evidence Code section 1235. Defendant does not cite or discuss section 1235.

Knipp's version of Mrs. Duckworth's statements was not admitted for the restricted purpose of impeaching Mrs. Duckworth, but as evidence of the statements' truth, that is, that Norman Freeman had twice been at the home of Annette Duckworth on the morning of the crime and had left in company with Foster (who had been identified by other evidence as defendant's crime partner). Had Mrs. Duckworth not previously denied her statements to Knipp, the latter's testimony would have been inadmissible hearsay. Manifestly the prosecutor did not elicit Mrs. Duckworth's version for its probative value but as a tool to unlock the evidentiary door to Knipp's conflicting version of Mrs. Duckworth's statements to him.

Evidence Code section 1235 declares: "Evidence of a statement made by a witness is not made inadmissible by the hearsay rule if the statement is inconsistent with his testimony at the hearing and is offered in compliance with Section 770." Section 1235 is designed to permit evidentiary use of a witness' inconsistent statement either to impeach him or as substantive evidence of the truth of the matters asserted. . . .

In some cases a witness' prior statement is offered by the opponent of the litigant who originally called him. More typically, a party calls a recanting, hostile witness as a prelude to the testimony of a subsequent witness who describes the conflicting declarations of the first. . . . The witness' recantation permits the inference that he has something to hide, and this inference provides the earlier version a measure of reliability.* The jury may choose which version to believe or reject both versions altogether. When a litigant intentionally brings in the declarant for the purpose of eliciting a predictably false version, he is not misusing section 1235 but utilizing it for the very purpose it is designed to fulfill—that is, to open the door to a second witness with a conceivably reliable indicator of the actual events. The technique conforms to the letter and spirit of section 1235, which supplies fact-finders with a formerly unavailable means for uncovering the truth.

---

* A parallel observation was voiced by the California Code Commission in its comments accompanying section 1235: ". . . The declarant is in court and may be examined and cross-examined in regard to his statements and their subject matter. In many cases, the inconsistent statement is more likely to be true than the testimony of the witness at the trial because it was made nearer in time to the matter to which it relates and is less likely to be influenced by the controversy that gave rise to the litigation. The trier of fact has the declarant before it and can observe his demeanor and the nature of his testimony as he denies or tries to explain away the inconsistency. Hence, it is in as good a position to determine the truth or falsity of the prior statement as it is to determine the truth or falsity of the inconsistent testimony given in court."

The record here shows that both Mrs. Duckworth and Investigator Knipp first testified outside the jury's presence as part of a prosecution offer of proof. Later, over defense objections, both testified before the jury as rebuttal witnesses for the prosecution. In view of their *voir dire* testimony, both the prosecution and district attorney knew what to expect. After Mrs. Duckworth had finished testifying before the jury, she was excused with the consent of both counsel. Although she was not in court when Knipp gave his version of his interview with her, she could have been made available for further cross-examination had defense counsel so elected. Section 1235 permits the prior inconsistent statements if offered in compliance with section 770. The latter, in effect, requires either that the declarant be provided an opportunity to explain or deny the statement or that he be kept available for further testimony. The first of these conditions was satisfied. Under these circumstances the court correctly permitted Knipp to testify.

Judgment affirmed.

PROBLEMS

7.7. Would *People v. Freeman* come out differently in federal court?

7.8. Wendy testifies before a grand jury that her brother Dan told her he had set fire to a post office. At Dan's subsequent federal trial for arson, the prosecution calls Wendy as a witness, but she denies ever hearing her brother admit to setting the fire. The prosecutor asks her, "Didn't you testify before a grand jury that Dan told you he had set fire to a post office?" Wendy denies having so testified. After Wendy leaves the stand, may the government introduce a transcript of her grand jury testimony?

7.9. Suppose the jury in Dan's trial deadlocks and the judge declares a mistrial. In a subsequent retrial, the government again calls Wendy as a witness, and she again denies ever hearing her brother say that he set fire to a post office. May the prosecutor again ask Wendy about her contrary testimony before the grand jury?

7.10. Dana is charged with bank robbery. At trial she claims mistaken identity and testifies that on the afternoon of the assault she was visiting her friend Alex. Alex has told the same story to government investigators, but they disbelieve him, partly because he was recently convicted of bank robbery in an unrelated case. Dana does not call Alex as a witness. The government calls Alex to the stand in its rebuttal case, and he corroborates Dana's account. May the prosecutor now ask him about the bank robbery conviction? What if the prior conviction were for perjury?

D. BIAS AND INCAPACITY

There are no special rules regarding impeachment for bias or incapacity, but each of these modes of impeachment can afoul of other, more general rules of evidence.

Impeachment for bias consists of proving that a witness (or hearsay declarant) has a reason to lie or to slant his or her testimony. Examples include showing that an expert witness is being paid to testify, eliciting testimony that the witness is romantically involved with the party for whom he or she has testified, and—as in the Supreme Court decision excerpted below—demonstrating that the witness is in the same prison gang as the party for whom he or she has testified.

Impeachment for incapacity consists of demonstrating that the memory or perception of the witness is unreliable. The classic example is showing that the witness has bad eyesight, but incapacity can be mental as well as physical. A witness can be impeached, for example, by showing that he or she suffers from delusions. But evidence of mental incapacity is easily subject to abuse, and for that reason is often ruled inadmissible, as the materials below illustrate. The problem is that evidence of mental incapacity often can be used to cast aspersions on the character of the witness, and more particularly on aspects of character other than honesty—precisely the kind of character impeachment disallowed by F.R.E. 608. Vigilant courts take care not to allow such character impeachment in the guise of evidence of incapacity, and disallow incapacity evidence when the actual probative force of the evidence seems predominantly or exclusively to concern the defendant's character.

UNITED STATES v. ABEL

469 U.S. 45 (1984)

Justice REHNQUIST delivered the opinion of the Court.

. . . Respondent John Abel and two cohorts were indicted for robbing a savings and loan in Bellflower, Cal., in violation of 18 U.S.C. §§2113(a) and (d). The cohorts elected to plead guilty, but respondent went to trial. One of the cohorts, Kurt Ehle, agreed to testify against respondent and identify him as a participant in the robbery.

Respondent informed the District Court at a pretrial conference that he would seek to counter Ehle's testimony with that of Robert Mills. Mills was not a participant in the robbery but was friendly with respondent and with Ehle, and had spent time with both in prison. Mills planned to testify that after the robbery Ehle had admitted to Mills that Ehle intended to implicate respondent falsely, in order to receive favorable treatment from the Government. The prosecutor in turn disclosed that he intended to discredit Mills' testimony by calling Ehle back to the stand and eliciting from Ehle the fact that respondent, Mills, and Ehle were all members of the "Aryan Brotherhood," a secret prison gang that required its members always to deny the existence of the organization and to commit perjury, theft, and murder on each member's behalf.

Defense counsel objected to Ehle's proffered rebuttal testimony as too prejudicial to respondent. After a lengthy discussion in chambers the District Court decided to permit the prosecutor to cross-examine Mills about the gang, and if Mills denied knowledge of the gang, to introduce Ehle's rebuttal testimony concerning the tenets of the gang and Mills' and respondent's membership in it. The District Court held that the probative value of Ehle's rebuttal testimony outweighed its prejudicial effect, but that respondent might be entitled to a limiting instruction if his counsel would submit one to the court.

At trial Ehle implicated respondent as a participant in the robbery. Mills, called by respondent, testified that Ehle told him in prison that Ehle planned to implicate respondent falsely. When the prosecutor sought to cross-examine Mills concerning membership in the prison gang, the District Court conferred again with counsel outside of the jury's presence, and ordered the prosecutor not to use the term "Aryan Brotherhood" because it was unduly prejudicial. Accordingly, the prosecutor asked Mills if he and respondent were members of a "secret type of prison organization" which had a creed requiring members to deny its existence and lie for each other. When Mills denied knowledge of such an organization the prosecutor recalled Ehle.

Ehle testified that respondent, Mills, and he were indeed members of a secret prison organization whose tenets required its members to deny its existence and "lie, cheat, steal [and] kill" to protect each other. The District Court sustained a defense objection to a question concerning the punishment for violating the organization's rules. Ehle then further described the organization and testified that "in view of the fact of how close Abel and Mills were" it would have been "suicide" for Ehle to have told Mills what Mills attributed to him. Respondent's counsel did not request a limiting instruction and none was given.

The jury convicted respondent. On his appeal a divided panel of the Court of Appeals reversed. . . . We hold that the evidence showing Mills' and respondent's membership in the prison gang was sufficiently probative of Mills' possible bias towards respondent to warrant its admission into evidence. Thus it was within the District Court's discretion to admit Ehle's testimony, and the Court of Appeals was wrong in concluding otherwise.

Both parties correctly assume, as did the District Court and the Court of Appeals, that the question is governed by the Federal Rules of Evidence. But the Rules do not by their terms deal with impeachment for "bias," although they do expressly treat impeachment by character evidence and conduct, Rule 608, by evidence of conviction of a crime, Rule 609, and by showing of religious beliefs or opinion, Rule 610. Neither party has suggested what significance we should attribute to this fact. Although we are nominally the promulgators of the Rules, and should in theory need only to consult our collective memories to analyze the situation properly, we are in truth merely a conduit when we deal with an undertaking as substantial as the preparation of the Federal Rules of Evidence. In the case of these Rules, too, it must be remembered that Congress extensively reviewed our submission, and considerably revised it.

Before the present Rules were promulgated, the admissibility of evidence in the federal courts was governed in part by statutes or Rules, and in part by case law. This Court had held in *Alford v. United States*, 282

U.S. 687 (1931), that a trial court must allow some cross-examination of a witness to show bias. This holding was in accord with the overwhelming weight of authority in the state courts as reflected in Wigmore's classic treatise on the law of evidence. *See id.* at 691, citing 3 J. Wigmore, Evidence § 1368 (2d ed. 1923). Our decision in *Davis v. Alaska*, 415 U.S. 308 (1974), holds that the Confrontation Clause of the Sixth Amendment requires a defendant to have some opportunity to show bias on the part of a prosecution witness.

With this state of unanimity confronting the drafters of the Federal Rules of Evidence, we think it unlikely that they intended to scuttle entirely the evidentiary availability of cross-examination for bias. One commentator, recognizing the omission of any express treatment of impeachment for bias, prejudice, or corruption, observes that the Rules "clearly contemplate the use of the above-mentioned grounds of impeachment." E. Cleary, McCormick on Evidence § 40, p. 85 (3d ed. 1984). Other commentators, without mentioning the omission, treat bias as a permissible and established basis of impeachment under the Rules. 3 D. Louisell & C. Mueller, Federal Evidence § 341, p. 470 (1979); 3 J. Weinstein & M. Berger, Weinstein's Evidence § 607[03] (1981).

We think this conclusion is obviously correct. Rule 401 defines as "relevant evidence" evidence having any tendency to make the existence of any fact that is of consequence to the determination of the action more probable or less probable than it would be without the evidence. Rule 402 provides that all relevant evidence is admissible, except as otherwise provided by the United States Constitution, by Act of Congress, or by applicable rule. A successful showing of bias on the part of a witness would have a tendency to make the facts to which he testified less probable in the eyes of the jury than it would be without such testimony.

The correctness of the conclusion that the Rules contemplate impeachment by showing of bias is confirmed by the references to bias in the Advisory Committee Notes to Rules 608 and 610, and by the provisions allowing any party to attack credibility in Rule 607, and allowing cross-examination on "matters affecting the credibility of the witness" in Rule 611(b). The Courts of Appeals have upheld use of extrinsic evidence to show bias both before and after the adoption of the Federal Rules of Evidence.

. . . Ehle's testimony about the prison gang certainly made the existence of Mills' bias towards respondent more probable. Thus it was relevant to support that inference. Bias is a term used in the "common law of evidence" to describe the relationship between a party and a witness which might lead the witness to slant, unconsciously or otherwise, his testimony in favor of or against a party. Bias may be induced by a witness' like, dislike, or fear of a party, or by the witness' self-interest. Proof of bias is almost always relevant because the jury, as finder of fact and weigher of credibility, has historically been entitled to assess all evidence which might bear on the accuracy and truth of a witness' testimony. The "common law of evidence" allowed the showing of bias by extrinsic evidence, while requiring the cross-examiner to "take the answer of the witness" with respect to less favored forms of impeachment.

. . . Respondent argues that even if the evidence of membership in the prison gang were relevant to show bias, the District Court erred in permitting a full description of the gang and its odious tenets. Respondent contends that the District Court abused its discretion under Federal Rule of Evidence 403, because the prejudicial effect of the contested evidence outweighed its probative value. In other words, testimony about the gang inflamed the jury against respondent, and the chance that he would be convicted by his mere association with the organization outweighed any probative value the testimony may have had on Mills' bias.

Respondent specifically contends that the District Court should not have permitted Ehle's precise description of the gang as a lying and murderous group. Respondent suggests that the District Court should have cut off the testimony after the prosecutor had elicited that Mills knew respondent and both may have belonged to an organization together. This argument ignores the fact that the *type* of organization in which a witness and a party share membership may be relevant to show bias. If the organization is a loosely knit group having nothing to do with the subject matter of the litigation, the inference of bias arising from common membership may be small or nonexistent. If the prosecutor had elicited that both respondent and Mills belonged to the Book of the Month Club, the jury probably would not have inferred bias even if the District Court had admitted the testimony. The attributes of the Aryan Brotherhood—a secret prison sect sworn to perjury and self-protection—bore directly not only on the *fact* of bias but also on the *source* and *strength* of Mills' bias. The tenets of this group showed that Mills had a powerful motive to slant his testimony towards respondent, or even commit perjury outright.

A district court is accorded a wide discretion in determining the admissibility of evidence under the Federal Rules. Assessing the probative value of common membership in any particular group, and weighing any factors counseling against admissibility is a matter first for the district court's sound judgment under Rules 401 and 403 and ultimately, if the evidence is admitted, for the trier of fact.

Before admitting Ehle's rebuttal testimony, the District Court gave heed to the extensive arguments of counsel, both in chambers and at the bench. In an attempt to avoid undue prejudice to respondent the court ordered that the name "Aryan Brotherhood" not be used. The court also offered to give a limiting instruction concerning the testimony, and it sustained defense objections to the prosecutor's questions concerning the punishment meted out to unfaithful members. These precautions did not prevent *all* prejudice to respondent from Ehle's testimony, but they did, in our opinion, ensure that the admission of this highly probative evidence did not *unduly* prejudice respondent. We hold there was no abuse of discretion under Rule 403 in admitting Ehle's testimony as to membership and tenets.

Respondent makes an additional argument based on Rule 608(b). That Rule allows a cross-examiner to impeach a witness by asking him about specific instances of past conduct, other than crimes covered by Rule 609, which are probative of his veracity or "character for truthfulness or untruthfulness." The Rule limits the inquiry to cross-examination of the witness, however, and prohibits the cross-examiner from introducing extrinsic evidence of the witness' past conduct.

Respondent claims that the prosecutor cross-examined Mills about the gang not to show bias but to offer Mills' membership in the gang as past conduct bearing on his veracity. This was error under Rule 608(b), respondent contends, because the mere fact of Mills' membership, without more, was not sufficiently probative of Mills' character for truthfulness. Respondent cites a second error under the same Rule, contending that Ehle's rebuttal testimony concerning the gang was extrinsic evidence offered to impugn Mills' veracity, and extrinsic evidence is barred by Rule 608(b).

. . . It seems clear to us that the proffered testimony with respect to Mills' membership in the Aryan Brotherhood sufficed to show potential bias in favor of respondent; because of the tenets of the organization described, it might also impeach his veracity directly. But there is no rule of evidence which provides that testimony admissible for one purpose and inadmissible for another purpose is thereby rendered inadmissible; quite the contrary is the case. It would be a strange rule of law which held that relevant, competent evidence which tended to show bias on the part of a witness was nonetheless inadmissible because it also tended to show that the witness was a liar.

We intimate no view as to whether the evidence of Mills' membership in an organization having the tenets ascribed to the Aryan Brotherhood would be a specific instance of Mills' conduct which could not be proved against him by extrinsic evidence except as otherwise provided in Rule 608(b). It was enough that such evidence could properly be found admissible to show bias.

The judgment of the Court of Appeals is
Reversed.

UNITED STATES v. SASSO

59 F.3d 341 (2d Cir. 1995)

KEARSE, Circuit Judge:

[Defendants Robert Sasso, Jr., and Anthony Armienti were convicted of trafficking in illegal firearms. Among the witnesses against them was Armienti's former girlfriend Kristine Kramer, who testified both to incriminating statements made by Armienti and to observations she made of both defendants.] At an in limine hearing outside the presence of the jury, it was revealed that in 1988, a truck that Kramer was driving accidentally struck and killed a fellow worker. Kramer testified that she became depressed and twice visited a psychiatrist for counseling. Shortly after these two visits, Kramer's family physician prescribed the antidepressant drug Prozac, which Kramer took "on and off" during the following year. Defendants sought permission to bring these facts out in the presence of the jury. . . . [The trial court denied the request.]

We see no abuse of discretion here. In light of the nature of Kramer's condition, i.e., a not-unpredictable depression resulting from her involvement in a specific catastrophic event, the fact that her depression was relatively recent did not necessarily suggest that condition had any probative value. Further, there was no indication that the accident in which she was involved in 1988 had put her in a delusional state or that any medications prescribed through 1990 or beginning in October 1992 would have affected her ability to perceive events or to understand what was said to her from July 1991, when she first met Armienti, until June 1992, when their intimate relationship ended. Indeed, there was no evidence that Kramer received or ingested any mood-altering drugs during the period in which she was involved with Armienti.

Chnapkova v. Koh, [985 F.2d 79, 81 (2d Cir. 1993),] on which defendants principally rely to support their contention that the evidence should have been admitted, is entirely distinguishable. In that case, the plaintiff claimed to have been disfigured in plastic surgery, and we held that it was an abuse of discretion for the trial court to exclude evidence that she believed, inter alia, that " 'people were laughing at her' " and were talking about her " 'on the T.V. & radio,' " 985 F.2d at 80 n.1 (quoting hospital records of the plaintiff's statements). That history of paranoid and delusional behavior indicated that the plaintiff suffered problems of perception, and her perceptions were directly related to the subject matter of the suit. Here, there was no indication that Kramer was delusional or paranoid, or had any difficulties in memory or perception. . . . The judgments of conviction are affirmed.

HENDERSON v. DETELLA

97 F.3d 942 (7th Cir. 1996)

ILANA DIAMOND ROVNER, Circuit Judge.

[An Illinois jury found Ladell Henderson guilty of murder and attempted murder, based in part on the testimony of Mona Chavez, who witnessed the murder and was the victim of the attempted murder. The trial judge refused to allow the defense to elicit testimony from an acquaintance of Chavez, Quintin Jones, that he had repeatedly seen her use drugs. The conviction was upheld on appeal, and Henderson's petition for federal habeas relief was rejected by the district court.]

Chavez's testimony was crucial to the state's case against Henderson. The use of narcotics can, obviously, affect the ability of a witness to perceive, to recall, and to recount the events she has observed. Whether Chavez may have been under the influence of narcotics at the time of the offense (or at some other pertinent time) was thus an appropriate subject of inquiry and impeachment.

But we agree that Henderson was not deprived of his right to confront the witnesses against him when the trial court barred the testimony of Quintin Jones. Had the proffer of Jones' testimony established that Chavez was using narcotics within the time frame of the events to which she testified, it might have been improper and prejudicial to Henderson to exclude the testimony. Instead, however, Jones was held up as a witness who would testify simply that he had known Chavez to use drugs on many occasions; we do not know when those occasions were in reference to the murder of Leonard and the attempted murder of Chavez. It is thus not at all clear that the testimony was probative of Chavez's ability to recognize and identify the individual who committed the offense. *See United States v. Robinson*, 956 F.2d 1388, 1398 (7th Cir.), *cert. denied*, 506 U.S. 1020 (1992) (testimony as to witness' drug use properly excluded where voir dire did not establish that it affected the witness' memory of relevant events). Absent a connection to Chavez's cognitive abilities, Jones' testimony would have served only to impeach her character, a purpose we have repeatedly deemed improper. Under these circumstances, we see no error, and certainly none rising to the level of a constitutional deprivation, in the decision to bar Jones from testifying on this topic. . . . The district court's decision to deny Henderson's petition for a writ of habeas corpus was therefore correct.

E. SPECIFIC CONTRADICTION

Like impeachment for incapacity or impeachment for bias, impeachment by specific contradiction is governed by no special provisions of the Federal Rules of Evidence or its state counterparts. There is a judge-made restriction on such impeachment, though, most commonly called the "collateral evidence rule." Sometimes it is referred to as the "specific contradiction rule."

The collateral evidence rule is confusing for reasons other than its varying names. The first problem is that it generally applies only to impeachment by specific contradiction, and the distinction between this mode of impeachment and others can be elusive. Impeachment by specific contradiction consists of demonstrating that some particular part of what a witness has testified to is false, and then suggesting that this gives the jury reason to disregard the remainder of the testimony. Sometimes this mode of impeachment is simply called "impeachment by contradiction." It is best to avoid that terminology, because it makes it easy to confuse this mode of impeachment with impeachment with prior inconsistent statements, which is sometimes referred to as "impeachment by self-contradiction."

The collateral evidence rule, it its most common formulation, bars extrinsic impeachment by specific contradiction on a "collateral matter." Here as elsewhere, "extrinsic" impeachment means impeachment through evidence other than testimony elicited from the witness being impeached. Because the collateral evidence rule applies only to extrinsic evidence, it does not restrict the ability of a party to impeach a witness by eliciting testimony on cross-examination contradicting part of the witness's earlier testimony.

The trickiest term in the collateral evidence rule is "collateral." Collateral in this context does not simply mean peripheral. It has a narrower, technical meaning. As the materials below explain, the classic test for a "collateral matter" under the collateral evidence rule asks whether the fact in question could be proven for any purpose *other* than contradicting the witness. A fact is collateral only if it fails this test. The materials below also explain the traditional rationale for the collateral evidence rule: to avoid the risk that the trial will be derailed by inquiry into side issues.

SIMMONS, INC. v. PINKERTON'S, INC.

762 F.2d 591 (7th Cir. 1985)

CUDAHY, Circuit Judge.

... Simmons, a manufacturer of residential and commercial bedding, owned a warehouse in Munster, Indiana, which it used as a regional distribution center for its products. In order to protect the warehouse, Simmons entered into a contract with defendant Pinkerton's, a national company providing investigative and security services, under which Pinkerton's agreed to provide uniformed guard protection for the warehouse 24 hours a day, 7 days a week. ... [A fire broke out at the warehouse and caused extensive damage. The Indiana Fire Marshal's Office concluded the fire had been set as an "attention getter" by William Hayne, a Pinkerton employee assigned to guard the warehouse.] Simmons then brought this diversity action against Pinkerton's, and against the National Surety Corporation as surety for Pinkerton's. ...

Pinkerton's ... argues that the district court erred in admitting Hayne's testimony that he falsely told a Pinkerton's investigator that he had taken and passed a polygraph examination regarding the circumstances of the fire. After the fire, Pinkerton's asked Hayne to take a lie detector test in Chicago. He took the test, but apparently it was inconclusive for extraneous reasons. Hayne then agreed to take a second test in Indiana, but failed to make arrangements to do so. Nevertheless, Hayne later told a Pinkerton's investigator that he had taken the second test in Indiana and had passed it. At trial, over Pinkerton's objection, Simmons' attorney elicited from Hayne his admission that he had lied about this matter. ...

Although "the rule in the Seventh Circuit is clear" that admission or exclusion of polygraph evidence is within the sound discretion of the trial judge, *United States v. Rumell*, 642 F.2d 213, 215 (7th Cir. 1981), for various reasons this discretion has most often been exercised in favor of exclusion, in this circuit, *See id.* at 215, as well as in others, *deVries v. St. Paul Fire and Marine Ins. Co.*, 716 F.2d 939, 945 n. 8 (1st Cir. 1983). Several circuits apparently exclude polygraph results entirely, *id.* Indeed, because of the perceived danger of prejudice, some courts also exclude evidence of a person's willingness or unwillingness to take a polygraph examination, *id.* at 944-45. For these reasons, Pinkerton's argues, it would have been error to admit the results of any polygraph that Hayne took as substantive evidence of the cause of the fire at the warehouse. The trial court did not admit Hayne's testimony as substantive evidence, however, but rather admitted it under Federal Rule of Evidence 608(b) to impeach Hayne's credibility through cross-examination about a specific instance of his conduct (his lie about the polygraph test) bearing on his character for truthfulness or untruthfulness. Pinkerton's contends that this was an improper basis for admission, because "a witness may not be impeached by contradiction as to collateral or irrelevant matters elicited on cross-examination," *United States v. Lambert*, 463 F.2d 552, 557 (7th Cir. 1972). Since the test for whether a matter is collateral is "whether the party seeking to introduce it for purposes of contradiction would be entitled to prove it as part of his case," *id.*, and since Simmons presumably could not introduce evidence of the polygraph examination as a substantive part of its case, Pinkerton's concludes that the "collateral evidence rule" precludes Simmons from impeaching Hayne in any manner that included a reference to whether he took a polygraph test, or whether he passed such a test.

We disagree. Assuming, arguendo, that testimony relating to the polygraph exam was inadmissible as substantive evidence, Pinkerton's has failed to note distinctions between this case and the authority on which it relies which seem to make the collateral evidence rule completely inapplicable here. The rule apparently was developed in conjunction with a particular type of impeachment—impeachment by contradiction. Impeachment by contradiction simply involves presenting evidence that part or all of a witness' testimony is incorrect. Thus if an eyewitness to an auto accident testifies that the car that caused the accident was red, impeachment by contradiction relies on evidence that the car actually was yellow. The inference to be drawn is not that the witness was lying, but that the witness made a mistake of fact, and so perhaps her testimony may contain other errors and should be discounted accordingly.

Of course, a particular misstatement may or may not be probative of the witness' general accuracy, depending on the circumstances, and thus may or may not be worth the time it takes to establish it. For this reason the collateral evidence rule developed. In the above example, assuming the color of the car was not directly relevant to any substantive issue in the case (e.g., if the identity of the car were stipulated), it presumably would not be worth the fact finder's time to entertain a "mini-trial" on the issue of the car's color, simply to prove that the witness was mistaken as to this fact. Thus, while the accuracy of a witness' perception or memory can always be tested through traditional cross-examination techniques, the collateral evidence rule limits the extent to which the witness' testimony about non-essential matters may be contradicted by extrinsic proof. In short, if a matter is collateral (that is, if it could not be introduced into evidence as substantive proof) then it cannot be proven simply to contradict the witness' testimony for impeachment purposes. 3 J. Weinstein and M. Berger, Weinstein's Evidence ¶ 607[05], 607-61-607-72 (1984).

But the collateral evidence rule does not, as Pinkerton's contends, limit the scope of all types of impeachment by cross-examination to only those matters that could be proven as a substantive part of a case; rather it merely precludes extrinsic evidence of certain facts that would impeach by contradiction. Various types of impeachment are allowed, despite the recognition that the subject-matter of the impeachment could not be used substantively, precisely because a witness' credibility is always an important consideration. Impeachment by prior inconsistent statement is one example; another is the type of impeachment at issue here—an attack on a witness' character for truthfulness through cross-examination as to specific instances of the witness' previous conduct (which, of course, have not been the subject of his direct examination).

Federal Rule of Evidence 608(b), which governs this type of impeachment, is exactly tailored to strike the balance that the collateral evidence rule was designed to achieve with respect to impeachment by contradiction. Rule 608(b) allows cross-examination of a witness about specific instances of her past conduct, if probative of truthfulness or untruthfulness, but prohibits the proof of such conduct by extrinsic evidence. Thus, as with the collateral evidence rule, a relevant fact bearing on the witness' credibility— in this case, that he has lied in the past or acted in some other manner that casts doubt on veracity—may, in the discretion of the trial judge, be considered sufficiently important and probative to be elicited on cross-examination; yet, because of the dangers of confusion, prejudice, waste of time, and so on, that would be inherent if a "mini-trial" on the existence of that fact were allowed, extrinsic evidence of the matter is prohibited.[7]

Applying these principles to the testimony at issue here, it becomes obvious that the collateral evidence rule—in one sense now incorporated into Rule 608(b)—does not prohibit it. The testimony concerned an incident in which Hayne lied about having taken a polygraph examination. Whether or not Hayne took such a test or whether or not he passed may not have been admissible as substantive evidence. Nevertheless, in the discretion of the court, the "specific instance of conduct" in which he lied was, understandably, considered probative of his character for truthfulness or untruthfulness. Therefore, it was proper to allow Simmons to inquire about the incident while cross-examining Hayne. Of course, had Hayne denied the lie, the bar on the use of extrinsic evidence of specific instances of conduct to attack credibility in Rule 608(b) would have prohibited Simmons from proving the lie through the testimony of other witnesses. This sort of proof, however, was not offered. Clearly, the testimony carried some danger of prejudice, and just as clearly the trial court was obligated to balance this risk against the probative value of the testimony. The court did so, and we think it properly exercised its discretion in deciding that the testimony could be elicited under Rule 608(b). . . . For the foregoing reasons the judgment is Affirmed.

---

7. Indeed, even under the collateral evidence test, impeachment by contradiction of a witness' testimony generally would not be considered collateral—and thus would be allowed—where the impeaching matter indicates the witness' character for untruthfulness. See 3 J. Weinsteind & M. Berger, Weinstein's Evidence ¶ 607[05], 607-65 (1984).

UNITED STATES v. COPELIN

996 F.2d 379 (D.C. Cir. 1993)

MIKVA, Chief Judge:

Warren Ricardo Copelin appeals his conviction on one count of unlawful distribution of cocaine. . . . Vanessa Moore, an undercover District of Columbia police officer, pre-recorded the serial numbers of three bills and used them to purchase two rocks of crack cocaine, totalling .144 gram, from a man she maintains was Mr. Copelin. The man who sold her the crack produced the drugs from a brown medicine bottle. After making the purchase, Officer Moore broadcast a radio lookout and description of the suspect, and, within a few minutes, an arrest team stopped Mr. Copelin. Shortly thereafter, Officer Moore identified Mr. Copelin as the man who sold her drugs. When the arrest team officers searched Mr. Copelin, they found he possessed the pre-recorded currency. At the scene of the arrest, one of the officers found a brown medicine bottle containing 5.634 grams of cocaine base lying on the ground.

Mr. Copelin was charged with the unlawful distribution of crack cocaine, in connection with the two rocks he allegedly sold the officer, and with possession with intent to distribute in excess of five grams of crack cocaine, in connection with the drugs contained in the bottle. At trial, Mr. Copelin contended that he had not made the sale. He argued that Officer Moore was mistaking him for a man named David Bailey, with whom he was playing dice around the time of the sale. Mr. Copelin and his corroborating witnesses testified that they had seen Mr. Bailey repeatedly leave the dice game to engage in transactions. They further testified that money was rapidly changing hands during the game. . . .

Mr. Copelin's evidentiary claims concern a colloquy that occurred during the government's cross-examination of him at trial. The prosecutor asked him whether he knew that Mr. Bailey, the man Mr. Copelin contends actually made the sale, was in fact engaging in drug transactions during the dice game.

> *Q:*   All right. And did you ever see him engage in a transaction where you knew it for sure?
> *A:*   I would see money change hands, but other than seeing the actual drugs or anything, no, I haven't noticed.
> *Q:*   You didn't see any actual drugs?
> *A:*   No, sir.
> *Q:*   Would you know what they looked like if you saw them?
> *A:*   Yes. It's advertised on TV, too, sometimes in the commercials.
> *Q:*   You see drugs advertised on TV?
> *A:*   Yes, you know, on news or something like that.
> *Q:*   And that's the only time you've ever seen drugs?
> *A:*   Roughly, yes.
> *Q:*   Roughly?
> *A:*   Yes.

The prosecutor then requested a bench conference, during which he sought permission from the court to cross-examine Mr. Copelin as to his positive drug tests while he was on pretrial release.

The defendant tested positive for cocaine on three separate occasions and I believe that provides a reasonable basis to assume that he has seen cocaine.... He's made a bald denial that he has ever seen cocaine aside from on TV right here on the stand. I believe that's false and as a result, I propose to cross-examine him on this, but I wanted to ask the Court about it in advance.

Over the objection of defense counsel, the trial judge, without explanation, permitted the prosecutor to proceed with this line of questioning.

> *Q:*   Now, Mr. Copelin, isn't it true that as a condition of your release pending trial in this case, you were required to report to the Pretrial Services Administration for drug testing?
> *A:*   Yes.
> *Q:*   And isn't it true that you tested positive for cocaine on June 13th, 1991?
> *A:*   Yes.
> *Q:*   And you tested positive for cocaine on June 14th, 1991.
> *A:*   Yes.
> *Q:*   And you tested positive for cocaine on June 21st, 1991?
> *A:*   I don't recall that one.
> *Q:*   You don't recall that one?
> *A:*   No, sir.
> *Q:*   But despite having tested positive for cocaine on at least two occasions, you're telling the ladies and gentlemen of the jury that you have never seen cocaine except on television?
> *A:*   It could be anywhere. I never seen it, never used it.

The government then went on to pursue other issues.... Mr. Copelin argues that the district court should not have allowed the government to question him as to the positive drug tests. As an initial matter, however, he concedes, as he must, that although "prior bad acts" evidence is not admissible to show a defendant's propensity to commit the crime at issue, there are circumstances under which a court may admit such evidence. Rule 404(b) of the Federal Rules of Evidence states:

Evidence of other crimes, wrongs, or acts is not admissible to prove the character of a person in order to show action in conformity therewith. It may, however, be admissible for other purposes, such as proof of motive, opportunity, intent, preparation, plan, knowledge, identity, or absence of mistake or accident. ...

Although it is not one of the listed permissible purposes, an attempt to impeach through contradiction a defendant acting as a witness is indisputably a legitimate reason to introduce evidence of other crimes or wrongs.... If "bad acts" evidence is offered for this reason, it is admissible unless "its probative value is substantially outweighed by the danger of unfair prejudice, confusion of the issues, or misleading the jury or by considerations of undue delay, waste of time, or needless presentation of cumulative evidence." Fed. R. Evid. 403.

Mr. Copelin . . . claims that the government's method of impeachment violated the ban on the use of extrinsic evidence to impeach by contradiction on collateral matters. It is true that this Circuit generally follows the rule that "a witness may not be impeached by extrinsic evidence (contradiction by another witness or evidence) on a collateral issue." *United States v. Tarantino*, 846 F.2d 1384, 1409 (D.C. Cir. 1988), *cert. denied*, 488 U.S. 840 (1988). . . . However, the rule disallowing the use of extrinsic evidence to impeach a witness as to a collateral matter is irrelevant to this case, because Mr. Copelin was impeached by his own statements on cross-examination, not by the testimony of another witness or by physical evidence. "[C]ases upholding a court's exclusion of *extrinsic* evidence offered to impeach a witness, on the ground of the issue's being 'collateral,' do not govern the scope of cross examination itself." *United States v. Stock*, 948 F.2d 1299, 1302 (D.C. Cir. 1991). . . .

When Mr. Copelin testified that the did not actually see David Bailey selling drugs, it was not entirely unnatural for the government to explore the basis for this response by inquiring whether Mr. Copelin had the ability to recognize drugs in the first place. . . . It may well be that the trial judge would have sustained timely objections by defense counsel to the prosecutor's questions concerning Mr. Copelin's ability to recognize drugs. Mr. Copelin's attorney did not issue any such objections, however, so in reviewing this aspect of the cross-examination, we are limited to correcting "plain errors." Fed. R. Crim. P. 52(b). The plain error exception to the contemporaneous objection requirement should be used sparingly, only for "particularly egregious errors," *United States v. Frady*, 456 U.S. 152, 163 (1982), that "seriously affect the fairness, integrity or public reputation of judicial proceedings." *United States v. Atkinson*, 297 U.S. 157, 160 (1936). The district court's failure to squelch the government's disputed line of questioning on its own initiative was certainly not plain error, if it was error at all. . . . [Reversed on other grounds.)

KEVIN C. MCMUNIGAL & CALVIN WILLIAM SHARPE, REFORMING EXTRINSIC IMPEACHMENT

33 Conn. L. Rev. 363, 385-388 (2001)

No Federal Rule of Evidence explicitly addresses extrinsic contradiction of a witness by others. Federal courts dealing with this area of extrinsic impeachment often invoke the common law's collateral contradiction rule. Some federal courts, though, reject the collateral contradiction rule, using instead a case-by-case weighing approach under Rule 403. Federal courts also diverge on recognition of an exception to the collateral contradiction rule for statements by a witness made on direct rather than cross-examination.

The collateral contradiction rule . . . seems simple and clear: extrinsic evidence offered to contradict a witness on a collateral matter is automatically excluded. And the test most often used for distinguishing a collateral from a non-collateral matter, formulated by Wigmore, is easy to state: evidence is not collateral if the contradictory fact could have been shown for any purpose independent of the contradiction. The application of this definition, though, has resulted in "difficulty and dispute," and the boundary between collateral and noncollateral issues "is often indistinct when the collateral test is applied to the facts of a particular case." [4 Jack B. Weinstein & Margaret A. Berger, Weinstein's Federal Evidence, § 607.06[3][a], at 607-676 (Joseph M. McLaughlin ed., 2d ed. 2000)] . . .

At its core, the collateral contradiction rule is based on categorical rejection of a particular theory of relevance to support admission of extrinsic contradiction evidence. . . . All contradiction evidence seeks to establish that a witness' testimony was inaccurate on some point. One theory of relevance which may be offered in support of contradiction evidence holds that the fact that the witness was inaccurate on one point, regardless of its subject, makes it more probable that he was inaccurate on other points critical to the case. . . . This relevance theory, sometimes described by the Latin phrase, "*falsus in uno, falsus in omnibus*," draws a sort of propensity inference concerning inaccuracies in testimony. It seeks to build an inferential bridge from what may be an insignificant inaccuracy to some more significant inaccuracy in the witness' testimony. This transitive inaccuracy relevance theory is typically considered sufficient to support intrinsic impeachment evidence—the cross-examiner is allowed to ask the witness about possible inaccuracy on any point in her testimony subject to Rule 403. The central thrust of the collateral contradiction rule is a categorical rejection of the transitive inaccuracy relevance theory as adequate to support the admission of extrinsic evidence.

PROBLEMS

7.11. Abraham Lincoln's most famous performance as a trial lawyer came during his defense of William "Duff" Armstrong in 1858:

Armstrong stood accused of the drunken murder of Preston Metzker in the vicinity of a camp meeting on an August night the previous year. Lincoln, as a friend of Armstrong's parents, volunteered to defend him, though he rarely took capital cases. The chief witness for the prosecution said the light of the moon at 10:00 p.m. enabled him to see the defendant strike the victim with "a slung shot" that killed him. Lincoln, in rebuttal, introduced in evidence an almanac showing there was very little moonlight at the hour in question; and this, it was said, secured Armstrong's acquittal. Newspapers publicized the story after Lincoln's nomination in 1860.

Before long Democratic newspapers were claiming that the almanac Lincoln had introduced was for the wrong year. In 1872 Lamon's Life flatly asserted he had won the trial by trickery. An English law book, Ram on Facts, subsequently cited Lincoln's action in the case an instance of the commission of fraud. As a young attorney, Ambram Bergen, who later became a judge in Kansas, had witnessed the trial in the Beards-town courtroom; he testified in

1898 that the correct almanac had been introduced, and moreover that the jury foreman later swore in an affidavit that he had personally verified the year of the almanac. Unfortunately, the almanac supposed to have been used had disappeared. But Boy Scouts later, and repeatedly, verified the dimness of the light at the same spot in the lunar period. The novelist Edward Eggleston, in 1887, offered a fictional treatment of the Armstrong case in The Graysons: A Story of Illinois. He moved the trial back twenty years and freely altered the facts while, of course, keeping Lincoln the hero. Toward the end of his life Armstrong told his own story. Lincoln had been right: there was no moon. "But it was light enough for everybody to see the fight. The fight took place in front of one of the bars, and each bar had two or three candles on it. I had no slungshot. . . . It was only a fist fight, and if I killed 'Pres' Metzker I killed him with my naked fist."

Merrill D. Peterson, *Lincoln in American Memory* 95 (1994)*; *see also, e.g.*, Albert A. Woldman, *Lawyer Lincoln* 111-116 (1936).

Should the almanac have been excluded pursuant to the collateral evidence rule? Under the hearsay rule?

7.12. Suppose a truck collides with a motorcycle and the motorcyclist sues the truck driver. Ethan testifies that he saw the accident while waiting for a bus, and that the truck was speeding. Ethan previously told an insurance adjuster that he saw the accident while waiting to meet a friend—at least, so the adjuster recalls. When asked on cross-examination about his conversation with the adjuster, Ethan insists he told the adjuster he was waiting for a bus. In order to impeach Ethan, may the truck driver elicit testimony from the adjuster that Ethan said he saw the accident while waiting for a friend?

F. REHABILITATION

Rehabilitation is the opposite of impeachment. Impeachment is the introduction of evidence that suggests a witness's testimony lacks credibility. Rehabilitation is the introduction of evidence that suggests a witness's testimony in fact is worthy of belief. Just as there are five classic modes of impeachment—dishonesty, inconsistency, bias, incapacity, and specific contradiction—so one can describe five modes of rehabilitation—honesty, consistency, disinterest, capacity, and what might be called "specific corroboration." The Federal Rules of Evidence and their state counterparts contain special restrictions on only two of the possible modes of rehabilitation: "character for truthfulness" and prior consistent statements. But those special restrictions draw on and partially codify a general, common-law rule against rehabilitating a witness before the witness has been impeached, a practice generally and pejoratively referred to as "bolstering." Courts tend to apply the general rule against bolstering—often justified as an application of balancing under F.R.E. 403 or C.E.C. 352— to *all* forms of rehabilitation, not just to "character for truthfulness" and prior consistent statements. All rehabilitation, in other words, generally must follow impeachment. That is why it is called "rehabilitation."

When you read the materials that follow it is worth asking what justifies this general prohibition of bolstering. The traditional explanation, as you will see, is that bolstering drags out trials and invites the jury to take what a witness says on faith. But not everyone finds that that explanation convincing.

1. In General

UNITED STATES v. LINDEMANN

85 F.3d 1232 (7th Cir. 1996)

CUMMINGS, Circuit Judge.

"Charisma," a show horse, died in its stall on the night of December 15, 1990. The insurance company that had issued a policy on Charisma's life concluded that the death was the result of natural causes and paid the $250,000 value of the policy. Subsequently, the Federal Bureau of Investigation uncovered an alleged conspiracy between Tommy Burns and Barney Ward to kill horses for pay, allowing the horses' owners to collect insurance proceeds. Burns gave the FBI information indicating that George Lindemann, Jr. ("Lindemann"), a partial owner of Charisma, had arranged the horse's death in order to gain the proceeds of its life insurance policy. Lindemann was tried and convicted of three counts of wire fraud in violation of 18 U.S.C. § 1343. He appeals that conviction and we affirm.

. . . [Burns testified against Lindemann at trial, and Lindemann] challenges the admission of evidence regarding Burns' cooperation with the government on other cases. During Burns' cross-examination, Lindemann attacked the credibility of his testimony by suggesting that he would not have gotten a plea deal if he hadn't come up with the name of a "big fish" like Lindemann. Naturally, the government wanted to offer evidence to rebut Lindemann's assertion. Specifically, it wanted to explain to the jury that Lindemann's indictment and Burns' cooperation were the result of a much larger investigation involving the killing of 15 horses, including Charisma. Thus the government elicited from Burns the following testimony:

> *Q:* Now, Mr. Burns, when the federal agents came down to Florida after you were arrested for killing a horse, Streetwise, they asked you a lot of questions about your crimes; is that right?
> *A:* Yes, they did.
> *Q:* Were those agents focused on George Lindemann?
> *A:* No, they weren't. They basically focused on Helen Brach.
> *Q:* During the course of your cooperation, Mr. Burns, you cooperated against other wealthy people; isn't that right?
> *A:* Oh yeah.
> *Q:* And you've cooperated, have you not, Mr. Burns, with respect to other famous equestrians?
> *A:* Yes, I have. . . .

Q: Is George Lindemann a big part of your cooperation or a small part of your cooperation?
A: They never treated him like he was a big part.
Q: In fact, Mr. Burns, you told the government about many, many people that you killed horses for. To your knowledge, how many people did you discuss with the government, roughly?
A: 30.
Q: And how many of those people have pleaded guilty?
A: 90 percent of them.

Immediately following this testimony, the court instructed the jury as follows:

> This testimony may be considered by you solely for the purpose of understanding the scope of Tom Burns' cooperation with the government. The fact that other subjects in the investigation may have pled guilty must not be considered by you to infer that the defendants are, therefore, guilty of the crimes with which they are charged.

. . . Lindemann argues that Burns' testimony was inadmissible because it was essentially "bolstering." "Bolstering" is the practice of offering evidence solely for the purpose of enhancing a witness's credibility before that credibility is attacked. Such evidence is inadmissible because it "has the potential for extending the length of trials enormously, . . . asks the jury to take the witness's testimony on faith, . . . and may . . . reduce the care with which jurors listen for inconsistencies and other signs of falsehood or inaccuracy." *United States v. LeFevour*, 798 F.2d 977, 983 (7th Cir. 1986). Once a witness's credibility has been attacked, however, the non-attacking party is permitted to admit evidence to "rehabilitate" the witness. *United States v. McKinney*, 954 F.2d 471, 478 (7th Cir. 1992), *certiorari denied*, 506 U.S. 1023 (1992).

Lindemann's suggestion that Burns falsely implicated him to obtain a plea deal was certainly an attack on the credibility of Burns' testimony. More specifically, it was an attempt to show that Burns had a bias. . . . Thus Lindemann was perfectly entitled to suggest his theory that Burns was lying about Lindemann in order to better the parameters of his plea deal. However, the direct consequence of the attack was that the government was entitled to introduce evidence to rehabilitate Burns on the issue.

The Federal Rules of Evidence specifically address the bolstering/rehabilitation aspect of only two of the five attack methods: Character for truthfulness and prior inconsistent statements.[8] The admissibility of evidence regarding a witness's bias, diminished capacity, and contradictions in his

---

8. Following the traditional rule against bolstering, Fed. R. Evid. 608 states that evidence of truthful character is admissible only after the character of the witness for truthfulness has been attacked. . . ." Furthermore, Rule 608 provides specific limitations on the admissibility of rehabilitation evidence: Once a witness's character for truthfulness has been attacked, evidence is admissible "in the form of opinion or reputation" (608(a)) or non-extrinsic evidence elicited on cross-examination (608(b)). Fed. R. Evid. 801(d)(1)(B) contains the bolstering/rehabilitation rule by defining as nonhearsay only those prior consistent statements that are offered "to rebut an express or implied charge" against a witness of "recent fabrication or improper influence or motive."

testimony is not specifically addressed by the Rules, and thus admissibility is limited only by the relevance standard of Rule 402. Therefore, because the attack at issue was on Burns' bias, and not on his character for truthfulness in general, Lindemann's contention that the limitations of Rule 608 should have applied is incorrect. Moreover, because bias is not a collateral issue, it was permissible for evidence on this issue to be extrinsic in form. *United States v. Brown*, 547 F.2d 438 (8th Cir. 1977) (extrinsic evidence admissible to rebut evidence of bias); *see also United States v. Beauchamp*, 986 F.2d 1, 4 (1st Cir. 1993); *United States v. Capozzi*, 883 F.2d 608, 615 (8th Cir. 1989), *certiorari denied*, 495 U.S. 918 (1990); *United States v. James*, 609 F.2d 36, 46 (2d Cir. 1979), *certiorari denied*, 445 U.S. 905 (1980).

Here we conclude that the admission of evidence regarding Burns' cooperation in other cases was relevant. The evidence specifically rebutted the allegation that Burns was biased out of self-interest in Lindemann's case: Burns' successful participation in numerous other cases meant that at the time he was negotiating over his plea deal, he had lots of information to use as bargaining chips. That fact was relevant under the standards of Fed. R. Evid. 402 because it made less probable the assertion that Burns was lying in Lindemann's case out of self-interest. Finally, the district court immediately warned the jury that it was not to infer Lindemann's guilt from the fact that other indicted individuals had pleaded guilty. Thus the evidence was used only to assess Burns' credibility, not as evidence of Lindemann's guilt.

In conclusion, because Lindemann attacked the credibility of Burns' testimony by asserting that Burns had a bias in Lindemann's case, the government was permitted to rebut that assertion by introducing evidence of its own. Furthermore, because that evidence was relevant according to Fed. R. Evid. 402, the district court's decision to admit it was not an abuse of discretion. . . . Affirmed.

2. Character for Truthfulness

[F.R.E. 608; C.E.C. §790]

ADVISORY COMMITTEE NOTE TO F.R.E. 608

. . . Character evidence in support of credibility is admissible under the rule only after the witness' character has first been attacked, as has been the case at common law. The enormous needless consumption of time which a contrary practice would entail justifies the limitation. Opinion or reputation that the witness is untruthful specifically qualifies as an attack under the rule, and evidence of misconduct, including conviction of crime, and of corruption also fall within this category. Evidence of bias or interest does not. McCormick § 49; 4 Wigmore §§ 1106, 1107. Whether evidence in the form of contradiction is an attack upon the character of the witness must depend upon the circumstances. McCormick § 49. Cf. 4 Wigmore §§ 1108, 1109. . . .

BEARD v. MITCHELL

604 F.2d 485 (7th Cir. 1979)

SPRECHER, Circuit Judge.

Plaintiff, Eloise Beard, appeals from a jury verdict finding the defendant, Roy Martin Mitchell, not guilty of depriving her deceased brother of rights secured by the United States Constitution. . . . On May 17, 1972, Jeff Beard was abducted and brutally murdered by Stanley Robinson, a Chicago police officer. An F.B.I. informant, William O'Neal accompanied Robinson on the night of the murder. Robinson was convicted of the crime in 1973. In 1975 plaintiff brought this suit against Roy Martin Mitchell, an F.B.I. agent who participated in the investigation of Robinson's activities. Plaintiff alleges that Mitchell's reckless conduct of the Robinson investigation resulted in the deprivation of Jeff Beard's constitutional rights, giving rise to a *Bivens* action for damages. The plaintiff contends that liability could be premised on Mitchell's reckless training and use of an informant, O'Neal, whose conduct allegedly caused Beard's death. Further plaintiff maintains that liability could be premised on Mitchell's failure to arrest Robinson prior to the murder or to take other preventive action. . . .

The trial judge permitted Kocoras, the Assistant U.S. Attorney assigned to the Robinson case, to testify at trial that defendant Mitchell had a reputation for truthfulness. The plaintiff contends that this was an impermissible use of reputation evidence under Rule 608(a) of the Federal Rules of Evidence. The plaintiff concedes that she introduced prior inconsistent statements by Mitchell as a means of attacking his credibility but maintains that Rule 608 does not permit the admission of this type of evidence to counter impeachment accomplished by prior inconsistent statements.

Rule 608(a)(2) provides that "evidence of truthful character is admissible only after the character of the witness for truthfulness has been attacked by opinion or reputation evidence *or otherwise*." (Emphasis added.) The use of prior inconsistent statements may constitute an attack on truthfulness. The Supreme Court noted in *United States v. Hale*, 422 U.S. 171, 176 (1975) that "[a] basic rule of evidence provides that prior inconsistent statements may be used to impeach the credibility of a witness." Thus we can not conclude that the trial judge abused his discretion in allowing the testimony. . . . [Affirmed.]

UNITED STATES v. DANEHY

680 F.2d 1311 (11th Cir. 1982)

PER CURIAM

Thomas Danehy appeals his conviction under 18 U.S.C. §§ 2, 111, and 1114 for forcibly resisting, opposing, impeding, and interfering with Coast Guardsmen while they were engaged in the performance of their duties. [The government charged Danehy with trying to ram a Coast Guard boat with his fishing boat and then resisting Coast Guard officers who boarded his boat and arrested him. Danehy testified at trial and denied the allegations.]

Danehy claims that . . . he should have been allowed to introduce evidence of his reputation for truthfulness as his credibility had been attacked. We disagree.

We addressed precisely this issue in *United States v. Jackson*, 588 F.2d 1046, 1055 (5th Cir. 1979). There, as here, the "attack" on the defendant's credibility consisted of a vigorous cross-examination and the pointing out by the prosecutor of discrepancies between the defendant's testimony and that of other witnesses. This does not call into question the reputation of the defendant for truthfulness. The mere fact that a witness is contradicted by other evidence in a case does not constitute an attack upon his reputation for truth and veracity. *Kauz v. United States*, 188 F.2d 9 (5th Cir. 1951).

Danehy claims that under Rule 404 of the Federal Rules of Evidence an accused may always bring forth evidence of a pertinent character trait and that his reputation for truth is pertinent in the instant case. We reject this line of reasoning. Since Danehy is trying to offer evidence to bolster himself as a witness rather than to show a trait of character that is pertinent to the crime charged, it is Federal Rule of Evidence 608, not 404, that governs. Rule 608 specifically states that "evidence of truthful character is admissible only after the character of the witness for truthfulness has been attacked by opinion or reputation evidence or otherwise." Government counsel pointing out inconsistencies in testimony and arguing that the accused's testimony is not credible does not constitute an attack on the accused's reputation for truthfulness within the meaning of Rule 608. Thus, Danehy may not attempt to bolster his testimony by evidence as to his reputation for truthfulness. Therefore, the district court properly denied Danehy's request to call witnesses to testify to his reputation for truthfulness. . . . [Reversed on other grounds.]

UNITED STATES v. DRURY

396 F.3d 1303 (11th Cir. 2005)

MARCUS, Circuit Judge:

[Dr. Carl] Drury appeals his convictions for violating the federal murder-for-hire statute, 18 U.S.C. § 1958, and for possessing a firearm in connection with a crime of violence, in violation of 18 U.S.C. § 924(c). [Drury hired an undercover agent of the Bureau of Alcohol, Tobacco, and Firearms to kill his wife, and he provided the agent with a gun.] . . . Drury's basic defense at trial was that the whole murder-for-hire scheme was merely an ATF role-playing exercise. . . . Drury denied ever actually intending to have his wife killed. . . .

Drury . . . challenges the district court's exclusion of evidence of his truthful character. Drury claims that the government attacked his credibility at trial, entitling him to introduce rehabilitative evidence pursuant to

Federal Rule of Evidence 608(a)(2). Rule 608(a)(2) provides that "evidence of truthful character is admissible only after the character of the witness for truthfulness has been attacked by opinion or reputation evidence or otherwise."

Drury does not suggest that the government presented any opinion or reputation evidence about his character, but argues that his character was "otherwise" attacked. He offers as the basis for this contention a series of scattered questions asked by the prosecutor during cross-examination of Drury. Among the examples of what Drury cites as the prosecution's "credibility-laden questions" are these: "Are you telling us that you told an arresting officer that you wanted to make a statement and he wouldn't let you?"; "Are you saying that he hushed you up?"; "Is that what you want this jury to believe?"; "You don't think the officer had any reason to think that you were trying to offer him a bribe?"; and "Is that what you are telling us?" Based on these and several other remarks of similar tenor, Drury sought to introduce testimony from six witnesses prepared to attest to his truthful character. . . .

An "attack" that consists only of "Government counsel pointing out inconsistencies in testimony and arguing that the accused's testimony is not credible does not constitute an attack on the accused's reputation for truthfulness within the meaning of Rule 608." *United States v. Daneby*, 680 F.2d 1311, 1314 (11th Cir. 1982). However, that is precisely the sort of "attack" Drury claims the prosecution to have launched during its cross-examination. Because such an attack is insufficient to authorize rehabilitation under Rule 608, we have little trouble concluding that the district court did not abuse its discretion in excluding Drury's proffered reputation-for-truthfulness testimony. . . . AFFIRMED.

UNITED STATES v. MURRAY

103 F.3d 310 (3d Cir. 1997)

ALITO, Circuit Judge:

Appellant Michael Murray was convicted following a jury trial of an intentional killing in furtherance of a continuing criminal enterprise ("CCE") in violation of 21 U.S.C. § 848(e)(1)(A); conspiracy to distribute in excess of five kilograms of cocaine in violation of 21 U.S.C. §§ 846 and 841(a)(1); and distribution of and possession with intent to distribute cocaine in violation of 21 U.S.C. § 841(a)(1). [Among the witnesses against Murray was a police informant named Richard Brown.] After Murray cross-examined Brown, the government called Lt. John Goshert, a Harrisburg police officer, to testify in support of Brown's reliability. Murray objected to Goshert's testimony on the ground that "the character of [Brown] for truthfulness" had not been "attacked by opinion or reputation evidence or otherwise," Fed. R. Evid. 608(a), and that even if it had, Lt. Goshert's testimony violated Fed. R. Evid. 608(b)'s proscription on proof of specific instances of conduct by extrinsic evidence. The court overruled Murray's objection.

. . . It is true that Murray did not present any opinion or reputation evidence to impeach Brown, but Murray's counsel performed an extended and vigorous cross-examination of Brown that exposed Brown's various illegal and sordid activities. Murray's counsel questioned Brown about his long-standing and heavy drug use, his acquaintance with many Harrisburg drug dealers, his apparent under-the-table tax-free compensation for his work as an informant, his convictions for drug possession and theft of services, his unlawful carrying of an unlicensed firearm, his concealment of his drug use from his friend and contact in the Harrisburg police department, and his prior inconsistent statements to the grand jury. In view of this questioning, the opinion or reputation testimony given by Lt. Goshert fell within the language of Rule 608(a)(2) permitting the introduction of such evidence to support a witness' credibility when his character for truthfulness has been "otherwise" attacked.

Murray's more persuasive argument is founded upon Rule 608(b)'s prohibition on proving specific instances of a witness' conduct by extrinsic evidence. Once Brown's character for truthfulness was attacked by Murray's counsel, the government was entitled to attempt to rehabilitate Brown by calling a witness to give opinion or reputation testimony as to Brown's character for truthfulness. But the government was not entitled to present "extrinsic evidence" of "specific instances" of Brown's conduct "for the purpose of . . . supporting [his] credibility." Fed. R. Evid. 608(b). Lt. Goshert's testimony was as follows:

> *Q:* Lieutenant Goshert, do you know an individual by the name of Richard Brown?
> *A:* Yes, I do.
> *Q:* Have you ever used Mr. Brown as a confidential informant?
> *A:* On numerous occasions, the Harrisburg Police has utilized him.
> *Q:* As a result pf [sic] your using Richard Brown as a confidential informant, have you made any cases?
> *A:* Yes, we have.
> *Q:* Do you have an idea of approximately how many?
> *A:* In excess of 65. 65, 66 something like that.
> *Q:* And search warrants, have you obtained search warrants based on his information?
> *A:* Yes, we have numerous times.
> *Q:* How long a period of time have you been dealing with Mr. Brown?
> *A:* Since 1988.
> *Q:* Based on your dealings with Mr. Brown and the cases you said that he has made, can you give us your opinion as to his reputation for being a reliable individual?
> *A:* He is extremely reliable.
> *Q:* In terms of the accuracy of the information?
> *A:* Yes.

This testimony, in our view, included "extrinsic evidence" of Brown's character for truthfulness. *United States v. McNeill*, 887 F.2d 448, 453

(3d Cir. 1989) ("Extrinsic evidence is evidence offered through other witnesses rather than through cross-examination of the witness himself or herself."), *cert. denied*, 493 U.S. 1087 (1990). Murray argues that Lt. Goshert's quantification of the cases that Brown had "made" constituted evidence of "specific instances" of Brown's conduct and thus should have been excluded under Rule 608(b). The government contends that Lt. Goshert's testimony was proper as foundation for his opinion as to Brown's character for truthfulness. In support of the admission of Lt. Goshert's testimony in the district court, the government argued that "[t]here has got to be some basis for the jury to know how he can give that opinion as to his reputation. And by letting the jury know they have a close working relationship over a period of time and that they have been involved in all of these incidents, then there is a basis for him giving that opinion." We agree that Lt. Goshert's testimony that the Harrisburg police had used Brown as a confidential informant on "numerous occasions" since 1988 was necessary to establish that he had a basis on which to offer his opinion as to Brown's character for truthfulness. However, his testimony that Brown had "made" 65 or 66 cases was more specific than can be justified as necessary to establish a foundation.

United States v. Taylor, 900 F.2d 779 (4th Cir. 1990) presented a situation extremely similar to the instant case. In *Taylor* as in this case, the government's fortunes depended in large part on the credibility of an informant, and the government called a law enforcement officer to testify as to the informant's reliability. The officer testified that the informant "had acted as a buyer for the government on 15 to 18 drug buys," that he "had given reliable information in a particular case which resulted in the seller's conviction," and that "several others either pleaded guilty or were convicted as a result of [the informant's] testimony." The court held that it was error to admit evidence that the informant's testimony had resulted in convictions in other cases. Lt. Goshert's testimony was substantially identical, and we conclude that its admission contravened Rule 608(b). . . . [Reversed on these and other grounds.]

PROBLEMS

7.13. The plaintiff in a medical malpractice case calls a physician as an expert witness. The physician admits on cross-examination that she is being paid $5,000 for her testimony. Can the plaintiff now call a witness to testify that the physician is honest or has a reputation for honesty?

7.14. The prosecution in a shoplifting case calls a department store employee who testifies that she saw the defendant, while in a dressing room, cut price tags from clothing and stuff the clothing in her shopping bag. On cross-examination, defense counsel suggests that it would have been impossible for the witness to see what she claims to have seen through the slats of the dressing room door. Can the prosecution now call the employee's supervisor to testify that, in the supervisor's opinion, the employee would not lie under oath?

3. Prior Consistent Statements

[F.R.E. 801(d)(1), C.E.C. §§791, 1236]

TOME v. UNITED STATES

513 U.S. 150 (1995)

Justice KENNEDY delivered the opinion of the Court, except as to Part IIB.

Various Federal Courts of Appeals are divided over the evidence question presented by this case. At issue is the interpretation of a provision in the Federal Rules of Evidence bearing upon the admissibility of statements, made by a declarant who testifies as a witness, that are consistent with the testimony and are offered to rebut a charge of a "recent fabrication or improper influence or motive." Fed. Rule Evid. 801(d)(1)(B). The question is whether out-of-court consistent statements made after the alleged fabrication, or after the alleged improper influence or motive arose, are admissible under the Rule.

I

Petitioner Tome was charged in a one-count indictment with the felony of sexual abuse of a child, his own daughter, aged four at the time of the alleged crime. The case having arisen on the Navajo Indian Reservation, Tome was tried by a jury in the United States District Court for the District of New Mexico, where he was found guilty of violating 18 U.S.C. §§ 1153, 2241(c), and 2245(2)(A) and (B).

Tome and the child's mother had been divorced in 1988. A tribal court awarded joint custody of the daughter, A.T., to both parents, but Tome had primary physical custody. In 1989 the mother was unsuccessful in petitioning the tribal court for primary custody of A.T., but was awarded custody for the summer of 1990. Neither parent attended a further custody hearing in August 1990. On August 27, 1990, the mother contacted Colorado authorities with allegations that Tome had committed sexual abuse against A.T.

The prosecution's theory was that Tome committed sexual assaults upon the child while she was in his custody and that the crime was disclosed when the child was spending vacation time with her mother. The defense argued that the allegations were concocted so the child would not be returned to her father. At trial A.T., then 6½ years old, was the Government's first witness. For the most part, her direct testimony consisted of one- and two- word answers to a series of leading questions. Cross-examination took place over two trial days. The defense asked A.T. 348 questions. On the first day A.T. answered all the questions posed to her on general, background subjects.

The next day there was no testimony, and the prosecutor met with A.T. When cross-examination of A.T. resumed, she was questioned about those conversations but was reluctant to discuss them. Defense counsel then began questioning her about the allegations of abuse, and it appears she was reluctant at many points to answer. As the trial judge noted, however, some of the defense questions were imprecise or unclear. The judge expressed his concerns with the examination of A.T., observing there were lapses of as much as 40-55 seconds between some questions and the answers and that on the second day of examination the witness seemed to be losing concentration. The trial judge stated, "We have a very difficult situation here."

After A.T. testified, the Government produced six witnesses who testified about a total of seven statements made by A.T. describing the alleged sexual assaults: A.T.'s babysitter recited A.T.'s statement to her on August 22, 1990, that she did not want to return to her father because he "gets drunk and he thinks I'm his wife"; the babysitter related further details given by A.T. on August 27, 1990, while A.T's mother stood outside the room and listened after the mother had been unsuccessful in questioning A.T. herself; the mother recounted what she had heard A.T. tell the babysitter; a social worker recounted details A.T. told her on August 29, 1990, about the assaults; and three pediatricians, Drs. Kuper, Reich, and Spiegel, related A.T.'s statements to them describing how and where she had been touched by Tome. All but A.T.'s statement to Dr. Spiegel implicated Tome. (The physicians also testified that their clinical examinations of the child indicated that she had been subjected to vaginal penetrations. That part of the testimony is not at issue here.)

A.T.'s out-of-court statements, recounted by the six witnesses, were offered by the Government under Rule 801(d)(1)(B). The trial court admitted all of the statements over defense counsel's objection, accepting the Government's argument that they rebutted the implicit charge that A.T.'s testimony was motivated by a desire to live with her mother. The court also admitted A.T.'s August 22d statement to her babysitter under Rule 803(24), and the statements to Dr. Kuper (and apparently also to Dr. Reich) under Rule 803(4) (statements for purposes of medical diagnosis). The Government offered the testimony of the social worker under both Rules 801(d)(1)(B) and 803(24), but the record does not indicate whether the court ruled on the latter ground. No objection was made to Dr. Spiegel's testimony. Following trial, Tome was convicted and sentenced to 12 years' imprisonment.

On appeal, the Court of Appeals for the Tenth Circuit affirmed, adopting the Government's argument that all of A.T.'s out-of-court statements were admissible under Rule 801(d)(1)(B) even though they had been made after A.T.'s alleged motive to fabricate arose. The court reasoned that "the pre-motive requirement is a function of the relevancy rules, not the hearsay rules" and that as a "function of relevance, the pre-motive rule is clearly too broad . . . because it is simply not true that an individual with a motive to lie always will do so. . . . Rather, the relevance of the prior consistent statement is more accurately determined by evaluating the strength of the motive to lie, the circumstances in which the statement is made, and the declarant's demonstrated propensity to lie." Applying this balancing test to A.T.'s first statement to her babysitter, the Court of Appeals determined that although A.T. might have had "some motive to lie, we do not believe that it is a particularly strong one." The court held that the District Judge had not abused his discretion in admitting A.T.'s out-of-court statements. It did not analyze the probative quality of A.T.'s six other out-of-court statements, nor did it reach the admissibility of the statements under any other rule of evidence.

We granted certiorari and now reverse.

II

The prevailing common-law rule for more than a century before adoption of the Federal Rules of Evidence was that a prior consistent statement introduced to rebut a charge of recent fabrication or improper influence or motive was admissible if the statement had been made before the alleged fabrication, influence, or motive came into being, but it was inadmissible if made afterwards. As Justice Story explained: "[W]here the testimony is assailed as a fabrication of a recent date, . . . in order to repel such imputation, proof of the *antecedent* declaration of the party may be admitted." *Ellicott v. Pearl*, 35 U.S. (10 Pet.) 412, 439 (1836) (emphasis added). See also *People v. Singer*, 300 N.Y. 120, 124-125, 89 N.E.2d 710, 712 (1949).

McCormick and Wigmore stated the rule in a more categorical manner: "[T]he applicable principle is that the prior consistent statement has no relevancy to refute the charge unless the consistent statement was made before the source of the bias, interest, influence or incapacity originated." E. Cleary, McCormick on Evidence § 49, p. 105 (2d ed. 1972) (hereafter McCormick). See also 4 J. Wigmore, Evidence § 1128, p. 268 (J. Chadbourn rev. 1972) (hereafter Wigmore) ("A consistent statement, at a *time prior* to the existence of a fact said to indicate bias . . . will effectively explain away the force of the impeaching evidence" (emphasis in original)). The question is whether Rule 801(d)(1)(B) embodies this temporal requirement. We hold that it does.

A

. . . Rule 801 defines prior consistent statements as nonhearsay only if they are offered to rebut a charge of "recent fabrication or improper influence or motive." Fed. Rule Evid. 801(d)(1)(B). Noting the "troublesome" logic of treating a witness' prior consistent statements as hearsay at all (because the declarant is present in court and subject to cross-examination), the Advisory Committee decided to treat those consistent statements, once the preconditions of the Rule were satisfied, as nonhearsay and admissible as substantive evidence, not just to rebut an attack on the witness' credibility. See Advisory Committee's Notes on Fed. Rule Evid. 801(d)(1). A consistent statement meeting the requirements of the Rule is thus placed in the same category as a declarant's inconsistent statement made under oath in another proceeding, or prior identification testimony, or admissions by a party opponent.

The Rules do not accord this weighty, nonhearsay status to all prior consistent statements. To the contrary, admissibility under the Rules is confined to those statements offered to rebut a charge of "recent fabrication or improper influence or motive," the same phrase used by the Advisory Committee in its description of the "traditiona[l]" common law of evidence, which was the background against which the Rules were drafted. Prior consistent statements may not be admitted to counter all forms of impeachment or to bolster the witness merely because she has been discredited. In the present context, the question is whether A.T.'s out-of-court statements rebutted the alleged link between her desire to be with her mother and her testimony, not whether they suggested that A.T.'s in-court testimony was true. The Rule speaks of a party rebutting an alleged motive, not bolstering the veracity of the story told.

This limitation is instructive, not only to establish the preconditions of admissibility but also to reinforce the significance of the requirement that the consistent statements must have been made before the alleged influence, or motive to fabricate, arose. That is to say, the forms of impeachment within the Rule's coverage are the ones in which the temporal requirement makes the most sense. Impeachment by charging that the testimony is a recent fabrication or results from an improper influence or motive is, as a general matter, capable of direct and forceful refutation through introduction of out-of-court consistent statements that predate the alleged fabrication, influence, or motive. A consistent statement that predates the motive is a square rebuttal of the charge that the testimony was contrived as a consequence of that motive. By contrast, prior consistent statements carry little rebuttal force when most other types of impeachment are involved. McCormick § 49, p. 105 ("When the attack takes the form of impeachment of character, by showing misconduct, convictions or bad reputation, it is generally agreed that there is no color for sustaining by consistent statements. The defense does not meet the assault" (footnote omitted)); see also 4 Wigmore § 1131, p. 293 ("The broad rule obtains in a few courts that consistent statements may be admitted *after* impeachment of any sort—in particular after any impeachment by *cross-examination*. But there is no reason for such a loose rule" (footnote omitted)).

There may arise instances when out-of-court statements that postdate the alleged fabrication have some probative force in rebutting a charge of fabrication or improper influence or motive, but those statements refute the charged fabrication in a less direct and forceful way. Evidence that a witness made consistent statements after the alleged motive to fabricate arose may suggest in some degree that the in-court testimony is truthful, and thus suggest in some degree that that testimony did not result from some improper influence; but if the drafters of Rule 801(d)(1)(B) intended to countenance rebuttal along that indirect inferential chain, the purpose of confining the types of impeachment that open the door to rebuttal by introducing consistent statements becomes unclear. If consistent statements are admissible without reference to the timeframe we find imbedded in the Rule, there appears no sound reason not to admit consistent statements to rebut other forms of impeachment as well. Whatever objections can be leveled against limiting the Rule to this designated form of impeachment and confining the rebuttal to those statements made before the fabrication or improper influence or motive arose, it is clear to us that the drafters of Rule 801(d)(1)(B) were relying upon the common-law temporal requirement. . . . The language of the Rule, in its concentration on rebutting charges of recent fabrication or improper influence or motive to the exclusion of other forms of impeachment, as well as in its use of wording that follows the language of the common-law cases, suggests that it was intended to carry over the common-law premotive rule.

B

Our conclusion that Rule 801(d)(1)(B) embodies the common-law premotive requirement is confirmed by an examination of the Advisory Committee's Notes to the Federal Rules of Evidence. We have relied on those well-considered Notes as a useful guide in ascertaining the meaning of the Rules. See, *e.g.*, *Huddleston v. United States*, 485 U.S. 681, 688 (1988); *United States v. Owens*, 484 U.S. 554, 562 (1988). Where, as with Rule 801(d)(1)(B), "Congress did not amend the Advisory Committee's draft in any way . . . the Committee's commentary is particularly relevant in determining the meaning of the document Congress enacted." *Beech Aircraft Corp. v. Rainey*, 488 U.S. 153, 165-166, n. 9 (1988). The Notes are also a respected source of scholarly commentary. Professor Cleary was a distinguished commentator on the law of evidence, and he and members of the Committee consulted and considered the views, criticisms, and suggestions of the academic community in preparing the Notes.

The Notes disclose a purpose to adhere to the common law in the application of evidentiary principles, absent express provisions to the contrary. Where the Rules did depart from their common-law antecedents, in general the Committee said so. See, *e.g.*, Notes on Rule 804(b)(4) ("The general common law requirement that a declaration in this area must have been made *ante litem motam* has been dropped, as bearing more appropriately on weight than admissibility"); Rule 804(b)(2) ("The exception is the familiar dying declaration of the common law, expanded somewhat beyond its traditionally narrow limits"); Rule 804(b)(3) ("The exception discards the common law limitation and expands to the full logical limit"). The Notes give no indication, however, that Rule 801(d)(1)(B) abandoned the premotive requirement. The entire discussion of Rule 801(d)(1)(B) is limited to the following comment:

> "Prior consistent statements traditionally have been admissible to rebut charges of recent fabrication or improper influence or motive but not as substantive evidence. Under the rule they are substantive evidence. The prior statement is consistent with the testimony given on the stand, and, if the opposite party wishes to open the door for its admission in evidence, no sound reason is apparent why it should not be received generally."

Throughout their discussion of the Rules, the Advisory Committee's Notes rely on Wigmore and McCormick as authority for the common-law approach. In light of the categorical manner in which those authors state the premotive requirement, it is difficult to imagine that the drafters, who noted the new substantive use of prior consistent statements, would have remained silent if they intended to modify the premotive requirement. As we observed with respect to another provision of the Rules, "[w]ith this state of unanimity confronting the drafters of the Federal Rules of Evidence, we think it unlikely that they intended to scuttle entirely [the common-law requirement]." *United States v. Abel*, 469 U.S. 45, 50 (1984). Here, we do not think the drafters of the Rule intended to scuttle the whole premotive requirement and rationale without so much as a whisper of explanation.

Observing that Edward Cleary was the Reporter of the Advisory Committee that drafted the Rules, the Court has relied upon his writings as persuasive authority on the meaning of the Rules. See *Daubert v. Merrell Dow Pharmaceuticals, Inc.*, 509 U.S. 579 (1993); *Abel, supra*, at 51-52. Cleary also was responsible for the 1972 revision of McCormick's treatise, which included an examination of the changes introduced by the proposed federal rules to the common-law practice of impeachment and rehabilitation. The discussion, which occurs only three paragraphs after the treatise's categorical description of the common-law premotive rule, also lacks any indication that the proposed rules were abandoning that temporal limitation. See McCormick § 50, p. 107.

Our conclusion is bolstered by the Advisory Committee's stated "unwillingness to countenance the general use of prior prepared statements as substantive evidence." See Notes on Rule 801(d)(1). Rule 801(d), which "enumerates three situations in which the statement is excepted from the category of hearsay," *ibid.*, was expressly contrasted by the Committee with Uniform Rule of Evidence 63(1) (1953), "which allows *any* out-of-court statement of a declarant who is present at the trial and available for cross-examination." Notes on Rule 801(d)(1) (emphasis added). When a witness presents important testimony damaging to a party, the party will often counter with at least an implicit charge that the witness has been under some influence or motive to fabricate. If Rule 801 were read so that the charge opened the floodgates to any prior consistent statement that satisfied Rule 403, as the Tenth Circuit concluded, the distinction between rejected Uniform Rule 63(1) and Rule 801(d)(1)(B) would all but disappear.

That Rule 801(d)(1)(B) permits prior consistent statements to be used for substantive purposes after the statements are admitted to rebut the existence of an improper influence or motive makes it all the more important to observe the preconditions for admitting the evidence in the first place. The position taken by the Rules reflects a compromise between the views expressed by the "bulk of the case law . . . against allowing prior statements of witnesses to be used generally as substantive evidence" and the views of the majority of "writers . . . [who] ha[d] taken the opposite position." *Ibid.* That compromise was one that the Committee candidly admitted was a "judgment . . . more of experience than of logic." *Ibid.*

"A party contending that legislative action changed settled law has the burden of showing that the legislature intended such a change." *Green v. Bock Laundry Machine Co.*, 490 U.S. 504, 521 (1989) (applying that presumption in interpreting Federal Rule of Evidence 609). Nothing in the Advisory Committee's Notes suggests that it intended to alter the common-law premotive requirement.

C

The Government's final argument in favor of affirmance is that the common-law premotive rule advocated by petitioner is inconsistent with the Federal Rules' liberal approach to relevancy and with strong academic criticism, beginning in the 1940's, directed at the exclusion of out-of-court statements made by a declarant who is present in court and subject to cross-examination. This argument misconceives the design of the Rules' hearsay provisions.

Hearsay evidence is often relevant. . . . That certain out-of-court statements may be relevant does not dispose of the question whether they are admissible.

. . . To be sure, certain commentators in the years preceding the adoption of the Rules had been critical of the common-law approach to hearsay, particularly its categorical exclusion of out-of-court statements offered for substantive purposes. General criticism was directed to the exclusion of a declarant's out-of-court statements where the declarant testified at trial. As an alternative, they suggested moving away from the categorical exclusion of hearsay and toward a case-by-case balancing of the probative value of particular statements against their likely prejudicial effect. The Advisory Committee, however, was explicit in rejecting this balancing approach to hearsay:

"The Advisory Committee has rejected this approach to hearsay as involving too great a measure of judicial discretion, minimizing the predictability of rulings, [and] enhancing the difficulties of preparation for trial." Advisory Committee's Introduction to Article VIII.

. . . The statement-by-statement balancing approach advocated by the Government and adopted by the Tenth Circuit creates the precise dangers the Advisory Committee noted and sought to avoid: It involves considerable judicial discretion; it reduces predictability; and it enhances the difficulties of trial preparation because parties will have difficulty knowing in advance whether or not particular out-of-court statements will be admitted.

D

The case before us illustrates some of the important considerations supporting the Rule as we interpret it, especially in criminal cases. If the Rule were to permit the introduction of prior statements as substantive evidence to rebut every implicit charge that a witness' in-court testimony results from recent fabrication or improper influence or motive, the whole emphasis of the trial could shift to the out-of-court statements, not the in-court ones. The present case illustrates the point. In response to a rather weak charge that A.T.'s testimony was a fabrication created so the child could remain with her mother, the Government was permitted to present a parade of sympathetic and credible witnesses who did no more than recount A.T.'s detailed out-of-court statements to them. Although those statements might have been probative on the question whether the alleged conduct had occurred, they shed but minimal light on whether A.T. had the charged motive to fabricate. At closing argument before the jury, the Government placed great reliance on the prior statements for substantive purposes but did not once seek to use them to rebut the impact of the alleged motive.

We are aware that in some cases it may be difficult to ascertain when a particular fabrication, influence, or motive arose. Yet, as the Government concedes, a majority of common-law courts were performing this task for well over a century, and the Government has presented us with no evidence that those courts, or the judicial circuits that adhere to the rule today, have been unable to make the determination. Even under the Government's hypothesis, moreover, the thing to be rebutted must be identified, so the date of its origin cannot be that much more difficult to ascertain. By contrast, as the Advisory Committee commented, the Government's approach, which would require the trial court to weigh all of the circumstances surrounding a statement that suggest its probativeness against the court's assessment of the strength of the alleged motive, would entail more of a burden, with no guidance to attorneys in preparing a case or to appellate courts in reviewing a judgment.

III

Courts must be sensitive to the difficulties attendant upon the prosecution of alleged child abusers. In almost all cases a youth is the prosecution's only eyewitness. But "[t]his Court cannot alter evidentiary rules merely because litigants might prefer different rules in a particular class of cases." *United States v. Salerno*, 505 U.S. 317, 322 (1992). When a party seeks to introduce out-of-court statements that contain strong circumstantial indicia of reliability, that are highly probative on the material questions at trial, and that are better than other evidence otherwise available, there is no need to distort the requirements of Rule 801(d)(1)(B). If its requirements are met, Rule 803(24) exists for that eventuality. We intimate no view, however, concerning the admissibility of any of A.T.'s out-of-court statements under that section, or any other evidentiary principle. These matters, and others, are for the Court of Appeals to decide in the first instance.

Our holding is confined to the requirements for admission under Rule 801(d)(1)(B). The Rule permits the introduction of a declarant's consistent out-of-court statements to rebut a charge of recent fabrication or improper influence or motive only when those statements were made before the charged recent fabrication or improper influence or motive. These conditions of admissibility were not established here.

The judgment of the Court of Appeals for the Tenth Circuit is reversed, and the case is remanded for further proceedings consistent with this opinion.

Justice SCALIA, concurring in part and concurring in the judgment.

I concur in the judgment of the Court, and join its opinion except for Part II-B. That Part, which is devoted entirely to a discussion of the Advisory Committee's Notes pertinent to Rule 801(d)(1)(B), gives effect to those Notes not only because they are "a respected source of scholarly commentary," but also because they display the "purpose" or "inten[t]" of the draftsmen.

I have previously acquiesced in, see, *e.g., Beech Aircraft Corp. v. Rainey*, 488 U.S. 153 (1988), and indeed myself engaged in, see *United States v. Owens*, 484 U.S. 554, 562 (1988), similar use of the Advisory Committee Notes. More mature consideration has persuaded me that is wrong.

Having been prepared by a body of experts, the Notes are assuredly per-
suasive scholarly commentaries—ordinarily the most persuasive—
concerning the meaning of the Rules. But they bear no special authorita-
tiveness as the work of the draftsmen, any more than the views of Alexander
Hamilton (a draftsman) bear more authority than the views of Thomas
Jefferson (not a draftsman) with regard to the meaning of the Constitution.
It is the words of the Rules that have been authoritatively adopted—by this
Court, or by Congress if it makes a statutory change. See 28 U.S.C. §§ 2072,
2074 (1988 ed. and Supp. IV). In my view even the adopting Justices'
thoughts, unpromulgated as Rules, have no authoritative (as opposed to
persuasive) effect, any more than their thoughts regarding an opinion
(reflected in exchanges of memoranda before the opinion issues) authoritatively demonstrate the meaning of that opinion. And the same for the
thoughts of congressional draftsmen who prepare statutory amendments to
the Rules. Like a judicial opinion and like a statute, the promulgated Rule
says what it says, regardless of the intent of its drafters. The Notes are, to be
sure, submitted to us and to the Members of Congress as the thoughts of the
body initiating the recommendations, see § 2073(d); but there is no certainty that either we or they read those thoughts, nor is there any procedure
by which we formally endorse or disclaim them. That being so, the Notes
cannot, by some power inherent in the draftsmen, change the meaning that
the Rules would otherwise bear. . . .

Justice Breyer, with whom The Chief Justice, Justice O'Connor, and
Justice Thomas join, dissenting.

The basic issue in this case concerns not hearsay, but relevance. As the
majority points out, the common law permitted a lawyer to rehabilitate a
witness (after a charge of improper motive) by pointing to the fact that the
witness had said the same thing earlier—but only if the witness made the
earlier statement before the motive to lie arose. . . . The majority believes
that a hearsay-related rule, Federal Rule of Evidence 801(d)(1)(B), codifies
this absolute timing requirement. I do not. Rule 801(d)(1)(B) has nothing
to do with relevance. Rather, that Rule carves out a subset of prior consistent
statements that were formerly admissible only to rehabilitate a witness
(a nonhearsay use that relies upon the fact that the statement was made).
It then says that members of that subset are "not hearsay." This means that,
if such a statement is admissible for a particular rehabilitative purpose (to
rebut a charge of recent fabrication or improper influence or motive), its
proponent now may use it substantively, for a hearsay purpose (i.e., as
evidence of its truth), as well.

. . . [O]ne can find a hearsay-related reason why the drafters might have
decided to restrict the Rule to a particular category of prior consistent statements. Juries have trouble distinguishing between the rehabilitative and
substantive use of the kind of prior consistent statements listed in Rule
801(d)(1)(B). Judges may give instructions limiting the use of such prior
consistent statements to a rehabilitative purpose, but, in practice, juries
nonetheless tend to consider them for their substantive value. . . . It is possible that the Advisory Committee made them "nonhearsay" for that reason,
i.e., as a concession "more of experience than of logic." Advisory

Committee's Notes on Fed. Rule Evid. 801(d)(1)(B) (also noting that the witness is available for cross-examination in the courtroom in any event). If there was a reason why the drafters excluded from Rule 801(d)(1)(B)'s scope other kinds of prior consistent statements (used for rehabilitation), perhaps it was that the drafters concluded that those other statements caused jury confusion to a lesser degree. On this rationale, however, there is no basis for distinguishing between premotive and postmotive statements, for the confusion with respect to each would very likely be the same.

. . . I would read the Rule's plain words to mean exactly what they say: If a trial court properly admits a statement that is "consistent with the declarant's testimony" for the purpose of "rebut[ting] an express or implied charge . . . of recent fabrication or improper influence or motive," then that statement is "not hearsay," and the jury may also consider it for the truth of what it says.

Assuming Rule 801(d)(1)(B) does not codify the absolute timing requirement, I must still answer the question whether, as a relevance matter, the common-law statement of the premotive rule stands as an absolute bar to a trial court's admission of a postmotive prior consistent statement for the purpose of rebutting a charge of recent fabrication or improper influence or motive.

. . . [T]here are sound reasons here for permitting an exception to the timing rule where circumstances warrant. For one thing, one can find examples where the timing rule's claim of "no relevancy" is simply untrue. A postmotive statement is relevant to rebut, for example, a charge of recent fabrication based on improper motive, say, when the speaker made the prior statement while affected by a far more powerful motive to tell the truth. A speaker might be moved to lie to help an acquaintance. But, suppose the circumstances also make clear to the speaker that only the truth will save his child's life. Or, suppose the postmotive statement was made spontaneously, or when the speaker's motive to lie was much weaker than it was at trial. In these and similar situations, special circumstances may indicate that the prior statement was made for some reason other than the alleged improper motivation; it may have been made not because of, but despite, the improper motivation. Hence, postmotive statements can, in appropriate circumstances, directly refute the charge of fabrication based on improper motive, not because they bolster in a general way the witness' trial testimony, but because the circumstances indicate that the statements are not causally connected to the alleged motive to lie.

. . . Trial judges may find it easier to administer an absolute rule. Yet, there is no indication in any of the cases that trial judges would, or do, find it particularly difficult to administer a more flexible rule in this context. And, there is something to be said for the greater authority that flexibility grants the trial judge to tie rulings on the admissibility of rehabilitative evidence more closely to the needs and circumstances of the particular case. Furthermore, the majority concedes that the premotive rule, while seemingly bright line, poses its own administrative difficulties.

This Court has acknowledged that the Federal Rules of Evidence worked a change in common-law relevancy rules in the direction of flexibility. See *Daubert v. Merrell Dow Pharmaceuticals, Inc.*, 509 U.S. 579 (1993). Article IV of the Federal Rules, which concerns relevance, liberalizes the rules for admission of relevant evidence. The Rules direct the trial judge generally to admit all evidence having "any tendency" to make the existence of a material fact "more probable or less probable than it would be without the evidence." Fed. Rules Evid. 401, 402. The judge may reject the evidence (assuming compliance with other rules) only if the probative value of the evidence is substantially outweighed by its tendency to prejudice a party or delay a trial. Rule 403. The codification, as a general matter, relies upon the trial judge's administration of Rules 401, 402, and 403 to keep the barely relevant, the time wasting, and the prejudicial from the jury. . . . Perhaps there are other circumstances in which categorical common-law rules serve the purposes of Rules 401, 402, and 403, and should, accordingly, remain absolute in the law. But, for the reasons stated above, this case, like *Daubert*, does not present such a circumstance. Thus, considered purely as a matter of relevancy law (and as though Rule 801(d)(1)(B) had not been written), I would conclude that the premotive rule did not survive the adoption of the Rules.

. . . Accordingly, I would hold that the Federal Rules authorize a district court to allow (where probative in respect to rehabilitation) the use of postmotive prior consistent statements to rebut a charge of recent fabrication or improper influence or motive (subject of course to, for example, Rule 403). Where such statements are admissible for this rehabilitative purpose, Rule 801(d)(1)(B), as stated above, makes them admissible as substantive evidence as well (provided, of course, that the Rule's other requirements, such as the witness' availability for cross-examination, are satisfied). In most cases, this approach will not yield a different result from a strict adherence to the premotive rule for, in most cases, postmotive statements will not be significantly probative. And, even in cases where the statement is admitted as significantly probative (in respect to rehabilitation), the effect of admission on the trial will be minimal because the prior consistent statements will (by their nature) do no more than repeat in-court testimony.

In this case, the Court of Appeals, applying an approach consistent with what I have described above, decided that A.T.'s prior consistent statements were probative on the question of whether her story as a witness reflected a motive to lie. There is no reason to reevaluate this factbound conclusion. Accordingly, I would affirm the judgment of the Court of Appeals.

UNITED STATES v. SIMONELLI

237 F.3d 19 (1st Cir. 2001)

LYNCH, Circuit Judge.

Peter Simonelli, a successful business man, was convicted by a jury of filing false federal income tax returns for the years 1991 and 1992, of aiding and abetting the filing of false tax returns for his company, Eastford Tool and Die Co., Inc., and of conspiracy. . . . Simonelli complains about the prosecution's use of . . . grand jury testimony [by his former accountant, Baker,] to bolster Baker's credibility on redirect by showing that Baker made statements to the grand jury consistent with his trial testimony, after Baker on cross-examination had been shown to have made some statements to the grand jury inconsistent with his trial testimony. . . .

The issue of when prior consistent statements can be used to rehabilitate a witness, rather than as substantive evidence, has its complications. Before the Supreme Court decision in *Tome v. United States*, 513 U.S. 150 (1995), most but not all circuits had held that although prior consistent statements could not be used for the truth of the statement if the conditions in Rule 801(d) were not met, the Rule did not displace the common law rule that prior consistent statements could be introduced in certain situations to rehabilitate a witness. Usually, this situation occurred when the other consistent statements came from the same document or transcript and pertained to the same supposedly inconsistent statement. The policies behind Rule 106, the rule of completeness, were used, in part, to justify admissibility. . . .

Since *Tome*, this court has adverted to but not decided the issue of whether prior consistent statements may be admissible, when the conditions of Rule 801 are not met, if they are not offered for their truth but only as to credibility following impeachment through prior inconsistent statements. One reason for caution is that the line between substantive use of prior statements and their use to buttress credibility on rehabilitation is one which lawyers and judges draw but which may well be meaningless to jurors. . . . [But we] now join the majority view, well expressed by the Fourth Circuit in *United States v. Ellis*, 121 F.3d 908 (4th Cir. 1997), *cert. denied*, 522 U.S. 1068 (1998), that "where prior consistent statements are not offered for their truth but for the limited purpose of rehabilitation, . . . Rule 801(d)(1)(B) and its concomitant restrictions do not apply." When the prior statements are offered for credibility, the question is not governed by Rule 801.

That Rule 801 does not preclude admissibility does not establish that there is a basis for admissibility. . . . Here neither the rule of completeness nor the common law doctrine of admissibility of prior consistent statements justified the admission of all of the evidence. . . . We see little basis for admissibility of the questioning about Baker's grand jury testimony that went beyond the setting of context, explanation, and completeness for the answers he gave on cross about his inconsistent answers to the grand jury. There is no rule admitting all prior consistent statements simply to bolster the credibility of a witness who has been impeached by particulars. *See Tome*, 513 U.S. at 157 ("Prior consistent statements may not be admitted to counter all forms of impeachment or to bolster the witness merely because she has been discredited."). There was certainly some discretion in the trial judge, as the boundaries for what is needed for completeness may be unclear. But beyond that, the introduction of prior grand jury statements on redirect was not really for rehabilitation. The government was just presenting again the testimony it presented on direct, this time through the testimony about statements to the grand jury.

For much the same reason, though, the error in admitting some prior statements, standing alone, is harmless. The evidence was cumulative and the line between what was useful for completeness and what went beyond is a judgment call. At most the evidence was an extra helping of what the jury had heard before. Sometimes, of course, that extra helping can be so prejudicial as to warrant a new trial. Not here. There was strong evidence of guilt and some improper repetition of testimony through what a witness said to a grand jury, in a generalized effort to bolster the witness, mattered little. . . . The conviction and sentence are *affirmed*.

PROBLEM

7.15. In a bank robbery case, a teller who saw the robber testifies that he had a moustache. On cross-examination, the teller admits that two days after the robbery he told a police detective that the robber had no facial hair. The prosecution then calls the bank manager and seeks to have her testify that, several hours after the robbery, the teller told the bank manager that the robber had "a bushy moustache." Is this testimony admissible?

8

COMPETENCE

"At the time of the incident, I was employed in the Dunbar house as a pet."

A. IN GENERAL

The terms "competence" and "competency" are used in two different ways in evidence law. Sometimes—most often in older cases—the terms often are synonyms for "admissibility": Proof is "competent" if it should be allowed into evidence. Today the terms are used not to describe *evidence* but to describe *witnesses*: a witness is "competent" if he or she is allowed to testify. The subject of this chapter is competence in this modern sense.

Two or three centuries ago, many categories of potential witnesses were excluded as incompetent: children, felons, atheists, the mentally infirm, parties to the lawsuit, and so on. Most of these rules have now been abolished. The modern view is that practically anyone should be allowed to testify, and the jury should judge a witness's credibility for itself.

It is worth noting that this vote of confidence in the jury is highly specific. It is limited to the jury's ability to size up witnesses by listening to them, watching their demeanor, and assessing their performance under cross-examination. We do not have the same degree of confidence in the *general* ability of jurors to identify good and bad evidence; otherwise we would not keep all the complicated rules of evidence that were examined in the other chapters of this book. We could do with evidence law generally what we have done with the old rules of competence: junk them and instead rely on the jury to sort wheat from chaff. But we have not done that. We trust jurors to sort good *witnesses* from bad much more than we trust their general ability to sort good *evidence* from bad.

In part this is testament to the extraordinary faith our system places in *vive voce* evidence—faith, that is, that truth is best found by hearing from witnesses in open court. The old, restrictive rules of competence rules reflected a degree of fear concerning *vive voce* evidence, or at least a belief that hearing from certain witnesses was likely to impede rather than advance the search for truth. The modern, relaxed rules of competence are, in a sense, the flip side of the hearsay ban. The hearsay rule expresses our worries about how the jury will handle secondhand evidence; the relaxed rules of competence express our confidence in the jury's ability to handle firsthand evidence. In the words of one scholar, "the jury is the system's lie detector." George Fisher, *The Jury's Rise as Lie Detector*, 107 Yale L.J. 575, 708 (1997).

[F.R.E. 601; C.E.C. §700]

JAMES B. THAYER, SELECT CASES ON EVIDENCE AT THE COMMON LAW

1070 (1892)

Fortescue (De Laud. c. 26), who has the earliest account (about 1470) of witnesses testifying regularly to the jury, gives no information as to any ground for challenging them. But Coke, a century and a third later, makes certain qualifications of the assertion of the older judges, that "they had not seen witnesses challenged." He mentions as grounds of exclusion, legal infamy, being an "infidel," of non-sane memory, "not of discretion," a party interested, "or the like." And he says that "it hath been resolved by the justices [in 1612] that a wife cannot be produced either against or for her husband, *quia sunt duœ animœ in carne una*." He also points out that "he that challengeth a right in the thing in demand cannot be a witness."

Here are the outlines of the subsequent tests for the competency of witnesses. They were much refined upon, particularly the excluding ground of interest; and great inconveniences resulted. At last in the fourth and fifth decades of the present century, in England, nearly all objections to competency were abolished, or turned into matters of privilege. Similar changes, a little later, were widely made in this country.

ROSEN v. UNITED STATES

245 U.S. 467 (1918)

Mr. Justice Clarke delivered the opinion of the court.

. . . Rosen and Wagner were indicted in the District Court of the United States for the Eastern District of New York with one Broder for conspiring to buy and receive certain checks and letters which had been stolen from "duly authorized depositories for mail matter of the United States," and which were known to the accused to have been so stolen. Broder pleaded guilty, and when he was afterwards called as a witness for the Government the objection was made that he was not competent to testify for the reason that, as was admitted by the Government, he had theretofore pleaded guilty to the crime of forgery in the second degree, in the Court of General Sessions, in the County and State of New York, had been sentenced to imprisonment, and had served his sentence. The objection was overruled and Broder was permitted to testify. This ruling was assigned as error in the Circuit Court of Appeals, where it was affirmed, and it is now assigned as error in this court. . . .

For the validity of the claim that Broder was disqualified as a witness by his sentence for the crime of forgery, the plaintiffs in error rely upon *United States v. Reid*, 12 How. 361, decided in 1852. In that case it was held that the competency of witnesses in criminal trials in United States courts must be determined by the rules of evidence which were in force in the respective States when the Judiciary Act of 1789 was passed, and the argument in this case is, that by the common law as it was administered in New York in 1789 a person found guilty of forgery and sentenced was thereby rendered incompetent as a witness until pardoned, and that, therefore, the objection to Broder should have been sustained.

While the decision in *United States v. Reid*, has not been specifically overruled, its authority must be regarded as seriously shaken by the decisions in *Logan v. United States*, 144 U.S. 263-301, and in *Benson v. United States*, 146 U.S. 325.

The Benson Case differed from the Reid Case only in that in the former the witness whose competency was objected to was called by the Government while in the latter he was called by the defendant. The testimony of the witness was admitted in the one case but it was rejected in the other, and both judgments were affirmed by this court—however forty years had intervened between the two trials. . . . In the almost twenty years which have elapsed since the decision of the Benson Case, the disposition of courts and of legislative bodies to remove disabilities from witnesses has continued, as that decision shows it had been going forward before, under dominance of the conviction of our time that the truth is more likely to be arrived at by hearing the testimony of all persons of competent understanding who may seem to have knowledge of the facts involved in a case, leaving the credit and weight of such testimony to be determined by the jury or by the court, rather than by rejecting witnesses as incompetent, with the result that this principle has come to be widely, almost universally, accepted in this country and in Great Britain.

Since the decision in the Benson Case we have significant evidence of the trend of congressional opinion upon this subject in the removal of the disability of witnesses convicted of perjury, Rev. Stats., § 5392, by the enactment of the Federal Criminal Code in 1909 with this provision omitted and § 5392 repealed. This is significant, because the disability to testify, of persons convicted of perjury, survived in some jurisdictions much longer than many of the other common-law disabilities, for the reason that the offense concerns directly the giving of testimony in a court of justice, and conviction of it was accepted as showing a greater disregard for the truth than it was thought should be implied from a conviction of other crime.

Satisfied as we are that the legislation and the very great weight of judicial authority which have developed in support of this modern rule, especially as applied to the competency of witnesses convicted of crime, proceed upon sound principle, we conclude that the dead hand of the common-law rule of 1789 should no longer be applied to such cases as we have here, and that the ruling of the lower courts on this first claim of error should be approved. . . .

It results that the judgments of the Circuit Court of Appeals must be Affirmed.

[Justices Van Devanter and McReynolds dissented.]

ADVISORY COMMITTEE NOTE TO F.R.E. 601

This general ground-clearing eliminates all grounds of incompetency not specifically recognized in the succeeding rules of this Article. Included among the grounds thus abolished are religious belief, conviction of crime, and connection with the litigation as a party or interested person or spouse of a party or interested person. With the exception of the so-called Dead Man's Acts, American jurisdictions generally have ceased to recognize these grounds.

The Dead Man's Acts are surviving traces of the common law disqualification of parties and interested persons. They exist in variety too great to convey conviction of their wisdom and effectiveness. These rules contain no provision of this kind. . . .

No mental or moral qualifications for testifying as a witness are specified. Standards of mental capacity have proved elusive in actual application. A leading commentator observes that few witnesses are disqualified on that ground. Weihofen, Testimonial Competence and Credibility, 34 Geo. Wash. L. Rev. 53 (1965). Discretion is regularly exercised in favor of allowing the testimony. A witness wholly without capacity is difficult to imagine. The question is one particularly suited to the jury as one of weight and credibility, subject to judicial authority to review the sufficiency of the evidence. 2 Wigmore §§ 501, 509. Standards of moral qualification in practice consist essentially of evaluating a person's truthfulness in terms of his own answers about it. Their principal utility is in affording an opportunity on voir dire examination to impress upon the witness his moral duty. This result may, however, be accomplished more directly, and without haggling in terms of legal standards, by the manner of administering the oath or affirmation under Rule 603.

Admissibility of religious belief as a ground of impeachment is treated in Rule 610. Conviction of crime as a ground of impeachment is the subject of Rule 609. Marital relationship is the basis for privilege under Rule 505. Interest in the outcome of litigation and mental capacity are, of course, highly relevant to credibility and require no special treatment to render them admissible along with other matters bearing upon the perception, memory, and narration of witnesses.

UNITED STATES v. LIGHTLY

677 F.2d 1027 (4th Cir. 1982)

ERVIN, Circuit Judge:

On December 19, 1979, Terrance McKinley, an inmate at Lorton Reformatory in northern Virginia, sustained serious stab wounds from an assault in his cell. Two of McKinley's fellow inmates, Randy Lightly and Clifton McDuffie, were investigated, but only Lightly was formally charged. McDuffie was not indicted by the grand jury because a court appointed psychiatrist found him incompetent to stand trial and criminally insane at the time of the offense. He is presently confined in a mental hospital.

On May 22, 1980, Lightly was convicted of assault with intent to commit murder, and sentenced to ten years' imprisonment to run consecutively with the sentence he already was serving. . . . The government's case included testimony from the victim, Terrance McKinley, inmates Harvey Boyd and Robert Thomas, and McKinley's treating physician, Dr. Lance Weaver, which indicated that McDuffie and Lightly cornered McKinley in his cell and repeatedly stabbed him with half pairs of scissors. Lightly received a severe cut on his hand in the assault. Lightly's account of the stabbing was that he was walking along cell block three when he saw McDuffie and McKinley fighting in McKinley's cell. Lightly said he went into the cell to stop the fight and while he was pulling McDuffie off of McKinley, McDuffie turned around and cut him. His testimony was corroborated by three other inmates.

The defense also attempted to have McDuffie testify. McDuffie would have testified that only he and not Lightly had assaulted McKinley. The court ruled McDuffie incompetent to testify because he had been found to be criminally insane and incompetent to stand trial, and was subject to hallucinations.[1] We believe this was error and that Lightly is entitled to a new trial.

Every witness is presumed competent to testify, Fed. R. Evid. 601, unless it can be shown that the witness does not have personal knowledge of the matters about which he is to testify, that he does not have the capacity to recall, or that he does not understand the duty to testify truthfully. This rule applies to persons considered to be insane to the same extent that it applies to other persons. *United States v. Lopez*, 611 F.2d 44 (4th Cir. 1979); *Shuler v. Wainwright*, 491 F.2d 1213, 1223 (5th Cir. 1974). In this case, the testimony of McDuffie's treating physician indicated that McDuffie had a sufficient memory, that he understood the oath, and that he could communicate what he saw. The district judge chose not to conduct an in camera examination of McDuffie. On this record, it was clearly improper for the court to disqualify McDuffie from testifying. . . .

McDuffie's potential testimony would have substantially corroborated Lightly's testimony. His disqualification from testifying, therefore, cannot be considered harmless error. In finding Lightly entitled to a new trial on this ground, we decline to rule on the other issues he raised in this appeal. REVERSED and REMANDED.

B. PERSONAL KNOWLEDGE

Almost all restrictions on competence have now been eliminated. But not all. Among the few restrictions that remain is the rule requiring that a witness testify from personal knowledge. Even this rule is relaxed for witnesses testifying as experts—a topic taken up in the next chapter. For all other witnesses, though, the personal knowledge requirement is yet another manifestation of our system's faith in *vive voce* evidence. It works in conjunction with the hearsay rule to limit trial testimony, generally, to firsthand accounts.

Without the personal knowledge requirement, the hearsay rule could be easily evaded. Instead of testifying, "I heard that Oliver was dealing cocaine out of his apartment," a witness could just say, "Oliver was dealing cocaine out of his apartment"—thereby avoiding reference to any out-of-court statements. Conversely, the personal knowledge requirement could do little work without the hearsay rule. A witness limited to recounting his or her firsthand experience could still testify, "Two months ago, here

1. McDuffie believed that "Star Child" told him to kill McKinley because McKinley and Hodge, who apparently was a prison administrator, were going to kill him.

is what happened to me: I was told by some mutual friends that Oliver was dealing cocaine out of his apartment."

One problem raised by the personal knowledge requirement, explored in the materials below, is that deciding whether a witness has personal knowledge very often involves deciding whether to *believe* the witness. Suppose a witness claims to have seen the defendant fleeing the bank after it was robbed, but defense counsel suggests on cross-examination that the witness was too far away to see clearly—or, worse, was nowhere near the bank the day it was robbed. Does the judge need to resolve this matter in order to determine whether the employee is competent to testify? If the answer were yes, judges would in essence wind up deciding whether witnesses should be believed, the job our system generally entrusts to juries. So the personal knowledge of a witness is assessed under a sufficiency standard.

[F.R.E. 602; C.E.C. §702]

ADVISORY COMMITTEE NOTE TO F.R.E. 602

". . . [T]he rule requiring that a witness who testifies to a fact which can be perceived by the senses must have had an opportunity to observe, and must have actually observed the fact" is a "most pervasive manifestation" of the common law insistence upon "the most reliable sources of information." McCormick § 10, p. 19. These foundation requirements may, of course, be furnished by the testimony of the witness himself; hence personal knowledge is not an absolute but may consist of what the witness thinks he knows from personal perception. 2Wigmore § 650. It will be observed that the rule is in fact a specialized application of the provisions of Rule 104(b) on conditional relevancy.

This rule does not govern the situation of a witness who testifies to a hearsay statement as such, if he has personal knowledge of the making of the statement. Rules 801 and 805 would be applicable. This rule would, however, prevent him from testifying to the subject matter of the hearsay statement, as he has no personal knowledge of it.

The reference to Rule 703 is designed to avoid any question of conflict between the present rule and the provisions of that rule allowing an expert to express opinions based on facts of which he does not have personal knowledge.

UNITED STATES v. HICKEY

917 F.2d 901 (6th Cir. 1990)

MILBURN, Circuit Judge.

This case involves an appeal by Quinn Hickey from his jury conviction in a drug conspiracy case. . . . Hickey, along with eighteen co-defendants, was charged with numerous counts of conspiracy to distribute cocaine in violation of 21 U.S.C. §§ 841(a)(1) & 846, and use of a communication facility to facilitate a crime in violation of 21 U.S.C. § 843(b). A jury trial commenced on September 8, 1988, and several of Hickey's co-defendants, including Bayron Moreno, were found guilty. However, the jury was unable to reach a verdict as to Hickey, and the court declared a mistrial as to him. Hickey was retried and found guilty on one of the conspiracy charges and two of the communications charges.

An investigation of drug trafficking in the Saginaw, Michigan, area soon centered on Jack Ventimiglia as his residence appeared to be the main terminal for considerable cocaine distribution. Ventimiglia was arrested and, pursuant to a plea agreement, testified for the government against several of his associates including Quinn Hickey.

Ventimiglia is a self-confessed cocaine addict, and his testimony at the trial was characterized by the district court as the words of a "loose cannon." In a lengthy cross-examination, defense counsel was able to expose Ventimiglia's cocaine addiction, his claimed lack of memory, his uncertainty as to details, and several inconsistencies in his testimony. In ruling on the defendant's motion for a judgment of acquittal, the district court stated that Ventimiglia's testimony alone would not support a guilty verdict; however, the district court denied the motion because the government had introduced, apart from Ventimiglia's testimony, "substantial circumstantial evidence that would tend to support the fact [that] Hickey was, in part, a seller."

. . . Hickey argues that the district court committed reversible error in allowing the jury to hear and consider the testimony of Ventimiglia. . . . After pointing out Ventimiglia's drug addiction and inconsistencies in Ventimiglia's testimony, Hickey argues that there was a "total lack of sufficient or supportive evidence to substantiate the findings that these witnesses had personal knowledge of the critical events in this prosecution upon which to base their testimony." This is not the first case in which we have faced an argument that the testimony of Jack Ventimiglia should be excluded. In *United States v. Moreno*, 899 F.2d 465 (6th Cir. 1990), we rejected an argument by Hickey's co-defendant in the first trial that inconsistencies in Ventimiglia's testimony, in light of his admitted drug addiction, showed that he was incompetent to testify.

In *Moreno* we relied upon *United States v. Ramirez*, 871 F.2d 582 (6th Cir.), *cert. denied*, 493 U.S. 841 (1989), a case which recognized that in some cases the ability of a witness might be so impaired that he cannot satisfy the personal knowledge requirement of Federal Rule of Evidence 602. . . . What we did not mention in *Ramirez* was the fact that the threshold of Rule 602 is low.

Rule 602 provides, in relevant part, that "[a] witness may not testify to a matter unless evidence is introduced sufficient to support a finding that the witness has personal knowledge of the matter." Testimony should not be excluded for lack of personal knowledge unless no reasonable juror could believe that the witness had the ability and opportunity to perceive the event that he testifies about. Weinstein, *Weinstein's Evidence* § 602[02], at 602-8 to 11 (1988). . . . Despite the fact that Ventimiglia's testimony may have been, in large part, unbelievable to some and in spite of the possibility that his perception was sometimes impaired, a reasonable or rational juror could believe that Ventimiglia and the other prosecution witnesses perceived the course of events to which they testified. Accordingly, we hold that the district court did not abuse its discretion in permitting Ventimiglia's testimony or the testimony of the other prosecution witnesses. . . . [T]he judgment of conviction is AFFIRMED. . . .

C. OATH OR AFFIRMATION

Aside from personal knowledge, the only other general prerequisite for competence is that the witness swear an oath to tell the truth—or make some similar commitment to providing honest testimony. Within limits, courts are flexible about the precise form of the commitment.

One lingering controversy concerns whether the requirement that every witness take an oath or its equivalent includes a requirement that the witness understand and appreciate the oath. More specifically, there is controversy regarding whether children should be allowed to testify without some inquiry to determine whether they understand and appreciate what it means to promise to tell the truth.

Another question worth keeping in mind as you read the materials below: given the general liberalization of rules of competence, and given the difficulties encountered in applying the oath requirement, why is that requirement retained at all?

[F.R.E. 603; C.E.C. §§701, 710]

UNITED STATES v. WARD

989 F.2d 1015 (9th Cir. 1993)

FLETCHER, Circuit Judge:

Wallace Ward appeals his conviction of three counts of attempt to evade income tax in violation of 26 U.S.C. § 7201 and three counts of failure to file income taxes in violation of 26 U.S.C. § 7203. . . . Ward is the president of I & O Publishing Company, a mail-order house and publisher located in Boulder City, Nevada. The prosecution presented evidence at trial that despite having substantial income, neither I & O nor Ward filed tax returns or paid income taxes for the years 1983, 1984 and 1985.

On March 29, 1990 a grand jury indicted Ward on three counts each of tax evasion and failure to file income tax returns. Ward chose to represent himself at trial. On July 9, 1990, Ward filed a "Motion to Challenge the Oath," which proposed an alternative oath that replaced the word "truth" with the phrase "fully integrated Honesty." The oath would read, "Do you affirm to speak with fully integrated Honesty, only with fully integrated Honesty and nothing but fully integrated Honesty?" For reasons we will not attempt to explain, Ward believes that honesty is superior to truth. Magistrate Lawrence R. Leavitt ruled on August 2, 1990 that "the oath or affirmation which has been administered in courts of law throughout the United States to millions of witnesses for hundreds of years should not be required to give way to the defendant's idiosyncratic distinctions between truth and honesty." The district court overruled Ward's objections to the magistrate's order on August 28, 1990, and again on October 8, 1990. Ward pursued an interlocutory appeal on the issue, which was dismissed for lack of jurisdiction.

A three-day trial commenced on February 11, 1991. Ward made a lengthy opening statement and actively cross-examined government witnesses. At a sidebar during the second day of trial, Ward offered to take both the standard oath and his oath. The prosecutor was amenable to the compromise, but the district court refused to allow it. "This is an oath that has been used for a very long time," the district court said, "And I'm not going to establish a precedent where someone can come in and require the court to address that matter differently." At the close of the government's case on the third day of trial, Ward asked once again to testify under his oath. The judge again refused, saying "[T]he oath has been used for a very long time. . . . That's the oath that will be administered." Ward did not testify and presented no witnesses. The jury convicted Ward of all counts after an hour's deliberation.

. . . The court's interest in administering its precise form of oath must yield to Ward's First Amendment rights. To begin with, there is no constitutionally or statutorily required form of oath. Federal Rule of Evidence 603 requires only that a witness "declare that the witness will testify truthfully, by oath or affirmation administered in a form calculated to awaken the witness' conscience and impress the witness' mind with the duty to do so." The advisory committee notes to Rule 603 explain that "the rule is designed to afford the flexibility required in dealing with religious adults, atheists, conscientious objectors, mental defectives, and children. Affirmation is simply a solemn undertaking to tell the truth; no special verbal formula is required."

. . . Our cases have routinely held that it is reversible error for a district court to prevent a party from testifying solely on the basis of the party's religiously-based objections to the form of the oath. In *Gordon v. State of Idaho*, 778 F.2d 1397 (9th Cir. 1985), a plaintiff in a § 1983 action professed religious objections to oath or affirmation, offering instead to say "I understand that I must tell the truth. I agree to testify under penalty of perjury." Using First Amendment analysis requiring that government use the "least restrictive means" to its ends when free exercise [of religion] is at stake, we held that it was an abuse of discretion for the district court to insist upon the standard oath and to dismiss plaintiff's case for failure to present evidence. Criminal trials additionally implicate the defendant's Fifth Amendment right to testify. . . . [*See, e.g.,*] *Moore v. United States*, 348 U.S. 966 (1955) (per curiam) (criminal defendant with religious objections to the word "solemnly" in the oath must be allowed to testify).

. . . While oaths including the familiar "truth, whole truth, and nothing but the truth" formulation date back at least to the seventeenth century, see 6 Wigmore, Evidence § 1818(2) (Chadbourne rev. 1976), the principle that the form of the oath must be crafted in a way that is meaningful to the witness also predates our constitution. In *Omichund v. Barker*, 1 Atk. 22, 45 (1744), Lord Chief Judge Willes wrote, "It would be absurd for [a non-Christian witness] to swear according to the Christian oath, which he does not believe; and therefore, out of necessity, he must be allowed to swear according to his own notion of an oath." See also *Atcheson v. Everitt*, 1 Cowp. 382, 389 (1776) (Mansfield, L.C.J.) ("[A]s the purpose of [the oath] is to bind his conscience, every man of every religion should be bound by that form which he himself thinks will bind his own conscience most").

This case has an odd twist in that the defendant offered to take the traditional "truth" oath, but only if he were permitted to also take his "fully integrated honesty" oath. In Ward's view, as best we can state it, only his oath expressed a commitment to the abstract purity of absolute "fully integrated honesty" that must be extracted from anyone before that person's word can be relied upon. The standard "truth" oath was so much surplusage—distasteful, wrong, but not necessarily a mortal sin to take.

His own oath superimposed on the traditional one would have taken nothing away from the commitment to tell the truth under penalties of perjury and, indeed, in the defendant's mind imposed upon him a higher duty. Under these circumstances the district court clearly abused its discretion in refusing the oath and preventing the defendant's testimony. We do not have a case where the witness offers to swear only to a cleverly worded oath that creates loopholes for falsehood or attempts to create a safe harbor for perjury as in *United States v. Fowler*, 605 F.2d 181, 185 (5th Cir. 1979), *cert. denied*, 445 U.S. 950 (1980), where the court properly refused testimony from a defendant who would not say so much as "I state that I will tell the truth in my testimony," and was willing to say only "I am a truthful man" or "I would not tell a lie to stay out of jail." Ward's "attempt[] to express a moral or ethical sense of right and wrong," [*Welsh v. United States*, 398 U.S. 333, 340 (1970)], coupled with the de rigueur fervor, brings his beliefs squarely within those safeguarded by the free exercise clause.

Ward also seeks to vindicate what he perceives to be his right to have all his witnesses sworn to his oath. This he cannot do. Ward has no standing to assert the First or Fifth Amendment rights of others. Ward also alleges numerous trial errors which we need not consider in light of our grant of a new trial.

REVERSED and REMANDED.

UNITED STATES v. ALLEN J.

127 F.3d 1292 (10th Cir. 1997)

BRORBY, Circuit Judge.

Allen J. appeals his adjudication of juvenile delinquency in the United States District Court for the District of New Mexico. In a non-jury trial held on September 11, 12, and 16, 1996, the district court adjudged Allen J. a juvenile delinquent pursuant to the Federal Juvenile Delinquency Act, 18 U.S.C. § 5031, et seq., after finding he had committed Aggravated Sexual Abuse in violation of 18 U.S.C. §§ 2241(a), and 2246(2)(A) by knowingly using force to engage in a sex act with a juvenile. The case was in federal court because both Allen J. and the victim are Indians and because the incident took place within the Navajo Nation Indian Reservation in New Mexico. See 18 U.S.C. § 3231. The district court placed Allen J. on probation until he reaches the age of twenty-one and required, among other things, completion of sex offender and substance abuse treatment at a youth facility. . . . The only issue Allen J. raises on appeal is whether the trial court erred in finding the victim competent to testify.

. . . Allen J. states the test for determining the competency of a child witness is found in *United States v. Spoonhunter*, 476 F.2d 1050 (10th Cir. 1973). In *Spoonhunter*, this Circuit applied the test for determining the competency of a child witness established by the Supreme Court in *Wheeler v. United States*, 159 U.S. 523 (1895). In that case, the Court held competency "depends on the capacity and intelligence of the child, [the child's] appreciation of the difference between truth and falsehood, as well as of [the child's] duty to tell the former." This determination was to be left primarily in the hands of the trial courts. The Court, however, warned trial courts to take care when excluding witnesses, in order to avoid "staying the hand of justice."

Both *Wheeler* and *Spoonhunter*, however, pre-date the enactment of Fed. R. Evid. 601 and 18 U.S.C. § 3509.[2] For this reason, the *Wheeler* test this court has relied upon for years no longer completely states the applicable

---

2. Rule 601 was enacted in 1975, and § 3509 was enacted in 1990. [18 U.S.C. § 3509(c) reads in substance as follows: "(1) Nothing in this subsection shall be construed to abrogate rule 601 of the Federal Rules of Evidence. (2) A child is presumed to be competent. (3) A competency examination regarding a child witness may be conducted by the court only upon written motion and offer of proof of incompetency by a party. (4) A competency examination regarding a child may be conducted only if the court determines, on the record, that compelling reasons exist. A child's age alone is not a compelling reason. (5) The only persons who may be permitted to be present at a competency examination are the judge; the attorney for the Government; the attorney for the defendant; a court reporter; and persons whose presence, in the opinion of the court, is necessary to the welfare and wellbeing of the child, including the child's attorney, guardian ad litem, or adult attendant. (6) A competency examination regarding a child witness shall be conducted out of the sight and hearing of a jury. (7) Examination of a child related to competency shall normally be conducted by the court on the basis of questions submitted by the attorney for the Government and the attorney for the defendant including a party acting as an attorney pro se. The court may permit an attorney but not a party acting as an attorney pro se to examine a child directly on competency if the court is satisfied that the child will not suffer emotional trauma as a result

standard for determining the competency of a child witness, although it may inform any examinations taking place pursuant to 18 U.S.C. § 3509(c) and may help explain the type of evidence necessary to demonstrate a compelling reason for such an examination.

... We agree with the district court's conclusion that the evidence offered by Allen J. . . . did not constitute a "compelling reason" to hold a § 3509(c) competency examination. To counter the presumption favoring competency, Allen J. asserted the victim suffers mild mental retardation, possibly due to Fetal Alcohol Syndrome, which caused her to repeat first grade. As the district court correctly pointed out, even if the victim only had the mental development of a much younger child, she would still be competent to testify. The evidence offered by Allen J. did not begin to show the victim had such severe problems she could not "understand and answer simple questions" 18 U.S.C. § 3509(c)(8), or "underst[and] the difference between truth and falsehood, and the consequences of falsehood, and what was required by the oath," *Spoonhunter*, 476 F.2d at 1054.

When the victim was called to testify, the court asked her a series of questions seeking to confirm she understood the importance of the oath. These questions included: "Do you understand what it is to tell the truth?" and "Do you know the difference between the truth and a lie?" The victim did not respond to the judge's questioning. (The court then asked the prosecutor to try questioning the witness. The prosecutor began with simple questions ("[W]hat is your last name?", "How old are you?", and "Where do you live?"), which the victim answered. After about thirty questions along these lines, almost all of which the victim was able to answer correctly, the prosecutor shifted to questions relating to the difference between the truth and lies. Among other questions, the prosecutor asked the victim if she understood she had promised to tell the truth in court, to which the victim responded affirmatively. After this series of questions, which established the victim knew the difference between a truth and a lie, knew she was to tell the truth in court, and knew she would be punished if she told a lie, the court directed the prosecutor to proceed to the heart of her case.)[3] Defense counsel objected repeatedly

---

of the examination. (8) The questions asked at the competency examination of a child shall be appropriate to the age and developmental level of the child, shall not be related to the issues at trial, and shall focus on determining the child's ability to understand and answer simple questions. (9) Psychological and psychiatric examinations to assess the competency of a child witness shall not be ordered without a showing of compelling need." For purposes of the statute, the term "child" is defined to include any person under the age of 18 "who is or is alleged to be" either "a victim of a crime of physical abuse, sexual abuse, or exploitation" or "a witness to a crime committed against another person." 18 U.S.C. § 3509(a)(2)(A).]

3. This initial questioning of the victim, during which the court satisfied itself the victim understood the need to be truthful in her statements, was not a competency examination pursuant to 18 U.S.C. § 3509(c). Fed. R. Evid. 603 requires every witness to declare he or she will testify truthfully. In addition to confirming for the court the victim understood the oath, the initial questioning of the victim also served "to awaken the witness' conscience and impress the witness' mind with the duty to [testify truthfully]," as required by Rule 603. The type of questions asked by the prosecutor along this line, and the answers given by the victim, were comparable to examinations approved in *Spoonhunter*, 476 F.2d at 1054, and *Wheeler*, 159 U.S. at 524. For this reason, to the extent Allen J.'s argument may be construed to be an

throughout this process and throughout the remainder of the victim's testimony.

Allen J. essentially bases his appeal on several instances in the victim's testimony where she had difficulty answering questions. The victim did not respond to the trial judge's questioning. She gave wrong answers to some of counsel's questions (e.g., she said she was eleven, when she was thirteen), and she gave nonsensical answers to others (e.g., she answered "true" to the question "is it good or bad to tell a lie?"). In addition, she apparently paused for long periods of time before answering some questions.

Any inconsistencies in the victim's story or problems with her testimony, however, raise questions of credibility, not competence. . . . The credibility of a witness is a question to be determined by the trier of fact, not this court. . . . We find nothing in the record demonstrating the district court abused its discretion in permitting the victim in this case to testify. The decision of the district court is, therefore, AFFIRMED.

VICTOR GOLD, DO THE FEDERAL RULES OF EVIDENCE MATTER?

25 Loy. L.A. L. Rev. 909 (1992)

Some authorities have resurrected common law mental and moral competency requirements in the guise of interpreting Rules 602 and 603. Some courts read Rule 602 as imposing a mental capacity requirement, suggesting that witnesses lack personal knowledge unless they can comprehend their observations to an extent that makes their testimony trustworthy. Similarly, many courts establish a moral capacity requirement by concluding that the oath or affirmation requirement of Rule 603 cannot be satisfied unless the witness appreciates the nature of truth and the duty to tell the truth.

On its face, Rule 602 does not justify excluding testimony on the ground that a witness lacks the mental capacity to make testimony trustworthy. The Rule requires no more than that the trier of fact find there is evidence "sufficient to support a finding" that the witness has personal

---

appeal based on Rule 603, we find the district court did not err and fully complied with the requirements of is up to the jury, not the judge, to decide if the witness is trustworthy. Rule 603 likewise imposes no moral capacity requirement. The Rule requires only that the witness perform the mechanical act of taking an oath or affirmation in a form calculated to awaken the witness's conscience and impress his or her mind with the legal duty to tell the truth. Nothing in the Rule suggests that the witness must in fact have his or her conscience awakened and mind so impressed. A member of the Advisory Committee reports that the Committee specifically considered and rejected imposition of any standard of moral qualification. Further, in his testimony before Congress in support of Rule 601, the Reporter for the Federal Rules made the point that the very presence of the oath or affirmation requirement in Rule 603 diminished the need for competency evaluations of the sort conducted at common law. It is ironic then that Rule 603 has been turned into a vehicle for undermining Rule 601's general statement that every witness is competent.

knowledge. This standard should be satisfied if a reasonable juror or judge could believe that the witness perceived the matters testified to. Based on the Rule's standard, it is up to the jury, not the judge, to decide if the witness is trustworthy. Rule 603 likewise imposes no moral capacity requirement. The Rule requires only that the witness perform the mechanical act of taking an oath or affirmation in a form calculated to awaken the witness's conscience and impress his or her mind with the legal duty to tell the truth. Nothing in the Rule suggests that the witness must in fact have his or her conscience awakened and mind so impressed. A member of the Advisory Committee reports that the Committee specifically considered and rejected imposition of any standard of moral qualification. Further, in his testimony before Congress in support of Rule 601, the Reporter for the Federal Rules made the point that the very presence of the oath or affirmation requirement in Rule 603 diminishes the need for competency evaluations of the sort conducted at common law. It is ironic then that Rule 603 has been turned into a vehicle for undermining Rule 601's general statement that every witness is competent.

PROBLEMS

8.1. The key prosecution witness in a criminal trial admits on cross-examination that he has been surreptitiously consuming opium throughout his testimony. The defense attorney asks the judge to strike the witness's testimony on grounds of competence. Should the request be granted?

8.2. The defendant in a civil case wishes to testify. He swears to tell "the truth and nothing but the truth," but will not swear or promise to tell "the whole truth." He explains that "no one ever knows the whole truth about anything." Defense counsel objects to the plaintiff's testimony on grounds of competence. How should the judge rule?

8.3. The defendant in an automobile accident case calls the plaintiff's five-year-old son, who was four at the time of the accident. The plaintiff claims her son is incompetent to testify, because his memory of the accident is too vague, because testifying about it would traumatize him, and because he does not understand what it means to swear or to promise to tell the truth. How should the judge respond?

D. DEAD MAN STATUTES

Many states have so-called "dead man statutes," which bar parties to a lawsuit from testifying about certain transactions or incidents, if the other participant is now dead. The idea is to stop a litigant from taking advantage of the fact that the other person is no longer around to object. Dead man statutes are remnants of the much broader disqualification that used to apply to all parties, and they are unpopular with scholars, who tend to view them as relics of an older, less enlightened time. The drafters of the Federal Rules of Evidence chose not to include any such provision, but Congress added the second sentence of Rule 601 specifically to ensure that state dead man statutes would operate in any federal case governed by state substantive law.

REPORT OF THE HOUSE JUDICIARY COMMITTEE

H.R. Rep. No. 93-650 (1974)

Rule 601 as submitted to the Congress provided that "Every person is competent to be a witness except as otherwise provided in these rules." One effect of the Rule as proposed would have been to abolish age, mental capacity, and other grounds recognized in some State jurisdictions as making a person incompetent as a witness. The greatest controversy centered around the Rule's rendering inapplicable in the federal courts the so-called Dead Man's Statutes which exist in some States. Acknowledging that there is substantial disagreement as to the merit of Dead Man's Statutes, the Committee nevertheless believed that where such statutes have been enacted they represent State policy which should not be overturned in the absence of a compelling federal interest. The Committee therefore amended the Rule to make competency in civil actions determinable in accordance with State law with respect to elements of claims or defenses as to which State law supplies the rule of decision. . . .

McCORMICK ON EVIDENCE

§65, at 1:313-16 (Kenneth S. Broun, ed., 6th ed. 2006)

By far the most drastic common law incompetency rule was the doctrine excluding testimony by parties to the lawsuit and all persons having a direct pecuniary or proprietary interest in the outcome. . . . It is almost unbelievable that the rule continued in force in England until the middle of the 19th century, and in this country for a few decades longer. In England, the reform was sweeping, and no shred of disqualification remains in civil cases.

In this country, however, the reformers were forced to accept a compromise. An objection was raised with respect to controversies over consensual transactions, such as contracts, or other events such as traffic accidents where one party died but the other survived. The thrust of the objection was that fraud might result if the surviving parties or interested persons could testify about the transaction or the event. The survivor could still testify although death had sealed the adverse party's lips. . . . Accordingly, statutes in numerous states still provide that the common law disqualification of parties and interested persons is abolished, with the single exception that they remain disqualified to testify concerning a transaction or communication with a person since deceased in a suit prosecuted or defended by the decedent's executor or administrator. However, there is often a proviso by statute or case law that the surviving party or interested person may testify if called by the adversary, that is, the decedent's executor or administrator. . . . The practical consequence of these statutes comes into play when a survivor has rendered services, furnished goods, or lent money to a person whom he trusted without an independent, corroborating witness or admissible written evidence. The survivor is helpless if the other dies and the representative of his estate declines to pay. The survivor's mouth may even be closed in an action arising from a fatal automobile collision, or a suit on a note or account which the survivor paid in cash without obtaining a receipt.

. . . [M]ost commentators agree that the expedient of refusing to listen to the survivor is, in Bentham's words, "blind and brainless." In seeking to avoid injustice to one side, the statutory drafters ignored the equal possibility of creating injustice to the other. The survivor's temptation to fabricate a claim or defense is evident enough—so obvious indeed that any jury should realize that his story must be evaluated cautiously. In case of fraud, a searching cross-examination will often reveal discrepancies in the "tangled web" of deception. In any event, the survivor's disqualification is more likely to disadvantage the honest than the dishonest survivor. A litigant who would resort to perjury will hardly hesitate at suborning a third person, who would not be disqualified, to swear to the false story.

Legislators and courts are gradually coming to see the stupidity of the traditional survivors' evidence acts, and adopting liberalizing changes. A few states provide that the survivor may testify, but his testimony will not support a judgment unless the testimony is corroborated by other evidence. Others authorize the trial judge to permit the survivor to testify when it appears that his testimony is necessary to prevent injustice. Both of these solutions have reasonably apparent drawbacks which are avoided by a third type of statute. The third type of statutory scheme sweeps away the disqualification entirely and allows the survivor to testify without restriction. However, the scheme evenhandedly minimizes the danger of injustice to the decedent's estate by admitting any relevant writings or oral statements by the decedent, both of which would ordinaily be excluded as hearsay.

ALABAMA CODE §12-21-163

In civil actions and proceedings, there must be no exclusion of any witness because he is a party or interested in the issue tried, except that no person having a pecuniary interest in the result of the action or proceeding shall be allowed to testify against the party to whom his interest is opposed as to any transaction with, or statement by, the deceased person whose estate is interested in the result of the action or proceeding or when such deceased person, at the time of such transaction or statement, acted in any representative or fiduciary relation whatsoever to the party against whom such testimony is sought to be introduced, unless called to testify thereto by the party to whom such interest is opposed or unless the testimony of such deceased person in relation to such transaction or statement is introduced in evidence by the party whose interest is opposed to that of the witness or has been taken and is on file in the case. No person who is an incompetent witness under this section shall make himself competent by transferring his interest to another.

CALIFORNIA EVIDENCE CODE §1261

(a) Evidence of a statement is not made inadmissible by the hearsay rule when offered in an action upon a claim or demand against the estate of the declarant if the statement was made upon the personal knowledge of the declarant at a time when the matter had been recently perceived by him and while his recollection was clear.

(b) Evidence of a statement is inadmissible under this section if the statement was made under circumstances such as to indicate its lack of trustworthiness.

E.   COMPETENCE AND THE CONSTITUTION

The old, restrictive rules of competence are now greatly disfavored. The modern attitude finds expression not just in the widespread abandonment of those rules, but also in decisions finding lingering restrictions on competence constitutionally suspect when applied to witnesses called by a criminal defendant, and especially suspect when applied to testimony from the criminal defendant himself or herself.

ROCK v. ARKANSAS

483 U.S. 44 (1987)

Justice BLACKMUN delivered the opinion of the Court.

The issue presented in this case is whether Arkansas' evidentiary rule prohibiting the admission of hypnotically refreshed testimony violated petitioner's constitutional right to testify on her own behalf as a defendant in a criminal case.

Petitioner Vickie Lorene Rock was charged with manslaughter in the death of her husband, Frank Rock, on July 2, 1983. . . . When police arrived on the scene they found Frank on the floor with a bullet wound in his chest. . . . According to the testimony of one of the investigating officers, petitioner told him that "she stood up to leave the room and [her husband] grabbed her by the throat and choked her and threw her against the wall and . . . at that time she walked over and picked up the weapon and pointed it toward the floor and he hit her again and she shot him."

Because petitioner could not remember the precise details of the shooting, her attorney suggested that she submit to hypnosis in order to refresh her memory. Petitioner was hypnotized twice by Doctor Bettye Back, a licensed neuropsychologist with training in the field of hypnosis. Doctor Back interviewed petitioner for an hour prior to the first hypnosis session, taking notes on petitioner's general history and her recollections of the shooting. Both hypnosis sessions were recorded on tape. Petitioner did not relate any new information during either of the sessions, but, after the hypnosis, she was able to remember that at the time of the incident she had her thumb on the hammer of the gun, but had not held her finger on the trigger. She also recalled that the gun had discharged when her husband grabbed her arm during the scuffle. As a result of the details that petitioner was able to remember about the shooting, her counsel arranged for a gun expert to examine the handgun. . . . That inspection revealed that the gun was defective and prone to fire, when hit or dropped, without the trigger's being pulled.

When the prosecutor learned of the hypnosis sessions, he filed a motion to exclude petitioner's testimony. The trial judge held a pretrial hearing on the motion and concluded that no hypnotically refreshed testimony would be admitted. The court issued an order limiting petitioner's testimony to "matters remembered and stated to the examiner prior to being placed under hypnosis." At trial, petitioner introduced testimony by the gun expert, but the court limited petitioner's own description of the events on the day of the shooting to a reiteration of the sketchy information in Doctor Back's notes. The jury convicted petitioner on the manslaughter charge and she was sentenced to 10 years' imprisonment and a $10,000 fine.

On appeal, the Supreme Court of Arkansas rejected petitioner's claim that the limitations on her testimony violated her right to present her defense. The court concluded that "the dangers of admitting this kind of testimony outweigh whatever probative value it may have," and decided to follow the approach of States that have held hypnotically refreshed testimony of witnesses inadmissible *per se.* . . .

At this point in the development of our adversary system, it cannot be doubted that a defendant in a criminal case has the right to take the witness stand and to testify in his or her own defense. This, of course, is a change from the historic common-law view, which was that all parties to litigation, including criminal defendants, were disqualified from testifying because of their interest in the outcome of the trial. The principal rationale for this rule was the possible untrustworthiness of a party's testimony. Under the common law, the practice did develop of permitting criminal defendants to tell their side of the story, but they were limited to making an unsworn statement that could not be elicited through direct examination by counsel and was not subject to cross-examination.

[B]y the end of the second half of the 19th century, all States except Georgia had enacted statutes that declared criminal defendants competent to testify. Congress enacted a general competency statute in the Act of Mar. 16, 1878, and similar developments followed in other common-law countries. Thus, more than 25 years ago this Court was able to state:

> "In sum, decades ago the considered consensus of the English-speaking world came to be that there was no rational justification for prohibiting the sworn testimony of the accused, who above all others may be in a position to meet the prosecution's case." *Ferguson v. Georgia*, 365 U.S. [570,] 582 [(1961)].

The right to testify on one's own behalf at a criminal trial has sources in several provisions of the Constitution. It is one of the rights that "are essential to due process of law in a fair adversary process." *Faretta v. California*, 422 U.S. 806, 819 n. 15 (1975). The necessary ingredients of the Fourteenth Amendment's guarantee that no one shall be deprived of liberty without due process of law include a right to be heard and to offer testimony. . . .

The right to testify is also found in the Compulsory Process Clause of the Sixth Amendment, which grants a defendant the right to call "witnesses in his favor," a right that is guaranteed in the criminal courts of the States by the Fourteenth Amendment. *Washington v. Texas*, 388 U.S. 14, 17-19 (1967). Logically included in the accused's right to call witnesses whose testimony is "material and favorable to his defense," *United States v. Valenzuela-Bernal*, 458 U.S. 858, 867 (1982), is a right to testify himself, should he decide it is in his favor to do so. In fact, the most important witness for the defense in many criminal cases is the defendant himself. There is no justification today for a rule that denies an accused the opportunity to offer his own testimony. Like the truthfulness of other witnesses, the defendant's veracity, which was the concern behind the original common-law rule, can be tested adequately by cross-examination. . . .

The opportunity to testify is also a necessary corollary to the Fifth Amendment's guarantee against compelled testimony. In *Harris v. New York*, 401 U.S. 222, 230 (1971), the Court stated: "Every criminal defendant is privileged to testify in his own defense, or to refuse to do so." . . .

The question now before the Court is whether a criminal defendant's right to testify may be restricted by a state rule that excludes her posthypnosis testimony. This is not the first time this Court has faced a constitutional challenge to a state rule, designed to ensure trustworthy evidence, that interfered with the ability of a defendant to offer testimony. In *Washington v. Texas*, 388 U.S. 14 (1967), the Court was confronted with a state statute that prevented persons charged as principals, accomplices, or accessories in the same crime from being introduced as witnesses for one another. The statute, like the original common-law prohibition on testimony by the accused, was grounded in a concern for the reliability of evidence presented by an interested party. . . .

As the Court recognized, the incompetency of a codefendant to testify had been rejected on nonconstitutional grounds in 1918, when the Court, refusing to be bound by "the dead hand of the common-law rule of 1789," stated:

> " '[T]he conviction of our time [is] that the truth is more likely to be arrived at by hearing the testimony of all persons of competent understanding who may seem to have knowledge of the facts involved in a case, leaving the credit and weight of such testimony to be determined by the jury or by the court. . . . ' " 388 U.S., at 22, quoting *Rosen v. United States*, 245 U.S. 467, 471 (1918).

The Court concluded that this reasoning was compelled by the Sixth Amendment's protections for the accused. In particular, the Court reasoned that the Sixth Amendment was designed in part "to make the testimony of a defendant's witnesses admissible on his behalf in court." 388 U.S., at 22.

With the rationale for the common-law incompetency rule thus rejected on constitutional grounds, the Court found that the mere presence of the witness in the courtroom was not enough to satisfy the Constitution's Compulsory Process Clause. By preventing the defendant from having the benefit of his accomplice's testimony, "the State *arbitrarily* denied him the right to put on the stand a witness who was physically and mentally capable of testifying to events that he had personally observed, and whose testimony would have been relevant and material to the defense." (Emphasis added.) *Id.* at 23.

Just as a State may not apply an arbitrary rule of competence to exclude a material defense witness from taking the stand, it also may not apply a rule of evidence that permits a witness to take the stand, but arbitrarily excludes material portions of his testimony. In *Chambers v. Mississippi*, 410 U.S. 284 (1973), the Court invalidated a State's hearsay rule on the ground that it abridged the defendant's right to "present witnesses in his own defense." . . .

Of course, the right to present relevant testimony is not without limitation. . . . But restrictions of a defendant's right to testify may not be arbitrary or disproportionate to the purposes they are designed to serve. In applying its evidentiary rules a State must evaluate whether the interests served by a rule justify the limitation imposed on the defendant's constitutional right to testify.

The Arkansas rule enunciated by the state courts does not allow a trial court to consider whether posthypnosis testimony may be admissible in a particular case; it is a *per se* rule prohibiting the admission at trial of any defendant's hypnotically refreshed testimony on the ground that such testimony is always unreliable. Thus, in Arkansas, an accused's testimony is limited to matters that he or she can prove were remembered *before* hypnosis. This rule operates to the detriment of any defendant who undergoes hypnosis, without regard to the reasons for it, the circumstances under which it took place, or any independent verification of the information it produced.

In this case, the application of that rule had a significant adverse effect on petitioner's ability to testify. It virtually prevented her from describing any of the events that occurred on the day of the shooting, despite corroboration of many of those events by other witnesses. Even more importantly, under the court's rule petitioner was not permitted to describe the actual shooting except in the words contained in Doctor Back's notes. The expert's description of the gun's tendency to misfire would have taken on greater significance if the jury had heard petitioner testify that she did not have her finger on the trigger and that the gun went off when her husband hit her arm.

In establishing its *per se* rule, the Arkansas Supreme Court simply followed the approach taken by a number of States that have decided that hypnotically enhanced testimony should be excluded at trial on the ground that it tends to be unreliable. Other States that have adopted an exclusionary rule, however, have done so for the testimony of *witnesses*, not for the testimony of a *defendant*. The Arkansas Supreme Court failed to perform the constitutional analysis that is necessary when a defendant's right to testify is at stake.

Although the Arkansas court concluded that any testimony that cannot be proved to be the product of prehypnosis memory is unreliable, many courts have eschewed a *per se* rule and permit the admission of hypnotically refreshed testimony. Hypnosis by trained physicians or psychologists has been recognized as a valid therapeutic technique since 1958, although there is no generally accepted theory to explain the phenomenon, or even a consensus on a single definition of hypnosis. See Council on Scientific Affairs, Scientific Status of Refreshing Recollection by the Use of Hypnosis, 253 J.A.M.A. 1918, 1918-1919 (1985) (Council Report). The use of hypnosis in criminal investigations, however, is controversial, and the current medical and legal view of its appropriate role is unsettled.

Responses of individuals to hypnosis vary greatly. The popular belief that hypnosis guarantees the accuracy of recall is as yet without established foundation and, in fact, hypnosis often has no effect at all on memory. The most common response to hypnosis, however, appears to be an increase in both correct and incorrect recollections. Three general characteristics of hypnosis may lead to the introduction of inaccurate memories: the subject becomes "suggestible" and may try to please the hypnotist with answers the subject thinks will be met with approval; the subject is likely to "confabulate," that is, to fill in details from the imagination in order to make an answer more coherent and complete; and, the subject experiences "memory hardening," which gives him great confidence in both true and false memories, making effective cross-examination more difficult. See generally M. Orne et al., Hypnotically Induced Testimony, in Eyewitness Testimony: Psychological Perspectives 171 (G. Wells & E. Loftus, eds., 1984); Diamond, Inherent Problems in the Use of Pretrial Hypnosis on a Prospective Witness, 68 Calif. L. Rev. 313, 333-342 (1980). Despite the unreliability that hypnosis concededly may introduce, however, the procedure has been credited as instrumental in obtaining investigative leads or identifications that were later confirmed by independent evidence. . . .

The inaccuracies the process introduces can be reduced, although perhaps not eliminated, by the use of procedural safeguards. One set of suggested guidelines calls for hypnosis to be performed only by a psychologist or psychiatrist with special training in its use and who is independent of the investigation. See Orne, The Use and Misuse of Hypnosis in Court, 27 Int'l J. Clinical and Experimental Hypnosis 311, 335-336 (1979). These procedures reduce the possibility that biases will be communicated to the hypersuggestive subject by the hypnotist. Suggestion will be less likely also if the hypnosis is conducted in a neutral setting with no one present but the hypnotist and the subject. Tape or video recording of all interrogations, before, during, and after hypnosis, can help reveal if leading questions were asked. Such guidelines do not guarantee the accuracy of the testimony, because they cannot control the subject's own motivations or any tendency to confabulate, but they do provide a means of controlling overt suggestions.

The more traditional means of assessing accuracy of testimony also remain applicable in the case of a previously hypnotized defendant. Certain information recalled as a result of hypnosis may be verified as highly accurate by corroborating evidence. Cross-examination, even in the face of a confident defendant, is an effective tool for revealing inconsistencies. Moreover, a jury can be educated to the risks of hypnosis through expert testimony and cautionary instructions. Indeed, it is probably to a defendant's advantage to establish carefully the extent of his memory prior to hypnosis, in order to minimize the decrease in credibility the procedure might introduce.

We are not now prepared to endorse without qualifications the use of hypnosis as an investigative tool; scientific understanding of the phenomenon and of the means to control the effects of hypnosis is still in its infancy. Arkansas, however, has not justified the exclusion of *all* of a defendant's testimony that the defendant is unable to prove to be the product of prehypnosis memory. A State's legitimate interest in barring unreliable evidence does not extend to *per se* exclusions that may be reliable in an individual case. Wholesale inadmissibility of a defendant's testimony is an arbitrary restriction on the right to testify in the absence of clear evidence by the State repudiating the validity of all posthypnosis recollections. The State would be well within its powers if it established guidelines to aid trial courts in the evaluation of posthypnosis testimony and it may be able to show that testimony in a particular case is so unreliable that exclusion is justified. But it has not shown that hypnotically enhanced testimony is always so untrustworthy and so immune to the traditional means of evaluating credibility that it should disable a defendant from presenting her version of the events for which she is on trial.

In this case, the defective condition of the gun corroborated the details petitioner remembered about the shooting. The tape recordings provided some means to evaluate the hypnosis and the trial judge concluded that Doctor Back did not suggest responses with leading questions. Those circumstances present an argument for admissibility of petitioner's testimony in this particular case, an argument that must be considered by the trial court. Arkansas' *per se* rule excluding all posthypnosis testimony infringes impermissibly on the right of a defendant to testify on his own behalf.

The judgment of the Supreme Court of Arkansas is vacated, and the case is remanded to that court for further proceedings not inconsistent with this opinion.

[Chief Justice Rehnquist filed a dissenting opinion.]

PROBLEM

8.4. Section 795(a) of the California Evidence Code provides as follows:

The testimony of a witness is not inadmissible in a criminal proceeding by reason of the fact that the witness has previously undergone hypnosis for the purpose of recalling events which are the subject of the witness' testimony, if all of the following conditions are met:

(1) The testimony is limited to those matters which the witness recalled and related prior to the hypnosis.
(2) The substance of the prehypnotic memory was preserved in written, audiotape, or videotape form prior to the hypnosis.
(3) The hypnosis was conducted in accordance with all of the following procedures:
    (A) A written record was made prior to hypnosis documenting the subject's description of the event, and information which was provided to the hypnotist concerning the subject matter of the hypnosis.
    (B) The subject gave informed consent to the hypnosis.
    (C) The hypnosis session, including the pre- and post-hypnosis interviews, was videotape recorded for subsequent review.
    (D) The hypnosis was performed by a licensed medical doctor, psychologist, licensed clinical social worker, or a licensed marriage, family and child counselor experienced in the use of hypnosis and independent of and not in the presence of law enforcement, the prosecution, or the defense.
(4) Prior to admission of the testimony, the court holds a hearing . . . at which the proponent of the evidence proves by clear and convincing evidence that the hypnosis did not so affect the witness as to render the witness' prehypnosis recollection unreliable or to substantially impair the ability to cross-examine the witness concerning the witness' prehypnosis recollection. . . .

The California courts have not applied § 795(a) to the testimony of criminal defendants. *See People v. Aguilar*, 2667 Cal. Rptr. 879 (Cal. App. 1990). If so applied, would the statute be constitutional? Is the statute constitutional as applied to other witnesses called by criminal defendants?

F. JUDGES, JURORS, AND LAWYERS

Although almost everyone who is not a very young child is now competent to testify, three important categories of incompetence remain: judges, jurors, and lawyers generally may not testify in the cases in which they serve. The disqualification of judges as witnesses leads to little litigation and little controversy, as does the rule prohibiting a juror from testifying before the jury of which he or she is a member. But there is a good deal of controversy as well as frequent litigation about the ability of jurors to testify in a *post-trial* hearing to set aside the verdict because of irregularities involving the jury. And there is uncertainty about the status and proper contours of the so-called "advocate-witness" rule, which bars attorneys from appearing both as witnesses and attorneys in the same proceeding.

[F.R.E. 605, 606; C.E.C. §§703, 704, 1150]

ADVISORY COMMITTEE NOTE TO F.R.E. 605

In view of the mandate of 28 U.S.C. § 455 that a judge disqualify himself in "any case in which he . . . is or has been a material witness," the likelihood that the presiding judge in a federal court might be called to testify in the trial over which he is presiding is slight. Nevertheless the possibility is not totally eliminated.

The solution here presented is a broad rule of incompetency, rather than such alternatives as incompetency only as to material matters, leaving the matter to the discretion of the judge, or recognizing no incompetency. The choice is the result of inability to evolve satisfactory answers to questions which arise when the judge abandons the bench for the witness stand. Who rules on objections? Who compels him to answer? Can he rule impartially on the weight and admissibility of his own testimony? Can he be impeached or cross-examined effectively? Can he, in a jury trial, avoid conferring his seal of approval on one side in the eyes of the jury? Can he, in a bench trial, avoid an involvement destructive of impartiality? The rule of general incompetency has substantial support. See Report of the Special Committee on the Propriety of Judges Appearing as Witnesses, 36 A.B.A.J. 630 (1950); cases collected in Annot. 157 A.L.R. 311; McCormick § 68, p. 147; Uniform Rule 42; California Evidence Code § 703; Kansas Code of Civil Procedure § 60-442; New Jersey Evidence Rule 42. Cf. 6 Wigmore § 1909, which advocates leaving the matter to the discretion of the judge, and statutes to that effect collected in Annot. 157 A.L.R. 311.

The rule provides an "automatic" objection. To require an actual objection would confront the opponent with a choice between not objecting, with the result of allowing the testimony, and objecting, with the probable result of excluding the testimony but at the price of continuing the trial before a judge likely to feel that his integrity had been attacked by the objector.

ADVISORY COMMITTEE NOTE TO F.R.E. 606

Subdivision (a). The considerations which bear upon the permissibility of testimony by a juror in the trial in which he is sitting as juror bear an obvious similarity to those evoked when the judge is called as a witness. The judge is not, however in this instance so involved as to call for departure from usual principles requiring objection to be made; hence the only provision on objection is that opportunity be afforded for its making out of the presence of the jury.

Subdivision (b). Whether testimony, affidavits, or statements of jurors should be received for the purpose of invalidating or supporting a verdict or indictment, and if so, under what circumstances, has given rise to substantial differences of opinion. The familiar rubric that a juror may not impeach his own verdict, dating from Lord Mansfield's time, is a gross oversimplification. The values sought to be promoted by excluding the evidence include freedom of deliberation, stability and finality of verdicts, and protection of jurors against annoyance and embarrassment. McDonald v. Pless, 238 U.S. 264 (1915). On the other hand, simply putting verdicts beyond effective reach can only promote irregularity and injustice. The rule offers an accommodation between these competing considerations.

The mental operations and emotional reactions of jurors in arriving at a given result would, if allowed as a subject of inquiry, place every verdict at the mercy of jurors and invite tampering and harassment. The authorities are in virtually complete accord in excluding the evidence. As to matters other than mental operations and emotional reactions of jurors, substantial authority refuses to allow a juror to disclose irregularities which occur in the jury room, but allows his testimony as to irregularities occurring outside and allows outsiders to testify as to occurrences both inside and out. However, the door of the jury room is not necessarily a satisfactory dividing point, and the Supreme Court has refused to accept it for every situation. Mattox v. United States, 146 U.S. 140 (1892).

Under the federal decisions the central focus has been upon insulation of the manner in which the jury reached its verdict, and this protection extends to each of the components of deliberation, including arguments, statements, discussions, mental and emotional reactions, votes, and any other feature of the process. Thus testimony or affidavits of jurors have been held incompetent to show a compromise verdict, Hyde v. United States, 225 U.S. 347, 382 (1912); a quotient verdict, McDonald v. Pless, 238 U.S. 264 (1915); speculation as to insurance coverage, Holden v. Porter, 405 F.2d 878 (10th Cir. 1969); Farmers Coop. Elev. Ass'n v. Strand, 382 F.2d 224, 230 (8th Cir. 1967), cert. denied 389 U.S. 1014; misinterpretation of instructions, Farmers Coop. Elev. Ass'n v. Strand, supra; mistake in returning verdict, United States v. Chereton, 309 F.2d 197 (6th Cir. 1962); interpretation of guilty plea by one defendant as implicating others, United States v. Crosby, 294 F.2d 928, 949 (2d Cir. 1961). The policy does not, however, foreclose testimony by jurors as to prejudicial extraneous information or influences injected into or brought to bear upon the deliberative process. Thus a juror is recognized as competent to testify to statements by the bailiff or the introduction of a prejudicial newspaper account into the jury room, Mattox v. United States, 146 U.S. 140 (1892). See also Parker v. Gladden, 385 U.S. 363 (1966).

This rule does not purport to specify the substantive grounds for setting aside verdicts for irregularity; it deals only with the competency of jurors to testify concerning those grounds. Allowing them to testify as to matters other than their own inner reactions involves no particular hazard to the values sought to be protected. The rule is based upon this conclusion. It makes no attempt to specify the substantive grounds for setting aside verdicts for irregularity. . . .

TANNER v. UNITED STATES

483 U.S. 107 (1987)

Justice O'CONNOR delivered the opinion of the Court.

[Petitioners William Conover, a procurement manager at an electric utility, and Anthony Tanner, a contractor hired by the utility, were charged with conspiracy and mail fraud in connection with payments Tanner made to Conover, allegedly in exchange for favorable treatment by the utility.] A 6-week trial resulted in a hung jury and a mistrial was declared. [On retrial,] Conover was convicted on all counts; Tanner was convicted on all but count three.

The day before petitioners were scheduled to be sentenced, Tanner filed a motion, in which Conover subsequently joined, seeking continuance of the sentencing date, permission to interview jurors, an evidentiary hearing, and a new trial. According to an affidavit accompanying the motion, Tanner's attorney had received an unsolicited telephone call from one of the trial jurors, Vera Asbul. Juror Asbul informed Tanner's attorney that several of the jurors consumed alcohol during the lunch breaks at various times throughout the trial, causing them to sleep through the afternoons. The District Court continued the sentencing date, ordered the parties to file memoranda, and heard argument on the motion to interview jurors. The District Court concluded that juror testimony on intoxication was inadmissible under Federal Rule of Evidence 606(b) to impeach the jury's verdict. The District Court invited petitioners to call any nonjuror witnesses, such as courtroom personnel, in support of the motion for new trial. Tanner's counsel took the stand and testified that he had observed one of the jurors "in a sort of giggly mood" at one point during the trial but did not bring this to anyone's attention at the time.

. . . Following the hearing the District Court filed an order stating that "[o]n the basis of the admissible evidence offered I specifically find that the motions for leave to interview jurors or for an evidentiary hearing at which jurors would be witnesses is not required or appropriate." The District Court also denied the motion for new trial.

While the appeal of this case was pending before the Eleventh Circuit, petitioners filed another new trial motion based on additional evidence of jury misconduct. In another affidavit, Tanner's attorney stated that he received an unsolicited visit at his residence from a second juror, Daniel Hardy. Despite the fact that the District Court had denied petitioners' motion for leave to interview jurors, two days after Hardy's visit Tanner's attorney arranged for Hardy to be interviewed by two private investigators. The interview was transcribed, sworn to by the juror, and attached to the new trial motion. In the interview Hardy stated that he "felt like . . . the jury was on one big party." Hardy indicated that seven of the jurors drank alcohol during the noon recess. Four jurors, including Hardy, consumed between them "a pitcher to three pitchers" of beer during various recesses. Of the three other jurors who were alleged to have consumed alcohol, Hardy stated that on several occasions he observed two jurors having one or two mixed drinks during the lunch recess, and one other juror, who was also the foreperson, having a liter of wine on each of three occasions. Juror Hardy also stated that he and three other jurors smoked marijuana quite regularly during the trial. Moreover, Hardy stated that during the trial he observed one juror ingest cocaine five times and another juror ingest cocaine two or three times. One juror sold a quarter pound of marijuana to another juror during the trial, and took marijuana, cocaine, and drug paraphernalia into the courthouse. Hardy noted that some of the jurors were falling asleep during the trial, and that one of the jurors described himself to Hardy as "flying." Hardy stated that before he visited Tanner's attorney at his residence, no one had contacted him concerning the jury's conduct, and Hardy had not been offered anything in return for his statement. Hardy said that he came forward "to clear my conscience" and "[b]ecause I felt . . . that the people on the jury didn't have no business being on the jury. I felt . . . that Mr. Tanner should have a better opportunity to get somebody that would review the facts right."

The District Court, stating that the motions "contain supplemental allegations which differ quantitatively but not qualitatively from those in the April motions," denied petitioners' motion for a new trial. The Court of Appeals for the Eleventh Circuit affirmed.

. . . Petitioners argue that the District Court erred in not ordering an additional evidentiary hearing at which jurors would testify concerning drug and alcohol use during the trial. Petitioners assert that, contrary to the holdings of the District Court and the Court of Appeals, juror testimony on ingestion of drugs or alcohol during the trial is not barred by Federal Rule of Evidence 606(b). Moreover, petitioners argue that whether or not authorized by Rule 606(b), an evidentiary hearing including juror testimony on drug and alcohol use is compelled by their Sixth Amendment right to trial by a competent jury.

By the beginning of this century, if not earlier, the near-universal and firmly established common-law rule in the United States flatly prohibited the admission of juror testimony to impeach a jury verdict. See 8 J. Wigmore, Evidence § 2352, pp. 696-697 (J. McNaughton rev. ed. 1961) (common-law rule, originating from 1785 opinion of Lord Mansfield, "came to receive in the United States an adherence almost unquestioned").

Exceptions to the common-law rule were recognized only in situations in which an "extraneous influence," *Mattox v. United States*, 146 U.S. 140, 149 (1892), was alleged to have affected the jury. In *Mattox*, this Court held admissible the testimony of jurors describing how they heard and read prejudicial information not admitted into evidence. The Court allowed juror testimony on influence by outsiders in *Parker v. Gladden*, 385 U.S. 363, 365 (1966) (bailiff's comments on defendant), and *Remmer v. United States*, 347 U.S. 227, 228-230 (1954) (bribe offered to juror). See also *Smith v. Phillips*, 455 U.S. 209 (1982) (juror in criminal trial had submitted an application for employment at the District Attorney's office). In situations that did not fall into this exception for external influence, however, the Court adhered to the common-law rule against admitting juror testimony to impeach a verdict. *McDonald v. Pless*, 238 U.S. 264 (1915); *Hyde v. United States*, 225 U.S. 347, 384 (1912).

Lower courts used this external/internal distinction to identify those instances in which juror testimony impeaching a verdict would be admissible. The distinction was not based on whether the juror was literally inside or outside the jury room when the alleged irregularity took place; rather, the distinction was based on the nature of the allegation. Clearly a rigid distinction based only on whether the event took place inside or outside the jury room would have been quite unhelpful. For example, under a distinction based on location a juror could not testify concerning a newspaper read inside the jury room. Instead, of course, this has been considered an external influence about which juror testimony is admissible. See *United States v. Thomas*, 463 F.2d 1061 (CA7 1972). Similarly, under a rigid locational distinction jurors could be regularly required to testify after the verdict as to whether they heard and comprehended the judge's instructions, since the charge to the jury takes place outside the jury room. Courts wisely have treated allegations of a juror's inability to hear or comprehend at trial as an internal matter. See *Government of the Virgin Islands v. Nicholas*, 759 F.2d 1073 (CA3 1985); *Davis v. United States*, 47 F.2d 1071 (CA5 1931) (rejecting juror testimony impeaching verdict, including testimony that jurors had not heard a particular instruction of the court).

Most significant for the present case, however, is the fact that lower federal courts treated allegations of the physical or mental incompetence of a juror as "internal" rather than "external" matters. In *United States v. Dioguardi*, 492 F.2d 70 (CA2 1974), the defendant Dioguardi received a letter from one of the jurors soon after the trial in which the juror explained that she had "eyes and ears that . . . see things before [they] happen", but that her eyes "are only partly open" because "a curse was put upon them some years ago". Armed with this letter and the opinions of seven psychiatrists that the letter suggested that the juror was suffering from a psychological disorder, Dioguardi sought a new trial or in the alternative an evidentiary hearing on the juror's competence. The District Court denied the motion and the Court of Appeals affirmed. The Court of Appeals noted "[t]he strong policy against any post-verdict inquiry into a juror's state of mind," and observed:

> "The quickness with which jury findings will be set aside when there is proof of tampering or external influence, . . . parallel the reluctance of courts to inquire into jury deliberations when a verdict is valid on its face. . . . Such exceptions support rather than undermine the rationale of the rule that possible *internal* abnormalities in a jury will not be inquired into except 'in the gravest and most important cases.' " *Id.*, at 79, n. 12, quoting *McDonald v. Pless, supra*, 238 U.S., at 269 (emphasis in original).

The Court of Appeals concluded that when faced with allegations that a juror was mentally incompetent, "courts have refused to set aside a verdict, or even to make further inquiry, unless there be proof of an adjudication of insanity or mental incompetence closely in advance . . . of jury service", or proof of "a closely contemporaneous and independent post-trial adjudication of incompetency." See also *Sullivan v. Fogg*, 613 F.2d 465, 467 (CA2 1980) (allegation of juror insanity is internal consideration); *United States v. Allen*, 588 F.2d 1100, 1106, n. 12 (CA5 1979) (noting "specific reluctance to probe the minds of jurors once they have deliberated their verdict"); *United States v. Pellegrini*, 441 F. Supp. 1367 (ED Pa. 1977), *aff'd*, 586 F.2d 836 (CA3), *cert. denied*, 439 U.S. 1050 (1978) (whether juror sufficiently understood English language was not a question of "extraneous influence"). This line of federal decisions was reviewed in *Government of the Virgin Islands v. Nicholas, supra*, in which the Court of Appeals concluded that a juror's allegation that a hearing impairment interfered with his understanding of the evidence at trial was not a matter of "external influence."

Substantial policy considerations support the common-law rule against the admission of jury testimony to impeach a verdict. As early as 1915 this Court explained the necessity of shielding jury deliberations from public scrutiny:

> "[L]et it once be established that verdicts solemnly made and publicly returned into court can be attacked and set aside on the testimony of those who took part in their publication and all verdicts could be, and many would be, followed by an inquiry in the hope of discovering something which might invalidate the finding. Jurors would be harassed and beset by the defeated party in an effort to secure from them evidence of facts which might establish misconduct sufficient to set aside a verdict. If evidence thus secured could be thus used, the result would be to make what was intended to be a private deliberation, the constant subject of public investigation—to the destruction of all frankness and freedom of discussion and conference". *McDonald v. Pless*, 238 U.S., at 267-268.

The Court's holdings requiring an evidentiary hearing where extrinsic influence or relationships have tainted the deliberations do not detract from, but rather harmonize with, the weighty government interest in insulating the jury's deliberative process. See *Smith v. Phillips*, 455 U.S. 209 (1982) (juror in criminal trial had submitted an application for employment at the District Attorney's office); *Remmer v. United States*, 347 U.S. 227 (1954) (juror reported attempted bribe during trial and was subjected to investigation). The Court's statement in *Remmer* that "[t]he integrity of jury proceedings must not be jeopardized by unauthorized invasions," could also be applied to the inquiry petitioners seek to make into the internal processes of the jury.

There is little doubt that postverdict investigation into juror misconduct would in some instances lead to the invalidation of verdicts reached after irresponsible or improper juror behavior. It is not at all clear, however, that the jury system could survive such efforts to perfect it. Allegations of juror misconduct, incompetency, or inattentiveness, raised for the first time days, weeks, or months after the verdict, seriously disrupt the finality of the process. See, e.g., *Government of Virgin Islands v. Nicholas, supra*, at 1081 (one year and eight months after verdict rendered, juror alleged that hearing difficulties affected his understanding of the evidence). Moreover, full and frank discussion in the jury room, jurors' willingness to return an unpopular verdict, and the community's trust in a system that relies on the decisions of laypeople would all be undermined by a barrage of postverdict scrutiny of juror conduct. See Note, Public Disclosures of Jury Deliberations, 96 Harv. L. Rev. 886, 888-892 (1983).

Federal Rule of Evidence 606(b) is grounded in the common-law rule against admission of jury testimony to impeach a verdict and the exception for juror testimony relating to extraneous influences. See *Government of Virgin Islands v. Gereau*, 523 F.2d 140, 149, n. 22 (CA3 1975); S. Rep. No. 93-1277, p. 13 (1974) (observing that Rule 606(b) "embodied long-accepted Federal law").

. . . Petitioners have presented no argument that Rule 606(b) is inapplicable to the juror affidavits and the further inquiry they sought in this case, and, in fact, there appears to be virtually no support for such a proposition. See 3 D. Louisell & C. Mueller, Federal Evidence § 287, pp. 121-125 (1979) (under Rule 606(b), "proof to the following effects is excludable . . . : . . . that one or more jurors was inattentive during trial or deliberations, sleeping or thinking about other matters"); cf. Note, *Impeachment of Verdicts by Jurors of Evidence* 606(b), 4 Wm. Mitchell L. Rev. 417, 430-431, and n. 88 (1978) (observing that under Rule 606(b), "juror testimony as to . . . juror intoxication probably will be inadmissible"; note author suggests that "[o]ne possibility is for the courts to determine that certain acts, such as a juror becoming intoxicated outside the jury room, simply are not within the rule," but cites no authority in support of the suggestion). Rather, petitioners argue that substance abuse constitutes an improper "outside influence" about which jurors may testify under Rule 606(b). In our view the language of the Rule cannot easily be stretched to cover this circumstance. However severe their effect and improper their use, drugs or alcohol voluntarily ingested by a juror seems no more an "outside influence" than a virus, poorly prepared food, or a lack of sleep.

In any case, whatever ambiguity might linger in the language of Rule 606(b) as applied to juror intoxication is resolved by the legislative history of the Rule. In 1972, following criticism of a proposed rule that would have allowed considerably broader use of juror testimony to impeach verdicts, the Advisory Committee drafted the present version of Rule 606(b). . . . This

Court adopted the present version of Rule 606(b) and transmitted it to Congress.

The House Judiciary Committee described the effect of the version of Rule 606(b) transmitted by the Court as follows:

> "As proposed by the Court, Rule 606(b) limited testimony by a juror in the course of an inquiry into the validity of a verdict or indictment. He could testify as to the influence of extraneous prejudicial information brought to the jury's attention (e.g. a radio newscast or a newspaper account) or an outside influence which improperly had been brought to bear upon a juror (e.g. a threat to the safety of a member of his family), but he could not testify as to other irregularities which occurred in the jury room. Under this formulation a quotient verdict could not be attacked through the testimony of juror, *nor could a juror testify to the drunken condition of a fellow juror which so disabled him that he could not participate in the jury's deliberations.*"
> H.R. Rep. No. 93-650, pp. 9-10 (1973) (emphasis supplied).

The House Judiciary Committee, persuaded that the better practice was to allow juror testimony on any "objective juror misconduct", amended the Rule so as to comport with the more expansive versions proposed by the Advisory Committee in earlier drafts,* and the House passed this amended version.

The Senate Judiciary Committee did not voice any disagreement with the House's interpretation of the Rule proposed by the Court, or the version passed by the House. Indeed, the Senate Report described the House version as "considerably broader" than the version proposed by the Court, and noted that the House version "would permit the impeachment of verdicts by inquiry into, not the mental processes of the jurors, but what happened in terms of conduct in the jury room." S. Rep. No. 93-1277, p. 13 (1974). With this understanding of the differences between the two versions of Rule 606(b)—an understanding identical to that of the House—the Senate decided to reject the broader House version and adopt the narrower version approved by the Court. The Senate Report explained:

"[The House version's] extension of the ability to impeach a verdict is felt to be unwarranted and ill-advised.

"The rule passed by the House embodies a suggestion by the Advisory Committee of the Judicial Conference that is considerably broader than the final version adopted by the Supreme Court, which embodied long-accepted Federal law. Although forbidding the impeachment of verdicts by inquiry into the jurors' mental processes, it deletes from the Supreme Court version the proscription against testimony 'as to any matter or statement occurring during the course of the jury's deliberations.' This deletion

---

*The House version, which adopted the earlier Advisory Committee proposal, read as follows: "Upon an inquiry into the validity of a verdict or indictment, a juror may not testify concerning the effect of anything upon his or any other juror's mind or emotions as influencing him to assent to or dissent from the verdict or indictment or concerning his mental processes in connection therewith. Nor may his affidavit or evidence of any statement by him indicating an effect of this kind be received for these purposes." H.R. 5463, 93d Cong., 2d Sess. (1974).

would have the effect of opening verdicts up to challenge on the basis of what happened during the jury's internal deliberations, for example, where a juror alleged that the jury refused to follow the trial judge's instructions or that some of the jurors did not take part in deliberations.

"Permitting an individual to attack a jury verdict based upon the jury's internal deliberations has long been recognized as unwise by the Supreme Court. . . .

"As it stands then, the rule would permit the harassment of former jurors by losing parties as well as the possible exploitation of disgruntled or otherwise badly-motivated ex-jurors.

"Public policy requires a finality to litigation. And common fairness requires that absolute privacy be preserved for jurors to engage in the full and free debate necessary to the attainment of just verdicts. Jurors will not be able to function effectively if their deliberations are to be scrutinized in post-trial litigation. In the interest of protecting the jury system and the citizens who make it work, rule 606 should not permit any inquiry into the internal deliberations of the jurors." *Id.*, at 13-14.

The Conference Committee Report reaffirms Congress' understanding of the differences between the House and Senate versions of Rule 606(b): "[T]he House bill allows a juror to testify about objective matters occurring during the jury's deliberation, such as the misconduct of another juror or the reaching of a quotient verdict. The Senate bill does not permit juror testimony about any matter or statement occurring during the course of the jury's deliberations." H.R. Conf. Rep. No. 93-1597, p. 8 (1974). The Conference Committee adopted, and Congress enacted, the Senate version of Rule 606(b).

Thus, the legislative history demonstrates with uncommon clarity that Congress specifically understood, considered, and rejected a version of Rule 606(b) that would have allowed jurors to testify on juror conduct during deliberations, including juror intoxication. This legislative history provides strong support for the most reasonable reading of the language of Rule 606(b)—that juror intoxication is not an "outside influence" about which jurors may testify to impeach their verdict.

Finally, even if Rule 606(b) is interpreted to retain the common-law exception allowing post-verdict inquiry of juror incompetence in cases of "substantial if not wholly conclusive evidence of incompetency," *Dioguardi*, 492 F.2d, at 80, the showing made by petitioners falls far short of this standard. The affidavits and testimony presented in support of the first new trial motion suggested, at worst, that several of the jurors fell asleep at times during the afternoons. The District Court Judge appropriately considered the fact that he had "an unobstructed view" of the jury, and did not see any juror sleeping. . . . The juror affidavit submitted in support of the second new trial motion was obtained in clear violation of the District Court's order and the court's local rule against juror interviews, MD Fla. Rule 2.04(c); on this basis alone the District Court would have been acting within its discretion in disregarding the affidavit. In any case, although the affidavit of juror Hardy describes more dramatic instances of misconduct, Hardy's allegations of incompetence are meager. Hardy stated that the alcohol consumption he engaged in with three other jurors did not leave any of them intoxicated. ("I told [the prosecutor] that we would just go out and get us a pitcher of beer and drink it, but as far as us being drunk, no we wasn't.") The only allegations concerning the jurors' ability to properly consider the evidence were Hardy's observations that some jurors were "falling asleep all the time during the trial," and that his own reasoning ability was affected on one day of the trial. These allegations would not suffice to bring this case under the common-law exception allowing post-verdict inquiry when an extremely strong showing of incompetency has been made.

Petitioners also argue that the refusal to hold an additional evidentiary hearing at which jurors would testify as to their conduct "violates the sixth amendment's guarantee to a fair trial before an impartial and competent jury." . . . As described above, long-recognized and very substantial concerns support the protection of jury deliberations from intrusive inquiry. Petitioners' Sixth Amendment interests in an unimpaired jury, on the other hand, are protected by several aspects of the trial process. The suitability of an individual for the responsibility of jury service, of course, is examined during voir dire. Moreover, during the trial the jury is observable by the court, by counsel, and by court personnel. Moreover, jurors are observable by each other, and may report inappropriate juror behavior to the court before they render a verdict. Finally, after the trial a party may seek to impeach the verdict by nonjuror evidence of misconduct. Indeed, in this case the District Court held an evidentiary hearing giving petitioners ample opportunity to produce nonjuror evidence supporting their allegations.

In light of these other sources of protection of petitioners' right to a competent jury, we conclude that the District Court did not err in deciding, based on the inadmissibility of juror testimony and the clear insufficiency of the nonjuror evidence offered by petitioners, that an additional post-verdict evidentiary hearing was unnecessary. . . . [Remanded in part on other grounds.]

Justice MARSHALL, with whom Justice BRENNAN, Justice BLACKMUN, and Justice STEVENS join, [dissenting in relevant part].

. . . I readily acknowledge the important policy considerations supporting the common-law rule against admission of jury testimony to impeach a verdict, now embodied in Federal Rule of Evidence 606(b): freedom of deliberation, finality of verdicts, and protection of jurors against harassment by dissatisfied litigants. See, e.g., *McDonald v. Pless*, 238 U.S. 264, 267-268 (1915); Advisory Committee's Notes on Fed. Rule Evid. 606(b). It has been simultaneously recognized, however, that "simply putting verdicts beyond effective reach can only promote irregularity and injustice." *Ibid.* If the above-referenced policy considerations seriously threaten the constitutional right to trial by a fair and impartial jury, they must give way.

In this case, however, we are not faced with a conflict between the policy considerations underlying Rule 606(b) and petitioners' Sixth Amendment rights. . . . Because petitioners' claim of juror misconduct and incompetency involves objectively verifiable conduct occurring prior to deliberations, juror testimony in support of the claims is admissible under Rule 606(b).

. . . As the Court emphasizes, the debate over two proposed versions of the Rule—the more restrictive Senate version ultimately adopted and the permissive House version, focused on the extent to which jurors would be permitted to testify as to what transpired *during the course of the deliberations themselves*. Similarly, the Conference Committee Report, quoted by the Court, compares the two versions solely in terms of the admissibility of testimony as to matters occurring during, or relating to, the jury's deliberations: "[T]he House bill allows a juror to testify about objective matters occurring during the jury's deliberation, such as the misconduct of another juror or the reaching of a quotient verdict. The Senate bill does not permit juror testimony about any matter or statement occurring *during the course of the jury's deliberations*." H.R. Conf. Rep. No. 93-1597, p. 8 (1974) (emphasis added). The obvious conclusion, and the one compelled by Rule 601, is that both versions of Rule 606(b) would have permitted jurors to testify as to matters not involving deliberations. The House Report's passing reference to juror intoxication during deliberations is not to the contrary. Reflecting Congress' consistent focus on the deliberative process, it suggests only that the authors of the House Report believed that the Senate version of Rule 606(b) did not allow testimony as to juror intoxication during deliberations.

. . . Even if I agreed with the Court's expansive construction of Rule 606(b), I would nonetheless find the testimony of juror intoxication admissible under the Rule's "outside influence" exception. As a common-sense matter, drugs and alcohol are outside influences on jury members. . . . The Court suggests that, if these are outside influences, "a virus, poorly prepared food, or a lack of sleep" would also qualify. Distinguishing between a virus, for example, and a narcotic drug is a matter of line-drawing. Courts are asked to make these sorts of distinctions in numerous contexts; I have no doubt they would be capable of differentiating between the intoxicants involved in this case and minor indispositions not affecting juror competency.

. . . The Court acknowledges that "postverdict investigation into juror misconduct would in some instances lead to the invalidation of verdicts reached after irresponsible or improper juror behavior," but maintains that "[i]t is not at all clear . . . that the jury system could survive such efforts to perfect it." Petitioners are not asking for a perfect jury. They are seeking to determine whether the jury that heard their case behaved in a manner consonant with the minimum requirements of the Sixth Amendment. If we deny them this opportunity, the jury system may survive, but the constitutional guarantee on which it is based will become meaningless.

I dissent.

PEOPLE v. FLEISS

No. B093373 (Cal. Ct. App. 2d Dist., May 28, 1996)

ORTEGA, Associate Justice.

. . . Defendant Heidi Lynne Fleiss was convicted by a jury of three counts of pandering. The panel was deadlocked on two other pandering counts and acquitted Fleiss of a single count of providing cocaine. [Fleiss had been arrested in 1995 on suspicion of running a high-priced prostitution ring that catered to Hollywood glitterati.]

Fleiss brought a motion for a new trial, in support of which five jurors [Sheila Mitrowski, Lorraine Estrada, Zina Alvavi, Henry Gipson, and Joseph Lechuga] filed declarations dated December 10, 1994. These are similar and deal with discussions about relative penalties, entrapment, stubbornness of some of the jurors, deliberation difficulties, and misunderstanding of the entrapment instructions. Joseph Lechuga says he and several jurors had discussed the case outside the deliberation room with other jurors absent. He did not think Fleiss had a fair trial because two jurors "presumed her guilty before the foreperson was even selected."

Soon thereafter, the Los Angeles *Daily Journal* published an article saying that the District Attorney's Office was looking into whether the jurors should be held in contempt or be charged with criminal violations. On December 21, 1994, Mitrowski, Alavi, and Gipson filed declarations saying they had read the *Daily Journal* article, in light of which they were unable to provide the defense further information.

On February 16, 1995, Mitrowski, Gipson, Estrada, and Lechuga testified on their request for immunity, which the trial court granted. The court granted Alavi . . . immunity on February 21, 1995, after she testified in support of her motion.

Alavi executed a declaration dated February 22, 1995. Shortly after returning from the noon recess on Tuesday, the first day of deliberations, "one juror immediately and spontaneously stated 'Let's just hang the bitch.'" That juror "essentially refused to deliberate with respect to the case. At times he laid on the couch in the jury room." Alavi described two days of deliberations where the panel split into two factions.

On Thursday, Alavi, Mitrowski, Gipson, and Estrada began to speculate about the potential punishment faced by Fleiss. They deduced that pandering convictions would probably lead to probation and that the drug charge was the most serious. They agreed they "must obtain Ms. Fleiss' acquittal on the narcotics charge." On Friday, a juror said he wanted five pandering convictions in exchange for his not guilty vote on the drug charge. Alavi, Mitrowski, Gipson, and Estrada agreed to vote guilty on three pandering counts. Alavi says she would not have voted to convict on any pandering charge "had the other jurors refused to vote not guilty on the narcotics charge." She specifically states that she traded guilty votes for the vote of not guilty on the drug charge.

Mitrowski executed a February 23, 1995, declaration, which generally mirrors Alavi's. On Thursday, Mitrowski and Gipson discussed potential punishment. The same day, the two discussed punishment with Alavi. The three agreed to try to get an acquittal on the drug charge. . . . The next day, Mitrowski, Alavi, Gipson, and Estrada agreed "to vote guilty on three pandering counts in hopes of persuading other jurors to acquit Ms. Fleiss on the narcotics offense." Mitrowski concludes, "I regret that I agreed to and did trade my guilty vote on the pandering counts in exchange for a not guilty vote on the narcotics offense."

Estrada's February 23, 1995, declaration recounts much the same detail as Alavi's and Mitrowski's. On Thursday, Estrada, Mitrowski, Gipson, "and possibly Joseph Lechuga," speculated on the punishment involved. . . . Friday, Estrada agreed with the others "to vote guilty on three pandering counts in hopes of persuading other jurors to acquit Ms. Fleiss on the narcotics offense." Like Mitrowski, Estrada concludes, "I regret that I agreed to and did trade my guilty vote on the pandering counts in exchange for a not guilty vote on the narcotics offense."

Gipson executed a declaration February 23, 1995. On Thursday morning, outside the courthouse, he and Mitrowski discussed punishment, concluding that the drug charge carried the more severe penalty. Gipson had Thursday lunch with Alavi and Mitrowski. They discussed punishment and agreed they "must obtain Ms. Fleiss' acquittal on the narcotics charge." . . . Gipson says he agreed with Alavi, Mitrowski, and Estrada "to vote guilty on three pandering counts in hopes of persuading other jurors to acquit Ms. Fleiss on the narcotics offense." Gipson also regrets that he "agreed to and did trade [his] guilty vote on the pandering counts in exchange for a not guilty vote on the narcotics offense."

Two jurors [Alavi and Mitrowski] testified. [Their testimony essentially reiterated the statements made in their declarations.] At the end of Mitrowski's testimony, the prosecutor said if the court did not want to hear more testimony, he would be willing to submit on Alavi's and Mitrowski's testimony. The court immediately excused Estrada and Gipson.

Counsel argued the matter. The prosecutor's position was that the declarations and testimony revealed nothing more than jurors who were attempting to improperly impeach a verdict with which they had become disenchanted. He attacked their credibility, arguing that the declarations were obviously all prepared by the same person and suggesting that the information in the declarations had been fed to the jurors. He argued that the evidence did not show an actual agreement to trade votes, but rather showed jurors who engaged in an improper mental process in order to arrive at their votes. Since a juror's mental process is not admissible to impeach the verdict, the argument goes, a juror's subsequent unhappiness with his vote does not call for a new trial.

The trial court denied Fleiss' motion for a new trial. The court concluded there had been misconduct, but that it was not prejudicial. . . . [T]he court referred to *People v. Blau* (1956) 140 Cal. App. 2d 193, and said the case was "still viable and . . . appears to be on point." The trial court read *Blau* as holding "that this type of compromise did not constitute prejudicial misconduct." . . .

In *Blau* several defendants were charged with one count of conspiracy to commit theft and falsify corporate records, and two counts of grand theft. Two, Blau and Fisher, were convicted of the conspiracy and two counts of petty theft. "On their motion for a new trial appellants submitted an affidavit of one of the jurors in which she stated that the verdict was the result of a compromise; some of the jurors who were inclined to vote in favor of Mays' guilt voted for his acquittal when other jurors who were in favor of acquittal of the appellants agreed to vote in favor of the guilt of Blau and

Fisher of a lesser offense." (*People v. Blau, supra*, 140 Cal. App. 2d at p. 217.) The *Blau* trial court denied the motion for new trial and the appellate court affirmed.

. . . While the evidence presented in this record is subject to varying interpretations, the circumstances shown by the record persuade us that the trial court accepted that interpretation showing bartering had occurred. . . . *Blau* did not hold that bartering votes is not prejudicial misconduct. Without discussion, the appellate panel merely stated the rule then in existence that "[j]urors may not impeach their verdict by affidavit that it was the result of compromise, or for other irregularity other than that it was arrived at by chance." In *People v. Hutchinson* (1969) 71 Cal. 2d 342, the California Supreme Court discussed Evidence Code section 1150, which became operative in 1967, well after the 1956 *Blau* decision. That section limits "impeachment evidence to proof of overt conduct, conditions, events, and statements. . . . This limitation prevents one juror from upsetting a verdict of the whole jury by impugning his own or his fellow jurors' mental processes or reasons for assent or dissent. The only improper influences that may be proved under section 1150 to impeach a verdict, therefore, are those open to sight, hearing, and the other senses and thus subject to corroboration." (*People v. Hutchinson, supra*, 71 Cal. 2d at pp. 349-350.)

Accordingly, in the instant matter, evidence of discussions in response to one juror's demand for guilty votes in exchange for his not guilty vote was admissible and provides sufficient basis to justify the trial court's conclusion that some members of this jury traded their votes.

That trading votes constitutes prejudicial misconduct is not reasonably open to debate. Such malfeasance strikes at the heart of the justice system. All citizens have two opportunities to participate directly in their representative government—voting and jury service. Both are to be taken seriously and engaged in responsibly. The involved jurors in this case took their solemn duty to impartially dispense justice and turned it into advocacy for a cause. All parties in the justice system are entitled to know what the rules of engagement are and should be able to count on those rules being followed. This was supposed to be a trial, not an auction. The jurors involved in this misconduct committed a transgression worse than those with which Fleiss was charged. Through no fault of the court, the litigants, or their representatives, those jurors turned this serious proceeding into a farce. This verdict resulted not from the evidence, but from extraneous and improper considerations.

Fleiss was entitled to a trial by a jury of 12 persons. A jury is defined as "[a] certain number of men and women selected according to law and sworn . . . to inquire of certain matters of fact, and declare the truth upon evidence to be laid before them." (Black's Law Dict. (5th ed. 1979) p. 768, col. 1.) Certain members of Fleiss' panel violated their oaths, ignored the evidence, abandoned their duty to seek the truth, and turned deliberations into a bazaar. These jurors did not act as a jury. Fleiss did not truly receive a trial by jury. The guilty verdicts rendered by this panel cannot stand. . . . The judgment is reversed. The matter is remanded for further proceedings.

UNITED STATES v. EWING

979 F.2d 1234 (7th Cir. 1992)

COFFEY, Circuit Judge.

[Henry Lee Ewing was convicted of drug trafficking and sentenced to fifteen months in prison. Police executing a search warrant at his home had found cocaine packaged in plastic bags, along with various other evidence of drug trafficking, including two composition notebooks with incriminating notations.]

Ewing maintains that the district court committed reversible error in not allowing his attorney, Renee E. Schooley, an assistant federal public defender, to testify about allegations that the Government tampered with the evidence used against him. Specifically, Ewing claims that the two composition notebooks found in his dining room did not have his name written on them when they were seized by the police during the search of his house. The two notebooks did have Ewing's name written on them when they were introduced at trial as evidence of his drug trafficking enterprise. Ewing's attorney was prepared to testify that six weeks before trial, when she and a paralegal from her office, Abigail Stottlar, examined the evidence gathered by the Alton police against Ewing and stored at the Alton police station, Ewing's name did not appear on either composition notebook.

Under the Illinois Rules of Professional Conduct, adopted by the United States District Court for the Southern District of Illinois as its own legal ethics code, a lawyer may not be both witness and counsel in the same case, except in exceptional circumstances. Rule 3.7 of the Illinois Rules provides, in pertinent part, that:

"(a) A lawyer shall not accept or continue employment in contemplated or pending litigation if the lawyer knows or reasonably should know that the lawyer may be called as a witness on behalf of the client, except that the lawyer may undertake the employment and may testify: (1) if the testimony will relate to an uncontested matter; (2) if the testimony will relate to a matter of formality and the lawyer reasonably believes that no substantial evidence will be offered in opposition to the testimony; (3) if the testimony will relate to the nature and value of legal services rendered in the case by the lawyer or the firm to the client; or (4) as to any other matter, if refusal to accept or continue the employment would work substantial hardship on the client."*

"The advocate-witness rule, which articulates the professional impropriety of assuming the dual role of advocate and witness in a single proceeding, has deep roots in American law." *United States v. Johnston*, 690

---

* [Ed. *Cf.* ABA Model Rule of Professional Conduct 3.7: "(a) A lawyer shall not act as an advocate at a trial in which the lawyer is likely to be a necessary witness except where: (1) The testimony related to an uncontested issue; (2) the testimony related to the nature and value of legal services rendered in the case; or (3) disqualification of the lawyer would work substantial hardship on the client. (b) A lawyer may act as an advocate in a trial in which another lawyer in the lawyer's firm is likely to be called as a witness unless precluded from doing so by Rule 1.7 or Rule 1.9 [pertaining to conflicts of interest]."]

F.2d 638, 642 (7th Cir. 1982) (en banc). "That counsel should avoid appearing both as advocate and witness except under special circumstances is beyond question." *United States v. Morris*, 714 F.2d 669, 671 (7th Cir. 1983).

> "The recognized rationales for forbidding counsel to appear as a witness are: . . . it eliminates the possibility that the attorney will not be a fully objective witness, . . . it reduces the risk that the trier of fact will confuse the roles of advocate and witness and erroneously grant testimonial weight to an attorney's arguments, . . . it reflects a broad concern that the administration of justice not only be fair, but also appear fair. . . ."

Id. "This rule, however, does not render an advocate incompetent as a witness, but merely *vests the trial court with discretion* to determine whether counsel may appear as a witness without withdrawing from the case." *Id.* (emphasis added). In *Johnston*, we considered whether a district court abused its discretion in refusing to allow a government prosecutor to testify at a pretrial suppression hearing. We concluded that allowing an advocate to testify "is a situation to be avoided if possible, but . . . will be permitted in extraordinary circumstances and for compelling reasons, usually where the evidence is not otherwise available." *See also United States v. Fogel*, 901 F.2d 23, 26 (4th Cir.), *cert. denied*, 498 U.S. 939 (1990) ("Courts have generally frowned on" allowing counsel to testify, but when "the testimony is important and no other witness would be able to supply it, then such testimony may be allowed.")

Our review of the instant record convinces us that the district court did not abuse its discretion in refusing to allow Ewing's counsel to testify about the alleged evidence tampering. Stottlar, the defense counsel's paralegal, testified before the jury that she and defense counsel examined the evidence against Ewing at the Alton police station on August 30, 1991, six weeks before trial. Stottlar explained that she and defense counsel focused on the composition notebooks in their examination of the evidence because "[w]e were specifically looking to see if they had Henry Ewing's name on them at the time." Defense counsel then asked Stottlar, "[a]nd on August 30, 1991, did they [the composition notebooks] have Henry Ewing's name on them." "No," answered Stottlar. Immediately following the Government's brief cross examination of Stottlar, the district court gave the jury the following instruction:

> "Ladies and gentlemen, you have just heard the testimony of Abigail Stottlar regarding her trip to the Alton Police Department for the purpose of viewing physical evidence, some or all of which has been admitted in this case.
>   "You have heard the testimony also that Renee Schooley, attorney for the defendant herein, accompanied Miss Stottlar and also examined the physical evidence.
>   "For reasons that are of no concern to you, I have ruled that Renee Schooley cannot testify in this case."

Defense counsel requested this instruction to clear up any confusion the jurors might have had as to why she did not also testify about her examination of the evidence along with her paralegal. Immediately following this instruction, the defendant called a handwriting analyst, William H. Store, who testified that Henry Ewing did not write the words "Henry Ewing" which appeared on the front of the two composition notebooks introduced at trial.

As the district court observed, the defendant was able to place before the jury his evidence supporting the claim that his name was written on the composition notebooks after they had been seized by police. Stottlar's testimony provided Ewing's most powerful evidence that tampering had allegedly occurred. Schooley's testimony, although it would have served to corroborate Stottlar's story, would have been, as the district court noted, cumulative. Given the strong presumption against allowing counsel to testify as a witness, and the fact that the defendant was able to present Stottlar's critical eyewitness testimony, it was not an abuse of discretion for the district court to rule that Schooley's testimony would have been cumulative and thus that it would not be allowed.[4]

. . . Ewing's conviction and sentence are AFFIRMED.

PROBLEMS

8.5. Following her client's conviction, an attorney receives a letter from one of the jurors, admitting that the jury treated the deliberations "as a joke" and spent the entire time "singing camp songs." A courtroom deputy who sat outside the jury room tells the lawyer that throughout the deliberations he heard laughter and boisterous singing. In support of his motion for a new trial, the defendant seeks to introduce the letter and to have both the juror and the deputy testify. The prosecutor argues none of the evidence is admissible. How should the judge rule?

8.6. Because the prosecutor's office is on the same hallway as the jury room, the defense attorney suspects that the prosecutor may have heard the laughter and singing. She wishes to call him to stand and examine him under oath. The prosecutor objects, citing the advocate-witness rule. How should the judge respond?

8.7. At the beginning of a civil trial, the judge instructs the jurors not to talk to anyone about the case while it is proceeding, including the lawyers.

---

4. One obvious solution to the problem would have been for Schooley to withdraw as defense counsel and then testify that Ewing's name was not on the composition notebooks when she examined them. The record on appeal contains no indication that defense counsel ever offered to withdraw from representation. In her brief and at oral argument, defense counsel asserted that she was prepared to withdraw from representation and have another attorney from the public defender's office replace her. She also claims that a potential replacement attorney was present in the district court's chambers when the matter was being discussed, and that the district court was aware of her willingness to withdraw. Schooley asserts that she did not make a formal offer to withdraw because the district court indicated that if she took the stand, the entire public defender's office would be disqualified from representing Ewing "which would mean that we would have to recess the trial for I don't know how long to make other arrangements. . . ."

During the trial one of the jurors passes the plaintiff's attorney in the hall-way and says, "You've got 'em running!" The attorney reports the remark to the judge and opposing counsel. May the judge question the juror under oath about the incident? May the judge question the juror under oath about the juror's continued ability to be fair and open-minded?

9

Opinions, Experts, and Scientific Evidence

"It is my considered opinion that drowning occurred due to a faulty room humidifier."

A. Lay Opinions

Many older cases allowed only expert witnesses to offer opinions and limited all other witnesses to testifying about "facts," not inferences or conclusions. All witnesses, moreover, were often barred from expressing opinions on the "ultimate issues" to be decided by the jury. Modern evidence law largely abandons these restrictions. Lay witnesses—i.e., witnesses who do not testify based on some special expertise—are free to offer opinions, even on ultimate issues. To be admissible, though, the opinions expressed by a lay witness must be helpful to the jury, and—critically—they must be based on the witness's own firsthand observations.

[F.R.E. 701, 704; C.E.C. §§800, 805]

ADVISORY COMMITTEE NOTE TO F.R.E. 701

. . . Witnesses often find difficulty in expressing themselves in language which is not that of an opinion or conclusion. While the courts have made concessions in certain recurring situations, necessity as a standard for permitting opinions and conclusions has proved too elusive and too unadaptable to particular situations for purposes of satisfactory judicial administration. McCormick §11. Moreover, the practical impossibility of determining by rule what is a "fact," demonstrated by a century of litigation of the question of what is a fact for purposes of pleading under the Field Code, extends into evidence also. 7 Wigmore §1919. The rule assumes that the natural characteristics of the adversary system will generally lead to an acceptable result, since the detailed account carries more conviction than the broad assertion, and a lawyer can be expected to display his witness to the best advantage. If he fails to do so, cross-examination and argument will point up the weakness. If, despite these considerations, attempts are made to introduce meaningless assertions which amount to little more than choosing up sides, exclusion for lack of helpfulness is called for by the rule.

ADVISORY COMMITTEE NOTE TO F.R.E. 704

. . . The older cases often contained strictures against allowing witnesses to express opinions upon ultimate issues, as a particular aspect of the rule against opinions. The rule was unduly restrictive, difficult of application, and generally served only to deprive the trier of fact of useful information. 7 Wigmore §§1920, 1921; McCormick §12. The basis usually assigned for the rule, to prevent the witness from "usurping the province of the jury," is aptly characterized as "empty rhetoric." 7 Wigmore §1920, p. 17. . . . Many modern decisions illustrate the trend to abandon the rule completely. . . .

Under Rules 701 and 702, opinions must be helpful to the trier of fact, and Rule 403 provides for exclusion of evidence which wastes time. These provisions afford ample assurances against the admission of opinions which would merely tell the jury what result to reach, somewhat in the manner of the oath-helpers of an earlier day. They also stand ready to exclude opinions phrased in terms of inadequately explored legal criteria. Thus the question, "Did T have capacity to make a will?" would be excluded, while the question, "Did T have sufficient mental capacity to know the nature and extent of his property and the natural objects of his bounty and to formulate a rational scheme of distribution?" would be allowed. McCormick §12.

UNITED STATES v. MELING

47 F.3d 1546 (9th Cir. 1995)

KOZINSKI, Circuit Judge.

[Joseph Meling was convicted of six counts of product tampering and sentenced to life in prison. The charges were that Meling had attempted to poison his wife by giving her Sudafed laced with cyanide, and then had tried to cover his tracks by putting cyanide in five packages of Sudafed and leaving them on drug store shelves—killing two people before the manufacturer could implement a nationwide recall.]

When his wife collapsed from the poison, Meling phoned 911 and feigned hysteria, then melodramatically vowed to the paramedic who arrived on the scene that he would beat the ambulance to the hospital. . . . Meling contends the district court erred in admitting the lay opinion testimony of the 911 operator and paramedic, both of whom testified that Meling was feigning his grief shortly after the poisonings. . . .

Lay opinion testimony is admissible if it is " 'rationally based on the perception of the witness' and . . . helpful to the jury in acquiring a 'clear understanding of the witness' testimony or the determination of a fact in issue.' " [*United States v*]. *Simas*, 937 F.2d [459, 464 (9th Cir. 1991)] (quoting Fed. R. Evid. 701). Paramedics are trained to respond quickly in emergency situations, and while treating Meling's wife, the paramedic had ample time to form the impression that Meling was feigning grief. The 911 operator's testimony was rationally based on her perception of Meling's agitation during his emergency call and, though a tape of the conversation was played in full, the jury was not in the same position as the 911 operator to compare Meling's behavior with that of other emergency callers or to assess whether it was abnormal. *Compare United States v. LaPierre*, 998 F.2d 1460, 1465 (9th Cir. 1993) (witness who has no previous exposure to the defendant is no better situated than the jury to identify the defendant from a surveillance photograph) *with [United States v.] Jackson*, 688 F.2d [1121, 1125 (7th Cir. 1982)] (eyewitness identification testimony is helpful to the jury, even if surveillance photographs are available, "because it is based upon [the eyewitness'] opportunity to compare the person in the bank surveillance photograph with every person she had ever met, whereas the jury could only compare the person in the surveillance photographs to the defendant"). . . . AFFIRMED.

GOVERNMENT OF THE VIRGIN ISLANDS v. KNIGHT

989 F.2d 619 (3d Cir. 1993)

COWEN, Circuit Judge.

While Henry Knight repeatedly struck Andreas Miller's head with a pistol, the gun discharged and killed Miller. . . . The jury found Knight guilty of voluntary manslaughter, possession of a firearm during the commission of a crime of violence, and possession of a firearm by a felon. . . . [T]he district court found Knight to be a habitual criminal and sentenced him to ten years imprisonment on all counts. . . .

Knight argues that it was reversible error to exclude an eyewitness' and an investigating officer's testimony that the firing of the gun was an accident. . . . Although we agree that the district court committed error by excluding the eyewitness' lay opinion, this error did not prejudice the defendant and therefore does not warrant a reversal of his conviction.

Federal Rule of Evidence 701 states:

If the witness is not testifying as an expert, the witness' testimony in the form of opinions or inferences is limited to those opinions or inferences which are (a) rationally based on the perception of the witness and (b) helpful to a clear understanding of the witness' testimony or the determination of a fact in issue.

The requirement that a lay opinion be rationally based on the witness' perception requires that the witness have firsthand knowledge of the factual predicates that form the basis for the opinion. The district court properly excluded the investigating police officer's opinion because he did not observe the assault. In contrast, the eyewitness obviously had first-hand knowledge of the facts from which his opinion was formed.

Having met the firsthand knowledge requirement of Rule 701(a), the eyewitness' opinion was admissible if it would help the jury to resolve a disputed fact. The "modern trend favors admissibility of opinion testimony." . . . If circumstances can be presented with greater clarity by stating an opinion, then that opinion is helpful to the trier of fact. Allowing witnesses to state their opinions instead of describing all of their observations has the further benefit of leaving witnesses free to speak in ordinary language.

In this case, an eyewitness' testimony that Knight fired the gun accidentally would be helpful to the jury. The eyewitness described the circumstances that led to his opinion. It is difficult, however, to articulate all of the factors that lead one to conclude a person did not intend to fire a gun. Therefore, the witness' opinion that the gunshot was accidental would have permitted him to relate the facts with greater clarity, and hence would have aided the jury. Based on an assessment of the witness' credibility, the jury then could attach an appropriate weight to this lay opinion.

Although the district court should not have excluded this opinion, the exclusion of the opinion was harmless error as it did not prejudice Knight. To find an error harmless, a court must be able to say that it is highly probable that the error did not contribute to the jury's judgment of conviction. *Government of the Virgin Islands v. Toto*, 529 F.2d 278, 284 (3d Cir. 1976). The eyewitness was permitted to describe fully the circumstances that led to his opinion—he stated that Knight never pointed the gun at the victim and never threatened to shoot the victim. Further, Knight himself testified that although he intended to assault Miller, the discharge of the gun was accidental, and defense counsel argued this theory to the jury. The jury could infer from these circumstances that the shooting was accidental.

The opinion of an unbiased eyewitness certainly may be viewed by a jury as more credible than the opinion of a criminal defendant. In this case, however, only a modicum of evidence was necessary to prove the accident theory of the defense because the prosecution barely disputed that the shooting was an accident. Indeed, the government all but conceded this point. During the government's closing argument, the prosecutor himself stated, "[The gunshot] may have been an accident. . . . [The beating] resulted in an unintentional, perhaps—probably unintentional and perhaps accidental discharge of that gun." Under these circumstances, the trial court's ruling could not have significantly prejudiced Knight and a reversal of the conviction is not warranted. . . .

ROBINSON v. BUMP

894 F.2d 758 (5th Cir. 1990)

Duhe, Circuit Judge.

This is a diversity negligence action brought by the estate and family of Willie Robinson against Willis Harris, MTD Products, and Henry Bump. The Robinsons appeal from a judgment denying relief against MTD and Bump.

MTD Products employed Henry Bump to operate an eighteen-wheel tractor-trailer rig. [After a car driven by Harris collided with the truck, Bump lost control and hit Robinson's car, killing Robinson and three other family members.] The jury found that Harris' negligence caused the accident but that Bump was not negligent. . . .

Battle, driver of the car following Bump, was called to testify for Bump and MTD. He testified that Bump was "in total control" of the truck until it was struck by the Harris vehicle. The appellants argue that this testimony constituted either a legal conclusion or an opinion on an ultimate issue. We review for abuse of discretion.

Rule 701 of the Federal Rules of Evidence permits a non-expert to testify in the form of an inference providing the inference is "rationally based on the perception of the witness" and "helpful to a clear understanding of the witness' testimony or the determination of a fact in issue." Under Rule 704 testimony in the form of an inference is "not objectionable because it embraces an ultimate issue to be decided by the trier of fact." . . .

While it is doubtful Battle was reciting anything more than his observations, the testimony was clearly admissible as an inference of a lay witness. Battle had every opportunity to observe the truck's movement, the movement of a truck is rationally connected to the control of its driver, and the testimony was helpful in allowing the jury to assess Bump's negligence. We find no abuse of discretion in allowing the testimony. . . . The judgment is Affirmed.

ADVISORY COMMITTEE NOTE TO 2000 AMENDMENT TO F.R.E. 701

Rule 701 has been amended [by the addition of subsection (c)] to eliminate the risk that the reliability requirements set forth in Rule 702 will be evaded through the simple expedient of proffering an expert in lay witness clothing. . . . The amendment is not intended to affect the "prototypical example[s] of the type of evidence contemplated by the adoption of Rule 701 relat[ing] to the appearance of persons or things, identity, the manner of conduct, competency of a person, degrees of light or darkness, sound, size, weight, distance, and an endless number of items that cannot be described factually in words apart from inferences." *Asplundh Mfg. Div. v. Benton Harbor Eng'g*, 57 F.3d 1190, 1196 (3d Cir. 1995). . . .

The amendment incorporates the distinctions set forth in *State v. Brown*, 836 S.W.2d 530, 549 (1992), a case involving former Tennessee Rule of Evidence 701, a rule that precluded lay witness testimony based on "special knowledge." In *Brown*, the court declared that the distinction between lay and expert witness testimony is that lay testimony "results from a process of reasoning familiar in everyday life," while expert testimony "results from a process of reasoning which can be mastered only by specialists in the field." The court in *Brown* noted that a lay witness with experience could testify that a substance appeared to be blood, but that a witness would have to qualify as an expert before he could testify that bruising around the eyes is indicative of skull trauma. That is the kind of distinction made by the amendment to this Rule.

UNITED STATES v. PEOPLES

250 F.3d 630 (8th Cir. 2001)

WOLLMAN, Chief Judge.

Cornelius Peoples and Xavier Lightfoot were convicted of aiding and abetting the murder of a federal government witness in violation of 18 U.S.C. §§[1512] and 1111. [The victim, Jovan Ross, was Lightfoot's housemate, and had cooperated with the investigation of Lightfoot for bank robbery.] . . . Although Ross had no substantial information implicating Peoples in criminal activity, the government argued that Peoples believed that his involvement would be discovered if Ross continued to cooperate with law enforcement. . . .

Special Agent Joan Neal, the FBI case agent in charge of the investigation of Ross's murder, testified in connection with [surreptitiously recorded] conversations between Peoples and Lightfoot. Drawing on her investigation, Agent Neal gave her opinion regarding the meaning of words and phrases used by the defendants during those conversations. Her testimony was not limited to coded, oblique language, but included plain English words and phrases. She did not personally observe the events and activities discussed in the recordings, nor did she hear or observe the conversations as they occurred. Agent Neal's testimony included her opinions about what the defendants were thinking during the conversations, phrased as contentions supporting her conclusion, repeated throughout her testimony, that the defendants were responsible for Ross's murder.

At various points during her testimony, Agent Neal asserted that Peoples went to Ross's house to murder Ross, that he had paid "the killers to do the job," that Peoples's various comments about being in need of money revolved around his debt to hit men, and that both defendants had sought confirmation of Ross's death. She asserted that during the course of her investigation she had uncovered hidden meanings for apparently neutral words; for example, she testified that when one of the defendants referred to buying a plane ticket for Ross, he in fact meant killing Ross. In short, as the recordings of the Peoples/Lightfoot conversations were played for the jury, Agent Neal was allowed to offer a narrative gloss that consisted almost entirely of her personal opinions of what the conversations meant. During several hours of testimony alternating with recorded conversation, Agent Neal made the argument that the defendants had conspired to hire someone to kill Ross, had tendered substantial sums as a partial payment, and then had become anxious when Ross's death was not publicly reported. During direct examination, the prosecutor referred to Agent Neal's statements both as Agent Neal's contentions and as the contentions of the government.

The following excerpts are examples of Agent Neal's testimony. After a recording of Lightfoot requesting a loan was played, Agent Neal stated, "I contend [Lightfoot] is needing a loan to pay the hit man to actually murder Ross." Peoples made repeated references in the taped conversations to "lost and found situations." Agent Neal stated, "When he discusses lost and found, I believe he is talking about no one had found the body yet. It's just a lost situation until somebody finds the body." After the jury heard a recording of Peoples saying, "I done already gave my loot," Agent Neal stated, "I contend that he has already paid the killers to do the job." In response to conversations that related to the burglary of Ross's house, Agent Neal testified, "I believe [Peoples] was there to actually murder Ross at the time."

Both before and during trial, the defendants objected to the admission of Agent Neal's testimony. The government responded by arguing that Agent Neal's contentions constituted lay opinions admissible under Rule 701 of the Federal Rules of Evidence. Stating that it was "possible though not certain" that Agent Neal's testimony was admissible under Rule 701, the district court ruled that her contentions were being admitted as "snippets of early argument from the witness stand" and not as evidence.

Federal Rule of Evidence 602 requires that a witness have personal knowledge of the matters about which she testifies, except in the case of expert opinions. Rule 701 adds that testimony in the form of lay opinions must be rationally based on the perception of the witness. When a law enforcement officer is not qualified as an expert by the court, her testimony is admissible as lay opinion only when the law enforcement officer is a participant in the conversation, has personal knowledge of the facts being related in the conversation, or observed the conversations as they occurred. Lay opinion testimony is admissible only to help the jury or the court to understand the facts about which the witness is testifying and not to provide specialized explanations or interpretations that an untrained layman could not make if perceiving the same acts or events.[1]

1. Although not in effect at the time of trial, the 2000 revisions to Rules 701 and 702 emphasize this distinction between lay and expert opinion testimony. See Fed. R. Evid. 701 advisory committee's note to 2000 Amendments.

Law enforcement officers are often qualified as experts to interpret intercepted conversations using slang, street language, and the jargon of the illegal drug trade. *See, e.g., United States v. Delpit*, 94 F.3d 1134, 1144 (8th Cir. 1996) (police officer gave expert testimony interpreting slang and drug codes in connection with recorded telephone calls); *United States v. Plunk*, 153 F.3d 1011, 1017 (9th Cir. 1998) (police officer gave expert testimony based on his specialized knowledge of narcotics code terminology); *United States v. Earls*, 42 F.3d 1321, 1324-25 (10th Cir. 1994) (expert testimony was proper to show that defendants were speaking in code). What is essentially expert testimony, however, may not be admitted under the guise of lay opinions. Such a substitution subverts the disclosure and discovery requirements of Federal Rules of Criminal Procedure 26 and 16 and the reliability requirements for expert testimony as set forth in *Daubert v. Merrell Dow Pharmaceuticals, Inc.*, 509 U.S. 579 (1993) and *Kumho Tire Co. v. Carmichael*, 526 U.S. 137 (1999).

Agent Neal lacked first-hand knowledge of the matters about which she testified. Her opinions were based on her investigation after the fact, not on her perception of the facts. Accordingly, the district court erred in admitting Agent Neal's opinions about the recorded conversations. The court's instructions to the jury that Agent Neal's opinions constituted argument rather than evidence finds no warrant in the Federal Rules of Evidence and could not serve to render admissible that which was inadmissible testimony. . . .

The erroneous admission of testimony is not harmless when there is a significant possibility that the testimony had a substantial impact on the jury. . . . Agent Neal's testimony so invaded the province of the jury that we cannot with confidence say that there was no significant possibility that it had substantial impact on the jury. Accordingly, we must set aside the convictions. . . .

UNITED STATES v. AYALA-PIZARRO

407 F.3d 25 (1st Cir. 2005)

LYNCH, Circuit Judge.

Luis Daniel Ayala-Pizarro was convicted, after a four-day jury trial, of possession with intent to distribute 153 decks of heroin and of knowingly possessing a firearm in furtherance of a drug trafficking crime. . . . Ayala argues that the district court erred in permitting an arresting officer to cross the line from being a fact witness to being an expert witness when the officer testified about drug distribution points and how they operate as well as how heroin is normally packaged for distribution at these points. . . .

Officer Mulero, one of the arresting officers, testified that he arrested Ayala at 2 p.m. on a Wednesday afternoon on Melilla Street in Loiza, Puerto Rico, near a house known to be a drug point. Officer Mulero and the other arresting officer . . . observed Ayala and another man, Luis Vazquez Alvarez, at the right-hand corner of the house. Ayala and Vazquez did not see the officers, but the officers saw both men and that they were armed with firearms. Indeed, Ayala was trying to cock his gun, a Cobrai Model M11, nine millimeter caliber semiautomatic assault weapon, at the time. The officers then detained and arrested the two men. A search of Ayala turned up 153 aluminum-foil covered decks of heroin from his left pocket; his companion had $250. The officers arrested three other men standing nearby; each had a revolver. Experts determined that the heroin weighed 10.94 grams. An expert also testified that Ayala's gun was functioning and capable of firing in semiautomatic mode, and that its serial number was obliterated.

At trial, when the government asked Officer Mulero about his experience with drug points, as a lead-in to Mulero's testimony that Ayala was arrested at a known drug point, defense counsel objected, arguing that this was expert testimony and that because the government had not given notice of expert testimony from Mulero under Fed. R. Crim. P. 16(a)(1)(G), the witness could not so testify.* At a subsequent bench conference, the government made a proffer that the witness would also testify that the particular packaging of the drugs seized showed they were packaged for distribution. Defense counsel countered that the testimony about the nature of the packaging was even more clearly expert testimony. The court ruled that the testimony that Melilla Street was a known drug point was permissible lay testimony. As to the packaging issue, the court ruled it needed to hear foundational evidence and allowed the testimony subject to a motion to strike.

Officer Mulero then testified as to how drug points work generally, stating:

> Basically one individual loads the drug while the other one collects the money, and then you have [men] who are armed and just waiting around in the event other gangs might come by and take action, and then you have others as vigilantes to see if the cops come.

*[Fed. R. Crim. P. 16(a)(1)(G) provides: "At the defendant's request, the government must give to the defendant a written summary of any testimony that the government intends to use under Rules 702, 703, or 705 of the Federal Rules of Evidence during its case-in-chief at trial. If the government requests discovery under subdivision (b)(1)(C)(ii) and the defendant complies, the government must, at the defendant's request, give to the defendant a written summary of testimony that the government intends to use under Rules 702, 703, or 705 of the Federal Rules of Evidence as evidence at trial on the issue of the defendant's mental condition. The summary provided under this subparagraph must describe the witness's opinions, the bases and reasons for those opinions, and the witness's qualifications."

Fed. R. Crim. P. 16(b)(1)(C) provides: "The defendant must, at the government's request, give to the government a written summary of any testimony that the defendant intends to use under Rules 702, 703, or 705 of the Federal Rules of Evidence as evidence at trial, if (i) the defendant requests disclosure under subdivision (a)(1)(G) and the government complies; or (ii) the defendant has given notice under Rule 12.2(b) of an intent to present expert testimony on the defendant's mental condition. This summary must describe the witness's opinions, the bases and reasons for those opinions, and the witness's qualifications."—Ed.]

Mulero testified about his experience with Melilla Street as a drug point. He also testified that he had made previous seizures of heroin at drug points, and that the heroin was typically packed in aluminum decks. Officer Mulero was then asked about the packaging of the drugs he seized from the defendant, and replied that the heroin was packaged "[i]n a shape or manner of a deck." . . .

On appeal, Ayala argues that he is entitled to a new trial because two parts of Mulero's testimony, first about how drug points operate and, second, about how heroin is packaged, could only be given by an expert and the government failed to give notice that Officer Mulero would testify as an expert. . . .

We agree with the government that neither type of testimony was expert testimony at all, but was admissible as lay witness testimony under Fed. R. Evid. 701, even after the amendments to the two rules in December 2000. The pre-amendment version of Rule 701 required lay opinion testimony to be "rationally based on the perception of the witness" and "helpful to a clear understanding of the witness' testimony or the determination of a fact in issue." In 2000, Rule 701 was amended to include the additional requirement that testimony admitted under the rule "not [be] based on scientific, technical, or other specialized knowledge within the scope of Rule 702." As the advisory committee's notes explain, this amendment was intended "to eliminate the risk that the reliability requirements set forth in Rule 702 will be evaded through the simple expedient of proffering an expert in lay witness clothing." . . .

We have noted that "[t]he line between expert testimony under Fed. R. Evid. 702 . . . and lay opinion testimony under Fed. R. Evid. 701 . . . is not easy to draw." *United States v. Colon Osorio,* 360 F.3d 48, 52-53 (1st Cir. 2004). Indeed, the same witness—for example, a law enforcement officer—may be qualified to "provide both lay and expert testimony in a single case." *See* Fed. R. Evid. 701, advisory committee's note (citing *United States v. Figueroa-Lopez,* 125 F.3d 1241, 1246 (9th Cir. 1997)). In this case, however, the testimony did not cross the line to become expert testimony.

As to the testimony about how drug points operate, Officer Mulero stated that he had investigated, patrolled, or made arrests at drug points on more than 100 occasions. His testimony stated what occurred at those drug points. This testimony was based on the requisite personal knowledge under Fed. R. Evid. 602 and also met the requirements of Fed. R. Evid. 701, because it was based on "particularized knowledge that the witness [had] by virtue of his . . . position" as a police officer assigned to patrol the neighborhood. Fed. R. Evid. 701, advisory committee's note.

Before the 2000 amendments, we had repeatedly noted that "the modern trend favors the admission of [lay] opinion testimony provided it is well founded on personal knowledge and susceptible to cross-examination." *See United States v. Vega-Figueroa,* 234 F.3d 744, 755 (1st Cir. 2000) (quoting *United States v. Paiva,* 892 F.2d 148, 157 (1st Cir. 1989)). While the 2000 amendments subject testimony falling within the scope of Rule 702 to heightened reliability requirements and rules governing pre-trial disclosure, Officer Mulero's testimony does not trigger these additional safeguards. It required no special expertise for Officer Mulero to conclude, based on his observations, that places which sell drugs are often protected by people with weapons. The defense could hardly be surprised by Mulero's testimony that Ayala was arrested at a drug point, nor was Ayala disabled from testing the reliability of Mulero's perceptions through cross-examination.

As to the packaging, the officer simply testified to his experience on prior drug arrests that the heroin seized at drug points was "basically packed in . . . aluminum decks," and that in this case the drugs were packaged "[i]n a shape or manner of a deck." The agent's testimony as to what he saw is not expert testimony. The jury was left to draw its own conclusions as to the contents and purpose of the decks, undoubtedly assisted by the fact that the 153 decks seized in this case, when tested, in fact contained heroin. . . .

The conviction is *affirmed.* . . .

B. EXPERT TESTIMONY

Trial lawyers and trial judges have long felt that witnesses with specialized skills or knowledge can often offer helpful testimony even if they have no firsthand knowledge of the facts in a particular case. Therefore expert witnesses, unlike lay witnesses, are allowed to offer opinions based in whole or in part on information they have received secondhand, as long as the information is of a kind typically relied upon by experts in the field, and as long as the witness is truly drawing on some special skill or knowledge, as opposed to making judgments the jury could just as easily make itself.

During the past several decades, as more and more trials have involved scientific or technical issues, expert testimony has become increasingly common and increasingly important. It has also grown increasingly controversial. There is widespread concern that experts can be hired to say almost anything, and that juries are too easily bamboozled by charlatans. One solution might be for judges rather than parties to select expert witnesses. Judges in fact are authorized to appoint experts, but they rarely do—largely, perhaps, because the practice fits poorly with our system's general delegation of investigation and witness selection to the parties and their lawyers.

The Federal Rules of Evidence now try to prevent shoddy expert testimony in a different way: they require a trial judge to exclude expert testimony unless the judge concludes it is "reliable." This requirement codifies the holdings of three cases decided by the Supreme Court in the 1990s: *Daubert v. Merrell Dow Pharmaceuticals, Inc.*, 509 U.S. 579 (1993), *General Electric Co. v. Joiner*, 522 U.S. 136 (1997), and *Kumho Tire Co. v. Carmichael*, 526 U.S. 137 (1999). Each of these decisions is excerpted below, along with materials illustrating more traditional limitations on expert testimony.

1. Permissible Subjects and Scope

[F.R.E. 702, 703, 705, 706; C.E.C. §§801-804]

ADVISORY COMMITTEE NOTE TO F.R.E. 702

An intelligent evaluation of facts is often difficult or impossible without the application of some scientific, technical, or other specialized knowledge. The most common source of this knowledge is the expert witness, although there are other techniques for supplying it.

Most of the literature assumes that experts testify only in the form of opinions. The assumption is logically unfounded. The rule accordingly recognizes that an expert on the stand may give a dissertation or exposition of scientific or other principles relevant to the case, leaving the trier of fact to apply them to the facts. Since much of the criticism of expert testimony has centered upon the hypothetical question, it seems wise to recognize that opinions are not indispensable and to encourage the use of expert testimony in non-opinion form when counsel believes the trier can itself draw the requisite inference. The use of opinions is not abolished by the rule, however. It will continue to be permissible for the experts to take the further step of suggesting the inference which should be drawn from applying the specialized knowledge to the facts. See Rules 703 to 705.

Whether the situation is a proper one for the use of expert testimony is to be determined on the basis of assisting the trier. "There is no more certain test for determining when experts may be used than the common sense inquiry whether the untrained layman would be qualified to determine intelligently and to the best possible degree the particular issue without enlightenment from those having a specialized understanding of the subject involved in the dispute." Ladd, Expert Testimony, 5 Vand. L. Rev. 414, 418 (1952). When opinions are excluded, it is because they are unhelpful and therefore superfluous and a waste of time. 7 Wigmore §1918.

The rule is broadly phrased. The fields of knowledge which may be drawn upon are not limited merely to the "scientific" and "technical" but extend to all "specialized" knowledge. Similarly, the expert is viewed, not in a narrow sense, but as a person qualified by "knowledge, skill, experience, training or education." Thus within the scope of the rule are not only experts in the strictest sense of the word, e.g., physicians, physicists, and architects, but also the large group sometimes called "skilled" witnesses, such as bankers or landowners testifying to land values.

HATCH v. STATE FARM FIRE & CASUALTY CO.

930 P.2d 382 (Wyo. 1997)

THOMAS, Justice.

[State Farm Fire & Casualty Co. refused to pay for the damage caused by a fire in the Hatch family's house, because the company concluded that Frank Hatch had started the fire. Hatch was charged with arson, but the jury found him not guilty. The Hatches then sued State Farm for breaching its duty of good faith and fair dealing in resolving their policy claim, and for intentional infliction of emotional distress. A jury found for State Farm, and the Hatches appealed. The Supreme Court of Wyoming affirmed.]

. . . In the course of their case in chief, the Hatches offered the discovery deposition testimony of an expert witness, Carrol M. Cloyd (Cloyd), into evidence pursuant to Wyo. R. Civ. P. 32 because Cloyd had died before the trial. At the deposition, Cloyd had been qualified as an expert on insurance industry standards for good faith and fair dealing in the investigation and handling of insurance claims. . . . A major issue about Cloyd's testimony concerned questions he was asked about State Farm complying with the standard it had established by its advertising. According to the Hatches' theory, State Farm had engaged in an advertising campaign that features the slogan, "Like a good neighbor, State Farm is there." [The trial judge excluded] testimony from Cloyd as to whether, in his opinion, State Farm's actions complied with the standard expected of good faith and fair dealing and "a good neighbor." . . .

The questions and answers in Cloyd's deposition went beyond the industry standard for good faith and fair dealing in the investigation and handling of insurance claims. They purported to provide his opinion with respect to an extraneous and non-legal standard. The provision in Wyo. R. Evid. 702, concerning opinions of experts offering "specialized knowledge" that "will assist the trier of fact," does not justify such testimony. Cloyd's opinion, as to whether the advertising established a standard and on how a "good neighbor" would act, required no specialized knowledge, nor could it have assisted the jury in understanding the evidence or determining any of the facts in issue. It properly was excluded. His opinion as to how a "good neighbor" would act was beyond the realm of his expertise. . . .

ADVISORY COMMITTEE NOTE TO F.R.E. 703

Facts or data upon which expert opinions are based may, under the rule, be derived from three possible sources. The first is the firsthand observation of the witness with opinions based thereon traditionally allowed. A treating physician affords an example. . . . The second source, presentation at the trial, also reflects existing practice. The technique may be the familiar hypothetical question or having the expert attend the trial and hear the testimony establishing the facts. . . . The third source contemplated by the rule consists of presentation of data to the expert outside of court and other than by his own perception. In this respect the rule is designed to broaden the basis for expert opinions beyond that current in many jurisdictions and to bring the judicial practice into line with the practice of the experts themselves when not in court. Thus a physician in his own practice bases his diagnosis on information from numerous sources and of considerable variety, including statements by patients and relatives, reports and opinions from nurses, technicians and other doctors, hospital records, and X rays. Most of them are admissible in evidence, but only with the expenditure of substantial time in producing and examining various authenticating witnesses. The physician makes life-and-death decisions in reliance upon them. His validation, expertly performed and subject to cross-examination, ought to suffice for judicial purposes.

The rule also offers a more satisfactory basis for ruling upon the admissibility of public opinion poll evidence. Attention is directed to the validity of the techniques employed rather than to relatively fruitless inquiries whether hearsay is involved.

If it be feared that enlargement of permissible data may tend to break down the rules of exclusion unduly, notice should be taken that the rule requires that the facts or data "be of a type reasonably relied upon by experts in the particular field." The language would not warrant admitting in evidence the opinion of an "accidentologist" as to the point of impact in an automobile collision based on statements of bystanders since this requirement is not satisfied.

ADVISORY COMMITTEE NOTE TO 2000 AMENDMENT TO F.R.E. 703

Rule 703 has been amended to emphasize that when an expert reasonably relies on inadmissible information to form an opinion or inference, the underlying information is not admissible simply because the opinion or inference is admitted. . . . The amendment provides a presumption against disclosure to the jury of information used as the basis of an expert's opinion and not admissible for any substantive purpose, when that information is offered by the proponent of the expert. In a multi-party case, where one party proffers an expert whose testimony is also beneficial to other parties, each such party should be deemed a "proponent" within the meaning of the amendment.

STATE v. LEWIS

235 S.W.3d 136 (Tenn. 2007)

WADE, J.

[Sabrina Lewis was convicted of criminally negligent homicide and facilitation of attempted aggravated robbery in connection with the failed robbery of an antiques store, during which the store's owner, Gary Finchum, was fatally shot. When a police detective arrived at the scene, Finchum] described his assailant as a "young male black" and showed the detective a blue, "floppy" hat that he had left behind. . . .

Dr. Terry Melton, a forensic scientist specializing in mitochondrial DNA analysis, testified that her laboratory performed an analysis on hairs taken from the floppy hat found at the scene. After comparing the DNA profile of the hair with the DNA of the Defendant's sons, Eton and Todd Bryant, she determined that neither individual could be excluded as the contributor of the hair. She explained that individuals with the same mother share an identical mitochondrial DNA profile, not only with each other but also with their maternal relatives. Dr. Melton, who testified that the mitochondrial DNA profile excluded 99.94% of the North American population, confirmed that the hair sample was completely consumed during testing and pointed out that the same mitochondrial DNA profile would also be found in the Defendant, her sisters and brothers, her sister's children, and her mother, that is, all of the maternal relatives of Eton and Todd Bryant. During cross-examination, Dr. Melton acknowledged that a co-worker . . . actually performed the mitochondrial DNA testing. . . . The Defendant complains that she was denied the opportunity to confront the person who "actually manipulated the sample." . . .

Dr. Melton testified that she analyzed the laboratory work that was performed by her colleague, Dr. Kimberly Nelson. She explained:

> [I]n our laboratory, we use the model of the FBI, which is that we have technicians who do the bench work and those technicians are not testifying personnel. They do the laboratory work.
> Dr. Nelson and I do all the data analysis and supervise the work of the technicians, so that is our standard procedure.
>   . . .
> She [Dr. Nelson] performed exactly as a technician would in this case. Sometimes when we get very busy, she will do some laboratory work and she's qualified to do that, but typically, she does not do laboratory work. She and I analyze the data, write the reports, and testify.

In our view, Dr. Melton's testimony concerning the DNA test did not violate the Defendant's right to confrontation. Dr. Melton, who evaluated the data gathered by Dr. Nelson, admittedly based her testimony upon the hearsay contained within that data. Rule 703 of the Tennessee Rules of Evidence provides, however, that

> [t]he facts or data in the particular case upon which an expert bases an opinion or inference may be those perceived by or made known to the expert at or before the hearing. If of a type reasonably relied upon by experts in the particular field in forming opinions or inferences upon the subject, the facts or data need not be admissible in evidence. The court shall disallow testimony in the form of an opinion or inference if the underlying facts or data indicate lack of trustworthiness.

Because the Defendant does not contend that the data was untrustworthy or otherwise not of a type generally relied on in the field of mitochondrial DNA analysis, it is our view that Dr. Melton's testimony was admissible under Rule 703.

[Nor did] Dr. Melton's testimony . . . violate the Defendant's right of confrontation. In *United States v. Henry*, 472 F.3d 910 (D.C. Cir. 2007), the United States Court of Appeals for the District of Columbia held that "*Crawford* . . . did not involve expert witness testimony and thus did not alter an expert witness's ability to rely on (without repeating to the jury) otherwise inadmissible evidence in formulating his opinion under Federal Rule of Evidence 703." Id. at 914 (footnote omitted). Other jurisdictions have reached similar conclusions. *See, e.g., United States v. Lombardozzi*, No. 04-0380-CR (2d Cir. July 11, 2007); *United States v. Adams*, 189 Fed. Appx. 120, 124 (3d Cir. 2006); *United States v. Stone*, 222 F.R.D. 334, 339 (E.D. Tenn. 2004). Indeed, one author has observed that "[m]ost courts have concluded that the Confrontation Clause is satisfied if the defendant has an opportunity to cross-examine the expert because his opinion is in evidence—not the underlying facts." Ross Andrew Oliver, Note, *Testimonial Hearsay as the Basis for Expert Opinion: The Intersection of the Confrontation Clause and Federal Rule of Evidence 703 After* Crawford v. Washington, 55 Hastings L.J. 1539, 1540 (2004). This is true "even if the expert relied on hearsay to form the basis of his opinion." *Id.* at 1555.

Here, the data gathered by Dr. Nelson was not admitted into evidence. The jury did not hear her "testimony." Dr. Melton's expert opinion was an evaluation of the data. She did not communicate any out-of-court statement made by Dr. Nelson. In consequence, it is our view that the trial court did not err by admitting the testimony. . . . [Affirmed.]

REPORT OF THE SENATE JUDICIARY COMMITTEE
S. Rep. 98-225 (1983)

The purpose of this amendment [adding section (b) to F.R.E. 704] is to eliminate the confusing spectacle of competing expert witnesses testifying to directly contradictory conclusions as to the ultimate legal issue to be found by the trier of fact. Under this proposal, expert psychiatric testimony would be limited to presenting and explaining their diagnoses, such as whether the defendant had a severe mental disease or defect and what the characteristics of such a disease or defect, if any, may have been. The basis for the limitation on expert testimony in insanity cases is ably stated by the American Psychiatric Association:

> . . . When . . . "ultimate issue" questions are formulated by the law and put to the expert witness who must then say "yea" or "nay," then the expert witness is required to make a leap in logic. He no longer addresses himself to medical concepts but instead must infer or intuit what is in fact unspeakable, namely, the probable relationship between medical concepts and legal or moral constructs such as free will. . . . Juries find themselves listening to conclusory and seemingly contradictory testimony that defendants are either "sane" or "insane" or that they do or do not meet the relevant legal test for insanity. This state of affairs does considerable injustice to psychiatry and, we believe, possibly to criminal defendants. . . . Psychiatrists, of course, must be permitted to testify fully about the defendant's diagnosis, mental state and motivation (in clinical and common sense terms) at the time of the alleged act so as to permit the jury or judge to reach the ultimate conclusion about which they and only they are expert. Determining whether a criminal defendant was legally insane in a matter for legal fact-finders, not for experts.

Moreover, the rationale for precluding ultimate opinion psychiatric testimony extends beyond the insanity defense to any ultimate mental state of the defendant that is relevant to the legal conclusion sought to be proved. The Committee has fashioned its Rule 704 provision to reach all such "ultimate" issues, e.g., premeditation in a homicide case, or lack of predisposition in entrapment.

2. Reliability

a. Court-Appointed Experts

ADVISORY COMMITTEE NOTE TO F.R.E. 706

The practice of shopping for experts, the venality of some experts, and the reluctance of many reputable experts to involve themselves in litigation, have been matters of deep concern. Though the contention is made that court appointed experts acquire an aura of infallibility to which they are not entitled, the trend is increasingly to provide for their use. While experience indicates that actual appointment is a relatively infrequent occurrence, the assumption may be made that the availability of the procedure in itself decreases the need for resorting to it. The ever-present possibility that the judge may appoint an expert in a given case must inevitably exert a sobering effect on the expert witness of a party and upon the person utilizing his services.

LEBLANC v. PNS STORES, INC.

Civ. A. No 96-2764 (E.D. La. Oct. 21, 1996)

LIVAUDAIS, District Judge.

Defendant PNS Stores has filed this motion pursuant to Rule 706 of the Federal Rules of Evidence seeking a court-appointed physician. . . . This matter arises out of slip and fall accident that took place at MacFrugal's Department Store on August 4, 1995. . . . [D]efendant wishes to have the Court appoint a physician of its choice to conduct an orthopedic and/or neurological examination of plaintiff. . . .

[T]he enlistment of court-appointed experts pursuant to Federal Rule of Evidence 706 is not commonplace. See F.R.E. 706, Advisory Comm. Note; *In re Joint E. & S. Dists. Asbestos Litigation*, 830 F. Supp. 686 (E. & S. D.N.Y. 1993). In fact, "Rule 706 should be reserved for exceptional cases in which the ordinary adversary process does not suffice." *Id.* at 693. . . .

It is the opinion of this Court that defendant has not demonstrated the necessity of appointing an independent physician. Defendant has been provided with the medical records of plaintiff since the filing of this motion. . . . Although Rule 706 is discretionary with the district court, it is appropriate only in rare circumstances and cannot be utilized as an alternative to communication and the adversary process. [Motion denied.]

JOHN SHEPARD WILEY JR., TAMING PATENT: SIX STEPS FOR SURVIVING SCARY PATENT CASES

50 UCLA L. Rev. 1413, 1427-1428, 1437 (2002)

[T]he truly striking thing about the power to appoint expert witnesses is how rarely most judges use it. Federal Rule of Evidence 706 has been around since 1975. Its precursors are decades older. . . . [E]mpirical research shows, however, that only 20 percent of a 1988 sample of district judges had ever appointed a 706 expert. . . . This reluctance hardly stems from judicial affection for battling partisan experts. From the perspective of discovering truth, the presentations of adversarial experts have been problematic for a long time. The partisan expert witness has enormous potential as a weapon of pure advocacy. Excellent trial lawyers know this potential. They risk disadvantage and even defeat if they do not wring every drop of advocacy power from their retained experts. In the process, the search for truth can suffer. An expert witness can be the advocate's strongest ally. The expert can speak directly to judge and jury with a demeanor chosen for Walter Cronkite—like sincerity. The expert's motivation can be prompted by ample compensation and guaranteed through careful selection. For the advocate, finding and selecting experts can be a momentous event in the litigation process. Resume horsepower is useful, but better yet is a compelling personal communication style married to the proper attitude. What is the proper attitude? It can be a subtle thing, perhaps detected through give-and-take on casual and seemingly irrelevant issues during a private telephone call or a relaxed interview in a comfortable office. For the trial lawyer puzzling over whether to retain this expert, a core question is whether the expert will become a team player. At some deep level, will the expert come to embrace the cause of the client? Experts with the proper attitude willingly deploy their potentially awesome experience and intelligence in the advocate's service. The result is unlikely to involve lying or deception, if for no other reason than such conduct rarely survives cross-examination. The result is, however, likely to be highly partisan. And the highly partisan character of expert testimony can imperil the search for truth. When one trial lawyer tells a colleague in an unguarded moment that the lawyer is in the process of "shopping for an expert," we should reflect on how accurate this phrase truly is. As a result, there have been serious doubts about the adequacy of adversarial experts for a century or more.

Judges know about these problems with retained experts. Why then have they usually made so little use of court-appointed experts? . . . [T]here are two main reasons: Most judges have no personal experience with court experts, and the parties rarely, if ever, suggest the possibility. The lawyers have no interest in mentioning this alternative, because they are doing everything they can to control the litigation. The appointment of a court expert represents a dramatic loss of control. This stranger is unknown and is likely to be influential. He or she is not supposed to have the client's best interests at heart. This prospect is not just unattractive; it is positively threatening.

b. Judicial Screening of Party-Approved Experts

i. Introduction

For decades, observers of American trials have worried that it is too easy to find an expert to say almost anything, and that experts, no matter how foolish or partisan, come draped with a mantle of authority that gives their testimony tremendous and often unwarranted weight with jurors.

F.R.E. 706(a) illustrates one long-standing response to this problem: authorizing trial judges to appoint their own experts. But as we have seen, this authorization is rarely used. When Judge Livaudais wrote in the *Leblanc* decision, excerpted above, that court-appointed experts should not be used "as an alternative to . . . the adversary process," he voiced a discomfort that many if not most American trial judges probably share—a discomfort with factfinding under the control of the judge rather than the parties. American judges do not *want* to become European-style inquisitors. That is not the legal culture in which they have been raised, and it is not what they are used to.

So federal evidence law has taken a different approach to the problem of partisan or otherwise unreliable experts. Instead of trial judges recruiting their own experts, trial judges have been instructed to scrutinize the expert testimony offered by the parties to make sure that it is "reliable." This requirement was first imposed by the Supreme Court in a 1993 decision excerpted below, *Daubert v. Merrell Dow Pharmaceuticals, Inc.* In order to understand *Daubert*, it may help to have some background about the doctrine it displaced—the "general acceptance" test first articulated in a 1923 decision by the United States Court of Appeals for the District of Columbia Circuit, *Frye v. United States.*

James Alphonso Frye was charged with murder. His lawyer sought to introduce evidence that a crude, early predecessor of the modern polygraph had shown that Frye was telling the truth when he said he was innocent. The machine used on Frye measured his blood pressure while he was asked questions about the crime. As the D.C. Circuit explained, "The theory seems to be that truth is spontaneous, and comes without conscious effort, while the utterance of a falsehood requires a conscious effort, which is reflected in the blood pressure." This business about truth coming naturally but fabrication taking effort should ring a bell: it is the same theory, more or less, that underlies the excited utterance and present sense impression exceptions to the hearsay rule. (And it turns out also to be pretty much the same theory underlying modern polygraph tests.)

The D.C. Circuit disallowed the testimony. In language that proved enormously influential, the court said that "while courts will go a long way in admitting expert testimony deduced from a well-recognized scientific principle or discovery, the thing from which the deduction is made must be sufficiently established to have gained general acceptance in the particular field in which it belongs." This criterion—"general acceptance"— soon became the dominant test in American courtrooms for the admissibility of scientific evidence. It is still the test in many states today. But it has been displaced in federal courts, and in the courts of most states, by the very different standard the U.S. Supreme Court first announced in *Daubert*.

ii. The *Daubert* Revolution

DAUBERT v. MERRELL DOW PHARMACEUTICALS, INC.

509 U.S. 579 (1993)

Justice BLACKMUN delivered the opinion of the Court.

... Petitioners Jason Daubert and Eric Schuller are minor children born with serious birth defects. They and their parents sued respondent in California state court, alleging that the birth defects had been caused by the mothers' ingestion of Bendectin, a prescription antinausea drug marketed by respondent. Respondent removed the suits to federal court on diversity grounds.

After extensive discovery, respondent moved for summary judgment, contending that Bendectin does not cause birth defects in humans and that petitioners would be unable to come forward with any admissible evidence that it does. In support of its motion, respondent submitted an affidavit of Steven H. Lamm, physician and epidemiologist, who is a well-credentialed expert on the risks from exposure to various chemical substances. Doctor Lamm stated that he had reviewed all the literature on Bendectin and human birth defects—more than 30 published studies involving over 130,000 patients. No study had found Bendectin to be a human teratogen (*i.e.*, a substance capable of causing malformations in fetuses). On the basis of this review, Doctor Lamm concluded that maternal use of Bendectin during the first trimester of pregnancy has not been shown to be a risk factor for human birth defects.

Petitioners did not (and do not) contest this characterization of the published record regarding Bendectin. Instead, they responded to respondent's motion with the testimony of eight experts of their own, each of whom also possessed impressive credentials. These experts had concluded that Bendectin can cause birth defects. Their conclusions were based upon "in vitro" (test tube) and "in vivo" (live) animal studies that found a link between Bendectin and malformations; pharmacological studies of the chemical structure of Bendectin that purported to show similarities between the structure of the drug and that of other substances known to cause birth defects; and the "reanalysis" of previously published epidemiological (human statistical) studies.

The District Court granted respondent's motion for summary judgment. The court stated that scientific evidence is admissible only if the principle upon which it is based is " 'sufficiently established to have general acceptance in the field to which it belongs.' " The court concluded that petitioners' evidence did not meet this standard. Given the vast body of epidemiological data concerning Bendectin, the court held, expert opinion which is not based on epidemiological evidence is not admissible to establish causation. Thus, the animal-cell studies, live-animal studies, and chemical-structure analyses on which petitioners had relied could not raise by themselves a reasonably disputable jury issue regarding causation. Petitioners' epidemiological analyses, based as they were on recalculations of data in previously published studies that had found no causal link between the drug and birth defects, were ruled to be inadmissible because they had not been published or subjected to peer review.

The United States Court of Appeals for the Ninth Circuit affirmed. Citing *Frye v. United States*, 293 F. 1013, 1014 (1923), the court stated that expert opinion based on a scientific technique is inadmissible unless the technique is "generally accepted" as reliable in the relevant scientific community. The court declared that expert opinion based on a methodology that diverges "significantly from the procedures accepted by recognized authorities in the field . . . cannot be shown to be 'generally accepted as a reliable technique.' "

The court emphasized that other Courts of Appeals considering the risks of Bendectin had refused to admit reanalyses of epidemiological studies that had been neither published nor subjected to peer review. Those courts had found unpublished reanalyses "particularly problematic in light of the massive weight of the original published studies supporting [respondent's] position, all of which had undergone full scrutiny from the scientific community." Contending that reanalysis is generally accepted by the scientific community only when it is subjected to verification and scrutiny by others in the field, the Court of Appeals rejected petitioners' reanalyses as "unpublished, not subjected to the normal peer review process and generated solely for use in litigation." The court concluded that petitioners' evidence provided an insufficient foundation to allow admission of expert testimony that Bendectin caused their injuries and, accordingly, that petitioners could not satisfy their burden of proving causation at trial. . . .

In the 70 years since its formulation in the *Frye* case, the "general acceptance" test has been the dominant standard for determining the admissibility of novel scientific evidence at trial. Although under increasing attack of late, the rule continues to be followed by a majority of courts, including the Ninth Circuit.

The *Frye* test has its origin in a short and citation-free 1923 decision concerning the admissibility of evidence derived from a systolic blood pressure deception test, a crude precursor to the polygraph machine. In what has become a famous (perhaps infamous) passage, the then Court of

Appeals for the District of Columbia described the device and its operation and declared:

> "Just when a scientific principle or discovery crosses the line between the experimental and demonstrable stages is difficult to define. Somewhere in this twilight zone the evidential force of the principle must be recognized, and while courts will go a long way in admitting expert testimony deduced from a well-recognized scientific principle or discovery, *the thing from which the deduction is made must be sufficiently established to have gained general acceptance in the particular field in which it belongs*." 293 F., at 1014 (emphasis added).

Because the deception test had "not yet gained such standing and scientific recognition among physiological and psychological authorities as would justify the courts in admitting expert testimony deduced from the discovery, development, and experiments thus far made," evidence of its results was ruled inadmissible. *Id.*

The merits of the *Frye* test have been much debated, and scholarship on its proper scope and application is legion. Petitioners' primary attack, however, is not on the content but on the continuing authority of the rule. They contend that the *Frye* test was superseded by the adoption of the Federal Rules of Evidence. We agree.

. . . [T]here is a specific Rule that speaks to the contested issue. Rule 702, governing expert testimony, provides:

> "If scientific, technical, or other specialized knowledge will assist the trier of fact to understand the evidence or to determine a fact in issue, a witness qualified as an expert by knowledge, skill, experience, training, or education, may testify thereto in the form of an opinion or otherwise."

Nothing in the text of this Rule establishes "general acceptance" as an absolute prerequisite to admissibility. Nor does respondent present any clear indication that Rule 702 or the Rules as a whole were intended to incorporate a "general acceptance" standard. The drafting history makes no mention of *Frye*, and a rigid "general acceptance" requirement would be at odds with the "liberal thrust" of the Federal Rules and their "general approach of relaxing the traditional barriers to 'opinion' testimony." *Beech Aircraft Corp. v. Rainey*, 488 U.S. [153, 169 (1988)] (citing Rules 701 to 705). See also Weinstein, Rule 702 of the Federal Rules of Evidence is Sound; It Should Not Be Amended, 138 F.R.D. 631 (1991) ("The Rules were designed to depend primarily upon lawyer-adversaries and sensible triers of fact to evaluate conflicts"). Given the Rules' permissive backdrop and their inclusion of a specific rule on expert testimony that does not mention " 'general acceptance,' " the assertion that the Rules somehow assimilated *Frye* is unconvincing. *Frye* made "general acceptance" the exclusive test for admitting expert scientific testimony. That austere standard, absent from, and incompatible with, the Federal Rules of Evidence, should not be applied in federal trials.

That the *Frye* test was displaced by the Rules of Evidence does not mean, however, that the Rules themselves place no limits on the admissibility of purportedly scientific evidence. Nor is the trial judge disabled from screening such evidence. To the contrary, under the Rules the trial judge must ensure that any and all scientific testimony or evidence admitted is not only relevant, but reliable.

The primary locus of this obligation is Rule 702, which clearly contemplates some degree of regulation of the subjects and theories about which an expert may testify. "*If scientific*, technical, or other specialized *knowledge will assist the trier of fact* to understand the evidence or to determine a fact in issue" an expert "may testify *thereto*." (Emphasis added.) The subject of an expert's testimony must be "scientific . . . knowledge."[2] The adjective "scientific" implies a grounding in the methods and procedures of science. Similarly, the word "knowledge" connotes more than subjective belief or unsupported speculation. The term "applies to any body of known facts or to any body of ideas inferred from such facts or accepted as truths on good grounds." Webster's Third New International Dictionary 1252 (1986). Of course, it would be unreasonable to conclude that the subject of scientific testimony must be "known" to a certainty; arguably, there are no certainties in science. See, *e.g.*, Brief for Nicolaas Bloembergen et al. as *Amici Curiae* 9 ("Indeed, scientists do not assert that they know what is immutably 'true'—they are committed to searching for new, temporary, theories to explain, as best they can, phenomena");Brief for American Association for the Advancement of Science et al. as *Amici Curiae* 7-8 ("Science is not an encyclopedic body of knowledge about the universe. Instead, it represents a *process* for proposing and refining theoretical explanations about the world that are subject to further testing and refinement" (emphasis in original)). But, in order to qualify as "scientific knowledge," an inference or assertion must be derived by the scientific method. Proposed testimony must be supported by appropriate validation—*i.e.*, "good grounds," based on what is known. In short, the requirement that an expert's testimony pertain to "scientific knowledge" establishes a standard of evidentiary reliability.[3]

Rule 702 further requires that the evidence or testimony "assist the trier of fact to understand the evidence or to determine a fact in issue." This condition goes primarily to relevance. "Expert testimony which does not relate to any issue in the case is not relevant and, ergo, non-helpful." 3 Weinstein & Berger[, Weinstein's Evidence] §702[02], p. 702-18 [(1988)]. See also *United States v. Downing*, 753 F.2d 1224, 1242 (CA3 1985) ("An additional consideration under Rule 702—and another aspect of relevancy—is whether expert testimony proffered in the case is sufficiently tied to the facts of the case that it will aid the jury in resolving a factual dispute"). The consideration has been aptly described by Judge Becker as one of "fit." *Ibid*. "Fit" is not always obvious, and scientific validity for one purpose is not necessarily scientific validity for other, unrelated purposes.

2. Rule 702 also applies to "technical, or other specialized knowledge." Our discussion is limited to the scientific context because that is the nature of the expertise offered here.

3. We note that scientists typically distinguish between "validity" (does the principle support what it purports to show?) and "reliability" (does application of the principle produce consistent results?). . . . [O]ur reference here is to evidentiary reliability—that is, trustworthiness. . . . In a case involving scientific evidence, evidentiary reliability will be based upon scientific validity.

The study of the phases of the moon, for example, may provide valid scientific "knowledge" about whether a certain night was dark, and if darkness is a fact in issue, the knowledge will assist the trier of fact. However (absent creditable grounds supporting such a link), evidence that the moon was full on a certain night will not assist the trier of fact in determining whether an individual was unusually likely to have behaved irrationally on that night. Rule 702's "helpfulness" standard requires a valid scientific connection to the pertinent inquiry as a precondition to admissibility.

That these requirements are embodied in Rule 702 is not surprising. Unlike an ordinary witness, see Rule 701, an expert is permitted wide latitude to offer opinions, including those that are not based on firsthand knowledge or observation. See Rules 702 and 703. Presumably, this relaxation of the usual requirement of firsthand knowledge—a rule which represents "a 'most pervasive manifestation' of the common law insistence upon 'the most reliable sources of information,' " Advisory Committee's Notes on Fed. Rule Evid. 602 (citation omitted)—is premised on an assumption that the expert's opinion will have a reliable basis in the knowledge and experience of his discipline.

Faced with a proffer of expert scientific testimony, then, the trial judge must determine at the outset, pursuant to Rule 104(a), whether the expert is proposing to testify to (1) scientific knowledge that (2) will assist the trier of fact to understand or determine a fact in issue.[4] This entails a preliminary assessment of whether the reasoning or methodology underlying the testimony is scientifically valid and of whether that reasoning or methodology properly can be applied to the facts in issue. We are confident that federal judges possess the capacity to undertake this review. Many factors will bear on the inquiry, and we do not presume to set out a definitive checklist or test. But some general observations are appropriate.

Ordinarily, a key question to be answered in determining whether a theory or technique is scientific knowledge that will assist the trier of fact will be whether it can be (and has been) tested. "Scientific methodology today is based on generating hypotheses and testing them to see if they can be falsified; indeed, this methodology is what distinguishes science from other fields of human inquiry." Green[, *Expert Witnesses and Sufficiency of the Evidence in Toxic Substances Litigation: The Legacy of* Agent Orange *and Bendectin Litigation*, 86 Nw. U. L. Rev. 643,] 645 [(1992)]. See also C. Hempel, Philosophy of Natural Science 49 (1966) ("[T]he statements constituting a scientific explanation must be capable of empirical test"); K. Popper, Conjectures and Refutations: The Growth of Scientific Knowledge 37 (5th ed. 1989) ("[T]he criterion of the scientific status of a theory is its falsifiability, or refutability, or testability")(emphasis deleted).

---

4. Although the Frye decision itself focused exclusively on "novel" scientific techniques, we do not read the requirements of Rule 702 to apply specially or exclusively to unconventional evidence. Of course, well-established propositions are less likely to be challenged than those that are novel, and they are more handily defended. Indeed, theories that are so firmly established as to have attained the status of scientific law, such as the laws of thermodynamics, properly are subject to judicial notice under Federal Rule of Evidence 201.

Another pertinent consideration is whether the theory or technique has been subjected to peer review and publication. Publication (which is but one element of peer review) is not a *sine qua non* of admissibility; it does not necessarily correlate with reliability, see S. Jasanoff, The Fifth Branch: Science Advisors as Policymakers 61-76 (1990), and in some instances well-grounded but innovative theories will not have been published, see Horrobin, The Philosophical Basis of Peer Review and the Suppression of Innovation, 263 JAMA 1438 (1990). Some propositions, moreover, are too particular, too new, or of too limited interest to be published. But submission to the scrutiny of the scientific community is a component of "good science," in part because it increases the likelihood that substantive flaws in methodology will be detected. See J. Ziman, Reliable Knowledge: An Exploration of the Grounds for Belief in Science 130-133 (1978); Relman & Angell, How Good Is Peer Review?, 321 New Eng. J. Med. 827 (1989). The fact of publication (or lack thereof) in a peer reviewed journal thus will be a relevant, though not dispositive, consideration in assessing the scientific validity of a particular technique or methodology on which an opinion is premised.

Additionally, in the case of a particular scientific technique, the court ordinarily should consider the known or potential rate of error, see, *e.g., United States v. Smith*, 869 F.2d 348, 353-54 (CA7 1989) (surveying studies of the error rate of spectrographic voice identification technique), and the existence and maintenance of standards controlling the technique's operation, see *United States v. Williams*, 583 F.2d 1194, 1198 (CA2 1978) (noting professional organization's standard governing spectrographic analysis), cert. denied, 439 U.S. 1117 (1979).

Finally, "general acceptance" can yet have a bearing on the inquiry. A "reliability assessment does not require, although it does permit, explicit identification of a relevant scientific community and an express determination of a particular degree of acceptance within that community." *United States v. Downing*, 753 F.2d, at 1238. See also 3 Weinstein & Berger §702[03], pp. 702-41 to 702-42. Widespread acceptance can be an important factor in ruling particular evidence admissible, and "a known technique which has been able to attract only minimal support within the community," *Downing*, 753 F.2d, at 1238, may properly be viewed with skepticism.

The inquiry envisioned by Rule 702 is, we emphasize, a flexible one. Its overarching subject is the scientific validity and thus the evidentiary relevance and reliability—of the principles that underlie a proposed submission. The focus, of course, must be solely on principles and methodology, not on the conclusions that they generate.

Throughout, a judge assessing a proffer of expert scientific testimony under Rule 702 should also be mindful of other applicable rules. Rule 703 provides that expert opinions based on otherwise inadmissible hearsay are to be admitted only if the facts or data are "of a type reasonably relied upon by experts in the particular field in forming opinions or inferences upon the subject." Rule 706 allows the court at its discretion to procure the assistance of an expert of its own choosing. Finally, Rule 403 permits the exclusion of relevant evidence "if its probative value is substantially outweighed by the danger of unfair prejudice, confusion of the issues, or misleading the jury. . . ." Judge Weinstein has explained: "Expert evidence can be both powerful and quite misleading because of the difficulty in evaluating it. Because of this risk, the judge in weighing possible prejudice against probative force under Rule 403 of the present rules exercises more control over experts than over lay witnesses." Weinstein, 138 F.R.D., at 632.

We conclude by briefly addressing what appear to be two underlying concerns of the parties and *amici* in this case. Respondent expresses apprehension that abandonment of "general acceptance" as the exclusive requirement for admission will result in a "free-for-all" in which befuddled juries are confounded by absurd and irrational pseudoscientific assertions. In this regard respondent seems to us to be overly pessimistic about the capabilities of the jury and of the adversary system generally. Vigorous cross-examination, presentation of contrary evidence, and careful instruction on the burden of proof are the traditional and appropriate means of attacking shaky but admissible evidence. See *Rock v. Arkansas*, 483 U.S. 44, 61 (1987). Additionally, in the event the trial court concludes that the scintilla of evidence presented supporting a position is insufficient to allow a reasonable juror to conclude that the position more likely than not is true, the court remains free to direct a judgment, Fed. Rule Civ. Proc. 50(a), and likewise to grant summary judgment, Fed. Rule Civ. Proc. 56. . . . These conventional devices, rather than wholesale exclusion under an uncompromising "general acceptance" test, are the appropriate safeguards where the basis of scientific testimony meets the standards of Rule 702.

Petitioners and, to a greater extent, their *amici* exhibit a different concern. They suggest that recognition of a screening role for the judge that allows for the exclusion of "invalid" evidence will sanction a stifling and repressive scientific orthodoxy and will be inimical to the search for truth. See, *e.g.*, Brief for Ronald Bayer et al. as *Amici Curiae*. It is true that open debate is an essential part of both legal and scientific analyses. Yet there are important differences between the quest for truth in the courtroom and the quest for truth in the laboratory. Scientific conclusions are subject to perpetual revision. Law, on the other hand, must resolve disputes finally and quickly. The scientific project is advanced by broad and wide-ranging consideration of a multitude of hypotheses, for those that are incorrect will eventually be shown to be so, and that in itself is an advance. Conjectures that are probably wrong are of little use, however, in the project of reaching a quick, final, and binding legal judgment—often of great consequence—about a particular set of events in the past. We recognize that, in practice, a gatekeeping role for the judge, no matter how flexible, inevitably on occasion will prevent the jury from learning of authentic insights and innovations. That, nevertheless, is the balance that is struck by Rules of Evidence designed not for the exhaustive search for cosmic understanding but for the particularized resolution of legal disputes.

. . . [T]he judgment of the Court of Appeals is vacated, and the case is remanded for further proceedings consistent with this opinion.

[Chief Justice Rehnquist filed an opinion concurring in part and dissenting in part.]

GENERAL ELECTRIC CO. v. JOINER

522 U.S. 136 (1997)

Chief Justice REHNQUIST delivered the opinion of the Court.

[While working as an electrician for the City of Thomasville, Georgia, respondent Robert Joiner came into frequent contact with fluids in the city's electrical transformers. Fluids in some of the transformers were later found to contain polychlorinated biphenyls (PCBs). After Joiner contracted lung cancer, he sued General Electric and Westinghouse Electric, the manufacturers of the transformers, and Monsanto, which had manufactured PCBs. The case was removed to federal court.]

The District Court ruled that there was a genuine issue of material fact as to whether Joiner had been exposed to PCB's. But it nevertheless granted summary judgment for petitioners because . . . the testimony of Joiner's experts had failed to show that there was a link between exposure to PCB's and small-cell lung cancer. The court believed that the testimony of respondent's experts to the contrary did not rise above "subjective belief or unsupported speculation." Their testimony was therefore inadmissible.

The Court of Appeals for the Eleventh Circuit reversed. It held that "[b]ecause the Federal Rules of Evidence governing expert testimony display a preference for admissibility, we apply a particularly stringent standard of review to the trial judge's exclusion of expert testimony." Applying that standard, the Court of Appeals held that the District Court had erred in excluding the testimony of Joiner's expert witnesses. The District Court had made two fundamental errors. First, it excluded the experts' testimony because it "drew different conclusions from the research than did each of the experts." The Court of Appeals opined that a district court should limit its role to determining the "legal reliability of proffered expert testimony, leaving the jury to decide the correctness of competing expert opinions." Second, the District Court had held that there was no genuine issue of material fact as to whether Joiner had been exposed to furans and dioxins. This was also incorrect, said the Court of Appeals, because testimony in the record supported the proposition that there had been such exposure. . . .

We have held that abuse of discretion is the proper standard of review of a district court's evidentiary rulings. Indeed, our cases on the subject go back as far as *Spring Co. v. Edgar*, 99 U.S. 645, 658 (1879), where we said that "[c]ases arise where it is very much a matter of discretion with the court whether to receive or exclude the evidence; but the appellate court will not reverse in such a case, unless the ruling is manifestly erroneous." The Court of Appeals suggested that *Daubert* somehow altered this general rule in the context of a district court's decision to exclude scientific evidence. But *Daubert* did not address the standard of appellate review for evidentiary rulings at all. . . .

[W]hile the Federal Rules of Evidence allow district courts to admit a somewhat broader range of scientific testimony than would have been admissible under *Frye*, they leave in place the "gatekeeper" role of the trial judge in screening such evidence. A court of appeals applying "abuse-of-discretion" review to such rulings may not categorically distinguish between rulings allowing expert testimony and rulings disallowing it. . . . On a motion for summary judgment, disputed issues of fact are resolved against the moving party—here, petitioners. But the question of admissibility of expert testimony is not such an issue of fact, and is reviewable under the abuse-of-discretion standard.

We hold that the Court of Appeals erred in its review of the exclusion of Joiner's experts' testimony. In applying an overly "stringent" review to that ruling, it failed to give the trial court the deference that is the hallmark of abuse-of-discretion review.

We believe that a proper application of the correct standard of review here indicates that the District Court did not abuse its discretion. Joiner's theory of liability was that his exposure to PCB's and their derivatives "promoted" his development of small-cell lung cancer. In support of that theory he proffered the deposition testimony of expert witnesses. Dr. Arnold Schecter testified that he believed it "more likely than not that Mr. Joiner's lung cancer was causally linked to cigarette smoking and PCB exposure." Dr. Daniel Teitelbaum testified that Joiner's "lung cancer was caused by or contributed to in a significant degree by the materials with which he worked."

Petitioners contended that the statements of Joiner's experts regarding causation were nothing more than speculation. Petitioners criticized the testimony of the experts in that it was "not supported by epidemiological studies . . . [and was] based exclusively on isolated studies of laboratory animals." Joiner responded by claiming that his experts had identified "relevant animal studies which support their opinions." He also directed the court's attention to four epidemiological studies on which his experts had relied.

The District Court agreed with petitioners that the animal studies on which respondent's experts relied did not support his contention that exposure to PCB's had contributed to his cancer. The studies involved infant mice that had developed cancer after being exposed to PCB's. The infant mice in the studies had had massive doses of PCB's injected directly into their peritoneums[5] or stomachs. Joiner was an adult human being whose alleged exposure to PCB's was far less than the exposure in the animal studies. The PCB's were injected into the mice in a highly concentrated form. The fluid with which Joiner had come into contact generally had a much smaller PCB concentration of between 0-to-500 parts per million. The cancer that these mice developed was alveologenic adenomas; Joiner had developed small-cell carcinomas. No study demonstrated that adult mice developed cancer after being exposed to PCB's. One of the experts admitted that no study had demonstrated that PCB's lead to cancer in any other species.

Respondent failed to reply to this criticism. Rather than explaining how and why the experts could have extrapolated their opinions from these seemingly far-removed animal studies, respondent chose "to proceed as if the only issue [was] whether animal studies can ever be a proper

_____

5. The peritoneum is the lining of the abdominal cavity.

foundation for an expert's opinion." Of course, whether animal studies can ever be a proper foundation for an expert's opinion was not the issue. The issue was whether *these* experts' opinions were sufficiently supported by the animal studies on which they purported to rely. The studies were so dissimilar to the facts presented in this litigation that it was not an abuse of discretion for the District Court to have rejected the experts' reliance on them.

The District Court also concluded that the four epidemiological studies on which respondent relied were not a sufficient basis for the experts' opinions. The first such study involved workers at an Italian capacitor[6] plant who had been exposed to PCBs. Bertazzi, Riboldi, Pesatori, Radice, & Zocchetti, Cancer Mortality of Capacitor Manufacturing Workers, 11 American Journal of Industrial Medicine 165 (1987). The authors noted that lung cancer deaths among ex-employees at the plant were higher than might have been expected, but concluded that "there were apparently no grounds for associating lung cancer deaths (although increased above expectations) and exposure in the plant." Given that Bertazzi et al. were unwilling to say that PCB exposure had caused cancer among the workers they examined, their study did not support the experts' conclusion that Joiner's exposure to PCB's caused his cancer.

The second study followed employees who had worked at Monsanto's PCB production plant. J. Zack & D. Musch, Mortality of PCB Workers at the Monsanto Plant in Sauget, Illinois (Dec. 14, 1979) (unpublished report). The authors of this study found that the incidence of lung cancer deaths among these workers was somewhat higher than would ordinarily be expected. The increase, however, was not statistically significant and the authors of the study did not suggest a link between the increase in lung cancer deaths and the exposure to PCB's.

The third and fourth studies were likewise of no help. The third involved workers at a Norwegian cable manufacturing company who had been exposed to mineral oil. Ronneberg, Andersen, & Skyberg, Mortality and Incidence of Cancer Among Oil-Exposed Workers in a Norwegian Cable Manufacturing Company, 45 British Journal of Industrial Medicine 595 (1988). A statistically significant increase in lung cancer deaths had been observed in these workers. The study, however, (1) made no mention of PCB's and (2) was expressly limited to the type of mineral oil involved in that study, and thus did not support these experts' opinions. The fourth and final study involved a PCB-exposed group in Japan that had seen a statistically significant increase in lung cancer deaths. Kuratsune, Nakamura, Ikeda, & Hirohata, Analysis of Deaths Seen Among Patients with Yusho—A Preliminary Report, 16 Chemosphere, Nos. 8/9, p. 2085 (1987). The subjects of this study, however, had been exposed to numerous potential carcinogens, including toxic rice oil that they had ingested.

Respondent points to *Daubert*'s language that the "focus, of course, must be solely on principles and methodology, not on the conclusions that they generate." He claims that because the District Court's disagreement was with the conclusion that the experts drew from the studies, the District

6. A capacitor is an electrical component that stores an electric charge.

Court committed legal error and was properly reversed by the Court of Appeals. But conclusions and methodology are not entirely distinct from one another. Trained experts commonly extrapolate from existing data. But nothing in either *Daubert* or the Federal Rules of Evidence requires a district court to admit opinion evidence that is connected to existing data only by the *ipse dixit* of the expert. A court may conclude that there is simply too great an analytical gap between the data and the opinion proffered. That is what the District Court did here, and we hold that it did not abuse its discretion in so doing. . . . We accordingly reverse the judgment of the Court of Appeals and remand this case for proceedings consistent with this opinion.

[Justice Breyer filed a concurring opinion. Justice Stevens filed an opinion concurring in part and dissenting in part.]

KUMHO TIRE COMPANY, LTD. v. CARMICHAEL

526 U.S. 137 (1999)

Justice Breyer delivered the opinion of the Court.

. . . On July 6, 1993, the right rear tire of a minivan driven by Patrick Carmichael blew out. In the accident that followed, one of the passengers died, and others were severely injured. In October 1993, the Carmichaels brought this diversity suit against the tire's maker and its distributor, whom we refer to collectively as Kumho Tire, claiming that the tire was defective. The plaintiffs rested their case in significant part upon deposition testimony provided by an expert in tire failure analysis, Dennis Carlson, Jr., who intended to testify in support of their conclusion.

Carlson's depositions relied upon certain features of tire technology that are not in dispute. A steel-belted radial tire like the Carmichaels' is made up of a "carcass" containing many layers of flexible cords, called "plies," along which (between the cords and the outer tread) are laid steel strips called "belts." Steel wire loops, called "beads," hold the cords together at the plies' bottom edges. An outer layer, called the "tread," encases the carcass, and the entire tire is bound together in rubber, through the application of heat and various chemicals. See generally, *e.g.*, J. Dixon, Tires, Suspension and Handling 68-72 (2d ed. 1996). The bead of the tire sits upon a "bead seat," which is part of the wheel assembly. That assembly contains a "rim flange," which extends over the bead and rests against the side of the tire. See M. Mavrigian, Performance Wheels & Tires 81, 83 (1998) (illustrations).

Carlson's testimony also accepted certain background facts about the tire in question. He assumed that before the blowout the tire had traveled far. (The tire was made in 1988 and had been installed some time before the Carmichaels bought the used minivan in March 1993; the Carmichaels had driven the van approximately 7,000 additional miles in the two months they had owned it.) Carlson noted that the tire's tread depth, which was 11/32 of an inch when new, had been worn down to depths that ranged from 3/32 of an inch along some parts of the tire, to nothing at all along others. He conceded that the tire tread had at least two punctures which had been inadequately repaired.

Despite the tire's age and history, Carlson concluded that a defect in its manufacture or design caused the blow-out. He rested this conclusion in part upon three premises which, for present purposes, we must assume are not in dispute: First, a tire's carcass should stay bound to the inner side of the tread for a significant period of time after its tread depth has worn away. Second, the tread of the tire at issue had separated from its inner steel-belted carcass prior to the accident. Third, this "separation" caused the blowout.

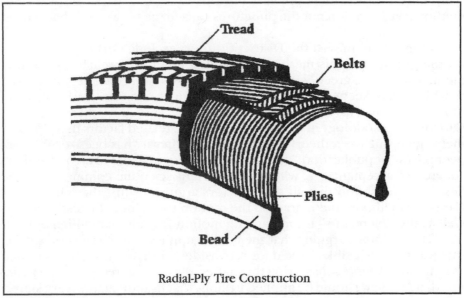

Radial-Ply Tire Construction

A. Markovich, How To Buy and Care For Tires 4 (1994).

Carlson's conclusion that a defect caused the separation, however, rested upon certain other propositions, several of which the defendants strongly dispute. First, Carlson said that if a separation is *not* caused by a certain kind of tire misuse called "overdeflection" (which consists of under-inflating the tire or causing it to carry too much weight, thereby generating heat that can undo the chemical tread/carcass bond), then, ordinarily, its cause is a tire defect. Second, he said that if a tire has been subject to sufficient overdeflection to cause a separation, it should reveal certain physical symptoms. These symptoms include (a) tread wear on the tire's shoulder that is greater than the tread wear along the tire's center; (b) signs of a "bead groove," where the beads have been pushed too hard against the bead seat on the inside of the tire's rim; (c) sidewalls of the tire with physical signs of deterioration, such as discoloration; and/or (d) marks on the tire's rim flange. Third, Carlson said that where he does not find *at least two* of the four physical signs just mentioned (and presumably where there is no reason to suspect a less common cause of separation), he concludes that a manufacturing or design defect caused the separation.

Carlson added that he had inspected the tire in question. He conceded that the tire to a limited degree showed greater wear on the shoulder than in the center, some signs of "bead groove," some discoloration, a few marks on the rim flange, and inadequately filled puncture holes (which can also cause heat that might lead to separation). But, in each instance, he testified that the symptoms were not significant, and he explained why he believed that they did not reveal overdeflection. For example, the extra shoulder wear, he said, appeared primarily on one shoulder, whereas an overde-flected tire would reveal equally abnormal wear on both shoulders. Carlson concluded that the tire did not bear at least two of the four overdeflection symptoms, nor was there any less obvious cause of separation; and since neither overdeflection nor the punctures caused the blowout, a defect must have done so.

Kumho Tire moved the District Court to exclude Carlson's testimony on the ground that his methodology failed Rule 702's reliability require-ment. The court agreed with Kumho that it should act as a *Daubert*-type reliability "gatekeeper," even though one might consider Carlson's testi-mony as "technical," rather than "scientific." The court then examined Carlson's methodology in light of the reliability-related factors that *Daubert* mentioned, such as a theory's testability, whether it "has been a subject of peer review or publication." the "known or potential rate of error," and the "degree of acceptance . . . within the relevant scientific community." The District Court found that all those factors argued against the reliability of Carlson's methods, and it granted the motion to exclude the testimony (as well as the defendants' accompanying motion for summary judgment).

The plaintiffs, arguing that the court's application of the *Daubert* fac-tors was too "inflexible," asked for reconsideration. And the Court granted that motion. After reconsidering the matter, the court agreed with the plain-tiffs that *Daubert* should be applied flexibly, that its four factors were simply illustrative, and that other factors could argue in favor of admissibility. It conceded that there may be widespread acceptance of a "visual-inspection method" for some relevant purposes. But the court found insufficient indi-cations of the reliability of

> "the component of Carlson's tire failure analysis which most concerned the Court, namely, the methodology employed by the expert in analyzing the data obtained in the visual inspection, and the scientific basis, if any, for such an analysis."

It consequently affirmed its earlier order declaring Carlson's testimony inadmissible and granting the defendants' motion for summary judgment.

The Eleventh Circuit reversed. . . . It noted that "the Supreme Court in *Daubert* explicitly limited its holding to cover only the 'scientific context,' " adding that "a *Daubert* analysis" applies only where an expert relies "on the application of scientific principles," rather than "on skill-or experience-based observation." It concluded that Carlson's testimony, which it viewed as relying on experience, "falls outside the scope of *Daubert*," that "the district court erred as a matter of law by applying *Daubert* in this case". . . .

In *Daubert*, this Court held that Federal Rule of Evidence 702 imposes a special obligation upon a trial judge to "ensure that any and all scientific testimony . . . is not only relevant, but reliable." The initial question before us is whether this basic gatekeeping obligation applies only to "scientific" testimony or to all expert testimony. We, like the parties, believe that it applies to all expert testimony.

For one thing, Rule 702 itself . . . makes no relevant distinction between "scientific" knowledge and "technical" or "other specialized" knowledge. It makes clear that any such knowledge might become the subject of expert testimony. In *Daubert*, the Court specified that it is the Rule's word "knowledge," not the words (like "scientific") that modify that word, that "establishes a standard of evidentiary reliability." Hence, as a matter of language, the Rule applies its reliability standard to all "scientific," "technical," or "other specialized" matters within its scope. We concede that the Court in *Daubert* referred only to "scientific" knowledge. But as the Court there said, it referred to "scientific" testimony "because that [wa]s the nature of the expertise" at issue.

Neither is the evidentiary rationale that underlay the Court's basic *Daubert* "gatekeeping" determination limited to "scientific" knowledge. *Daubert* pointed out that Federal Rules 702 and 703 grant expert witnesses testimonial latitude unavailable to other witnesses on the "assumption that the expert's opinion will have a reliable basis in the knowledge and experience of his discipline." The Rules grant that latitude to all experts, not just to "scientific" ones.

Finally, it would prove difficult, if not impossible, for judges to administer evidentiary rules under which a gatekeeping obligation depended upon a distinction between "scientific" knowledge and "technical" or "other specialized" knowledge. There is no clear line that divides the one from the others. Disciplines such as engineering rest upon scientific knowledge. Pure scientific theory itself may depend for its development upon observation and properly engineered machinery. And conceptual efforts to distinguish the two are unlikely to produce clear legal lines capable of application in particular cases. Cf. Brief for National Academy of Engineering as *Amicus Curiae* 9 (scientist seeks to understand nature while the engineer seeks nature's modification); Brief for Rubber Manufacturers Association as *Amicus Curiae* 14-16 (engineering, as an "applied science," relies on "scientific reasoning and methodology"); Brief for John Allen et al. as *Amici Curiae* 6 (engineering relies upon "scientific knowledge and methods").

Neither is there a convincing need to make such distinctions. Experts of all kinds tie observations to conclusions through the use of what Judge Learned Hand called "general truths derived from . . . specialized experience." Hand, Historical and Practical Considerations Regarding Expert Testimony, 15 Harv. L. Rev. 40, 54 (1901). And whether the specific expert testimony focuses upon specialized observations, the specialized translation of those observations into theory, a specialized theory itself, or the application of such a theory in a particular case, the expert's testimony often will rest "upon an experience confessedly foreign in kind to [the jury's] own." *Ibid*. The trial judge's effort to assure that the specialized testimony is reliable and relevant can help the jury evaluate that foreign experience, whether the testimony reflects scientific, technical, or other specialized knowledge.

We conclude that *Daubert*'s general principles apply to the expert matters described in Rule 702. The Rule, in respect to all such matters, "establishes a standard of evidentiary reliability." . . .

The petitioners ask more specifically whether a trial judge determining the "admissibility of an engineering expert's testimony" *may* consider several more specific factors that *Daubert* said might "bear on" a judge's gate-keeping determination. . . . Emphasizing the word "may" in the question, we answer that question yes.

Engineering testimony rests upon scientific foundations, the reliability of which will be at issue in some cases. See, e.g., Brief for Stephen Bobo et al. as *Amici Curiae* 23 (stressing the scientific bases of engineering disciplines). In other cases, the relevant reliability concerns may focus upon personal knowledge or experience. As the Solicitor General points out, there are many different kinds of experts, and many different kinds of expertise. See Brief for United States as *Amicus Curiae* 18-19, and n. 5 (citing cases involving experts in drug terms, handwriting analysis, criminal *modus operandi*, land valuation, agricultural practices, railroad procedures, attorney's fee valuation, and others). Our emphasis on the word "may" thus reflects *Daubert*'s description of the Rule 702 inquiry as "a flexible one." *Daubert* makes clear that the factors it mentions do *not* constitute a "definitive checklist or test." And *Daubert* adds that the gatekeeping inquiry must be "tied to the facts" of a particular "case." We agree with the Solicitor General that "[t]he factors identified in *Daubert* may or may not be pertinent in assessing reliability, depending on the nature of the issue, the expert's particular expertise, and the subject of his testimony." Brief for United States as *Amicus Curiae* 19. The conclusion, in our view, is that we can neither rule out, nor rule in, for all cases and for all time the applicability of the factors mentioned in *Daubert*, nor can we now do so for subsets of cases categorized by category of expert or by kind of evidence. Too much depends upon the particular circumstances of the particular case at issue. . . .

The trial court must have the same kind of latitude in deciding *how* to test an expert's reliability, and to decide whether or when special briefing or other proceedings are needed to investigate reliability, as it enjoys when it decides *whether or not* that expert's relevant testimony is reliable. Our opinion in *Joiner* makes clear that a court of appeals is to apply an abuse-of-discretion standard when it "review[s] a trial court's decision to admit or exclude expert testimony." That standard applies as much to the trial court's decisions about how to determine reliability as to its ultimate conclusion. Otherwise, the trial judge would lack the discretionary authority needed both to avoid unnecessary "reliability" proceedings in ordinary cases where the reliability of an expert's methods is properly taken for granted, and to require appropriate proceedings in the less usual or more complex cases where cause for questioning the expert's reliability arises. Indeed, the Rules seek to avoid "unjustifiable expense and delay" as part of their search for "truth" and the "jus[t] determin[ation]" of proceedings. Fed. Rule Evid. 102. Thus, whether *Daubert*'s specific factors are, or are not, reasonable measures of reliability in a particular case is a matter that the law grants the trial judge broad latitude to determine. And the Eleventh Circuit erred insofar as it held to the contrary.

We further explain the way in which a trial judge "may" consider *Daubert*'s factors by applying these considerations to the case at hand, a matter that has been briefed exhaustively by the parties and their 19 *amici.* The District Court did not doubt Carlson's qualifications, which included a master's degree in mechanical engineering, 10 years' work at Michelin America, Inc., and testimony as a tire failure consultant in other tort cases. Rather, it excluded the testimony because, despite those qualifications, it initially doubted, and then found unreliable, "the methodology employed by the expert in analyzing the data obtained in the visual inspection, and the scientific basis, if any, for such an analysis." ...

[T]he transcripts of Carlson's depositions support both the trial court's initial uncertainty and its final conclusion. Those transcripts cast considerable doubt upon the reliability of both the explicit theory (about the need for two signs of abuse) and the implicit proposition (about the significance of visual inspection in this case). Among other things, the expert could not say whether the tire had traveled more than 10, or 20, or 30, or 40, or 50 thousand miles, adding that 6,000 miles was "about how far" he could "say with any certainty." The court could reasonably have wondered about the reliability of a method of visual and tactile inspection sufficiently precise to ascertain with some certainty the abuse-related significance of minute shoulder/center relative tread wear differences, but insufficiently precise to tell "with any certainty" from the tread wear whether a tire had traveled less than 10,000 or more than 50,000 miles. And these concerns might have been augmented by Carlson's repeated reliance on the "subjective[ness]" of his mode of analysis in response to questions seeking specific information regarding how he could differentiate between a tire that actually had been overdeflected and a tire that merely looked as though it had been. They would have been further augmented by the fact that Carlson said he had inspected the tire itself for the first time the morning of his first deposition, and then only for a few hours. (His initial conclusions were based on photographs.)

Moreover, prior to his first deposition, Carlson had issued a signed report in which he concluded that the tire had "not been . . . overloaded or underinflated," not because of the absence of "two of four" signs of abuse, but simply because "the rim flange impressions . . . were normal." That report also said that the "tread depth remaining was 3/32 inch," though the opposing expert's (apparently undisputed) measurements indicate that the tread depth taken at various positions around the tire actually ranged from .5/32 of an inch to 4/32 of an inch, with the tire apparently showing greater wear along *both* shoulders than along the center.

Further, in respect to one sign of abuse, bead grooving, the expert seemed to deny the sufficiency of his own simple visual-inspection methodology. He testified that most tires have some bead groove pattern, that where there is reason to suspect an abnormal bead groove he would ideally "look at a lot of [similar] tires" to know the grooving's significance, and that he had not looked at many tires similar to the one at issue.

Finally, the court, after looking for a defense of Carlson's methodology as applied in these circumstances, found no convincing defense. Rather, it found (1) that "none" of the *Daubert* factors, including that of "general acceptance" in the relevant expert community, indicated that Carlson's testimony was reliable; (2) that its own analysis "revealed no countervailing factors operating in favor of admissibility which could outweigh those identified in *Daubert*; and (3) that the "parties identified no such factors in their briefs." For these three reasons *taken together*, it concluded that Carlson's testimony was unreliable.

Respondents now argue to us, as they did to the District Court, that a method of tire failure analysis that employs a visual/tactile inspection is a reliable method, and they point both to its use by other experts and to Carlson's long experience working for Michelin as sufficient indication that that is so. But no one denies that an expert might draw a conclusion from a set of observations based on extensive and specialized experience. Nor does anyone deny that, as a general matter, tire abuse may often be identified by qualified experts through visual or tactile inspection of the tire. . . . [T]he question before the trial court was specific, not general. The trial court had to decide whether this particular expert had sufficient specialized knowledge to assist the jurors "in deciding the particular issues in the case." 4 J. McLaughlin. Weinstein's Federal Evidence §702.05[1], p. 702-33 (2d ed. 1998). . . .

The particular issue in this case concerned the use of Carlson's two-factor test and his related use of visual/tactile inspection to draw conclusions on the basis of what seemed small observational differences. We have found no indication in the record that other experts in the industry use Carlson's two-factor test or that tire experts such as Carlson normally make the very fine distinctions about, say, the symmetry of comparatively greater shoulder tread wear that were necessary, on Carlson's own theory, to support his conclusions. Nor, despite the prevalence of tire testing, does anyone refer to any articles or papers that validate Carlson's approach. Compare Bobo, Tire Flaws and Separations, in Mechanics of Pneumatic Tires 636-637 (S. Clark ed. 1981): C. Schnuth et al., Compression Grooving and Rim Flange Abrasion as Indicators of Over-Deflected Operating Conditions in Tires, presented to Rubber Division of the American Chemical Society, Oct. 21-24, 1997; J. Walter & R. Kiminecz, Bead Contact Pressure Measurements at the Tire-Rim Interface, presented to Society of Automotive Engineers, Feb. 24-28, 1975. Indeed, no one has argued that Carlson himself, were he still working for Michelin, would have concluded in a report to his employer that a similar tire was similarly defective on grounds identical to those upon which he rested his conclusion here. Of course, Carlson himself claimed that his method was accurate, but, as we pointed out in *Joiner*, "nothing in either *Daubert* or the Federal Rules of Evidence requires a district court to admit opinion evidence that is connected to existing data only by the *ipse dixit* of the expert."

. . . The District Court did not abuse its discretionary authority in this case. Hence, the judgment of the Court of Appeals is
Reversed.

[Justice Scalia filed a concurring opinion. Justice Stevens filed an opinion concurring in part and dissenting in part.]

iii. The Current Legal Landscape

ADVISORY COMMITTEE NOTE TO
2000 AMENDMENT TO F.R.E. 702

Rule 702 has been amended in response to *Daubert v. Merrell Dow Pharmaceuticals, Inc.*, 509 U.S. 579 (1993), and to the many cases applying *Daubert*, including *Kumho Tire Co. v. Carmichael*, 119 S. Ct. 1167 (1999). . . .

A review of the caselaw after *Daubert* shows that the rejection of expert testimony is the exception rather than the rule. *Daubert* did not work a "seachange over federal evidence law," and "the trial court's role as gate-keeper is not intended to serve as a replacement for the adversary system." *United States v. 14.38 Acres of Land Situated in Leflore County, Mississippi*, 80 F.3d 1074, 1078 (5th Cir. 1996). . . .

ELEANOR SWIFT, ONE HUNDRED YEARS OF
EVIDENCE LAW REFORM: THAYER'S TRIUMPH
88 Cal. L. Rev. 2468, 2469, 2472-2473 (2000)

Taken together, *Joiner* and *Kumho Tire* cordon off an area of judicial decision making at the trial court level that is exceedingly complex and difficult, and now appears to be practically immune from appellate review. It is difficult to imagine any choice of, or application of, *Daubert* factors that would be held to be erroneous. . . . Consistency and predictability in the trial court's method of making decisions about the reliability of expert testimony, and in the outcomes of those decisions, will be lost. Imagine the same expert offering the same type of scientific testimony, based upon the same sources of knowledge, in a series of cases. It will be possible under *Kumho Tire* for successive trial courts to select different *Daubert* factors, to apply them differently, and thus to reach different, inconsistent outcomes, admitting or excluding the same expertise. Under the abuse of discretion standard of review, appellate courts will uphold these inconsistent results. Indeed such inconsistency is inevitable under the opinion of the Court in *Kumho Tire*, which emphasizes that the Court will not refine *Daubert* into a categorical rule for application in "subsets of cases categorized by category of expert or by kind of evidence."

DAVID L. FAIGMAN, DAVID H. KAYE, MICHAEL J. SAKS & JOSEPH SANDERS, HOW GOOD IS GOOD ENOUGH? EXPERT EVIDENCE UNDER DAUBERT AND KUMHO

50 Case W. Res. L. Rev. 645, 656-657 (2000)

Despite some dicta in *Daubert* stating that the test embodied by Rule 702 is a more liberal one than *Frye*, when compared to the general acceptance test, the *Daubert* test requires more from some fields and less from others depending on the state of the knowledge being offered. . . . *Daubert* is more liberal when the expert evidence is solid, but on the cutting edge, and therefore not yet generally accepted. Presumably, this is the category Justice Blackmun had in mind when comparing the two tests. On the other hand, *Frye* is more liberal when what is offered is unsound expert evidence that nevertheless has become "generally accepted" in its field. This is the category that judges have encountered in numerous cases in the wake of *Daubert*, and found themselves puzzled about why a supposedly more liberal standard was leading them toward exclusion of evidence that long has been admitted without question.

The *Frye* test required faith to be placed in various fields and their practitioners, and inevitably made the courts more accepting of speculative, pseudo and sloppy science, but it had the appearance of being easier for judges to administer. *Daubert* requires that fields justify their claims, and this places a heavy cognitive burden on judges. The essential requirement of *Daubert* and its progeny is that to avoid exclusion, experts must offer the courts more than unsupported assertions; they must offer evidence about the basis of their asserted expertise sufficient to enable a judge to conclude that their expert testimony will provide dependable information to the factfinder. . . . We think all of this makes good sense. It should help insure that expert evidence will be more often informative than misleading.

RICHARD D. FRIEDMAN, "E" IS FOR ECLECTIC: MULTIPLE PERSPECTIVES ON EVIDENCE

87 Va. L. Rev. 2029, 2050-2052 (2001)

[I]n the realm of expert evidence as in that of hearsay, it is a mistake to make admissibility depend on a determination of reliability. . . . [W]e do not yet have any good basis for confidence that judges will do a significantly better job than juries in sorting out the wheat from the chaff . . . [so we] should not accept readily the premises that juries will tend to be led astray by bad expertise and that courts can help set them aright by filtering out bad expert evidence from good. . . .

[W]hen expert evidence is troublesome, the difficulty is likely to be not that the evidence is too unreliable to warrant admissibility, but that the plaintiff's case is, at least arguably, too weak as a matter of law to support a judgment. . . . This was true in each case in the Supreme Court's recent trilogy on expert evidence—*Daubert* itself . . . ; *General Electric Co. v. Joiner* . . . ; and *Kumho Tire Co. v. Carmichael.* . . . In each of these cases, the methods used by the experts were open to question—as is often so in cases involving expert testimony—and the conclusions they reached were dubious. But in none of them was the evidence worthless. . . . [T]he law of admissibility has been called on to carry weight that should be borne—if at all—by the law of sufficiency. . . . [I]f the court believes that control of the jury is necessary, it should exercise that control less by ruling the expert evidence inadmissible and more by ruling that, even given that evidence, the plaintiff does not have enough evidence to support a judgment.

MARSH v. VALYOU

977 So. 2d 533 (Fla. 2007)

Per Curiam

After sustaining injuries in four separate car accidents between August 1995 and January 1998, the petitioner, Jill Marsh, filed a negligence action against a series of four defendants [including Robert Valyou and Avis Rent-A-Car]. She claimed the accidents caused fibromyalgia, which is a "syndrome of widespread pain, a decreased pain threshold, and characteristic symptoms including non-restorative sleep, fatigue, stiffness, mood disturbance, irritable syndrome, headache, paresthesias, and other, less common features." . . . Frederick Wolfe, et al., *The Fibromyalgia Syndrome: A Consensus Report on Fibromyalgia and Disability,* 23 J. Rheumatology 534, 534 (1996) [hereinafter *Consensus Report*].

Avis moved to preclude Marsh from presenting expert testimony that the accidents caused her fibromyalgia, arguing that the testimony did not meet the *Frye* standard for admissibility because the premise that trauma can cause fibromyalgia had not been generally accepted in the scientific community. The trial court held a *Frye* hearing and, after reviewing numerous documents related to fibromyalgia and hearing arguments of counsel, granted the motion. . . . Marsh then announced she had no claims apart from fibromyalgia [and a related syndrome], and the trial court entered summary judgment. Petitioner appealed. . . .

Despite the Supreme Court's decision in *Daubert,* we have since repeatedly reaffirmed our adherence to the *Frye* standard for admissibility of evidence. . . . Other states have adhered to *Frye* as well. *See, e.g.,* [Charles Alan Wright & Victor James Gold, *Federal Practice and Procedure* §6266 (1997)] (noting that many states have adopted *Daubert,* but others have declined to do so); [David E. Bernstein & Jeffrey D. Jackson, *The Daubert Trilogy in the States,* 44 Jurimetrics 351, 356 (2004)] (noting that *Frye* "remains the rule in a significant minority of states"). . . .

Under *Frye,* "[t]he proponent of the evidence bears the burden of establishing by a preponderance of the evidence the general acceptance of the underlying scientific principles and methodology." *Castillo v. E.I.*

Du Pont Du Nemours & Co., 854 So. 2d 1264, 1268 (Fla. 2003). We review *Frye* issues de novo, with general acceptance considered as of the time of the appeal. *Id.* "By definition, the *Frye* standard *only applies* when an expert attempts to render an opinion that is based upon *new or novel scientific techniques*." *U.S. Sugar Corp. v. Henson,* 823 So. 2d 104, 109 (Fla. 2002) (emphasis added). . . .

The expert medical causation testimony at issue here is not "new or novel." The American College of Rheumatology published classification criteria for fibromyalgia in 1990. *Consensus Report, supra*. . . . Marsh's experts based their diagnoses and opinions about the cause of her fibromyalgia on a review of her medical history, clinical physical examinations, their own experience, published research, and differential diagnosis. . . . Experts routinely form medical causation opinions based on their experience and training. . . . And there is always the possibility that two experts may reach dissimilar opinions based on their individual experience. However, a disagreement among experts does not transform an ordinary opinion on medical causation into a new or novel principle subject to *Frye*. . . . Because testimony causally linking trauma to fibromyalgia is based on the experts' experience and training, it is "pure opinion" admissible without having to satisfy *Frye*.

Marsh's experts did not base their opinions on new or novel scientific tests or procedures, and Respondents did not challenge the patient history, examination methods, clinical practices, or other methodologies upon which they did rely. . . . Instead, Respondents challenged the experts' *conclusions* that trauma caused Marsh's fibromyalgia. However, as we stated in *U.S. Sugar*, "[u]nder *Frye,* the inquiry must focus only on the general acceptance of the scientific principles and methodologies upon which an expert relies in rendering his or her opinion. Certainly the opinion of the testifying expert need not be generally accepted as well. . . . [O]nce the *Frye* test is satisfied through proof of general acceptance of the basis of an opinion, the expert's opinions are to be evaluated by the finder of fact and are properly assessed as a matter of weight, not admissibility." . . .

Trial courts must resist the temptation to usurp the jury's role in evaluating the credibility of experts and choosing between legitimate but conflicting scientific views. . . . A challenge to the conclusions of Marsh's experts as to causation, rather than the methods used to reach those conclusions, is a proper issue for the trier of fact. For these reasons, we hold that *Frye* does not apply to testimony of a causal link between trauma and fibromyalgia. . . .

[Moreover, even] if subject to *Frye,* testimony linking trauma to fibromyalgia satisfies it. The purpose of *Frye* is to ensure the reliability of expert testimony. . . . Numerous published articles and studies recognize an association between trauma and fibromyalgia. Respondents' own expert testified that he has seen situations where he thought trauma indirectly led to fibromyalgia. A lack of studies conclusively demonstrating a causal link between trauma and fibromyalgia and calls for further research do not preclude admission of the testimony. . . .

Frye does not require unanimity. While the precise etiology of fibromyalgia may not be fully understood, we hold that Marsh has sufficiently demonstrated the reliability of her experts' testimony, and the trial court erred in excluding it. . . . [Reversed.]

ANSTEAD, J., specially concurring.
. . . There are courts that have addressed the exact question of expert testimony linking physical trauma to fibromyalgia and found it admissible pursuant to the rule announced in *Daubert*. . . . I would hold that *Frye* has been superseded by the adoption of Florida's Evidence Code, and that under the relevancy standard contained in the code the expert opinion evidence in question was admissible. Hence, I concur in the majority's decision.

CANTERO, J., dissenting.
. . . I would hold that expert testimony causally linking trauma to fibromyalgia is subject to, and fails, the *Frye* test. . . . Whether trauma can ever cause fibromyalgia is a subject of much debate, and therefore the view that it can has not been generally accepted. I cannot agree with the majority that the jury should be left to sort out contentious and complex disputes about medical causation where experts in the relevant scientific community have been unable to agree. . . . [T]he majority decision turns the courtroom into a laboratory. . . . I respectfully dissent.

PROBLEM

9.1. Would the testimony at issue in *Marsh* be admissible in federal court? One commentator has suggested that "[t]he choice is not between easy *Frye* and difficult *Daubert*; it is between strict and lax scrutiny." Mike Redmayne, *Expert Evidence and Criminal Justice* 113 (2001). Is he right?

C. CURRENT CONTROVERSIES IN SCIENTIFIC EVIDENCE

Generally speaking . . . the more complex the scientific issues subject to proof, the more difficult it becomes to elucidate it through conventional partisan advocacy designed to win the day in the court. . . . [T]he scientization of proof is likely to exacerbate the presently minor frictions within traditional procedural arrangements. Their further deterioration should be considered likely on this ground alone.

Mirjan R. Damaška, *Evidence Law Adrift* (1997)

The following materials illustrate and discuss how the rules of evidence have been applied to several particularly controversial kinds of scientific proof: polygraph results; expert testimony regarding human psychology; probabilistic evidence; DNA testing; and "traditional" forensic sciences such as fingerprinting and handwriting examination.

1. Lie Detection

[C.E.C. §351.1]

STATE v. PORTER

698 A.2d 739 (Conn. 1997)

BORDEN, Justice.

. . . The defendant's home in Norwich was destroyed by a fire on July 20, 1992. The defendant was subsequently charged with two counts of arson. . . . Before trial, the defendant retained Leighton Hammond, a polygrapher, to conduct a polygraph examination to determine whether the defendant was telling the truth when he claimed that he had no guilty knowledge of, and had not participated in, the burning of his home. . . . The pertinent test questions asked of the defendant were: (1) "Did you set fire to your home?"; (2) "Did you tell even one lie, in your statement to the Norwich Police?"; and (3) "Do you know for sure, if any person deliberately set fire to your home?" In the opinion of Hammond, the defendant was telling the truth when he answered "no" to each of these questions.

The defendant then moved that the trial court admit the results of the polygraph examination. After a hearing, the trial court denied the defendant's motion, stating that it was not the place of a trial court to reconsider Connecticut's traditional per se ban on the admissibility of polygraph evidence.

Following a jury trial, at which the defendant did not testify, he was convicted of arson. . . . The Appellate Court affirmed. . . . This certified appeal followed. . . .

Because *Daubert* was premised on an interpretation of a federal rule of evidence, its rejection of *Frye* is not binding authority on state courts. Nonetheless, subsequent to the *Daubert* decision, several states that had theretofore followed *Frye* reconsidered the issue and adopted the *Daubert* standard. . . . [A]t present, Connecticut nominally follows the *Frye* rule. A closer examination of our precedent, however, reveals that on many occasions we have declined to apply *Frye* when considering expert scientific testimony. . . . It is clear that we have been moving toward a validity standard for a number of years. We believe that it is time to complete that process, and that "the *Daubert* [reliability] approach will provide structure and guidance to what has until now been a potentially confusing and sparsely defined area of legal analysis in our state jurisprudence." *Taylor v. State*, 889 P.2d 319, 329 (Okla. Crim. App. 1995). Accordingly, we conclude that the *Daubert* approach should govern the admissibility of scientific evidence in Connecticut. . . . In doing so, we follow in the footsteps of the many jurisdictions that, both before and after the *Daubert* decision, have chosen to reject the *Frye* standard as an absolute prerequisite to the admissibility of scientific evidence.[7] . . .

---

7. We recognize that, to date, most of the states that have rejected *Frye* and have adopted a *Daubert* approach have state evidentiary codes that contain an analogue to rule 702 of the Federal Rules of Evidence, which Connecticut lacks, and that this fact

We now turn to the defendant's claim that Connecticut should abandon its traditional per se rule against the admission of polygraph evidence at trial. . . . Without deciding, we will assume, for the purposes of this opinion, that polygraph evidence satisfies the admissibility threshold established by *Daubert*. After reviewing the case law and the current, extensive literature on the polygraph test, however, we are convinced that the prejudicial impact of polygraph evidence greatly exceeds its probative value. Accordingly, we see no reason to abandon our well established rule of exclusion, and we conclude that polygraph evidence should remain per se inadmissible in all trial court proceedings in which the rules of evidence apply, and for all trial purposes, in Connecticut courts. . . .

Modern polygraph theory rests on two assumptions: (1) there is a regular relationship between deception and certain emotional states; and (2) there is a regular relationship between those emotional states and certain physiological changes in the body that can be measured and recorded. J. Tarantino, Strategic Use of Scientific Evidence (1988), §6.01. These physiological changes include fluctuations in heart rate and blood pressure, rate of breathing, and flow of electrical current through the body, and they are measured by a cardiosphygmograph, a pneumograph and a galvanometer, respectively. *Id.* These instruments, bundled together, form the basis of most modern polygraphs.

There is no question that a high quality polygraph is capable of accurately measuring the relevant physical characteristics. United States Congress, Office of Technology Assessment, "Scientific Validity of Polygraph Testing: A Review and Evaluation—A Technical Memorandum" (1983) (OTA Memorandum), reprinted in 12 Polygraph 198, 201 (1983). Even polygraph advocates, however, acknowledge that "[n]o known physiological response or pattern of responses is unique to deception." D. Raskin, "The Polygraph in 1986: Scientific, Professional and Legal Issues Surrounding Application and Acceptance of Polygraph Evidence," 1986 Utah L. Rev. 29, 31 (1986). Indeed, "there is no reason to believe that lying produces distinctive physiological changes that characterize it and only it. . . . [T]here is no set of responses—physiological or otherwise—that humans omit only when lying or that they produce only when telling the truth. . . . No doubt when we tell a lie many of us experience an inner turmoil, but we experience similar turmoil when we are falsely accused of a crime, when we are anxious about having to defend ourselves against accusations, when we are questioned about sensitive topics—and, for that matter, when we are elated or otherwise emotionally stirred." (Citation

---

often plays some role in their decisions. We also recognize that with the exception of Georgia and, now, Connecticut, every other state without a rule 702 analogue—Alabama, California, Illinois, Maryland and New York—currently operates under a *Frye* standard. We note, however, that three of these states—Alabama, Illinois and Maryland—simply have not addressed the issue. Thus, only two of the states without a rule 702 analogue—New York and California—have expressly rejected *Daubert* and have retained *Frye*. See *People v. Leahy,* 8 Cal. 4th 587, 595 (1994); *People v. Wesley,* 83 N.Y.2d 417, 423 (1994). Moreover, although California ostensibly still follows *Frye* the California Supreme Court has implicitly recognized the imprudence of the strict "general acceptance" standard by holding that "general acceptance" does not require unanimity, a consensus of opinion, or even majority support by the scientific community." *People v. Leahy,* supra, at 601. . . .

omitted.) B. Kleinmuntz & J. Szucko, "On the Fallibility of Lie Detection," 17 Law & Society Rev. 85, 87 (1982). Thus, while a polygraph machine can accurately gauge a subject's *physiological* profile, it cannot, on its own, determine the nature of the underlying *psychological* profile. "The instrument cannot itself detect deception." OTA Memorandum, supra, [at 196,] statement of John Gibbons, Director of Office of Technology Assessment.

The polygraph examiner, therefore, is responsible for transforming the output of a polygraph machine from physiological data into an assessment of truth or deception. See, e.g., P. Giannelli, "Forensic Science: Polygraph Evidence: Part I," 30 Crim. L. Bull. 262, 264 (1994). This mission actually involves two separate tasks. First, the examiner must design and implement a polygraph test in such a way that the physiological data produced is properly linked to a subject's deceptiveness, and not just to his nervousness or other unrelated emotional responses. Id., 263. Second, even if the data produced *is* linked to a subject's deception, the examiner must interpret the data, that is grade the test, correctly. Id., 264.

The "control question test" is the polygraph method most commonly used in criminal cases to link physiological responses to deception. See, e.g., C. Honts & M. Perry, "Polygraph Admissibility: Changes and Challenges," 16 Law & Hum. Behav. 357 (1992). The control question test is based on the theory that fear of detection causes psychological stress. Under that test, therefore, the "polygraph instrument is measuring the fear of detection *rather than deception per se.*" (Emphasis added.) OTA Memorandum, supra, [at 201].

In the control question test procedure, the polygrapher first conducts a pretest interview with the subject wherein the accuracy and reliability of the polygraph are emphasized. This is done to aggravate the deceptive subject's fear of detection while calming the innocent subject, which is crucial given that the test's efficacy is based entirely on the subject's emotional state. All exam questions are then reviewed with the subject, in order to minimize the impact of surprise on the test results and to ensure that the subject understands the questions. The actual control question test consists of a sequence of ten to twelve questions, repeated several times. There are three categories of questions: neutral; relevant; and control. All questions are formulated by the polygrapher conducting the examination based on a review of the facts of the case.

A neutral question is entirely nonconfrontational and is designed to allow the polygrapher to get a baseline reading on the subject's physiological responses. A neutral question addresses a subject's name, age, address, or similar topic.

A relevant question is accusatory and directed specifically at the subject under investigation. "For example, in an assault investigation, a relevant question might be: 'On May 1, 1986, did you strike Mr. Jones (the alleged victim) with any part of your body?'" J. Tarantino, supra, §6.09.

A control question concerns "an act of wrongdoing of the same general nature as the main incident under investigation," and is designed to be "one to which the subject, in all probability, will lie or to which his answer will be of dubious validity in his own mind." J. Rat & F. Inbau, Truth and Deception (2d Ed. 1977) p. 28. Control questions "cover many years in the prior life of the subject and are deliberately vague. Almost anyone would have difficulty answering them truthfully with a simple 'No.' " D. Raskin, supra, [at 34]. In an assault case, a control question might be: "Did you ever want to see anyone harmed?" J. Tarantino, supra, §6.09. Although few people honestly could deny these control questions categorically, they are "presented to the subject in a manner designed to lead him to believe that admissions would negatively influence the examiner's opinion and that strong reactions to those questions during the test would produce a deceptive result." D. Raskin, supra, [at 34].

The theory behind the control question test is that "the truthful person will respond more to the control questions than to the relevant questions because they represent a greater threat to that person. For the same reason the deceptive person will respond more to the relevant questions than to the control questions." P. Giannelli, supra, [at 266-267]. Thus, in order for the test to work properly, both truthful and deceptive examinees must have particular mind sets during the exam. "The innocent examinee [must fear] that the polygraph examiner will pick up his deception [on the control question] and incorrectly conclude that he is also being deceptive about the relevant question." J. Tarantino, supra, §6.09. As a result, the innocent subject's physiological responses to the control question, stemming from this fear, will be greater than those to the relevant question, which the subject can answer honestly. A guilty subject, however, will be more worried about having his crime and deception exposed by the relevant question than he is about any control question issues. Accordingly, his physiological responses—prompted by his fear of detection—will be greater with regard to the relevant question than to the control question.

Under the control question test, the absolute measure of the subject's physiological responses to each question is unimportant. For example, the mere fact that a subject has a strong response to a relevant question can simply be indicative of nervousness and does not, by itself, indicate deception. Instead, the polygrapher looks to the *relative* strength of the responses to the control and relevant questions in order to determine truth or deception. The art of the polygrapher lies in composing control and relevant questions that elicit the appropriate relative responses from truthful and deceitful parties.

A control question exam ordinarily pairs relevant and control questions with some neutral questions interspersed. For example, a typical progression would be:

"1. (Neutral) Do you understand that I will ask only the questions we have discussed?
"2. (Pseudo-Relevant) Regarding whether you took that ring, do you intend to answer all of the questions truthfully?
"3. (Neutral) Do you live in the United States?
"4. (Control) During the first twenty-four years of your life, did you ever take something that did not belong to you?

"5. (Relevant) Did you take a ring from the Behavioral Sciences Building on July 1, 1985?

"6. (Neutral) Is your name Joanne?

"7. (Control) Between the ages of ten and twenty-four, did you ever do anything dishonest or illegal?

"8. (Relevant) Did you take that diamond ring from a desk in the Behavioral Sciences Building on July 1?

"9. (Neutral) Were you born in the month of February?

"10. (Control) Before 1984 did you ever lie to get out of trouble or to cause a problem for someone else?

"11. (Relevant) Were you in any way involved in the theft of that diamond ring from the Behavioral Sciences Building last July?" D. Raskin, supra, [at 36].

The entire sequence is normally gone through three times, after which the examiner scores the result to attempt to reach a determination of truthfulness or deception.

The most common technique for scoring polygraph charts is pure numerical grading. In the most prevalent numerical system, the polygrapher assigns a numerical value along the range of -3 to $+3$ to each pair of relevant and control questions. A score of $+3$ indicates a much stronger reaction to the control question than to the relevant question and, therefore, truthfulness; a score of -3 indicates a much stronger reaction to the relevant question and, therefore, deception; and a score of 0 indicates that there was no significant difference in response. The examiner considers only the polygraph chart in assigning these scores; no consideration is given to any subjective impressions regarding the subject's truthfulness that the examiner develops over the course of the exam. The scores for all question pairs in all three sequences are then totaled. If the sum is $+6$ or greater, the subject is classified as truthful; if the sum is -6 or lower, the subject is classified as deceptive; scores of -5 to $+5$ are deemed inconclusive. Computers are sometimes used to give more precise numerical scores to polygraph charts.

If an analysis of the first three charts produces inconclusive results, the examiner will often repeat the question sequence twice more. After that, however, further repetitions are generally considered meritless, as the subject will have become habituated to the test questions and, therefore, will no longer have sufficiently strong emotional responses for polygraph purposes.[8] Id., 37-40.

_____

8. The other main type of polygraph examination used in criminal matters is the guilty knowledge test. The guilty knowledge test "does not attempt to determine whether the [subject] is lying but, rather, whether he or she possesses guilty knowledge, that is, whether the [subject] recognizes the correct answers, from among several equally plausible but incorrect alternatives, to certain questions relating to a crime. For example, escaping through an alley a bank robber drops and leaves behind his hat. A likely suspect is later apprehended and, while attached to the polygraph, he is interrogated as follows: "1. 'The robber in this case dropped something while escaping. If you are that robber, you will know what he dropped. Was it: a weapon? a face mask? a sack of money? his hat? his car keys?' . . .

We now examine the validity of the results produced by the polygraph test.[9] The word "validity" has two meanings in the polygraph context: for the purposes of this discussion, they will be labeled "accuracy" and "predictive value." Courts generally do not specify to which concept they are referring when they address polygraph issues. Maintaining this distinction is essential, however, if one is to evaluate fairly the validity of the polygraph test.

The "accuracy" of the polygraph test itself has two components: *sensitivity* and *specificity*. The polygraph's sensitivity is its ability to tell that a guilty person is, in fact, lying. If the polygraph test had a 90 percent sensitivity, then it would correctly label a deceptive subject as being deceptive 90 percent of the time. Thus, the test would incorrectly label a deceptive subject as being truthful 10 percent of the time; this mislabeling is called a "false negative" error. The polygraph's specificity is its ability to tell that an innocent person is, in fact, being truthful. If the polygraph test had an 80 percent specificity, then it would label a truthful subject as being truthful 80 percent of the time. The test would thus incorrectly label a truthful subject as being deceptive 20 percent of the time; this mislabeling is called a "false positive" error. It is generally agreed in the literature, by both advocates and critics, that polygraphs have greater sensitivity than specificity; that is, that false positives outnumber false negatives. See, e.g., C. Honts & M. Perry, supra, [at 362]; see also *United States v. Galbreth*, 908 F. Supp. 877, 885 (D.N.M. 1995).

There is wide disagreement, however, as to what the sensitivity and specificity values actually are for a well run polygraph exam. Dozens of studies of polygraph accuracy have been conducted. They fall into two

---

"Unlike the control question test, the accuracy of the guilty knowledge test does not depend upon the nature or degree of the subject's emotional concern. The physiological variables employed are not intended to measure emotional response but, rather, to signal the cognitive processes involved in the recognition of the correct alternative." D. Lykken, "The Case Against Polygraph Testing," in The Polygraph Test (A. Gale ed., 1988) pp. 111, 121-23.

"The guilty knowledge test assumes that the guilty subject will have a greater physical response to the 'significant alternative' than would a subject without any guilty knowledge." J. Tarantino, supra, §6.13. Advocates claim that the primary advantage of the guilty knowledge test is that recognition can be more directly measured by physiological data than can truth or deception. D. Lykken, "The Case Against Polygraph Testing," supra. For the guilty knowledge test to work, however, there must be "concealed knowledge" that only the guilty party would know and recognize. This requirement greatly limits the number of cases in which the test can be utilized. P. Giannelli, supra. In any event, although the guilty knowledge test does have its advocates; D. Lykken, "The Case Against Polygraph Testing," supra; B. Kleinmuntz & J. Szucko, supra; the guilty knowledge test's validity is as hotly debated as that of the control question test. C. Honts & M. Perry, supra; D. Raskin, supra (many guilty people can pass guilty knowledge test). Because the validity of the guilty knowledge test is so uncertain, and because all of the prejudicial effects of allowing control question test evidence apply to guilty knowledge test evidence as well . . . we conclude that guilty knowledge test evidence must also be excluded from use in our courts.

9. Although courts generally use the word "reliability" when discussing the polygraph test . . . the concept to which the courts are referring is actually the test's "validity." In the polygraph context, reliability and validity have specialized meanings. Reliability refers only to reproducibility of results, or consistency, while validity relates to the test's actual ability to do what it claims to do, namely, detect deception. Reliability is important, but the polygraph debate really centers around the test's validity.

basic types, namely, laboratory simulations of crimes[10] and field studies based on data from polygraph examinations in actual criminal cases.[11] P. Giannelli, supra, [at 270-273]. The variance in expert opinion regarding polygraph accuracy arises from disagreements as to which methods and which studies within each method are methodologically valid. C. Honts & M. Perry, supra, [at 360].

Polygraph supporters base their accuracy estimates on both laboratory simulation and field studies. These advocates acknowledge that field studies are theoretically preferable for establishing the polygraph test's field accuracy, but they conclude that serious methodological difficulties inherent in such studies, such as establishing the actual guilt or innocence of the study subjects, make most of these studies unreliable. They think, however, that laboratory studies, when designed to approximate field conditions and when carefully conducted, *can* provide useful and valid data. David Raskin, perhaps the foremost polygraph advocate in the United States, recently reviewed the literature on polygraph studies and concluded that eight laboratory studies and four field studies of the control question test polygraph technique were methodologically valid. D. Raskin, "The Scientific Status of Research on Polygraph Techniques," in West Companion to Scientific Evidence 2 (Faigman et al. eds., forthcoming 1996), cited in C. Honts & B. Quick, "The Polygraph in 1995: Progress in Science and the Law," 71 N.D. L. Rev. 987, 995, 1018-19 (1995). The laboratory studies that Raskin cites, taken together, indicate that the polygraph test has an 89 percent sensitivity rate and a 91 percent specificity rate; the field studies give an 87 percent sensitivity and a 59 percent specificity. Id. Other studies indicate higher levels of accuracy. The United States Department of Defense, although acknowledging that more research needs to be done, concluded after a thorough review of the literature that there was no "data suggesting that the various polygraph techniques and applications . . . have high false positive or high false negative error rates." United States Department of Defense, The Accuracy and Utility of Polygraph Testing (1984) p. 63.

Critics, however, view the existing body of polygraph studies quite differently. First, although polygraph detractors agree with the advocates that most field studies are invalid due to methodological concerns, they disagree as to which tests *are* valid. David Lykken, a prominent polygraph critic, has concluded from the field tests he deems valid that the polygraph

10. "The most accepted type of laboratory study simulates a real crime in which subjects are randomly assigned to guilty and innocent treatment conditions. . . . Guilty subjects enact a realistic crime, and innocent subjects are merely told about the nature of the crime and do not enact it. All subjects are motivated to produce a truthful outcome, usually by a substantial cash bonus for passing the test." (Citations omitted.) D. Raskin, "Does Science Support Polygraph Testing?," in The Polygraph Test (A. Gale ed., 1988) pp. 96, 99.

11. "The best available method for field research uses cases in which suspects were administered polygraph tests after which their guilt or innocence was established when the guilty person confessed. Other polygraph examiners are then asked to make diagnoses based solely on the polygraph charts from those tests without knowledge of the guilt or innocence of the subjects or the opinions of the original examiners. The decisions from these blind analyses are then compared to the confession criterion to estimate the accuracy of the polygraph tests." D. Raskin, supra [at 44].

has a sensitivity of 84 percent and a specificity of only 53 percent. D. Lykken, "The Validity of Tests: Caveat Emptor," 27 Jurimetrics 263, 264 (1987). Another critic has concluded that reliable field studies indicate that there is "little or no case" for using the polygraph, and that "polygraph lie detection adds nothing positive to conventional approaches to interrogation and assessment." D. Carroll, "How Accurate Is Polygraph Lie Detection?," in The Polygraph Test (A. Gale ed., 1988) pp. 19, 28. After its own thorough review of the polygraph field studies, the United States Office of Technology Assessment concluded that "the cumulative research evidence suggest[s] that . . . the polygraph test detects deception better than chance, but with significant error rates." OTA Memorandum, supra, [at 200].

Moreover, polygraph critics argue that laboratory simulation studies are almost completely invalid. They point out that, although the accuracy of the control question test turns entirely on the subject having the "right" emotional responses, the emotional stimuli in the laboratory are completely different from those in the field. D. Carroll, supra, [at 24]. "In the mock crime paradigm . . . it is likely that volunteer subjects regard the experience as a kind of interesting game. Those persons instructed to commit the mock crime and to lie during the test no doubt feel a certain excitement, but not the guilt or fear of exposure that a real thief feels when tested for the police. Volunteers assigned to the innocent group have no reason at all to fear the relevant questions; they are not suspected of any wrongdoing and they will not be punished or defamed even if the test goes awry. On the other hand, the control questions used in laboratory studies . . . unlike the relevant questions, do refer to real-world events and, presumably, have the same embarrassing or disturbing effect on volunteer subjects that they have on criminal suspects. This is probably the reason why mock crime studies typically show a much lower rate of false positive errors than do studies of actual criminal interrogation in the field. Innocent suspects often fail police-administered tests . . . because they find the relevant questions more disturbing than the control questions, since they know they are in real jeopardy in respect to the accusations contained in the relevant questions while the controls involve no comparable risk. For the volunteer laboratory subject, this balance is reversed." D. Lykken, "The Case Against Polygraph Testing," in The Polygraph Test (A. Gale ed., 1988) pp. 111, 114-15. Raskin has admitted that these concerns with laboratory simulations are significant. . . .

Even if one accepts Raskin's field study estimates of accuracy over those of the polygraph critics, polygraph evidence is of questionable validity. Raskin's 87 percent sensitivity indicates a 13 percent false negative rate. In other words, 13 percent of those who are in fact deceptive will be labeled as truthful. Moreover, Raskin's 59 percent specificity indicates a 41 percent false positive rate. In other words, 41 percent of subjects who are, in fact, truthful will be labeled as deceptive.

. . . The actual *probative value* of polygraph evidence as a signifier of guilt or innocence, moreover, is even more questionable. This is because sensitivity, for example, only tells how likely a polygraph is to label accurately a person as deceptive *given that* the person really is lying. At trial, however, we would not yet know that a subject is deceptive—indeed, making that determination may be the entire point of the trial. Knowing how accurately the polygraph test labels deceptive people as deceptive is not, therefore, directly helpful. We are instead interested in a related, but distinct, question: how likely is it that a person really is lying given that the polygraph labels the subject as deceptive? This is called the "predictive value positive." Similarly, at trial we are not directly interested in the polygraph test's specificity, but rather in its "predictive value negative": how likely is it that a subject really is truthful given that the polygraph labels the subject as not deceptive?

Predictive value positive and predictive value negative depend on the sensitivity and specificity of the polygraph test, but also turn on the "base rate"[12] of deceptiveness among the people tested by the polygraph.[13] Unfortunately, no reliable measure of this base rate currently exists

12. The term "base rate" refers to the prevalence of a condition among the relevant tested population. In the context of the polygraph test, the base rate is the percentage of people who submit to a polygraph exam who are, in fact, deceptive on the exam. If, out of every 100 people who take a polygraph test, we could empirically demonstrate that fifty are, in fact, giving deceptive responses, then the base rate of deception would be 50 percent.

The base rate is important because it can greatly accentuate the impact of the false positive and false negative rates arising from any given specificity and sensitivity values. If one assumes base rates progressively higher than 50 percent, then, by definition, the number of deceptive examinees increases and the number of honest examinees decreases. A logical consequence is that, even holding specificity and sensitivity rates constant, as the base rate increases the number of false negatives (the labeling of deceptive subjects as truthful) also rises and the number of false positives (the labeling of truthful subjects as deceptive) falls, because only deceptive subjects produce false negatives and only truthful subjects produce false positives. Likewise, if one were to assume base rates progressively lower than 50 percent, then, even holding sensitivity and specificity constant, as the base rate falls the number of false positives will necessarily rise and the number of false negatives will fall. For example, a very low base rate would dramatically emphasize the problem of false positives, even if sensitivity and specificity were both relatively high. Suppose that the polygraph has a sensitivity of 90 percent (and thus a false negative rate of 10 percent) and a specificity of 80 percent (and thus a false positive rate of 20 percent), and that the base rate of deception is 10 percent. If 100 subjects are tested, then the 10 percent base rate signifies that ten subjects are deceptive and ninety are truthful. Given the specificity of 80 percent, seventy-two of the ninety truthful subjects will be labeled accurately as truthful (80 percent of ninety is seventy-two); the remaining eighteen truthful subjects will be mislabeled as deceptive due to the 20 percent false positive rate. Similarly, given the sensitivity of 90 percent, nine of the ten deceptive subjects will be labeled accurately as deceptive (90 percent of ten is nine); the remaining deceptive subject will be mislabeled as truthful due to the 10 percent false negative rate. These results can be summarized as follows:

	Innocent	Guilty
Pass	72	1
Fail	18	9

"A hundred people are tested: 81 percent are correctly classified; 90 percent of the guilty fail; 80 percent of the innocent pass. And yet of these who fail, only one in three is guilty." S. Blinkhorn, "Lie Detection as a Psychometric Procedure," in The Polygraph Test (A. Gale ed., 1988) pp. 29, 34.

13. Predictive value positive (PVP) and predictive value negative (PVN) are determined by an equation involving the polygraph test's sensitivity and specificity, and the base rate of

if, indeed, one is possible at all. Raskin has claimed, on the basis of an analysis of a United States Secret Service study and on the basis of his own empirical experience, that only about 40 to 60 percent of criminal defendants who are willing to submit to polygraph tests are actually guilty. D. Raskin, supra, [at 59-60]. If a base rate of about 50 percent were correct, then, using Raskin's own field derived figures of 87 percent sensitivity and 59 percent specificity, the predictive value positive of the polygraph test would only be 68 percent and the predictive value negative would be 82 percent. That is, even if we were to agree with all of Raskin's figures, we should only be 68 percent confident that a subject really is lying if the subject fails a polygraph exam, and only 82 percent confident that the subject is being truthful if the subject passes. Therefore, although the probative value of the polygraph test may be greater than that of a coin toss, it is not significantly greater, especially for failed tests.

Furthermore, the 50 percent base rate that Raskin posits is far from universally accepted. "[T]he figures for [the base rate] that [Raskin] pull[s] out of the hat should not be taken as firm." D. Kaye, "The Validity of Tests: Caveant Omnes," 27 Jurimetrics J. 349, 357 (1987). Lykken posits, albeit with as equally sparse evidence as Raskin, that the base rate of guilt among people volunteering for a polygraph exam is 80 percent. D. Lykken, [The Validity of Tests], supra, [at 268]. Using this base rate, the polygraph test's predictive value positive is 89 percent and its predictive value negative is 53 percent. Lykken's base rate, therefore, makes a failed test more probative than it is under Raskin's base rate, but makes a passed test much less probative.

The *specific* predictive value positive and predictive value negative figures generated by a particular set of assumptions, however, is not the significant point for the legal determination of whether to admit polygraph evidence. The point is that, given the complete absence of reliable data on base rates, we have no way of assessing the probative value of the polygraph test. Under one set of assumptions, a failed test has some significance, while a passed test does not; under another, the situation is reversed. The figures are further muddied when one recalls that the sensitivity and specificity of the polygraph are also hotly debated.

Countermeasures are also a concern with regard to polygraph validity. A countermeasure is any technique used by a deceptive subject to induce a

---

deception among the tested population. Mathematically, the relationship among these concepts is expressed as follows:

$$PVP = \frac{\Pi\eta}{\Pi(\eta + \theta - 1) + (1 - \theta)}$$

$$\text{and:} \quad PVN = \frac{\theta(1 - \Pi)}{\theta(1 - \Pi) + \Pi(1 - \eta)}$$

where: Π = the base rate of deception among people who choose to take the polygraph exam;
η = the polygraph test's sensitivity; and
θ = the polygraph test's specificity.
See D. Kaye, "The Validity of Tests: Caveant Omnes," 27 Jurimetrics J. 349 (1987).

false negative result and thereby pass the test. For a countermeasure to work on the control question test, all it must do is "change the direction of the differential reactivity between the relevant and control questions. . . ." G. Gudjonsson, "How to Defeat the Polygraph Tests," in The Polygraph Test (A. Gale ed., 1988) pp. 126, 127.

It may be true that "subjects *without special training* in countermeasures are unable to beat the polygraph test, even if they have been provided with extensive information and suggestions on how they might succeed. . . ."[14] (Citation omitted; emphasis added.) D. Raskin, "Hofmann, Hypnosis, and the Polygraph," 3 Utah B.J. 7, 8 (1990); G. Gudjonsson, [supra, at 135], Yet as one polygraph supporter, Charles Honts, concedes, "studies have indicated that [expert-conducted] training in specific point countermeasures designed to increase [physiological responses to control questions] is effective in producing a substantial number of false negative outcomes. . . ." C. Honts & B. Quick, supra, [at 1001]. Specifically, "[s]ubjects in these studies were informed about the nature of the control question test and were trained to recognize control and relevant questions. Countermeasure subjects were then instructed to employ a countermeasure (e.g., bite their tongue, press their toes to the floor, or count backward by seven) during the control question zones of a control question test. In one study, none of the guilty subjects who received this brief training was correctly detected. . . . Across all of the studies more than 50% of the decisions on countermeasures subjects were incorrect." (Citation omitted.) C. Honts & M. Perry, supra, [at 274]. Although we share Honts' hope that "the required [expert] training is . . . difficult to obtain"; C. Honts & B. Quick, supra; we question whether such is the case and whether it would remain the case if polygraph examination of witnesses became common, especially given the apparent brevity and simplicity of the training in question.

[T]he probative value of polygraph evidence is very low, even if it satisfies *Daubert* . . . [We] conclude that any limited evidentiary value that polygraph evidence does have is substantially outweighed by its prejudicial effects. . . . The most significant, and fundamental, problem with allowing polygraph evidence in court is that it would invade the fact-finding province of the jury. The jury has traditionally been the sole arbiter of witness credibility. Indeed, an underlying premise of our legal system is that the jury is capable in this regard. Accordingly, we generally disallow expert testimony as to witness credibility when the subject matter of the testimony "is within the knowledge of jurors and expert testimony [therefore] would not assist them. . . ." *State v. Kemp*, 199 Conn. 473 (1986); *State v. Boscarino*, 204 Conn. 714 (1987) (expert testimony on reliability of eyewitness identifications properly excluded).

14. But see D. Lykken, [The Validity of Tests,] supra, [at 267] ("As it happens, there is a simple, easily learned technique with which a guilty person can 'beat' the control question test. In one informal prison study, twenty-seven inmates accused of violating prison rules were given some fifteen minutes of instruction in this method [by a fellow inmate, based on information provided by Lykken] before reporting for a test concerned with the alleged infraction. Although all twenty-seven privately admitted their guilt, twenty-four of them managed to pass the polygraph.").

A determination of whether a witness is telling the truth is well within the province of all jurors' understanding and abilities. . . . [P]olygraph evidence so directly abrogates the jury's function that its admission is offensive to our tradition of trial by jury. . . . It violates the premise of this entire system to allow a single person—the polygrapher—to label a witness as honest or as dishonest based solely on the same type of indirect evidence that we generally maintain takes an entire jury to evaluate. . . .

We . . . are convinced of the continued wisdom of our long established rule of polygraph inadmissibility. . . . If, at some future date, *substantial* evidence indicates that some polygraph or other lie detection technique has reached a sufficiently high level of validity that the probative value of such evidence potentially outweighs its prejudicial impact, we may be forced to revisit this issue. . . . The judgment of the Appellate Court is affirmed.

UNITED STATES v. SCHEFFER

523 U.S. 303 (1998)

Justice Thomas announced the judgment of the Court and delivered the opinion of the Court with respect to Parts I, II-A, and II-D. . . .

This case presents the question whether Military Rule of Evidence 707, which makes polygraph evidence inadmissible in court-martial proceedings, unconstitutionally abridges the right of accused members of the military to present a defense. We hold that it does not.

I

In March 1992, respondent Edward Scheffer, an airman stationed at March Air Force Base in California, volunteered to work as an informant on drug investigations for the Air Force Office of Special Investigations (OSI). His OSI supervisors advised him that, from time to time during the course of his undercover work, they would ask him to submit to drug testing and polygraph examinations. In early April, one of the OSI agents supervising respondent requested that he submit to a urine test. Shortly after providing the urine sample, but before the results of the test were known, respondent agreed to take a polygraph test administered by an OSI examiner. In the opinion of the examiner, the test "indicated no deception" when respondent denied using drugs since joining the Air Force.

On April 30, respondent unaccountably failed to appear for work and could not be found on the base. He was absent without leave until May 13, when an Iowa state patrolman arrested him following a routine traffic stop and held him for return to the base. OSI agents later learned that respondent's urinalysis revealed the presence of methamphetamine.

Respondent was tried by general court-martial on charges of using methamphetamine, failing to go to his appointed place of duty, wrongfully

absenting himself from the base for 13 days, and, with respect to an unrelated matter, uttering 17 insufficient funds checks. He testified at trial on his
own behalf, relying upon an "innocent ingestion" theory and denying that
he had knowingly used drugs while working for OSI. On cross-examination,
the prosecution attempted to impeach respondent with inconsistencies
between his trial testimony and earlier statements he had made to OSI.

Respondent sought to introduce the polygraph evidence in support
of his testimony that he did not knowingly use drugs. The military
judge denied the motion, relying on Military Rule of Evidence 707, which
provides, in relevant part:

> "(a) Notwithstanding any other provision of law, the results of a polygraph
> examination, the opinion of a polygraph examiner, or any reference to an
> offer to take, failure to take, or taking of a polygraph examination, shall not be
> admitted into evidence."

. . . Respondent was convicted on all counts and was sentenced to a
bad-conduct discharge, confinement for 30 months, total forfeiture of all
pay and allowances, and reduction to the lowest enlisted grade. The Air
Force Court of Criminal Appeals affirmed in all material respects. . . .

By a 3-to-2 vote, the United States Court of Appeals for the Armed
Forces reversed. Without pointing to any particular language in the Sixth
Amendment, the Court of Appeals held that "[a] per se exclusion of polygraph evidence offered by an accused to rebut an attack on his credibility, . . . violates his Sixth Amendment right to present a defense." . . . We
granted certiorari, and we now reverse.

II

A defendant's right to present relevant evidence is not unlimited, but
rather is subject to reasonable restrictions. See *Taylor v. Illinois*, 484 U.S.
400, 410 (1988); *Rock v. Arkansas*, 483 U.S. 44, 55 (1987); *Chambers v.
Mississippi*, 410 U.S. 284, 295 (1973). . . . [S]tate and federal rulemakers
have broad latitude under the Constitution to establish rules excluding
evidence from criminal trials. Such rules do not abridge an accused's
right to present a defense so long as they are not "arbitrary" or "disproportionate to the purposes they are designed to serve." *Rock, supra*, at 56 . . .

A

State and federal governments unquestionably have a legitimate
interest in ensuring that reliable evidence is presented to the trier of fact
in a criminal trial. Indeed, the exclusion of unreliable evidence is a principal
objective of many evidentiary rules. See, e.g., Fed. Rule Evid. 702; Fed. Rule
Evid. 802; Fed. Rule Evid. 901; see also *Daubert v. Merrell Dow Pharmaceuticals, Inc.*, 509 U.S. 579, 589 (1993).

The contentions of respondent and the dissent notwithstanding, there
is simply no consensus that polygraph evidence is reliable. To this day, the
scientific community remains extremely polarized about the reliability of
polygraph techniques. . . . Some studies have concluded that polygraph

tests overall are accurate and reliable. . . . Others have found that polygraph tests assess truthfulness significantly less accurately—that scientific field studies suggest the accuracy rate of the "control question technique" polygraph is "little better than could be obtained by the toss of a coin," that is, 50 percent. . . .

This lack of scientific consensus is reflected in the disagreement among state and federal courts concerning both the admissibility and the reliability of polygraph evidence. Although some Federal Courts of Appeal have abandoned the per se rule excluding polygraph evidence, leaving its admission or exclusion to the discretion of district courts under *Daubert*, see, e.g., *United States v. Posado*, 57 F.3d 428, 434 (CA5 1995); *United States v. Cordoba*, 104 F.3d 225, 228 (CA9 1997), at least one Federal Circuit has recently reaffirmed its per se ban, see *United States v. Sanchez*, 118 F.3d 192, 197 (CA4 1997), and another recently noted that it has "not decided whether polygraphy has reached a sufficient state of reliability to be admissible." *United States v. Messina*, 131 F.3d 36, 42 (CA2 1997). Most States maintain per se rules excluding polygraph evidence. New Mexico is unique in making polygraph evidence generally admissible without the prior stipulation of the parties and without significant restriction. Whatever their approach, state and federal courts continue to express doubt about whether such evidence is reliable. . . .

The approach taken by the President in adopting Rule 707—excluding polygraph evidence in all military trials—is a rational and proportional means of advancing the legitimate interest in barring unreliable evidence. Although the degree of reliability of polygraph evidence may depend upon a variety of identifiable factors, there is simply no way to know in a particular case whether a polygraph examiner's conclusion is accurate, because certain doubts and uncertainties plague even the best polygraph exams. Individual jurisdictions therefore may reasonably reach differing conclusions as to whether polygraph evidence should be admitted. We cannot say, then, that presented with such widespread uncertainty, the President acted arbitrarily or disproportionately in promulgating a per se rule excluding all polygraph evidence. . . .

B

It is equally clear that Rule 707 serves a second legitimate governmental interest: Preserving the court members' core function of making credibility determinations in criminal trials. A fundamental premise of our criminal trial system is that "the *jury* is the lie detector." *United States v. Barnard*, 490 F.2d 907, 912 (CA9 1973) (emphasis added), cert. denied, 416 U.S. 959 (1974). Determining the weight and credibility of witness testimony, therefore, has long been held to be the "part of every case [that] belongs to the jury, who are presumed to be fitted for it by their natural intelligence and their practical knowledge of men and the ways of men." *Aetna Life Ins. Co. v. Ward*, 140 U.S. 76, 88 (1891).

By its very nature, polygraph evidence may diminish the jury's role in making credibility determinations. . . . Unlike other expert witnesses who testify about factual matters outside the jurors' knowledge, such as the analysis of fingerprints, ballistics, or DNA found at a crime scene, a polygraph expert can supply the jury only with another opinion, in addition to its own, about whether the witness was telling the truth. Jurisdictions, in promulgating rules of evidence, may legitimately be concerned about the risk that juries will give excessive weight to the opinions of a polygrapher, clothed as they are in scientific expertise and at times offering, as in respondent's case, a conclusion about the ultimate issue in the trial. Such jurisdictions may legitimately determine that the aura of infallibility attending polygraph evidence can lead jurors to abandon their duty to assess credibility and guilt. Those jurisdictions may also take into account the fact that a judge cannot determine, when ruling on a motion to admit polygraph evidence, whether a particular polygraph expert is likely to influence the jury unduly. For these reasons, the President is within his constitutional prerogative to promulgate a *per se* rule that simply excludes all such evidence. . . .

D

. . . [T]he court members heard all the relevant details of the charged offense from the perspective of the accused, and the Rule did not preclude him from introducing any factual evidence. Rather, respondent was barred merely from introducing expert opinion testimony to bolster his own credibility. Moreover, in contrast to the rule at issue in *Rock*, Rule 707 did not prohibit respondent from testifying on his own behalf; he freely exercised his choice to convey his version of the facts to the court-martial members. We therefore cannot conclude that respondent's defense was significantly impaired by the exclusion of polygraph evidence. Rule 707 is thus constitutional under our precedents. . . . The judgment of the Court of Appeals is reversed.

JUSTICE KENNEDY . . . concurring in part and concurring in the judgment.

. . . The continuing, good-faith disagreement among experts and courts on the subject of polygraph reliability counsels against our invalidating a *per se* exclusion of polygraph results or of the fact an accused has taken or refused to take a polygraph examination. . . . Given the ongoing debate about polygraphs, I agree the rule of exclusion is not so arbitrary or disproportionate that it is unconstitutional. . . .

[I]t seems the principal opinion overreaches when it rests its holding on the additional ground that the jury's role in making credibility determinations is diminished when it hears polygraph evidence. I am in substantial agreement with Justice STEVENS' observation that the argument demeans and mistakes the role and competence of jurors in deciding the factual question of guilt or innocence. In the last analysis the principal opinion says it is unwise to allow the jury to hear "a conclusion about the ultimate issue in the trial." I had thought this tired argument had long since been given its deserved repose as a categorical rule of exclusion. . . . The principal opinion is made less convincing by its contradicting the rationale of Rule 704 and the well considered reasons the Advisory Committee recited in support of its adoption.

JUSTICE STEVENS, dissenting.

. . . The constitutional requirement that a blanket exclusion of potentially unreliable evidence must be proportionate to the purposes served by the rule obviously makes it necessary to evaluate the interests on both sides of the balance. Today the Court all but ignores the strength of the defendant's interest in having polygraph evidence admitted in certain cases. As the facts of this case illustrate, the Court is quite wrong in assuming that the impact of Rule 707 on respondent's defense was not significant because it did not preclude the introduction of any "factual evidence" or prevent him from conveying "his version of the facts to the court-martial members." Under such reasoning, a rule that excluded the testimony of alibi witnesses would not be significant as long as the defendant is free to testify himself. But given the defendant's strong interest in the outcome—an interest that was sufficient to make his testimony presumptively untrustworthy and therefore inadmissible at common law—his uncorroborated testimony is certain to be less persuasive than that of a third-party witness. A rule that bars him "from introducing expert opinion testimony to bolster his own credibility" unquestionably impairs any "meaningful opportunity to present a complete defense"; indeed, it is sure to be out-come-determinative in many cases. . . .

There are a host of studies that place the reliability of polygraph tests at 85% to 90%. While critics of the polygraph argue that accuracy is much lower, even the studies cited by the critics place polygraph accuracy at 70%. Moreover, to the extent that the polygraph errs, studies have repeatedly shown that the polygraph is more likely to find innocent people guilty than vice versa. Thus, exculpatory polygraphs—like the one in this case—are likely to be more reliable than inculpatory ones.

Of course, within the broad category of lie detector evidence, there may be a wide variation in both the validity and the relevance of particular test results. Questions about the examiner's integrity, independence, choice of questions, or training in the detection of deliberate attempts to provoke misleading physiological responses may justify exclusion of specific evidence. But such questions are properly addressed in adversary proceedings; they fall far short of justifying a blanket exclusion of this type of expert testimony.

There is no legal requirement that expert testimony must satisfy a particular degree of reliability to be admissible. Expert testimony about a defendant's "future dangerousness" to determine his eligibility for the death penalty, even if wrong "most of the time," is routinely admitted. *Barefoot v. Estelle*, 463 U.S. 880, 898-901 (1983). Studies indicate that handwriting analysis, and even fingerprint identifications, may be less trustworthy than polygraph evidence in certain cases. And, of course, even highly dubious eyewitness testimony is, and should be, admitted and tested in the crucible of cross-examination. The Court's reliance on potential unreliability as a justification for a categorical rule of inadmissibility reveals that it is "overly pessimistic about the capabilities of the jury and of the adversary system generally. Vigorous cross-examination, presentation of contrary evidence, and careful instruction on the burden of proof are the traditional and appropriate means of attacking shaky but admissible evidence." *Daubert*, 509 U.S., at 596. . . .

There is, of course, some risk that some "juries will give excessive weight to the opinions of a polygrapher, clothed as they are in scientific expertise." In my judgment, however, it is much more likely that juries will be guided by the instructions of the trial judge concerning the credibility of expert as well as lay witnesses. . . . Common sense suggests that the testimony of disinterested third parties that is relevant to the jury's credibility determination will assist rather than impair the jury's deliberations. As with the reliance on the potential unreliability of this type of evidence, the reliance on a fear that the average jury is not able to assess the weight of this testimony reflects a distressing lack of confidence in the intelligence of the average American. . . .

The Government's concerns would unquestionably support the exclusion of polygraph evidence in particular cases, and may well be sufficient to support a narrower rule designed to respond to specific concerns. In my judgment, however, those concerns are plainly insufficient to support a categorical rule that prohibits the admission of polygraph evidence in all cases, no matter how reliable or probative the evidence may be. Accordingly, I respectfully dissent.

PROBLEM

9.2. California Evidence Code §351.1 provides that "the results of any polygraph examination, the opinion of a polygraph examiner, or any reference to an offer to take, failure to take or taking of a polygraph examination shall not be admitted into evidence in any criminal proceeding . . . unless all parties stipulate to the admission of such results." In 1994, Nicole Brown and her friend Ronald Goldman were stabbed to death. Brown's ex-husband, former football star O.J. Simpson, was charged with the murders. The prosecution sought to have Simpson's friend Ronald Shipp testify about remarks Simpson allegedly had made to Shipp the day after the murders. According to Shipp, Simpson had said that the police wanted him to take a lie detector test, but that Simpson was unsure whether to agree. Shipp said that Simpson had explained his reluctance by admitting, with a "kind of chuckle[]," that he "had a lot of dreams about killing her." The trial judge ruled that Shipp could recount what Simpson had said about his dreams, but that §351.1 required redaction of the reference to a lie detector test. Shipp then testified that Simpson had said "jokingly" that he had "had some dreams of killing her"; no mention was made of the request to take a lie detector test. At the conclusion of the trial, the judge instructed the jurors that they should disregard Shipp's testimony about Simpson's statement if they concluded "that the statement referred to subconscious thoughts while asleep," but should give the testimony "the weight to which you feel it is entitled" if they concluded that Simpson had made the statement and that "the statement referred to an expression of a desire or an expectation." *See* Gerald F. Uelmen, *The O.J. Files: Evidentiary Issues in a Tactical Context* 12-13, 20-21, 24-25 (1998). Did the judge handle this matter properly? (Simpson was acquitted of the murders but later found liable for the killings in a civil action for wrongful death.)

2. Social Science Evidence

UNITED STATES v. SMITHERS

212 F.3d 306 (6th Cir. 2000)

MARBLEY, District Judge.

Appellant James Smithers was convicted of bank robbery in violation of 18 U.S.C. §2113(a). [Three eyewitnesses identified Smithers as the robber at trial, although two had earlier failed to select his picture in a photospread. The trial judge refused to allow the defense to call an expert witness, Solomon Fulero, to testify about the general factors that may affect eyewitness accuracy. Fulero's testimony, according to the defense proffer, would have focussed on the following issues:] (1) "detail salience" (the fact that eyewitnesses tend to focus on unusual characteristics of people they observe); (2) the relationship between the time that has passed since observing the event and the accuracy of recalling it; (3) the effect of post-identification events on memory; (4) the fact that when one person both prepares and administers a photo spread, the likelihood of misidentification increases; (5) the "conformity effect" (the fact that witnesses' memories are altered by talking about the event with each other after it occurs); and (6) the relationship between a witness's confidence in her recollection and its accuracy. Regarding the issue of detail salience, the proffer stated that "[h]ad Mr. Smithers been the robber, the eyewitnesses would have observed and been able to recall the large scar on Mr. Smithers' [sic] neck." [Two of the witnesses testified at trial that they did not notice that the robber had any distinguishing features.] . . .

. . . Courts' treatment of expert testimony regarding eyewitness identification has experienced a dramatic transformation in the past twenty years and is still in a state of flux. Beginning in the early 1970's, defense attorneys began to bring expert testimony into the courtroom. Then, courts were uniformly skeptical about admitting such testimony, elaborating a host of reasons why eyewitness experts should not be allowed to testify. In the first case to address the issue, *United States v. Amaral*, 488 F.2d 1148 (9th Cir. 1973), the Ninth Circuit held that the district court did not err in excluding expert testimony regarding eyewitness identification because cross-examination was sufficient to reveal any weaknesses in the identifications. After that decision, a series of cases rejected similar evidence for a variety of reasons. *See, e.g., United States v. Purham*, 725 F.2d 450, 454 (8th Cir. 1984) (finding the question is within the expertise of jurors); *United States v. Thevis*, 665 F.2d 616, 641 (5th Cir. 1982) (reasoning that identification was adequately addressed through cross-examination): *United States v. Sims*, 617 F.2d 1371,

1375 (9th Cir. 1980); *United States v. Fosher*, 590 F.2d 381, 383 (ruling that the testimony would be prejudicial).

This trend shifted with a series of decisions in the 1980's, with the emerging view that expert testimony may be offered, in certain circumstances, on the subject of the psychological factors which influence the memory process. *See, e.g., United States v. Moore*, 786 F.2d 1308, 1313 (5th Cir. 1986) (finding that "[i]n a case in which the sole testimony is casual eyewitness identification, expert testimony regarding the accuracy of that identification is admissible and properly may be encouraged . . ."): *United States v. Downing*, 753 F.2d 1224, 1232 (3d Cir. 1985) (reasoning that "expert testimony on eyewitness perception and memory [should] be admitted at least in some circumstances"); *United States v. Smith*, 736 F.2d 1103, 1107 (6th Cir. 1984) ("The day may have arrived, therefore, when Dr. Fulero's testimony can be said to conform to a generally accepted explanatory theory"). State court decisions also reflect this trend. *See, e.g., State v. Buell*, 22 Ohio St. 3d 124, 489 N.E.2d 795 (1986) (overruling per se rule and holding expert testimony admissible to inform jury about factors generally affecting memory process). Indeed, several courts have held that it is an abuse of discretion to exclude such expert testimony. *See, e.g., United States v. Stevens*, 935 F.2d 1380, 1400-01 (3d Cir. 1991) (reversing and remanding for new trial): *Smith*, 736 F.2d at 1107 (holding error harmless in light of other inculpatory evidence); *Downing*, 753 F.2d at 1232 (holding error harmless in light of other inculpatory evidence); *State v. Chapple*, 135 Ariz. 281, 660 P.2d 1208 (1983) (reversing and remanding for new trial). This jurisprudential trend is not surprising in light of modern scientific studies which show that, while juries rely heavily on eyewitness testimony, it can be untrustworthy under certain circumstances.[15]

---

15. A plethora of recent studies show that the accuracy of an eyewitness identification depends on how the event is observed, retained and recalled. *See generally* Roger v. Handberg, *Expert Testimony on Eyewitness Identification: A New Pair of Glasses for the Jury*, 32 Am. Crim. L. Rev. 1013, 1018-22 (1995). Memory and perception may be affected by factors such as:

(1) the retention interval, which concerns the rate at which a person's memory declines over time; (2) the assimilation factor, which concerns a witness's incorporation of information gained subsequent to an event into his or her memory of that event; and (3) the confidence-accuracy relationship, which concerns the correlation between a witness's confidence in his or her memory and the accuracy of that memory. Other relevant factors include: (4) stress; (5) the violence of the situation; (6) the selectivity of perception; (7) expectancy; (8) the effect of repeated viewings; (9) and the cross-racial aspects of identification, that is where the eyewitness and the actor in the situation are of different racial groups.

Alan K. Stetler, *Particular Subjects of Expert and Opinion Evidence*, 31A Am. Jur. Expert §371 (1989). Accordingly, "a jury should consider several factors in judging the accuracy of an eyewitness identification. Social science data suggests, however, that jurors are unaware of several scientific principles affecting eyewitness identifications." Handberg, *supra*, at 1022. In fact, because many of the factors affecting eyewitness impressions are counter-intuitive, many jurors' assumptions about how memories are created are actively wrong. . . . One study has estimated that half of all wrongful convictions result from false identifications. *See* Elizabeth F. Loftus, *Ten Years in the Life of an Expert Witness*, 10 Law &

. . . We find that the district court abused its discretion in excluding Dr. Fulero's testimony, without first conducting a hearing pursuant to *Daubert*. . . . Under *Daubert*, a trial court should consider: (1) whether the reasoning or methodology underlying the expert's testimony is scientifically valid; and (2) whether that reasoning or methodology properly could be applied to the facts at issue to aid the trier of fact. The district court, in neglecting to undertake a *Daubert* analysis, failed to take these factors into consideration. Indeed, the district court did not make *any* determination as to this expert's scientific reasoning or methodology. We find that if the district court had given this issue proper consideration, it may have deemed Dr. Fulero's testimony scientifically valid.

. . . Tellingly, this Court has already accredited Dr. Fulero's science and methodology. In *Smith*, this Court not only noted the jurisprudential movement toward admitting psychological studies of eyewitness experts in general, but praised the qualifications and scientific methods of this same expert witness, Dr. Fulero. In addition, the district court could have concluded that this testimony—describing psychological factors such as detail salience, the conformity effect, the dynamics of photo identifications and the confidence-accuracy relationships—could have been applied to the facts at issue in this case. Information about the effects of detail salience would bear on the witnesses' failure to notice Smithers's conspicuous scar; evidence about the conformity effect would apply to [the ability of two of the eyewitnesses] to identify Smithers only after they had spoken with [the third]; the suggestibility of photo identifications created and administered by a single person would apply to the procedures . . . used [in this case]; and explaining the lack of correlation between confidence and accuracy would bear upon the credibility of all of the eyewitnesses. Had the district court conducted a proper evaluation of this testimony, we believe it may have found that Dr. Fulero's testimony met the first requirement of the *Daubert* test.

The trial court should have next considered whether the proposed expert testimony was relevant to the task at hand and would aid the trier of fact. The district court did, to some extent, discuss this second *Daubert* prong (even if it did not explicitly note that it was doing so), by stating that "a jury can fully understand" its "obligation to be somewhat skeptical of eyewitness testimony." This point addresses whether the testimony would "aid the trier of fact." The court's statement, however, is simply wrong, and the district court, on remand, should reconsider this factor. As noted above, jurors tend to be unduly receptive to, rather than skeptical of, eyewitness testimony. . . . Today, there is no question that many aspects of perception

---

Hum. Behav. 241, 243 (1986) (citing a 1983 Ohio State University doctoral dissertation). And "[i]t has been estimated that more than 4,250 Americans per year are wrongfully convicted due to sincere, yet woefully inaccurate eyewitness identifications." Andre A. Moenssens et al., Scientific Evidence in Civil and Criminal Cases §19.15, at 1171-72 (4th ed. 1995) (citing *United States v. Wade*, 388 U.S. 218 (1967)). A principal cause of such convictions is "the fact that, in general, juries are unduly receptive to identification evidence and are not sufficiently aware of its dangers." Patrick M. Wall, Eye-Witness Identification in Criminal Cases §19 (1965). . . .

and memory are not within the common experience of most jurors, and in fact, many factors that affect memory are counter-intuitive. . . .

. . . [E]yewitness testimony was the crucial, if not the sole basis for Smithers's conviction. The district court in this case concluded that "[a]dmission of Dr. Fulero's testimony in this case is almost tantamount to the Court declaring the defendant not guilty as a matter of law. . . . absent the eyewitness testimony I don't think there's enough here to go to the jury." The lower court did not seem to realize that eyewitness expert testimony is most appropriate in such situations. . . .

The district court should have conducted a hearing under *Daubert* and analyzed the evidence to determine whether Dr. Fulero's proffered testimony reflects scientific knowledge, and whether the testimony was relevant and would have aided the trier of fact. . . . [Reversed and remanded.]

BATCHELDER, Circuit Judge, dissenting.

. . . The trepidation with which nearly all appellate courts have treated this subject is representative of a broader reluctance, which I share, to admit the expert testimony of social scientists with the same deference given to the testimony of those in the physical sciences. I do not seek to discredit the value of these researchers' work; the ever-expanding psychological disciplines have done much in the past several decades to explode commonly held misconceptions and enrich our understanding of human behaviors. As even those courts most opposed to admitting the testimony in court have acknowledged, those benefits include an enhanced insight into the fallibility of eyewitness identification that can inform our trial procedures. The difficulty arises in treating psychological theories as if they were as demonstrably reliable as the laws of physics. Conclusions reached by applying the laws of all but the most theoretical of physical sciences to a particular set of facts are verifiable through replication; disagreements between dueling experts in the physical sciences (e.g., accident reconstructionists or DNA experts) typically focus on the data to which the scientific method is applied, which is subject to objective analysis. The certainty of the testimony of social scientists, however, is limited by the nature of their field. They typically base their opinions on studies of small groups of people under laboratory conditions; those studies are then interpreted and extrapolated to predict the likelihood that another person under similar but non-controlled conditions will manifest similar behavior. Each step of this analysis—the choice of sample and control groups, the conditions under which they are observed, the cause and nature of the observed behavior, and the likelihood that the observed behavior will be replicated by a different person in a non-controlled setting—is influenced by the personal opinion of the individual expert. Nor will there be much similarity between the persons typically studied by social scientists and the witnesses in any given criminal trial. The studies are virtually always based on college students or other readily available test subjects in a controlled environment (which are the most easily measurable), not individuals involved in real world incidents such as actual robbery victims. *See, e.g., United States v. Hines*, 55 F. Supp. 2d 62, 72 (D. Mass. 1999) (assessing relevance of studies of college students);

Brian L. Cutler and Steven D. Penrod, *Assessing the Accuracy of Eye-Witness Identifications*, in Handbook of Psychology in Legal Contexts 193 (R. Bull and D. Carson ed. 1995) (Attachment E to Smithers's Motion *in Limine*) ("Most of what is known about the psychology of eye-witness memory has been acquired through laboratory experiments"). The limits of social science testimony were aptly expressed in *Gacy v. Welborn*, 994 F.2d 305, 313-14 (7th Cir. 1993):

> Social science has challenged many premises of the jury system. Students of the subject believe, for example, that jurors give too much weight to eyewitness evidence and not enough weight to other kinds. Still, the ability of jurors to sift good evidence from bad is an axiom of the system, so courts not only permit juries to decide these cases but also bypass the sort of empirical findings that might help jurors reach better decisions. Juries have a hard time distinguishing "junk science" from the real thing, but aside from some tinkering with the expert testimony admitted at trial, this shortcoming has been tolerated. Jurors reach compromise verdicts, although they aren't supposed to. Juries return inconsistent verdicts, representing irrational behavior or disobedience to their instructions. Juries act in ways no reasonable person would act. This is the standard for granting judgment notwithstanding the verdict in a civil case, or acquittal after verdict in a criminal case, or reducing an award of damages, and there are plenty of occasions for these post-verdict correctives. Yet for all of this, courts do not discard the premises of the jury system, postulates embedded in the Constitution and thus, within our legal system, unassailable. This shows up in a striking fact about the Supreme Court's treatment of social science: of the 92 cases between 1970 and 1988 addressing issues of evidence and trial procedure, not one relied on the extensive body of evidence about jurors' conduct.

No psychological study will ever bear directly on the specific persons making an eyewitness identification in court; psychological experts will always be forced to extrapolate from studies done on other people and opine on the relevance such data might have to the facts at hand. Cross-examination of the identifying witnesses, on the other hand, will always provide more relevant testimony, because by definition the inquiry is limited to what the eye-witnesses themselves saw and experienced. Indeed, to a certain extent, lawyers are abdicating their own roles when they seek to rely on experts instead of cross-examination to discredit an eyewitness identification. *See* [*United States v. Amaral*, 488 F.2d 1148, 1153 (9th Cir. 1973)] ("Our legal system places primary reliance for the ascertainment of truth on the test of cross-examination. . . . It is the responsibility of counsel during cross-examination to inquire into the witness' opportunity for observation, his capacity for observation, his attention and interest and his distraction or division of attention"). The witness's cross-examination testimony can then be framed as the defendant chooses in closing argument to maximize its potential to undermine the identification. What the defendant is unable to establish by these means—e.g., the counter-intuitive concept suggested by psychological research that confidence in one's recollection does not necessarily reflect accuracy—can be ably communicated by the court in its jury instructions. Instructions have an advantage over experts in that they can be informed by advances in social science research while communicating only those theories that are relevant to the facts of the case, and avoiding the extra delay and expense of producing and rebutting expert testimony, all without the imprimatur of scientific reliability that accompanies expert testimony. Certainly the utility of jury instructions in these situations was aptly demonstrated in this case, where the district court skillfully addressed Smithers's concerns by adopting an instruction specifically tailored to explain the possible deficiencies of the identifications in this case. In any event, given the utility of cross-examination and jury instructions combined, it is little wonder that the vast majority of appellate cases have found the choice of these mechanisms over expert testimony, even if the expert may have some particular insight that would not be otherwise revealed, not to be an abuse of the district court's broad discretion under *Kumho Tire, Daubert*, and Rule 702. . . .

STATE v. COLEY

32 S.W.3d 831 (Tenn. 2000)

BIRCH, J., delivered the opinion of the court. . . .

. . . At trial, Eddie L. Coley, Jr., the defendant, sought to introduce expert testimony concerning eyewitness identification; at the State's objection, the trial court refused to admit the testimony. . . . The intermediate court affirmed his conviction and sentence. . . . We accepted review in this case to determine the admissibility of expert testimony concerning eyewitness identification. We hold that the testimony proffered here is inadmissible under Tenn. R. Evid. 702 and that the trial court, therefore, properly excluded the testimony of Coley's expert witness.

[Coley was convicted of aggravated robbery. The critical issue was identification. The prosecution relied heavily on pre-trial and in-court identifications of Coley by two eyewitnesses. Coley offered an alibi.]

Coley desired to adduce the testimony of Michael G. Johnson, Ph.D., J.D., an expert in the field of eyewitness identification. The State objected to Johnson's testimony on the ground that it would not assist the jury in deciding the identification issue. The trial court agreed and refused to admit Johnson's testimony. . . . The proffered testimony included information covering the following topics: 1. the process of eyewitness identification; 2. the relationship between stress and memory of an event; 3. cross-racial identification; 4. the confidence the witnesses have in the accuracy of their identifications and the actual accuracy of their identifications; 5. the effect of time on the accuracy of memory; and 6. the suggestibility of the photographic line-up used in this case. . . .

Though the admissibility of each expert's testimony generally rests within the sound discretion of the trial judge, Tennessee courts have, on occasion, excluded specific categories of expert testimony. *See State v. Ballard*, 855 S.W.2d 557, 561-63 (Tenn. 1993). . . . In *Ballard*, we held that expert testimony concerning symptoms of post-traumatic stress syndrome exhibited by victims of child abuse was inadmissible. In reaching this conclusion we reasoned that:

> [i]n the context of the criminal trial, expert scientific testimony solicits the danger of undue prejudice or confusing the issues or misleading the jury because of its aura of special reliability and trustworthiness. This "special aura" of expert scientific testimony, especially testimony concerning personality profiles of sexually abused children, may lead a jury to abandon its responsibility as a fact finder and adopt the judgment of the expert. Such evidence carries strong potential to prejudice a defendant's cause by encouraging a jury to conclude that because the children have been identified by an expert to exhibit behavior consistent with post-traumatic stress syndrome, brought on by sexual abuse, then it is more likely that the defendant committed the crime. Testimony that children exhibit symptoms or characteristics of post-traumatic stress syndrome should not suffice to confirm the fact of sexual abuse. The symptoms of the syndrome are "not like a fingerprint in that it can clearly identify the perpetrator of a crime." Expert testimony of this type invades the province of the jury to decide on the credibility of witnesses.

Here, as in *Ballard*, we are presented with testimony of a general nature designed to affect the juror's decision on the credibility of witnesses. Using the *Ballard* rationale, expert testimony concerning eyewitness identification "solicits the danger of undue prejudice or confusing the issues or misleading the jury. . . ." As a result, it may "lead a jury to abandon its responsibility as fact finder and adopt the judgment of the expert," rather than "assist" the jury in making its own determination of credibility. . . .

Though we have not specifically addressed the issue of the admissibility of expert evidence concerning the reliability of eyewitness testimony, the Court of Criminal Appeals has articulated several reasons for excluding such evidence. In *State v. Ward*, 712 S.W.2d 485, 487 (Tenn. Crim. App. 1986), the court stated,

> We are of the opinion that there are too many variables involved including individual power of observation, individual reaction to stress or the threat of violence, the visual acuity of a particular witness, as well as numbers of general, common factors unamenable to charting and categorizing.

And in *State v. Wooden*, 658 S.W.2d 553, 556 (Tenn. Crim. App. 1983), the court found the following:

> To admit such testimony in effect would permit the proponent's witness to comment on the weight and credibility of opponents' witnesses and open the door to a barrage of marginally relevant psychological evidence. Moreover, we conclude, as did the trial judge, that the problems of perception and memory can be adequately addressed in cross-examination and that the jury can adequately weigh these problems through common-sense evaluation.

In other jurisdictions as well, an overwhelming majority of courts have upheld the trial court's finding that the testimony is inadmissible. These courts have provided many reasons for excluding this type of expert testimony. For example, some courts have upheld the exclusion because such testimony is unhelpful and simply offers generalities. As the Nebraska Supreme Court has noted:

> the knowledge of behavioral scientists, such as psychologists, is probabilistic, couched in terms of averages, standard deviations, curves, and differences between groups. A court, however, is not concerned with the average eyewitness' reliability but with the reliability of the specific eyewitness before it, who may vary from the average in probabilistic but ultimately unknown ways. It is not the research behavioral social scientist who is in a position to assess a specific witness' reliability; the jury, which views the witness as an individual, is best able to collectively determine, on the basis of common human experience as yet unsurpassed by laboratory research, how to weigh what an individual witness has to say.

State v. Trevino, 230 Neb. 494, 432 N.W.2d 503, 520 (1988).

Other courts have excluded this type of testimony because " '[s]uch expert testimony will not aid the jury because it addresses an issue of which the jury is already generally aware, and it will not contribute to their understanding of the particular dispute.' " *United States v. Hall*, 165 F.3d 1095, 1104 (7th Cir. 1999)] (quoting *United States v. Hudson*, 884 F.2d 1016, 1024 (7th Cir. 1989)). Thus, the " 'reliability of eyewitness identification is within the knowledge of jurors and expert testimony generally would not assist them. . . .' " [*State v. McClendon*, 730 A.2d 1107, 1114 (Conn. 1999).]

In excluding expert testimony concerning eyewitness identification, courts have also noted that the "minimal probative value of the proffered expert testimony is outweighed by the danger of juror confusion." [*United States v. Kime*, 99 F.3d 870, 884 (8th Cir. 1996).] Such testimony has the potential to confuse and mislead the jury and create prolonged trials by battles of experts.

Finally, courts have reasoned that this testimony invades the province of the jury by evaluating witness credibility. Rather than permit experts to testify in such cases, usurping a function traditionally left to juries, courts have found that "juries may be made to understand psychological factors which affect the accuracy of an identification when these factors are brought to light at cross-examination and during closing argument." *State v. Percy*, 156 Vt. 468, 595 A.2d 248, 252 (1990). Thus, "jurors using common sense and their faculties of observation can judge the credibility of an eyewitness identification, especially since deficiencies or inconsistencies in an eyewitness's testimony can be brought out with skillful examination." [*United States v. Smith*, 156 F.3d 1046, 1053 (10th Cir. 1998)] (quoting [*United States v. Harris*, 995 F.2d 532, 535 (4th Cir. 1993)]). Courts have also reasoned that along with cross-examination, jury instructions specifically tailored to cases involving eyewitness identification sufficiently aid the jury in determining the credibility of the witnesses. As the Kansas Supreme Court has reasoned:

> we have concluded that requiring trial courts to admit this type of expert evidence is not the answer to the [eyewitness identification] problem. We believe that the problem can be alleviated by a proper cautionary instruction to the jury which sets forth the factors to be considered in evaluating

eyewitness testimony. Such instruction, coupled with vigorous cross-examination and persuasive argument by defense counsel dealing realistically with the shortcomings and trouble spots of the identification process, should protect the rights of the defendant and at the same time enable the courts to avoid problems involved in the admission of expert testimony on this subject.

State v. Gaines, 260 Kan. 752, 926 P.2d 641, 647 (1996) (quoting *State v. Warren*, 230 Kan. 385, 635 P.2d 1236 (1981)).

. . . [W]e find that expert testimony concerning eyewitness identification simply offers generalities and is not specific to the witness whose testimony is in question. Moreover, we are of the opinion that the subject of the reliability of eyewitness identification is within the common understanding of reasonable persons. Therefore, such expert testimony is unnecessary. It may mislead and confuse, and it could encourage the jury to abandon its responsibility as fact-finder. Such responsibility is a task reserved for and ably performed by the jury, aided by skillful cross-examination and . . . jury instruction . . . when appropriate. For these reasons, we find that general and unparticularized expert testimony concerning the reliability of eyewitness testimony, which is not specific to the witness whose testimony is in question, does not substantially assist the trier of fact. Thus, we hold that such testimony is inadmissible under Tenn. R. Evid. 702 and that the trial court, therefore, properly excluded Johnson's testimony.

We recognize that we are in the minority of jurisdictions which find such testimony per se inadmissible, rather than leaving the determination of admissibility to the discretion of the trial court. Nonetheless, we are convinced that a per se rule of exclusion is appropriate. First, leaving the admissibility of this type of expert testimony to the discretion of the trial court would require us, at least implicitly, to reject the sound reasoning of *Ballard*. Second, the rules of evidence from those jurisdictions which leave the admissibility of expert testimony concerning eyewitness identification to the discretion of the trial court require, as does Fed. R. Evid. 702, only that expert testimony "assist the trier of fact." Under Tenn. R. Evid. 702, however, expert testimony is admissible only if it "*substantially* assists the trier of fact." (Emphasis added.) Thus, Tenn. R. Evid. 702 requires a greater showing of probative force than the federal rules of evidence or the rules of evidence from those states that have followed the federal rules, making the per se exclusion appropriate. . . . The judgment of the Court of Criminal Appeals is, therefore, affirmed on the separate grounds stated herein.

STATE v. KINNEY

762 A.2d 833 (Vt. 2000)

DOOLEY, J.

Defendant Steven Kinney was convicted by a jury on charges of kidnapping, aggravated sexual assault, and lewd and lascivious behavior. He was sentenced to two concurrent terms of forty-years-to-life imprisonment and one concurrent term of four-to-five-years imprisonment. . . .

The State called Dr. Jan Tyler to testify about rape trauma syndrome and the characteristics and conduct of rape victims. . . . Dr. Tyler testified that rape trauma syndrome is associated with post-traumatic stress disorder—that is, it is a set of behaviors and symptoms experienced by victims of trauma. She explained that victims of severe trauma commonly experience symptoms such as nightmares, anxiety, and fear as a result of the trauma. Victims of rape, in particular, may experience symptoms such as difficulty in interpersonal relationships, guilt, shame, and sexual dysfunction.

Dr. Tyler also testified that studies have shown that victims of rape are more likely to resist their attacker by making verbal protests than by struggling or screaming, and that victims are less likely to resist if force is used or threatened. Furthermore, she said that it is not unusual for victims to delay in reporting a rape, especially if the attacker is an acquaintance, and that a rape victim may be more likely to report to a friend first, rather than to someone with whom she is having an intimate relationship. This delay in reporting is related to the feelings of guilt and shame experienced due to the trauma of the rape. Dr. Tyler then testified to statistics regarding the rate of false reporting of rape. Finally, she testified that, although she had no statistics, she thought it would not be unusual for a victim of rape to fall asleep immediately after the assault, due to the physical exertion and psychological responses to the trauma such as denial and withdrawal. . . .

[M]ost of the evidence offered by the expert, not including that about the rate of false reporting, is of the type we have found admissible in *State v. Catsam*, 148 Vt. 366, 534 A.2d 184 (1987), and its progeny, with respect to child sexual abuse. *Catsam* involved expert evidence describing post-traumatic stress disorder suffered by child victims of sexual assault. We held such evidence was admissible to help the jury understand the evidence because "[t]he unique psychological effects of sexual assault on children place the average juror at a disadvantage in understanding the behavior of the victim." We amplified on the theory of admissibility in [*State v. Gokey*, 574 A.2d 766 (Vt. 1990)]:

> "Profile or syndrome evidence is evidence elicited from an expert that a person is a member of a class of persons who share a common physical, emotional, or mental condition. [T]he condition must be one that is generally recognized in the field." Profile evidence is typically admitted in evidence to assist the jury in understanding "superficially bizarre behavior" of a putative victim, such as a child's ambivalence about pursuing a sexual abuse complaint, or a child's recantation of an earlier accusation. In these situations, the expert's testimony may be useful to dispel misconceptions about the behavior of victims of certain crimes and to show that the conduct of the complaining witness, however seemingly unusual, is consistent with the profile. The function of the testimony is thus primarily rehabilitative, where behaviors such as delay in reporting, recantation, or a continued relationship with the alleged abuser may be mistaken as impeaching the credibility of the child.

Once we ruled such evidence is admissible in *Catsam*, and followed with decisions defining the outside contours of admissibility, PTSD evidence involving child victims became admissible in the trial courts. . . . The admissibility standard continues despite the intervening issuance of the *Daubert* decision, and the adoption of its holding in *State v. Brooks*, 162 Vt. 26, 30, 643 A.2d 226, 229 (1993), and [*State v. Streich*, 163 Vt. 331, 342, 658 A.2d 38, 46 (1995)]. . . . The basic thrust of *Daubert* is that the widely-accepted standard of novel scientific and technical evidence, announced first in *Frye v. United States*, 293 F. 1013 (D.C. Cir. 1923), did not survive the adoption of Federal Rule of Evidence 702, which contains a more flexible standard of reliability and relevancy. Largely because we had adopted F.R.E. 702 as V.R.E. 702, we adopted the *Daubert* standard as our own.

We affirmed the admission of PTSD evidence in *Catsam* under V.R.E. 702 using a flexible standard of admissibility that is fully consistent with *Daubert*. . . . Our emphasis in *Catsam* was on whether the expert evidence of PTSD, and related explanations of the typical behavior of child sexual assault victims, would "assist the trier of fact to understand the evidence." V.R.E. 702. We also drew on decisions from other states to show the evidence was reliable. . . . [S]cientific or technical evidence which is novel to us is frequently not novel to many other state and federal courts. To the extent the evaluation of these courts is complete and persuasive, we can affirmatively rely upon it in reaching our own decision. . . .

We concur with the trial court that expert evidence of rape trauma syndrome and the associated typical behavior of adult rape victims is admissible to assist the jury in evaluating the evidence, and frequently to respond to defense claims that the victim's behavior after the alleged rape was inconsistent with the claim that the rape occurred. As with child sexual abuse victims, the jury may be at a loss to understand the behavior of a rape victim. See D. McCord, *The Admissibility of Expert Testimony Regarding Rape Trauma Syndrome in Rape Prosecutions*, 26 B.C. L. Rev. 1143, 1177 (1985) (discussing the use of rape trauma syndrome to explain unusual behavior of the victim); *People v. Hampton*, 746 P.2d 947, 952 (Colo. 1987) (admitting expert testimony on rape trauma syndrome to explain delay in reporting); *Rivera v. State*, 840 P.2d 933, 938-39 (Wyo. 1992) (same); *Terrio v. McDonough*, 16 Mass. App. Ct. 163, 450 N.E.2d 190, 198 (1983) (explaining that it would not be remarkable for rape victim to return to scene with attacker or feel safe in his company after the event). For example, the defense made much of the fact that defendant's parents were close by when the sexual contact took place but heard no signs of a struggle, that the victim appeared to be sleeping peacefully in defendant's bed the next morning, and that she failed to immediately tell her boyfriend she had been raped. Dr. Tyler's testimony explained why a rape victim might exhibit these behaviors.

For the purpose the evidence was used here, it is sufficiently reliable to be admitted. See, e.g., *People v. Taylor*, 75 N.Y.2d 277, 552 N.E.2d 131, 134-35 (1990). Rape trauma syndrome is professionally recognized as a type of post-traumatic stress disorder, and the behavioral characteristics of rape victims has been the subject of numerous professional studies. See generally Note, *"Lies, Damned Lies, and Statistics"? Psychological Syndrome Evidence in the Courtroom After Daubert*, 71 Ind. L.J. 753, 760-61 (1996). As the trial court noted in this case, Dr. Tyler was prepared to address some of the studies that formed the bases for her opinions if the defendant raised them in cross-examination.

We note that the evidence here was of a type that the danger of improper usage or excessive prejudice was at a minimum. The expert never interviewed the victim and offered no opinion whether the victim suffered from rape trauma syndrome or exhibited any of the behavior of a rape victim.[16] Thus, there was little risk that Dr. Tyler would be seen as a truth detector.

We do not, however, have the same view of the expert's testimony about the incidence of false reporting by rape victims. The prosecutor asked Dr. Tyler whether "there are any data on the issue of false reporting that you are aware of?" She answered:

> False reporting, the percentages are very low. About two percent. That's about the same as any other crime that's committed. In other words, the number of people who would report a burglary that didn't happen is about the same as people who would report a rape, with one difference. The statistics for the rape include those reports that are made and then either withdrawn by the victim for whatever reason, either they were false or there's a fear of going through the legal system, or they're being pressured by other persons. Those also include reports that the police will not arrest on because they don't feel they have enough evidence. And they also include those that don't get to trial because the prosecutor feels it's not a winnable case. So when you get down to literal false reporting of this really never happened, it's very small.

In short, Dr. Tyler testified that at least 98% of the rapes reported actually occurred.

In *State v. Percy*, [507 A.2d 955 (Vt. 1986)], a rape case in which defendant claimed amnesia caused by insanity and consent of the victim, three psychiatrists testified for the State that rapists typically claim consent or amnesia. We reversed defendant's conviction in part because of the admission of this testimony. We concluded that explanations or excuses offered by other rapists were not relevant, and, in any event, the prejudicial effect of the testimony outweighed the probative value because the jury could have convicted defendant because "he fit the mold" and not because of the evidence in the case.

Similarly, in *Catsam*, we found inadmissible an expert's opinion that child victims of sexual abuse do not make up stories of the abuse. As in this case, the evidence was offered as part of the expert's explanation of the

---

16. In a twist, defendant suggests that Dr. Tyler's testimony was inadmissible because she did not address whether the victim suffered from the syndrome and did not tie the syndrome to the testimony on the common behavior of rape victims, some of which related to how victims react during the rape before any syndrome developed. We reiterate the point of *State v. Wetherbee*, [594 A.2d 390, 394 (Vt. 1991)], that the opinions of experts who have examined the victim are much more likely to be seen as vouching for the victim's story than the opinions of experts who have never examined the victim. Moreover, the common behaviors of rape victims are directly related to the rape trauma syndrome in the sense that the stress reaction creates a profile. This testimony has been the least controversial of the expert evidence related to rape trauma syndrome. Some courts and commentators have concluded that rape trauma syndrome evidence should be admissible solely for this purpose. . . .

typical behavior of victims. We concluded that the expert testimony was tantamount to an expert opinion that the victim was telling the truth and that it invaded the proper role of the jury. . . .

Dr. Tyler's testimony on the rate of false reporting clearly went over the line as explained in *Percy* and *Catsam*. The jury could infer from her testimony that scientific studies have shown that almost no woman falsely claims to have been raped and convict defendant on that basis.

Although the evidence of the incidence of false reporting of rape accusations was inadmissible and prejudicial, [defendant failed to preserve this issue for appeal]. . . . We cannot conclude that failure to exclude the inadmissible expert testimony caused a miscarriage of justice in this case. Accordingly, we find no plain error. . . . *Affirmed*.

D. MICHAEL RISINGER, NAVIGATING EXPERT RELIABILITY: ARE CRIMINAL STANDARDS OF CERTAINTY BEING LEFT ON THE DOCK?

64 Alb. L. Rev. 99 (2000)

In its general meaning, all "syndrome" means is a group of symptoms or signs typical of an underlying cause or disease. In regard to physical illnesses with established causal agents, the concept of syndrome is uncontroversial. With regard to behavioral or psychological manifestations where the "cause" may commonly be constructed partly from the symptoms themselves, the notion of "syndrome" is more controversial. These problems are compounded by ethical restrictions on experimental research into behavioral syndromes, making most of the data utilized in their identification necessarily the product of inherently less reliable methodology. This is further complicated by the fact that many of those involved in both supplying the initial "data" and in analyzing it and constructing it into theories may wear two hats: researchers looking for empirically defensible constructs of reality, and therapists committed to helping their patients regardless of the objective reality of the patients' particular accounts. To this is sometimes added a third role, social policy advocate for the groups to which the patients are perceived to belong. It is not surprising that the result of all this is not always the most dependable science, especially in its forensic applications.

In a sense, any mental condition listed in any version of the [American Psychiatric Association's] Diagnostic and Statistical Manual is a "syndrome", and testimony concerning such syndromes has been part of the evidence proffered by criminal defendants on issues of insanity and diminished capacity since long before the first such manual. Nevertheless, the first asserted condition commonly associated with the modern controversy over "syndrome" evidence, "Rape Trauma Syndrome," surfaced in the psychological literature in 1974, in civil courtrooms in 1978, and criminal courtrooms in 1979. Then, spurred by the publication of Lenore Walker's influential, if empirically thin, 1979 book *The Battered Woman* (wherein was coined the phrase "battered woman syndrome"), and by the 1980 issuance of the DSM-III, which promoted the phenomenon of post traumatic stress effects to a full scale disorder, Battered Woman Syndrome and Post Traumatic Stress Disorder (PTSD) followed Rape Trauma Syndrome into the courtroom, trailed not long after by Child Sexual Abuse Accommodation Syndrome (CSAAS).

When used as defense-proffered evidence on insanity, diminished capacity or mens rea questions . . . these asserted "syndromes" seem to have been held to fairly low dependability standards, which was in keeping with the fairly lax foundational standards of the period. . . . [Syndrome evidence] has been generally received in most jurisdictions when so proffered by criminal defendants.

It was not long before prosecutors too found use for such testimony; however, not limited to state-of-mind issues, but bearing upon the brute fact issues of the happening of the crime or the identity of the perpetrator, and that presented a different set of jurisprudential problems. . . . [B]y the time of the decision in *Daubert*, certain general approaches to such prosecution evidence had already begun to work themselves out. A minority of jurisdictions allowed prosecutors to use some or all syndrome evidence pretty openly in very specific proof of the objective elements of the crime. In typical cases, the experts would interview the victim, evaluate their rendition and affect, then conclude that they demonstrated the syndrome and therefore had been the victim of battering, rape, or child molestation. The expert would generally not be allowed to explicitly say that the victim was truthful, or to identify the perpetrator of the crime, but the diagnostic finding not only provided evidence of the actus reus, but by implication corroborated the veracity, and to a lesser degree, the accuracy of the victim's rendition.

The majority of jurisdictions would not go so far. They have held that syndrome evidence was not admissible to prove the existence of the crime, but could be used in cases where there was a delay in reporting the crime, or some other detail of the victim's situation, which common assumptions might cause one to overvalue in discounting the victim's testimony. In those cases (and such conditions were commonly present) the expert would be allowed to explain the aspects of the syndrome that accounted for such a delay, and also normally to opine on whether the characteristics of the victim were consistent with the syndrome. And, beyond this, virtually every jurisdiction allowed expert testimony in such circumstances if the expert did not evaluate the individual victim, but testified as a clear and unambiguous educational expert summarizing what the expert claimed was known to science about the syndrome. Checking the available research to see if the empirical record supported such assertions was done haphazardly at best.

CHRISTOPHER SLOBOGIN, DOUBTS ABOUT *DAUBERT*: PSYCHIATRIC ANECDATA AS A CASE STUDY
57 Wash. & Lee. L. Rev. 919, 940-941 (2000)

Somewhat surprisingly, *Daubert* initially had little impact on the admissibility of behavioral science testimony in criminal cases. Despite the suspect reliability of such testimony, the proportion of cases in *Daubert* jurisdictions admitting expert evidence about such subjects as mental disorders, syndromes, intent, dangerousness, and child sex abuse victims either remained the same or actually increased in the first five years after that decision as compared to the five years prior to *Daubert*. Most courts . . . avoided taking a hard look at the scientific credentials of psychiatric opinion evidence, either by explicitly classifying it or by implicitly treating it as specialized knowledge, thus exempting it from *Daubert*'s threshold for "scientific" testimony.

After *Kumho* that tactic is no longer available, at least in federal court. *Daubert*'s reliability requirement now clearly applies to all expert testimony. The question remains as to how courts should define reliability in the criminal context.

3. Probabilistic Evidence

a. A Probability Primer

Expert testimony purporting to apply the laws of probability has long been a source of particular concern and puzzlement, both for courts and for commentators. In one sense, of course, all proof is probabilistic; that is why Rule 401 of the Federal Rules of Evidence treats evidence as relevant as long as it tends to make some material fact "more probable or less probable" than it otherwise would be. But ordinarily the probabilities assessed in trials are left unquantified. When experts try to attach numbers to these probabilities, special difficulties arise.

The difficulties are not chiefly mathematical. In most cases the underlying mathematics is relatively uncomplicated, involving nothing more sophisticated than high-school algebra. The difficulties are philosophical: they pertain to how numerical probabilities should be understood, and for what purposes they may properly be employed. To understand those issues, and to follow the arguments that courts and commentators have made about them, it helps to be familiar with some basic concepts of mathematical probability.

Mathematicians and statisticians typically use the expression "$P(X)$" to stand for the probability of X, and the expression "$P(\sim X)$" to stand for the probability of the opposite—"not X." They define probabilities to run from zero to one: something that is impossible has a probability of zero, and something that is certain has a probability of one. And, by definition, $P(X)$ and $P(\sim X)$ add up to one, no matter what X is. So, for example, if we pick a playing card at random from a standard deck of 52 cards, and if X is "picking the jack of hearts," then:

$$P(X) \;=\; 1/52$$
$$P(\sim X) \;=\; 51/52$$
$$\text{and} \quad P(X) \,+\, P(\sim X) \;=\; (1/52) \,+\, (51/52) \;=\; (52/52) \;=\; 1$$

In everyday conversation, the terms "probability" and "odds" are often used interchangeably. But mathematicians and statisticians use the terms to refer to two different figures, albeit figures that each can be calculated from the other. When mathematicians and statisticians speak of the "odds" of something, they mean the probability of that thing, divided by the opposite probability. So, for example, the probability of picking of the jack of hearts from a standard deck of 52 playing cards—what we have been calling "P(X)"—is 1/52. The *odds* of picking the jack of hearts can therefore be calculated as follows:

$$P(X) \div P(\sim X) = (1/52) \div (51/52) = 1/51$$

This may make intuitive sense if you read the fraction as "1 to 51." Since there is one card that is the jack of hearts and 51 cards that are not, the odds of picking the jack of hearts are 1 to 51. Similarly, if the probability of something (say, a coin landing heads) is 1/2, then the odds are "1 to 1," which mathematically is 1/1, or 1.

A little bit more terminology: the expression "P(X|Y)" commonly refers to something called a "conditional probability"—in this case, the conditional probability of X given Y. If X is "picking the jack of hearts," and Y is "picking a jack," then P(X|Y) is the probability of picking the jack of hearts *if we know* that we have picked a jack. Since there are four jacks, and we have an equal chance of picking any of them, P(X|Y) in this example is 1/4. On the other hand, the conditional probability of Y given X—i.e., P(Y|X)—is one. If we know that we have picked the jack of hearts, then we necessarily know that we have picked a jack.

Sometimes knowing one thing tells us nothing about the probability of some other thing. Knowing that we have picked a jack from an ordinary deck of 52 playing cards, for example, tells us nothing about the suit of the card we have selected. We can express this mathematically. If Y is "picking a jack," and Z is "picking a heart," then:

$$P(Y|Z) = P(Y) = 1/13$$
$$\text{and } P(Z|Y) = P(Z) = 1/4$$

When, as in this example, P(Y|Z) = P(Y), and P(Z|Y) = P(Z), mathematicians say that the probabilities of Y and Z are "independent."

Some important conclusions follow from all these definitions. First, independent probabilities can be multiplied together to calculate a so-called "joint probability"—i.e., the probability of two different things both happening. For example, the joint probability of picking a jack and picking a heart—i.e., the probability of picking the jack of hearts—can be calculated as follows:

$$P(X) = P(Y \text{ and } Z) = P(Y) \times P(Z) = (1/4) \times (1/13) = 1/52$$

where, again, X is "picking the jack of hearts," Y is "picking a jack," and Z is "picking a heart." This is sometimes called the "product rule."

The product rule works, though, only if Y and Z are independent. We could stop Y and Z from being independent—we could make them "dependent"—by removing some cards from the deck. Suppose we remove the jack of clubs and the jack of spades, leaving only 50 cards—13 of which are hearts, two of which are jacks, and one of which is the jack of hearts. Now P(Y), the probability of randomly picking a jack, is 2/50 rather than 1/13, and the P(Z), the probability of picking a heart, is 13/50 rather than 1/4. And P(Y and Z), the probability of picking the jack of hearts, is 1/50, or 0.02. But

$$P(Y) \times P(Z) = (2/50) \times (13/50) = 0.0104$$

and therefore

$$P(Y \text{ and } Z) \neq P(Y) \times P(Z)$$

There is a more general version of the product rule, though, that works even when the underlying probabilities are dependent rather than independent. Here it is:

$$P(Y \text{ and } Z) = P(Y) \times P(Z|Y)$$

In the case of our 50-card deck, P(Z | Y)—the probability of picking a heart given that we have picked a jack—is 1/2, because there are only two jacks left in the deck, and one of them is the jack of hearts. So:

$$P(Y \text{ and } Z) = P(Y) \times P(Z|Y) = (2/50) \times (1/2) = 1/50$$

Because P(Y and Z) must be the same as P(Z and Y), we can also run the calculation the other way:

$$P(Y \text{ and } Z) = P(Z) \times P(Y|Z)$$

For the 50-card deck, P(Y | Z)—the probability of picking a jack given that we have picked a heart—is 1/13, because all 13 hearts are left in the deck. So:

$$P(Y \text{ and } Z) = P(Z) \times P(Y|Z) = (13/50) \times (1/13) = 1/50$$

Remember, when probabilities are independent—as they for picking a jack and picking a heart out of a standard, 52-card deck—P(Z | Y) = P(Z) and P(Y | Z) = P(Y). So when probabilities are independent, the more general version of the product rule reduces to the simpler version presented earlier:

$$P(Y \text{ and } Z) = P(Y) \times P(Z|Y) = P(Y) \times P(Z)$$

You may have noticed, perhaps with annoyance, that so far we have said nothing about what a probability *is*—all we have discussed is how they can be calculated. That is because mathematicians and statisticians have never been able to agree about what probabilities are. Mathematicians generally have contented themselves with describing how probabilities behave, whatever they actually represent. Among statisticians, on the other hand, there is a longstanding debate about what probability values mean. Some statisticians argue that a probability is simply a long-term frequency: the probability of picking the jack of hearts from a standard deck of playing cards is 1/52, they say, because if we repeat the experiment thousands of times, we will pick the jack of hearts roughly one out of every 52 times. Statisticians holding this view, sometimes called "frequentists," argue that the mathematical theory of probability, at least in its traditional form, cannot meaningfully be applied to probabilities of the sort typically at issue in a trial—e.g., the probability that a particular criminal defendant robbed a particular bank.

But other statisticians disagree. They argue that probabilities can be understood to represent subjective degrees of confidence. For statisticians of this school, sometimes called "subjectivists," it makes perfect sense to say, for example, "there is a 99% probability that the defendant robbed the bank." That simply means that we are as confident that the defendant robbed the bank as we would be of randomly drawing the jack of hearts from an imaginary deck of 100 cards, 99 of which are the jack of hearts.

Statisticians who take this view are sometimes also called "Bayesians," because they often make use of a formula called Bayes' Rule or Bayes' Theorem, after Thomas Bayes, an eighteenth-century English clergyman and statistician who focussed attention on it. The formula, which can be derived from the basic rules of probability discussed above, is as follows:

$$[P(A|B) \div P(\sim A|B)] = [P(A) \div P(\sim A)] \times [P(B|A) \div P(B|\sim A)]$$

Notice that the first term on the right side of the equation—$[P(A) \div P(\sim A)]$—simply represents the odds of A, as defined above. The term on the left side of the equation—$[P(A \mid B) \div P(\sim A \mid B)]$—represents the "conditional odds" of A given B, i.e., what the odds of A become if we take B as a given. So the formula can be rewritten like this:

$$\text{odds}(A|B) = \text{odds}(A) \times [P(B|A) \div P(B|\sim A)]$$

If A is some fact being litigated—say, whether the defendant robbed the bank—and B is a piece of evidence—say, the robber was the same height as the defendant—then Bayes' Theorem provides, some statisticians believe, a method for calculating the probability of the litigated fact in light of the evidence. All we need to know, or at least be able to estimate, is what the probability of guilt would be *without* the evidence, and the ratio of two conditional probabilities: the probability that the height would match if the defendant were guilty (which presumably is one), and the probability that the height would match if the defendant were innocent (which will depend on how unusual the defendant's height is). All of this makes sense, though, only if it makes sense to quantify the probability of the defendant's guilt, and to combine that number mathematically with probabilities derived from long-term frequencies (like how often a man selected at random would be approximately 6 feet tall). Reverend Bayes thought it did, and so do many statisticians today—but many others do not.

b. "Trial by Mathematics"

PEOPLE v. COLLINS

438 P.2d 33 (Cal. 1968)

SULLIVAN, Justice.

We deal here with the novel question whether evidence of mathematical probability has been properly introduced and used by the prosecution in a criminal case. While we discern no inherent incompatibility between the disciplines of law and mathematics and intend no general disapproval or disparagement of the latter as an auxiliary in the fact-finding processes of the former, we cannot uphold the technique employed in the instant case.... Mathematics, a veritable sorcerer in our computerized society, while assisting the trier of fact in the search for truth, must not cast a spell over him. We conclude that on the record before us defendant should not have had his guilt determined by the odds and that he is entitled to a new trial. We reverse the judgment.

A jury found defendant Malcolm Ricardo Collins and his wife defendant Janet Louise Collins guilty of second degree robbery. Malcolm appeals from the judgment of conviction. Janet has not appealed.[17]

On June 18, 1964, about 11:30 a.m., Mrs. Juanita Brooks, who had been shopping, was walking home along an alley in the San Pedro area of the City of Los Angeles. She was pulling behind her a wicker basket carryall containing groceries and had her purse on top of the packages. She was using a cane. As she stooped down to pick up an empty carton, she was suddenly pushed to the ground by a person whom she neither saw nor heard approach. She was stunned by the fall and felt some pain. She managed to look up and saw a young woman running from the scene. According to Mrs. Brooks the latter appeared to weigh about 145 pounds, was wearing "something dark," and had hair "between a dark blond and a light blond," but lighter than the color of defendant Janet Collins' hair as it appeared at trial. Immediately after the incident, Mrs. Brooks discovered that her purse, containing between $35 and $40, was missing.

About the same time as the robbery, John Bass, who lived on the street at the end of the alley, was in front of his house watering his lawn. His attention was attracted by 'a lot of crying and screaming' coming from the alley. As he looked in that direction, he saw a woman run out of the alley and enter a yellow automobile parked across the street from him. He was unable to give the make of the car. The car started off immediately and pulled wide around another parked vehicle so that in the narrow street it passed within six feet of Bass. The latter then saw that it was being driven by a male Negro, wearing a mustache and beard. At the trial Bass identified defendant as the driver of the yellow automobile. However, an attempt was

17. Hereinafter, the term "defendant" is intended to apply only to Malcolm, but the term "defendants" to Malcolm and Janet.

made to impeach his identification by his admission that at the preliminary hearing he testified to an uncertain identification at the police lineup shortly after the attack on Mrs. Brooks, when defendant was beardless. . . .

At the seven-day trial the prosecution experienced some difficulty in establishing the identities of the perpetrators of the crime. The victim could not identify Janet and had never seen defendant. The identification by the witness Bass, who observed the girl run out of the alley and get into the automobile, was incomplete as to Janet and may have been weakened as to defendant. There was also evidence, introduced by the defense, that Janet had worn light-colored clothing on the day in question, but both the victim and Bass testified that the girl they observed had worn dark clothing.

In an apparent attempt to bolster the identifications, the prosecutor called an instructor of mathematics at a state college. Through this witness he sought to establish that, assuming the robbery was committed by a Caucasian woman with a blond ponytail who left the scene accompanied by a Negro with a beard and mustache, there was an overwhelming probability that the crime was committed by any couple answering such distinctive characteristics. The witness testified, in substance, to the "product rule," which states that the probability of the joint occurrence of a number of mutually independent events is equal to the product of the individual probabilities that each of the events will occur.[18] Without presenting any statistical evidence whatsoever in support of the probabilities for the factors selected, the prosecutor then proceeded to have the witness assume probability factors for the various characteristics which he deemed to be shared by the guilty couple and all other couples answering to such distinctive characteristics.[19]

18. In the example employed for illustrative purposes at the trial, the probability of rolling one die and coming up with a "2" is 1/6, that is, any one of the six faces of a die has one chance in six of landing face up on any particular roll. The probability of rolling two "2"s in succession is $1/6 \times 1/6$, or 1/36, that is, on only one occasion out of 36 double rolls (or the roll of two dice), will the selected number land face up on each roll or die.

19. Although the prosecutor insisted that the factors he used were only for illustrative purposes—to demonstrate how the probability of the occurrence of mutually independent factors affected the probability that they would occur together—he nevertheless attempted to use factors which he personally related to the distinctive characteristics of defendants. In his argument to the jury he invited the jurors to apply their own factors, and asked defense counsel to suggest what the latter would deem as reasonable. The prosecutor himself proposed the individual probabilities set out in the table below. Although the transcript of the examination of the mathematics instructor and the information volunteered by the prosecutor at that time create some uncertainty as to precisely which of the characteristics the prosecutor assigned to the individual probabilities, he restated in his argument to the jury that they should be as follows:

	Characteristic	*Individual Probability*
A.	Partly yellow automobile	1/10
B.	Man with mustache	1/4
C.	Girl with ponytail	1/10
D.	Girl with blond hair	1/3
E.	Negro man with beard	1/10
F.	Interracial couple in car	1/1000

In his brief on appeal defendant agrees that the foregoing appeared on a table presented in the trial court.

Applying the product rule to his own factors the prosecutor arrived at a probability that there was but one chance in 12 million that any couple possessed the distinctive characteristics of the defendants. Accordingly, under this theory, it was to be inferred that there could be but one chance in 12 million that defendants were innocent and that another equally distinctive couple actually committed the robbery. Expanding on what he had thus purported to suggest as a hypothesis, the prosecutor offered the completely unfounded and improper testimonial assertion that, in his opinion, the factors he had assigned were "conservative estimates" and that, in reality "the chances of anyone else besides these defendants being there, . . . having every similarity, . . . is somewhat like one in a billion."

Objections were timely made to the mathematician's testimony on the grounds that it was immaterial, that it invaded the province of the jury, and that it was based on unfounded assumptions. The objections were "temporarily overruled" and the evidence admitted subject to a motion to strike. When that motion was made at the conclusion of the direct examination, the court denied it, stating that the testimony had been received only for the "purpose of illustrating the mathematical probabilities of various matters, the possibilities for them occurring or re-occurring." . . .

As we shall explain, the prosecution's introduction and use of mathematical probability statistics injected two fundamental prejudicial errors into the case: (1) The testimony itself lacked an adequate foundation both in evidence and in statistical theory; and (2) the testimony and the manner in which the prosecution used it distracted the jury from its proper and requisite function of weighing the evidence on the issue of guilt, encouraged the jurors to rely upon an engaging but logically irrelevant expert demonstration, foreclosed the possibility of an effective defense by an attorney apparently unschooled in mathematical refinements, and placed the jurors and defense counsel at a disadvantage in sifting relevant fact from inapplicable theory.

We initially consider the defects in the testimony itself. As we have indicated, the specific technique presented through the mathematician's testimony and advanced by the prosecutor to measure the probabilities in question suffered from two basic and pervasive defects—an inadequate evidentiary foundation and an inadequate proof of statistical independence. First, as to the foundation requirement, we find the record devoid of any evidence relating to any of the six individual probability factors used by the prosecutor and ascribed by him to the six characteristics as we have set them out in footnote 10, ante. To put it another way, the prosecution produced no evidence whatsoever showing, or from which it could be in any way inferred, that only one out of every ten cars which might have been at the scene of the robbery was partly yellow, that only one out of every four men who might have been there wore a mustache, that only one out of every ten girls who might have been there wore a ponytail, or that any of the other individual probability factors listed were even roughly accurate.[20]

---

20. We seriously doubt that such evidence could ever be compiled since no statistician could possibly determine after the fact which cars, or which individuals, "might" have been present at the scene of the robbery; certainly there is no reason to suppose that the human

The bare, inescapable fact is that the prosecution made no attempt to offer any such evidence. Instead, through leading questions having perfunctorily elicited from the witness the response that the latter could not assign a probability factor for the characteristics involved,[21] the prosecutor himself suggested what the various probabilities should be and these became the basis of the witness' testimony (see fn. 10, ante). It is a curious circumstance of this adventure in proof that the prosecutor not only made his own assertions of these factors in the hope that they were "conservative" but also in later argument to the jury invited the jurors to substitute their "estimates" should they wish to do so. We can hardly conceive of a more fatal gap in the prosecution's scheme of proof. A foundation for the admissibility of the witness' testimony was never even attempted to be laid, let alone established. His testimony was neither made to rest on his own testimonial knowledge nor presented by proper hypothetical questions based upon valid data in the record. . . .

But, as we have indicated, there was another glaring defect in the prosecution's technique, namely an inadequate proof of the statistical independence of the six factors. No proof was presented that the characteristics selected were mutually independent, even though the witness himself acknowledged that such condition was essential to the proper application of the "product rule" or "multiplication rule." To the extent that the traits or characteristics were not mutually independent (e.g. Negroes with beards and men with mustaches obviously represent overlapping categories), the "product rule" would inevitably yield a wholly erroneous and exaggerated result even if all of the individual components had been determined with precision. (Siegel, Nonparametric Statistics for the Behavioral Sciences (1956) 19; see generally Harmon, Modern Factor Analysis (1960).)

In the instant case, therefore, because of the aforementioned two defects—the inadequate evidentiary foundation and the inadequate proof of statistical independence—the technique employed by the prosecutor could only lead to wild conjecture without demonstrated relevancy to the issues presented. It acquired no redeeming quality from the prosecutor's statement that it was being used only "for illustrative purposes" since, as we shall point out, the prosecutor's subsequent utilization of the mathematical testimony was not confined within such limits.

We now turn to the second fundamental error caused by the probability testimony. Quite apart from our foregoing objections to the specific technique employed by the prosecution to estimate the probability in question, we think that the entire enterprise upon which the prosecution embarked, and which was directed to the objective of measuring the likelihood of a random couple possessing the characteristics allegedly

and automotive populations of San Pedro, California, include all potential culprits—or, conversely, that all members of these populations are proper candidates for inclusion. Thus the sample from which the relevant probabilities would have to be derived is itself undeterminable. (See generally, Yaman, Statistics, An Introductory Analysis (1964), ch.I.)

21. The prosecutor asked the mathematics instructor: "Now, let me see if you can be of some help to us with some independent factors, and you have some paper you may use. Your specialty does not equip you, I suppose, to give us some probability of such things as a yellow car as contrasted with any other kind of car, does it? . . . I appreciate the fact that you can't assign a probability for a car being yellow as contrasted to some other car, can you? A. No, I couldn't."

distinguishing the robbers, was gravely misguided. At best, it might yield an estimate as to how infrequently bearded Negroes drive yellow cars in the company of blonde females with ponytails.

The prosecution's approach, however, could furnish the jury with absolutely no guidance on the crucial issue: *Of the admittedly few such couples, which one, if any, was guilty of committing this robbery?* Probability theory necessarily remains silent on that question, since no mathematical equation can prove beyond a reasonable doubt (1) that the guilty couple in fact possessed the characteristics described by the People's witnesses, or even (2) that only *one* couple possessing those distinctive characteristics could be found in the entire Los Angeles area.

As to the first inherent failing we observe that the prosecution's theory of probability rested on the assumption that the witnesses called by the People had conclusively established that the guilty couple possessed the precise characteristics relied upon by the prosecution. But no mathematical formula could ever establish beyond a reasonable doubt that the prosecution's witnesses correctly observed and accurately described the distinctive features which were employed to link defendants to the crime. Conceivably, for example, the guilty couple might have included a light-skinned Negress with bleached hair rather than a Caucasian blonde; or the driver of the car might have been wearing a false beard as a disguise; or the prosecution's witnesses might simply have been unreliable.[22]

The foregoing risks of error permeate the prosecution's circumstantial case. Traditionally, the jury weighs such risks in evaluating the credibility and probative value of trial testimony, but the likelihood of human error or of falsification obviously cannot be quantified; that likelihood must therefore be excluded from any effort to assign a number to the probability of guilt or innocence. Confronted with an equation which purports to yield a numerical index of probable guilt, few juries could resist the temptation to accord disproportionate weight to that index; only an exceptional juror, and indeed only a defense attorney schooled in mathematics, could successfully keep in mind the fact that the probability computed by the prosecution can represent, *at best*, the likelihood that a random couple would share the characteristics testified to by the People's witnesses—*not necessarily the characteristics of the actually guilty couple.*

As to the second inherent failing in the prosecution's approach, even assuming that the first failing could be discounted, the most a mathematical computation could ever yield would be a measure of the probability that a random couple would possess the distinctive features in question. In the present case, for example, the prosecution attempted to compute the probability that a random couple would include a bearded Negro, a blonde girl with a ponytail, and a partly yellow car; the prosecution urged that this probability was no more than one in 12 million. Even accepting this

22. In the instant case, for instance, the victim could not state whether the girl had a ponytail, although the victim observed the girl as she ran away. The witness Bass, on the other hand, was sure that the girl whom he saw had a ponytail. The demonstration engaged in by the prosecutor also leaves no room for the possibility, although perhaps a small one, that the girl whom the victim and the witness observed was, in fact, the same girl.

conclusion as arithmetically accurate, however, one still could not conclude that the Collinses were probably *the* guilty couple. . . .

Again, few defense attorneys, and certainly few jurors, could be expected to comprehend this basic flaw in the prosecution's analysis. Conceivably even the prosecutor erroneously believed that his equation established a high probability that no other bearded Negro in the Los Angeles area drove a yellow car accompanied by a ponytailed blonde. In any event, although his technique could demonstrate no such thing, he solemnly told the jury that he had supplied mathematical proof of guilt.

Sensing the novelty of that notion, the prosecutor told the jurors that the traditional idea of proof beyond a reasonable doubt represented "the most hackneyed, stereotyped, trite, misunderstood concept in criminal law." He sought to reconcile the jury to the risk that, under his "new math" approach to criminal jurisprudence, "on some rare occasion . . . an innocent person may be convicted." "Without taking that risk," the prosecution continued, "life would be intolerable . . . because . . . there would be immunity for the Collinses, for people who chose not to be employed to go down and push old ladies down and take their money and be immune because how could we ever be sure they are the ones who did it?"

In essence this argument of the prosecutor was calculated to persuade the jury to convict defendants whether or not they were convinced of their guilt to a moral certainty and beyond a reasonable doubt. Undoubtedly the jurors were unduly impressed by the mystique of the mathematical demonstration but were unable to assess its relevancy or value. Although we make no appraisal of the proper applications of mathematical techniques in the proof of facts, we have strong feelings that such applications, particularly in a criminal case, must be critically examined in view of the substantial unfairness to a defendant which may result from ill conceived techniques with which the trier of fact is not technically equipped to cope. We feel that the technique employed in the case before us falls into the latter category.

We conclude that the court erred in admitting over defendant's objection the evidence pertaining to the mathematical theory of probability and in denying defendant's motion to strike such evidence. . . . After an examination of the entire cause, including the evidence, we are of the opinion that it is reasonably probable that a result more favorable to defendant would have been reached in the absence of the above error. The judgment against defendant must therefore be reversed. . . .

ROGER C. PARK, EVIDENCE SCHOLARSHIP, OLD AND NEW
75 Minn. L. Rev. 849, 855-856 (1991)

Among American law professors, scholarly interest in probability theory received its most significant boost from a celebrated case, *People v. Collins*, a 1968 decision of the California Supreme Court. . . . The *Collins* case inspired an article in the *Harvard Law Review* arguing that although *Collins* was correct on its facts, experts in other cases properly might use probability theory, in particular Bayes' Theorem, to aid the jury in making identification decisions.[23] The authors suggested a hypothetical case in which the defendant is accused of murdering his girlfriend. A partial palm-print was found on the knife that was used in the murder. It matches the defendant's palm. Yet the palmprint would also match the palm of one in a thousand people chosen at random, which means that in a metropolitan area hundreds of people would have the same palmprint characteristics. How is the jury to use that one in a thousand figure? Bayes' Theorem, which provides a way of determining how an evaluation of probability based upon initial evidence should be modified in light of additional evidence, could serve as a guide to the jury. If the trier of fact believed that the prior probability of defendant's guilt (before taking the palmprint into account) was 25%, Bayes' Theorem indicates that the trier should believe the posterior probability of guilt (after taking the palmprint into account) is 99.9%. The method often yields higher probabilities than intuition would yield. For example, if the prior probability is 25% and the frequency of the palmprint is one in a hundred, the posterior probability of guilt is 97%.

The proposition that the jury should be instructed about Bayes' Theorem attracted the attention of a talented and resourceful debater, Laurence Tribe, then a young assistant professor at the Harvard Law School.[24] Tribe pointed out a host of problems. It would be difficult for jurors who are not familiar with formal probabilities to arrive at a consistent understanding of what they are supposed to do in formulating a prior probability. There is also a danger of the jury "dwarfing soft variables," that is, that the jury might overlook issues that cannot be quantified as it became mesmerized with those that could. Moreover, uncertainty about predicate facts can require the jury to make so many quantification decisions about so many issues that use of the theorem would be more confusing than helpful.

Although Tribe's view seems to have carried the day with regard to the use of Bayes' Theorem in instructing the jury, the debate did stimulate interest in Bayes' Theorem and probability theory. It has spawned a considerable body of scholarship that explores how probability theory might be used as a means of proof or as a way to help scholars model and evaluate trial processes.

STATE v. SPANN

617 A.2d 247 (N.J. 1993)

PER CURIAM.

Defendant, Joseph M. Spann, was convicted of sexual assault, a second-degree crime under *N.J.S.A.* 2C:14-2c(3). The statute criminalizes sexual

23. Finkelstein & Fairley, *A Bayesian Approach to Identification Evidence*, 83 Harv. L. Rev. 489, 501-09 (1970).

24. See Tribe, *Trial by Mathematics: Precision and Ritual in the Legal Process*, 84 Harv. L. Rev. 1329 (1971).

penetration when the defendant has supervisory or disciplinary power, by virtue of his "legal, professional or occupational status" and when the victim is "on probation or parole, or is detained in a hospital, prison or other institution. . . ." Defendant was a corrections officer at the Salem County Jail, where the victim was incarcerated on a detainer from the Immigration and Naturalization Service. . . . The challenged evidence was that defendant was the father of the victim's child, conception clearly having occurred while she was imprisoned. . . . The evidence consisted of blood and tissue tests, including human leukocyte antigen (HLA) tissue tests used to prove not that defendant was or was not *excluded* as the father but that he *was* the father. The specific item of that proof objected to by counsel was the State expert's opinion, based on those tests, that the "probability" of defendant's paternity was 96.55%. Obviously, that probability opinion, if improperly admitted, was highly prejudicial. . . . The expert's quantitative description of the percentage, expressed in non-mathematical terms (known as the "verbal predicate"), was that it was "very likely" defendant was the father. As stated by the prosecutor in summation, "guilt . . . is proved to a mathematical certainty . . . by carefully applying an objective scientific technique to the hard facts of this case."

The expert, testifying that the probability of defendant's paternity was 96.55%, knew absolutely nothing about the facts of the case other than those revealed by the blood and tissue tests of defendant, the victim, and the child, and that defendant was the accused.

Until relatively recently, blood-grouping tests to establish paternity were admissible only to exculpate the accused in paternity cases. *N.J.S.A.* 2A:83-3 (repealed by New Jersey Parentage Act, *L.* 1983, *c.* 17, §23). Science had proven, and there is apparently no question about the validity of the proposition and certainly none raised in this case, that certain blood specimens completely exclude others. Thus, blood specimen "X," found at the scene of the crime and presumably that of the criminal, cannot come from an accused who has blood specimen "Y." Similarly, blood specimens from mother and child that conclusively determine that only a man with blood specimen "X" could be the father eliminate a man with blood specimen "Y." In such cases, if the accused's blood was excluded, he was innocent; in paternity disputes, he was not the father. In New Jersey paternity cases, this limited use of blood tests, to prove only that defendant was *not* the father, was codified in 1939. On the other hand, however, if the blood specimen was of the kind that *could* have come from the purported father, the evidence was apparently inadmissible to prove paternity.

The lack of probative force of this evidence for the purpose of proving paternity was thought to warrant its exclusion. Its identifying factor, the fact for instance that 50% of the population, including the accused, have blood that could have produced a specimen matching that of the father, was deemed too insignificant to justify admission if offered as independent proof of paternity, *i.e.*, sufficient proof by itself. Even though insignificantly probative, it nevertheless was admissible as "a link in the chain of evidence" in criminal trials, just as the alleged assailant's blond hair is used against a blond defendant. *See State v. Beard*, 16 *N.J.* 50, 58-59 (1954) (holding type O—the victim's blood type and also the most common type—blood stains on defendant's clothing admissible as "link in the chain of evidence"); *see also State v. Alexander*, 7 *N.J.* 585, 593-94 (1951) (allowing evidence of defendant's blood type at murder trial for purpose of showing it was of the same type as blood found on the murder weapon), *cert. denied*, 343 *U.S.* 908 (1952).

With the advent of multiple tests of blood samples, geneticists were sometimes able to exclude up to 72% of the population from certain blood types, *i.e.* given that kind of sample, those tests conclusively demonstrated that the sample could have come from only a limited portion of the population—28% of it. And with the discovery and development of HLA tissue testing—a test not of blood alone but of tissues of all kinds—the combination of blood and tissue testing, and on many occasions HLA testing alone, very often brought the exclusionary percentage to 95% and higher. In contrast to earlier blood-group testing, which had limited utility in identifying rare blood types, the advanced HLA systems enable geneticists to identify a rare blood type "in virtually every case."[25]

When the portion of the population excluded ran as high as, *e.g.*, 98%, it became intuitively obvious that if only 2% of the population could produce that sample and defendant was part of the 2%, it was not only consistent with his guilt, but tended to prove it—here that he was the father. Tests of blood and tissue samples started to be admitted not only to prove exclusion but also to prove paternity. With an estimated one out of every six children born out of wedlock in this country, testimony revealing the probability of paternity becomes important, to society in general and to the welfare system in particular. Prodded by federal laws aimed at identifying fathers for child-support purposes where children received welfare benefits, New Jersey amended its parentage laws, for the first time allowing the court to require blood or genetic tests in contested paternity cases and to compel such tests when requested by a party. Whenever HLA tests are ordered by the court, they are admissible in evidence to establish "the positive probability of parentage." *N.J.S.A.* 9:17-51e. Moreover, "evidence

---

25. HLA types correspond to molecules, known as antigens because they react to specific antibodies found in blood as well as on all cells. The production of these antigens is directed by closely-linked genes, known as haplotypes, which are almost always passed as a unit from parent to child and exhibit a substantial number of variations in human population. . . . To illustrate how the HLA system works in identifying paternity: The child in this case had phenotypes (observable traits corresponding to some set of underlying genotypes) A2 A28 B45 B53, and the mother had HLA types A28 A30 B53 B61. These symbols refer to distinct antigens expressed by genes at two locations (the A locus and the B locus) in the human genome. These two genes, located next to one another on the same chromosome, typically are inherited as a haplotype, one from each parent. Thus, the child receives one pair of A and B genes from both the mother and from the father. Because the mother and child have types A28 B53, the child must have inherited the haplotype A2 B45 from the father. Any man who did not possess this obligatory haplotype (A2 B45) could be excluded as a possible father. The HLA test showed that defendant's phenotype was A2 A28 B35 B45, making him a possible father because he possessed the obligatory haplotype. The expert in this case testified that after factoring in the results of the HLA and other blood tests, the probability of exclusion was derived by consulting a table of haplotype frequencies that showed that only 1% of the relevant male population have the inculpatory blood and tissue type, and that the father is found only in that group. Thus, 99% of the relevant male population is excluded and could not be the father.

relating to paternity may include . . . genetic or blood tests, weighted in accordance with evidence, if available, of the statistical probability of the alleged father's paternity". *N.J.S.A.* 9:17-52.

Precisely that kind of positive proof of paternity was used in this criminal case, as it had been in prior civil paternity cases without objection. The State's expert stated that the blood and tissue samples, combined with statistical data reflecting the number of men with the relevant genes, excluded 99% of the North American black male population as possible fathers. In other words, only 1% of the presumed relevant population had the type of blood and tissue that the father must have had, and further, defendant was included within that 1%.

In calculating a final probability of paternity percentage, the expert relied in part on this 99% probability of exclusion. She also relied on an assumption of a 50% prior probability that defendant was the father. This assumption, not based on her knowledge of any evidence whatsoever in the case, placed the odds of defendant being the father—wholly apart from the blood-tissue test—at fifty-fifty. The fifty-fifty odds are usually expressed as "defendant being no more or less likely of being the father than any other man chosen at random." The claim of the victim (that defendant is the father) and the claim of the accused (that he is not) ostensibly are given equal weight. Or, as the expert stated in this case, "everything is equal . . . he may or may not be the father of the child." Based on the various tests, and the fifty-fifty assumption, the expert concluded that "[t]he likelihood of this woman and this man producing this child with all of the genetic makeup versus this woman with a random male out of the black population . . . [results in] a probability of paternity [of] 96.55 percent."[26]

This figure was conveyed to the jury to mean what it says—this man is the father, or at least it is 96.55% probable that he is. It is not intended to and does *not* mean that he is part of a small group who *might* be the father (1%—and if there are 100,000 men in the relevant population, that "small group" adds up to 1,000 men). It means that even though there may be 1,000 others who fit the bill, he *is* the father—the odds are not 999 to 1 against the possibility of his being the father, but a 96.55% probability that he *is*. If credited, the opinion is enormously persuasive.

The expert's opinion was based on a mathematical combination of three factors: the expert's assumed probability that defendant was as likely as any other man to be the father; the "probability" that a guilty suspect would have the required blood type (the probability here is 1, *i.e.*, 100%, for whoever was "guilty," namely, the father, *must* have that blood type); and the probability that any man chosen at random would have that blood type (here 1%). Using a mathematical formula (Bayes' Theorem) apparently universally-accepted as valid in conventional probability analysis, the expert calculated the probability of paternity by multiplying the assumed odds (fifty-fifty, such odds being expressed as "1") by the relative likelihood of

---

26. The expert nowhere explained how she specifically arrived at the calculation that led to the "probability of paternity" figure. Our understanding of the mathematics suggests that the actual exclusionary figure used was not 1% but rather 3.57%. Had she in fact used a 1% exclusionary figure, the probability of paternity would have been 99.01%, not 96.55%.

paternity as shown by the tests, called a "likelihood ratio" and calculated by dividing the probability of the incriminating results being found in a guilty suspect (1.0) divided by the probability that they will be found in an innocent suspect (.01). This multiplication $(1 \times 1/.01)$ gives the new odds: 100. Since odds of 100 means a probability of 100 out of 101 chances (odds of 3, for instance, means 3 to 1 or three out of four chances, a probability of .75), the probability thus calculated would be 99.01%. In fact, as noted above, the probability of paternity figure was 96.55%. Essentially, the formula the expert actually used included an exclusionary factor of 3.57% (not 1%) and would look something like the following:

$$
\begin{array}{ccccc}
1 & \times & 1/.0357 & = & 28 \\
\text{(prior odds)} & & \text{(likelihood ratio)} & & \text{(new odds)}
\end{array}
$$

The odds of 28 are the equivalent of a probability of 96.55%.

The reports of blood and tissue testing labs fairly regularly use this mathematical formula, calculating the probability of paternity figure based on the fifty-fifty assumption (that assumption sometimes referred to as the "prior probability," to convey the sense that it is the probability of defendant being the father based on all of the evidence in the case *prior* to any consideration of the blood and tissue test evidence). Many of the experts who testify concerning the lab results also use the fifty-fifty assumption, following Joint Guidelines formulated in 1976 by the American Medical Association (A.M.A.) and the Section on Family Law of the American Bar Association (A.B.A.).

On cross-examination defense counsel brought out the fact that the probability of paternity percentage was based on that fifty-fifty assumption. The expert described it as a "neutral" assumption. Since it supposedly favored neither the accused nor the victim, the expert said it gave the contention of each side (mother and purported father) equal weight and eliminated any subjectivity from the opinion. Her characterization of the evidence was that its "purely objective" nature was "one of the beauties of the test"; that it "makes no assumption other than everything is equal"; and that "the jury simply has objective information." According to her testimony, there was no taking of sides, no judgment on the facts of the case. Defense counsel saw it differently. Counsel noted that even if it were conclusively proven that defendant had been out of the country at the time when conception could have occurred, this expert still would have concluded that the probability defendant was the father was 96.55%. Counsel's observation was correct; the expert's opinion had no relation whatsoever to the facts of the case. . . .

Although the jury learned, in cross-examination of the expert, of the expert's assumption of a 50% prior probability that defendant was the father, the clear impression given by the expert was that it was somehow a "scientific" assumption, an accepted part of a scientific calculation, "objective," "neutral," "fair." It is no such thing—although it is often, indeed apparently almost regularly, used by forensic experts testifying in paternity matters. While counsel could have demonstrated this inherent lack of neutrality through fuller cross-examination, we think that his objections to the introduction of the probability of paternity percentage on that ground were well founded, fairly clearly stated, and should have been sustained.

More than that, we conclude that even if not objected to sufficiently by counsel, the expert's opinion on probability of paternity did not satisfy the most fundamental requirement of expert testimony: its ability to aid the jury in its deliberations. *See State v. Kelly,* 97 *N.J.* 178, 209 (1984). Moreover, as presented, the testimony "create[d] [a] substantial danger of . . . misleading the jury." *Evid. R. 4; see also Fed. R. Evid.* 403. In this criminal case, the jury had no idea what to do with the probability of paternity percentage if its own estimate of probabilities (the prior probability of paternity as estimated by the jury apart from blood and tissue tests) was different from .5. There was neither guidance from the expert nor specific instructions from the trial court regarding this crucial aspect of the probability of paternity opinion. Was the jury supposed to reject the expert's opinion, or was that opinion still of scientific value because of its alleged "objectivity"? Was the expert's opinion valid even if the jury disagreed with the assumption of .5? If the jury concluded that the prior probability was .4 or .6, for example, the testimony gave them no idea of the consequences, no idea of what the impact (of such a change in the prior probability) would be on the formula that led to the ultimate opinion of probability of paternity. . . .

There is no contention in this case by defendant that the probability of paternity thus computed is inadmissible as such (at oral argument defense counsel said that the probability of paternity opinion was admissible if the *jury itself* found that the prior probability was .5). We therefore could conclude this opinion with the implicit holding above, namely, that a probability of paternity opinion is admissible but only if the expert notes that the calculations leading to that opinion use as one of the critical factors an assumed prior probability of paternity of .5. While this .5 assumed prior probability clearly is neither neutral nor objective, rather than prohibiting an expert witness from describing it as such, we would leave it to counsel to challenge this characterization through cross-examination. However, a jury should be required to use its own estimate of the prior probability of paternity, one based on all of the evidence in the case *other than* the scientific evidence arising from the blood and tissue tests; a prior probability, in other words, based on facts of which the expert has absolutely no knowledge— the facts of the case as they would exist were there no scientific tests, no scientific reports, and no expert. Furthermore, the expert's testimony should be required to include an explanation to the jury of what the probability of paternity would be for a varying range of such prior probabilities, running, for example, from .1 to .9.

On this last point, we note that a similar approach, initially suggested by Professors Ellman and Kaye, [Mark Ellman & David Kaye, *Probabilities and Proof: Can HLA and Blood Group Testing Prove Paternity?,*] 54 *N.Y.U. L. Rev.* [1131,] 1152-58 [(1979)], has been adopted by the Supreme Court of Oregon. *Plemel v. Walter, 303 Or.* 262 (1987). In that case, the court held that an expert who testifies regarding a probability of paternity "should present calculations based on [varying] assumed prior probabilities of 0, 10, 20, 30, 40, 50, 60, 70, 80, 90 and 100 percent." Such an approach ensures that the jury's attention will be focused on the other evidence in the case and that it will not be misled by the expert's assumption of a prior probability of .5. *Ibid.*

Other courts have challenged the use of the fifty-fifty assumption. Indeed some courts have rejected the use of the probability of paternity statistic altogether on the grounds that the assigned .5 prior probability renders the statistic unreliable. . . .

Because the issue was neither tried nor raised before us, we do not decide whether the probability of paternity opinion, based on Bayes' Theorem, is sufficiently reliable to warrant its use in criminal cases to prove paternity. Its use in civil paternity proceedings appears to have legislative authorization. *See N.J.S.A.* 9:17-52c (permitting evidence "of the statistical probability of the alleged father's paternity"). Opinions based on Bayes' Theorem, however, are far from universally accepted for forensic purposes, especially in criminal cases. . . . [W]e leave the determination of the admissibility of the probability of paternity opinion to the trial court after a full hearing of the matter.

Without meaning to foreclose examination of any issue that the trial court deems relevant in making the admissibility determination, we suggest that the precise issue is rather narrow. We believe, from our readings, that Bayes' Theorem, when applied in conventional probability analysis, is practically universally accepted as valid—certainly sufficiently accepted to conform to any requirement of "general acceptance in the relevant scientific community." *See Probability and Inference in the Law of Evidence* ix (Peter Tillers and Eric D. Green eds., 1988) ("[E]ven the most rigorous critics of Bayesianism do not argue that Bayes' Theorem is invalid"). . . . What is not at all clear is its general acceptance for the purpose of converting what is essentially a nonmathematical conclusion of a prior probability of guilt into a higher probability through the use of the formula.

The controversy, rather than the "general acceptance," concerning the use of the probability of paternity opinion and Bayes' Theorem of formula—indeed the evidentiary use of Bayes' Theorem at all—is best reflected in the scholarly articles on this issue. See generally D.H. Kaye, *Presumptions, Probability and Paternity, 30 Jurimetrics J.* 323 (1990); C.C. Li & A. Chakravarti, *An Expository Review of Two Methods of Calculating the Paternity Probability, 43 Am. J. Hum. Genetics* 197 (1988); L. Jonathan Cohen, *The Role of Evidential Weight in Criminal Proof, 66 B.U. L. Rev.* 635 (1986); Lea Brilmayer, *Second-Order Evidence and Baysian Logic, 66 B.U. L. Rev.* 673 (1986); Stephen Fienberg & Mark J. Schervish, *The Relevance of Bayesian Inference for the Presentation of Evidence and for Legal Decisionmaking, 66 B.U. L. Rev.* 771 (1986); Leonard J. Jaffee, *Of Probativity and Probability: Statistics, Scientific Evidence, and the Calculus of Chance at Trial, 46 U. Pitt. L. Rev.* 925 (1985); Craig R. Callen, *Notes on a Grand Illusion: Some Limits on the Use of Bayesian Theory in Evidence Law, 57 Ind. L. Rev.* 1 (1982); Michael O. Finkelstein & William B. Fairley, *A Bayesian Approach to Identification Evidence, 83 Harv. L. Rev.* 489 (1970). The intensity and complexity of the dispute is mind boggling on occasion for those other than mathematical experts. Indeed, even the experts have difficulty with it. . . .

The disagreement on the subject is such as to prevent us from reaching any conclusion about "general acceptance." What is needed is what the trial court will have: examination and cross-examination on that issue. It boils down to this: you have a mathematical formula that invariably works in converting a mathematical statistical probability into a new probability by using in that formula new information about the matter, here the likelihood ratio based on the blood-tissue tests. The question is whether the formula produces reliable results when it is applied to a jury's conclusion about the prior probability—for instance when a jury, let us say in this case, concludes that even without the blood-tissue tests it believes defendant is guilty, that he is the father, and it quantifies that belief by saying that it is 60% probable that he is the father. Ordinarily, a 60% probability means that out of ten chances, the event in question will occur six times, but not the four other times. But what does a 60% probability mean in this case other than the strength of the jury's belief in guilt? That is just the beginning of the argument.

One of the ends of the argument is the meaning of the ultimate figure—here that the probability of paternity is 96.55%. The expert translates that into "very likely," based on the verbal predicate set forth in the Joint AMA-ABA Guidelines. To a layman, 96.55% probability seems to correspond to something much stronger, highly likely, almost certain. But how is the jury to relate that percentage to the governing standard: "beyond a reasonable doubt"?

The formula is helpful, if one considers it helpful, because it tells the jury in mathematical terms just how strongly the blood-tissue tests may be deemed to point in the direction of paternity—here, converting an assumed probability of 50% into one of 96.55%. If valid, the expert's opinion performs a service in helping the jury in such a case, for jurors presumably will have great difficulty in figuring out the significance of the likelihood ratio. Put differently, although the jury will intuitively and logically understand that the exclusion of 99 out of every 100 males as possible fathers increases the likelihood that defendant is the father, the jury will have difficulty in assessing just how *much* that likelihood is increased. . . .

The fundamental objections to the use of Bayes' Theorem to establish probability of paternity are both mathematical and jurisprudential. The mathematical objections are suggested above: they raise doubts about the validity of applying a formula designed for statistical probabilities to an assessment of proofs by the jury that, although it can be expressed as a probability, is in fact simply a statement of the strength, or weakness, of the jury's belief in a fact, forced into the mold of a statement of probability. The "prior probability" that is the basis for the Bayes' Theorem calculation is truly no prior probability at all so far as the jury is concerned. Jurors simply believe, at whatever stage of the proceedings they have to make the assessment, that defendant is guilty or not, and have varying degrees of confidence in that belief. If forced to—and they will be, if Bayes' Theorem is admitted—they can express that degree of confidence as a "prior probability," the defendant's probability of guilt is 80% 50% or 10%. The question remains whether Bayes' Theorem, when applied to such a non-statistical probability estimate, is likely to yield reliable results. . . .

The jurisprudential objection is different. It says that even if reliable, this factfinding method should not be used by juries except in the most unusual situations, or where the law explicitly requires a calculation of probabilities. In criminal cases, those objections go beyond the possibility of confusing or overwhelming the jury with mathematical complexities. They go to the heart of the jury's function—the finding of guilt beyond a reasonable doubt. . . .

Although some of these issues, both mathematical and jurisprudential, may ultimately become issues of law for this Court, we prefer to commit their resolution initially to the trial court where they will be subjected to adversarial testing. We are inclined to believe that appropriate jury instructions can cure all of them, or at least diminish their risk to the point that the advantages of the expert's calculation outweigh these risks, assuming the opinion is otherwise admissible. . . . We remand the matter for a new trial in accordance with this opinion.

UNITED STATES v. VEYSEY

334 F.3d 600 (7th Cir. 2003)

POSNER, Circuit Judge.

John Veysey appeals from his conviction, after a jury trial, and sentence of 110 years in prison for mail and wire fraud, arson, and the related offense of felony by fire. The facts are amazing, but we shall resist the temptation to recount them at length. In 1991 Veysey set fire to his house and inflated the claim that he then filed with his insurer. The insurer paid, and the house was rebuilt. The following year Veysey married a woman named Kemp, increased the insurance on the house, removed the valuable contents of the house, along with himself and his wife, and then cut the natural-gas line inside the house, causing the house to fill up with gas and explode spectacularly, utterly destroying it. He grossly exaggerated the value of the property allegedly lost in the explosion—some did not exist and some he had removed before the explosion. The insurance company (a different one) paid, and he used part of the proceeds to buy another house. The next year he tried to kill his wife by driving his van with her in it into a river. When that failed he killed her by poisoning her, and collected $200,000 in the proceeds of insurance policies on her life. He placed personal ads in newspapers, seeking to meet women. He became engaged to one of the women he met through his ads, named Donner, but broke his engagement after failing to procure a $1 million policy on her life. He then took up with a Ms. Beetle. This was in 1996 and the same year he burned down his house, again submitting an inflated estimate of the loss and receiving substantial proceeds from the insurance company (a different one, again). He then married Beetle, and they moved into a rented house. She insured her life for $500,000 with him as beneficiary. One night in 1998, after drugging her, he set fire to the house, hoping to kill both her and their infant son, on whom he had also taken out a life insurance policy and who was in the house with her. They were rescued, and soon afterwards Veysey and Beetle divorced. The house was rebuilt and Veysey persuaded a woman named Hilkin to move in with him after she had accumulated some $700,000 in life insurance and named him as the primary beneficiary. He apparently intended to murder her, but he was arrested before his plans matured. There is more, but these are the highlights. . . .

[Veysey objects] to testimony by an actuary, Charles L. McClenahan, that the probability of four residential fires occurring by chance during the 106 months between April 1989 (when Veysey bought the first house that he is known to have set fire to) and January 1998 (when he set fire to his last house) was only one in 1.773 trillion; he described this as a conservative estimate. We can imagine two distinct grounds for Veysey's objection to the actuary's evidence. The first, which, though the stronger, Veysey's lawyer has not made—and in fact expressly disclaimed, when pressed, at argument—is that the calculation was based on implicit assumptions that are untenable.

A simplified version of what the actuary did is that he first determined the number of serious residential fires in the United States over the interval in which houses occupied by Veysey caught fire four times (with "serious" defined as a fire that caused a loss equal to or greater than 20 percent of the amount of fire insurance on the house, and so defined serious fires are 5.3 percent of all residential fires), then divided that number by the number of houses in the United States, and finally multiplied the resulting probability by itself four times. Suppose (we are using hypothetical figures for the sake of simplicity) the probability that a specific house would have caught fire during the 106-month interval were one in 1,000. Then, on the assumption of independence (an important qualification, discussed next), the probability that two specific houses would have caught fire during the interval would be one in a million (1/1,000 × 1/1,000), the probability that three specific houses would have caught fire would be one in a billion, and the probability that four would have caught fire would be one in a trillion.

This simplified calculation does modest violence to the actuary's method, as the mathematics of repeatable events is somewhat complex. When the actuary divided the number of fires by the number of houses, the resulting quotient was not *really* the probability of a fire happening to a specific house, but an input into a formula designed to assess the probability of a repeated event, in this case a serious fire in a series of Veysey's dwellings. But as with our simple version, the actuary's actual computation assumed that the probabilities of each of a person's multiple fires are independent of each other—that the fact that you had a fire at one time or in one of your houses would not affect the probability that you would have a second fire in that house or a fire in your next house. The assumption was not defended by the actuary, and is unrealistic. . . . A fire in a house or in an apartment is likely to be the result, at least in part, of carelessness on the part of the occupant, implying that he is more likely to have another fire than a person who has never had a fire (though against this it can be argued that someone who has experienced a fire will be more careful to avoid a repetition—once burned is twice shy). Moreover, even if the assumption of independence were defensible, the actuary's calculation would be flawed by his failure to limit the reference group to residences comparable in design, materials, age, value, region, and other factors relevant to the likelihood of a fire in Veysey's residences.

But Veysey as we have said does not object to the actuary's methodology. His objection is that the actuary usurped the jury's function by testifying in effect that Veysey was guilty of the crimes with which he was charged *way* beyond a reasonable doubt, as the probability of his innocence was not 1 or 2 or 5 percent or whatever might be thought the implicit probability of innocence sufficient to prevent a finding of guilt beyond a reasonable doubt, but, if the actuary was believed, a mere .0000000000564 percent. Veysey's counsel goes so far as to argue that statistical evidence should never be admissible to establish an element of a crime. Fingerprint or DNA evidence is admissible, he acknowledges, but the jury must not be told what the probability is that such evidence actually establishes the proposition for which it is introduced, such as that the defendant's fingerprints were on the murder weapon.

In making this argument Veysey's counsel is gesturing toward an academic literature . . . that argues that judges and jurors, because they lack knowledge of statistical theory, are both overawed and easily deceived by statistical evidence . . . and toward decisions, such as *Smith v. Rapid Transit,* 317 Mass. 469 (1945), that refuse to permit a case to go to a jury on purely statistical evidence. In *Smith* the court held that it "was not enough" "that mathematically the chances somewhat favor the proposition that a bus of the defendant caused the accident."

Suppose, to consider a well-known hypothetical variant of *Smith,* that a person is hit by a bus, and it is known that 51 percent of the buses on the road where he was hit are owned by Bus Company *A* and 49 percent by Bus Company *B.* He sues *A* and asks for judgment on the basis of this statistic alone; he presents no other evidence. If the defendant also presents no evidence, should a jury be permitted to award judgment for the plaintiff? The law answers "no." But this is not because of doubt about the evidentiary value of statistical evidence. The true source of disquiet in the example, we believe, is the tacit assumption that the statistic concerning the ownership of the buses is the only evidence the plaintiff can obtain. If it is his only evidence, the inference to be drawn is not that there is a 51 percent probability that it was a bus owned by *A* that hit him but that he either investigated and discovered that it was actually a bus owned by *B* (which might be judgment-proof and so not worth suing), or that he has simply not bothered to conduct an investigation. In either event he should lose, in the first case obviously and in the second because a court should not be required to expend any of its scarce resources of time and effort on a case until the plaintiff has conducted a sufficient search to indicate that an expenditure of public resources is reasonably likely to yield a social benefit.

But if both bus companies had been determined to be negligent, so that the only issue was which had hit the plaintiff, then in many states the 51/49 ratio of *A*'s to *B*'s buses would be enough for a judgment against *A*— indeed against *A* and *B.* See *Sindell v. Abbott Laboratories,* 26 Cal. 3d 588 (1980); *Summers v. Tice,* 33 Cal. 2d 80 (1948); *Krist v. Eli Lilly & Co.,* 847 F.2d 293, 300 (7th Cir. 1990). Or if the ratio of buses owned by *A* to those owned by *B* were much higher than 51/49, the case against allowing "naked" statistical evidence to carry the plaintiff's burden of production on the issue of liability (rather than only causation) would be weakened. The law recognizes this not only in the obvious cases of fingerprint and DNA evidence, the admissibility of which depends on the improbability that two different people would have the same fingerprint or DNA signature, but also in the law's adoption of such presumptions as that a properly addressed, stamped, and mailed letter will reach the addressee. This is a purely statistical presumption because it is applied without regard to the particulars of the case beyond those required to satisfy the conditions of the presumption; and yet it can determine the outcome.

"All evidence is probabilistic—statistical evidence merely explicitly so," *Riordan v. Kempiners*, 831 F.2d 690, 698 (7th Cir. 1987) . . . , because nothing with which the law deals is metaphysically certain. Statistical evidence is merely probabilistic evidence coded in numbers rather than words. "Nothing about the nature of litigation in general, or the criminal process in particular, makes anathema of additional information, whether or not that knowledge has numbers attached. After all, even eyewitnesses are testifying only to probabilities (though they obscure the methods by which they generate those probabilities)—often rather lower probabilities than statistical work insists on." *Branion v. Gramly*, [855 F.2d 1256, 1264 (7th Cir. 1988)]. An eyewitness does not usurp the jury's function if he testifies that he is *positive* that he saw the defendant strike a match, and it would make no difference if he said that he is "99 percent" positive. The significant question would be the accuracy of the estimate. The actuary's one in 1.7 trillion estimate in this case probably was inaccurate, but not because it was a statistic. The issue of its accuracy has been waived, however, and in any event the error in its introduction was harmless; the other evidence against the defendant was overwhelming. . . . AFFIRMED.

PROBLEM

9.3   A century before *People v. Collins*, the most famous mathematician in the United States, Benjamin Peirce, testified as an expert in *Robinson v. Mandell*, a federal diversity lawsuit over a disputed will. Sylvia Ann Howland died in 1865 with an estate worth more than $2 million. In a will dated 1863, Howland left roughly half her wealth to various individuals and institutions, and directed that the remainder be held in trust for the benefit of her niece, Hetty Robinson, with the principal distributed at Robinson's death to certain distant relatives. Robinson came forward with an earlier will leaving the entire estate to her and—on a second, separately signed page—invalidating all subsequent wills. The executor, Thomas Mandell, rejected the second page as a forgery. Robinson sued. Peirce and his son, the logician Charles Sanders Peirce, testified for the estate.

At his father's direction, Charles had compared forty-two known signatures of Howland, superimposing two at a time and counting how many of the thirty downstrokes in each signature overlapped. He testified that, on average, six of the downstrokes—one out of five—matched up. But when the signature on the first page of the earlier will, which both sides agreed was genuine, was compared with the signature on the second page, which the estate suggested Robinson had simply traced, all thirty of the downstrokes coincided. Following his son to the stand, Benjamin Peirce testified that the probability that all thirty downstrokes would coincide in two signatures by Howland was $(1/5)^{30}$, or 1 divided by 2,666,000,000,000,000,000,000. "So vast improbability," he added, "is practically an impossibility. Such evanescent shadows of probability cannot belong to actual life. They are unimaginably less than those least things which the law cares not for." Accordingly, Peirce concluded, "the coincidence which has occurred here must have had its origin in an intention to produce it. It is utterly repugnant to sound reason to attribute this coincidence to any cause but design." *See* Louis Menand, *The Metaphysical Club* 163-176 (2001); Paul Meier & Sandy Zabell, *Benjamin Peirce and the Howland Will*, 75 J. Am. Stat. Ass'n 497 (1980); *The Howland Will Case*, 4 Am. L. Rev. 625 (1870). (Ultimately, the court ruled for the estate without reaching the allegations of forgery. No one other than Robinson had seen Howland sign the second page, and a federal "dead man" statute made parties to a suit over a will incompetent unless called by the other side or ordered by the court to testify. So there was a simple failure of proof. *See Robinson v. Mandell*, 20 F. Cas. 1027 (C.C.D. Mass. 1868) (No. 11,959).)

Would Benjamin Peirce's testimony be admissible today in federal court? He appears to have made an arithmetic error: $(1/5)^{30}$ is actually 1 divided by 9.313×10^{20}, not 1 divided by 2.666×10^{21}. Would the mistake affect the admissibility of his testimony?

c. DNA Testing

JONATHAN J. KOEHLER, DNA MATCHES AND STATISTICS: IMPORTANT QUESTIONS, SURPRISING ANSWERS

76 Judicature 222 (1993)

Since its introduction at trial in a Florida case in 1987, DNA profiling evidence has been used to find against defendants in more than a thousand criminal and civil cases. . . . DNA is a long double-stranded molecule found in the chromosomes carried in the nuclei of all cells. It contains the genetic code that provides the blueprint for life. A typical DNA identification in criminal cases compares the DNA found in blood, semen, or hairs left at a crime scene with the DNA found in blood samples taken from the suspect. . . . When scientists declare a DNA match between a person and an evidentiary trace, they are saying that the person might be the source of that trace. In other words, the person cannot be excluded as a possible source. But a match report does not necessarily mean the suspect is the source of the trace, or even that one can determine a probability that the matching person is the source. . . .

The probability that accompanies a reported DNA match is the theoretical likelihood that a randomly selected person from the general population (or from the population of certain large ethnic or racial groups) would genetically match the trace evidence as well as the defendant. This probability, which may be referred to as the "random match probability," often (but not always) helps fact finders assess the probative significance of a match.

It is important to be clear about what the random match probability does not reflect. It does not tell us the "source probability," the likelihood that the defendant is the source of the trace, and it certainly does not tell us the "guilt probability," the likelihood that the defendant committed the crime in question. . . .

Three probabilities [thus should be distinguished]:

Random Match Probability: The probability that a person selected at random from a particular population would match the trace evidence as well as the suspect. A random match probability of .001 indicates that the trace evidence would match about 10 people in a population of 10,000 and would not match the remaining 9,990 people. Based on the genetic test alone, each of the 10 matchees is a possible source of the trace, while all of the 9,990 nonmatchees may be excluded as possible sources.

Source Probability: The probability that the suspect is the source of the recovered trace evidence. The source probability is not, simply, one minus the random match probability, as many people seem to believe. The source probability is affected by the random match probability, but it is also affected by an estimate of the number of other people who might be the source, their relation to the suspect, and the particular circumstances surrounding the trace evidence.

Guilt Probability: The probability that the suspect is guilty of the crime in question. This computation requires an estimate of both the strength of the genetic matching evidence and the strength of the nongenetic evidence in the case. Genetic evidence that supports an inference of guilt can be offset by nongenetic evidence that supports an inference of innocence. Likewise, genetic evidence that supports an inference of innocence (e.g., hairs recovered from a crime scene that do not match those of the suspect) may be offset by nongenetic evidence that supports an inference of guilt (e.g., credible eyewitness testimony that places the suspect at the crime scene).

UNITED STATES v. SHEA

957 F. Supp. 331 (D.N.H. 1997), aff'd, 159 F.3d 37 (1st Cir. 1998)

BARBADORO, District Judge.

Two men wearing masks and gloves broke into the Londonderry branch of the First New Hampshire Bank about an hour after closing on August 4, 1995. One of the robbers apparently cut himself when he entered the building, as bloodstains were discovered inside the bank and in a stolen minivan believed to have been used as a getaway vehicle.

The government later charged Anthony Shea with the robbery and proposed to base its case in part on expert testimony comparing Shea's DNA with DNA extracted from several of the bloodstains. The government's expert, a forensic scientist employed by the FBI, used a method of DNA analysis known as Polymerase Chain Reaction ("PCR"), in determining that Shea has the same DNA profile as the person who left several of the blood stains at the crime scene and in the getaway vehicle. The expert also concluded that the probability of finding a similar profile match if a DNA sample were drawn randomly from the Caucasian population is 1 in 200,000.

Shea moved to exclude the DNA evidence prior to trial. . . . After holding an evidentiary hearing and carefully considering Shea's arguments, I denied his motion to exclude. Shea subsequently was convicted of attempted bank robbery and several related charges. In this opinion, I explain why I admitted the DNA evidence. . . .

DNA, an acronym for deoxyribonucleic acid, is the chemical blueprint for life. Most human cells other than reproductive cells contain identical copies of a person's DNA. Although 99.9% of human DNA does not vary from person to person, no two persons other than identical twins have the same DNA. [National Research Council, *The Evaluation of Forensic DNA Evidence* (1996)("NRC II")], at 63.

Human DNA is organized into 23 pairs of chromosomes and each chromosome contains a DNA molecule. DNA molecules have a double stranded helical structure that can be envisioned as a spiral staircase. [National Research Council, *DNA Technology in Forensic Science* (1992) ("NRC I")], at 2. Running between the two sugar-phosphate strands forming the handrails of the staircase are millions of steps comprised of two loosely bound nitrogen bases. Each step is referred to as a base pair. There are four types of bases: adenine (A), thymine (T), guanine (G), and cytosine (C). A's ordinarily pair only with T's, and C's ordinarily pair only with G's. Thus, if the sequence of bases on one side of a DNA molecule is known, the corresponding sequence of bases on the other side can be deduced. The arrangement of base pairs in chromosomal DNA comprises the genetic code that differentiates humans from non-humans and makes every person unique. [Elaine J. Mange and Arthur P. Mange, *Basic Human Genetics* (1994)], at 19-20.

In total, the DNA molecules in the 23 pairs of human chromosomes contain approximately 3.3 billion base pairs. Most of the base pairs are arranged in the same sequence in all humans. NRC II, *supra*, at 62-63. However, every DNA molecule has regions known as polymorphic sites where variability is found in the human population. Each possible arrangement of base pairs that occurs at a polymorphic site is referred to as an allele. Alleles can result from differences in a single base pair, differences in multiple base pairs, or differences in the number of base pairs that comprise a site.

The combination of alleles from corresponding sites on a chromosome pair is sometimes referred to as the site's genotype. NRC II, *supra*, at 216. One allele for each single locus genotype is inherited from each parent. If both parents contribute the same type of allele, the child's genotype is considered to be homozygous. If each parent contributes a different type of allele, the child's genotype is considered to be heterozygous. To illustrate, if only two alleles for a locus are found in the population, A and a, two homozygous genotypes, AA and aa, and one heterozygous genotype, Aa, will be found in the population. Although an individual's genotype consists of either two copies of the same allele or one copy of each of two different alleles, many different alleles may be found in the population for a single locus. NRC II, *supra*, at 15.

PCR and Restriction Fragment Length Polymorphism ("RFLP")[27] are the two methods most often used in forensic DNA typing. In this case, the government relies exclusively on PCR. PCR . . . has two aspects, amplification and allele identification.

PCR amplification is a process for making many copies of selected portions of a DNA sample. . . . The amplification process is repeated many times. . . . Eventually, enough copies of the shorter segments are produced to permit the amplified alleles to be identified. Mange, *supra*, at 288. [The alleles are identified either through the use of strips containing probes to which only certain alleles will bind, or through electrophoresis, which segregates alleles based on the rate at which they migrate through a gel placed in an electrical field.] . . . PCR is a very potent process which can result in the amplification of very small amounts of DNA. Accordingly, special care must be taken to minimize the possibility that samples become contaminated though mishandling. . . .

The PCR analysis conducted in this case allegedly demonstrates that Shea's DNA matches DNA extracted from several of the bloodstains at seven studied sites. To put this finding in context, the government offered evidence that the probability of finding a similar match if a DNA sample were drawn randomly from the Caucasian population is 1 in 200,000. This random match probability essentially expresses the expected frequency of the observed DNA profile in a pertinent population.

The process of calculating a random match probability begins with a determination of the allele frequencies comprising the DNA profile. An allele frequency is simply a statement of relative proportion that is customarily expressed as a decimal fraction.[28] Genotype frequencies are calculated by squaring the frequency of the single allele comprising each homozygous genotype (P2) and by doubling the product of the two allele frequencies comprising each heterozygous genotype (2PiPj).[29] NRC I, *supra*, at 4; NRC II, *supra*, at 92. The law of genetics that permits genotype frequencies

27. RFLP targets sites on DNA molecules that are known to have different lengths because of variations in the number of times that a sequence of base pairs is repeated. Such sites are referred to as Variable Number Tandem Repeats ("VNTRs"). RFLP uses restriction enzymes to cut DNA into fragments at the boundaries of a studied site. The relative lengths of the alleles for the site are then identified by a process known as gel electrophoresis. Mange, *supra*, at 306; NRC II, *supra*, at 65-67. . . .

28. The sum of the allele frequencies for a site totals 1. Thus, if a site has two alleles with equal frequencies, each allele will have a frequency of .5.

29. For example, if a site has two alleles with equal frequencies, A and a, the genotype frequencies will be: AA = .25 (or .5 × .5); aa = .25 (or .5 × .5); and Aa = .5 (or 2(.5 × .5)). The product of allele frequencies for heterozygous genotypes must be doubled because the genotype Aa can be comprised either of an A from the father and an a from the mother, or vice versa.

to be determined in this way under proper conditions is called the Hardy-Weinberg law.[30] Mange, *supra*, at 408-11. Once genotype frequencies are determined, the probability of a random match of genotypes at multiple sites is calculated by multiplying the frequencies of the sample's genotypes at each site.[31]

The rule that the joint probability of multiple independent events can be determined by multiplying the frequencies of the individual events is known as the product rule. Mange, *supra*, at 61. The product rule can be applied reliably in the manner described above only if the estimate of allele frequencies is reasonably accurate and the conditions in the population approximate what are known as Hardy-Weinberg equilibrium and linkage equilibrium.

Because it is not practical to test an entire population, allele frequencies are derived from databases of DNA samples. If these databases do not accurately reflect the distribution of alleles in the population—either because the sample size is too small or because of a bias in the way in which samples were selected for inclusion—the calculation of a random match probability may be unreliable. NRC I, *supra*, at 10.

Hardy-Weinberg equilibrium is the state in which genotype frequencies can be calculated reliably using the Hardy-Weinberg law. Hardy-Weinberg equilibrium will exist for a large population if there is approximately random mating within the population, a negligible amount of biased mutation occurs in the alleles comprising the genotypes under study, migration is limited and unbiased, and natural selection is insignificant. Large deviations from Hardy-Weinberg equilibrium make it difficult to reliably determine genotype frequencies from allele frequencies. Mange, *supra*, at 410-411.

The product rule can be used reliably only if the events considered in a joint probability calculation are independent.[32] Thus, to the extent that genotypes at multiple sites are linked, it becomes more difficult to calculate a random match probability using the product rule. Linkage equilibrium exists in a population when alleles comprising the genotypes at one site are not associated with the alleles comprising genotypes at other sites. NRC II, *supra*, at 106. If Hardy-Weinberg equilibrium persists in a population over

30. The distribution of alleles in a population will occur in Hardy-Weinberg proportions under appropriate conditions because genotypes are formed in accordance with the first law of genetics. This law, which is also known as the law of segregation, recognizes that observable traits are the product of two alleles which are segregated in reproductive cells so that a child inherits one allele from each parent. Mange, *supra*, at 52-53.

31. Thus, if a sample has three genotypes with equal frequencies of .5, the probability of a random match will be 1 in 8 ($.5 \times .5 \times .5 = .125$ or 1/8).

32. *People v. Collins*, [438 P.2d 33 (Cal. 1968)], is frequently cited as an example of how dependence skews the results obtained by using the product rule. In that case involving eyewitness identification, the prosecutor applied the product rule to variables that were not independent. The prosecutor used individual probabilities of a man with mustache (25%), a Negro man with beard (10%), a girl with ponytail (10%), a girl with blond hair (33%), a partly yellow automobile (10%) and an interracial couple in car (001%), and using the product rule arrived at a 1 in 12 million random match probability. Because the characteristics were not independent, the product rule yielded a drastically exaggerated result.

several generations, the population will approach linkage equilibrium.[33] NRC II, *supra*, at 27. Linkage equilibrium will be approached more quickly for sites on different chromosomes than for sites on the same chromosome, and widely spaced sites on the same chromosome will approach linkage equilibrium more quickly than sites that are close together. NRC II, *supra*, at 64, 106. Whereas Hardy-Weinberg equilibrium will produce alleles in Hardy-Weinberg proportions after a single generation, it takes several generations before linkage equilibrium is approached. NRC II, *supra*, at 106.

Hardy-Weinberg equilibrium and linkage equilibrium are rarely attained in real populations, most significantly because real populations are finite and contain subgroups that are perpetuated by non-random mating. Accordingly, debate about whether the product rule can be used reliably often focuses on the power of the statistical methods used to detect deviations from Hardy-Weinberg equilibrium and linkage equilibrium and the adequacy of the measures that are used to account for potential deviations. . . .

Shea's challenges to the DNA evidence fall into three categories. First, he argues that the FBI's PCR testing protocols contain errors and omissions that render the methodology suspect. Second, he contends that the product rule cannot be used to calculate the probability of a random match because the databases on which the calculation is based are too small. Finally, he asserts that the government should be barred from informing the jury of the probability of a random match because it will mislead the jury. I address each class of contentions in turn.

A. PCR TYPING PROTOCOLS

The PCR Typing methods used by the FBI in this case readily satisfy Rule 702's reliability requirement. First, although PCR is a relatively new technology, it is based on sound scientific methods and it has quickly become a generally accepted technique in both forensic and non-forensic settings. Perhaps the strongest evidence on this point is the conclusion reached by the National Research Council's Committee on Forensic DNA Science that "the molecular technology [on which PCR is based] is thoroughly sound and . . . the results are highly reproducible when appropriate quality-control methods are followed."[34] NRC II, *supra*, at 23; *see also*

---

33. Linkage equilibrium for sites on different chromosomes is possible under proper conditions because of the second law of genetics. This law, which is also known as the law of independent assortment, holds that chromosome pairs sort randomly during the process of reproductive cell formation. Mange, *supra*, at 518. . . . Linkage equilibrium also is possible under proper conditions for sites on the same chromosome because of a phenomenon known as crossing over. Crossing over occurs when corresponding parts of a chromosome pair are exchanged during the production of reproductive cells. If equilibrium conditions persist in a population over a number of generations, crossing over will result in the independence in the population of genotypes on the same pair of chromosomes. Mange, *supra*, at 47, 196; NRC II, *supra*, at 64.

34. The general acceptance of PCR technology is further underscored by the fact that at least two federal circuit courts and at least 16 state courts have approved the admission of expert testimony based on PCR analysis. . . .

Mange, *supra*, at 287 (noting PCR's "widespread and growing applications [in the field of molecular biology]"). Second, the tests used to type each of the 7 sites examined in this case were validated in a carefully constructed series of experiments and the results were later published in peer-reviewed publications.[35] Finally, the FBI followed detailed testing protocols and quality control procedures in this case that conform to industry standards.[36]

Notwithstanding the considerable evidence supporting a finding that the FBI's PCR test methods are scientifically valid, Shea argues that the DNA evidence must be excluded because the FBI's PCR tests will produce an unacceptably high percentage of erroneous results even if evidence samples are properly handled and the tests are properly performed. Shea bases this argument primarily on the testimony of Dr. Donald Riley. Dr. Riley claims that the FBI's testing protocols could result in typing errors because the testing protocols specify incorrect amplification and typing temperatures. He also states that this problem is particularly significant with the amplification and typing of the DQ Alpha region. Because the control probes for both the DQ Alpha and Polymarker tests are intended to detect DQ Alpha alleles, Dr. Riley theorizes, the FBI's testing protocols could produce erroneous results on both tests.

I reject Dr. Riley's testimony for two reasons. First, although he claimed that he has tested his theory, he has not subjected his conclusions to peer review, nor has he described his test methods in sufficient detail to permit a conclusion that they are scientifically valid. Second, even if the testing protocols specify the wrong amplification and typing temperatures, Dr. Riley has offered no scientific support for his theory that this methodological flaw could produce false positive signals at the control probes on the DQ Alpha and Polymarker test strips. In the face of such poorly supported testimony, I have no difficulty in finding that the published validation studies relied on by the government persuasively establish the evidentiary reliability of the FBI's PCR testing protocols.[37]

Shea also argues that the DNA evidence should be excluded because PCR cannot reliably detect mixtures of more than one person's DNA. The government concedes that a mixture theoretically could result in the

35. Catherine Theisen Comey and Bruce Budowle, *Validation Studies on the Analysis of the HLA DQ? Locus Using the Polymerase Chain Reaction*, 36 Journal of Forensic Sciences 1633 (1991); Bruce Budowle, et al., *Validation and Population Studies of the Loci LDLR, GYPA, HBGG, D7S8, and Gc (PM loci), and HLA-DQ? Using a Multiplex Amplification and Typing Procedure*, 40 Journal of Forensic Sciences 45 (1995); Susan Cosso and Rebecca Reynolds, *Validation of the AmpliFLP D1S80 PCR Amplification Kit for Forensic Casework Analysis According to TWGDAM Guidelines*, 40 Journal of Forensic Sciences 424 (1995).

36. The DNA Identification Act of 1994, 42 U.S.C.A. §14131(a) (West 1995), requires the Director of the FBI to convene an advisory board to develop quality assurance standards for DNA testing. Until such standards are developed and approved by the Director, the FBI is obligated to follow standards developed by the Technical Working Group on DNA Analysis Methods (TWGDAM), a group comprised of analysts working in government and private laboratories. The FBI's PCR testing protocols and quality control standards conform to TWGDAM guidelines.

37. I express no opinion concerning the admissibility of Dr. Riley's trial testimony on this point because the government did not seek to exclude his testimony pursuant to Rule 702.

declaration of a false match. However, Richard Guerrieri, one of the government's expert witnesses, testified that such errors are exceedingly unlikely because an examiner will be able to identify a mixture from observable differences in the relative strengths of the signals indicated on the PCR test strips, except in extremely unusual circumstances. I reject Shea's argument because I find Mr. Guerrieri's testimony persuasive on this point.

Shea next argues that the DNA evidence must be excluded because the government did not establish that the FBI laboratory has an acceptably low PCR error rate.[38] Testing errors can occur either because a test has inherent limitations or because the people involved in collecting, handling or testing samples are not sufficiently skilled. *See* Edward J. Imwinkelried, *Coming to Grips with Scientific Research in Daubert's "Brave New World": The Courts' Need to Appreciate the Evidentiary Differences Between Validity and Proficiency Studies*, 61 Brook. L. Rev. 1247 (1995) (explaining the difference between a validation study which evaluates whether a test produces accurate results if performed properly and a proficiency study which evaluates a laboratory's ability to correctly perform the test). A laboratory's error rate is a measure of its past proficiency that is of limited value in determining whether a test has methodological flaws. Since Rule 702's reliability requirement focuses on the validity of the test rather than the proficiency of the tester, the absence of a laboratory error rate will rarely be dispositive if the rest of the evidence establishes that the test has been properly validated. In this case, the government produced substantial persuasive evidence to support its claim that its PCR tests are reliable. Accordingly, the absence of a known PCR error rate for the FBI laboratory does not warrant the exclusion of the government's evidence.

Shea [also] challenges the reliability of the DNA evidence by pointing to several alleged deficiencies in the FBI's evidence handling and quality control procedures. Shea contends that the FBI laboratory mishandled the evidence by packaging the dried blood samples in individual paper coin envelopes and storing them together. Dr. Riley theorizes that this practice is fatally flawed because DNA from one sample could migrate through a paper coin envelope and contaminate other similarly packaged samples. Shea also contends that the laboratory's quality control procedures are deficient because substrate control samples[39] were not taken and a positive control sample[40] was not tested for each possible allele. The government responds

---

38. Mr. Guerrieri testified that the FBI's PCR laboratory follows TWGDAM standards by requiring its PCR examiners to submit to two open external proficiency tests and one blind proficiency test per year. Although he claims that no FBI examiner has ever failed a PCR proficiency test, he stated that the FBI does not calculate a laboratory error rate because its current proficiency testing program does not produce enough samples to serve as the basis for calculating a meaningful error rate and it would be impractical to develop a proficiency testing program that could produce a meaningful calculation. *See generally*, NRC II, *supra*, at 85-86 (discussing difficulties in attempting to calculate a laboratory error rate).

39. A substrate control tests the substance from which a sample is obtained. For example, if an evidentiary blood sample is obtained from a steering wheel, a substrate control would test a different part of the steering wheel to detect DNA from another source which would compromise the evidentiary sample.

40. A positive control is DNA of a known type. The FBI uses positive controls, but does not use a positive control for each positive allele.

by noting that Shea failed to produce any scientific evidence to support Dr. Riley's contamination theory and by explaining that the laboratory's quality control procedures conform to industry standards.

I need not address the merits of Shea's arguments. Instead, I join the many courts that have addressed similar issues by concluding that because such arguments concern the way in which a method is applied in a particular case rather than the validity of the method, they affect the weight that should be given to the evidence rather than its admissibility. . . .

B. RANDOM MATCH PROBABILITY

The government's estimate of a 1 in 200,000 random match probability is based primarily on information drawn from a PCR database comprised of DNA profiles for 148 Caucasians, 145 African Americans, 94 Southeastern Hispanics, and 96 Southwestern Hispanics.[41] Bruce Budowle, et al., *Validation and Population Studies of the Loci LDLR, GYPA, HBGG, D7S8, and Gc (PM loci), Procedure*, 40 Journal of Forensic Sciences 45, 50 (1995). Shea contends that this database is simply too small to be used reliably in estimating random match probabilities with the product rule.

The government cites a study published in a peer-reviewed journal to refute Shea's claim. *Id.* This study analyzes the government's database using several statistical tests in an effort to identify significant departures from Hardy-Weinberg and linkage equilibrium. The study states that the distribution of the various genotypes found at the 7 loci at issue in this case meet Hardy-Weinberg expectations and exhibit little evidence of deviation from linkage equilibrium. Accordingly, it concludes that "[t]he data demonstrate that valid estimates of a multiple locus profile frequency can be derived for identity testing purposes using the product rule under the assumption of independence." *Id.* at 53.

Notwithstanding the study cited by the government, legitimate questions can be raised concerning the reliability of a random match probability that is estimated with the product rule from a database as small as the one used here. Because such databases are comprised of a limited number of samples, the possibility of random error ordinarily must be considered.[42]

41. Data is collected for separate racial groups because significant population substructuring is known to exist for such groups. The NRC II report recommends that random match probabilities should be calculated for all potentially applicable racial groups when the race of the perpetrator is unknown. NRC II, *supra*, at 122. However, the report also recognizes that it may be appropriate to provide only the estimate for the major racial group that gives the largest probability of a match. NRC II, *supra*, at 114. . . . The government informed the jury only of the random match probability estimate for Caucasians since the match probability is highest for this group. Shea did not challenge the government's position on this point.

42. Random error is error that can occur by chance because a database does not contain the entire population being studied. Daniel L. Rubinfeld, *Reference Guide on Multiple Regression, in Moore's Federal Practice: Reference Manual on Scientific Evidence* 415, 466 (1994).

Further, legitimate questions can be raised concerning the power of existing statistical methods to detect deviations from Hardy-Weinberg and linkage equilibrium when small databases are used. If random error is not accounted for and if the likely potential effects of factors such as population substructuring are not identified and addressed, a random match probability estimated with the product rule may be unreliable.

The recently released NRC II report addresses these issues by acknowledging the potential for error and suggesting several ways to conservatively account for the problem. First, the report describes alternatives adjustments to the product rule to account for the systematic over-representation of homozygous genotypes that is caused by undetected population substructuring.[43] NRC II, *supra*, at 99-100. If, as is the case with most PCR-based systems, the method used to identify alleles does not present significant ambiguity, the report recommends that homozygous frequencies be determined by using $P2 + P(1 - P)\theta$ rather than by P2 where P is the allele frequency and θ is the percentage of excess homozygosity that is expected because of undetected population substructuring. *Id.* at 122. After examining empirical data from several sources, the report concludes that a θ value of .01 will conservatively address the likely potential systematic effect of undetected population substructuring except for cases involving small, isolated populations, where a θ value of .03 may be appropriate. *Id.* at 122. If an allele identification system such as one based on VNTRs is used where there is a potential that a heterozygous genotype may be misidentified as homozygous, the report recommends that homozygous genotype frequencies be calculated using 2P rather than P2. *Id.* at 122. The report concludes that these two methods will account in a conservative way for the likely systematic effect of undetected population substructuring. *Id.*

Undetected population substructuring and random error can also affect individual random match probability calculations in ways that are difficult to predict. NRC II, *supra*, at 112. Thus, the NRC II report also suggests a way of qualifying random match probability estimates to account for such uncertainties. After considering empirical data comparing genotype frequencies observed in a number of aggregate population databases with genotype frequencies found in known regional and ethnic subpopulation databases, the report concludes that likely uncertainties caused by random error and undetected population substructuring can be conservatively accounted for if the database used in calculating the random match probability contains samples from "at least several hundred persons" and the estimate obtained by using the product rule is qualified by stating that the true value is likely to be within a factor of 10 above or below the estimated value.[44] *Id.* at 156.

---

43. Substructuring also usually produces an under-representation of heterozygous genotype frequencies from those that would be predicted using the Hardy-Weinberg law. NRC II, *supra*, at 122. Since this effect will tend to favor defendants, however, the report does not recommend any adjustment to the formula used to estimate heterozygous genotype frequencies.

44. The report notes that the uncertainty can be greater for very small profile frequencies. *Id.* at 160. . . .

The government agreed to adjust its random match probability estimate in the manner suggested in the NRC II report.[45] Accordingly, I consider whether the method used by the government's expert in estimating the probability of a random match, when adjusted in accordance with the recommendations contained in the NRC II report, satisfies *Daubert*'s reliability standard.

Shea relies primarily on the testimony of Dr. William Shields in claiming that the FBI's methodology for estimating the probability of a random match is unreliable even if it is adjusted to conform to the recommendations contained in the NRC II report. Dr. Shields challenged the FBI's methodology by claiming that: (1) a θ value of .01 is insufficient to capture the likely systematic effects of population substructuring; (2) the NRC II's recommended factor of 10 correction is based on VNTR data that cannot reliably be applied to the PCR loci at issue here; and (3) the PCR database used in this case is too small, even when judged by the standards of the NRC II report, for the factor of 10 correction to account for potential error. . . .

Whether the adjustments to the product rule suggested in the NRC II report are sufficiently conservative and whether a database of 148 is of sufficient size to serve as the basis for a reliable random match probability estimate are important questions about which population geneticists can legitimately disagree. However, Rule 702 does not require scientific consensus. The government has produced a peer-reviewed study using accepted statistical methods to support its position that the estimation of a random match probability from the database used in this case will produce a reliable result. It has further qualified its estimate in accordance with the recommendations of a distinguished committee of scientists and academicians that included leading population geneticists as members. Under these circumstances, the concerns raised by Dr. Shields affect the weight that should be given to the evidence rather than its admissibility. . . .

C. JUROR CONFUSION

Evidence that a defendant's DNA profile matches DNA extracted from an evidence sample suggests that the defendant cannot be excluded as a potential contributor, but it is of little value, standing alone, in proving the defendant's guilt. Giving the jury a random match probability estimate for the profile is one way of helping it assess the potential significance of a DNA profile match. However, because such evidence also has the potential to

45. The genotypes for the D1S80 site and 5 of the remaining 6 sites examined in this case were found to be heterozygous. When the genotype frequency for the single homozygous locus is recalculated using a θ value of .01, it does not significantly affect the government's random match probability estimate because the FBI routinely rounds down when calculating the probability of a random match and that rounding process more than captured the effect of the adjustment that needed to be made to the single homozygous genotype frequency. When the NRC II's factor of 10 adjustment is applied to the random match probability estimate, it results in a range of possible results of from 1 in 20,000 to 1 in 2,000,000.

mislead, Rule 403 requires that the probative value of the evidence must be carefully balanced against the danger of unfair prejudice.

Shea argues that a jury would be so overwhelmed by evidence of a random match probability that it could not properly assess the possibility that a profile match is false unless a laboratory or industry error rate is calculated and combined with the random match probability estimate. Shea bases this argument on the following reasoning: (1) a random match probability estimate is meaningless if the declared DNA profile match is false; (2) the best evidence of whether a match is false in a particular case is the laboratory's false match error rate; (3) if the laboratory's false match error rate cannot be determined, the next best evidence is the industry's false match error rate; (4) jurors cannot understand the significance of a laboratory's error rate unless it is combined with the random match probability estimate. Because the FBI laboratory does not calculate a PCR false match error rate and the government refuses to combine what Shea suggests is the industry's PCR error rate with the random match probability estimate, Shea argues that the estimate is inherently misleading.

I reject Shea's argument because it is built on several flawed premises. First, I cannot accept Shea's contention that a laboratory or industry error rate is the best evidence of whether a test was properly performed in a particular case. Juries must decide whether a particular test was performed correctly based on all of the relevant evidence. This determination can never be precisely quantified because it will often depend in part on subjective factors such as the credibility of the person who performed the test. At best, evidence of a laboratory's past proficiency should be considered as one of several factors in making this important judgment.[46] *See* NRC II, *supra*, at 85-86 ("[t]he risk of error in any particular case depends on many variables (such as the number of samples, redundancy in testing, and analyst proficiency), and there is no simple equation to translate these variables into the probability that a reported match is spurious"). Shea's method for dealing with the probability of a false match is thus seriously flawed because it would deprive the jury of the opportunity to determine the probability of a false match based on all of the pertinent evidence.

Second, I am unconvinced by Shea's claim that a jury cannot properly assess the potential of a false match unless a false match error rate is calculated and combined with the random match probability estimate. Shea relies on testimony and research conducted by Dr. [Jonathan] Koehler to support this contention. Although Dr. Koehler's research suggests that jurors could become confused if evidence of a false match error rate and a random match probability estimate are presented with little or no explanation, it does not support Shea's broader contention that jurors cannot be made to understand such evidence even if it is properly explained.

---

46. The parties assume that error rate information is admissible at trial. This assumption may well be incorrect. Even though a laboratory or industry error rate may be logically relevant, a strong argument can be made that such evidence is barred by Fed. R. Evid. 404 because it is inadmissible propensity evidence. Imwinkelreid, *supra*, at 1271-81. I need not determine whether error rate information is ever admissible, however, because the point is not essential to my analysis, and the government did not object to Shea's effort to introduce error rate information at trial.

See NRC II, *supra*, at 199 (noting that "[t]he argument that jurors will make better use of a single figure for the probability that an innocent suspect would be reported to match never has been tested adequately"). In a real trial setting, the parties are given an opportunity to explain the significance of statistical evidence through expert testimony. Further, if a trial judge concludes that jurors could be confused by statistical evidence, the judge can deliver carefully crafted instructions to insure that the evidence is properly understood. Notwithstanding Dr. Koehler's research, I am confident that the concerns Shea raises can be properly addressed through expert testimony and, if necessary, clarifying jury instructions.

Shea next argues that a random match probability estimate is inherently misleading because the jury inevitably will confuse the probability of a random match with the potentially very different probability that the defendant is not the source of the matching samples. This type of incorrect reasoning is often referred to as the fallacy of the transposed conditional, or the prosecutor's fallacy. NRC II, *supra*, at 133. The probability of a random match is the conditional probability of a random match given that someone other than the defendant contributed the evidence sample. The potentially different probability that someone other than the defendant contributed the sample given the existence of a match can only be determined by considering all of the evidence in the case.[47] Shea argues, based on research conducted by Dr. Koehler, that the jury will inevitably confuse these two probabilities.

Although I acknowledge that a jury could become confused concerning the meaning and potential significance of a random match probability estimate, I am confident that the risk of confusion is acceptably small if the concept is properly explained. Moreover, because such an estimate can be extremely valuable in helping the jury appreciate the potential significance of a DNA profile match, it should not be excluded merely because the concept requires explanation. . . . Accordingly, I denied the defendant's motion. . . .

JONATHAN J. KOEHLER, ON CONVEYING THE PROBATIVE VALUE OF DNA EVIDENCE: FREQUENCIES, LIKELIHOOD RATIOS, AND ERROR RATES

67 U. Colo. L. Rev. 859, 866, 869-875, 884 (1996)

In most cases, the possibility of laboratory error is substantially larger than the possibility of a coincidental match. This is not because DNA laboratory work is particularly sloppy or unreliable. Instead, it is because the chance of a coincidental match is usually small. . . .

---

47. To illustrate how these two probabilities can be very different, consider a hypothetical case where: (1) the defendant's DNA profile is correctly found to match DNA left by the perpetrator at the crime scene during the commission of the crime; (2) the random match probability estimate for the observed DNA profile is 1 in 1,000,000; and (3) undisputed evidence establishes that the defendant did not commit the crime. In this hypothetical case, the random match probability estimate is 1 in 1,000,000 even though the probability that someone other than the defendant contributed the evidence sample is 1.

In courtrooms throughout the country, DNA experts have testified that false positive matches in DNA profiling are "impossible." However, a review of proficiency test data indicates not only that errors are possible but that they have occurred in a variety of laboratories. . . . Most of the errors that arise in proficiency tests appear to be due to human errors (e.g., mislabeling, contamination, interpretive error, etc.) rather than to technical errors in the DNA typing process itself. But it does not justify unmitigated enthusiasm about the accuracy of DNA evidence. Fact-finders need to be aware of the chances that some error will occur rather than the chance that a particular error, or a particular type of error, will occur. . . .

The claim that proficiency test data cannot be used to estimate case-specific error rates is . . . unpersuasive. The argument runs roughly as follows: At best, proficiency test data provide an indication of a general, industry-wide error rate in DNA typing. But the specific testing features associated with each laboratory and each test render the industry-wide error rate irrelevant to any given case. . . .

No one would argue that the unique testing features associated with a particular laboratory in a particular case should be ignored when these features are demonstrably related to a reduced error rate. But it is a fallacy to believe that the fact that such individuating features may exist denies relevance to industry-wide error-rate estimates. . . . [I]gnoring the industry-wide DNA error-rate statistics because there exist favorable individuating features in this laboratory or in this test will produce overly optimistic estimates of the chance that the laboratory did not make an error in the instant case. Because favorable individuating features always exist (e.g., the analyst is experienced, the analyst was observed, the samples were clean, the results were double-checked, etc.), extreme caution must be exercised before concluding that the chance of error in the instant case is lower than the chance of error in the industry as a whole. It cannot be that every laboratory in the industry has an error rate that is less than the industry-wide average. Yet this is exactly the claim that is made every time laboratory personnel reject the industry-wide figures and argue that their own error rate is substantially less or zero. . . .

If a sufficiently reliable set of such data were available, it would indeed be reasonable to use these data rather than the industry-wide figures. The problem, however, is that few laboratories have participated in enough high quality proficiency tests to permit computation of reliable error-rate estimates. Even error-free performance on a small number of proficiency tests will not ordinarily provide a sufficiently reliable basis for replacing the industry-wide error-rate estimates. This elementary principle is poorly understood by many attorneys and judges.[48]

48. See, e.g., Transcript at 19-20, Commonwealth of Virginia v. Antonio Hodges, No. 2542 & 2543, (Cir. Ct. of The City of Norfolk June 16, 1995) (voir dire of Jonathan Koehler by Arthur Karp):

Q: Well, tell me what you know about how errors are made in processing DNA?
A: I'm not here to comment at all about how errors are made in the processing of DNA. I'm here to comment on the inferential significance of errors that have been committed.
Q: What errors have been committed?

Suppose a laboratory makes ten correct match calls out of ten tries on proficiency tests. Based on these data, one may be 95% "confident" that the laboratory's error rate is somewhere between 0 and 26%. In other words, error rates of 0%, 5%, 10%, 20%, and 25% are all consistent with these data (i.e., zero errors in ten tries). If a laboratory participated in 100 tests without error then we could be 95% confident that its error rate is between 0% and 3%.

Even when errors are not made, proficiency testing at the individual laboratory level would have to be quite extensive to produce error-rate estimates that are substantially below current estimates. Unless and until such extensive testing has been completed, industry-wide error rates should be used when estimating a DNA laboratory's match report error rate. . . .

When scientifically defensible estimates of laboratory error rates are not incorporated into likelihood ratios or related quantitative indexes of probative value, the numbers that jurors receive may exaggerate the strength of the DNA evidence. The possibility of human error imposes practical boundaries on the probative value of DNA evidence. To be sure, estimating the frequency of errors in case work is tricky. But the difficulty of doing so does not justify the production of likelihood ratios that are based on the false assumption that errors do not occur. . . .

The DNA Wars have moved to a different level during the past few years. At one time, debate centered around biological and genetic issues. Today, the most controversial issues are statistical, as the new debate focuses on ways to convey the probative value of DNA evidence to jurors. . . .

The appropriate resolution of these issues is critical to ensure the accurate and appropriate use of DNA evidence in our courts. Therefore, courts should require that (a) experts speak only of "reported" DNA matches, (b) reported matches should only be considered evidence that suspects are the source of the recovered genetic material, and (c) error-rate estimates should be included in a calculation of likelihood ratios. . . .

[E]ven if agreement is reached on these thorny issues, thornier psychological issues must also be addressed. How do people process quantitative evidence in general and likelihood ratio and frequency information in particular? Can jurors be taught to aggregate different types of quantitative evidence and to give it the weight that it deserves? These psychological

---

A: Well, there have been some errors committed in proficiency tests.

Q: By the Virginia lab?

A: No, not that I'm aware of.

Q: Well, tell me what you can say about the implications of error rates for a laboratory that doesn't make errors?

A: Well, there is an assumption implicit in your question, [that] the lab doesn't make errors. . . . If there was such a thing as a zero error rate, which I categorically reject and which any scientist should categorically reject, then I really wouldn't have much to say about errors. . . .

Comment by the Court: We are not going into proficiency tests where there were errors when there is no evidence that the Virginia lab had any errors. Okay.

questions may yet turn out to be the most important of all. If people do not process quantitative information effectively, and if we continue to inundate jurors with statistical data without bothering to train them in the use of such information, then much of the debate over what the right numbers are will have been a waste of time.

ERIN MURPHY, THE NEW FORENSICS: CRIMINAL JUSTICE, FALSE CERTAINTY, AND THE SECOND GENERATION OF SCIENTIFIC EVIDENCE
95 Cal. L. Rev. 721, 767-774 (2007)

Advocates of DNA typing . . . suggest that the rigors of DNA science will spare it from the embarrassments that plagued traditional forensic sciences. . . . [But] many of the characteristics that make second-generation [forensic] sciences [including not only DNA typing but also data mining, electronic location tracking, and biometric scanning] so appealing in fact places them at equal, if not greater, risk for error. . . .

[T]he technical complexity of second-generation techniques make[s] close and continuous judicial scrutiny of their methodological soundness less likely. Judges confronting sophisticated scientific evidence must invest greater intellectual and material resources to conduct a comprehensive examination of second-generation techniques. Even well-meaning judges may struggle to comprehend complicated scientific or mathematical principles, and the heightened likelihood of error may discourage a court from delving too deeply into such complicated scientific knowledge.

Judicial reluctance, however, only renders the initial hearings on a new technique more decisive, since few later judges will retread the treacherous path—especially if it is only to risk arriving at a result suspiciously contrary to that reached earlier. Yet at the initial stages, second-generation methodologies, with their requirements of mechanical sophistication and specialized technical knowledge, are even less likely to have withstood the scrutiny of an independent community of auditors. Indeed, the general rigor of second-generation sciences may also lend them an air of "mystic infallibility" that discourages critical inspection, and the existence of "real world" analogues, notwithstanding that the nonforensic applications in fact deploy meaningfully different methodologies, may bolster this sense. A judge who thinks that cell phones or GPS satellites or iris scans or DNA tests generally work in the world may be less inclined to question whether, when put to forensic purposes, the methodological underpinnings remain sound.

The high volume of second-generation cases only exacerbates this impulse. Resource constraints may ultimately persuade the "amateur scientists" of the bench, particularly those inclined to intellectual timidity with regard to sophisticated scientific techniques, to lean heavily upon the "law-like" status of other courts' rulings rather than spend precious time deciphering a seemingly legitimate methodology. Of course, the more that forensic evidence is approved in cases in which the defendant admits guilt and the evidence goes unexamined, the more it affirms the belief that this kind of evidence is typically trustworthy and reliable.

But even an intellectually entrepreneurial judge willing to fully exercise her gatekeeper role under *Daubert* might not find much help from the adversarial parties. . . . [D]efense attorneys, like judges, may find themselves susceptible to the temptation simply to trust the integrity of the evidence, thus making the case seem insurmountable or "open-and-shut." Many lawyers will reasonably conclude that it requires too great an effort, and reaps too little a reward, to study such evidence in the hopes of uncovering a flawed methodological approach. And the more technically complex the evidentiary form, the more likely it becomes that even a well-meaning attorney may be incapable of comprehending the science regardless of the effort she expends. After all, not every attorney can be expected to master the methodological details of facial recognition software or DNA amplification and testing. Similarly, the seeming (or actual) impenetrability of the technique may discourage the attorney from conducting a thorough inspection for errors in its application. . . .

[E]ven assuming a judge receptive to such a challenge, a defense attorney capable and well-resourced enough to pursue one, and an expert available for appointment, it remains unlikely that the expert could undertake the examination necessary to truly safeguard the integrity of the evidence. That is because the mechanical sophistication and technical complexity of this evidence all but forecloses independent research. The infrastructure necessary for true methodological testing is simply lacking. At the same time, the database-dependency of second-generation sciences, and the privacy and proprietary secrets concerns they raise, effectively prohibit access to the material necessary for independent research. Manufacturers of DNA typing kits, cell phone or search engine technologies, or biometric scanning software may bristle at disclosing broadly the technology underlying their particular techniques, even under a court "gag" order. Similarly, the relinquishment of data stored indiscriminately in databanks for exploratory purposes—whether iris patterns, DNA profiles, or cell records—understandably raises legitimate concerns about personal privacy. The database dependency of second-generation technologies also means that scrutiny of these techniques for case-specific errors in application itself requires access to large volumes of data, which may not be feasibly disclosed, or feasibly reviewed, in every case. . . .

[T]he very qualities that make second-generation technologies so desirable make it all the more likely they will never encounter adversarial scrutiny of any kind. And while this lack of scrutiny is troubling on its face, it becomes all the more troubling when considered in light of the very real possibility that, given the investigative power of these technologies, in many cases they may be the only actual evidence of the defendant's guilt.

4. Traditional Forensic Science

MICHAEL J. SAKS & JONATHAN J. KOEHLER, WHAT DNA "FINGERPRINTING" CAN TEACH THE LAW ABOUT THE REST OF FORENSIC SCIENCE

13 Cardozo L. Rev. 361, 362-364 (1991)

[M]ore is known about the strengths and weaknesses of DNA finger-printing evidence than about most of the other, older, and more widely used forms of forensic science evidence. . . . To be sure, handwriting identification, ballistics, toolmarks, fingerprints, and the like have become familiar fixtures in American courts, but none has undergone scrutiny even remotely resembling that to which DNA typing is being subjected. . . .

The accuracy of "identification techniques" (including DNA typing) is based on statistical principles and inference. Unfortunately, the statistical reasoning required is often casual and intuitive, rather than explicit and rigorous. In all of these respects, research testing the claims of DNA identification, however youthful that research may be, has already outdistanced most of what has been done for its more senior forensic science relatives. One likely reason is that most forensic sciences have no academic or industrial counterpart disciplines. In most other fields (agriculture, chemistry, engineering, medicine, psychology, zoology, etc.), academic counterparts exist and perform the lion's share of research. Because many forensic sciences have no knowledge-producing counterparts elsewhere in society, and because they address a question that few if any basic sciences have any interest in (namely, unique identification), they suffer from a handicapping isolation. As a result, the handful of seminal works in a forensic science field, some of them generations old, a few of them approaching their centennials, remain the principal works to which contemporary analysts turn. Continual refinement and reexamination of assumptions do not occur. In some forensic science fields, one is happy to find a handful of empirical studies, or even a single study, rigorously testing some basic premise or applied technique. . . .

UNITED STATES v. FUJII

(N.D. Ill., No. 00 CR 17, Sept. 25, 2000)

[GOTTSCHALL, District Judge].

Defendant Fujii has moved in limine to exclude the testimony of the government's handwriting expert, Karen Ann Cox. The government proposes to call Ms. Cox to identify the defendant as the writer of certain handprinted immigration forms submitted at John F. Kennedy International Airport in New York in December 1999 in connection with the fraudulent entry of two Chinese nationals. . . . [T]he court held a *Daubert* hearing . . . [and] concludes that, at least in the peculiar circumstances of this case, Ms. Cox's testimony is inadmissible. . . .

Since the *Daubert* decision, a number of courts have scrutinized the field of handwriting analysis under its standards with differing results. Prior to *Kumho*, the Sixth Circuit affirmed a district court decision allowing handwriting identification testimony, relying largely on Evidence Rule 901. *United States v. Jones*, 107 F.3d 1147, 1158-60 (6th Cir. 1997). Since *Kumho*, a number of district courts have excluded expert opinions on handwriting identification, while sometimes permitting handwriting experts to testify about handwriting itself to assist the jury in making its own determination. . . . *But see United States v. Paul*, 175 F.3d 906, 910-11 (11th Cir.), *cert. denied*, 120 S. Ct. 535 (1999).

Handwriting analysis does not stand up well under the *Daubert* standards. Despite its long history of use and acceptance, validation studies supporting its reliability are few, and the few that exist have been criticized for methodological flaws. Further, as discussed in [*United States v. Hines*, 55 F. Supp. 2d 62 (D. Mass. 1999)], there has been no peer review by an unbiased and financially disinterested community of practitioners and academics; the acceptance of handwriting identification expertise has been largely driven by handwriting experts. It[s] potential rate of error is almost entirely unknown. In the study relied on by the government's expert . . . a sample of 105 forensic document examiners and 41 laypeople were tested; 38% of the laypeople made an incorrect match while only 6.5% of the experts made an incorrect match. But according to the evidence presented to this court, there are few if any other studies in existence that tend to validate the reliability of handwriting analysis. The defense expert in this case testified to studies that have undermined some of handwriting analysis' key principles, such as its principle that no two people write exactly alike. Of course, on the [test of] general acceptance, handwriting analysis scores high.

This court need not weigh in on this question, however, for whether handwriting analysis *Per se* meets the *Daubert* standards, its application to this test poses more significant problems. . . . Typical handwriting analysis involves cursive writing, and there record is devoid of evidence that there is even a recognized field of expertise in the identification of handprinting. While Ms. Cox testified that many of the documents she examines at the INS involve handprinting, and while she testified that in her prior employment with ATF, she was tested in identifying handprinting, "erred," studied, was retested and passed, the court has no idea whether there is a recognized and accepted expertise in identifying handprinted documents, let alone whether Ms. Cox is an expert in this putative field. Michael Saks, who testified for the defense, testified that he was aware of only one study of the reliability of handprinting identification, and in that study, only 13% of the handwriting experts tested got the right answer; 45% identified the wrong person.

The reliability of handprinting identification, however, is only part of the problem. The government has offered no evidence that Ms. Cox's expertise extends to making an identification of handprinting when the handprinter[s] in question are native Japanese writers. Neither the government's expert, Ms. Cox, nor the defendant's witness, Mr. Saks, is aware of any studies attempting to validate handprinting (or event handwriting) identification of the writings of foreign-trained writers. Following the hearing, the defense submitted the affidavit of Mark Litwicki, Director of Loyola University's English as a Second Language program. Mr. Litwicki avers that he has had extensive experience examining the handwriting styles of foreign students, including Japanese students, as he has taught many Japanese students in this country. He further avers that he spent two years teaching English to Japanese students in Japan and is "especially familiar with the manner in which Japanese-trained writers make the characters of the English alphabet." Mr. Litwicki avers that the Japanese language requires its students to spend a good deal of time learning to write several thousand Japanese characters, that uniformity of characters is "an important and valued principle of Japanese handwriting," that Japanese students "spend many years attempting to maximize the uniformity of their writing" and that "Japanese-trained writers also tend to write English characters in a very uniform manner". Mr. Litwicki concludes, "In my opinion, it would be very difficult for an individual not familiar with the English handwriting of Japanese writers to identify the subtle dissimilarities in the handwriting of individual writers". . . . There is no evidence in the record that Ms. Cox has such expertise or has even considered the problem Mr. Litwicki has pointed out. . . . [T]he court grants the defendant's motion.

MICHAEL J. SAKS, BANISHING IPSE DIXIT: THE IMPACT OF *KUMHO TIRE* ON FORENSIC IDENTIFICATION SCIENCE

57 Wash. & Lee L. Rev. 879, 888-889, 899-900 (2000)

[T]he history of the admission of forensic identification science in American courts is remarkably barren of serious examinations of the data (or lack of data) underlying the claims of various fields. The pre-*Daubert* courts generally paid so little attention to the theoretical and empirical support on which an asserted expertise might stand that post-*Daubert* courts will often have no choice but to start over at the beginning. This is certainly true concerning the early admissibility of fingerprint expert evidence. . . . From the beginning, the uniqueness of fingerprint patterns was so widely assumed that it never seemed necessary to prove it. . . . Ironically, Henry Faulds, one of the pioneers of the use of fingerprints in the field of criminal identification, complained that "the popular fiction, that no two fingers can be alike" was being treated as "a sober fact of the highest scientific certainty" for no other reason than that people kept repeating that "fact". . . . Once courts accepted fingerprint identification, proponents of other asserted fields of forensic science availed themselves of the law's principal tool of reasoning: analogy. Every other field could claim that the phenomenon central to its claimed expertise was "just like fingerprints". . . .

SIMON A. COLE, SUSPECT IDENTITIES: A HISTORY OF FINGERPRINTING AND CRIMINAL IDENTIFICATION

260-261, 281-286, 302 (2001)

[E]ven the contention that no two complete single fingerprint patterns are exactly alike did not address the issue fundamental to forensic identification: How great is the likelihood that a latent fingerprint impression might mistakenly be matched to the wrong source finger? . . .

Two different strategies developed during the postwar period for dealing with the uncertainty about how small a partial latent fingerprint fragment could be before the chance of accidental matching with another source finger became too great. The first strategy, which found its most pronounced expression in Britain, was essentially to err on the side of caution by mandating an overly conservative number of matching ridge characteristics, or "points of similarity", as the threshold for identification. . . . The second strategy, which found its most prominent expression in North America, was to do away with point standards altogether and rely instead on the expert judgment of trained, experienced examiners. . . . Since minimum standards were not based on empirical evidence but were merely estimates aimed at providing a margin of safety against error, American examiners suggest that they were profoundly unscientific and therefore undermined latent fingerprint identification's status as a forensic science. In their place, American examiners proposed what was essentially a floating standard based on the expert judgment of the examiner.

. . . [T]he first external proficiency tests on American police fingerprint laboratories [were performed in 1995]. The results were astonishing. Only 44 percent of the tested examiners scored perfectly. Six of the 156 examiners reported false negatives—that is, they failed to identify matching prints. But the consequences of a false negative—possibly allowing a guilty person to escape conviction—paled in comparison with the consequences of a false positive, in which an innocent person could (and, given the power of fingerprint evidence, probably would) be falsely convicted of a crime. Thirty-four examiners, 22 percent of the total, reported false positives. . . . The 1996 test yielded somewhat better news. Only 3 percent of the laboratories reported false positives. In the 1997 test 16 of 204 examiners reported false positives, and in the 1998 test 14 of 219 participants (around 6 percent) reported false positives. These rates were still far too high . . . to support the long-standing contention that errors in latent fingerprint identification were impossible. . . .

Soon, however, it was American examiners' turn to point out that they did not have a monopoly on incompetence or malfeasance. In April 1997 Scotland Yard admitted that its examiners had erroneously matched a latent print from the scene of a burglary . . . with that of a suspect. . . . In December 1998 the British courts freed Danny McNamee, who had been convicted of building a nail bomb for the Irish Republican Army that killed four British cavalrymen and seven horses in 1982. McNamee's fingerprints had been matched with latent prints found on tape and a battery used in the bomb, but, on appeal, 14 expert witnesses disagreed as to the value of the prints. . . . In the spring of 1999 Detective Constable Shirley McKie of the Strathclyde Police in Scotland was tried in Glasgow for allegedly tampering with evidence in a murder investigation. [Scottish investigators tied McKie to a fingerprint found in the murder victim's home, which McKie claimed she had never entered. Two American fingerprint examiners testified that the prints did not match]. A jury acquitted McKie of the charges. . . . [T]he Scottish examiners had labeled 16 "points of similarity" between two prints that the American examiners insisted did not match. [Other experts have since agreed with the American examiners' conclusion, but Scottish authorities remain convinced the print is McKie's. Britain abandoned the 16-point standard on January 1, 2001.] . . .

Legal scholars and forensic scientists [have] suggested . . . that fingerprint evidence might not be able to meet the *Daubert* criteria. In a 1997 legal practice guide, forensic scientist David Stoney concluded that "the criteria for absolute identification in fingerprint work are subjective and ill-defined. They are the products of probabilistic intuitions widely shared among fingerprint examiners, not of scientific research". . . . It now seems at least possible, if not likely, that a variety of forces—the internal divisions within the fingerprint profession itself, the changing notion of science promoted by the *Daubert* decision, and the far more statistically and methodologically sophisticated example being set by DNA evidence—may conspire to have fingerprint identification declared legally unscientific. . . . Paradoxically, "DNA fingerprinting", which initially derived much of its credibility by way of analogy with fingerprinting, may now be undermining its role model.

UNITED STATES v. LLERA PLAZA

188 F. Supp. 2d 549 (E.D. Pa. 2002)

POLLAK, District Judge.

In the government's list of witnesses expected to be called at the upcoming trial, on drug and murder charges, of . . . Carlos Ivan Llera Plaza [and two co-defendants], there are four Federal Bureau of Investigation (FBI) fingerprint examiners and one FBI fingerprint specialist. [The defendants filed a motion to] bar the testimony of these anticipated witnesses, . . . [and the] government responded with [motion to admit the testimony]. The principal question posed by the defendants' motion and the government's counter-motion was whether, as the government contended, fingerprint identification evidence is sufficiently reliable to meet the standards for expert testimony set by Rule 702 of the Federal Rules of Evidence as explicated by the Supreme Court in *Daubert v. Merrell Dow Pharmaceuticals, Inc*, 509 U. S. 579(1993) and reaffirmed in *Kumbo Tire Co., Ltd. v. Carmichael*, 526 U. S. 137(1999). . . . By stipulation of the parties, the evidence with respect to these questions consisted of a copy of the transcript of a five-day hearing addressed to the same question presided over by my colleague Judge Joyner, in 1999, in *United States v. Mitchell*, Cr. No. 96-407.

On January 7, 2002, I filed an opinion and order addressed to the defendants' motion and the government's counter-motion. . . . I considered whether the ACE-V fingerprint identification system employed by the FBI sufficiently conforms to the *Daubert* standards of reliability laid down by the Court as guidelines in determining the admissibility of expert testimony under Rule 702. First I described the four fingerprint examination procedures—"analysis", "comparison," "evaluation," and "verification,"—for which "ACE-V" is an acronym: "analysis" by an initial fingerprint examiner of the observable distinctive patterns of a latent print; "comparison" by the examiner of the latent print patterns with those of a rolled print; "evaluation" by the examiner of these compared patterns with a view to determining whether the prints are, or are not, impressions made by the same finger or palm; and "verification" by a second examiner who repeats the analysis, comparison and evaluation steps in order to verify, or not, the initial examiner's finding. Next I identified the four *Daubert* factors of scientific reliability relied on by both the government and the defendants as touchstones of Rule 702 admissibility: (1) whether the technique on which the proffered expert testimony is premised "can be (and has been) tested"; (2) whether the technique has been "subjected to peer review and publication"; (3) "the known or potential rate of error . . . and the existence and maintenance of standards controlling the technique's operation"; and (4) "general acceptance." Based on the *Mitchell* record, I came to the following conclusions with respect to ACE-V's conformity to the *Daubert* factors:

> The one *Daubert* factor that ACE-V satisfies in significant fashion is the fourth factor: ACE-V has attained general acceptance within the American fingerprint examiner community. . . . But the caveat must be added that, in the court's view, the domain of knowledge occupied by fingerprint examiners should be described, in Rule 702 terms, by the word "technical," rather than by the word "scientific," the word the government deploys. . . . [T]he court finds that ACE-V does not adequately satisfy the "scientific" criterion of testing (the first *Daubert* factor) or the "scientific" criterion of "peer review" (the second *Daubert* factor). Further, the court finds that the information of record is unpersuasive, one way or another, as to ACE-V's "scientific" rate of error (the first aspect of *Daubert*['s] third factor), and that, at the critical evaluation stage, ACE-V does not operate under uniformly accepted "scientific" standards (the second aspect of *Daubert*'s third factor).

The substance of my ruling was as follows:

> . . . This court will permit the government to present testimony by fingerprint examiners who, suitably qualified as "expert" examiners by virtue of training and experience, may (1) describe how the rolled and latent fingerprints at issue in this case were obtained, (2) identify and place before the jury the fingerprints and such magnifications thereof as may be required to show minute details, and (3) point out observed similarities (and differences) between any latent print and any rolled print the government contends are attributable to the same person. What such expert witnesses will not be permitted to do is to present "evaluation" testimony as to the "opinion"

(Rule 702) that a particular latent print is in fact the print of a particular person. The defendants will be permitted to present their own fingerprint experts to counter the government's fingerprint testimony, but defense experts will also be precluded from presenting "evaluation" testimony. Government counsel and defense counsel will, in closing arguments, be free to argue to the jury that, on the basis of the jury's observation of a particular latent print and a particular rolled print, the jury may find the existence, or the non-existence, of a match between the prints.

. . . [On the government's motion,] I agreed to reconsider the January 7 ruling [and to hold an evidentiary hearing]. . . . The hearing was held on February 25, 26 and 27. . . .

Properly to determine whether an FBI fingerprint examiner operates at a proper level of intellectual rigor when she comes to court as an expert witness, it becomes necessary . . . to reexamine the grounds on which I found that ACE-V did not satisfy three of the *Daubert* factors and only marginally met the fourth ("general acceptance" by the fingerprint community, which I deemed not a "scientific community"). . . .

(A) "PEER REVIEW" AND "GENERAL ACCEPTANCE"

. . . The fact that fingerprint specialists are not "scientists," and hence that the forensic journals in which their writings on fingerprint identification appear are not "scientific" journals in *Daubert*'s peer review sense, does not seem to me to militate against the utility of the identification procedures employed by fingerprint specialists, whether on the witness stand or at the disaster site. By the same token, I conclude that the fingerprint community's "general acceptance" of ACE-V should not be discounted because fingerprint specialists—like accountants, vocational experts, accident-reconstruction experts, appraisers of land or of art, experts in tire failure analysis, or others—have "technical, or other specialized knowledge" (Rule 702), rather than "scientific . . . knowledge" (*id.*), and hence are not members of what *Daubert* termed a "scientific community."

(B) "TESTING"

. . . Disagreeing with contentions that the "verification" phase of ACE-V constitutes *Daubert* "testing," or, in the alternative, that a century of litigation has been a form of "adversarial" testing that meets *Daubert*'s criteria, I concluded in the January 7 opinion that *Daubert*'s testing factor was not met, and I have found no reason to depart from that conclusion.

(C) "RATE OF ERROR" AND "STANDARDS CONTROLLING THE TECHNIQUE'S OPERATION"

The last *Daubert* question to be addressed is whether *Daubert*'s third factor—"the known or potential rate of error . . . and the existence and maintenance of standards controlling the technique's operation"—offers support for fingerprint identification testimony. . . .

(I) "RATE OF ERROR"

. . . The defense witnesses succeeded in raising real questions about the adequacy of the proficiency tests taken annually by certified FBI fingerprint examiners. It may be that further inquiry by qualified forensic specialists and persons versed in skills-testing will answer those questions in the FBI's favor. But on the present record I conclude that the proficiency tests are less demanding than they should be. To the extent that this is the case, it would appear that the tests can be of little assistance in providing the test makers with a discriminating measure of the relative competence of the test takers. But the defense witnesses offered not a syllable to suggest that certified FBI fingerprint examiners as a group, or any individual examiners among them, have not achieved at least an *acceptable* level of competence. The record shows that over the years there have been at least a few instances in which fingerprint examiners, here and abroad, have made identifications that have turned out to be erroneous. . . . But [the defense presented no evidence of] erroneous identifications attributable to FBI examiners. . . . I conclude, therefore, on the basis of the limited information in the record as expanded, that there is no evidence that the error rate of certified FBI fingerprint examiners is unacceptably high.

(II) "STANDARDS CONTROLLING THE TECHNIQUE'S OPERATION"

The January 7 opinion found that three aspects of ACE-V manifested an absence of generally accepted controlling standards: (a) there appeared to be no agreed qualification standards for fingerprint examiners; (b) jurisdictions varied widely with respect to the minimum number of Galton points [i.e., matching ridge characteristics] required for finding a "match"; (c) the ultimate "evaluation" judgment was termed "subjective." On reviewing these issues on the basis of the expanded record I reach the following conclusions:

(a) Whatever may be the case for other law enforcement agencies, the standards prescribed for qualification as an FBI fingerprint examiner are clear: To be hired by the FBI as a fingerprint trainee, one must be a college graduate, preferably with some training in one of the physical sciences; to become a certified fingerprint examiner, the trainee must complete the FBI's two-year in-house training program which winds up with a three-day certifying examination. The uniformity and rigor of these FBI requirements provide substantial assurance that, with respect to certified FBI fingerprint examiners, properly controlling qualification standards are in place and are in force.

(b) . . . The absence of a Galton minimum under FBI auspices, as against maintenance of a high Galton threshold in the United Kingdom, the jurisdiction whose police first systematized fingerprint identification for law enforcement purposes, could be perceived as troublesome—*i.e.*, connoting a lack of rigor in FBI standards. However . . . there is no longer any significant lack of harmony between the FBI's fingerprint identification standards and those that prevail in English courtrooms. . . . [O]ver the course of years, a consensus was arrived at in the United Kingdom that there was no scientific rationale for insisting on some minimum number of "similar ridge characteristics". . . . Though a number of other countries may still observe Galton point minima, the fact that England has, after many years of close study, moved to the position which prevails in Canada and which the FBI has long subscribed to, leads me to conclude that there is sufficient uniformity within the principal common law jurisdictions to satisfy *Daubert*.

(c) In the January 7 opinion, the aspect of the *Daubert* inquiry into "the existence and maintenance of standards controlling the technique's operation" that was of greatest concern was the acknowledged subjectivity of the fingerprint examiner's stated opinion that a latent print and a known exemplar are both attributable to the same person. Government witnesses . . . described the "match" opinion as "subjective," and [a] defense witness . . . agreed. I concluded that "[w]ith such a high degree of subjectivity, it is difficult to see how fingerprint identification—the matching of a latent print to a known print—is controlled by any clearly describable set of standards to which most examiners prescribed." On further reflection, I disagree with myself. . . . [T]here are many situations in which an expert's manifestly subjective opinion . . . is regarded as admissible evidence in an American courtroom: a forensic engineer's testimony that a bottom-fire nailer's defective design caused an unintended "doublefire," resulting in injury to the plaintiff, *Lauzon v. Senco Products*, 270 F.3d 681 (8th Cir. 2001); an electrical engineer's testimony that fire in a clothes drier was caused by a thermostat malfunction, *Maryland Casualty Co. v. Therm-O-Disc*, 137 F.3d 780 (4th Cir. 1998); a marketing researcher's testimony as to consumer interpretations of advertising claims, the testimony being based on a market survey of consumers, *Southland Sod Farms v. Stover Seed Co.*, 108 F.3d 1134 (9th Cir. 1997). In each instance the expert is operating within a vocational framework that may have numerous objective components, but the expert's ultimate opinion is likely to depend in some measure on experiential factors that transcend precise measurement and quantification. As compared with the degree of subjectiveness inherent in one or more of the foregoing examples of expert opinion testimony, the subjective ingredients of opinion testimony presented by a competent fingerprint examiner appear to be of substantially more restricted compass. . . .

In sum, contrary to the view expressed in my January 7 opinion, I am now persuaded that the standards which control the opining of a competent fingerprint examiner are sufficiently widely agreed upon to satisfy *Daubert*'s requirements. . . .

[T]he one *Daubert* factor which is both pertinent and unsatisfied is the first factor—"testing." *Kumho Tire* . . . instructs district courts to "consider the specific factors identified in *Daubert* where they are reasonable measures of the reliability of expert testimony." Scientific tests of ACE-V—*i.e.*, tests in the *Daubert* sense—would clearly aid in measuring ACE-V's reliability. But, as of today, no such tests are in hand. The question, then, is whether, in the absence of such tests, a court should conclude that the ACE-V fingerprint identification system, as practiced by certified FBI fingerprint examiners, has too great a likelihood of producing erroneous results to be admissible as evidence in a courtroom setting. There are respected authorities who, it appears, would render such a verdict. In a recent OpEd piece in *The New York Times*, Peter Neufeld and Barry Scheck, who direct Cardozo Law School's Innocence Project, have this to say:

> No one doubts that fingerprints can, and do, serve as a highly discriminating identifier, and digital photographic enhancement and computer databases now promise to make fingerprint identification more useful than ever before. But to what degree incomplete and imperfect fingerprints can be reliably used to identify individuals requires more scientific examination. . . . Forensic science has rarely been subjected to the kind of scrutiny and independent verification applied to other fields of applied and medical science. Instead, analysts testifying in courts about fingerprint analysis, bite marks, handwriting comparisons and the like have often argued that in their field the courtroom itself provided the test. . . . As the National Institutes of Health finance basic scientific research, the National Institute of Justice should put money into verification and validation before a technique of identification is admitted into court.

     . . . [T]here is no evidence that certified FBI fingerprint examiners present erroneous identification testimony, and as a corollary, that there is no evidence that the rate of error of certified FBI fingerprint examiners is unacceptably high. With those findings in mind, I am not persuaded that courts should defer admission of testimony with respect to fingerprinting— which Professors Neufeld and Scheck term "[t]he bedrock forensic identifier of the 20th century"—until academic investigators financed by the National Institute of Justice have made substantial headway on a "verification and validation" research agenda. For the National Institute of Justice, or other institutions both public and private, to sponsor such research would be all to the good. But to postpone present in-court utilization of this "bedrock forensic identifier" pending such research would be to make the best the enemy of the good. . . .

     I have concluded that arrangements which, subject to careful trial court oversight, are felt to be sufficiently reliable in England, ought likewise to be found sufficiently reliable in the federal courts of the United States, subject to similar measures of trial court oversight. In short, I have changed my mind. . . .

     Accordingly, in an order filed today accompanying this opinion, this court grants the government's motion for reconsideration of the January 7 order; vacates the January 7 order; denies the defendants' Motion to Preclude the United States from Introducing Latent Fingerprint Evidence; and grants the government's Motion in Limine to Admit Latent Prints.

     At the upcoming trial, the presentation of expert fingerprint testimony by the government, and the presentation of countering expert fingerprint testimony by any of the defendants . . . will be subject to the court's oversight prior to presentation of such testimony before the jury, with a view to insuring that any proposed expert witness possesses the appropriate expert qualifications and that fingerprints offered in evidence will be of a quality arguably susceptible of responsible analysis, comparison and evaluation.

JENNIFER McMENAMIN, JUDGE BARS USE
OF FINGERPRINTS IN MURDER TRIAL
Balt. Sun, Oct. 23, 2007

A Baltimore County judge has ruled that fingerprint evidence, a main-stay of forensics for nearly a century, is not reliable enough to be used against a homicide defendant facing a possible death sentence—a finding that national experts described yesterday as unprecedented and potentially far-reaching.

Baltimore County Circuit Judge Susan M. Souder's order bars prose-cutors from using at trial the partial fingerprints lifted from the Mercedes of a Security Square Mall merchant who was fatally shot last year during an attempted carjacking at the shopping center. Prosecutors say the finger-prints—as well as those found in a stolen Dodge Intrepid in which witnesses said the shooter fled the mall parking lot—link a 23-year-old Baltimore man to the killing.

In her ruling, Souder outlined the long history of fingerprinting as a crime-solving tool but says that such history "does not by itself support the decision to admit it." . . .

The technology has come under scrutiny in recent years.

Stephan Cowans, a Boston man who spent six years in prison for the shooting of a police sergeant, was released in 2004 after the discovery that the fingerprint used to convict him was not his.

That same year, the FBI mistakenly linked Brandon Mayfield, an Oregon lawyer, to a fingerprint lifted off a plastic bag of explosive detona-tors found in Madrid after commuter train bombings there killed 191 people. Two weeks after Mayfield's arrest, Spanish investigators traced the fingerprint to an Algerian man.

The U.S. Justice Department issued a formal apology last year to Mayfield and awarded him $2 million.

Souder, the Baltimore County judge, referred repeatedly in her opin-ion to that case, as well as a March 2006 report from the Justice Depart-ment's internal investigators on the FBI's handling of the matter.

In the Mayfield case, three FBI fingerprint examiners and an independent court-appointed fingerprint analyst determined that the fingerprint on the bag of detonators belonged to the Oregon attorney.

"Up to that point, [the government] had maintained that if you have a competent examiner, the technique of fingerprinting can't produce a misidentification. Mayfield exposed that as a fallacy," said Robert Epstein, an assistant federal defender in Philadelphia who in 1998 was among the first lawyers to challenge the reliability of latent fingerprint identifications.

In the Baltimore County murder case, defense attorneys challenged the admissibility of fingerprint evidence that linked Rose to the killing Jan. 5, 2006, of Warren T. Fleming, the owner of a Cingular Wireless store at Security Square Mall. . . . "The state is correct that fingerprint evidence has been used in criminal cases for almost a century," Souder, the judge, wrote in her decision. "While that fact is worthy of consideration, it does not prove reliability. For many centuries, perhaps for millennia, humans thought that the earth was flat."

DAVID A. SKLANSKY & STEPHEN C. YEAZELL, COMPARATIVE LAW WITHOUT LEAVING HOME: WHAT CIVIL PROCEDURE CAN TEACH CRIMINAL PROCEDURE, AND VICE VERSA

94 Geo. L.J. 683, 728-731 (2006)

Ever since evidence law emerged as an integrated, systematic body of doctrine in the late 1800s and early 1900s, it has treated criminal and civil cases largely alike. . . . When efforts to codify evidence law began in earnest in the mid-twentieth century, the codifiers never proposed separate sets of rules for criminal and civil cases, and apparently never even considered doing so. . . . On the state level as well as the federal level, evidence law today is dominated by codes that apply to both civil and criminal cases. . . .

Of course there are exceptions to this general pattern of evidence rules spanning the civil-criminal divide. Some evidence rules apply only in criminal cases or only in civil cases. . . . [And not] all variations in evidence law across the criminal-civil divide are explicit. Judges are widely believed to apply the character evidence ban, for example, less strictly in civil cases than in criminal cases. . . . [But special evidence] rules for civil or criminal cases, whether express or unstated, are customarily viewed with skepticism. And that skepticism can be and has been a powerful force for reform.

The most striking recent example pertains to expert testimony. A decade ago the Supreme Court directed trial judges to begin screening expert testimony for "reliability," a mandate since codified in Federal Rule of Evidence 702. The new requirement was announced and elaborated by the Court in a series of civil cases, and it responded to concerns specifically focused on civil litigation—the widespread complaints about "junk science" in the courtroom. But the Court drew no distinction between civil and criminal cases. It would have been awkward to do so, because the Court justified the requirement of "reliability" as a gloss on the provisions of the Federal Rules of Evidence governing relevance and expert testimony, and those rules, like most other provisions of the Federal Rules of Evidence, themselves drew no distinction between civil and criminal cases. Nonetheless, lower courts, perhaps reading between the lines of the *United States Reports*, have assessed the "reliability" of expert testimony in civil cases much more rigorously than in criminal cases. Until quite recently, forensic science evidence—fingerprinting; ballistics, handwriting identification, hair analysis, bite mark identification, etc.—received something of a free pass, even when there was little or no proof of its reliability.

The double standard for the admissibility of expert testimony led some observers to grow skeptical of both the possibility and the wisdom of unified rules of evidence. But the resignation was unwarranted. The formal equivalence of treatment of expert testimony in civil and criminal trials is slowly and belatedly making itself felt in the courtroom. Forensic science evidence that has gone unquestioned for decades is suddenly under scrutiny. For example, several trial judges have excluded or significantly limited expert testimony by handwriting examiners—something that virtually never happened up until a few years ago. Even fingerprint examiners have come under pressure, from scholars if not yet from courts, to testify with more care and to qualify their claims of 100% accuracy. It is hard not to see this as an improvement. It is also hard to believe that it would have happened so rapidly were it not for the presumption, however loose, that rules of evidence announced in civil cases should also apply in criminal trials.

10

PRIVILEGES

"And, because a princess can't be forced to testify against her prince, they lived happily ever after."

A. IN GENERAL

Privilege rules differ from other rules of evidence in four important ways.

First, privileges are not just rules of admissibility. They govern not just whether particular evidence can be introduced at trial, but also whether disclosure of certain information can be compelled *before* trial. Indeed, the procedural context in which privileges most often are encountered is not an objection to the introduction of evidence at trial, but an objection to compelled disclosure, either through a grand jury subpoena or in the process of civil discovery.

Second, some evidentiary privileges—those that pertain to confidential communications with lawyers and certain other professionals—parallel rules of professional responsibility that impose duties of confidentiality. Usually the contours of the privilege and the duty of confidentiality coincide. But not always. The attorney-client privilege, in particular, is conceptually distinct from, and does not always coincide with, the duty of confidentiality you study in a course on professional responsibility.

Third, as the materials below explain, privileges differ from other rules of evidence in their purpose. Most other rules of evidence aim, at least in part, to improve the accuracy of factfinding. Privileges do not. In fact, it is widely acknowledged that privileges undermine the factfinding process and impair its accuracy. Privileges exist not because of their effect on factfinding but in spite of it. They are typically justified on the ground that they serve some goal outside the litigation process, most often the protection of some relationship that is thought to be socially beneficial and to require confidentiality.

Fourth and finally, privileges are not codified in the F.R.E., for reasons explained in the materials below. The sole provision of the F.R.E. that addresses privileges, Rule 501, directs federal courts to continue to develop and to apply a federal common law of privileges—except with respect to civil claims or defenses as to which state law provides the rule of decision. For those issues—typically (although not always) the claims and defenses raised in diversity cases—Rule 501 treats privileges the way that the second sentence of F.R.E. 601 treats competence: as, in effect, a matter of substance rather than procedure.

[F.R.E. 501; C.E.C. §911]

McCORMICK ON EVIDENCE

§72 (Kenneth S. Broun, ed., 6th ed. 2006)

The overwhelming majority of all rules of evidence have as their ultimate justification some tendency to promote the objectives set forward by the conventional witness' oath, the presentation of "the truth, the whole truth, and nothing but the truth." Thus such prominent exclusionary rules as the hearsay rule, the opinion rule, the rule excluding bad character as evidence of crime, and the original documents (or "Best Evidence") rule, have as their common purpose the elucidation of the truth, a purpose that these rules seek to effect by operating to exclude evidence which is unreliable or which is calculated to prejudice or mislead.

By contrast the rules of privilege, of which the most familiar are the rule protecting against self-incrimination and those shielding the confidentiality of communications between husband and wife, attorney and client, and physician and patient, are not designed or intended to facilitate the fact-finding process or to safeguard its integrity. Their effect instead is clearly inhibitive; rather than facilitating the illumination of truth, they shut out the light. . . . Their warrant is the protection of interests and relationships which, rightly or wrongly, are regarded as of sufficient social importance to justify some sacrifice of availability of evidence relevant to the administration of justice.

CHRISTOPHER B. MUELLER & LAIRD C. KIRKPATRICK, EVIDENCE

§5.6 (3d ed. 2003)

As originally proposed, Article V of the Federal Rules of Evidence would have codified the law of privileges into 13 rules. Nine of the proposed rules defined specific privileges: required reports, lawyer-client, psychotherapist-patient, spousal testimony, communications to clergymen, political vote, trade secrets, secrets of state, and identity of an informer. Another rule provided that only those privileges set forth in Article V or other act of Congress could be recognized by the federal courts, thereby superseding the common law of privileges. The three remaining rules addressed procedural incidents of the privileges such as waiver by voluntary disclosure, protection of privileged matter disclosed under compulsion, and prohibition of adverse inferences or adverse comment regarding a party's assertion of a privilege.

When the proposed rules were considered by Congress, Article V turned out to be particularly controversial for a number of reasons. First, it did not include some privileges such as the physician-patient, spousal communications, and journalist privilege, thereby arousing the opposition of supporters of those privileges. Second, proposed Rule 509 redefined the scope of secrets of state and official information privileges, an exceedingly sensitive issue for Congress because the rules were being considered at the time of the Watergate affair. Third, the proposed privilege rules would have applied even in diversity cases and other cases where state law supplied the rule of decision, thereby overriding state law governing privileges.

Unable to resolve the controversies surrounding proposed Article V, Congress ultimately rejected the attempt to codify the federal law of privileges. . . . The legislative history makes clear that congressional rejection of proposed Article V was not to be construed as disapproval of the specific privileges contained therein. Congress intended to leave privilege law where it had found it but not to freeze the evolution of the federal common law with respect to creation, modification, or repeal of specific privileges. Congress did, however, remove privileges from the general rulemaking power of the Supreme Court and adopted legislation providing that no formal rules of privilege promulgated by the Court could become effective until approved by Act of Congress. [28 U.S.C. §2074(b).]

B. ATTORNEY-CLIENT PRIVILEGE

[C.E.C. §§912, 950-962]

1. Introduction

It makes sense to start the study of privileges with the attorney-client privilege for several reasons. As the Supreme Court notes in the decision excerpted below, the attorney-client privilege is among the oldest privileges for confidential communications. It is the model, in many ways, for most other professional privileges. It is probably the most heavily litigated privilege. It may be the most zealously defended privilege, in part because, since most judges started out as lawyers, it hits close to home. Nonetheless, the privilege has always been controversial. Critics keep noting that it offers tremendous assistance to wrongdoers—and that it coincides suspiciously well with the professional interests of the bar. So before you get enmeshed in the intricacies of the privilege—its elements and its exceptions—it is worth considering the big picture. Why do we have an attorney-client privilege, and should we stick with it?

SWIDLER & BERLIN v. UNITED STATES

524 U.S. 399 (1998)

Chief Justice REHNQUIST delivered the opinion of the Court.

Petitioner, an attorney, made notes of an initial interview with a client shortly before the client's death. The Government, represented by the Office of Independent Counsel, now seeks his notes for use in a criminal investigation. We hold that the notes are protected by the attorney-client privilege.

This dispute arises out of an investigation conducted by the Office of the Independent Counsel into whether various individuals made false statements, obstructed justice, or committed other crimes during investigations of the 1993 dismissal of employees from the White House Travel Office. Vincent W. Foster, Jr., was Deputy White House Counsel when the firings occurred. In July, 1993, Foster met with petitioner James Hamilton, an attorney at petitioner Swidler & Berlin, to seek legal representation concerning possible congressional or other investigations of the firings. During a 2-hour meeting, Hamilton took three pages of handwritten notes. One of the first entries in the notes is the word "Privileged." Nine days later, Foster committed suicide.

In December 1995, a federal grand jury, at the request of the Independent Counsel, issued subpoenas to petitioners Hamilton and Swidler & Berlin for, inter alia, Hamilton's handwritten notes of his meeting with Foster. Petitioners filed a motion to quash, arguing that the notes were protected by the attorney client privilege. [The district court denied the summons, but the Court of Appeals reversed.]

The attorney client privilege is one of the oldest recognized privileges for confidential communications. *Upjohn Co. v. United States*, 449 U.S. 383, 389 (1981); *Hunt v. Blackburn*, 128 U.S. 464, 470 (1888). The privilege is intended to encourage "full and frank communication between attorneys and their clients and thereby promote broader public interests in the observance of law and the administration of justice." *Upjohn, supra*, at 389. The issue presented here is the scope of that privilege; more particularly, the extent to which the privilege survives the death of the client. Our interpretation of the privilege's scope is guided by "the principles of the common law . . . as interpreted by the courts . . . in the light of reason and experience." Fed. Rule Evid. 501; *Funk v. United States*, 290 U.S. 371 (1933).

The Independent Counsel argues that the attorney-client privilege should not prevent disclosure of confidential communications where the client has died and the information is relevant to a criminal proceeding. There is some authority for this position. One state appellate court, *Cohen v. Jenkintown Cab Co.*, 238 Pa. Super. 456, 357 A.2d 689 (1976), and the Court of Appeals below have held the privilege may be subject to posthumous exceptions in certain circumstances. . . .

But other than these two decisions, cases addressing the existence of the privilege after death—most involving the testamentary exception—uniformly presume the privilege survives, even if they do not so hold. . . . [The cases] view testamentary disclosure of communications as an exception to the privilege: "[T]he general rule with respect to confidential communications . . . is that such communications are privileged during the testator's lifetime and, also, after the testator's death unless sought to be disclosed in litigation between the testator's heirs." [*United States v. Osborn*, 561 F.2d 1334, 1340 (CA9 1977).] The rationale for such disclosure is that it furthers the client's intent.[2]

. . . Commentators on the law also recognize that the general rule is that the attorney-client privilege continues after death. *See, e.g.*, 8 Wigmore, Evidence §2323 (McNaughton rev. 1961); Frankel, The Attorney-Client Privilege After the Death of the Client, 6 Geo. J. Legal Ethics 45, 78-79 (1992); 1 J. Strong, McCormick on Evidence §94, p. 348 (4th ed. 1992). Undoubtedly, as the Independent Counsel emphasizes, various commentators have criticized this rule, urging that the privilege should be abrogated after the client's death where extreme injustice would result, as long as disclosure would not seriously undermine the privilege by deterring client communication. See, *e.g.*, C. Mueller & L. Kirkpatrick, 2 Federal Evidence §199, at 380-381 (2d ed. 1994); Restatement (Third) of the Law Governing Lawyers §127, Comment d (Proposed Final Draft No. 1, Mar. 29, 1996). But even these critics clearly recognize that established law supports the

2. About half the States have codified the testamentary exception by providing that a personal representative of the deceased can waive the privilege when heirs or devisees claim through the deceased client (as opposed to parties claiming against the estate, for whom the privilege is not waived). . . .

continuation of the privilege and that a contrary rule would be a modification of the common law. See, *e.g.*, Mueller & Kirkpatrick, supra, at 379;
Restatement of the Law Governing Lawyers, supra, §127, Comment c; 24
C. Wright & K. Graham, Federal Practice and Procedure §5498, p. 483
(1986).

Despite the scholarly criticism, we think there are weighty reasons that
counsel in favor of posthumous application. Knowing that communications
will remain confidential even after death encourages the client to communicate fully and frankly with counsel. While the fear of disclosure, and the
consequent withholding of information from counsel, may be reduced if
disclosure is limited to posthumous disclosure in a criminal context, it
seems unreasonable to assume that it vanishes altogether. Clients may be
concerned about reputation, civil liability, or possible harm to friends or
family. Posthumous disclosure of such communications may be as feared as
disclosure during the client's lifetime.

The Independent Counsel suggests, however, that his proposed
exception would have little to no effect on the client's willingness to confide
in his attorney. He reasons that only clients intending to perjure themselves
will be chilled by a rule of disclosure after death, as opposed to truthful
clients or those asserting their Fifth Amendment privilege. This is because
for the latter group, communications disclosed by the attorney after the
client's death purportedly will reveal only information that the client himself would have revealed if alive.

The Independent Counsel assumes, incorrectly we believe, that the
privilege is analogous to the Fifth Amendment's protection against self-
incrimination. But as suggested above, the privilege serves much broader
purposes. Clients consult attorneys for a wide variety of reasons, only one of
which involves possible criminal liability. Many attorneys act as counselors
on personal and family matters, where, in the course of obtaining the
desired advice, confidences about family members or financial problems
must be revealed in order to assure sound legal advice. The same is true of
owners of small businesses who may regularly consult their attorneys about
a variety of problems arising in the course of the business. These confidences may not come close to any sort of admission of criminal wrongdoing, but nonetheless be matters which the client would not wish divulged.

The contention that the attorney is being required to disclose only
what the client could have been required to disclose is at odds with the
basis for the privilege even during the client's lifetime. In related cases, we
have said that the loss of evidence admittedly caused by the privilege is
justified in part by the fact that without the privilege, the client may not
have made such communications in the first place. . . . This is true of disclosure before and after the client's death. Without assurance of the privilege's posthumous application, the client may very well not have made
disclosures to his attorney at all, so the loss of evidence is more apparent
than real. In the case at hand, it seems quite plausible that Foster, perhaps
already contemplating suicide, may not have sought legal advice from
Hamilton if he had not been assured the conversation was privileged.

The Independent Counsel additionally suggests that his proposed
exception would have minimal impact if confined to criminal cases, or,

as the Court of Appeals suggests, if it is limited to information of substantial importance to a particular criminal case.[3] However, there is no case authority for the proposition that the privilege applies differently in criminal and civil cases, and only one commentator ventures such a suggestion, see Mueller & Kirkpatrick, *supra*, at 380-381. In any event, a client may not know at the time he discloses information to his attorney whether it will later be relevant to a civil or a criminal matter, let alone whether it will be of substantial importance. Balancing ex post the importance of the information against client interests, even limited to criminal cases, introduces substantial uncertainty into the privilege's application. For just that reason, we have rejected use of a balancing test in defining the contours of the privilege. See *Upjohn*, 449 U.S., at 393 . . .

In a similar vein, the Independent Counsel argues that existing exceptions to the privilege, such as the crime-fraud exception and the testamentary exception, make the impact of one more exception marginal. However, these exceptions do not demonstrate that the impact of a posthumous exception would be insignificant, and there is little empirical evidence on this point.[4] The established exceptions are consistent with the purposes of the privilege, see *Glover*, 165 U.S., at 407-408; *United States v. Zolin*, 491 U.S. 554, 562-563 (1989), while a posthumous exception in criminal cases appears at odds with the goals of encouraging full and frank communication and of protecting the client's interests. A "no harm in one more exception" rationale could contribute to the general erosion of the privilege, without reference to common law principles or "reason and experience."

Finally, the Independent Counsel, relying on cases such as *United States v. Nixon*, 418 U.S. 683, 710 (1974), and *Branzburg v. Hayes*, 408 U.S. 665 (1972), urges that privileges be strictly construed because they are inconsistent with the paramount judicial goal of truth seeking. But both *Nixon* and *Branzburg* dealt with the creation of privileges not recognized by the common law, whereas here we deal with one of the oldest recognized

---

3. Petitioner, while opposing wholesale abrogation of the privilege in criminal cases, concedes that exceptional circumstances implicating a criminal defendant's constitutional rights might warrant breaching the privilege. We do not, however, need to reach this issue, since such exceptional circumstances clearly are not presented here.

4. Empirical evidence on the privilege is limited. Three studies do not reach firm conclusions on whether limiting the privilege would discourage full and frank communication. Alexander, The Corporate Attorney Client Privilege: A Study of the Participants, 63 St. John's L. Rev. 191 (1989); Zacharias, Rethinking Confidentiality, 74 Iowa L. Rev. 352 (1989); Comment, Functional Overlap Between the Lawyer and Other Professionals: Its Implications for the Privileged Communications Doctrine, 71 Yale L.J. 1226 (1962). These articles note that clients are often uninformed or mistaken about the privilege, but suggest that a substantial number of clients and attorneys think the privilege encourages candor. Two of the articles conclude that a substantial number of clients and attorneys think the privilege enhances open communication, Alexander, supra, at 244-246, 261, and that the absence of a privilege would be detrimental to such communication, Comment, 71 Yale L.J., supra, at 1236. The third article suggests instead that while the privilege is perceived as important to open communication, limited exceptions to the privilege might not discourage such communication, Zacharias, supra, at 382, 386. Similarly, relatively few court decisions discuss the impact of the privilege's application after death. This may reflect the general assumption that the privilege survives—if attorneys were required as a matter of practice to testify or provide notes in criminal proceedings, cases discussing that practice would surely exist.

privileges in the law. And we are asked, not simply to "construe" the privilege, but to narrow it, contrary to the weight of the existing body of caselaw.

It has been generally, if not universally, accepted, for well over a century, that the attorney-client privilege survives the death of the client in a case such as this. While the arguments against the survival of the privilege are by no means frivolous, they are based in large part on speculation— thoughtful speculation, but speculation nonetheless—as to whether posthumous termination of the privilege would diminish a client's willingness to confide in an attorney. In an area where empirical information would be useful, it is scant and inconclusive.

Rule 501's direction to look to "the principles of the common law as they may be interpreted by the courts of the United States in the light of reason and experience" does not mandate that a rule, once established, should endure for all time. But here the Independent Counsel has simply not made a sufficient showing to overturn the common law rule embodied in the prevailing caselaw. Interpreted in the light of reason and experience, that body of law requires that the attorney client privilege prevent disclosure of the notes at issue in this case. The judgment of the Court of Appeals is

Reversed.

[Justice O'Connor filed a dissenting opinion, joined by Justice Scalia and Justice Thomas.]

JEREMY BENTHAM, RATIONALE OF JUDICIAL EVIDENCE
5:302-304 (1827)

English judges have taken care to exempt the professional members of the partnership from so unpleasant an obligation as that of rendering service to justice. . . . When, in consulting with a law adviser, attorney or advocate, a man has confessed his delinquency, or disclosed some fact which, if stated in court, might tend to operate in proof of it, such law adviser is not to be suffered to be examined as to any such point. The law adviser is neither to be compelled, nor so much as suffered, to betray the trust thus reposed in him. Not suffered? Why not? Oh, because to betray a trust is treachery; and an act of treachery is an immoral act.

An immoral sort of act, is that sort of act, the tendency of which is, in some way or other, to lessen the quantity of happiness in society. In what way does the supposed cause in question tend to the production of any such effect? The conviction and punishment of the defendant, he being guilty, is by the supposition an act the tendency of which, upon the whole, is beneficial to society. . . .

But if such confidence, when reposed, is permitted to be violated, and if this be known (which, if such be the law, it will be), the consequence will be, that no such confidence will be reposed. Not reposed?—Well: and if it be not, wherein will consist the mischief? The man by the supposition is guilty;

if not, by the supposition there is nothing to betray: let the law adviser say every thing he has heard, every thing he can have heard from his client, the client cannot have anything to fear from it. That it will often happen that in the case supposed no such confidence will be reposed, is natural enough: the first thing the attorney or advocate will say to his client, will be,— Remember that, whatever you say to me, I shall be obliged to tell, if asked about it. What, then will be the consequence? That a guilty person will not in general be able to derive quite so much assistance from his law adviser, in the way of concocting a false defence, as he may do at present.

WILLIAM H. SIMON, THE KAYE, SCHOLER AFFAIR: THE LAWYER'S DUTY OF CANDOR AND THE BAR'S TEMPTATIONS OF EVASION AND APOLOGY

23 Law & Soc. Inquiry 243 (1998)

For three years, lawyers from the New York firm of Kaye, Scholer, Fierman, Hays, & Handler devoted themselves to keeping the government off the back of Charles Keating while he engaged in financial and political exploits that eventuated in criminal convictions for Keating and several of his associates, billions of dollars in civil liability for Keating and a larger group of associates, formal criticism by the United States Senate of five of its members, and a loss to the federal banking insurance system estimated at $3.4 billion. . . . Succeeding Keating to ownership of the defunct Lincoln Savings & Loan, the banking agencies found themselves with access to records of confidential communications between the Keating crowd and the Kaye Scholer lawyers and, from this intimate vantage point, concluded that some of the lawyers' conduct went beyond the legitimate bounds of representation. The Office of Thrift Supervision (OTS) charged the lawyers with misconduct in a case the firm settled for $41 million and injunctive relief.

. . . The rationale for confidentiality with respect to ongoing or anticipated wrongful behavior is that it induces people to seek legal advice. But a person who intends to abide by the law in any event does not need this inducement. The key question is thus why it is important to induce people who think they might be inclined to violate the law to seek legal advice. Of course, such a person might learn something from the lawyer—say the size of the penalty—that would deter her from illegality. On the other hand, she might learn something that had the opposite effect. (Maybe the penalty will turn out to be lower than she expected.) So a key part of the bar's argument is that inducing people with a shaky commitment to law abidingness to seek legal advice is good because it gives their lawyers an opportunity to dissuade them from illegal conduct. The drafters of the Model Rules [of Professional Conduct] consider this practice so potent, they tell us, "Based upon experience, lawyers know that almost all clients follow the advice given, and the law is upheld (1983, Rule 1.6, comment, ¶ 3)."

Presumably the drafters were given pause by the chorus of ridicule with which many greeted OTS's suggestion that Kaye Scholer had a duty to exhort Lincoln's officers and directors to mend their ways. No one suggests that Kaye Scholer tried to dissuade the Lincoln people; the defense has been that it would have been transparently pointless for them to do so. . . . Lincoln thus appears to be an example of a case in which a rule abrogating confidentiality would not have had any bad effects. Very likely Keating would have refrained from seeking legal assistance. If OTS is right in suggesting Kaye Scholer exacerbated Lincoln's frauds, then it would have been a good thing for society if Keating had never retained the firm; even if OTS is wrong, there might not have been any social costs to depriving Keating of representation.

Of course, this is only one example. It is, however, a very large example, and one suspects one could find others among the aggressive S&L failures. Moreover, since the bar has yet to give us any specific examples of circumstances in which the confidentiality rule for ongoing and future acts provided positive social benefits, I'd say these cases were sufficient to shift the burden of going forward.

BENJAMIN H. BARTON, DO JUDGES SYSTEMATICALLY FAVOR THE INTERESTS OF THE LEGAL PROFESSION?

58 Ala. L. Rev. 453 (2008)

[M]any legal outcomes can be explained, and future cases predicted, by asking a very simple question: is there a plausible legal result in this case that will significantly affect the interests of the legal profession (positively or negatively)? If so, the case will be decided in the way that offers the best result for the legal profession. . . .

One of the oldest and most ingrained examples . . . is the [way in which] the attorney-client privilege has been accorded a unique and vaunted position among all professional privileges. . . . [T]he primacy of the attorney-client privilege—in comparison to other privileges like those accorded physicians, spouses, or clergy—cannot be justified solely jurisprudentially. Instead, the difference is most likely the inherent sympathy that judges have had for the importance of the attorney-client relationship. . . .

It is also worth noting what an exceptional product the attorney-client privilege allows lawyers to sell to clients. In conjunction with extremely tight professional confidentiality rules and norms, the attorney-client privilege offers clients protection for almost all disclosures. . . . If you are concerned at all about later confidentiality in court and need someone to talk to, you would be well advised to choose a lawyer.

2. Elements of the Privilege

Application of the attorney-client privilege typically requires four things: (a) a communication, (b) in confidence, (c) between a lawyer and client, (d) in the course of provision of professional legal services. In practice, analysis of the four elements often overlaps.

a. Communication

UNITED STATES v. KENDRICK

331 F.2d 110 (4th Cir. 1964)

PER CURIAM.

This is an appeal from the District Court's decision denying, after hearing, the petitioner's motion under 28 U.S.C.A. §2255 to vacate an illegal sentence on the grounds that the petitioner was incompetent to stand trial. . . . [In November 1960] he was tried and sentenced to seven years for three thefts from interstate commerce committed between July and September of that year. The substance of his allegations in the present action is . . . that at his trial in November of 1960 he was insane and suffering from amnesia; that as a result of his disabilities he was not competent to stand trial.

. . . We do not agree with the petitioner that the testimony of his trial counsel should have been excluded at the post-conviction hearing on the basis of the attorney-client privilege. . . . Communications made in confidence by a client to his attorney are protected by the attorney-client privilege. It is the substance of the communications which is protected, however, not the fact that there have been communications. Excluded from the privilege, also, are physical characteristics of the client, such as his complexion, his demeanor, his bearing, his sobriety and his dress. Such things are observable by anyone who talked with the client, and there is nothing, in the usual case, to suggest that the client intends his attorney's observations of such matters to be confidential. In short, the privilege protects only the client's confidences, not things which, at the time, are not intended to be held in the breast of the lawyer, even though the attorney-client relation provided the occasion for the lawyer's observation of them. *See generally* VIII Wigmore, Evidence (McNaughton Revision) §2306.

Here the attorney testified to just such nonconfidential matters. Petitioner, the attorney testified, was responsive, readily supplied the attorney with his version of the facts and the names of other people involved, was logical in his conversation and his reasoning, and appeared to know and understand everything that went on before and during the trial. No mention was made of the substance of any communication by client to attorney; the witness testified only about his client's cooperativeness and awareness.

All of the matters to which the attorney testified are objectively observable particularizations of the client's demeanor and attitude. Made at a time when neither client nor lawyer manifested any reason to suppose they were confidential, they were not within the privilege. . . . [Reversed on other grounds.]

TORNAY v. UNITED STATES

840 F.2d 1424 (9th Cir. 1988)

EUGENE A. WRIGHT, Circuit Judge:

. . . Stephen and Galene Tornay were the subject of an investigation by the Internal Revenue Service to determine their federal tax liability for tax years 1978 through 1983. The IRS sought to establish tax liability on a net worth, net expenditure basis. It issued summonses to three Oregon attorneys, whom the Tornays had retained in connection with a 1983 criminal conviction, for information regarding fees paid. When the attorneys complied with the summonses, the Tornays discharged them.

The Tornays also retained Seattle attorney Robert Wayne, their present counsel. [The IRS subsequently issued a summons to Wayne, seeking "information concerning the date, amount and form of legal fees paid to and trust funds deposited with Wayne by the Tornays during 1983."] Wayne failed to comply with the summons and continues to do so. The Tornays petitioned to quash. . . . The Tornays insist that they will discharge Wayne if he is forced to comply with the summons. [The district court denied the petition, and the Tornays appealed.]

The purpose of the attorney-client privilege is to encourage full disclosure to attorneys so they are able to render effective legal assistance. 8 J. Wigmore, Evidence §§2291-92 (McNaughton rev. 1961). Because "the privilege has the effect of withholding relevant information from the fact-finder, it applies only where necessary to achieve its purpose. Accordingly, it protects only those disclosures—necessary to obtain informed legal advice—which might not have been made absent the privilege." *Fisher v. United States*, 425 U.S. 391, 403 (1976).

We have said repeatedly, as the Tornays concede, that fee information generally is not privileged. Payment of fees is incidental to the attorney-client relationship, and does not usually involve disclosure of confidential communications arising from the professional relationship.

The Tornays argue that, in light of an exception to this rule, the privilege is applicable to information concerning fees paid to Wayne. The genesis of their argument is *Baird v. Koerner*, 279 F.2d 623 (9th Cir. 1960).

Baird involved several clients who directed their attorney to tender anonymously to the IRS delinquent tax payments and interest. The IRS issued a summons requiring counsel to identify his clients. We concluded that disclosure of the clients' identity was protected by the attorney-client privilege . . . because identifying the clients would be tantamount to conveying a privileged communication in which the clients disclosed their delinquent tax liabilities.

. . . *Baird* and its progeny do not apply here. The Tornays' identity was known to the IRS. The agency sought only the amount, date and form of the payments to Wayne. . . . The Tornays have not demonstrated the existence of exceptional circumstances that would make disclosure tantamount to revealing a confidential communication. . . .

. . . The Tornays argue that the privilege must be applied because the IRS summons has interfered with the attorney-client relationship. They say the primary reason for discharging their Oregon attorneys was their compliance with the IRS summonses. They presented two experienced defense lawyers who testified that: (1) a client is less forthcoming if he knows that his attorney might be called as a witness against him, and (2) a subpoena to a lawyer hinders the development of a defense because it distracts the lawyer.

We apply the attorney-client privilege only when necessary to effectuate its limited purpose of encouraging complete disclosure by the client. We are not persuaded that its purpose will be furthered by extending the privilege to information regarding fees paid by a client.

We do not believe that clients, knowing that their attorney may be compelled to testify about the amount, date, and form of fees paid, would be inhibited from disclosing fully information needed for effective legal representation. Nor do we accept a generalization that clients feel less free to disclose once it becomes apparent that their attorney's testimony may cause adverse results. The Tornays' voluntary discharge of their Oregon attorneys does not show that disclosure of fee information established a barrier to the free flow of information, nor does the possibility that an attorney may be required to expend time and resources to comply with a summons.

Some prospective clients, arguably, may decide not to retain counsel for legal services if they could be implicated by expenditures for those services. This is not, however, a sufficient justification to invoke the privilege. The privilege is not to immunize a client from liability stemming from expenditures for legal services. Its purpose is only to encourage persons who choose to be represented by counsel, despite the consequences of that choice, to confer candidly and openly with their attorney. The district court was correct in ruling that the attorney-client privilege was inapplicable. It did not abuse its discretion by denying the petition to quash. . . . The judgment is Affirmed.

b. In Confidence

UNITED STATES v. GANN

732 F.2d 714 (9th Cir. 1984)

Alarcon, Circuit Judge:

[Defendant Terry Gann was convicted of illegally possessing a sawed-off shotgun.] On April 28, 1982, the United States National Bank in Portland, Oregon was robbed of approximately $800 in currency and $18,000 in travelers' checks by Patrick Dussault. Dussault was observed fleeing in a yellow Mustang driven by Gann.

On May 19, 1982, warrants were issued for the search of Gann's home and of a 1972 green Vega automobile registered in his name. . . . After the agents found the bag containing the shotgun and shotgun ammunition in Gann's car, Detective Fantz of the Portland Police bureau decided to arrest him. Gann was in the house talking on the telephone in the presence of several law enforcement officers who were searching the house. One of the agents told Detective Fantz: "I think he is talking to his lawyer." Detective Fantz waited in the room in order to arrest Gann as soon as he got off the phone. Detective Fantz heard Gann state: "Looks like I'm going to have to go downtown," followed by the words "ex-con in possession, I guess." The government later introduced these statements to prove that Gann had knowledge of the shotgun and ammunition found in his vehicle. . . .

Because Gann knew, or should have known, that third parties were present, his attorney-client privilege claim must fail. The burden of proving that the privilege applies is upon the party asserting it. Here, Gann cannot show that his conversation with his attorney was made in confidence. The statement in question was made with the knowledge that he was surrounded by officers searching his residence. There is no evidence that Detective Fantz purposely positioned himself by the phone so that he could eavesdrop on a privileged communication. The evidence shows, instead, that the officer merely walked into the room and waited for Gann to complete his call. . . . The judgment is AFFIRMED.

UNITED STATES v. EVANS

113 F.3d 1457 (7th Cir. 1997)

CUMMINGS, Circuit Judge.

The trial of Jesse Evans, a Chicago alderman indicted on charges of racketeering (including acts of extortion, accepting bribes, and official misconduct), filing false tax returns, and obstruction of justice, is presently pending in the district court. This interlocutory appeal requires us to review an order of that court granting the government's pretrial motion *in limine* to admit certain testimony by attorney James Koch, which Evans asserts is protected by the attorney-client privilege. . . .

In early January 1996, news reports revealed that Alderman Evans had been targeted in a federal corruption investigation of City officials. . . . After learning that his long-time friend and occasional client had been implicated in the investigation, attorney John Holden, who is also a Chicago police officer, contacted Evans and spoke with him about Evans' interviews with FBI agents. In the aftermath of this meeting, Holden arranged for and scheduled Evans to meet with three criminal defense attorneys so that Evans could explain his situation, seek legal advice, and decide which of the three attorneys, if any, to retain. On January 8, 1996, after scheduling an appointment on Evans' behalf with attorney James Koch, Holden took Evans to Koch's office where the three conferred. . . .

The attorney-client privilege shields only those communications by a client to an attorney that were intended to be confidential. Thus as a general matter, the attorney-client privilege will not shield from disclosure statements made by a client to his or her attorney in the presence of a third party who is not an agent of either the client or attorney. See 8 Wigmore, Evidence

§2311 ("One of the circumstances by which it is commonly apparent that the communication is not confidential is the *presence of a third person* who is not the agent of either client or attorney."). . . .

Evans attempts to avoid this general rule by arguing that Holden was present at the meeting with Evans and Koch in his capacity as Evans' attorney. . . . [T]he district judge recognized that resolution of this capacity issue turned on a credibility determination . . . and she resolved the issue by crediting Koch's testimony. Koch expressly testified that Holden stated that he was present at the meeting *not* as an attorney, but as a personal friend of Evans and as a potential character witness. . . .

. . . Evans is not aided by cases holding that the presence of a third party at an attorney-client consultation does not defeat the privilege where the third party's presence was needed to make the conference possible or to assist the attorney in rendering legal services. Beyond stating the general rule, Evans has failed to carry his burden of proving that Holden's presence was necessary to accomplish the objective of his consultation. Evans' only showing on this score lies in Holden's discredited testimony that he was present at the meeting in order to advise Evans as to the relative abilities of the several defense attorneys who were to be consulted. Giving effect to the district court's factual findings, we must conclude that Holden was present merely as a friend and potential character witness. This is plainly insufficient to establish the necessity of Holden's presence. . . .

For the foregoing reasons, the district court's order granting the government's motion to admit Mr. Koch's testimony is affirmed.

UNITED STATES v. LAWLESS

709 F.2d 485 (7th Cir. 1983)

GRANT, Senior District Judge.

The Respondent-Appellee, J. Martin Lawless, an attorney in Peoria, Illinois, was retained by the co-executors of the estate to prepare the federal estate tax return of Edna E. Dieken, deceased. [The IRS sought by summons to obtain from Lawless all documents relating to or used in the preparation of the return. Lawless cited attorney-client privilege and refused to comply. After reviewing the disputed documents in camera, the district court ruled that two of them were privileged because "they were the type of information which I think the client is privileged to furnish to his attorney and not have the attorney disclose to the extent they were used in the preparation of the return." The government appealed.]

. . . When information is transmitted to an attorney with the intent that the information will be transmitted to a third party (in this case on a tax return), such information is not confidential. *Colton v. United States*, 306 F.2d 633, 638 (2d Cir. 1962), *cert. denied*, 371 U.S. 951 (1963).

The respondent argues that the information transmitted to him, as the attorney preparing the tax return, but which was not disclosed on the return, is protected by the privilege. If the client transmitted the information so that it might be used on the tax return, such a transmission destroys any expectation of confidentiality which might have otherwise existed. . . . Following the precedence of other Circuits . . . this Court now finds that information transmitted for the purpose of preparation of a tax return, though transmitted to an attorney, is not privileged information.

The holding of the district court is reversed and the documents are returned to the district court for enforcement proceedings consistent with this opinion.

SMITHKLINE BEECHAM CORP. v. APOTEX CORP.

193 F.R.D. 530 (N.D. Ill. 2000)

BOBRICK, United States Magistrate Judge.

Before the court is the motion of defendants Apotex Corporation, Apotex Inc., and Torpharm, Inc. to compel the production of certain documents listed in the privilege log of plaintiffs Smithkline Beecham Corporation and Beecham Group, Inc. [Plaintiffs sued defendants for infringing plaintiffs' patent to an antidepressant drug.]

. . . [W]hen information is transmitted to an attorney with the intent that it be transmitted to a third party, the material is not privileged. *United States v. Lawless*, 709 F.2d 485, 487 (7th Cir. 1983). In the end, however, the question is: does the document in question reveal, directly or indirectly, the substance of a confidential attorney-client communication.

. . . Courts have struggled with the application of the attorney-client privilege to the practice of patent law. It was not until 1963, that the Supreme Court established that patent practice—advising clients as to patentability, drafting specifications and claims, preparation of arguments to establish patentability, etc.—was the practice of law. *Sperry v. Florida*, 373 U.S. 379 (1963). Since that time courts have either considered patent attorneys to be conduits of information between a client and the Patent Office, where the lack of expectation of confidentiality doomed the application of the privilege, *see, e.g. Jack Winter, Inc. v. Koratron Co.*, 50 F.R.D. 225, 228 (N.D. Cal. 1970), or have rejected the conduit theory, and held that nearly all communications between client and patent attorney are requests for legal advice in that they pertain to assessment of patentability, and preparation and prosecution of the patent application. *Knogo Corp. v. U.S.*, 213 U.S.P.Q. 936, 939-41 (1980). Courts have also attempted to draw a line between technical and legal information which, in the context of patent law, is not a line easily drawn. *See, e.g. In re Spaulding Sports Worldwide*, 203 F.3d 800, 806 n. 3 (Fed. Cir. 2000) (collecting cases). . . .

In *Spalding*, the Federal Circuit discussed the application of the privilege to materials that were substantially technical, but produced in a legal setting: "It is enough that the overall tenor of the document indicates that it is a request for legal advice or services. . . . [A]n attorney cannot evaluate patentability or prepare a competent patent application without knowing the prior art and obtaining the relevant technical information from the inventors." 203 F.3d at 806; *see also* [*McCook Metals L.L.C. v. Alcoa Inc.*, 192 F.R.D. 242, 254 (N.D. Ill. 2000)] (following Federal Circuit law with respect to materials unique to patent law). Accordingly, we find such documents, described as prepared in order to allow attorneys to assess patentability and sift information to prepare applications, to be immune from discovery under the attorney-client privilege. . . .

c. Between Attorney and Client

UNITED STATES v. KOVEL

296 F.2d 918 (2d Cir. 1961)

FRIENDLY, Circuit Judge.

. . . Kovel is a former Internal Revenue agent having accounting skills. Since 1943 he has been employed by Kamerman & Kamerman, a law firm specializing in tax law. A grand jury in the Southern District of New York was investigating alleged Federal income tax violations by Hopps, a client of the law firm; Kovel was subpoenaed to appear on September 6, 1961, a few days before the date, September 8, when the Government feared the statute of limitations might run. The law firm advised the Assistant United States Attorney that since Kovel was an employee under the direct supervision of the partners, Kovel could not disclose any communications by the client of the result of any work done for the client, unless the latter consented; the Assistant answered that the attorney-client privilege did not apply to one who was not an attorney.

. . . [Questioned before the grand jury about his communications with Hopps, Kovel declined to answer on the ground of privilege. His refusal was relayed to the district court.] The court held him in contempt, sentenced him to a year's imprisonment, ordered immediate commitment and denied bail. Later in the day, the grand jury having indicted, Kovel was released until September 12, at which time, without opposition from the Government, I granted bail pending determination of this appeal.

Here the parties continue to take generally the same positions as below—Kovel, that his status as an employee of a law firm automatically made all communications to him from clients privileged; the Government, that under no circumstances could there be privilege with respect to communications to an accountant. The New York County Lawyers' Association as amicus curiae has filed a brief generally supporting appellant's position.

Decision under what circumstances, if any, the attorney-client privilege may include a communication to a nonlawyer by the lawyer's client is the resultant of two conflicting forces. One is the general teaching that "The investigation of truth and the enforcement of testimonial duty demand the restriction, not the expansion, of these privileges," 8 Wigmore, Evidence (McNaughton Rev. 1961), §2192, p. 73. The other is the more particular lesson "That as, by reason of the complexity and difficulty of our law, litigation can only be properly conducted by professional men, it is absolutely necessary that a man . . . should have recourse to the assistance of professional lawyers, and . . . it is equally necessary . . . that he should be able to place unrestricted and unbounded confidence in the professional agent, and that the communications he so makes to him should be kept secret . . . ," Jessel, M.R. in *Anderson v. Bank*, 2 Ch. D. 644, 649 (1876). Nothing in the policy of the privilege suggests that attorneys, simply by placing accountants, scientists or investigators on their payrolls and maintaining them in their offices, should be able to invest all communications by clients to such persons with a privilege the law has not seen fit to extend when the latter are operating under their own steam. On the other hand, in contrast to the Tudor times when the privilege was first recognized, see 8 Wigmore, Evidence, §2290, the complexities of modern existence prevent attorneys from effectively handling clients' affairs without the help of others; few lawyers could now practice without the assistance of secretaries, file clerks, telephone operators, messengers, clerks not yet admitted to the bar, and aides of other sorts. "The assistance of these agents being indispensable to his work and the communications of the client being often necessarily committed to them by the attorney or by the client himself, the privilege must include all the persons who act as the attorney's agents." 8 Wigmore, Evidence, §2301

Indeed, the Government does not here dispute that the privilege covers communications to non-lawyer employees with "a menial or ministerial responsibility that involves relating communications to an attorney." We cannot regard the privilege as confined to "menial or ministerial" employees. Thus, we can see no significant difference between a case where the attorney sends a client speaking a foreign language to an interpreter to make a literal translation of the client's story; a second where the attorney, himself having some little knowledge of the foreign tongue, has a more knowledgeable non-lawyer employee in the room to help out; a third where someone to perform that same function has been brought along by the client; and a fourth where the attorney, ignorant of the foreign language, sends the client to a non-lawyer proficient in it, with instructions to interview the client on the attorney's behalf and then render his own summary of the situation, perhaps drawing on his own knowledge in the process, so that the attorney can give the client proper legal advice. All four cases meet every element of Wigmore's famous formulation, §2292, "(1) Where legal advice of any kind is sought (2) from professional legal adviser in his capacity as such, (3) the communications relating to that purpose, (4) made in confidence (5) by the client, (6) are at his instance permanently protected (7) from disclosure by himself or by the legal adviser, (8) except the protection be waived," save (7); literally, none of them is within (7) since the disclosure is not sought to be compelled from the client or the lawyer. Yet §2301 of Wigmore would clearly recognize the privilege in the first case and the Government goes along to that extent; §2301 would also recognize the privilege in the second case and §2311 in the third unless the circumstances negated confidentiality. We find no valid policy reason for a different result in the fourth case, and we do not read Wigmore as thinking there is. Laymen consulting lawyers should not be expected to anticipate niceties perceptible only to judges—and not even to all of them.

This analogy of the client speaking a foreign language is by no means irrelevant to the appeal at hand. Accounting concepts are a foreign language to some lawyers in almost all cases, and to almost all lawyers in some cases. Hence the presence of an accountant, whether hired by the lawyer or by the client, while the client is relating a complicated tax story to the lawyer, ought not destroy the privilege, any more than would that of the linguist in the second or third variations of the foreign language theme discussed above; the presence of the accountant is necessary, or at least highly useful, for the effective consultation between the client and the lawyer which the privilege is designed to permit. By the same token, if the lawyer has directed the client, either in the specific case or generally, to tell his story in the first instance to an accountant engaged by the lawyer, who is then to interpret it so that the lawyer may better give legal advice, communications by the client reasonably related to that purpose ought fall within the privilege; there can be no more virtue in requiring the lawyer to sit by while the client pursues these possibly tedious preliminary conversations with the accountant than in insisting on the lawyer's physical presence while the client dictates a statement to the lawyer's secretary or is interviewed by a clerk not yet admitted to practice. What is vital to the privilege is that the communication be made in confidence for the purpose of obtaining legal advice from the lawyer. If what is sought is not legal advice but only accounting service, as in *Olender v. United States*, 210 F.2d 795, 805-806 (9 Cir. 1954), or if the advice sought is the accountant's rather than the lawyer's, no privilege exists. We recognize this draws what may seem to some a rather arbitrary line between a case where the client communicates first to his own accountant (no privilege as to such communications, even though he later consults his lawyer on the same matter, *Gariepy v. United States*, 189 F.2d 459, 463 (6 Cir. 1951)), and others, where the client in the first instance consults a lawyer who retains an accountant as a listening post, or consults the lawyer with his own accountant present. But that is the inevitable consequence of having to reconcile the absence of a privilege for accountants and the effective operation of the privilege of client and lawyer under conditions where the lawyer needs outside help. We realize also that the line we have drawn will not be so easy to apply as the simpler positions urged on us by the parties—the district judges will scarcely be able to leave the decision of such cases to computers; but the distinction has to be made if the privilege is neither to be unduly expanded nor to become a trap.

. . . The judgment is vacated and the cause remanded for further proceedings consistent with this opinion.

UNITED STATES v. McPARTLIN

595 F.2d 1321 (7th Cir. 1979)

TONE, Circuit Judge.

The appellants were convicted, in a nine-week jury trial, of conspiring to violate the wire and travel fraud statutes and of substantive violations of those statutes.

The indictment charged that defendant Frederick B. Ingram, chairman of the board of the Louisiana-based Ingram Corporation, had paid defendant Robert F. McPartlin, an Illinois legislator, defendant Valentine Janicki, a trustee for the Metropolitan Sanitary District, and others more than $900,000 to secure for the Ingram Corporation a multi-million dollar sludge-hauling contract with the District. . . . William J. Benton, vice president of Ingram Corporation, was an unindicted co-conspirator who played a major role in the conspiracy and testified as a witness for the prosecution.

. . . Throughout the period covered by the indictment, Benton kept diaries, or appointment calendars, in which he made notes concerning meetings and telephone conversations, naming the persons involved and often recording the substance of the conversations. The Benton diaries figured prominently in the government's case, for they corroborated much of his testimony.

. . . An investigator acting for Frederick Ingram's counsel twice interviewed McPartlin with the consent of the latter's counsel for the purpose of determining whether there was a basis for challenging the truth of some of the diary entries. In the second of these interviews McPartlin made certain statements, which Ingram argues tend to support his defense. At trial, when Ingram offered evidence of these statements, McPartlin's counsel objected on the ground, inter alia, of the attorney-client privilege, and the court, after an in camera hearing, sustained the objection. . . .

McPartlin was entitled to the protection of the attorney-client privilege, because his statements were made in confidence to an attorney for a codefendant for a common purpose related to both defenses. They were made in connection with the project of attempting to discredit Benton, a project in which Ingram and McPartlin and their attorneys were jointly engaged for the benefit of both defendants. Ingram acknowledges that communications by a client to his own lawyer remain privileged when the lawyer subsequently shares them with co-defendants for purposes of a common defense. The common-defense rule, which is not as narrow as Ingram contends, has been recognized in cases spanning more than a century. Uninhibited communication among joint parties and their counsel about matters of common concern is often important to the protection of their interests. In criminal cases it can be necessary to a fair opportunity to defend. Therefore, waiver is not to be inferred from the disclosure in confidence to a co-party's attorney for a common purpose.

. . . Ingram argues that the co-defendants' defenses must be in all respects compatible if the joint-defense privilege is to be applicable. The cases do not establish such a limitation, and there is no reason to impose it. . . . The privilege protects pooling of information for any defense purpose common to the participating defendants. Cooperation between defendants in such circumstances is often not only in their own best interests but serves to expedite the trial or, as in the case at bar, the trial preparation.

Ingram also seems to argue that the communication was not privileged because it was made to an investigator rather than an attorney. The investigator was an agent for Ingram's attorney, however, so it is as if the communication was to the attorney himself. "It has never been questioned that the privilege protects communications to the attorney's . . . agents . . . for rendering his services." 8 Wigmore, Evidence §2301 at 583 (McNaughton rev. 1961); *cf. United States v. Kovel*, 296 F.2d 918, 921-922 (2d Cir. 1961) (client's communications to an accountant employed by his attorney).

Nor was it, as Ingram contends, fatal to the privilege that McPartlin made the statement, in effect, to Ingram's attorney rather than his own. When the Ingram and McPartlin camps decided to join in an attempt to discredit Benton, the attorney for each represented both for purposes of that joint effort. The relationship was no different than it would have been if during the trial the Ingram and McPartlin attorneys had decided that Ingram's attorney would cross-examine Benton on behalf of both, and during cross-examination McPartlin passed Ingram's attorney a note containing information for use in the cross-examination. The attorney who thus undertakes to serve his client's co-defendant for a limited purpose becomes the co-defendant's attorney for that purpose. [Affirmed.]

PASTERIS v. ROBILLARD

121 F.R.D. 18 (D. Mass. 1988)

JOYCE L. ALEXANDER, United States Magistrate.

[Marie and Stanley Pasteris sued Gary and Sharon Robillard for injuries Marie suffered when she fell down a flight of stairs at the Robillard's home. The plaintiffs sought discovery of Gary Robillard's transcribed statement to his insurance company. The defendants objected on grounds of attorney-client privilege.]

. . . The attorney-client privilege protects certain communications between client and attorney. The privilege applies only if the person to whom the communication was made is a member of the bar of a court, or his subordinate, and in connection with this communication is acting as a lawyer. *United States v. United Shoe Machinery Corporation*, 89 F. Supp. 357, 358 (D. Mass.1950). Absent this element, the privilege cannot be invoked. Defendants do not contend that Mr. Robillard's statement was made to an attorney. *United States v. Wilson*, 798 F.2d 509, 512-13 (1st Cir. 1986). Therefore, the statement, to merit protection, must have been given to a subordinate of an attorney who was acting as a lawyer when the statement was made.

Defendants state that Mr. Robillard's insurance policy requires his insurance company to defend him. Further, defendants aver that the insurance policy, running from defendants to the insurance company, requires that the insured cooperate with his insurer. Defendants conclude that the statement was given by Mr. Robillard to his insurer to assist the insurer, and the attorney it would retain to defend Mr. Robillard. Notwithstanding the insurance company's obligation to defend and Mr. Robillard's duty to cooperate, defendants do not advance facts showing that the person to whom the communication was made—presumably, i.e., an employee of the insurance company—was actually a subordinate of an attorney or that the individual taking the statement on behalf of the insurance company was acting as an attorney. Thus, defendants cannot invoke the attorney-client privilege. . . . So ORDERED.

UPJOHN CO. v. UNITED STATES

449 U.S. 383 (1981)

Justice REHNQUIST delivered the opinion of the Court.

. . . Petitioner Upjohn Co. manufactures and sells pharmaceuticals here and abroad. In January 1976 independent accountants conducting an audit of one of Upjohn's foreign subsidiaries discovered that the subsidiary made payments to or for the benefit of foreign government officials in order to secure government business. The accountants so informed petitioner, Mr. Gerard Thomas, Upjohn's Vice President, Secretary, and General Counsel. Thomas is a member of the Michigan and New York Bars, and has been Upjohn's General Counsel for 20 years. He consulted with outside counsel and R. T. Parfet, Jr., Upjohn's Chairman of the Board. It was decided that the company would conduct an internal investigation of what were termed "questionable payments." As part of this investigation the attorneys prepared a letter containing a questionnaire which was sent to "All Foreign General and Area Managers" over the Chairman's signature. The letter began by noting recent disclosures that several American companies made "possibly illegal" payments to foreign government officials and emphasized that the management needed full information concerning any such payments made by Upjohn. The letter indicated that the Chairman had asked Thomas, identified as "the company's General Counsel," "to conduct an investigation for the purpose of determining the nature and magnitude of any payments made by the Upjohn Company or any of its subsidiaries to any employee or official of a foreign government." The questionnaire sought detailed information concerning such payments. Managers were instructed to treat the investigation as "highly confidential" and not to discuss it with anyone other than Upjohn employees who might be helpful in providing the requested information. Responses were to be sent directly to Thomas. Thomas and outside counsel also interviewed the recipients of the questionnaire and some 33 other Upjohn officers or employees as part of the investigation.

On March 26, 1976, the company voluntarily submitted a preliminary report to the Securities and Exchange Commission on Form 8-k disclosing certain questionable payments. A copy of the report was simultaneously submitted to the Internal Revenue Service, which immediately began an investigation to determine the tax consequences of the payments. Special agents conducting the investigation were given lists by Upjohn of all those interviewed and all who had responded to the questionnaire. On November 23, 1976, the Service issued a summons pursuant to 26 U.S.C. §7602 demanding production of:

> "All files relative to the investigation conducted under the supervision of Gerard Thomas to identify payments to employees of foreign governments

and any political contributions made by the Upjohn Company or any of its affiliates since January 1, 1971 and to determine whether any funds of the Upjohn Company had been improperly accounted for on the corporate books during the same period.

"The records should include but not be limited to written questionnaires sent to managers of the Upjohn Company's foreign affiliates, and memorandums or notes of the interviews conducted in the United States and abroad with officers and employees of the Upjohn Company and its subsidiaries."

The company declined to produce the documents specified in the second paragraph on the grounds that they were protected from disclosure by the attorney-client privilege and constituted the work product of attorneys prepared in anticipation of litigation. On August 31, 1977, the United States filed a petition seeking enforcement of the summons under 26 U.S.C. §§7402(b) and 7604(a) in the United States District Court for the Western District of Michigan. That court adopted the recommendation of a Magistrate who concluded that the summons should be enforced. Petitioners appealed to the Court of Appeals for the Sixth Circuit which rejected the Magistrate's finding of a waiver of the attorney-client privilege, but agreed that the privilege did not apply "[t]o the extent that the communications were made by officers and agents not responsible for directing Upjohn's actions in response to legal advice . . . for the simple reason that the communications were not the 'client's.' " . . . In a concluding footnote the court stated that the work-product doctrine "is not applicable to administrative summonses issued under 26 U.S.C. §7602."

Federal Rule of Evidence 501 provides that "the privilege of a witness . . . shall be governed by the principles of the common law as they may be interpreted by the courts of the United States in light of reason and experience." The attorney-client privilege is the oldest of the privileges for confidential communications known to the common law. 8 J. Wigmore, Evidence §2290 (McNaughton rev. 1961). Its purpose is to encourage full and frank communication between attorneys and their clients and thereby promote broader public interests in the observance of law and administration of justice. The privilege recognizes that sound legal advice or advocacy serves public ends and that such advice or advocacy depends upon the lawyer's being fully informed by the client. As we stated last Term in *Trammel v. United States*, 445 U.S. 40, 51 (1980): "The lawyer-client privilege rests on the need for the advocate and counselor to know all that relates to the client's reasons for seeking representation if the professional mission is to be carried out." And in *Fisher v. United States*, 425 U.S. 391, 403 (1976), we recognized the purpose of the privilege to be "to encourage clients to make full disclosure to their attorneys." This rationale for the privilege has long been recognized by the Court, see *Hunt v. Blackburn*, 128 U.S. 464, 470 (1888) (privilege "is founded upon the necessity, in the interest and administration of justice, of the aid of persons having knowledge of the law and skilled in its practice, which assistance can only be safely and readily availed of when free from the consequences or the apprehension of disclosure"). Admittedly complications in the application of the privilege arise when the client is a corporation, which in theory is an artificial creature of the law, and not an individual; but this Court has assumed that the privilege applies when the client is a corporation, *United States v. Louisville & Nashville R. Co.*, 236 U.S. 318, 336 (1915), and the Government does not contest the general proposition.

The Court of Appeals, however, considered the application of the privilege in the corporate context to present a "different problem," since the client was an inanimate entity and "only the senior management, guiding and integrating the several operations, . . . can be said to possess an identity analogous to the corporation as a whole." The first case to articulate the so-called "control group test" adopted by the court below, *Philadelphia v. Westinghouse Electric Corp.*, 210 F. Supp. 483, 485 (ED Pa.), *petition for mandamus and prohibition denied sub nom General Electric Co. v. Kirkpatrick*, 312 F.2d 742 (CA3 1962), *cert denied*, 372 U.S. 943 (1963), reflected a similar conceptual approach:

> "Keeping in mind that the question is, Is it the corporation which is seeking the lawyer's advice when the asserted privileged communication is made?, the most satisfactory solution, I think, is that if the employee making the communication, of whatever rank he may be, is in a position to control or even to take a substantial part in a decision about any action which the corporation may take upon the advice of the attorney, . . . then, in effect, *he is (or personifies) the corporation* when he makes his disclosure to the lawyer and the privilege would apply." (Emphasis supplied.)

Such a view, we think, overlooks the fact that the privilege exists to protect not only the giving of professional advice to those who can act on it but also the giving of information to the lawyer to enable him to give sound and informed advice. The first step in the resolution of any legal problem is ascertaining the factual background and sifting through the facts with an eye to the legally relevant. See ABA Code of Professional Responsibility, Ethical Consideration 4-1:

> "A lawyer should be fully informed of all the facts of the matter he is handling in order for his client to obtain the full advantage of our legal system. It is for the lawyer in the exercise of his independent professional judgment to separate the relevant and important from the irrelevant and unimportant. The observance of the ethical obligation of a lawyer to hold inviolate the confidences and secrets of his client not only facilitates the full development of facts essential to proper representation of the client but also encourages laymen to seek early legal assistance."

See also *Hickman v. Taylor*, 329 U.S. 495, 511 (1947).

In the case of the individual client the provider of information and the person who acts on the lawyer's advice are one and the same. In the corporate context, however, it will frequently be employees beyond the control group as defined by the court below—"officers and agents . . . responsible for directing [the company's] actions in response to legal advice"—who will possess the information needed by the corporation's lawyers. Middle-level—and indeed lower-level—employees can, by actions within the scope of their employment, embroil the corporation in serious legal difficulties, and it is only natural that these employees would have the relevant information needed by corporate counsel if he is adequately to advise the client with respect to such actual or potential difficulties. . . .

The control group test adopted by the court below thus frustrates the very purpose of the privilege by discouraging the communication of relevant information by employees of the client to attorneys seeking to render legal advice to the client corporation. The attorney's advice will also frequently be more significant to noncontrol group members than to those who officially sanction the advice, and the control group test makes it more difficult to convey full and frank legal advice to the employees who will put into effect the client corporation's policy. . . .

The narrow scope given the attorney-client privilege by the court below not only makes it difficult for corporate attorneys to formulate sound advice when their client is faced with a specific legal problem but also threatens to limit the valuable efforts of corporate counsel to ensure their client's compliance with the law. In light of the vast and complicated array of regulatory legislation confronting the modern corporation, corporations, unlike most individuals, "constantly go to lawyers to find out how to obey the law," Burnham, The Attorney-Client Privilege in the Corporate Arena, 24 Bus. Law. 901, 913 (1969), particularly since compliance with the law in this area is hardly an instinctive matter, see, e. g., *United States v. United States Gypsum Co.*, 438 U.S. 422, 440-441 (1978) ("the behavior proscribed by the [Sherman] Act is often difficult to distinguish from the gray zone of socially acceptable and economically justifiable business conduct"). The test adopted by the court below is difficult to apply in practice, though no abstractly formulated and unvarying "test" will necessarily enable courts to decide questions such as this with mathematical precision. But if the purpose of the attorney-client privilege is to be served, the attorney and client must be able to predict with some degree of certainty whether particular discussions will be protected. An uncertain privilege, or one which purports to be certain but results in widely varying applications by the courts, is little better than no privilege at all. The very terms of the test adopted by the court below suggest the unpredictability of its application. The test restricts the availability of the privilege to those officers who play a "substantial role" in deciding and directing a corporation's legal response. Disparate decisions in cases applying this test illustrate its unpredictability. Compare, e.g., *Hogan v. Zletz*, 43 F.R.D. 308, 315-316 (ND Okla. 1967), *aff'd in part sub nom. Natta v. Hogan*, 392 F.2d 686 (CA10 1968) (control group includes managers and assistant managers of patent division and research and development department), with *Congoleum Industries, Inc. v. GAF Corp.*, 49 F.R.D. 82, 83-85 (ED Pa. 1969), *aff'd*, 478 F.2d 1398 (CA3 1973) (control group includes only division and corporate vice presidents, and not two directors of research and vice president for production and research).

The communications at issue were made by Upjohn employees[1] to counsel for Upjohn acting as such, at the direction of corporate

---

1. Seven of the eighty-six employees interviewed by counsel had terminated their employment with Upjohn at the time of the interview. Petitioners argue that the privilege should nonetheless apply to communications by these former employees concerning activities during their period of employment. Neither the District Court nor the Court of Appeals had occasion to address this issue, and we decline to decide it without the benefit of treatment below.

superiors in order to secure legal advice from counsel. As the Magistrate found, "Mr. Thomas consulted with the Chairman of the Board and outside counsel and thereafter conducted a factual investigation to determine the nature and extent of the questionable payments *and to be in a position to give legal advice to the company with respect to the payments*." (Emphasis supplied.) Information, not available from upper-echelon management, was needed to supply a basis for legal advice concerning compliance with securities and tax laws, foreign laws, currency regulations, duties to shareholders, and potential litigation in each of these areas. The communications concerned matters within the scope of the employees' corporate duties, and the employees themselves were sufficiently aware that they were being questioned in order that the corporation could obtain legal advice. The questionnaire identified Thomas as "the company's General Counsel" and referred in its opening sentence to the possible illegality of payments such as the ones on which information was sought. A statement of policy accompanying the questionnaire clearly indicated the legal implications of the investigation. The policy statement was issued "in order that there be no uncertainty in the future as to the policy with respect to the practices which are the subject of this investigation." It began "Upjohn will comply with all laws and regulations," and stated that commissions or payments "will not be used as a subterfuge for bribes or illegal payments" and that all payments must be "proper and legal." Any future agreements with foreign distributors or agents were to be approved "by a company attorney" and any questions concerning the policy were to be referred "to the company's General Counsel." This statement was issued to Upjohn employees worldwide, so that even those interviewees not receiving a questionnaire were aware of the legal implications of the interviews. Pursuant to explicit instructions from the Chairman of the Board, the communications were considered "highly confidential" when made, and have been kept confidential by the company. Consistent with the underlying purposes of the attorney-client privilege, these communications must be protected against compelled disclosure.

The Court of Appeals declined to extend the attorney-client privilege beyond the limits of the control group test for fear that doing so would entail severe burdens on discovery and create a broad "zone of silence" over corporate affairs. Application of the attorney-client privilege to communications such as those involved here, however, puts the adversary in no worse position than if the communications had never taken place. The privilege only protects disclosure of communications; it does not protect disclosure of the underlying facts by those who communicated with the attorney:

> "[T]he protection of the privilege extends only to *communications* and not to facts. A fact is one thing and a communication concerning that fact is an entirely different thing. The client cannot be compelled to answer the question, 'What did you say or write to the attorney?' but may not refuse to disclose any relevant fact within his knowledge merely because he incorporated a statement of such fact into his communication to his attorney."
> *Philadelphia v. Westinghouse Electric Corp.*, 205 F. Supp. 830, 831.

Here the Government was free to question the employees who communicated with Thomas and outside counsel. Upjohn has provided the IRS with a list of such employees, and the IRS has already interviewed some 25 of them. While it would probably be more convenient for the Government to secure the results of petitioner's internal investigation by simply subpoenaing the questionnaires and notes taken by petitioner's attorneys, such considerations of convenience do not overcome the policies served by the attorney-client privilege. As Justice Jackson noted in his concurring opinion in *Hickman v. Taylor*, 329 U.S., at 516: "Discovery was hardly intended to enable a learned profession to perform its functions . . . on wits borrowed from the adversary."

Needless to say, we decide only the case before us, and do not undertake to draft a set of rules which should govern challenges to investigatory subpoenas. Any such approach would violate the spirit of Federal Rule of Evidence 501. See S. Rep. No. 93-1277, p. 13 (1974) ("the recognition of a privilege based on a confidential relationship . . . should be determined on a case-by-case basis"). While such a "case-by-case" basis may to some slight extent undermine desirable certainty in the boundaries of the attorney-client privilege, it obeys the spirit of the Rules. At the same time we conclude that the narrow "control group test" sanctioned by the Court of Appeals, in this case cannot, consistent with "the principles of the common law as . . . interpreted . . . in the light of reason and experience," Fed. Rule Evid. 501, govern the development of the law in this area.

Our decision that the communications by Upjohn employees to counsel are covered by the attorney-client privilege disposes of the case so far as the responses to the questionnaires and any notes reflecting responses to interview questions are concerned. The summons reaches further, however, and Thomas has testified that his notes and memoranda of interviews go beyond recording responses to his questions. To the extent that the material subject to the summons is not protected by the attorney-client privilege as disclosing communications between an employee and counsel, we must reach the ruling by the Court of Appeals that the work-product doctrine does not apply to summonses issued under 26 U.S.C. §7602.

The Government concedes, wisely, that the Court of Appeals erred and that the work-product doctrine does apply to IRS summonses. This doctrine was announced by the Court over 30 years ago in *Hickman v. Taylor*, 329 U.S. 495 (1947). In that case the Court rejected "an attempt, without purported necessity or justification, to secure written statements, private memoranda and personal recollections prepared or formed by an adverse party's counsel in the course of his legal duties." The Court noted that "it is essential that a lawyer work with a certain degree of privacy" and reasoned that if discovery of the material sought were permitted

> "much of what is now put down in writing would remain unwritten. An attorney's thoughts, heretofore inviolate, would not be his own. Inefficiency, unfairness and sharp practices would inevitably develop in the giving of legal advice and in the preparation of cases for trial. The effect on the legal profession would be demoralizing. And the interests of the clients and the cause of justice would be poorly served."

The "strong public policy" underlying the work-product doctrine was reaffirmed recently in *United States v. Nobles*, 422 U.S. 225, 236-240 (1975), and Has been substantially incorporated in Federal Rule of Civil Procedure 26(b)(3).[7] . . . While conceding the applicability of the work-product doctrine, the Government asserts that it has made a sufficient showing of necessity to overcome its protections. The Magistrate apparently so found.

. . . It is clear that the Magistrate applied the wrong standard when he concluded that the Government had made a sufficient showing of necessity to overcome the protections of the work-product doctrine. The Magistrate applied the "substantial need" and "without undue hardship" standard articulated in the first part of Rule 26(b)(3). The notes and memoranda sought by the Government here, however, are work product based on oral statements. If they reveal communications, they are, in this case, protected by the attorney-client privilege. To the extent they do not reveal communications, they reveal the attorneys' mental processes in evaluating the communications. As Rule 26 and *Hickman* make clear, such work product cannot be disclosed simply on a showing of substantial need and inability to obtain the equivalent without undue hardship.

While we are not prepared at this juncture to say that such material is always protected by the work-product rule, we think a far stronger showing of necessity and unavailability by other means than was made by the Government or applied by the Magistrate in this case would be necessary to compel disclosure. Since the Court of Appeals thought that the work-product protection was never applicable in an enforcement proceeding such as this, and since the Magistrate whose recommendations the District Court adopted applied too lenient a standard of protection, we think the best procedure with respect to this aspect of the case would be to reverse the judgment of the Court of Appeals for the Sixth Circuit and remand the case to it for such further proceedings in connection with the work-product claim as are consistent with this opinion.

Accordingly, the judgment of the Court of Appeals is reversed, and the Case remanded for further proceedings.

[Chief Justice Burger filed an opinion concurring in part and concurring in the judgment.]

---

7. This provides, in pertinent part: "[A] party may obtain discovery of documents and tangible things otherwise discoverable under subdivision (b)(1) of this rule and prepared in anticipation of litigation or for trial by or for another party or by or for that other party's representative (including his attorney, consultant, surety, indemnitor, insurer, or agent) only upon a showing that the party seeking discovery has substantial need of the materials in the preparation of his case and that he is unable without undue hardship to obtain the substantial equivalent of the materials by other means. In ordering discovery of such materials when the required showing has been made, the court shall protect against disclosure of the mental impressions, conclusions, opinions, or legal theories of an attorney or other representative of a party concerning the litigation."

d. To Facilitate Legal Service

HUGHES v. MEADE

453 S.W.2d 538 (Ky. 1970)

CLAY, Commissioner.

This is an original proceeding for a writ of prohibition against the Honorable N. Mitchell Meade, Judge of the Fayette Circuit Court. Petitioner, an attorney, seeks to restrain the respondent from enforcing a contempt ruling entered against him because of his refusal to answer a question as a witness in a criminal trial. Petitioner was not a party to, nor did he represent anyone as an attorney in such proceeding.

The proceeding in which he was called as a witness was the trial of one Williams on a criminal charge involving the theft of an IBM typewriter. Petitioner had participated in the return of an IBM typewriter to the Lexington Police Department. [He refused to disclose who had hired him to return it.] It Is his contention that his information was a privileged communication under KRS 421.210(4), and the trial court improperly sought to compel him to disclose it. That subsection of the statute provides (insofar as pertinent): "No attorney shall testify concerning a *communication* made to him, *in his professional character*, by his client, or his advice thereon without the Client's consent. . . ." (Emphasis added.)

This statutory provision generally conforms to the common law policy and principle of attorney-client privilege (developed since 1800) and it is generally recognized in the United States. See 8 Wigmore, Evidence §2291 (McNaughton rev. 1961). This same author thus phrases the principle (page 554): "(1) Where legal advice of any kind is sought (2) from a professional legal adviser in his capacity as such, (3) the communications relating to that purpose, (4) made in confidence (5) by the client, (6) are at his instance permanently protected (7) from disclosure by himself or by the legal adviser, (8) except the protection be waived."

. . . In line with those limitations, it is generally held that the identity of a client is not a privileged communication. *United States v. Page* (C.A.2 1944), 144 F.2d 778, 782, *cert den.* 323 U.S. 752 (1944); *Behrens v. Hironimus* (C.A.4 1948), 170 F.2d 627, 628; *Colton v. United States* (C.A.2 1962), 306 F.2d 633, 637; *NLRB v. Harvey* (C.A.4 1965), 349 F.2d 900. . . . This general rule, however, like most others, is subject to exception under unusual circumstances. In the following cases the identity of the client was held within the scope of the privilege. *Ex parte McDonough*, 170 Cal. 230 (1915); *Baird v. Koerner* (C.A.9 1960), 279 F.2d 623; *In Re Kaplan*, 8 N.Y.2d 214 (1960); and *Tillotson v. Boughner* (C.A.7 1965), 350 F.2d 663.

In the above cases the attorney-client relationship was clearly established, and the acts performed were closely interrelated with the rendering of professional service. In *McDonough* the attorney had been employed by an undisclosed client to defend a criminal charge against another person. In *Baird* the attorney had turned over to the government a sum of money which some taxpayers, in consultation with the attorney, had determined was due and owing as unpaid income taxes. The court observed that the only reason for obtaining information concerning the clients' identities was for the purpose of prosecution. *Tillotson* involved facts similar to those in *Baird*. In *Kaplan* the attorney had been retained to pass on to a public investigating body certain information concerning certain apparent wrongdoing by municipal authorities. It was here observed that since the information had been given, the client's name deserved and needed protection.

As noted in the foregoing cases, the transactions about which information had been given constituted in essence the performance of a legal service. On the other hand, if the act in question fairly cannot be said to fall within the scope of professional employment, the privilege cannot be invoked. As said in 97 C.J.S. Witnesses §280, page 793: "Neither is there any privilege as to communications with reference to a matter in which the attorney acts, not in his professional capacity, but merely as an agent or attorney in fact, or in which the attorney acts merely as a depositary or as a trustee, particularly where he has instructions to deliver the instrument deposited to a third person, or abstracter of titles."

. . . Returning to the facts of this case, it is the opinion of the majority of the court that whether or not a bona fide attorney-client relationship existed between the petitioner and the undisclosed person, the principal transaction involved, i.e., the delivery of stolen property to the police department, was not an act in the professional capacity of petitioner nor was it the rendition of a legal service. He was acting as an agent or conduit for the delivery of property which was completely unrelated to legal representation. While repose of confidence in an attorney is something much to be desired, to use him as a shield to conceal transactions involving stolen property is beyond the scope of his professional duty and beyond the scope of the privilege. . . . The petition for a writ of prohibition is denied.

UNITED STATES v. DAVIS

636 F.2d 1028 (5th Cir. 1981)

WISDOM, Circuit Judge:

[Attorney Craig Davis appealed from a judgment enforcing an IRS summons requiring him to produce documents relating to the tax liability of his client.] The summons to Davis requests the workpapers he produced in the course of preparing Howard's tax returns and the tax records upon which they were based. Neither category of documents is privileged, because although preparation of tax returns by itself may require some knowledge of the law, it is primarily an accounting service. Communications relating to that service should therefore not be privileged, even though performed by a lawyer. *Olender v. United States*, 9 Cir. 1954, 210 F.2d 795, 805-06; *Canaday v. United States*, 8 Cir. 1966, 354 F.2d 849, 857. Some courts have suggested, to the contrary, that tax return preparation and tax advice is sufficiently "legal" in nature to trigger the privilege. *See*

Colton v. United States, 2 Cir. 1962, 306 F.2d 633, 637, *cert. denied*, 1963, 371 U.S. 951. These services, however, are typically performed by accountants, and since there is no accountant-client privilege under federal law, there is no doubt that the papers summoned here would not be privileged if Howard had had a professional accountant prepare his returns. *Couch v. United States*, 1973, 409 U.S. 322, 335; *Falsone v. United States*, 5 Cir. 1953, 205 F.2d 734, *cert. denied*, 1953, 346 U.S. 864. It would make little sense to permit a taxpayer to invoke a privilege merely because he hires an attorney to perform the same task. The summons to Davis must therefore be enforced in its entirety. [Affirmed.]

UNITED STATES v. ROWE

96 F.3d 1294 (9th Cir. 1996)

KOZINSKI, Circuit Judge.

After learning of possible irregularities in attorney W. Lee McElravy's Handling of client funds, the senior partner at his San Diego law firm, Charles E. Rowe, asked two young associates to investigate McElravy's conduct. Rowe also wrote to the State Bar, asking it to "take appropriate action" against McElravy. A grand jury investigating McElravy later subpoenaed the associates; the government hoped to question them about their conversations with Rowe. Appellants argued that the conversations were protected by the attorney-client privilege.

The attorney-client privilege can exist only after a client consults an attorney, 24 Charles A. Wright & Kenneth W. Graham, Jr., *Federal Practice and Procedure: Evidence* §5473, at 105-08 (1986), "for the purpose of facilitating the rendition of professional legal services." *Id.* at 110.

The district judge, although expressing considerable unease about her ruling, held that appellants had not shown these requirements were met. According to the judge, who had spoken to the associates in camera, "Basically, they were trusted young associates [who] were asked to do some leg work and come up with information. . . . They were . . . helping out." The judge noted that the associates were never told they were working as the firm's attorneys; that they didn't bill the firm or record hours expended on the firm's behalf; and that, because they were far less experienced than Rowe, "they were certainly taking direction from him." The judge issued an order compelling the associates to testify. Rowe and the firm, as probable holders of the privilege, appeal.

The government argues that, in assigning the associates to investigate McElravy, Rowe was not a client consulting an attorney. It further argues that the type of investigative work performed by the associates does not qualify as "professional legal services." We review these mixed questions of fact and law de novo. . . .

1. Attorney-client relationship. Rowe assigned the associates to perform services on behalf of the firm. They were, effectively, in-house counsel. In determining the existence of a privilege, "no attempt [is] made to

distinguish between 'inside' and 'outside' counsel. . . ." 2 Jack B. Weinstein et al., *Weinstein's Evidence* ¶503(a)(2)[01], at 503-30 (1996). *See also* 1 Scott N. Stone & Robert K. Taylor, *Testimonial Privileges* §1.10, at 1-35 (2d ed. 1993) ("Judge Wyzanski in United States v. United Shoe Machinery Corp. [89 F. Supp. 357, 360 (D. Mass. 1950)] established the principle that the attorney-client privilege will apply to confidential communications concerning Legal matters made between a corporation and its house counsel. . . . *This Principle has been followed with virtual unanimity by American courts.*" (emphasis added; footnote deleted)).

Several months after the associates began their investigation, Rowe turned the matter over to outside counsel. The associates thereafter conducted their activities under the direction of this outside counsel. The district court found, and the government now concedes, that the associates' communications with members of the firm after outside counsel was hired were privileged. However, the pre- and post-hiring distinction finds no support in Commentary or caselaw. The hiring of outside counsel is, obviously, an indication that litigation is anticipated and, therefore, that professional legal services are required. However, in this case, it is clear that, because litigation was anticipated, professional legal services were sought from day one.

2. *Professional legal services.* The government also argues that the associates were engaged in fact-finding, rather than the rendering of "professional legal services." It states: "The two associates collected facts for Rowe. They did not render any legal advice. . . ." . . .

Although some commentators, including Wright & Graham, continue to distinguish between fact-finding and lawyering,[2] federal judges cannot. In *Upjohn Co. v. United States*, 449 U.S. 383 (1981), a law firm was retained to investigate wrongdoing within the client corporation. The question on appeal—which has vexed courts before and since—was the definition of "client" in the corporate setting. Whether conversations undertaken in the course of fact-finding can be privileged was never questioned by the Court. See Wright & Graham, *supra*, §5478, at 228 ("The issue was ignored in the Court's opinion."). In fact, the *Upjohn* Court observed, "The first step in the Resolution of any legal problem is ascertaining the factual background and sifting through the facts with an eye to the legally relevant." 449 U.S. at 390-91. Thus, "the privilege exists to protect not only the giving of professional advice to those who can act on it but also the giving of information to the lawyer to enable him to give sound and informed advice." *Id.*

Prior to *Upjohn*, "in claiming the protection of the attorney-client privilege [t]he corporation ha[d] the burden of showing that the communication was made for the purpose of securing *legal* advice. . . ." *In re Grand Jury Subpoena*, 599 F.2d 504, 510 (2d Cir. 1979) (quoting *Weinstein's Evidence* ¶503 (b)[04], at 503-45 (emphasis in original)). Where the

---

2. "The better view would seem to be that investigative work is not 'professional legal services' and that no privilege applies where the lawyer's primary function is as a detective." Wright & Graham, supra, §5478, at 229. Wright and Graham are, of course, mistaken on this score.

attorney was asked for business (as opposed to legal) counsel, no privilege attached. . . . *Upjohn* did not eliminate this distinction. What it did do is make clear that fact-finding which pertains to legal advice counts as "professional legal services." . . .

3. The government argues that upholding the privilege in this case would reward a law firm just for being a law firm because another type of company that uses its own employees to investigate internal wrong-doing would not get the benefit of the privilege. But a firm whose employees are physicians or computer programmers would probably not use its own employees to investigate legal wrong-doing; they would likely hire lawyers to do the job. Here, the firm happens to have employees who are lawyers, which made it easier for the senior partner to "hire" a lawyer—he needed only walk down the hall. This, however, did not change the fact that he asked lawyers—not secretaries, paralegals, librarians or other of the firm's employees—to conduct the investigation. And, having chosen to hand the job over to lawyers, he is justified in expecting that communications with these lawyers will be privileged. If a doctor, by analogy, consults one of his own partners for diagnosis of a personal health problem, their conversations are protected by the doctor-patient privilege. That patient happens to have easier access to doctors than most people; Rowe had easier access to lawyers. Neither is stripped of the privilege because hiring the professional was convenient.

We are not unmindful that the attorney-client privilege, like all privileges, can impede fact-finding. . . . Nor are we unaware of academic criticism that the privilege allegedly gives unjustified protection to entrenched interests. . . . Nonetheless, we have no doubt that, under existing caselaw, the activities here meet the "attorney-client" and "professional legal services" requirements for the privilege.

4. Finally, the government argues that, even if we were to find the existence of communications between a client and an attorney relating to the rendering of professional legal services, the crime or fraud exception may defeat the privilege. In the alternative, it argues, the privilege has been waived by appellants. These are questions for the district court on remand. REVERSED.

PROBLEMS

10.1. Shortly after meeting with his lawyer on a separate matter, Dan is arrested for driving while intoxicated. At his trial, the prosecutor calls Dan's lawyer to the stand and asks her whether Dan appeared inebriated during their meeting. Dan objects on grounds of privilege. How should the judge rule?

10.2. Carolyn hires an accountant and tells him at their first meeting that she has not filed tax returns for the past five years because she could never find the time. She asks him whether he thinks she needs a lawyer, and he says yes. Are Carolyn's remarks to her accountant privileged?

10.3. The president of a chemical manufacturing company suspects that some of his employees are illegally disposing hazardous wastes. He hires a private detective firm to investigate. Are his conversations with the firm privileged? What about the conversations of his employees? Would the answers be different if he hired a law firm instead of a private detective firm? What if he hired a private detective firm, but the person he dealt with at the firm was a lawyer?

10.4. Craig wishes to become a U.S. citizen. Fred advertises his services as an "expert in immigration law." Craig hires Fred to help him complete the naturalization application. Contrary to Craig's belief, Fred is not a lawyer. Are Craig's confidential conversations with Fred privileged?

10.5. Colleen meets in her office with her lawyer. No one else is present, and they close the door. But their conversation is overheard by a window washer working outside the office immediately below Colleen's. Can Colleen prevent the window washer from testifying about what he heard?

10.6. From his desk at work, Collin sends his lawyer an e-mail message seeking legal advice. Collin's employer randomly monitors e-mail messages sent to and from Collin's workplace, in order to ensure the computer system is not misused. Collin was informed of the monitoring when he joined the company, but has forgotten about it. As it happens, Collin's employer does not read his message to his lawyer. Is the message privileged? Would the answer be different if the employer *did* read the message?

3. Waiver

Information protected by the attorney-client privilege, or any other privilege, loses its protection if the privilege is "waived." Waiver can be accomplished by any of a variety of actions inconsistent with a continuing intention to keep the protected communication confidential. The attorney-client privilege is held by the client, not the attorney, so in theory only the client can waive it. In practice, though, the privilege is often deemed waived because of actions by the attorney, on the ground that the attorney was acting as the agent of the client.

UNITED STATES v. BERNARD

877 F.2d 1463 (10th Cir. 1989)

BRORBY, Circuit Judge.

Mr. Bernard appeals the judgment entered following his conviction of sixty-two criminal violations including [the making of illegal nominee loans.] . . . Two of these nominee loans were made to Mr. Treat. At trial, the government called Mr. Treat as a witness against the defendant. The gist of the testimony was that Mr. Treat had asked Mr. Bernard about the legality of making a nominee loan. Mr. Treat testified that Mr. Bernard told him that he (Mr. Bernard) had verified the legality of such a loan with an attorney, Mr. Tom Nally. . . . Later in the trial, the court ruled that Mr. Bernard waived his attorney-client privilege "in regard to the loans made by Bernard to Treat" and permitted the government to call Mr. Nally as a witness. Mr. Nally testified that Mr. Bernard was his client. He denied even discussing the question of the legality of nominee loans with his client.

. . . Mr. Bernard willingly sacrificed his attorney-client confidentiality and privilege by voluntarily disclosing the confidential communication to Mr. Treat. Any voluntary disclosure by the client is inconsistent with the attorney-client relationship and waives the privilege. Mr. Bernard did this in an effort to convince Mr. Treat that the proposed nominee loan was lawful and proper. Mr. Bernard, having revealed the purported conversation between himself and his counsel in an effort to induce Mr. Treat to engage in a nominee loan, cannot later claim the protection of the attorney-client privilege. . . . AFFIRMED.

TASBY v. UNITED STATES

504 F.2d 332 (8th Cir. 1974)

GIBSON, Chief Judge.

Johnnie Tasby appeals his jury conviction of making a false material declaration in violation of 18 U.S.C. §1623. He was sentenced to a term of three years' imprisonment to run consecutively to the term he is now serving. This prosecution arises from Tasby's testimony given under oath during two previous court proceedings. In the first proceeding Tasby was convicted of interstate kidnapping. This was affirmed on appeal. Subsequently, Tasby brought a petition for post-conviction relief pursuant to 28 U.S.C. 2255 which was denied after a hearing in the district court. This denial was affirmed on appeal.

At his original kidnapping trial Tasby testified in his own behalf. This occurred only after a record was made establishing through Tasby's own testimony that his attorney, Mr. Peek, had advised him not to take the stand, had explained to him the possible consequences of taking the stand, and that Tasby still wished to testify.

In the later §2255 proceeding Tasby claimed the ineffective assistance of counsel. In support of this claim Tasby testified that he did not wish to take the stand at the original trial. Further he stated that Mr. Peek had never advised him not to take the stand, alleging that he was coerced into taking the stand by Mr. Peek's statements that he would get 25 years to life if he did not testify. [Peek testified to the contrary at Tasby's trial for making a false material declaration.]

. . . We find no violation of the attorney-client privilege in the facts of this case. It has long been the law that a client may waive protection of the privilege, either expressly or impliedly. *Blackburn v. Crawfords*, 70 U.S. (3 Wall.) 175, 194 (1865). One of the circumstances which may support a conclusion of a waiver is an attack by the client upon his attorney's conduct which calls into question the substance of their communications. A client has a privilege to keep his conversations with his attorney confidential, but that privilege is waived when a client attacks his attorney's competence in giving legal advice, puts in issue that advice and ascribes a course of action to his attorney that raises the specter of ineffectiveness or incompetence. Here, the confidentiality of the attorney-client relationship was breached by Tasby. Surely a client is not free to make various allegations of misconduct and incompetence while the attorney's lips are sealed by invocation of the attorney-client privilege. Such an incongruous result would be inconsistent with the object and purpose of the attorney-client privilege and a patent perversion of the rule. When a client calls into public question the competence of his attorney, the privilege is waived. *Laughner v. United States*, 373 F.2d 326 (5th Cir. 1967); *Sherman v. United States*, 261 F. Supp. 522, 531 (D. Haw.), *aff'd* 383 F.2d 837 (9th Cir. 1966); *see Pruitt v. Peyton*, 243 F. Supp. 907 (E.D. Va. 1965); *United States v. Butler*, 167 F. Supp. 102 (E.D. Va. 1957), *aff'd* 260 F.2d 574 (4th Cir. 1958).

Tasby at the §2255 hearing attacked the representation of his attorney, thereby putting into question the substance of his communications with Tasby. We think this establishes Tasby's waiver of the privilege. In the present proceeding, Mr. Peek's testimony was relevant and material as to the truth or falsity of Tasby's prior declarations and the trial court was not in error in allowing Mr. Peek to testify. . . . Judgment of conviction affirmed.

HOLLINS v. POWELL

773 F.2d 191 (8th Cir. 1985)

FLOYD R. GIBSON, Senior Circuit Judge.

The defendants, the City of Wellston and Robert Powell, appeal from a judgment entered by the district judge upon a jury verdict finding them liable for violating the plaintiffs'—Margie Hollins', Mamie Wallace's, Annette McNeil's and Lloyd Brown's—constitutional rights. [Powell was the mayor of Wellston. The plaintiffs were city housing commissioners, appointed by Powell's predecessor. Powell questioned the legality of their appointments and named his own commissioners. When the plaintiffs nonetheless assembled for a regularly scheduled meeting and tried to conduct business, Powell had them arrested.]

Before trial, the plaintiffs sought to depose the City's attorney. The City filed a motion to quash the deposition, with an alternative request for a protective order, and the plaintiffs filed a motion to compel the deposition. The district court granted the plaintiffs' motion, noting that it appeared the City and Powell would raise advice of counsel as a defense, and held that the attorney-client privilege would be waived under those circumstances. The district court based its observations on the pleadings and the plaintiffs' assertions. Because the defendants had not yet raised advice of counsel as a defense, the court granted them seven days from entry of the order to inform the court whether the communications with the attorney would be part of the defense. The defendants failed to file a motion for reconsideration.

The City argues that because the district court erred by granting the motion to compel the deposition, it also erred in overruling the City's objection to the attorney's testimony at trial. We disagree. The district court properly granted the motion to compel and, although we do so for a different reason than did the district court, we hold that the defendants had waived the attorney-client privilege by the time the attorney was called as a witness.

Because the plaintiffs have sued the defendants for a violation of federal law, the federal law of privilege applies to this issue. Fed. R. Evid. 501. Initially, we note that the party who claims the benefit of the attorney-client privilege has the burden of establishing the right to invoke its protection. The defendants clearly failed to meet this burden as far as the deposition of the attorney is concerned. They adduced no evidence to support their assertion of the privilege. Thus, the district court did not err by granting the plaintiffs' motion to compel the deposition.

During the attorney's deposition, the City objected whenever it perceived that a question covered by the privilege was asked, and then instructed the attorney to answer the question. The plaintiffs argue that by proceeding in this manner the defendants waived the privilege. Under the circumstances of this case, the defendants preserved their right to claim the privilege at trial as to those questions to which they had objected. Had the defendants interrupted the deposition every time it objected to a question on the basis of privilege, and sought a protective order from the district court, they would have been violating the court's previous order. Thus, we reject the contention that the defendants waived the privilege during the deposition. Nonetheless, we hold that the defendants did waive the privilege during trial.

A client may waive the attorney-client privilege, and may do so either expressly or by implication. Waiver will be implied when a client has testified concerning portions of the attorney-client communication.

On plaintiffs' direct examination of him, Powell testified as to the substance of his conversations with the City's attorney, as well as to the substance of his conversations with his own attorney. This testimony occurred before the City's attorney was called as a witness. Because the City's attorney failed to object to the plaintiffs' relevant questions of Powell, it waived the attorney-client privilege. Thus, we need not determine whether the district court erred by relying on its pretrial order in overruling the City's objection to the attorney's testimony, for the privilege had been waived by that time. . . . [Judgment affirmed.]

IN RE VON BULOW

828 F.2d 94 (2d Cir. 1987)

CARDAMONE, Circuit Judge:

Petitioner Claus von Bulow seeks a writ of mandamus directing the United States District Court for the Southern District of New York (Walker, J.) to vacate its discovery order of February 12, 1987, granting plaintiff the right to discover certain conversations between petitioner and his attorneys. . . . On July 6, 1981 petitioner was indicated by a Newport County, Rhode Island, grand jury on two counts of assault with intent to murder for allegedly injecting his wife Martha von Bulow with insulin causing her to lapse into an irreversible coma. After a widely publicized jury trial, von Bulow was convicted on both counts on March 16, 1982. In April 1982 petitioner retained Harvard law professor Alan M. Dershowitz to represent him on appeal. In May 1982 von Bulow was sentenced to 30-years' imprisonment, but granted bail pending appeal. On April 27, 1984 the Rhode Island Supreme Court reversed both convictions, and upon retrial, he was acquitted on June 10, 1985.

Shortly after the acquittal, petitioner's wife, by her next friends, Alexander Auersperg and Annie Laurie Auersperg-Kneissal, Martha von Bulow's children from a prior marriage (plaintiff), commenced this civil action in federal court against petitioner alleging common law assault, negligence, fraud, and RICO violations. These claims arose out of the same facts and circumstances as the Rhode Island criminal prosecution.

In May 1986 Random House published a book entitled *Reversal of Fortune—Inside the von Bulow Case*, authored by attorney Dershowitz, which chronicles the events surrounding the first criminal trial, the successful appeal, and von Bulow's ultimate acquittal. After obtaining an advance copy of the book, plaintiff's counsel notified petitioner on April 23, 1986 that it would view publication as a waiver of the attorney-client privilege. Von Bulow's counsel responded that no waiver had occurred and that, accordingly, he would not act to stop the book's publication. After the book was released, von Bulow and attorney Dershowitz appeared on several television and radio shows to promote it.

Plaintiff then moved to compel discovery of certain discussions between petitioner and his attorneys based on the alleged waiver of the attorney-client privilege with respect to those communications related in the book. In order to avoid piecemeal rulings on each communication, counsel stipulated in July 1986 as to those controversial subjects appearing in *Reversal of Fortune*. On February 12, 1987 the United States District Court for the Southern District of New York (Walker, J.) found a waiver of the attorney-client privilege and ordered von Bulow and his attorneys to comply with discovery requested by plaintiff.

. . . By allowing publication of confidential communications in his attorney's book *Reversal of Fortune*, petitioner was held to have waived his attorney-client privilege. In reaching that conclusion, the district court considered the following facts. First, petitioner knew of, consented to, and actually encouraged attorney Dershowitz's plans to write a book providing an "insider look" into his case. Second, petitioner was warned before publication that such an act might trigger a waiver and, yet, took no active measures to preserve his confidences. Third, after publication, petitioner joined his attorney in enthusiastically promoting the book on television and radio shows. Based on these key facts, the district court determined that von Bulow had waived his attorney-client privilege.

Petitioner argues that this holding is erroneous because only the client—and not his attorney—may waive the privilege. Of course, the privilege belongs solely to the client and may only be waived by him. An attorney may not waive the privilege without his client's consent. Hence, absent a client's consent or waiver, the publication of confidential communications by an attorney does not constitute a relinquishment of the privilege by the client. *See, e.g., Schnell v. Schnall*, 550 F. Supp. 650, 653 (S.D.N.Y. 1982) (no waiver of attorney-client privilege where attorney testified at SEC hearing without presence or authorization of client). *See also Wigmore*, Evidence §2325, at 633 (McNaughton rev. ed. 1961) (attorney's voluntary disclosures remain privileged unless impliedly authorized by client).

A client may nonetheless by his actions impliedly waive the privilege or consent to disclosure. And an attorney may, in appropriate circumstances, possess "an implied authority to waive the privilege on behalf of his client." [Drimmer v. Appleton, 628 F. Supp. 1249, 1251 (S.D.N.Y. 1986)]; Wigmore, supra, §2325. Moreover, it is the client's responsibility to insure continued confidentiality of his communications. In *In re Horowitz*, 482 F.2d 72 (2d Cir.), *cert. denied*, 414 U.S. 867 (1973), Judge Friendly, speaking for the Court, warned: "[I]t is not asking too much to insist that if a client wishes to preserve the privilege under such circumstances, he must take some affirmative action to preserve confidentiality."

Applying these principles, it is quite clear that in finding that von Bulow waived his privilege the district court did not abuse its discretion. In light of petitioner's acquiescence in and encouragement of *Reversal of Fortune*'s publication, Judge Walker properly concluded that von Bulow consented to his attorney's disclosure of his confidences and effectively waived his attorney-client privilege. Our discussion now turns to examine the breadth of that waiver.

The district court held that plaintiffs were entitled to discover "the entire contents of all conversations from which Dershowitz published extracts in *Reversal of Fortune.*" The four relevant conversations between von Bulow and his attorneys were their initial one, and the ones regarding the bail hearing, appellate strategy, and von Bulow's decision to testify on his own behalf. Under that ruling, plaintiff is permitted to discover those parts of the four Identified conversations not made public in the book. Petitioner argues that the district court's holding improperly broadened the fairness doctrine to include extrajudicial disclosures and that, accordingly, the discovery order cannot stand. We agree.

. . . [T]he district judge based his decision on an extension of "[t]he principle that disclosure of a portion of a privileged conversation entitles an adversary to discovery of the matters discussed in the remainder of the conversation. . . ." The court reasoned that where reputation is at stake in a major case, it is tried today before the bar of public opinion, as well as in a courtroom. Judge Walker believed it unfair to permit a party to make use of privileged information as a sword with the public, and then as a shield in the courtroom. Thus, the trial judge found what is generally called a "waiver by implication", *see* Wigmore, supra, §2327, at 635, based on fairness considerations.

These considerations—which underlie "the fairness doctrine"—aim to prevent prejudice to a party and distortion of the judicial process that may be caused by the privilege-holder's selective disclosure during litigation of otherwise privileged information. Under the doctrine the client alone controls the privilege and may or may not choose to divulge his own secrets. But it has been established law for a hundred years that when the client waives the privilege by testifying about what transpired between her and her attorney, she cannot thereafter insist that the mouth of the attorney be shut. *Hunt v. Blackburn,* 128 U.S. 464, 470-71 (1888). From that has grown the rule that testimony as to part of a privileged communication, in fairness, requires production of the remainder. McCormick On Evidence §93, at 194-95 (2d ed. 1972).

Yet this rule protecting the party, the factfinder, and the judicial process from selectively disclosed and potentially misleading evidence does not come into play when, as here, the privilege-holder or his attorney has made extra-judicial disclosures, and those disclosures have not subsequently been placed at issue during litigation. In fact, the cases finding, as the district court did here, implied waivers on account of fairness involved material issues raised by a client's assertions during the course of a judicial proceeding. . . .

Applying the fairness doctrine, we hold therefore that the extrajudicial disclosure of an attorney-client communication—one not subsequently used by the client in a judicial proceeding to his adversary's prejudice—does not waive the privilege as to the undisclosed portions of the communication. Hence, though the district court correctly found a waiver by von Bulow as to the particular matters actually disclosed in the book, it was an abuse of discretion to broaden that waiver to include those portions of the four identified conversations which, because they were not published, remain secret. . . .

The district court next ruled that von Bulow's waiver extended to subject matter areas related to the published conversations with Dershowitz. This "subject matter waiver", which allows the attacking party to reach all privileged conversations regarding a particular subject once one privileged conversation on that topic has been disclosed, is simply another form of the waiver by implication rule discussed above. Like the "implied waiver", the subject matter waiver also rests on the fairness considerations at work in the context of litigation. *See Smith* [*v. Alyeska Pipeline Serv. Co.,* 538 F. Supp. 977, 979 (D. Del. 1982)] ("It would be unfair to allow a client to assert the attorney-client privilege and prevent disclosure of damaging communications while allowing the client to disclose other selected communications solely for self-serving purposes.")

For this reason, it too has been invoked most often where the privilege-holder has attempted to use the privilege as both "a sword" and "a Shield" or where the attacking party has been prejudiced at trial. . . . For example, in *Weil v. Investment/Indicators, Research & Management, Inc.,* 647 F.2d 18 (9th Cir. 1981), the Ninth Circuit held that the client had waived its attorney-client privilege "only as to communications about the matter actually disclosed" because the disclosure occurred early in the proceedings, was made to opposing counsel rather than to the court, and was not demonstrably prejudicial to other party. Professor Wigmore's formulation of the subject matter waiver rule also contemplates the testimonial use of privileged information in the courtroom: "The client's offer of his own or the attorney's testimony as to a specific communication to the attorney is a waiver as to all other communications to the attorney on the same matter." Wigmore, supra, §2327, at 638.

But where, as here, disclosures of privileged information are made extrajudicially and without prejudice to the opposing party, there exists no reason in logic or equity to broaden the waiver beyond those matters actually revealed. Matters actually disclosed in public lose their privileged status because they obviously are no longer confidential. The cat is let out of the bag, so to speak. But related matters not so disclosed remain confidential. Although it is true that disclosures in the public arena may be "one-sided" or "misleading", so long as such disclosures are and remain extrajudicial, there is no legal prejudice that warrants a broad court-imposed subject matter waiver. The reason is that disclosures made in public rather than in court—even if selective—create no risk of legal prejudice until put at issue in the litigation by the privilege-holder. Therefore, insofar as the district court broadened petitioner's waiver to include related conversations on the same subject it was in error.

. . . [T]he petition for a writ of mandamus is granted and the district court is directed to vacate its discovery order of February 12, 1987.

CHRISTOPHER B. MUELLER & LAIRD C. KIRKPATRICK, EVIDENCE

§5.29 (3d ed. 2003)

There has been confusion in the cases whether inadvertent disclosure should be addressed as a problem of failed confidentiality or as a matter of waiver. The two issues are analytically distinct. The confidentiality requirement generally focuses on the intent of the communicator at the time the communication was made not to disclose the communication to persons who are outside the privilege. The client's subsequent conduct bears on confidentiality only to the extent that it provides circumstantial evidence of the client's intent at the time the communication was made.

Waiver focuses on whether the holder "voluntarily" disclosed or consented to disclosure of the privileged matter. Waiver occurs only after the making of a *confidential* communication—the privilege does not attach if the communication was not confidential. As a practical matter, similar standards have tended to evolve under both lines of analysis. If the holder did not take reasonable steps to protect against interception at the time the communication was made, the privilege is denied because of lack of confidentiality. If the holder (or the attorney acting as his agent) did not take reasonable steps to protect against subsequent disclosure, the privilege is lost on grounds of waiver.

4. Crime-Fraud Exception

Even when all the elements of the attorney-client privilege are satisfied and there is no basis for finding a waiver, the privilege has traditionally been limited by several exceptions. Among the most of important is the "crime-fraud" exception, which applies when an attorney's services are obtained for purposes of furthering a future crime or fraud, regardless whether the attorney is aware of that purpose.

UNITED STATES v. ZOLIN

491 U.S. 554 (1989)

Justice BLACKMUN delivered the opinion of the Court.

This case arises out of the efforts of the Criminal Investigation Division of the Internal Revenue Service (IRS) to investigate the tax returns of L. Ron Hubbard, founder of the Church of Scientology (the Church), for the calendar years 1979 through 1983. . . . In the course of its investigation, the IRS sought access to 51 documents that had been filed with the Clerk of the Los Angeles County Superior Court in connection with a case entitled *Church of Scientology of California v. Armstrong*, No. C420 153. The *Armstrong* litigation involved, among other things, a charge by the Church that one of its former members, Gerald Armstrong, had obtained by unlawful means documentary materials relating to Church activities, including two tapes. Some of the documents sought by the IRS had been filed under seal.

The IRS, by its Special Agent Steven Petersell, served a summons upon the Clerk on October 24, 1984, pursuant to 26 U.S.C. §7603, demanding that he produce the 51 documents.[4] The tapes were among those listed. On November 21, IRS agents were permitted to inspect and copy some of the summoned materials, including the tapes.

On November 27, the Church and Mary Sue Hubbard, who had intervened in *Armstrong*, secured a temporary restraining order from the United States District Court for the Central District of California. The order required the IRS to file with the District Court all materials acquired on November 21 and all reproductions and notes related thereto, pending disposition of the intervenors' motion for a preliminary injunction to bar IRS use of these materials. By order dated December 10, the District Court returned to the IRS all materials except the tapes and the IRS' notes reflecting their contents.

On January 18, 1985, the IRS filed in the District Court a petition to enforce its summons. . . . Respondents asserted the [attorney-client] privilege as a bar to disclosure of the tapes. The IRS argued, among other things, however, that the tapes fell within the crime-fraud exception to the attorney-client privilege, and urged the District Court to listen to the tapes in the course of making its privilege determination. . . . After oral argument and an evidentiary hearing, . . . the District Court ruled that respondents

4. The current Clerk of the Superior Court, Frank S. Zolin, is a named respondent in this case, but did not participate in briefing or argument before the Court of Appeals or before this Court. We use the term "respondents" to refer to Mary Sue Hubbard and the Church, the only active respondents in this Court.

had demonstrated that [the tapes] contain confidential attorney-client communications, that the privilege had not been waived, and that "[t]he 'fraud-crime' exception to the attorney-client privilege does not apply. The quoted excerpts tend to show or admit past fraud but there is no clear indication that future fraud or crime is being planned." On this basis, the court held that the Clerk "need not produce its copy of the tapes pursuant to the summons." The District Court denied the IRS' motion for reconsideration, rejecting the IRS' renewed request that the court listen to the tapes *in toto.* . . .

[The Court of Appeals agreed with respondents that] "the Government's evidence of crime or fraud must come from sources independent of the attorney-client communications recorded on the tapes" . . . On the basis of its review of the "independent evidence," the Court of Appeals affirmed the District Court's determination that the IRS had failed to establish the applicability of the crime-fraud exception.

. . . The attorney-client privilege must necessarily protect the confidences of wrongdoers, but the reason for that protection—the centrality of open client and attorney communication to the proper functioning of our adversary system of justice—"ceas[es] to operate at a certain point, namely, where the desired advice refers *not to prior wrongdoing*, but to *future wrongdoing*." 8 Wigmore, §2298, p. 573 (emphasis in original); see also *Clark v. United States*, 289 U.S. 1, 15 (1933). It is the purpose of the crime-fraud exception to the attorney-client privilege to assure that the "seal of secrecy," *ibid.*, between lawyer and client does not extend to communications "made for the purpose of getting advice for the commission of a fraud" or crime. *O'Rourke v. Darbishire*, [1920] A.C. 581, 604 (P.C.).

The District Court and the Court of Appeals found that the tapes at issue in this case recorded attorney-client communications and that the privilege had not been waived when the tapes were inadvertently given to Armstrong. 809 F.2d, at 1417 (noting that Armstrong had acquired the tapes from L. Ron Hubbard's personal secretary, who was under the mistaken impression that the tapes were blank). These findings are not at issue here. Thus, the remaining obstacle to respondents' successful assertion of the privilege is the Government's contention that the recorded attorney-client communications were made in furtherance of a future crime or fraud.

. . . We consider first the question whether a district court may ever honor the request of the party opposing the privilege to conduct an *in camera* review of allegedly privileged communications to determine whether those communications fall within the crime-fraud exception. We conclude that no express provision of the Federal Rules of Evidence bars such use of *in camera* review, and that it would be unwise to prohibit it in all instances as a matter of federal common law.

At first blush, two provisions of the Federal Rules of Evidence would appear to be relevant. Rule 104(a) provides: "Preliminary questions concerning the qualification of a person to be a witness, *the existence of a privilege*, or the admissibility of evidence shall be determined by the court. . . . In making its determination it is not bound by the rules of evidence *except those with respect to privileges*." (Emphasis added.) Rule 1101(c) provides: "The rule with respect to privileges applies at all stages of all actions, cases, and proceedings." Taken together, these Rules might be read to establish that in a summons-enforcement proceeding, attorney-client communications cannot be considered by the district court in making its crime-fraud ruling: to do otherwise, under this view, would be to make the crime-fraud determination without due regard to the existence of the privilege.

Even those scholars who support this reading of Rule 104(a) acknowledge that it leads to an absurd result.

> "Because the judge must honor claims of privilege made during his preliminary fact determinations, many exceptions to the rules of privilege will become 'dead letters,' since the preliminary facts that give rise to these exceptions can never be proved. For example, an exception to the attorney-client privilege provides that there is no privilege if the communication was made to enable anyone to commit a crime or fraud. There is virtually no way in which the exception can ever be proved, save by compelling disclosure of the contents of the communication; Rule 104(a) provides that this cannot be done." 21 C. Wright & K. Graham, Federal Practice & Procedure: Evidence §5055, p. 276 (1977) (footnote omitted).

We find this Draconian interpretation of Rule 104(a) inconsistent with the Rule's plain language. The Rule does not provide by its terms that all materials as to which a "clai[m] of privilege" is made must be excluded from consideration. In that critical respect, the language of Rule 104(a) is markedly different from the comparable California evidence rule, which provides that "the presiding officer may not require disclosure of information *claimed to be privileged* under this division in order to rule on the claim of privilege." Cal. Evid. Code Ann. §915(a) (West Supp. 1989) (emphasis added).[10] There is no reason to read Rule 104(a) as if its text were identical to that of the California rule. . . .

Having determined that Rule 104(a) does not prohibit the *in camera* review sought by the IRS, we must address the question as a matter of the federal common law of privileges. See Rule 501. We conclude that a complete prohibition against opponents' use of *in camera* review to establish the applicability of the crime-fraud exception is inconsistent with the policies underlying the privilege.

---

10. A good example of the effect of the California rule is provided by the record in this case. While the disputed matters were being briefed in Federal District Court, the State Superior Court held a hearing on a motion by Government attorneys seeking access to materials in the *Armstrong* case for ongoing litigation in Washington, D.C. The transcript of the hearing was made part of the record before the District Court in this case. Regarding the tapes, the Government argued to the Superior Court that the attorney-client conversations on the tapes reflect the planning or commission of a crime or fraud. That claim was supported by several declarations and other extrinsic evidence. The Government noted, however, that "the tape recordings themselves would . . . be the best evidence of exactly what was going on." The intervenors stressed that, as a matter of California law, "you can't show the tapes are not privileged by the contents." The Superior Court acknowledged the premise that "you can't look at the conversation itself to make [the crime-fraud] determination," and concluded that the extrinsic evidence was not sufficient to make out a prima facie case that the crime-fraud exception applies.

We begin our analysis by recognizing that disclosure of allegedly privileged materials to the district court for purposes of determining the merits of a claim of privilege does not have the legal effect of terminating the privilege. Indeed, this Court has approved the practice of requiring parties who seek to avoid disclosure of documents to make the documents available for *in camera* inspection, see *Kerr v. United States District Court for Northern District of Cal.*, 426 U.S. 394, 404-405 (1976), and the practice is well established in the federal courts. Respondents do not dispute this point: they acknowledge that they would have been free to request *in camera* review to establish the fact that the tapes involved attorney-client communications, had they been unable to muster independent evidence to serve that purpose.

Once it is clear that *in camera* review does not destroy the privileged nature of the contested communications, the question of the propriety of that review turns on whether the policies underlying the privilege and its exceptions are better fostered by permitting such review or by prohibiting it. In our view, the costs of imposing an absolute bar to consideration of the communications *in camera* for purpose of establishing the crime-fraud exception are intolerably high.

"No matter how light the burden of proof which confronts the party claiming the exception, there are many blatant abuses of privilege which cannot be substantiated by extrinsic evidence. This is particularly true ... of ... situations in which an alleged illegal proposal is made in the context of a relationship which has an apparent legitimate end." Note, The Future Crime or Tort Exception to Communications Privileges, 77 Harv. L. Rev. 730, 737 (1964). A *per se* rule that the communications in question may never be considered creates, we feel, too great an impediment to the proper functioning of the adversary process. . . .

We turn to the question whether *in camera* review at the behest of the party asserting the crime-fraud exception is *always* permissible, or, in contrast, whether the party seeking *in camera* review must make some threshold showing that such review is appropriate. In addressing this question, we attend to the detrimental effect, if any, of in camera review on the policies underlying the privilege and on the orderly administration of justice in our courts. We conclude that some such showing must be made.

Our endorsement of the practice of testing proponents' privilege claims through *in camera* review of the allegedly privileged documents has not been without reservation. This Court noted in *United States v. Reynolds*, 345 U.S. 1 (1953), a case which presented a delicate question concerning the disclosure of military secrets, that "examination of the evidence, even by the judge alone, in chambers" might in some cases "jeopardize the security which the privilege is meant to protect." Analogizing to claims of Fifth Amendment privilege, it observed more generally: "Too much judicial inquiry into the claim of privilege would force disclosure of the thing the privilege was meant to protect, while a complete abandonment of judicial control would lead to intolerable abuses."

The Court in *Reynolds* recognized that some compromise must be reached. . . . [I]t declined to "go so far as to say that the court may automatically require a complete disclosure to the judge before the claim of privilege will be accepted in any case." We think that much the same result is in order here.

A blanket rule allowing *in camera* review as a tool for determining the applicability of the crime-fraud exception, as *Reynolds* suggests, would place the policy of protecting open and legitimate disclosure between attorneys and clients at undue risk. There is also reason to be concerned about the possible due process implications of routine use of *in camera* proceedings. Finally, we cannot ignore the burdens *in camera* review places upon the district courts, which may well be required to evaluate large evidentiary records without open adversarial guidance by the parties.

There is no reason to permit opponents of the privilege to engage in groundless fishing expeditions, with the district courts as their unwitting (and perhaps unwilling) agents. . . . Indeed, the Government conceded at oral argument (albeit reluctantly) that a district court would be mistaken if it reviewed documents *in camera* solely because "the government beg[ged it]" to do so, "with no reason to suspect crime or fraud." We agree.

In fashioning a standard for determining when *in camera* review is appropriate, we begin with the observation that "*in camera* inspection . . . is a smaller intrusion upon the confidentiality of the attorney-client relationship than is public disclosure." Fried, Too High a Price for Truth: The Exception to the Attorney-Client Privilege for Contemplated Crimes and Frauds, 64 N.C. L. Rev. 443, 467 (1986). We therefore conclude that a lesser evidentiary showing is needed to trigger *in camera* review than is required ultimately to overcome the privilege. The threshold we set, in other words, need not be a stringent one.

We think that the following standard strikes the correct balance. Before engaging in *in camera* review to determine the applicability of the crime-fraud exception, "the judge should require a showing of a factual basis adequate to support a good faith belief by a reasonable person," *Caldwell v. District Court*, 644 P.2d 26, 33 (Colo. 1982), that *in camera* review of the materials may reveal evidence to establish the claim that the crime-fraud exception applies.

Once that showing is made, the decision whether to engage in *in camera* review rests in the sound discretion of the district court. The court should make that decision in light of the facts and circumstances of the particular case, including, among other things, the volume of materials the district court has been asked to review, the relative importance to the case of the alleged privileged information, and the likelihood that the evidence produced through *in camera* review, together with other available evidence then before the court, will establish that the crime-fraud exception does apply. The district court is also free to defer its *in camera* review if it concludes that additional evidence in support of the crime-fraud exception may be available that is *not* allegedly privileged, and that production of the additional evidence will not unduly disrupt or delay the proceedings.

. . . Because the Court of Appeals employed a rigid independent evidence requirement . . . we vacate its judgment on this issue and remand the case for further proceedings consistent with this opinion. On remand, the Court of Appeals should consider whether the District Court's refusal to listen to the tapes *in toto* was justified by the manner in which the IRS presented and preserved its request for *in camera* review. In the event the Court of Appeals holds that the IRS' demand for review was properly preserved, the Court of Appeals should then determine, or remand the case to the District Court to determine in the first instance, whether the IRS has presented a sufficient evidentiary basis for *in camera* review, and whether, if so, it is appropriate for the District Court, in its discretion, to grant such review.

It is so ordered.

C. SPOUSAL PRIVILEGES

There are two widely recognized spousal privileges. One is a privilege against disclosure of confidential spousal communications. It closely resembles the attorney-client privilege, except that it protects confidential communications between spouses during the course of a marriage, rather than confidential communications between an attorney and a client during the course of an attorney-client relationship. The second spousal privilege is the privilege against adverse spousal testimony. It is structured quite differently from the attorney-client privilege, and it was the subject of the Supreme Court decision reproduced below.

[C.E.C. §§970-987]

TRAMMEL v. UNITED STATES

445 U.S. 40 (1980)

Mr. Chief Justice BURGER delivered the opinion of the Court.

We granted certiorari to consider whether an accused may invoke the privilege against adverse spousal testimony so as to exclude the voluntary testimony of his wife. This calls for a re-examination of *Hawkins v. United States*, 358 U.S. 74 (1958).

I

On March 10, 1976, petitioner Otis Trammel was indicted with two others, Edwin Lee Roberts and Joseph Freeman, for importing heroin into the United States from Thailand and the Philippine Islands and for conspiracy to import heroin in violation of 21 U.S.C. §§952(a), 962(a), and 963. The indictment also named six unindicted co-conspirators, including petitioner's wife Elizabeth Ann Trammel.

According to the indictment, petitioner and his wife flew from the Philippines to California in August 1975, carrying with them a quantity of heroin. Freeman and Roberts assisted them in its distribution. Elizabeth Trammel then traveled to Thailand where she purchased another supply of the drug. On November 3, 1975, with four ounces of heroin on her person, she boarded a plane for the United States. During a routine customs search in Hawaii, she was searched, the heroin was discovered, and she was arrested. After discussions with Drug Enforcement Administration agents, she agreed to cooperate with the Government.

Prior to trial on this indictment, petitioner moved to sever his case from that of Roberts and Freeman. He advised the court that the Government intended to call his wife as an adverse witness and asserted his claim to a privilege to prevent her from testifying against him. At a hearing on the motion, Mrs. Trammel was called as a Government witness under a grant of use immunity. She testified that she and petitioner were married in May 1975 and that they remained married.[1] She explained that her cooperation with the Government was based on assurances that she would be given lenient treatment.[2] She then described, in considerable detail, her role and that of her husband in the heroin distribution conspiracy.

After hearing this testimony, the District Court ruled that Mrs. Trammel could testify in support of the Government's case to any act she observed during the marriage and to any communication "made in the presence of a third person"; however, confidential communications between petitioner and his wife were held to be privileged and inadmissible. The motion to sever was denied.

At trial, Elizabeth Trammel testified within the limits of the court's pretrial ruling; her testimony, as the Government concedes, constituted virtually its entire case against petitioner. He was found guilty on both the substantive and conspiracy charges and sentenced to an indeterminate term of years pursuant to the Federal Youth Corrections Act, 18 U.S.C. §5010(b).

In the Court of Appeals petitioner's only claim of error was that the admission of the adverse testimony of his wife, over his objection, contravened this Court's teaching in *Hawkins v. United States, supra*, and therefore constituted reversible error. The Court of Appeals rejected this contention. It concluded that Hawkins did not prohibit "the voluntary testimony of a spouse who appears as an unindicted co-conspirator under grant of immunity from the Government in return for her testimony."

II

The privilege claimed by petitioner has ancient roots. Writing in 1628, Lord Coke observed that "it hath beene resolved by the Justices that a wife cannot be produced either against or for her husband." 1 E. Coke, A Commentarie upon Littleton 6b (1628). See, generally, 8 J. Wigmore, Evidence

---

1. In response to the question whether divorce was contemplated, Mrs. Trammel testified that her husband had said that "I would go my way and he would go his."

2. The Government represents to the Court that Elizabeth Trammel has not been prosecuted for her role in the conspiracy.

§2227 (McNaughton rev. 1961). This spousal disqualification sprang from two canons of medieval jurisprudence: first, the rule that an accused was not permitted to testify in his own behalf because of his interest in the proceeding; second, the concept that husband and wife were one, and that since the woman had no recognized separate legal existence, the husband was that one. From those two now long-abandoned doctrines, it followed that what was inadmissible from the lips of the defendant-husband was also inadmissible from his wife.

Despite its medieval origins, this rule of spousal disqualification remained intact in most common-law jurisdictions well into the 19th century. See *id.*, §2333. It was applied by this Court in *Stein v. Bowman*, 13 Pet. 209, 220-223 (1839), in *Graves v. United States*, 150 U.S. 118 (1893), and again in *Jin Fuey Moy v. United States*, 254 U.S. 189, 195 (1920), where it was deemed so well established a proposition as to "hardly requir[e] mention." Indeed, it was not until 1933, in *Funk v. United States*, 290 U.S. 371, that this Court abolished the testimonial disqualification in the federal courts, so as to permit the spouse of a defendant to testify in the defendant's behalf. *Funk*, however, left undisturbed the rule that either spouse could prevent the other from giving adverse testimony. *Id.*, at 373. The rule thus evolved into one of privilege rather than one of absolute disqualification. See J. Maguire, Evidence, Common Sense and Common Law 78-92 (1947).

The modern justification for this privilege against adverse spousal testimony is its perceived role in fostering the harmony and sanctity of the marriage relationship. Notwithstanding this benign purpose, the rule was sharply criticized. Professor Wigmore termed it "the merest anachronism in legal theory and an indefensible obstruction to truth in practice." 8 Wigmore §2228, at 221. The Committee on Improvements in the Law of Evidence of the American Bar Association called for its abolition. 63 American Bar Association Reports 594-595 (1938). In its place, Wigmore and others suggested a privilege protecting only private marital communications, modeled on the privilege between priest and penitent, attorney and client, and physician and patient. See 8 Wigmore §2332 et seq.[5]

These criticisms influenced the American Law Institute, which, in its 1942 Model Code of Evidence advocated a privilege for marital confidences, but expressly rejected a rule vesting in the defendant the right to exclude all adverse testimony of his spouse. In 1953 the Uniform Rules of Evidence, drafted by the National Conference of Commissioners on Uniform State Laws, followed a similar course; it limited the privilege to confidential communications and "abolishe[d] the rule, still existing in some states, and largely a sentimental relic, of not requiring one spouse to testify against the other in a criminal action." Several state legislatures enacted similarly patterned provisions into law.

---

5. This Court recognized just such a confidential marital communications privilege in *Wolfle v. United States,* 291 U.S. 7 (1934), and in *Blau v. United States*, 340 U.S. 332 (1951). In neither case, however, did the Court adopt the Wigmore view that the communications privilege be substituted in place of the privilege against adverse spousal testimony. The privilege as to confidential marital communications is not at issue in the instant case; accordingly, our holding today does not disturb *Wolfle* and *Blau*.

In *Hawkins v. United States*, 358 U.S. 74 (1958), this Court considered the continued vitality of the privilege against adverse spousal testimony in the federal courts. There the District Court had permitted petitioner's wife, over his objection, to testify against him. With one questioning concurring opinion, the Court held the wife's testimony inadmissible; it took note of the critical comments that the common-law rule had engendered but chose not to abandon it. Also rejected was the Government's suggestion that the Court modify the privilege by vesting it in the witness-spouse, with freedom to testify or not independent of the defendant's control. The Court viewed this proposed modification as antithetical to the widespread belief, evidenced in the rules then in effect in a majority of the States and in England, "that the law should not force or encourage testimony which might alienate husband and wife, or further inflame existing domestic differences."

Hawkins, then, left the federal privilege for adverse spousal testimony where it found it, continuing "a rule which bars the testimony of one spouse against the other unless both consent." Accord, *Wyatt v. United States*, 362 U.S. 525, 528 (1960).[7] However, in so doing, the Court made clear that its decision was not meant to "foreclose whatever changes in the rule may eventually be dictated by 'reason and experience.' "

III

A

The Federal Rules of Evidence acknowledge the authority of the federal courts to continue the evolutionary development of testimonial privileges in federal criminal trials "governed by the principles of the common law as they may be interpreted . . . in the light of reason and experience." Fed. Rule Evid. 501. The general mandate of Rule 501 was substituted by the Congress for a set of privilege rules drafted by the Judicial Conference Advisory Committee on Rules of Evidence and approved by the Judicial Conference of the United States and by this Court. That proposal defined nine specific privileges, including a husband-wife privilege which would have codified the *Hawkins* rule and eliminated the privilege for confidential marital communications. In rejecting the proposed Rules and enacting Rule 501, Congress manifested an affirmative intention not to freeze the law of privilege. Its purpose rather was to "provide the courts

---

7. The decision in *Wyatt* recognized an exception to *Hawkins* for cases in which one spouse commits a crime against the other. This exception, placed on the ground of necessity, was a longstanding one at common law. See Lord Audley's Case, 123 Eng. Rep. 1140 (1631); 8 Wigmore §2239. It has been expanded since then to include crimes against the spouse's property, see *Herman v. United States*, 220 F.2d 219, 226 (CA4 1955), and in recent years crimes against children of either spouse, *United States v. Allery*, 526 F.2d 1362 (CA8 1975). Similar exceptions have been found to the confidential marital communications privilege. See 8 Wigmore §2338.

with the flexibility to develop rules of privilege on a case-by-case basis," 120 Cong. Rec. 40891 (1974) (statement of Rep. Hungate), and to leave the door open to change. See also S. Rep. No. 93-1277, p. 11 (1974); H.R. Rep. No. 93-650, p. 8 (1973).[8]

Although Rule 501 confirms the authority of the federal courts to reconsider the continued validity of the *Hawkins* rule, the long history of the privilege suggests that it ought not to be casually cast aside. That the privilege is one affecting marriage, home, and family relationships— already subject to much erosion in our day—also counsels caution. At the same time, we cannot escape the reality that the law on occasion adheres to doctrinal concepts long after the reasons which gave them birth have disappeared and after experience suggest the need for change. This was recognized in *Funk* where the Court "decline[d] to enforce . . . ancient rule[s] of the common law under conditions as they now exist." 290 U.S., at 382. For, as Mr. Justice Black admonished in another setting, "[w]hen precedent and precedent alone is all the argument that can be made to support a court-fashioned rule, it is time for the rule's creator to destroy it." *Francis v. Southern Pacific Co.*, 333 U.S. 445, 471 (1948) (dissenting opinion).

B

Since 1958, when *Hawkins* was decided, support for the privilege against adverse spousal testimony has been eroded further. Thirty-one jurisdictions, including Alaska and Hawaii, then allowed an accused a privilege to prevent adverse spousal testimony. 358 U.S., at 81, n. 3 (STEWART, J., concurring). The number has now declined to 24.[9] In 1974, the National Conference on Uniform State Laws revised its Uniform Rules of Evidence, but again rejected the Hawkins rule in favor of a limited privilege for confidential communications. That proposed rule has been enacted in Arkansas, North Dakota, and Oklahoma—each of which in 1958 permitted

8. Petitioner's reliance on 28 U.S.C. §2076 for the proposition that this Court is without power to reconsider *Hawkins* is ill-founded. That provision limits this Court's statutory rulemaking authority by providing that rules "creating, abolishing, or modifying a privilege shall have no force or effect unless . . . approved by act of Congress." It was enacted principally to insure that state rules of privilege would apply in diversity jurisdiction cases unless Congress authorized otherwise. In Rule 501 Congress makes clear that §2076 was not intended to prevent the federal courts from developing testimonial privilege law in federal criminal cases on a case-by-case basis "in light of reason and experience"; indeed Congress encouraged such development.

9. Eight States provide that one spouse is incompetent to testify against the other in a criminal proceeding. . . . Sixteen States provide a privilege against adverse spousal testimony and vest the privilege in both spouses or in the defendant-spouse alone. . . . Nine States entitle the witness-spouse alone to assert a privilege against adverse spousal testimony. . . . The remaining 17 States have abolished the privilege in criminal cases. . . . In 1901, Congress enacted a rule of evidence for the District of Columbia that made husband and wife "competent but not compellable to testify for or against each other," except as to confidential communications. This provision, which vests the privilege against adverse spousal testimony in the witness-spouse, remains in effect. See 31 Stat. 1358, §§1068, 1069, recodified as D.C. Code §14-306 (1973).

an accused to exclude adverse spousal testimony.[10] The trend in state law toward divesting the accused of the privilege to bar adverse spousal testimony has special relevance because the laws of marriage and domestic relations are concerns traditionally reserved to the states. See *Sosna v. Iowa*, 419 U.S. 393, 404 (1975). Scholarly criticism of the Hawkins rule has also continued unabated.

C

Testimonial exclusionary rules and privileges contravene the fundamental principle that " 'the public . . . has a right to every man's evidence.' " United States v. Bryan, 339 U.S. 323, 331 (1950). As such, they must be strictly construed and accepted "only to the very limited extent that permitting a refusal to testify or excluding relevant evidence has a public good transcending the normally predominant principle of utilizing all rational means for ascertaining truth." *Elkins v. United States*, 364 U.S. 206, 234 (1960)(Frankfurter, J., dissenting). Accord, *United States v. Nixon*, 418 U.S. 683, 709-710 (1974). Here we must decide whether the privilege against adverse spousal testimony promotes sufficiently important interests to outweigh the need for probative evidence in the administration of criminal justice.

It is essential to remember that the *Hawkins* privilege is not needed to protect information privately disclosed between husband and wife in the confidence of the marital relationship—once described by this Court as "the best solace of human existence." *Stein v. Bowman*, 13 Pet., at 223. Those confidences are privileged under the independent rule protecting confidential marital communications. *Blau v. United States*, 340 U.S. 332 (1951); see n. 5, *supra*. The *Hawkins* privilege is invoked, not to exclude private marital communications, but rather to exclude evidence of criminal acts and of communications made in the presence of third persons.

No other testimonial privilege sweeps so broadly. The privileges between priest and penitent, attorney and client, and physician and patient limit protection to private communications. These privileges are rooted in the imperative need for confidence and trust. The priest-penitent privilege recognizes the human need to disclose to a spiritual counselor, in total and absolute confidence, what are believed to be flawed acts or thoughts and to receive priestly consolation and guidance in return. The lawyer-client privilege rests on the need for the advocate and counselor to know all that relates to the client's reasons for seeking representation if the

---

10. In 1965, California took the privilege from the defendant-spouse and vested it in the witness-spouse, accepting a study commission recommendation that the "latter [was] more likely than the former to determine whether or not to claim the privilege on the basis of the probable effect on the marital relationship." See Cal. Evid. Code Ann. §§970-973 (West 1966 and Supp. 1979) and 1 California Law Revision Commission, Recommendation and Study Relating to the Marital "For and Against" Testimonial Privilege at F-5 (1956). Support for the common-law rule has also diminished in England. In 1972, a study group there proposed giving the privilege to the witness-spouse, on the ground that "if [the wife] is willing to give evidence . . . the law would be showing excessive concern for the preservation of marital harmony if it were to say that she must not do so." Criminal Law Revision Committee, Eleventh Report, Evidence (General) 93.

professional mission is to be carried out. Similarly, the physician must know all that a patient can articulate in order to identify and to treat disease; barriers to full disclosure would impair diagnosis and treatment.

The *Hawkins* rule stands in marked contrast to these three privileges. Its protection is not limited to confidential communications; rather it permits an accused to exclude all adverse spousal testimony. As Jeremy Bentham observed more than a century and a half ago, such a privilege goes far beyond making "every man's house his castle," and permits a person to convert his house into "a den of thieves." 5 Rationale of Judicial Evidence 340 (1827). It "secures, to every man, one safe and unquestionable and ever ready accomplice for every imaginable crime." *Id.*, at 338.

The ancient foundations for so sweeping a privilege have long since disappeared. Nowhere in the common-law world—indeed in any modern society—is a woman regarded as chattel or demeaned by denial of a separate legal identity and the dignity associated with recognition as a whole human being. Chip by chip, over the years those archaic notions have been cast aside so that "[n]o longer is the female destined solely for the home and the rearing of the family, and only the male for the marketplace and the world of ideas." *Stanton v. Stanton*, 421 U.S. 7, 14-15 (1975).

The contemporary justification for affording an accused such a privilege is also unpersuasive. When one spouse is willing to testify against the other in a criminal proceeding—whatever the motivation—their relationship is almost certainly in disrepair; there is probably little in the way of marital harmony for the privilege to preserve. In these circumstances, a rule of evidence that permits an accused to prevent adverse spousal testimony seems far more likely to frustrate justice than to foster family peace.[12] Indeed, there is reason to believe that vesting the privilege in the accused could actually undermine the marital relationship. For example, in a case such as this the Government is unlikely to offer a wife immunity and lenient treatment if it knows that her husband can prevent her from giving adverse testimony. If the Government is dissuaded from making such an offer, the privilege can have the untoward effect of permitting one spouse to escape justice at the expense of the other. It hardly seems conducive to the preservation of the marital relation to place a wife in jeopardy solely by virtue of her husband's control over her testimony.

IV

Our consideration of the foundations for the privilege and its history satisfy us that "reason and experience" no longer justify so sweeping a rule as that found acceptable by the Court in *Hawkins*. Accordingly, we

---

12. It is argued that abolishing the privilege will permit the Government to come between husband and wife, pitting one against the other. That, too, misses the mark. Neither *Hawkins*, nor any other privilege, prevents the Government from enlisting one spouse to give information concerning the other or to aid in the other's apprehension. It is only the spouse's testimony in the courtroom that is prohibited.

conclude that the existing rule should be modified so that the witness-spouse alone has a privilege to refuse to testify adversely; the witness may be neither compelled to testify nor foreclosed from testifying. This modification—vesting the privilege in the witness-spouse—furthers the important public interest in marital harmony without unduly burdening legitimate law enforcement needs.

Here, petitioner's spouse chose to testify against him. That she did so after a grant of immunity and assurances of lenient treatment does not render her testimony involuntary. *Cf. Bordenkircher v. Hayes*, 434 U.S. 357 (1978). Accordingly, the District Court and the Court of Appeals were correct in rejecting petitioner's claim of privilege, and the judgment of the Court of Appeals is

Affirmed.

Mr. Justice Stewart, concurring in the judgment.

Although agreeing with much of what the Court has to say, I cannot join an opinion that implies that "reason and experience" have worked a vast change since the *Hawkins* case was decided in 1958. . . . The fact of the matter is that the Court in this case simply accepts the very same arguments that the Court rejected when the Government first made them in the *Hawkins* case in 1958. I thought those arguments were valid then, and I think so now.

The Court is correct when it says that "[t]he ancient foundations for so sweeping a privilege have long since disappeared." But those foundations had disappeared well before 1958; their disappearance certainly did not occur in the few years that have elapsed between the *Hawkins* decision and this one. To paraphrase what Mr. Justice Jackson once said in another context, there is reason to believe that today's opinion of the Court will be of greater interest to students of human psychology than to students of law.

PROBLEMS

10.7. The prosecutor in a robbery case seeks to have the defendant's ex-wife testify that the defendant confessed his guilt to her while they were still married. The ex-wife is willing to testify, but the defendant objects. Is the testimony admissible?

10.8. The prosecutor in a murder case seeks to have the defendant's wife testify that, the night of the victims' deaths, the defendant came home with a bloody shirt. The defendant and his wife were living together at the time but were not yet married. They married the following week. One month later, the defendant fled the country. He was captured and extradited fifteen years later. The prosecution offers to prove that, while a fugitive, the defendant lived with a woman and did not communicate with his wife or their children or provide them with financial support. The defendant's wife does not wish to testify against him. May she be compelled to do so?

D. OTHER PRIVILEGES

[C.E.C. §§990-1070]

McCORMICK ON EVIDENCE

§76.2 (Kenneth S. Broun, ed., 6th ed. 2006)

[A]ll states possess some form of husband-wife, and attorney-client privilege. All afford some protection to certain government information. Most, though not all, allow at least a limited privilege to communications between physician and patient. In addition several other privileges are worthy of specific mention.

Though probably not recognized at common law, a privilege protecting confidential communications between clergymen and penitents has now been adopted in all 50 states. Wigmore's seemingly grudging acceptance of the privilege perhaps reflects the difficulty of justifying its existence on exclusively utilitarian grounds, since at least where penitential communications are required or encouraged by religious tenets, they are likely to continue to be made irrespective of the presence or absence of evidentiary privilege. A firmer ground appears available in the inherent offensiveness of the secular power attempting to coerce an act violative of religious conscience. Implementing a decent regard for religious convictions while at the same time avoiding making individual conscience the ultimate measure of testimonial obligation has proved to be attended by some difficulties. Early statutory forms of the privilege undertook to privilege only penitential communications "in the course of discipline enjoined by the church" to which the communicant belongs. This limitation, however, has been urged to be unduly, perhaps unconstitutionally, preferential to the Roman Catholic and a few other churches. The statutes have, accordingly, generally been broadened. Uniform Rule of Evidence 505, as promulgated in 1974, is typical in extending the privilege generally to "confidential communication[s] by a person to a clergyman in his professional character as a spiritual advisor."

The states are split on the question of who can waive the clergyman penitent privilege. Some provide that the privilege belongs only to the communicant, others provide that it belongs to the clergy member and still others hold that it belongs to both.

One of the most persistently advocated privileges for many years . . . has been one shielding journalists from being testimonially required in court to divulge the identities of news sources. The rationale asserted for this privilege is analogous to that underlying the long-standing governmental informer's privilege* and is exclusively utilitarian in character. Thus, it is contended that the news sources essential to supply the public's need for

---

*[Ed. See the discussion of the informant's privilege in United States v. Green, 670 F.2d 1148 (D.C. Cir. 1981): "One limitation on a defendant's right to cross-examine Government witnesses is the 'informer's privilege,' which allows the Government to refuse to disclose the identity of a person who has furnished information about criminal activities. . . . Long recognized at common law, the informer's privilege serves important individual and societal

information will be "dried up" if their identities are subject to compelled disclosure. Numerous attempts to have the privilege enacted by federal statute have failed, and it is not one of those privileges incorporated into the Revised Uniform Rules of Evidence (1974). Moreover, the argument that a journalist's privilege is constitutionally to be implied from the First Amendment guarantee of a free press was seemingly rejected by the Supreme Court in Branzburg v. Hayes [408 U.S. 665 (1972)]. However, taking note that this rejection did not command an absolute majority of the Court, a substantial number of lower federal courts have undertaken to recognize a qualified journalist's privilege that may be penetrated by appropriate showings on the part of the party desiring the privileged information. Though occasionally referred to as a common law creation, despite *Branzburg*, the privilege has generally been said to derive from the First Amendment. Some form of privilege for journalists has been created by statute, or in a few cases by judicial decision, in a substantial number of states. A few state courts have also found the privilege to be implied by state constitutional provision. Unlike other professional privileges, it is generally conceived as belonging to the journalist, to be claimed or waived irrespective of the wishes of the news source.

Communications to accountants are privileged in perhaps a third of the states. . . . In recent years much attention has been bestowed upon the plight of the rape victim, and some sort of sexual assault victim-counselor privilege has been created by statute or court decision in a substantial number of states. . . . Even broader acceptance has been achieved by the principle that protection by evidentiary privilege is necessary for the deliberations of medical review committees.

There is occasional recognition of privilege for communications to confidential clerks, stenographers and other "employees" generally, school teachers, school counselors, participants in group psychotherapy, nurses, marriage counselors, private detectives, and social workers. A privilege for parent-minor child communications has been recommended but has received little judicial approval. Privileges for scientific researcher-subject and self-critical analysis have fared only somewhat better.

An attempt to obtain recognition of a federal privilege protecting against disclosure of confidential peer review materials of academic institutions has been rejected by the Supreme Court [in *University of Pennsylvania v. EEOC*, 493 U.S. 182 (1990)].

---

interests in protecting the anonymity of citizens who cooperate in law enforcement. The privilege protects the informer and his family from possible physical harm or from other potential undesirable consequences. Moreover, the availability of the privilege preserves the usefulness of those who have aided the police in law enforcement and may encourage other citizens to supply information concerning the commission of crimes." Nonetheless, "[t]he Supreme Court in . . . Roviaro v. United States, 353 U.S. 53 (1957) . . . held that at trial the informer's privilege is limited by 'the fundamental requirements of fairness. Where the disclosure of an informer's identity, or of the contents of his communication, is relevant and helpful to the defense of an accused, or is essential to a fair determination of a cause, the privilege must give way.' " Id.]

JAFFEE v. REDMOND

518 U.S. 1 (1996)

Justice STEVENS delivered the opinion of the Court.

After a traumatic incident in which she shot and killed a man, a police officer received extensive counseling from a licensed clinical social worker. The question we address is whether statements the officer made to her therapist during the counseling sessions are protected from compelled disclosure in a federal civil action brought by the family of the deceased. Stated otherwise, the question is whether it is appropriate for federal courts to recognize a "psychotherapist privilege" under Rule 501 of the Federal Rules of Evidence.

I

Petitioner is the administrator of the estate of Ricky Allen. Respondents are Mary Lu Redmond, a former police officer, and the Village of Hoffman Estates, Illinois, her employer during the time that she served on the police force. Petitioner commenced this action against respondents after Redmond shot and killed Allen while on patrol duty.

On June 27, 1991, Redmond was the first officer to respond to a "fight in progress" call at an apartment complex. As she arrived at the scene, two of Allen's sisters ran toward her squad car, waving their arms and shouting that there had been a stabbing in one of the apartments. Redmond testified at trial that she relayed this information to her dispatcher and requested an ambulance. She then exited her car and walked toward the apartment building. Before Redmond reached the building, several men ran out, one waving a pipe. When the men ignored her order to get on the ground, Redmond drew her service revolver. Two other men then burst out of the building, one, Ricky Allen, chasing the other. According to Redmond, Allen was brandishing a butcher knife and disregarded her repeated commands to drop the weapon. Redmond shot Allen when she believed he was about to stab the man he was chasing. Allen died at the scene. Redmond testified that before other officers arrived to provide support, "people came pouring out of the buildings," and a threatening confrontation between her and the crowd ensued.

Petitioner filed suit in Federal District Court alleging that Redmond had violated Allen's constitutional rights by using excessive force during the encounter at the apartment complex. The complaint sought damages under 42 U.S.C. §1983 and the Illinois wrongful death statute. At trial, petitioner presented testimony from members of Allen's family that conflicted with Redmond's version of the incident in several important respects. They testified, for example, that Redmond drew her gun before exiting her squad car and that Allen was unarmed when he emerged from the apartment building.

During pretrial discovery petitioner learned that after the shooting Redmond had participated in about 50 counseling sessions with Karen

Beyer, a clinical social worker licensed by the State of Illinois and employed at that time by the Village of Hoffman Estates. Petitioner sought access to Beyer's notes concerning the sessions for use in cross-examining Redmond. Respondents vigorously resisted the discovery. They asserted that the contents of the conversations between Beyer and Redmond were protected against involuntary disclosure by a psychotherapist-patient privilege. The district judge rejected this argument. Neither Beyer nor Redmond, however, complied with his order to disclose the contents of Beyer's notes. At depositions and on the witness stand both either refused to answer certain questions or professed an inability to recall details of their conversations.

In his instructions at the end of the trial, the judge advised the jury that the refusal to turn over Beyer's notes had no "legal justification" and that the jury could therefore presume that the contents of the notes would have been unfavorable to respondents. The jury awarded petitioner $45,000 on the federal claim and $500,000 on her state-law claim.

The Court of Appeals for the Seventh Circuit reversed and remanded for a new trial. Addressing the issue for the first time, the court concluded that "reason and experience," the touchstones for acceptance of a privilege under Rule 501 of the Federal Rules of Evidence, compelled recognition of a psychotherapist-patient privilege. . . . The Court of Appeals qualified its recognition of the privilege by stating that it would not apply if "in the interests of justice, the evidentiary need for the disclosure of the contents of a patient's counseling sessions outweighs that patient's privacy interests." Balancing those conflicting interests, the court observed, on the one hand, that the evidentiary need for the contents of the confidential conversations was diminished in this case because there were numerous eyewitnesses to the shooting, and, on the other hand, that Officer Redmond's privacy interests were substantial. Based on this assessment, the court concluded that the trial court had erred by refusing to afford protection to the confidential communications between Redmond and Beyer.

The United States courts of appeals do not uniformly agree that the federal courts should recognize a psychotherapist privilege under Rule 501. . . . Because of the conflict among the courts of appeals and the importance of the question, we granted certiorari. We affirm.

II

Rule 501 of the Federal Rules of Evidence authorizes federal courts to define new privileges by interpreting "common law principles . . . in the light of reason and experience." . . . The Rule thus did not freeze the law governing the privileges of witnesses in federal trials at a particular point in our history, but rather directed federal courts to "continue the evolutionary development of testimonial privileges." *Trammel v. United States*, 445 U.S. 40 (1980).

The common-law principles underlying the recognition of testimonial privileges can be stated simply. " 'For more than three centuries it has now been recognized as a fundamental maxim that the public . . . has a right to every man's evidence. When we come to examine the various claims of exemption, we start with the primary assumption that there is a general duty to give what testimony one is capable of giving, and that any exemptions which may exist are distinctly exceptional, being so many derogations from a positive general rule.' " *United States v. Bryan*, 339 U.S. 323 (1950) (quoting 8 J. Wigmore, Evidence §2192 (3d ed. 1940)). Exceptions from the general rule disfavoring testimonial privileges may be justified, however, by a " 'public good transcending the normally predominant principle of utilizing all rational means for ascertaining the truth.' " *Trammel*, quoting *Elkins v. United States*, 364 U.S. 206 (1960) (Frankfurter, J., dissenting).

Guided by these principles, the question we address today is whether a privilege protecting confidential communications between a psychotherapist and her patient "promotes sufficiently important interests to outweigh the need for probative evidence. . . ." *Trammel*. Both "reason and experience" persuade us that it does.

III

Like the spousal and attorney-client privileges, the psychotherapist-patient privilege is "rooted in the imperative need for confidence and trust." *Trammel*. Treatment by a physician for physical ailments can often proceed successfully on the basis of a physical examination, objective information supplied by the patient, and the results of diagnostic tests. Effective psychotherapy, by contrast, depends upon an atmosphere of confidence and trust in which the patient is willing to make a frank and complete disclosure of facts, emotions, memories, and fears. Because of the sensitive nature of the problems for which individuals consult psychotherapists, disclosure of confidential communications made during counseling sessions may cause embarrassment or disgrace. For this reason, the mere possibility of disclosure may impede development of the confidential relationship necessary for successful treatment.[3] . . . By protecting confidential communications between a psychotherapist and her patient from involuntary disclosure, the proposed privilege thus serves important private interests.

Our cases make clear that an asserted privilege must also "serve public ends." *Upjohn Co. v. United States*, 449 U.S. 383 (1981). Thus, the purpose of the attorney-client privilege is to "encourage full and frank communication between attorneys and their clients and thereby promote broader public interests in the observance of law and administration of justice." *Ibid.* And the spousal privilege, as modified in *Trammel*, is justified because it "furthers the important public interest in marital harmony," *id.* The psychotherapist privilege serves the public interest by facilitating the provision of appropriate treatment for individuals suffering the effects of a mental or

---

3. See studies and authorities cited in the Brief for American Psychiatric Association et al. as Amici Curiae and the Brief for American Psychological Association as Amicus Curiae.

emotional problem. The mental health of our citizenry, no less than its physical health, is a public good of transcendent importance.[4]

In contrast to the significant public and private interests supporting recognition of the privilege, the likely evidentiary benefit that would result from the denial of the privilege is modest. If the privilege were rejected, confidential conversations between psychotherapists and their patients would surely be chilled, particularly when it is obvious that the circumstances that give rise to the need for treatment will probably result in litigation. Without a privilege, much of the desirable evidence to which litigants such as petitioner seek access—for example, admissions against interest by a party—is unlikely to come into being. This unspoken "evidence" will therefore serve no greater truth-seeking function than if it had been spoken and privileged.

That it is appropriate for the federal courts to recognize a psychotherapist privilege under Rule 501 is confirmed by the fact that all 50 States and the District of Columbia have enacted into law some form of psychotherapist privilege. We have previously observed that the policy decisions of the States bear on the question whether federal courts should recognize a new privilege or amend the coverage of an existing one. See *Trammel; United States v. Gillock*, 445 U.S. 360 (1980). Because state legislatures are fully aware of the need to protect the integrity of the factfinding functions of their courts, the existence of a consensus among the States indicates that "reason and experience" support recognition of the privilege. In addition, given the importance of the patient's understanding that her communications with her therapist will not be publicly disclosed, any State's promise of confidentiality would have little value if the patient were aware that the privilege would not be honored in a federal court. Denial of the federal privilege therefore would frustrate the purposes of the state legislation that was enacted to foster these confidential communications. . . .

The uniform judgment of the States is reinforced by the fact that a psychotherapist privilege was among the nine specific privileges recommended by the Advisory Committee in its proposed privilege rules. In *United States v. Gillock*, our holding that Rule 501 did not include a state legislative privilege relied, in part, on the fact that no such privilege was included in the Advisory Committee's draft. The reasoning in *Gillock* thus supports the opposite conclusion in this case. . . .

Because we agree with the judgment of the state legislatures and the Advisory Committee that a psychotherapist-patient privilege will serve a "public good transcending the normally predominant principle of utilizing all rational means for ascertaining truth," *Trammel*, we hold that confidential communications between a licensed psychotherapist and her patients in

---

4. This case amply demonstrates the importance of allowing individuals to receive confidential counseling. Police officers engaged in the dangerous and difficult tasks associated with protecting the safety of our communities not only confront the risk of physical harm but also face stressful circumstances that may give rise to anxiety, depression, fear, or anger. The entire community may suffer if police officers are not able to receive effective counseling and treatment after traumatic incidents, either because trained officers leave the profession prematurely or because those in need of treatment remain on the job.

the course of diagnosis or treatment are protected from compelled disclosure under Rule 501 of the Federal Rules of Evidence.[5]

IV

All agree that a psychotherapist privilege covers confidential communications made to licensed psychiatrists and psychologists. We have no hesitation in concluding in this case that the federal privilege should also extend to confidential communications made to licensed social workers in the course of psychotherapy. The reasons for recognizing a privilege for treatment by psychiatrists and psychologists apply with equal force to treatment by a clinical social worker such as Karen Beyer. Today, social workers provide a significant amount of mental health treatment. See, e.g., U.S. Dept. of Health and Human Services, Center for Mental Health Services, Mental Health, United States, 1994; Brief for National Association of Social Workers et al. as Amici Curiae (citing authorities). Their clients often include the poor and those of modest means who could not afford the assistance of a psychiatrist or psychologist, *id.* (citing authorities), but whose counseling sessions serve the same public goals.[6] Perhaps in recognition of these circumstances, the vast majority of States explicitly extend a testimonial privilege to licensed social workers. We therefore agree with the Court of Appeals that "drawing a distinction between the counseling provided by costly psychotherapists and the counseling provided by more readily accessible social workers serves no discernible public purpose."

We part company with the Court of Appeals on a separate point. We reject the balancing component of the privilege implemented by that court and a small number of States. Making the promise of confidentiality contingent upon a trial judge's later evaluation of the relative importance of the patient's interest in privacy and the evidentiary need for disclosure would eviscerate the effectiveness of the privilege. As we explained in *Upjohn,* if the purpose of the privilege is to be served, the participants in the confidential conversation "must be able to predict with some degree of certainty whether particular discussions will be protected. An uncertain privilege, or one which purports to be certain but results in widely varying applications by the courts, is little better than no privilege at all."

---

5. Like other testimonial privileges, the patient may of course waive the protection.

6. The Judicial Conference Advisory Committee's proposed psychotherapist privilege defined psychotherapists as psychologists and medical doctors who provide mental health services. This limitation in the 1972 recommendation does not counsel against recognition of a privilege for social workers practicing psychotherapy. In the quarter-century since the Committee adopted its recommendations, much has changed in the domains of social work and psychotherapy. See generally Brief for National Association of Social Workers et al. as Amici Curiae (and authorities cited). While only 12 States regulated social workers in 1972, all 50 do today. Over the same period, the relative portion of therapeutic services provided by social workers has increased substantially. See U.S. Dept. of Health and Human Services, Center for Mental Health Services, Mental Health, United States, 1994.

These considerations are all that is necessary for decision of this case. A rule that authorizes the recognition of new privileges on a case-by-case basis makes it appropriate to define the details of new privileges in a like manner. Because this is the first case in which we have recognized a psychotherapist privilege, it is neither necessary nor feasible to delineate its full contours in a way that would "govern all conceivable future questions in this area." *Id.*[7] . . . The conversations between Officer Redmond and Karen Beyer and the notes taken during their counseling sessions are protected from compelled disclosure under Rule 501 of the Federal Rules of Evidence. The judgment of the Court of Appeals is affirmed.

Justice SCALIA, with whom THE CHIEF JUSTICE joins as to Part III, dissenting.

The Court has discussed at some length the benefit that will be purchased by creation of the evidentiary privilege in this case: the encouragement of psychoanalytic counseling. It has not mentioned the purchase price: occasional injustice. That is the cost of every rule which excludes reliable and probative evidence—or at least every one categorical enough to achieve its announced policy objective. In the case of some of these rules, such as the one excluding confessions that have not been properly "Mirandized," see *Miranda v. Arizona*, 384 U.S. 436 (1966), the victim of the injustice is always the impersonal State or the faceless "public at large." For the rule proposed here, the victim is more likely to be some individual who is prevented from proving a valid claim—or (worse still) prevented from establishing a valid defense. The latter is particularly unpalatable for those who love justice, because it causes the courts of law not merely to let stand a wrong, but to become themselves the instruments of wrong.

In the past, this Court has well understood that the particular value the courts are distinctively charged with preserving—justice—is severely harmed by contravention of "the fundamental principle that "'the public . . . has a right to every man's evidence.'" *Trammel v. United States*, 445 U.S. 40, 50 (1980) (citation omitted). Testimonial privileges, it has said, "*are not lightly created nor expansively construed*, for they are in derogation of the search for truth." *United States v. Nixon*, 418 U.S. 683, 710 (1974) (emphasis added). Adherence to that principle has caused us, in the Rule 501 cases we have considered to date, to reject new privileges, see *University of Pennsylvania v. EEOC*, 493 U.S. 182 (1990) (privilege against disclosure of academic peer review materials); *United States v. Gillock*, 445 U.S. 360 (1980) (privilege against disclosure of "legislative acts" by member of state legislature), and even to construe narrowly the scope of existing privileges, see, e.g., *United States v. Zolin*, 491 U.S. 554, 568-570 (1989) (permitting in camera review of documents alleged to come within crime-fraud exception to attorney-client privilege); *Trammel*, supra

---

7. Although it would be premature to speculate about most future developments in the federal psychotherapist privilege, we do not doubt that there are situations in which the privilege must give way, for example, if a serious threat of harm to the patient or to others can be averted only by means of a disclosure by the therapist.

(holding that voluntary testimony by spouse is not covered by husband-wife privilege). The Court today ignores this traditional judicial preference for the truth, and ends up creating a privilege that is new, vast, and ill defined. I respectfully dissent.

I

The case before us involves confidential communications made by a police officer to a state-licensed clinical social worker in the course of psychotherapeutic counseling. Before proceeding to a legal analysis of the case, I must observe that the Court makes its task deceptively simple by the manner in which it proceeds. It begins by characterizing the issue as "whether it is appropriate for federal courts to recognize a 'psychotherapist privilege,'" and devotes almost all of its opinion to that question. Having answered that question (to its satisfaction) in the affirmative, it then devotes less than a page of text to answering in the affirmative the small remaining question whether "the federal privilege should also extend to confidential communications made to licensed social workers in the course of psychotherapy."

Of course the prototypical evidentiary privilege analogous to the one asserted here—the lawyer-client privilege—is not identified by the broad area of advice giving practiced by the person to whom the privileged communication is given, but rather by the professional status of that person. Hence, it seems a long step from a lawyer-client privilege to a tax advisor-client or accountant-client privilege. But if one recharacterizes it as a "legal advisor" privilege, the extension seems like the most natural thing in the world. That is the illusion the Court has produced here: It first frames an overly general question ("Should there be a psychotherapist privilege?") that can be answered in the negative only by excluding from protection office consultations with professional psychiatrists (i.e., doctors) and clinical psychologists. And then, having answered that in the affirmative, it comes to the only question that the facts of this case present ("Should there be a social worker-client privilege with regard to psychotherapeutic counseling?") with the answer seemingly a foregone conclusion. At that point, to conclude against the privilege one must subscribe to the difficult proposition, "Yes, there is a psychotherapist privilege, but not if the psychotherapist is a social worker." . . .

II

To say that the Court devotes the bulk of its opinion to the much easier question of psychotherapist-patient privilege is not to say that its answer to that question is convincing. . . . Effective psychotherapy undoubtedly is beneficial to individuals with mental problems, and surely serves some larger social interest in maintaining a mentally stable society. But merely mentioning these values does not answer the critical question: are they of such importance, and is the contribution of psychotherapy to them so distinctive, and is the application of normal evidentiary rules so destructive to psychotherapy, as to justify making our federal courts occasional instruments of injustice? On that central question I find the Court's analysis insufficiently convincing to satisfy the high standard we have set for rules that "are in derogation of the search for truth." *United States v. Nixon*, 418 U.S. 683 (1974).

When is it, one must wonder, that the psychotherapist came to play such an indispensable role in the maintenance of the citizenry's mental health? For most of history, men and women have worked out their difficulties by talking to, *inter alios*, parents, siblings, best friends and bartenders—none of whom was awarded a privilege against testifying in court. Ask the average citizen: Would your mental health be more significantly impaired by preventing you from seeing a psychotherapist, or by preventing you from getting advice from your mom? I have little doubt what the answer would be. Yet there is no mother-child privilege.

How likely is it that a person will be deterred from seeking psychological counseling, or from being completely truthful in the course of such counseling, because of fear of later disclosure in litigation? And even more pertinent to today's decision, to what extent will the evidentiary privilege reduce that deterrent? The Court does not try to answer the first of these questions; and it cannot possibly have any notion of what the answer is to the second, since that depends entirely upon the scope of the privilege, which the Court amazingly finds it "neither necessary nor feasible to delineate." If, for example, the psychotherapist can give the patient no more assurance than "A court will not be able to make me disclose what you tell me, unless you tell me about a harmful act," I doubt whether there would be much benefit from the privilege at all. That is not a fanciful example, at least with respect to extension of the psychotherapist privilege to social workers. See Del. Code Ann., Tit. 24, §3913(2) (1987); Idaho Code §54-3213(2) (1994).

Even where it is certain that absence of the psychotherapist privilege will inhibit disclosure of the information, it is not clear to me that that is an unacceptable state of affairs. Let us assume the very worst in the circumstances of the present case: that to be truthful about what was troubling her, the police officer who sought counseling would have to confess that she shot without reason, and wounded an innocent man. If (again to assume the worst) such an act constituted the crime of negligent wounding under Illinois law, the officer would of course have the absolute right not to admit that she shot without reason in criminal court. But I see no reason why she should be enabled both not to admit it in criminal court (as a good citizen should), and to get the benefits of psychotherapy by admitting it to a therapist who cannot tell anyone else. And even less reason why she should be enabled to deny her guilt in the criminal trial—or in a civil trial for negligence—while yet obtaining the benefits of psychotherapy by confessing guilt to a social worker who cannot testify. It seems to me entirely fair to say that if she wishes the benefits of telling the truth she must also accept the adverse consequences. To be sure, in most cases the statements to the psychotherapist will be only marginally relevant, and one of the purposes of the privilege (though not one relied upon by the Court) may be simply to spare patients needless intrusion upon their privacy, and to spare psychotherapists needless expenditure of their time in deposition and trial.

But surely this can be achieved by means short of excluding even evidence that is of the most direct and conclusive effect.

The Court confidently asserts that not much truth-finding capacity would be destroyed by the privilege anyway, since "without a privilege, much of the desirable evidence to which litigants such as petitioner seek access . . . is unlikely to come into being." If that is so, how come psychotherapy got to be a thriving practice before the "psychotherapist privilege" was invented? Were the patients paying money to lie to their analysts all those years? Of course the evidence-generating effect of the privilege (if any) depends entirely upon its scope, which the Court steadfastly declines to consider. And even if one assumes that scope to be the broadest possible, is it really true that most, or even many, of those who seek psychological counseling have the worry of litigation in the back of their minds? I doubt that, and the Court provides no evidence to support it.

The Court suggests one last policy justification: since psychotherapist privilege statutes exist in all the States, the failure to recognize a privilege in federal courts "would frustrate the purposes of the state legislation that was enacted to foster these confidential communications." This is a novel argument indeed. A sort of inverse pre-emption: the truth-seeking functions of federal courts must be adjusted so as not to conflict with the policies of the States. This reasoning cannot be squared with *Gillock*, which declined to recognize an evidentiary privilege for Tennessee legislators in federal prosecutions, even though the Tennessee Constitution guaranteed it in state criminal proceedings. Moreover, since, as I shall discuss, state policies regarding the psychotherapist privilege vary considerably from State to State, no uniform federal policy can possibly honor most of them. If furtherance of state policies is the name of the game, rules of privilege in federal courts should vary from State to State, a la *Erie*.

The Court's failure to put forward a convincing justification of its own could perhaps be excused if it were relying upon the unanimous conclusion of state courts in the reasoned development of their common law. It cannot do that, since no State has such a privilege apart from legislation. What it relies upon, instead, is "the fact that all 50 States and the District of Columbia have [1] enacted into law [2] some form of psychotherapist privilege." Let us consider both the verb and its object: The fact [1] that all 50 States have enacted this privilege argues not for, but against, our adopting the privilege judicially. At best it suggests that the matter has been found not to lend itself to judicial treatment—perhaps because the pros and cons of adopting the privilege, or of giving it one or another shape, are not that clear; or perhaps because the rapidly evolving uses of psychotherapy demand a flexibility that only legislation can provide. At worst it suggests that the privilege commends itself only to decisionmaking bodies in which reason is tempered, so to speak, by political pressure from organized interest groups (such as psychologists and social workers), and decisionmaking bodies that are not overwhelmingly concerned (as courts of law are and should be) with justice.

And the phrase [2] "some form of psychotherapist privilege" covers a multitude of difficulties. . . . To rest a newly announced federal common-law psychotherapist privilege, assertable from this day forward in all federal

courts, upon "the States' unanimous judgment that some form of psychotherapist privilege is appropriate," is rather like announcing a new,
immediately applicable, federal common law of torts, based upon the
States' "unanimous judgment" that some form of tort law is appropriate.
In the one case as in the other, the state laws vary to such a degree that the
parties and lower federal judges confronted by the new "common law" have
barely a clue as to what its content might be.

III

Turning from the general question that was not involved in this case to
the specific one that is: The Court's conclusion that a social-worker psychotherapeutic privilege deserves recognition is even less persuasive. In
approaching this question, the fact that five of the state legislatures that
have seen fit to enact "some form" of psychotherapist privilege have elected
not to extend any form of privilege to social workers, ought to give one
pause. So should the fact that the Judicial Conference Advisory Committee
was similarly discriminating in its conferral of the proposed Rule 504
privilege. . . .

A licensed psychiatrist or psychologist is an expert in psychotherapy—
and that may suffice (though I think it not so clear that this Court should
make the judgment) to justify the use of extraordinary means to encourage
counseling with him, as opposed to counseling with one's rabbi, minister,
family or friends. One must presume that a social worker does not bring this
greatly heightened degree of skill to bear, which is alone a reason for not
encouraging that consultation as generously. Does a social worker bring to
bear at least a significantly heightened degree of skill—more than a minister
or rabbi, for example? I have no idea, and neither does the Court. . . .

Another critical distinction between psychiatrists and psychologists,
on the one hand, and social workers, on the other, is that the former
professionals, in their consultations with patients, do nothing but psychotherapy. Social workers, on the other hand, interview people for a
multitude of reasons. . . . Thus, in applying the "social worker" variant of
the "psychotherapist" privilege, it will be necessary to determine whether
the information provided to the social worker was provided to him in his
capacity as a psychotherapist, or in his capacity as an administrator of
social welfare, a community organizer, etc. Worse still, if the privilege is
to have its desired effect (and is not to mislead the client), it will presumably be necessary for the social caseworker to advise, as the conversation with his welfare client proceeds, which portions are privileged and
which are not. . . .

[A]lthough the Court is technically correct that "the vast majority of
States explicitly extend a testimonial privilege to licensed social workers,"
that uniformity exists only at the most superficial level. No State has adopted
the privilege without restriction; the nature of the restrictions varies enormously from jurisdiction to jurisdiction; and 10 States . . . effectively reject the
privilege entirely. It is fair to say that there is scant national consensus even as
to the propriety of a social-worker psychotherapist privilege, and none

whatever as to its appropriate scope. In other words, the state laws to which the Court appeals for support demonstrate most convincingly that adoption of a social-worker psychotherapist privilege is a job for Congress. . . .

. . . In its consideration of this case, the Court was the beneficiary of no fewer than 14 amicus briefs supporting respondents, most of which came from such organizations as the American psychiatric Association, the American psychoanalytic Association, the American Association of State Social Work Boards, the Employee Assistance Professionals Association, Inc., the American Counseling Association, and the National Association of Social Workers. Not a single amicus brief was field in support of petitioner. That is no surprise. There is no self-interested organization out there devoted to pursuit of the truth in the federal courts. The expectation is, however, that this Court will have that interest prominently—indeed, primarily—in mind. Today we have failed that expectation, and that responsibility. It is no small matter to say that, in some cases, our federal courts will be the tools of injustice rather than unearth the truth where it is available to be found. The common law has identified a few instances where that is tolerable. Perhaps Congress may conclude that it is also tolerable for the purpose of encouraging psychotherapy by social workers. But that conclusion assuredly does not burst upon the mind with such clarity that a judgment in favor of suppressing the truth ought to be pronounced by this honorable Court. I respectfully dissent.

IN RE GRAND JURY

103 F.3d 1140 (3d Cir. 1997)

GARTH, Circuit Judge:

Three appeals presenting the same critical issue are before us. One appeal originated in the District Court of the Virgin Islands at docket number 95-7354. The other two appeals pertaining to the same Delaware defendant originated in the District Court of Delaware at docket numbers 96-7529 and 96-7530. We scheduled oral argument in all three appeals on the same day inasmuch as they raised the same question—should this court recognize a parent-child privilege? . . .

In the Virgin Islands case, the grand jury sitting in St. Croix subpoenaed the father of the target of the grand jury investigation as a witness. At the time of the alleged transactions, the [witness's] son was eighteen years old. . . . The father, a former FBI agent, lived with his wife and son in St. Croix. . . . [B]ased on his belief that the grand jury intended to question him about conversations that he had had with his son, the father moved to quash the subpoena, asserting that those conversations were privileged from disclosure under Fed. R. Evid. 501.

The father testified, at a hearing before the district court, that he and his son "ha[d] an excellent relationship, very close, very loving relationship." He further testified that if he were coerced into testifying against his son, "[their] relationship would dramatically change and the closeness that [they] have would end. . . ." The father further explained that the subpoena would impact negatively upon his relationship with his son:

> I will be living under a cloud in which if my son comes to me or talks to me, I've got to be very careful what he says, what I allow him to say. I would have to stop him and say, "you can't talk to me about that. You've got to talk to your attorney." It's no way for anybody to live in this country.

. . . [The district court denied] the father's motion to quash. On the same day, the district court granted the targeted son's motion to intervene and then stayed its order which denied the quashing of the father's subpoena pending any appeal. The court's memorandum opinion and order, although clearly sympathetic with the plight of the subpoenaed father, "regretfully decline[d] to recognize [a parent-child] privilege" because the Third Circuit had yet to address the issue and "every United States Court of Appeals that has confronted this question has declined to recognize the parent-child privilege."

In the Delaware case, a sixteen year old minor daughter was subpoenaed to testify before the grand jury, as part of an investigation into her father's participation in an alleged interstate kidnapping of a woman who had disappeared. . . . [The day before she was scheduled to testify,] a motion to quash subpoena was made by counsel for the daughter and her mother, as well as by separate counsel for the father. The motion sought to bar the testimony of the daughter claiming a parent-child privilege which would cover testimony and confidential communications. . . . [The district court denied the motion and ordered the daughter to testify.] She refused to testify and was found in contempt. The district court then stayed the imposition of sanctions during the pendency of these appeals. . . .

The central question in these appeals is one of first impression in this court: should we recognize a parent-child testimonial privilege? Appellants argue that recognition is necessary in order to advance important public policy interests such as the protection of strong and trusting parent-child relationships; the preservation of the family; safeguarding of privacy interests and protection from harmful government intrusion; and the promotion of healthy psychological development of children. These public policy arguments echo those advanced by academicians and other legal commentators in the myriad of law review articles discussing the parent-child testimonial privilege.

Although legal academicians appear to favor adoption of a parent-child testimonial privilege, no federal Court of Appeals and no state supreme court has recognized such a privilege. We too decline to recognize such a privilege . . .

Federal Rule of Evidence 501 provides that "the privilege of a witness . . . shall be governed by the principles of the common law as they may be interpreted by the courts of the United States in the light of reason and experience." No such principle, interpretation, reason or experience has been drawn upon here.

It is true that Congress, in enacting Fed. R. Evid. 501, "manifested an affirmative intention not to freeze the law of privilege. Its purpose rather was to 'provide the courts with the flexibility to develop rules of privilege on a case-by-case basis,' and to leave the door open to change." *Trammel v. United States*, 445 U.S. 40, 47 (1980) (quoting 102 Cong. Rec. 40,891 (1974) (statement of Rep. William Hungate)). In doing so, however, we are admonished that privileges are generally disfavored; that "'the public . . . has a right to every man's evidence'"; and that privileges are tolerable "only to the very limited extent that permitting a refusal to testify or excluding relevant evidence has a public good transcending the normally predominant principle of utilizing all rational means for ascertaining truth." [*Trammel*, 445 U.S. at 50].

In keeping with these principles, the Supreme Court has rarely expanded common-law testimonial privileges. Following the Supreme Court's teachings, other federal courts, including this court, have likewise declined to exercise their power under Rule 501 expansively. *See, e.g., United States v. Schoenheinz*, 548 F.2d 1389, 1390 (9th Cir. 1977) (declining to recognize an employer-stenographer privilege); *In re Grand Jury Impaneled on January* 21, 1975, 541 F.2d 373, 382 (3d Cir. 1976) (declining to recognize a required-reports privilege).

Neither the appellants nor the dissent has identified any principle of common law, and hence have proved no interpretation of such a principle. Nor has the dissent or the appellants discussed any common-law principle in light of reason and experience. Accordingly, no basis has been demonstrated for this court to adopt a parent-child privilege.

The Supreme Court's most recent pronouncement in the law of privileges, *Jaffee v. Redmond*, 116 S. Ct. 1923 (1996), which recognized a psychotherapist-patient privilege, supports the conclusion that a privilege should not, and cannot, be created here. . . . The *Jaffee* Court emphasized that a court, in determining whether a particular privilege "'promotes sufficiently important interests to outweigh the need for probative evidence,'" must be guided by "reason and experience." Specifically, the *Jaffee* Court instructed that a federal court should look to the "experience" of state courts: "[T]he policy decision of the States bear on the question [of] whether federal courts should recognize a new privilege or amend the coverage of an existing one."

Notably, in recognizing a psychotherapist-patient privilege, the Supreme Court relied on the fact that all fifty states had enacted some form of a psychotherapist privilege. The *Jaffee* Court explained that "it is appropriate to treat a consistent body of policy determinations by state legislatures as reflecting both 'reason' and 'experience.'" Here, by contrast, only four states have deemed it necessary to protect from disclosure, in any manner, confidential communications between children and their parents. . . . New York state courts have recognized a limited parent-child privilege, and Idaho and Minnesota have enacted limited statutory privileges protecting confidential communications by minors to their parents. In Massachusetts . . . minor children are statutorily disqualified from testifying against their parents in criminal proceedings. . . .

The policy determinations of these four states do not constitute a "consistent body of policy determinations by state[s]" supporting recognition of a parent-child privilege. Indeed, if anything, the fact that the over-whelming majority of states have chosen not to create a parent-child privilege supports the opposite conclusion: "reason and experience" dictate that federal courts should refuse to recognize a privilege rejected by the vast majority of jurisdictions.

The *Jaffee* Court also relied on the fact that the psychotherapist-patient privilege was among the nine specific privileges recommended by the Advisory Committee on Rules of Evidence in 1972. . . . [T]he parent-child privilege, like the state legislative privilege rejected in [*United States v. Gillock*, 445 U.S. 360 (1980)], was not among the enumerated privileges submitted by the Advisory Committee. Although this fact, in and of itself, is not dispositive with respect to the question as to whether this court should create a privilege, it strongly suggests that the Advisory Committee, like the majority of state legislatures, did not regard confidential parent-child communications sufficiently important to warrant "privilege" protection.

. . . In *In re Grand Jury Investigation*, 918 F.2d 374 (3d Cir. 1990) (Becker, J.), we adopted a clergy-communicant privilege. We did so, however, only after examining the state and federal precedents addressing the issue of a clergy-communicant privilege and after determining that these precedents, on balance, weighed in favor of recognizing such a privilege. . . . Moreover, like the *Jaffee* Court and perhaps in anticipation of *Jaffee*'s instructions, Judge Becker considered the "reason and experience" of the state legislatures and of the Advisory Committee. First, Judge Becker, writing for a unanimous panel, noted that "virtually every state has recognized some form of a clergy-communicant privilege." In addition, Judge Becker posited that "the proposed rules prove a useful reference point and offer guidance in defining the existence and scope of evidentiary privileges in the federal courts." . . . Judge Becker then concluded that "[t]he inclusion of the clergy-communicant privilege in the proposed rules, taken together with its uncontroversial nature, strongly suggests that [that] privilege is, in the words of the Supreme Court, 'indelibly ensconced' in the American common law." Judge Becker also provided a detailed exegesis of the historical development of the clergy-communicant privilege, stressing that common-law tradition, as reflected in practice and case law, supported recognition of such a privilege.

In contrast, the parent-child privilege sought to be recognized here is of relatively recent vintage, and is virtually no more than the product of legal academicians. Unlike, for example, the attorney-client privilege, which is "the oldest" common-law privilege, *see United States v. Zolin*, 491 U.S. 554, 562 (1989); *Upjohn Co. v. United States*, 449 U.S. 383, 389 (1981), the parent-child privilege lacks historical antecedents.

Furthermore, an analysis of the four Wigmore factors, which Judge Becker used to buttress this court's disposition in *In re Grand Jury Investigation*, does not support the creation of a privilege. Dean Wigmore's four-factor formula requires satisfaction of all four factors in order to establish a privilege:

(1) The communications must originate in a confidence that they will not be disclosed.

(2) This element of confidentiality must be essential to the full and satisfactory maintenance of the relation between the parties.

(3) The relation must be one which in the opinion of the community ought to be sedulously fostered.

(4) The injury that would inure to the relation by the disclosure of the communications must be greater than the benefit thereby gained for the correct disposal of litigation.

In re Grand Jury Investigation, 918 F.2d at 384 (quoting 8 John H. Wigmore, Evidence §2285 (J. McNaughton rev. ed. 1961)).

At least two of Wigmore's prerequisite conditions for creation of a federal common-law privilege are not met under the facts of these cases. We refer to the second and fourth elements of the Wigmore test.

First, confidentiality—in the form of a testimonial privilege—is not essential to a successful parent-child relationship, as required by the second factor. A privilege should be recognized only where such a privilege would be indispensable to the survival of the relationship that society deems should be fostered. For instance, because complete candor and full disclosure by the client is absolutely necessary in order for the attorney to function effectively, society recognizes an attorney-client privilege. Without a guarantee of secrecy, clients would be unwilling to reveal damaging information. As a corollary, clients would disclose negative information, which an attorney must know to prove effective representation, only if they were assured that such disclosures are privileged.

In contrast, it is not clear whether children would be more likely to discuss private matters with their parents if a parent-child privilege were recognized than if one were not. It is not likely that children, or even their parents, would typically be aware of the existence or non-existence of a testimonial privilege covering parent-child communications. On the other hand, professionals such as attorneys, doctors and members of the clergy would know of the privilege that attends their respective profession, and their clients, patients or parishioners would also be aware that their confidential conversations are protected from compelled disclosure.[8]

Moreover, even assuming arguendo that children and their parents generally are aware of whether or not their communications are protected from disclosure, it is not certain that the existence of a privilege enters into whatever thought processes are performed by children in deciding whether or not to confide in their parents. Indeed, the existence or nonexistence of a parent-child privilege is probably one of the least important considerations in any child's decision as to whether to reveal some indiscretion, legal or illegal, to a parent. Moreover, it is unlikely that any parent would choose to

---

8. Notably, the Advisory Committee on the Rules of Evidence reached a similar conclusion with respect to a marital communications privilege. The Advisory Committee explained: "[Proposed Rule 505] recognizes no privilege for confidential communications [between spouses]. . . . [It cannot] be assumed that marital conduct will be affected by a privilege for confidential communications of whose existence the parties in all likelihood are unaware. The other communication privileges, by way of contrast, have as one party a professional person who can be expected to inform the other of the existence of the privilege."

deter a child from revealing a confidence to the parent solely because a federal court has refused to recognize a privilege protecting such communications from disclosure.

Finally, the proposed parent-child privilege fails to satisfy the fourth condition of the Wigmore test. As explained above, any injury to the parent-child relationship resulting from non-recognition of such a privilege would be relatively insignificant. In contrast, the cost of recognizing such a privilege is substantial: the impairment of the truth-seeking function of the judicial system and the increased likelihood of injustice resulting from the concealment of relevant information. . . .

An even more compelling reason for rejecting a parent-child privilege stems from the fact that the parent-child relationship differs dramatically from other relationships. This is due to the unique duty owing to the child from the parent. A parent owes the duty to the child to nurture and guide the child. This duty is unusual because it inheres in the relationship and the relationship arises automatically at the child's birth.

If, for example, a fifteen year old unemancipated child informs her parent that she has committed a crime or has been using or distributing narcotics, and this disclosure has been made in confidence while the child is seeking guidance, it is evident to us that, regardless of whether the child consents or not, the parent must have the right to take such action as the parent deems appropriate in the interest of the child. That action could be commitment to a drug rehabilitation center or a report of the crime to the juvenile authorities. This is so because, in theory at least, juvenile proceedings are undertaken solely in the interest of the child. We would regard it intolerable in such a situation if the law intruded in the guise of a privilege, and silenced the parent because the child had a privilege to prevent disclosure.

This results in the analysis that any privilege, if recognized, must be dependent upon both the parent and child asserting it. However, in such a case, the privilege would disappear if the parent can waive it. It follows therefore that, if a child is able to communicate openly with a parent and seeks guidance from that parent, the entire basis for the privilege is destroyed if the child is required to recognize that confidence will be maintained only so long as the parent wants the conversation to be confidential. If, however, the parent can waive the privilege unilaterally, the goal of the privilege is destroyed. . . . [A]n effective parent-child privilege requires that the parent's lips be sealed, but such a sealing would be inexcusable in the parent-child relationship. No government should have that power.

. . . [In any event,] the legislature, not the judiciary, is institutionally better equipped to perform the balancing of the competing policy issues required in deciding whether the recognition of a parent-child privilege is in the best interests of society. Congress, through its legislative mechanisms, is also better suited for the task of defining the scope of any prospective privilege. Congress is able to consider, for example, society's moral, sociological, economic, religious and other values without being confined to the evidentiary record in any particular case. Thus, in determining whether a parent-child privilege should obtain, Congress can take into consideration a host of facts and factors which the judiciary may be unable to consider.

These considerations are also relevant to determining whether the privilege, if it is to be recognized, should extend to adult children, adopted children or unemancipated minors.

Among additional factors that Congress could consider are other parameters of familial relationships. Does "parent" include step-parent or grandparent? Does "child" include an adopted child, or a step-child? Should the privilege extend to siblings? Furthermore, if another family member is present at the time of the relevant communication is the privilege automatically barred or destroyed?

. . . In short, if a new privilege is deemed worthy of recognition, the wiser course in our opinion is to leave the adoption of such a privilege to Congress. . . . Sympathy alone cannot justify the creation of a new and unprecedented privilege which does not meet the standards set by Congress, the Supreme Court and this court.

Accordingly, we will affirm [the district courts' orders].

MANSMANN, Circuit Judge, concurring and dissenting.

I write separately because I am convinced that the testimonial privilege issue raised by the Virgin Islands appeal is substantially different from that presented in the Delaware appeals and should be resolved in favor of the targeted son. The Virgin Islands appeal, which challenges the denial of a motion to quash a grand jury subpoena, requires that we confront an issue of first impression in our circuit: should we make available to a parent and child an evidentiary privilege which could be invoked to prevent compelling that parent to testify regarding confidential communications made to the parent by his child in the course of seeking parental advice and guidance? It appears that this precise question is one of first impression in the federal courts.

Because I conclude that the public good at issue, the protection of strong and trusting parent-child relationships, outweighs the government's interest in disclosure, I would exercise the authority granted to the federal courts by Congress under Rule 501 of the Federal Rules of Evidence and would recognize a limited privilege. Accordingly, I respectfully dissent. . . .

MIRJAN R. DAMAŠKA, EVIDENCE LAW ADRIFT

12-13, 77-78 (1997)

Rules rejecting probative information for the sake of values unrelated to the pursuit of truth are clearly not limited to the world of Anglo-American justice. A piquant example is testimonial privileges: not only are they widespread on the Continent, but they often assume broader forms—much more encompassing than in the law of any common law country. Thus, in addition to refusing to answer self-incriminating questions, in many European jurisdictions witnesses can refuse to answer questions potentially capable of incriminating members of their family. Some countries go even further and dispense witnesses from the duty to answer any question likely to dishonor them or expose them to direct financial loss. Other countries grant parties in civil litigation a general dispensation from the duty to testify. Indeed, so expansive are some of these testimonial privileges that one wonders how the lawgivers' promises can be kept without seriously harming the interests of justice.

. . . The short answer is that Continental privileges are not invoked nearly so often as Anglo-American lawyers would expect. Prominent among the reasons is the paucity of contact between prospective witnesses and litigants' lawyers. . . . The pretrial collection of evidence is here primarily the job of the judge or some other official. Although counsel for the parties are not prohibited from conducting investigations, their contacts with prospective witnesses are disfavored. If revealed, these contacts are likely to diminish the credibility of the witness's testimony. Preparing witnesses for court is strongly disapproved and may in some countries come dangerously close to tampering with evidence. For all these reasons, lawyers conduct few factual investigations on their own, largely limiting themselves to conveying investigative leads to the official in charge of proof-taking.

11

PHYSICAL EVIDENCE

"The proof was in the pudding, but the pudding was ruled inadmissible as evidence."

Most trial evidence takes the form of testimony from a witness. But most trials also involve at least some physical evidence—i.e., tangible exhibits such as documents, photographs, contraband, weapons, etc. Physical evidence is subject to many of the same rules as testimonial evidence. The Documents generally are inadmissible if they contain hearsay; guns generally are inadmissible if they serve only to demonstrate the defendant's violent character. But physical evidence also may need to satisfy two more specialized rules.

First, all physical evidence must be *authenticated*. That is to say, the party offering the evidence must provide sufficient evidence to allow the factfinder to conclude that the evidence is genuine. As the materials in the first portion of this chapter explain, authentication is best understood as a specific application of a more principle of evidence law: conditional relevance. Indeed, the rules follow the practice of trial lawyers in referring to the "authentication" not just of physical evidence, but also of certain *testimony* raising problems of conditional relevance—for example, testimony recounting conversations in which the opposing party is alleged to have participated.

Second, certain physical evidence—and certain forms of testimony— may be rendered inadmissible by the *best evidence rule*, which is the subject of the second part of this chapter. Unlike the requirement of authentication, which applies quite broadly, the best evidence rule has a narrow scope. In its modern formulation, the best evidence rule does *not* require, as a general matter, that a party introduce the best evidence available on any given point. Instead, it requires only that a party seeking to prove the content of a document introduce the original—and even that requirement has several significant exceptions.

Most physical evidence qualifies as what is sometimes called "real evidence": items that allegedly played some role in or were generated by the events in dispute. But lawyers often generate charts, photographs, diagrams, models, or video presentations specifically for trial, to clarify their case or to make it more vivid. "Demonstrative evidence" of this kind is usually thought subject to neither the requirement of authentication nor the best evidence rule. As the materials in the third and final part of this chapter demonstrate, demonstrative evidence is increasingly powerful and increasingly important, but courts and rulemakers remain unsure how to regulate it, or even whether to think of it as "evidence."

In discussing either "real" or "demonstrative" evidence, it is important to distinguish between introducing an exhibit and merely "marking" it. We touched on this in Chapter One. The basic point is that a traditional, uncodified rule of trial practice requires any physical exhibit used during the trial to be marked. "Marking" means both physical labeling of the exhibit (usually with a sticker that says something like "Plaintiff's Exhibit 2" or "People's Exhibit 7B") and making it part of the formal record of the case (i.e., turning over custody of the exhibit to the court and keeping it with the documents and other materials available to reviewing courts). Exhibits must be marked even if they are never introduced into evidence but are used solely, for example, to refresh the recollection of a forgetful witness. But an exhibit that is merely marked cannot be relied upon by the jury in reaching a verdict. In order to serve this role, the marked exhibit must be introduced into evidence.

A. AUTHENTICATION

[F.R.E. 901-903; C.E.C. §§1400-1454]

ADVISORY COMMITTEE NOTE TO F.R.E. 901

Authentication and identification represent a special aspect of relevancy. Thus a telephone conversation may be irrelevant because on an unrelated topic or because the speaker is not identified. The latter aspect is the one here involved. Wigmore describes the need for authentication as "an inherent logical necessity."

This requirement of showing authenticity or identity falls in the category of relevancy dependent upon fulfillment of a condition of fact and is governed by the procedure set forth in Rule 104(b).

... The treatment of authentication and identification [in subdivision (b)] draws largely upon the experience embodied in the common law and in statutes to furnish illustrative applications of the general principle set forth in subdivision (a). The examples are not intended as an exclusive enumeration of allowable methods but are meant to guide and suggest, leaving room for growth and development in this area of the law. ...

It should be observed that compliance with requirements of authentication or identification by no means assures admission of an item into evidence, as other bars, hearsay for example, may remain.

UNITED STATES v. LONG

857 F.2d 436 (8th Cir. 1988)

HEANEY, Circuit Judge.

Thaddeus Adonis Long and Edward Larry Jackson appeal from their convictions on a number of counts for their involvement in a check forging and bank fraud scheme. We affirm their convictions on all counts.

... At trial, Long called his fiancee, Mary Statten, as a witness. On direct examination, she briefly mentioned a contract Long signed prior to coming to Minnesota, which, according to her, led her and Long to believe he was participating in a legitimate business venture. The government did not object to her mentioning the contract. On cross-examination, the government questioned her quite extensively about the contract. She replied that the contract involved Thermo-Dynamics and that Jackson had hired Long for six months for $40,000 as a promoter. She indicated that Long had probably brought the contract with him to Minnesota. On re-direct examination, Statten identified an exhibit as the contract of employment. The government and Jackson objected to the exhibit as hearsay. The trial court sustained the objection.

At a side bar conference, Long's counsel argued that the exhibit was not being offered for its truth but rather to show Long's state of mind, as the best evidence of the agreement about which Statten testified on direct examination, or as a response to the government's cross-examination which implied that the contract was a recent fabrication. The trial court questioned whether the contract had been authenticated.

On appeal, the government only argues that the trial court did not abuse its discretion in excluding the contract because it had not been authenticated. To authenticate a document, the proponent need only prove a rational basis for the claim that the document is what the proponent asserts it to be. ... This may be done with circumstantial evidence.

For the purpose of attempting to bolster Statten's testimony, we see no reason why the contract was insufficiently authenticated. The government contends that Statten was not a party or a signatory to the document or witness to its preparation. The question of authenticity here, however, is not whether the contract was an authentic contract between Jackson and Long but whether it reasonably could be the document which Statten claims she saw and read at the airport. The defense did not have to prove the contract's reliability and accuracy. This was a matter for the jury to determine after examining all the evidence.[2] Thus, the document was authenticated as the document which Statten claims she saw and read.

Any error which occurred, however, was harmless. The contract was introduced to bolster Statten's testimony that Long thought he was entering a legitimate business enterprise. Other evidence strongly indicated that Long had not unwittingly entered the fraud scheme. Long used various aliases and false forms of identification; he did nothing that could be construed as a legitimate business activity while in Minnesota; and the cash he withdrew from the bank was for his personal use. We, therefore, find no reversible error. . . .

BRUTHER v. GENERAL ELECTRIC CO.

818 F. Supp. 1238 (S.D. Ind. 1993)

Barker, District Judge.

On January 31, 1989, Plaintiff was electrocuted while changing a light bulb at his place of employment, Rexnord, Inc., in Madison, Indiana. . . . According to Plaintiff, when he attempted to unscrew the bulb from its socket, the glass envelope separated from the base, exposing his right hand to an electrical current. As a result of the ensuing shock, Plaintiff apparently sustained permanent, disabling injuries; he now seeks recovery from Defendant under the full gamut of theories available in a product liability action: strict liability, negligence, breach of warranty, and failure to warn. Mrs. Bruther also seeks compensation from the Defendant for the loss of "support, services, society, love and affection and comfort of her husband. . . ."

Defendant has moved for summary judgment on . . . [the ground that] Plaintiff cannot authenticate the bulb that he wishes to introduce into evidence. . . .

Under Federal Rule of Evidence 901(a): "The requirement of authentication or identification as a condition precedent to admissibility is satisfied by evidence sufficient to support a finding that the matter in question is what its proponent claims." F.R.E. 901(a). The rationale behind this Rule is

2. There is the danger that such documentary evidence may be given undue weight by a jury. As Weinstein and Berger observe, "[r]eal proof often has enormous apparent probative force because the lay trier may lose sight of the fact that its connection to a party may depend upon the credibility of an authenticating witness." J. Weinstein and M. Berger, Weinstein's Evidence, ¶901(a)[01], at 901-19 (1983). We believe, however, such a problem should be confronted under Rule 403, which states that relevant evidence may be excluded "if its probative value is substantially outweighed by the danger of unfair prejudice, confusion of the issues, or misleading the jury. . . ."

that absent a showing that the evidence is what the proponent alleges, it has no relevance.

Defendant believes that Plaintiff is unable to authenticate the bulb that he seeks to introduce into evidence because of the lack of identifying marks on the bulb, and the existence of a gap in the chain of custody which developed immediately after the accident occurred. Apparently, no one at Rexnord took care to safeguard the bulb after Plaintiff was injured. While Howard Goodin, an employee at Rexnord, [testified in deposition that he] later removed the bulb from the socket, see Goodin Deposition at 50, it is unclear what became of the bulb after that time. It was only after Mr. James, Plaintiff's counsel, asked to examine the bulb that Don Riley, the plant safety manager, began to look for it. (The exact dates of these events are unknown.) Mr. Riley found a broken bulb in a small cabinet next to the site where the accident occurred. Although he cannot positively identify the bulb as the one that was involved in the accident, Mr. Riley [testified in deposition that he] believes, with some reservations, that it is the bulb in question because "[w]e wouldn't keep broken bulbs; so if it was there, it had a specific purpose to be there." In addition, the record indicates that only six people had access to the area where the accident occurred and the cabinet where the bulb was found. As concerns the brand of the bulb, Plaintiff states in his affidavit [that two weeks before the accident he had installed General Electric bulbs in the sockets where he was working at the time of the accident, and that to the best of his knowledge no other brand of bulbs were ever used in those sockets].

The Court finds that the evidence in the record is "sufficient" within the meaning of F.R.E. 901 to support a finding that the bulb in question is the bulb that caused Plaintiff's injuries, and that the bulb was manufactured by Defendant. Of course this holding is limited only to the issue whether Plaintiff has met the threshold burden of producing enough evidence to support his allegations; the determination whether the bulb in fact is what the Plaintiff claims it is must be made by the jury when it acts in its appointed role as finder of fact. Given, however, the limited access to the area where the injury occurred and where the bulb was found to the site of the accident, Mr. Riley's statement that Rexnord would not keep a broken bulb unless there was a reason to do so, and Plaintiff's own statement that he had installed, just two weeks prior to the accident, a G.E. light bulb in the same socket where the bulb that caused Plaintiff's injuries was located, a jury considering these factors reasonably could conclude that the bulb in question is the bulb that came apart and caused Plaintiff injury.

The Defendant's arguments to the contrary are unpersuasive. Besides a frontal assault on the sufficiency of Plaintiff's evidence (i.e. that no one can directly identify the bulb), Defendant makes much ado about lapses in the chain of custody, and tries to persuade the Court that because the bulb in question is nondescript, akin to a blood sample, "the chain of custody requirement must be followed to the letter . . ." to satisfy F.R.E. 901. That rule requires nothing of the sort. Rule 901 regulates the admissibility of evidence. The slightest research on the law in this circuit concerning the effect of gaps in the chain of custody reveals that "any discrepancies in the chain of custody go to the weight of the evidence, not its admissibility." *See U.S. v. L'Allier*, 838 F.2d 234, 242 (7th Cir. 1988), *citing, United States v.*

Shackleford, 738 F.2d 776, 785 (7th Cir. 1984). Consequently, it is the jury, and not the Court, which must evaluate the significance of Plaintiff's inability to account for the bulb following the accident. . . .

Because there remain genuine issues of material fact in this case, Defendant's motion for summary judgment is DENIED. . . .

UNITED STATES v. CASTO

889 F.2d 562 (5th Cir. 1989)

CLARK, Chief Judge:

Diana Casto appeals her conviction in the United States District Court for the Western District of Texas on one count of conspiracy to possess with intent to distribute methamphetamine . . . and two counts of aiding and abetting in the unlawful distribution of methamphetamine. . . .

Casto contends that a break in the chain of custody pertinent to Government Exhibits Two, Three, Four, and Five, the packages of methamphetamine sold to the undercover agents by [codefendant Melinda] Gutierrez, should have rendered these exhibits inadmissible. Shortly after Officer Martinez seized the packages, they were sealed and sent to a Drug Enforcement Agency laboratory in Dallas, Texas. Over two months later the packages were tested by Frank Medina, a forensic chemist at the lab. Medina found that the packages contained methamphetamine. He then sent the packages back to Martinez, who held custody of them until trial. During the period between the arrival of the packages at the laboratory and Medina's testing, the packages were kept in a vault where a technician had placed them upon their arrival at the laboratory.

Martinez and Medina testified at trial as to their custody of the packages, but the technician did not testify. According to Casto the trial judge erred by disregarding this evidentiary flaw and allowing the packages into evidence. We disagree.

A trial judge is correct in allowing physical evidence to be presented to the jury as long as a reasonable jury could decide that the evidence is what the offering party claims it to be. Fed. R. Evid. 901. Any question as to the authenticity of the evidence is then properly decided by the jury. Thus, a break in the chain of custody affects only the weight and not the admissibility of the evidence. The trial court was correct to admit the packages of methamphetamine. . . . AFFIRMED.

UNITED STATES v. GRANT

967 F.2d 81 (2d Cir. 1992)

PER CURIAM:

Sharon Grant appeals from her conviction, following a jury trial, on charges of conspiracy to import heroin, importation of heroin, and possession of heroin with intent to distribute it in violation of 21 U.S.C. §§841(a)(1), 952(a), and 963. . . . Grant contends that the government failed to prove that the packages imported by [her travelling companion Gene] Kirven . . . contained heroin. She points out that the government did not establish an airtight chain of custody over the packages from the time they were seized at the airport until the time they were tested in the laboratory by the government's chemist. Instead, the testimony and documents introduced at trial indicated that the packages were signed out of an airport vault on January 9, 1991 and not signed into the Drug Enforcement Agency's laboratory until January 23, 1991. There is nothing in the record to indicate what happened to the packages in the interim. From this lapse, Grant contends that there was insufficient evidence to establish that the laboratory tested the same substance that Kirven carried to the airport. Grant then argues that without the lab test, there was not sufficient evidence from which any reasonable jury could find that the packages contained heroin. We disagree.

We first note that this is not a typical "chain of custody" case. Chain of custody is usually an issue where a party attempts to introduce a piece of physical evidence. . . . In this case we need not determine whether the drugs were properly authenticated since the government did not offer the drugs themselves into evidence. Instead, the government presented the testimony of the chemist who analyzed the package. There is no need to authenticate the testimony of live witnesses.

This is not to say that the government's failure to establish a chain of custody is unimportant. In order to be admissible, the testimony of a live witness must be relevant, that is, must have a "tendency to make the existence of any fact that is of consequence to the determination of the action more probable or less probable than it would be without the evidence." Fed. R. Evid. 401. In order for the chemist's testimony to be relevant, there must be some likelihood that the substance tested by the chemist was the substance seized at the airport. The government's failure to establish a chain of custody from the moment the substance was seized to the time it was subjected to laboratory analysis makes this less likely, and thus casts some doubt on the admissibility of the chemist's testimony.

However, Grant did not object to the chemist's testimony at trial and does not assert here that the testimony should have been excluded. Even if Grant had pursued this argument, we doubt it would be successful, given the broad discretion afforded district courts in making relevancy determinations. . . . [W]e affirm her conviction and sentence in all respects.

PROBLEMS

11.1. Julia sues Samantha for injuries Julia suffered when her car was hit by Samantha's. Julia's lawyer wants to show the jury a photograph taken of Julia after the accident, to demonstrate the extent of her injuries. Does the photograph need to be authenticated? If so, how could that requirement be satisfied?

11.2. Clyde sues his torts professor, Harold, for slander, alleging that Harold said falsely during one of his lectures that Clyde had bribed his way into law school. Clyde's lawyer seeks to introduce an audiotape of the lecture. Does the tape need to be authenticated? If so, how could that requirement be satisfied?

B. THE BEST EVIDENCE RULE

Students studying for the bar exam are sometimes taught a rule of thumb: on a multiple-choice question, the best evidence rule is always the wrong answer. This is at best an exaggeration (the bar examiners are too tricky for any rule like this to work reliably), but it captures an important truth. Despite its grand name, the best evidence rule does very little work today.

There was a time when the best evidence rule meant what its name suggests: only the best evidence available on a particular question was admissible. As you will see, some judges and scholars still think that principle deserves to be followed. But prevailing law has made the best evidence rule a shadow of its former self. The rule is defined today to apply only in a narrow category of cases, and it is further hemmed in by a series of sweeping exceptions.

[F.R.E. 1001-1008; C.E.C. §§250-260, 1520-1523]

1. Scope and Purpose

JOHN H. LANGBEIN, HISTORICAL FOUNDATIONS OF THE LAW OF EVIDENCE: A VIEW FROM THE RYDER SOURCES

96 Colum. L. Rev. 1168 (1996)

... Written sometime before the author's death in 1726, Geoffrey Gilbert's treatise on *The Law of Evidence* was not published until 1754 ... [but] became the most influential eighteenth-century book on evidence, going through seven editions in the hands of revisers. Although prefaced with some analytic discussion, Gilbert's book was essentially an abridgment—a law-finder that collected precedents, mostly from published yearbooks and law reports, but also from the juristic literature, including Coke, Hale, and Hawkins.

Gilbert arranged his treatise on the distinction between written and unwritten evidence, but written evidence occupied virtually all the book. As Twining has observed, "Gilbert tried to subsume all the rules of evidence under a single principle, the 'best evidence rule,' " a notion that is oriented to documentary authenticity. Among the topics concerning written evidence that Gilbert reviews are record versus nonrecord evidence, statutes, sealed versus unsealed instruments, proving copies when originals are lost, proving prior verdicts, proving chancery proceedings and depositions, evidencing wills, and the receipt of manorial court rolls. He continues with the complex rules governing proof of deeds, then bills of exchange and negotiable instruments.

The later eighteenth-century writers on evidence, Bathurst and Buller, followed Gilbert's emphasis on the best evidence rule as the organizing principle of the law of evidence. As late as 1806, a North Carolina court still proclaimed the view: "There is but one decided rule in relation to evidence, and that is, that the law requires the best evidence."

MEYERS v. UNITED STATES

171 F.2d 800 (D.C. Cir. 1949)

WILBUR K. MILLER, Circuit Judge.

Bleriot H. Lamarre and the appellant, Bennett E. Meyers, were jointly indicted for violating the District of Columbia statute which denounces perjury and subornation thereof. Three counts of the indictment charged Lamarre with as many separate perjuries in his testimony before a subcommittee of a committee of the United States Senate constituted to investigate the national defense program, and three more counts accused Meyers of suborning the perjuries of his codefendant.

Lamarre pleaded guilty to all three charges when he was arraigned on December 19, 1947, a few days after the return of the indictment. Meyers entered a plea of not guilty and was tried before a jury in the District Court of the United States for the District of Columbia. . . . Having been found guilty under each of the three counts against him, he appeals.

[Meyers was an army officer and the founder of Aviation Electric Corporation, which became a subcontractor on government work. Lamarre was the company's president.] In order to ascertain what connection, if any, the appellant had with Aviation Electric, the subcommittee subpoenaed Lamarre, who testified on Saturday, October 4, and Monday, October 6, in 1947. That testimony brought about the indictment which was the genesis of the case now before us.

. . . William P. Rogers, chief counsel to the senatorial committee, who had examined Lamarre before the subcommittee and consequently had heard all the testimony given by him before that body, was permitted to testify as to what Lamarre had sworn to the subcommittee. Later in the trial the government introduced in evidence a stenographic transcript of Lamarre's testimony at the senatorial hearing.

In his brief here the appellant characterizes this as a "bizarre procedure" but does not assign as error the reception of Rogers' testimony. The dissenting opinion, however, asserts it was reversible error to allow Rogers to testify at all as to what Lamarre had said to the subcommittee, on the theory that the transcript itself was the best evidence of Lamarre's testimony before the subcommittee.

That theory is, in our view, based upon a misconception of the best evidence rule. As applied generally in federal courts, the rule is limited to cases where the contents of a writing are to be proved. Here there was no attempt to prove the contents of a writing; the issue was what Lamarre had said, not what the transcript contained. The transcript made from shorthand notes of his testimony was, to be sure, evidence of what he had said, but it was not the only admissible evidence concerning it. Rogers' testimony was equally competent, and was admissible whether given before or after the transcript was received in evidence. Statements alleged to be perjurious may be proved by any person who heard them, as well as by a reporter who recorded them in shorthand.

A somewhat similar situation was presented in *Herzig v. Swift & Co.*, 146 F.2d 444, decided by the United States Court of Appeals for the Second Circuit in 1945. In that case the trial court had excluded oral testimony concerning the earnings of a partnership on the ground that the books of account were the best evidence. After pointing out the real nature and scope of the best evidence rule,[12] the court said, ". . . Here there was no attempt to prove the contents of a writing; the issue was the earnings of a partnership, which for convenience were recorded in books of account after the relevant facts occurred. Generally, this differentiation has been adopted by the courts. On the precise question of admitting oral testimony to prove matters that are contained in books of account, the courts have divided, some holding the oral testimony admissible, others excluding it. The federal courts have generally adopted the rationale limiting the 'best evidence rule' to cases where the contents of the writing are to be proved. We hold, therefore, that the district judge erred in excluding the oral testimony as to the earnings of the partnership."

. . . As we have pointed out, there was no issue as to the contents of the transcript, and the government was not attempting to prove what it contained; the issue was what Lamarre actually had said. Rogers was not asked what the transcript contained but what Lamarre's testimony had been. . . . Since we perceive no prejudicial error in appellant's trial, the judgment entered pursuant to the jury's verdict will not be disturbed.

Affirmed.

PRETTYMAN, Circuit Judge (dissenting).

. . . I realize that there is a line of authority that (absent or incompetent the original witness) a bystander who hears testimony or other conversation may testify as to what was said, even though there be a stenographic report. And there is a line of cases which holds that a stenographic transcript is not

---

12. In doing so the court quoted with approval the following statement from McKelvey, Evidence, 604, 5th Ed., 1944: "In its modern application, the best evidence rule amounts to little more than the requirement that the contents of a writing must be proved by the introduction of the writing itself, unless its absence be satisfactorily accounted for." See also 4 Wigmore, Evidence, §§1174, 1177-1182, 3d Ed., 1940.

the best evidence of what was said. There is also a legal cliche that the best evidence rule applies only to documentary evidence. The trial judge in this case was confronted with that authority, and a trial court is probably not the place to inaugurate a new line of authority. But I do not know why an appellate court should perpetuate a rule clearly outmoded by scientific development. I know that courts are reluctant to do so. I recognize the view that such matters should be left to Congress. But rules of evidence were originally judge-made and are an essential part of the judicial function. I knew of no reason why the judicial branch of Government should abdicate to the legislative branch so important a part of its responsibility.

I am of opinion, and quite ready to hold, that the rules of evidence reflected by the cases to which I have just referred are outmoded and at variance with known fact, and that the courts ought to establish a new and correct rule. The rationale of the so-called "best evidence rule" requires that a party having available evidence which is relatively certain may not submit evidence which is far less certain. The law is concerned with the true fact, and with that alone; its procedures are directed to that objective, and to that alone. It should permit no procedure the sole use of which is to obscure and confuse that which is otherwise plain and certain.

. . . The doctrine that stenographic notes are not the best evidence of testimony was established when stenography was not an accurate science. . . . But we have before us no such situation. Stenographic reporting has become highly developed, and official stenographic reports are relied upon in many of the most important affairs of life. . . . In the present instance, at least, no one has disputed the correctness of the transcript.

. . . Given both (1) an accurate stenographic transcription of a witness' testimony during a two-day hearing and (2) the recollection of one of the complainants as to the substance of that testimony, is the latter admissible as evidence in a trial of the witness for perjury? I think not. To say that it is, is to apply a meaningless formula and ignore crystal clear actualities. The transcript is, as a matter of simple, indisputable fact, the best evidence. The principle and not the rote of the law ought to be applied. . . .

ADVISORY COMMITTEE NOTES TO F.R.E. 1001-1002

In an earlier day, when discovery and other related procedures were strictly limited, the misleading named "best evidence rule" afforded substantial guarantees against inaccuracies and fraud by its insistence upon production or original documents. The great enlargement of the scope of discovery and related procedures in recent times has measurably reduced the need for the rule. Nevertheless important areas of usefulness persist: discovery of documents outside the jurisdiction may require substantial outlay of time and money; the unanticipated document may not practically be discoverable; criminal cases have built-in limitations on discovery. . . .

The rule [set forth in F.R.E. 1002] is the familiar one requiring production of the original of a document to prove its contents, expanded to include writings, recordings, and photographs, as defined in Rule 1001(1) and (2), supra.

Application of the rule requires a resolution of the question whether contents are sought to be proved. Thus an event may be proved by nondocumentary evidence, even though a written record of it was made. If, however, the event is sought to be proved by the written record, the rule applies. For example, payment may be proved without producing the written receipt which was given. Earnings may be proved without producing books of account in which they are entered. McCormick §198; 4 Wigmore §1245. Nor does the rule apply to testimony that books or records have been examined and found not to contain any reference to a designated matter.

The assumption should not be made that the rule will come into operation on every occasion when use is made of a photograph in evidence. On the contrary, the rule will seldom apply to ordinary photographs. In most instances a party wishes to introduce the item and the question raised is the propriety of receiving it in evidence. Cases in which an offer is made of the testimony of a witness as to what he saw in a photograph or motion picture, without producing the same, are most unusual. The usual course is for a witness on the stand to identify the photograph or motion picture as a correct representation of events which he saw or of a scene with which he is familiar. In fact he adopts the picture as his testimony, or, in common parlance, uses the picture to illustrate his testimony. Under these circumstances, no effort is made to prove the contents of the picture, and the rule is inapplicable.

On occasion, however, situations arise in which contents are sought to be proved. Copyright, defamation, and invasion of privacy by photograph or motion picture falls in this category. Similarly as to situations in which the picture is offered as having independent probative value, e.g. automatic photograph of bank robber. . . . The most commonly encountered of this latter group is of course, the X ray, with substantial authority calling for production of the original.

It should be noted, however, that Rule 703, supra, allows an expert to give an opinion based on matters not in evidence, and the present rule must be read as being limited accordingly in its application. Hospital records which may be admitted as business records under Rule 803(6) commonly contain reports interpreting X rays by the staff radiologist, who qualifies as an expert, and these reports need not be excluded from the records by the instant rule.

The reference to Acts of Congress is made in view of such statutory provisions as 26 U.S.C. §7513, photographic reproductions of tax returns and documents, made by authority of the Secretary of the Treasury, treated as originals, and 44 U.S.C. §399(a), photographic copies in National Archives treated as originals.

UNITED STATES v. GONZALES-BENITEZ

537 F.2d 1051 (9th Cir. 1976)

KENNEDY, Circuit Judge:

Aida Gonzales-Benitez and Ambrosio Hernandez-Coronel were convicted for importing and distributing heroin. . . . Appellants contend the trial court erred in permitting testimony that related their conversations with the informers during a certain meeting in a motel room in Arizona. They claim that since the conversations were recorded on tapes, the tapes themselves, and not testimony of one of the participants, were the "best evidence" of the conversations. We are puzzled that this argument should be advanced so seriously and would not consider it if attorneys for both appellants had not argued the point so strenuously both in their briefs and in the court below. Certainly the trial court was correct in dismissing the objection out of hand.

The appellants simply misconstrue the purpose and effect of the best evidence rule. The rule does not set up an order of preferred admissibility, which must be followed to prove any fact. It is, rather, a rule applicable only when one seeks to prove the contents of documents or recordings. Fed. R. Evid. 1002. Thus, if the ultimate inquiry had been to discover what sounds were embodied on the tapes in question, the tapes themselves would have been the "best evidence."

However, the content of the tapes was not in itself a factual issue relevant to the case. The inquiry concerned the content of the conversations. The tape recordings, if intelligible,[2] would have been admissible as evidence of those conversations. But testimony by the participants was equally admissible and was sufficient to establish what was said. . . .

AFFIRMED.

DALE A. NANCE, THE BEST EVIDENCE PRINCIPLE

73 Iowa L. Rev. 227, 227-229, 295 (1988)

[T]here exists, even today, a principle of evidence law that a party should present to the tribunal the best evidence reasonably available on a litigated factual issue. This principle is not absolute, and in particular circumstances other considerations may override it or excuse its nonsatisfaction. Nevertheless, it is a general principle that manifests itself in a wide variety of concrete rules governing the trial process. In fact, it provides an organizing principle within the law of evidence. Consequently, it is improper for a court to reason from the premise, explicit or implicit, that there is no such principle. Unfortunately, such a premise has been widely professed by modern commentators and is regularly employed by the courts.

The case of *United States v. Gonzales-Benitez* illustrates the problem. . . .The point is not that the appellants in that case should have prevailed, but simply that the court's treatment of their argument was inadequate. The court should have considered whether the trial court had and abused a discretion to deny admission of the testimony pursuant to a general best evidence principle. At the very least, the court should have

---

2. We note that the reason the tapes were not introduced here was that the recording quality was so poor that the court translator was unable to understand and translate them.

justified its implicit assumption that the phrase "best evidence" could only refer, in the context of this case, to the original document rule.

. . . [P]utting aside the rules, such as those governing privileges, which are said to serve extrinsic social policies, the remaining evidentiary rules are more plausibly attributable to the epistemic concerns of a tribunal encountering the adversarial presentation of evidence than to judicial concerns about the irrational behavior of weak-minded lay jurors. . . . This view understands at least a significant number of the rules of evidence as designed to protect the tribunal as a truth-finding, and thereby dispute-resolving, forum by imposing educative restraints and disciplinary sanctions upon litigants who would otherwise deprive the tribunal of the best, reasonably available evidence on a given issue. Although these measures may or may not be maximally conducive to the ascertainment of truth in the instant case, it is contemplated and hoped that their imposition will contribute in the long run not only to accurate fact-finding but also to a deserved public respect for the legal system.

. . . [F]airness to litigants requires that determinations of the use of the coercive power of the state be made on the best reasonably available evidence. Respect for the tribunal demands that it not be placed in the position of making such determinations upon evidence of lesser quality. In the final analysis, it must also be said that truth has intrinsic value, knowledge is a common good, and the presentation of the best reasonably available evidence is a crucial part of the participation in that good by persons who utilize the judicial system. . . . In any event, and this is most important, it seems impossible to understand fully the present system without reference to that principle. Certainly, then, appeals to it cannot reasonably be dismissed as no more than the invocation of a mistaken or outmoded idea.

2. Exceptions

ADVISORY COMMITTEE NOTES TO F.R.E. 1003-1008

When the only concern is with getting the words or other contents before the court with accuracy and precision, then a counterpart serves equally as well as the original, if the counterpart is the product of a method which insures accuracy and genuineness. . . . Therefore, if no genuine issue exists as to authenticity and no other reason exists for requiring the original, a duplicate is admissible under [F.R.E. 1003]. . . .

Basically the rule requiring the production of the original as proof of contents has developed as a rule of preference: if failure to produce the original is satisfactorily explained, secondary evidence is admissible. [F.R.E. 1004] specifies the circumstances under which production of the original is excused.

The rule recognizes no "degrees" of secondary evidence. While strict logic might call for extending the principle of preference beyond simply preferring the original, the formulation of a hierarchy of preferences and a procedure for making it effective is believed to involve unwarranted complexities. Most, if not all, that would be accomplished by an extended scheme of preferences will, in any event, be achieved through the normal motivation of a party to present the most convincing evidence possible and the arguments and procedures available to his opponent if he does not. . . .

Public records call for somewhat different treatment. Removing them from their usual place of keeping would be attended by serious inconvenience to the public and to the custodian. As a consequence judicial decisions and statutes commonly hold that no explanation need be given for failure to produce the original of a public record. McCormick §204; 4 Wigmore §§1215-1228. This blanket dispensation from producing or accounting for the original would open the door to the introduction of every kind of secondary evidence of contents of public records were it not for the preference given certified or compared copies. Recognition of degrees of secondary evidence in this situation is an appropriate *quid pro quo* for not applying the requirement of producing the original. . . .

Most preliminary questions of fact in connection with applying the rule preferring the original as evidence of contents are for the judge, under the general principles announced in Rule 104, *supra*. Thus, the question whether the loss of the originals has been established, or of the fulfillment of other conditions specified in Rule 1004 . . . is for the judge. However, questions may arise which go beyond the mere administration of the rule preferring the original and into the merits of the controversy. For example, plaintiff offers secondary evidence of the contents of an alleged contract, after first introducing evidence of loss of the original, and defendant counters with evidence that no such contract was ever executed. If the judge decides that the contract was never executed and excludes the secondary evidence, the case is at an end without ever going to the jury on a central issue. The latter portion [F.R.E. 1008] is designed to insure treatment of these situations as raising jury questions. The decision is not one for uncontrolled discretion of the jury but is subject to the control exercised generally by the judge over jury determinations. See Rule 104(b), *supra*.

UNITED STATES v. STOCKTON

968 F.2d 715 (8th Cir. 1992)

McMillan, Circuit Judge.

Gary Wayne Badley and William D. Stockton . . . appeal from final judgments entered in the United States District Court for the Western District of Missouri, upon jury verdicts, finding them guilty of involvement in a conspiracy to manufacture methamphetamine. . . .

During a search of [co-defendant Terry] Appleby's residence in Thayer, Kansas, photographs were taken of "miscellaneous papers" and these photographs were introduced at trial (Exhibits 74-H and 74-I). According to Stockton, the government provided no reason why the originals could not be produced, and, therefore, the district court's admission of the photographs violated the Best Evidence Rule.

. . . We hold that the Best Evidence Rule does apply in this situation, but that the photographs were properly admitted as duplicates under Fed. R. Evid. 1003. While the government is correct that the Best Evidence Rule does not usually apply to photographs, this case is one of "those relatively rare instances in which [the photographs'] contents are sought to be proved." John W. Strong et al., *McCormick on Evidence* §232, at 65 (4th ed. 1992).[7] During the government's case-in-chief, Harley Sparks, a special agent with the DEA, testified to the contents of the photographs and specifically read from the photographs. Therefore, the contents of the photographs were at issue in this case.

These photographs are not the original documents and therefore violate Fed. R. Evid. 1002. But the analysis does not end there because Fed. R. Evid. 1003 allows duplicates to be introduced in the same manner as originals "unless (1) a genuine question is raised as to the authenticity of the original or (2) in the circumstances it would be unfair to admit the duplicate in lieu of the original." This rule allows photocopies or carbon copies to be introduced in lieu of the original documents unless there is a genuine challenge to the authenticity of the document. We see no distinction between a photocopy and the photographs used in this case. Photographs of notes were taken by DEA agents during a lawful search and one of the agents testified to contents of the photographs. No question was raised below as to the authenticity of the photographs so that exception is not at issue in this case. We hold, therefore, that the district court did not abuse its discretion in admitting the photographs which were admissible as duplicates in lieu of the original documents pursuant to Fed. R. Evid. 1003.

. . . Accordingly, we affirm the judgments of the district court.

UNITED STATES v. STANDING SOLDIER

538 F.2d 196 (8th Cir. 1976)

Webster, Circuit Judge.

Victor Standing Solider appeals his conviction of assault with intent to kill. . . . [Following Standing Soldier's arrest, he signed a written statement of his involvement. Later his jailer gave Captain Gerald Hill of the Bureau of Indian Affairs Police] a note allegedly written by the appellant, stating that

---

7. The government argues that the Best Evidence Rule does not apply to photographs because they are demonstrative evidence. For example, in *United States v. Alexander,* 415 F.2d 1352, 1357 (7th Cir. 1969), *cert. denied*, 397 U.S. 1014 (1970), the Best Evidence Rule did not apply to a photograph of stolen mail because "[t]he photograph was introduced to show the quantity of mail seized at the time of arrest and not for the purpose of demonstrating anything about the contents of the particular letters." The photographs introduced in the present case were introduced to prove the contents of the writings which they represented, and, therefore, the Best Evidence Rule is applicable.

he wanted to talk. Apparently, the note was lost by tribal or federal authorities, but Captain Hill produced a typewritten copy at trial from which he testified. . . . The District Court permitted testimony concerning the note after Captain Hill testified that he had compared the signature on the note with that of appellant on the signed statement he had made and found them to be the same. . . .

Captain Hill . . . testified that he had attempted to locate the original note by contacting the criminal investigator and the FBI, but had been unable to find it, although he thought that it probably did still exist. . . . Fed. R. Evid. 1004(1) provides that the "original is not required, and other evidence of the contents of a writing . . . is admissible if . . . [a]ll originals are lost or have been destroyed, unless the proponent lost or destroyed them in bad faith." There being no evidence of bad faith on the part of the government and the original having been lost, the District Court properly permitted Captain Hill's oral testimony concerning the note. . . . The Federal Rules of Evidence recognize no "degrees" of secondary evidence and thus there was no requirement that the copy be introduced in preference to the oral testimony. See Fed. R. Evid. 1000, Notes of Advisory Committee. . . . The judgment of conviction is accordingly affirmed.

SEILER v. LUCASFILM, LTD.

808 F.2d 1316 (9th Cir. 1987)

FARRIS, Circuit Judge.

Lee Seiler, a graphic artist and creator of science fiction creatures, alleged copyright infringement by George Lucas and others who created and produced the science fiction movie "The Empire Strikes Back." . . . Seiler contends that he created and published in 1976 and 1977 science fiction creatures called Garthian Striders. In 1980, George Lucas released The Empire Strikes Back, a motion picture that contains a battle sequence depicting giant machines called Imperial Walkers. In 1981 Seiler obtained a copyright on his Striders, depositing with the Copyright Office "reconstructions" of the originals as they had appeared in 1976 and 1977.

Seiler contends that Lucas' Walkers were copied from Seiler's Striders which were allegedly published in 1976 and 1977. Lucas responds that Seiler did not obtain his copyright until one year after the release of The Empire Strikes Back and that Seiler can produce no documents that antedate The Empire Strikes Back.

Because Seiler proposed to exhibit his Striders in a blow-up comparison to Lucas' Walkers at opening statement, the district judge held an evidentiary hearing on the admissibility of the "reconstructions" of Seiler's Striders. Applying the "best evidence rule," Fed. R. Evid. 1001-1008, the district court found at the end of a seven-day hearing that Seiler lost or destroyed the originals in bad faith under Rule 1004(1) and that consequently no secondary evidence, such as the post-Empire Strikes Back reconstructions, was admissible. In its opinion the court found specifically that

Seiler testified falsely, purposefully destroyed or withheld in bad faith the
originals, and fabricated and misrepresented the nature of his reconstructions. The district court granted summary judgment to Lucas after the evidentiary hearing. . . .

The best evidence rule embodied in Rules 1001-1008 represented a
codification of longstanding common law doctrine. Dating back to 1700,
the rule requires not, as its common name implies, the best evidence in
every case but rather the production of an original document instead of a
copy. Many commentators refer to the rule not as the best evidence rule but
as the original document rule.

Rule 1002 states: "To prove the content of a writing, recording, or
photograph, the original writing, recording, or photograph is required,
except as otherwise provided in these rules or by Act of Congress." Writings
and recordings are defined in Rule 1001 as "letters, words, or numbers, or
their equivalent, set down by handwriting, typewriting, printing, photostat-
ing, photographing, magnetic impulse, mechanical or electronic recording,
or other form of data compilation."

The Advisory Committee Note supplies the following gloss:

> Traditionally the rule requiring the original centered upon accumulations of
> data and expressions affecting legal relations set forth in words and figures.
> This meant that the rule was one essentially related to writings. Present day
> techniques have expanded methods of storing data, yet the essential form
> which the information ultimately assumes for usable purposes is words and
> figures. Hence the considerations underlying the rule dictate its expansion to
> include computers, photographic systems, and other modern developments.

Some treatises, whose approach seems more historical than rigorously analytic, opine without support from any cases that the rule is limited to words
and figures. 5 Weinstein's Evidence (1983), ¶1001(1)[01] at 1001-11; 5
Louisell & Mueller, §550 at 285.

We hold that Seiler's drawings were "writings" within the meaning of
Rule 1001(1); they consist not of "letters, words, or numbers" but of "their
equivalent." To hold otherwise would frustrate the policies underlying the
rule and introduce undesirable inconsistencies into the application of the
rule.

In the days before liberal rules of discovery and modern techniques of
electronic copying, the rule guarded against incomplete or fraudulent
proof. By requiring the possessor of the original to produce it, the rule
prevented the introduction of altered copies and the withholding of originals. The purpose of the rule was thus long thought to be one of fraud
prevention, but Wigmore pointed out that the rule operated even in
cases where fraud was not at issue, such as where secondary evidence is
not admitted even though its proponent acts in utmost good faith. Wigmore
also noted that if prevention of fraud were the foundation of the rule, it
should apply to objects as well as writings, which it does not. 4 Wigmore,
Evidence §1180 (Chadbourn rev. 1972).

The modern justification for the rule has expanded from prevention of
fraud to a recognition that writings occupy a central position in the law.
When the contents of a writing are at issue, oral testimony as to the terms of

the writing is subject to a greater risk of error than oral testimony as to events or other situations. The human memory is not often capable of reciting the precise terms of a writing, and when the terms are in dispute only the writing itself, or a true copy, provides reliable evidence. . . . [T]he importance of the precise terms of writings in the world of legal relations, the fallibility of the human memory as reliable evidence of the terms, and the hazards of inaccurate or incomplete duplication are the concerns addressed by the best evidence rule. . . .

Viewing the dispute in the context of the concerns underlying the best evidence rule, we conclude that the rule applies. McCormick summarizes the rule as follows:

> In proving the terms of a writing, where the terms are material, the original writing must be produced unless it is shown to be unavailable for some reason other than the serious fault of the proponent.

McCormick on Evidence §230, at 704. The contents of Seiler's work are at issue. There can be no proof of "substantial similarity" and thus of copyright infringement unless Seiler's works are juxtaposed with Lucas' and their contents compared. Since the contents are material and must be proved, Seiler must either produce the original or show that it is unavailable through no fault of his own. Rule 1004(1). This he could not do.

The facts of this case implicate the very concerns that justify the best evidence rule. Seiler alleges infringement by The Empire Strikes Back, but he can produce no documentary evidence of any originals existing before the release of the movie. His secondary evidence does not consist of true copies or exact duplicates but of "reconstructions" made after The Empire Strikes Back. In short, Seiler claims that the movie infringed his originals, yet he has no proof of those originals.

The dangers of fraud in this situation are clear. The rule would ensure that proof of the infringement claim consists of the works alleged to be infringed. Otherwise, "reconstructions" which might have no resemblance to the purported original would suffice as proof for infringement of the original. Furthermore, application of the rule here defers to the rule's special concern for the contents of writings. Seiler's claim depends on the content of the originals, and the rule would exclude reconstituted proof of the originals' content. Under the circumstances here, no "reconstruction" can substitute for the original.

Seiler argues that the best evidence rule does not apply to his work, in that it is artwork rather than "writings, recordings, or photographs." He contends that the rule both historically and currently embraces only words or numbers. Neither party has cited us to cases which discuss the applicability of the rule to drawings.

To recognize Seiler's works as writings does not, as Seiler argues, run counter to the rule's preoccupation with the centrality of the written word in the world of legal relations. Just as a contract objectively manifests the subjective intent of the makers, so Seiler's drawings are objective manifestations of the creative mind. The copyright laws give legal protection to the objective manifestations of an artist's ideas, just as the law of contract protects through its multifarious principles the meeting of minds evidenced in the contract. Comparing Seiler's drawings with Lucas' drawings is no different in principle than evaluating a contract and the intent behind it. Seiler's "reconstructions" are "writings" that affect legal relations; their copyrightability attests to that.

A creative literary work, which is artwork, and a photograph whose contents are sought to be proved, as in copyright, defamation, or invasion of privacy, are both covered by the best evidence rule. See McCormick, §232 at 706 n. 9; Advisory Committee's Note to Rule 1002; 5 Louisell & Mueller, §550 at 285 n. 27. We would be inconsistent to apply the rule to artwork which is literary or photographic but not to artwork of other forms. Furthermore, blueprints, engineering drawings, architectural designs may all lack words or numbers yet still be capable of copyright and susceptible to fraudulent alteration. In short, Seiler's argument would have us restrict the definitions of Rule 1001(1) to "words" and "numbers" but ignore "or their equivalent." We will not do so in the circumstances of this case.

Our holding is also supported by the policy served by the best evidence rule in protecting against faulty memory. Seiler's reconstructions were made four to seven years after the alleged originals; his memory as to specifications and dimensions may have dimmed significantly. Furthermore, reconstructions made after the release of The Empire Strikes Back may be tainted, even if unintentionally, by exposure to the movie. Our holding guards against these problems. . . .

As we hold that the district court correctly concluded that the best evidence rule applies to Seiler's drawings, Seiler was required to produce his original drawings unless excused by the exceptions set forth in Rule 1004. The pertinent subsection is 1004(1), which provides:

> The original is not required, and other evidence of the contents of a writing, recording, or photograph is admissible if—(1) Originals lost or destroyed. All originals are lost or have been destroyed, unless the proponent lost or destroyed them in bad faith

In the instant case, . . . the trial judge found that the reconstructions were inadmissible under the best evidence rule as the originals were lost or destroyed in bad faith. This finding is amply supported by the record.

Seiler argues on appeal that regardless of Rule 1004(1), Rule 1008 requires a trial because a key issue would be whether the reconstructions correctly reflect the content of the originals. Rule 1008 provides:

> When the admissibility of other evidence of contents of writings, recordings, or photographs under these rules depends upon the fulfillment of a condition of fact, the question whether the condition has been fulfilled is ordinarily for the court to determine in accordance with the provisions of rule 104. However, when an issue is raised (a) whether the asserted writing ever existed, or (b) whether another writing, recording, or photograph produced at the trial is the original, or (c) whether other evidence of contents correctly reflects the contents, the issue is for the trier of facts to determine as in the case of other issues of fact.

Seiler's position confuses admissibility of the reconstructions with the weight, if any, the trier of fact should give them, after the judge has ruled that they are admissible. Rule 1008 states, in essence, that when the admissibility of evidence other than the original depends upon the fulfill-ment of a condition of fact, the trial judge generally makes the determina-tion of that condition of fact. The notes of the Advisory Committee are consistent with this interpretation in stating: "Most preliminary questions of fact in connection with applying the rule preferring the original as evidence of contents are for the judge ... thus the question of ... fulfill-ment of other conditions specified in Rule 1004 ... is for the judge." In the instant case, the condition of fact which Seiler needed to prove was that the originals were not lost or destroyed in bad faith. Had he been able to prove this, his reconstructions would have been admissible and then their accu-racy would have been a question for the jury. In sum, since admissibility of the reconstructions was dependent upon a finding that the originals were not lost or destroyed in bad faith, the trial judge properly held the hearing to determine their admissibility. . . .

AFFIRMED.

PROBLEMS

11.3. Consider the following fact pattern from 1991 Multistate Bar Examination: "Paulsen Corporation sued Dorr for ten fuel oil deliveries not paid for. Dorr denied that the deliveries were made. At trial, Paulsen calls its office manager, Wicks, to testify that Paulsen employees always record each delivery in duplicate, give one copy to the customer, and place the other copy in Paulsen's files; that he (Wicks) is the custodian of those files; and that his examination of the files before coming to court revealed that the ten deliveries were made."* Is Wick's testimony about what the invoices show admissible?

11.4. Law enforcement officers spotted Vincent Bennett's boat in U.S. waters near the Mexican border, sailing north, away from the border. They boarded the boat and eventually discovered 1,500 pounds of marijuana hidden inside it. Bennett was convicted of importing marijuana into the United States, based in part on testimony from one of the officers that he found a global positioning device on the boat, which included a "back-track" feature indicating where the device (and presumably the boat) had been. The officer testified that when he activated the backtrack feature, the device plotted the boat's journey earlier that day from Mexican territorial waters several miles south of the U.S. border. At trial and again on appeal, Bennett challenged this testimony on grounds of hearsay and best evidence. Should either of these objections have been sustained? (The Ninth Circuit gave its answer in *United States v. Bennett*, 363 F.3d 947, 953-954 (2004).)

11.5. In *United States v. Workinger*, 90 F.3d 1409 (1996), the Ninth Circuit affirmed the defendant's conviction for tax evasion, and rejected his hearsay, authentication and best evidence objections to a transcript of a sworn statement he had given years earlier to his former wife's attorney. "Although no court reporter was present, Workinger affirmed that he would

*Copyright © 1995 by the National Conference of Bar Examiners. All rights reserved.

696   Chapter 11.   Physical Evidence

tell the truth and the conversation was tape-recorded." The attorney, apparently following his standard practice, erased the tape after having it transcribed. The government called the secretary who transcribed the tape; she testified that she had listened to it "over and over" to make sure the transcript was accurate. The government also called the lawyer who took the statement; he testified that "to the best of his recollection" the transcript accurately reflected what the defendant had said.

All members of the appellate panel agreed that the trial court was right to admit the transcript, but they disagreed about why. Writing for the majority, Judge Fernandez rejected the hearsay objection on the ground that "Workinger's statements in the transcript were admissions of a party-opponent," and therefore were not hearsay under Fed. R. Evid. 801(d)(2)(a). He further reasoned that the testimony from the attorney and the secretary "certainly met the minimum requirements for authentication." But he found the best evidence rule applicable to the case, because the content of the tape was at issue:

> It is true that, ultimately, the transcript of the tape was intended to reflect the content of the conversation that took place. But, more proximately, it was intended to reflect the content of the tape itself. When Johnson's secretary was given the tape and told to transcribe it, what she did was prepare a document which purported to indicate what she heard on the tape. But if somebody wanted to know the content of that tape, it itself *was* the best evidence of that.

Nonetheless Judge Fernandez found the transcript admissible under Fed. R. Evid. 1004(1), because the tape was unavailable through no fault of the government.

Concurring separately, Judge Kozinski argued that the best evidence rule was entirely inapplicable, because "the government did not seek, by introducing the transcript, to prove the content of the tapes but to prove what was said at the deposition itself." He explained:

> The transcript here was admissible not because it accurately reflected the tape, but because . . . the attorney for the defendant's ex-wife, testified that it accurately reflected *the deposition*. Without this testimony from someone who was present, I'm not at all sure the transcript would have been admissible since, as the majority notes, the transcriber was not present when the testimony was given and thus could not authenticate the transcript as an accurate reflection of what was said at the deposition.

Who had the better of this argument?

C. DEMONSTRATIVE EVIDENCE

There is no law to learn with regard to demonstrative evidence. The *absence* of specific rules about demonstrative proof is, in fact, one of the three key things to understand about this topic. The other two are the continuing conceptual confusion about demonstrative evidence and the rapid increase in the prevalence and sophistication of this kind of proof.

McCORMICK ON EVIDENCE

§212 (John W. Strong, ed., 5th ed. 1999)

There is a type of evidence which consists of things, e.g., weapons, whiskey bottles, writings, and wearing apparel, as distinguished from the assertions of witnesses (or hearsay declarants) about things. . . . [Such] evidence may be classified as to whether the item offered did or did not play an actual and direct part in the incident or transaction giving rise to the trial. Objects offered as having played such a direct role, e.g., the alleged weapon in a murder prosecution, are commonly called "real" or "original" evidence and are to be distinguished from evidence which played no such part but is offered for illustrative or other purposes. It will be readily apparent that when real evidence is offered an adequate foundation for admission will require testimony first that the object offered is *the* object which was involved in the incident, and further that the condition of the object is substantially unchanged. . . . It should, however, always be borne in mind that foundational requirements are essentially requirements of logic, and not rules of art. Thus, e.g., even a radically altered item of real evidence may be admissible if its pertinent features remain unaltered.

. . . It is today increasingly common to encounter the offer of tangible items which are not themselves contended to have played any part in the history of the case, but which are instead tendered for the purpose of rendering other evidence more comprehensible to the trier of fact. Examples of types of items frequently offered for purposes of illustration and clarification include models, maps, photographs, charts, and drawings. If an article is offered for these purposes, rather than as real or original evidence, its specific identity or source is generally of no significance whatever. Instead, the theory justifying admission of these exhibits requires only that the item be sufficiently explanatory or illustrative of relevant testimony in the case to be of potential help to the trier of fact. Whether the admission of a particular exhibit will in fact be helpful, or will instead tend to confuse or mislead the trier, is a matter commonly viewed to be within the sound discretion of the trial court.

JENNIFER L. MNOOKIN, THE IMAGE OF TRUTH: PHOTOGRAPHIC EVIDENCE AND THE POWER OF ANALOGY

10 Yale J.L. & Human. 1, 5, 43-44, 64-65, 70 (1998)

In the 1850s and before, legal evidence usually consisted of words—spoken testimony, written depositions, contracts, deeds, and the like. Those few images present in court were often those that had received explicit legal sanction, such as county-approved maps and surveys in land dispute cases, or drawings and diagrams in patent cases. When unofficial drawings were used, they were not thought to be evidence. Only with the advent of photography were these broader kinds of visual representations conceptualized as evidence, their evidentiary value deemed significant enough to be fought over, their improper inclusion or exclusion deemed worthy grounds for appeal. Indeed, by the end of the century, the use of visual evidence had blossomed, and images of many sorts, from photographs to diagrams to three-dimensional models, were frequently used in an effort to persuade the jury. Visual representation, not limited to photography, had become a significant persuasive technique in the courtroom. Now, an attorney or witness could not only locate evidence, but could create it himself. He could represent his side of the story with an elaborate visual image prepared especially for the lawsuit. These forms of visual evidence were especially persuasive because jurors and judges could see the evidence for themselves. To put it crudely, judicial response to the photograph brought into existence that category of proof we now know as "demonstrative evidence."

. . . [T]he prevailing judicial approach to the photograph was to align it, by analogy, with maps, models, and diagrams. All of these were viewed as constructed visual aids that a witness could use to illustrate his testimony. These visual representations were viewed not as independent evidence but as illustrative evidence that could aid a witness in communicating his point. The justification for allowing such representations at all was that some matters were more easily explained visually than orally; therefore, witnesses should be allowed to use images whenever the use would clarify their points. . . . In other words, a photograph, map, model, or diagram could be used as evidence as long as an attesting witness proclaimed it a correct representation. The visual aid was evidence in the sense that it was the witness's own description in visual rather than oral form. The visual representation itself, however, was not to serve as proof that the witness's description was accurate, nor as independent or corroborative evidence. It was merely the witness's testimony rendered visually.

. . . And yet, despite this doctrinal declaration, it proved impossible for the photograph not to be understood as evidence. The photograph was conceptually viewed as evidence almost from the moment of its invention—it was "a witness on whose testimony the most certain conclusions may be confidently founded." The sheer force of doctrine alone could not keep the photograph secure in a box labeled "illustration"; the strong realist conception could not simply be left behind at the courthouse door. A major consequence of linking photographs to models, maps, and diagrams was that all of these forms of representation began to acquire the sheen of evidence.

. . . Demonstrative evidence has continued to hover awkwardly on the boundary between illustration and proof. In their analysis of the topic, Robert Brain and Daniel Broderick described the tremendous conceptual confusion that still besets "demonstrative evidence," pointing out that "there is not even a settled definition of the term." Some commentators define demonstrative evidence to include all evidence that consists of "things" rather than testimony, "all phenomena which can convey a relevant firsthand sense impression to the trier of fact." Others limit its definition to those displays "principally used to illustrate or explain other testimonial, documentary, or real proof . . . a visual (or other sensory) aid." Some definitions deem it substantive, independent evidence, while others insist it serves merely the secondary, derivative purpose of illustration.

UNITED STATES v. WEEKS

919 F.2d 248 (5th Cir. 1990)

EDITH H. JONES, Circuit Judge:

Defendant-appellant Danny Michael Weeks was convicted after a jury trial of two counts of kidnapping, two counts of interstate transportation of a stolen vehicle, and one count each of carrying a firearm during a crime of violence and possessing a firearm as a convicted felon. . . . We affirm. . . .

Weeks . . . contends that the district court erred in allowing the government to display a firearm to the jury even though it was not connected to Weeks. We agree with the government that the court did not abuse its discretion in permitting the display. Two of the six crimes charged in the indictment involved a firearm. Although the revolver was not the actual firearm used by the defendant, it belonged to a government firearms expert and was identified by kidnap victim Mayeaux as looking similar to the weapon that Weeks took from the trunk of her car and used during the offenses. The court did not admit the firearm into evidence—which would have allowed the jury to examine it during deliberations—but allowed it to be displayed for "demonstrative purposes only." Finally, the court instructed the jury that the revolver they had seen was merely a model similar to the one used in the crime. Weeks also claims that the government displayed the weapon in an inflammatory manner that unfairly prejudiced him. At trial, defense counsel objected because the prosecutor "clicked [the gun] and tried it again, emphasizing the use of it. It inflames the jury panel. I would object to him trying to point the gun and play with the handle, and he clicks it so it's that much more intimidating." The prosecutor disputed this characterization, stating that "[t]he gun's chamber was open. The barrel was open, Your Honor. As I walked toward the witness, the barrel closed." The court responded: "Next time keep it closed." From the cold record, we are unable to determine what actually happened, but the district court evidently accepted the government's version. The firearm display does not constitute reversible error. . . .

UNITED STATES v. HUMPHREY

279 F.3d 372 (6th Cir. 2002)

MOORE, Circuit Judge.

Defendant-Appellant Cheryl Ann Humphrey ("Humphrey") appeals her jury conviction and sentence for one count of embezzling bank funds, in violation of 18 U.S.C. §656, and five counts of making false entries in bank records with the intent to defraud, in violation of 18 U.S.C. §1005. . . . From 1975 to 1996, Humphrey was employed as a bank and vault teller for Hamilton Bank, later known as SunTrust Bank ("Bank"), of Johnson City, Tennessee. . . .

Humphrey claims that the district court abused its discretion in admitting 107 coin bags as demonstrative evidence. At trial, the Government introduced as Government Exhibit 6a a vault cash form dated May 21, 1996, and verified by Humphrey that showed an inventory of $214,167.45 in loose coin. The Government also introduced a videotape dated May 21, 1996, that showed the area inside the Bank's vault where loose coin was stored. The purpose of the demonstrative evidence was to show the jury what 107 coin bags would look like and to establish that the vault did not contain that many coin bags. Six of the 107 bags were filled with coins; the remainder were stuffed with styrofoam peanuts to the approximate size of the bags filled with coins.

Defense counsel objected to the demonstration, arguing that the evidence was prejudicial because the bags filled with styrofoam were bigger than those filled with coins. The district court thought otherwise. After hearing from an expert witness who stated that the bags filled with styrofoam were representative of and "about the same size" in volume as the bags filled with coins, the district court admitted the exhibit, noting that defense counsel could raise this issue on cross-examination. Defense counsel proceeded to do so. Witnesses for the Government later testified that they did not see that much loose coin in the Bank's vault on May 21, 1996, or on any other day.

Under Federal Rule of Evidence 403, evidence that is relevant "may be excluded if its probative value is substantially outweighed by the danger of unfair prejudice." In admitting the coin bags into evidence, the district court did not expressly weigh their probative value against the danger of unfair prejudice, but it did recognize that the Government wanted the jury to see what the bags would look like in the Bank's vault. Reviewing this evidentiary decision, we are not persuaded that the district court abused its discretion. . . . [Convictions affirmed.]

ROLAND v. LANGLOIS

945 F.2d 956 (7th Cir. 1991)

HARLINGTON WOOD, JR., Circuit Judge.

[Seeking damages for injuries he suffered when a carnival ride hit him in the head, Douglas Roland and his wife sued the operator of the ride and the carnival company. Following a judgment for defendants, the Rolands appealed.]

. . . [T]he district court admitted a life-size model [of a portion of the fence surrounding the ride,] offered by the defendants. . . . The district court has wide discretion in these matters . . . and we can find no abuse of that discretion on this record. . . . [T]he plaintiffs' principal complaint is that the model was not completely accurate. There is no requirement that demonstrative evidence be completely accurate, however, and the evidence was admitted only on the express condition that the jury be alerted to the perceived inaccuracies. Having reviewed the record in this case, moreover, and having struggled to familiarize ourselves with the scene of the accident, we agree with the district court that the benefits from the use of a life-size model were not substantially outweighed by the danger of unfair prejudice. *See* Fed. R. Evid. 403. . . . AFFIRMED.

UNITED STATES v. WOOD

943 F.2d 1048 (9th Cir. 1991)

O'SCANNLAIN, Circuit Judge:

Wood appeals his conviction for tax evasion. . . . Wood urges that the district court erred in admitting into evidence a summary chart prepared by the government's expert, while excluding from evidence a summary chart prepared by the defense expert.

Bob Marcinek, an agent with the Internal Revenue Service, testified as an expert on behalf of the government. Marcinek testified as to his opinion of Wood's tax liability, which he summarized in two charts. The government moved to admit the charts into evidence; the motion was granted without objection.

The defense offered its own expert, Larry Richter, to testify about Wood's tax liability. During the course of his testimony, Richter filled in a chart outlining his version of the correct tax calculations. Thereafter, Wood moved to admit the chart into evidence. The government objected, claiming that the chart was a "misapplication of the law." The district court sustained the government's objection. However, the court permitted Wood to use the chart during closing arguments, so long as the figures concerning business loss deductions were masked.

"When considering the admissibility of exhibits of this nature, it is critical to distinguish between charts or summaries *as evidence* and charts or summaries *as pedagogical devices.*" *Pierce v. Ramsey Winch Co.*, 753 F.2d 416, 431 (5th Cir. 1985). Charts and summaries as evidence are governed by Federal Rule of Evidence 1006, which permits the introduction of charts, summaries, or calculations "of voluminous writings, recordings, or photographs which cannot conveniently be examined in court." In contrast, charts or summaries of testimony or documents already admitted into evidence are merely pedagogical devices, and are not evidence themselves. *See Pierce*, 753 F.2d at 431; *see also United States v. Poschwatta*, 829 F.2d 1477, 1481 (9th Cir. 1987)(describing such summary charts as "testimonial aids"), *cert. denied*, 484 U.S. 1064 (1988).

We have long held that such pedagogical devices should be used only as a testimonial aid, and should not be admitted into evidence or otherwise be used by the jury during deliberations. *See United States v. Soulard*, 730

F.2d 1292, 1300 (9th Cir. 1984). . . . *But see Poschwatta*, 829 F.2d at 1481 (concluding that "[a]lthough the better practice may have been for the court to allow the charts to be used as testimonial aids only," court did not abuse its discretion in admitting charts into evidence). Thus, the district court's refusal to admit Richter's charts into evidence, standing alone, was not error. . . . Nonetheless, we agree with Wood that the disparate treatment between the government's summary charts and that of the defendant warrants explanation. Such explanation is readily apparent from the record. In *Soulard*, we explained that "[t]he trial court . . . should carefully examine the summary charts to determine that everything contained in them is supported by the proof." Richter offered only one reason for his calculation of Wood's "gains or losses": that Wood operated a trade or business, and thus, he was eligible for a business loss deduction. . . . [T]his analysis is incomplete; Wood was not entitled to a business loss deduction unless the property loss was held by Wood "primarily for sale to customers in the ordinary course of his trade or business." I.R.C. §1221(1). Richter presented no evidence that Wood had customers. Thus, the chart was not supported by the proof. The district court did not err in masking the unsupported portion or in declining to admit the chart into evidence. . . . AFFIRMED.

BANNISTER v. TOWN OF NOBLE, OKLAHOMA

812 F.2d 1265 (10th Cir. 1987)

TACHA, Circuit Judge.

In this appeal we review a jury verdict for Bannister, a Texas resident, in a diversity suit alleging negligence against the Town of Noble, Oklahoma, for personal injuries arising out of a one-car accident which occurred in Oklahoma. . . . Noble contends that the district court abused its discretion by admitting into evidence three videotapes. The district court viewed the videotapes before admitting them into evidence.

The first videotape Noble challenges is a "Day in the Life" film. Such films purport to show how an injury has affected the daily routine of its victim. Typical "Day in the Life" films show the victim in a variety of everyday situations, including getting around the home, eating meals, and interacting with family members. These films are prepared solely to be used as evidence in litigation concerning the injury. Such evidence is often desired because "films illustrate, better than words, the impact the injury had had on the plaintiff's life." *Grimes v. Employers Mut. Liab. Ins. Co.*, 73 F.R.D. 607, 610 (D. Alaska 1977). Noble argues that Bannister's "Day in the Life" videotape was unduly prejudicial within the meaning of Fed. R. Evid. 403 and thus inadmissible. . . .

We have held that "the prejudicial effect of a videotape is to be decided on a case by case basis." *Durflinger v. Artiles*, 727 F.2d 888, 894 (10th Cir. 1984). . . . In the present case, the district court examined the film and concluded that it accurately portrayed the daily routine of the plaintiff and that it was not unduly prejudicial. We have reviewed the film as well.

The film shows Bannister getting around school, getting into his car, pumping gasoline for his car, and performing several different tasks in his home. Although there are a couple of scenes that show Bannister conducting activities that he would be unlikely to do frequently, the film as a whole demonstrates Bannister's adaptation to his injury. We hold that the district court did not abuse its discretion in admitting the film depicting a "Day in the Life" of Clifford Bannister.

Noble next argues that the district court abused its discretion in admitting into evidence a videotape which shows a car like the one involved in the accident approaching an inclined ramp, becoming airborne, and landing. The film shows the jump three times, each time from a different angle. Bannister offered the videotape not as a reenactment, but as a demonstration showing the trajectory of this type of car with this type of suspension system. Noble argues that the film is not a demonstration but an attempted recreation of the accident and that there are substantial dissimilarities between the film event and the actual accident; thus, the film should have been excluded as unduly prejudicial.

We have approved the admission of filmed evidence "not meant to depict the actual event of the accident but rather to show mechanical principles" upon a showing that "the experiments were conducted under conditions that were at least similar to those which existed at the time of the accident." *Brandt v. French*, 638 F.2d 209, 212 (10th Cir. 1981). But "[d]emonstrations of experiments used to merely illustrate the principles in forming expert opinion do not require strict adherence to the facts." *Id.* "[W]hen experiments do not simulate the actual events at issue, the jury should be instructed that the evidence is admitted for a limited purpose or purposes." *Robinson v. Audi NSU Auto Union Aktiengesellschaft*, 739 F.2d 1481, 1484 (10th Cir. 1984). . . .

In the present case, Bannister offered the videotape not as a recreation but as a demonstration of certain principles. The district court viewed the film and then admitted it for this limited purpose. The district court instructed the jury that

> [T]he film is not being introduced for the purpose of attempting to recreate the accident involved in this case. The Plaintiff does not contend that the film reenacts the accident. . . . The film is introduced only to demonstrate certain physical principles. . . . You're instructed not to consider this film as a reenactment of the accident.

We find no abuse of discretion.

Noble also argues that the district court erred when it allowed Bannister to show a videotape to the jury during closing argument. The videotape was edited to show portions of the "Day in the Life" tape, the demonstration tape, and a portion of a taped deposition of one of Bannister's doctors. We first note that the district court has a great deal of discretion in controlling arguments of counsel. Furthermore, a judgment should not be set aside unless it is clear that the closing argument has unduly aroused the sympathy of the jury thereby influencing the verdict. All of the videotapes used to make the closing argument tape had been properly admitted into evidence during the course of the trial. In addition, the district court viewed the videotape prior to allowing it to be shown to the jury. We have also reviewed the tape. We find that the district court did not abuse its discretion. . . . AFFIRMED.

ROBERT D. BRAIN & DANIEL J. BRODERICK, THE DERIVATIVE USE OF DEMONSTRATIVE EVIDENCE: CHARTING ITS PROPER EVIDENTIARY STATUS

25 U.C. Davis L. Rev. 957, 961-966, 1027(1992)

Under common law regulation of evidence, the propriety of a witness's use of some sort of demonstrative exhibit was simply assumed by most American trial judges and trial lawyers. . . . Contemporary jurists and lawyers continue to share the historical vision that demonstrative proof can be used at trial as a matter of right, subject only to the discretion of the trial judge to preclude individual exhibits that are unfairly prejudicial, inaccurate, incomplete, or cumulative. Undoubtedly this is due, in large part, to the fact that no evidence code in use today provides any specific direction for the admission or use of demonstrative exhibits at trial. Hence, the focus today of any case in which the use of demonstrative evidence is an issue continues to be an extremely fact-specific discussion of whether a particular photograph is too gory, a certain chart too incomplete, or a specific graph too misleading, and not on what standards govern generally the use of demonstrative exhibits. . . .

Within the last ten years, the nature of demonstrative evidence has changed in kind, not just in degree. With the advent of relatively low-cost but powerful computers and sophisticated computer graphics software, demonstrative proof has changed from the "state-of-the-art" brightly colored charts and nascent day-in-the-life films of the early 1980's to professionally produced movies, imprinted on laser discs, dramatically depicting, for example, an expert's opinion of what the pilot saw from the cockpit during the last fifteen minutes before an airplane crash, or the causes of a complicated accident at a hexane production plant. Within the next decade or so, even these types of demonstrative exhibits will seem tame, as then-state-of-the-art demonstrative proof will be even more powerful. . . . The font of judicial discretion is no longer a reliable source for easy and predictable rulings regarding the use of newer demonstrative evidence, for the change in the very essence of this proof has pushed aside any boundaries that might have been formed as a result of a shared normative vision of "unfair prejudice" between bench and bar.

Another reason for a current reexamination of demonstrative evidence has to do with the ever-increasing emphasis in modern trials on lay and expert opinion testimony. More and more often, testimonial evidence at trials is not limited to just percipient witnesses, but also includes witnesses who are asked their opinions about why something happened or how something works. As a result, modern lawyers are increasingly turning to demonstrative evidence to make these opinions understandable to triers of fact. Hence, demonstrative evidence's role in trial is no longer a "secondary" one. In a trial of any complexity, where opinion testimony is important, demonstrative evidence is becoming ever more crucial to rational decision-making and enlightened jury deliberation.

Yet another reason for undertaking an in-depth study of demonstrative evidence is that the introduction of demonstrative proof at trial has been rendered illegitimate. This is because, as a matter of definitional logic, demonstrative evidence does not and cannot meet the test of relevance required under modern evidence rules for admission at trial. For example, to be admissible under the Federal Rules of Evidence, a piece of evidence must be relevant, and to be relevant, a piece of evidence must make the existence of a fact of consequence in the action more or less probable than it would be without that evidence. No piece of demonstrative evidence can meet this test. The only purpose of demonstrative evidence is to illustrate or clarify previously admitted other evidence. It has no independent effect on the determination of the existence of a fact of consequence, other than its helpfulness as an illustrative aid to another, independently relevant piece of substantive evidence. That is, a diagram of an apartment that has been burglarized does not, in and of itself, make it any more or less probable that the defendant was the one who committed the crime; it only clarifies previous testimony as to what the apartment looked like. Demonstrative evidence's relevance is thus derivative and different from that of admissible substantive evidence. Hence, when modern courts allow demonstrative exhibits to be used at trial based on traditional relevance tests, they do so illegitimately, without sufficient theoretical support.

. . . [T]he lack of a well-defined evidential theory of demonstrative evidence has fostered inconsistency among trial courts on how demonstrative exhibits are to be treated at trial. Some courts treat demonstrative exhibits exactly like they do substantive exhibits, by formally admitting them into evidence and allowing the jury to view the exhibits during deliberations. Other courts admit demonstrative exhibits into a twilight zone reserved for "demonstrative purposes only," apparently indicating that such exhibits can be identified for the record but must be precluded from use by the jury during deliberations. Still other courts admit demonstrative exhibits "for limited purposes," but nevertheless permit the jury to view the exhibits during deliberations. Finally, some courts explicitly refuse to "admit" demonstrative exhibits into evidence at all, but allow witnesses to refer to them during testimony. Even among those courts, however, there is a difference of opinion—with some permitting the jury to view this unadmitted evidence during deliberations, while others do not. . . . Modern evidence codes need to be modified to account for the derivative relevance of demonstrative evidence and to regulate the use of demonstrative evidence at trial. . . .

12

BURDENS, PRESUMPTIONS, AND JUDICIAL NOTICE

"Not guilty, because puppies do these things."

A. BURDENS AND PRESUMPTIONS IN CIVIL CASES

The rules regarding presumptions, like the rules regarding relevance, continue to be influenced strongly by the thinking of James Bradley Thayer, who taught and wrote about evidence law at the beginning of the twentieth century. Surveying nineteenth-century evidence cases, Thayer noticed that judges often talked about facts being "presumed" but did not make clear what they meant. It seemed obvious that a presumption was a kind of legal relationship between two facts: the fact giving rise to the presumption ("the basic fact") and the fact being presumed ("the presumed fact"). But what exactly was the relationship?

Thayer thought the answer required distinguishing between two kinds of burdens borne by one party or the other in every lawsuit: the burden of persuasion and the burden of production. The burden of persuasion is the burden to satisfy the trier of fact, typically the jury, that a particular proposition has been demonstrated to a particular level of certainty. The principal burden of persuasion in a criminal trial, for example, requires the prosecution to prove the elements of the offense "beyond a reasonable doubt." Similarly, the burden of persuasion with regard to elements of a civil claim typically rests with the plaintiff. Instead of "beyond a reasonable doubt," though, the standard of proof required in a civil case is typically "preponderance of the evidence." In certain classes of civil cases involving particularly high stakes— e.g., civil commitment, or proceedings to set aside election results—an intermediate standard of "clear and convincing evidence" is applied.

Ordinarily, the burden of persuasion carries with it a more basic burden to produce some evidence. If a party has the burden to persuade the jury that a given fact is true, it typically also has the burden to produce some evidence of that fact. Otherwise the adverse party will be entitled to a directed verdict or to a dismissal of charges. Thayer distinguished this "burden of production" from the ultimate burden of persuasion, and he thought that presumptions should be understood to shift the first but not the second. For example, judges often said that a properly mailed letter is presumed to have been received. Thayer thought the presumption should operate only if there is no evidence the letter was not received. Once any such evidence is presented, Thayer argued that the presumption should drop out of the case and have no further effect.

This seemed silly to a later scholar, Edmund Morgan. He argued that presumptions should shift both the burden of production *and* the burden of proof. He thought, for example, that juries should be instructed to assume that any letter that had been properly mailed had been received, unless they were affirmatively convinced by the evidence that the letter had *not* been received.

Many current controversies regarding presumptions boil down to disagreements between followers of Thayer and followers of Morgan. But the boiling down can be hard to do. Professors Charles Alan Wright and Kenneth Graham, in their leading treatise on federal practice and procedure, call presumptions "a sea of technicality that defies logical analysis." Surveying this body of doctrine in 1941, no less a lawyer than Judge Learned Hand declared with exasperation that courts "have mixed it up until nobody can tell what on earth it means." Whether things have improved since then is debatable. The law of presumptions today has few fans.

[F.R.E. 301, 302; C.E.C. §§110, 115, 500, 550, 600-670]

IN RE YODER CO.

758 F.2d 1114 (6th Cir. 1985)

Cornelia G. Kennedy, Circuit Judge.

In this Chapter 11 proceeding the Bankruptcy Court affirmed by the District Court, held that Mark S. Bratton's products liability claim for the loss of four fingers was barred for failure to timely file a proof of claim. Bratton contends that his claim should not be barred because he did not receive notice of the latest date for filing proofs of claim.

In 1981, Yoder filed a petition requesting relief under Chapter 11 of the Bankruptcy Code. At that time Bratton's products liability suit against Yoder was pending in a Michigan state court. Bratton's claim was listed as a "contingent, unliquidated and disputed" claim in the amended schedule of assets and liabilities filed by Yoder. The Bankruptcy Court issued an order setting July 13, 1981 as the last date for creditors to file proofs of claim against Yoder (the "bar date").

Bratton filed a proof of claim on March 15, 1982, about eight months after the bar date. Yoder applied to the Bankruptcy Court for an order expunging certain products liability claims, including Bratton's. Following a hearing on Yoder's application, at which Bratton was represented, the Bankruptcy Court found that Bratton had been sent sufficient notice of the bar date and that Bratton's failure to file timely proof of claim was not due to excusable neglect. Bratton's claim was therefore barred. The District Court affirmed, and Bratton appeals.

. . . Bratton's address on the amended schedule of assets and liabilities, the list which Yoder's employee testified was used to prepare the labels [for mailing notices of the bar date], was that of his attorney, A.T. Ornstein. Ornstein testified that he had not received notice of the bar date. Attorneys for two other listed products liability claimants also represented that they and their clients had not received notices of the bar date.

The Bankruptcy Court made a factual finding that notice of the bar date had been sent to Ornstein. The Court did not discuss its reasons for this finding or explain how it weighed the evidence, although the evidence concerning mailing was far from undisputed. . . . We do not need to decide whether the finding that notice was mailed was clearly erroneous, however, because we hold that the Bankruptcy Court abused its discretion in holding that Bratton did not file a late proof of claim as a result of excusable neglect. This holding was based on the closely related finding that Bratton's attorney received the notice, which we hold to be clearly erroneous.

Rule 906(b) of the Rules of Bankruptcy Procedure provides that a time period may be extended if failure to act in time "was the result of excusable neglect." . . . [N]onreceipt of notice would clearly constitute excusable neglect. The Bankruptcy Court's determination that no excusable neglect existed was based entirely on its finding that notice was received at Bratton's attorney's law firm. We thus turn to the question of whether this finding of receipt was clearly erroneous.

The Bankruptcy Court relied mainly on a presumption of receipt that it held arose from evidence that the notice was properly mailed. The common law has long recognized a presumption that an item properly mailed was received by the addressee. *Hagner v. United States*, 285 U.S. 427 (1932). The presumption arises upon proof that the item was properly addressed, had sufficient postage, and was deposited in the mail. *Simpson v. Jefferson Standard Life Insurance Co.*, 465 F.2d 1320, 1323 (6th Cir. 1972). For purposes of this discussion, we will assume that the presumption of receipt did arise.

The District Court held that the presumption had not been rebutted, reasoning that "testimony amounting to a mere denial that a properly mailed notice was not received is insufficient to rebut the presumption of receipt."[5] This statement is inconsistent with prior decisions of this Circuit. In *McKentry v. Secretary of HHS*, 655 F.2d 721 (6th Cir. 1981), the plaintiff and her attorney both filed affidavits that they had not received a notice of reconsideration from the Department of HHS. This Court held that this would have been sufficient evidence of non-receipt to rebut the presumption of mailing, had it arisen. In *Baldwin v. Fidelity Phoenix Fire Insurance Co.*, 260 F.2d 951, 953 (6th Cir. 1958), there was evidence that a notice had been sent to an insurance company and to one of its agents. The agent testified that he had not received the notice. This Court held that the evidence was sufficient to support the jury's finding that notice was not received by the insurance company or the agent. These decisions are in consonance with the general proposition that a presumption is rebutted "upon the introduction of evidence which would support a finding of the nonexistence of the presumed fact." 10 Moore's Federal Practice ¶301.04[2] (2d ed.). Testimony of non-receipt, standing alone, would be sufficient to support a finding of non-receipt; such testimony is therefore sufficient to rebut the presumption of receipt.

The next question is whether the presumption, once rebutted, retains any effect.[7] The Bankruptcy Court found that it was "entitled to presume that notice has been received once a proper mailing is made, even though the intended recipient testifies that the notice never really came." The Bankruptcy Court reasoned as follows:

> According to the note of the Advisory Committee on Proposed Rules, Federal Rule 301 rejects the so-called "bursting bubble" theory, under which a presumption vanishes upon the introduction of evidence that negates the existence of the presumed fact. According to the Federal Rule, when evidence is put forth negating the fact that the presumption tends to support, the presumption still continues and is evidence to be weighed and considered with all of the other evidence in the case.

Federal Rule of Evidence 301 provides in part:

> [A] presumption imposes on the party against whom it is directed the burden of going forward with evidence to rebut or meet the presumption, but does not shift to such party the burden of proof in the sense of the risk of non-persuasion, which remains throughout the trial upon the party on whom it was originally cast.

A brief review of the history of this rule will aid in evaluating the Bankruptcy Court's reasoning. Before adoption of the Federal Rules of Evidence there were two major theories concerning the effect of a presumption once rebuttal evidence is admitted. Under the Thayer or "bursting

---

5. To support the proposition that testimony of non-receipt does not rebut the presumption of receipt, the District Court relied on *In re Majors*, 19 B.R. 275 (Bankr. M.D. Tenn. 1982); *In re Torres*, 15 B.R. 794 (Bankr. E.D.N.Y. 1981); and *In re Heyward*, 15 B.R. 629 (Bankr. E.D.N.Y. 1981). These decisions are inconsistent with the common law views of presumptions and the law of this Circuit.

7. The fact sought to be established by the presumption is an element of a claim or defense to be determined under federal bankruptcy law, not state law. Federal law is therefore determinative of the effect of the presumption. Cf. Fed. R. Evid. 302.

bubble" theory a presumption vanishes entirely once rebutted, and the question must be decided as any ordinary question of fact.[8] Under a later theory, proposed by Morgan, a presumption shifts the burden of proving the nonexistence of the presumed fact to the opposing party.

The version of Rule 301 that was proposed by the Advisory Committee, accepted by the Supreme Court, and submitted to Congress adopted the Morgan view.[10] That rule, however, was not enacted by Congress. The Advisory Committee notes, on which the Bankruptcy Court relied, that reject the "bursting bubble" theory pertain to the proposed rule, which was not enacted, and are thus of little help in interpreting the final rule.

The House of Representatives adopted a rule espousing an interme-diate view, which would allow a rebutted presumption to be considered evidence of the fact presumed.[11] The Senate criticized the House rule on the ground that it made no sense to call a presumption evidence, and adopted the present language of Rule 301, which was adopted by the Conference Committee and enacted into law.

Most commentators have concluded that Rule 301 as enacted embo-dies the Thayer or "bursting bubble" approach. *See, e.g.*, 10 Moore's Federal Practice ¶301.04[4.-1] (2d ed.); 1 Weinstein's Evidence 301-12; IX Wigmore on Evidence §2493h (Chadbourn rev. 1981). *Contra* 21 C. Wright & K. Graham, Federal Practice and Procedure §§5121, 5122, 5126.[13] At least two other circuit courts have expressly agreed. *Reeves v. General Foods*

---

8. The facts giving rise to the presumption often give rise to an inference that remains and may still be considered by the factfinder. See IX Wigmore on Evidence §2491 (Chad-bourn rev. 1981) ("[T]he legal consequence [of the presumption] being removed, the infer-ence, as a matter of reasoning, may still remain. . . .").

10. The text of the proposed rule was as follows: "In all cases not otherwise provided for by Act of Congress or by these rules a presumption imposes on the party against whom it is directed the burden of proving that the nonexistence of the presumed fact is more probable than its existence."

11. The House version of the rule was as follows: "In all civil actions and proceedings not otherwise provided for by Act of Congress or by these rules, a presumption imposes on the party against whom it is directed the burden of going forward with the evidence, and, even though met with contradicting evidence, a presumption is sufficient evidence of the fact presumed, to be considered by the trier of the facts."

13. Professors Wright and Graham interpret Rule 301 as providing that a rebutted presumption still suffices to carry the issue to the jury, which should be instructed that it may infer the presumed fact. 21 C. Wright & K. Graham, Federal Practice and Procedure §5122 at p. 572. This interpretation differs from the bursting bubble theory only in the effect given an "illogical" presumption, i.e., one where the facts giving rise to the presumption do not logically give rise to an inference that the presumed fact exists. See id. §5126 at pp. 609-11, 609 n. 22. According to Wright and Graham, once an illogical presumption was rebutted the presumption would still have the effect of requiring that the question be sent to the jury with instructions that it may infer the presumed fact. Under the bursting bubble theory a rebutted illogical presumption would have no effect and the only evidence on the question would be the rebuttal evidence, which would be conclusive. However, in the case of a "logical" presumption, such as the presumption of receipt involved here, the jury would be allowed to consider the inference naturally drawn from the facts establishing the pre-sumption whether or not the presumption is given any effect after rebuttal. Wright and Graham's interpretation would therefore have no effect on the present case.

Wright and Graham's conclusion that Rule 301 rejects the bursting bubble theory is based primarily on the Conference Committee's statement that: "If the adverse party does offer evidence contradicting the presumed fact, the court cannot instruct the jury that it may

Corp., 682 F.2d 515, 522 n. 10 (5th Cir. 1982); *Legille v. Dann*, 544 F.2d 1, 6-7 (D.C. Cir. 1976). The Thayer view is consistent with the language of Rule 301, which provides only that a presumption shifts "the burden of going forward with evidence to rebut or meet the presumption." Accordingly, we hold that a presumption under Rule 301 has no probative effect once rebutted. The Bankruptcy Court therefore erred in considering the presumption as evidence of receipt.

The only other evidence of receipt expressly considered by the Bankruptcy Court was that "Mr. Bratton's law firm did receive and respond to the notice setting debtor's objection to his claim for hearing." However, there was no evidence that the notices of the hearing were sent to the same addresses as were the notices of the bar date, which were sent more than a year earlier. The testimony was that no copy of the address labels made up for the bar date notices was kept, so a copy of those labels could not have been used to mail the later notices of the hearing on debtor's objections to claims. That Bratton received notice of the hearing is therefore not evidence that he received notice of the bar date.

The Bankruptcy Court erred in relying upon the presumption and notice of the hearing to establish receipt. Had it properly considered all the evidence it would have had to find that Bratton had not received notice. . . . The evidence other than Ornstein's testimony that he did not receive the notice is at best neutral. If the Bankruptcy Court had considered all the evidence without relying on a presumption and still found that notice was received, it would have been clearly erroneous. Non-receipt is sufficient ground for excusable neglect, and it is clear from the lower court opinions that had those courts found non-receipt the claim would have been allowed.

Accordingly, the judgment of the District Court is reversed and the case remanded for reversal of the Bankruptcy Court order expunging Bratton's claim.

LAW REVISION COMMISSION COMMENT TO CALIFORNIA EVIDENCE CODE §601

For several decades, courts and legal scholars have wrangled over the purpose and function of presumptions. The view espoused by Professors

---

presume the existence of the presumed fact from proof of the basic facts. *The court may, however, instruct the jury that it may infer the existence of the presumed fact from proof of the basic facts.*" Id. §5121 n. 27 (emphasis added). The emphasized portion of this quotation is not inconsistent with the bursting bubble theory. Nothing in the legislative history indicates that Congress was concerned with the distinction between "logical" and "illogical" presumptions. The statement that the jury may be instructed to consider an inference is most naturally read as permitting such an instruction when called for by the existence of a logical inference. An "inference" not based on logic is not an inference at all, but a presumption. Jurors would have no way to decide how much weight to give an "inference" drawn from a fact that their own logic tells them has no relevance to the question to be decided. The sentence immediately preceding the emphasized portion of the Conference Committee's report clearly indicates that the jury should not be allowed to apply a presumption once rebutted.

Thayer and Wigmore, accepted by most courts, and adopted by the American Law Institute's Model Code of Evidence, is that a presumption is a preliminary assumption of fact that disappears from the case upon the introduction of evidence sufficient to sustain a finding of the nonexistence of the presumed fact. In Professor Thayer's view, a presumption merely reflects the judicial determination that the same conclusionary fact exists so frequently when the preliminary fact exists that, once the preliminary fact is established, proof of the conclusionary fact may be dispensed with unless there is actually some contrary evidence:

> Many facts and groups of facts often recur, and when a body of men with a continuous tradition has carried on for some length of time this process of reasoning upon facts that often repeat themselves, they cut short the process and lay down a rule. To such facts they affix, by a general declaration, the character and operation which common experience has assigned to them. [Thayer, Preliminary Treatise on Evidence 326 (1898).]

Professors Morgan and McCormick argue that a presumption should shift the burden of proof to the adverse party. Morgan, Some Problems of proof 81 (1956); McCormick, Evidence §317 at 671-672 (1954). They believe that presumptions are created for reasons of policy and argue that, if the policy underlying a presumption is of sufficient weight to require a finding of the presumed fact when there is no contrary evidence, it should be of sufficient weight to require a finding when the mind of the trier of fact is in equilibrium, and, *a fortiori*, it should be of sufficient weight to require a finding if the trier of fact does not believe the contrary evidence.

The classification of presumptions in the Evidence Code is based on a third view suggested by Professor Bohlen in 1920. Bohlen, The Effect of Rebuttable Presumptions of Law Upon the Burden of Proof, 68 U. Pa. L. Rev. 307 (1920). Underlying the presumptions provisions of the Evidence Code is the conclusion that the Thayer view is correct as to some presumptions, but that the Morgan view is right as to others. The fact is that presumptions are created for a variety of reasons, and no single theory or rationale of presumptions can deal adequately with all of them. Hence, the Evidence Code classifies all rebuttable presumptions as either (1) presumptions affecting the burden of producing evidence (essentially Thayer presumptions), or (2) presumptions affecting the burden of proof (essentially Morgan presumptions). . . .

CHRISTOPHER B. MUELLER & LAIRD C. KIRKPATRICK, EVIDENCE

§3.4 (3d ed. 2003)

Many terms are used to describe presumptions, and some are redundant or conflicting or have shifting meanings. . . .

Conclusive or irrebuttable presumptions. Substantive law sometimes borrows the language of presumptions. Under the Coal Mine Health and Safety Act of 1969, for example, a miner shown by X-ray or other clinical evidence to have pneumoconiosis (black lung disease) is "irrebuttably presumed" to be totally disabled, and the presumption "operates conclusively to establish entitlement to benefits." [*See* 30 U.S.C. §921] Under a California statute, it was irrebuttably presumed that a husband was the father of a child born to his wife during marriage (absent proof that they did not cohabit or that he was impotent), and the presumption still cannot be rebutted by ordinary evidence (testimony denying intercourse or evidence that the wife had intercourse with another). [*See* Cal. Evid. Code §621 (requiring finding of paternity unless blood tests indicate otherwise).] These legal rules are really not presumptions as the term is ordinarily understood but substantive principles expressed in the language of presumptions.

Mandatory presumptions or presumption of law. Generally these terms refer to the true presumption. . . . A presumption controls decision if unopposed, so in jury-tried cases an instruction is in order and in bench trials the judge has no option but to find the presumed fact. "Mandatory" is redundant, and "presumption" by itself conveys the intended meaning.

Permissive presumption, inference, presumption of fact. These terms usually refer to conclusions that are permitted but not required. The term "inference" is a better word to describe what is happening here. . . . Inference instructions amount to judicial comment on the evidence, almost nudging or inviting the jury to draw a conclusion. . . . [7]

PROBLEMS

12.1. Section 641 of the California Evidence Code, classified as a Thayer presumption, provides that "[a] letter correctly addressed and properly mailed is presumed to have been received in the ordinary course of mail." Suppose a California tenant slips in the hallway of her apartment building and breaks her collarbone. She files a diversity suit against her out-of-state landlord for medical costs and lost wages. To prove negligence, the tenant testifies that three weeks before the accident she mailed the landlord a correctly addressed, properly stamped letter complaining that the hallway was slippery. The landlord testifies he never received the letter. The tenant asks the judge to instruct the jury that, if they conclude that her letter was correctly addressed and properly mailed, they must find that it was received in the ordinary course of the mail. Should the judge give the instruction?

12.2. Section 667 of the California Evidence Code, classified as a Morgan presumption, provides that "[a] person not heard from in five years is presumed to be dead." Suppose a testator in California leaves his house to his son, Saul, for the duration of the Saul's life, but provides that on Saul's death the property will go to the State of California. Six years later the state sues Saul's wife, who is living in the house, for possession. The state introduces evidence that no one has heard from Saul for the past five years.

---

7. Inference instructions are discouraged in many states, used sparingly in others, and sometimes disallowed altogether. Even federal judges may be reluctant to give inference instructions, but they have some latitude to comment on evidence.

The defendant testifies that she received a telephone call from Saul eight months ago. What instruction, if any, should the judge give the jury regarding the presumption?

12.3. Section 636 of the California Evidence Code, classified as a Thayer presumption, provides that "[t]he payment of earlier rent or installments is presumed from a receipt for later rent or installments." Suppose a California construction company buys a bulldozer from an out-of-state vendor. The bulldozer repeatedly breaks down, and five years after the purchase the construction company brings a federal diversity action against the vendor, alleging breach of warranty. The plaintiff introduces the purchase contract, which calls for payment in four annual installments, and a receipt for payment of the fourth installment. The defendant claims in its pleadings that the first three installments were never paid, but introduces no evidence to this effect and does not challenge the authenticity of the receipt. Is the plaintiff entitled to a directed verdict on the question of its payments for the bulldozer?

B. Burdens and Presumptions in Criminal Cases

The rules regarding burdens and presumptions in criminal cases can be even more puzzling than the parallel rules for civil cases. This is partly because of confusing terminology—distinguishing, for example, between "mandatory" and "permissive" presumptions. As the treatise excerpt at the end of the previous section explained, *all* true presumptions—including both Thayer presumptions and Morgan presumptions—are "mandatory" in the sense used by the Supreme Court.

The operation of presumptions in criminal cases is also complicated by the constitutional requirement that the prosecution shoulder the burden of proving guilt "beyond a reasonable doubt." As you will see, the Supreme Court has construed this requirement to prohibit shifting the burden of persuasion to a criminal defendant with regard to any element of the offense. But, as the following cases also demonstrate, the Court has found it difficult to reach agreement regarding the proper reach of that prohibition.

PATTERSON v. NEW YORK

432 U.S. 197 (1977)

Mr. Justice WHITE delivered the opinion of the Court.

. . . After a brief and unstable marriage, the appellant, Gordon Patterson, Jr., became estranged from his wife, Roberta. Roberta resumed an association with John Northrup, a neighbor to whom she had been engaged prior to her marriage to appellant. On December 27, 1970, Patterson borrowed a rifle from an acquaintance and went to the residence of his father-in-law. There, he observed his wife through a window in a state of semiundress in the presence of John Northrup. He entered the house and killed Northrup by shooting him twice in the head.

Patterson was charged with second-degree murder. In New York there are two elements of this crime: (1) "intent to cause the death of another person"; and (2) "caus[ing] the death of such person or of a third person." N.Y. Penal Law §125.25 (McKinney 1975). Malice aforethought is not an element of the crime. In addition, the State permits a person accused of murder to raise an affirmative defense that he "acted under the influence of extreme emotional disturbance for which there was a reasonable explanation or excuse."

New York also recognizes the crime of manslaughter. A person is guilty of manslaughter if he intentionally kills another person "under circumstances which do not constitute murder because he acts under the influence of extreme emotional disturbance." Appellant confessed before trial to killing Northrup, but at trial he raised the defense of extreme emotional disturbance.

The jury was instructed as to the elements of the crime of murder. Focusing on the element of intent, the trial court charged:

> "Before you, considering all of the evidence, can convict this defendant or anyone of murder, you must believe and decide that the People have established beyond a reasonable doubt that he intended, in firing the gun, to kill either the victim himself or some other human being. . . .
>
> "Always remember that you must not expect or require the defendant to prove to your satisfaction that his acts were done without the intent to kill. Whatever proof he may have attempted, however far he may have gone in an effort to convince you of his innocence or guiltlessness, he is not obliged, he is not obligated to prove anything. It is always the People's burden to prove his guilt, and to prove that he intended to kill in this instance beyond a reasonable doubt."

The jury was further instructed, consistently with New York law, that the defendant had the burden of proving his affirmative defense by a preponderance of the evidence. The jury was told that if it found beyond a reasonable doubt that appellant had intentionally killed Northrup but that appellant had demonstrated by a preponderance of the evidence that he had acted under the influence of extreme emotional disturbance, it had to find appellant guilty of manslaughter instead of murder.

The jury found appellant guilty of murder. Judgment was entered on the verdict, and the Appellate Division affirmed. While appeal to the New York Court of Appeals was pending, this Court decided *Mullaney v. Wilbur*, 421 U.S. 684 (1975), in which the Court declared Maine's murder statute unconstitutional. Under the Maine statute, a person accused of murder could rebut the statutory presumption that he committed the offense with "malice aforethought" by proving that he acted in the heat of passion on sudden provocation. The Court held that this scheme improperly shifted the burden of persuasion from the prosecutor to the defendant and was therefore a violation of due process. In the Court of Appeals appellant urged that

New York's murder statute is functionally equivalent to the one struck down in Mullaney and that therefore his conviction should be reversed.

The Court of Appeals rejected appellant's argument, holding that the New York murder statute is consistent with due process. The Court distinguished Mullaney on the ground that the New York statute involved no shifting of the burden to the defendant to disprove any fact essential to the offense charged since the New York affirmative defense of extreme emotional disturbance bears no direct relationship to any element of murder. . . . We affirm.

. . . [I]t is normally "within the power of the State to regulate procedures under which its laws are carried out, including the burden of producing evidence and the burden of persuasion," and its decision in this regard is not subject to proscription under the Due Process Clause unless "it offends some principle of justice so rooted in the traditions and conscience of our people as to be ranked as fundamental." *Speiser v. Randall*, 357 U.S. 513, 523 (1958); *Leland v. Oregon*, 343 U.S. 790, 798 (1952); *Snyder v. Massachusetts*, 291 U.S. 97, 105 (1934).

In determining whether New York's allocation to the defendant of proving the mitigating circumstances of severe emotional disturbance is consistent with due process, it is therefore relevant to note that this defense is a considerably expanded version of the common-law defense of heat of passion on sudden provocation and that at common law the burden of proving the latter, as well as other affirmative defenses indeed, "all . . . circumstances of justification, excuse or alleviation" rested on the defendant. 4 W. Blackstone, Commentaries *201; M. Foster, Crown Law 255 (1762); *Mullaney v. Wilbur*. This was the rule when the Fifth Amendment was adopted, and it was the American rule when the Fourteenth Amendment was ratified. *Commonwealth v. York*, 50 Mass. 93 (1845).

In 1895 the common-law view was abandoned with respect to the insanity defense in federal prosecutions. *Davis v. United States*, 160 U.S. 469 (1895). This ruling had wide impact on the practice in the federal courts with respect to the burden of proving various affirmative defenses, and the prosecution in a majority of jurisdictions in this country sooner or later came to shoulder the burden of proving the sanity of the accused and of disproving the facts constituting other affirmative defenses, including provocation. *Davis* was not a constitutional ruling, however, as *Leland v. Oregon* made clear.

At issue in *Leland v. Oregon* was the constitutionality under the Due Process Clause of the Oregon rule that the defense on insanity must be proved by the defendant beyond a reasonable doubt. Nothing that *Davis* "obviously establish[ed] no constitutional doctrine," the Court refused to strike down the Oregon scheme, saying that the burden of proving all elements of the crime beyond reasonable doubt, including the elements of premeditation and deliberation, was placed on the State under Oregon procedures and remained there throughout the trial. To convict, the jury was required to find each element of the crime beyond a reasonable doubt, based on all the evidence, including the evidence going to the issue of insanity. Only then was the jury "to consider separately the issue of legal sanity per se. . . ." This practice did not offend the Due Process Clause even though among the 20 States then placing the burden of proving his insanity on the defendant, Oregon was alone in requiring him to convince the jury beyond a reasonable doubt.

In 1970, the Court declared that the Due Process Clause "protects the accused against conviction except upon proof beyond a reasonable doubt of every fact necessary to constitute the crime with which he is charged." *In re Winship*, 397 U.S. 358, 364 (1970). Five years later, in *Mullaney v. Wilbur*, 421 U.S. 684, 95 S. Ct. 1881, 44 L. Ed. 2d 508 (1975), the Court further announced that under the Maine law of homicide, the burden could not constitutionally be placed on the defendant of proving by a preponderance of the evidence that the killing had occurred in the heat of passion on sudden provocation. The Chief Justice and Mr. Justice Rehnquist, concurring, expressed their understanding that the *Mullaney* decision did not call into question the ruling in *Leland v. Oregon* with respect to the proof of insanity.

Subsequently, the Court confirmed that it remained constitutional to burden the defendant with proving his insanity defense when it dismissed, as not raising a substantial federal question, a case in which the appellant specifically challenged the continuing validity of *Leland v. Oregon*. This occurred in *Rivera v. Delaware*, 429 U.S. 877 (1976), an appeal from a Delaware conviction which, in reliance on *Leland*, had been affirmed by the Delaware Supreme Court over the claim that the Delaware statute was unconstitutional because it burdened the defendant with proving his affirmative defense of insanity by a preponderance of the evidence. The claim in this Court was that *Leland* had been overruled by *Winship* and *Mullaney*. We dismissed the appeal as not presenting a substantial federal question.

We cannot conclude that Patterson's conviction under the New York law deprived him of due process of law. The crime of murder is defined by the statute, which represents a recent revision of the state criminal code, as causing the death of another person with intent to do so. The death, the intent to kill, and causation are the facts that the State is required to prove beyond a reasonable doubt if a person is to be convicted of murder. No further facts are either presumed or inferred in order to constitute the crime. The statute does provide an affirmative defense that the defendant acted under the influence of extreme emotional disturbance for which there was a reasonable explanation which, if proved by a preponderance of the evidence, would reduce the crime to manslaughter, an offense defined in a separate section of the statute. It is plain enough that if the intentional killing is shown, the State intends to deal with the defendant as a murderer unless he demonstrates the mitigating circumstances.

Here, the jury was instructed in accordance with the statute, and the guilty verdict confirms that the State successfully carried its burden of proving the facts of the crime beyond a reasonable doubt. Nothing in the evidence, including any evidence that might have been offered with respect to Patterson's mental state at the time of the crime, raised a reasonable doubt about his guilt as a murderer; and clearly the evidence failed to convince the jury that Patterson's affirmative defense had been made out. It seems to us that the State satisfied the mandate of *Winship* that it prove beyond a reasonable doubt "every fact necessary to constitute the crime with which [Patterson was] charged."

In convicting Patterson under its murder statute, New York did no more than *Leland* and *Rivera* permitted it to do without violating the Due Process Clause. Under those cases, once the facts constituting a crime are established beyond a reasonable doubt, based on all the evidence including the evidence of the defendant's mental state, the State may refuse to sustain the affirmative defense of insanity unless demonstrated by a preponderance of the evidence.

The New York law on extreme emotional disturbance follows this pattern. This affirmative defense, which the Court of Appeals described as permitting "the defendant to show that his actions were caused by a mental infirmity not arising to the level of insanity, and that he is less culpable for having committed them," does not serve to negative any facts of the crime which the State is to prove in order to convict of murder. It constitutes a separate issue on which the defendant is required to carry the burden of persuasion; and unless we are to overturn *Leland* and *Rivera*, New York has not violated the Due Process Clause, and Patterson's conviction must be sustained.

We are unwilling to reconsider *Leland* and *Rivera*. But even if we were to hold that a State must prove sanity to convict once that fact is put in issue, it would not necessarily follow that a State must prove beyond a reasonable doubt every fact, the existence or nonexistence of which it is willing to recognize as an exculpatory or mitigating circumstance affecting the degree of culpability or the severity of the punishment. Here in revising its criminal code, New York provided the affirmative defense of extreme emotional disturbance, a substantially expanded version of the older heat-of-passion concept; but it was willing to do so only if the facts making out the defense were established by the defendant with sufficient certainty. The State was itself unwilling to undertake to establish the absence of those facts beyond a reasonable doubt, perhaps fearing that proof would be too difficult and that too many persons deserving treatment as murderers would escape that punishment if the evidence need merely raise a reasonable doubt about the defendant's emotional state. It has been said that the new criminal code of New York contains some 25 affirmative defenses which exculpate or mitigate but which must be established by the defendant to be operative.[10]

---

10. The State of New York is not alone in this result: "Since the Model Penal Code was completed in 1962, some 22 states have codified and reformed their criminal laws. At least 12 of these jurisdictions have used the concept of an 'affirmative defense' and have defined that phrase to require that the defendant prove the existence of an 'affirmative defense' by a preponderance of the evidence. Additionally, at least six proposed state codes and each of the four successive versions of a revised federal code use the same procedural device. Finally, many jurisdictions that do not generally employ this concept of 'affirmative defense' nevertheless shift the burden of proof to the defendant on particular issues." Low & Jeffries, DICTA: Constitutionalizing the Criminal Law?, 29 Va. Law Weekly, No. 18, p. 1 (1977) (footnotes omitted).

Even so, the trend over the years appears to have been to require the prosecution to disprove affirmative defenses beyond a reasonable doubt. See W. LaFave & A. Scott, Criminal Law §8, p. 50 (1972); C. McCormick, Evidence §341, pp. 800-802 (2d ed. 1972). The split among the various jurisdictions varies for any given defense. Thus, 22 jurisdictions place the

The Due Process Clause, as we see it, does not put New York to the choice of abandoning those defenses or undertaking to disprove their existence in order to convict of a crime which otherwise is within its constitutional powers to sanction by substantial punishment.

. . . It is said that the common-law rule permits a State to punish one as a murderer when it is as likely as not that he acted in the heat of passion or under severe emotional distress and when, if he did, he is guilty only of manslaughter. But this has always been the case in those jurisdictions adhering to the traditional rule. It is also very likely true that fewer convictions of murder would occur if New York were required to negative the affirmative defense at issue here. But in each instance of a murder conviction under the present law New York will have proved beyond a reasonable doubt that the defendant has intentionally killed another person, an act which it is not disputed the State may constitutionally criminalize and punish. If the State nevertheless chooses to recognize a factor that mitigates the degree of criminality or punishment, we think the State may assure itself that the fact has been established with reasonably certainty. To recognize at all a mitigating circumstance does not require the State to prove its nonexistence in each case in which the fact is put in issue, if in its judgment this would be too cumbersome, too expensive, and too inaccurate.[11]

. . . This view may seem to permit state legislatures to reallocate burdens of proof by labeling as affirmative defenses at least some elements of the crimes now defined in their statutes. But there are obviously constitutional limits beyond which the States may not go in this regard. "[I]t is not within the province of a legislature to declare an individual guilty or presumptively guilty of a crime." *McFarland v. American Sugar Rfg. Co.*, 241 U.S. 79, 86 (1916). The legislature cannot "validly command that the finding of an indictment, or mere proof of the identity of the accused, should create a presumption of the existence of all the facts essential to guilt." *Tot v. United States*, 319 U.S. 463, 469 (1943). . . .

Mullaney . . . held that a State must prove every ingredient of an offense beyond a reasonable doubt, and that it may not shift the burden of proof to the defendant by presuming that ingredient upon proof of the

---

burden of proving the affirmative defense of insanity on the defendant, while 28 jurisdictions place the burden of disproving insanity on the prosecution. Note, Constitutional Limitations on Allocating the Burden of Proof of Insanity to the Defendant in Murder Cases, 56 B.U. L. Rev. 499, 503-505 (1976).

11. The drafters of the Model Penal Code would, as a matter of policy, place the burden of proving the nonexistence of most affirmative defenses, including the defense involved in this case, on the prosecution once the defendant has come forward with some evidence that the defense is present. The drafters recognize the need for flexibility, however, and would, in "some exceptional situations," place the burden of persuasion on the accused.

"Characteristically these are situations where the defense does not obtain at all under existing law and the Code seeks to introduce a mitigation. Resistance to the mitigation, based upon the prosecution's difficulty in obtaining evidence, ought to be lowered if the burden of persuasion is imposed on the defendant. Where that difficulty appears genuine and there is something to be said against allowing the defense at all, we consider it defensible to shift the burden in this way." ALI Model Penal Code s 1.13, Comment, p. 113 (Tent. Draft No. 4, 1955).

Other writers have recognized the need for flexibility in allocating the burden of proof in order to enhance the potential for liberal legislative reforms. . . .

other elements of the offense. . . . Such shifting of the burden of persuasion with respect to a fact which the State deems so important that it must be either proved or presumed is impermissible under the Due Process Clause.

. . . [A] killing became murder in Maine when it resulted from a deliberate, cruel act committed by one person against another, "suddenly without any, or without a considerable provocation." Premeditation was not within the definition of murder; but malice, in the sense of the absence of provocation, was part of the definition of that crime. Yet malice, i.e., lack of provocation, was presumed and could be rebutted by the defendant only by proving by a preponderance of the evidence that he acted with heat of passion upon sudden provocation. In *Mullaney* we held that however traditional this mode of proceeding might have been, it is contrary to the Due Process Clause as construed in *Winship*.

As we have explained, nothing was presumed or implied against Patterson; and his conviction is not invalid under any of our prior cases. The judgment of the New York Court of Appeals is

Affirmed.

Mr. Justice POWELL, with whom Mr. Justice BRENNAN and Mr. Justice MARSHALL join, dissenting.

. . . The test the Court today establishes allows a legislature to shift, virtually at will, the burden of persuasion with respect to any factor in a criminal case, so long as it is careful not to mention the nonexistence of that factor in the statutory language that defines the crime. The sole requirement is that any references to the factor be confined to those sections that provide for an affirmative defense. . . . What *Winship* and *Mullaney* had sought to teach about the limits a free society places on its procedures to safeguard the liberty of its citizens becomes a rather simplistic lesson in statutory draftsmanship. Nothing in the Court's opinion prevents a legislature from applying this new learning to many of the classical elements of the crimes it punishes. It would be preferable, if the Court has found reason to reject the rationale of *Winship* and *Mullaney*, simply and straightforwardly to overrule those precedents. . . .

COUNTY COURT OF ULSTER COUNTY v. ALLEN

442 U.S. 140 (1979)

Mr. Justice STEVENS delivered the opinion of the Court.

A New York statute provides that, with certain exceptions, the presence of a firearm in an automobile is presumptive evidence of its illegal possession by all persons then occupying the vehicle. . . . Four persons, three adult males (respondents) and a 16-year-old girl (Jane Doe, who is not a respondent here), were jointly tried on charges that they possessed two loaded handguns, a loaded machinegun, and over a pound of heroin found in a Chevrolet in which they were riding when it was stopped for speeding on the New York Thruway shortly after noon on March 28, 1973.

The two large-caliber handguns, which together with their ammunition weighed approximately six pounds, were seen through the window of the car by the investigating police officer. They were positioned crosswise in an open handbag on either the front floor or the front seat of the car on the passenger side where Jane Doe was sitting. Jane Doe admitted that the handbag was hers. The machinegun and the heroin were discovered in the trunk after the police pried it open. The car had been borrowed from the driver's brother earlier that day; the key to the trunk could not be found in the car or on the person of any of its occupants, although there was testimony that two of the occupants had placed something in the trunk before embarking in the borrowed car. The jury convicted all four of possession of the handguns and acquitted them of possession of the contents of the trunk.

Counsel for all four defendants objected to the introduction into evidence of the two handguns, the machinegun, and the drugs, arguing that the State had not adequately demonstrated a connection between their clients and the contraband. The trial court overruled the objection, relying on the presumption of possession created by the New York statute. Because that presumption does not apply if a weapon is found "upon the person" of one of the occupants of the car, the three male defendants also moved to dismiss the charges relating to the handguns on the ground that the guns were found on the person of Jane Doe. Respondents made this motion both at the close of the prosecution's case and at the close of all evidence. The trial judge twice denied it, concluding that the applicability of the "upon the person" exception was a question of fact for the jury.

At the close of the trial, the judge instructed the jurors that they were entitled to infer possession from the defendants' presence in the car. He did not make any reference to the "upon the person" exception in his explanation of the statutory presumption, nor did any of the defendants object to this omission or request alternative or additional instructions on the subject.

. . . [Following affirmance of their convictions, the defendants] filed a petition for a writ of habeas corpus in the United States District Court for the Southern District of New York contending that they were denied due process of law by the application of the statutory presumption of possession. The District Court issued the writ, holding that . . . the mere presence of two guns in a woman's handbag in a car could not reasonably give rise to the inference that they were in the possession of three other persons in the car.

The Court of Appeals for the Second Circuit affirmed, . . . [concluding] that the statute is unconstitutional on its face because the "presumption obviously sweeps within its compass (1) many occupants who may not know they are riding with a gun (which may be out of their sight), and (2) many who may be aware of the presence of the gun but not permitted access to it." . . .

Inferences and presumptions are a staple of our adversary system of factfinding. It is often necessary for the trier of fact to determine the existence of an element of the crime—that is, an "ultimate" or "elemental" fact—from the existence of one or more "evidentiary" or "basic" facts.

The value of these evidentiary devices, and their validity under the Due Process Clause, vary from case to case, however, depending on the strength of the connection between the particular basic and elemental facts involved and on the degree to which the device curtails the factfinder's freedom to assess the evidence independently. Nonetheless, in criminal cases, the ultimate test of any device's constitutional validity in a given case remains constant: the device must not undermine the factfinder's responsibility at trial, based on evidence adduced by the State, to find the ultimate facts beyond a reasonable doubt. *See In re Winship*, 397 U.S. 358, 364; *Mullaney v. Wilbur*, 421 U.S. [684], 702-703 n. 31.

The most common evidentiary device is the entirely permissive inference or presumption, which allows—but does not require—the trier of fact to infer the elemental fact from proof by the prosecutor of the basic one and which places no burden of any kind on the defendant. In that situation the basic fact may constitute prima facie evidence of the elemental fact. . . . Because this permissive presumption leaves the trier of fact free to credit or reject the inference and does not shift the burden of proof, it affects the application of the "beyond a reasonable doubt" standard only if, under the facts of the case, there is no rational way the trier could make the connection permitted by the inference. For only in that situation is there any risk that an explanation of the permissible inference to a jury, or its use by a jury, has caused the presumptively rational factfinder to make an erroneous factual determination.

A mandatory presumption is a far more troublesome evidentiary device. For it may affect not only the strength of the "no reasonable doubt" burden but also the placement of that burden; it tells the trier that he or they must find the elemental fact upon proof of the basic fact, at least unless the defendant has come forward with some evidence to rebut the presumed connection between the two facts.[16] In this situation, the Court has generally examined the presumption on its face to determine the extent to which the basic and elemental facts coincide. To the extent that the trier of fact is forced to abide by the presumption, and may not reject it based on an independent evaluation of the particular facts presented by the State, the analysis of the presumption's constitutional validity is logically divorced from those facts and based on the presumption's

---

16. This class of more or less mandatory presumptions can be subdivided into two parts: presumptions that merely shift the burden of production to the defendant, following the satisfaction of which the ultimate burden of persuasion returns to the prosecution; and presumptions that entirely shift the burden of proof to the defendant. The mandatory presumptions examined by our cases have almost uniformly fit into the former subclass, in that they never totally removed the ultimate burden of proof beyond a reasonable doubt from the prosecution.

To the extent that a presumption imposes an extremely low burden of production— e.g., being satisfied by "any" evidence—it may well be that its impact is no greater than that of a permissive inference, and it may be proper to analyze it as such. *See generally Mullaney v. Wilbur*, 421 U.S. 684, 703 n. 31.

In deciding what type of inference or presumption is involved in a case, the jury instructions will generally be controlling, although their interpretation may require recourse to the statute involved and the cases decided under it. . . .

accuracy in the run of cases.[17] It is for this reason that the Court has held it irrelevant in analyzing a mandatory presumption, but not in analyzing a purely permissive one, that there is ample evidence in the record other than the presumption to support a conviction.

Without determining whether the presumption in this case was mandatory, the Court of Appeals analyzed it on its face as if it were. In fact, it was not. . . . The trial judge's instructions make it clear that the presumption was merely a part of the prosecution's case,[19] that it gave rise to a permissive inference available only in certain circumstances, rather than a mandatory conclusion of possession, and that it could be ignored by the jury even if there was no affirmative proof offered by defendants in rebuttal.[20] The judge explained that possession could be actual or constructive,

17. . . . [T]his point is illustrated by *Leary v. United States*[, 395 U.S. 6 (1969)]. In that case, Dr. Timothy Leary, a professor at Harvard University, was stopped by customs inspectors in Laredo, Tex., as he was returning from the Mexican side of the international border. Marihuana seeds and a silver snuffbox filled with semirefined marihuana and three partially smoked marihuana cigarettes were discovered in his car. He was convicted of having knowingly transported marihuana which he knew had been illegally imported into this country in violation of 21 U.S.C. §176a (1964 ed.). That statute included a mandatory presumption: "possession shall be deemed sufficient evidence to authorize conviction [for importation] unless the defendant explains his possession to the satisfaction of the jury." Leary admitted possession of the marihuana and claimed that he had carried it from New York to Mexico and then back.

Mr. Justice Harlan for the Court noted that under one theory of the case, the jury could have found direct proof of all of the necessary elements of the offense without recourse to the presumption. But he deemed that insufficient reason to affirm the conviction because under another theory the jury might have found knowledge of importation on the basis of either direct evidence or the presumption, and there was accordingly no certainty that the jury had not relied on the presumption. The Court therefore found it necessary to test the presumption against the Due Process Clause. Its analysis was facial. Despite the fact that the defendant was well educated and had recently traveled to a country that is a major exporter of marihuana to this country, the Court found the presumption of knowledge of importation from possession irrational. It did so, not because Dr. Leary was unlikely to know the source of the marihuana, but instead because "a majority of possessors" were unlikely to have such knowledge. Because the jury had been instructed to rely on the presumption even if it did not believe the Government's direct evidence of knowledge of importation (unless, of course, the defendant met his burden of "satisfying" the jury to the contrary), the Court reversed the conviction.

19. "It is your duty to consider all the testimony in this case, to weigh it carefully and to test the credit to be given to a witness by his apparent intention to speak the truth and by the accuracy of his memory to reconcile, if possible, conflicting statements as to material facts and in such ways to try and get at the truth and to reach a verdict upon the evidence." Tr. 739-740.

"To establish the unlawful possession of the weapons, again the people relied upon the presumption and, in addition thereto, the testimony of Anderson and Lemmons who testified in their case in chief." *Id.*, at 744.

"Accordingly, you would be warranted in returning a verdict of guilt against the defendants or defendant if you find the defendants or defendant was in possession of a machine gun and the other weapons and that the fact of possession was proven to you by the People beyond a reasonable doubt, and an element of such proof is the reasonable presumption of illegal possession of a machine gun or the presumption of illegal possession of firearms, as I have just before explained to you." *Id.*, at 746.

20. "Our Penal Law also provides that the presence in an automobile of any machine gun or of any handgun or firearm which is loaded is presumptive evidence of their unlawful possession.

"In other words, these presumptions or this latter presumption upon proof of the presence of the machine gun and the hand weapons, you may infer and draw a conclusion

but that constructive possession could not exist without the intent and ability to exercise control or dominion over the weapons.[21] He also carefully instructed the jury that there is a mandatory presumption of innocence in favor of the defendants that controls unless it, as the exclusive trier of fact, is satisfied beyond a reasonable doubt that the defendants possessed the handguns in the manner described by the judge.[22] In short, the instructions plainly directed the jury to consider all the circumstances tending to support or contradict the inference that all four occupants of the car had possession of the two loaded handguns and to decide the matter for itself without regard to how much evidence the defendants introduced. . . .

As applied to the facts of this case, the presumption of possession is entirely rational. Notwithstanding the Court of Appeals' analysis, respondents were not "hitchhikers or other casual passengers," and the guns were neither "a few inches in length" nor "out of [respondents'] sight." The argument against possession by any of the respondents was predicated solely on the fact that the guns were in Jane Doe's pocketbook. But several circumstances—which, not surprisingly, her counsel repeatedly emphasized in his questions and his argument—made it highly improbable that she was the sole custodian of those weapons.

Even if it was reasonable to conclude that she had placed the guns in her purse before the car was stopped by police, the facts strongly suggest that Jane Doe was not the only person able to exercise dominion over them. The two guns were too large to be concealed in her handbag. The bag was consequently open, and part of one of the guns was in plain view, within easy access of the driver of the car and even, perhaps, of the other two respondents who were riding in the rear seat.

---

that such prohibited weapon was possessed by each of the defendants who occupied the automobile at the time when such instruments were found. The presumption or presumptions is effective only so long as there is no substantial evidence contradicting the conclusion flowing from the presumption, and the presumption is said to disappear when such contradictory evidence is adduced." *Id.*, at 743.

"The presumption or presumptions which I discussed with the jury relative to the drugs or weapons in this case need not be rebutted by affirmative proof or affirmative evidence but may be rebutted by any evidence or lack of evidence in the case." *Id.*, at 760.

21. "As so defined, possession means actual physical possession, just as having the drugs or weapons in one's hand, in one's home or other place under one's exclusive control, or constructive possession which may exist without personal dominion over the drugs or weapons but with the intent and ability to retain such control or dominion." *Id.*, at 742.

22. "[Y]ou are the exclusive judges of all the questions of fact in this case. That means that you are the sole judges as to the weight to be given to the evidence and to the weight and probative value to be given to the testimony of each particular witness and to the credibility of any witness." *Id.*, at 730.

"Under our law, every defendant in a criminal trial starts the trial with the presumption in his favor that he is innocent, and this presumption follows him throughout the entire trial and remains with him until such time as you, by your verdict, find him or her guilty beyond a reasonable doubt or innocent of the charge. If you find him or her not guilty, then, of course, this presumption ripens into an established fact. On the other hand, if you find him or her guilty, then this presumption has been overcome and is destroyed." *Id.*, at 734.

"Now, in order to find any of the defendants guilty of the unlawful possession of the weapons, the machine gun, the .45 and the .38, you must be satisfied beyond a reasonable doubt that the defendants possessed the machine gun and the .45 and the .38, possessed it as I defined it to you before." *Id.*, at 745.

Moreover, it is highly improbable that the loaded guns belonged to Jane Doe or that she was solely responsible for their being in her purse. As a 16-year-old girl in the company of three adult men she was the least likely of the four to be carrying one, let alone two, heavy handguns. It is far more probable that she relied on the pocketknife found in her brassiere for any necessary self-protection. Under these circumstances, it was not unreasonable for her counsel to argue and for the jury to infer that when the car was halted for speeding, the other passengers in the car anticipated the risk of a search and attempted to conceal their weapons in a pocketbook in the front seat. The inference is surely more likely than the notion that these weapons were the sole property of the 16-year-old girl.

Under these circumstances, the jury would have been entirely reasonable in rejecting the suggestion—which, incidentally, defense counsel did not even advance in their closing arguments to the jury—that the handguns were in the sole possession of Jane Doe. Assuming that the jury did reject it, the case is tantamount to one in which the guns were lying on the floor or the seat of the car in the plain view of the three other occupants of the automobile. In such a case, it is surely rational to infer that each of the respondents was fully aware of the presence of the guns and had both the ability and the intent to exercise dominion and control over the weapons. The application of the statutory presumption in this case therefore comports with the standard laid down in *Tot v. United States*, 319 U.S. [463, 467 (1943)], and restated in *Leary v. United States*, 395 U.S. [6, 36 (1969)]. For there is a "rational connection" between the basic facts that the prosecution proved and the ultimate fact presumed, and the latter is "more likely than not to flow from" the former. . . .

The judgment is reversed. . . .

[Chief Justice Burger filed a concurring opinion. Justice Powell filed a dissenting opinion, joined by Justice Brennan, Justice Stewart, and Justice Marshall.]

SANDSTROM v. MONTANA

442 U.S. 510 (1979)

Mr. Justice BRENNAN delivered the opinion of the Court.

The question presented is whether, in a case in which intent is an element of the crime charged, the jury instruction, "the law presumes that a person intends the ordinary consequences of his voluntary acts," violates the Fourteenth Amendment's requirement that the State prove every element of a criminal offense beyond a reasonable doubt.

On November 22, 1976, 18-year-old David Sandstrom confessed to the slaying of Annie Jessen. Based upon the confession and corroborating evidence, petitioner was charged on December 2 with "deliberate homicide," Mont. Code Ann. §45-5-102 (1978), in that he "purposely or knowingly caused the death of Annie Jessen." At trial, Sandstrom's attorney informed the jury that, although his client admitted killing Jessen, he did not do so "purposely or knowingly," and was therefore not guilty of "deliberate homicide" but of a lesser crime. The basic support for this contention was the testimony of two court-appointed mental health experts, each of whom described for the jury petitioner's mental state at the time of the incident. Sandstrom's attorney argued that this testimony demonstrated that petitioner, due to a personality disorder aggravated by alcohol consumption, did not kill Annie Jessen "purposely or knowingly."

The prosecution requested the trial judge to instruct the jury that "[t]he law presumes that a person intends the ordinary consequences of his voluntary acts." Petitioner's counsel objected, arguing that "the instruction has the effect of shifting the burden of proof on the issue of" purpose or knowledge to the defense, and that "that is impermissible under the Federal Constitution, due process of law." . . . The instruction was delivered, the jury found petitioner guilty of deliberate homicide, and petitioner was sentenced to 100 years in prison.

Sandstrom appealed to the Supreme Court of Montana, again contending that the instruction shifted to the defendant the burden of disproving an element of the crime charged, in violation of *Mullaney v. Wilbur*, [421 U.S. 684 (1975),] *In re Winship*, 397 U.S. 358 (1980), and *Patterson v. New York*, 432 U.S. 197 (1977). The Montana court conceded that these cases did prohibit shifting the burden of proof to the defendant by means of a presumption, but held that the cases "do not prohibit allocation of *some* burden of proof to a defendant under certain circumstances." Since in the court's view, "[d]efendant's sole burden . . . was to produce *some* evidence that he did not intend the ordinary consequences of his voluntary acts, not to disprove that he acted 'purposely' or 'knowingly,' . . . the instruction does not violate due process standards as defined by the United States or Montana Constitution. . . ." . . . We reverse.

The threshold inquiry in ascertaining the constitutional analysis applicable to this kind of jury instruction is to determine the nature of the presumption it describes. See *Ulster County Court v. Allen*, 442 U.S. 140 (1979). That determination requires careful attention to the words actually spoken to the jury, see *id.*, for whether a defendant has been accorded his constitutional rights depends upon the way in which a reasonable juror could have interpreted the instruction.

Respondent argues, first, that the instruction merely described a permissive inference—that is, it allowed but did not require the jury to draw conclusions about defendant's intent from his actions—and that such inferences are constitutional. These arguments need not detain us long, for even respondent admits that "it's possible" that the jury believed they were required to apply the presumption. Sandstrom's jurors were told that "[t]he law presumes that a person intends the ordinary consequences of his voluntary acts." They were not told that they had a choice, or that they might infer that conclusion; they were told only that the law presumed it. It is clear that a reasonable juror could easily have viewed such an instruction as mandatory.

In the alternative, respondent urges that, even if viewed as a mandatory presumption rather than as a permissive inference, the presumption did not conclusively establish intent but rather could be rebutted. On this view, the instruction required the jury, if satisfied as to the facts which trigger the presumption, to find intent *unless* the defendant offered evidence to the contrary. Moreover, according to the State, all the defendant had to do to rebut the presumption was produce "some" contrary evidence; he did not have to "prove" that he lacked the required mental state. Thus, "[a]t most, it placed a *burden of production* on the petitioner," but "did not shift to petitioner the *burden of persuasion* with respect to any element of the offense. . . ." Again, respondent contends that presumptions with this limited effect pass constitutional muster.

We need not review respondent's constitutional argument on this point either, however, for we reject this characterization of the presumption as well. Respondent concedes there is a "risk" that the jury, once having found petitioner's act voluntary, would interpret the instruction as automatically directing a finding of intent. Moreover, the State also concedes that numerous courts "have differed as to the effect of the presumption when given as a jury instruction without further explanation as to its use by the jury," and that some have found it to shift more than the burden of production, and even to have conclusive effect. Nonetheless, the State contends that the only authoritative reading of the effect of the presumption resides in the Supreme Court of Montana. And the State argues that by holding that "[d]efendant's sole burden under instruction No. 5 was to produce *some* evidence that he did not intend the ordinary consequences of his voluntary acts, not to disprove that he acted 'purposely' or 'knowingly,'" (emphasis added), the Montana Supreme Court decisively established that the presumption at most affected only the burden of going forward with evidence of intent—that is, the burden of production.[5]

The Supreme Court of Montana is, of course, the final authority on the legal weight to be given a presumption under Montana law, but it is not the final authority on the interpretation which a jury could have given the instruction. If Montana intended its presumption to have only the effect described by its Supreme Court, then we are convinced that a reasonable juror could well have been misled by the instruction given, and could have believed that the presumption was not limited to requiring the defendant to satisfy only a burden of production. Petitioner's jury was told that "*[t]he law presumes* that a person intends the ordinary consequences of his voluntary acts." They were not told that the presumption could be rebutted, as the Montana Supreme Court held, by the defendant's simple presentation of "some" evidence; nor even that it could be rebutted at all. Given the common definition of "presume" as "to suppose to be true without proof," Webster's New Collegiate Dictionary 911 (1974), and given the lack of qualifying instructions as to the legal effect of the presumption,

5. For purposes of argument, we accept respondent's definition of the production burden when applied to a defendant in a criminal case. We note, however, that the burden is often described quite differently when it rests upon the prosecution. See United States v. Vuitch, 402 U.S. 62, 72 n. 7 (1971) ("evidence from which a jury could find a defendant guilty beyond a reasonable doubt"); C. McCormick, Evidence §338, p. 790, and n. 33 (2d ed. 1972), p. 101, and n. 34.1 (Supp. 1978). We also note that the effect of a failure to meet the production burden is significantly different for the defendant and prosecution. When the prosecution fails to meet it, a directed verdict in favor of the defense results. Such a consequence is not possible upon a defendant's failure, however, as verdicts may not be directed against defendants in criminal cases.

we cannot discount the possibility that the jury may have interpreted the instruction in either of two more stringent ways.

First, a reasonable jury could well have interpreted the presumption as "conclusive," that is, not technically as a presumption at all, but rather as an irrebuttable direction by the court to find intent once convinced of the facts triggering the presumption. Alternatively, the jury may have interpreted the instruction as a direction to find intent upon proof of the defendant's voluntary actions (and their "ordinary" consequences), unless *the defendant* proved the contrary by some quantum of proof which may well have been considerably greater than "some" evidence—thus effectively shifting the burden of persuasion on the element of intent. . . . [A]lthough the Montana Supreme Court held to the contrary in this case, Montana's own Rules of Evidence expressly state that the presumption at issue here may be overcome only "by a preponderance of evidence contrary to the presumption." Montana Rule of Evidence 301(b)(2). Such a requirement shifts not only the burden of production, but also the ultimate burden of persuasion on the issue of intent.

We do not reject the possibility that some jurors may have interpreted the challenged instruction as permissive, or, if mandatory, as requiring only that the defendant come forward with "some" evidence in rebuttal. However, the fact that a reasonable juror could have given the presumption conclusive or persuasion-shifting effect means that we cannot discount the possibility that Sandstrom's jurors actually did proceed upon one or the other of these latter interpretations. And that means that unless these kinds of presumptions are constitutional, the instruction cannot be adjudged valid.[8] It is the line of cases urged by petitioner, and exemplified by *In re Winship*, 397 U.S. 358 (1970), that provides the appropriate mode of constitutional analysis for these kinds of presumptions.

In *Winship*, this Court stated: "Lest there remain any doubt about the constitutional stature of the reasonable-doubt standard, we explicitly hold that the Due Process Clause protects the accused against conviction except upon proof beyond a reasonable doubt *of every fact* necessary to constitute the crime with which he is charged" (emphasis added). Accord, *Patterson v. New York*, 432 U.S., at 210. The petitioner here was charged with and convicted of deliberate homicide, committed purposely or knowingly, under Mont. Code Ann. §45-5-102(a) (1978). It is clear that under Montana law, whether the crime was committed purposely or knowingly is a fact necessary to constitute the crime of deliberate homicide. Indeed, it was the lone element of the offense at issue in Sandstrom's trial, as he confessed to causing the death of the victim, told the jury that knowledge and purpose were the only questions he was controverting, and introduced evidence solely on those points. Moreover, it is conceded that proof of defendant's "intent" would be sufficient to establish this element. Thus, the question before this Court is whether the challenged jury instruction had the effect of relieving the State of the burden of proof enunciated in *Winship* on the critical question of petitioner's state of mind. We conclude that under either

---

8. Given our ultimate result in this case, we do not need to consider what kind of constitutional analysis would be appropriate for other kinds of presumptions.

of the two possible interpretations of the instruction set out above, precisely that effect would result, and that the instruction therefore represents constitutional error. . . . Accordingly, the judgment of the Supreme Court of Montana is reversed, and the case is remanded for further proceedings not inconsistent with this opinion.

[Justice Rehnquist filed a concurring opinion, joined by Chief Justice Burger.]

PROBLEMS

12.4. A federal statute passed in 1984 purports to impose on criminal defendants "the burden of proving the defense of insanity by clear and convincing evidence." 18 U.S.C. §17(b). Is this statute constitutional?

12.5. In January 1980, police in Santa Cruz, California, executed a search warrant at a second-hand store called Betty Boop's Junque Shop and found a variety of stolen property. The proprietors of the store were prosecuted for receiving stolen property. The elements of the offense are receiving property that has been stolen, and knowing the stolen nature of the property at the time of receiving it. The trial judge instructed the jury on the elements of the offense, the presumption of innocence, and the definition of reasonable doubt.

Relying on a statutory presumption, the judge also instructed the jury that if it found (1) that the defendants were dealers in second-hand merchandise, (2) that they had bought or received property under circumstances that should have prompted a reasonable inquiry regarding whether the seller had a legal right to sell it, and (3) that they had failed to make such an inquiry, "then you shall presume that defendants bought or received such property knowing it to have been stolen unless from all the evidence you have reasonable doubt that defendants knew the property was stolen."

When the jury asked regarding the presumption, and the judge responded as follows: "There are two kinds of presumptions. One is a conclusive presumption that if you have the presumption, that's it, you don't go any further. This isn't that kind of presumption. It's what's called a rebuttable presumption, because you have the presumption, presume to know that the property was stolen, but they can go forward and raise a reasonable doubt that they actually knew that. So you still do have that question. Basically, it boils down to are you satisfied that they acquired the property or retained the property knowing it was stolen, or do you have a reasonable doubt."

Did these instructions violate the federal Constitution? (The California Supreme Court gave its answer in *People v. Roeder*, 189 Cal. Rptr. 501 (1983).)

C. JUDICIAL NOTICE

Like presumptions, judicial notice is a topic that seems straightforward enough until one tries to set down some rules about it. Everyone agrees that there are some facts that should not have to be proved, because they cannot reasonably be disputed—like the fact that December 5, 1999, was a Sunday. And no one wants judges or jurors to ignore everything they know about the world from their experiences outside the courtroom. The difficult questions are, first, where to draw the lines and, second, how much of the line-drawing can usefully be accomplished through rules of general application.

Judicial notice should be distinguished from two other mechanisms for establishing facts without evidence. The first of these mechanisms is sometimes called "jury notice"; the Advisory Committee Note excerpted below refers to it as reliance on "non-evidence facts." The idea is that there are certain facts that do not need to be proved because they are part of the background understanding of the world that the trier of fact brings to the case. The example the Advisory Committee gives is the usual meaning and connotations of the word "car"—i.e., the fact that when people say "car," they usually mean an automobile, the fact that most automobiles have internal combustion engines and pneumatic tires, and so on. Other examples might be the fact that sadness sometimes makes people cry or the fact that apples grow on trees.

The second common mechanism for establishing facts without evidence and without judicial notice is a stipulation. A long-standing feature of our litigation system allows the parties to agree to certain facts and have the jury instructed to take them as proven, without introducing any evidence. This is another aspect of the extensive control that parties exert over factfinding in our system. We saw it in operation in *Old Chief v. United States*, excerpted in Chapter Two.

Much of the work you might think has to be done by judicial notice is really done by these other two mechanisms. This means that there is a role for judicial notice only with respect to facts about which the parties do *not* stipulate, and which do *not* represent such common knowledge that we can assume the jury knows them without being told. This might lead you to wonder why we even need a doctrine of judicial notice. After all, if facts are not so obvious that all jurors know them, and they are not matters about which the parties agree, why not just require proof? This is a good question, and it is worth keeping in mind as you read the cases and commentary excerpted below.

One other point is worth noting at the outset. Rule 201 of the Federal Rules of Evidence, which addresses judicial notice, leans heavily on a distinction between "adjudicative facts" and "legislative facts." Rule 201 regulates judicial notice of the former but not of the latter. In practice, however, the two categories of facts are often difficult to tell apart, and courts do not always even try—partly because, as you will see, the restrictions that F.R.E. 201 imposes on judicial notice of adjudicative facts are in many ways very similar to the restrictions that courts impose, as a matter of federal common law, on judicial notice of legislative facts. (The major exception is the wishy-washy jury instruction that Rule 201 tells trial judges to use when they deliver judicial notice of any fact in a criminal case.)

Whether the distinction between adjudicative and legislative facts assists sensible thinking about judicial notice remains an open question. Some states, like California, ignore the distinction entirely in their own evidence codes.

[F.R.E. 201; C.E.C. §§450-460]

ADVISORY COMMITTEE'S NOTE TO F.R.E. 201

This is the only evidence rule on the subject of judicial notice. It deals only with judicial notice of "adjudicative" facts. No rule deals with judicial notice of "legislative" facts. . . .

Adjudicative facts are simply the facts of the particular case. Legislative facts, on the other hand, are those which have relevance to legal reasoning and the lawmaking process, whether in the formulation of a legal principle or ruling by a judge or court or in the enactment of a legislative body. The terminology was coined by Professor Kenneth Davis in his article An Approach to Problems of Evidence in the Administrative Process, 55 Harv. L. Rev. 364, 404-407 (1942). . . .

The usual method of establishing adjudicative facts is through the introduction of evidence, ordinarily consisting of the testimony of witnesses. If particular facts are outside the area of reasonable controversy, this process is dispensed with as unnecessary. A high degree of indisputability is the essential prerequisite.

Legislative facts are quite different. As Professor Davis says:

> "My opinion is that judge-made law would stop growing if judges, in thinking about questions of law and policy, were forbidden to take into account the facts they believe, as distinguished from facts which are 'clearly . . . within the domain of the indisputable.' Facts most needed in thinking about difficult problems of law and policy have a way of being outside the domain of the clearly indisputable." A System of Judicial Notice Based on Fairness and Convenience, supra, at 82.

An illustration is Hawkins v. United States, 358 U.S. 74 (1958), in which the Court refused to discard the common law rule that one spouse could not testify against the other, saying, "Adverse testimony given in criminal proceedings would, we think, be likely to destroy almost any marriage." This conclusion has a large intermixture of fact, but the factual aspect is scarcely "indisputable." . . .

Professor Morgan gave the following description of the methodology of determining domestic law:

> "In determining the content or applicability of a rule of domestic law, the judge is unrestricted in his investigation and conclusion. He may reject the propositions of either party or of both parties. He may consult the sources of pertinent data to which they refer, or he may refuse to do so. He may make an independent search for persuasive data or rest content with what he has or what the parties present. . . . [T]he parties do no more than to assist; they control no part of the process." Morgan, Judicial Notice, 57 Harv. L. Rev. 269, 270-271 (1944).

This is the view which should govern judicial access to legislative facts. It renders inappropriate any limitation in the form of indisputability, any formal requirements of notice other than those already inherent in affording opportunity to hear and be heard and exchanging briefs, and any requirement of formal findings at any level. . . .

Similar considerations govern the judicial use of non-adjudicative facts in ways other than formulating laws and rules. Thayer described them as a part of the judicial reasoning process.

"In conducting a process of judicial reasoning, as of other reasoning, not a step can be taken without assuming something which has not been proved; and the capacity to do this with competent judgment and efficiency, is imputed to judges and juries as part of their necessary mental outfit." Thayer, Preliminary Treatise on Evidence 279-280 (1898).

As Professor Davis points out, A System of Judicial Notice Based on Fairness and Convenience, in Perspectives of Law 69, 73 (1964), every case involves the use of hundreds or thousands of non-evidence facts. When a witness in an automobile accident case says "car," everyone, judge and jury included, furnishes, from non-evidence sources within himself, the supplementing information that the "car" is an automobile, not a railroad car, that it is self-propelled, probably by an internal combustion engine, that it may be assumed to have four wheels with pneumatic rubber tires, and so on. The judicial process cannot construct every case from scratch, like Descartes creating a world based on the postulate *Cogito, ergo sum*. These items could not possibly be introduced into evidence, and no one suggests that they be. Nor are they appropriate subjects for any formalized treatment of judicial notice of facts.

Another aspect of what Thayer had in mind is the use of non-evidence facts to appraise or assess the adjudicative facts of the case. Pairs of cases from two jurisdictions illustrate this use and also the difference between non-evidence facts thus used and adjudicative facts. In People v. Strook, 347 Ill. 460, 179 N.E. 821 (1932), venue in Cook County had been held not established by testimony that the crime was committed at 7956 South Chicago Avenue, since judicial notice would not be taken that the address was in Chicago. However, the same court subsequently ruled that venue in Cook County was established by testimony that a crime occurred at 8900 South Anthony Avenue, since notice would be taken of the common practice of omitting the name of the city when speaking of local addresses, and the witness was testifying in Chicago. People v. Pride, 16 Ill. 2d 82, 156 N.E.2d 551 (1951). And in Hughes v. Vestal, 264 N.C. 500, 142 S.E.2d 361 (1965), the Supreme Court of North Carolina disapproved the trial judge's admission in evidence of a state-published table of automobile stopping distances on the basis of judicial notice, though the court itself had referred to the same table in an earlier case in a "rhetorical and illustrative" way in determining that the defendant could not have stopped her car in time to avoid striking a child who suddenly appeared in the highway and that a nonsuit was properly granted. Ennis v. Dupree, 262 N.C. 224, 136 S.E.2d 702 (1964). It is apparent that this use of non-evidence facts in evaluating the adjudicative facts of the case is not an appropriate subject for a formalized judicial notice treatment.

In view of these considerations, the regulation of judicial notice of facts by the present rule extends only to adjudicative facts.

What, then, are "adjudicative" facts? Davis refers to them as those "which relate to the parties," or more fully:

"When a court or an agency finds facts concerning the immediate parties— who did what, where, when, how, and with what motive or intent—the court or agency is performing an adjudicative function, and the facts are conveniently called adjudicative facts. . . .

"Stated in other terms, the adjudicative facts are those to which the law is applied in the process of adjudication. They are the facts that normally go to the jury in a jury case. They relate to the parties, their activities, their properties, their businesses." 2 Administrative Law Treatise 353.

With respect to judicial notice of adjudicative facts, the tradition has been one of caution in requiring that the matter be beyond reasonable controversy. This tradition of circumspection appears to be soundly based, and no reason to depart from it is apparent. As Professor Davis says:

"The reason we use trial-type procedure, I think, is that we make the practical judgment, on the basis of experience, that taking evidence, subject to cross-examination and rebuttal, is the best way to resolve controversies involving disputes of adjudicative facts, that is, facts pertaining to the parties. The reason we require a determination on the record is that we think fair procedure in resolving disputes of adjudicative facts calls for giving each party a chance to meet in the appropriate fashion the facts that come to the tribunal's attention, and the appropriate fashion for meeting disputed adjudicative facts includes rebuttal evidence, cross-examination, usually confrontation, and argument (either written or oral or both). The key to a fair trial is opportunity to use the appropriate weapons (rebuttal evidence, cross-examination, and argument) to meet adverse materials that come to the tribunal's attention." A System of Judicial Notice Based on Fairness and Convenience, in Perspectives of Law 69, 93 (1964).

The rule proceeds upon the theory that these considerations call for dispensing with traditional methods of proof only in clear cases. . . . In accord with the usual view, judicial notice may be taken at any stage of the proceedings, whether in the trial court or on appeal. . . .

UNITED STATES v. GOULD

536 F.2d 216 (8th Cir. 1976)

GIBSON, Chief Judge.

Defendants, Charles Gould and Joseph Carey, were convicted of conspiring to import . . . and actually importing . . . cocaine from Colombia, South America, into the United States in violation of the Controlled Substances Import and Export Act. 21 U.S.C. §951 et seq. (1970). [The statute prohibits the importation of "any controlled substance in schedule I or II."]

. . . The evidence persuasively showed that defendants and David Miller enlisted the cooperation of Miller's sister, Barbara Kenworthy, who agreed to travel to Colombia with defendants and smuggle the cocaine into the United States by placing it inside two pairs of hollowed-out platform shoes. . . . The success of the importation scheme was foiled when, upon Ms. Kenworthy's arrival to the Miami airport from Colombia, a customs agent insisted upon X-raying the cocaine-laden shoes. Approximately two pounds of cocaine were discovered and seized by customs officials. . . .

Defendants do not challenge the sufficiency of the evidence but contend that the District Court erred in . . . improperly taking judicial notice and instructing the jury that cocaine hydrochloride is a schedule II controlled substance. . . . Schedule II controlled substances, for the purpose of the Controlled Substances Import and Export Act, [include, *inter alia,*] . . . "Coca leaves and any salt, compound, derivative, or preparation of coca leaves, and any salt, compound, derivative, or preparation thereof which is chemically equivalent or identical with any of these substances, except that the substances shall not include decocainized coca leaves or extraction of coca leaves, which extractions do not contain cocaine or ecgonine." 21 U.S.C. §812 (1970); *see* 21 C.F.R. §1308.12 (1975).

At trial, two expert witnesses for the Government testified as to the composition of the powdered substance removed from Ms. Kenworthy's platform shoes at the Miami airport. One expert testified that the substance was comprised of approximately 60 percent cocaine hydrochloride. The other witness stated that the white powder consisted of 53 percent cocaine.[3] There was no direct evidence to indicate that cocaine hydrochloride is a derivative of coca leaves. In its instructions to the jury, the District Court stated: "If you find the substance was cocaine hydrochloride, you are instructed that cocaine hydrochloride is a schedule II controlled substance under the laws of the United States."

Our inquiry . . . is twofold. We must first determine whether it was error for the District Court to take judicial notice of the fact that cocaine hydrochloride is a schedule II controlled substance. Secondly, if we conclude that it was permissible to judicially notice this fact, we must then determine whether the District Court erred in instructing the jury that it must accept this fact as conclusive.

The first aspect of this inquiry merits little discussion. . . . It is apparent that courts may take judicial notice of any fact which is "capable of such instant and unquestionable demonstration, if desired, that no party would think of imposing a falsity on the tribunal in the face of an intelligent adversary." IX J. Wigmore, Evidence §2571, at 548 (1940). The fact that cocaine hydrochloride is derived from coca leaves is, if not common knowledge, at least a matter which is capable of certain, easily accessible and indisputably accurate verification. *See* Webster's Third New International Dictionary 434 (1961). Therefore, it was proper for the District Court to judicially notice this fact. Our conclusion on this matter is amply supported by the weight of judicial authority. . . .

Our second inquiry involves the propriety of the District Court's instruction to the jurors that this judicially noticed fact must be accepted as conclusive by them. Defendants, relying upon Fed. R. Ev. 201(g), urge that the jury should have been instructed that it could discretionarily accept or reject this fact. . . . [4]

3. It is not significant that one expert witness testified that the substance contained cocaine hydrochloride and the other testified that it was comprised in part of cocaine. The fact that cocaine hydrochloride contains cocaine is common knowledge. *United States v. Sims,* 529 F.2d 10, 11 (8th Cir. 1976).

4. In the proposed federal Rules of Evidence, forwarded by the Supreme Court of the United States to Congress on February 5, 1973, rule 201(g) did not draw this distinction between civil and criminal cases. The proposed rule 201(g) provided that "(t)he judge shall instruct the jury to accept as established any facts judicially noticed." Congress disagreed

It is clear that the reach of rule 201 extends only to adjudicative, not legislative, facts. Fed. R. Ev. 201(a). Consequently, the viability of defendants' argument is dependent upon our characterization of the fact judicially noticed by the District Court as adjudicative, thus invoking the provisions of rule 201(g). In undertaking this analysis, we note at the outset that rule 201 is not all encompassing. "Rule 201 . . . was deliberately drafted to cover only a small fraction of material usually subsumed under the concept of 'judicial notice.' " 1 J. Weinstein, Evidence ¶201(01) (1975).

The precise line of demarcation between adjudicative facts and legislative Facts is not always easily identified. Adjudicative facts have been described as . . . "facts concerning the immediate parties who did what, where, when, how, and with what motive or intent the court. . . . Stated in other Terms, the adjudicative facts are those to which the law is applied in the process Of adjudication. They are the facts that normally go to the jury in a jury Case. They relate to the parties, their activities, their properties, their businesses." 2 K. Davis, Administrative Law Treatise §15.03, at 353 (1958).

Legislative facts, on the other hand, do not relate specifically to the activities or characteristics of the litigants. A court generally relies upon legislative Facts when it purports to develop a particular law or policy and thus Considers material wholly unrelated to the activities of the parties. . . . 2 K. Davis, Administrative Law Treatise, *supra* at §15.03. Legislative facts are established Truths, facts or pronouncements that do not change from case to Case but apply universally, while adjudicative facts are those developed in a Particular case.

Applying these general definitions, we think it is clear that the District Court in the present case was judicially noticing a legislative fact rather than an adjudicative fact. . . . The fact that cocaine hydrochloride is a derivative of coca leaves is a universal fact that is unrelated to the activities of the parties to this litigation. . . . [Accordingly,] rule 201(g) is inapplicable. The District Court was not obligated to inform the jury that it could disregard the judicially noticed fact. In fact, to do so would be preposterous, thus permitting juries to make conflicting findings on what constitutes controlled substances under federal law. . . . The judgment of conviction is affirmed.

UNITED STATES v. LEWIS

833 F.2d 1380 (9th Cir. 1987)

ALARCON, Circuit Judge:

The government appeals from the district court's order suppressing a Confession on motion of defendant Jerri C. Lewis in this bank robbery prosecution. . . . [Lewis argued her confession] was involuntary because

---

with this unqualified rule requiring mandatory instructions in all cases. It was feared that requiring the jury to accept a judicially noticed adjudicative fact in a criminal case might infringe upon the defendants' Sixth Amendment right to a trial by jury. H. Rep. No. 93-650, 93d Cong., 1st Sess. 6-7 (1973), reprinted in 4 U.S. Code Cong. & Admin. News pp. 7075, 7080 (1974). Consequently, Congress adopted the present text of rule 201(g) which requires a mandatory instruction in civil cases but a discretionary instruction in criminal cases.

she was a "heroin addict suffering from the effects of drug withdrawal [and] was questioned in her hospital bed hours after she had awakened from a general anesthetic administered during surgery."

[In rejecting the prosecutor's claim that the confession was voluntary,] the court then made the following comment:

> Well, you see, I can't go with you on that. One of the reasons why, and I am frank to say, I am influenced by personal experience. I mean, I represent to you that I have never been a heroin addict and I have never experienced what it is like to come out from under heroin, but I have come out from under an anesthetic. And people have told me that—and I seem to be perfectly all right—and people have told me that I said the most incredible things during the few first six hours or so after I came out of a general anesthetic. And I have had the same experience related by other people.
>
> You are not accountable for what you do or say for quite a number of hours after you come out of a general anesthetic. So I cannot find that a person who is both withdrawing from heroin and coming out from under a general anesthetic and is under arrest and confronted by FBI agents is in a position to make a voluntary and knowing statement at that time.

. . . We begin our discussion of the applicable law with the statement of an obvious principle. The trial judge in this matter was not a competent witness to Lewis' condition. "The judge presiding at the trial may not testify in that trial as a witness. No objection need be made in order to preserve the point." Fed. R. Evid. 605.

. . . Lewis contends for the first time on appeal that the trial judge properly relied on his personal experience based on the court's power to take judicial notice of adjudicative facts under Rule 201 of the Federal Rules of Evidence. This argument is unpersuasive.

A trial judge is prohibited from relying on his personal experience to support the taking of judicial notice. "It is therefore plainly accepted that the judge is not to use from the bench, under the guise of judicial knowledge, that which he knows *only as an individual* observer outside of court." 9 J. Wigmore, Evidence in Trials at Common Law §2569, at 723 (J. Chabourn rev. Ed. 1981) (emphasis in original).

In relying on his "personal knowledge" the trial judge did not advise the parties he was taking judicial notice of Lewis' condition at the time she spoke to the agents on October 21, 1986. Furthermore, the trial judge did not rely on facts "generally known within the territorial jurisdiction of the trial court or . . . capable of accurate and ready determination by resort to sources whose accuracy cannot reasonably be questioned." Fed. R. Evid. 201(b). Instead, he looked solely to his own reaction to an anesthetic. The record is silent concerning the nature of his illness, the surgical procedure performed upon the trial judge, the type and amount of anesthetic administered to him, or its general effect on a patient. Announcement on the record of the fact that a court is taking judicial notice is necessary to accord a party the "opportunity to be heard as to the propriety of taking judicial notice and the tenor of the matter noticed." Fed. R. Evid. 201(e).

Lewis relies on *Bey v. Bolger*, 540 F. Supp. 910 (E.D. Pa. 1982) for the proposition that "[c]ourts have also taken judicial notice of commonly known health facts." In *Bey*, the district court took judicial notice in a written memorandum setting forth the basis for its ruling in cross motions for partial summary judgment that a person suffering hypertension is susceptible to stroke, heart attack or other physical ailment. Thus, in *Bey*, the parties were given an opportunity to ask the court to reconsider the propriety of taking judicial notice of the effect of hypertension. Furthermore, the trial judge in *Bey* did not indicate to the parties that he was relying on his personal experience with hypertension.

The trial judge's reliance in the instant matter on facts known to him from his personal experience denied the government the opportunity to test the basis for the court's opinion concerning the effect of an anesthetic on a person's freedom of choice through the usual methods that assure trustworthiness in our adversarial system of justice. The prosecutor was denied the opportunity to contrast the nature of the illness or injury suffered by the judge with Lewis' abscessed shoulder, the amount of anesthesia administered to each, or the actual statements made by the judge which others characterized as "incredible" with the responses made by the defendant in this matter. . . . REVERSED AND REMANDED.

CARLEY v. WHEELED COACH

991 F.2d 1117 (3d Cir. 1993)

COWEN, Circuit Judge.

Plaintiff Mary Carley appeals the grant of summary judgment dismissing her claim for personal injuries caused by an alleged design defect in an ambulance manufactured by defendant Wheeled Coach Industries, Inc. ("Wheeled Coach"). . . . [Carley, an emergency medical technician, was injured when the ambulance rolled over. Wheeled Coach contended that it was immune from liability because the ambulance had been manufactured pursuant to a contract with the United States General Services Administration, and the GSA knew as much about any design problems as the company.] The district court took judicial notice "of the fact that the government conducts numerous crashworthiness tests, and the well known rollover problems of vehicles having a high center of gravity." The court [therefore] concluded that . . . Wheeled Coach could not have been more aware than the government of the ambulance's tendency to rollover. We disagree. . . . The facts judicially noticed by the district court are not beyond reasonable dispute and therefore do not satisfy Rule 201(b).

The government may perform various tests on vehicles, but the quantity and nature of those tests are not matters of common knowledge, nor are they readily provable through a source whose accuracy cannot reasonably be questioned. Likewise, the district court could not have determined, beyond reasonable dispute, that the rollover propensities of vehicles with high centers of gravity are well known. Most people probably know little, if anything, about how high centers of gravity cause vehicular accidents. The facts judicially noticed by the district court are not the kind of readily ascertainable facts that satisfy Rule 201(b). *See, e.g., Policeman's Benevolent Ass'n v. Washington Twp.*, 850 F.2d 133, 137 (3d Cir. 1988) (court of appeals took judicial notice of township's police regulations), cert. denied,

490 U.S. 1004, 109 S. Ct. 1637, 104 L. Ed. 2d 153 (1989); *Government of the Virgin Islands v. Testamark*, 528 F.2d 742, 743 (3d Cir. 1976) (no error to take judicial notice of court records indicating defendant's prior conviction). *But see Town Sound & Custom Tops, Inc. v. Chrysler Motors Corp.*, 959 F.2d 468, 494-95 n. 40 (3d Cir.) (court could not take judicial notice that standardizing of autosound systems was prevalent in the automotive industry), *cert. denied*, 506 U.S. 868 (1992).

Aside from the judicially noticed facts, there is no evidence on record showing that Wheeled Coach warned the GSA about dangers in its ambulance that were known to Wheeled Coach but not to the GSA. . . . We therefore will reverse the grant of summary judgment and remand the case to the district court. . . .

UNITED STATES v. BOWERS

660 F.2d 527 (5th Cir. 1981)

Per Curiam:

Pok Sin Bowers was convicted, following a jury trial in the district court, for cruelty to a child in violation of the Georgia child abuse statute, Ga. Code Ann. §26-2801(b) (1980), as it applies to a federal reservation through the Assimilative Crimes Act, 18 U.S.C. §13 (1976). . . . Appellant asserts that the court committed reversible error in taking judicial notice that "Fort Benning, Georgia, is on land which is property of the United States and is under the jurisdiction of [the] United States." The alleged vice in this instruction is the court's failure to inform the jurors that they were not bound to accept the noticed fact. Appellant cites Fed. R. Evid. 201(g). . . .

Rule 201 "governs only judicial notice of adjudicative facts," and not legislative facts. Consequently, appellant's argument turns on the characterization of the fact judicially noticed. The Eighth Circuit has observed that

> Legislative facts are established truths, facts or pronouncements that do not change from case to case but apply universally, while adjudicative facts are those developed in a particular case.

United States v. Gould, 536 F.2d 216, 220 (8th Cir. 1976). The fact that Fort Benning is under federal jurisdiction is a well established fact appropriate for judicial notice. Unlike an adjudicative fact, this fact does not change from case to case but, instead, remains fixed. Consequently, the court committed no error in failing to instruct the jury it could disregard the judicially noticed fact. . . . Affirmed.

UNITED STATES v. BELLO

194 F.3d 18 (1st Cir. 1999)

Lipez, Circuit Judge.

Jesus Bello appeals his conviction and sentence for assaulting a fellow prisoner in the Metropolitan Detention Center in Guaynabo, Puerto Rico

("MDC-Guaynabo") in violation of 18 U.S.C. §113(a)(6). Bello claims that the court erred in taking judicial notice of the jurisdictional element of the offense, namely, that MDC-Guaynabo was within the territorial jurisdiction of the United States.

. . . By its terms, Rule 201 applies only to adjudicative facts, and the parties and the court assumed that the jurisdictional element at issue here involved an adjudicative rather than a legislative fact. They assumed correctly. Whether a fact is adjudicative or legislative depends not on the nature of the fact—e.g., who owns the land—but rather on the use made of it (*i.e.*, whether it is a fact germane to what happened in the case or a fact useful in formulating common law policy or interpreting a statute) and the same fact can play either role depending on context. *See* Fed. R. Evid. 201, Advisory Committee's note ("Adjudicative facts are simply the facts of the particular case. Legislative facts, on the other hand, are those which have relevance to legal reasoning and the lawmaking process. . . ."). Where the prison sits is an element of the offense and unquestionably an adjudicative fact,[4] and we review the trial court's decision to take judicial notice under Rule 201 for abuse of discretion.

. . . [J]udicial notice was proper pursuant to Rule 201(b)(2), based on "sources whose accuracy cannot reasonably be questioned." Indeed, "[g]eography has long been peculiarly susceptible to judicial notice for the obvious reason that geographic locations are facts which are not generally controversial and thus it is within the general definition contained in Fed. R. Evid. 201(b). . . ." *United States v. Piggie*, 622 F.2d 486, 488 (10th Cir. 1980). . . . The government submitted to the court official government maps, letters from Army officials, and various legislative acts of Puerto Rico, all tending to show that MDC-Guaynabo was within the jurisdiction of the United States. . . .

The instruction offered by the court was as follows:

> Even though no evidence has been introduced about it in your presence, I believe that the fact that the Metropolitan Detention Center is within a land reserved for the use of the United States and under its exclusive jurisdiction . . . is of such common knowledge and can be so accurately and readily determined from the Metropolitan Detention Center officials that it cannot reasonably be disputed. You may, therefore, reasonably treat this fact as proven even though no evidence has been presented on this point before you.

---

4. Some other Courts of Appeals have held that Rule 201 is not applicable to judicial notice that a place is within the "special maritime and territorial jurisdiction of the United States," finding this to be a "legislative fact" beyond the scope of Rule 201. *See United States v. Hernandez-Fundora*, 58 F.3d 802, 811 (2d Cir. 1995); *United States v. Bowers*, 660 F.2d 527, 531 (5th Cir. 1981); *see also* II Kenneth Culp Davis & Richard J. Pierce, *Administrative Law Treatise*, §10.6, at 155 (3d. ed.1994) ["Whether 123 C Street is inside or outside the city is a question about 123 C Street, not about a party. The question whether X lives in the city is a question of adjudicative fact, but, even though X lives at 123 C Street, the fact that that address is within the city is not an adjudicative fact."]. *But see* Wright & Graham, *Federal Practice & Procedure* §5103 n. 16 (1999 Supp.) ("One court has resolved the problem by a dubious holding that the fact that Fort Benning is under the jurisdiction of the United States is a legislative fact," citing *Bowers*).

As with any fact presented in the case, however, the final decision whether or
not to accept it is for you to make and you are not required to agree with me.

This instruction . . . complied entirely with the dictates of the rule. . . . [10]
. . . *Affirmed.*

PROBLEMS

12.6. Suppose a calendar manufacturer sues a rival for patent infringement, based in part on the fact that the rival's calendar, like the one the
plaintiff has recently patented, is secured to the wall by a punched hole at
the top. The defendant asks the court to take judicial notice of the fact that
calendars have had this feature for many years, and the plaintiff objects.
How should the court rule?

12.7. Suppose a spectator at a minor league baseball game gets hit by a
line drive and sues the ballpark for negligence, alleging failure to post adequate warnings. The ballpark asks the judge to take judicial notice of the fact
that the hazard of being hit by a ball at a professional baseball game is well
known, and the plaintiff objects. How should the judge rule?

12.8. Suppose a criminal defendant moves to suppress evidence found
during a patdown search and alleges the police lacked reason to suspect he
was armed. The government proves the police had reason to suspect the
defendant was selling cocaine and asks the judge to take judicial notice of
the fact that drug dealers often carry weapons. The defendant objects. How
should the judge rule?

12.9. In a prosecution for robbery of a federally insured bank, suppose
the government asks the judge to instruct the jury that Bank of America—a
branch of which the defendant is alleged to have robbed—is federally
insured. The defendant objects. What instruction, if any, should the
judge give? What if the defendant is alleged to have robbed a branch of
Coast Federal Bank, and the government asks the court to take judicial
notice of the fact that federal law requires any bank with "Federal" in its
name to be federally insured?

12.10. For purposes of determining the admissibility of DNA identification evidence, can a court take judicial notice of the general reliability of
the technology employed, without holding an evidentiary hearing? (Several
courts have said yes. *See United States v. Beasley*, 102 F.3d 1440, 1447 (8th
Cir. 1996); *United States v. Martinez*, 3 F.3d 1191, 1197 (8th Cir. 1993),
cert. denied, 510 U.S. 1062 (1994); *United States v. Jakobetz*, 955 F.2d 786,
799 (2d Cir. 1992); *United States v. Shea*, 957 F. Supp. 331, 347 (D.N.H.
1997), *aff'd*, 159 F.3d 37 (1st Cir. 1998).)

---

10. It . . . remains unsettled whether 201(g)'s non-conclusive standard, permitting a
jury to disregard judicial notice in a criminal case, is constitutionally compelled. "With the
exception of Nevada, all of the states with modern codes make judicial notice binding on the
jury in all cases, criminal as well as civil." 21 Wright & Graham, *Federal Practice & Procedure*
§5111 n. 17, at 533. . . .

TABLE OF CASES

Excerpted cases are in italics.

TABLE OF RULES, STATUTES, AND CONSTITUTIONAL PROVISIONS

INDEX